THE CAMBRIDGE ANCIENT HISTORY

EDITORS

VOLUME XI

LONDON
Cambridge University Press
FETTER LANE

NEW YORK · TORONTO
BOMBAY · CALCUTTA · MADRAS
Macmillan

TOKYO
Maruzen Company Ltd

THE
CAMBRIDGE
ANCIENT HISTORY

VOLUME XI

THE IMPERIAL PEACE

A.D. 70—192

EDITED BY

S. A. COOK, Litt.D., F.B.A.

F. E. ADCOCK, M.A., F.B.A.

M. P. CHARLESWORTH, M.A.

CAMBRIDGE

AT THE UNIVERSITY PRESS

1936

PRINTED IN GREAT BRITAIN

PREFACE

VOLUME TEN ended with a year of civil war and rebellion within the Empire. In this volume is described a speedy recovery of security and stability under the Flavian emperors, followed by a century in which, despite wars of conquest and wars of defence, there was in general peace and a sense of security. This fact is reflected in the title which we have chosen, 'The Imperial Peace.' At the end of the volume an attempt has been made to sum up the main characteristics of the period under review and to indicate the transition to Volume Twelve. There, too, is given the connection with the preceding volume which would otherwise have been described at this point.

The first nine chapters of this volume contain, on the one hand, the narrative of events, domestic and foreign, in the reigns of the several emperors, and, on the other, an account of the northern and eastern peoples that were in closest touch with the Empire. They include, also, the rise of Christianity, which is described at the point at which it takes shape as a definite factor in the life of the Empire. While, in this volume, the influence of Oriental and Western religions finds record in so far as it is relevant for Imperial policy or for the life of the provinces, the general religious development of paganism within the Empire is reserved for Volume Twelve, where its range and significance can be seen as a whole. There follows next a chapter which sums up the development of the Principate and of the Imperial administration (Chap. x); and this leads on to an estimate of what Roman rule meant for the world of the Empire (Chap. xi). The complement to this is to be found in the next five chapters, which provide a survey of those groups of provinces which were, and were to be, important in Imperial history. In this survey the emphasis is bound to fall unevenly because of the incidence of the ancient evidence, but we hope that the balance of West and East has been properly preserved. Where, as with Sicily, Sardinia, Corsica and Cyprus, it did not seem possible to isolate enough evidence to provide a picture with significance, we have been content to have occasional references but no systematic description. The social life of Rome and Italy has been set somewhat later in the volume because it becomes most intelligible after the Latin literature of the period has been described (Chap. xviii). The last main section of the

13694

volume (Chaps. XVII–XXI) has for its theme the intellectual and
artistic achievements of the Empire concluding with a review of
Roman Classical Law from the time of Augustus onwards.

The chief characteristic of this phase of the Roman Empire is
its wide diversity despite an underlying unity, and this diversity is
fully reflected in the international character of research into its
history. There is hardly a European country that has not claimed
as its especial province some area of the Empire, together with an
appreciation of the whole. We have, therefore, to record an
obligation to the research of many countries as well as a more
particular debt to those of their scholars who have contributed to
the present volume. Professor Weber has written on Hadrian
and the Antonines, Professor Keil on the Greek provinces,
Dr Stade on Roman Germany, Professor Rodenwaldt on Imperial art, M. Albertini on Spain, Africa and Gaul, M. Cumont
on the frontier provinces of the East, Professor Romanelli on
Crete and Cyrenaica, Professor Alföldi of Budapest on the Getae
and Dacians and the Danube provinces. Dr Ekholm of Uppsala
has described the peoples of Northern Europe. Professor
Rostovtzeff, to whose work on the Empire every contributor is
much indebted, has written on the Sarmatae and Parthians. Of
English scholars, Mr Charlesworth and Mr Syme have dealt
with the Flavians, Mr Longden with Nerva and Trajan, Dr
Streeter with the rise of Christianity, Professor Collingwood with
Britain, Dr Idris Bell with Egypt, Mr Sandbach with Greek
Literature, Philosophy and Science, Mr Sikes with Latin Litera-
ture, Dr Wight Duff with Social Life in Rome and Italy, and
Professor Buckland with Classical Roman Law. To Professor
Last we owe the two central chapters, those on the Principate and
Imperial Administration and on Rome and the Empire. The
Conclusion to the volume is by Professor Adcock, the Appendix
on Sources by Mr Charlesworth, the Notes at the end of the
volume are by Mr Longden and M. Cumont.

In the construction of the bibliographies, which are due to the
several contributors, account has been taken of material already
provided in Volume Ten which in some respects anticipated the
present volume. Detailed surveys of ancient sources have been
made less necessary by an increase in documentation, desirable in
view of the peculiarly wide range of the evidence. The extent to
which inscriptions replace literary sources is reflected in the Index
of Passages. In the bibliographies, especially in those that refer
to the several provinces and to the peoples outside the Empire, we are
indebted to contributors for the great pains which they have taken

in the assembling, selection and arrangement of their material·
We venture to hope that they will be rewarded by the due gratitude of other scholars engaged on these fields of study. These
will not fail to realize that completeness is unattainable within the
limits of a single volume, and that reference must at times be
made to the collections of bibliographical material which are cited.
The maps are intended to assist the reading of the text, and not
to form in themselves a complete atlas of the ancient world in this
period. In such matters as the use of 'Empire' and 'empire' and
the employment of italics to mark technical terms we have
followed the practice described in the Preface to Volume Ten.
For any apparent or real inconsistencies the responsibility lies
with the Editors, not with the contributors, who, in these and
other formal details, have at times sacrificed their own preferences
to the general uniformity of the volume.

The first duty of the Editors is to thank the contributors for
their co-operation and for the help which they have generously
given on questions allied to the subjects of their chapters. Other
scholars, also, have kindly assisted us with information on special
topics. In the planning of the volume we have, besides our debt
to the scheme drawn up by the late Professor Bury, an especial
reason to be grateful for advice from Professors Last, Rostovtzeff
and Weber, though responsibility rests entirely on our shoulders.
On several matters connected with this volume we have also had
the benefit of the opinion of Professor N. H. Baynes, who has
consented to act with us as an Editor of Volume Twelve. We
welcome his accession, which will ensure that the join with the
Cambridge Medieval History, to which, indeed, he was a contributor,
will be expertly made, and the plan on which Volume Twelve is
already being prepared is in the main due to him. Mr Charlesworth would record his indebtedness to Professors J. G. C.
Anderson and A. D. Nock, for reading through his chapter in
proof and for many helpful suggestions. Professor Romanelli
wishes to acknowledge the courtesy of Signora M. Guarducci in
allowing him to see the proofs of her volume of *Inscriptiones
Creticae* before its publication. Professor Rodenwaldt has to thank
Professor Keil for information about his researches at Ephesus.
Professor Buckland would express his debt to Professor de Zulueta
for his assistance.

The Table showing the Parthian Dynasty has been constructed
by Professor Adcock in consultation with Professor Rostovtzeff.
In the drawing-up of the Chronological Table, which has involved a reading of the proofs, the Editors would gratefully

acknowledge once more the vigilant assistance of Mr G. B. A. Fletcher. In the preparation of maps Dr Ekholm supplied material for Map 2 and Mr Syme for Map 4; Map 16, which is repeated from Volume Ten, is due to Dr Bell; Map 7 is based on a map constructed by Mrs D. W. Brogan with her kind permission and that of the Royal Archaeological Institute of Great Britain and Ireland. For the construction of the other maps Mr Charlesworth is responsible, but he has had the benefit of advice from contributors on certain points. For the plans that accompany this volume we acknowledge the courtesy of the publishers of E. Lugli's *Classical Monuments of Rome* for Plan 1, of the Reale Accademia dei Lincei for Plan 2, of the Ufficio Antichità e Belle Arti of the Governatorato of Rome for Plan 3. We have to thank Mr C. T. Seltman for his assistance with the plans and his co-operation in the illustrations to this volume. These will appear in Volume of Plates V (illustrating Volumes Eleven and Twelve), which he is preparing for publication at the same time as the latter volume. We have further to acknowledge translations by Mr S. J. Charleston, Mr H. Sykes Davies, Mr Fletcher, Mr G. T. Griffith, Mr A. H. J. Knight, Mr Seltman and Mr D. E. W. Wormell.

The Index to Maps and the Index of Passages are the work of Mr B. Benham, who is also in part responsible for the General Index, together with Mrs B. Goulding Brown and Mr W. H. Swift, to all of whom we owe a debt for their care in a task of much complexity. We have omitted from the General Index many single entries which seemed to us not needed, and if any omissions are observed with regret the fault rests with the Editors. Finally, we have once more to express our gratitude to the Staff of the University Press for their unfailing skill and helpfulness.

We have chosen to place on the cover the head of Hadrian, the most notable personality in the period covered by the volume. The medallion is reproduced by the kind permission of the Staatl. Muënzkabinett, Kaiser Friedrich Museum in Berlin.

S.A.C.
F.E.A.
M.P.C.

August, 1936

TABLE OF CONTENTS

CHAPTER I

THE FLAVIAN DYNASTY

By M. P. Charlesworth, M.A.

Fellow of St John's College and Laurence Reader in Ancient
History in the University of Cambridge

CHAPTER II

THE PEOPLES OF NORTHERN EUROPE:
THE GETAE AND DACIANS

By G. EKHOLM, Dozent in the University of Uppsala, and A. ALFÖLDI, Professor
of the Ancient History and Archaeology of the Hungarian territory
in the University of Budapest[1]

[1] Sections I–V are by Dr Ekholm, sections VI and VII by Professor Alföldi.

CONTENTS

CHAPTER III

THE SARMATAE AND PARTHIANS

By M. ROSTOVTZEFF, Hon. Litt.D. (Cantab.), Hon. D.Litt. (Oxon.),
Hon. Litt.D. (Wisconsin)
Professor of Ancient History in Yale University

CHAPTER IV

FLAVIAN WARS AND FRONTIERS

By RONALD SYME, M.A.
Fellow of Trinity College, Oxford

CONTENTS

CHAPTER V

NERVA AND TRAJAN

By R. P. LONGDEN, M.A.
Student and Censor of Christ Church, Oxford

CHAPTER VI

THE WARS OF TRAJAN

By R. P. LONGDEN

CHAPTER VII

THE RISE OF CHRISTIANITY

By B. H. STREETER, M.A., D.D., F.B.A.

Provost of The Queen's College, Oxford, formerly Canon of Hereford

CHAPTER VIII

HADRIAN

By Wilhelm Weber
Professor of Ancient History in the University of Berlin

CHAPTER IX

THE ANTONINES

By Wilhelm Weber

CHAPTER X

THE PRINCIPATE AND THE ADMINISTRATION

By Hugh Last, M.A.

Fellow of Brasenose College, and Camden Professor of Ancient History in the
University of Oxford, formerly Fellow of St John's College, Oxford

CHAPTER XI

ROME AND THE EMPIRE

By HUGH LAST

CHAPTER XII

THE LATIN WEST: AFRICA, SPAIN AND GAUL

By E. ALBERTINI

Professor at the Collège de France

CHAPTER XIII

THE LATIN WEST: BRITAIN, ROMAN GERMANY, THE DANUBE LANDS

By R. G. COLLINGWOOD, M.A., F.S.A., F.B.A., Waynflete Professor of Metaphysical Philosophy in the University of Oxford, K. STADE, Second Director of the Römisch-Germanische Kommission of the German Archaeological Institute, and A. ALFÖLDI[1]

[1] Section I is by Professor Collingwood, section II by Dr Stade, section III by Professor Alföldi.

CHAPTER XIV

THE GREEK PROVINCES

By J. KEIL

Professor of Ancient History in the University of Greifswald

CHAPTER XV

THE FRONTIER PROVINCES OF THE EAST

By FRANZ CUMONT, Hon. Litt.D. (Cantab. and Dublin), Hon. D.Litt. (Oxon.),
Hon. LL.D. (Aberdeen)

CHAPTER XVI

EGYPT, CRETE AND CYRENAICA

By H. IDRIS BELL, C.B., M.A., Hon. D.Litt. (Wales and Michigan), F.B.A., Keeper of Manuscripts in the British Museum, and P. ROMANELLI, Professor of the Archaeology of Roman Africa in the Royal University of Rome[1]

CHAPTER XVII

GREEK LITERATURE, PHILOSOPHY AND SCIENCE

By F. H. SANDBACH, M.A.

Fellow of Trinity College, Cambridge, and University Lecturer in Classics

[1] Section I is by Dr Bell, sections II–IV by Professor Romanelli.

CHAPTER XVIII

LATIN LITERATURE OF THE SILVER AGE

By E. E. SIKES, M.A.

President of St John's College, Cambridge

CHAPTER XIX

SOCIAL LIFE IN ROME AND ITALY

By J. WIGHT DUFF, M.A., D.Litt., LL.D., Hon. D.Litt. (Durham), F.B.A.,
Hon. Fellow of Pembroke College, Oxford, Emeritus Professor of Classics,
Armstrong College (in the University of Durham), Newcastle-upon-Tyne

CHAPTER XX

ART FROM NERO TO THE ANTONINES

By G. RODENWALDT

Professor of Classical Archaeology in the University of Berlin

CHAPTER XXI

CLASSICAL ROMAN LAW

By W. W. BUCKLAND, LL.D., Hon. D.C.L. (Oxon.), Hon. LL.D. (Edinburgh and Harvard), F.B.A., Fellow of Gonville and Caius College and Regius Professor of Civil Law in the University of Cambridge

CONTENTS

LIST OF MAPS, PLANS, STATUES, ETC.

CHAPTER I

THE FLAVIAN DYNASTY

I. THE NEW EMPEROR

SEPTEMBER in the year 70 marked the hundredth anniversary of the battle of Actium. The victor in that battle had succeeded in a task which had baffled his predecessors: he had discovered a form of government which secured continuance for the Roman domination of the Mediterranean world, and had given to the peoples of that world a century of undisturbed peace. But though the solution that Augustus devised—the Principate—had many admirable features, which were to endure and develop, his determination to retain that Principate in his own family had proved unfortunate. Two generations after Augustus' death found the nobles terrorized and the armies disgusted: the last of the line, Nero, had by his behaviour merely succeeded in getting himself feared by the army-commanders and despised as a mountebank by the common soldier. Yet the revolt which broke out in 68 was against the Princeps, not against the Principate: the rival armies were quite ready to see their own general *princeps*. Republicanism, as a political creed, was dead save among a few theorists: even Piso's conspiracy had aimed, not at overthrowing the system, but at substituting some other man for Nero.

Thus the main portion of Augustus' great work stood firm. The Principate must remain, and there must be a *princeps*; all that was needed was a suitable person. But the three candidates who in the twelve months between July 69 and July 70 had great-

Note. The only substantial continuous literary sources for the years 70 to 96 are Suetonius, *Divus Vespasianus, Divus Titus* and *Domitianus* (cited as *Vesp., Tit., Dom.*), and Dio LXV–VII Boissevain (which are not entire but preserved in epitome and excerpts). Book IV of Tacitus' *Histories* includes events in Rome during the last days of December 69 and the first half of the year 70, the twenty-six chapters of Book V give an account of the rebellion in Judaea and the Batavian revolt, but the rest is lost. Occasional references to contemporary events occur in the poets Silius Italicus, Statius, Martial and Juvenal, and in the prose-writers Frontinus, Quintilian and the younger Pliny. This paucity of literary material enhances the value of the epigraphic and numismatic evidence, though as a rule this is more useful for the history of the provinces and the frontiers than for internal history. As Suetonius and Dio Cassius underlie so much of this chapter, and their accounts are in comparatively small compass, reference to them for statements of fact is only given on controversial points or in stressing an opinion.

ness thrust upon them, unlike though they were in character and outlook, were unfortunate in having one notable similarity, an entire unsuitability for the post. The fourth candidate, Vespasian, while not a man of outstanding genius or originality, did possess the necessary insight and determination to survive. Some sketch of his career and character must form the prelude to any account of the work he did.

Vespasian was born at Reate, in the Sabine hill-country, in A.D. 9. His family, with generations of hard farming stock behind it, was respectable but not distinguished: in his early years he gained the patronage of Narcissus, served with credit in Germany and in Britain, obtained the consulship in 51 and a pro-consulship after. Then he fell on poverty and evil days; he was forced to mortgage his estates to his more brilliant brother, Flavius Sabinus; worse, he offended Nero by falling asleep at one of his recitals. He was living in obscurity when in 66 Nero unexpectedly offered him the command of three legions to put down the revolt that had broken out in Judaea. The offer seems strange, but Vespasian had proved his competence as a soldier, and his lack of birth and wealth were positive recommendations to Nero; he could never be a danger; the prophecy of the Jew Josephus that he would one day become emperor seemed laughable to Vespasian himself. Yet within twelve months it was justified, for on 1 July of 69 he was hailed as Imperator by the legions at Alexandria and on 3 July by the army in Judaea. Five months later the murder of Vitellius removed his only rival, and the Senate duly acknowledged his accession.

Of his soldierly ability there could be no doubt, and this was perhaps the most important immediate qualification: the armies accepted him and he could hold them in check. Important for the future was the fact that he had sons and heirs[1], Titus, now thirty years old, and Domitian, who was eighteen; thus a dynastic succession was possible. Next came a certain dogged courage: once convinced a thing must be done he would carry on stubbornly and resolutely against all obstacles. Nor was he a man dependent upon and gullible by subordinates; he was no aristocrat, extravagant and unaware of the value of money, but one who had known poverty, learnt to drive a hard bargain and to manage an estate frugally. Yet his farming ancestry had not made

---

[1] His wife, Flavia Domitilla, died before 69: he took as concubine, Caenis, a freedwoman of Antonia, and treated her *paene iustae uxoris loco*. Such treatment scandalized Domitian (Suetonius, *Dom.* 12, 3): Dio (LXV, 14) asserts that she gained wealth by selling honours and preferments.

him a boor: he could quote Homer or Menander appositely, turn a jest in Greek or Latin, and was often able (like Abraham Lincoln) to tide over an unpopular measure or an awkward situation with a joke[1]. Informing all his actions was an unconquerable common-sense and grip of realities: few men can have been so completely normal and sensible.

Even so the task that confronted the new emperor was formidable. Though the Civil War was ended the loyalty and morale of the armies had been shaken badly. There was a danger that the legionaries might learn to do what they did in the third century, dictate the form of rule and set up rulers as they pleased; how that danger was turned aside will be seen (pp. 393 *sqq.*). Revolts, too, were still raging, in the West of the Batavi, in the East of the Jews; Pontus, Britain and Mauretania were in a disturbed state; in Africa two of the chief cities, Oea and Leptis, were conducting a war of their own (in which the Garamantes had readily joined), while on the north-eastern frontier barbarians—Dacians, Roxolani and Sarmatae—had seized the opportunity to cross the Danube and harry Roman territory. Besides the tasks of repression and defence it was essential to repair the material loss caused by the Civil War; for this money was plainly needed, yet there was the ominous fact that the guardians of the Aerarium, anxious at the depleted state of their treasury, were calling loudly for retrenchment. Most urgent of all, the moral and psychological damage of the war must be set right, and a healthy tone of confidence given to the whole Empire.

The task, though large, was compassable. Unlike Augustus, Vespasian had not to devise a new system. There had been a serious breakdown in the machinery, but no more; once the armies had been recalled to discipline, once the civil population had been nursed back to confidence, all that was called for was the patient competence of the mechanic. This competence Vespasian possessed: his qualities were just those necessary, and though he was already sixty years old, it was a robust and sane old age, strikingly different from the misanthropy of Tiberius and the invalidism of Claudius. With the Flavian dynasty the Roman Empire has reached a happier period: the glitter and extravagance of life under the Julio-Claudians vanish, and Roman history becomes in growing measure the story not of a court but of the peoples inhabiting a vast empire and learning to enjoy a common civilization.

---

[1] Instances abound in Suetonius' *Life*. His falling asleep over Nero's performance does not prove beyond doubt a lack of artistic perception.

II. ROME AND THE EMPEROR

Vespasian began as a usurper. His position could not be sure till the Senate and People of Rome had confirmed the choice of the legions, had done for him what they had done for Galba, Otho and Vitellius. On 22 December, A.D. 69, the day after Vitellius' death, the Senate met and expressed its will that all the usual powers should be conferred on the victor; this resolution was then passed by the People[1]. It should be noted that it was not only the *imperium proconsulare maius* and the *tribunicia potestas* that were thus conferred: Augustus had needed, in addition to these, certain special powers from time to time, and exemption occasionally from laws; many of these powers and exemptions were now included *en bloc* in the law, as (for example) the right of convening the Senate and bringing business before it, or the right of *commendatio*. But Vespasian's competence was more comprehensive; the right of *commendatio* granted to him was apparently unlimited, and he had the right of advancing the pomerium whenever he thought fit[2]. Naturally, all acts done by or authorized by him before this date were validated. Thus he was now legally secured and could take his place as the lawful successor to the deified Augustus, to Tiberius and Claudius[3].

The most urgent need was action to allay panic and to restore confidence to a distressed world. While he was at Alexandria during the early summer of 70, Vespasian worked miraculous cures upon a blind man and upon a maimed man: the whole East should know that the power of the gods was upon him, and that he and his son Titus were the men, foretold in prophecy, who should come from Judaea to rule the world[4]. In the West, his chief lieutenant, Mucianus, who arrived in Rome late in December 69, took power out of the hands of Antonius Primus and of the soldiery he could no longer control. He put to death the infant son of Vitellius, and another possible rival, Calpurnius Galerianus, and

---

[1] Dessau 244. Hence the enactment, while referred to as a *lex*, is couched in the form of a *senatus consultum*. For a fuller discussion of its constitutional implications see below, pp. 404 *sqq.* It should be noted that Vespasian counted his tribunician years from 1 July 69.

[2] The titles of *Pontifex Maximus* and *Pater Patriae* were given later; they do not appear on a diploma of 6 March 70, though they do on one of 5 April; H. C. Newton, *The Epigraphical Evidence for the Reigns of Vespasian and Titus*, 1901, nos. 30 and 31.

[3] These three emperors alone are cited for precedents, Gaius, Nero, Galba, Otho and Vitellius being omitted: it is noticeable that Claudius is not called Divus. [4] Tacitus, *Hist.* IV, 81; and cf. V, 13.

quickly restored some semblance of law and order. The new dynasty was represented by the young Domitian. A proclamation restored full civic status to all who had been convicted of *maiestas* under Nero or his successors, and from the Senate various commissions were appointed—to adjudicate upon claims for damage caused by the war, to make suggestions for greater economy in administration, and to search for copies of those old treaties and laws which had perished in the burning of the Capitol[1]. As a sign to the whole world that the Roman power was unshaken the restoration of the Capitoline Temple was to be begun, and on 21 June 70 the foundation stone was laid amid general rejoicing. The revolts in East and West were to be put down: two good generals, Annius Gallus and Petilius Cerialis, were to deal with the Batavi, while it was learnt that the Emperor was leaving his own son, Titus, in Palestine to bring the Jewish rebellion to a speedy close (vol. x, pp. 847, 861).

Thus, though Vespasian did not reach Rome till about October 70, he had already manifested unmistakably that he stood for order and peace, and on his arrival he confirmed these signs. He himself took a hand in clearing the site for the new Capitol, and tradition cherished the picture of the plebeian Emperor carting away rubbish on his shoulder[2]. He began the reduction of the Praetorian Guards from sixteen cohorts to the original nine. By the end of the year he could announce that the revolts of the Batavi and Jews had been crushed, and could close ceremonially, like Augustus, the Temple of Janus; the Senate voted to him and to Titus a triumph for the capture of Jerusalem. Coins and altars mirror something of the joy and thankfulness that was felt. A whole series of dedications from this eventful year has been preserved— to the Victory of Vespasian, to the *Pax Augusta*, and to 'the lasting peace brought by the house of Vespasian and his sons[3].' The bronze coinage hailed Vespasian as 'Champion of the People's Freedom' and celebrated 'The Loyalty of the Armies,' 'The Restoration of Liberty,' 'The Fairness of the Emperor,' 'The People's Good Fortune' and other similar topics[4]. Most significant, perhaps, of all the coin-types for its message was that which depicted in symbol and promised in its legend 'The Eternity of the Roman People.'

---

[1] Tacitus, *Hist.* IV, 40: over three thousand such State documents were ultimately copied and replaced, Suetonius, *Vesp.* 8, 5.

[2] This seems the best way to reconcile Tacitus, *Hist.* IV, 53 and Suetonius, *Vesp.* 8 (with which cf. Dio LXV, 10).

[3] For these dedications see Dessau 6049–52.

[4] See Mattingly-Sydenham, *The Roman Imperial Coinage*, II, pp. 66–76.

It was essential to convince the world of two things, one that the succession was provided for and secure, second that the soldiers and the Praetorians would be under control. Vespasian kept his two sons assiduously before the public eye, though the elder was naturally more favoured: with Titus he held the ordinary consulship in 70, 72, 74, 75, 76, 77 and 79, while though Domitian only held the ordinary consulship with his father once—in 71—he was *consul ordinarius* with L. Valerius Catullus Messallinus in 73, and suffect consul in 75, 76, 77 and 79. Coins displayed the brothers, elder and younger, as 'Principes Juventutis,' and both bore the title Caesar[1], a title which henceforward indicates an heir to the throne. Titus was still further advanced: on his return from the East, in the spring of 71, he received the proconsular imperium, and was made partner with his father in tribunician power, which he held continuously from 1 July in that year, and in the year 73–4 he shared the censorship with Vespasian. He was allowed to write and sign letters and edicts in his father's name, and in the Senate he often acted as quaestor to him; Suetonius does not exaggerate when he claims that he played the part of colleague and guardian of the Empire[2]. Though Domitian's position was lower, he yet held the consulship six times, and on inscriptions his name appeared frequently coupled with those of his father and brother.

There can be no doubt as to the significance of this. Apart from the prestige that this large number of consulships bestowed on his family, Vespasian made two things clear. One was that the stability of the government was assured: there was no lack of heirs, heirs who were being properly trained and were gaining ample political experience; it would take more than one man's assassination to produce a break in the succession. Secondly the future rulers were to be Flavians, for no other family would be so well fitted. 'My sons shall succeed me, or no one,' he declared: it was a choice between the rule of his family or anarchy[3].

Another danger point had been the legionaries. By the new régime the soldiers were kept in hand and in a good state of discipline, under extremely able commanders, some of whom may

[1] For the coins see Mattingly-Sydenham, *op. cit.* II, pp. 80, 82, 97, 98; for inscriptions see *e.g.* Dessau 246, 259.

[2] Suetonius, *Tit.* 6 and 7: cf. Philostratus, *Vita Apoll.* VI, 30.

[3] Suetonius, *Vesp.* 25: cf. Dio LXV, 12. The date and occasion are doubtful: for a view connecting it with 'the philosophic opposition' see Rostovtzeff, *Storia economica e sociale*, pp. 131–3 and notes. See further p. 9.

have been related to the ruling house. The Praetorians had proved unruly in the past, and the examples of Sejanus and of Nymphidius Sabinus showed that their Prefect might easily cherish undesirable ambitions; they were now placed under the sole control of Titus[1]. It was a generous but bold step, for rumours had already circulated about Titus' supposed ambitions in the East; it was said he had let the army salute him as *imperator* after the capture of Jerusalem, and issued coins on which that title was given him; he was alleged to have attended the Apis Ceremony, and in the course of the ritual to have placed a diadem upon his head[2]. None of these things need have weighed heavily with Vespasian, and the confidence the father placed in his son was fully repaid: Titus was faithful and vigilant, over-vigilant indeed according to our sources. For there were still disaffected elements to form a nucleus for the 'continual conspiracies' which Suetonius records, and it would have been sheer folly to run risks.

Presumably these conspiracies—of which we have no details except of one in 79—aimed at murdering Vespasian and his sons and at setting up a new *princeps* in his place. There was opposition, however, from another quarter, more vocal and more stressed in our sources, though the danger from it was smaller. The focus of this opposition was a small coterie of Republican-minded senators, led by Helvidius Priscus, and supported by such men as Arulenus Rusticus and Junius Mauricus. From the start they had determined to magnify the importance of the Senate and to minimize the part of the *princeps*: possibly they imagined that Vespasian, conscious of his humble origin, could be overawed by the *patres*; if so they were soon undeceived. But in the first few weeks they made themselves prominent. On the question of choosing members for an embassy to the Emperor, Helvidius Priscus demanded that they should be chosen for merit by their fellows on oath, rather than by lot, as was usual. When the praetors complained of the poverty of the State and the consul designate advised that this should be reserved for the Princeps to deal with, Helvidius was insistent that the Senate alone should tackle the problem, and he demanded that the restoration of the Capitol

---

[1] The previous Prefect was M. Arrecinus Clemens (Tacitus, *Hist.* IV, 68), who was also related to Vespasian.

[2] Suetonius, *Tit.* 5, 2: see Mattingly-Sydenham, *op. cit.* II, p. 56. The discovery of the new Apis often led to great popular excitement and enthusiasm (cf. S.H.A. *Hadr.* 12, 1), and Titus' action could easily be misinterpreted.

should be carried out by the State and Vespasian merely invited to assist[1].

These heroics did not win approval, and common-sense prevailed. But on some other matters senators were inclined to prove difficult. Many of them—C. Cassius Longinus, Helvidius Priscus, Q. Paconius Agrippinus, and Musonius Rufus—had suffered humiliation and exile under Nero, and some could not forget it. Cassius Longinus was wiser, devoting the remainder of his life to those legal studies in which he had already acquired fame (p. 822 sq.); Paconius Agrippinus was prepared to serve under a new and better *princeps*[2]; but the others were eager for revenge. Musonius Rufus attacked a Neronian informer, P. Egnatius Celer, and gained his condemnation. Heartened by this, Helvidius turned on the redoubtable Eprius Marcellus himself, while Junius Mauricus asked Domitian to throw open the Imperial archives and disclose the names of the informers. But though the body of senators, in new-found fervour, took an oath that they had done nothing to harm any man's life or goods, vindictiveness was not to be allowed play: both Domitian and Mucianus urged a general amnesty, the accusation against Marcellus was dropped, and he himself presently promoted to the governorship of Asia[3].

Thus Helvidius' day of glory was short: the Senate soon returned to a more submissive attitude. For the next few years, however, Helvidius was a thorn in the side of the ruling house. By his family connections he belonged to the irreconcilables; his wife Fannia was a daughter of the Thrasea Paetus, whom Nero had put to death, and a grand-daughter of the Caecina Paetus who had joined in a conspiracy against Claudius (vol. x, pp. 730 sq. and 671); his conduct must have been deliberate. He insulted Vespasian in word and act, refusing him his titles and reviling him. Vespasian asked him not to come to the Senate-House, if he meant simply to disagree with him and abuse him, but Helvidius persisted[4]. Indeed he went further: 'he attacked monarchical systems and praised republican, and to the people he openly advocated revolution[5].' The upshot could not be doubtful: placable though he was, Vespasian could not offer himself as a perpetual target for insult, and could not allow a senator

---

[1] Tacitus, *Hist.* IV, 9.

[2] Inscriptions from Cyrene show him acting as legate of Vespasian between July and December 71: *Ann. épig.* 1919, nos. 91–3.

[3] See R. K. McElderry in *J.R.S.* III, 1913, p. 116.

[4] Epictetus, *Diss.* (ed. Schenkl[2]), I, 2, 19–24.

[5] Dio LXV, 12, 2.

to preach sedition. On some charge, unknown to us, he was banished and, shortly after, put to death, though Vespasian was extremely reluctant and even tried to recall the executioners.

Helvidius, indeed, was one of the few victims of Vespasian's reign, and some others may conveniently be mentioned with him. The Emperor had to face savage attacks from a class of people called variously in our sources 'philosophers,' 'Stoics' and 'Cynics.' The last term seems the truer: at this time there arose again a class of itinerant moralists, who preached anarchy, inveighed against all rulers, and gloried in an utter unconventionality and indecency. Few of these can have been Stoics, for the Stoics had no objection to monarchy *per se*, only to bad monarchs, whereas these mob-orators were against all rule and order. So irritating and insulting did their attacks become that Mucianus, enraged, persuaded Vespasian in 71 to banish not only Cynics but all *astrologi* and *philosophi* from Rome: among others Demetrius the Cynic and C. Tutilius Hostilianus, a Stoic, had to leave the city[1].

This opposition may then be termed 'philosophic,' but there is no direct evidence for what has been sometimes assumed— that it aimed at replacing a hereditary Principate by one based upon election. It would not be easy to disentangle the Republican and the Cynic elements in Helvidius Priscus, but one thing seems clear, that he was utterly opposed to *any* form of Principate, whether hereditary or elective. The Cynics went even further: while Helvidius may have advocated a return to some form of the old Republic, they were against all government and all holders of power. For generations they continued their exasperating attacks on the Emperors: Lucian records that Peregrinus actually abused and insulted the gentle Antoninus Pius himself—who took no notice—until at last the Prefect of the City drove him from Rome[2]. It was unfortunate that these extravagances should bring the name of philosophy into disrepute, but they did: not only do Quintilian and Tacitus express their grave disapproval, but Dio Chrysostom and Lucian inveigh against the Cynics, who will do anything for publicity, while two

---

[1] Dio LXV, 13, 1–2; for Hostilianus see Fr. Bücheler in *Rhein. Museum*, LXIII, 1908, p. 194: Musonius Rufus, who was no revolutionary, and who advocated the sage's marrying and taking a part in public life, was exempted, but must have been banished later since Jerome records his recall by Titus.

[2] Lucian, *de morte Peregrini*, 18. The present writer is here indebted to his friend, Mr D. R. Dudley, for the use of his unpublished thesis, *The History of Cynicism*.

Greek writers, who—be it observed—had both held official posts, Appian and Cassius Dio, are severest of all in their strictures[1]. The average Roman had never had much taste for academic discussion; when the Cynics combined this with anarchic and subversive doctrine Roman official opinion was bound to be hostile.

Even to these Cynics Vespasian showed tolerance, if exile from Rome instead of flogging or execution can be counted as tolerance. He refused to put them to death, and when Demetrius continued his attacks and railings from outside Rome merely replied, 'You are doing your utmost to get yourself killed by me, but I don't kill dogs for barking.' But the Cynics succeeded in placing the Emperor in a difficult position; his patience was not inexhaustible, and a few years later their determined efforts at martyrdom met their reward.

Politically the most important achievement of the early years was the censorship which Vespasian and Titus held in 73–4. A century before, Augustus had had to fill the gaps caused among the patrician ranks by war and the proscriptions, and to reward merit or service to himself by promotion to the Senate; Vespasian had a like task. The number of patrician families had shrunk considerably, partly owing to natural causes, partly to persecution, while civil war and confiscation had also depleted the Senate. There is no doubt that Vespasian, at the very beginning of his reign, had irregularly given men senatorial rank to secure their loyalty: but the great work of restoration waited until his censorship. His policy was at once prudent and liberal: he was the first to adlect provincials *inter patricios*; the soundness of his choice is shown by three names—M. Ulpius Traianus, M. Annius Verus, and Cn. Julius Agricola[2]. Men of merit, whether Italian or provincial, found their careers forwarded, and thus C. Antius A. Julius Quadratus, L. Baebius Avitus, and C. Fulvius Lupus Servilianus were adlected *inter praetorios*[3]: among others added to the Senate, were an Ephesian, Tib. Julius Celsus Polemae-anus, a Galatian, C. Caristanius Fronto, and L. Antonius

---

[1] Quintilian, *Inst. Orat.* XI, 1, 35 and cf. XII, 2, 6; Tacitus, *Hist.* IV. 5 and Dio Chrys. *Or.* XXXII, 9–10; Lucian, *de morte Peregrini*, 17, *Vitarum Auctio*, 10, *Demonax*, 48 are examples; Appian, *Mithr.* 28; Dio LXV, 13. It may be noted that Dio in LII, 36 makes Maecenas warn Augustus against 'philosophers' because they may cause revolutions; this is almost certainly a later view and not Augustan.

[2] B. Stech, *Senatores Romani...*, p. 184: add to his list P. Calvisius Ruso L. Julius Frontinus, H. Dessau in *J.R.S.* III, 1913, p. 301.

[3] Stech, *op. cit.* p. 185 *sq.*

Saturninus[1]. All these men were to play a considerable part—Antonius Saturninus a sinister one—in the two generations after 70. After completing the work of the censorship Vespasian not only advanced the pomerium—like Augustus and Claudius before him—but was able also to dedicate the Temple of Peace, in which he placed the spoils of the Jewish campaign: the Roman People could regard him now as conqueror, peace-bringer, and restorer of the State.

Within six years from his accession Vespasian had restored peace and order, stabilized the financial system (pp. 13 *sqq.*), created new patrician families and refilled the Senate, and secured the succession for his family. From 75 to 79 there is little to record, though one or two items stand out. During the Jewish War one of the client-kings who had helped prominently was M. Julius Agrippa II (see vol. x, p. 752); Titus fell violently in love with his sister Berenice. In 75 the brother and sister visited Rome and were greeted with great honour: Agrippa was granted the praetorian *insignia* and Berenice was lodged in the Palatium. Possibly, imagining that she was going to be Titus' wife, Berenice behaved arrogantly: we know she held her own court in Rome, for Quintilian records that he had pleaded before her[2]. The memory of Cleopatra was not dead, many Romans honestly dreaded a union between Titus and an Oriental princess. Some Cynic preachers managed to slip back into Rome, and denounced the marriage and the ruling house; one of them, Diogenes, was caught and flogged, another, Heras, was executed. Such a punishment may represent a hardening in the governmental attitude towards 'philosophers,' or merely the personal exasperation of Titus. But the mischief was done, the marriage made impossible, and Titus must let Berenice depart 'invitus invitam.'

In legislation Vespasian was content to confirm or carry further the measures of Augustus or Claudius, and to correct anomalies. One method of evading the provisions of the Augustan marriage laws had been by creating trusts (*fideicommissa*) instead of making legacies: the *S.C.* Pegasianum of 73 put a stop to this by extending to *fideicommissa* the same restrictions with regard to *caelibes* and *orbi* as attached to inheritance under the Augustan law[3] (see vol. x, p. 454). A law of Claudius had forbidden money-lenders to make

---

[1] Stech, *op. cit.* p. 186; add Dessau 9485. For an Eastern king, Alexander (possibly the son of Tigranes V of Armenia), who was adlected, see Dessau 8823. [2] Quintilian, *Inst. Orat.* IV, I, 19.

[3] Gaius II, 286, 286a. The *S.C.* was so called after the celebrated jurist, Pegasus, who rose to be Prefect of the City later.

loans to a young man against his father's death (vol. x, p. 694): a
S.C. Macedonianum, apparently passed in this period, strengthened
this by directing that no action was to be given to such a creditor
even though the father had since died[1]. Apart from this we hear
of little, save that Vespasian abolished one anomaly in the mass
of rules relating to the status of children of parents of unequal
status by declaring that, in accordance with *ius gentium*, the
children of a slave mother must themselves be slaves and the
property of her owner[2].

There is little more to chronicle, though two events darkened
the last year of Vespasian's reign. Orosius[3] records that a plague
visited Rome and carried off many victims, and this is our only
notice of what may have been a serious disaster. The second
event was a conspiracy formed against him by two of his trusted
friends, A. Caecina Alienus, the general, and Eprius Marcellus,
the orator and ex-governor of Asia (pp. 8, 18). Conceivably it was
a move by those who saw Vespasian was ageing, and feared the
rule of Titus, but that can be only conjecture. The vigilance of
Titus discovered the plot, but only just in time: Caecina, arrested
as he was leaving the palace after dinner, was found to be carrying
on him a speech for delivery to the soldiers, and was executed out
of hand; Marcellus was given a form of trial and committed
suicide[4]. The danger must have been pressing, but that is all we
know.

In the late spring of 79 Vespasian's health, till then untroubled,
began to break. Even so he insisted on carrying on with business,
and neither his courage nor his humour failed him. He refused
to be put out by reported omens, light-heartedly referring their
significance to others; when his final illness struck him he jested,
'Vae, puto, deus fio.' On June 24 he struggled to his feet to
die as he said an *imperator* should, 'standing,' and collapsed. He
died as a soldier; his jest came true in his deification as Divus
Vespasianus.

---

[1] Bruns, *Fontes*[7], 57. The *S.C.* was called after the name of the money-
lender whose villainies provoked it: it is usually dated to this reign by comparison with Suetonius, *Vesp.* 11. Other instances in which Vespasian
carried further Claudian legislation are to be found in Suetonius, *Vesp.* 11,
where he apparently re-enacted the *S.C.* Claudianum (vol. x, p. 693), and
in *Cod. Just.* VIII, 10, 2, where he apparently reiterated, with some modifications, the *S.C.* Hosidianum against demolition of buildings (vol. x, p. 695).

[2] Gaius I, 85.   [3] VII, 9, 11.

[4] Dio LXV, 16, 3; Suetonius, *Tit.* 3.

III. RE-ORGANIZATION: FINANCIAL AND PROVINCIAL

The longest remembered[1] though the least popular part of Vespasian's task was the hardest—the creation of financial stability. Fortunately he was well fitted for the part. A man of simple tastes himself, with no mind for display, he put an abrupt end to the ostentatious extravagance of the court of Claudius or Nero; a tone of greater moderation and of frugality spread from the *princeps* downwards to all classes[2]. But parsimony and retrenchment alone were insufficient, what was needed was more money; that meant increased taxation, and Vespasian grappled firmly with the problem. At the very outset the officials in charge of the Aerarium had complained that funds were low (p. 3); when Mucianus began dismissing the Vitellian veterans from the Praetorian Guard, so great was the amount of cash needed to pay their pensions that one suggestion made was that a special loan of sixty million sesterces should be raised by private subscription[3]. No one could fail to be aware of the gravity of the situation and Vespasian was wisely frank: startling though it might be he announced that he would have to collect no less than forty thousand million sesterces in order to make the State solvent again.

This immense estimate has naturally caused questioning. To one of the earlier commentators, Budé, it appeared so vast that he proposed to emend it to four thousand million. One thing seems clear, that the sum Vespasian named was a capital sum and not the required yearly revenue. Though the extent of the Empire was larger, and though prices may have risen a little, it is inconceivable that the expenses of its administration alone demanded a revenue one hundred times as large as that of the Aerarium in Augustus' day (400,000,000 sesterces)[4]. The revenues of the Empire had increased amazingly during a century of peace and security: Egypt alone now produced well over five hundred million sesterces[5]; it is the only province for which we possess a reliable figure, but if we bear in mind the great prosperity and wealth of such regions as Africa, Spain, Gaul and Syria, we may reasonably conclude that the total revenue accruing might be at

---

[1] See, for example, S.H.A. *Tyr. Trig. Victorinus*, 6: 'Victorino...neminem aestimo praeferendum...non in gubernando aerario Vespasianum....'

[2] Tacitus, *Ann.* III, 56.   [3] Tacitus, *Hist.* IV, 47.

[4] See the calculations of T. Frank in *J.R.S.* XXIII, 1933, p. 143.

[5] See M. Bang, *Die Steuern dreier römischen Provinzen*, in Friedländer, *Darstellungen aus der Sittengeschichte Roms*, 9 and 10 ed., IV, p. 297.

least five times as much as the Egyptian, that is some two thousand five hundred million sesterces. Financial figures in ancient history, especially when derived from manuscripts and not from stone or bronze, are notoriously untrustworthy, but it looks as though the sum that Vespasian named was less than twenty times the annual revenue of the Empire and that it could be obtained without undue harshness or pressure. The most immediate use for the money would be to help the devastated areas in North Italy and Gaul: in addition the increased number of legions and the extensive frontier schemes initiated by the Flavians would call for large sums (chap. IV); finally, there were ambitious and grandiose building schemes for Rome, for the people must be amused and fed and kept contented. But immediate needs were not all: it is a reasonable assumption that the sane and cautious Vespasian meant to establish a definite capital fund which could produce a yearly income, and that some portion of the forty thousand million was destined for this. Whether any special taxes were to be devoted to this fund—as Augustus had arranged for the *Aerarium militare*—we cannot tell.

There is no doubt, however, that taxation was considerably increased and sometimes even doubled: but it is fair to remember that many of the provinces had made such strides in prosperity that the earlier assessment was on the low side and they could afford to contribute more. A glance at Gaul will show how fortunes had risen. Caesar had imposed on the country a tribute of forty million sesterces; in the Julio-Claudian period C. Julius Secundus left to the town of Burdigala two million sesterces, and the colony of Lugdunum on one occasion offered the State four million; under Nero the Arverni could afford to pay the sculptor Zenodorus, for a colossal statue of Mercury, the sum of forty million[1]. Considerable changes in provincial organization took place under Vespasian; while some were due to military needs, as the incorporation of the kingdom of Commagene in Syria or the formation of the new large province of Galatia-Cappadocia (p. 140), many were obviously designed to increase revenue. One such change is typical of Vespasian's shrewdness. When Nero gave freedom and immunity to Greece he compensated the Senate, whose province it had been, by giving it Sardinia and Corsica. Vespasian had little of Nero's philhellene sentiment: convinced by their internal quarrels that the Greeks 'had lost the art of

[1] C. Julius Secundus, *C.I.L.* XIII, 596–600: Lugdunum, Tacitus, *Ann.* XVI, 13: the Arverni, Pliny, *N.H.* XXXIV, 45. It should be mentioned that in these two last passages the reading is not certain.

liberty,' and annoyed by outbreaks and riots, he took even this freedom away from them. But Achaea was impoverished and could make no great contribution to the revenue, so Vespasian graciously returned it to the Senate, and took over again the fertile and wealthy territory of Sardinia and Corsica[1]. For like reasons, doubtless, Vespasian deprived Rhodes and Byzantium and Samos of liberty and assigned them to provinces, Rhodes and Samos to Asia and Byzantium to Bithynia-Pontus. There is evidence for considerable re-organization in this region: an inscription shows that in Domitian's reign there was a *provincia Hellesponti* controlled by a financial procurator, while a passage in Festus speaks of a *provincia insularum* being established[2]. (If this is correct Rhodes and Samos may have been incorporated in this new *provincia insularum*.) The Lycian cities had always been turbulent; though deprived of freedom by Claudius (vol. x, p. 680), they may have regained it under Nero, but Vespasian deprived them of it finally, and made them into a province to which he added Pamphylia[3]. Most of these changes appear to have taken place in the first years of his reign, by 73–4[4], and all must have meant definite increases to the Imperial exchequer.

In addition new taxes were imposed, though here again we possess little detailed information[5]. We should probably assign to the early years the first organization of three special treasuries, the *fiscus Judaicus*, the *fiscus Alexandrinus*, and the *fiscus Asiaticus*. The *fiscus Judaicus* simply appropriated to the Capitoline Temple the two drachmas which every Jew used to pay annually to the Temple at Jerusalem: as the number of Jews in the Empire was something near five million the revenue brought in was considerable. On whom the taxes that filled the two other chests were imposed and what they brought in we do not know, though it has been conjectured that the *fiscus Alexandrinus* was connected with the Egyptian corn-supply[6].

[1] Pausanias VII, 17, 4; Philostratus, *Vita Apoll.* v, 41; for the evidence about Corsica see Newton, *op. cit.* p. 61 *sq.*

[2] Suetonius, *Vesp.* 8, 4; Dessau 1374; Festus, *Brev.* 10; see also McElderry, *op. cit.* p. 119 *sq.*

[3] The evidence is very confused: see Suetonius, *Claud.* 25 and *Vesp.* 8. The creation of the province of Lycia-Pamphylia is wrongly ascribed to Claudius by Dio LX, 17, 3: Pamphylia before Vespasian's reign had gone with Galatia, Tacitus, *Hist.* II, 9 (p. 590).

[4] Pliny, *N.H.* IV, 46, suggests that Byzantium held its freedom till 77.

[5] One new tax, the so-called *vectigal urinae*, is mentioned by Suetonius in a later chapter (*Vesp.* 23, 3) to illustrate a jest of Vespasian's.

[6] See Hirschfeld, *Die kais. Verwaltungsbeamte*[2], pp. 369 *sqq.* and P.-W. *s.v.* Fiscus (Rostowzew).

Besides increasing taxation and improving organization (which included some control of the tax-collecting companies) the Emperor kept a strict watch on public property: public land which had been unlawfully occupied, whether in Italy or the provinces, he won back for the State[1]. He even tackled the problem of *subsiciva*, that is, land that had been left unallotted in a colony. These *subsiciva* were of two kinds, either plots lying outside the centuriation or supposedly uncultivable pieces within it; being unassigned, they were still technically public property though, naturally enough, in course of time they had been occupied. Vespasian began to reclaim this land from the squatters: his action roused indignation, and deputations came from all Italy. Vespasian compromised characteristically; there should be no more confiscations, but he kept what he had already taken[2].

The raising of money is an ungrateful task, and Vespasian's imposition of taxation and efficient methods made him a natural target for attacks and lampoons. The Alexandrians were quick to find a nickname for him, and our sources have plenty of anecdotes which show him as a man who never disdained to make economies or profits however small. But though Vespasian used every device to extort money, he was no miser, and he did not spend on himself; rather he spent generously and wisely on the defence and stability of the Empire and encouraged culture. He was never tyrannical in his exactions, and where people could show reason for immunity or special treatment, he secured it to them: thus, after due investigation, he confirmed to the Vanacini, of northern Corsica, the *beneficia* that Augustus had granted[3]. Needy but deserving senators were supported by yearly grants, and he encouraged education and the arts by the establishment of professorial chairs and by handsome donations to poets and literary men. Quintilian was appointed to the chair of Latin Rhetoric, the poet Saleius Bassus was rewarded with 500,000 sesterces. This official encouragement of education was followed by individuals and communities alike: we find the younger Pliny endowing a school at Comum, and teachers visited and were often given permanent appointments in provincial towns. Typical of the enhanced position of teachers is the fact that Vespasian

---

[1] For control of tax-collection see Hirschfeld, *op. cit.*, p. 82 *sq.*: for public land in Italy see Newton, *op. cit.*, nos. 75 and 76: in Cyrene, *Ann. épig.* 1919, nos. 91–3, and *Corpus Agrimensorum Rom.* (ed. C. Thulin), I, p. 85.

[2] *Corpus Agrimensorum Rom.* I, p. 41. See the remarks of Heitland in *Agricola*, p. 272. Titus tried to continue the confiscations.

[3] Bruns, *Fontes*[7], 80.

was ready to grant them immunity from taxation and freedom from having soldiers billeted upon them[1].

Money was allotted freely to public works and improvements, both in Rome and in the provinces. One great symbolic achievement was the new temple of Capitoline Juppiter, completed in 71, but Rome could also boast of the Temple of Peace, the Colosseum, and other buildings; provincial capitals such as Antioch benefited too, and bridges and roads were constructed over the whole Empire[2]. Small provincial towns received benefactions and recorded them gratefully. Occasionally the inscription points a moral, as when the town of Cadyanda in Lycia declares that 'the Emperor Vespasian built the bath-house out of money rescued for the city by him[3]'; more often it is simply a commemoration of the benefaction, but there is scarcely a province that did not benefit from the imperial care and generosity.

Equally important was the work of romanization, which Vespasian did his utmost to promote. He granted Latin rights to the whole of Spain, and henceforward there were no longer *peregrini* there, but only the two grades of citizenship[4]. This generous measure must have entailed a work of re-organization lasting over years—it has been reckoned that some four hundred new charters were required—but its wisdom cannot be questioned: apart altogether from the fact that it gave Vespasian a new recruiting-ground (p. 496), it encouraged a vigorous local municipal life and was a fitting reward to a region that had been under Roman sway for nearly three hundred years and had already made considerable contributions to literature. In other provinces, usually in mountainous or less developed regions, progress was helped by the foundation of new colonies; to mention a few names only, in Africa Ammaedara, in Northern Spain Flaviobriga, in Switzerland Aventicum, in Pannonia Sirmium and Siscia, in Moesia Scupi, in Thrace Deultum and Flaviopolis, and in Syria Caesarea received new settlers and became centres for the spread of civilization[5].

---

[1] See *Dig.* L, 4, 18,30; Bruns, *Fontes*[7], 112; and the new inscriptions from Pergamum which are discussed by R. Herzog in *Sitz. d. preuss. Akad.* XXXII, 1935, p. 967.

[2] See Newton, *op. cit.* pp. 50–4 and 61–70.

[3] No attempt is made here to catalogue all the cities which benefited: for Cadyanda see *I.G.R.R.* III, 507, of which a better text is given in *Tit. Asiae Min.* II, 651.

[4] Pliny, *N.H.* III, 30. On the whole topic see R. K. McElderry in *J.R.S.* VIII, 1918, p. 53.

[5] For a fuller list see the articles in P.-W. *s.vv.* Coloniae and T. Flavius Vespasianus, cols. 2681 *sqq.*

Throughout the Empire Vespasian encouraged *municipia* too, while in some of the Western provinces the appointment of officials, subordinate to the governor, to assist him in judicial administration, the *legati iuridici*, implies an increase in litigation which is usually regarded as a sign of advancing civilization. In fact the provinces were steadily progressing: Spain and Narbonensis had already contributed their quota of men to the Senate and to the magistracies, and it is significant that in the year 80 for the first time an African, Q. Pactumeius Fronto, achieved the consulship.

Where necessary Vespasian took strong measures to secure efficient control: thus it seems likely that he made the Senate accept as governor for the province of Asia the wealthy but unpopular Eprius Marcellus, and that he retained him there for three years, during which a number of administrative alterations were made (see above, p. 8, n. 3). However distasteful Marcellus may have been to the more Republican-minded senators, his ability was undoubted, his wealth set him above the temptations that might have attacked another governor, and he possessed previous experience of the region. As far as we can judge—the evidence is not abundant—Vespasian's appointments were good: throughout his whole reign we hear only of one accusation for extortion, against C. Julius Quadratus Bassus, ex-quaestor of Bithynia, and in the end he was acquitted[1]. He insisted certainly on a high standard of efficiency: a young dandy who came, reeking with scent, to thank him for an appointment, he rebuked with the words 'I would sooner you smelt of garlic' and cancelled his appointment. His officials, generals and governors, formed a new aristocracy of service, for the old aristocracy of birth had either died out or been killed by the Julio-Claudians; they had the good sense to carry on the administration of the Empire, whatever the emperor, and were ready (in Eprius Marcellus' phrase) 'to admire the old times but fall in with the present.'

Fortunately for this new aristocracy of service Vespasian was a man like themselves—keen, energetic, shrewd—whom they could admire and under whom they were willing to serve. A more moderate tone set in: not only did Vespasian cut down the feverish extravagance of Julio-Claudian times, but he also achieved a greater simplicity at court. He laughed at the flatterers who tried to find him a heroic ancestry, and he pruned away much of the

---

[1] Pliny, *Ep.* IV, 9. The alleged practice of Vespasian, of appointing greedy procurators whose ill-gotten gains he could later appropriate (Suetonius, *Vesp.* 16, 2), sounds apocryphal.

formality that had been growing up; there were no longer grades
of admission to the imperial presence, for Vespasian made himself
equally accessible to all[1]. He abolished too the custom of searching
all who were admitted to the presence[2]; Claudius, mindful of the
assassination of Gaius, had first introduced it, Vespasian was
sufficiently confident to dispense with it. He did not fear the
consequences of assassination, for he had provided against them:
he even forgave conspirators freely, jokingly remarking that they
were fools not to realize what a burden of cares the Principate
carried[3]. 'It will be hard,' judges Suetonius, 'to find one instance
of an innocent person being punished, unless when he was away
and knew nothing of it or at least against his will or when he had
been misled[4].' Here was a real clemency and tolerance, utterly
different from the much-lauded *Clementia* of Nero. He won
men over to serve under him because he did not spare himself,
and worked as hard as he asked others to work. Two of his predecessors he obviously regarded with admiration, Augustus and
Claudius. We have already noted how much of his legislation
aimed at developing and safeguarding the laws of these two statesmen: it is significant that much of his coinage deliberately copies
the coinage of Augustus, and that he placed his amphitheatre in
the middle of the City because he was informed that Augustus had
intended to build one there, significant too that he completed the
Temple of Divus Claudius on the Caelian, and restored his cult.
It was a fitting reward that he should take his place next after
them on the roll of deified emperors; that, after Divus Augustus
and Divus Claudius, Divus Vespasianus should be handed down
to the gratitude of posterity.

IV. TITUS

Vespasian dead Titus succeeded as a matter of course; on the
24th June 79 he became *princeps*, and that same day received the
titles of Pontifex Maximus and Pater Patriae. He had one child,
Julia, a girl of about thirteen, but no son; his brother Domitian
was bound to be his heir, and Titus protested he should be his
partner and his successor. But he did nothing to confirm his
protestations: Domitian remained as before Princeps Juventutis;
he held a consulship in 80 with his brother but he received no
share of proconsular imperium and no grant of tribunician power.

---

[1] See Pliny, *N.H.* XXXIII, 41, who praises Vespasian 'aequaliter publi-
cando principem.'   [2] Dio LX, 3, 3.
[3] Aurelius Victor, *Caes.* IX, 3.   [4] Suetonius, *Vesp.* 15.

There was a lack of sympathy between Titus and his assertive and ambitious brother and nothing could heal it. It was plain that he distrusted him; Domitian retorted by complaining that Titus had tampered with Vespasian's will and by assiduously undermining him.

Men had dreaded Titus' accession, remembering his ruthlessness, his extravagance, and his affair with Berenice, but he completely falsified their expectations. There were no executions, no trials for *maiestas*; on the contrary informers were publicly scourged and then sold into slavery or banished to those islands to which they had often sent victims. Court life remained on the same modest level as in his father's day. Berenice, who apparently returned to Rome, he again dismissed. In the enthusiastic accounts which have come down he stands out as the ideal *princeps*, solicitous for the welfare of all and loved by his people. Under forty when he succeeded, handsome, brilliant and gracious, the stormer of Jerusalem, the favourite of the soldiers, fluent both in Greek and in Latin, equally adept in the arts of peace and war, all that he did only increased his popularity and esteem; when he died after a little over two years' rule he had become (in Suetonius' phrase) 'amor ac deliciae generis humani.'

The little we know of his laws and actions reveals a paternal and equitable spirit. He put a stop to two evil practices; the first was one by which informers who had failed to net their victim on a charge under one law tried under another, the second was one by which they tried to invalidate a dead man's testamentary dispositions by challenging his right to free status. The first Titus prohibited altogether, the second he forbade after a term of years had passed; this term was fixed by Nerva and by Marcus Aurelius later at five years[1].

He showed a like kindly spirit in meeting two disasters which befell Italy. The first was a fire at Rome, which destroyed, among other buildings, the Porticus Octaviae with its libraries, the Iseum, and the recently restored temple of Capitoline Juppiter and so made a large rebuilding programme necessary. The second was the famous eruption of Vesuvius on August 24 A.D. 79, which overwhelmed Pompeii and Herculaneum. Here he showed, as Suetonius records, 'not only the anxious care of a *princeps* but the love of a father.' He had senators appointed by lot to act as *curatores* for the ruined district, and assigned the property of those

---

[1] Suetonius, *Tit.* 8, 5; cf. *Dig.* XL, 15, 1 and 4. Titus also abolished one of the two praetors whom Claudius had put in charge *de fideicommissis*. *Dig.* 1, 2, 32.

who died intestate to the relief of distress. It was in this eruption
that a friend of Titus lost his life, the elder Pliny: he went
impelled by scientific curiosity about the phenomena of the eruption, he stayed to rescue panic-stricken fugitives; 'quod studioso
animo inchoaverat, obit maximo[1].'

The games that Titus gave at the opening of the Colosseum
were lavish and splendid, lasting a hundred days; his benefactions
were frequent and liberal. Tradition remembered with praise a
remark of his at the close of a day when he could not remember
any benefit conferred—'Friends, I have lost a day!' Some ancient
critics and most modern have seized upon this characteristic and
drawn from it the generalizations that, had he lived longer, he
might have been a second Nero, and that his liberality drained the
Treasury. Both seem ill-founded: by his dismissal of Berenice
and the frugality of his private life he showed he could control
himself, and the evidence for wastefulness is not strong. True,
by one edict he confirmed all *beneficia* granted by his predecessors
to corporations or individuals; but it may be remarked that any
beneficia that had passed the critical scrutiny of Vespasian must
have been well-deserved, and that all succeeding emperors followed Titus' equitable practice. The fact too that he reclaimed
some of the *subsiciva* suggests that he had all his father's financial
shrewdness, and had no intention of wasting public money.

Loved though he was, he had to face the danger of conspiracies.
Yet we hear that he forgave all plotters, even promoted some.
It was partly a wise clemency, partly fatalistic composure. Himself
a soldier, knowing his family had come to power by the strangest
of destinies, he felt—like the Illyrian soldier-emperors of two
centuries later—that 'empire was a gift of Fate!'[2] But against his
own brother this could not avail him, though he remonstrated
with him with tears. Whether Domitian assisted him out of life,
as various traditions assert, cannot be told, but he certainly did
not lack the will to do so. Titus was attacked by a fever and died
in his father's country-house at Reate on September 13, 81. His
death was greeted by a spontaneous outburst of mourning and
affection, such as were manifested for few rulers, and his deification naturally followed. One discordant note alone sounds through
the chorus of praise and that was from the Jews, who, hating the
destroyer of their Temple, ascribed to him an agonizing end; to
the rest of the world he was Divus Titus, undeniably to be
reckoned among the good rulers that Rome had enjoyed.

[1] Pliny, *Ep.* vi, 16, 9.　　　[2] Aurelius Victor, *Caes.* x, 4.

V. DOMITIAN: THE COURT AND THE ARISTOCRACY

The death of Titus left no doubt as to his successor, and Domitian galloped away from his death-bed to be acclaimed as *Imperator* by the Praetorians that very day (13 September, 81). The Senate made no difficulty about conferring upon him all the usual powers: from September 14 Domitian counted his years of tribunician power, and by the end of the autumn he had also accepted the titles of Pontifex Maximus and Pater Patriae, and had conferred upon his wife Domitia the title of Augusta.

He was a man of very different stamp from his brother. Born in 51, he had lived through days when his father was out of favour at court and so had known poverty and neglect: there is nothing to show that he had received a good education, and throughout his reign he was content to let others draft his letters, speeches and edicts. In the critical autumn of 69 he had been besieged upon the Capitol, and had only escaped by disguising himself as a follower of Isis. Then, for a few months before the return of his father, as representative of the ruling house he had suddenly enjoyed power: he used it to the full, issuing commissions and making appointments so widely that Vespasian said it was a mercy that his son did not send a successor to him. But with the advent of his father things altered: though he rode behind the chariot of Vespasian and Titus on their triumph, though he was allowed to hold the consulship seven times, though he was given the titles 'Princeps Juventutis' and Caesar and was plainly destined for succession some day, that day was to be far off. Vespasian refused all his petitions to be sent campaigning: he gave him no share in tribunician power nor in real responsibility. Domitian retired and turned to the consolations of poetry: his enthusiasm was probably genuine enough—throughout his whole life Minerva was his patroness and things Greek his passion—but there is nothing beyond the flattery of his dependents to suggest that he achieved greatness in literature, and we need not regret the disappearance of his poem on Titus' Jewish War or of his tract on The Care of the Hair[1]. Minerva was, after all, goddess of other things besides Literature, and what Domitian wanted most was glory in war and a controlling hand in administration. Power and consciousness of power—things for which he had longed—were his at last, and he meant to use them to the full.

---

[1] For his poetry see Pliny, *N.H. praef.* 5, and Quintilian, *Inst. Orat.* x, 1, 91.

It will be convenient to relate briefly affairs at Rome and in the court-circle down to the time of his assassination, and then to consider his administrative and legislative record. But at the outset the reader must be warned that the study of his reign is hedged about with difficulties. The epigraphic evidence is scanty, and contemporary literary sources, especially the poets, mostly sustain a fortissimo of adulation. In notable contrast those who survived him, such as Pliny and Tacitus, give full vent to their loathing. The short Life of Domitian by Suetonius, though it embodies material of great value and maintains a more balanced tone than might be expected, has little hint of chronology and is marred by some unaccountable omissions. Book LXVII of Dio Cassius, which is mainly preserved in Xiphilinus, affords a chronological framework, it is true, but, apart from that, little more than the conventional tradition. Generally speaking this tradition looked upon him as but one more instance of a ruler ruined by power, and placed him in the class of Gaius or Nero.

Much of this is exaggerated, yet a large residuum of truth remains. Domitian was in some ways unfortunate. His claim to rule rested not on the rescue of an empire from ruin or on any overwhelming prestige, but simply on the fact that he was a son of the divine Vespasian. But twelve years was not enough to root the Flavian dynasty deep, and Divus Vespasianus could not bequeath to his descendants the same veneration as Divus Augustus. If Domitian had possessed a less autocratic temper or a more genial personality he might have secured power for his family. But though endowed with a fair share of the ability and shrewdness of his father he lacked the good humour that can render efficiency palatable. A student of astrology, given to spending long hours in solitude, grim and ironic, treating with contempt even those he invited to his table, a lover of austere legalism and archaic correctness, his constant reading was the records of Tiberius' reign, and the two men had much in common. But whereas hesitation and uncertainty led Tiberius on into false positions, Domitian knew his own mind from the start; what fills Tacitus and Pliny with horror is no occasional act of vengeance or outburst of passion, but the fact that Domitian's cruelty was calculated and deliberate, conceived and carried out in pursuit of a definite aim.

That aim was the unconcealed exaltation of the Princeps into a ruler pre-eminent over Senate, People and Army, and the consequent lowering of all to the grade of ministers and servants. Domitian held the consulship frequently: from 82 to 88 consecutively he was consul ordinarius, then in 90, 92 and 95. It might be merely the continuation of the policy of his father and brother, but it resulted in his holding the office seventeen times, more often than any *princeps* before. But the consulship alone did not give him all the prestige he sought. In the early years of his reign disturbances on the middle Rhine offered him the chance of that military fame and those victories for which he longed so ardently (p. 162). But while detractors belittled his conquests and mocked at his victories as sham, he used them eagerly to enhance his eminence still further. After his triumph in late 83 he assumed the cognomen Germanicus, and issued coins announcing it and proclaiming his conquest of Germany[1]; henceforth he wore the dress of a *triumphator* even in the Senate-House, and was attended by twenty-four lictors. On the model of his father he was given *censoria potestas*, apparently early in 85, but instead of resigning after eighteen months he continued in the exercise of power with the title of *censor perpetuus*[2], and thus possessed permanently absolute and undisguised control over the personnel of the Senate, a control which he did not hesitate to use. The commemoration of his victories was to pass into the calendar, for September and October were renamed Germanicus and Domitianus[3]; these titles were certainly used during his reign, though they did not outlast his death.

In private affairs he showed himself equally autocratic. He had destined his cousin T. Flavius Sabinus as his partner for the consulship of 82; at the election in 81, the herald, by an unlucky slip, announced him not as consul but as Imperator. At the moment Domitian took no action, but he would not endure even the suspicion of an equal, and before the end of 84 he had got rid of Sabinus, on an unknown charge[4]. It was rumoured that his wife Domitia had a lover in Paris, the dancer; Domitian killed

[1] Suetonius, *Dom.* 13, 3. Dessau 1997 shows that the cognomen Germanicus had been taken by 3 September, 84. For coins of 84 and 85 with legends GERMANICUS and of 85 with GERMANIA CAPTA see Mattingly-Sydenham, *op. cit.* II, p. 159 *sq.* and p. 186.

[2] The title of CENSOR PERPETUUS on coins of late 85, Mattingly-Sydenham, *op. cit.* II, p. 161 *sq.*

[3] No certain instance of the use occurs till A.D. 87–8, *P. Genav. Lat.* I, Recto II. c, 9.

[4] Perhaps on the ground of conspiracy; if so, the senators whose exile Jerome records in 83–4 may have been suspected accomplices, and perhaps Xiphilinus 219, 8 is a muddled recollection of this. Sabinus' death involved the disgrace and banishment of his friend and counsellor, Dio of Prusa: Dio Chrys. *Or.* XIII, 1.

him and divorced Domitia, probably in 83. In her place he now took the widow of Sabinus, his own niece, Julia, though not as wife but as mistress[1]; but it would seem that about a year later he took back his divorced wife, and the two women lived together with him in the palace.

Further ostentation of his power and position followed. The suppression in 86 of a revolt of the Nasamones in Africa afforded him the opportunity of declaring to the Senate 'I have ended the existence of the Nasamones,' and from now onwards courtiers and poets greeted him as 'Master and God'; it is just possible that he used this style himself (p. 41). More display came when, in this same year he instituted four-yearly games, upon the Greek model, in honour of Capitoline Juppiter; Rome was to have its Olympian games, with contests in literature, in chariot-racing, and in athletics. Over them he himself presided, in Greek dress, wearing a golden crown with medallions of Juppiter, Juno, and Minerva embossed upon it, while his fellow-judges wore crowns upon which among these gods his own effigy appeared as well[2]. Into the Quinquatria, the festival sacred to Minerva, he also introduced literary contests, and he celebrated these yearly at his villa upon the Alban Mount (p. 34). By these foundations he honoured the two deities, Juppiter and Minerva, whom he most respected, and in whose honour he had built temples in Rome, and he perhaps hoped to impose something of Greek refinement upon the Roman populace. But by this, like Nero, he simply alienated the aristocracy; we have only to read Pliny's approval of the abolition of similar games at Vienna in Gaul[3], to appreciate how deep would be the feeling against such practices being introduced into the capital.

Nor was the situation abroad favourable. In 84 or 85 Agricola was recalled, wisely, in view of events in the North-East, but a source of discontent to those who shared Agricola's views: in 86 the newly-consolidated Dacian kingdom inflicted a crushing blow upon a Roman army (see p. 170 sq.), which the boasted annihilation of the Nasamones could hardly offset. Dissatisfaction at last began to issue in plots against this second Nero; on September 22 in 87 the Arval Brethren are found sacrificing 'ob detecta scelera nefariorum[4].' It was probably the first serious danger Domitian had encountered, and trials may have lasted

---

[1] For the date of these occurrences see J. Janssen, *C. Suetoni Tranquilli Vita Domitiani*, p. 54 *sq.* (on c. 10, 2).

[2] Suetonius, *Dom.* 4, 4.   [3] Pliny, *Ep.* IV, 22.

[4] *C.I.L.* VI, p. 515, l. 61.

some time[1], but we have no details of any plot and cannot profitably conjecture the names of the conspirators.

October of the year 88 witnessed the holding of Ludi Saeculares, by which Domitian not only celebrated the passing of one more *saeculum* in Rome's long history, but perhaps intended to impress on men's minds the coming of a new and glorious Flavian Age. His coinage shows how great a stress he laid upon the celebration, and it is even possible that he deliberately anticipated the date—for one hundred and ten years after the Augustan celebration would have brought them to 93—because he was anxious to give the Roman People at this time a spectacle at once solemn and heartening: if not, his mathematicians were badly out in their reckoning. But if Domitian dreamed that the celebration would have an edifying effect on the Empire he was to have a rough awakening. Scarcely were they over when alarming news reached the capital: L. Antonius Saturninus, the legate of Upper Germany, had been acclaimed as *Imperator* by the legions at Moguntiacum and was in open revolt (p. 172). The danger was urgent: Saturninus had been in correspondence with others, he had summoned barbarian tribes to assist him, it might be the beginning of a movement such as had overthrown Nero, and in the depth of winter (mid-January, 89) Domitian hastened northwards.

But before he had got far the danger had collapsed, thanks to the promptitude and loyalty of L. Appius Maximus Norbanus, the legate of Lower Germany, and by the end of January the Senate was already proclaiming fervent thanksgivings and vows for the safe return of the Princeps[2]. But Domitian did not return: he continued his march to Moguntiacum and there made inquisition. Though Maximus, with a courage that does him credit, had burned Saturninus' correspondence, some of Saturninus' accomplices were known and more were suspected; there were executions, the extremest tortures were used to extract confession or information, and of those found guilty two alone obtained pardon. Saturninus' head was sent to Rome to be exhibited on the Rostra, and Domitian soon after turned eastwards to deal with an invasion of the Iazyges (p. 176).

It had been a great deliverance: in Rome itself the usual vows were made and poets execrated the dead traitor. A less usual

[1] The notice in Jerome under the eighth year of Domitian, 88/9, *plurimos nobilium in exilium mittit atque occidit* may refer to a continuation of these trials, or, more likely, it records the results of the suppression of Saturninus.

[2] The dates are known from the vows of the Arval Brethren, *C.I.L.* VI, p. 517.

memorial arose in the South of Italy, where a citizen of Beneventum dedicated in his native town a temple to Isis, 'the great
mistress of Beneventum,' with obelisks in front of it which
Domitian had ordered to be fetched from Egypt; the whole
temple, apparently, was an *ex voto* for the safety and return of the
Emperor[1]. But neither Italian deities nor foreign goddesses could
relieve his suspicious mind, for the conspiracy of Saturninus had
given him a shock from which he never recovered. From 89 his
rule became more tyrannical, since he saw conspirators and rivals
around him everywhere. He began to listen favourably to *delatores*
and to those who played upon his fears, and once an emperor was
willing to listen there were not lacking men to inform. Chief
among these were M'. Aquilius Regulus, A. Didius Gallus
Fabricius Veiento, and the blind L. Valerius Catullus Messallinus,
but there were others whose names have been handed down to
infamy, a rhetorician Pompeius, a dancer Latinus, and a so-called
'philosopher' Seras.

Aided by these creatures Domitian struck blow after blow
against those who seemed for any reason formidable. By an edict
in 89 he banished philosophers and astrologers from Rome[2], and
during the next years he steadily eliminated the objects of his
fear or resentment. He dared not trust influential generals or
governors: C. Vettulenus Civica Cerialis, a proconsul of Asia, was
charged with conspiracy and executed even during his tenure of
office, probably in 90[3], and a governor of Britain, Sallustius
Lucullus, was put to death for allowing a new kind of lance to
be named after him instead of after the Emperor[4]. Men of
ability and reputation withdrew from public life; Sextus Julius

[1] O. Marucchi in *Not. degli Scavi*, 1904, p. 118; A. Erman in *Röm.
Mitt.* VIII, 1893, p. 210 and in *Zeits. f. ägypt. Sprache und Altertumskunde*,
XXXIV, 1896, p. 149.

[2] But the mention of the 'philosopher' Seras among the informers, and
the approval Domitian officially bestowed on Flavius Archippus, another
'philosopher' who was not above acting as *delator* (see Pliny, *Ep.* x, 58 [66]
and 81 [85]), suggests that Domitian had no objection to 'philosophers'
who fell in with his views, only to those who preached sedition. In much
the same way Statius or Martial can with impunity praise Cato, whereas a
suspect could not. If only the exact words of the enactment had been preserved our information on the interpretation to be put on 'philosophers'
would be far better.

[3] It was shortly before Agricola's turn to draw lots for Asia and Africa
(Tacitus, *Agric.* 42), and at this time proconsulship normally came about fifteen years after consulship (see R. Heberdey in *Jahreshefte*, VIII, 1905, p. 236).

[4] Suetonius, *Dom.* 10. The date may be any year between 85 and 96;
that adopted here seems most likely to the present writer.

Frontinus went unemployed, C. Julius Cornutus Tertullus lived in retirement, Herennius Senecio held no post after the quaestorship; Agricola, who had been living unobtrusively at Rome since his return from Britain, was not allowed to proceed to the governorship of Syria, which Domitian had hinted should be his, and did not dare let his name go forward for the province of Asia[1]. Seventy years experience of *maiestas* had supplied informers with a stock of useful precedents and had taught them how easily trivial matters could be worked into serious accusations, but some of the charges are so vaguely recorded that it is impossible to give any detailed account.

The fate of Mettius Pompusianus is typical: he was rumoured to have an imperial horoscope, and to possess a map of the whole empire; he had made from Livy a collection of speeches by kings and generals, and had given some of his slaves hated names like Mago or Hannibal. The fatuity of such charges is reminiscent of those brought in the earliest years of Tiberius (vol. x, p. 628), but there was no Tiberius presiding to dismiss them with scorn; instead, Pompusianus was driven into exile on Corsica, and in 91 he was executed. His disgrace appears to have involved other members of his clan, for M. Mettius Rufus, who had been appointed Prefect of Egypt in 89, disappears from records at this date and his name has been erased on some documents, while his son Mettius Modestus, who had dared to revile the notorious informer Regulus, was sent into exile[2]. This same year too, a distinguished noble, M'. Acilius Glabrio, was first compelled to fight in the arena at Domitian's Alban villa, and when he emerged successful, was exiled; a rhetorician called Maternus was executed for reciting an exercise against tyranny[3], and we ought probably to assign to this same period the execution of another rhetorician, Hermogenes of Tarsus, who was killed for lampoons against the Emperor, while his slave-copyists were crucified. Even provincials were not safe, for it is nearly certain that the trial and

[1] Tacitus, *Agric.* 40 and 42. Domitian probably sent to Syria P. Valerius Patruinus (*Ann. épig.* 1927, no. 44): possibly P. Calvisius Ruso L. Julius Frontinus was the proconsul chosen for Asia (H. Dessau in *J.R.S.* III, 1913, p. 301).

[2] The connection is not certain but seems highly probable; see A. Stein, *Die römische Ritterstand*, pp. 337 *sqq.* Pliny, *Ep.* I, 5, 6, shows that Mettius Modestus had been exiled before the trial of Arulenus Rusticus.

[3] Dio LXVII, 12. He may be one with Curiatius Maternus, a speaker in the *Dialogus de claris oratoribus*, where the discussion recorded is presumed to have taken place late in Vespasian's reign. A man who had written tragedies on themes such as Cato and Domitius could easily be accused.

execution, on an unknown charge, of the wealthy Athenian Hipparchus, the grandfather of Herodes Atticus, falls within these years[1]. His vast landed estates were confiscated, and though some funds may have escaped, his property must have meant a considerable accession to the imperial chest.

These cases can be dated with some approach to certainty: there remain other victims about whom little is known beyond the name, for though the nature of the charge is sometimes indicated the date is quite obscure. To have been a friend of the Emperor was no protection: M. Arrecinus Clemens had been for a brief space Prefect of the Praetorians to Vespasian (p. 7, n. 1), yet though he was then a favourite of Domitian, he was one of those condemned to death. C. Julius Bassus, another friend, suffered relegation and was not restored till after Domitian's fall. Salvidienus Orfitus was first exiled on a charge of conspiracy and then put to death, while L. Salvius Otho Cocceianus was executed because he had celebrated the birthday of his uncle, Otho, as a day of rejoicing.

Such is a part of that melancholy roll of sufferers, of which a full list was afterwards drawn up by various writers. But the effects of this policy of terrorism had so far been limited in range. The city-populace had its shows and games and was supplied with food, and Domitian had been able to gratify it by the sight of two triumphs in November 89 (p. 175). The legionaries, too, were satisfied by the victories gained and by the re-assertion of Roman supremacy in war, and their loyalty was confirmed by the recent rise in pay, one-third as much again, which their Imperator had awarded them, and by the generous grants of immunity from various taxes and burdens which veterans received[2]. The persecution fell mainly upon the Senatorial and upper classes, and how they felt is well shown by Pliny's account of his visit to Q. Corellius Rufus[3]. Rufus had been legate of Upper Germany in 82, and was doubtless a fair sample of the administrative class; in old age and retirement, though racked by pain, he clung to life, 'so that I can survive that brigand for one day at least.'

Yet in fairness to Domitian it should be recorded that his administration, as will be seen later (p. 39), was keen and

[1] See P. Graindor, *Un milliardaire antique*, pp. 12–17. He is perhaps the man recorded in Dio Chrys. *Or.* VII, 11 *sq.*

[2] For an example see a papyrus in Mitteis-Wilcken, *Grundzüge und Chrest.* I, ii, no. 463: an improved text is offered by F. Schehl in *Aegyptus*, XIII, 1933, p. 136. The date of this is between Sept. 88 and Sept. 89, and must fall after the suppression of Saturninus.

[3] Pliny, *Ep.* I, 12.

efficient; evil he may have been, but his servants were acknowledged to be good[1], and many of the men who were to hold
distinguished positions under Trajan served their apprenticeship
under Domitian. Tacitus and the younger Pliny are famous
examples; but there were many others, men who though they
might disapprove of the reigning *princeps* yet realized the necessity of a Principate. There is nothing to confirm the suggestions
of Domitian's enemies that he was ruled by favourites or freedmen: his secretaries, Claudius, Epaphroditus, and Abascantus,
were kept in their place and did not dominate his councils[2]. Nor
were the informers secure; though these later prosecutions stand
in singular contrast to the principle that Domitian had enunciated
at first—'a *princeps* who does not punish informers encourages
them'—he was not under their thumb; Veiento, Regulus and
Mettius Carus survived his reign, but Arrecinus Clemens and
Baebius Massa, who had been informers, were punished. It would
be truer to say that Domitian's anti-Senatorial policy brought him,
just as it had brought Nero, into conflict with opposition; against
that opposition he might rely on informers, or use soldiers as
agents-provocateurs (p. 41), but all whom he used were alike his
servants, and he was alone responsible for his policy.

It was upon the remnants of the Republican opposition that
the next blow fell. Though during the second half of 92 Domitian
had been absent from Rome, superintending the campaigns against
the Suebi and Sarmatae (p. 176 *sq.*), by January of 93 he had returned. But no action was taken immediately: he waited till after
the death of Agricola (23 August, 93) and then in the winter of
93 and during 94 he launched his attack. The first victim was
apparently the younger Helvidius Priscus, son of the revolutionary (p. 7). Though a consular he was living in retirement,
but he had written a farce about Paris and Oenone which Domitian
interpreted as a satire upon his own relations to his wife. Whatever
the charges preferred—whether treasonable libel or abstention
from duties—the matter was represented as urgent and dangerous,
and troops lined the Senate-House: his accuser Publicius Certus,
a man of praetorian rank, obtained his condemnation and actually
helped to drag the condemned man away[3]. The next victim was
Junius Arulenus Rusticus, who had published a panegyric upon

---

[1] S.H.A. *Alex. Sev.* 65. See below, p. 41.
[2] Claudius had probably succeeded Pallas in the post of *a rationibus* in 55;
under Domitian he fell into disfavour and was exiled, Statius, *Silv.* III,
154 *sqq.* and Martial VI, 83; for the fate of Epaphroditus see p. 32.
[3] It was this action, an ex-praetor laying hands upon an ex-consul, which
aroused such horror; Pliny, *Ep.* IX, 13, 2 and Tacitus, *Agric.* 45.

Thrasea Paetus; for this he was condemned and executed, and his book, like that of Cremutius Cordus (vol. x, p. 630), was ordered to be burnt. With these two the destiny of a third man, Herennius Senecio, was too closely linked for him to escape; he had not held any official post after the quaestorship, but he had written a Life of the elder Helvidius Priscus at the request of his widow Fannia and he was an enemy of Regulus; Mettius Carus acted as prosecutor, he was condemned and executed, and his book banned. Though these three alone were killed, heavy punishment fell on their relatives and members of their circle: Fannia, for instigating Senecio to write the life of her husband, had her estates confiscated and suffered relegation, as did her mother the aged Arria (widow of Thrasea Paetus), together with another member of the group, Verulana Gratilla, and the brother of Rusticus, Junius Mauricus. Finally, by a *senatus consultum* in 95[1], Domitian drove all philosophers not only from Rome but from Italy, and so teachers and preachers such as Artemidorus (the son-in-law of Musonius), or Epictetus, left Italy to wander or to find a home elsewhere.

On the 1st of January, 95, Statius, with the bold vision vouchsafed to minor poets, could discern his emperor 'rising with the new sun, among the mighty stars, yet more brilliant than them and greater than the early dawn-star[2].' Domitian might well have been satisfied as he surveyed the world beneath his feet: there was peace in the Empire, the Dacian king had acknowledged his overlordship and sent his brother Diegis to accept the diadem from his hands (p. 176), the temples were full of statues of him in gold and silver dedicated by his admirers[3], and he had so terrorized the Senators that he had them subservient to his will whenever he appeared in the Senate-House. One more group yet remained to stir his suspicions, and this group involved his own family. Flavius Clemens, a cousin of Domitian, was married to the Emperor's niece, Domitilla; he was an easy-going, slothful creature who had so far kept in favour; indeed Domitian, despairing of an heir of his own, about the year 90 had proclaimed two of their children as his successors, had given them the names of Vespasian and Domitian, and had appointed Quintilian to be their tutor[4]. In 95 Clemens was *consul ordinarius* for some four

---

[1] For the date here adopted see W. Otto, *Sitz. bay. Akad.* 1919, no. 10 (esp. pp. 43–54) and 1923, no. 4. The *senatus consultum* is referred to by Gellius, *N.A.* xv, 11, 4.

[2] Statius, *Silv.* iv, 1, 3 *sqq.*   [3] Pliny, *Pan.* 52, 3 and 4.

[4] For the date see Janssen, *op. cit.* p. 72.

months, but scarcely had he resigned his office when, with his wife and with several others, he was called upon to answer an accusation of neglect of the State religion (*atheotes*). It may be that this accusation was due to their being favourers of Jewish or Christian rites (p. 42), but whatever the precise implications attaching to the word *atheotes*, it proved fatal to Clemens and to the exiled Acilius Glabrio, for both were executed; Domitilla was spared but sent into exile. There may have been others involved but these are the only names that have come down to us.

Unimportant though Clemens was, his murder sealed the fate of his murderer; if a creature 'contemptissimae inertiae' could be so treated, who was safe from attack? Not the Praetorian Prefects, for Domitian put them on trial even while they were in office, so that T. Petronius Secundus, the Prefect of Egypt, was summoned early in the year 96 to take up the vacant post with a certain Norbanus[1]. Not the palace freedmen, for the Emperor, with senseless cruelty, ordered the execution of his *a libellis* Epaphroditus, because some twenty-seven years before he had helped Nero to commit suicide. Flattery and abasement before the 'Master and God' seemed the only way of escape[2]; even moderate men were not immune from suspicion, for—as was subsequently discovered—Domitian had received and filed informations against both Pliny and Nerva. The suspense and dread of the last few months must have been appalling, and it could be ended only by Domitian's death. For their common safety all parties, Domitia herself, the two new Praetorian Prefects, Entellus the successor of Epaphroditus, Parthenius the chamberlain, and various minor officials of the palace, joined in a plot. But first they must find another *princeps*, for there must be no civil war and no rival claimants, and so they approached Cocceius Nerva, an elderly, amiable and distinguished jurist of some literary pretensions (p. 188 *sq.*). His natural fears of a trap were overcome; he consented and the plot could proceed.

It was by now September. The conspirators secured the instrument they needed in a freedman Stephanus. He had been a procurator of Domitilla and had her exile to avenge; more, he had been accused of misappropriating money and could hope for little mercy if Domitian heard his case. Tradition speaks of omens

[1] Petronius appears to have been in Egypt till April of 96 (J. Lesquier, *L'armée romaine d'Égypte*, p. 512); his appointment, Dio LXVII, 15.

[2] Dio LXVII, 13 mentions a certain Juventius Celsus (presumably the Juventius Celsus of Pliny, *Ep.* VI, 5, 4), who was accused of conspiracy and only escaped by worshipping Domitian.

and of warnings enough to put the dullest on their guard: perhaps
Domitian had some intimation of his peril. There was no time
to lose, and on September 16 Stephanus attacked him, under the
pretence of handing him a paper. Into the details of the last
scene and the ferocious joy of the narrators there is no need to
enter; the tyrant was killed, Stephanus was dispatched by those
who rushed to help their master, the other and more prudent
conspirators escaped unscathed for the moment, and Nerva was
proclaimed *princeps* that very day. Domitian's body was burned
privately by his nurse, Phyllis, who laid the ashes in the temple
of the Gens Flavia that he himself had built. Already the Senate
was condemning his memory, and men were pulling down his
statues; she mingled the ashes with those of his niece, Julia,
Titus' daughter, so that they might rest undisturbed.

VI. ADMINISTRATION AND LEGISLATION

Thus far we have seen Domitian mainly in his relations with
the Senatorial class: they regarded him, with reason, as a persecutor and their description of him as a tyrant has prevailed.
There is, however, another side to consider, how he administered
the Empire.

In the capital his first task was to feed the populace and keep
it contented, and this he achieved. Three times he distributed
congiaria, amounting in all to 225 denarii a head, the last one
apparently in 93; he also gave games, wild-beast hunts, races and
a mimic naval battle, and for these purposes he erected two schools
for gladiators, and constructed a *naumachia* by the Tiber. But
he was eager to offer the people more refined amusements than
these; the Capitoline *Agon* which he founded included contests
(in the Greek manner) not only in sport but in literature, and
for these he built a Stadium and an Odeum in the Campus
Martius. Building suited well his taste for display and magnificence; besides, the death of Titus and the fire of the year 80
had left much work unfinished and much to repair and reconstruct. In consequence the achievement of his principate in
building was solid and splendid. He restored the Saepta, rebuilt
the temples of Sarapis and of Isis (in front of which he placed
obelisks specially brought from Egypt[1]), the Pantheon, and the
Baths of Agrippa, and the Porticus Octaviae (with its libraries),
all of which had been damaged; to fill the libraries he sought for
books far and wide, even sending scribes to Alexandria to copy

[1] See O. Marucchi in *Bull. Com. Arch.* XLV, 1918, p. 103.

rare ones. In addition to work on the Colosseum (p. 778 *sq.*) he completed the Baths that Titus had begun and his temple to Vespasian, which now became the temple of the deified Vespasian and the deified Titus, and he also dedicated in the Campus Martius a colonnade, the Divorum Porticus, containing two shrines to their memory. Between the Forum Augusti and the new Forum Pacis, he swept away the untidy Argiletum and constructed a Forum of his own, which was later appropriated by Nerva (p. 781). On the Quirinal he built a temple to the Gens Flavia, and on the Capitol, from which he had escaped in 69, disguised and in humiliation, he erected in gratitude a huge temple to 'Juppiter the Guardian' with an image of the god holding him in his lap[1]. Most splendid of all was the restored temple of Juppiter Optimus Maximus on the Capitol, which with its columns of Pentelic marble, its doors plated with gold, and its gilded tiles, was one of the wonders of the world[2]. But Domitian was determined, like Nero, to be properly housed; in Rome the architect Rabirius spent eleven years refashioning the imperial palaces, and on the Alban Mount, in the early years of his reign, there arose a magnificent villa, with theatre and amphitheatre close by, overlooking the waters of the Alban Lake, upon which, in summer, the imperial barge could float in unbroken calm and silence[3]. Detractors complained that Rome was shaken by the weight of the lorry-loads that rumbled through the city and that vast sums were poured out on his private pleasure. Yet much of the money was not spent upon these or on display alone; apart from the temples, prosaic but useful work was certainly carried out by his engineers upon the water-system of Rome, and granaries for the storage of corn and spices and pepper were built. Still it cannot be denied that this huge programme of building was costly: the gold-work of the Capitoline Temple alone accounted for 12,000 talents, and during the twelve years between 81 and 93—for that year seems to mark the completion of the programme—enormous sums must have been expended.

On that important aspect of an emperor's policy, the financial, we have little accurate information though plenty of assertion. Domitian had no intention of doing things shabbily: his constant

[1] Tacitus, *Hist.* III, 74: Suetonius, *Dom.* 5. Coins with the legend JUPPITER CUSTOS were minted in 86 (Mattingly-Sydenham, *op. cit.* II, p. 194).

[2] Plutarch, *Publicola*, 15. Coins with the legend CAPIT. RESTIT. were struck in 82 (Mattingly-Sydenham, *op. cit.* II, p. 182).

[3] Pliny, *Pan.* 82. See, for the modern excavations, the articles by Lugli cited in the Bibliography.

instruction to his agents was 'ne quid sordide facerent.' But to add to the cost of buildings and shows, there were the increased pay of the soldiers and wars between 81 and 93 to finance, while no new sources of revenue had been tapped. Money must have been needed; whence did it come? To Pliny the Younger, writing in the reaction that followed Domitian's death, Domitian was a monster of rapacity, whose lavish grants to the populace were drawn from murder and confiscation. Suetonius, more detached and writing a little later, notes a deterioration in Domitian's character and is inclined to explain it by the hypothesis that 'contrary to his natural disposition lack of funds made him predatory and fear made him cruel,' and this explanation seems more reasonable.

From the start, however, he had all his father's financial shrewdness. Though in Italy and Rome he was lenient enough at first (p. 38), elsewhere taxes were gathered in strictly. The Nasamones in Africa are said to have revolted because of the exactions of the collectors, and the poll-tax upon Jews was rigorously enforced, giving rise to many malicious prosecutions[1]. Other sums, too, went to enrich the Imperial chest: Frontinus declares that Domitian appropriated to it the income that accrued from the aqueducts[2]; Pliny avers that any means was employed to rake money into the Fiscus—prosecutions under obsolescent laws (such as the Lex Voconia of 168 b.c.), trials for *maiestas* with subsequent confiscations, the encouragement of slaves to lay information against their masters, and so on[3]. On one point we can certainly trace a definite hardening, for those condemned to *relegatio* no longer retained their property but forfeited it to the Fiscus[4]. Apart from that the evidence is not overwhelming, for in the last years of the reign, when prosecutions followed each other fast, most of Domitian's building programme had been carried out, the wars in the North were over, and expenses should therefore have fallen[5]. It may well be that under Domitian the process of centralizing the finances of the Empire initiated by Claudius (vol. x, p. 687) was being carried still further, but we must not overlook the possibility that these trials and confiscations were not the result of an economic need, but were rather part

---

[1] Dio LXVII, 4, 6; Suetonius, *Dom.* 12, 2. Hence the propaganda-legend on Nerva's coins FISCI JUDAICI CALUMNIA SUBLATA (p. 191).

[2] Frontinus, *de aquaeductibus*, 118.

[3] Pliny, *Pan.* 42. Yet in the one recorded instance where a slave accused his master, Domitian punished him, Josephus, *Vita* [76], 429.

[4] *Dig.* XLVIII, 22, 1.　　　　[5] R. Syme in *J.R.S.* xx, 1930, pp. 65–70.

of a definite political purpose, that purpose being the complete crippling, financial and moral, of the aristocratic opposition. In the present state of the evidence, however, it would be unwise to pronounce definitely, for we have no means of judging the Emperor's intentions: we can only view, through the glass of a hostile tradition, his actions. In fairness to Domitian it must be noted that, however great the financial stringency, he did not take the fatally easy step (that Nero had taken and that Trajan was to take) of debasing the coinage; indeed recent researches suggest that he raised it somewhat above the Neronian level[1].

But in spite of all that Domitian spent on pleasing the populace he was never its servant, like Nero; he would allow it spectacles and shows, but he disapproved of mimes and farces and forbade actors to appear in public. It was a step that Tiberius would have applauded (vol. x, p. 648), and it is amusing to watch the efforts Pliny makes to minimize a measure of which he approved but which a tyrant had ordained[2]. It well illustrates the rigorous and reformatory side of his character, and leads to a consideration of Domitian's own legislation and of his attitude towards jurisdiction. An archaic severity pervades much of it, whether it be the revival of half-forgotten laws or the enactment of new ones. One salutary enactment came early, a veto on the practice of castration, and he followed this up later by restrictions on child-prostitution and other such practices[3]. He enforced the provisions of the Lex Scantinia, which imposed a fine upon those found guilty of un-natural vice, and he put some restrictions upon prostitutes: they were deprived of the right to ride in a litter, and were not allowed to accept legacies or inheritances, in effect were reduced to the status of freedwomen[4]. It was an easy and grateful task for his enemies to retort that he himself was tainted by most of the vices that he burned to repress, but even a glance at the poems of Martial and Juvenal suggests that Rome badly needed such legislation, and much of it was re-enacted by succeeding emperors.

Some phrases in contemporary poets imply that he enforced

[1] G. Mickwitz in *Arctos*, III, 1933/34, p. 1.
[2] Pliny, *Pan.* 46.
[3] Suetonius, *Dom.* 7; Dio LXVII, 2, 3; Ammian. Marc. XVIII, 4, 5. Possibly it was a reform of his censorship, Statius, *Silv.* IV, 3, 13; for later measures see Martial IX, 5 (6) and 7 (8).
[4] Suetonius, *Dom.* 12 and 8, 3. It may be noted that in the Coptos tariff-table (*O.G.I.S.* 674), belonging to his reign, the landing-tax for prostitutes is extremely high, 120 drachmae.

the provisions of the Lex Julia de adulteriis[1], and where his
religious sense was shocked as well he showed himself implacable.
A case of adultery by Vestal Virgins had been overlooked by his
more charitable father and brother, but in 83 when three Vestals
were found guilty, their lovers were relegated and they themselves
merely allowed to choose their mode of death. Seven years later
he had grown austerer still: the Chief Vestal, Cornelia, was
guilty; her lovers (save one, Valerius Licinianus) were beaten to
death with rods, and Cornelia was condemned to be buried alive.
It was, indeed, the traditional punishment, but the infliction of
it sent a thrill of horror through the City, and men whispered
that Domitian had merely gratified his cruelty[2].

As an upholder of the hierarchical order of society he tried to
discourage over-indulgence to slaves and easy manumission; thus
he warned the court of the *recuperatores* that they must not grant
to a claimant the free status to which he pretended, except on
convincing proof, and he went so far as to restore to his former
master an escaped slave who had actually risen to centurion's rank.
Two decisions of his, preserved in the *Digest*, show a harshness
of temper typical of him and quite out of touch with the humaner
trend of the times; the first, a *senatus consultum*, ordained that if
a man could prove that there had been fraudulent or collusive
manumission of a slave, he could own that slave in future; the
second laid down that if a slave, on some charge, had been put in
chains awaiting trial, the usual pardons and remissions granted
by the Senate on days of public rejoicing should not apply to him;
he could not be loosed even though his master should offer bail,
and the trial must be carried through[3]. It was a measure that
wrung a protest from the equitable Papinian, yet it is likely
enough that throughout Domitian plumed himself on being a
supporter of the Augustan Roman tradition, and many of his
actions hark back to the first *princeps*. He paraded an anxiety
to uphold the dignity and status of the different orders. As in
Augustus' time, authors of lampoons against noted men and
women were severely punished and their writings burnt. A certain
Rustius Caepio had directed in his will that a sum of money
should be paid to senators as they entered the Curia; it was a prac-

---

[1] Statius, *Silv.* v, 2, 102; Martial vi, 2 and 7.

[2] Pliny, *Ep.* iv, 11; Suetonius, *Dom.* 8; Dio lxvii, 3 (though he does not
mention Cornelia).

[3] *Dig.* xl, 16, 1; xlviii, 3, 2, 1. What view Domitian took in the letters
he sent to a legate 'de agnoscendis liberis et restitutione natalium' (Pliny,
Ep. x, 72 [77]) or about *threptoi* (*ib.* 75 [79]) we do not know.

tice possible and frequent in small municipalities, but Domitian cancelled the order, as not befitting the dignity of the Senate of Rome. Herein he was undoubtedly right, as in his other provisions for public order and decency; to the Equites he again secured their coveted fourteen rows of seats in the theatre, and he insisted that Roman citizens must, on public occasions, wear the distinctive Roman dress, the toga.

At the beginning of his reign he displayed a lenity and generosity over money-matters which Suetonius candidly admits. There was to be none of the cheese-paring policy of his father; the Fiscus was full and there was no need to hunt out long-standing debts; those more than five years old were cancelled, and in future an informer must bring his charge within a year and was liable to exile if he failed to prove his charge. Malicious accusations, even though they might bring gain to the Fiscus, he severely discouraged. By constant attendance at the courts, like Tiberius or Claudius before him, he secured the impartial administration of justice against influence or bribery; indeed judges who took bribes found themselves degraded. He refused to accept a legacy if the testator had left children alive, and in his treatment of the problem of *subsiciva*, he showed the same liberal attitude[1]. To evict occupiers after long undisturbed possession, as his father and Titus had done, was extremely unfair; to leave things as they were would subject them to the vexatious attentions of informers. He took the wise and generous step of granting the *subsiciva* in freehold to the occupiers[2], and solved the problem for good.

A second incursion into agrarian matters was not so helpful. Like others in his time he was struck by the predominance of vine over wheat in Italy and elsewhere, and feared a possible shortage of corn supplies. His remedy was drastic; by an edict he forbade the planting of any more vines in Italy, while in the provinces existing vineyards were to be reduced by one half and the ground given over to wheat-growing[3]. Suetonius adds that he did not follow the edict up vigorously: it would certainly have had to face considerable opposition and possibly it was not introduced in some provinces at all, but it is thought[4] that in Northern

---

[1] Probably his notice was first attracted to the problem by a dispute between Falerii and Firmum which he settled in 82: Bruns, *Fontes*[7], 82.

[2] Suetonius, *Dom.* 9, 3: cf. *Corpus Agrimensorum Rom.* I, pp. 41, 97.

[3] Suetonius, *Dom.* 7, 2 and 14, 2; Statius, *Silv.* IV, 3, 11; Philostratus, *Vita Apoll.* VI, 42.

[4] M. Rostovtzeff, *Soc. and Econ. Hist.* p. 189 and p. 545 (more fully in Ital. ed. p. 237 *sq.*).

and Central Gaul and to a certain extent in the Danubian provinces it was put into effect.

About his administration of the provinces there is little that can
be affirmed, for evidence is singularly lacking, and it may be that
Nerva and Trajan have absorbed some of the credit due to him.
Following the condemnation of his memory many of his monuments were overthrown and mention of him erased, and this
makes knowledge difficult. Suetonius[1] records his deliberate
opinion that 'he gave such attention to controlling magistrates
in the City and governors in the provinces that they were never
more just or more moderate; since his death we have seen many
of them accused on every kind of charge.' In this strict control
of his helpers he resembled his model Tiberius. The only recorded
trial, however, is that of Baebius Massa, the proconsul of Baetica,
prosecuted by the whole province, which chose Pliny and Herennius Senecio as its advocates: Massa had been an informer, but
Domitian put no obstacles in the way, and in 93 he was duly
tried and condemned[2]. Similar was his treatment of an avaricious
aedile; he made the tribunes hale him before the court of the
Senate on a charge of extortion.

The regular routine work was conducted smoothly: in Italy
roads were mended and improved[3], and in the provinces, especially
in Asia Minor, the road-system was kept in a high state of efficiency[4]; the repairs recorded here show how all-important was
swift communication between the Danubian and the Eastern
armies. Over the whole Empire generally the work of romanization was going on steadily, and there is no need to note
Domitian's contribution in each province, for he was simply
carrying on the task left him by his father. As might be expected
from his disposition, he showed a marked sympathy for the cities
of Greece. He allowed Corinth to mint money again, he held
the office of Archon Eponymus at Athens, in 84 he undertook
to repair the temple of Apollo at Delphi, and in 93 he rebuilt
for Megalopolis at his own expense a colonnade that had been
burnt down[5]. Equally keen was his interest in the historic cities
of Greek Asia Minor, such as Rhodes and Ephesus; he apparently

---

[1] Suetonius, *Dom.* 8, 2.

[2] Pliny, *Ep.* III, 4, 4; VII, 33.

[3] Repairs on the Via Appia, Statius, *Silv.* IV, 3; Dio LXVII, 14 (*c.* A.D. 95):
the Via Latina, Statius, *Silv.* IV, 4, 60.

[4] *C.I.L.* III, 312, 318 and 14184[48]: *I.G.R.R.* IV, 1194 and 1598.

[5] Corinthian coinage, Head, *Hist. Num.*[2] p. 404; Athens, *I.G.* III, 461 A,
654; Delphi, Ditt.[3] 821 A and C; Megalopolis, *Ann. épig.* 1893, no. 128.

extended the boundaries of the temple of Ephesian Artemis, and in that city there stood his own temple with a colossal cult-statue[1]. Apart from one or two isolated dedications, as that from the *Koinon* of the Lycians or from Smyrna[2], little remains in the peninsula to record his principate. To the south-east, the little client-kingdom of Chalcis was absorbed into the province of Syria in the year 92, and the principality of Emesa suffered the same fate; Judaea remained quiet. In Egypt we find a canal being dug to connect the Nile with Alexandria, a few dedications and the tariff-table at Coptos, but that is all[3]. On many even of these monuments the abhorred name has been obliterated: others probably endured even worse treatment, flung down and shattered to pieces.

The personnel sent out to govern these provinces was good; many who afterwards attained high places under Trajan or Hadrian had already been employed by Domitian. To mention a few names—T. Avidius Quietus, P. Calvisius Ruso Julius Frontinus, C. Caristanius Fronto, Tacitus himself, and the two Asiatic senators, Tib. Julius Celsus Polemaeanus and C. Antius A. Julius Quadratus, all held commands or governorships in his reign[4]. Good fortune has preserved for us an admirable edict issued by one of his governors, L. Antistius Rusticus, who was legate of the enlarged province of Galatia-Cappadocia between 84 and 94. Owing to a severe winter and scarcity of corn the price of wheat had soared high in the city of Antioch-by-Pisidia, and in answer to a petition from its Senate Rusticus orders a general declaration of all grain in store to be made by all the inhabitants, who must be prepared (after making reasonable deductions) to sell the surplus at a price to be fixed by him. The price, 'as it is most unfair that men should make a profit from the hunger of their fellow-citizens,' is fixed at a little above the normal[5]. The only complaint that could justly be made was that Domitian gave some of the highest offices to knights and freedmen; thus he included

---

[1] Rhodes: *I.G.R.R.* IV, 1130; 1151; 1152; Ditt.³ 819. Ephesus: *Arch. Anz.* Beiblatt, 1933, col. 43, and 1931–2, cols. 58 *sqq.* A fragment of a letter to Chios, *I.G.R.R.* IV, 931. For cities called after Domitian see also Ptol. v, 7, 5, Head², p. 656, and Malalas, x, p. 266, 12.

[2] *I.G.R.R.* III, 548 and IV, 1393b.

[3] *I.G.R.R.* I, 1099, 1183; for dedications see 1138, 1243–4, and 1287–9.

[4] A convenient summary in Stech, *op. cit.*: Avidius Quietus, Ditt.³ 822, Caristanius Fronto, Dessau 9485, Calvisius Ruso, *J.R.S.* III, 1913, p. 301.

[5] See *J.R.S.* XIV, 1924, p. 180 (=*Ann. épig.* 1925, no. 126).

knights as well as senators in his *consilium*, he placed his Praetorian Prefect, Cornelius Fuscus, at the head of the legions in the Dacian War, and doubtless his emergency order to a procurator, C. Minicius Italus, to take charge of the province of Asia upon the death of a proconsul, caused scandal among the nobility[1]. But to that the answer is that most of these were energetic and trustworthy men, and that their choice was a concession to efficiency like the sending of the Greek-born Senators to positions of trust in the Eastern, though not in the Western, provinces. As his successors approved his choice of governors, so they continued in office his capable secretary Cn. Octavius Titinius Capito[2], who held the post of Latin secretary under both Nerva and Trajan.

A final topic remains, his deification. Both Suetonius and Dio assert that he styled himself 'Master and God' and liked to be so addressed[3]. Inscriptions, naturally enough, bear no trace of this, but the fact that in 89 Martial can speak of an 'edictum domini deique nostri,' and the scornful remarks of Pliny and Dio Chrysostom later leave no doubt that in the second half of his reign Domitian did accept a form of address which implied his divinity and mastership[4]. In fact he was moving, though with greater deliberation and more calculated policy, along the path that Gaius and Nero had already trodden. As god-monarch of the Roman realm, placed above all both in appearance and in fact[5], he needed no Senate to partner him but only ministers and servants; hence the opposition of the Senatorial order and its pitiless suppression.

Terrorism certainly flourished during the last years: even soldiers could be used as spies and *agents-provocateurs*. An interesting passage in Epictetus deals with the theme of how confidence begets confidence[6]: it proceeds—

That is how imprudent men are trapped by soldiers in Rome. A soldier in civilian dress comes and sits by you and begins by abusing Caesar, whereupon you, regarding the fact that he began the abuse as a sort of guarantee

---

[1] For the career of C. Minicius Italus see Dessau 1374.

[2] For Capito's career see Dessau 1448.

[3] Suetonius, *Dom.* 13, 2; Dio LXVII, 4, 7 (dated 85–6). The text here reproduces in a condensed form the argument of an article published by the writer in *Harv. Theol. Rev.* XXVIII, 1935, p. 5, especially pp. 32–5; it is not possible to give all the references here.

[4] Martial V, 8, 1, with which cf. X, 72, 3 (written after Domitian's death); Pliny, *Pan.* 2 and 52: Dio Chrys. *Or.* XLV, 1.

[5] A. Alföldi, *Röm. Mitt.* L, 1935, pp. 1 *sqq.* (esp. pp. 103 *sq.* and 128 *sq.*).

[6] Epictetus, *Diss.* IV, 13, 5.

of trustworthiness, say all that you yourself feel; the next moment you are bound and being led away.

Such a passage implies quite definitely that the masses as well as the nobles could fall victims on charges of treason. And Domitian's assertiveness seems to have introduced a new practice: for three generations men had been accustomed to take an oath by the genius of the Princeps, but always voluntarily and not as an official form; during his reign we find for the first time men swearing in public documents by the genius of the living Emperor, while those who wished to flatter him began to make sacrifices to his genius. It looks as though Domitian seized upon this voluntary action and turned it into a test of loyalty: a man suspected or accused might now save himself and prove his loyalty by offering sacrifice before the image of the *princeps*; if he refused he could then be charged with *atheotes* (p. 32). Dio Cassius notes the increasing number of trials for this offence in the last years[1], and this charge not only served possibly to get rid of obstinate and Republican-minded people, but it brought Domitian into conflict with the Jews and the Christians, neither of whom could acknowledge his divinity. An Emperor who demanded worship from his subjects might one day, like Gaius, demand it of the Jews too, and revoke existing edicts of tolerance. Jewish tradition relates that, about 95, the Senate was deliberating on a decree expelling all Jews from the boundaries of the Empire, and that a famous rabbi, Gamaliel II, with some friends, made a hurried winter journey to Rome to avert the threatened persecution[2]. Christian tradition too branded Domitian as a persecutor, who sought out the kindred of Jesus Christ and punished adherents of the new religion. It is curious, certainly, that Flavius Clemens was claimed as an adherent both by Jews and Christians, and that archaeological evidence suggests that both Domitilla and Acilius Glabrio, who were punished apparently for *atheotes*, were, if not Christian, at least favourably inclined towards the sect (p. 255). We cannot doubt that in the last three or four years both Jews and Christians, as well as Romans, had much to fear from an Emperor who could demand worship of himself as a proof of loyalty. But the dagger of Stephanus put an end to their fears as to the fears of others. The last ruler of the Flavian house perished without an adult

---

[1] Dio LXVII, 14, 1, 2.

[2] For the Jewish references see *Harv. Theol. Rev.* XXVIII, 1935, p. 34. Suetonius, *Dom.* 12, 2, may mean that Roman proselytes were liable to punishment, but the passage is very doubtful; Jews who had evaded payment of the tax were punished presumably for evasion and not for being Jews.

heir. For twenty-seven years the family had directed Roman affairs: it remains to estimate their achievement.

Martial, writing some years after Domitian was safely out of the way, dismisses his reign curtly as almost counterbalancing the good that Vespasian and Titus had done:

'Flavia gens quantum tibi tertius abstulit heres,
    Paene fuit tanti non habuisse duos'.

Yet his verdict merely shows that he had not lost the art of pleasing those in power: indeed, once 'liberty' was the order of the day some of the unlikeliest people invested in busts of Brutus and Cassius.[1] To agree with Martial would be utterly unjust. Domitian's cruelty to a certain class was real and terrible, but it was limited in its incidence: he paraded absolutism, giving to the imperial position the airs of divinity and the pomp of a despot; apart from that he did little to undo and much to forward the work of his father, and that work was a great one. To take defence first: for some two hundred years Rome had been accustomed to enlarge her territories by the conquest of the barbarian: now, in the background, forces were moving and gathering that would call a halt to Roman aggression and test her defences; in the two succeeding chapters the reader will see something of the strength of the peoples that lay outside, to the East and North of Rome's boundaries. The frontiers needed attention: the development of a more scientific defence-line, the provision of better communications, the disciplining of the legions under experienced commanders (of which an account will be found in the fourth chapter), were among the most enduring things that Vespasian and his sons did.

While the empire was protected against attacks from without the Flavians strove hard to improve its internal stability. Finance was set on a better basis, the administrative machine was made to run more smoothly, and an aristocracy of office, recruited from good provincial as well as Italian stock, was created to help control it. There were few famous Republican families left by the end of the first century, and still fewer believers in a Republican system: the Flavians established the Principate more firmly, and in the new aristocracy they and their successors found a class that was willing to co-operate with them. It is worth observing with what care Vespasian chose his officers: whether it was Petilius Cerialis, or Julius Agricola, or Q. Paconius Agrippinus, all had

_____

[1] As, for example, Cn. Octavius Titinius Capito; Pliny, *Ep.* I, 17.

had previous experience of the provinces to which they were sent. He was not afraid to employ men of Eastern origin to help administer the Eastern regions: Tib. Julius Celsus Polemaeanus and C. Antius Julius Quadratus were adlected by him to the Senate (p. 10), and afterwards held important posts. Traditional Roman sentiment may have felt some resentment at such appointments, especially at the loud fanfares with which they were celebrated in the East—'in all time', records one inscription, 'he was fifth from the whole of Asia to enter the Senate, and from Miletus and the rest of Ionia the first and only'[1]—but of the generous wisdom of such a policy we can feel no doubt. And Vespasian knew well how to reward good service with office and honours and was shrewd enough to point the contrast between his predecessors' treatment of such officials and his own.[2]

Within the framework of the Empire thus defended and served by more capable officials the process of romanization was going steadily on. The foundation of colonies, the granting of municipal rights, the encouragement of education (whether by the creation of professorial chairs and endowment of new schools, or by the immunities and privileges granted to teachers), were all instruments of this process, and this work was simply continued and developed by succeeding emperors.

Most important, perhaps, of all the Flavian achievement, was the restoration of confidence. Had the anarchy of 69 not been quickly suppressed, Mediterranean civilization might have been badly shaken: 'the empire was adrift and in danger,' judges Suetonius: it was brought back to safety. The steps taken to control the armies are related more fully elsewhere (pp. 395 *sqq.*); here we need only record that they succeeded. Vespasian and Titus had both led armies, and Domitian was wise enough to go in person to the scene of action and so had the troops devoted to him. What danger there may have been that the Empire should become the prize or plaything of armies or generals was averted, and the legal basis of the Principate remained civilian. To all the provinces and peoples comprising the Empire the Flavian dynasty restored that confidence in the lasting strength of Rome, in her *aeternitas*, which had tottered for a while; such was the

[1] For these Oriental Senators see C. S. Walton, *J.R.S.* xix, 1929, p. 28; for the inscription quoted see A. M. Woodward, *B.S.A.* xxviii, 1926–7, p. 120 (ironically enough we do not know the name of the man).

[2] See, for example, Dessau 986, where Vespasian, in moving the grant of *ornamenta triumphalia* to Ti. Plautius Silvanus Aelianus, condemns by implication Nero's tardiness in recognizing merit.

message of the coins that promised AETERNITAS and linked that promise to the Princeps. A striking example of this sentiment has survived in an inscription from Acmonia in Phrygia.[1] The town had received by the will of a rich citizen a considerable benefaction: Senate and People ordain how the money is to be spent; then comes the clause—'and this decree is to be guaranteed by the eternity of the empire of the Romans.' Belief in the eternal lasting power of Rome was restored, and with it belief in the foresight and loving care (*providentia*) of the emperor. This unceasing anxiety for the welfare of the peoples of the empire was an aspect on which some early rulers, such as Augustus and Claudius, had already laid stress; from now on it grew more prominent still. It was that 'principis sollicitudo' of which Suetonius speaks in recording Titus' activities after the eruption of Vesuvius; from the time of the Flavians *Providentia* (or its Greek equivalent *Pronoia*) comes to be looked on as a natural attribute of the good Princeps; to that loving care all, Senate, People and subjects look for safety and deliverance.[2] Materially and morally, in strength and in confidence, the Flavians restored a shaken realm, and that is their great achievement.

[1] *I.G.R.R.* IV, 661.
[2] See M. P. Charlesworth in *Harv. Theol. Rev.* XXIX, 1936, pp. 107 *sqq.*

CHAPTER II

THE PEOPLES OF NORTHERN EUROPE
THE GETAE AND DACIANS

I. THE EARLIEST AGES

THE difficulties that beset attempts to determine when man first appeared on any part of our globe, are increased in the case of Northern Europe by its repeated glacial periods. It may be presumed that by far the greater part of the traces of man which probably existed from interglacial times have been completely obliterated by the destructive action of the ice on the earth's surface. It is therefore significant that the most northerly dwelling-place finds of indisputable Early-Palaeolithic character in Germany lie outside the latest North European ice-cap[1], which is considered to fall in the Magdalenian period of West Europe. No decisive evidence that the Baltic districts also were inhabited as early as the last interglacial epoch has yet been advanced, but it is possible that it may be forthcoming from certain parts of the Scandinavian peninsula. Geologists have, indeed, proved that parts of Norway, particularly the coastal districts from Bergen to Lofoten, were not entirely covered by the latest land-ice. It has also been conjectured that the very ancient North-Norwegian Komsa culture discovered during recent years has its origins in the interglacial epoch. It is, however, worthy of mention that finds which are probably still older than the Komsa dwelling-places found hitherto have been made on the west coast of Sweden. These finds are thought to belong to the period about 9000 B.C. If it cannot yet be regarded as certain that the Komsa culture represents an immigration from the south, it is true of the Lyngby culture[2], ascribed to the Mesolithic Age, which is represented above all by picks or axes of reindeer horn and is undoubtedly that of a hunting people who followed in the tracks of the reindeer the receding ice-edge over the tundras of Northern Europe.

It is still not known to what race the bearers of the Komsa and Lyngby cultures belonged, as there are no skeleton remains from that period, nor has any direct connection been traced between

[1] See map 1 in E. Wahle, *Deutsche Vorzeit*.
[2] Ebert, *Reallexikon*, VII, pp. 324 *sqq.*

MAP 2

I   INGAEVONES
II ISTAEVONES
III HERMINONES

L. Ladoga

GULF OF BOTHNIA

GULF OF FINLAND

Aestii Fenni

Suiones

Gotland I.

Teutoni

Cimbri

Bornholm I.

Anglii
Aviones
Varini
Reudigni
Rugii
R. Persante
Gepidae
Gotones
R. Passarge

Langobardi
Burgundiones

I

R. Ems

Semnones

R. Oder

R. Vistula

52

II

R. Weser

R. Elbe

Vandali

R. Rhine

III

Silingae

Marcomanni   Cotini

Osi

R. Danube   Quadi

Anartii

MAP TO ILLUSTRATE
THE PEOPLES OF
NORTHERN EUROPE

Scales

0 50 100 150 200 250

English miles

0 50 100   200   300

Kilometres

The names marked * were added
to the map after the Index to
Maps was printed and should
be inserted in it. For the West-
Germani see map 4, facing p. 131.

that settlement and the one immediately following it, also Mesolithic, called the Maglemose culture[1] after a place in Seeland.
During the Ancylus period when the Baltic was a fresh-water
inland lake, this culture extended over its North German and
East Baltic shores and, above all, the Scandinavian peninsula.
There is a find of skeleton remains of this age from Stångenäs[2]
in Bohuslän (Sweden), which are ascribed to the Nordic race and
so mark their first appearance in prehistory. The settlement
attested by the kitchen-middens on the shores of the Litorina-
Tapes Sea is a direct development of this civilization. This is also
true of the numerous Neolithic Age dwelling-places which are
characterized particularly by an abundance of pottery.

At the beginning of the North European Neolithic Age (which
is placed by Montelius, probably too early, about 4000 B.C.) a
culture with agriculture and cattle-raising appears here. The
Megalithic graves characteristic of one of the main groups of a
later stage in the new civilization are regarded as barbaric imitations of the built graves of the Orient which reached Scandinavia
by way of the coasts of North Africa and Western Europe. They
certainly came here by way of England, and they have also been
interpreted as evidence of an immigration from the west. This
question must still be regarded as unsettled. On the other hand
it must be taken as established that the Megalithic grave culture
of the Baltic regions is associated with that of Western Europe
and has its centre on the Danish Islands. The German and Dutch
Megalithic graves may probably be regarded as simplified
descendants of the Nordic ones. Strong influence from the north
can also be traced in the German-Dutch Megalithic grave culture.
Certain types of tools and weapons and the abundant pottery
attest this affinity[3].

Scandinavia and North Germany also show common features
in the second main group of the agricultural civilization of the
Stone Age—that of the single graves. Opinions vary greatly as
to the interpretation of these conditions. On the one hand this
culture, which is marked by beautiful battle-axes and pottery of
a definite type, is taken to be a Scandinavian culture group which
spread over adjacent parts of the continent. According to another
theory it is due to a wave of culture from the south, brought by
the Indo-Europeans who migrated into the country at that time.
A third school identifies the Nordic race (*Homo europaeus*) with
the Indo-Germanic primitive people who spread from South

[1] Ebert, *Reallexikon*, VII, pp. 344 *sqq.*　　　[2] *Ib.* XII, pp. 386 *sqq.*
[3] *Ib.* IX, pp. 44 *sqq.*

Scandinavia, or that region together with North-West Germany, beginning as early as the Stone Age. Where the truth lies it is at present impossible to decide[1]. The fact that in Scandinavia— apart from its northernmost parts inhabited by Lapps and Finns— no names of places or of natural features are met with which are not of Indo-European origin, deserves very serious attention. They invite a comparison with other very different conditions found, for example, in Greece. It is thus not impossible that Tacitus was right in thinking that the Germani were the original inhabitants of their country, and it is a tenable view that the North German and Scandinavian agriculturalists of the Later Stone Age are largely directly descended from the nomads who occupied the land when the ice receded. In any event, it is probably right to describe the inhabitants of Scandinavia and North Germany between Weser-Aller and the lower Oder (or Vistula)[2] during the Later Stone Age as proto-germanic.

It is more difficult to determine whether the original home of the Germanic people included the East Baltic countries. Western Finland and parts of the former Russian Baltic provinces exhibit a Stone Age culture which, in general, shows considerable resemblances to the Scandinavian—though here Megalithic graves are not found. Nevertheless, the paucity of the skeleton material from this period—entirely lacking in Finland—makes it impossible to draw any certain conclusions (see below, p. 65). But it has been assumed both by philologists and archaeologists that the Swedish-speaking inhabitants of the present day in Finland derive from the Stone Age. The 'comb-pottery' on the other hand, which is richly represented in Eastern Europe and also in countries north and south of the Gulf of Finland, is ascribed in general to Finnish and Baltic tribes.

Conditions during the Bronze Age (which in Scandinavia began

[1] Among the abundant literature on these questions see the following recent works: J. Pokorny in *Wörter und Sachen*, XII, 1929, pp. 309 *sqq.*; O. Rydbeck, 'The earliest settling of man in Scandinavia,' *Acta archaeologica*, I, 1930, pp. 55 *sqq.*; O. Menghin, *Weltgeschichte der Steinzeit*; E. Lewy in *Zeitschr. f. vergl. Sprachwissenschaft*, LVIII, 1931, pp. 1 *sqq.*; P. Kretschmer, 'Die Urgeschichte der Germanen und die germanische Lautverschiebung,' in *Wien. Prähist. Zeitschr.* XIX, 1932, pp. 269 *sqq.*; E. von Eickstedt, *Rassenkunde und Rassengeschichte der Menschheit*; H. Güntert, *Der Ursprung der Germanen: Kultur und Sprache*, IX, 1934. See also the present writer's review of the discussion in H. Lundborg and F. J. Linders, *The racial character of the Swedish nation*, pp. 27 *sqq.* and *Rassenkunde des schwedischen Volkes*, pp. 35 *sqq.*

[2] See K. Jazdzewski's map in *Praehist. Zeitschr.* XXIII, 1932, p. 79.

c. 1800 B.C.[1]) agree with those of the Later Stone Age in so far as the centre of culture lay in Denmark, and still more markedly than before. At the same time the boundary towards the south is still more sharply drawn than during the Stone Age. Foreign influences are more pronounced in North Germany than in Scandinavia, and on the Continent the way is less prepared for the development of a national culture. Even in this period, however, traces of Scandinavian influences in North Germany appear partly in the shape of imported goods and partly in the development and forms of the remains. But the competition of the southern metal cultures was too strong, and during the Bronze Age northern influences do not extend over the continent as they did earlier. On the other hand, Nordic cultures gain in the East some compensation for what is lost in the South. South-West Finland may now be described as a province of Central-Swedish culture. In a lesser degree Swedish influences extend even to the countries south of the Gulf of Finland, and clear traces of it are found as far east as the regions of Oka and the upper Volga.

Although the continental part of Germanic territory with its largely heterogeneous culture seems less markedly an outward fringe of Scandinavia, its civilization shows great vitality. The spread of Late Bronze Age razors of Nordic type and certain clay vessels has been adduced as evidence of the expansion of this culture and its bearers towards the Rhine during that period (see vol. VII, p. 66). The rise of the East-German culture group ('*Grossendorfkultur*') with its centre in Pommerellen (the district between the Vistula and the Persante) is also of great importance. Its strongly local character indicates that it is deeply rooted and tells against the theory that it marks an invasion moving from West to East. But it is rich and vigorous and exercises a considerable influence, especially on the Bronze Age of Eastern Scandinavia.

The end of the Bronze Age, at the middle of the first millennium B.C., shows a cultural weakening in Northern Europe. This continues during the early centuries of the Iron Age when it is characterized by great paucity of finds, and it does not cease until the second century B.C. This decline has been attributed to various causes, such as the Celtic migrations on the continent, which interrupted communications with the metal exporting countries. That an interruption of this kind actually did play a part is con-

---

[1] This date (Montelius) is accepted by Gordon Childe, *Wien. Prähist. Zeitschr.* XIII, 1926, pp. 38 *sqq.*; according to several Scandinavian and German scholars it is three or four centuries too early.

firmed by the fact that the beginning of the renascence seems to coincide with the exploitation of the native bog-ore iron in the middle of the second century. It has also been maintained by men of science that a deterioration of climate[1] occurred in Europe during these centuries. The view that this was a factor in the cultural depression finds some support in the repeated emigrations from Scandinavia which can be assigned to this period— those of the Vandals, the Burgundians, the Goths, and others. That these peoples were of Scandinavian origin is attested by their own traditions, their ethnic names, their house-forms, the evidence of philology and archaeological data, while the fact that these ethnic names appear in Tacitus as those of continental Germanic tribes indicates that their emigration to the continent must have begun before the end of the first century B.C.

II. THE ENTRANCE INTO HISTORY OF THE NORTHERN PEOPLES

The *Germania* of Tacitus marks the entrance into history of the North-European peoples. But long before his time isolated glimpses are caught of them[2]. The name of a Scandinavian people (the Teutones) is first met with in Pytheas. This Greek from Massilia, who made a journey to Britain at the beginning of the fourth century B.C., mentions Thule, lying six days journey to the north of Britain. That country has been identified as the northern part of Norway (vol. VII, p. 53). Information about the continental part of Germania in other authors may be traced to his work, which has itself perished. The first more detailed description of a North-European people is Polybius' picture of the Bastarnae (see further, p. 59), whose connection with the Germani, however, it was left for the elder Pliny to elucidate. The first writer to realize that the Germani were a people by itself, separable from Celts and Scythians, was Posidonius (135–51 B.C.), in his lost continuation of Polybius' historical work. It is from his writings that classical authors chiefly derive their pictures of the violent attacks of the Cimbri and the Teutones—the first sign of the 'blonde peril' threatening the Roman Empire. Important information about the Germani—though sometimes hard to interpret—is also contained in Caesar's *Gallic War*. To the decades

---

[1] Ebert, *Reallexikon*, VII, pp. 6 *sqq.*
[2] For older vaguer notices, not based on autopsy, see L. Schmidt, *Geschichte der deutschen Stämme*, I², pp. 1 *sqq.*

immediately before and after the beginning of the Christian era belong three sources concerning northern Europe that supplement each other—Augustus' short presentation in his *Res Gestae* of the most important results of his foreign policy[1], Velleius' detailed description of Tiberius' campaigns[2], and Strabo's geographical work[3]. Augustus and Strabo mention the Cimbri, but on the whole the Elbe is still the boundary of the world as known to the Romans. The summary of the geographical knowledge of the time presented by Pomponius Mela shortly before the middle of the first century A.D., mentions the Sinus Codanus and its island world north of the Elbe. He is here probably referring only to the southern part of the west coast of Jutland[4]. Pliny shows himself considerably better informed in his *Natural History*, in which five main Germanic tribes are enumerated. Of the countries north of the Baltic he mentions the island of Scadinavia, a word which is probably akin to the name of the Swedish province Skåne (Scania), and may be assumed to refer to the southern portion of the Scandinavian peninsula.

In the knowledge of North Europe among the civilized people of his time Tacitus' *Germania* marks a great advance. The work, the original title of which is assumed to have been *De situ et origine Germanorum*, is one of the earliest works known to us wholly devoted to the presentation of a geographico-ethnographical subject.

From the first chapter of the *Germania* we can conclude that the shifting towards the south which the distribution of the Scandinavian tribes indicates (see above, p. 50) was paralleled among the Germanic people on the continent. This becomes clear when the contents of that chapter are compared with the evidence of archaeological research. In the middle of the last millennium B.C., when the southern boundary between the Germani and the Celts is easy to trace, thanks to the entirely different burial customs of the two peoples, the Germani practising cremation, the Celts inhumation, the conditions in the Saale districts afford clear evidence. The territory of the Germani does not extend farther south than the Harz and the Celts still occupy Thuringia[5]. In the time of Tacitus, however, the Germani's southern boundary lies along the Danube.

He gives the Rhine as the western boundary of the Germani,

---

[1] 26.   [2] II, 105 *sqq.*   [3] VII, 290 *sqq.*
[4] L. Weibull, *Scandia*, VII, 1934, pp. 89 *sqq.*
[5] See vol. VII, p. 69 and the maps *Mannus, Erg.-Bd.* IV, 1925, pl. XIII; VII, 1929, pl. I; VIII, 1931, pl. I.

though he himself states[1] that the Mattiaci (around Wiesbaden) were clients of Rome and that the area in the angle between the Rhine and the Danube (*agri decumates*) lay within the boundaries of the Roman Empire[2]. The statement that the Rhine was the Germani's western boundary is also misleading in so far as it ignores the tribes living west of the Rhine, some of whom Tacitus himself enumerated[3]. Efforts have been made to decide from archaeological evidence when these *Germani cisrhenani* mentioned by Caesar occupied Eastern Gaul, and a number of grave-finds have been interpreted as indicating that the Germani passed the lower Rhine as early as in the middle of the last century B.C. (see vol. VII, p. 67).

Tacitus' statement must be taken to refer to the political boundary between the Roman Empire and free Germania. For the rest, there are many signs that this boundary was not exclusively political, and that before the close of the first century A.D. the Romans had made a considerable advance in their endeavour to merge the foreign element into the body of the community. It is probable that the task of absorbing the western Germanic tribes into the Roman Empire was facilitated by the fact that the people there were not unmixed. Caesar's statements about the Belgae[4] indicate that the Celts had not been entirely driven out, but had largely remained in the country. It is difficult to decide whether the Germani west of the Rhine had simply become celticized, as some scholars have assumed. The grave finds are rather scanty, and in addition the two cultures are fairly similar—even that of free Germania shows strong Celtic influence during the closing centuries of the pre-Christian era. The fact that the cremation-grave culture, which was so vigorous at that time, becomes general in these districts shows that in this respect the Germani set the fashion. But as regards the period following Caesar's conquest of Gaul, it is certain that no cultural expansion, either Celtic or Germanic, went on here, but rather a fusion with romanizing tendencies. The archaeological material points unmistakably in this direction. All the commodities which reach England, West Germany and Scandinavia especially from the mouth of the Rhine after the end of the second century, are provincial Roman in character. As a further sign that the Rhine Germani of this period are separated from their fellow-tribes reference may be made to the fact that of the Germanic fibulae which are found in such profusion only a single group is really represented

[1] *Germ.* 29.   [2] For the Germans within the Empire see below, pp. 526 *sqq.*
[3] *Germ.* 28–9.   [4] *B.G.* II, 4.

here[1]. This may indicate that even in Tacitus' time the Rhine
was not only a political but also an ethnographical boundary,
along which classical culture encountered Germanic.

Thus at the time of Tacitus there lived west of the Rhine a
number of Germanic tribes, who undoubtedly formed an important element in the population of these areas. Both Tacitus'
account and the archaeological facts referred to above suggest
that they were in culture, though not in speech, largely denation-
alized. Even though a number of tribes still proudly asserted
their Germanic origin[2] we need not assume the existence of a
Germania irredenta groaning beneath the Roman yoke. The real
description of the Germani by Tacitus thus begins with his
account of *Germania libera*, the regions east of the Rhine.

III. THE 'FREE' GERMANI OF THE CONTINENT

In his account of these 'free' Germanic tribes in the west he begins
with the Chatti living in what is now Hessen, whom he describes
in considerable detail and extols for their military virtues. The
Tencteri and the Usipetes on the right bank of the Rhine, who are
said to have been skilled horsemen, receive similar praise. After
a short mention of some other tribes, come the Frisii. These
people, who inhabited the coast-lands between the Rhine and the
Ems, had joined the Romans at the same time as the Batavi and
did them great service during the campaigns of Drusus and
Germanicus. By a revolt in A.D. 28, provoked by the severity of
the tax-collectors, they made themselves independent, were again
subdued in 46–47, but joined the revolt of the Batavi in 69–70
and regained their freedom. Tacitus has not much to say about
the Frisii, but a good deal can be discovered from archaeological
evidence. The finds which can be referred to them practically all
come from remains of the artificial mounds on which they built
their villages (Terpen). The oldest go back to the La Tène period,
while several of the later ones contain a considerable quantity
of both native and imported (Roman) pottery from the early
Empire. To a smaller extent, also, metal objects are met with,
among them Roman bronze vessels. These Roman wares in
Terpen may be regarded as the earliest evidence for the Frisii as
traders. The transportation of cattle up the Rhine by the Frisii
is attested in literature from the end of the third century[3]. As has
been seen, there was considerable export of provincial Roman

---

[1] See O. Almgren, *Mannus-Bibliothek*, XXXII, 1923, map II.   [2] *Germ.* 28.
[3] H. Wilkens, *Hansische Geschichtsblätter*, XIV, 1908, p. 310.

wares from the mouth of the Rhine at the end of the second century, and it must be assumed that this was chiefly in Frisian ships[1]. The Terpen finds attest connections between this people and the Romans as early as the first century, and it may be assumed that this trade began at the time when their waters were directly connected with the Rhine by the canal built by Drusus in 12 B.C. (vol. x, p. 362).

After the Frisii a brief reference is made to their neighbours on the east, the Chauci at the estuary of the Weser—now traced in archaeological material[2]—and on the south the Cherusci, Arminius' renowned tribe, who, however, by the time of Tacitus had lost much of their power to their more warlike neighbours, the Chatti. Next come the Cimbri, whose name evokes gloomy reflections on what the Romans had to endure from the Germani —'tam diu Germania vincitur'. The position of their home-country is not precisely stated, but their name is found in the present Danish place-name Himmerland, the district south of Limfjorden. The home of the Teutones, their comrades in arms (who are not mentioned by Tacitus), is also definitely known now. It is to be found in Thy, north-west of Limfjorden. Archaeological evidence of these two peoples has now been found in traces of extensive abandoned agricultural areas, obviously deserted in prehistoric times, and a fortified place in the moor at Borre[3].

Great interest attaches to the account of the Suebi, the collective name for a number of tribes—indeed, according to Tacitus, all except those dealt with above. This is a single use of the name[4]; Pliny (p. 56) and Tacitus himself elsewhere[5] give to it a more restricted meaning. The Suebi are generally made to include the tribes in Mecklenburg, Brandenburg, Saxony and Thuringia[6]. Their habitation is traced in the name Schwaben. The fact that Suebi are placed also on the Eider indicates, perhaps, that they, like many other peoples, were invaders from Scandinavia[7]. The next chapter, that about the Semnones round the Havel and the Spree, who consider themselves the leading tribe among the Suebi, gives clear information as to the nature of this tribal alliance. In a sacred

---

[1] On the Frisian trade to Scandinavia during the later prehistoric period see E. Wadstein, *Saga-Book of the Viking Society*, xi, 1933, pp. 5 *sqq.*

[2] K. Waller, *Mannus*, xxv, 1933, pp. 40 *sqq.*

[3] G. Hatt, *Acta archaeologica*, ii, pp. 117 *sqq.*; J. Bröndsted, *Tilskueren*, 1935.

[4] Cf. his name *Suebicum mare* for the Baltic Sea (*Germ.* 45); P.W. *s.v.* Suebi, col. 567.   [5] *Germ.* 2.

[6] Schmidt, *op. cit.* p. 85.   [7] P.W. *s.v.* Suebi, col. 569.

grove in the territory of the Semnones representatives of all the
Suebi assemble at fixed times for collective religious observances
which include human sacrifices. The Langobardi, so renowned
later, also belong to the Suebi, living north-west of the Semnones,
in what is now Lüneburg, at the beginning of the century[1] and
probably also in the time of Tacitus. According to their own
traditions, they migrated from Scandinavia. It has been assumed
that they came from the Swedish provinces Skåne or Halland[2]
but spent a short time in Gotland before they landed in Germany,
a theory which receives some support from the fact that the Gotland
archaeological material from the pre-Roman Iron Age is strongly
influenced from North-West Germany. North-German burial
places of a certain type are unanimously ascribed to the Langobardi: the men's burial places with weapons (Nienbüttel, Rieste,
Körchow, etc.), and the women's without weapons (Darzau).
These burial customs are interpreted as indicating Woden-cult[3]
and their connection with the Suebi has been disputed.

Another kind of cult-association of a similar nature to that of
the Suebi is mentioned as existing north of the Langobardi, and
more detailed information about the nature and object of the cult
is given. The goddess *Nerthus*, identified by Tacitus with *terra
mater*[4], is carried round in procession at certain times of the year
in a covered waggon drawn by cows, and worshipped by the
people with festive joy and with the laying aside of weapons.
Here we have obviously the female representative in the twin
deity of fertility, which is known to us from the Mediterranean
countries and the Orient, whence this cult spread over the world.
The old German form of the name Nerthus corresponds to the
Icelandic Njorðr, the Swedish Njord, which is, however, the name
of the male deity. The Nerthus-worshipping tribes are identified
with the Ingaevones mentioned by Tacitus[5], but it may be observed that Nerthus also was worshipped in Scandinavia, to judge
from several place-names, e.g. Närtuna in Uppland[6]. Among the
seven peoples enumerated by Tacitus are to be noted the Angli,
with their original tribal centre on the peninsula Angel in East
Slesvig, and their neighbours on the south-west, the Reudigni who
occupied the territory of the Chauci by the lower Elbe towards

[1] Vell. Pat. II, 106.   [2] W. Schulz, *Mannus*, XXIV, 1932, p. 226.
[3] Schulz, *op. cit.* p. 223.
[4] *Germ.* 40. On Nerthus see H. M. Chadwick, *The Origin of the
English Nation*, chap. x.   [5] *Germ.* 2; see Hoops, *Reallexikon*, p. 181.
[6] Pliny (*N.H.* IV, 96) mentions Inguaeones as inhabitants of Scandinavia and calls them *gens prima in Germania*.

the end of the second century, and who are probably identical with the Saxons[1]. On Ptolemy's map (A.D. 150) the Saxons are placed on the right bank of the lower Elbe, in the Lauenburg. The types of remains, characteristic of both these peoples, which are to be met with in England and mark the Anglo-Saxon invasion, belong however to a later period than the one dealt with here. A considerable West-Germanic tribe in this region whose name does not appear in Tacitus is that of the Franks. This name is therefore assumed to have arisen later to designate a tribal association inhabiting the district between the Rhine and the Ems and composed of the Bructeri, Ampsivarii and others[2]. It is thought that this group appears in Tacitus as the Istaevones.

After the diversion to the north which the description of the Nerthus people implies, Tacitus turns southward and goes now from west to east. The first people dealt with are the Hermunduri, who lived south of the Chatti. Philologists associate their name with the first element of the name Thüringerwald, the mountain country forming part of their tribal territory[3]. The name of this tribe has also been connected with that of the Herminones, and it has been assumed that we must seek in these districts the third of the tribal confederations mentioned by Tacitus[4]. This is confirmed by the fact that, according to Pliny[5], the Herminones inhabit the interior of Germania and consist, *inter alia*, of Suebi, Hermunduri, Chatti and Cherusci. That the territory of the Hermunduri, or the tribes allied to them, extended far southward is indicated by what Tacitus says about their trade with the Roman province of Raetia, a trade which was not confined only to the neighbouring river, the Danube, but penetrated far into the Roman Empire. The privileged position enjoyed by the Hermunduri in this respect was the reward for their conduct during the critical period in the first century A.D. (vol. x, p. 619). They had taken no part in the war against Rome led by Arminius and the Cherusci.

While only vague glimpses of the Hermunduri are caught both in literature and archaeological material we are, on the other hand, well informed about the Marcomanni and the Quadi. The first references to the Marcomanni are found in Caesar[6], where they are mentioned as forming part of Ariovistus' army. It is assumed that at that time they lived between the Main and the Danube in the territory evacuated by the Helvetii. When the Romans

---

[1] P.W. *s.v.* Reudigni, col. 701.   [2] P.W. *s.v.* Franci, col. 83.
[3] See Schütte, *Our Forefathers*, II, p. 152.
[4] *Germ.* 2.   [5] *N.H.* IV, 100 (Hermiones).   [6] *B.G.* I, 51.

occupied the country west of the Rhine and were obviously preparing to cross the river and subdue the Germani, the Marcomanni found their position insecure, and under the leadership of their king, Maroboduus, they marched eastward into Bohemia, large parts of which they conquered in the last decade B.C. Maroboduus, who seems to have been possessed of some statesmanship, obtained great influence in Central Germany during the next two decades, and became leader of a tribal alliance which is said to have extended from the Elbe to the Vistula. His power was broken by a defeat at the hands of the Cherusci under Arminius in A.D. 17, and after the Goths, under the leadership of the exiled Marcomannic nobleman Catualda, invaded Bohemia in A.D. 19, Maroboduus' empire collapsed, and he himself ended his days in exile in Ravenna A.D. 35 (vol. x, p. 782 *sq.*).

The *Germania* gives only vague indications of the relations between the Marcomanni and the Romans: 'raro armis nostris, saepius pecunia iuvantur, nec minus valent'[1]. But in the *Annals*[2] Tacitus makes a statement which, short as it is, is illuminating, and affords an explanation of one of the most important factors in the Germanic culture of the Earlier Empire. When Catualda conquered Maroboduus' capital, he found there sutlers and merchants from the Roman provinces who had immigrated thither 'from greed of gain.' It is clearly possible that there was some sort of commercial agreement, as Tacitus suggests, which entitled Roman merchants and other traders to settle and do business within the boundaries of the Marcomannic kingdom. The leading cultural rôle of Bohemia within the Germanic world at this time is explained in this way. As a transit country for Italian exports to Northern Europe it had been of importance as early as the beginning of the Bronze Age. Further, as the Romans gained control of Carnuntum, first as a summer camp and later as a fortress (vol. x, p. 804), the town became a staple place for trade with Northern Europe. It is of still greater importance that Bohemia now became the centre of a particularly vigorous culture built up of Germanic, West-Celtic, Boian, provincial-Roman and purely Italian elements[3]. It was this culture, characterized by certain fibulae, buckles, mounts for drinking-horns, etc., which sets its stamp on the whole of the archaeological material of Northern Europe during the beginning of the first century. In view of the dominating importance of this culture of the Marcomanni, its bearers—the last people in the West-Germanic group

---

[1] 42.   [2] II, 62.   [3] See Volume of Plates v, 4.

dealt with by Tacitus—must also be given a prominent position during the Earlier Empire which can only be compared to that of the Goths during the Later.

Tacitus' description[1] of the East Germanic and non-Germanic peoples together occupies only about half the space devoted to the West Germani. This indicates that the information he could obtain about these tribes, which were farthest away from the Roman boundaries, was somewhat scanty. Herein probably lies also the explanation—which will be dealt with in more detail later—why the author's own speculations about these peoples were given freer scope than before. In spite of their paucity and other shortcomings these notes are of great importance, since they comprise the oldest extant historical detail about several peoples. It is therefore assumed that Tacitus had access to some now lost written source, or, more probably, to verbal information from some traveller. In this connection the Roman knight who visited the amber coast has been suggested (see below, p. 65). After having mentioned by way of introduction four little known tribes, one of which (the Osi) is generally considered to be Illyrian, he discusses in somewhat more detail the Lugian group who are said to occupy the largest area. The tribes enumerated here are also practically unknown to history. Of ethnographical interest are the particulars about the Harii—possibly identical with the Hirri mentioned by Pliny[2]—that they have black shields, blacken their bodies and choose dark nights for their battles. The information about the Naharvali—that in their territory they had a sacred grove where ancient rites were performed—suggests that within their tribal group they played the same part as the Semnones among the West Germani, and that thus these Lugii also were associated in a common cult. Beyond the Lugii dwell the Gotones (Goths), and in the coast regions (of the Baltic) the Rugii and the Lemovii, all of whom are curtly described as 'distinguished by their round shields, short swords and obedience to their kings.' With regard to the shields, however, it is to be observed that over the whole of the Germanic territory, besides the predominant round shape, other types of shields, both oval and many-sided, for example hexagonal, are also met with[3]. On the other hand, the statement that the short (one-edged) sword[4] is

---

[1] *Germ.* 43–6.

[2] In *N.H.* IV, 97; Schmidt, *op. cit.* p. 102, identifies the Harii with Pliny's Charini.

[3] M. Jahn, *Mannus-Bibliothek*, XVI, 1916, pp. 199 *sqq.*

[4] See Volume of Plates V, 10, *g.*

specially characteristic of the East Germani at that time is correct. But the contrast to which Tacitus alludes between the West-Germanic long and the East-Germanic short swords belongs to the end of the pre-Roman epoch. In Tacitus' time also the West Germani used short swords, but only two-edged of Roman *gladius* type although with certain native features[1]. As the Burgundians and Vandals do not appear among the tribes enumerated here, though the latter are mentioned elsewhere[2] it has been assumed that they are included in the Lugii[3]. Of the Germanic people on the continent (i.e. not in Scandinavia) mention is also made of the Veneti and Peucini or Bastarnae. Their nationality is stated with a certain hesitation as they are said to resemble the Sarmatae.

In the description of the continental Germanic tribes, the statements about the Bastarnae deserve special interest, as they are the Germanic tribe with whom the classical peoples had come into contact previously, and who thereby first made their appearance in history. As early as the end of the third century B.C. they are said to have appeared in the company of the Sciri at the estuary of the Danube, where during the following centuries they were allies of Rome's enemies, until they suffered a decisive defeat at the hands of M. Crassus in 29 B.C. (vol. x, p. 117 *sq.*). Earlier Roman sources regard them as Celts or Scythians, and their Celtic nationality has also been maintained by modern scholars, but their Germanic origin may be regarded as established[4]. The reliefs of them which can be studied on Trajan's Column show Germanic types with the characteristic knot of hair[5]. This detail, as well as their grave-culture, has caused surprise, since these features are looked upon as particularly West-Germanic. The explanation lies perhaps in the fact that the Bastarnae were a continental Germanic tribe, whereas the specific East-Germanic culture was created by people who immigrated from Scandinavia. The Bastarnae may be considered to have been the first Germanic people to have moved down towards the Black Sea from the Baltic, and their road thither is indicated by the name for the Carpathians, Alpes Bastarnicae,

---

[1] Jahn, *ib.* Abb. 146.   [2] *Germ.* 2.

[3] Pliny (*N.H.* IV, 99) includes in the Vandals Burgundiones, Varinnae, Charini and Gutones.

[4] R. Much in Hoops, *Reallexikon, s.v.* Bastarnen and elsewhere. The discussion on the Bastarnae is reviewed by Richthofen in *Wien. Prähist. Zeitschr.* XIX, 1932, pp. 127 *sqq.*; see also Schmidt, *op. cit.* pp. 86 *sqq.*

[5] See Volume of Plates v, 2, *a, b.* On the reliefs on the Adamclisi monument, see Schmidt, *op. cit.* pp. 93 *sqq.*

known from classical sources. It has been assumed[1] that theirs
was the peculiar culture which, at the beginning of the Iron Age,
had spread over Pommerellen, and is characterized by stone cist-
graves filled with pottery—sometimes as many as thirty vessels,
many of them face-urns. This culture has been declared to be a
direct continuation of the *Grossendorfkultur* in the same district
from the Later Bronze Age (p. 49). The cause of the departure
of the Bastarnae from the shores of the Baltic has been sought
in the immigrations from Scandinavia in the closing centuries of
the pre-Christian era.

Among the Scandinavian peoples who were the earliest to
move to the south coast of the Baltic are numbered the Vandals,
mentioned first by Pliny[2] under the name of Vandili. Their name
has been associated with the Danish place-name Vendsyssel, Jutland, north of Limfjorden, which area is supposed to have been
their original home, an assumption which receives some support
from the fact that one of the Vandal tribes bore the name Silingae,
a name probably connected with Saelund, the old form of Sjaelland
(Seeland). That in the time of Tacitus Jutland at any rate had
connections with East Germany appears from the ornamentation
of the Jutland pottery (meander or meander-like patterns with
continuous lines[3]), which agrees with what is found on the pottery
in that area, whereas in the adjacent West-German territory these
patterns consist of dotted lines made with a little toothed wheel[4].
In Silesia, which obtained its name from the Silingae, and where
both the latter and other Vandalic tribes thus lived, pottery has
been found from as early as the first century B.C., closely corresponding to that in Denmark and Sweden. The researches of
recent years[5] have succeeded in tracing with fair certainty from
the archaeological material (house-foundations, burial customs,
pottery) the movement of the Vandals to the continent during the
second century B.C. The name of the Vandals used to be associated
with the face-urn culture, but that does not square with the results
of most recent research, as we have seen above, and their line of
immigration was not the Vistula but the Oder.

A closer study of burial culture and types of remains has made
possible more definite conclusions with reference to the other
East-German peoples enumerated by Tacitus. In western Further
Pomerania and round the bend of the river Vistula a group of
burial grounds can be distinguished, characterized by 'Brand-

[1] E. Petersen, *Vorgeschichtliche Forschungen*, II, 2.
[2] *N.H.* IV, 99.   [3] See Volume of Plates V, 6, *m.*
[4] *Ib.* 6, *a.*   [5] B. von Richthofen, in *Altschlesien*, III, 1931, pp. 21 *sqq.*

grubengraber'[1] with girdle-hook[2] and an abundance of weapons, among them ornamented spearheads. Rondsen[3], lying within the area last mentioned, is typical of these burial grounds. As the same burial practice obtained in Bornholm in the centuries immediately preceding the birth of Christ, the burial grounds of this type on the mainland have been associated with the Burgundiones also mentioned by Pliny (p. 59, n. 3), who are assumed to have migrated from Bornholm (*Borghundarholmr*) in the second century B.C. East and north of the Burgundian territory referred to, in Pomerania, burial grounds with *Brandschüttungsgräber*[4] and several skeleton graves appear towards the end of the pre-Roman period. The Rugii ('rye-eaters') first mentioned by Tacitus are placed here, and this is supported by a statement in Jordanes[5], according to whom the Goths after their landing on German soil—this is nowadays placed in the first century B.C.—first attacked the Ulmerugi (*i.e.* the Rugii on the island), which probably refers to that section of the Rugii who had settled in the delta of the Vistula. The name of the island of Rügen has also been correctly associated with that of the Rugii[6]. Some of the Rugii are assumed to have been settled at the estuary of the Oder. There is agreement among Scandinavian scholars that the Rugii come from Rogaland in south-west Norway. In view of the fact that a find in Rogaland (the Avaldsnesgrave) from about A.D. 300 contains a remarkable number of Roman imported goods and that similar goods are also found in abundance in connection with skeleton-graves in the estuary of the Oder and on the Danish islands, it has been suggested[7] that the Rugii migrated from their native country to the mouth of the Oder and Vistula with the Danish isles as an intermediate station. Thus the appearance of Roman imported goods in Scandinavia[8] was largely due to the Rugii's trade with their kinsmen in Denmark and West Norway. After the successful invasion of the Goths (see above) their allies the Gepidae settled down at the delta of the Vistula as neighbours to the Rugii; east and south of them lived the Goths. The Gothic-Gepidae area is characterized by burial places with both skeleton and cremation graves, a form of burial well known from South Sweden—especially Östergöt-

---

[1] Cremation pit graves not containing cinerary urns, Ebert, *Reallexikon*, II, pp. 122 *sqq.*   [2] See Volume of Plates v, 6, *g.*
[3] Ebert, *Reallexikon*, XI, p. 155.
[4] Cremation pit graves containing urns, Ebert, *Reallexikon*, II, pp. 123 *sqq.*   [5] *Getica*, IV, 26 M.   [6] Schmidt, *op. cit.* p. 118.
[7] By Almgren, *Mannus*, x, 1918, pp. 1 *sqq.* Cf. Kossinna, *Mannus-Bibliothek*, L, 1932, p. 227.   [8] Volume of Plates v, 8, 10.

land and Västergötland—during this period. This has been interpreted as a proof that the Goths came from Götaland[1], part of the
mainland of Sweden, not as had been previously supposed from
Gotland. Their name has been interpreted as the people on the
Gutälven (Göta älv—the Göta River). South of the region occupied by the Burgundians, Rugii and Goths a culture-group with
urn-graves, *Brandschüttungsgräber*, and weapons is still to be found
under the Empire—during this period weapons cease to be found
in the northern area—in Silesia, Poland and West Russia. This
widely spread culture[2] is considered to have been that of the
Vandals (see above) and a little area in Silesia with skeleton-
graves is referred to the Silingae.

In this outline of the distribution of peoples, which refers to the
conditions immediately before and after the birth of Christ,
certain changes may be traced as we pass to the second century A.D. At that time a vigorous expansion of Gothic culture
in various directions may be observed. The lower reaches of the
Passarge had formed the eastern limit of the spread of the Goths
in the main area of East Prussia[3]. In Samland, the peninsula
between the Frisches Haff and the Kurisches Haff, and also in
Natangen at the base of this peninsula, burial places now appear
which indicate Gothic immigration, although the native culture—
ascribed to the Aestii of Tacitus—is still prevalent. Towards the
middle of the second century the Rondsen type of burial place is
no longer found at the bend of the Vistula and is replaced by a
mixed grave-culture—that of the Goths, marking their advance
southwards as they drive out the Burgundians, whose burial places
now appear farther towards the south-west.

IV. SCANDINAVIA AND THE EAST BALTIC

To his account of the continental Germanic tribes Tacitus adds
a description of the Suiones[4], the only people in the *Germania*
who can with absolute certainty be stated to have lived on the
Scandinavian peninsula[5]. The following chapter deals with the
Sitones, and contains a digression about a northern sea which
must be the Gulf of Bothnia[6]. These two chapters are among the

---

[1] B. Nerman, *K. Vitterhets Historie och Antikvitets Akademiens Handlingar*, III, 1, 5, 1924, p. 49.   [2] See the map in *Mannus*, XXII, 1930, p. 288.
[3] See the map *ib.* XXIV, 1932, p. 562.   [4] *Germ.* 44.
[5] For Tacitus' Lemovii, identified with Ptolemy's Leuonoi, see P.W.,
Suppl. V, col. 549, E. Wadstein, *Göteborgs högskolas årsskrift*, XXXI, 1925,
p. 198, and G. Kossinna, *Mannus-Bibliothek*, L, 1932, pp. 234 *sqq.*
[6] According to E. Hjärne, *Svearne enligt Tacitus* (forthcoming).

most difficult to interpret in the work. They also seem to constitute
a curious mixture of correct facts, misunderstood statements, and
the author's subjective speculations on the information he had
obtained. It has been impossible to check his statement that the
Suiones were especially strong at sea, and therefore its accuracy
has been called into question. During the last ten years, however,
there have been discovered in the province of Uppland, where
the original home of the Swedes must be sought, very many burial
places from the next two centuries A.D., characterized particularly
by upright stones[1], so that there can be no doubt that the province
was thickly populated at that time. The Swedes originally formed
only a small part of this population, having as their nearest neighbours, so it has been assumed, the Danes, who had not yet migrated
southwards. The Swedes had at that time obviously achieved hegemony, and possibly also extended their kingdom round Lake Mälar.
Tacitus' description of their ships as of the same shape fore and
aft, and with oars that could be moved and used on either side,
gives a good picture of the Scandinavian boat as we know it from
the centuries before Christ[2], until the Viking period.

Though certain parts of this chapter now receive satisfactory
archaeological confirmation, others do not. Thus, the strange
statement that in times of peace weapons were not worn by the
men but were kept in some sort of arsenal under the custody of a
slave is probably due to a confusion with the sacred peace observed
at sacrificial feasts, when weapons were laid aside (p. 55). Nor,
undoubtedly, is the emphasis laid on the strength of the royal
power quite justified[3], but should be viewed in connection with
the statement about its increase to be noted among the Goths[4]
and the degenerate form of it among the Sitones[5]. The power of
the king of the Suiones can no more have been independent of the
will of the people than that of the king of any other Germanic
people, but he possibly had somewhat greater authority. This may
be ascribed partly to his character as commander of a mighty fleet,
partly due to his position, which dates from very early times and
may have lasted even till Tacitus' day, as chief priest and representative on earth of a god of fertility belonging, like Nerthus, to
the god family of the Wanes (Vanir). In a fertile country particularly suitable for agriculture and cattle-raising, it must be assumed
that this god occupied an unusually dominant position. Finally,

---

[1] Swedish *bautastenar*. See Volume of Plates v, 14, *a*.
[2] Cf. the boat found at Hjortspring on the Alsen; Ebert, *Reallexikon*, v,
p. 332.
[3] *Germ.* 44.   [4] *Ib.* 44.   [5] *Ib.* 45.

reference may be made to the circumstances mentioned below (p. 75), which indicate that as early as during the first century after Christ the power of the Suiones was somewhat greater than that of the usual Germanic tribal kingdoms.

Immediately adjoining the Suiones lived the Sitones, who only differed from their neighbours in that their ruler was a woman[1]. Opinions as to the proper interpretation of these statements have been very conflicting. One suggestion[2] is that the name in question refers to the traders who moved from the valley of Lake Mälar to the coast of the Bothnian Gulf and there became in part dependent on the Finnish Quains known from a later time at the upper part of that water. The resemblance between this name and the old Norse word *kvæn* (woman, wife) is said to have given rise to the statement about the degenerate gynaecocracy. This theory is supported by the circumstance that Adam of Bremen also mentions a *terra feminarum* lying north of the Swedes.

In comparison with the abundant information about the continental Germanic peoples contained in Tacitus, particulars about the Scandinavian countries are more than scanty. They still lay too far beyond the periphery of the known world. It seems strange that even Denmark, which lay nearest and already possessed a flourishing culture, should have been unknown, for its civilization was characterized by just the abundance of Roman imports and Roman-Marcomannic influences[3], the expression of lively, even if not direct, connections with the Roman Empire. During the centuries after Tacitus this importation of Roman goods increases still more and now comes also by way of the mouth of the Rhine. The geographical work of Ptolemy from the middle of the second century A.D., which is largely based on the accounts of travelling merchants, contains the first detailed particulars about South Scandinavia. At this time also Denmark's star rises in the firmament of history. From the haze which has hitherto surrounded the Sinus Codanus (see p. 51) appear the contours of the 'Cimbrian peninsula' (Jutland), and four islands lying to the east of it, of which the largest and the most easterly is obviously to be identified with the Scandinavian peninsula. Among the seven tribes on Jutland enumerated by Ptolemy[4], it is thought that at least four can be located with the help of place-names. On the largest Scandia island are also mentioned seven different tribes, among whom the inhabitants of the Hedmark,

[1] *Germ.* 45.   [2] E. Hjärne, *Fornvännen*, XII, 1917, pp. 147.
[3] See Volume of Plates v, 8.
[4] G. Schütte, *Ptolemy's maps*, pp. 144 *sqq.*

the Lapps in the north, and the Goths (Γοῦται) in the south have
been identified. According to another interpretation[1] Ptolemy's
Chaidinoi does not allude to the inhabitants of Hedmark but to
those of the western part of the Swedish province Småland.
Among the other tribe-names of Ptolemy's map glimpses are
perhaps also caught of several territories in the province Skåne.

In addition to the tribes about whose ethnographical connection with the Germani there is no doubt, Tacitus also deals shortly
with some other peoples of Northern Europe. The Aestii living
on the amber coast east of the mouth of the Vistula, whom for his
part he regards as Germani, are described fairly fully[2]. The reason
why Tacitus is so well informed about this people is undoubtedly
to be sought in the fact that the Romans were in direct contact
with them through the amber trade, attested by Pliny's story of
the noble sent out by Nero to procure amber for the Roman arena[3].
According to Tacitus the Aestii resemble the Suebi in appearance and customs, but their language is nearer that of the Britons.
The last-mentioned statement must be accepted with reserve,
since Tacitus cannot have been in a position to decide this question,
but it is reasonable to conclude that the language of the Aestii
differed materially from that of the Germani. Modern investi-
gators have held conflicting opinions as to whether the Aestii were
a Germanic or a Baltic people, but in general the latter assumption
has been accepted. According to old sources, this people inhabited
a very large area—presumably the whole coast up to the Gulf of
Finland. This is corroborated by the circumstance that they bequeathed their name to the West Finnish tribe who inhabit the
south coast of the same bay at the present time. However, certain
philological conclusions, among them those dealing with a number
of place-names, also indicate that Germani inhabited the East
Baltic area at a very early date. It also receives some support from
the skeleton material from prehistoric times found in these countries. From this it appears that the earlier inhabitants of the
countries south of the Gulf of Finland represent to a considerable
extent the Nordic race (p. 48)[4]. Whether they are the original
inhabitants or immigrants cannot yet be decided.

After the short statement about the Sitones referred to above
Tacitus comes in his last chapter to the Veneti, Fenni and
Bastarnae, about whose nationality he expresses some doubt. In
the case of the Bastarnae this was unjustified, as has been shown

[1] E. Wadstein, *op. cit.* pp. 195 *sqq.*   [2] *Germ.* 45.
[3] *N.H.* XXXVII, 45; see vol. X, pp. 415, 418 *sqq.*
[4] Ebert, *Reallexikon*, I, p. 342.

above (p. 59); as regards the Veneti it has been shown that this name is undoubtedly identical with that of the Wends, later used by the Germani to designate the Slavs. But as a West Finnish tribe has inherited the name Estians (see above), the Slavs have succeeded an Illyrian people in the possession of the name Veneti. That in the *Germania* the Slavs are referred to is indicated by the fact that Tacitus places them between the Bastarnae and the Finns. This agrees with the supposed situation of the original home of the Slavs, immediately south of the Balts—the upper Dniester south of the Pripet marsh. The original home of the Finns is now placed in the region of Moscow.

The description of the Fenni which concludes Tacitus' work is one of its most discussed parts. They are described as 'notably brutal, miserably poor: they have no weapons, no horses, no homes, herbs serve them for food, hides for clothes, the ground for their couch. Their only hope lies in their arrows, which they point with bone, because they have no iron.' This description of a nomadic people in a very low state of civilization has been declared by some scholars to be so untrue of the Finns that it must refer to the Lapps. This theory is supported by the fact that the modern Norwegian name for the Lapps is still ' Finner,' and the Lapps are found mentioned under that name in classical and medieval literature (Ptolemy, Procopius, Jordanes, Adam of Bremen). Although, however, it is not known how far south the Finnish-speaking, but probably independent, Lappish race[1] had penetrated in the time of Tacitus, it is certain they never lived south of the Gulf of Finland, and to judge from the context in which they are mentioned Tacitus' Fenni must be placed there. But in the period before the birth of Christ Finnish tribes lived there, to whom therefore the statements in the *Germania* probably refer. The territory between the Gulf of Finland, Lake Ladoga and the Dvina is no longer to be regarded as the original home of the Finns: it has been shown[2] that the Finnish language lacks words for forest and for a number of forest animals and also for certain fish found in the Baltic regions and for the crayfish, from which the conclusion is drawn that their original home must be sought in the Moscow district. From this centre Finnish peoples spread along the Gulf of Finland to the Baltic as early as the middle of the last millennium B.C., and may thus be assumed to have lived at least in Esthonia and Northern Latvia in the time of Tacitus. It

[1] K. B. Wiklund in Ebert, *Reallexikon*, III, pp. 367 *sqq.*
[2] By Wiklund, *op. cit.* III, pp. 369 *sqq.*

is also worth observing that there is found in Latvia an extremely primitive culture, ascribed to the pre-Roman Iron Age, characterized particularly by bone and horn implements. The cultural stage attained by its bearers does not appear to contradict that ascribed by Tacitus to the Finns and the scantiness of metal is a feature consistent with the East Finnish Bronze Age, which is ascribed to a Finnish people who spread from the original home at an earlier stage than the southern tribes. It is also probable that this bone culture might have persisted till the time of Tacitus. It is true that in Esthonia, Latvia and the Memel district of Lithuania, a rich Iron-Age culture is also found[1], but it does not begin before the second century. It bears a strong East-Germanic impress, and is undoubtedly to be ascribed to influences from that quarter. North of the Dvina this culture was probably shared by a mixture of Germanic-Baltic-Finnish peoples, south of the same river, more particularly by Baltic tribes, about whose period of immigration however the most conflicting opinions are held[2]. This culture is thought to have been carried to Western Finland by a Finnish migration across the Gulf of Finland, which, however, cannot be traced farther back than to the second century A.D. Nevertheless in connection with the assumption that Tacitus' Fenni really refers to the Finns it must be noticed that this description is largely conventional and therefore of very little value as ethnographical evidence.

As regards Finland—of which a glimpse is caught in Tacitus' description, if the Sitones are rightly to be regarded as the Germanic inhabitants of this country— only a single archaeological find from the first century A.D. is known, a Roman wine-ladle from south Österbotten, certainly imported by way of Sweden[3]. With the second century begins the invasion from the south which gives a marked East-Baltic impress to the Finnish archaeological material. But that the Finns found there a Scandinavian population, even though a rather scanty one, and received from it significant cultural impulses, appears from about 400 ancient Norse loan-words in the Finnish language, among them the names for king, prince, rule, judge, fine, and the like[4].

---

[1] See Volume of Plates v, 18.

[2] According to C. Engel, *Führer durch die vorgeschichtl. Sammlung des Dommuseums*, Riga, 1933, p. 35, the Baltic people entered this area as early as 2000 years B.C.; cf. Ebert, *Reallexikon*, I, pp. 341.

[3] See Volume of Plates v, 18, *d*. Nor is this find securely dated, as snch ladles in Scandinavia also belong to the second century of our era.

[4] K. B. Wiklund, *Fornvännen*, XXVIII, 1933, pp. 91 *sqq*.

V. THE *GERMANIA* AND THE CIVILIZATION
OF THE GERMANI

The information about the non-Germanic peoples in North Europe which we can obtain from Tacitus and other classical writers is comparatively insignificant. We are best informed about the Germani, the most important source being Tacitus' work. It is true that this work has lost some of its authority owing to the penetrating criticisms of such scholars as Georg Wissowa, Eduard Norden and A. Schroeder. It has been shown that the *Germania* is a late representative of a long succession of geographical-ethnographical works by Greek and Roman authors. In the statements of these works about the various peoples can be discerned a long series of 'ethnographical migration motives.' Thus one of Tacitus' statements about the Germani is met with in the Hippocratic Corpus referring to the Scythians, another in Herodotus, where it refers to the Persians, and so on. It has also been shown that, directly and indirectly, Tacitus must have availed himself largely of other sources, such as Posidonius, Caesar, Livy and Pliny. A further weakness in the work, though a very explicable one, is that the Roman author, who had himself seen the dark sides of civilization at close quarters—the reign of terror under Domitian—sometimes unconsciously idealizes in his description of the unspoiled children of nature. As has been shown, this 'ethnographical romanticism,' despite its Rousseauist character, is also old and ultimately has its roots in the Stoic conception of the baleful influence of culture on mankind. Closely connected with this is the fact that in the interpretation of Germanic customs and conceptions—marriage, religion, government, various forms of punishment, and the like—points of view are adopted which are Tacitus' own, not those of the people he is describing. By the side of this subjectivity the aestheticizing tendency asserts itself as a weakness from the scientific point of view. The tendency of the author, the trained rhetorician, towards epigrammatic acerbity not infrequently degenerates into incomprehensibility; his taste for effective points with which to conclude a section in the book, and his seeking after the artistic welding of the various parts, sometimes impair the work. But in spite of this and other weaknesses touched upon later, Tacitus' work is still a document of inestimable value for our knowledge of the early history of the Germani. What it has lost in authority through the critical research of recent decades it has gained through the results

of archaeological research which, more often than not, confirm
its statements with surprising emphasis. Hardly any other people
has had the good fortune to be introduced into history by an
author at once so penetrating and so kindly disposed.

The introductory chapters in the *Germania* may in their
general character be from Pliny, as Norden has sought to show,
the contents being largely derived from Book xx of his lost work
on the Germanic Wars. However that may be, this part of Tacitus'
book contains much information not to be gained from other
sources. This includes his notes about the tribal saga of the
Germani and about the origin of their name, which only the
Tungri are said originally to have borne. The interpretation of
this has been the subject of much dispute. The general opinion is
that the name was originally that of a tribe, which was later given
to the whole people as the result of the prominence of its bearers
as conquerors[1]. Tacitus gives no explanation of the name Germani
—indeed, he seems to have had little interest in etymology—and
the question must still be considered unsolved; there is not even
unanimous agreement to what language the name belongs[2].

After the description of the physical characteristics of the
Germani, a description which proves to be largely in agreement
with Posidonius' account of the Celts, the author turns to the
nature and features of the country. Here, as elsewhere in the
book, geographical conditions are touched upon very briefly. The
natural features of Germania are stated to be varied, but in general
the country is covered with gloomy forests and horrible swamps.
This exaggeration is echoed in Tacitus' account of the battle of
the Teutoburgerwald and of Germanicus' campaign along the
marshy coasts of the North Sea. At the same time, however, it
is indicated that the marshy parts of the country lie nearest to
Gaul, while those lying along the Danube boundary are higher.
Further the country is said to produce grain but to be unsuitable
for fruit-growing. Cattle-breeding is carried on extensively, but
the cattle are small and hornless. Probably they belonged to the
'mountain breed' which still to-day predominates in the north
of Scandinavia.

In this country the Germani lived in scattered farms and
villages, in houses roughly built of wood. In Jutland and Gotland
particularly, a large number of house-foundations from the first
centuries of our era are known, which give us an idea of the type
of buildings of that time—rectangular houses with the entrance

[1] Schmidt, *op. cit.* p. 43.
[2] Ebert, *Reallexikon*, IV, pp. 274 *sqq.*; Schmidt, *op. cit.* p. 8.

on one of the short sides in Gotland[1], or on one of the long sides in Jutland. Also more primitive dwellings, half underground, are mentioned by Tacitus, and survive even now in several countries. The dress for men of all classes was a mantle, held together by a fibula, or for lack of a fibula, by a thorn. The extremely rich development of the fibula in Germanic territory[2] accords excellently with this statement. The wealthier had also close-fitting undergarments. Roman reliefs, as well as sculptures and statuettes, show us the normal Germanic costume of that period[3]. It appears from these that the dress had been greatly changed since the Bronze Age[4], above all by the adoption of long trousers— which are supposed to have been borrowed from one of the horse-riding peoples in South-East Europe. Among their objects of luxury were furs, sometimes brought from distant countries in the most northerly parts of Europe. The women's clothing was similar in character. As regards the relations between the sexes, monogamy was the rule and matrimony, which was entered into fairly late, was held sacred[5]. Adultery was rare and was severely punished. The children grew up 'naked and dirty' and no difference was made between those of the free-born and the serfs. The women occupied a highly honoured position. In peace woman was the man's adviser, even credited with a prophetic instinct; in wartime she urged him on to combat, and wavering armies had stood firm at the adjurations of their womenfolk.

Tribal and family feeling were very strong among the Germani, and they were loyal to each other both in friendship and enmity. Family revenge was an imperative duty on every man, but the vendetta was not implacable. Even murder could be expiated by fines, a principle preserved in the Germanic laws which were codified much later. Indeed reconciliation between families was almost a social necessity in view of the temperament of the Germani and their forms of social intercourse. Extensive hospitality was practised, and feasts often finished with fights and bloodshed. As a drink Tacitus mentions a fermented beverage prepared from barley and wheat[6]. Wine was probably imported in much larger

[1] See Volume of Plates v, 16.   [2] *Ib.* 4, 6, 8, 10, 20.   [3] *Ib.* 2, *b*, *c*.
[4] Ebert, *Reallexikon*, vi, pl. 95; new evidences in *Nordiske Fortidsminder*, ii, 5–6, 1935.   [5] But see Hoops, *Reallexikon*, pp. 214 *sqq.*
[6] At Skudstrup in Slesvig have been found two drinking horns with remains of a beverage brewed from German wheat (*Praehist. Zeitschr.* xxii, 1931, pp. 180 *sqq.*). The drink which once filled the horns at Juellinge was something between beer and a home-made wine (*Nordiske Fortidsminder*, ii, p. 54).

quantities than the Roman author was aware of (p. 72). Dice-throwing was also a favourite amusement of the Germani. This statement is well corroborated by the archaeological material; from the first century A.D. until the time of the Vikings, dice and gaming-men—the older ones of glass, the later ones of bone—frequently recur in the furnishings of the men's graves[1].

The reason why so much time could be devoted to social life and amusements is that peaceful work was considered unworthy of a freeman[2], who therefore left it to the women and serfs. The chief industries were cattle-raising and farming. The latter was of a primitive character, and the description of the methods employed is particularly difficult to interpret. It is a debated question whether it was on communal lines, as described in Caesar's *Gallic War*[3]. It has been argued by Fustel de Coulanges and others[4] that Caesar's statements refer to the exceptional circumstances prevailing among the invading tribes, but that otherwise full ownership of land existed among the Germani.

As regards trade, Tacitus' statements are rather calculated to give the impression that the Germani had little interest in it, but it is observed that furs were obtained from the far distant North. Of Roman goods for which the Germani were eager only wine is mentioned, and this is said not to have penetrated farther than to the tribes on the frontier. They amassed capital in the form of herds of cattle and placed little value on precious metals in general. The tribes in the interior of Germania traded chiefly by barter, and only those nearest to the borders used money. For practical reasons they preferred silver. Most in favour were *serrati* and *bigati*, the full-weight denarii of the Republic.

Many of these statements are well founded. The large part played in the economy of the Germani by cattle-rearing is reflected in the fact that the word in the Germanic languages for cattle during ancient times (Got. *faihu*, old Norse *fæ*) also denotes property in general. It is also true that money came into use comparatively late and coins struck before Nero's depreciation of the coinage (A.D. 63) were most in demand. Over 500 Republican denarii from free Germania and also many such coins from the Empire before Nero are certainly extant. A number of German hoards show, however, that these coins continued to be introduced

---

[1] See Volume of Plates v, 10, *m–o*.

[2] *Pigrum quin immo et iners videtur sudore adquirere quod possis sanguine parare* (14).

[3] IV, 1; VI, 22.

[4] See A. Dopsch, *Wirtschaftliche und soziale Grundzüge...*, I, p. 59.

right up to the time when Trajan withdrew them (A.D. 107)[1]. This anxiety to secure coin of good quality contradicts Tacitus' statement about the indifference of the Germani to precious metals. The beautiful gold ornaments, which give evidence of great technical skill[2], also point in the same direction. The enormous quantities of gold which the continental tribes demanded from the Roman Empire during the period of migrations, and the tributes in silver which the Vikings imposed on Western Europe, also show plainly that the desire for money was far from foreign to the Germani of those times. An interest in trade must also have been long established among them. As early as the Stone Age the South Scandinavians carried on an extensive export of flint implements and amber. The latter attained still greater importance during the Bronze Age for the purpose of barter for metals (bronze and gold). During the first period of the Northern Iron Age trade with foreign countries suffered a great set-back, but during the last century before Christ connections with Italy began. This is proved, for instance, by the importation of bronze *situlae* dating from the La Tène period, no less than fifteen having been found in Hanover alone, while five had found their way to Scandinavia. There are no statistics to show the extent of the Roman imports into the continental portion of free Germania but it was undoubtedly considerable. Of Roman and provincial Roman wares the Scandinavian countries show more than 500 vessels of bronze, about 260 of glass and half-a-dozen of silver[3]. These figures go to show that the Germani could appreciate the products of the Roman metal industries far more than Tacitus' statements would lead us to suppose. The considerable proportion of *trullae* (wine-ladles) among the bronze vessels indicates that wine had also penetrated far beyond the frontiers of free Germania, probably as early as the time of Tacitus.

Just as Tacitus pays too little attention to the trade of the Germani with the Roman Empire, he also fails to recognize their receptivity of Roman culture. As early, however, as the Later Stone Age, they had shown themselves extremely susceptible to cultural influences from abroad. During the Bronze and Early Northern Iron Ages a decided increase in these influences in connection with the metal import is observed, which reaches its height during the first two centuries A.D. They certainly remained unacquainted with the highest expressions of Roman culture, such

[1] S. Bolin, *R.G.K. Ber*. xix, 1929, p. 130.
[2] See Volume of Plates v, 6, 8, 10, 20.
[3] *Ib.* 8, 10, 12; G. Ekholm, *Acta archaeologica*, vi, 1935, pp. 49 *sqq.*

as literature, art, and the like, but the imported Roman goods and the marked classical forms of the native antiquities are so characteristic of the epoch that Scandinavian archaeologists call it the 'Roman Iron Age.' With regard to the group which is far the most numerously represented—the fibulae—they are certainly not, as was formerly assumed, imports from the Empire, but their forms were strongly affected by classical taste. This applies in general to all the Germanic forms of ornaments, implements, earthenware vessels, belonging to these two centuries. The gold ornaments in particular attest an independent development of the filigree technique copied from the classical peoples, perhaps the Etruscans[1]. As also during the Bronze Age, it is in the Scandinavian countries that the technique of metal-work reaches its zenith[2]. The great absorption of Roman culture by the Germani is also remarkable, because it contrasts with the indifference of the Scotch and Irish, who appear to have remained unaffected by it.

In view of the fact that the best goods of foreign and native extraction are almost entirely taken from graves, a reservation must also be made against Tacitus' statements about the simple burial custom of the Germani. The burial-mounds with cremated bones and few objects which he describes are characteristic especially of the districts of the Lower Rhine, whence indeed he got much of his information about the Germani. But in other parts of free Germania graves of another type with more abundant furniture are met with. Before the beginning of the Christian era isolated skeleton-graves had begun to make their appearance, probably as a result of Celtic influences. At first their adornment had been quite simple, but during the first century of our era grave objects were often very abundant. The inhumation flat graves in particular often contain rich deposits either of native earthenware vessels or of imported wares of bronze, glass or occasionally of silver[3]. It is mainly in this type of grave that the imported Roman goods referred to above are found.

As has been indicated above, Tacitus' account of the religious conditions must also be read with a certain scepticism[4]. The explanation given of the lack of images and temples reflects his own personal ideas. The real cause may be sought in the fact that the Germani had not yet got quite beyond their original nature-worshipping stage. During the Bronze Age they had still worshipped the divine powers, mainly in the shape of axes and other symbols. A number of small statuettes of a naked woman are

[1] Almgren, *Mannus-Bibliothek*, XXXII, 1923, pp. 123 *sqq.*
[2] See Volume of Plates v, 8, 10.   [3] *Ib.* 12.   [4] *Germ.* 9.

found from the end of this period, probably representing a goddess of fertility—possibly the same as Tacitus' Nerthus—and in the time of Tacitus the divine world is entirely anthropomorphized. The chief gods mentioned in the *Germania*, Mercury, Hercules and Mars, are identified in various ways, but usually as Woden (Odin), Donar (Tor) and Tiu (Tyr). The cult of the war-god Woden is traced in the burial customs of several West-Germanic tribes (p. 55), whereas the Scandinavian peoples at this time worshipped predominantly the Wanes (Vanir), the divine family of Nerthus. But the Germani had not yet reached the stage of images and temples, and all kinds of magic, the interpretation of signs and other primitive customs, still constituted part of their religion. There was a priesthood, but the father of the family also had certain religious duties.

The most interesting chapters in Tacitus' work are those that deal with the political and social structure of the Germanic peoples. At the same time they are among the hardest to interpret, not from the point of view of language, but as regards their contents. In short, sometimes enigmatic, sentences a number of problems are touched upon which are still not entirely solved. This is the more remarkable in that discussions about them take up by far the greater part of the literature which has appeared in connection with Tacitus' work. It is now universally agreed that the Germanic community was based on the family. During the time of Tacitus and much later, the Germanic State was of the nature of an alliance of families and constituted a rather loose association of a number of small territories. These Tacitus calls *pagi* and says that each is ruled by a prince (*princeps*). The bond of union within each state is the national assembly (the *Thing*) and the king (*rex*), who possesses very limited powers[1]. The terminological difference between *princeps* and *rex* made by Tacitus and other classical authors is, however, assumed to be foreign to the Germani. These statements do not entitle us to make a distinction between monarchical and republican forms of government[2]. Among the Scandinavians at any rate all princes seem as a rule to have borne the name of king. The most varied opinions have been expressed about the origin of the power of the kings among the Germani. According to some scholars, it is very ancient, according to others comparatively late and developed from other offices such as that of general. The three distinctive functions of the king—as generalissimo, supreme judge and chief priest—suggest its

[1] *Germ.* 11–14.
[2] K. Müllenhoff, *Deutsche Altertumskunde*, IV, pp. 184 *sqq.*

great antiquity because they indicate that the office ultimately has its roots in the authority of the head of the family.

In Tacitus' statement about the Suiones[1] we get a glimpse of another kind of kingship, embracing several *civitates*. A number of facts indicate that this strongly sacral kingship arose out of the old kingship under influences coming from the Mediterranean countries in connection with the cult of the fertility goddess[2]. It can be assumed that, as in Egypt and India also, the King and Queen of the Suiones were looked upon as the hypostases of the male and female forms of that twin deity of fertility. Nevertheless even kingships such as those of the Suiones must be assumed to have been somewhat loosely welded monarchies, most nearly of the same character as the tribal associations on the continent (referred to above), whose cult was chiefly the bond that held them together. But the over-kingship common to the states of the Suiones is remarkable, nothing corresponding to it being mentioned elsewhere, though it is alleged that this sacral Uppsala-kingship was the model at the founding of the all-Norwegian dominion during the ninth century. Whether it also influenced the development of this institution among other Germanic peoples it is not yet possible to decide. But it should be observed that the word *king* is proved to be of North-Germanic origin and further that it is absent in the Gothic—Ulfila's term is *þiudans*—and that in the West-Germanic languages it is borrowed from the North[3].

According to Tacitus the kings were chosen for their noble birth, which probably referred to divine origin which was usually claimed by the dynasties of the Germani. As the history of the Germani shows, kingship was so strictly confined to certain families that in practice it was hereditary—even though not in the direct line. The power of the king was limited. The love of liberty was strongly developed and the Germani submitted to authority unwillingly. By the side of the king there was a council of princes, who settled minor matters and had the right to prepare more important ones before they were laid before the national assembly, which had the right of decision, in certain cases (matters of life

---

[1] *Germ.* 44.

[2] See the present writer in *Historisk tidskrift*, XLVI, 1926, pp. 326 *sqq.*

[3] The old view, that the Germanic words for *king* have connection with Old-Norse *kyn*, family, may now be abandoned. The Old-Norse *KonungR* has its root in *kona*, woman, wife, here alluding to a fertility goddess and is to be interpreted as *the mate of the goddess*, a new and important testimony for the sacral character of this kingship. O. von Friesen, *Saga och sed*, 1932–1934, pp. 15 *sqq.* and Chadwick, *op. cit.* p. 252.

and death), also jurisdiction. The members of the Thing, which was composed of all free men, received the proposals with a murmur of disapproval or an assenting clash of weapons.

The democratic features of the Germanic method of government were counterbalanced by certain aristocratic ones. Although the serfs were well treated—some of them seem to have been in a position almost resembling bond tenants—sharp distinctions were drawn between them and the men who had been freed, and between these and the real freeborn. The nobility (*nobiles*) had the greatest influence in the Thing, and a certain order of precedence was observed in the division of land[1]. The power of the aristocracy was very much strengthened by the chieftains' surrounding themselves with large armed body-guards (*comitatus*) of freemen and youths. The institution of body-guards with their cultivation of the virtues of war and their glorification of the bond of loyalty between the chieftain and his men appears to be a forerunner of the chivalry of the Middle Ages and seems to have had a close analogy among the Celts (vol. VII, p. 72). It had the effect of weakening the power of the king, but at the same time undoubtedly helped strongly to accentuate the warlike traits in both peoples. Campaigns and the booty they produced were necessary for the maintenance of the body-guards and in turn the *comitatus* often formed the nucleus of new kingdoms in the time of the great migration.

The military system of the Germani is also a subject which Tacitus dwells on fully[2]. Their military organization, the disposition of the army, and their method of fighting, as well as their weapons, are described in detail. Weapons are seldom laid aside, and as in Rome a youth assumed the toga on coming of age, so among the Germani he was given a shield and lance. When speaking of the Cimbri, Tacitus takes the opportunity to give a survey of the struggles of the Romans with the Germanic peoples and strongly emphasizes their character as Rome's most dangerous enemy[3]. It can hardly be doubted that an expansion of the Germani was to Tacitus the great danger that still threatened the Roman Empire. To him the internal dissension among the Germanic peoples was the only bright side of this picture. To warn and enlighten his fellow-countrymen and to some extent also for the purpose of their self-examination, he published in A.D. 98— at the time when Trajan was present on the banks of the Rhine for the purpose of settling frontier questions—his book about the vigorous, brave and moral but rapacious and bellicose people who inhabited the wide countries of free Germania.

---

[1] *Germ.* 26.   [2] *Ib.* 6–8.   [3] *Ib.* 37.

VI. THE GETAE AND THE DACIANS

There is both linguistic and archaeological evidence for an early settlement of Thracian peoples in Transylvania and the eastern Carpathians, and in the adjacent steppes beyond to the north of the Danube estuary and the Black Sea. By the eighth and seventh centuries B.C., it would seem, the Thracians had achieved a strong and stable political organization, as appears from the remarkable fact that only the earliest and latest stages of Illyrian iron culture succeeded in penetrating into the lands to the east of the central Danube, where in the intervening period the traditional bronze culture continued to flourish. This significant separation from and contrast with the west, where Illyrian influence was predominant, clearly points to the existence of a unified system of government among the Thracian settlers, a system which crumbled before the onslaught of the immigrant hordes from the remote north-east. It is even possible that this first unification of northern Thrace was itself the achievement of an invading wave of pre-Scythian horse-riding shepherds—the mare-milkers of Homer. For in this district traces have been found of a horse-riding people who coalesced with the northern Thracians at a time contemporary with the later Hallstatt age, and who have been identified with the Cimmerians. The *trique-trum*[1], which combines the parts of various animals into one composition, the animal form with body twisted backwards, and the Shaman crown, from the find at Mikhalkowo, suffice to prove that the users of this type of ornamentation came from the home of the North-Asiatic animal style[2]. The wealth in gold of the Transylvanian Agathyrsi, which Herodotus[3] emphasizes, is pre-Scythian and dates from this early period in the land's history.

Archaeology shows that Transylvania again changed masters in the sixth century B.C. A similar series of articles to the early Scythian finds from South Russia often occurs here, especially in the valley of the Marisus (Maros). The Scythian types and their

---

[1] See Volume of Plates v, 22, *a, b*.

[2] Conversely these motifs show that the animal style had an individual development in South Russia, and possessed a basis of typical themes before the Scythian invasion. A collection of the horse-riding nomadic elements in this group of monuments is given in the work of S. Gallus and T. Horváth on the emergence of the horse-riding people in Hungary (in the series *Dissertationes Pannonicae*, to appear in 1936).

[3] IV, 104.

ornamentation have an archaic flavour[1], and do not share the development which occurred in South Russia under Greek influence.
The intrusion of local elements reflects the gradual absorption
of the Scythian conquerors by the native Thracian population.
We learn more about this process in Herodotus. The Agathyrsi
of the Marisus basin, of whom he writes, had their place in the
original tribal organization of the Scythians; they constituted one
of the three parts into which the Scythian people was divided for
military and political purposes, and which also formed the framework of their religious institutions[2]. Moreover, the tribal name
of this people and also of its original king Spargapeithes is
genuinely Scythian. All that emerges from Herodotus' conflicting
statements is that the Agathyrsian conquest in Transylvania dates
back to the sixth century. The aloofness of the Agathyrsi during
Darius' Scythian expedition is in keeping with the isolation reflected in the archaeological remains, and also with the singularity
which has repeatedly characterized this country, cut off as it is
by mountains on every side. As early as Herodotus the effects
of Thracian influence were profound: in two generations the
exogamy of the horse-riding shepherds had sufficed to bring about
a large measure of assimilation between rulers and subjects. An
illuminating parallel in later times is provided by the rapid
germanization of the ruling aristocracy of the Huns.

We have much less information concerning the consequences
of the next great invasion of the lands to the north of the Danube.
We know that the Celts penetrated to Hungary at about the same
time as they invaded Italy, but their arrival in Transylvania was
somewhat later, if we may trust the archaeological evidence. It
would seem, indeed, that intermittent advances were made as
early as the fourth century, but there was no real invasion until
some hundred years later, when the La Tène culture finally
established itself here (vol. VII, p. 65). The names of tribes and
settlements preserved in Ptolemy attest further Celtic immigration in the Getic East, Galicia, and Bessarabia; they also throw
light on the migrations of the third century.

The Celts, like the Scythians, exercised a repressive influence
on the primitive inhabitants of the eastern Carpathians (p. 80),
but they neither destroyed them nor drove them out. Subsequently

[1] Cf. M. Rostowzew, *Skythien und der Bosporus*, I, p. 534.

[2] Cf. the present writer's lecture on metal-working and kingship in
Northern Asia, at present printed in Hungarian only in *Magyar Nyelv*, XXVIII,
1932, pp. 205 *sqq*. The importance of the sacred hearth-fire of the kings,
and the name *paradāta* (cf. H. Lommel, *Die Yašts des Awesta*, p. 170) of
the kingly house link early Scythian legend with Iranian theology.

these older races became known to the neighbouring Greeks, who established the fact that the complex of peoples in northern Thrace which had supplied much human material for the Athenian slave-market in the fourth century B.C. was composed of two main elements, Dacians and Getae. Since, however, the Greeks had more to do with the Getae, who were their immediate neighbours, they applied this name to all the peoples of northern Thrace, to the confusion both of ancient and of modern writers. In spite of this it is possible to delimit with some accuracy the territories occupied by the Dacians and the Getae. The former were not confined to Transylvania, but were distributed over an area reaching westwards as far as the central Danube, and northwards beyond the Carpathians to the Vistula. Agrippa's map of the world marked these northerly Dacians, and the place-names ending in *-dava* (the Dacian for settlement) which occur over an area extending as far as Podolia confirm the accuracy of his authorities. We have from various sources a considerable number of tribal names[1]. It must have been in early times that the collection of tribes in the Carpathians, cut off as they were by their geographical environment from the other branches of their race, became differentiated as the special group of Dacian Getae, even though the name Dacian is unknown to the Greek world before the fourth century. The Getae proper had settled to the east and south of the Carpathians. The Dniester was the limit of the really populous area, but they extended far beyond, since Thracian nomenclature occurs in the personal and place-names of the Bosporan kingdom. To the south the Getic region of settlement extended along both banks of the Danube[2], and was bounded by the mountain barrier of the Balkan range. The Dacians and Getae spoke the same language—a Thracian dialect.

It is natural that our Greek authorities should make earlier and more frequent mention of those Getae who lived to the south of the Danube, between the lower reaches of the river and the Balkan massif, than of the others. The complexity of this mountainous area was reflected in the diversity of the tribes inhabiting it, which remained isolated units, and in spite of their common origin and great personal bravery failed to achieve national unity[3], and in

[1] The tribal names, derived from place-names, in Ptolemy, have more evidential value than is usually supposed: he attests a similar name formation for Moesia, and his information here, as in the case of the north Dacian and Getic tribal territories, may go back to the time before the conquest.

[2] Strabo II, 117; II, 128; VII, 295; VII, 305.

[3] E. Roesler, *Sitz.-Ber. d. Wien. Akad.* XLIV, 1863, p. 163 *sq.*

consequence were severely handled and oppressed by their more powerful neighbours. A few words must suffice to describe their sufferings which lasted for centuries. The Scythians not only made plundering raids into their territory, but settled there permanently from the sixth century onwards, as the growing Scythian influence on these Getae shows (p. 86 *sq.*). Subsequently Darius during his Scythian expedition devastated their country, and in the following centuries their kings were successively subjects of the Odrysians, the Scythian Atheas, Philip of Macedon, and Lysimachus. First Celtic hordes, then the Bastarnae and the Sarmatae ravaged their territory, but in the first century B.C. they were still strong enough to oppose the generals of Rome, after Mithridates had sought to master them. In 73 M. Lucullus defeated them, but shortly afterwards, at about the middle of the century, the southern Getae were incorporated in Burebista's great Dacian kingdom. About the time of Caesar's death, however, this dangerous unification of the northern Thracians broke down, and when M. Crassus, after 30 B.C., brought order into these regions we hear of several petty kingdoms of the Getae. The territories of Roles and Dapyx were situated on the frontier district between northeastern Bulgaria and Roumania[1], while Zyraxes ruled to the south of the Dobrudja[2]. Their strength was broken and their subjects were incorporated in the Roman Empire (vol. x, p. 117 *sq.*).

Still harder was the fate of the other Getae, who inhabited the plains to the north of the Danube and the Black Sea and so were exposed to the attacks of immigrant peoples. We know little of their fate under the Cimmerians and Scythians; the shift of the Scythian centre of power to the vicinity of the Danubian delta must have seriously lessened their political freedom. This change did not, however, destroy them utterly: when Alexander the Great crossed the Danube and defeated them they showed themselves to be an independent people of great bravery (vol. vi, p. 355). Their military power is best illustrated by the defeats they shortly afterwards inflicted on Macedonian generals of repute. Zopyrion, for example, failed ignominiously against them, and Lysimachus fared no better (vol. vi, p. 394, vii, p. 82). Lysimachus' opponent, Dromichaetes, was supported by contingents from many tribes of Wallachia and South Russia; but the military strength of the

---

[1] Cf. C. Patsch, in *Sitz.-Ber. d. Wien. Akad.* 214, 1932, I, pp. 77 *sqq.*
[2] P. Kretschmer (*Glotta*, XXIV, 1935, p. 45) suggests that Zyraxes may mean the prince of the Zyras river. These dynasts may have been Dacian princely families introduced by Burebista. See below, p. 82.

Getae was later shattered by the mass migrations of the Sciri and Bastarnae, who by about 230 B.C. must have begun to make definite inroads into Getic possessions, since their territory extended at that time as far as the shores of the Black Sea[1]. Nevertheless, Oroles, the king of the Getae, despite early defeats, contrived to hold his own in the face of these enemies[2]. It is, however, clear from the numerous military undertakings of the Bastarnae in the Balkans, and from their attacks on the Greek cities on the north coast of the Black Sea, that the Getae in the second century B.C. could make little headway against such opponents, and the prominent part played by the Bastarnae in the campaigns and armies of Mithridates shows that this critical situation persisted. The Germanic Sciri were cowed by the Dacians (after 60 B.C.), and the Bastarnae were subdued by Crassus in 29–8 B.C., but neither of these happenings was of much help to the Getae, as yet a new enemy arose to oppress them. For the break-up of the kingdoms of Mithridates and Burebista opened the way westwards to the Sarmatae (p. 92 *sq.*). It is not improbable that the mass migration of the Bastarnae with all their belongings to Moesia in 29 B.C. was due to the beginning of Sarmatian pressure. Certainly from 16 B.C. onwards Roman generals frequently came into contact with them[3], and Ovid in his exile could frequently observe them in the neighbourhood of Tomi. They also crossed to the right bank of the Danube. It is therefore not surprising that the Getae on the Black Sea coast vanish from the stage of history under the Empire.

While the peoples of the steppes to the east of the Black Sea had cut each other's throats, the Dacians in the rocky fastness of Transylvania grew stronger. Although they too were weakened by wars, yet even before the king who was to be the founder of their power came to the throne, a representative of the Greek city Dionysopolis on the shores of the Black Sea found it advisable

---

[1] Cf. L. Schmidt, *Geschichte der deutschen Stämme bis zum Ausgange der Völkerwanderung*[2], I, p. 87.

[2] Oroles was not a Dacian but a Getic king, as is clear from the fact that Trogus (Prol. xxxII) dates the beginnings of Dacian power from the time of Burebista, *i.e.* knows nothing of a successful predecessor; but he describes the Getae as predecessors of the Dacians. This has obscured Justin's excerpt, xxxII, 3, 16: *Daci quoque suboles Getarum sunt, qui cum Orole rege adversus Bastarnas male pugnassent*, etc.—*qui* must be taken as referring to the Getae.

[3] Dio LIV, 20, 3. Patsch, *op. cit.* pp. 83, 92 *sqq.* suggests that the Sarmatae of the sources are really Bastarnae, but this interpretation appears to the present writer to be inadmissible.

to appear at the Dacian court. In the ten years 61–51 B.C. came the great expansion that was achieved under Burebista[1]. The chronological order of his conquests is uncertain; they made him the dominant ruler to the north of the Danube and also in Thrace. Eastwards he succeeded in utterly crushing the Bastarnae —at a later date their fortresses were still in the hands of Dacian petty princes[2]. The brave resistance of the Greek cities in the north-west corner of the Black Sea was in vain: most of them were plundered, many razed to the ground, and they never recovered from this terrible blow. About 55 B.C.[3], it would seem, Burebista turned against Thrace, devastating and in part subduing the country as far as Macedonia and Roman Illyria. Farther west-wards he conquered the powerful Celtic tribe of the Scordisci between the Save and the Morava, and made them his allies, presumably for his next war, in the course of which he almost destroyed the Boii[4] and Taurisci. The Boii were recent immigrants who had driven the Dacians beyond the Theiss. By their victory the Dacians recovered the Hungarian central plain, and took possession of Slovakia.

The sudden emergence of so powerful a kingdom, which could mobilize a force 200,000 strong in the rear of Macedonia and Italy, presented a challenge to the chief power of the ancient world, which must sooner or later be taken up. Although the death of Burebista and the collapse of the power he had built postponed the day of reckoning, the future of the Dacians re-mained dependent on their relations with Rome.

All along the borders of the civilized world there stretched a belt of turbulent peoples who were ignorant of the restraining influences of civilization but were eager to gain for themselves the riches it had produced. Wherever Rome broke the power of a Hellenistic State she destroyed at the same time a bulwark of defence against these frontier peoples[5]. Thus when she destroyed the Macedonian State she inherited its enemies in the north. The raids of the Balkan tribes enticed their northern neighbours

---

[1] Patsch, *op. cit.* p. 51 has rightly stressed the fact that after 49 his aggression ceased.

[2] Pointed out by G. Zippel, *Die röm. Herrschaft in Illyrien*, p. 216 *sq.*

[3] Cf. Patsch, *op. cit.* p. 49.

[4] Observe, however, that the son of the defeated king Critasirus ruled after him (cf. W. Kubitschek, *Jahreshefte*, IX, 1906, pp. 70 *sqq.*) and the Boii also re-appear often in Imperial times.

[5] F. Altheim, *Epochen der römischen Geschichte*, II, pp. 163, 175. V. Pârvan, *Dacia*, p. 156.

the Dacians into joining in the game. In 112 and 109 B.C. the
Dacians are found in alliance with the Scordisci against Roman
generals[1]; in 75 they assist the Dardani against Scribonius Curio[2],
who follows them along the valley of the Morava or Timok as
far as the Danube, but then falls back, being unprepared for an
advance into the primeval forest of the Dacian mountain ranges.
But Rome's frontier defences were presently crippled by the
extreme internal strain of the civil wars, and the astonishingly
rapid spread of Burebista's power in every direction is largely due
to Roman weakness. Burebista negotiated with Pompey before
Pharsalus, but did not give him any real assistance; and this only
strengthened Caesar's determination to come to a final reckoning
with this opponent (vol. ix, p. 715). His great expeditionary force
had already been set in motion; the young Octavian was to leave
his studies at Apollonia to join Caesar's staff. But the Ides of March
intervened. The Dacian king himself lost his life at about the
same time, and his empire broke up into four principalities.

Through the advance of the Empire's frontier to the Danube
the problem of Dacia assumed a different aspect in Augustus'
reign. From a point near Vienna to the river mouth, the Dacian
and Roman frontiers marched side by side, and the Dacians had
to be taught to cease their encroachments on the Roman bank.
Siscia, captured in 35 B.C., was to have served as Octavian's base
of operations for a great Dacian campaign[3]. The clash with
Antony, however, prevented an active offensive: indeed, the initiative lay with the Dacians, for, since the decisive action in the
civil wars took place in the Balkan peninsula, each of the rival
opponents was constrained to attempt to draw on the military
resources of the Dacians for his own uses. Antony accused
Octavian of having planned to win King Cotiso's support by
a matrimonial alliance; but the Dacians, after fruitless negotiations
with the ruler of the West, favoured Antony. The prince Dicomes
promised him numerous troops, but proved unable to keep his
promise; another prince, Scorylo, wished to maintain peace—the
truth was that internal rivalries prevented all from any active
participation. The most powerful of these dynasts was Cotiso[4],

---

[1] Brandis in P. W. s.v. Dacia, col. 1956 sq.

[2] F. Münzer in P. W. s.v. Scribonius Curio (10), col. 864.

[3] See, however, vol. x, p. 84.

[4] A. von Premerstein (*Jahreshefte*, xxix, 1934, p. 66 sq.) would separate
the *Coson* of Suetonius (= the ΚΟΣΩΝ of the coins) from the *Cotiso* of Horace
and Florus but the two forms of the name may clearly be due to a half-way
form Κόζων.

the ruler of Transylvania, whose armies were still a frequent menace to the security of Moesia and Pannonia. The astonishing number of his gold staters which have been found is in itself sufficient evidence of a prosperous reign. They were probably made for him by coin-designers from Olbia[1]. The fear of the Dacians at Rome in the years after Actium is vividly reflected in the relevant passages of Horace and Virgil, and there was a general sigh of relief when Cotiso's armies were defeated.

The solution of the Dacian question was in fact a very difficult matter for the Roman State—not because the Dacians were a match for Rome, as has been suggested, but because Transylvania, the inaccessible mountain land of the Dacians, lay outside the natural frontier line on which the Romans based their plans of conquest, namely, the line of the Danube. Incorporation in the Empire was not accordingly a part of imperial policy, but the Romans concentrated on reprisals for raids, and on various methods of isolating the Dacians from the regions bordering on the river. This could not be achieved without military activity. The reports preserved of these measures are very defective[2]. It is quite by chance that we learn from a fragmentary inscription that some general (presumably M. Vinicius, cos. 19 B.C.) penetrated into Dacia in the lower Danubian region, and defeated an army of Dacians and Bastarnae, while at the same time his legate in the North-West of Dacia carried out a punitive expedition against the Osi, Cotini, Anartii, and others, perhaps in revenge for the Dacian invasion of 10 B.C. A second important expedition against the Dacians was led by Cn. Cornelius Lentulus (cos. 18 B.C.) apparently in the later years of Augustus' reign. He succeeded in driving back the Dacians and Sarmatae from the north bank of the stream. Aelius Catus, perhaps in co-operation with him, transplanted 50,000 Dacians from the north bank to Moesia. Through this aggressive action the Romans also succeeded in splitting one of the most powerful Dacian principalities into two parts[3]. One of these offensives was important enough in the Emperor's eyes to merit mention in his Res Gestae.

Strabo maintains that the Dacians were pacified by these measures, but this was not the case—they remained a thorn in

---

[1] Cf. M. von Bahrfeldt, Über die Goldmünzen des Dakerkönigs ΚΟΣΩΝ.

[2] See for these operations vol. x, p. 366 sq. and the works cited in the bibliography, ib. p. 940, to which may now be added A. von Premerstein, op. cit. above.

[3] Strabo VII, 304.

the side of the Empire to the end[1]. From year to year they made
small raids across the Danube: the Appuli of the Marisus valley,
for example, frequently penetrated as far as the Greek cities of
the Black Sea in their search for booty. On two occasions, in
10 B.C. and A.D. 11, the solemn closing of the temple of Janus
by Augustus was prevented by dangerous Dacian incursions.
Moreover the Dacians combined with rebellious Pannonians to
ravage in Moesia (A.D. 6) and we learn from Ovid of serious disturbances in the last years of Augustus' reign.

Rome's hard-won victories failed, therefore, to impose tranquillity. Tiberius, however, here as elsewhere, followed the policy
formulated by his predecessor: he concentrated on keeping the
Dacians away from the immediate vicinity of the river. Indeed
he may well have been responsible for transferring the Iazyges,
the westernmost tribe of the Sarmatians, from the estuary of the
Danube to the Hungarian plain[2] in order to cut off the Dacians
from the Danubian border of Pannonia. Under subsequent emperors the pressure of the Roxolani[3], who were akin to the
Iazyges and sought to follow them, stirred up the Dacians on the
border of Moesia. Possibly these Roxolani initiated that 'incipient
revolt of the Sarmatae,' which Plautius Silvanus[4] suppressed under
Nero (Vol. x, pp. 775 sqq.) and in which the Dacians and Bastarnae
were concerned on one side or the other. A hundred thousand
barbarians were transplanted to the Roman side of the Danube by
Silvanus; he was given absolute power in organizing the country
adjoining the *limes*, and made himself felt as far as the Crimea.
But the gap thus created gave the Roxolani still more room for
their restless movements. And when in the confusion that followed

[1] Strabo, VII, 305. It is not due to chance that there is no mention of
Dacian allegiance in the *Res Gestae*, as Pârvan, *Getica*, p. 92 noted. Cf.
further Horace, *Od.* II, 20, 17 *sqq.*

[2] The immigration of the Iazyges was against the wishes of the Dacians
as the words *pulsi ab iis Daci* in Pliny *N.H.* IV, 80 show; no one who reflects
how the legates dealt with the frontier peoples at that time will imagine that
they came without permission from the governor of Pannonia.

[3] Some suppose that they remained near the Black Sea, but we know from
Dio (LXXII, 19, 2) that under Marcus Aurelius they had permission to com-
municate with the Iazyges through the province of Dacia, *i.e.* across the
Aluta, and so could not have been far away. Jordanes, *Getica*, XII, 74 M,
following an ancient authority, says: *nam Iazyges ab Aroxolanis Aluta tantum
fluvio segregantur*.

[4] Dessau 986. Cf. Patsch, *op. cit.* pp. 164 *sqq.*, H. Dessau, *Jahreshefte*,
XXIII, 1926, pp. 346 *sqq.*, V. Pârvan, *Getica*, pp. 103 *sqq.*, L. Halkin, *L'Antiquité class.* III, 1934, p. 145.

Nero's death the Dacians attacked Moesia, not they but the Roxolani were the most dangerous disturbers of the peace[1] (p. 168). The revival of Dacian power begins under the Flavians.

VII. DACIAN CIVILIZATION

About the time when Trogus announces the 'incrementa Dacorum per Burobusten regem[2],' we see Dacian civilization beginning to bear an individual stamp of its own. Before this period the Dacians and Getae constituted merely a province of the Thracian, Scythian and Celtic cultures which were coloured to a greater or less extent from their contact with the supreme achievements of Greek civilization.

Scythian influence in this region has been generally underestimated, although (especially since the researches of Minns and Rostovtzeff) the fundamental modification which it caused even in the Greek coastal cities has been clearly demonstrated. On the Thracians it is also very marked, especially among the more northerly tribes (see above, vol. VIII, pp. 557 sqq.). Thus Bulgaria is rich in finds of Scythian art-products, and the crossing of Thracian and Scythian stock through intermarriage is well attested[3]. In Homer the Thracian allies of the Trojans still fight with war chariots, whereas Thucydides knows them as mounted archers of the Scythian type, just like the Getae. The long Thracian cavalry cape (ib. p. 543) is also borrowed from the Scythians, as are several of their customs, notably to induce perspiration and complete unconsciousness resembling sleep by means of the fumes from grains of hemp thrown on heated flat stones[4]. Among the Getae and Dacians, who were much more open to this influence, its effects were still more profound. This has been demonstrated by linguistic evidence[5]: even the name of the Getae is the abbreviated form of a Scythian title, which appears to have originally designated an upper class among the Scythians. The name Danus, applied to the central and upper Danube, is Scythian[6], and so is

---

[1] According to Tacitus (*Hist.* IV, 4) Mucianus received the *insignia triumphalia* on account of his *in Sarmatas expeditio*, which cannot be interpreted as referring to successes against the Dacians. The repulse of Dacian attacks is mentioned as a duty of the Moesian garrisons (in A.D. 66) by Josephus, *Bell. Jud.* II, [16, 4], 369.

[2] *Prol.* XXXII.

[3] *E.g.* Herodotus, IV, 80. Apoll. Rhod. IV, 320. Strabo VII, 296.

[4] W. Tomaschek, *Die alten Thraker*, I, p. 123 sq.; II, I, p. 11 n. 11.

[5] Kretschmer, *op. cit.* pp. 37 sqq.

[6] *Ib.* pp. 1 sqq.

even the name of the chief Getic deity Zalmoxis[1]. The explanations
given by Porphyry[2] of this word's original meaning are by no
means unconvincing[3]. He translates it 'bearskin' and 'strange
man,' and the two interpretations are complementary. The first
takes us back to the cult of the bearskin prevalent among the
North-Asiatic hunting peoples, and the second is a typical secret
name for the bear among the same races. The cult of the bearskin
belongs to a very primitive cultural stratum among the nomads:
the sacred trio of bearskins[4] apparently corresponds to a triple
social division of the people, just as in the next stage of development the two animal ancestors correspond to a double social
division. The Scythians still preserved a threefold tribal organization when they reached the Black Sea region, and the Agathyrsi
comprised one of the three units (see above, p. 78). The threefold
structure has also a matriarchal aspect with the goddess of the
hearth Tabiti, who organizes the life of the community, at its
centre; the worship of Hestia (κοινὴ Ἑστία) of the Getae may
correspond to this (Vol. viii, p. 550). The bear-father in heaven,
on the lofty mountain peak, the withdrawal of Zalmoxis to the
(world-) cave, and the predominant part played by the belief in
immortality[5] may all belong to this order of ideas. The Scythians
also introduced the knowledge of iron weapons among the Dacians,
but the marked Iranian influence is not attributable to the
Scythians alone. The Iazyges and the Roxolani were the Getans'
instructors in the use of the phalanx of heavy-armed cavalry
(p. 99), and were in general a contributory factor in prolonging
Iranian influence down to Imperial times. Hence the Thracian
horseman divinity retained his original character[6], and the dragon
remained the national banner of the Dacian troops[7].

Greek influence on the northern Thracians was naturally more
indirect and far more superficial, though there was a strong
demand for the excellent Greek manufactures which were bartered
in exchange for raw materials and slaves. There was a considerable
market for the products of Greek industry among the Getae—and
also to the north of the Danube, where Istros and the neighbouring

[1] Kretschmer, *op. cit.* p. 43 *sq.*
[2] *Vita Pythag.* 14, 15.
[3] Cf. also Tomaschek, *op. cit.* ii, 1, p. 10, n. 11.
[4] G. Boroffka, 25 *Jahre Römisch-Germanische Kommission*, pl. xii;
A. Alföldi, *Arch. Anz.* 1931, p. 403 *sq.*
[5] Kretschmer, *op. cit.* p. 43 *sq.*
[6] M. Rostovtzeff, *Mém. prés. à l'Acad. d. Inscr.* xiii, 2, 1923, p. 405.
[7] Tomaschek, *op. cit.* i, 1893, 120; Pârvan, *op. cit.* pp. 519 *sqq.*

cities controlled the supply[1], but in the mountainous regions of Dacia the imports were slight indeed. The great bronze hydria from Bene is evidence that even in the sixth century such splendid manufactures could penetrate as far as Slovakia, just as, conversely, scanty reports concerning the inhabitants of Transylvania reached the Greeks at this early stage. But in the classical period this exchange of commodities was very small. A few of the fibulae found at Marosvásárhely and elsewhere may date back to this era, but the flow of trade did not really quicken until there came a moderate development in the Hellenistic age. Greek palmettes on Dacian spiral silver armlets, copies of Megarian tankards from the Wittenberg near Segesvár[2], and especially the circulation of Greek coins[3], attest this tendency. In the third and second centuries Dacians accustomed themselves to a monetary system, and used the silver coinage of Philip II and especially the gold of his son and of Lysimachus. Numerous tetradrachms from the first Macedonian administrative region and from Thasos also penetrated into the land. The vast number of drachmas from Apollonia and Dyrrachium, however, herald the approach of a time when Dacia will be a Roman sphere of influence, since these cities were used by Rome as military and trading centres. Yet coins from the Black Sea coastal cities are also found.

It was much easier for the Thracians to assimilate the La Tène culture with which they were brought into immediate proximity through the Celtic conquests. Whereas in earlier times this culture in Transylvania as elsewhere shows a striking uniformity, from the second century B.C. it develops in its own way into a special Dacian branch, which affords a parallel to the tendency towards unification in the political sphere, since the civilization of Moldavia and Wallachia, as of Transylvania, is uniform in character[4]. On the ornaments, mostly of silver, and the other typical articles, special Dacian characteristics emerge; while the Macedonian and Thasian tetradrachms are replaced by primitive imitations minted locally. A very impressive monument to this Dacian culture, and at the same time characteristic of its strange aristocratic flavour, is to be found in its fortresses. Few of these have as

---

[1] V. Pârvan, *Pénétration hellén. et hellénist. dans la vallée du Danube*, Bull. de la sect. hist. de l'Acad. Roumaine x, 1923.

[2] J. Nestor, 22*tes Ber. R.G. Kom.*, p. 160, n. 656. See Vol. of Plates v, 22, *c, d*.

[3] E. Gohl, *Numizmatikai Közlöny*, XXI–XXII, 1922–1923 (1924), pp. 4 *sqq.*; V. Pârvan, *Dacia*, pp. 99 *sqq.*

[4] For the best survey see Nestor, *op. cit.* pp. 155 *sqq.*

yet been examined[1], but their number and the skill with which
they have been constructed are striking in themselves. The walls
are unusual: the outer and inner faces are built of squared blocks
of hewn limestone held together by wooden ties, while the centre
is packed with rubble and earth; in Gradište it is reported that
the blocks of stone bear Greek letters. These walls were built
to a certain height only, a superstructure of sun-baked brick
being added. The laborious levelling of platforms among the rocks,
the transport of the heavy building materials into the mountain
ranges, the construction of huge circular edifices—whether they
were of practical utility (perhaps as granaries) or served a religious
purpose is not yet determined[2]—these, and many other achievements increase our respect for the builders of these strongholds.
Great treasures of gold coins which came to light in these fastnesses reflect their owners' wealth.

The prestige of the kings was upheld by the great authority
of the high priest, whose position doubtless resulted from a
partition of the functions originally discharged by the priest-king.
The leading aristocrats were called *pilleati*, the free warriors
capillati (a title reminiscent of the Ostrogothic *capillati*): the
sculpture of the Trajanic age has preserved typical portraits of
both classes, which reveal the masculine arrogance of their
character. In time of peace the Dacians practised cattle-breeding,
and agriculture where there were plains to make it possible. In
time of war they fought as infantry, and were feared for their
scythe-like *falces*, whereas among the Getae cavalry predominated;
both peoples were famed for archery.

At the same period at which friction with Rome began, in other
words after the occupation of Macedonia, the cultural influence
of Rome also became more strongly felt. Roman imports on the
sites of Dacian settlements (such as Campanian bronze ware from
the first century of our era), and also a list of Dacian botanical
names originally written in Latin[3] are evidence of this. And, in
particular, the lively circulation of Roman denarii from the second
century B.C. onwards, and the local copying of these issues,
show that the Dacians could adopt the superior Roman culture.
The enemies which Rome had to face after the thorough-going
extermination of the Dacians were far more dangerous because
they were wholly unfamiliar with Roman civilization.

[1] See Nestor, *op. cit.* p. 170 for the literature on this.
[2] Cf. *ib.* pp. 170 *sqq.* B. Götze, *Arch. Anz.* 1935, pp. 348 *sqq.* (The
writer is indebted for this reference to N. Láng.)
[3] Tomaschek, *op. cit.* 2, 1, pp. 22 *sqq.*

THE PARTHIAN DYNASTY IN THE TIME OF THE ROMAN EMPIRE

Kings	Sharers or rivals of the Royal power
Phraates IV. 38/7–3/2 B.C.	Tiridates[1]. 32/1, 28/7 B.C.
Phraataces (Phraates V, son of above). and Musa. 3/2 B.C.–A.D. 4.	(Phraates (?) V[2].)
	Mithridates. c. 12–9 B.C.[3]
Orodes III (II in traditional list. See vol. IX, p. 613).	
Vonones I. A.D. 8/9–11/2. (Son of Phraates IV.)	

Atropatene Branch (see p. 107)

Artabanus III. 10/11–40.	Vonones I[4].
Vardanes. 40/1[5].	Phraates.
Gotarzes. 41–51.	Tiridates. 36.
	(? Cinnamus[6].)
	Vardanes. 42–4.
Vonones II. 51.	Meherdates. 49[7].
Vologases I[8]. 51–77. Coins 51–4, 60–7.	Vardanes or son of Vardanes. Coins 54–8[9].
Vologases II. 77–9[10].	
Pacorus II. 77–96 or later.	
	Vologases (II). 79.
	Artabanus (IV). Coins 79–81[10].
Osroes. 106–(?) 130[11]. Coins to 127/8.	Vologases (II). 121–(?) 130.
Vologases II. (?) 130–47.	Mithridates[12].
Vologases III. 148–91.	
Vologases IV. 190/1–208/9.	
Vologases V. 208/9. Coins 208–21.	
Artabanus V. 227[13].	
Artavasdes. 228[14].	

The evidence of the literary sources can be in part supplemented or controlled by that of coins, especially of the silver tetradrachms of the kings which bear a year and month of the Seleucid Era. But the issue of tetradrachms was irregular, and the kings' portraits which they also bear cannot always be identified. The actual names of the kings, as distinct from the traditional royal title, are rarely given before the middle of the second century. The chronology of the Parthian kings is therefore hypothetical and controversial; see for a different reconstruction R. H. McDowell, *Coins from Seleucia on the Tigris*, p. 237.

[1] See vol. X, pp. 79 and n. 2, 261.

[2] See W. W. Tarn, *Mél. Glotz*, II, pp. 831 sqq. This Phraates may, however, be Phraataces.

[3] Attested only by Josephus, *Ant.* XVI [8, 4], 253.

[4] The efforts of Vonones, son of Phraates, against his rival Artabanus were prolonged and sometimes successful. Witness the coins with the legend βασιλεὺς Ὀνώνης νικήσας Ἀρτάβανον.

[5] On Vardanes and Gotarzes see vol. X, p. 754.

[6] Josephus (*Ant.* XX [3, 2–3], 54–69) is the only evidence for this pretender, and the whole story may be invented by the Jewish writer to glorify Izates, the Jewish convert on the throne of Adiabene, who is said to have restored Artabanus (p. 112 sq.).

[7] Vol. X, p. 755.   [8] *Ib.* p. 755 sq.

[9] There are three groups of coins, of which those of 54–8 differ from those of 51–4, and both from those of 60–7 (see Volume of Plates v, 124, *d–f*). Those of 54–8 are here attributed to Vardanes or a son of Vardanes, the other two to Vologases I.

[10] The history of the Parthian kings after Vologases I is confused. The numismatic evidence shows that Vologases I was succeeded by Pacorus II and Vologases II. In 79 Pacorus ruled alone, and was faced by a usurper Artabanus IV, whom he probably removed in A.D. 82. After the death of Pacorus (the date of which is unknown) began a period of anarchy which ended with the accession of Osroes (A.D. 106), who from 121 shared his rule with Vologases II, his successor in A.D. 130.

[11] On coins of 106 appears (on a set of drachmae and bronze coins) a head that must be Osroes (Volume of Plates v, 124, *g*), who may have come to the throne then after a period of disorder. The coins of Pacorus cannot be traced after A.D. 96.

[12] Perhaps co-ruler with Vologases II or king of a vassal-State in the East, as his coins are mainly found there.

[13] There are no dated coins of Artabanus V. With his death begins the dynasty of Sasan the Persian.   [14] Perhaps son of Artabanus V. Some coins struck at Seleuceia are extant.

CHAPTER III

THE SARMATAE AND PARTHIANS

I. SARMATIAN ORIGINS AND EXTERNAL HISTORY

FOR centuries the Sarmatae together with the Scythians ruled over the steppes of South Russia and thus affected the life of the Hellenistic world. For centuries, later, they were the dangerous and dreaded enemies of the Roman Empire. They shared with their allies, the Germans, and with their cousins, the Parthians, the reputation of being a match for the Romans in war and of never having been conquered by them. On the contrary, in the time of the late Roman Empire, they took their part in its conquest by the barbarians.

The name Sarmatae first appears in our literary tradition at the end of the fourth century B.C. in Pseudo-Scylax and Eudoxus of Cnidus in the form Syrmatae. Pseudo-Scylax regards them as different from the Sauromatae of earlier historians and geographers. The same name—slightly changed to Sarmatae—is used by Polybius and the sources of Strabo, as a special designation for a group of tribes not identical with the Sauromatae of Herodotus. But this distinction between the ancient Sauromatae and the new Sarmatae never took firm root. Most of the Greek and Latin authors of the late Hellenistic and Imperial periods used the two names interchangeably and applied freely to the Sarmatae of their own times what Hecataeus, Herodotus and other early authors had to say of the Sauromatae. This confusion is explained by the fact that the two names were probably only different spellings of the same Iranian name—perhaps Sauruma[1], as well as by the history of the classical Sauromatae and the post-classical Sarmatae.

According to the Iranian tradition the Sauromatae were a half-Iranian people, akin to the Scythians, who lived in the sixth to the fourth centuries B.C. beyond the Don and on the shores of the Sea of Azov. One of their main characteristics, and one which

---

[1] Suggested by Marquart; cf. H. H. Schaeder in *Abh. Gött. Ges.* III, 10 pp. 50 *sqq.*

impressed the Greeks, was the important part played by women in their social and political life—they were called 'ruled by women' (γυναικοκρατούμενοι). Since this feature is common in the life of the Anatolians and foreign to the Iranians—both to the Scythians of Herodotus and later the Sarmatians of Hellenistic and Roman times—it is very probable that the Sarmatians were a mixture of Iranian and Maeotian tribes, and that some of them adopted the peculiar social and political structure of the Maeotians, their so-called *gynaecocracy*. Archaeological evidence proves that the regions between the Don and the Volga and between the Volga and the river Ural were inhabited by a group of Scythian tribes from the seventh to the third century B.C. Some of them—those nearest to the Don and the Sea of Azov—show in their culture, as reflected in their tombs (the necropolis of Elizavetovskaia), foreign non-Scythian and non-Greek elements together with a strong Greek influence. There is no doubt—though we have no trustworthy tradition to prove it— that Sauromatian tribes often crossed the Don and engaged in war with their nominal overlords, the Scythians, who formed a strong State from the seventh to the third century B.C. between the Don and the Dnieper and farther south in the Crimea, and on the Kuban. Traces of these Eastern Scythians have been found in graves of the Scythian period in the region of the Dnieper.

One of the most important and probably most hellenized Scytho-Maeotian tribes were the Jazamatae or Jaxamatae, whose queen was Tirgatao, the romantic heroine of a semi-historical Scythian novel (vol. VIII, p. 564 *sq*.). They figure in older geographers like Hecataeus and in writers dependent on them, but in the Hellenistic period, they disappear from the tradition almost completely. On the other hand, Polybius[1] mentions the Sarmatians with their king, Gatalas, as an important State, somewhere north of the Crimea, and Polyaenus reports another story of a queen-Amazon—this time of the Sarmatians—Amage (vol. VIII, p. 581). A little later, the Hellenistic sources of Strabo speak of a powerful tribe, the Iazyges, the vanguard of the Sarmatians, whose original home, according to the sources of Ammianus Marcellinus, was the region near the Sea of Azov. Later writers inform us that they steadily advanced toward the west and before the middle of the first century A.D. passed through the regions occupied by the Bastarnae and the Dacians and occupied the plains between the Danube and the Theiss, where they continued to reside for centuries as neighbours of the Roman Empire. Some

[1] xxv, 6, 13, referring to 179 B.C.

of their graves in this new home, few of which have been explored, have contents, such as funeral chariots, which are foreign to the Sarmatian graves in South Russia, and suggest rather the habits of the Pontic Scythians. It is possible, therefore, that the Iazyges are to be identified with the Jazamatae[1] and a reconstruction of their history may be attempted. Sometime before 179 B.C. the Jazamatae were driven out of their native country near the Sea of Azov and then conquered a part of the steppes between the Don and the Dnieper. While there, they played an active part, especially in the life of the Scythian Empire. Then they advanced again to the west, and since they were part of the Sauromatae of the early tradition they were the first to receive the name of Sarmatae.

This advance at the end of the second century B.C. was probably caused by the appearance in South Russia of Iranian tribes who moved westwards in great numbers, and were given the same general name Sarmatae. The tradition used by Strabo names two groups of these tribes, one in the west, another in the east, in the steppes of the northern Caucasus. The former group is mentioned by Artemidorus of Ephesus and Posidonius[2] in their *diathesis* (distribution) of peoples on the north-west shore of the Black Sea, and by the historians of Mithridates; the latter appears in the tradition which is connected with Pompey's conquest of the East[3]. In the first group the leading part is played by the Roxolani. This powerful tribe steadily advanced on the heels of the Iazyges and finally occupied the regions north of them. Still later, they probably drove the Iazyges out from their former home between the Don and the Dnieper. While there, they took an active part in the Mithridatic wars in the Crimea (vol. IX, p. 231). The second group consisted mainly of two tribes—the Aorsi and the Siracians, the latter living close to the Kuban valley in the south-eastern part of the North Caucasian steppes, the former more to the north and west, near the Don and the Sea of Azov. Strabo mentions them twice[4], both times in connection with each other. They played an important part in the history of Pharnaces, the son of Mithridates, as his faithful and strong allies, the Aorsi being by far the stronger. Both tribes appear again in the reign of Claudius, now as enemies of each other (vol. x, p. 753). The Siracians are still found in these parts in A.D. 193, but the Aorsi are not mentioned in any trustworthy historical or geographical source after

[1] K. Müllenhoff, *Deutsche Altertumskunde*, III, p. 39.
[2] *ap.* Strabo VII, 305 *sq.*   [3] *Ib.* XI, 492, 497 *sq.*
[4] *Ib.* 492, 506.

the first century. In their stead the Alani appear as the leading Sarmatian tribe.

The provenance of the Aorsi and Alani is known. The Chinese *Annals (or History) of the Former Han*, in describing the western countries, mention to the north of Sogdiana an important tribe with the name An-ts'ai or Yen-ts'ai (vol. IX, p. 585). Since the time of Chang Ch'ien at least, the Yen-ts'ai lived near the Aral Sea. The *Annals* describe them as a strong nomadic tribe (100,000 archers), subject to Sogdiana (K'ang-chü). The northern Chinese silk route ran through their country. The same description with some unimportant changes and additions is repeated by the *Annals of the Later Han*, with the new fact, that in this period the 'Kingdom of Yen-ts'ai changed its name to that of A-lani.' This statement is confirmed by the record of the Wei (*Wei-lio*) with the addition that at the time of this record (third century A.D.) the Yen-ts'ai who 'formerly were dependent from time to time to a certain extent upon K'ang-chü are no longer dependent upon them.' It is generally agreed that the Aorsi of the western sources are the Yen-ts'ai of the Chinese *Annals*, and that some time after A.D. 25 a new tribe got the upper hand of them and gave their own name of Alani to the whole confederacy of nomads which they controlled. It is no accident that the name 'Aorsi' disappears from western sources in the second half of the first century A.D. while that of 'Alani' takes its place (perhaps as early as A.D. 35)[1]. It is, therefore, very probable that the great movement of peoples of the second half of the second century B.C., which so greatly changed the life of the East (vol. IX, p. 582), pushed to the west a group of nomadic tribes (perhaps related to the Yüeh-chih). These tribes were very little known to the Chinese, since they spread north and west of the Aral Sea. But they formed apparently a powerful nomadic State which extended far into Siberia on the north and reached the steppes of South Russia in the late second century B.C.: one of the tribes, the Roxolani, occupied the steppes between the Don and the Dnieper, while others, under the name Aorsi, held the regions beyond the Don.

The Siracians belonged to a different stock who maintained their independence against both the Aorsi and the Alani. Tribes of their name are found in Hyrcania and a part of Armenia near a group of Sacae. It is, indeed, probable that they were a branch of the Sacae who pushed on to the steppes north of the Caucasus at the time of their great migration (vol. IX, p. 583). They may, then, have appeared there at the same time as the Aorsi from the

[1] Josephus, *Ant.* XVIII [4, 4], 97. Cf. vol. X, p. 777 nn. 4 and 5.

north[1]. Some of them (? the Aspurgiani) penetrated the Kuban valley and played an important part in the history of the Bosporan kingdom from the reign of Augustus onwards (vol. x, p. 268).

In the first two centuries A.D. the Alani sought to expand south and west, in the South at the expense of Parthia and the Roman province of Cappadocia (A.D. 35, 72–3, 134–5). It may also have been their pressure that thrust the Roxolani on the Iazyges, so that both these became repeatedly dangerous to Rome on the Danube, as has been described elsewhere (vol. x, p. 775). It was probably about the end of Tiberius' reign that the Iazyges passed through the country of the Dacians and occupied the area between the Theiss and the Danube (see above, p. 85). The Roxolani remained in the east, a potential danger to the Empire the more if, as *c.* A.D. 62, they joined forces with the Dacians and the Bastarnae at the mouth of the Danube. The inscription set up to Plautius Silvanus[2], the general who checked this movement, suggests that yet more powerful and dangerous tribes, of whom the Romans knew little, stood behind these peoples. Again and again both Iazyges and Roxolani appeared on the military horizon of Rome before, in 179/80, Marcus Aurelius earned the title of Sarmaticus that was to be borne by many later emperors. In the third century the Roxolani seem to have been absorbed into the coalition formed by the Goths and the Alani, while the Iazyges remained a separate people and were active in the struggle on the Danube frontier under the late Empire.

In the first and second centuries the Romans did not come into direct contact with the most powerful of the Sarmatians, the Aorsi and Alani, except for a moment in A.D. 49, when they allied themselves with the King of the Aorsi to facilitate their support of a Roman candidate to the throne of Bosporus. On the other hand, these Sarmatians of the North Caucasian steppes and of the Don evoked the vigilance of Rome, for they, with the Scythians of the Crimea, were the most dangerous enemies of the Bosporan kingdom, the client-state that served Rome's interests in the far north-east.

No wars between the Alani and the Bosporan kingdom are mentioned in the many inscriptions which celebrate the military

---

[1] If Θρακῶν is corrected to Σιράκων in Diodorus xx, 22, 4 they appeared north of the Caucasus at least as early as the fourth century B.C. The name of the king in Diodorus, Aripharnes, is a good Iranian name, and the strength of the tribe agrees with accounts of the time of Claudius. Archaeological evidence does not conflict with the earlier date.

[2] Dessau 986; see vol. x, pp. 775 and 806 *sq.*

achievements of the Bosporan kings of the first and second centuries A.D. The Scythians were apparently more aggressive, for wars against them were frequent, and in order to save Chersonesus the Romans were forced to occupy it with troops, to strengthen its fortifications and to build against the Scythians a regular *limes* across the Crimea, comparable to a similar fortified line built across their own peninsula by the Bosporan kings. Against the piracy of the Scythians both the Bosporan kings and Rome kept a flotilla on the Black Sea (vol. x, p. 775). The lack of any direct mention of wars between Bosporus and the Alani may, however, be an accident. In the reign of Antoninus Pius the Alani were restless and probably threatened the Bosporan kingdom (p. 336). In A.D. 193 we hear of a war of Sauromates II against the Siracians[1], who may have been at that time vassals of the Alani, and we know, both from coins and inscriptions, that Tanaïs on the Don and the Greek cities of the Taman peninsula were repeatedly fortified by the Bosporan king, at least from the days of Domitian. This may be combined with the mention in two inscriptions of a regular service of interpreters of the Bosporan kingdom, who were in charge of diplomatic relations between Bosporus and the Alani—an important official of Bosporus has the title 'Chief interpreter of the Alani' ($\dot{\alpha}\rho\chi\epsilon\rho\mu\eta\nu\epsilon\dot{\upsilon}\varsigma$ $\tau\hat{\omega}\nu$ 'A$\lambda\alpha\nu\hat{\omega}\nu$)[2]. And yet the Alani never made real efforts to become masters of the Greek cities of the Black Sea. In their attitude toward them they were very tolerant and very liberal. This attitude is certainly to be explained, not only by the support which the Romans gave to the Bosporus, but also by the desire of the Alani to have in the Greek cities trustworthy commercial agents for their trade with the West and to use them as centres of supply for the products of Greek industry, of which some of them were very fond.

Friendly relations between the Alani and the Bosporan kingdom and Olbia, which was at times under the control of the Bosporan kings, are also attested by the peaceful penetration of Sarmatians into the Greek cities of Bosporus, which led to the gradual iranization of the Bosporan kingdom. Hundreds of residents in these Greek cities now bear Sarmatian names, and all of them wear Sarmatian dress and use Sarmatian weapons. Last but not least, the ruling dynasty of Bosporus itself assumes an ever more Iranian aspect. Along with Thracian dynastic names appears

---

[1] *Ios. P. E.* II, no. 423.

[2] *Bull. Comm. Arch.* 40, p. 112 no. 28; *Ios. P. E.* II, p. 296, no. 86[2]; cf. *I.G.R.R.* I, 261—a Bosporan interpreter at Rome.

a new name—Sauromates, which may reflect the fact that many subjects of the Bosporan king were Sarmatian. The figure of the king on horseback, adoring the supreme god, as it appears on the coins of Bosporus in the second century A.D., is almost exactly the same as the figure of the king on contemporary Parthian and Graeco-Sacian coins[1]. In the third century the grave of a Bosporan king or noble was not much different from that of an Alan of the same rank. So strong a sarmatization would be impossible, were not relations between the Alani and the Bosporus both constant and friendly.

With the third century the situation changed. The Alani, who maintained constant relations with the Germanic tribes that were gradually occupying the valley of the Dnieper, became merged with the Germans, or rather, became a part of the Gothic-Alanic kingdom of South Russia. Thus they came to be neighbours of the Romans, and they took part in most of the enterprises of the Goths, Suebi and Vandals against the Empire. In the south of Russia, Olbia and Tanaïs were destroyed, and Panticapaeum became a Gotho-Sarmatian city. Later centuries were to witness the gradual advance of the Goths, Vandals and Alani to France, to Spain and finally to Africa.

II. SARMATIAN SOCIETY, WARFARE AND ART

Very little is known of the organization of Sarmatian political life. There are kings and barons, the *skeptouchoi*, and it may be assumed that the Sarmatians, like all the Iranians, had a kind of monarchical feudal State. Our sources are unanimous in regarding all the Sarmatian tribes, with the exception of the Siracians, as nomads leading a pastoral life and breeding great numbers of cattle. Their small, swift horses were famous in the Roman world. In a well-known inscription found at Apta[2] on the Durance the Emperor Hadrian praises and commemorates his 'Borysthenes Alanus Caesareus Veredus' that 'flew' with him over swamps and hills of Tuscany as he hunted the wild boar.

There is no doubt that the Sarmatians were Iranians—near relations of the Scythians. The descendants of the Alani—the Ossetes in the Northern Caucasus—still speak an Iranian language and most of the non-Greek names in the Bosporan cities, especially in Tanaïs in Imperial times, are Iranian. The Sarmatian aristocracy was probably very rich. Through the empire of the Aorsi-Alani, which

---

[1] Volume of Plates v, 124 *a, b, c.*
[2] *C.I.L.* xii, 1122, *a*, ll. 1–6; cf. Dio lxix, 10, 2.

occupied vast regions to the north of the Caspian and Aral Seas and included the eastern part of the South Russian steppes, there ran an important caravan road connecting the Greek cities of the Black Sea with China, witness its description in the Chinese sources and the many Chinese articles, especially mirrors, which have been found in Sarmatian graves and at Panticapaeum (fragments of silk stuffs of Chinese workmanship of the second century A.D.). Furthermore, according to Strabo[1], many Indian and Babylonian products passed through Media and Armenia across the Caucasus into the regions occupied by the Aorsi and thence probably to the harbours of the Bosporan kingdom. Strabo meant probably the important trade-routes, one of which ran from India through Parthia to the Oxus and from there to the Caspian, the other from Babylonia along the Tigris and the Euphrates.

Since the Greeks and Romans met the Sarmatians mostly on the field of battle, their information on the military equipment, strategy and tactics of the Sarmatae is much more complete than on their religious[2], social and economic life, of which we know practically nothing. A combination of the descriptions of the Sarmatian army given by Strabo, Josephus, Tacitus, Arrian, Pausanias and Ammianus Marcellinus gives a picture which is very similar to that of the Parthian, Armenian and Iberian armies given by the same and other writers. The dominant feature is the prominent part played in the army by a body of heavy cataphracts with metal helmets, whose chief weapons were long heavy lances and swords, the bow being subsidiary. This body of mailed knights mounted on armoured steeds was made up, according to Tacitus[3], of members of the Sarmatian aristocracy, while the main body of the army was formed by light-armed bowmen, protected by leather corselets and leather caps. A like combination of heavy cavalry in close formation and swarms of nimble archers existed earlier in the steppes of Russia, at the time of the Scythian domination. But the new system was then in its beginnings, and the new type of a mailed phalanx had not yet been created. Who deserves the credit of having used it first, we do not know. It

---

[1] XI, 506. Strabo adds that the Aorsi ἐχρυσοφόρουν διὰ τὴν ἐμπορίαν.

[2] The Sarmatians were probably Mazdaeans. Ammianus Marcellinus (XIX, 11, 10) says that before battle they shouted 'Marha, Marha.' This name appears in a poem in honour of a Parthian governor as that of the supreme god. Fr. Cumont, C. R. Ac. Inscr. 1931, pp. 278 sqq. But E. Benveniste (Journ. Asiat. 221, 1931, pp. 135 sqq.) identifies the battle-cry with the Persian 'merd u mard' ('man against man').

[3] Hist. I, 79; cf. Ann. VI, 35.

must have been a people controlling a certain supply of iron and bronze, which suits both the Aorsi, masters of the Ural mountains, of the Altai and of the Minussinsk region, and the Parthians, who got their iron and steel through Merv. It must be noted, however, that the resources of the Sarmatian tribes in iron were not very large, since Ammianus Marcellinus[1] describes the Sarmatae as wearing scale-armour, not of iron but of horn. A specimen of this armour dedicated in the temple of Asclepius at Athens moves Pausanias[2] to observe how skilfully they made good their deficiency in iron. The mode of fighting used by the Sarmatians was much the same as that of the Parthians: the *pièce de résistance* was the attack of the mailed, mounted phalanx, prepared and supported by the archers. Duels between the leaders of Iranian hosts in which the lasso and wrestling played an important part were common.

The picture given by classical authors is illustrated by many monuments of Graeco-Roman and Oriental art of the Hellenistic and Roman periods, as, for example, the figures of enemy cataphracts on the column of Trajan and similar figures on the arch of Galerius at Salonica. It is very probable that the first are meant to represent the equestrian phalanx of the Roxolani, while the second are the Sarmatian '*foederati*' of the army of Galerius in his Persian expedition (A.D. 296). No pictures of Sarmatian warriors appear on the objects found in their graves. But the Sarmatian military organization had a strong influence on that of the Bosporan kingdom in the first three centuries A.D. Many grave paintings[3] of this period at Panticapaeum show Panticapaean victories over their enemies, the Scythians and Taurians of the Crimea. These pictures are probably copies of parts of the monumental paintings which were dedicated by the Bosporan kings and their generals to commemorate these victories[4]. The Panticapaeans are represented either as a mounted phalanx or as single heroes charging their enemies[5], alone or at the head of their infantry. They always wear the complete equipment of a Sarmatian cataphract—long

[1] XVII, 2, 2.

[2] I, 21, 5–7. It may be noted that this type of armour has occasionally been found in South Russian graves.

[3] Volume of Plates v, 24, *a*.

[4] A picture of this kind is mentioned, for instance, as dedicated in a new temple, to commemorate a victory of Sauromates I (A.D. 96–123) over the Scythians; *Ios. P.E.* IV, no. 202.

[5] This combat between heroes is typical of Iranian art and mentality, and is a most common motive of Parthian and Sassanian art and of the great epics of the nomads of Asia.

scale-cuirass, conical scale-helmet, sword and a long, heavy lance[1], while their enemies are bare-headed, mounted archers of the Scythian type. The same Sarmatian equipment appears also on many Panticapaean grave-stelae and on a commemorative monument from Tanaïs. Even the Bosporan kings adopted it in the second century A.D., as is shown by their coins, and it appears also on pictures engraved on the rocks along the Yenisei river, pictures which probably represent the eastern Asiatic Aorsi-Alani. Finally may be mentioned a gold plaque found in Siberia, which represents a Sarmatian hunting a wild boar[2]. As he is hunting, not fighting, he wears the nomadic riding kaftan of leather and not the cuirass and is using the bow. But his long sword hangs down from the shoulder. The peculiar manner of wearing this sword which slides on a special *porte-épée*, appears over and over again on many monuments of Oriental art, for example in India, and swords with this *porte-épée* (mostly of jade) have been found in the Volga region and at Panticapaeum and in many Chinese and Korean graves of the Han period. The Yenisei pictures and the Siberian plaque may attest the extension of Sarmatian domination over large parts of Siberia as far as the Minussinsk region.

The evidence collected above, which bears on the history and life of the Sarmatians, is supported and completed by archaeological material. No cities or other settlements of the Sarmatians have been excavated. The Sarmatians were nomads and became sedentary city-dwellers only as emigrants who settled down in some of the Greek cities or as successors of earlier residents of the regions which the Sarmatians had conquered, for example, Uspa, the capital of the Siracians. The archaeological evidence for their life and art must be derived, therefore, from their graves. Very few of these have been systematically excavated. A small group in the region of the Ural river, some cemeteries along the lower Volga and a set of tumulus graves in the Kuban valley make up the list. The rest of our archaeological evidence comes from chance finds in various parts of the wide area inhabited by the Sarmatians—graves in Western Siberia, others in the region of the Don and the Donetz and burials in the region of the Dnieper and further to the

---

[1] This is typical also of the Parthian army (Volume of Plates iv, 26, *c*) and was borrowed in the second and third century A.D. by units of the Roman army. Two Roman sets of horse-armour of cataphracts, probably of the *cohors* xx Palmyrenorum, were recently found at Doura; see F. Brown in *Dura*, Rep. vi. A Parthian composite bow was found intact in 1934 at Irzi near Doura; see *Dura*, Reps. vii–viii.

[2] Volume of Plates v, 24, *b*.

west. The Sarmatian graves may be subdivided in chronological groups—Hellenistic, early Imperial and late Imperial. Some local peculiarities may also be noted. The most important local group is that of the early Hellenistic graves of the Taman peninsula of the Kuban valley, and of the region of the lower Don. The rich graves recently discovered in the Altai mountains and in Mongolia show the same general characteristics as the Eastern European and Siberian graves and certainly belong to the same time and to the same civilization. But whether the chieftains buried in these graves were Iranian or Mongolian princelings no one can say.

As regards the archaeological evidence for the nomadic graves of the Sarmatian period, which cannot here be described in detail, it will suffice to say that the armour and weapons found in them all coincide with those described in the literary and archaeological evidence analysed above. We find as especially typical the sword, the heavy lance and the various types of body-armour, the scale-cuirass, plate, ring or chain mail. The persistence of these makes these graves, whether the more modest or the more ambitious, a single group throughout the Hellenistic and early Imperial period, with certain chronological and local subdivisions. It is to be observed that the same equipment appears in Parthia, Armenia and Iberia, all Iranian or iranized countries. It penetrated also into China and India, but never appears there in the same pure form. Whether it was also used by the Mongolian nomads cannot as yet be said with confidence.

Archaeological evidence for the Sarmatian burials of the Volga and Kuban regions, which are identical in almost all details, is especially rich. It may be useful to quote a reconstruction of the picture of a typical Volga-Sarmatian tribesman (not a chieftain) derived from the objects found in scores of contemporary graves of this region. 'Dressed in a shirt and long trousers, which were adorned with small beads above and larger ones below, wearing a short overcoat which was fastened with a safety-pin on the right shoulder and a leather cap covered with bronze scales, his body protected by scale-armour and his feet by low, soft shoes, the Volga nomad appeared high on his horse, holding his small, curved bow. On a strap from his right shoulder, a red quiver, filled with long, painted arrows, hung down on his left side, while a sword—long or short—was fastened at his right side. A lance completed his military equipment[1].' This description may be compared with that of an average Roxolan given by Strabo[2]. The

---

[1] P. Rykov, *Das susslowsche Hügelgrabfeld*, p. 20 *sq.*   [2] VII, 306.

equipment of the chieftain was, of course, more ambitious and more complicated. The main point, however, is that this is entirely different from the ancient Iranian equipment of the Scythian warriors of the sixth to the fourth centuries B.C. (vol. III, pp. 197 *sqq.*). The typical Scytho-Persian dagger (*akinakes*), the short javelins, the *gorytus*, the Scythian bow, the triangular arrow-heads, the Greek helmet—all have disappeared completely and are never found in the Sarmatian graves.

Another typical feature of the Sarmatian graves is the complete change in artistic tastes and styles. The Sarmatians no doubt brought their own art with them from their Oriental home. One of the striking traits of the earlier eastern Sarmatian graves is the entire absence of imported Greek objects, which are so common in Pontic Scythian graves, an absence which persisted in the eastern branches of the Sarmatian stock, for example the Volga Sarmatians. Not that all the objects which these Sarmatians wore were home-made; some were imported, but none from Greece. Persia and China were the countries with which the eastern Sarmatians were in constant commercial relations. The picture is different for the western Sarmatians of the Kuban river and the Don, who were good customers of the Greek cities of the Black Sea. But even in the western Sarmatian graves the Greek objects are but a foreign addition to a nomadic Oriental stock.

So far as imports are concerned, one group of Sarmatian graves appears in a quite peculiar light. A number of Hellenistic graves of the Taman peninsula, the Kuban valley and the region of the lower Don have yielded, alongside the objects typical of the Sarmatian period, a large number of silver and gold phalerae, which took the place of the earlier Scythian plaques used for horse-trappings. These phalerae, and jewels found with them, show such similarity, both in style and subjects, to the earlier products of Graeco-Sacian art, that it must be assumed that the men who used them belonged to the same group as that which created the peculiar Graeco-Sacian art which is so closely related to early Parthian art. These Graeco-Sacian phalerae were apparently imported by the Siracians into South Russia and spread from there along the north shore of the Black Sea.

Our information regarding the Sarmatian type of art is scanty. The only objects of a more or less artistic character that the graves have yielded are of metal, the local pottery being very coarse and the better grades of pottery and glass imported. And yet even this scanty supply shows some features which are interesting in themselves and important from the point of view of the evolution of

art in both East and West. One of these features is the great love
of the Sarmatians for effects of colour: their arms and weapons,
their silver and gold plate, the metal plaques sewn on their garments are regularly adorned with rows and groups of inset coloured
stones. Instead of, or along with them, a peculiar type of enamel
is often used. Polychromy in jewelry and toreutics was all the
fashion of the day in the classical world of the Hellenistic period
in general, and this fashion was inherited by Roman art and is
especially noticeable in the provincial art of the Empire. It reached
the Hellenistic kingdoms both from Egypt and from the Semitic
and Iranian East, while the Roman provinces of central and
eastern Europe added to it Celtic features—polychrome metallurgy was age-old in the Celtic countries—and developed it in
their own way. Sarmatian polychrome jewelry and toreutics has,
however, its own *cachet* and its own development parallel to, and
independent of, the evolution of polychromy in the Near East
and in western Europe, and resembles that of the Parthian kingdom, India and China. A reflection of this eastern development
may be seen in the costumes, jewelry and silver and gold plate of
Palmyra (p. 130). This eastern branch of polychrome jewelry—
one of the peculiar features of it being enamel *cloisonné*—came
into touch with the western branch, both in Syria and in South
Russia and on the Danube. In the south this style was spread by
the Parthians and the Sassanian Persians, in the north by the
Sarmatians. It was the characteristic style of the North which was
in the main responsible for the gorgeous development of polychrome metallurgy in the period of the Migrations and in the early
Middle Ages, the Sassanian influence being merely subsidiary.

Still more characteristic is another feature of Sarmatian art—
its love for animal forms and its peculiar style of ornamentation
which is usually called the 'animal style.' This style had long
obtained in central Asia. It came with the Scythians to South
Russia where in the seventh to the fourth century B.C. it developed
in its own way. To this early Asiatic animal style the Sarmatian is
certainly closely related. Yet it is not a continuation of the Pontic
or Scythian branch of it; it marks a new period in the development
of the original animal style of Asia unaffected by Greek influence,
which was so strong in the later period of the Pontic or Scythian
variety. The Sarmatian animal style is at once vigorous and savage
and highly refined and stylized, though in a way different
from the earlier Scythian stylization of the animal forms. It combines, moreover, the polychrome and the animal style in a most
skilful and, at the same time, 'barbarous,' way.

The most important objects which represent the Sarmatian, *i.e.* neo-Asiatic, animal style come partly from Western Siberia, partly from South Russia (especially the region of the Don). They belong to the adornments of dresses and to horse-trappings of the great Sarmatian chieftains. On the other hand, the animal style is but poorly represented in more modest graves, both of the Kuban and of the Volga region. It was an art of the ruling aristocracy. Whether or not it was confined to the Iranian aristocracy, it is hard to say. In all probability it was the art of the ruling Asiatic families in general, since it is found so splendidly displayed in princely graves of Mongolia and of the Altai, which hardly belonged to Iranian tribal chieftains. It may have been imported into China, where the style was fashionable mostly on the borderlands for a time, by the Yüeh-chih, but more probably by the Huns, who for centuries were the nearest neighbours of the Chinese. In Siberia and in South Russia, however, the neo-Asiatic animal style was certainly patronized by the great chieftains of the Aorsi and the Alani, whom Strabo characterizes as 'wearers of gold' (p. 98, n. 1). On the other hand, it never became the mode among the Parthians or Sassanian Persians.

The development of western European art owes but little to this style. It certainly influenced the art of the upper Volga and Kama, and some elements of it perhaps penetrated into early Scandinavian art, which had its own native animal style. Some features of the late Gotho-Sarmatic polychrome art may be derived from the neo-Asiatic animal style and may have penetrated with the Goths, Alani and Vandals into western Europe. Another source of animal motives may have been the art of the later Mongolian invaders of western Europe—the Huns, the Avars, the Bulgars and the Magyars. But, on the whole the animal style of the Romanesque, Carolingian and Gothic periods must be regarded as only partly derived from these sources.

III. PARTHIA: FOREIGN POLICY

The Parthian Empire, as created by Mithridates II (vol. IX, pp. 584 *sqq.*), was surrounded by strong, warlike and ambitious rivals. To the west were Roman provinces and client-states and the independent Arab tribes of the Syrian desert. On the north to the west of the Caspian beyond the Armenians, Iberians and Albanians, who were all more or less under Parthian protectorate or influence, lay the powerful well-organized, well-armed and warlike Sarmatians, especially the Alani, who since their settle-

THE PARTHIAN EMPIRE

Scales

0   50 100   200   300

English miles

0 50 100   200   300   400   500

Kilometres

To face p. 105

ment in the Northern Caucasus took every opportunity to invade the Parthian lands through one of the two Caucasian Gates (Darial and Derbend), while to the east of the Caspian Parthia faced the many nomadic Iranian tribes known to the Western world under the general name of Scythians[1]. Farther to the east lay the successors of the Bactrian Greeks, the growing kingdom of the Yüeh-chih and Tokharians, which separated Parthia from the great Chinese Empire of the later Han, and finally, towards the south-east and south, the border-lands of India.

Of the struggles of the Parthians against their enemies in the north, the east and the south comparatively little is known. Where evidence is more ample is on the relations of Parthia and Rome, and this comes from Roman sources and represents the Roman point of view. Roman policy towards Parthia is the topic of other chapters, but at the cost of some repetition, it is worth while to attempt a reconstruction of the course of Parthian policy in its turn. When Parthia and Rome first faced each other it was as claimants to the heritage of the Seleucid monarchy. The prestige won by Pompey in the East was dimmed by the defeat of Crassus, Caesar's plans were cut short by his death, and Antony failed to avenge Crassus. His disastrous retreat, and the Parthian offensive into Syria that preceded it, convinced Augustus that Parthia was a serious enemy and inspired the Roman public at large with a lasting fear and respect for the Parthians[2]. But both Augustus and the Parthian king realized that, as defeat to either would be fatal, victory would not be without danger and would lead nowhere.

An expansion of the Roman Empire into Central Asia and India, though not impossible, meant a complete new orientation of the Roman Empire and its hellenization and orientalization. This was against the leading political Western ideas of Augustus. Equally the King Phraates was well aware that it was idle to dream of the conquest of Syria with the forces and organization of an Empire whose main task and main strength lay in the East and whose structure was perforce feudal and half-nomadic. On the other hand a *modus vivendi* promised good returns both for Parthia and Rome: regular caravan trade well-organized and well-protected was a source of income for both powers, inasmuch as it yielded large custom duties to their treasuries and brought prosperity both to Syria and Mesopotamia. Thus the *modus vivendi*

---

[1] Sacae, Massagetae, Dahae and the rest, according to Pliny: *multitudo innumera et quae cum Parthis ex aequo degat. N.H.* VI, 50; cf. VI, 112.

[2] Besides the Augustan poets, see Strabo XI, 515; Tacitus, *Ann.* XII, 10; Justin XLI, 1, 1.

came into being: the Euphrates as frontier, the development of the buffer-state of Palmyra as a centre of Partho-Roman exchange and perhaps a kind of commercial agreement between Parthia and Rome. The Parthians agreed to satisfy Roman honour by delivering up the standards and captives of Crassus and Antony, and Augustus in return ceased to support the pretender Tiridates and insured Parthia against future pretenders by keeping the dangerous princes of the Arsacid house in Rome (vol. x, pp. 260 *sqq.*). This understanding, reinforced by a later demonstration of Roman power, was kept and carried out by Tiberius. Especially successful was the mission of Germanicus, who probably made Roman influence in Palmyra stronger than before and regulated Palmyra's relations to Parthia and Rome. At the same time he entered, perhaps in the name of Palmyra, into diplomatic relations with some of those petty vassal dynasts of Parthia who held the keys to the great caravan roads leading to Syria and Asia Minor (vol. x, pp. 621, 747 n. 2).

However, there remained one question which urgently required regulation, the question of Armenia. It is unnecessary to point out the strategical importance of Armenia (vol. x, p. 260 *sq.*). An independent Armenia was unacceptable alike to the Romans and the Parthians, neither of whom had forgotten the power of Tigranes fifty years before. Armenia in the hands of the Romans meant for Parthia a constant threat to Mesopotamia and its flourishing caravan cities, and Mesopotamia was the key to Babylonia: to lose it was equivalent to the potential surrender of all the western satrapies of Parthia. On the other hand, Rome was not willing to leave Armenia to the Parthians, since it opened to them an easy access to the Black Sea, secured for them a supremacy over Iberia and Albania and thus the command of an important trade-route to the East, connected the Parthian Empire with the half-Iranian countries of Cappadocia, Pontus and Commagene, and made possible an alliance between the Parthians and their cousins the Sarmatians, the great rivals of Rome in the north-east. Thus the Armenian question became the chief obstacle to a lasting peace between the two Empires and led repeatedly to wars and diplomatic conflicts.

Augustus and Tiberius insisted upon solving the Armenian problem in the traditional Roman way, by making Armenia a Roman vassal-state under the rule of a hellenized client-king. Phraates accepted this solution and undermined by this his position in Parthia, since the leading aristocratic clans were bitterly opposed to it. This led to the elimination of Phraates' successor

Phraataces and to the downfall of the Arsacids of the Mithridatic line in Parthia[1]. The short rule of Vonones opened the eyes of the Parthians to the danger of becoming a hellenizing vassal-kingdom of Rome and led to a national Iranian reaction which gave the throne to Artabanus, a member of a collateral branch of the Arsacids connected with the home-land of the Parthians and with Hyrcania and Atropatene. It is characteristic of Artabanus' aspirations that he at once insisted on his own solution of the Armenian problem: the ruler of Armenia must be a member of the ruling house of Parthia, an Arsacid. Since, however, Vonones, the former king of Parthia, the rival of Artabanus, who once won a splendid victory over him, was now the actual king of Armenia, Artabanus, in order to eliminate this danger and to deprive Vonones of Roman support, was ready to accept for a while a compromise which was suggested by Germanicus. A neutral hellenized king ruled again over Armenia. But this compromise was not lasting. As soon as Artabanus, whose hands were for a while tied up by important wars in the East, felt free and strong again, he renewed his claim to rule over Armenia through a member of his house. He failed, however, a second time and in the same way. Instead of Vonones Tiberius used romanized Arsacids, first Phraates and then Tiridates, as his tools, and after this diversion Artabanus was forced again to give up his plan. The interview between Artabanus and Vitellius was one of the greatest diplomatic victories of Tiberius (vol. x, p. 749 *sq.*). Armenia was in the hands of a prince of the neighbouring Iberian dynasty, vassals of Rome.

However, no lasting peace could be established on such a basis. The Armenian question remained acute. It is characteristic of the urgency of this problem that Vardanes in his short rule was ready to raise it again and it is very probable that the episode of Meherdates whom Claudius put up as a pretender (vol. x, p. 755) was in one way or another connected with similar plans and aspirations of the Hyrcanian Gotarzes. No wonder, therefore, if Vologases I, in agreement with his brothers, raised the question again and did not shrink from long and bloody wars to gain a solution acceptable both to Rome and to Parthia. The solution, though a compromise, satisfied the vital interests of the Parthians. The brother of Vologases, Tiridates, became king of Armenia but he received his crown from the hands of Nero in Rome (vol. x, p. 773). Thus a *modus vivendi* was established for a while and lasted until the end of the Flavian dynasty.

[1] See List of Parthian kings, p. 90.

With Trajan the question became acute once more. The origin of the conflict between Trajan and Pacorus first and Osroes afterwards is unknown. But it is certain that it involved the question who was to be king of Armenia. Whether or not the trouble was complicated by an invasion of the Parthians into Syria is a matter of controversy and does not concern us here. Suffice it to say that Trajan decided to solve the Armenian problem in his own radical way: Armenia was to become a Roman province protected by Mesopotamia and Adiabene occupied by Roman garrisons, and Parthia was to be ruled by a Roman nominee, a client-king of Rome (p. 249).

The conquest of Mesopotamia by Trajan and his capture of the royal capital Ctesiphon produced a tremendous impression on the Parthians and certainly aroused a strong national reaction: witness the revolt of Mesopotamia and Adiabene under the leadership of members of the house of the Arsacids while Trajan was at Ctesiphon. The invasion of Trajan is mentioned as a kind of era by the chronicle of Arbela[1] and as late as A.D. 572, according to John of Ephesus[2], the Romans reminded the Sassanian Persians of Trajan and emphasized the fact that statues of him were still standing in Persia and the Persians were afraid of riding by them.

This national reaction was probably the chief reason why Hadrian restored the legitimate kings in Parthia and gave Mesopotamia back to them, controlling Armenia indirectly through vassal-kings[3]. Our scanty information on the time of Hadrian and Antoninus Pius does not reveal the conditions on which an understanding between Parthia and Rome was reached. It is not improbable, however, that in return for restoring the *status quo* Hadrian received important concessions. We hear that he did not exact tribute from Mesopotamia[4], which may mean that his right to do so was acknowledged, *i.e.* that the status of Mesopotamia was not exactly the same as before the war. The appointment of Parthamaspates as king of Edessa shows that the status of Armenia was to a certain extent extended to some minor kingdoms of Mesopotamia. This led to complications, and a new

---

[1] E. Sachau, *Bay. Abh.* 1915, 6, p. 43 *sq.*

[2] Ed. Schönfelder, pp. 251–3. It is probable that there were statues of Trajan in Parthia: witness the triumphal arch in his honour at Doura and the mention of the export of bronze statues to Parthia in the tariff of Palmyra (*I.G.R.R.* III, 1056; IV, 29 *sqq.*; *C. I. S.* II, 3, no. 3913).

[3] As the order to evacuate Doura is now known to have preceded the death of Trajan (see p. 617, n. 3, and M. Rostovtzeff in *C. R. Ac. Inscr.* 1935, pp. 285 *sqq.*), it was he who began the policy of concessions to Parthia.

[4] S. H. A. *Hadr.* 21, 12.

arrangement was achieved in 123 when the former dynasty was restored. It is also significant that, though King Osroes received back from Hadrian his daughter whom Trajan had captured, the royal throne was never sent back to Ctesiphon either by Hadrian or by Antoninus, as Hadrian had promised. This was probably regarded by the Parthians as a humiliating symbol of inferiority. The merchants of Palmyra never felt more at home in the great commercial cities of Parthia than in the times of Hadrian and Antoninus and statues of Roman emperors may even have stood in the Palmyrene quarter of the royal Parthian caravan-city of Vologasia[1]. In the time of Hadrian and later, Palmyra had detachments of her own desert police (mounted archers) in all the important towns of the Euphrates frontier with Parthia. Doura was one of these and Anath (Anah) another[2]. A strong Parthia was bound to resent Roman predominance, and more than once in the reigns of Hadrian and Antoninus the Roman Empire was threatened by a war on the eastern frontier (pp. 313, 345).

The break came with Vologases III. Conditions were troubled in the Parthian Empire in the last years of Osroes and during the rule of Vologases II. Rival rulers contested the throne of both of them[3]. Vologases III probably yielded to the pressure of public opinion and decided to put an end to the conditions created by Trajan's expedition. It was again the question of Armenia which led to the war, which started with the appointment of an Armenian king by Vologases and with two crushing defeats of the Roman governors of Cappadocia and Syria who tried to save the prestige of Rome in Armenia. The expeditions of Lucius Verus against Parthia began with the reconquest of Armenia in 163–4, followed by the occupation of Mesopotamia and an expedition against Ctesiphon—an exact repetition of Trajan's campaign.

The results of the three campaigns of Lucius were, however, not decisive (p. 349). The war ended in a compromise. Armenia remained a vassal-kingdom garrisoned by Rome; the most important Mesopotamian cities were also held by Roman forces and the Euphrates *limes* (or defence-system) was extended from Sura to points south of Doura, which last became a strong Roman fortress[4] (p. 618 *sq.*). But Vologases remained king at

1 Inscription of Palmyra, R. Mouterde and A. Poidebard in *Syria*, XII, 1931, pp. 101 *sqq.*
2 See F. Brown and M. Rostovtzeff in *C. R. Ac. Inscr.* 1935, pp. 300 *sqq.*
3 See List of Parthian kings, p. 90.
4 See M. Rostovtzeff in *Bull. Comm. Arch.* XXXIII, 1909, pp. 1 *sqq.* (Armenia); *Münch. Beit. zur Papyrusforschung*, XIX, 1934, pp. 351 *sqq.* (Doura).

Ctesiphon, and it was plain that another war could not be long delayed.

The next war began in the troubled time after the death of Commodus. The Parthians never became reconciled to the loss of Mesopotamia, and it was a revolt in Mesopotamia (Osrhoëne and Adiabene) that was the beginning of Septimius Severus' operations against Parthia which ended in the capture of Ctesiphon. This capture, however, was no more than a military demonstration intended to frighten Parthia and make Mesopotamia safe for Rome, for Severus never thought of extending the Roman province to include lower Mesopotamia. This new humiliation exasperated the Iranians and led to the first serious rising of vassal-kingdoms against the Arsacids. Persia and Media revolted, a fact which was unknown until the discovery of a local chronicle of Arbela[1].

The last phase of what was now the question for Rome and Parthia, the rival claim to Mesopotamia, was a new war that began in 215 under Caracalla, who sought to profit by the dynastic dissensions of Armenia and of Parthia. But fortune was not with Rome. Though Caracalla once captured the Armenian king Tiridates by treachery and once apparently secured his extradition from the Parthian king Vologases V[2], a less pliant rival of Vologases, Artabanus V, took his place on the throne of Parthia. The Roman general Theocritus was sent against Armenia but was defeated. Caracalla invaded Adiabene and part of Media but was then assassinated, and Artabanus inflicted two defeats on the new Emperor Macrinus. The Romans were compelled to save their province in Mesopotamia by paying a heavy indemnity and to see Tiridates king of Armenia even though, like his namesake of the time of Nero, he received his diadem from the Emperor.

It was a pitiful end to the efforts of the Roman Empire to reduce the Parthians to vassaldom. Parthia emerged victorious, and the recapture of Mesopotamia was a matter of time. Fate

---

[1] *Chron. of Arbela*, p. 56 *sq.*; cf. G. Messina, *La Cronaca di Arbela*, La Civiltà cattolica, LXXXIII, 1932, pp. 362 *sqq.* Coins found at Seleuceia (R. H. McDowell, *Coins from Seleucia on the Tigris*, p. 234 *sq.*) show that a national reaction replaced Vologases III by Vologases IV, his success being due to the support of Elymaïs.

[2] For these events we possess only the fragments of Dio LXXVIII, 12, 19; LXXIX, 25-7, 31. It is, however, possible that the replacement of Vologases by Artabanus prevented the extradition, and that Tiridates, having once escaped to Parthia, now escaped to Armenia so that the operations of Caracalla were intended to isolate that country.

decided that it was to be carried out not by the Arsacids but by the descendants of Sasan the Persian. A new revolt in Persis led by Ardashir put an end to the rule of the Arsacids in the Iranian lands and to the life of the last great Arsacid, Artabanus V, A.D. 227.

Closely connected with the Armenian and Caucasian problem was the problem of dealing with the various 'Sarmatian' tribes which, probably early in the first century A.D., formed a powerful kingdom under the rule of the Alani in the Northern Caucasus (p. 94). There are many episodes in Parthian history which were connected with the existence of this strong nomadic State in the eastern part of the steppes of South Russia. Thus Vonones, the rival of Artabanus III, tried to escape from his confinement in Cilicia to the Caucasus and then to 'consanguineum sibi regem Scytharum,' probably one of the Sarmatian kings (vol. x, p. 747). Then both Orodes, son of Artabanus, and Mithridates the Iberian used in their struggle for Armenia the help of 'Sarmatian' chiefs (vol. x, p. 748). Again in A.D. 75 during the rule of Vologases I the Alani invaded Media and Armenia. The danger was great, and Vologases asked Vespasian for help which, however, was refused (p. 143). Finally there was a great invasion in A.D. 134 which affected Albania, Gordyene, Media and even Cappadocia and was checked by the joint efforts of the historian Arrian[1], the governor of Cappadocia, and King Vologases II. The chronicle of Arbela gives a dramatic account of the struggle of Vologases and the Alani of which the hero is the pious satrap of Adiabene, Rakbakt, a convert to Christianity.

The other frontiers of Parthia were, no doubt, of little less importance than those on the west and north-west, but the tradition that has survived is almost silent about the wars and diplomatic exchanges of the Arsacids with the northern 'Scythians' and Massagetae, the Bactrian Kushans and the Indian neighbours of Parthia. We hear incidentally that a Phraates fled to the Scythians when Tiridates entered Ctesiphon in A.D. 36[2]. Those Scythians may be the Sacae, who at that time became masters of Sacastene (Drangiane) and of a part of the Punjab[3]. Then under Artabanus III, after his victory over Vonones and before his clash with Tiberius, we are told of Parthian victories against his neighbours[4]. What these are we cannot tell. They may be connected with the great events

---

[1] See his Ἔκταξις κατ' Ἀλανῶν.   [2] See vol. x, p. 749, n. 1.

[3] E. Herzfeld, *Archaeol. Mitt. aus Iran*, IV, 1932, p. 73.

[4] *fretus bellis quae secunda adversum circumiectas nationes exercuerat.* Tacitus, *Ann.* II, 31.

which happened about this time in Sacastene, the substitution of
the dynasty of Gundofarr, who may have belonged to the powerful
Parthian clan of the Surēn, for the former Sacian kings who were
already masters of large parts of the Punjab[1]. After Gundofarr his
immediate successors, Orthagnes, Abdagaeses and Pakores, may
have kept the kingdom intact for some time. It is, however,
certain that soon (though how soon is in doubt) the kingdom of
Gundofarr fell to pieces, the Punjab being gradually conquered
by the Bactrian Kushans while the southern parts of it down to
Barbarikon and Minnagara on the Indus were ruled by Parthian
satraps, who were busy fighting each other, until the last remnants
of Parthian rule were swept away by the Kushans. In the description of the West as it was between A.D. 25 and 125 which is contained in the Chinese *Annals of the Later Han* it is stated that the
Kushan king Kozulokadphises, who was the first to create a united
kingdom out of the principalities of the Yüeh-chih in Bactria,
'invaded Parthia and took hold of the territory of Kao-fu (Kabul).'
The date of this event is disputed, but it must be later than
the reign of Gundofarr.

The Kushan kingdom separated Parthia from China. But
though they had no common frontier, commercial relations between the two countries were of such importance to both of them
that diplomatic interchanges were frequent and regular. Embassies with presents and messages went to and fro, but China learnt
little from them: at least the description of Parthia (An-hsi) in the
Annals of the Later Han is short, vague and almost meaningless.

It is impossible to say how often the peace of the Parthian
Empire was disturbed by foreign invasions of its eastern borders.
But it can hardly have been a rare event in the life of Parthia, and
we may conjecture that the Arsacids had to devote as much atten-
tion to the East as they did to the West. For example, the conflict
between Izates, the pious Jewish proselyte of Adiabene, and
Vologases I, as told by Josephus[2] can hardly be historical fact.
The sudden retreat of Vologases after he received the alarming

---

[1] See Herzfeld, *op. cit.* pp. 98 *sqq.*, who would make the Parthian clan of
the Surēn the enemies of the Atropatene dynasty in Parthia and responsible for
Vonones and Tiridates as opponents of Artabanus. To the present writer it
seems more probable that the creation of Gundofarr's kingdom and the establishment of a Parthian dynasty in Sacastene, the Punjab and the Indus
valley was achieved by Artabanus and Gundofarr in concert. Later in
Gundofarr's reign his kingdom may have become practically independent
like Hyrcania and Persis, though it may have remained in name part of the
Parthian Empire. He took the title Great King of Kings.

[2] *Ant.* xx [4, 2], 81–91.

news of an invasion of the Dahae and Sacae into Parthyene savours of a miracle. The hand of God is seen in it. Yet the setting of the story must be regarded as probable, so that an invasion of the northern 'Scythians' was a phenomenon familiar to all the readers of Izates' history in the Parthian Empire.

Of much concern to the Parthian kings were their relations with the large nominally vassal kingdoms on the borders of Parthia. One of them was Sacastene, another Persis (see above, p. 111 *sq.*). There is no doubt that wars against such stubborn and powerful vassals happened frequently. The same is true of Hyrcania. We hear that in A.D. 58 a Hyrcanian king sent an embassy to Corbulo and offered his help (vol. x, p. 704). What was the status of Hyrcania later we do not know.

All told, it cannot be denied that the Arsacids were on the whole successful in their endeavour to defend the integrity and the independence of their empire. The Sassanians were more successful than their predecessors—their neighbours were not so strong— but their general policy was exactly the same as that of the Arsacids.

IV. PARTHIA: CONSTITUTION AND ADMINISTRATION

The leading feature of the Parthian State in the time of the Roman Empire was, as before, the feudal character of its empire (see vol. ix, pp. 588 *sqq.*). It continued to include the large, nominally vassal, kingdoms of Armenia, Media Atropatene, Hyrcania, Sacastene and Persis, of which Armenia and Media were ruled by members of the Arsacid house, the others retaining their own dynasties. These kingdoms had in all probability the same feudal structure as the other parts of the Parthian Empire and that empire itself, and this is borne out by later information about Armenia and Persis. Of these major kingdoms two only, Persis and Sacastene, struck their own coins. Next in rank came the minor kingdoms. We have information about some of them, especially Adiabene, Osrhoëne, Elymaïs and Spasinu Charax, which last may be the same as the kingdom of Mesene. These vassal-kingdoms might differ in rank. Thus Adiabene, whose king was granted the rights of a first-class vassal monarch by Artabanus III, of wearing the upright tiara and using the golden couch, was degraded to the second class by Vologases I when its king received a second-class insignia—the diadem, ring and sword of State. Adiabene never coined money, while both Mesene and Elymaïs had their own coinage. Strabo and Josephus, drawing upon local sources, enable us to form a good idea, for example, of the social structure of Adiabene[1]. At the death of a king his queen, according to Josephus, summons the *megistanes* (the heads of the powerful clans[2]), the satraps[3], and those in charge of the armed forces, comprising the middle and lower nobility[4].

Not very much different from the vassal-kingdoms were the satrapies or provinces of the Parthian Empire which were ruled not by kings but by satraps (*marzban* or *marzapan*), who were styled in the Greek version of their title *strategoi*[5]. Each satrapy had one or more ruling houses, whose heads were the feudal lords of many villages and cities. Such were the Surēn, who had large estates in Mesopotamia and perhaps became the ruling dynasty of Sacastene (p. 112), the Karēn of Media whose lands lay near Nihawand, the Gewpathran (or Geopothroi) of Hyrcania and the Mihrān of Media near Rhagae, who appear also as a ruling house in Iberia in the third century A.D.[6] Naturally enough, since the Parthian army consisted of retinues of feudal lords, the Parthian kings would appoint the heads of powerful clans to be governors of their several countries, thus making the position of a satrap almost a hereditary office. In Mesopotamia, for instance, most of the governors known to us have names which were probably hereditary in the clan of the Surēn—Monaeses, Abdagaeses, Sinnaces, Silaces. A Monaeses often appears active in Mesopotamia: it is possible that the Surēn who defeated Crassus had the name of Monaeses, next comes the Monaeses of Antony's time, then another Monaeses general of Vologases I in A.D. 64 and finally a Monaeses at Doura in A.D. 121. Equally frequent are the names Silaces and Sinnaces (in 88 B.C., in 53 B.C. and in the time of Tiberius and Artabanus) and there is a Sinnaca near Carrhae. These names appear, too, in the Acts of the Oriental Apostle Addai. To the same category of feudal lords probably belonged the Parthian governors and generals with Greek names like Hiero

---

[1] xvi, 745 *sq.*; *Ant.* xx [2], 17–33.

[2] Usually called συγγενεῖς in Greek, *vāspuhr* in Iranian.

[3] στρατηγοί and γενεάρχαι in Agathangelus i, p. 112, sect. 6.

[4] Iranian *vasurkan* and *azatan*.

[5] A document from Doura (of A.D. 121) gives in Greek translation the full title of one of these provincial governors: τῶν βατησα καὶ τ[ῶν συγγενῶν ἀνδ]ρῶν(?) παρ[απά]του καὶ στρατηγοῦ Μεσοποταμίας καὶ Παραποταμίας καὶ Ἀραβάρχου. The restorations are by Ensslin and Mlaker (*Phil. Woch.* 1933, cols. 268 *sq.* According to Mlaker παραπάτης may be a transliteration of pāhragbēd: 'head of the guard' (cf. ἀρκαπάτης).

[6] O. G. von Wesendonk, *The Georgian Chronicle K'art 'lis ts'hovreba* in *Klio*, xxi, 1927, pp. 125 *sqq.*

and Demonax of the time of Artabanus III. Beside the higher
nobility stood in each satrapy the middle and lower nobility, who
served in the army as officers and horsemen.

Within the satrapies there were many semi-independent units,
ethnical or urban. Such were the Arab phylarchs of Mesopotamia, who sometimes became masters of Greek and Oriental
cities and assumed the title of kings. The best known are the
kings of the Macedonian colony of Edessa, the Abgars. Of the
same type were Sporaces, the phylarch of Anthemusias and ruler
of the city of Batnae, Mannus the lord of Singara, Manisarus of
Gordyene and the kings who ruled in Hatra, all of the time of
Trajan. In the province of Babylonia, beside Mesene and Characene, there were many petty kingdoms, for instance that of Hadad-
nadin-akh[1] at Tello, and those of Nippur and perhaps Forat. The
same may be said of tyrants in the Greek cities, as Andromachus
in Carrhae and Apollonius at Zenodotium in 53 B.C. In this
connection the story of the ephemeral Jewish petty kingdom of
Babylonia, the robber kingdom of Asinai and Anilai, appears as
natural and cannot be used as evidence of anarchy marking the
last years of Artabanus' rule. The formation of a Jewish phylarchy
in Babylonia does not differ very much from the formation of the
phylarchy of Edessa or of Hatra. It is very probable that the
successful brothers were recognized by Artabanus in return for
a good round sum, and, like Abgar of Edessa in the time of
Pacorus II, they might have boasted of holding their land by
right of purchase ($\chi\acute{\omega}\rho\alpha$ $\acute{\omega}\nu\eta\tau\acute{\eta}$, p. 119).

The Greek cities of Macedonian origin which were not transformed into petty monarchies also formed self-governing units
within the satrapies (vol. IX, p. 595). Of their life and constitution
little is known. Of the many cities of this type[2] we have information about Seleuceia on the Tigris[3], the greatest and the richest of
them, about Seleuceia on the Eulaeus (Susa) and about Europus
(Doura). Babylon, Uruk and Nineveh probably belonged to the
same class. New and important evidence yielded by excavations
is shedding more and more light on Susa and Doura. It must not

---

[1] *C.I.S.* II, 1, 72.   [2] See Map 4 in vol. VII.

[3] On its constitution see vol. IX, p. 595. A recently discovered fragmentary inscription of the time of Antiochus II attests the existence at Seleuceia
of priests of the dynastic cult, of a *hieromnemon*, a *tamias* and an *agonothetes*.
It may be assumed that these continued under Parthia. See R. H. McDowell,
Stamped and inscribed objects from Seleucia on the Tigris, pp. 258 *sqq.* On
the vicissitudes of the city under Parthia and the effect of its party-warfare
on Parthian history see McDowell, *Coins from Seleucia on the Tigris*,
pp. 216 *sqq.*

be forgotten that when Parthia became the mistress of the Macedonian cities they were already military settlements with a population of soldiers who had a good military training and warlike spirit. All of them had large tracts of land assigned to them, and their residents were most of them well-to-do landowners who, in fighting the enemies of the Seleucids, were defending their own homes and their own privileged position. Under Parthia they retained their military and agricultural character. The Macedonian colonists remained masters of their own cities and owners of their allotments of land. Neither Seleuceia on the Eulaeus nor Europus on the Euphrates had Parthian garrisons, such as those that held other fortresses built by Parthia or of Oriental origin (*e.g.* Paliga to the north of Europus and probably the modern Amka to the south). The Greek cities were defended by their own residents, usually under Greek commanders. At Doura these belonged to the local aristocracy, where the offices of *strategos* and *epistates* or *strategos genearches* (the last probably meaning *ethnarches*) seem to have belonged to one particular family[1]. *Strategoi* and *epistatai* are also found at Babylon and Nineveh and probably at Uruk[2]. Whether they were appointed by the king or elected by the citizens is unknown; more probably, like the feudal lords of other cities, they were nominated by the king. One thing is certain, that they were subordinate to the provincial governors.

Alongside these military presidents there probably existed in all the Macedonian cities the regular machinery of a Greek city-state, with magistrates, *boule* and *demos*. *Bouleutai* are attested at Doura by several inscriptions, as are also *agoranomoi*, *chreophylakes* and *kerykes*. Two recently discovered parchments[3] give a very good picture of the composition of the 'royal court' ($\beta\alpha\sigma\iota\lambda\iota\kappa\grave{o}\nu$ $\delta\iota\kappa\alpha\sigma\tau\acute{\eta}\rho\iota o\nu$) at Doura with two or three 'royal judges,' an *eisagogeus* and a *praktor*. The judges were probably appointed by the king but belonged to the local aristocracy. Many of the governors of the cities and the judges bore court titles, and it is probable that some of these prominent Macedonians and Greeks were occasionally appointed governors of provinces and commanders of royal armies. The situation at Susa, the capital of the

[1] *Graffiti* found in 1935 in the house of the leading family of Doura, the Lysiae and Seleuci, confirm the view in the text, which in the main is that of J. Johnson, *Dura Studies*, 1932. Cf. M. Holleaux in *B.C.H.* LVII, 1933, p. 28, no. 1. M. Rostovtzeff in *J.H.S.* LV, 1935, p. 57.

[2] Babylon, *O.G.I.S.* 254; Nineveh, R. W. Hutchinson in *Archaeol.* LXXIX, 1929, pp. 140 *sqq.*

[3] *Dura*, Perg. 21 and 40.

province of that name, was somewhat different, and more like that of Artemita, the capital of the Chalonitis or of Sittacene. There have been found two new inscriptions, both of poems, carved in the time of Phraates IV on the base of a statue set up at Susa by the garrison of the city in honour of Zamaspes, the governor of Susiane. Zamaspes is praised as the great benefactor of the garrison (*akrophylakes*), the man who restored to prosperity the *kleroi* of these soldiers by irrigation works. It is evident that Zamaspes was the chief commander of the garrison of Susa and that the garrison consisted of *klerouchoi* of Macedonian origin, citizens of the city. This is confirmed by many inscriptions which speak of the garrison. Part of the garrison are called 'bodyguards,' possibly of the governor. Still more interesting is an inscription written on the base of another statue during the reign of Artabanus III. The statue was set up in honour of Hestiaeus, a distinguished citizen of Susa. The text shows that there were two representatives of the king in the city, one with a Greek, the other with an Iranian name[1]. Unfortunately their titles are not given: one may be the governor of the province, the other the commander of the garrison. Next to them come the magistrates of the city, two archons and a treasurer. The treasurer, Hestiaeus, is a highly honoured man, bearer of court titles, who was sent twice as ambassador probably to the king to discuss the affairs of the city. The *boule* and the *demos* take an active part in the life of the city. It is an interesting combination of royal control and self-government.

The feudal structure of the Parthian Empire was inherited by the Arsacids from the Achaemenids and was transmitted by them to the Sassanian kings. It is a characteristic feature of the great Iranian states of Asia, a form of government as widely spread as the Hellenistic form of centralized monarchy, which last was inherited by the Hellenistic monarchs from Egypt and Assyria and was ultimately transmitted by them to the Roman West. In a feudal monarchy there is always much unrest and insubordination, and strong kings always seek to curb the feudal lords and to establish a more centralized government. Such attempts were not unknown to the Arsacid monarchy. Roman sources frequently refer to them, since the Parthian nobles, when oppressed by the

---

[1] Fr. Cumont in *C. R. Ac. Inscr.* 1932, pp. 238 *sqq.*; M. Rostovtzeff in *Scientia*, LIII, 1933, p. 120 *sq.*; C. B. Welles, *Royal Correspondence in the Hellenistic Period*, no. 75, pp. 299 *sqq.* A. Wilhelm in *Anz. d. Wien. Akad.* 1934, pp. 45 *sqq.* Prof. Welles believes that the king is addressing the two archons of Susa.

kings, often tried in the first century A.D. to turn the tables by setting up a pretender with the help of Rome. In Rome these nobles regularly complained of 'atrocities,' as in the reigns of Phraates IV, of Artabanus III and of Gotarzes. The background of these atrocities was either the struggle of the king with a clan or party which opposed him or a struggle for a more centralized form of government in general.

Parallel to this struggle with the nobility went a like struggle with the vassal lords of smaller and larger kingdoms. This may be reflected in the coinage of the kingdom of Elymaïs. The coins of the hereditary dynasts of the Elymaïs (Kamnaskires) show, in the late first century, B.C. and in the first century A.D., such a deterioration of type that it may reasonably be supposed that at this time the dynasty had but a shadowy existence[1]. Later, at the end of the first century, a new dynasty appears with Parthian royal names (Orodes, Phraates and perhaps Osroes). It may be suggested that in the times of the Parthian kings Orodes, Phraates and Artabanus the old dynasty of Elymaïs may have lost its former importance and that finally the native kings were replaced by members of the Arsacid family. Coins reflect similar phenomena in the dynasty which was ruling in Spasinu Charax. After Attambelos III, that is, after A.D. 71–2, there is a gap in the sequence of Characene coins which lasts until 100–1. About the same time the list of Characene kings used by the source of the *Macrobioi* attributed to Lucian gives the name of Artabazus as restored to his throne by the Parthians. The name is foreign to the Characene dynasty and does not appear on the coins. It may be suggested that Artabazus was a Parthian nominee who ruled twice, each time for a short while. Being practically a Parthian governor he did not strike coins. He may have been appointed by Vologases I and restored by Pacorus II. After this episode the old dynasty was restored, probably for a very short time. It gave place later to a new dynasty with new Semitic names which used Aramaic exclusively on their coins. The relation in which this dynasty stood to the later Arsacids is not known.

Slight as is our knowledge of the history of the other lesser kingdoms, there are indications that intervention by Parthia or by Rome was not rare. In the time of Vologases I a conflict arose between Adiabene and Parthia which apparently led to a war, and in a later reign, probably that of Vologases II, Adiabene became

[1] A like phenomenon may be observed in the coins of Persis. Some scholars assume that there was a gap in this coinage coinciding with the reigns of Orodes and Phraates IV.

a satrapy instead of a kingdom. So at the time of Trajan the king of Edessa held his kingdom from Pacorus II by right of purchase (p. 115), whereas it seems to have been ruled before by the kings of Adiabene. He went over to the Romans and probably lost his life in the revolt of 116. Hadrian placed on the throne Parthamaspates, ruler of Osrhoëne, whom Trajan had sought to make king of Parthia. In 123 the former dynasty of Edessa was restored under Parthian overlordship only to become vassal to Rome after the expedition of L. Verus. It retained this status until Edessa was made a Roman provincial city by Caracalla[1].

We may finally observe attempts to control parts of the kingdom which became too strong and too independent in the relations between the Arsacids and the more considerable Greek cities of their kingdom. Seleuceia on the Tigris may serve as the best example. We hear that the city was strong enough to challenge the kings, and indeed rebellions of Seleuceia against the Arsacids were probably not uncommon. We may connect with them the autonomous coinage of the city in 88 B.C. and again in A.D. 14–15, the last perhaps connected with the reform of Seleuceia's constitution by Artabanus III, whereby power was given to a group of citizens which formed the *boule*. This encroachment on the democratic constitution of the city may have led to the recognition of the pretender Tiridates in the closing years of Artabanus and to the revolt against Artabanus which was put down after a long siege by Vardanes in A.D. 42–3. The vicissitudes of this struggle are reflected in the autonomous coins of the city in 39–40 and 41–2 and the city coins with the portrait of Vardanes and the figure of the *boule*.

The forces of this feudal empire continued to consist mainly of the private armies of the satraps and of the vassal kings, but the nucleus of the army was certainly the king's own troops, and a strong body of guards, largely foreigners, were always at hand in the palace. There were, besides, the garrisons of the Greek cities, though we never hear that Greeks were mobilized to form a field army. Sometimes in case of need the army was reinforced by mercenary units. The Parthian army was an array of horsemen— heavy *clibanarii* and cataphracts and light *sagittarii* recruited mostly from the lesser nobility of small landowners. They often used the lasso as well as the bow, spear and sword. None the less, the Parthian kings were not blind to the occasional need of infantry.

[1] Important evidence for the constitution and civilization of Edessa in the third century is provided by a parchment found at Doura but written at Edessa; A. R. Bellinger and C. B. Welles in *Yale Class. Stud.* v, 1935, pp. 95 *sqq.*

At times they called up their vassals from the mountains and formed strong armies of foot-soldiers. Thus according to the chronicle of Arbela an army of 20,000 foot was concentrated at Ctesiphon when the Alani invaded Parthia in A.D. 134. A new form of cavalry, perhaps borrowed from the Roman *dromedarii*, was the corps of cataphracts mounted on camels which was used by Artabanus V against Caracalla. Finally the introduction of new devices and especially of engines of war into the Parthian army is plausibly ascribed by Herodian to former Roman soldiers who, as captives or deserters, were incorporated in one capacity or another into the Parthian army. In addition, the Macedonian colonists of the Parthian cities had inherited a good training in the arts of war[1]. The Arsacids were not wild nomads in their warfare, and if they kept to their army of horse it was because it was a strong weapon well adapted to the needs of the Empire.

V. PARTHIA: ECONOMIC AND SOCIAL CONDITIONS

Of the economic and social life of the Parthian Empire we know very little. It doubtless varied from kingdom to kingdom, from satrapy to satrapy, from city to city. The most prominent feature is again the feudal structure of both social and economic life with the great feudatories leading, with the minor feudal lords holding cities and villages, with small free landowners cultivating their holdings and with bondmen working for both large and small landowners. Some estates were owned, according to Ammianus Marcellinus, by the Magi. The conditions of Mesopotamia may serve as an example. Isidore of Charax enumerates along the Euphrates a number of stations on the great commercial and military road. We find here a curious mixture of settlements: Macedonian colonies of which the best known is Doura-Europus, villages surrounding or adjacent to Parthian fortresses like Paliga, temples with their territories and their hereditary priests, smaller and larger villages. The documents found at Doura show that there were many villages in the territory of this city. The nucleus of the Greek cities was formed by the Macedonian colonists, well-to-do landowners, holders of their ancient *kleroi* which were hereditary in their families. Side by side with them may have lived Parthian dignitaries possessing larger or smaller estates and rich Semitic families engaged in trade and industry, owners of shops in the

---

[1] The Sassanians took over these methods from the Parthians, *e.g.* the art of taking cities by sapping and mining. For the details of the capture of Doura in A.D. 256 see *Dura*, Rep. VI (Du Mesnil du Buisson).

souks of the city and owners or leaseholders of parcels of cultivated land. Finally, there were many small landowners and tenants, and a number of slaves. Their relations to each other were regulated by laws which in Mesopotamia are Greek in character, perhaps with an admixture of Babylonian elements. No general regulations by the central power are noticeable in the few business documents which we possess, most of them from Doura and Babylonia. In Doura most of them are written in good Greek but the recent excavations have yielded also documents in Syriac (from Edessa), Palmyrene and Pahlavi (vol. ix, p. 589). In Babylonia the cuneiform script still obtains on the clay tablets as long as they last, while the parchment documents were probably written in Aramaic, the *lingua franca* of the time. In Atropatene both Greek and Pahlavi were used. The general impression is that the central government did not interfere with local economic, social and legal life. Whether as in the times of the Seleucids there existed taxes which were imposed and levied by the central government we do not know. We are equally ignorant how large were the payments of the various parts of the kingdom to the treasury of the central government, or how they were organized. It seems in one instance that the Arsacids were inclined to sell the right of collecting the taxes to the ruler of a given country or satrapy[1]. It is unfortunate that we are so poorly informed on one of the most important sources of revenue of the Arsacids, the customs duties levied from the caravans. Here again the most probable hypothesis is that the kings used their vassals to collect these dues and included them in the general tribute of the kingdoms, satrapies and cities.

The wealth of the Arsacids and of the richest vassal-kingdoms and cities of the Parthian Empire depended largely on the flourishing caravan trade between Parthia and China and India on one hand and Parthia and the Roman Empire on the other (pp. 122 *sqq.*). It is well known how important was the foreign commerce of the Roman Empire and how much attention was paid by the Chinese emperors of the Han dynasty to the development of their foreign trade with the North and the West. The excavations at Lou-lan in Chinese Turkestan and the Chinese historical records[2] give us an excellent picture of it. Both the Chinese and the Romans were eager to enter into direct relations with each other. But the Parthian kings and probably the Kushans and the Sogdians were too much interested in keeping the trade in their own hands to

---

[1] This is apparently the meaning of Arrian's statement (*Parth.* frag. 45 R.) that Pacorus II sold Osrhoëne to its king.

[2] *Annals of the Later Han*, 98, cf. *Annals of the Former Han*, 96.

allow Roman merchants and ambassadors to penetrate into China. On the contrary they tried hard to prevent any direct relations between the two countries. There are bitter complaints of them in the Chinese writers. And yet information about the great trade route and the two Empires of the West and of the East penetrated into the two countries through Parthian channels. Though the merchants of Palmyra never penetrated farther than the lowlands of Babylonia enterprising traders, probably Parthian subjects, tried to establish direct relations between China and Babylonia and perhaps between China and the Roman Empire. One of these was Maes Titianus, a Macedonian, who sent an expedition to China and gave the geographical material which this expedition collected to Marinus of Tyre, the main source of Ptolemy. Maes was certainly not from Palmyra, where no Macedonians are known. It is hard to believe that he was a Roman subject, for if he were, the Parthians would certainly have prevented him, as they prevented others, from penetrating into China. It is, therefore, probable that he belonged to one of the Macedonian colonies of the Parthian Empire, a rich merchant who had commercial relations both with China and the Roman Empire. The Chinese counterpart and contemporary of Maes was the agent of the general Pan-Ch'ao, Kan Ying by name, who according to the *Annals of the Later Han* penetrated as far as Spasinu Charax in his attempt to reach Ta-ch'in (the Syrian provinces of the Roman Empire and South Arabia[1]) and thus to establish direct relations between China and the 'Far West.' The Parthians frightened him by describing the horrors of a long sea voyage around Arabia. It was only by sea that the Romans were able to come into direct contact with China. Sporadic attempts are attested for A.D. 120 and then for A.D. 166 when an 'embassy' of Marcus Aurelius is recorded to have visited China.

The great land trade-routes which ran through Parthia connecting China and India with the West were certainly one of the chief concerns of the Arsacids. How successful they were in their control of them is shown by the fact that the Asiatic caravan roads described by Isidore of Charax and Ptolemy, which ended in Babylonia and from there ran up the Tigris and the Euphrates to the confines of the Roman Empire, were by far the most important arteries of commerce at that time, much more important than the Caspian route across the Caucasus or the steppe route to the north

[1] For the meaning of Ta-ch'in and Fu-lin in the Chinese sources see H. H. Schaeder, *Iranica* in *Gött. Abh.* III, 10, 1934, pp. 24 *sqq.* esp. p. 25 n. 1.

of the Caspian through the Aorsi (Alani). The Parthian roads rivalled the maritime route from India and Arabia to Spasinu Charax and Forat in supplying the Roman Empire with a large portion of its imports from China and India. Even with Egypt Parthia maintained lively trade connections, as may be seen from the relations between Palmyra and Egypt and the information which we have on Scythianus and Terebinthus, the forerunners of Mani in Egypt, and on the rapid spread of Manichaeism in Egypt[1].

To the caravan trade of Parthia three great cities, namely, Vologasia in Babylonia, Hatra in Mesopotamia and Palmyra in the Syrian desert owed their existence, while many other towns, among them Seleuceia, Babylon, Forat and lesser cities on the Tigris or Euphrates, such as Doura, not to mention Singara, Nisibis and Edessa, owed to it much of their prosperity. It is probable that the Arsacids viewed the advance of Seleuceia with an unfriendly eye and sought to direct the trade from Palmyra to Vologasia and Spasinu Charax[2]. Here, and at Babylon before Vologasia was founded, were the most important settlements of Palmyrene merchants. The founding of Vologasia and the almost contemporary creation of Ctesiphon as the royal residence and military centre of he Parthian Empire combined to undermine the prestige of Seleuceia.

What slight knowledge we possess of the organization of Parthian trade is mainly derived from Chinese sources. The traveller Chang Ch'ien declares that 'their market folk and merchants travel in carts and boats[3] to the neighbouring countries perhaps several thousand li distant,' and this is repeated in the *Annals of the Former Han*. These Annals stress the fact that such countries as Chi-pin (? Sacastene), K'ang-chü (Sogdiana) and Ta-wan (Ferghana) strove to keep on good terms with China chiefly because of their trade. To all these alike, including the Parthians, may be applied what is said of the people of Ta-wan, that 'they are clever traders and dispute about the division of a farthing.' The discoveries at Lou-lan, the military post and caravan station of China in Chinese Turkestan, and at Palmyra, the queen of the Syrian desert (p. 631), may be adduced to show how the wise Chinese

---

[1] C. Schmidt and H. J. Polotsky, *Ein Mani-Fund in Aegypten*. Sitz. d. Berl. Akad. 1933, 12; cf. E. Peterson in *Byz. Zeitschr.* XXXIV, 1934, p. 380.

[2] It is significant that in the many texts that speak of Palmyrene trade Seleuceia is probably mentioned only once and that for a very early date.

[3] The mention of carts, as in Palmyra, suggests the care taken of the great roads, while the boats may reflect not only maritime relations with Arabia and India but also the use of the great rivers, especially the Oxus.

in the East and the shrewd Semites in the West handed on their wares to Sogdian, Bactrian and Parthian traders, who carried on this commerce by the same methods as those from whom they thus received it.

VI. PARTHIA: RELIGION, LITERATURE, ART

The official religion of the Parthian royal house was Mazdaism, at least since the reign of Vologases I, who made a new edition of the *Avesta* and had it provided with a running commentary in Pahlavi[1]. Herein he was true to the great Iranian traditions of Atropatene, the home of his dynasty, and his brother Tiridates made clear his adhesion to Mazdaean tenets (vol. x, pp. 550, 772). In the Iranian Epos both Vologases (Vistaspa) and Tiridates (Spaniyād) appear as champions of the new religion against paganism. In all this we may perhaps detect a deliberate reaction against the syncretistic and Hellenistic tendencies of their predecessors, especially Phraates IV and Phraataces and the pretenders supported by Rome. On Parthian coins the titles *Theopater* and *Theos* disappear, while that of *Epiphanes*, which does not make so explicit a claim to divinity, persists. Indeed the title *Theos*, first used by Phraates III, was revived but once in this period and that for Musa, the mother of Phraataces[2]. The Greek poems found at Susa go farther in stressing the divine nature of Phraates IV than would have been acceptable to a good Zoroastrian even from his Greek subjects. The Parthian kings, it is true, never abandoned such elements of the official worship of the king as they inherited from the Achaemenids, but it appears not improbable that the last Arsacids of the old line had pressed this tendency too far, and that the dynasty from Atropatene marks a reaction to the older tradition. At the same time, the kings and probably the Magi, of whose organization in this period hardly anything is known, did not fail in reverence to their ancestral gods, whom they may have regarded as emanations of the great Ahura-Mazda. Chief among these was the Sun and Moon, and it is to be noted that coins of Persis, where the kings were notably orthodox Mazdaeans, show the symbol of the crescent moon on the royal tiara[3], as did the coins of the Sacastene kings and their successors the Kushans (vol. ix, pp. 593 *sqq.*).

---

[1] The *Dinkart*, iv, 24. The statement that these books with their commentaries existed by the second century A.D. is borne out by the fact that Mani, the contemporary of Artabanus V, is well acquainted with them.

[2] See Volume of Plates iv, 200, *d.*   [3] *Ib.* 8, *n.*

The religious beliefs of the masses of the people throughout the Parthian Empire are quite another matter. But evidence is lacking to decide how large a part of the Iranian population were Mazdaeans or what kind of Mazdaism, if any, was offered to them by the numerous and powerful Magi, the clergy of the Empire. Nor is it easy to tell how far Mazdaean and Iranian religion in general influenced the cults and faith of the non-Iranian subjects of Parthia. But one thing is certain, the Arsacids were no fanatics and did not seek to impose their own religion on their subjects. In Assyria, for instance, local cults persisted, and new temples were built to the ancient gods. The same is true of Doura, where even the Seleucid dynastic cults continued under Parthian rule[1], and of Susa. What we find in these Greek cities is not the introduction of Iranian cults and the building of fire-temples, but the supplementing of Greek cults by Semitic even among the inhabitants who still spoke Greek and had Greek names.

How far Iranian doctrine and practice affected the various Semitic religions is also a question. At Doura, for instance, where all the temples found are dedicated to gods with Semitic names, it is probable that a slight Iranian influence was perceptible, which through a kind of syncretism made it possible for Iranians to take part in the worship of Semitic gods. The Babylonian Bel and his acolytes, the gods of the Sun and the Moon, may well have been in one way or another identified with Ahura-Mazda and the corresponding Iranian gods of the pre-Zoroastrian Pantheon, one of whom was Mithra. The tolerance of the Parthian kings extended beyond the ancient worships of the Empire to proselytizing foreign religions, especially Judaism and Christianity. In Adiabene, if we may trust the Jewish tradition, they did not demur when the ruling dynasty embraced Judaism, and any persecution of the Christians in the same vassal-state was the work of the local Magi and not of the central government or its representatives.

Little is known of the intellectual life of the Parthian Empire. The citizens of the Greek cities kept intact their native language and probably gave to their children a Greek education or at least an education in Greek. Many citizens of Seleuceia on the Eulaeus (Susa) must have been fond of Greek poetry, to judge from the four poems that have been discovered there, and no doubt they studied the classical poets of Greece in order to be able themselves to compose. The excellent style of King Artabanus' letter to the magistrates of that city (p. 117 n. 1) shows that the Greek secretaries of the Parthian kings, who were probably of Mesopotamian

[1] See M. Rostovtzeff, *C. R. Ac. Inscr.* 1935, pp. 300 *sqq.*

origin, were well trained in schools which kept alive the Seleucid traditions of Greek rhetoric. A like familiarity with the Greek language and the same degree of education are shown by the much more modest scribes of Doura, who are found writing a correct Greek style as late as the second century A.D. The same is true for Media Atropatene. Literary and stylistic interests seem to have been keener in Babylonia than in upper Mesopotamia. No metrical inscriptions in Greek comparable to those of Susa have been found at Doura, and most of the non-official inscriptions show that the population at large—in this unlike the professional scribes —spoke a highly debased and semitized form of Greek.

The Greeks of the Parthian Empire did not lose their interest in learning. Apollodorus of Artemita, the late Hellenistic historian of Parthia, had successors of his own type, men who were born in Parthia but wrote for the educated people of the Graeco-Roman world. Such was Dionysius of Charax, the geographer, author of a description of the world, who wrote for Augustus a monograph on Parthia and Arabia (vol. x, p. 253). Such was another writer used by the elder Pliny, Isidore of Charax, whose date and identity are uncertain. We still possess his *Parthian Stations*, in which he describes the great military and caravan route down the Euphrates and across Parthia to India. It is a work doubtless based on Parthian official itineraries, and we have quotations from his other writings in Pliny, Athenaeus and the author of the *Macrobioi* (p. 118). The last quotation shows that he gave lists of kings of Parthia, Persis, Elymaïs, Spasinu Charax and the Yemen. The list of kings of Charax which goes down to a time which coincides with the gap in our numismatic evidence between A.D. 71/2 and 100/1 may be taken as evidence that Isidore was a contemporary of Pliny and not to be identified with Dionysius of Charax. Finally a similar work may have been used by Josephus, perhaps a *Parthica* written by a hellenized Jew of Mesopotamia in which special attention was paid to the destinies of the Jews and of the kings of Adiabene who were converts to Judaism. To the same class of Mesopotamian educated Greeks belonged Maes Titianus and his agents (p. 122).

Greek education and Greek learning certainly affected some of the natives, both Iranians and non-Iranians. The most splendid example is the great teacher Mani, who certainly had a good Greek philosophical training. But we are not entitled to ascribe exclusively to Greek influence the literary activity of those subjects of the Parthian kings who never received a Greek education. Thus it is improbable that the acquaintance with Parthian history of Abel the Teacher, the source of Mešihâ-zekha, who wrote about A.D. 550 a local ecclesiastical chronicle of Arbela, was derived from Greek works. It probably goes back to a Parthian chronicle or annals which embodied the official tradition of Parthian history. It may be assumed that similar chronicles existed in most of the vassal-kingdoms and formed with the Parthian annals the historical substructure of such works as the life of Addai, the apostle of Adiabene and Osrhoëne, and the lists of Arsacid kings which are found in Dionysius of Tellmahre for Osrhoëne and in Mar Abas and Moses of Choarene for Armenia, as well as those cited in the *Macrobioi*. It was probably not Greeks who kept the itineraries of the Parthian kingdom which were used by Isidore and the agents of Maes Titianus. All these semi-official, semi-literary records perished when the Sassanians replaced the Arsacids, and yet their memory survived—for the West in the works of Western historians, for the East in the epic poetry, whose most glorious heroes are reflections of the Arsacids and of their vassals.

More or less the same conditions prevailed with Parthian art. As in the field of religion we must clearly distinguish between the imperial art of the court and the Iranian art of the Arsacid period in general on the one hand and the art of the various non-Iranian kingdoms and satrapies of Parthia on the other. Both the Iranian, and what may be called the provincial, art of the Parthian Empire are very little known and studied, but an analysis of the extant monuments shows that the common view of Parthian art as a degeneration of Greek art is mistaken. A peculiar and original Iranian art, which included a flourishing imperial art, did exist and shows but very few Greek elements. This Iranian art exercised a strong influence both on the art of the non-Iranian parts of the empire and on that of its eastern neighbours, especially China. What we know of the provincial art of Parthia and its Iranian features is derived from the many objects found in North India and in Mesopotamia, especially in Babylonia, at Susa, at Hatra[1], at Assur and at Doura.

The greatest contribution that the Parthian Empire made to art was in the field of architecture. The excavations of the Parthian city of Assur and the study of the Parthian monuments there and at Hatra prove that the so-called *liwan*-palace with its peculiar plan and stucco decoration which is so typical for the Sassanian period is of Parthian origin. All the essential parts of the palace and all the peculiar features of its decoration are brilliantly exemplified in both cities, and they certainly had a deep

[1] See Volume of Plates iv, 20.

influence on Mesopotamian architecture of the same period as we find it in Babylon and at Doura. How far back we can trace the development of the *liwan*-palace in the pre-Parthian period it is difficult to say. The same is true of another peculiar form of Iranian architecture—the fire-temple. It is certain that the Sassanian fire-temples repeat the plan and the system of decoration of earlier temples of the same type.

It is beyond doubt that both sculpture and painting flourished in Iranian lands in the Parthian period. Very few monuments are extant, but they suffice to show that both religious and secular sculpture and painting were cultivated in the Parthian Empire by Iranian artists[1]. In the field of religious art may be adduced the religious paintings and sculptures of Doura and the religious sculptures of Palmyra, especially the recently discovered painted bas-reliefs of the temple of Bel[2]. They cannot be derived from either Greek or Assyrian art alone. Indeed, their style and composition show striking resemblances with those of scattered religious sculptures of the Parthian period in Iranian lands and of the impressive religious sculptures of Nimrud Dagh of half-Iranian Commagene in the first century B.C., both of which show many purely Achaemenid features[3]. It may, therefore, be suggested that the religious paintings and sculptures of Doura and Palmyra are to be regarded as products of late Iranian art which flourished in both Iranian and Syro-Anatolian regions in Hellenistic times and was ultimately a direct continuation of the late Graeco-Persian art of the fifth, fourth and third centuries B.C.[4]

The same is true of secular art. The portraits of the kings on the Parthian coins have always been regarded as products of genuine Greek art. Yet the style of these portraits is Graeco-Iranian rather than Greek, as is proved by a comparison with products of Graeco-Iranian toreutics in South Russia and with the Graeco-Iranian sculptures of Nimrud Dagh. A glance at the contemporary coins of the Hellenistic kings will suffice to show

---

[1] A close study of the paintings of the Synagogue at Doura will probably show that at least one part of them was painted by Iranian artists. Some of these are mentioned in Pahlavi *dipinti* of the Elijah and Esther scenes. See M. Rostovtzeff in *Röm. Quartalschrift*, XLII, 1934, p. 213 and *Dura*, Rep. VI (A. Pagliaro). Manichaeism, a genuine Parthian movement, was fond of pictures. See Andreas-Henning in *Sitz. d. Berl. Akad.* 1933, pp. 301 *sqq.*; Schaeder, *op. cit.* pp. 71 *sqq.*

[2] See Volume of Plates v, 26, *a, b*.   [3] *Ib.* iv, 30 *a, b*.

[4] Cf. for Asia Minor the Phrygian and Lycian sculptures and Graeco-Persian gems, for North Syria and Phoenicia the columns and sarcophagi of Sidon and Cyprus.

how deep is the difference between them and the coins of the Parthian dynasty. Far more Iranian are secular sculptures and paintings, most of which illustrate episodes in the heroic epos of Iran. The bas-relief of Bihistun which represents the duel between Gotarzes and Meherdates was certainly not the first of its kind and shows no connection with Greek art[1]. The same type of composition is found in South Russia in graves of the early Roman period in painting and in many *graffiti* and *dipinti* on the walls of temples and private houses in Doura[2]. The same is true of another favourite motive of epic art in general—the hunting-scene—which recurs in this Iranian treatment at Doura, on bas-reliefs of the Iranian border lands and in South Russia[3]. They must derive, like the compositions of religious art, from late Achaemenid art, for the same types of composition and the same style are found on the Graeco-Persian gems. Finally a third favourite motif of epic art—the banquet scene—is often found on monuments of the Parthian period, in the bone-carvings of Olbia, the silver cups of Sacastene, the paintings and sculptures of Palmyra, Babylonia and Doura. This, too, goes back to the art of the Achaemenid period.

It is not the composition only that is characteristic for the Iranian art of the Parthian period. The monuments mentioned above show stylistic peculiarities which set them in a class apart. Some of these are typical of Oriental art in general; others, however, are peculiar to the Parthian period. One of these last is the flying gallop, another the strict frontality of the human figures, next come the elongated proportions of the bodies, a peculiar schematic treatment of the folds of their dress, a far-reaching neglect of the study of the human body and a growing linearity in its representation. Some minor peculiarities like special treatment of eyes, hair, beards and moustaches are equally typical of Parthian art. But its most striking peculiarity is the way in which intense spiritual rather than intellectual life is reflected especially in the eyes. Of this the figures of the priests of the well-known Conon fresco at Doura[4] give a fine example, but the same trait is found in almost all the religious sculptures and paintings and in the portraits of this period both in the Iranian and the non-Iranian parts of the Parthian Empire.

Finally, though the minor arts of the Parthian period are little studied, here also Parthia created many new forms and devices.

---

[1] See Volume of Plates v, 28, *a*.   [2] *Ib.* iv, 26.
[3] *Ib.* v, 24, *a*. Hunting scenes appear with the same treatment and peculiarities (the flying gallop) in China of the Han period.
[4] See Volume of Plates v, 28, *b*.

The silver plate of this period presents new and peculiar features both in style and composition. A new type of plant-ornament takes hold of it, and figure compositions which show at the beginning strong Greek influences become gradually more and more iranized and use all the motives of the great secular art of Parthia: battles and hunting-scenes and banquets. A set of Sacian silver cups is especially rich and typical in its development[1]. The same is true of the jewels of the Parthian period, especially of those of heavy silver inset with coloured stones which characterize both Palmyrene and Gandhara sculpture (both men and women are represented wearing them) and of which two sets were found in Doura[2] and some examples at Taxila. They all go back to Greek originals but show a development and tendencies of their own which lead gradually to the creation of new types, such as large and massive round and trapezoidal fibulae, characteristic chains with medallions, amulets and the like. One of the most striking features of this jewelry is its fondness for polychromy, which seems to be an ancient peculiarity of Iranian jewelry and may have been borrowed from Iran by Syria, where it flourished in the late Hellenistic and the Roman period. Finally, the Mesopotamian countries use a special type of glazed pottery different both from the contemporary Egyptian and Hellenistic glazed pottery and from the similar ware of China. Both the forms and ornaments of the pots and the type of the glaze show that Mesopotamian pottery forms a class in itself which attained such a rich development later in the Sassanian and Arab periods[3]. It is worthy of note that glaze was used in the Parthian times not only for vases but also for various types of coffins. In conclusion it may be said that most of the types of composition and, in great measure, the style of Parthian art were inherited and developed by the artists of the Sassanian period. Sassanian art thus appears, not as a sudden renascence of what was Achaemenid, but as a natural continuation of the Iranian art of the Parthian period.

[1] See Volume of Plates v, 30, a.   [2] Ib. 30, b.   [3] Ib. 32.

MAP 4

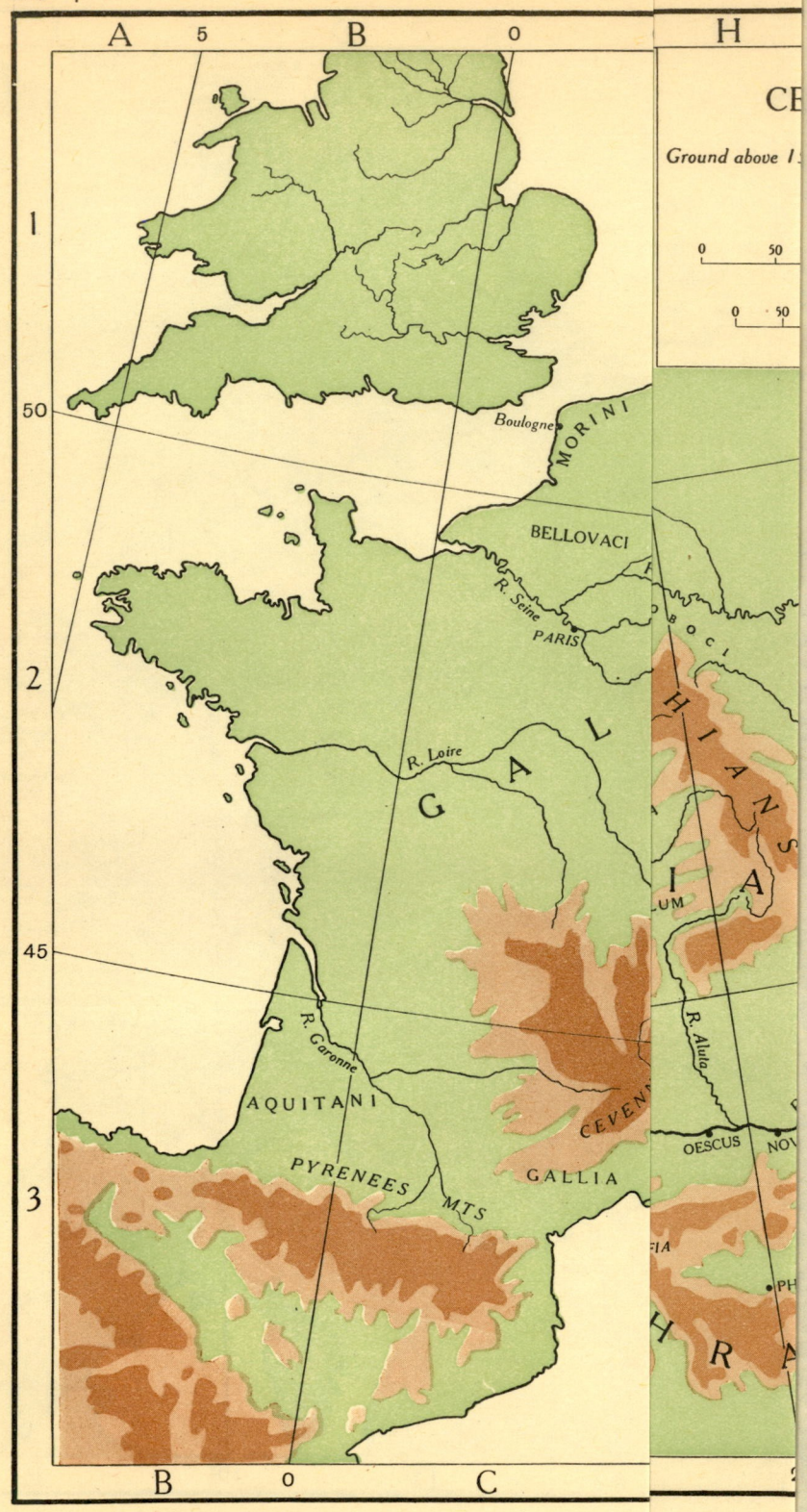

A 5 B 0 H

CE

Ground above 1

0 50

0 50

1

50

Boulogne MORINI

BELLOVACI

R. Seine

PARIS

2

R. Loire GALLIA

G

LUM

HIANS

A

CEVENN

45

R. Aluta

R. Garonne

OESCUS NOV

AQUITANI

PYRENEES GALLIA

3 MTS

FIA

PH

B 0 C HRA

CHAPTER IV

FLAVIAN WARS AND FRONTIERS

I. THE ARMY

NOBIS in arto et inglorius labor[1]. In comparison with the Republic, the history of the Empire is dull. Augustus meant that it should be: his aim was to substitute the routine of administration for the ruinous vicissitudes of domestic politics and foreign wars. Like Augustus, Vespasian made peace and order his watchword. But even now, enduring stability demanded further conquests: moreover the time had come to apply the lessons which the experience of the intervening years had gradually formulated.

The chief pre-occupation of the legions had hitherto been the control of the interior rather than the defence of the frontiers—indeed, of frontiers with their connotation of visible demarcation or organized defence it is perhaps too early to speak. What had once been a field army was becoming a garrison army. The age of Augustus had been familiar with groups of large field armies, sometimes comprising as many as five legions each: and pairs of legions were not infrequently brigaded together in single camps. As time goes on, the provincial armies tend to increase in number but diminish in size, while the legion slowly changes in character and function. With the legion become more sedentary, the practice develops of sending away for service in other provinces not whole legions as in the time of Augustus, but legionary detachments (*vexillationes*). This becomes a normal institution and heralds the establishment of field armies distinct from frontier troops. The legions of Augustus had been mobile units, their stations little better than marching-camps. Though the ramparts of earth become more massive and are reinforced with wooden beams, the defences of such a camp were not formidable either by nature or by art. The legions had commonly been established at positions that were strategically strong but tactically weak—it had not been expected that the camp of Vetera would ever be attacked[2]. The Flavian period witnessed extensive rebuildings in stone, but the process was neither contemporary nor uniform. From an early date the armies differed widely from province to province in composition, character and habits.

[1] Tacitus, *Ann.* IV, 32.   [2] Tacitus, *Hist.* IV, 23.

The auxiliary troops underwent an evolution more rapid and more complete. In the time of Augustus the operations of the army in the field had been seconded by 'tumultuary levies' of native warriors. Permanent auxiliary units certainly existed, above all of cavalry, as was to be expected: but in the course of the next fifty years the total of foot regiments was enormously increased as more and more native levies were converted into regular regiments and were dispatched to serve in countries other than those of their origin. In this way they acquired a definite status with definite terms of pay and service.

As active campaigning lapsed and a system of frontier defence evolved, the character and functions of the *auxilia* changed yet further. When these regiments occupied permanent forts strung out along a frontier which it was their duty to patrol and defend, it became necessary to create other light formations for the purposes of scouting and warfare. The *numeri* organized by Hadrian answered this function: and the irregular Moorish cavalry of Lusius Quietus and bands of *Astures symmachiarii* had already fought in the Dacian Wars of Trajan[1]. The auxiliary regiments had originally, like the legions, been stationed in encampments of earth, which, sooner or later, are replaced by forts of stone. The development was more rapid on the Rhine than on the Danube or in Britain—for the British army was one of the last to lose its mobile character.

Vespasian was the first ruler with military experience since Tiberius. His natural sagacity fortified him against the doctrinaire without weakening his preference for hard facts and clear outlines. Moreover, Vespasian had sons to succeed him: and though much that happened was due to chance or circumstances, there is some warrant for speaking of a Flavian policy in domestic and in foreign affairs, sober, practical, uninspired.

Vespasian's earliest task was the re-organization of the army and the restoration of discipline. The virtues of the soldiery had proved more deadly than their vices. The loyalty of the legions, divorced from a careless emperor and estranged by neglect, might attach itself with a devotion all the more intense to their commanders and their comrades. The fall of Nero was followed by a ruinous competition in which the German, Danubian and Eastern armies participated. Worse than this, Roman legions had been induced to take the oath of allegiance to the ' Imperium Galliarum '[2]:

---

[1] For *Astures symmachiarii*, cf. *Ann. épig.* 1926, no. 88. The *Mauri gentiles* of Lusius Quietus (S.H.A. *Hadr.* 5, 8) are represented on the Column of Trajan.   [2] See vol. x, p. 846.

but these were the shattered remnants of an army, weakened not only by defeat but by an infusion of local levies, without leaders and without hope in the universal confusion and apparent collapse of the Empire. With the restoration of authority, they were able as well as willing to repent. Legions which had disgraced their eagles and their honour had signed their own death-warrant: they were disbanded or fused with other legions—the result was the same, since in each case the soldiers appear to have been retained in service. This fate overtook four, or probably five, of the legions of the old Rhine army: I, IV Macedonica, XV Primigenia, XVI Gallica all disappear, while there is no certain trace of the survival of V Alaudae (see below, p. 171). Two of the legions, however, which as units had not been involved in the ignominy of their fellows, namely XXI Rapax and XXII Primigenia, were preserved and were stationed on the Rhine again, in Lower instead of in Upper Germany.

The abolition of four or five legions did not mean any reduction in the permanent legionary strength, which Nero had increased to twenty-eight by his creation of I Italica. This number was maintained by Vespasian, for he had at his disposal three formations of the Civil Wars, I Adiutrix, II Adiutrix, both recruited from the marines, and the legion (VII Gemina) which Galba had raised in Spain; and to these he added two new legions bearing his own family name, IV Flavia felix and XVI Flavia firma. More legions could hardly have been provided. In the first place there was the cost in money: Vespasian on his accession was confronted by an empty treasury, and though the financial situation improved enough for Domitian to increase the pay of the troops, that measure in itself constituted a permanent charge[1]. More serious, perhaps, than the financial difficulty was the scarcity of suitable recruits, hitherto a constant embarrassment.

Against these difficulties there were various imperfect remedies that might be invoked singly or together. When Augustus first regulated the conditions of military service and pay he fixed the term of years at sixteen: this he was subsequently compelled to raise to twenty, and by the time of the Antonines the period is one of twenty-five years. The introduction of this change is commonly attributed to Hadrian, but, like so many innovations, it may have

---

[1] After his war against the Chatti in 83 Domitian raised the pay by a third, from 225 to 300 denarii (Suetonius, *Dom.* 7; Dio LXVII, 3, 5). Later in his reign Domitian is alleged to have sought to reduce the size of the army (*Dom.* 12): but a statement of unrealized intentions is not very good historical evidence (cf. *J.R.S.* xx, 1930, p. 68).

begun in practice before it was applied as a regulation—Domitian's increase of the legionary pay may not have been an unmitigated bribe (see above, pp. 29, 133). Furthermore, whatever the nominal and legal term of discharge, soldiers frequently served beyond it, whether from choice or compulsion: and the maintenance of the legions below their full strength in times of peace was another attractive economy. Above all, a deficiency of legionary soldiers could be compensated by an increase of the auxiliary forces.

The provinces already paid a heavy contribution to the legions. Though there is no foundation for the belief that Italian recruiting ceases with Vespasian[1], a gradual change can be detected. From the time of Hadrian onwards the contribution of northern Italy and the more romanized parts of the Empire declines sharply; the provincial armies derive their recruits instead from local sources, from the children of the camps and the population of the adjacent regions. The legions more and more approximate to the *auxilia* in composition as well as in equipment and in length of service.

The auxiliary soldiers on the Rhine who had first followed the legions to war and rapine and then had defeated or dominated their depleted remnants were mainly Germanic or Gallic in origin, even when the regiments in which they served bore the names of Spanish or Dalmatian tribes. And though the rebellious *auxilia* were disbanded or dispersed and replaced by new formations, the old practice of local recruiting resumed its sway. Not that the regiments were ethnic units—this was only true of the Batavian *auxilia*, a new series of which was levied, and certain specialist formations such as Syrian bowmen. Though all the regiments distinguished with the Flavian name may not have been entirely new creations, it is clear that the army was considerably augmented by Vespasian and his sons.

So much for the armed forces of the frontier provinces. What of the reserves? Good communications would facilitate the transference of troops from frontier to frontier, and with the passing of time some of the provinces could dispense with all or most of the legions that garrisoned them. Spain had already surrendered two legions, Dalmatia one: and in the future the Flavian policy of organization and pacification might be expected to yield similar results. There were also the Italian fleets, which had already enriched the army with two legions. Nor should the garrison of the city of Rome be forgotten. Inflated by the soldiery of Vitellius, the Praetorian Cohorts were reduced by Vespasian to the number

[1] As held by Mommsen, *Ges. Schriften*, VI, p. 37, and developed by M. Rostovtzeff, *Soc. and Econ. Hist. of the Roman Empire*, pp. 103 and 510 *sq*.

of nine[1]: and there were four Urban Cohorts[2]. To historians and moralists the Praetorians are a subject of disparagement as well as distaste. Their loyalty to Otho had been signalized by valour rather than discipline; but in the wars of Domitian the Guard was chastened by service on the frontiers. They were resentful after his assassination, but a year elapsed before they sought to avenge their Emperor and their honour (see below, p. 196).

Of the discipline of the army in general, it is difficult to speak when the evidence is partisan as well as imperfect[3]. If the sudden ordeal of the Danubian wars found officers and men unprepared, it schooled them by adversity and turned the army into the formidable fighting-machine which proved its worth under Trajan.

The first duty of an army, however, is not to make war but to prevent war. The Empire was large enough: such extension as it might require was modest—consolidation rather than conquest. Vespasian therefore recognized the limits imposed upon the Roman dominions by nature or by policy and proceeded to make them more definite and more secure.

A description of the system of frontier defence in the Roman Empire might appear to belong more naturally to the history of Hadrian, the emperor with whose name it is linked in a fashion so intimate and so enduring; but to trace the design and the process of which the work of Hadrian is but the culmination, not the origin, demands an earlier beginning. Bold innovation and rapid change are foreign to the slow and almost casual development of the imperial system. In his organization of the army and of the defences of the Empire, Hadrian returns to the sober and peaceful policy of the Flavians which had been deserted by the energy and the ambition of the warlike emperor whose damaged inheritance he received and repaired (see below, p. 312 *sq.*).

On the frontiers of the Empire what has most impressed the imagination of posterity is the visible barrier that separated the world of civilization from the outer regions, the mound of earth, the stone wall, the wooden palisade: the frontiers which these works protected had existed before them and might have existed

---

[1] Dessau 1993. A tenth cohort was soon added, probably by Domitian (*Ann. épig.* 1930, no. 16).

[2] In addition the cities of Lugdunum and Carthage had each a cohort for garrison.

[3] Pliny (*Ep.* VIII, 14, 7) complains of the poor state of discipline at the time when he served as a military tribune (*c.* A.D. 80): that was in a Syrian legion. Pliny praises Trajan as the restorer of military discipline (*Pan.* 18): that was after Nerva.

without them. The recognition of the need for definiteness in the drawing of the frontiers and the most decisive steps towards its achievement were due to the emperors of the Flavian House.

Once Britain had been dealt with, it might have appeared that this modest ideal was near to attainment. Before Vespasian died, twenty imperatorial salutations were recorded in his titles, one short of the total of Augustus. This comparison gives point to a contrast. The time of Augustus had been the epic age of the Roman army. The conquests—or rather the annexations—of the Flavians were not intended to provide a theatre for brilliant exploits of strategy. A slow process of subjugation is consummated by driving roads and establishing fortified posts: the spade steadily supersedes the sword.

Great generals are as much out of place as under the successors of Augustus. The sudden crisis on the Danube in the reign of Domitian, however, made more exacting claims. How far they were satisfied, it is difficult to say[1]. As in other branches of the imperial administration, the needs of the armies and the provinces were met by an increasing measure of specialization. There were many senators like the younger Pliny whose service as a military tribune had been brief and superficial, and who were subsequently not placed in command of a legion. Others, however, might pass through a long course of training and hope at last to govern the great military provinces—not the surviving heirs of Republican families or the descendants of Augustan consuls, for such men were systematically excluded, but a newer nobility, not infrequently of equestrian parentage and provincial origin. It is significant that the longest known period of military service of young senators occurs in the reign of Vespasian. Trajan, the future emperor, passed ten *stipendia* as a military tribune[2]. Nor had military technique fallen behind. As before, it had adapted itself to changing needs. With the Romans it had never been a theoretical study, but embodied the lessons of experience, formed and transmitted in the camps, and seldom recorded in writing. The technical accomplishments, like the geographical knowledge, of Roman military men, were wider and deeper than anything revealed in the manuals composed by Greek professors or retired generals. The reader of the *Strategemata* of Frontinus would never infer that their author had consummated the conquest of Wales.

Frontinus and Agricola are typical of the age that produced

[1] Tacitus, *Agric.* 41—the *inertia et formido* of the generals, a theme expanded by Pliny, *Pan.* 18.
[2] Pliny, *Pan.* 15.

them and the age that needed them. All the arts of a biographer could not invest such a man with a brilliance alien to his character and achievements. And it might have been feared that the Flavian period as a whole would be barren and uninspiring. The reign of Domitian, however, in foreign as in domestic policy, belied this fear and gave the historian full scope for his peculiar talents. But the masterpiece of Tacitus breaks off with the submission of Civilis. It is not only the splendour of Tacitean rhetoric that has perished. Most of the facts are gone beyond recall. It is with the utmost difficulty that even a bare outline, let alone a coherent and credible narrative, can be reconstructed. Other evidence, of different kinds, must be invoked. Inscriptions have revealed names and facts—and even whole wars—that were hitherto unknown; and, especially with the aid of the stamped tiles manufactured in such numbers by the soldiers, the movements of legions can often be traced and related to facts—or conjectures—of history. Many military sites have been identified and some have been systematically excavated: and the study of the finds of coins and pottery has often permitted a very close dating. But it will not be forgotten that the archaeological as well as the literary record is fragmentary and incomplete. The earliest testimony of epigraphy or archaeology is not always the earliest that ever existed, and silence may be a lying advocate.

These difficulties, everywhere present, are most apparent when the subject is a slow advance or a peaceful re-organization that offered no incidents worth recording for their own sake or for purposes of misrepresentation. Before the wars on the northern frontiers are narrated—the most important as well as the most dramatic chapter of the foreign policy of the Flavian Emperors—it will be necessary to sketch in outline the uneventful annals of the eastern provinces and of northern Africa.

II. THE EASTERN FRONTIER

The claim of the Romans to dispose as they pleased of Armenia had proved not only distasteful to the inhabitants of that country and provocative to Parthia, but a source of trouble to themselves.

The reign of Nero witnessed a series of campaigns, or rather of manœuvres. A Roman army was induced to capitulate: it was allowed to depart. Corbulo marched, impressive and unopposed, through the length and breadth of Armenia. As national prestige and 'historical' claims had been pledged on both sides, it was no less remarkable than fortunate that good sense was allowed to prevail. A compromise was reached, by which a prince of the Parthian royal house was to rule in Armenia, but was to receive his investiture from Rome (see above, vol. x, p. 772).

In the East as elsewhere the policy of Vespasian was not so much an innovation as an open recognition, to the last consequences, of a changed situation. The Romans had resigned control, direct or indirect, over Armenia. The abandonment of this sphere of influence was followed by the substitution of Roman provincial government in certain dependent kingdoms that had indubitably belonged to the Empire. A new frontier called for a new system of defence.

Hitherto the only legionary armies stationed in the East had been the two legions of Egypt and the four in Syria. The Syrian like the Egyptian troops enjoyed no great repute as soldiers. If a vigorous effort was intended or threatened, the European armies were called upon to supply fighting troops: in the time of Nero no fewer than three legions had been summoned from the Danubian lands, the source that fed in later days the campaigns of Trajan, of Verus and of Septimius Severus. On the line of the Euphrates itself where a Parthian invasion would come—if it ever came— none of the legions seem to have been permanently posted. Nor is it likely that the army of Syria was equipped with auxiliary regiments in the proportion of the warlike provinces of the West and North—there was little prospect of operations in the field, there was as yet no organized system of frontier defence. At need, the levies of the dependent princes were available.

The Parthian War of Nero and the insurrection in Judaea had necessitated the establishment of two temporary commands. They were made permanent by Vespasian. For one army of four legions in Syria Vespasian substituted three armies, in Syria, Cappadocia and Judaea, with a total of six legions. By the end of the reign of Hadrian no fewer than eight legions were strung out along the eastern frontier from Satala in the north to Bostra in Arabia.

To maintain order in Judaea one of the legions employed by Titus, X Fretensis, was left at Jerusalem. This lightened the task of the army of Syria, now reduced to three legions: and the area of that province was at the same time extended and consolidated. All the dependent principalities were not, it is true, at once dissolved. Between the new province of Judaea and the southern borders of Syria a large region, Batanea, Trachonitis, Peraea and part of Galilee, remained under the rule of Agrippa II until his death (c. A.D. 93)[1]: and farther to the east and south-east the kingdom of the Nabataean Arabs preserved its independence down to

[1] Cf. P.W., s.v. M. Iulius Agrippa II.

the time of Trajan. The exact limits of the province of Syria on the south are uncertain. Sohaemus, the prince of Emesa, was still reigning in 72, but he may before long have relinquished the throne amicably and with honour[1]. Aristobulus may have continued for a time to hold the neighbouring principality of Chalcis in the Lebanon[2]. Midway between Damascus and the bank of the Euphrates lay the city of Palmyra, in a fertile oasis. It had long remained aloof and secure, independent of the rival empires of Rome and Parthia and profiting by their discord[3]. There was no sudden annexation of Palmyra and so no date for it: there was a gradual process of tightening control and final absorption (see below, p. 859). One of the stages of this process probably belongs to the Flavian period. A milestone set up in the year 75 by M. Ulpius Traianus, the governor of Syria, has been discovered at Aracha, some twenty miles east of Palmyra[4]. The road on which it stood ran from Palmyra to Aracha, thence north-eastwards to the station of Sura on the Euphrates—and may have served to mark the frontier of Syria. It would therefore appear that Vespasian had taken in hand the delimitation of the frontier of Syria on the south and south-east. The comparatively late date at which the Romans incorporated territories like Palmyra and Arabia with their promise of rich profit from the caravan trade illustrates how indifferent on the whole was their frontier policy to economic advantages. A livelier interest in that subject might be deduced from the character of Vespasian.

A delimitation of the frontier of Syria between the Lebanon and the Euphrates was probably accompanied by a stricter watch upon the Euphrates itself, along the bank of which river the province of Syria now received an added extension to the north; for though Syria lost Cilicia Campestris, which together with Cilicia Aspera was converted into a separate province under a legate of praetorian standing, it gained Commagene. The deposition of Antiochus IV, the ruler of that region, was decreed, on a flimsy pretext—he was alleged to have entertained treasonable negotiations with Parthia. In the course of the year 72 the governor of Syria, Caesennius Paetus, accompanied by the legion VI Ferrata and the levies of the kings Sohaemus and Aristobulus, entered the territory of Commagene and marched upon the capital city of Samosata. Conscious of innocence or of impotence, Antiochus would offer no resistance. His sons, Epiphanes and Callinicus, displayed more spirit. They took up arms and engaged the Roman forces. But the

[1] Dessau 8958.   [2] *Pros. Imp. Rom.*[2] I, no. 1052.
[3] Pliny, *N.H.* v, 88.   [4] *Ann. épig.* 1933, no. 205.

despair of the king rendered their cause hopeless. They escaped to Parthia. Vologases received the princes with honour, but did not refuse to yield them up when a centurion called Velius Rufus arrived bearing the mandate of Vespasian. Thus ended the Bellum Commagenicum, if we may use the fine name of an inscription[1].

In this way the bounds of the province of Syria were defined and regulated. Its eastern frontier was the river Euphrates from the great gorge above Samosata as far down as the neighbourhood of Sura: that frontier was now to be firmly defended. Of the important passages across the river into Mesopotamia, Samosata as well as Zeugma was now in Roman hands, and both, it is to be presumed, were held by legions. From the time of Hadrian onwards Samosata was certainly garrisoned by XVI Flavia firma, then one of the Syrian legions, but still in Cappadocia under the Flavian emperors. The evidence about the Syrian army in this period is, however, so scanty that it cannot be proved whether or no the legion VI Ferrata, which occupied Samosata in 72, subsequently remained there[2]. IV Scythica was certainly the legion stationed nearest to Antioch, the capital of Syria—either at Cyrrhus or at Zeugma. The other, III Gallica, if not itself at Zeugma or Samosata, was perhaps at Raphaneae in the south, near Emesa, its station in the second century.

In the north a comprehensive change, initiated in the time of Nero, was recognized and completed. For the conduct of operations in Armenia a separate command had been instituted in Cappadocia. The post to which Corbulo was first appointed, and which Caesennius Paetus subsequently held, appears to have been the combined governorship of Cappadocia and Galatia. Vespasian placed a consular legate in charge of a vast Anatolian province extending north-eastwards from the confines of Asia and Pamphylia to the coast of Pontus and the upper reaches of the Euphrates. On the south Galatia lost some territory to the newly-formed province of Lycia-Pamphylia: but the various regions that in the course of time had come to be included in the province of Galatia, namely Pisidia, Isauria, Lycaonia, Paphlagonia, Galatia, and Galatic Pontus, were now united to Cappadocia. But this was not all—in 64–5 Nero had annexed Pontus Polemoniacus, and in 72 Armenia Minor was also added to the new province[3]. The Cappa-

---

[1] Josephus, Bell. Jud. VII [7, 1–3], 219–43; Dessau 9198, 9200.
[2] Cf. R. K. McElderry, C.Q. III, 1909, p. 52. The legion at Samosata might, however, have been III Gallica, cf. Dessau 8903.
[3] Fr. Cumont in Anatolian Studies presented to Sir. W. M. Ramsay, pp. 109–19.

docian army, as for brevity and convenience it may be called, comprised two legions. The one, XII Fulminata, guarded the important crossing of the Euphrates at Melitene, whither it had been dispatched by Titus in A.D. 70. The other legion of the army of Cappadocia was XVI Flavia firma, a new creation of Vespasian[1]. It may be assumed that Satala, to the north, in Armenia Minor (the camp of the legion XV Apollinaris from the time of Hadrian onwards) had a Flavian origin. The coasts of the Black Sea were now subjected to a closer control by the Romans[2]; and the port of Trapezus was of manifest value for an army in Cappadocia[3]. Satala, lying on the road that ran eastwards to Elegeia (near Erzerûm), was a position of considerable strategic importance.

For the leisurely processes of diplomacy was now substituted the presence of Roman legions and the threat of instant action. It was not enough, however, to station legions commanding the entrances to Armenia and ready to invade it. It was necessary to link the camps of the Cappadocian army with each other, with the army of Syria and with the provinces in the rear. The absence of good communications had been sorely felt in the time of Nero. In the event of war, Danubian troops would again be required, and, for their passage, roads, especially in the north. The Flavian emperors undertook a comprehensive programme of construction and repair all over Asia Minor[4]. The work was prosecuted under Nerva and Trajan.

Of the communications between west and east the most northerly— the great Pontic highroad from Bithynia coming by Phazimon and Neocaesarea to Nicopolis and thence to the fortress of Satala— now recovered the military importance which it had lost since the Mithridatic Wars[5]. This road was also accessible in various ways

---

[1] The governor of Cappadocia-Galatia was of consular standing, and so there must have been a garrison of two legions (Tacitus, *Hist.* II, 81; Suetonius, *Vesp.* 8).

[2] Josephus, *Bell. Jud.* II [16, 4], 366 *sq.*—the dramatic date of the speech is A.D. 66, but Flavian rather than Neronian conditions may be reflected (see above, vol. x, p. 775 *sq.*). [3] Tacitus, *Ann.* XIII, 39.

[4] Dessau 253, near Prusa; 263, Dorylaeum–Ancyra; 268, Ancyra; 8904, Nicopolis–Satala; *C.I.L.* III, 12218, Lystra–Derbe; 14184[48], south-east of Ancyra, on the road to Caesarea Mazaca.

[5] For this road, cf. J. A. R. Munro, *J.H.S.* XXI, 1901, pp. 52–66. Between the Halys and Nicopolis there are four milestones of Nerva and one of Nerva or Trajan (Munro, *op. cit.* p. 63; *C.I.L.* III, 12158–9; 14184[23]; 14184[32–3]). East of Nicopolis, however, there is a milestone from which the name of Domitian appears to have been erased (F. Cumont, *Studia Pontica*, II, p. 325): and the milestone of A.D. 76 from Melik–Sherif

from Ancyra, for example, through Amasia or Pontic Comana; moreover from Ancyra a road ran due east by Tavium to Sebasteia where it branched, eastwards by Nicopolis to Satala, south-eastwards to Melitene. Farther to the south, the main eastward route from Caesarea Mazaca through Arabissus to Melitene may not have been neglected, though evidence of its construction and use as a military road at this time is lacking[1].

It has been maintained that the engineers of the Flavians prepared the conquests of Trajan[2]: but it does not follow that the Flavian emperors were designing a war of conquest. Whatever their policy, roads were required. Moreover, the policy which Vespasian inherited from Nero gave a promise of lasting peace. It depended upon mutual tolerance and the recognition of a common interest. If conciliation were not interpreted as weakness, the honour and the advantage of Rome were alike secured. The vicissitudes of Armenian affairs enliven and adorn the pages of Tacitus, to him a welcome relief from the monotony and the degradation of domestic politics. But it all mattered very little. The policy of Augustus and of his successors may have appeared irresolute, that of the Flavian emperors unheroic. Yet one fact remains. Between Ventidius' victory at Gindarus and the second year of Marcus Aurelius two centuries elapsed. In that space of time no Parthian was ever seen west of the Euphrates save as a hostage or a captive. Parthia was not a well-organized power, capable of conducting a sustained war and formidable in offence. Though the Arsacid might affect the title of 'King of Kings' he could not count upon obedience among his vassals or the concord of his family: and even when not wholly incapacitated by domestic feuds or civil strife the Parthians were hampered by the absence of a standing army and by their ignorance of the art of siege-warfare. A prince of the house of Herod warned the Jews that it was vain to expect aid from Parthia[3]. Such hopes were more suitably enshrined in apocalyptic literature than admitted to any rational calculation of policy.

Nor was it certain that Rome would resume the habit of aggression. The memory of Crassus and the influence of poets and historians exalted Parthia to an equal and a rival of the Roman Empire:

(Dessau 8904) probably belongs to that road. Extensive repairs under Nerva and in the early years of Trajan are attested by numerous milestones on the roads Ancyra–Tavium, Tavium–Amasia and Gangra–Amasia.

[1] Cf. J. G. C. Anderson, *J.H.S.* xvii, 1897, pp. 27–8.
[2] Cumont, *op. cit.* p. 115.
[3] Josephus, *Bell. Jud.* ii [16, 4], 379 and 389.

but it was the part of prudence to ignore the temptation presented by Parthian weakness and a popular war. Moreover, the common interest of Rome and Parthia in the preservation of peace was now cemented by a common danger, the pressure of the Sarmatian Alani from beyond the Caucasus. Whatever may have been the nature of the projects conceived but abandoned by Nero, they would have involved action with rather than action against Parthia; and Vologases was disposed to extend to Vespasian the favour with which he had regarded Nero. In the crisis of 69 Vologases had offered the aid of his horsemen to Vespasian, and several years later (*c.* A.D. 75) he suggested concerted measures to repress and punish the Alani who had been harrying his dominions. The Alani had been let loose on Media by enemies of Parthia, the Hyrcanians. After over-running Media they swept through Armenia on their return, all but capturing Tiridates, the prince of Armenia, by their dexterity in the use of the lasso[1]. Roman territory does not seem to have been violated on this occasion[2]. Vespasian declined the invitation of Vologases and thereby deprived his younger son of that opportunity for a military command and military glory which he so ardently desired[3]. Rome took her own measures to avert any invasion that might threaten from across the Caucasus through the Darial Pass, and in A.D. 75 Roman troops were building a fort at Harmozica near Tiflis in the client-kingdom of the Iberians[4].

Vologases took offence. His resentment may have been further inflamed by the extension of Roman control over Palmyra about this time. A threat of hostilities was countered and averted in some way or other by M. Ulpius Traianus, and a diplomatic success was commemorated by the dispatch of a 'Parthian laurel' to Rome[5]. In this achievement the studied vagueness of a pane-gyrist associated the son of the governor, then serving as a military tribune in one of the Syrian legions. Thwarted, like Domitian, of an Eastern war in his youth, in his old age he was to have his revenge.

Fate had forged the Parthians a weapon, if they cared to use it.

[1] Josephus, *Bell. Jud.* VII [7, 4], 244–51 (in A.D. 72).
[2] Josephus is silent, and nothing can be got from Suetonius' statement about Cappadocia *propter assiduos barbarorum incursus* (*Vesp.* 8).
[3] Suetonius, *Dom.* 2; Dio LXV, 15, 3 (A.D. 75); *B.M. Cat. R. Emp.* II, p. 42.   [4] Dessau 8795.
[5] Pliny, *Pan.* 14. For a bloodless 'Parthian laurel,' cf. Tacitus, *Ann.* XIII, 9. The elder Trajan was awarded the *ornamenta triumphalia* (Dessau 8970). Hostilities with Parthia in the Flavian period are disproved by Tacitus, *Hist.* I, 2. Cf. Aurelius Victor, *Epit.* IX, 12, *rex Parthorum Vologaesus metu solo in pacem coactus est*; *Caes.* IX, 10, *ac bello* (*ab illo,* Gutschmid) *rex Parthorum Vologaesus in pacem coactus.*

The sudden and mysterious disappearance of Nero encouraged a belief that he was alive and would return, a belief still prevalent as late as the time of Trajan and shared by pagan, Jew and Christian. In this fertile soil of superstition a crop of impostors sprang up and throve upon the affection or the terror that the name of Nero had inspired over all the East. The first of them arose in the year 69: he was quickly suppressed. Of the others—the total is unknown— two secured a place in history before the Flavian dynasty went the way of the Julio-Claudians. In the hopes of the Jews the end of the Empire and the last days were to be heralded by a Parthian invasion: and it was not unreasonable to conjecture that Nero was lurking in Parthia. Composers of Sibylline oracles developed this attractive theme—according to one forecast there would appear at the time of an eruption of Vesuvius 'the exiled man of Rome lifting up a mighty sword, crossing the river Euphrates with many tens of thousands[1].' Prophecy is often no more than a sanguine interpretation of contemporary history. In the early months of the brief reign of Titus a certain Terentius Maximus claiming to be Nero gathered a company of followers in Asia, advanced to the bank of the Euphrates and took refuge with Artabanus IV, who made preparations to restore him[2]. Of this there was no danger. Weakened by the permanent loss of Hyrcania, and by the death of the able Vologases (c. 77?), Parthia was a prey to internal dissensions for many years[3]. Artabanus did not rule over all the Parthian dominions, and it was some time before Pacorus succeeded in establishing a precarious unity. A favourable but transient conjuncture presented itself towards the end of the year 88 or early in 89[4]. The energies of Rome were engaged in a Dacian war; a great conspiracy and the armed rising of Antonius Saturninus revealed the insecurity of Domitian[5]. Dacia and Parthia may indeed have been in negotiation, as they were some years later, against their common enemy (below, p. 239): but the Parthians needed no encouragement if they could embarrass Rome without risk to themselves. A Nero was certain to be available—Terentius Maximus if he was still with them, or another, and so the Parthians are found giving vigorous support to a false Nero and threatening war. But the crisis passed, and before long they were induced

[1] *Orac. Sibyll.* IV, 130–9.   [2] Dio LXVI, 19, 3 b–c (Boissevain).
[3] *B.M. Cat. Parthia*, pp. lvi–lvii.
[4] Suetonius, *Nero*, 57; Tacitus, *Hist.* I, 2. A diploma of November 7, 88 (*Ann. épig.* 1927, no. 44), attests a concentration of auxiliary troops in Syria.
[5] Below, p. 172. It was about this time that a proconsul of Asia was put to death, Tacitus, *Agric.* 42; Dessau 1374.

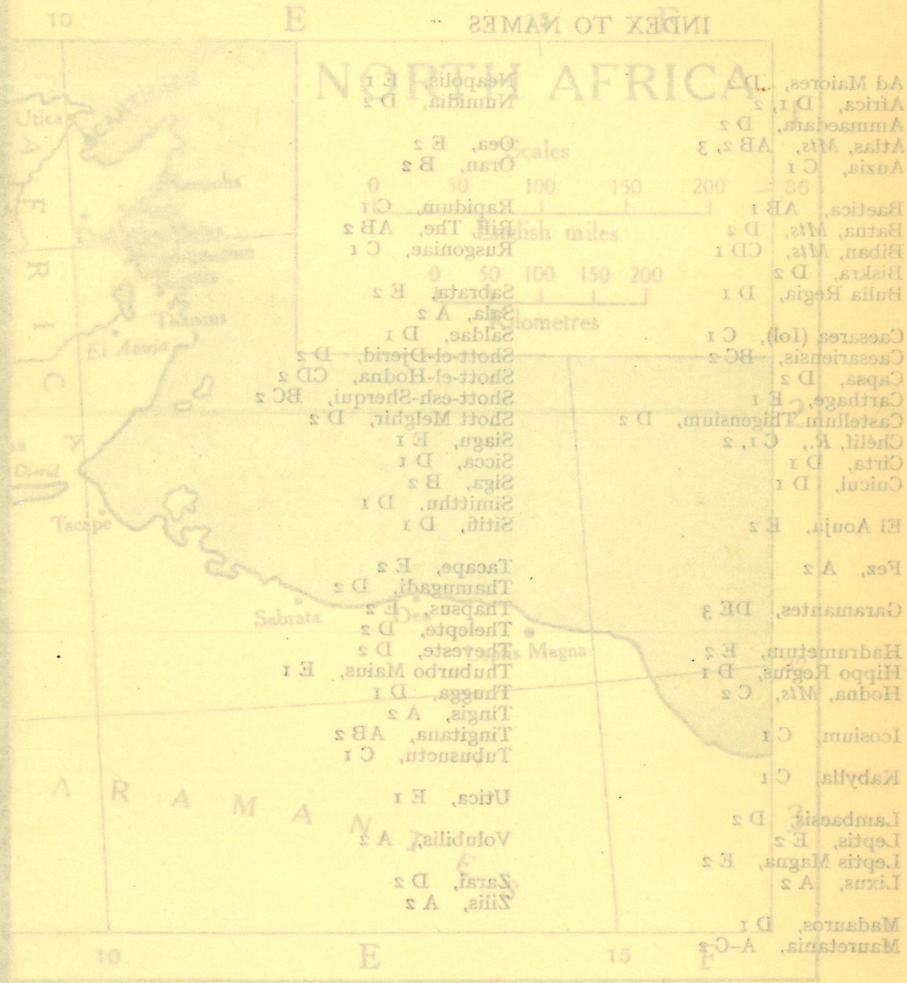

MAP 5

to surrender their guest[1]. The failure of these impostors did not dispel, but may have modified, the belief that Nero lived and must return.

III. AFRICA

Until Hadrian, no emperor chose to visit Africa in person or send thither a son or a colleague; and in the interval of confusion from the fall of Nero to the triumph of the Flavian cause the decision was fought out in other lands: all that the African provinces endured was a brief notoriety, rather than any serious disturbance or damage. Save for a few notices that might appear to concern geography rather than history, the literary record lapses again into silence. But that silence is no measure of the importance of Africa—in the fifty years that followed, these wide territories were the theatre of events, or rather of processes, without some consideration of which no study of imperial policy in its relation to native races and frontier defence could be other than defective and misleading.

In the trouble they gave to the Roman administration, the tribes of the desert itself could not be compared with those of the plateau of Numidia and the tangled mountains of Mauretania. Where the frontier faced the desert, it seems to have been most easily watched and most secure. In the year 70 the Garamantes had been persuaded to participate in the dissensions between Oea and Leptis, two of the cities of Tripolitania. Retribution was not long delayed. Though they hoped to baffle pursuit by covering up the wells as they fled, a Roman column penetrated their territory by a new route[2]. Relations of friendship were now renewed, as can be inferred from the record of two distant expeditions preserved by Ptolemy the geographer[3]. Septimius Flaccus who had come with troops to Garama advanced a three-months' journey beyond it into the land of the Ethiopians, and a certain Julius Maternus of Leptis, perhaps a merchant rather than a soldier, went even farther. Accompanied by the king of the Garamantes, he travelled for four months and came to Agisymba, 'the assembling-place of the rhinoceros,' probably Lake Tchad.

North-east from the Garamantes and south and east of Leptis dwelt another desert tribe, the Nasamones, who revolted in 85 or

[1] Suetonius, *Nero*, 57; Statius, *Silv.* IV, 3, 110, *Eoae citius venite laurus.*
[2] Tacitus, *Hist.* IV, 49–50; Pliny, *N.H.* V, 38.
[3] Ptol. I, 8, 4–5.

86, at a time when the Romans were hampered by serious embarrassments in another part of northern Africa, in Mauretania (see below, p. 149). The legate of the army of Numidia defeated them with great carnage, and Domitian was able to announce to the Senate that the Nasamones had ceased to exist[1]. The cause of this disturbance is assigned to discontent with Roman fiscal methods, an assertion which naturally cannot be verified. Yet here as elsewhere the Romans may well have been seeking to restrict the independence and freedom of movement of a nomad tribe. However that may be, it is certain that by the early years of Trajan's reign there had been a considerable advance on the other side of the Shott-el-Djerid, to the south of the great mountain massif of the Aurès. This was the complement to the moving forward of the legion from Theveste to Lambaesis: and the result was the encirclement of the Aurès.

The Roman province of Africa remained quite small. The legion III Augusta, commanded by a *legatus* independent of the proconsul, seems to have been stationed at first at Ammaedara, some twenty miles north-east of Theveste, whither it was transferred early in the Flavian period[2]. Of any kind of definite frontier in Africa it is still too early to speak: for the greater part of the century the zone of Roman control might be roughly represented by a line bending eastwards and southwards from the territory of Cirta to Ammaedara and from Ammaedara curving again by way of Thelepte to Capsa[3]. There may have been here and there a few fortified posts, garrisoned by legionary detachments or auxiliary regiments: but in Africa as in Illyricum and elsewhere the Romans at first relied largely upon a method of maintaining peace which was more economical than an intensive military occupation or an organized system of frontier defence. Native tribes were left in the charge of their own chieftains or placed under the supervision of a Roman military official[4].

---

[1] Zonaras XI, 19 = Dio LXVII, 4, 6–7 (Boissevain). The general's name was Flaccus, perhaps Cn. Suellius Flaccus (S. Gsell, *I.L. Al.* 1, 3002). The date comes from Eusebius, 84/5 in the Armenian version, 85/6 in Jerome.

[2] F. de Pachtere, 'Les camps de la troisième légion en Afrique au premier siècle de l'empire,' *C.R. Ac. Inscr.* 1916, pp. 273 *sqq.*; Gsell, *op. cit.* 1, p. 286. Ammaedara yielded a number of early military gravestones, to which are now to be added five more, *Ann. épig.* 1927, nos. 38–42.

[3] Cf. R. Cagnat, *L'armée romaine d'Afrique*[2], pp. 582 *sqq.*

[4] Examples of these officers are provided by the following inscriptions belonging to the period from Nero to Hadrian: Dessau 1418, 1435, 2721, 9195.

The Roman rule was often welcome to an agricultural population, to whom it brought protection from their enemies, the predatory pastoral tribes of the mountain and the steppe. The latter were regarded by the Romans as beyond the pale of civilization, and in the interests of peace it was necessary either to exterminate them or to compel them to change their habits. Because of seasonal variations, the pastoral peoples must wander over wide tracts in search of subsistence for their flocks and herds. The Romans required land for colonial foundations: it was won at the expense of the nomads, who were themselves compelled to resort to agriculture if they were to survive at all within their restricted limits. As the Romans in the Flavian period moved steadily forward south and west over the plateau of Numidia, the shepherd and the herdsman retired before the peasant, and a broad zone was redeemed for agriculture and for civilization. The Musulamii especially suffered for the benefit of colonies, imperial domains and private estates[1]. Most conspicuous but not alone among the foundations of the Flavians may be mentioned the military colonies of Madauros and Ammaedara. The work proceeded apace. Nerva founded a colony at Sitifi in old Numidian land just inside the frontier of Mauretania, and Theveste received colonists from Trajan when the legion departed. The clearest indication of the extent of the advance that had been made in these years is revealed by Trajan's colony of Thamugadi, a long way to the west of Theveste and only twelve miles short of the legionary camp of Lambaesis. Thamugadi was founded in A.D. 100, and the legion III Augusta co-operated in the building[2]. For this reason it would be preferable to date the transference of the legionary camp from Theveste to Lambaesis near the beginning rather than the end of the reign of Trajan[3].

When the legion was encamped at Ammaedara or Theveste, it covered the fertile territory of proconsular Africa behind it and kept watch over the Musulamii. Its transference to Lambaesis marked a momentous change. At Lambaesis the legion was within striking distance of the difficult country in the south-east of Mauretania: and it now became possible to construct a chain of

[1] Cf., *e.g.*, Dessau 5958–9. There are numerous inscriptions from the years 102–5.

[2] Dessau 6841.

[3] Until de Pachtere (*op. cit.*) showed that Ammaedara had been a legionary camp it was necessary to postulate an intermediate stage between Theveste and Lambaesis in order to explain Hadrian's remarks to the troops (Dessau 2487).

forts to Zarai, thirty miles south of Sitifi, continuous (and perhaps contemporaneous) with the outer line of defence of that part of Mauretania. More important than this, Lambaesis, lying between the mountains of Batna in the west and the Aurès on the south-east, commanded the entrance to the defile of El Kantara leading southwards to Biskra on the edge of the desert. The encirclement of the Aurès proceeded simultaneously from the other side: in the early years of Trajan a line of posts was erected between the Aurès and the Shotts running from east to west, from the station Ad Maiores to Biskra[1]. In this way the Aurès was isolated. It was not, however, penetrated and occupied until a generation had elapsed. The completion of this process provided an admirable frontier on the south and west and enabled the provinces of Africa and Numidia to develop unhindered the prosperity which was one of the most imposing memorials of the Roman peace.

Mauretania was very different. Ever since the two Roman provinces of Caesariensis and Tingitana had been substituted for a native kingdom, unrest was endemic and recurrent. Numidia received an adequate frontier on the south, facing the Sahara. In Mauretania, however, the Roman power even at its greatest extension in the third century did not cover the wide plateau of southern Algeria: worse than that, there remained within the nominal limits of the province of Caesariensis many regions that were really unsubdued. The irregular and broken character of the land and the absence of natural lines of communication or of demarcation made it difficult for the Romans to draw a single and continuous frontier. In different parts of the country they were compelled to build both parallel and transverse chains of fortified posts for the purpose of isolating and controlling refractory regions like the mountains of Kabylia north of Sitifi. When the term frontier is applied to Mauretania it merely means the southernmost line of forts. In Hadrian's time, when the frontier of Mauretania was continuous with that of Numidia, it appears to have run from Zarai westwards between the mountains of Biban and those of the Hodna to Auzia and Rapidum, and thence to the valley of the Chélif[2]. But beyond Oran the western frontier of Caesariensis is ill-defined.

[1] *C.I.L.* VIII, 2478; 2479 = 17971, of A.D. 105, building-inscriptions of the fort of Ad Maiores. To the same year belong two milestones of the road leading westwards in the direction of Biskra, *C.I.L.* VIII, 22348–9. South-east of Ad Maiores, Castellum Thigensium had already been occupied as early as A.D. 83, *C.I.L.* VIII, 23165.

[2] The fort of Rapidum was probably built in A.D. 122, *C.I.L.* VIII, 20833. There is no earlier evidence about this frontier.

It was separated from Tingitana by the mountains of the Riff, which throughout the centuries have maintained their independence of all empires down to the year 1925. The Romans who were able to subjugate regions like Asturia or Isauria left the Riff alone and did not even seek to isolate it effectively by penetrating into the interior behind it and securing a line of communications between Caesariensis and Tingitana. Even when, as not infrequently happened, the two provinces were placed under the charge of a single governor, he had to travel from the one to the other by sea; by land, there was no route, no common frontier. Tingitana itself was a tiny province with a coast-line running from Tangier to Rabat: it was shaped like a triangle with its base on the Atlantic and its apex at Fez. Though isolated from Caesariensis, Tingitana was close to Baetica: in the fourth century it is reckoned as one of the Spanish provinces[1].

Even in times of comparative peace Mauretania required a large army of occupation—larger than that of Numidia: there is adequate evidence of its presence[2]. Besides the regular auxiliary regiments there was a dangerous abundance of native levies, serving under chieftains of their own such as the notorious Lusius Quietus (see below, p. 228). Although policy counselled a minimum of interference, peace and order could not always be guaranteed by these methods. A Mauretanian rising, like all African wars in any age, was an affair of years. Of these perennial disturbances, the best known is the war which exercised the government of Pius for at least six years and brought to Mauretania troops from many provinces (see below, p. 336 sq.). But it does not stand alone. Under Trajan and under Hadrian there was trouble in Mauretania[3]: and it might have been expected that the emperors of the Flavian House with their conscious policy of consolidation and delimitation in the frontier provinces would have chosen to pay some attention to Mauretania even if they had not been compelled to.

The cause, extent and duration of Domitian's Mauretanian War are alike unknown. The presumption that such a war was neither brief nor easily terminated is an added difficulty in dating. At some time between 84 and 88, probably in 84–5, a certain Velius Rufus who held—or who had just been holding—the command of the urban cohort at Carthage led an expeditionary force drawn from the army of Numidia against rebel tribes in Mauretania[4]: and both

[1] Festus, *Brev.* 5.   [2] Tacitus, *Hist.* II, 58.
[3] Dessau 1352, a *procurator pro legato* of Tingitana in the time of Trajan.
[4] Dessau 9200. Coh. XIII urbana apparently went to the Danube as early as 85–6, cf. Dessau 2127.

Caesariensis and Tingitana were put in charge of a senatorial governor, Sentius Caecilianus[1]. To be successful, military operations in northern Africa demand the employment of many separate columns of troops. From the presence of an imperial legate and the analogy of the war of Pius it might be inferred that Velius Rufus' contingent was not the only reinforcement needed if Mauretania was to be pacified.

Spain is not usually reckoned among the frontier provinces of the Roman Empire. But even when the north-west of the peninsula had at last been subdued (19 B.C.), a large garrison remained in occupation. Though by the end of Nero's reign this had fallen to one legion, Vespasian did not contemplate any further reduction. After spending a few years in Upper Germany on its way back from Pannonia, the legion VII Gemina came to Spain and occupied the camp of León, well-placed to control the Cantabrians to the north and the Asturians to the west, and the already extensive network of roads that penetrated the wild Asturian land was amplified by the labours of the legionaries[2]. The southern frontier of Spain lay across the sea in Mauretania: and the protection of Spain was one of the reasons that moved Augustus to plant a dozen military colonies on or near the coasts of Mauretania, without as well as within the pillars of Hercules (vol. x, p. 346). In any crisis of the Empire in later days the pirates of the unconquered Riff were a perennial menace to the security of the rich and peaceful province of Baetica.

IV. CONQUEST IN BRITAIN

The accession of the Flavian House restored order in the Empire, and portended a change in Britain. *Magni duces, egregii exercitus, minuta hostium spes*: the work of conquest was renewed with vigour and consistently prosecuted for some fifteen years by able generals, Cerialis, Frontinus and Agricola, with the object of winning a shorter frontier in Britain and ultimately a reduction of the garrison. Where that frontier would run, exploration and time would show.

In contrast to other provinces of the Empire in this period, the written evidence for the history of Britain is both abundant and valuable. The survival of the biography of Agricola has secured to

[1] Dessau 8969. Sentius had previously been legate of Numidia (Gsell, *op. cit.* 1, 3950), a command which was probably subsequent to, and distinct from, the position which he held when he and Rutilius Gallicus set up terminal *cippi* along the Fossa Regia (Dessau 5955, probably *c.* 73.)
[2] A new road was made between Asturica and Bracara, Dessau 5833.

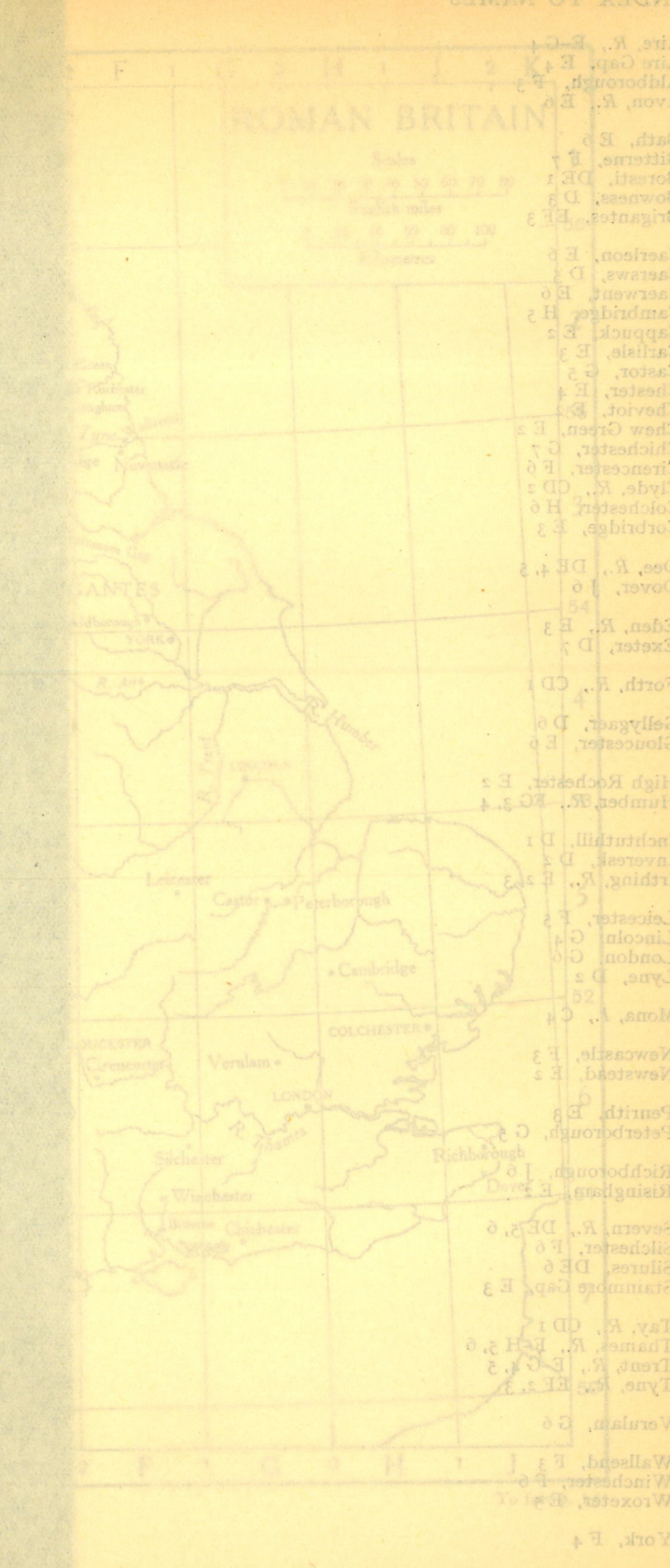

ROMAN BRITAIN

Scales

MAP 6

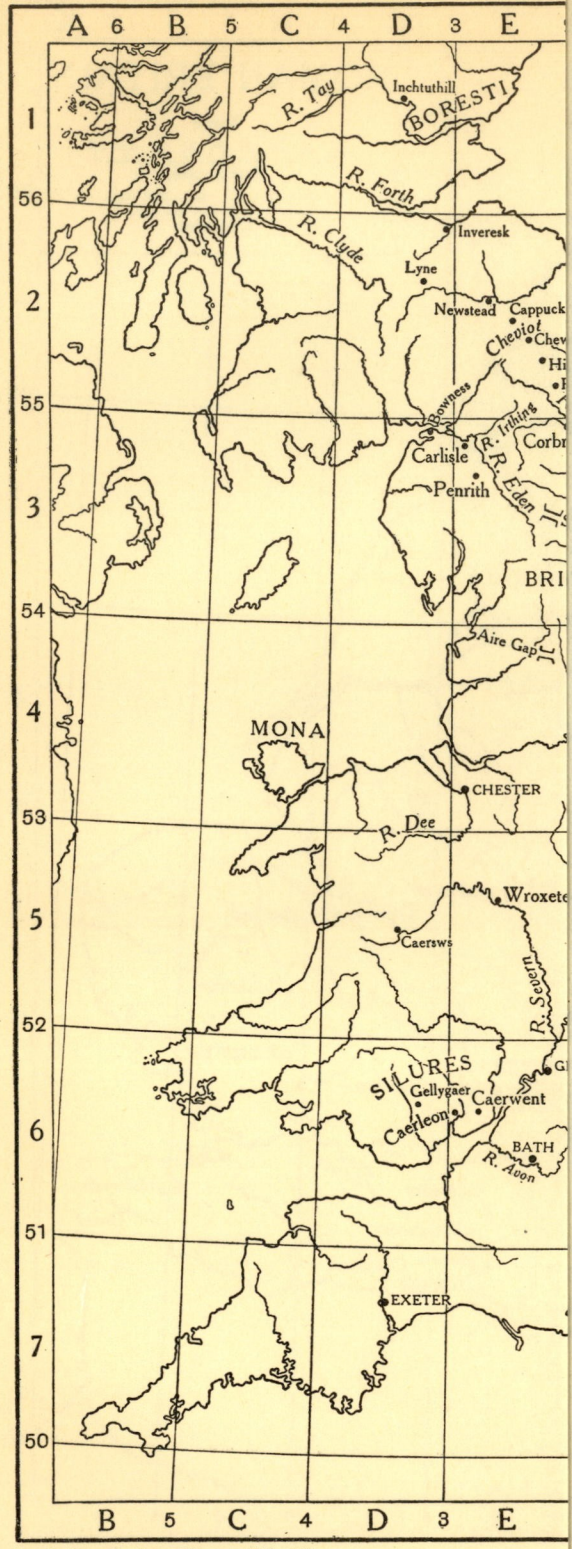

its subject that immortality of fame which the author so confidently predicted: otherwise, save for a lead pipe discovered at Chester and the brief and garbled remarks preserved by Cassius Dio the name of Agricola along with his exploits would have perished from human knowledge[1]. Of the space devoted by Tacitus to the narrative of the seven campaigns of Agricola, one-half is engrossed by a single battle and its preliminaries; and only six geographical names illustrate those campaigns, a tribe, a harbour, a mountain and three estuaries—of all these only two estuaries (Clota and Bodotria) can be identified. Tacitus may have known more than he has told: but it is also possible that he neither clearly understood nor accurately transmitted some of the information which he had derived from the conversation of his father-in-law[2]. Another danger besets the interpretation of the *Agricola*— it has the character of a funeral laudation.

What is lacking in Tacitus can be supplied, up to a point, by the results of archaeological research. One of the routes which the armies of Agricola followed in the invasion of Scotland can be traced beyond doubt. The sites of numerous forts have provided accurate evidence of the territory covered and the direction taken by his campaigns, and even an indication of the length of time during which some at least of his conquests in Scotland were subsequently maintained. South of the Cheviots, however, the archaeological evidence, while illustrating the methods by which the Flavian conquest was achieved, does not seem to be competent by itself to determine and delimit the shares of Cerialis, Frontinus and Agricola in the pacification of the Brigantian territory, and date yet more narrowly those forts which were presumably erected in the years 71–9, and are conveniently designated as 'Agricolan.'

The termination of the Batavian War late in A.D. 70 liberated for service in Britain a legion and a general. The army, weakened by the withdrawal of XIV Gemina, was restored to its former strength of four legions by the accession of II Adiutrix, and Cerialis soon arrived to take in hand the subjugation of the Brigantes. This tribe, or rather confederacy of tribes, was the most populous and most powerful in all the island[3]. The Romans had

[1] Dessau 8704 a; Dio XXXIX, 50, 4; LXVI, 20, 1–3.

[2] Cf. the problems, perhaps insoluble, presented by the estuary of Tanaus and by the fifth campaign.

[3] *Agric.* 17. The Brigantes did not constitute a unit comparable to the large Celtic tribes of Gaul and southern Britain: as in the north-west of Spain and among the Dalmatian tribes of Bosnia (with their numerous *decuriae*) a convenient name embraces a multitude of small communities.

come into contact with the Brigantes as early as A.D. 50; since then, however, they had intervened only to supplement the resources of their diplomacy and secure peace by supporting the authority of the queen Cartimandua over her turbulent subjects. In the end the queen was dethroned. A Roman expeditionary force was able to rescue but not to restore her. And so the Brigantian War began: conquest was inevitable sooner or later, for no Roman frontier could have been safe with the untamed Brigantes beyond it. The campaigns in which Cerialis battered and broke the power of this tribe were marked by many stubbornly contested battles. He departed to assume a second consulate in Rome in the year 74. His successor, Frontinus, was not doomed to inaction—he turned his attention to the west and by subjugating the Silures completed the long-delayed conquest of Wales.

Here and in many parts of the Brigantian country the Romans had to deal, not with an agricultural population which could be harried and circumvented if it were not amenable to intimidation, but with the difficulties of forest and mountain and the indomitable resistance of tribes as fierce and as tenacious as those which so long delayed the progress of conquest in north-western Spain and in Bosnia. It was necessary to pierce the land with roads and cover it with a network of fortified posts, occupying the valleys that lead into Wales and separating the mountain masses from each other[1]. This was the work of Frontinus in Wales. A single sentence is the only record of his activities—the subjugation of the Silures in South Wales: that would not be enough to justify the unworthy suspicion that he had neglected both northern Wales and northern England and had failed to consolidate or extend the gains of his predecessor. If the biographies of Cerialis and Frontinus were ever written, they have not been preserved.

In 77 or 78 a new governor, Cn. Julius Agricola, came to Britain, a province with which he was already familiar from his service as a military tribune and as a legionary legate[2]. Though it was late in the year, Agricola at once took the field, and crushed the Ordo-

---

[1] Among Flavian forts in Wales may be mentioned Caerhun, Caersws and Brecon. Originally earth-forts, they seem to have been refaced in stone in the time of Trajan, when several new forts were also built, for example Gellygaer. The legionary camp at Caerleon is an early Flavian foundation, at first with a rampart of clay and timber.

[2] It cannot be ascertained whether Agricola's term of office began in 77 or in 78. A complete summary of arguments that have been used will be found in Tacitus, *Agric.*, edd. Furneaux and Anderson, App. 1, pp. 166–73. The present writer has a preference for the year 78.

vices in North Wales. This was not all. A surprise attack delivered into his hands the island of Mona, the haunt of Druids.

The next year saw Agricola active in the north. By force and conciliation he induced a number of tribes that had hitherto maintained their independence to surrender hostages and endure forts and garrisons. The Romans in their conquests followed methods of classic simplicity. They first seized the most important lines of communication, so as to cut off the more rugged and inaccessible parts of a country which, being thus isolated and encircled, could subsequently be reduced with less trouble. The tribes which so readily submitted to Agricola in the course of a single year are not described as strangers to the Romans: they were evidently members of the Brigantian confederacy which Cerialis had shattered. Cerialis had transferred the camp of the legion IX Hispana from Lincoln to York. Unless he had already carried the arms of Rome far to the north, the events that follow are difficult to explain. In the next year (his third campaign) Agricola launches an invasion of Scotland. On any other hypothesis this would be foreign to his native caution and to the policy of which he was the heir and instrument. Cerialis' work must have been well done[1].

Between the Solway Firth and the mouth of the Tyne, the distance from sea to sea narrows to some sixty miles, and the valleys of the Irthing and the Tyne make a gap between the hill-country to the north and to the south of paramount strategic importance. Across this neck of land extends a perplexing variety of Roman frontier works, the wall of Hadrian, the flat-bottomed ditch erroneously called the Vallum, and a little to the south and apparently only from Carlisle to Corbridge a Roman road, the Stanegate. Of the date and purpose of this road, there is no definite evidence. Its construction has commonly been attributed to Agricola; and it is evident that to seize this line and provide it with a chain of forts must have been an integral part of the subjugation of northern England. The wall of Hadrian itself is not merely a defensive structure designed to ward off invaders from Scotland: one of its functions was to facilitate the control of the turbulent and ever-resurgent Brigantians (see *e.g.* below, p. 336). This being so, the line from Corbridge westwards to Carlisle might have been

---

[1] *Agric.* 17, *magnamque Brigantum partem aut victoria amplexus est aut bello.* This is not likely to be an exaggeration—on the contrary, given the character of the *Agricola*. As Tacitus has mentioned no tribe in northern England, or, for that matter, in southern Scotland, other than and distinct from the Brigantes, the northward extension both of the Brigantes and of the conquests of Cerialis is difficult to determine.

occupied even earlier than Agricola[1]; and the operations of Agricola's second campaign will have consisted in the reduction of peoples farther south which had already been isolated—perhaps in Cumberland and Westmorland. Even here he was probably content to secure a route northwards from Lancashire by way of Penrith to Carlisle, thus encircling the district of the Lakes. Roads from south to north, however, were not enough, and Agricola might be given the credit for building some, but not all, of the roads that pierced the Pennine Chain from east to west—the most important were those that used the Aire Gap and the Gap of Stainmore (the latter providing the line of communication between York and Carlisle). But here as elsewhere the predecessors of Agricola must not be defrauded.

Whether or no Agricola was the first to occupy the line of the Stanegate, here was a point at which the northward advance of the Romans might have stopped and a frontier might have been found, though Tacitus gives no hint of that possibility. But Agricola himself—or the men who advised the Emperor in the affairs of Britain—had decided otherwise.

In the third year Agricola opened up new country. His columns swept northwards and spread devastation as far as an estuary called the Tanaus: the following season he spent in securing his hold on the territory he had traversed in the previous year. To this end he established a chain of forts across the narrow isthmus between Clota and Bodotria (the Clyde and the Forth). If it were certain that Tacitus wrote with a clear conception of the operations which he describes it might appear that the mysterious estuary of Tanaus should be either identical with Clota or Bodotria, or at least not far distant from them. Much short of them it cannot be—it may rather even lie beyond them, for the line which Agricola drew in order to consolidate his gains need not be as far to the north as the farthest point that his scouts and raiders had reached the year before[2].

The advanced base which Agricola used for the invasion of

---

[1] Bushe-Fox believed that some of the pottery from Carlisle was pre-Agricolan (*Archaeologia*, LXIV, 1912–13, p. 311); cf., however, Haverfield and Atkinson, *Cumberland and West. Trans.* XVII, 1916–17, pp. 235–50.

[2] *Agric.* 22, *tertius expeditionum annus novas gentes aperuit, vastatis usque ad Tanaum (aestuario nomen est) nationibus.* The possibility that the Tanaus was the Tay has been summarily rejected by many critics on the ground that the Tay lies too far to the north (Anderson, *Tacitus, Agricola*, p. lvi and p. 106). Yet it is difficult to find a suitable estuary south of Clota and Bodotria.

Scotland appears to have been Corbridge on the Tyne, from which a Roman road (the continuation of Dere Street) runs northwards, accompanied in its course by the visible relics of many camps and forts, by Risingham, High Rochester and Chew Green (Makendon) across the Cheviots to the important position of Newstead near Melrose in the fertile valley of the Tweed. From Newstead there was a choice of routes, northwards across the Lammermuir Hills to Inveresk on the Firth of Forth, a few miles east of Edinburgh; or westwards up the Tweed past the small fort of Lyne (near Peebles) to the valley of the Clyde. But there was another route, to the west, by which troops could have been moved forward from the line of the Solway and the Tyne—the valley of the Clyde could be reached from Carlisle through Annandale. To deny Agricola's use of it would be rash; for he seems to have been able to convey a large Roman army far into Scotland.

It is only in the east, however, that there are certain traces of the passage of Agricola. At Cappuck some seven miles south-east of Newstead a tiny fort of earth has yielded early pottery. Newstead itself provides full evidence of repeated occupations and repeated rebuildings—the history of this site appears to fall into five periods of which three are earlier than the Antonine occupation of Scotland. The earliest fort was made of earth and, from its dimensions, was perhaps a winter camp for several auxiliary regiments. Of the forts constructed by Agricola across the isthmus between the Clyde and the Forth in his fourth campaign, many have been identified as small temporary posts near or beneath some of the stations of the Wall of Antoninus. They appear soon to have been evacuated —but not because Scotland was abandoned. On the contrary, the purpose of these forts was temporary and had already been served when Agricola decided to advance yet farther to the north.

The occupation of the isthmus between the Clyde and the Forth severed the south from the north and banished, as it were, the enemies of Rome into another island: to the south-west, however, extended a vast region as yet untouched, wild, barren and difficult of access, and subsequently neglected by the Romans in the period of the Antonine occupation of southern Scotland, though it was a danger, because it admitted invaders from Ireland. Yet these unpromising tracts were not entirely devoid of population—in a later age they harboured the savage Attacotti, suspected of cannibalism. Whether or not Agricola was to carry his conquest of the island yet farther, it was perhaps time for him now to satisfy his curiosity about the region which his advance had isolated. If this was indeed the purpose of the fifth campaign, the vagueness of

Tacitus does not permit it to be affirmed. Agricola made an expedition by sea. He encountered and defeated tribes hitherto unknown; he also marshalled troops on that part of the coast of Britain that looks towards Ireland.

That island had troubles of its own. An Irish prince took refuge with Agricola, the pretext for an intervention to which, so a sanguine observer might be tempted to believe, the natives would fall an easy prey. But Agricola did not choose, or was not permitted, to cross the narrow seas. In the years of his retirement at Rome he was often heard to say that a single legion supported by a few auxiliary regiments would have sufficed for the conquest and the retention of Ireland. It will be recalled that a similar estimate had once been entertained of the ease of a conquest of Britain[1].

Abandoning the seductive prospect of Ireland, in the sixth year Agricola resolved to prosecute his conquests among the peoples beyond the Firth of Forth. They gathered in force, and after assaults on some of the Roman fortified posts hung about the flank of the army, which marched in three columns of unequal strength. After a vain attack upon the weakest of these, the Caledonians broke and fled. Had they not been able to escape to the protection of their woods and marshes, the Roman victory, so Tacitus asserts, would have meant the end of the whole war; the troops of Agricola were all inspired with a new confidence. In spite of this favourable conjuncture, the operations of the year were not prosecuted.

The actions which are described as Roman victories do not always appear to have exercised a depressing influence upon their barbarian adversaries. No more dismayed than the warriors of Arminius after one of the memorable exploits of Germanicus, the Caledonians employed this respite to redouble their efforts. When Agricola again marched forth in the next year, the tribes had mustered under the command of a chieftain called Calgacus. They took up their station at the Mons Graupius. Here the armies met. After each side had been treated to one of those moral and patriotic discourses which generals—or at least historians—regarded as the indispensable preliminary to action, the clash came. The Caledonians were routed after sharp fighting. Agricola had been fortunate in his adversaries. The presence of a common danger induced the Caledonian tribes to compose their differences and combine their levies: had their experience of warfare against the Romans not been recent and superficial, they would have known that a pitched battle is not the most effective method of frustrating the advance of an army. Instead of reserving their efforts for

1 Strabo iv, 200.

guerrilla warfare in difficult country, for raids and surprise attacks on camps and convoys until winter or the shortage of food compelled the Romans to retreat, the Caledonians vainly spent their valour in a single disastrous battle.

The situation of the Mons Graupius must remain unknown, it is true: but the extent of Agricola's advance is sufficiently indicated by the existence of a large fortified post at Inchtuthill on the Tay, a dozen miles north of Perth, facing the gate of the Highlands—apparently the winter quarters for an army or a part of an army[1]. It may well have been occupied in the year before this campaign: and it was held subsequently. It is therefore by no means improbable that Agricola reached the neighbourhood of Aberdeen, for after the battle he marched farther and received hostages from a tribe called the Boresti. Dispatching the fleet on a voyage of exploration, Agricola now led his army back slowly towards winter quarters.

Such was the end of the seventh campaign (83 or 84). Agricola had now been in Britain for six years and a few months, a long term: he could hardly expect to have his governorship extended indefinitely. If the reports which Agricola sent to Rome conveyed the impression that the victory of the Mons Graupius was decisive and final, he had the less ground for surprise at being superseded. His work was done. This more than an emperor's jealousy of military success too great for a subject, or the needs of the Empire on another frontier determined his recall[2]. His services did not lack due recognition. On the motion of Domitian the Senate had voted Agricola the *ornamenta triumphalia*. He was still young—not over forty-four: and he may have hoped when he returned to Rome that further distinctions and further service might not be denied him: but the State had other generals, and the attitude of Domitian, even if not malevolent, was lacking in enthusiasm for the merit and talents of the conqueror of Britain. And so Agricola subsided into private life.

While Agricola was in Britain, the organization of the German frontier had been carried decisively forward by a war against the Chatti: and Domitian had celebrated late in 83 a triumph, the

---

[1] Cf. Sir G. Macdonald, 'The Agricolan Occupation of North Britain,' *J.R.S.* IX, 1919, pp. 111 *sqq.*

[2] It is true that the situation on the Danube may have appeared threatening earlier than A.D. 85 (see below, p. 169). A legion, II Adiutrix, was subsequently withdrawn from Britain (p. 171). For a weakening of the army of Britain in A.D. 83, while Agricola was still prosecuting his campaigns, cf. Dessau 1020; 9200 (p. 163).

derisory nature of which was before long to be revealed (so Tacitus affirms) when Agricola's glorious victory at the Mons Graupius evoked the damaging comparison[1].

V. THE ADVANCE IN GERMANY

The disturbances which the crisis of the year 69 had called forth did not long survive the triumph of the Flavian cause. The ignominious collapse of the 'Imperium Galliarum' was followed, not without serious fighting, by the termination of the Batavian War in the late autumn of A.D. 70. What the system of defence on the Lower Rhine now required was repair and re-organization: and so the composition, but not the size or function of the army was modified. The repentant Batavians returned to their old allegiance on the old terms. The Frisii, as before, were accessible to Roman influence. It was not intended, here or elsewhere, that the power of Rome should stop short at the frontier which she had chosen and fortified: and it might further be conjectured that the Tencteri and the Usipi, whose lands extended along the right bank of the Rhine from the Ruhr to the Lahn, showed themselves amenable.

Drastic measures were taken against the Bructeri, a confederation, who dwelt to the north of the Tencteri between the Lippe and the Ems. They had embraced the enterprises of Civilis with alacrity and with effect—the veneration in which their priestess Veleda was widely held was a powerful force on the side of the insurgents. Whether the Romans had dispatched punitive expeditions beyond the Rhine immediately after the end of the Batavian War is not known, but at some time in the years 75–78 Rutilius Gallicus defeated the Bructeri and secured the person of Veleda[2]. This did not reduce them to acquiescence. At a later date (which cannot more closely be determined) another governor of Lower Germany, Vestricius Spurinna, entered the territory of the Bructeri, and by the mere threat of war compelled them to take back a king whom they had driven out[3]. It may be to another aspect of the same incident that Tacitus is referring when he describes how in the presence of a Roman army and without the shedding of Roman blood, sixty thousand of the Bructeri were massacred by a coalition

---

[1] For the date of Domitian's triumph, see below, p. 164. This suggests that the seventh and last campaign of Agricola belongs to 84 rather than to 83.

[2] Statius, *Silv.* I, 4, 88–9; Dessau 9052 (a diploma of 15 April, 78).

[3] Pliny, *Ep.* II, 7, 2.

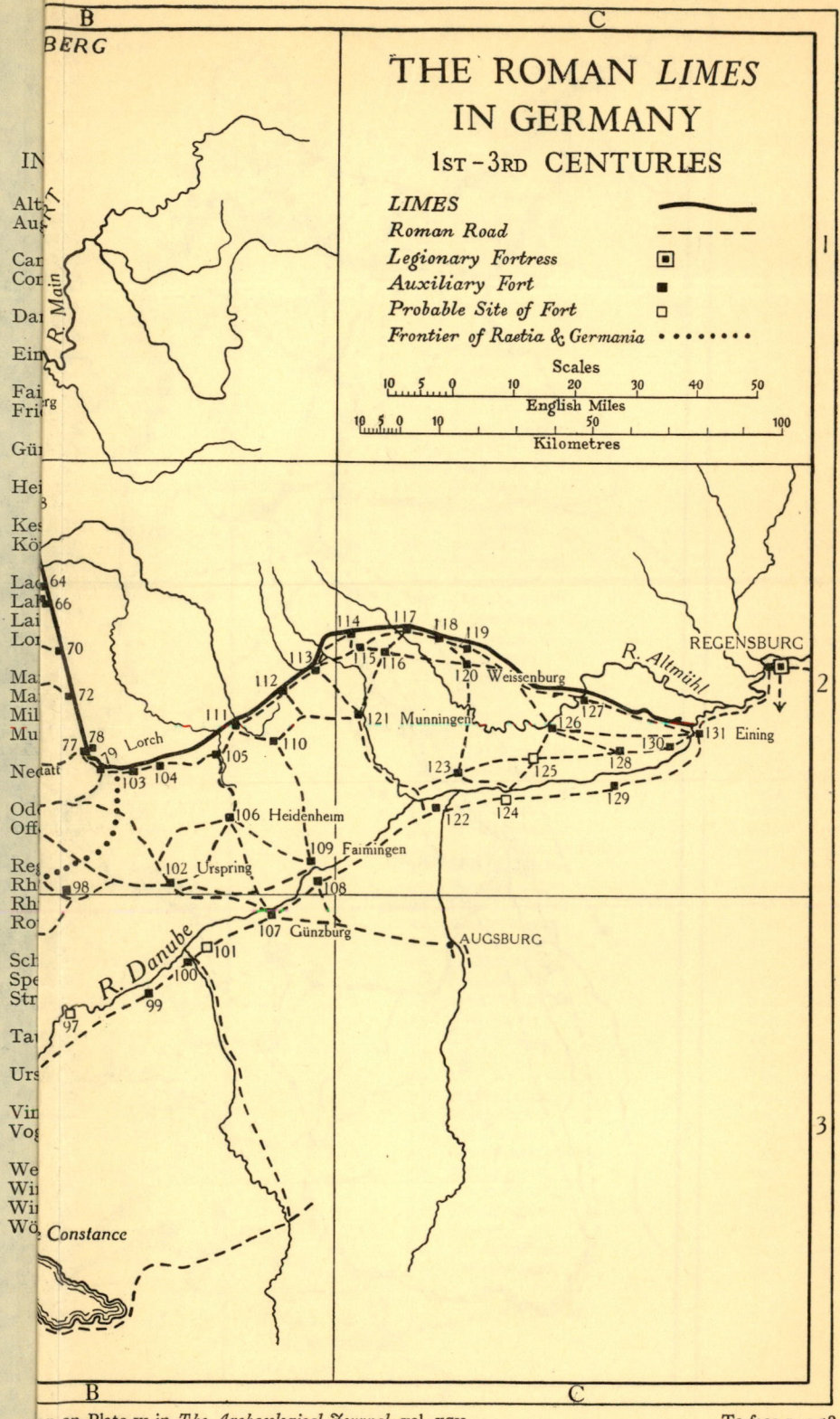

THE ROMAN *LIMES*
IN GERMANY
1ST–3RD CENTURIES

LIMES
Roman Road
Legionary Fortress
Auxiliary Fort
Probable Site of Fort
Frontier of Raetia & Germania

Scales
English Miles
Kilometres

KEY TO THE NUMBERED SITES

(other than those named on the map)

INDEX TO NAMES

of the neighbouring peoples[1]. It is evident that imperial policy had been pursuing its traditional methods with skill and with economy.

The line of the Rhine was guarded as before, but more firmly. Hitherto the forts occupied by the *auxilia* had been built of earth, strengthened with timber. A line of stone forts was now constructed, garrisoned by a new series of regiments, drawn from other provinces. Four new legions were brought to Lower Germany: and their camps too were built in stone. A new position, Noviomagus (Nymwegen), watching the island of the Batavians, was chosen for a legion and garrisoned by X Gemina: and the old double camp of Vetera was replaced by a stone fortress for one legion, XXII Primigenia. The other two legions, VI Victrix and XXI Rapax, occupied Novaesium and Bonna.

The army of Upper Germany likewise numbered four legions. I Adiutrix and XIV Gemina built for themselves a new stone fortress at Moguntiacum. Argentorate was occupied by VIII Augusta, Vindonissa by XI Claudia. But the forts of the auxiliary regiments southwards from Mainz at least were not rebuilt in stone. These positions were soon abandoned and the garrisons were transferred to the right bank of the Rhine.

The history of the advance of the Roman frontier in Germany beyond the Rhine and the Danube cannot be recovered, even in outline, from the fragments that have survived of literary records[2]. The details of the Roman military occupation beyond the Rhine have been won and co-ordinated by the thorough and continuous archaeological investigation of the last fifty years[3]. The evidence

[1] *Germ.* 33. The date of this episode—or of these episodes—baffles enquiry. Spurinna was voted a *statua triumphalis* on the motion of the emperor, probably Nerva, Pliny, *Ep.* II, 7, 1. But his age—he was over seventy—and other reasons make it difficult to believe that he was governor of Lower Germany in 97. That command probably belongs to an earlier date.

[2] For example, the campaign of Cornelius Clemens is nowhere recorded, and Dio (LXVII, 4, 1) does not mention the Chatti by name. The testimony of Frontinus, however, a soldier and an eye-witness of Domitian's war, is invaluable (*Strat.* I, 1, 8; 3, 10; II, 3, 23; 11, 7). The more important pieces of evidence, including inscriptions, will be cited where relevant.

[3] The results of the exploration of the frontier by the Limes-Kommission have been published in the monumental work *Der Obergermanisch-rätische Limes des Römerreiches* (O.R.L.) (not yet complete). Section A is devoted to the description of the different sections of the frontier, Section B to the forts. For the interpretation, cf. above all E. Fabricius, *P.W.*, *s.v.* Limes. For the military occupation of south-west Germany short of the line of the ultimate frontier, cf. F. Hertlein, *Die Römer in Württemberg*, I–III.

consists of inscriptions, stamped tiles of legions and auxiliary regiments, coins and pottery and, not least, the forts themselves, by reason of their situation and structure. This evidence varies enormously in extent and character from region to region: sometimes abundant and convergent, as in the Wetterau[1], sometimes scanty, as on the line of the Neckar and in the Raetian sector (see below, p. 166 *sq*.). History will not always be the loser if it prefers a generously wide margin to a date that is delusively definite.

So much for the methods of study. It remains to summarize the results. Across the Rhine from Moguntiacum the Mattiaci between the Taunus and the mouth of the Main appear to have remained in amicable dependence ever since the days of Augustus down to A.D. 69, when they yielded to the temptation of attacking Moguntiacum in alliance with the Chatti and the Usipi. After this brief interlude they returned to their allegiance. New forts of earth were established in this territory at Wiesbaden (Aquae Mattiacae) and at Hofheim, a few miles farther east. Southwards from Moguntiacum after a brief occupation such as is attested at Rheingönheim in the Palatinate opposite the old Neckar, the auxiliary regiments south of Mainz were transferred early in the reign of Vespasian from the left to the right bank of the Rhine. For Rheingönheim, which had probably housed a garrison of two regiments, were substituted forts at Ladenburg (Lopodunum) and at Neuenheim, on the Lower Neckar near Heidelberg[2]. To the north, between the Neckar and the Main, forts may have been established at Gross Gerau and Gernsheim[3], but there is no sufficient evidence: south of the Neckar, however, Baden-Baden was occupied, but the sites of most of the other new forts, like their predecessors on the left bank of the Rhine, are still a matter for conjecture.

In the extreme south-west of Germany, however, in the angle between the Upper Rhine and the sources of the Danube, the Roman advance is attested by more definite evidence and presents more decisive features. Across the Schwarzwald a road was constructed[4], running south-eastwards up the valley of the Kinzig to

---

[1] See below, p. 164 and p. 175.

[2] F. Sprater, *Die Pfalz unter den Römern*, I, p. 30.

[3] Fabricius, *op. cit.* col. 586.

[4] The milestone from Offenburg in the valley of the Kinzig (Dessau 5832) is unfortunately incomplete in its dating (*c.* 73–4) and in its indication of direction, *iter de[rectum ab Arge]ntorate in R[aetiam?]*. For *in R[aetiam]*, Domaszewski suggested *in r[ipam Danuvii]* (*Westdeutsche Zeitschr.* XXI, 1902, p. 201).

Rottweil (Arae Flaviae), and thence continued to the bank of the Danube near Tuttlingen or Laiz. In this way Rottweil was reached from the direction of the legionary camp of Argentorate. The advance had probably been a converging one, for another road came to Rottweil from the south, from Vindonissa by way of Schleitheim and Hüfingen. On the line of the road across the Schwarzwald forts were built at Offenburg, Waldmössingen and Rottweil: and it was further protected by posts at Sulz to the north and at Geislingen to the east.

The military operations of which this modest advance was the permanent but perhaps not the only result may be dated to the years 73–4. The governor of Upper Germany, Cn. Pinarius Cornelius Clemens, received the *ornamenta triumphalia* and two senators who held in succession the command over the auxiliary forces were also decorated[1]. Moreover, a fifth legion appears at this time to have been attached to the army of Upper Germany[2]. None the less, despite this imposing array, despite the decorations for service in the field, the campaign may have been more a display than an exertion of force. Numbers of troops would be needed, not merely to overawe opposition, but to provide the labour for roads and forts. In all the wide expanse of territory bounded by the Rhine and the Danube and extending north-eastwards to the lands of the Chatti and the Hermunduri there does not appear to have been a single large and formidable fighting tribe: the population—by no means as scanty as ancient accounts have been taken to imply—was mixed in origin, the relic of wars and migrations, and predominantly Celtic in civilization (see above, chap. 11).

This region does not enter into the history of the Augustan wars of conquest, and subsequently a strong and organized system of defence would have been superfluous. A reason for the advance will perhaps be discovered in the need for a shorter route of communication between the armies of the Rhine and the Danube— and thence, ultimately, an economy in troops. How far Vespasian intended the advance in southern Germany to proceed is unknown —before the end of his reign, several of the Raetian forts may have been transferred to the northern bank of the Danube (see below, p. 166). Be that as it may, the intervention of Domitian was vigorous and eventful.

---

[1] Dessau 997, cf. 1992 (a diploma of 21 May, 74); 990–1.
[2] VII Gemina, on its way back from Pannonia to Spain: Dessau 2729 (cf. 9052); *C.I.L.* XIII, 11542. Also tiles from Rheinzabern, *C.I.L.* XIII, 12167 [1–8].

VI. THE WAR AGAINST THE CHATTI

It did not require the fate of Nero to remind Domitian that his own security and the peace of the world demanded at the very least that an emperor should know and be known by his troops. In the course of A.D. 83, within two years of his accession, he came to Gaul under pretext of holding a census and suddenly appeared on the Rhine. The Chatti were already in arms: it was his design to forestall attack and to crush that powerful tribe[1].

On the west and south towards the Rhine and the Main their territory in Hessen-Nassau stretched as far as did the Hercynian forest—the name given at one time or another in antiquity to all or to almost any part of the forests of Central Europe. To the north their neighbours were the Cherusci, now fallen from their pride and reduced to dependence on Rome, to the south-east the Hermunduri of Franconia and Thuringia who, since their establishment in those regions by Domitius Ahenobarbus, had enjoyed and had repaid the favour which Rome extended to them. Here were allies against the Chatti: but it is not known whether Domitian commanded the active co-operation as well as the good will of the Cherusci or the Hermunduri when he proceeded against their enemies. Nothing is recorded save that, perhaps some years later, Domitian supported, though only with money, a king of the Cherusci whose explusion the Chatti had secured and whose return they sought to frustrate[2].

The triumph which Domitian celebrated over the Chatti was treated with derision. A tale once told of Gaius[3], a tale of slaves with dyed hair masquerading as German captives, was seasonably revived, and the battle of the Mons Graupius soon came to sharpen the contrast between real and spurious victories. It was not likely that Domitian's war would be signalized by any of those grandiose and sometimes futile battles, dear to a historian with a taste for the dramatic. The formidable Chatti, imitators of Roman discipline, and equipped, when they marched to war, with tools and supplies[4], were far too intelligent to be lured into a pitched battle.

The character of the Chatti and the nature of their land dictated the strategy that Domitian employed against them. Over a front of a hundred and twenty miles he drove military roads deep into the broken and wooded country that hitherto had secured them

---

[1] Frontinus, *Strat.* I, I, 8.
[2] Dio LXVII, 5, I.
[3] See vol. X, p. 660.
[4] Cf. Tacitus, *Germ.* 30.

immunity and thus opened access to their fortresses[1]. These were massive structures with ramparts of stone and timber, after the Gallic fashion, crowning the hilltops. A cluster of native hill-forts occupying spurs of the Taunus is to be seen not far south of the line which the Roman frontier subsequently followed; but whether any of them were occupied by the Chatti at this time is not known. Farther to the north, their land was dotted thickly with fortresses, such as the imposing Dünsberg near Giessen, or the Altenburg in the direction of Cassel[2]. The campaign of Domitian must have embraced much more than the territory that was to be annexed if that annexation were to be effective, permanent and secure.

Operations conceived on so large a scale and carried out with such thoroughness demanded the employment of many columns of troops. About the *auxilia*, details of a great concentration are lacking: but there is some evidence for the legions. It was about this time that Domitian raised a new legion, I Minervia: this he dispatched to the camp of Bonna in Lower Germany, withdrawing thence XXI Rapax for service against the Chatti. So for a time there were five legions in the army of Upper Germany. But not for long—the creation of I Minervia would liberate a German legion for service elsewhere, and I Adiutrix soon departed from the Rhine[3]: XXI Rapax took its place beside XIV Gemina in the camp of Moguntiacum. From Britain Domitian withdrew *vexillationes* of the four legions of that province[4]. These troops fought in the war under the command of their own tribunes of senatorial rank. They appear to have been retained for a time on the Continent. Velius Rufus (see above, pp. 140, 149) emerges into history again, between 83 and 85, as the commander of a force composed of *vexillationes* of nine legions[5]—the four from Britain and the five of Upper Germany. Tiles of most of these detachments have been discovered at Mirebeau-sur-Bèze (near Dijon) in the territory of

---

[1] Frontinus, *Strat.* 1, 3, 10; against this interpretation see *O.R.L.* A, Strecke 3, p. 45.

[2] The Altenburg has been identified with Mattium, the capital of the Chatti, cf. H. Hofmeister, *Die Chatten, I: Mattium. Die Altenburg bei Niedenstein.*

[3] Perhaps in 85–6 for the Dacian War (E. Ritterling, *P.W.*, *s.v.* Legio, col. 1388), or perhaps even earlier: cf. further p. 171, n. 4.

[4] Only IX Hispana is directly attested, Dessau 1025, cf., however, 9200.

[5] Dessau 9200, ...*praef. vexillariorum leg. VIIII: I Adiut., II Adiut., II Aug., VIII Aug., VIIII Hisp., XIIII Gem., XX Vic., XXI Rapac.* The name of the Upper German legion XI Claudia has been accidentally omitted. For the date of this command, cf. E. Ritterling, *Jahreshefte*, VII, 1904, Beiblatt cols. 23 *sqq.*

the Lingones[1]: and Domitian may have had his reasons for temporarily establishing a field-army under a soldier of tried worth and fidelity at this important strategic position. Yet even so, Velius Rufus may have employed his army elsewhere—operations designed to reinforce the security of the frontier of Lower Germany may well have been carried out in 83 or 84 as a complement to the crushing of the Chatti.

In the meantime Domitian had returned to Rome, conscious that he had earned the title of Germanicus which he assumed and the triumph which he celebrated shortly before the end of the year 83[2]. Moreover by his presence with the armies and in the field he had attached the soldiers to his person. Their spontaneous loyalty he rewarded and confirmed by raising their pay (p. 133).

Vigorous measures were taken for controlling the Chatti in the future. Along the crest of the High Taunus, north-westwards to the mouth of the Lahn and eastwards in a great sweep enclosing the region of the Wetterau as far as the Main in the vicinity of Hanau a chain of patrols was established. Wooden watch-towers were erected from four to seven hundred yards apart, and here and there, on or near the sites of the stone forts of Hadrian's day, tiny earth encampments of about seventy yards square. A salient is weak only if it is weakly held. In the plain below, between the Taunus and the Main, forts (at first of earth and timber) for cohorts and *alae* were established, at Wiesbaden, Hofheim, Heddernheim, Okarben and Friedberg, probably also at Höchst and at Frankfort. The eastern flank of this defensive system was secured by a stone fort at Kesselstadt (near Hanau) of unusual size, nearly four hundred yards square[3]: it was designed either to hold a legion (there was temporarily an additional legion in the army of Upper Germany) or a small army of auxiliary regiments. A network of roads linked these forts with each other and with positions on the outer line of patrols. If the Chatti came again, their approach would be at once detected and their advance checked by a rapid concentration of auxiliary troops, supported, in the last resort, by the two legions from Mainz. It is not impossible that to these defences was added the lesser security of a treaty (p. 174).

[1] *C.I.L.* XIII, 12539[1-6], especially 12539[1] = Dessau 2285, *vexil. legionum I VIII XI XIIII XXI.*

[2] Between 9 June 83 and 3 Sept. 84 Domitian received four fresh salutations (IV–VII, cf. *C.I.L.* III, pp. 1962–3). Britain, however, may claim one, or two, of these, and Mauretania must not be forgotten (p. 149). The triumph was probably celebrated, or at least voted, late in 83, for the cognomen *Germanicus* appears on hardly any of the coins of 83, but upon most of 84.

[3] *O.R.L.* B 24; G. Wolff, *Die südliche Wetterau,* p. 59.

In this way Domitian designed and created a new frontier beyond the Rhine between the Lahn and the Main. Of the territory so unequivocally claimed and so firmly grasped by Rome, little or none appears to have belonged originally to the Chatti. Even when they lay beyond the frontier of the Empire the friendly Mattiaci had been subject to Roman influence and control: their territory was now definitely annexed. The Usipi, however, to the north-west of the Mattiaci, were probably still outside the Empire. The Mattiaci were not the only native inhabitants of the land enclosed by Domitian's frontier. The region of the Wetterau had never been covered by forest: from neolithic times onwards its rich loess soil had supported a dense agricultural population, ever at the mercy of a stronger power. It might be conjectured that the Roman annexation was not unwelcome, bringing as it did protection from the raids and the exactions of the warlike Chatti. A tribe, the name of which cannot be identified, received compensation in money from Domitian when he erected forts in their territory[1].

Fertile land was thus acquired. Though economic considerations may have determined, here and elsewhere, the extent of the Roman annexations, they do not alone explain the purpose of those annexations. The region lying between Mainz and Hanau is of unique strategic importance, for so many routes of communication meet and cross in it. Northwards the Hessian Gap between Taunus and Vogelsberg provides the easiest approach to the Weser and to the Elbe—and conversely the easiest way by which a German invasion might reach the Rhine. The occupation of the Wetterau by a force based on Mainz practically cuts off North from South Germany. The significance and purpose of Domitian's measures is at once apparent. He pushed away from the Rhine the only formidable tribe in the neighbourhood of the frontier, and by creating beyond the Rhine an enlarged fortified zone to repel or control the Chatti, provided for the security of the whole frontier to the south. It is no accident that the crushing of the Chatti was soon followed by an advance in the south which won for Rome the valley of the Neckar and a still shorter line of communications between the armies of the Rhine and the Danube, roughly the line Mainz-Heidelberg-Stuttgart-Ulm.

In the early years of Vespasian the campaign of Cn. Pinarius Cornelius Clemens had brought the Romans to Rottweil, not far from the sources of the Neckar. The advance made by Domitian

---

[1] Frontinus, *Strat.* ii, 11, 7, *in finibus Cubiorum* [Ubiorum, Modius]: the chapter bears the heading *De dubiorum animis in fide retinendis* and the reading may be *dubiorum*.

did not proceed north-eastwards from Rottweil down the Neckar, but was a converging movement, from the plain of the Rhine eastwards to the middle course of the Neckar and from the Danube northwards and north-eastwards. For a time the two lines of forts, the German and the Raetian, seem to have overlapped in the south-west, even when in the last years of Domitian the easternmost forts of the Raetian line had been pushed forward almost to the ultimate line of the frontier. So much may be said of the advance in general. The details are mostly obscure.

In the first place, Raetia. The absence of a legionary garrison had an unhappy effect, not only upon the civilization of that province, but also upon the amount and quality of the historical and archaeological evidence. Nor is the material provided by the auxiliary forts of Raetia adequate to permit very close datings. The Danubian frontier of Raetia had long been neglected by the Roman government. Claudius posted forts along the southern bank of the Danube. Vespasian continued the work. Activity can be traced in the years 78–81. Now forts were constructed at Günzburg, a little east of Ulm, and at Eining, some twenty miles south-west of Regensburg[1]. This might have been thought to preclude any intention of an advance north of the Danube. Yet in A.D. 80 a fort appears beyond the Danube at Kösching, about fifteen miles to the west of Eining[2]. This fort can hardly have stood alone—it is probably a link in a chain of forts extending westwards a few miles beyond the northern bank of the Danube to Faimingen[3]. This advance in the eastern sector of the Raetian forts might indeed be explained by local conditions—the southern bank of the river, marshy for a long stretch, does not provide a good line of lateral communication. In any event, it was not long before a more decisive step was taken in the western sector of the frontier of Raetia between Faimingen and the most easterly of the forts (Geislingen) erected after the campaign of 72–4. Between the Danube and the upper reaches of the Neckar where that river runs parallel with the Danube extends a bare treeless plateau, rising gently from the Danube but descending abruptly to the Neckar— the Rauhe Alb, or Swabian Jura. Along the Alb, at points commanding the routes across it, runs a chain of forts, Lautlingen, Burladingen, Gomadingen, Donnstetten, Urspring. Such is the

---

[1] Vollmer, *Inscr. Bav. Rom.* 196, 331.   [2] *Ib.* 257.
[3] For this conjectural line of forts, cf. *O.R.L.* B 66 c (Faimingen), p. 27; F. Winkelmann, *R–G. K. Bericht*, XI, p. 29 *sq.* For the possibility of an earlier dating, cf. W. Barthel, *R–G. K. Bericht*, VI, p. 175.

Alb-Limes[1]. How it was prolonged eastward from Urspring is uncertain. Perhaps at first by way of Heidenheim to Faimingen and the hypothetical line of east-Raetian forts beyond the Danube as far east as Kösching: perhaps rather by a more northerly line, which extended almost as far to the north as the Raetian frontier in its ultimate form. This latter advance, embracing the forts Oberdorf, Munningen, Gnotzheim and Weissenburg, had been carried out before the end of Domitian's reign[2]; and it might even be contemporary with the Alb-Limes[3], which has been dated *c.* A.D. 85. The remains from the forts of the Alb-Limes are deplorably scanty. There are no inscriptions: the pottery from one of them, Burladingen, has suggested a date for its origin approximately five years earlier than Cannstatt on the Neckar.

As for the forts along the Neckar from Wimpfen southwards to Cannstatt and Köngen, the establishment of which was the complement of the moving forward of the Raetian forts, here too the evidence is by no means abundant. From the pottery, Cannstatt has been dated *c.* A.D. 90[4]. Yet, the evidence being what it is, a slightly earlier date in each case might not be excluded, *c.* 85 for Cannstatt and *c.* 80 for Burladingen[5]. Indeed, as both series of forts, the Alb-Limes and the positions on the Neckar, seem to be parts of the same process, a converging movement from the Rhine and from the Danube, they might be closely connected in time as well as in design. This advance in the south was not merely a sequel but a consequence of Domitian's victorious war against the Chatti and might therefore be presumed to have followed after no long interval. But the date affects only the speed at which the process was carried out, not the purpose, the methods or the result.

The Roman occupation of these territories proceeded quietly and peacefully: it had been carried a stage forward by the end of the reign of Domitian when the building of a chain of forts northwards from Wimpfen across the Odenwald to the Main established a junction with the southern end of Domitian's frontier[6]. In the

---

[1] On the Alb-Limes, cf. especially W. Barthel, *R–G. K. Bericht*, VI, pp. 176 *sqq.*; F. Hertlein, *Die Römer in Württemberg*, I, pp. 38 *sqq.*; G. Bersu, *Germania*, I, 1917, pp. 111 *sqq.* (Burladingen); *Württembergische Studien*, 1926, pp. 177 *sqq.* (Lautlingen).

[2] E. Fabricius, *O.R.L.* A, Strecke 13, p. 18.

[3] For this theory, cf. Fabricius, *loc. cit.*, and *P.W.*, *s.v.* Limes, col. 607 *sq.*

[4] P. Goessler, *Vor- und Frühgesch. von Stuttgart-Cannstatt*, p. 37.

[5] Cf. R. Rau, *Württembergische Geschichtsblätter*, 1932, pp. 47 *sqq.*; against this view, cf. *O.R.L.* A, Strecke 11, p. 35.

[6] For the dating of the Odenwald-Limes, cf. Fabricius, *P W*, *s.v.* Limes, col. 590 *sq.*; *O.R.L.* A, Strecke 10, pp. 33–6.

meantime, however, on another frontier the Empire had been subjected to the vicissitudes of a long and arduous contest.

VII. THE DACIAN WAR

In the course of A.D. 85 the Dacians crossed the Danube and harried the province of Moesia. The governor, Oppius Sabinus, was slain in battle, forts and their garrisons were overwhelmed: the camps of the legions, however, were successfully defended. Summoning reinforcements from different provinces, Domitian marched at once with the Guard and its prefect, Cornelius Fuscus, to the seat of war[1].

After more than a century of weakness and disunion, the tribes of the Dacians had come together again and formed a kingdom. This change is associated with the name of Decebalus. Whether his assumption of undivided supremacy in Dacia preceded or followed the invasion of Moesia is uncertain, but if that supremacy did not originate in the wars against Rome, it was confirmed by them[2]. About the causes of the conflict there can only be conjecture. The Romans had maintained a claim to suzerainty over many of the Transdanubian peoples and had intervened in their affairs[3]. The revival of Dacian power may have caused a clash of interests among the tribes in Wallachia between the Carpathians and the Danube and so have precipitated the crisis of A.D. 85.

Apart from the Dacians, a new and alarming enemy was surging against this frontier, Sarmatians from Moldavia and Bessarabia. In the winter of 67/8 the Roxolani cut to pieces an auxiliary cohort, and in the early spring of 69 they swept over the Danube again. Though the Roxolani were defeated, later in the same year a host of Dacians assaulted the legionary camps; nor is it likely

[1] The principal authorities for the Danubian Wars of A.D. 85–92 are: Dio LXVII, 5–7; 10; LXVIII, 9, 3; Jordanes, *Getica*, XIII, 76 M; Suetonius, *Dom.* 6; Tacitus, *Agric.* 41; Orosius VII, 10, 3–4; Eutropius VII, 23, 4. Martial and Statius are sometimes of great value for determining the date and the order of operations (*e.g. Silv.* I, 1, 79 *sqq.*; III, 3, 168 *sqq.*). For this purpose the imperatorial salutations are helpful. Domitian was *Imp.* IX on 5 Sept. 85, *Imp.* XI by 17 Feb. of 86, *Imp.* XII by 13 May (*C.I.L.* III, pp. 855–7). *Imp.* XIII and *Imp.* XIV occur on coins of 86 after 14 Sept. (*B.M. Cat. R. Emp.* II, p. 320). No salutations were recorded in 87. For the later wars, see below, p. 172, n. 1; p. 177. The relevant inscriptions are referred to in the course of the narrative.

[2] A certain Duras retired in his favour (Dio LXVII, 6, 1)—possibly the same as the Diurpaneus or Dorpaneus whom Orosius and Jordanes mention as the adversary of Fuscus.

[3] Dessau 986.

that the Sarmatians neglected this favourable opportunity. But Mucianus, on his way to Italy, repelled the invaders. The respite was only temporary. In the next year the Sarmatians defeated and killed the governor of Moesia, Fonteius Agrippa. His successor, Rubrius Gallus, restored order and sought to prevent the recurrence of these raids by the building of a number of forts[1].

What further provision was made by the government of Vespasian for the defence of the Danubian provinces is not known. No great changes appear to have been introduced[2]: Dalmatia still retained a legion, the new IV Flavia felix, stationed at Burnum. In Pannonia, XV Apollinaris returned from the East to Carnuntum; the other legion, XIII Gemina, garrisoned Poetovio, as before. The army of Moesia, raised to three legions by Claudius, but subsequently depleted by the demands of the East, was restored to its strength in the last year of Nero. Under Vespasian it comprised at least three legions, I Italica, V Macedonica and VII Claudia. As for their camps, VII Claudia was probably stationed at Viminacium, some forty miles east from Belgrade, V Macedonica at Oescus and I Italica at Novae, both facing the valley of the Aluta. A fourth legion and a consequent strengthening of the garrison are to be admitted if it is true that the legion V Alaudae survived after A.D. 70 (see p. 133, p. 171).

Before long more troops were sorely needed in Moesia and in Pannonia. The literary sources betray no trace of trouble on the Danube between A.D. 70 and 85, which, from the character of those sources, is in no way surprising. Signs of unrest can, however, be detected. In 82 three regiments detached from the army of Upper Germany were serving in Moesia[3]: they never after returned to the Rhine. The storm had long been gathering: though violent, it may not have been unheralded.

The first task that confronted Domitian and Fuscus was to expel the Dacians from Moesia and prevent their return. Only Dacians are named as the enemies of Rome in Domitian's war on the Lower Danube: but Sarmatians may well have seized the chance of plunder, as in 69/70, even if they were not acting in concert and in co-operation with the Dacians. To the measures taken against the invaders in the autumn and winter of 85 may belong the erection of the great vallum of earth in the Dobrudja. Where the Danube

---

[1] Josephus, *Bell. Jud.* VII [4, 3], 89–94.

[2] Cf. Ritterling, *P.W.*, *s.v.* Legio, under the several legions.

[3] Dessau 1995. Moreover, a comparison between three Pannonian diplomas of 80, 84 and 85 (*C.I.L.* III, pp. 854, 1963, 855) reveals an increase in the garrison of that province.

changes its course from east to north, it is barely forty miles distant
from the Black Sea. Here, running across the low and bare plateau
of the Dobrudja, roughly from Raşova to Constanţa, are to be seen
the remains of no fewer than three parallel lines of defence, more or
less continuous from the river to the sea, a stone wall, a small
vallum and a large vallum[1]. The latter is probably of Domitianic
date; it resembles a line of entrenchments for an army in the face
of an enemy rather than a fortified frontier: it might be conjectured
that a Roman army wintered in the Dobrudja and that a part of it
garrisoned the line of the vallum and its forts.

Some twelve miles to the south of the vallum, on the crown of
the plateau above the village of Adamclisi and visible from afar,
stand the massive ruins of the trophy which Trajan erected to
commemorate the conquest of Dacia: close beside the Tropaeum
Trajani is another monument, an altar bearing the names of soldiers
who had fallen in battle[2]. Neither the date of the erection of the
altar, nor the events it recorded, nor the purpose it was designed
to serve, can be ascertained[3]. Whatever it may be, the choice of the
site at least is not fortuitous—Adamclisi may have witnessed a
battle (perhaps the defeat of Oppius Sabinus) or the presence of a
Roman emperor. Adamclisi is a position of some strategic importance. It possesses—a rarity in the Dobrudja—a spring of water
and is the natural headquarters for an army holding the vallum.

It was not enough to have restored order in a Roman province.
Domitian resolved to send a punitive expedition across the Danube,
an operation which is probably to be dated to the early summer
of 86. Wherever it was that Fuscus bridged the river, his advance
into Dacia was soon arrested by a shattering defeat. Fuscus fell—
if he still retained the dash and vigour that had contributed to the

---

[1] C. Schuchhardt, *Die sogenannten Trajanswälle in der Dobrudscha*, Berl.
Abh. 1918; Fabricius, *P.W.*, *s.v.* Limes, cols. 647 *sqq.* Built on to the
vallum are two series of earth-forts, the first, at least thirty-five in number,
of cohort-size, the second, about twenty-eight, very small. The larger
forts were not occupied for long: they were replaced by the smaller posts,
some of which occupy a part of their area or utilize a section of their ramparts.

[2] Dessau 9107.

[3] Against the view of Cichorius that the altar marks the site of the
disaster of Fuscus, it is evident that Fuscus perished in Dacia (Tacitus,
Agric. 41; Martial VI, 76; Juvenal IV, 111). It is indeed far from certain
whether the altar could be brought into connection with Fuscus in any way
—even as a cenotaph. Across one of its faces, in large letters, run the words
[c]*ol. Pomp. domicil. Neapol. Ital., prae*[*f.*]. Yet it might be doubted whether
Pompeii was the colony of Fuscus—*idem pro Galba dux coloniae suae* (Tacitus,
Hist. II, 86).

winning of a civil war, they served him ill in the forests and mountains of Dacia. The army suffered further losses in its disastrous
retreat, and the booty captured by the Dacians included a military
standard—perhaps an eagle[1].

Tacitus withheld the total of the Roman dead, imitating the
patriotic reticence of certain earlier historians, and enhancing
thereby the disaster and the discredit of Domitian. The choice of
Fuscus the Prefect of the Guard as commander was Domitian's,
a natural choice if the Emperor himself was at the seat of war.
Tradition preserved the picture of Domitian slaying the innocent
and the helpless in Rome while on the frontiers his generals waged
disastrous wars[2]. None the less there is evidence that on this
occasion Domitian was not far from the scene of operations.
According to one account he took up his abode in a city of Moesia
and sent others against the enemy, for the most part with disastrous
results; moreover, rejecting Decebalus' overtures for peace, he
dispatched Fuscus against him, in reply to which Decebalus sent
a derisive message, offering to let the Roman army depart from
Dacia in return for a ransom[3]. If this be not all fiction, Domitian
was still in Moesia after Fuscus had crossed the Danube.

When Domitian returned to Rome it was not to celebrate the
triumph he had once expected: he arrived in time to inaugurate the
Capitoline Games in the summer of the year 86.

The Dacians were contented with a victory beyond their hopes.
But they were not to enjoy it for long. If the success which was
subsequently achieved is any measure, the Roman preparations
must have been thorough and comprehensive[4]. A second miscalculation would be fatal. Nor can diplomacy have been neglected

[1] Dio LXVIII, 9, 3, τὸ σημεῖον τὸ ἐπὶ Φούσκου ἁλόν. For the theory
that a legion, V Alaudae, perished with Fuscus, cf. E. Ritterling, *P.W.*, *s.v.*
Legio, cols. 1569 *sq.*; R. Syme, *J.R.S.* XVIII, 1928, p. 46. It might, however, be conjectured that the σημεῖον mentioned by Dio was a standard of
the Praetorian Guard.

[2] Orosius VII, 10, 3.

[3] Dio LXVII, 6, 3 and 5. Cf. further *ib.* 6, ἐπειδὴ οἱ μετὰ τοῦ Φούσκου
στρατευσάμενοι ἡγήσασθαι σφῶν αὐτῶν ἠξίωσαν, where Boissevain
suggests inserting ἐκεῖνον or reading αὐτόν for αὐτῶν. These passages
favour 86 against 87 as the date of the expedition.

[4] The legion IV Flavia felix had probably been transferred from Dalmatia
to Moesia in 85/6. I Adiutrix had departed from Germany soon after 83;
it is next heard of in Pannonia in 97 (Dessau 2720). II Adiutrix from
Britain fought in a Dacian War (Dessau 9193), probably Domitian's
(cf. E. Ritterling, *P.W.*, *s.v.* Legio, col. 1444), and apparently belongs to
the garrison of the Moesian provinces in 92 (Dessau 2719).

in the endeavour to isolate and encircle Decebalus. To the west in the great plains between Transylvania and the frontier of Pannonia extended the Sarmatae Iazyges, allies of Rome: but it is not known whether Rome could command their active co-operation, or had been able to buy the neutrality either of Dacian tribes in Wallachia or of Sarmatians farther to the east beyond the Lower Danube.

After a lull in 87 the war was resumed in 88 and prosecuted in the next year[1]. Its climax was signalized by a remarkable victory. A Roman army commanded by Tettius Julianus reached the plain of Caransebeş, facing the Iron Gates—perhaps after a converging approach in several columns. At a place called Tapae, where Trajan was to meet with indifferent success in his first campaign, a great battle and a great slaughter of Dacians ensued. Vezinas, next in power to Decebalus, was left for dead on the field. Julianus, however, did not march on Sarmizegethusa: he was baffled, it was alleged, by a Dacian stratagem. Other causes might be invoked, not least the difficult approach through the Iron Gates. If the battle of Tapae was fought in the autumn of 88, it might be supposed that the Romans remained in occupation of Dacian territory through the winter and prepared to consummate their triumph by a further advance in the direction of Sarmizegethusa by another route.

At Rome in the meantime Domitian had celebrated the Secular Games in September 88. But before he could come to the Danube to contemplate the achievement of his armies and receive in person the submission of Decebalus, a civil war had been fought on the Rhine, and on the Danube a rapid turn of fortune compromised and impaired the success that had been won in Dacia.

VIII. THE CIVIL WAR

On the first of January 89, Antonius Saturninus, the governor of Upper Germany, seized the deposited savings of the two legions wintering at Mainz and induced them to proclaim him emperor. A civil war had begun, likely to be no less eventful and ruinous than that which was still in all men's minds[2].

[1] Domitian became *Imp.* xv in 88, before 14 Sept. (*B.M. Cat. R. Emp.* II, p. 326). By 7 Nov., however, he is already *Imp.* xvII (*Ann. épig.* 1927, no. 44). The salutations xvIII–xxI were registered before 14 Sept. of 89, but cannot be closely dated or apportioned between the Dacian War, the Civil War and the expedition against the Marcomanni and Quadi.

[2] The reconstruction of the Civil War here adopted is in the main that proposed by E. Ritterling, *Westdeutsche Zeitschr.* xII, 1893, pp. 218 *sqq.* From a comparison with the events of A.D. 69 and from the date at which Domitian set out for the North (12 Jan., supplied by the *Acta fratrum Arv.,*

The conspirators—for there seems to have been a widespread conspiracy—had chosen their time with skill and were able to use the difficulties of the Empire for their own ends. The continuance of hostilities in Dacia tied down a considerable Roman army, and the East was disturbed: the Parthians supported—or had just been supporting—a false Nero with the threat of war (see above, p. 144). A civil war more than any other can be determined by promptness of decision and rapidity of movement. While Verginius yet wavered and all the West was in suspense, the cause of Nero had been far from hopeless. Courage might have saved him: cowardice or folly prevented him from joining the army which was mustering for him in northern Italy (vol. x, p. 739 *sq.*). The same dangers confronted Domitian. Upper Germany was in revolt. Lower Germany and Britain, too, for all that could yet be known, were in the plot—all the great military provinces of the West and a dozen legions. But Domitian displayed decision himself and expected it of others. Summoning, before it was too late, the Spanish legion VII Gemina, which its commander Trajan conducted with dutiful rapidity towards the seat of war[1], Domitian hastened with the Guard to northern Italy, there to concentrate his troops and, if necessary, fall back upon the Danubian armies. Everything promised a long and tenacious struggle, but the storm was dispelled as suddenly as it had gathered. Swift couriers had brought the ill news from Germany to Rome: by the twelfth day of the month Domitian was on his way to the north; on the twenty-fifth the tidings of victory, heralded by rumour and prodigies, were celebrated by the Arval Brethren.

On the Rhine events had moved swiftly. Miscalculation or misfortune ruined the designs of Saturninus. Maximus, the governor of Lower Germany, stood by Domitian, and his army won a victory against great odds. On the day of the battle a host of Germans was seen beyond the Rhine, intending to cross the frozen river to the help of Saturninus. A sudden thaw set in, and the Germans were frustrated. The scene of Saturninus' defeat is probably to be sought in the plain near Andernach, between Coblenz and Bonn. Saturninus was hastening northwards to win to

---

C.I.L. vi, 2066, p. 517), Ritterling inferred that the revolt broke out on 1 Jan. The other evidence is supplied by Martial iv, 11; ix, 84; Pliny, *Pan.* 14; Suetonius, *Dom.* 6 and 7; Dio lxvii, 11, 1–4; Aurelius Victor, *Epit.* xi, 10; Dessau 1006; *C.I.L.* xiii, 12168[7–9]; 12171[7]; 12173[16–18] (tiles of VIII Augusta).

[1] Pliny, *Pan.* 14, *cum legiones duceres seu potius (tanta velocitas erat) raperes.* There was only one legion in Spain at this time.

his cause or force by persuasion the army of Lower Germany, while the Germans in whose presence the armies fought were the Chatti who had descended from the upper reaches of the Lahn to the Neuwieder Becken opposite Coblenz and Andernach.

The news of the victory did not interrupt the march of Domitian. He came to the Rhine and punished the officers and accomplices of Saturninus with a severity as merciless as it was intelligible. Maximus had taken care to destroy the private papers of Saturninus, an action which will not have commended him to a suspicious and resentful emperor: the historian Dio praises him for disinterested virtue[1]. The treasonable designs of Saturninus can hardly have been matured without reference to the attitude of the commanders of the armies of Lower Germany and of Britain. By the former, he was deluded or repulsed, the latter may have been privy to the conspiracy—at least a governor of Britain, Sallustius Lucullus, is named amongst the senators whom Domitian put to death on trivial or spurious charges[2]. The army of Lower Germany had saved the Emperor and the Empire. The legions, I Minervia, VI Victrix, X Gemina, and XXII Primigenia, the auxiliary regiments and the Rhine fleet were honoured with the title *pia fidelis Domitiana*. Maximus later received a second consulate[3].

Rewards and privileges were showered upon the soldiery. But precautions were also taken. Domitian limited the sum of money that might be deposited at the headquarters of a legion, and abolished double camps[4]. XIV Gemina was left at Mainz, where it remained for three years longer. Its partner in treason and armed revolt, the notorious XXI Rapax, marched with Domitian when after a brief sojourn on the Rhine he set out for Pannonia.

Before his departure it is to be presumed that Domitian settled accounts with the Chatti. They agreed to respect the Roman frontier in the future, a transaction sanctioned by the imposition— or renewed imposition—of some kind of treaty[5]. There is evidence enough that the Chatti had been in arms and had broken into Roman territory. On the line of the frontier from the river Lahn to

---

[1] LXVII, 11, 1–2.   [2] Suetonius, *Dom.* 10.

[3] Dessau 1006, [. . .]*eliae/Appi Maximi/bis cos., confectoris belli Germanici.* The true form of his name is uncertain—L. Maximus (Dio LXVII, 11, 1); Norbanus (Martial IX, 84, 1); Norbanus Appius (Aurelius Victor, *Epit.* XI, 10, where Pichlmayr reads *Norbanus Lappius*). On this problem, cf. E. Ritterling, *P.W.*, *s.v.* Legio, col. 1458; *Fasti des röm. Deutschland unter dem Prinzipat*, p. 24.   [4] Suetonius, *Dom.* 6.

[5] Statius, *Silv.* III, 3, 168 (cf. I, 1, 27), *victis parcentia foedera Chattis*; cf. *J.R.S.* XXV, 1935, p. 96.

the Taunus the wooden watch-towers were all destroyed by fire[1]. In the Wetterau, the bath-houses of three at least of the forts, Okarben, Heddernheim and Hofheim, show traces of destruction[2]. It would appear that the Chatti had descended in two bands from their haunts beyond the Taunus, the one sweeping down the Wetterau stripped of its garrisons by Saturninus, the other making for the Neuwieder Becken opposite Coblenz. In the years immediately following, the damage caused in the Wetterau was made good by the construction of new bath-houses and perhaps of new forts as well. The incursion of the Chatti may well have had another immediate result. At some time in the late years of Domitian, the frontier was extended some twenty-five miles north-westward of the Lahn to enclose the Neuwieder Becken[3]. This was a region where many routes from the interior reached the bank of the Rhine: and it was now strongly occupied by the Romans, with no fewer than three forts[4].

The Chatti are said to have come as allies at the invitation of a Roman governor. This might be doubted, but it was an interpretation which could not be refuted after the event, and it had much to recommend it. Treason in the army and its associates in Rome were thereby branded with a deeper infamy and Domitian secured an opportunity and an excuse for celebrating a triumph later in the year *de Germanis*. Victory in a civil war was not the proper occasion for a Roman triumph. As it was, Domitian's double triumph over Chatti and Dacians presented certain equivocal features.

IX. PEACE WITH DACIA

The Roman victory at Tapae had reduced Decebalus to sore straits. He was saved by a catastrophic turn of fortune. Beyond the Danube from Bohemia eastwards to the borders of Transylvania the peoples that acknowledged the suzerainty of Rome and protected the frontier of Pannonia, the Marcomanni, the Quadi and the Sarmatae Iazyges, cast off their allegiance and prepared for war. 'Coortae in nos Sarmatarum ac Sueborum gentes.'

The Marcomanni and the Quadi failed to send help to Domitian in the Dacian War. He came to Pannonia from the Rhine in the spring of 89 and, after putting to death the members of an embassy of excuse and protestations (the second that they sent), made war

[1] E. Fabricius, *P.W.*, s.v. Limes, col. 587; *O.R.L.* A, Strecke 2, p. 29.
[2] *O.R.L.* B 25 a, p. 9; B 27, pp. 22, 62; B 29, p. 5.
[3] E. Fabricius, *P.W.*, s.v. Limes, col. 587; *O.R.L.* A, Strecke 1, p. 58.
[4] Namely Bendorf, Niederberg and Heddesdorf.

upon them. The brief notice in an epitome[1], the only record of this affair, fixes on Domitian the blame for an arrogant and unwise attack. If the circumstances were adequately known, his action might not appear to have been both criminal in its disregard for the law of nations and misguided in its object. Domitian refused to tolerate an affront to the majesty of Rome: but no emperor of the Flavian house had any liking for the risks and the costs of war if war could be avoided. If his was the aggression, it had a purpose —to forestall the attack of the Germans and avert a greater danger: it is unfortunate that the ulterior causes of this change of front of the German and Sarmatian allies of Rome on the middle Danube are beyond recovery.

The army which Domitian conducted or dispatched across the Danube met with a reverse, and the Iazyges allied themselves with their German neighbours, a peril not only to the Pannonian frontier but to the army in Dacia. The changed situation demanded a rapid decision. When Tiberius invaded Bohemia in A.D. 6, all Illyricum rose in his absence, and he was compelled to make terms with Maroboduus, recognizing him as a king and friend of the Roman People (vol. x, p. 368 sq.). Decebalus had been hard pressed[2]: he had asked for peace before, more than once, and even now that Germans and Sarmatians were in arms against his enemy he had no wish to continue the struggle. On both sides expediency prevailed and honour was saved. Decebalus gained Roman recognition, and more than that, the Roman support for which Maroboduus vainly hoped and vainly appealed. Domitian lent him skilled workmen and engineers and promised an annual subsidy. A well-grounded distrust prevented Decebalus from putting his valuable person in the power of Rome. At a ceremony of vicarious homage Diegis, a Dacian prince, received a diadem from the hands of Domitian[3]. In the course of the year the Emperor returned to Rome and celebrated with great pomp a double triumph over the Chatti and the Dacians.

There remained other enemies. Before, or just after, the termination of the war in Dacia, a column was detached from the army of occupation and sent north-westwards across the Banat of Temesvar to take the Iazyges in the rear; it was led by a soldier of tried merit, Velius Rufus[4]. Of the course taken by the war on

---

[1] Dio LXVII, 7, 1. [2] Ib. 7, 2, δεινῶς γὰρ ἐτεταλαιπώρητο.
[3] Ib. 7, 3; Martial v, 3. Fuscus had now been avenged and Dacia could be regarded as subject, Martial VI, 76.
[4] Dessau 9200. Cf. the inscription Dessau 2127, a centurion of Coh. XIII urbana decorated by Domitian.

the Pannonian front, nothing is known. Warfare might be supplemented by the resources of Roman diplomacy—either now or in the course of the next few years attempts were made to stir up the tribes in the rear of the recalcitrant Marcomanni and Quadi. Before now the Hermunduri had intervened in Bohemia to the advantage, if not with the encouragement, of the Romans: of their attitude at this time, however, there is no evidence. North of Bohemia in Saxony dwelt the Semnones, whose primacy among the Suebic tribes was consecrated by antiquity and religion: the visit which their king, accompanied by an influential priestess, paid to Domitian was hardly the result of chance or idle curiosity[1]. Domitian also entered into negotiations with the powerful Lugii in Silesia, to whose aid he sent a small force of cavalry[2]. By these means he sought to prevent the growth of a hostile power or confederacy with its centre in Bohemia—both the Semnones and the Lugii had once acknowledged the supremacy of Maroboduus —and he was able to isolate the Marcomanni and Quadi.

Despite the use of diplomacy and an increase of the garrison of Pannonia to a total of four legions (see below, p. 187), unrest prevailed along the middle course of the Danube, culminating in another Suebo-Sarmatian War[3]. In the early spring of the year 92 the Iazyges crossed the river. A Pannonian legion met the invaders and perished in the encounter[4]. It was probably XXI Rapax: a fitting end for a legion whose name and whose history were so intimately associated with scenes of violence and sedition. To replace this legion, Domitian summoned from Mainz its companion and associate in the recent civil war, XIV Gemina, and once again visited the endangered frontier. Detachments were drawn from the five legions of the Moesian provinces[5]. Whether Decebalus lent help against the Iazyges is, like almost everything else about the war, unknown. Domitian assumed one imperatorial salutation (XXII) and after an absence of eight months returned to Rome in January, 93[6]. He did not celebrate the triumph which a servile Senate was ready to decree, but contented himself with

---

[1] Dio LXVII, 5, 3.   [2] Ib. 5, 2.

[3] Dessau 1017, expedit(ione) Suebic(a) et Sarm(atica); 2719, bello Suebico it[em Sar]matico; C.I.L. XI, 5992, bellum Germ(anicum) et Sarmatic(um). It is uncertain whether the bellum Germanicum of Dessau 2710 and C.I.L. III, 7397 is this war or that of A.D. 89. On Dessau 1006, see above, p. 174, n. 3.

[4] Suetonius, Dom. 6; Tacitus, Agric. 41; Eutropius VII, 23, 4. For the identification with XXI Rapax, cf. E. Ritterling, P.W., s.v. Legio, col. 1789 sq.

[5] Dessau 2719.   [6] Martial IX, 31; VIII, 2; VIII, 8, etc.

depositing a wreath of laurel in the temple of Juppiter on the Capitol.

After this the Iazyges were kept in order—perhaps by fear of Dacia, their eternal enemy: but operations against the Germans in the autumn of the year 97 provided a happy omen for Nerva's adoption of Trajan and an additional name in the titles of each emperor[1].

X. THE FLAVIAN ACHIEVEMENT

The inglorious issue and, as it turned out, the delayed decision, of the Danubian crisis cannot obscure the achievement of the Flavian emperors in other lands. The re-organization of the eastern frontier and the pacification of northern Africa were matched by a great advance in Germany: solid results continued to be attained with an economy of men and of money that would have gratified Vespasian himself.

Nor was there less apparent cause for satisfaction in the state of Britain. Wales and northern England had been subjugated, and the Roman arms had been triumphantly carried far into Scotland. With the departure of Agricola, silence envelopes the island for nearly forty years. When the veil lifts again it reveals the presence of a Roman emperor in Britain and the construction of Roman frontier-works between the Solway and the Tyne. What had happened in the interval? Only archaeology can provide an answer; and that answer is still faint and faltering.

Perdomita Britannia et statim missa[2]. On the strength of this observation, it was long believed that all the conquests made by Agricola were immediately abandoned. There is exaggeration not merely in one member but in both members of the Tacitean phrase. The supersession of Agricola did not represent any change of policy with regard to Britain, for even had he remained a lull would presumably have followed the great advance initiated by his third campaign. Agricola's successor, whoever he was, was the author neither of an advance nor yet of a retreat.

The greater part of Agricola's gains in Scotland were held for some years, for that is the conclusion that appears to be indicated by the study both of the Roman coins found in Scotland and of the remains, structural and other, of certain military sites in Scotland, not merely Newstead and Camelon, but Ardoch and Inchtuthill, beyond the Forth[3]. A definite frontier has not been found and may

---

[1] Pliny, *Pan.* 8; Dessau 2720.   [2] Tacitus, *Hist.* 1, 2; cf. *Agric.* 10.
[3] Sir George Macdonald, *J.R.S.* IX, 1919, pp. 111 *sqq.*; *P.S.A. Scot.* LII, 1917–1918, pp. 203–76, and LVIII, 1923–4, pp. 325–9.

never have existed—for it is often misleading to apply that term to chains or groups of forts built for the purpose of penetrating and subjugating a refractory region[1]. How long the Romans kept their hold on southern Scotland is not known—a withdrawal in the early years of Trajan or even towards the end of Domitian's reign is not impossible[2]. In default of more evidence from Scotland, knowledge may be augmented by the result of excavation on or near the frontier-works of Hadrian, where there are forts or posts that are proved, either by their situation, their structure or their remains, to be earlier than the Wall of Hadrian and therefore perhaps contemporary with the Stanegate.

The occupation of the line between the Solway and the Tyne was a necessary part both of the conquest of the Brigantes and of their subsequent repression, for these recalcitrant tribes were to be heard of again. As in Mauretania, the Romans in Britain were unable to find a single and satisfactory line behind which peace could reign undisturbed. It is no accident that the only wars that troubled Pius, the most Antonine of emperors, were waged in Britain and in Mauretania (p. 336). Seen in its true light, the retention or the abandonment of Scotland has a local rather than an imperial significance—it concerns merely the depth of the military zone of control in northern Britain.

An advance in the north did not obviate the need for forts south of Hadrian's Wall and in Wales: the difficulties that confronted the Romans are indicated by the fact that it was necessary in the Antonine period to keep garrisons not merely along the more important of the roads across the Pennines at points like Bowes and Ilkley, but even on the southernmost fringe of the Brigantian territory, for example, at Brough in Derbyshire and at Templeborough. The civilizing methods of Agricola which extorted the grudging admiration of Tacitus[3] were pursued with success in the south. There was no place for them in the north. Beyond Aldborough there were no cities.

In peace or war the army of Britain was imposing in size, especially in its contingent of auxiliary regiments, indispensable for open warfare, of which there was abundance, and for garrisoning

[1] A Roman road with a number of small wooden signal towers at intervals on either side of it runs from the fort of Ardoch north-eastwards to the river Tay (cf. D. Christison, *P.S.A. Scot.* xxxv, 1900–1, pp. 15–43). The road may well be of Flavian date; but it is doubtful whether it marks a frontier and is not rather a line of penetration, that is, a *limes* in its original military sense (cf. below, p. 183).

[2] T. D. Pryce and E. Birley, *J.R.S.* xxv, 1935, pp. 59 *sqq.*; against their thesis, Sir G. Macdonald, *J.R.S.* xxv, 1935, pp. 187 *sqq.*   [3] *Agric.* 21.

forts. While Agricola was still in Britain, the legions had sent detachments for service in Germany (p. 163): and several years later, apparently in 86 or 88, II Adiutrix departed for ever to the Danube (above, p. 171). Three legions remained, II Augusta at Caerleon, IX Hispana at York, XX Valeria victrix at Chester[1]. For their tasks they were none too many, and they acquitted themselves nobly. Britain continued to be a fighting province, and her legions were thought worthy of comparison with the best in the Empire, the Danubian troops[2].

Germany, however, suffers a change and a degradation. For more than a century, from Domitian to Antoninus Caracalla, the peace of this frontier does not appear to have been seriously disturbed. The German armies decline in numbers and in prestige. They had been the arbiters of empire: they now no longer play a decisive or even an independent rôle.

It had long been desirable, and it now became possible, to reduce the formidable total of the legions stationed on the Rhine. To this frontier Domitian had brought his new legion I Minervia: but he had withdrawn in succession three legions, I Adiutrix, XXI Rapax and XIV Gemina. None of these ever returned to Germany, and after the departure of XIV Gemina to Pannonia in A.D. 92, the two German armies number three legions apiece[3]: in the course of the following generation each army surrenders yet another legion, and the camps of Vindonissa and Noviomagus are abandoned.

For Lower Germany the Rhine provided a secure frontier. The tribes beyond it had been persuaded or intimidated into submission. But that river no longer marked the eastern limit of Upper Germany. Shortly after 89 the frontier that had been won as a result of Domitian's war against the Chatti was prolonged northwards beyond the Lahn and touched the Rhine at Rheinbrohl, opposite the boundary of the two Germanies (p. 175). From this point a new frontier by land ran in an irregular line south-eastward to reach the Danube a little above Regensburg. At the death of Domitian it had probably not been clearly delimited along its

[1] The exact distribution of the legions of Britain when they still numbered four is not certain. Caerleon and York are early Flavian sites. As for Chester (also early Flavian?) it is not known whether or not it at first housed two legions. II Adiutrix has left traces both at Chester and at Lincoln.

[2] Herodian III, 7, 2.

[3] XXII Primigenia then came to Mainz, and VI Victrix, abandoning Novaesium, occupied Vetera. The distribution of the legions after that year is as follows: Noviomagus, X Gem. P.F.D.; Vetera, VI Victrix P.F.D.; Bonna, I Min. P.F.D.; Moguntiacum, XXII Prim. P.F.D.; Argentorate, VIII Aug.; Vindonissa, XI Claudia.

whole course. But the process may be described as completed. Indeed, such modifications as were made later, even the advance east of the Odenwald and the valley of the Neckar in the time of Antoninus Pius, bear a local rather than a general significance. There was a change, however, in the form of the defence—in the Antonine system all the forts were strung out on the line of the frontier itself. Hadrian erected a wooden palisade. Later (perhaps in the time of Caracalla) the Raetian frontier received a stone wall about eight feet high, Upper Germany, however, the mound and ditch known as the Pfahlgraben.

The Flavian advance had secured a route between the Rhine and the Danube, from Mainz by Stuttgart to Ulm[1]. It might indeed have been expected that the Roman advance would cut yet deeper into southern Germany, to incorporate the land of the Hermunduri in the valley of the Main and win not only a shorter frontier but a shorter line of communications from Mainz to Regensburg by way of Nuremberg. But this was not to be, and a salient of free Germany still faced the Roman frontier on the west and on the south. In this region south-west from the territories of the Hermunduri extended a broad belt of virgin forest[2]: it presented no threat to the Romans and promised no advantage from annexation.

To an advance of the Roman frontier in Germany and an annexation of territory beyond the Rhine there is a solitary reference in the imperfect records of history. In his account of the nations of Germany, Tacitus inserts, while refusing them the right to appear there, the inhabitants of a district which he designates as *decumates agri*[3]. They were Gauls and immigrants, subsequently annexed to the Empire—'mox limite acto promotisque praesidiis sinus imperii et pars provinciae habentur'. The meaning of this term is quite uncertain: it never recurs—and was perhaps obsolescent when Tacitus wrote, for the regions beyond the Rhine had become part of a province. The military territories of Upper and Lower Germany had not hitherto in official language been dignified with the name of provinces. That title appears for the first time in the reign of Domitian, an emperor enamoured of precision and uniformity. The change of title first attested in A.D. 90[4] may have

---

[1] Aurelius Victor (*Caes.* XIII, 3) assigns to Trajan the building of a road *per feras gentes quo facile ab usque Pontico mari in Galliam permeatur.*

[2] The 'fränkisches Nadelholzgebiet.'

[3] *Germ.* 29. On this passage see E. Norden, *Alt-Germanien*, pp. 137 *sqq.*

[4] Dessau 1015, cf. 1998.

followed close upon the suppression of the revolt of Saturninus: an earlier date is not excluded. However that may be, the new lands beyond the Rhine soon received an organization based upon tribal communities, such as already existed among the Mattiaci and the Suebi Nicretes: for the rest, however, the *civitates* appear to be new creations, with names derived from their locality, a fact which justifies Tacitus' refusal to number them among the nations of Germany. In the upper valley of the Neckar, indeed, around Sumelocenna (Rottenburg) a large region became Imperial domain-land[1]: but the natives subsequently developed into a self-governing community.

From the brief and confused remarks of two epitomators of a later age, this process of organization is sometimes assigned to Trajan[2], an emperor who is never allowed less than his due: but it may well go back to the institution of a province of Upper Germany in the time of Domitian. For Trajan there remained little or nothing to be done along or within the frontiers of Germany and Raetia; and no military activity is recorded. Even a remorseless panegyrist like Pliny the Younger must confess himself defeated.

The advance of the frontier in Germany and Raetia had been completed in its essentials by A.D. 96. The date at which certain forts were first established cannot always, it is true, be closely determined: whether some forts belong to the last years of Domitian, to the brief reign of Nerva, or to the beginning of that of his successor is a problem that belongs to topography rather than to history. The process of annexation was completed, so Tacitus records, by the drawing of a *limes*. This was the term which soon came to be applied to each and all of the frontiers of the Empire, at first perhaps only when they were lines of demarcation or defence on land, but later to rivers as well[3]. The original meaning of the word, a straight path, hence a boundary, might be taken to suggest that it developed by an easy and natural transition to signify the limit first of a province, then of an empire[4]. But this is not so:

---

[1] Dessau 4608; 7099; 7100. Dessau 8855 is difficult to interpret: it mentions a procurator χώρας [Σ]ομελοκεννησίας καὶ [...] ερλιμιτανῆς.

[2] Eutropius VIII, 2, 2; Orosius VII, 12, 2. Some of the communities in fact bear his name, e.g. the Civitas Ulpia Sueborum Nicretum (Dessau, 472, 532, 7104).

[3] Cf. especially the description of Hadrian's palisades (*S.H.A. Hadr.* 12, 6), *in plurimis locis in quibus barbari non fluminibus sed limitibus dividuntur, stipitibus magnis in modum muralis saepis funditus iactis atque conexis barbaros separavit.* Already in Tacitus we find the word applied to the frontier of the Danube (*Agric.* 41), *de limite imperii et ripa.*

[4] Lucan (I, 216) uses it of the Rubicon.

the word had also a narrower sense—it was a technical military term, designating the straight clear path along which a column of troops moved forward to attack in a battle or in a campaign. *Limites* were constructed to penetrate hostile territory and were subsequently maintained to control it. These military lines of penetration had been employed by the Romans in their invasion of Germany in Augustan days[1]: and Domitian operated in this way against the Chatti over a wide front[2]. A military road, accompanied in its course by fortified posts or watch-towers, might thus be used to isolate difficult territory and might sometimes correspond more or less to the limit of effective control. In northern England the Stanegate may have fulfilled this function for a time: and at an earlier date the Fosse Way was perhaps the earliest frontier of the Roman province of Britain[3].

The essential of a *limes*, then, is a road with watch-towers or forts along it. It is not necessary that it should be provided with any other defences. As has very properly been observed, the essential feature of Hadrian's Wall is not the stone wall itself, which is best regarded not as a barrier but as an elevated sentry-walk[4].

In this sense, all the *limites* of the frontier provinces of the Empire embody the same principle. But here the resemblance ends. Just as army varied from army in composition and functions, so did *limes* from *limes*. Great differences may indeed be observed along the same frontier at the same time. The system of defence designed by Domitian after the annexation of the Wetterau has already been described—a chain of watch-towers, with here and there a small post, running along the rim of the Taunus and sweeping around the north-east of the Wetterau, to join the river Main near Hanau. Here there was an enemy to be feared, the Chatti: and so the forts that housed the auxiliary regiments were situated in the rear. South of Hanau, however, things were different, and the regiments could be placed on the line of the frontier, for the patrolling of which they supplied the troops. This frontier followed the bank of the Main for some twenty miles, as far as Wörth, where it struck southwards, keeping to the line of a ridge, and descended to the Neckar at Wimpfen. Thence the Neckar provided the frontier as far as Cannstatt, with a chain of forts, constructed, like those on the rest of the *limes* south of Hanau, of earth. East of Cannstatt the point of junction with the *limes* of Raetia at this date is uncertain,

[1] Vell. Pat. II, 121; Tacitus, *Ann.* I, 50; II, 7.
[2] Cf. Frontinus, *Strat.* I, 3, 10.
[3] Cf. R. G. Collingwood, *J.R.S.* XIV, 1924, pp. 252 *sqq.*
[4] See Volume of Plates V, 34.

for the limit of the Roman advance had not yet been clearly marked by any natural or artificial line.

In the form which it was ultimately to receive, the Roman frontier in Germany was a visible and an imposing barrier. But none of the features which gave it this character, in Upper Germany the palisade of Hadrian and the later mound and ditch (the Pfahlgraben), in Raetia the palisade and then the stone wall, were present in the original scheme. This scheme, indeed, could have served its purpose adequately enough without them, for the new frontier was designed to be, not a line of defence, but a line of patrols, to watch the natives and prevent their crossing without leave the limit that Rome had set, whether that limit was a river or a line drawn across the dry land. This function is illustrated by the inscriptions which Commodus set up to commemorate his repairs along the Pannonian *limes* of the Danube—'ripam omnem burgis a solo extructis item praesidis per loca opportuna ad clandestinos latrunculorum transitus oppositis munivit[1].' Even before the Flavian re-organization of the frontiers of Germany and Raetia, it was the rule that natives should not cross the boundary rivers how and when they pleased[2]. This interdiction was now reinforced by a stricter control. The tranquillity of the frontier is illustrated by the fact that Hadrian transferred the garrisons from the forts in the Wetterau to the line of the *limes* itself: of a German invasion there appears to be no danger, and Roman soldiers usurp the duties of gendarmes and customs officials.

The full significance of the measures adopted by the Flavian emperors in Germany and of the changes thereby effected or portended was not at once apparent to contemporaries. In the year 98 Tacitus published his *Germania*. Of its character and purpose there has been much debate. Though it may very properly be denied that the tract was written to serve a moral or a political end, Tacitus would not be its author if it did not betray some indication of his personality and his opinions. At the time when the *Germania* was made public, Trajan was on the Rhine. A policy different from that of the Flavians might be deduced from his character and his career. From the earliest encounter of the Romans with the nations of Germany down to the second consulate of Trajan, more than two centuries of history had been filled with the record of their wars: and the latest triumph celebrated over them had been false and futile. ' Tam diu Germania vincitur[3].'

---

[1] Dessau 8913, etc.   [2] Tacitus, *Germ.* 41; *Hist.* IV, 64.
[3] Tacitus, *Germ.* 37.

It may be inferred that Tacitus hoped in secret for that conquest of Germany which he did not dare openly to advocate. He recounts how an offending people, the Bructeri, were pitilessly massacred by a confederacy of their neighbours for the advantage of Rome[1]. In the comments which this edifying spectacle has moved him to record, it is perhaps permissible to read, not so much solicitude for the future destiny of the Empire and hope that the enemies of Rome may ever be divided thus, as irony and indignation that so ignoble a policy should in the present be recommended. But Tacitus was deceived and disappointed: Trajan sought his laurels in other lands. Tacitus should have assigned more space and more significance to the Danubian Germans, the Marcomanni and the Quadi: he should have compiled for his contemporaries and for posterity some account of the peoples of Dacia and Sarmatia.

To the changed and calamitous situation on the Danube Tacitus had already in his biography of Agricola borne emphatic testimony —disaster upon disaster, continuous and unmitigated, four Roman defeats in Moesia, Dacia, Germany and Pannonia[2]. As later in the days of Marcus Aurelius, from Bohemia to the Pontus all was confusion. The needs of the Empire summoned Domitian three times to a frontier which no emperor before him had ever troubled to visit. He adopted the methods which tradition and common-sense recommended: he had not designed the conquest and annexation of Dacia, but had sent Fuscus and then Julianus across the river to restore the prestige of Rome and secure peace for the future by humbling and weakening Decebalus. It was now advisable to come to an understanding with Dacia: a strong Dacia, with a monarch who could keep his own subjects in order, and check the nomad tribes on either side, might become an integral part of the system of frontier defence. For this reason Domitian paid Decebalus a subsidy and lent him engineers to build forts. In a later age, when Rome could no longer hold and defend Dacia as a province, Aurelian yielded this territory to the Goths and acquired for Rome a century of peace along the Lower Danube. To choose, delimit and garrison a frontier is only a small part of frontier defence: more important are the relations with the tribes beyond it: instead of continuous unrest, of repeated punitive expeditions against an elusive or inaccessible enemy, empires before or since have not disdained to enlist by the payment of money the co-operation of the more civilized or the neutrality of the more turbulent tribes along their borders. Trajan subsidized the Sarmatae Roxolani

[1] Tacitus, *Germ.* 33.
[2] Tacitus, *Agric.* 41.

beyond the Lower Danube: in the first year of Hadrian they complained of a reduction of the money paid to them[1].

Rome had hitherto paid subsidies to the Marcomanni and Quadi; now Dacia occupied that privileged status. That a Roman victory in Dacia should have been followed by peace without conquest was distasteful or inexplicable to contemporaries who were more familiar with history as it appeared transfigured in literature than with the stern requirements and the sober methods of imperial frontier policy: and even if Domitian had not been detested and his memory condemned, the choice which he took must have appeared ignoble when confronted with the glorious achievements of an emperor who revived the wars and triumphs of ancient days. Yet it might be urged that a policy adopted in the face of a sudden emergency should only be judged with reference to that emergency. Time might have refuted Domitian's policy by its results: that it was folly and a failure is not at once proved by the fact that it was reversed by Trajan. Moreover, should the power of Decebalus appear to have been unduly augmented, the ephemeral empires and rapid ends of Burebista and of Maroboduus gave some grounds for confidence in an issue other than that of war and conquest.

The change in Roman foreign policy was accompanied by a re-organization of the defence of the long and imperilled frontier of the Danube. Though evidence is scanty, it is clear that ample compensation must have been made for the neglect that had prevailed hitherto. Additional auxiliary regiments and new forts would be required. The Column of Trajan depicts wooden watch-towers along the Danube, like those built by Domitian in the Taunus; and repairs were made on the road hewn in the rock on the southern bank of the Danube in the narrow gorge, called the Pass of Kazan[2], a road begun by Tiberius, but for which Trajan was to have the ultimate and enduring credit.

What can be inferred of the movements and distribution of the legions provides an indication of value. In the time of Vespasian six (or perhaps seven) legions comprised the garrison of the provinces of Dalmatia, Pannonia and Moesia (see p. 169): and two of these were still stationed in the interior. By the end of Domitian's reign there were probably nine. Three legions had arrived in succession from the Rhine, I Adiutrix, XIV Gemina and XXI Rapax, one from Britain, II Adiutrix: none went back, and one had perished.

Moesia had been divided in 85–6[3]. Uncertainty about the

---

[1] S.H.A. *Hadr.* 6, 8.   [2] Dessau 9373.   [3] *Ib.* 1005.

boundary between the two provinces contributes to the difficulty of determining which of the Moesian provinces had three legions, which two, for the total appears to have comprised five[1]. The camps of I Italica, V Macedonica and VII Claudia were probably, as before, Novae, Oescus and Viminacium: about the camps of the new arrivals, probably II Adiutrix and IV Flavia felix, there is no certain evidence[2].

As for Pannonia, the line of the Danube from Carnuntum (east of Vienna) to its confluence with the Save at Belgrade had long been neglected. The defection of the German and Sarmatian allies of Rome laid bare what was perhaps the most vulnerable section of the whole frontier, between Vienna and Budapest—in the time of Hadrian it was held by four legions, stationed at Vindobona, Carnuntum, Brigetio and Aquincum. By the end of Domitian's reign XIII Gemina had probably moved from Poetovio to Vindobona[3]; and XV Apollinaris garrisoned Carnuntum as before. There now appear, however, to have been two more legions in Pannonia, I Adiutrix and XIV Gemina, possibly at Brigetio and at Aquincum[4].

The garrisons of Britain and the German provinces have now fallen to three legions apiece, and Pannonia, with four legions, holds pride of place among the military provinces of the Empire. Long neglected, the Danube comes into its own, with nine legions as against six in the Rhine. By the time of Hadrian the Rhine armies have shrunk to four, and ten legions in the Danubian provinces attest and guarantee the importance of that frontier in peace and in war.

---

[1] Dessau 2719.

[2] Above, p. 171, n. 4. For a conjecture (quite insecure), cf. R. Syme in *J.R.S.* xviii, 1928, p. 49.

[3] Cf. E. Ritterling, *P.W.*, s.v. Legio, col. 1714 *sq.*

[4] Cf. *J.R.S.* xviii, 1928, p. 51. I Adiutrix fought against the Suebi in A.D. 97 (Dessau 2720). Brigetio and Aquincum may well be pre-Trajanic: for Aquincum, cf. the Domitianic building-inscription, *C.I.L.* iii, 14547[2]; for Brigetio, S. Paulovics, *Aevum*, viii, 1934, p. 246.

CHAPTER V

NERVA AND TRAJAN

I. NERVA

THE most embittered opponent of Domitian's rule could scarcely have desired a greater contrast to the murdered man than the ruler who succeeded him. The new emperor, M. Cocceius Nerva, was born at Narnia on November 8, probably in A.D. 30[1]: he was therefore nearly 66 at the date of his accession. His career as a private citizen is only partially known[2]. He had been a friend of Nero, who was inspired by his lyric pieces to christen him the Tibullus of his age; and as praetor designate in 65 he was rewarded with *ornamenta triumphalia* and other honours after the suppression of the Pisonian conspiracy. Yet these proofs of Nero's favour did not prevent Vespasian from choosing him as his colleague in the consulship for the critical year 71. From that date until his second consulship with Domitian in 91 his movements are unknown. Even during the Terror of 93–6 his part is obscure. There is, indeed, some evidence that he was in danger of his life[3]. But when after the tyrant's death it was a point of pride to have endured his threats, the new emperor would naturally be credited with his predecessor's hatred: and it is no long transition to Dio's statement that his danger made him all the readier to listen to the conspirators' advances.

Note. The chief literary sources for the principate of Nerva are:—Dio LXVII, 15–6; LXVIII, 1–4; Eutropius VIII, 1; Aurelius Victor, *Caes.* XII; XIII, 10; *Epit.* XII; Pliny, *Pan.* passim; *Ep.* I, 5, 12; II, 1, 7; III, 11; IV, 9, 11, 17, 22; VII, 31, 33; IX, 13; X, 8 (24), 58 (66). For inscriptions see the Bibliography and for coins see Mattingly and Sydenham, *The Roman Imperial Coinage*, II, pp. 220–33 and Volume of Plates V, 126.

[1] Fasti Philocal. et Silv. *C.I.L.* I², p. 255, 276 *sq.*; VI, 10050 = Dessau 5285, give the month and day; but the year is variously given in the records: cf. Dio ed. Boissevain III, p. 190.

[2] Dessau 273 adds a few further details to those given in the text.

[3] Aurelius Victor, *Caes.* XII (an unlikely legend); Dio LXVII, 15; Philostratus, *Vita Apoll.* VII, 8, 132 (cf. VIII, 7, 160). The two last can be harmonized into a plausible story; but the negative evidence of Suetonius is strong against his actual punishment, and Martial XII, 6 is unexpectedly colourless if Nerva had really been in serious danger (cf. V, 28; VIII, 70).

Whoever was responsible for it, the choice of such a man, placid though eloquent, nobly-born but over sixty years of age, to succeed to the Empire in a moment of crisis demands some explanation. On neither side was he descended from the Republican nobility[1]. His grandfather and father had alike been jurists of distinction, and the former, *Caesari familiarissimus*, accompanied Tiberius from Rome in A.D. 26 and remained with him until his own voluntary death in 33 (Vol. x, pp. 632, 640). His great-grand-father, also M. Cocceius Nerva, was consul in 36 B.C. and *XV vir sac. fac.* in 17 B.C. on the occasion of the Secular Games; and was himself the brother of a man even better known, L. Cocceius Nerva, consul in 39 B.C., who played an important part in securing the treaty of Brundisium between Octavian and Antony[2].

On his father's side, therefore, Nerva belonged to a family which (though no member of it is yet known to have held military command since the battle of Actium) had been eminent since the Civil Wars and had enjoyed the respect and friendship of the Julio-Claudian house. Through his mother's family, however, he could claim more exalted connections. Nerva's mother, Sergia Plautilla[3], was the daughter of that C. Octavius Laenas who succeeded his other grandfather as *curator aquarum* in A.D. 34[4]. Her brother married Rubellia Bassa, the great-grand-daughter of Tiberius through her father's marriage with Julia, the child of Drusus and Livilla, and this lady, Nerva's aunt, thus formed a link which related him to the Julio-Claudian family: in the veins of those cousins whom he passed over for the succession in 97 there ran the blood of Tiberius and of Octavia. So remote a connection may appear to be of small significance: but the prestige of the Julio-Claudian house remained high, and an inspection of their genealogical tree shows at once that the number of people who had even that degree of affinity to the family can, after the death of Nero, have been only extremely small[5].

Nerva was thus a man who was in different ways linked both on his father's and mother's side with the Julio-Claudian court; he had been, perhaps for this reason, the first private *consul ordinarius* under Vespasian; and his name would naturally be

---

[1] Eutropius VIII, 1, *nobilitatis mediae*.

[2] That the family had at some time been granted patrician rank is shown by Nerva's early appointment as salius Palatinus.

[3] Dessau 281.   [4] Frontinus, *de aquaeductibus*, 102.

[5] Nerva was the last of the emperors whose ashes were deposited in the Mausoleum of Augustus; cf. E. Groag, *Jahreshefte*, XXII, 1924, Beibl. col. 425 *sq.*

among the first to come to mind in the choice of an acceptable successor. The words of Dio prove beyond reasonable doubt that he had no sons to follow him[1]; and time would show where a younger and more vigorous heir might be found. The ancient writers are at one in emphasizing the kindliness of his disposition, and the fact, if it be correct, that he had held no important military or provincial command may not have appeared as a disadvantage. After all, the chaos of 69 had been the work of rival armies and their leaders; and such jealousies might not arise against a man who was not, and perhaps had never been, an army commander. Nor was his age, to senators at least, unwelcome. History had enforced the lesson that, however well disposed a *princeps* were on his accession, few men could withstand the temptations of unlimited power for long: an old emperor might die before he became dangerous. Lastly, the greatest present need was for a government which could conciliate all interests. Domitian, by whatever means, had won the favour of the army; but his policy towards other classes in the State was rapidly unbalancing the whole imperial administrative system.

The sources of evidence for the next sixteen months, the last of Nerva's life, are certainly meagre; but a reconstruction of the chronology is assisted by the accurate dates of the coin series, and with these the order of Dio's narrative is not seriously at variance. In foreign affairs the period was relatively uneventful, and it is the domestic programme of the government and its progressive decline that is important. In both two stages are at once discernible, the first covering the immediate reactions to Domitian's murder, and the second the year 97 when the new government initiated its own policy and its essential weakness had had time and opportunity to make itself felt.

No coup d'État, involving the violent death of an autocratic head of the State, can dispense with an initial period of danger and anxiety; the new régime, however, survived its birth-pangs unimpaired. A trace of the uncertainty of those days has been preserved in the rumour that Domitian was after all alive: but the positive assurance of the principal murderer proved sufficient to allay the fears of a resurrection. The attitude of the Praetorian Guard was more serious, but for the moment the danger passed: according to tradition both the Prefects Norbanus and Petronius had been privy to the plot, and Petronius at least was later to suffer for this suspicion. Abandoned by their leaders, the praetorians were silenced, though they continued to watch their opportunity

[1] Dio LXVIII, 4. Cf. Ausonius XXI, 2, 55 (ed. Schenkl).

for a rising. That the provincial armies hesitated to take the oath
we have no certain evidence, but prominent in the new coin issue
was the legend CONCORDIA EXERCITUUM, a piece of propaganda
that seldom appears but when it is needed, and had been in abey-
ance since Vespasian's issues of A.D. 69–70[1]. That the customary
donative was paid need not be doubted; the example of Galba
can hardly have been forgotten in circumstances so closely parallel.
For the moment, then, the troops were quiet, the oath was taken.
From the urban populace there was less to fear. It had received
the news with indifference, and a *congiarium* of the usual dimensions was at once distributed; this too Galba had omitted.

The remainder of the year was occupied with the return of the
exiles, the reaction against Domitian's informers, and the repeal
of his most unpopular measures. About the tyrant's death the
Senate at least had had no doubts[2]. His memory was damned, his
acts abolished[3]; the *infaustum vocabulum*, his name, was ordered
everywhere to be erased; his triumphal arches were pulled down
or converted to other uses: and with a howl of gratification the
Senate lent their hands to the work, as they saw the hated statues
crashing from their pedestals, rent, split and shattered by the axe
or melting in the flames[4]. A deplorable scene, but a measure of
the depths of humiliation and terror to which Domitian's mad
persecution had reduced the men from whom he continued to
recruit his most responsible lieutenants. After the vengeance
upon the dead came the vengeance upon the living. Many of the
informers, especially in the humbler classes, were condemned to
death at once. Everyone accused his enemies—*dumtaxat minores*—
and wild confusion ensued. Nerva held his hand, and his first
appointed consul Ti. Catius Fronto, himself a lawyer of distinction,
bitterly remarked that there might be worse things than tyranny.
Finally the Princeps intervened; the returned exiles were still far
from satisfied, but the storm of accusations died down[5]. Meanwhile
the principal sources of delation were sealed. The charge of
maiestas was temporarily suppressed and with it that of Judaism:
henceforth the Jewish tax was to be confined to Jews self-confessed.
These reforms were commemorated on coins of 96 bearing the
legends IUSTITIA AUGUST. and FISCI IUDAICI CALUMNIA SUBLATA;

---

[1] The trouble at one of the Danube camps witnessed by Dio Chrysostom
may well belong to this period; Philostratus, *Vitae Soph.* 1, 7, 1.

[2] Cf. Suetonius, *Dom.* 23.

[3] Nerva, however, confirmed his *beneficia* by an edict, quoted in Pliny,
Ep. x, 58 (66).　　　　　　　　　　　　　　[4] Pliny, *Pan.* 52.

[5] Aurelius Victor, *Epit.* XII. Cf. Pliny, *Ep.* IV, 22 and for the subsequent
punishment of the surviving informers by Trajan, *Pan.* 34–5.

of the types issued by the Imperial mint in this year only one—
MONETA AUGUST., which does not re-appear after 96—repeats a
Domitianic *motif*, and in the senatorial coinage the types are nearly
all new. The legend ROMA RENASCENS recalls the ROMA RESURGENS
of Vespasian (69–72), and LIBERTAS PUBLICA voices another and
similar echo. These, with types of Salus, Fortuna and Aequitas,
all emphasize Nerva's desire to blot out the past and foreshadow
the benevolent programme of the following year.

The year 97 opened with Nerva as consul, his colleague being
the veteran L. Verginius Rufus, who now entered upon his third
consulship at the age of eighty-two or three, after nearly thirty
years of retirement from active public life. The constructive
programme now introduced was planned almost entirely for the
benefit of Rome and Italy. There is indeed in coins of the year
a suggestion of a temporary corn shortage which Nerva met by
emergency measures[1]; but more serious steps than this were taken
to deal with the problem of poverty. A *lex agraria* voted the
provision by the State of lands to the value of 60 million sesterces
for allotment to poor citizens; and a senatorial commission was
put in charge of the purchase and distribution. This return to
Republican methods of dealing with the urban poor was re-inforced
by the adoption of a plan for the country towns of Italy which had
been already tested by private benefactors. The local evidence
for the working of the State alimentary scheme is nowhere earlier
than the succeeding principate and the system employed may have
been different under Nerva, but there is no doubt that it is to him
that its initiation was due (see p. 210)[2]. Further relief to Italy was
granted by the government's assumption of the costs of the *cursus
publicus*, which had hitherto been a serious burden on all who lived
along the main arterial roads[3]. The colony of Scolacium was refounded or re-inforced, and other Italian cities may have received
similar attention[4]. The modest programme of public works which
accompanied these measures reveals a similar imprint. In Rome,
little new building was begun; the Forum transitorium, dedicated
by Nerva, is a work for which the credit must be given to Domitian,
and Nerva's only original contribution appears to be some

---

[1] Mattingly and Sydenham, *op. cit.* no. 89 (p. 229). *Plebei urbanae
frumento constituto.*

[2] The suggestion (cf. J. Asbach, *Röm. Kaisertum und Verfassung*, pp. 188
sqq.) that it owed its origin to Domitian is hardly tenable.

[3] Imperial freedmen of this department first appear under Trajan: for his
attempt to improve its efficiency cf. Aurelius Victor, *Caes.* XIII, 6. Mattingly
and Sydenham, *op. cit.* no. 93 (p. 229). *Vehiculatione Italiae remissa.*

[4] Dessau 5750.

granaries[1]. The year 97, however, saw the appointment of Sex. Julius Frontinus to the *cura aquarum*, and the beginning of a thorough and, if we may believe its author, long overdue re-organization of the water system of Rome. The restoration of the Via Appia was put in hand (p. 207) and repairs were carried out on the Tiburtina and the road from Puteoli to Naples.

In the provinces Nerva, like his predecessors, is recorded to have tided some cities over their difficulties[2]; and the number of milestones bearing his name testifies perhaps to particular instructions to governors to review and improve the communications of their province[3]. But in general there is no doubt that Nerva's first aim lay nearer home in the restoration of Italian prosperity. There remain a few other reforms which probably belong to this year. The immunity from the 5 per cent. succession duty for near kin, which had previously been withheld from new citizens who won their rights by imperial grant or by way of Latinitas, was extended to them to cover inheritances from father to son[4], from mother to children and from children to mother. A special praetor was appointed to judge cases between the *fiscus* and private persons: and, as Pliny gratefully observes, 'saepius vincitur fiscus.' Laws were passed permitting cities to receive legacies, forbidding castration, and tightening up the table of kindred and affinity, this last no doubt with a reflection on the scandalous relations of Domitian and his niece.

These measures were not passed by Nerva without a conscious return to constitutional practice; and the programme of 97 is accompanied in the coin series by a new type bearing the legend PROVIDENTIA SENATUS. The scheme of land distribution was even embodied in a *lex agraria* and passed by the Comitia, the last recorded piece of legislation by that body. This policy, of social improvement and public utility, of honest government and equality before the law, reflects no doubt the aims not only of Nerva but of his immediate circle of friends, traditionalists like Verginius Rufus

---

[1] Dessau 1627. Perhaps also some alterations to the Colosseum; *C.I.L.* VI, 32254.

[2] Aurelius Victor, *Epit.* XII, 4. The evidence is meagre. The assistance to Citium in Cyprus at least belongs to 96 (Dessau 275, *I.G.R.R.* III, 976). Cf. *C.I.L.* III, 7146, 12041, 12238. Nerva founded the colony of Sitifis (Sétif) in Mauretania, and probably also that of Cuicul (Djemila) across the Numidian border (cf. R. Cagnat, *Musée Belge* XXVII, 1923, 115–6).

[3] They are especially numerous in the Eastern provinces, where the lines of communication behind the frontier were being steadily improved. Cf. *C.I.L.* III, 6896–7, 6899, 7192, 12158–9, 14184.

[4] Provided he was *in patria potestate*. See further, p. 213.

and lawyers like Catius Fronto together with a few, who, like the
younger Pliny, had been brought up under their influence. It
says no disparagement that it was pleasing to the Senate, that
Pliny could write of *reddita libertas* and Tacitus of the blending
of *res olim dissociabiles principatum ac libertatem*. Yet, however
admirable might be Nerva's principles and his programme, his
régime was bound to collapse if it could not keep the loyalty of
the troops: and over this his precarious hold might be loosened by
either of two events, a financial crisis resulting in arrears of pay,
or the ambition of a popular general.

The financial record of Nerva's government has been very
variously appraised. It has been lauded as masterly and damned
as extravagant and chaotic; both extreme views turn largely on
one known event. At some date within the reign the Senate
appointed a commission of five *minuendis publicis sumptibus*: this
took place during the last illness of Verginius Rufus, an illness
which Pliny describes as 'durior longiorque,' and which resulted
from breaking his thigh while rehearsing a speech of thanks to
Nerva. The speech belongs to Verginius' consulship at the
beginning of 97, and though we do not know at what point in
his illness the commission was nominated, it may most likely be
placed in the spring of that year. At least two of its members were
designated to second consulships by Nerva, and one of these,
Sex. Iulius Frontinus (who had continued throughout the year
as *curator aquarum*), succeeded him as Trajan's colleague in
January 98. The appointment of such a commission as this was
no innovation and there is no need to assume that it was a measure
of panic. But a glance at Nerva's situation shows at once that he
had cause for some anxiety. Suetonius says definitely of Domitian
that it was only by wholesale confiscation that he could replenish
a treasury compromised by the cost of his buildings, shows, and
increase in military pay: and, whatever his motive in confiscation,
the fact remains that money did so come in, and perhaps the extra
burden of the rise in pay was not seriously felt in his time. But
Nerva had suspended the charge of *maiestas* and returned what
remained of the confiscated property; and he was thus left without
the prospect of the considerable windfalls which had accrued to
Domitian's exchequer. His relief of certain taxes meant a further
though comparatively small drop in revenue; and besides these,
in 97 he launched his own programme. It was hardly an extravagant one. The only large immediate outlay was that involved by
the land-allotment scheme: but the 60 million sesterces which it
cost were a non-recurrent charge. Domitian's increase of pay

was costing an extra 60 millions every year, and while this may have been a justifiable reform, it cannot have escaped upsetting the balance of a treasury scarcely restored by the parsimony of Vespasian and already jeopardized by the expansive building schemes of Titus. Domitian in his turn had been a prolific builder and a lavish entertainer of the Roman populace; and he had left a fresh liability in the large annual subsidy with which he had pacified Decebalus in 89. Where was Nerva to retrench? Dio suggests that he met the expenses of the *lex agraria* by a sale of much of the personal estate which he inherited as *princeps*, and in other directions he economized as much as possible. Himself of frugal tastes, he reduced the expenses of the imperial court to a minimum. But to cut down the soldiers' pay (by far the largest item in the imperial budget) was suicide: to cancel the Dacian subsidy was to invite a war for which the time was not yet ripe. Since neither of these courses, nor the imposition of fresh taxation, was open to a new and inevitably uneasy government, it is hardly surprising that we hear of few positive results from the economy commission[1]. Nerva was compelled to postpone any serious innovation and content himself with minor economies in entertainment to the Roman populace, already conciliated by the payment of the customary *congiarium*[2] on accession, and provided for by the *lex agraria*. That the financial question was laid before the Senate is nothing remarkable: it is of a piece with the known policy of the reign.

Meanwhile, however, the signs of the government's political weakness were multiplying. Some time in 97, when Pliny attacked a senior ex-praetor, Publicius Certus, who had been prominent in securing the conviction of Helvidius Priscus in 93, his consular friends, sceptical, it may be, of the vitality of the régime, tried to dissuade him, saying that he had made himself a marked man to future emperors, and reminding him that Publicius had powerful friends, especially the governor of Syria 'qui tunc ad orientem

---

[1] If G. Mickwitz, *Arctos*, III, 1933–4, p. 1 is correct in maintaining that the standard weight of the denarius which had been raised under Domitian from 2·92 gr. to over 3·20, was reduced in 98 to its old level, this may have been one of the commission's recommendations: these would naturally not affect the coinage of 97.

[2] The sums realized by melting down the gold and silver statues of Domitian would help in this payment. In Nerva's short reign of 16 months it naturally bulks large, but to compare it to Domitian's total of such expenditure in 16 years is a *suggestio falsi*. His only other gift was apparently a bequest paid after his death.

amplissimum et famosissimum exercitum non sine magnis dubiis-
que rumoribus obtinebat[1].' These rumours, indeed, came to
nothing, but the story is good evidence of the feeling of insecurity
which succeeded the first few glorious months of *reddita libertas*.
The attempt of C. Calpurnius Crassus to undermine the loyalty of
the troops is significant only because of the mildness—in senatorial
eyes the culpable mildness—with which Nerva punished it. The
Emperor had sworn not to kill a senator, and in spite of plots he
kept his oath. But in the end it was not from senatorial ambition
that the gravest danger was to come. The praetorians had been
rebellious ever since Domitian's death: suppressed by their leaders
in 96, their dissatisfaction came to a head in the autumn of 97.
In the interval these unpopular leaders, or Norbanus at least,
had been superseded by the re-appointment of Casperius Aelianus,
who had already served a term as Prefect under Domitian. So
weak a move can only have been a desperate attempt at conciliation. But if this was Nerva's hope, it was vain. The praetorians
rose, with Casperius at their head, and demanded the surrender
of Domitian's murderers. Nerva attempted to resist and even
offered his own throat, but he was brushed aside and Petronius,
Parthenius and possibly others were put to death by the soldiers.
Casperius went further and even compelled the Emperor to return
thanks to the rebels before the assembled people for the execution
of those to whom he owed his throne.

Nerva's prestige in Rome had now suffered an irreparable blow,
and on the publication of the news the final collapse of his régime
could not be long delayed. He himself, deeply humiliated and
oppressed by ill-health, seems to have thought of abdication; but
if this is true he was persuaded by his friends to try the only
possible means of preventing civil war, by adopting at once as
heir one who could command the loyalty of the legionary troops
and could overawe the praetorians. The choice fell on M. Ulpius
Traianus, who, as commander of the army of Upper Germany, was
in the best position of any provincial governor to coerce the Roman
insurgents, and also, perhaps, to march on Rome on his own
account if some less accessible general were preferred to him.
What sort of pressure, if any, was put on Nerva to select Trajan
remains unknown[2]: Trajan never showed any personal respect

---

[1] *Ep.* IX, 13, 22. Possibly L. Javolenus Priscus (Dessau 1015).

[2] It cannot be recovered from Aurelius Victor, *Epit.* XIII, 7, which
assigns a part to Licinius Sura, a fellow Spaniard, who may have held at this
time an official position in Germany or Belgica; cf. Groag in P.W. *s.v.*
Licinius (167) Sura, col. 475 *sq.* Pliny (*Pan.* 5, 10) is explicit that Trajan
had long been the popular choice.

or affection for Nerva, rather the contrary. But if his strategic command was a potent factor, there might be other and more disinterested recommendations. He was now in the prime of life, and while his career had been spent almost entirely in military service, which had taken him, says Pliny, from end to end of the empire, there are grounds for supposing that during recent years he had suffered in silence at Rome like other senators[1]. He was thus a man, and one of the only men alive, who could both sympathize with the Senate and command the respect of the armies. That he was not related to Nerva, who passed over several possible heirs among his own kinsmen (p. 189), was not perhaps a disadvantage. His Spanish descent, on the other hand, might in easier circumstances have shocked the conservatives; but with the State crumbling—'ruens imperium super imperatorem'—they could not be too nice[2]. Moreover, of all provincials the Romans of Spain had long been recognized as second only to the Italian-born, and Trajan's father had himself been a much respected senator, an ex-consul and proconsul of Asia, and the holder of triumphal decorations[3]. Finally, whatever the reasons which prompted it, the choice was abundantly justified in the result. Not only was civil war averted, but the present discord was immediately stilled and the Empire entered upon a long period of practically unruffled internal harmony.

The formal adoption was carried through without delay. The Suebi had apparently been giving trouble again on the Upper Danube, and the welcome news of a victory gave Nerva his opportunity[4]. Having, as *pontifex maximus*, deposited the laurel from the despatch on the knees of the cult-statue of Juppiter, he turned to the assembled people and from the steps of the Capitol announced his adoption of Trajan. Unlike the furtive and irregular procedure followed in the case of Piso in 69, the ceremony, barring Trajan's absence, was performed with full legal forms. The conferment of honours followed in the Senate. Trajan was given the title of Caesar and the powers that marked a *consors imperii*[5]: Pliny compares his position to that of Titus in his

---

[1] Pliny, *Pan.* 44.   [2] Pliny, *Pan.* 5, 6.

[3] Spanish influence was strong at Rome at this time; among prominent representatives were Licinius Sura, M. Annius Verus, L. Julius Ursus Servianus and the notorious Marius Priscus.

[4] Pliny, *Pan.* 8. Cf. Dessau 2720, which records the decoration by Nerva of a tribune of leg. I *Adiutrix* for service in this war.

[5] On the problem of the dating of Trajan's *tribunicia potestas* cf. the works cited in the bibliography. His first year ran till autumn 98 and was then

father's life-time, and when, shortly after, Nerva took the title
of Germanicus for the victories over the Suebi, Trajan received
this title also. It was now the winter of 97. Nerva lived three
months longer, but he did not see his adopted son. Trajan remained on the frontier and did not visit Rome at all till 99,
though his hand may be seen in the appointments at this time of
his trusted friends Servianus and Sura to the command of Upper
and Lower Germany and perhaps in that of C. Pompeius Planta
to Egypt. The three months passed quietly. In January 98 Nerva
entered on his fourth and Trajan his second consulship; and on
the 25th of that month Nerva died of a feverish chill and Trajan
succeeded to the Empire.

The rule of Nerva has in the past been uncritically praised
by many historians. The sun of senatorial approval and the clear
sky at his death have made it too easy to forget the dark clouds
that hung over the greater part of the reign. Civil war was never
very far away and for a short while in the autumn of 97, when
Casperius was virtually master of Rome, it must have seemed to
many unescapable. Yet the Empire owed a debt to Nerva and the
small cabal of elderly nobles who formed his entourage. Of those
whose share is attested, Verginius Rufus was over 80, Vestricius
Spurinna 73, Corellius Rufus 68, Arrius Antoninus about 65,
Julius Frontinus about 60, Nerva himself 66[1]. They were confronted by difficulties which might well have conquered younger
and more active men. Most of them had been retired from public
life for many years, and to the serving army the best known of
them can have been little more than a name. But they succeeded:
the fact remains that civil war did not break out. The crisis
was tided over, and a new era opened. The series of adoptions
begun by Nerva may not have been founded on any principle[2],
may indeed have been a series of accidents, but the childlessness

followed by a short period, probably till Dec. 10, from which it was renewed
regularly. There are difficulties in any view but the inscriptions strongly
suggest a renewal date close to Jan. 1, while certain coins prove, if they
may be trusted, that it must be before the New Year.

[1] Behind these, two younger groups can be distinguished; the first consisting of lawyers and peaceful administrators like Pliny, Catius Fronto,
Sosius Senecio and Cornutus Tertullus, nearly all either actually or spiritually
related to the older group, the second of soldiers, largely of provincial origin,
like Trajan, Sura, Servianus, Cornelius Palma and the unknown of Dessau
1019 (? Annius Verus).

[2] There is nothing in Dio Chrysostom, the philosophic mouthpiece of
the Trajanic régime, to commend such a principle: indeed the suggestions
of *Or.* III, 119 seem even to favour a dynastic succession.

of the succeeding emperors at least preserved Rome for nearly
a hundred years from the whims of heredity; and a new standard
was set in the government. Empire and liberty were reconciled.
It was not the liberty of the Republic. That could now never
return and can hardly have been regretted by the existing Senate.
But the liberalism of Nerva was a reaction valuable and indeed
essential to the safe working of the administrative system. If
imperial forbearance did lead at first to a few cases of senatorial
misgovernment, the provinces benefited on the whole from the
assurance of peaceful conditions; and it is impossible to doubt
the accumulated evidence of the contentment and prosperity of
the Empire in the succeeding years.

II. TRAJAN: *PRINCEPS* AND *SENATUS*

The news of his accession reached Trajan at Cologne after a
race of messengers, won by his cousin and future successor
P. Aelius Hadrianus. The Emperor, however, despite popular
appeal[1], did not return to Rome at once. The removal of Aelianus
and the leaders of the praetorian outbreak was a sufficient assurance of peace at home and there was work to be completed on the
German frontier. The months since his adoption had given Trajan
time to think out an imperial policy, of which the leading idea,
shaped in part perhaps by the financial needs of the Empire, was
a rehandling of the Dacian problem. But even to re-assert Roman
prestige effectively on the middle and lower Danube demanded
careful preparation, and in particular an organization of the Rhine
and upper Danube provinces which should enable reinforcements
to be sent, if needed, for a Dacian campaign; and this, owing to
the progress made on these frontiers under the Flavians, it was
now possible to achieve. Trajan, therefore, contented himself with
letters of goodwill to the Senate, which included an oath to abstain
from tyranny, and a refusal of the title of *pater patriae*[2], and remained in the north until 99. In the spring of that year he set
out for Rome, and after a journey which was in deliberate contrast
to Domitian's exigent progressions, he entered the city on foot
amid enthusiastic demonstrations from all classes of the citizens.

---

[1] Martial x, 6; 7. Pliny, *Pan.* 22. Cf. for coins, P. L. Strack, *Die
Reichsprägung zur Zeit des Traians*, pp. 76–9 and Volume of Plates, v, 126.

[2] Pliny, *Pan.* 21, corroborated by its absence from coins. But see *ib.* 57
and Strack, *op. cit.* p. 20 *sq.* for evidence that he had accepted the title by
October 98. All coins, however, bear the title of *pontifex maximus*, Strack,
op. cit. p. 22, n. 50.

The difficulties which beset any attempt to summarize and appraise the events of Trajan's reign are, in the main, of two kinds. The first and greatest is the inadequacy of the literary sources. It is the historian deprived of their help who is least contemptuous of the value of Suetonius and the *Historia Augusta*, as he bitterly recalls the famous lament of Gibbon (who himself did not attempt the task) that he must 'collect the actions of Trajan from the glimmerings of an abridgement or the doubtful light of a panegyric.' The sixty-eighth book of Cassius Dio's history, as preserved mainly in the eleventh-century epitome of Xiphilinus, is indeed the corner-stone of any reconstruction of the reign; but it is not of a material which any prudent builder would choose. The *Panegyric* of Pliny, delivered during his consulship in 100, is a tolerable authority for events down to that date, and facts of importance can be gleaned from his letters, and especially from the official correspondence which he conducted with Trajan as governor of Bithynia in 111–113. For the rest the historian must be content with a sentence of Trajan's own commentaries on the Dacian war, a fable of the Emperor Julian, and a number of scattered references, most of them of doubtful value, and of a later age. He has, however, one advantage denied to Gibbon. The epigraphical evidence for the reign is comparatively abundant, and with the help of the coins[1] makes a fairly full chronological reconstruction possible. The second difficulty is one of judgment. Unlike Domitian, Trajan was popular with the class from which contemporary writers were drawn, and, unlike him, he was succeeded by one who, though in many ways the antithesis of himself, was favourable to his memory. The tradition is therefore almost wholly laudatory[2]. The example of Domitian and his own temperament preserved Trajan from the grosser forms of adulation; but flatterers soon found a way to please him too, and there are passages in the *Panegyric* of Pliny with which a Martial or a Statius would have been proud to charm Domitian's palate. Dio merely echoes the verdict of the contemporary tradition, and is, for example, at pains to gloss over even Trajan's private vices[3]. The praise of Trajan was the corollary of the vilification of Domitian, and there is no doubt that the pendulum swung too far. But a modern

---

[1] The evidence of the coins is particularly rich for this reign and has recently been brilliantly arranged and discussed by Strack, *op. cit.*

[2] For an exception see *Or. Sibyll.* xii; a Jew would have the best of reasons for not approving of Trajan.

[3] Drink and boys, Dio LXVIII, 7; Nerva was also reproached with *vinolentia*, Aurelius Victor, *Caes.* XIII, 10 (unsupported).

critic must be on his guard lest in redressing the balance he make the contrary error. Trajan was popular in his lifetime and his memory remained green, and that in an age which, like Tacitus' own, is *infensa virtutibus* is hard to forgive; for him, as for Agricola, his laudators have proved a *pessimum genus inimicorum*.

Early in September of the year 100, the younger Pliny, newly elected consul, rose in the Senate to render public thanks for his election. It was a great opportunity. The recent consulship of Trajan, the first since becoming emperor, had shed a brighter lustre on his successors in his year; and no doubt a splendid contribution was expected from an orator of Pliny's standing. The new consul apologized for his inadequacy, but he did not scamp his theme. For several hours the Senate listened while Pliny expounded the virtues of the reigning prince, the misdeeds of Domitian, and his ideals of the imperial government. The spirits of the reader, far removed from the circumstances of the time, may flag beneath the reiterations of his panegyric, but of his sincerity there can be no doubt; and for many of his facts there is evidence more concrete than his own polished phrases. At about the same time the philosopher Dio Chrysostom delivered before Trajan the first of his sermons upon kingship, in striking accord with the tone of Pliny's speech[1], and from a comparison of the two the ideals of the new régime emerge in sharp outline. Both paint the *princeps* as the first servant of the State, but neither is under any illusion as to the supremacy of his position over all other parties to the government. The difference between *dominatio* and *principatus*, stressed by both Dio and Pliny[2], lay in the distinction between a master and a leader. The spearhead of the hatred against Domitian had been not his power, but his misuse of it. It was the capacity for leadership which Trajan possessed and which Domitian so conspicuously lacked which enabled him to carry through many of Domitian's political aims with the approval and even at the request of the senators themselves.

The career of Trajan as a *privatus* had indeed simplified his task. His own choice of a soldier's life was no doubt responsible for the length of his service as a *tribunus militum* (see p. 136);

---

[1] The character of Dio's speech as a philosophical discourse precluded him from the direct address of Pliny, but he himself took care that his reference to Trajan should not be missed, *Or.* 1, 36.

[2] *E.g.* Dio Chrys. *Or.* 1, 22, cf. *Or.* III, 48; *Pan.* 2, 24, 45, 63–5. Pliny's address of Trajan as 'domine' in his letters should not be stressed as inconsistent. In the epistolary vocative it had probably become only the normal address of an inferior to a superior official. Cf. Dessau 5795. See p. 412, n. 8.

from his father's son no more than the statutory minimum would
have been required. He thus learnt the frontiers and the conditions of military service as a subordinate, and even later, though
he had personal knowledge of the tyranny in Rome[1], much of his
time had been spent abroad. Naturally easy of access, he had
already firmly planted his hold on the legions, and at the same
time his years of absence had set him a little apart from the gossip
and intrigue of senatorial circles at Rome: in Pliny's speech and
early letters, if one makes all allowances for the circumstances of
their composition, there is something of a stranger's tone. But
any doubts in Rome of his deportment were quickly resolved on
his arrival. He made no claims to divine honours and showed
himself as reluctant as the senators to participate in the ceremonies
of royalty. The swaying palanquin, with its imperious outriders,
the embracing of the emperor's feet, the kissing of his hand,
and all the degrading symbols of an Oriental monarchy (p. 43),
remained only as the memory of an evil dream. The palace, over
which Nerva had inscribed the words 'publicae aedes,' was so in
fact, in contrast to that 'specus' in which an 'inmanissima belua'
had licked the blood of his kinsmen and meditated the slaughter of
the chief men in the State. The chilly receptions at which Domitian
had disdained even to eat with his compulsory guests were replaced by friendly informal gatherings at which a man might say
what he liked and could attend or not as he pleased.

Trajan himself was far from greedy of worldly honours: the
fame he coveted was above trifles. The celebrated epigram of the
Emperor Constantine which described Trajan as a *herba parietaria*
has been used to convey a false impression since the days of
Ammianus Marcellinus, who first interpreted it to mean that
Trajan deliberately suppressed the memorials of earlier builders;
in the original phrase there is no more than a humorous reference
to the extent of his public works in Rome[2]. On the other hand,
in at least one case we have epigraphical evidence that he conformed to ordinary standards[3]; and his existing inscriptions show
an attitude the reverse of vainglorious. He had refused to hold
the consulship in absence in 99; his tenure in 100, attended with
a strict adherence to traditional forms habitually flouted by his
predecessors, was a natural corollary of his return, and he
signalized it by elevating in the same year two others to a like
number of consulships with himself. In 101 he was persuaded,

[1] *Pan.* 44, 72. See above, p. 197.
[2] Aurelius Victor, *Epit.* XLI, 13; Ammian. Marc. XXVII, 3, 7.
[3] *C.I.L.* VI, 1275, cf. D. R. Stuart, *Class. Phil.* III, 1908, p. 59.

according to Pliny for this reason among others, to hold a fourth: but he added only two more, in 103 after the first Dacian war and lastly in 112, the year of the inauguration of his forum. Thirteen salutations make a modest showing for a martial emperor beside the twenty-two of Domitian or the twenty-seven of Claudius, and as for the name of Optimus, already in public use by 100[1], he did not permit its inclusion among his official titles for nearly fifteen years: the titles of censor and *praefectus morum* he refused outright.

Trajan was wise. By his openheartedness and natural manners he won the love of the two most influential classes in the State: the soldiers and the Senate. His soldiers he knew to their nicknames and he commanded their unquestioning loyalty: to Pliny he was 'one of us,' and by a scrupulous observance of senatorial customs he bound their affection still more closely. He was thus enabled on the one hand to tighten the discipline of the army and on the other to pursue his political ends without serious discontent[2]. The Senate indeed recognized its incapacity to govern. Vastly changed in personnel since Julio-Claudian days, it now contained few of a type not ready to follow the imperial lead, content with the position of superior civil servant, and under Domitian it had still further lost its power of initiative. His reign left behind it a rising generation of senators unversed in the arts of government and unfitted for responsibility[3]. Time was needed for their recovery to a sense of their own dignity, before they could rise to high ideals of public service. Watched by Domitian, the provincial governors had behaved particularly well; to afford him just excuse for severity was simple suicide. But the indulgent policy of Nerva brought a quick reaction in a crop of provincial scandals. If the Senate had learnt anything from recent experience, it was a sense of solidarity. Menaced together and forced to pass sentence on each other against their judgment, they were in no mood for fresh convictions now, even if the offence were plainly proved; and weak or rapacious governors were not slow to take advantage of this expectation of leniency.

---

[1] *Pan.* 2, 91. Cf. R. P. Longden in *J.R.S.* XXI, 1931, p. 10, n. 4. For other examples of his modesty, see *e.g. Pan.* 20, 21, 24, 45, 52, 54–60, 83–4.

[2] Trace of conspiracies, in which apparently Crassus (p. 196) was again concerned, is found in Dio LXVIII, 5, 16; S.H.A. *Hadr.* 5. One of these attempts, perhaps that of Laberius Maximus, may have been serious enough to justify the award of the title *pia fidelis* to leg. I Adiutrix, cf. Ritterling, *P.W.*, *s.v.* legio, col. 1389.

[3] Cf. Tac. *Agr.* 3, Plin. *Ep.* VIII, 14.

During the next five years the services of Pliny as advocate were retained in at least four trials for provincial misgovernment[1]. In the first three the chief offenders had all received their nominations under Nerva; all were guilty of corruption and two at least, Marius Priscus (a Spaniard) in Africa and Caecilius Classicus (an African) in Spain, of callous brutality as well, while the iniquities of Julius Bassus in Bithynia are less clearly known since Pliny himself was for the defence on this occasion. The results were not re-assuring. Under Trajan's personal presidency in 100 the Senate did pass the harsher of the two sentences proposed on Priscus[2], but in other cases they were as complaisant as they dared. Classicus died before his trial, but in the subsequent proceedings against his subordinates senatorial defendants received marked favour, and Bassus though found guilty retained his full rights on the mere repayment of damages. The fourth case, also from Bithynia, ended in confusion and a promise from Trajan to investigate conditions in the province, a promise which ultimately matured in the special appointment of Pliny as an imperial governor. The criticism of these decisions even within the Senate aided Trajan's efforts to secure more capable administration without impairing senatorial prestige. Bithynia at least had been not only corruptly but inefficiently governed by men whose annual terms of office were inadequate for a proper understanding of its problems. The impunity of a few guilty proconsuls was a small matter if the Senate should voluntarily acquiesce in a closer imperial control of their provinces.

But it was not here alone that senatorial shortcomings were manifest. Their conduct of elections showed a like sacrifice of public interests to personal friendships and advantage, while some were even too worthless to discharge their duty with dignity. This was the upshot of depriving an assembly with still considerable legal rights and administrative duties of all actual responsibility. Their present unfitness and necessary dependence Pliny sadly admits, while he is not ashamed to appreciate the crumbs of government which Trajan let fall to the Senate[3]. Trajan's power, in fact, was no less complete than had been that of Domitian; only the spirit of its exercise was different. Not only had he renounced divine honours; he had admitted the supremacy of

---

[1] Pliny, *Ep.* II, 11; III, 9; IV, 9; V, 20; VII, 6, 10; for the dates, cf. A. von Premerstein, *Bay.S.B.* 1934, 3, pp. 72–86.

[2] Though even that was too mild; cf. Juvenal I, 49.

[3] Pliny, *Ep.* III, 20; IV, 25; cf. also III, 7; V, 13 (14); VI, 19; IX, 2.

the laws over the emperor's will[1]. He counted senators his friends
and recognized the influence of their prestige; and by consulting
them on imperial issues even while retaining the decision in his
own hands aimed at reconciling them to a position in some ways
parallel to that of his judicial *consilium*. His firm control of the
army banished fears of a military tyranny. Life and property
were safe. In short he had given the upper classes of the Roman
world a new deal: and they were prepared to follow his lead[2].

III. PUBLIC WORKS, FINANCE, SOCIAL POLICY

In his third oration on kingship Dio Chrysostom concludes
his account of the ideal ruler by the following summary of his
activities; 'he reviews an army, subdues a province, founds a city,
bridges rivers and builds roads.' Trajan's military career must
be the subject of a separate chapter: but a survey of the administration of one who earned a reputation as a great builder may
fairly begin with his public works. At Rome, the early years
were not spectacular. Pliny describes the Emperor as 'parcus in
aedificando'; though it is true that he is referring mainly to private
building for imperial use, of which Domitian had been lavish.
But beyond the vague mention of *porticus* and *delubra* he can
find nothing to record except the well-known restoration and
extension of the Circus Maximus[3]. It is possible that the repair
of the temple of Augustus, which is mainly, if not entirely, Domitian's work, was not completed till 101[4]: and tolerably certain
that a temple of Nerva was at least begun by 100[5]. Coins of 100
show a triumphal arch, which is now generally identified with
the so-called Arch of Drusus on the Via Appia, of which it perhaps commemorated the partial reconstruction completed in this

---

[1] *Nunc primum disco, non est 'princeps supra leges' sed 'leges supra principem,' idemque Caesari consuli quod ceteris non licet,* Pliny, *Pan.* 65.

[2] For the immense influence of the imperial example in both private and
public life, cf. Tacitus, *Ann.* III, 55; Pliny, *Pan.* 44, 45.

[3] The work was evidently not finished when Pliny wrote: Dessau 286,
which appears to record the same extension, belongs to 103; and with this
date the commemorative coins agree. Cf. Strack, *op. cit.* pp. 145 *sqq.*

[4] Platner-Ashby, pp. 62–3, 84. The Odeum too, which is called one
of Apollodorus' greatest achievements, may have undergone some changes,
though it is substantially Domitianic, Dio LXIX, 4, 1; cf. Pausanias, V,
12, 6.

[5] *Pan.* 11; Strack, *op. cit.* pp. 147 *sqq.*, thinks he can recognize it on coins
of about 103–4. A third unidentified temple is recorded on coins of the same
period.

year, just as the arch at Beneventum later marked the Via
Traiana. The other undertakings for which an early date is confirmed were of a more general utility. The series of terminal stones
of the years 101 and 103 bear witness to fresh activity in the
department of the *curator alvei et riparum Tiberis*, and in the
former year for the first time the addition *et cloacarum urbis* is
found in the title of the curator. The danger to Rome from flood,
which was the special concern of this office, was further met by
the construction of a canal to carry off the flood water; its precise
date and locality, however, are still uncertain[1]. Meanwhile a
similar energy was shown by the office of the *cura aquarum*.
Besides minor improvements, the Anio Novus was extended at
its source to tap fresh and better supplies, and the Marcia within
the city in order to serve the Aventine. These changes initiated
by Nerva were completed in the early years of Trajan's reign.

But the greater part by far of his work in Rome belongs to
the period between the Dacian and Parthian wars. In 109 the
Baths on the Oppian, the Aqua Traiana, and the Naumachia were
dedicated and opened to public use[2]. For the first of these Trajan's
great architect Apollodorus used a space adjoining the Baths of
Titus on the site of the former *domus aurea* of Nero[3]; the Naumachia were probably situated on the right bank of the Tiber
near the castle of S. Angelo and fed by the Aqua Traiana, which
brought water from the lake of Bracciano to serve mainly the
industrial quarter of Trastevere[4]. Other baths, adjoining his
house on the Aventine, were bequeathed to the Roman people
by Licinius Sura on his death about 110[5]. In 113 the temple of
Venus in the Forum of Caesar was re-opened[6]; but a theatre in the
Campus Martius which Hadrian is said to have pulled down probably never got beyond an early stage of construction[7]. All these
works were, however, dwarfed by the great Forum Traiani, the
largest and most splendid of the imperial Fora, and the marvel
of succeeding ages, which was dedicated by Trajan in January,

[1] Dessau 5797*a* (after 102). It was only partially successful, cf. Pliny,
Ep. VIII, 17.
[2] *Ann. épig.* 1934, no. 30, the new Fasti Ostienses, on which in general
cf. Ch. Hülsen, *Rh. Mus.* LXXXII, 1933, p. 362.
[3] Probably further damaged by fire in 104, Jerome, *Chron.* ad. ann. 2120.
[4] Dessau 290; Strack *op. cit.* pp. 192–4.
[5] Cf. Groag, in P.W. *s.v.* Licinius (167) Sura, col. 481 *sq.*
[6] *Ann. épig.* 1934, no. 30. The elaborate restoration of this temple may
have been at least begun by Domitian; see below, p. 781.
[7] S.H.A. *Hadr.* 9. A temple to Fortuna, mentioned only by Lydus
(*de mens.* IV, 7), is still unidentified.

112 (p. 781 *sq.*). The complete group of buildings filled a space
some five times as great as the Forum of Augustus, and contained
the Basilica Ulpia, two libraries, the Column of Trajan and the
temple of Trajan and Plotina, erected by Hadrian. The architect
of the group was Apollodorus. The forum itself, rectangular in
shape, was surrounded on three sides by a marble colonnade
pierced on the south-east by an entrance arch which was still in
process of construction during the Parthian wars. On the long
sides it was flanked by semicircular courts built against and into
the slope of the Capitoline and Quirinal hills. For the buildings
which surrounded these courts considerable excavation was
necessary, and it is probably this work which was proclaimed in
the dedicatory inscription at the base of the column[1]. The column
itself, 100 feet high[2] and of Parian marble, was entirely covered
by a spiral frieze commemorating the Dacian wars (p. 225);
it was surmounted by a statue of the Emperor, and afterwards
housed his ashes.

The communications of Italy, both external and internal, were
one of Trajan's main concerns in his attempt to buttress her
economic structure; and here, too, a similar distinction between
the earlier and later parts of his reign is apparent. The re-making
of the Via Appia, begun by Nerva, was continued and by 100 was
complete as far as the 48th milestone at Forum Appii. From this
point the difficulties were more serious and further work was
postponed. Milestones also record repairs on the Via Aemilia in
100, Puteolana in 102 (begun by Nerva), Sublacensis in 103–5
and Latina in 105 (restoration of a bridge over the Liris). More
substantial work was undertaken after the Dacian wars. The Via
Appia was completed by the building of a sound road through the
Pomptine marshes, the stretch from Forum Appii to Terracina,
in 110. The Via Salaria was repaired in 111, the Latina further
in 115, and a bridge on the Flaminia in the same year. In 108
a series of improvements was carried out on the Clodian-Cassian
group of roads leading through Etruria; these alterations bore
the title of Tres Traianae or Traiana Nova. Of greater significance, however, was the Via Traiana itself and the harbours
which Trajan built on both coasts of Italy. The Via Traiana
diverged from the Appia at Beneventum and ran through Canossa
and Bari to Brindisi. A road here had existed since Republican

---

[1] Dessau 294. The restoration of the inscription has been much disputed.
Cf. the references in Platner-Ashby, *op. cit.* pp. 238, 242.
[2] With the pedestal the total height was 128 feet.

times[1], but it was now entirely re-made and perhaps first numbered among the public roads of Italy at this time. The milestones, of which some thirty have been found, bear the date 109[2]. Of the harbours, that of Ostia, which alone is represented on the coins, was the most important. Trajan's work here was an extension and improvement of that of Claudius[3], which still failed to provide adequate shelter for shipping. An interior basin was excavated, hexagonal in shape, and surrounded with buildings; and round the two harbours, the Claudian and the Trajanic, a town grew up and ultimately became independent of Ostia, which itself shows traces of Trajanic work. Farther north new harbours at Centumcellae and Ancona, built after the Dacian wars, filled a need on both western and eastern coasts; the dedicatory arch at Ancona, of A.D. 115, bears words which echo the purpose of all Trajan's work in Italy, 'quod accessum Italiae, hoc etiam addito ex pecunia sua portu, tutiorem navigantibus reddidit[4].' Of rather less importance was a similar restoration at Terracina, connected with the earlier phase of the work on the Via Appia[5]. Between 115–7 reclamation was undertaken on the shores of the Fucine lake, and the Claudian drainage system was probably overhauled; and undated traces of fresh work or repairs to aqueducts are recorded from various parts of the peninsula[6].

The wealth of public buildings in the provinces reflects no doubt the influence of Trajan's example; but to determine his actual share is another matter. For not every dedication—in Trajan's case they were legion—marks gratitude for a particular beneficence[7].

---

[1] It was followed without approval by Horace in 37 B.C. (*Sat.* I, 5).

[2] It is not commemorated on coins before 112; but it is by no means a certain inference that it was not completed before that date. *C.I.L.* IX, 37 records a dedication to Trajan by the city of Brindisi in 110. The earliest known *curator* was Q. Roscius Caelius Pompeius Falco, between 110 and 116 (Dessau 1036). As a consular, he was probably the first holder of the office. For the course of the road see T. Ashby and R. Gardner, *B.S.R.* VIII, 1917, pp. 104–171.

[3] Vol. x, p. 689. The coins are not earlier than 112 (Strack, *op. cit.* p. 213).   [4] Dessau 298.

[5] Dessau 282 (before 103). It is perhaps this to which Pliny refers in *Pan.* 29. A new harbour at Ariminum is even more dubious (R. Paribeni, *Optimus Princeps*, II, p. 119).

[6] Centumcellae (contemporary with the harbour), Forum Clodium (probably about 109), Subiaco, Talamone near Orbetello (after 103) and perhaps Ravenna.

[7] The city of Lyttus in Crete, for example, put up at least one annually for years—and to Plotina and Marciana (Trajan's wife and sister) also, *I.G.R.R.* I, 982–999. The usual phrase is τῷ κτίστῃ τῆς οἰκουμένης: direct benefits are generally marked by τῷ ἰδίῳ κτίστῃ or the like.

The Bithynian letters of Pliny show how forward the Greek cities were themselves in building, and much was due also to private donors who would generally include the emperor in their dedications. We stand indeed on the threshold of an age of unparalleled generosity[1], in which rich men counted it an honour to spend money for the service of their city. This public spirit was directly fostered by the emperors, by example, exhortation and edict. Nerva made it legal for cities to receive legacies; Trajan enacted that what a man promised to his city he must perform, and the obligation descended to his heir. Where Trajan was himself concerned, his motive, as in Italy, was public utility—roads, bridges, harbours, aqueducts. Milestones bear witness to roadmaking in nearly every province, and their dates permit some narrower conclusions. In Spain, for example, they are especially numerous and early (98–105; but mostly 98–100). They reflect no doubt Trajan's interest in the land of his origin, and probably still more the needs which he had observed as a legionary legate under Domitian. Some roads, notably those from Asturica to Emerita (98–9) and to Caesaraugusta (100) seem to have been entirely re-made[2]. It is clear that orders to repair the Spanish road system were among the first which he issued as emperor.

The stones from the German provinces date from instructions given before his return to Rome in 99; the Numidian roads belong mostly to 100–1 and 104–5 and are a corollary of the founding of Thamugadi, the encirclement of the Aurès and the removal of the camp of leg. III Augusta to Lambaesis within this period (p. 147). The work in Cappadocia was a continuation of that of the Flavians and Nerva; in Arabia (p. 238), Dacia (p. 232) and Mesopotamia (p. 247) it was the natural result of annexation; and this applies indirectly to the other Danube provinces. The rest seems on the present evidence to have been merely the answer to general instructions to see that the efficiency of the roads was maintained. Among other works the great bridges at Drobetae over the Danube, built by Apollodorus about 104, and at Alcantara over the Tagus by Julius Lacer in 105 take precedence over others near Simitthu in Africa, in Spain and elsewhere; aqueducts are recorded at Iader in Dalmatia, Miletus, Smyrna, Antioch, and in Arabia and Egypt, and harbour works at Ephesus[3]: in Egypt an old canal between the Nile and Red Sea

[1] M. Rostovtzeff, *Soc. and Econ. Hist.* pp. 141 *sq.*, 522.

[2] Most but not all of the roads belong to the western and north-western parts of Spain.

[3] The presence at Ephesus at the time (103–114) of a man who had earlier been *prom. portuum prov. Sic.* may be noted, Dessau 7193.

was reopened to traffic, and acquired the name of 'Trajan's river[1].'
The private enterprise of the period, where it can be dated, belongs
mainly to the period between the Dacian and Parthian wars,
no doubt fulfilling many vows undertaken for the Emperor's
success in Dacia.

Something more drastic, however, than the mere improvement
of communications was needed to restore the prosperity of Italy
and to enable her to maintain her position of supremacy within
the empire; and the dominant character of the measures now
inaugurated was an interest in the rising generation. The creation
of trust funds for child maintenance was not a new thing in the
Roman world. At least as early as the principate of Claudius or
Nero, one T. Helvius Basila had provided a sum of 400,000
sesterces for maintenance grants at Atina and for the presentation
of 1000 sesterces to each child on coming of age[2]: and it is likely
that under the Flavians there were similar private benefactions
of which no record has survived. It may indeed have been in
Domitian's time that the younger Pliny made his provision for
the people of Comum[3]. His method was to saddle an estate of
his, worth half a million sesterces or more, with a perpetual
charge of 30,000 a year; and this sum, paid annually to the local
authority, was to be distributed in *alimenta* to free-born boys
and girls. The adoption of such a scheme by the State was one
of Nerva's remedial measures for Italy undertaken in A.D. 97.
The details and progress of his plan, however, are unknown,
and the first local evidence belongs to the principate of Trajan.

In A.D. 101 a grant was made to the Ligures Baebiani near
Beneventum, and in the same year the citizens of Florence co-opted
T. Pomponius Bassus as a patron of their municipality in return
for the way in which he had carried out similar duties as a commissioner in their district[4]. Pomponius re-appears in the so-called
Table of Veleia, which supplies fuller evidence of the system
employed[5]. The *fiscus* provided the funds in the form of credit
to local landowners, who charged certain of their estates in return
with a perpetual interest of 5 p.c. on the sum received from the
fiscus: this interest was used for maintenance grants to local
children in need. The scale of payments has been preserved:
boys received more than girls, sixteen sesterces a month against
twelve, and more than seven times as many were supported; such

---

[1] Ptol. IV, 5.   [2] Dessau 977.

[3] Pliny, *Ep.* I, 8; VII, 18.   [4] Dessau 6509, 6106.

[5] Dessau 6675, dated between 103–114, but incorporating the results of
at least one earlier scheme.

details, subject to a general recommendation from the government, were perhaps left to local initiative. The children of Rome were also assisted by enrolment in the lists of those qualified to receive the distributions of free corn within the city, and by A.D. 100 some five thousand had already been enrolled[1]. Pliny underlines the object of these grants, the encouragement of free Roman citizens to beget and bring up children, the *spes Romani nominis*. His special reference is to the City, but his sentiments have a wider application, and they find an echo in the monuments and on the coins of the reign. Already in the earlier years (but after 103) the Spes issue, both by Senate and *princeps*, refers to the hopes which were founded on the alimentary system[2], but from 108 onwards, Trajan's decennial year, when the first generation of recipients was already growing to manhood, the coins celebrate the scheme more directly in the series stamped ALIM(ENTATIO) ITAL(IAE) and ITAL(IA) REST(ITUTA), and in both it is the assistance to children which the design emphasizes. Two reliefs from the arch of Beneventum and one from a balustrade in the Forum Romanum illustrate the same theme (p. 788).

The united testimony of the evidence, written, sculptural, and numismatic, compels the inference that the main purpose of the alimentary scheme was the encouragement of population. But whether convenience was the only reason for the form of security chosen is more questionable. If the loans made to farmers were on easier terms than they could otherwise obtain, the system also provided valuable assistance to Italian agriculture. The rate of interest given on the Baebian table is $2\frac{1}{2}$ per cent., which is of course inordinately low, but it is possible that this represents a half-yearly payment; a 5 per cent. rate is quoted at Veleia. Even this, however, the farmers may have been glad to accept; Pliny's thirty thousand on an estate worth half a million indicates a rate of 6 per cent. and some Veleian landowners may indeed have found it difficult to obtain money on any practicable terms. This is, however, a conjecture based on the assumption that depression in Italian agriculture was widespread. The evidence of Pliny's letters and further enactments of Trajan indeed suggest that in certain districts at least this was so, and the absence of a proper circulation of capital was perhaps partly to blame[3]. In

---

[1] Pliny, *Pan.* 25–8. They also ranked for the receipt of *congiaria*.

[2] Cf. also the AETERNITAS issue, and Dessau 6106, *cura...qua aeternitati Italiae suae prospexit*.

[3] Pliny, who was a wealthy man and able to raise fresh capital at need, has no hesitation in continuing to purchase real estate; and the fact that he

that event, the provision of what amounted to cheap agricultural credits was an additional and important merit of the scheme. A rather different view would see here an attempt, concurrently with the effort to check depopulation, to restore the cultivation of the soil, and the evidence of early imperial grants comes from areas where *saltus* predominated. It is plain that some at least of the Veleian loans were taken up by rich men who could easily have raised capital in the open market, and it is possible that the credits were earmarked for land reclamation, and that direct encouragement was given to farmers to undertake this service to the community. The provisions of the Henchir Mettich inscription show Trajan's keenness on such work in his own African estates[1]. The progress of the distribution was gradual, nor was the scheme fully developed even locally at first. Either, as seems probable, the *fiscus* was enabled after the Dacian wars to provide funds on a more generous scale, or if the plan was made to depend on the willingness of the local farmers to accept the loans, the demand increased as its advantages were perceived or greater pressure was brought to bear. If the whole of Italy was provided for, the cost to the government must have been enormous; but in some places it was relieved by private generosity and no doubt the most necessitous areas were dealt with first. The expense of organization appears to have been borne by the local authority; at least at Veleia the whole of the cash returns were absorbed in the distributions themselves, and from now onwards the title of *quaestor alimentorum* appears among the local officials. A general control was, however, maintained by the central government, which delegated the duties where possible to the senatorial curators of the public roads.

If, among Trajan's measures for the recovery of Italy, *alimenta* and public works took pride of place, they did not stand alone. The obligation enforced on senators to have at least one-third of their capital invested in Italian land had the effect of at any rate temporarily raising the value of such property, though it is doubtful whether this was the Emperor's primary motive for the order[2]. Some Italian cities were probably reinforced by settlements of veterans[3] and it is possible that emigration from Italy

regards the estate previously mentioned as a desirable property in spite of its charge shows that from it at least a return higher than 6 per cent. might be expected.

[1] Bruns, *Fontes*[7] 114, cf. J. Carcopino, *Rev. Ét. Anc.* XXIII, 1921, p. 287.

[2] Pliny, *Ep.* VI, 19.   [3] Rostovtzeff, *op. cit.* p. 587, n. 6.

was forbidden[1]. Finally an attempt was made to check the mismanagement of their own affairs by Italian cities by the appointment of special curators (p. 219).

In the further assistance from the relief of certain taxes, the provincials as well as the Italians shared. The *aurum coronarium*, a provincial contribution on the accession of a new *princeps*, was remitted; and with a similar aim certain reliefs seem to have been made in the compulsory services and contributions levied from the provincials. The *fiscus* also renounced its claim to the goods of those condemned to relegation, and the virtual abolition of trials for *maiestas* deprived it of what had whether by accident or design been in the past a steady source of income. The exemptions from the succession duty which Nerva had made were further extended. Sons were now free whether *in patria potestate* or not, as were fathers, grand-parents and brothers. The minimum was raised and certain deductions allowed for in arriving at the net figure for assessment; and lastly the provisions were made retrospective, thus absolving a large number of recent heirs from accumulated debt. It is this, perhaps, which is commemorated on the second of the two balustrades in the Forum Romanum (see below, p. 788).

The citizens of Rome itself were the recipients of even greater indulgence. Pliny's emphasis in the *Panegyric* is proof of Trajan's concern with the proper working of the corn supply. The additional granaries of Nerva and his programme of public works had this end in view, and it was furthered by Trajan's improvements at Ostia. Meanwhile the situation was not such as to prevent him from relieving a serious famine in Egypt in 99 by calling on the accumulated grain reserves in Rome[2]. Special concessions were made to the bakers of the city, who were besides allowed to form a college (no doubt under close supervision) and the transporters may have received some though not all of these privileges[3]. The admission of children to the corn distributions

---

[1] If this is the right inference from S.H.A. *Marcus*, 11, 7, which remains very doubtful. Cf. Rostovtzeff, *op. cit.* p. 523, n. 34, and 585, n. 2; Ritterling, in P.W. *s.v.* legio, col. 1300.

[2] The duties of T. Flavius Macer, *curator frumenti comparandi in annona urbis factus a divo Nerva Traiano Aug.*, Dessau 1435, *Ann. épig.* 1922, no. 19, which seem to have been unusual, were perhaps connected with this failure, or more probably the disturbances in Egypt in 116–7.

[3] They were not exempted from the *tutela*. *Dig.* XXVII, 1, 17, 6. For the *pistores*, Aurelius Victor, *Caes.* XIII, 5; Gaius I, 34; Ulpian, *Frag. Vat.* 233. The formation of a college was not an unmixed advantage to them, since the government could control their operations more efficiently.

and *congiaria* has already been mentioned; the sum total of the latter, however, rose under Trajan to an unprecedented height, though even this was surpassed by later emperors. Trajan gave at least three *congiaria*, the first on his return to Rome in 99, the second and third in 102 and 107 after his two Dacian wars. The normal sum distributed on such occasions was 75 denarii a head to those qualified for grant, and the silence of Pliny proves that this sum was not exceeded in 99. The total of Trajan's generosity reached the figure, according to our only authority[1], of 650 denarii; but the first two distributions are recorded only in the senatorial coinage, while the third is accompanied by a special imperial issue with the motif of *Liberalitas*. It is a reasonable assumption that this, celebrating the final victory over Dacia and its annexation, completes the series and was of extraordinary size: the figures ran perhaps 75 in 99 and 102 and 500 in 107.

It is usual to condemn the *congiaria* off-hand as an unwarrantable indulgence to the pampered populace of Rome; there is, however, something to be said on the other side. The prevalence of poverty in Rome is an undeniable fact, and it is likely that it was amongst the free-born citizens that it was most widespread. The revival of land-allotment, which Nerva had attempted, had fatal practical objections, the monthly dole was a palliative and provided no permanent solution, while the small *congiaria* previously distributed were little better, welcome as no doubt they were. A substantial outright grant, however, if wisely expended, would enable many to rise above subsistence level, and like the *alimenta* it represented the hope of creating a population eventually independent of public charity. But if the figure given be correct, the cost would absorb some two-thirds of a year's total state revenue[2], and it must next be considered whether the state of the imperial exchequer could justify so large an expenditure at this time.

The bulk of expenditure so far recorded follows the Dacian wars. It is highly unlikely that any of the great works finished in 108–113 was begun before 106: without delays such as strikes and under the present direction of an eager author they would certainly be pushed on quickly. Their completion was signalized in nearly every case by extensive games, of which the new frag-

---

[1] Chronog. of 354 in Mommsen, *Chronica minora*, I, p. 146; and see below p. 216, n. 1.

[2] It may have been considerably more if Strack (*op. cit.* pp. 83–8) is right in maintaining that there were two lists and that a *congiarium* was received by many who were not qualified for the corn distributions.

ments of the Fasti Ostienses have provided some particulars. Dio (LXVIII, 15) relates that on Trajan's return to Rome in 107 public entertainments were held over a period of 123 days in which ten thousand gladiators took part and eleven thousand animals were killed. The celebrations of the next five years were scarcely less lavish. We know too little of the expense of the games to estimate the total cost with any accuracy: but it is noteworthy that in the eight exhibitions given by Augustus during his principate at different times, a total of about 10,000 gladiators took part. This figure was equalled by Trajan in the games of 107 alone, and between 106 and 114 over 23,000 performers appear to have fought[1]. The Emperor, whose favourite recreation was hunting, was notoriously fond of the games and his exhibitions no doubt added to his popularity; and besides these displays *ludi Herculei* were instituted at Rome, and founders of provincial games might be sure of the Emperor's approval[2].

This orgy of spending from 107 onwards, on buildings, games, *congiaria* (and probably a donative) and *alimenta* suggests very powerfully the recent acquisition of much ready money; and there is evidence available to confirm the suggestion. In the *de Magistratibus* (II, 28) Johannes Lydus quotes Trajan's doctor, T. Statilius Crito[3], who accompanied him to Dacia, for the statement that Trajan brought back 5 million pounds weight of gold, the double of silver, besides a prodigious quantity of other plunder and over 500,000 very bellicose prisoners with their arms. Crito is good authority, but these figures are frankly impossible; a simple palaeographical error has however been alleged for their multiplication tenfold in transmission[4]. Divided by ten, the results are still striking. The fifty thousand warlike prisoners may easily have provided for the shows; and in effect Trajan had received in addition a cash windfall of the value of 2250 million sesterces in gold alone, together with about 430 million in silver (on the existing standard) besides the worth of the other articles. This total, of at least 2700 million sesterces, is considerably greater

---

[1] If, however, the reference were to the number of appearances rather than of gladiators who fought, this total might be reduced in proportion to the rate of gladiatorial survival. The Dacian prisoners were of course a windfall for the purpose. See below, p. 216, n. 1.

[2] *I.G.R.R.* I, 446, Strack, *op. cit.* pp. 134–6. Cf. *I.G.R.R.* I, 146–50, Paribeni, *op. cit.* II, p. 49. For provincial games *e.g. I.G.R.R.* IV, 336 (Pergamum).

[3] *Jahreshefte* XXIII, 1926, Beibl. col. 263 = *Ann. épig.* 1928, no. 94.

[4] J. Carcopino, *Points de vue sur l'impérialisme romain*, pp. 73–86.

than the whole sum of disbursements recorded by Augustus in
the *Res Gestae*, and the expenditure of Trajan in the following
years sinks into proportion[1]. Further, there was reason to expect
a permanent rise in the income from the Dacian mines, which
were at once re-opened under the surveillance of imperial officials.
The acquisition of so great an amount of gold and the prospect
of a steady fresh supply caused a dislocation in the exchange
relations of the two precious metals. A papyrus seems to show
that in Egypt between 107–112 the price of gold fell in terms
of silver by about 4 per cent., and the prefect was asked to adjust
the rate of exchange between the drachma and the aureus[2]. This
represents a very large fall, but it gains support from the increase at about this time of the alloy in the denarius from 10 to
15 per cent[3]. There remain a few items of expenditure of which
the date is still uncertain. Chief among these are the two legions
XXX Ulpia and II Traiana, which it is natural to suppose were
raised for the Dacian wars, though a later date is not impossible
(p. 231): the double annexation of Dacia and Arabia would need
fresh garrisons. The new auxiliaries were all raised after the wars;
as for the *equites singulares*, if they were not a corps already
instituted by the Flavians, their introduction by Trajan belongs
probably to the early years[4].

The balance of evidence does in fact mark 107 as the turning-
point in the financial history of the reign. Trajan inherited from
Nerva if not an actual deficit at least the prospect of financial
difficulty once the reserve of Domitian's confiscations had been

---

[1] These figures, even divided, are disturbingly large and show a suspicious
roundness; and though it is certain that Trajan did receive much gold
from Dacia, it has been questioned whether Decebalus can have amassed
so large a hoard, to say nothing of the silver (the Dacian silver mines have
not been certainly located, O. Davies, *Roman Mines in Europe*, p. 206).
The totals of *congiaria* and of gladiators have also been suspected. But
although Johannes Lydus, the chronographer of 354, and Dio are each
severally authorities whose mathematics might be questioned, the cumulative
effect of their evidence (in Dio's case supported by the Fasti Ostienses) on
independent points is very great; and their figures have therefore been
retained, though they must be taken with reserve.

[2] P. Baden 37, F. Heichelheim in Klio xxv, 1932, p. 124; but cf.
Mickwitz, *op. cit.* p. 2; Davies, *op. cit.* p. 205.

[3] The recall of earlier money recorded by Dio LXVIII, 15 and dated by
him in this year is possibly connected with this change; but Dio's meaning
is obscure, and the whole question must await the results of further statistics.

[4] They were, however, only a thousand. Cf. Paribeni, *op. cit.* i,
pp. 187–90.

spent: he inherited also a new programme of Italian reconstruction. It was important to maintain confidence until new sources of revenue could be tapped, and this he achieved. Certain economies were effected. The donative to the troops was halved, the *congiarium* postponed for eighteen months. The renunciation of *aurum coronarium* was perhaps a necessity, since it had presumably been paid only a little over a year before. The schemes for Italian reconstruction went on slowly: but meanwhile an impression of security was being given; and with 107 an era of prosperity dawned for the *fiscus*. It did not set in Trajan's lifetime. His Eastern wars were no doubt costly and perhaps bore heavily on the provinces behind the frontier[1]; Hadrian's decision to renounce the territory annexed gave no chance for the conquests to pay for themselves: the Jewish revolt had devastated large areas even within the empire: yet it is on the whole to a prosperous world and a fair financial outlook that Hadrian succeeded.

The remaining legislation, which is here grouped together without special regard to the forms of particular enactments, is marked on the whole by humanity and a desire for efficiency and dispatch in the discharge of business. In criminal procedure, the conduct of trials was accelerated; possessors of *bona vacantia* could save half their illegal gains by confession (part of an attempt to check informers); anonymous accusations and leading questions were forbidden; defendants condemned in absence had a right to a retrial; and a special warning was issued against conviction in any case where the least doubt remained. On the other hand the existing practice of torture for servile witnesses was extended and, in the case of a master murdered in his own house, those whom he had freed during his life-time might be tortured along with his slaves and testamentary freedmen. Looking further afield, Trajan laid down that a parent who had maltreated his son must emancipate him and lost all rights over his inheritance, and that free-born children exposed at birth and brought up by the finder could claim their freedom without repaying the cost of their

---

[1] The requisitions for feeding troops and for the imperial journeys are often cited as having been disastrous (*e.g.* Rostovtzeff *op. cit.* p. 586, n. 5). This, however, is easily over-emphasized. The facts that C. Julius Severus fed certain forces billeted for the winter at Ancyra in 114, *I.G.R.R.* III, 173, and that a letter was written to Opramoas bidding him prepare for Trajan's reception at Rhodiapolis, *I.G.R.R.* III, 739 (iv, ch. 13), are no proof of the insolvency of the *fiscus* or that the cities concerned would otherwise have been ruined. Both were men of great wealth whose duty and perhaps pleasure it was to help in the prosecution of the war.

maintenance[1]. He also tightened the regulations of the *tutela* in the interests of minors and others subject to its provisions. The use of false weights was made punishable by relegation. A law was passed against *ambitus*, limiting the expenses of candidates for office. An advance in the matter of fidei-commissary manumission was marked by the S. C. *Rubrianum* which provided that if an heir did not obey the wishes of the testator and failed to appear when the slave applied to the praetor the slave was freed and the heir lost the rights of patronage; certain anomalies which arose from the working of this decree were subsequently rectified in the reign of Hadrian. However, if a Latin obtained full citizenship directly without his patron's consent, he lost his testamentary rights. In view of the recurrent difficulties about the wills of soldiers, which were often technically invalidated by the ignorance of the testator, Trajan decided that the wishes of the soldiers—*optimi fidelissimi commilitones*—where they could be ascertained, must be paramount and flaws in drafting overlooked. By another answer, however, he laid down that public holidays were no concern of the army. A further significant reply dealt with the practice of mutilating children to prevent them from being called up for levies; this no doubt belongs to one of the war periods. Lastly the well-known decision in the case of the Christians (p. 255 *sq.*) reflects a genuine endeavour to strike a compromise between discipline and humanitarianism.

IV. IMPERIAL ADMINISTRATION

The measures described above, mostly gathered from scattered references to Trajan in the Digest, must not be taken to include more than a small part of his legislation; they do assist, however, to fill in the picture of the man himself, which emerges much more fully from the Bithynian correspondence of Pliny[2]. The letters show a flexible disciplinarian; the replies are brief but pointed, and the reasons for each decision are fully explained. They prove in fact that Trajan was no mere warrior, but a man of serious purpose and very great administrative ability; and with a survey of his administrative changes this sketch of the internal history of his reign must conclude.

The presence of Pliny in Bithynia at all was due to the state of the province which was disclosed by investigations into the

---

[1] Pliny, *Ep.* x, 65–6 (71–2). The rule can hardly have been applied to Bithynia alone; though several replies in this correspondence show that Trajan was an opportunist in these matters, and its effectiveness has been doubted.

[2] *E.g. Ep.* 114 (115) *sq.*

case of Varenus Rufus (p. 204). Trajan took it over temporarily from the Senate with their consent and Pliny was sent out, probably in 111, as a *legatus pro praetore* directly responsible to the Emperor. The choice was a wise one. The finances of some of the cities were compromised, and Pliny had considerable financial experience. His personal uprightness was beyond question, and his legal training and love of detail, coupled with his philhellenism, made him ideally suitable for dealing with the many petty but complicated problems. His inexperience of provincial government was not necessarily a disadvantage: Trajan wanted a dependent and informative governor, and in Pliny he certainly got his man. The provision was continued, and after Pliny's death his old friend and colleague Cornutus Tertullus took his place, and held the position probably until the end of Trajan's reign.

A leading trouble in Bithynia had been the misgovernment of the cities, though it does not appear that there was a general financial crisis, and fresh public works were being freely inaugurated in the province with Pliny's approval. In their mismanagement, however, the Bithynian cities did not stand alone. Even earlier than his appointment a senatorial friend of his, by name Maximus, had been sent to Achaea 'ad ordinandum statum liberarum civitatium[1].' The emperors could always, of course, interfere in the affairs of a free city and even revoke its freedom by unilateral act, but an appointment such as that of Maximus was something of a novelty and rather shocking to Pliny's susceptibilities. He was given wider powers than those of merely overseeing the city finances, but he stands alone in his period: similar functions were exercised by the later officers known as *correctores*. The better known *curatores reipublicae* or *civitatis* also first come into prominence under Trajan, and pending further evidence he must be given responsibility for the institution[2]. The majority of contemporary instances belong to Italy, in whose welfare he had a particular interest[3]; in the provinces the governors were no doubt given instructions to take their own steps, and for Bithynia we can see the results, but Trajan's appointments occur at least in Gaul and the system spread rapidly throughout the empire,

---

[1] Pliny, *Ep.* VIII, 24; possibly Sex. Quinctilius Valerius Maximus (Dessau 1018). See further, p. 220.

[2] A *curator coloniarum et municipiorum* of the late 80's (Dessau 1017) *may* represent a similar commission and a *logistes* at Smyrna under Nerva (Philostratus, *Vitae Soph.* I, 19) a particular duty; but both examples can be explained otherwise. Cf. Ritterling, *Fasti d. Röm. Deutschland*, pp. 19, 87.

[3] The fullest particulars are furnished by Dessau 5918a of A.D. 113 from Caere in Etruria.

though in imperial provinces it was rare. The purpose of the institution was to prevent cities getting into debt through over-building or municipal corruption, and the degree of interference exercised at first was probably small[1]. If it were successful the gain to the Empire would be great, though only indirectly: and the dangerous uses to which the system was later put could not have been foreseen. It marked, however, a further step on the road to paternalism, the implications of which Trajan, whose letters show him solicitous for urban independence, probably did not clearly understand.

Among further innovations, the duties of C. Julius Proculus as *leg. Aug. p. p. region. Transpadanae* are obscure but the probable date of his appointment suggests a connection with the Dacian War; and he seems to have found no successor[2]. From the title held by C. Avidius Nigrinus in Achaea the province seems to have been removed, like Bithynia, from senatorial to imperial control, perhaps as a result of the experiment with Maximus[3]. About 114 the procurator of Thrace was replaced by a senator of praetorian rank, the jurist P. Juventius Celsus, and the change persisted[4]. An obvious explanation lies in the outbreak of the Parthian War, but no doubt the progress in civilization of Thrace, especially fostered by Trajan (p. 236), also warranted a rise in its provincial status. The annexation of Armenia caused the division of the Galatian-Cappadocian complex: henceforward Cappadocia and Armenia Minor were detached and formed a separate unit with Armenia Major[5].

The tendency already manifest under the Flavians for knights to replace freedmen in control positions in the civil service reached a further stage under Trajan. In his reign appears the first equestrian *a rationibus*, in the person of L. Vibius Lentulus, who held the office before 114; this man also appears to be the earliest known equestrian *procurator monetae* and *procurator a loricata*, the first of which posts he must have held in the nineties[6]. Another new equestrian office was the *procurator aquarum*; early in the reign the post was still held by freedmen. The process of trans-ference from tax farming to direct collection of the vectigalia was

[1] Cf. Pliny, *Ep.* x, 110 (111) *sqq.* for 'presents' on a large scale in Bithynia. Gifts to individuals were forbidden by Trajan.

[2] Dessau 1040. He was consul in 109 and quaestor probably in 96.

[3] Ditt.[3] 827, cf. *Pros. Imp. Rom.*[2] I, p. 286.

[4] For Celsus cf. *Pros. Imp. Rom.*[1] II, p. 255; he was succeeded by A. Platorius Nepos (Dessau 1052).   [5] Dessau 1041, 1338 and cf. p. 243.

[6] *Ann. épig.* 1913, no. 143; 1924, no. 81; cf. R. H. Lacey, *The Equestrian Officials of Trajan and Hadrian*, pp. 4, 50.

further developed and perhaps completed: but in their essentials these reforms belong to Flavian initiative[1].

In the real business of government, senatorial debates had little share; Trajan was master, but the most absolute autocrat needs good subordinates, and inscriptions tell us much about the personnel of Trajan's administration. As he worked hard himself, so he expected his intimate friends to do and numerous careers of the time, as of Cornutus Tertullus, Minicius Natalis, Pompeius Falco or Numisius Sabinus[2], show almost continuous employment in the imperial service. Nor were Orientals excluded from high positions; C. Antius A. Julius Quadratus of Pergamum was legate of Syria from about 101, Claudianus of Xanthus, the first senator from Lycia, commanded leg. II Traiana probably in the East, while C. Julius Berenicianus Alexander, the descendant of a 'King Alexander' admitted to the Senate by Vespasian, was perhaps a legionary legate in the Parthian campaign[3]; C. Julius Quadratus Bassus, honoured in Pergamum, served on Trajan's staff in both the Dacian and Parthian Wars, and rose to be one of the most distinguished men in the State[4]. It is possible, too, that both Ti. Claudius Livianus, *praefectus praetorio* for the greater part of the reign and throughout both Dacian and Parthian wars, and C. Claudius Severus, governor of Arabia from 111–115, were of Asiatic Greek descent[5].

Above this circle of hard-working administrators stood the particular intimates of the Princeps. First of these was L. Licinius Sura, thrice consul, a fellow Spaniard and contemporary, who had stood by Trajan in Germany and throughout the Dacian wars (see below). His great riches, and the Emperor's confidence, earned him enemies, whom his patronage of Hadrian did nothing to appease; but their attempt to estrange Trajan from him was a failure. His death about 110 was an evil day for Rome; he possessed great influence and he alone could have dissuaded the Emperor from the Parthian campaign; had he lived he would have seen the adoption of Hadrian placed beyond all doubt. Next to

---

[1] Dessau 7193–5 and *Ann. épig.* 1924, no. 80, show control officials under Trajan.   [2] Dessau 1024, 1029, 1036, 1038.

[3] In M. Pompeius Macrinus Theophanes, *Leg. leg.* VI Vict. about 96–7, Groag sees the first Greek legionary commander on the Rhine (*ap.* Ritterling, *op. cit.* p. 125). The family, however, though of Greek origin, had been settled in Rome for nearly a century.

[4] No identification of this man yet proposed is free from objections; cf. W. Weber, *Berl. Abh.* 1932, 5, pp. 57–95; R. Herzog, *Berl. S.B.* 1933, 10, pp. 408–415; A. von Premerstein, *Bay. S.B.* 1934, Heft 3.

[5] Cf. C. S. Walton in *J.R.S.* XIX, 1929, pp. 48, 59.

Sura and probably among his enemies mentioned by Dio came the
three consulars A. Cornelius Palma, L. Julius Ursus Servianus
and L. Publilius Celsus, who were as jealous of his influence with
Trajan, as they certainly were of the rise of Hadrian. All three
had given the Emperor distinguished service and were rewarded
with second consulships, and two at least with triumphal statues
in his Forum. It is not indeed fanciful to see in Trajan's un-
willingness to proceed to a formal adoption of Hadrian a reluctance
to offend this powerful group. There were thus divided parties
round the throne; and the succession of Hadrian brought matters
to a head. Servianus certainly survived—though he was put to
death by Hadrian in 136, in his ninetieth year—and was honoured
with a third consulship, the highest honour a private citizen could
obtain under the empire; but Palma and Celsus were executed in
118 and their fate was shared by Avidius Nigrinus and Lusius
Quietus, who had no doubt belonged to their faction (p. 303).

The career of the Moor Quietus illustrates Trajan's readiness to
favour a competent man whatever his origins: but it is probable
that his impetuousness was a dangerous influence in the Emperor's
later years when his hold of himself was less steady. The political
sympathies of Q. Sosius Senecio are less well known: he was a
patron of literature and the friend of Pliny and Plutarch; his
father-in-law was Julius Frontinus, and his son-in-law Pompeius
Falco, after a distinguished career under Trajan, was further
promoted by Hadrian. Senecio then probably belonged to the
party of Sura and Hadrian, which one may characterize as pacific
and perhaps opposed to the Parthian wars, in opposition to the
aggressive policy urged by the faction of Palma and Quietus. Still
less certain is the position of L. Neratius Priscus whom Trajan
was even said to have destined as his successor: he was, however,
primarily a lawyer and with Juventius Celsus a leader of the
Proculian school; and he was among the judicial counsellors of
both Trajan and Hadrian. It is possible that his influence lay
in this direction rather than that of politics. It is difficult to
estimate the share of these different men in shaping the policy
of Trajan's principate; and in view of his own strong character
we are justified in calling it the Emperor's own. One thing is
certain—the influence of Sura, and it is perhaps to his death that
we should attribute the deterioration of the last years.

CHAPTER VI

THE WARS OF TRAJAN

I. THE DANUBE

THE verdict of historians may be that in his work as an administrator lay Trajan's greatest service to the Roman State; but it is as a soldier that his reputation has endured. The later writers of antiquity, though as members of the Empire they gloried in his conquests, doubted of their wisdom and succeeding years have reinforced their doubt. But to Tacitus and his contemporaries the great days of the past seemed to have returned. The boundaries of the empire, which since Augustus had been 'defensum magis quam nobiliter ampliatum,' were being carried forward on every side; and under her ardent and inspiring leader Rome was recovering her confidence not only in internal peace but also in her imperial destiny. In Africa, though the Aurès massif was not yet wholly secured, its encirclement in Trajan's early years marked the arrival of Rome at the limit of settled habitation on the desert edge (p. 148), and the founding of Thamugadi and Lambaesis proclaimed the final achievement of Roman aims in Numidia. The Dacian problem ceased to exist and the further absorption of the Rumanian plains, now enclosed by the advanced posts of the Dacian province and of Scythia Minor, and the attainment of a firm line on the Sereth against westward migrations must have seemed only a matter of time. In 106, despite the concurrence of the second Dacian War, the annexation of Arabia was carried through with little fuss; and when in 116 the victorious Emperor reached the Persian Gulf and kept informing the Senate of his subjection of peoples of whose very existence they were ignorant, it is no marvel that their sense of proportion was overwhelmed. It is the task of this chapter to strike a balance between Trajan's martial exploits and to seek the causes which led him on a career of conquest which in the end was to prove a *damnosa hereditas* for the empire he sought to strengthen.

It was the Danube frontier that demanded first attention. The settlement of Domitian (p. 185 *sq.*), while in the circumstances it was perhaps the wisest temporary expedient, could hardly be a permanent solution, nor is there evidence that its author ever intended it for such. A policy of subsidy can only be so effectively used, as it has been in corners of the British Empire, where the recipients are numerically too weak or traditionally too disunited ever to constitute a serious menace to the neighbouring provinces. Elsewhere it can at best be a temporary measure, to tide over a period of general stress or to await better local conditions for a final settlement. But the Dacians were a united race, conscious of nationhood and thoroughly organized under a prince of genius. Like Mithridates, with whose career his own can bear comparison, Decebalus was fired by an unquenchable hate for Rome and dreamed like him of a wider union of Rome's enemies than was bounded by his mountain circle; and during the Trajanic wars he even made overtures to the Parthian king for a concerted plan against the common danger[1]. The death of Decebalus might have removed the immediate threat to the Roman peace; but a century and more of experience could tell that Dacia was a permanently dangerous neighbour, a focus for the union of all the middle and lower Danubian peoples, a *gens nusquam fida*, and an enemy to be reckoned with whenever, as in 69, necessity elsewhere weakened the garrisons and offered an opportunity. Conversely, the tenure by Rome of the Dacian mountain salient, a comparatively simple task, as the event showed, once the difficult conquest had been achieved, would hold the tribesmen apart and give security for the safe development of the Thracian and Moesian hinterland.

Some such answer, then, as Trajan's was dictated by the strategic needs of the Empire and would probably in any case have soon followed the completion of the German *limes*; and in the state of the evidence it is rash to pronounce upon the causes which fixed the declaration of war in 101. It may be Trajan judged that time could only make success more difficult, or that some lost event precipitated the conflict[2]; but to attack Decebalus at the height of his prestige, with the frontier re-organization scarcely complete and with troops many of whom had shared the bitter outcome of the previous war, was to try a dangerous hazard—how dangerous the history of the first campaigns amply shows: and in his early decision to invade, Trajan's own military ambitions and self-confidence were probably the dominant factor.

The day of his accession found him on the Rhine, where he had still work to do in composing the repercussions along the upper German frontier of the Suebic War of 97, which may even

[1] Pliny, *Ep.* x, 74 (16).
[2] Such as the conjectural encroachment of Decebalus on his neighbours, probable enough in itself, but an insecure deduction from Dio LXVIII, 9, 5.

itself have lingered into 98[1]. But in fact the immediate goal of
Rome in this area had been achieved already by the careful
planning of Domitian and his staff, and for the remaining details
the presence of the Emperor and of anything more than a skeleton
force was no longer necessary. Trajan was therefore soon free to
turn his attention farther east, and he spent the winter of 98–9
on the Danube frontier. The fruits of his visit appear in the construction of at least one new road (and probably more) in the
sector from which the advance of A.D. 101 proceeded, and it need
not be in doubt that he had already made up his mind for war, even
if he had not now designed the actual annexation of the Dacian
kingdom; and after a short period in Rome which coincided with
the delays of preparation rather than the necessity for his presence
in the capital, he left Italy in March, 101, to open his campaign[2].

The monographs which were written to describe the Dacian
wars have all perished, with the exception of one sentence of
Trajan's own *Dacian Commentaries*, and since the topographical
indications in Dio are of the slightest, the principal guide to the
course of the war is the Column of Trajan itself (p. 207) with its
spiral band of reliefs. The historical value of these sculptures has
been severely challenged, and it is true that without an adequate
written narrative it is likely to remain impossible to unlock their
secret to a demonstration; but that they do embody a chronological record which we should easily recognize if, like the public
for whom they were designed, we had other knowledge of the
events portrayed, is unquestionable, and an historian is entitled
to make the best use he may of their evidence. At the same time
the dangers of interpretation may be seen from the fact that were
it not for the positive identification of the first route depicted by
Trajan's own statement in his *Commentaries*, discussion of the
later campaigns would be almost useless, since this begins from
the knowledge that a different road was employed and the field
can be narrowed to an extent which makes further investigation reasonably worth while. It must, moreover, be admitted that
the details of the reliefs cannot always be closely pressed; patient
examination by a series of scholars building upon the original
researches of Cichorius[3] has established certain principles and
symbols evolved by the designer to clarify his record, but the
artist was never in bond to the historian, and it is, for example,

---

[1] *Ann. épig.* 1923, no. 28, a centurion decorated by Trajan alone for services
bello Germanico. Eutropius and Orosius refer obscurely to the work of re-
organization (p. 182).   [2] March 25, Dessau 5035.
[3] C. Cichorius, *Die Reliefs der Traianssäule*, I, 1896; II, 1900.

unprofitable to attempt to identify upon the Column particular minor incidents recorded by Dio or to deduce the composition of the armed forces from the units represented in the stone.

The general plan of the first campaign follows from Trajan's own comment 'Inde Berzobim, deinde Aizi processimus[1].' These two places lay on the most westerly of the roads into Dacia, which ran from Lederata on the Danube, near Viminacium, round the western outliers of the mountains to Tibiscum, whence a short march led to Tapae and the so-called Iron Gate pass into Dacia proper[2]. This route had already been used by Tettius Julianus in the uncompleted campaign of 88–9 (p. 172), and it presented obvious advantages. The base at Viminacium made an accessible centre for reinforcements and supplies, and the line of communications of the advancing army was short[3] and comparatively secure, since the Sarmatian Iazyges on its left flank were at this time friendly to Rome. This line, then, Trajan himself followed; but whether he was assisted by a parallel column using the second of the later Roman roads, which led from Tsierna, lower down the river, over a pass known as the Teregova Keys, to join the first at Tibiscum, is less certain. For this hypothesis the double bridging of the Danube shown by the sculptor was originally responsible[4], but its exponents disagreed over the base of the eastern force and the point of junction of the two expeditions; and more recent criticism has dismissed the theory of a double advance as a figment[5]. Nevertheless, even though the positive identifications on the Column break down, the use of the Teregova route in the first campaign remains a likely possibility. The two bridges are a natural means for the sculptor to indicate a simultaneous crossing of separate forces, and his failure to make their subsequent advance as clear as he does in the campaign of 106 accords with the recognized fact[6] that only as he progressed did he discover the full potentialities of his medium. The use of separate columns in penetrating difficult country and splitting the opposition at key points was obvious strategy, well known at the time; Dio's narrative of the following year shows certainly two and possibly three Roman units at work, and a similar division in

[1] Priscian, *Inst. Gram.* VI, 13 (Peter, *Hist. rom. rel.* II, p. 117).
[2] For the Dacian wars see Map 12 facing p. 554.
[3] The Peutinger Table gives the road distance from Lederata to Tibiscum as about 75–80 miles.
[4] Cichorius, *op. cit.* Scenes IV and V; Volume of Plates V, 36.
[5] *Imprimis*, Sir H. Stuart Jones in *B.S.R.* V, 1910, pp. 439 *sqq.*
[6] Stuart Jones, *op. cit.* p. 437.

106 is plain from the Column, while the fact, for what it is worth, that Trajan employed a double advance along the Tigris and Euphrates in 115 is some indication that it was a method of which he approved. Lastly, the cliff road constructed in 100 along the Danube bank facing Tsierna[1] forcibly suggests a special need at this point, since the previous road here left the river and went inland to rejoin it at Egeta; and this new section, a difficult engineering feat, may well have been designed to serve an attack by the Teregova route.

Before the Roman advance, whether double or single, the Dacian forces withdrew, adhering to the tactics which had proved successful against Fuscus in 86 (p. 170 sq.) and hoping to draw out the opposing line of communications and cut the enemy off in the mountains of Transylvania. The sculptures show abandoned fortresses, crops destroyed and hills empty save for a few spies. Despite the lack of opposition, however, Trajan moved forward cautiously, consolidating his advance at each point, and building roads, bridges, and forts as he went. Reaching Tibiscum without serious fighting, he paused before the attack on the main Dacian defences at the entrance to the Iron Gate pass. Here, at Tapae, the first pitched battle of the war took place. The sculptor represents it as a Roman victory[2]; but it seems to have failed in its objective. The defences were not forced, and as the campaigning season was now far spent Trajan contented himself with securing the Banat and maintaining his advanced position.

In the winter Decebalus, blockaded on the west, delivered his counter attack. As his objective he chose, as he had done before, Lower Moesia and summoned his allies or dependents the Sarmatian Roxolani from the Moldavian plain to join in the offensive. The two forces swam the river and gained at first considerable success. The exact locality of the raid is uncertain, since the Column shows only that it was considerably lower down the river than Drobetae, where Trajan was himself wintering, but the city of Nicopolis which he founded some miles south-east of Novae has been supposed to commemorate its repulse[3]. It was perhaps this eastern raid, and the propaganda value of his success against it which, together with the proved strength of the Iron Gate defences, determined Trajan upon a fresh line for his main assault in 102. His route in this year has been plausibly traced along the easternmost of the practical entries into Dacia, up the Aluta

---

[1] Dessau, 5863.　　[2] Cichorius, *Scene* XXIV; Volume of Plates v, 38, *a*.

[3] An alternative, but less probable, view would connect with it the great trophy built in 109 at Adamclisi in the Dobrudja (p. 234).

(Oltu) valley and through the mountain barrier by the comparatively broad and easy Red Tower pass[1]. Although by this road
the line of communications was much longer and weaker than in
the campaign of 101, the advance proceeded without molestation.
The prestige of the winter victories had paved its way, and it may
have been the defection of his allies, tired of the war, which
induced Decebalus to send at least two embassies to ask for peace.
Trajan rejected the first, but the second, containing as it did some
of the highest Dacian nobles, the *pileati*, was better received, and
the chief of staff and praetorian prefect, Licinius Sura and
Claudius Livianus, were sent to discuss terms. But the conditions
offered by Rome were too severe for Decebalus—still himself
undefeated—to accept; and the war went on.

Meanwhile Trajan continued his march and was enabled to penetrate the Red Tower pass before a Dacian army could be sent to
block it, and at Cedoniae (Sibiu) he stood inside the Carpathian
ring. From this point his objective, Sarmizegethusa, lay due west;
but the easiest access to it involved a descent north-west to
Apulum (Alba Julia) followed by a left-handed turn down the
valley of the Marisus, the principal river of Dacia. There were,
however, serious objections to following this route, for it exposed
his left flank to the series of Dacian fortresses on the spurs of the
Mühlbach mountains, and any disaster in his rear would leave
him trapped in the Marisus valley and at the mercy of Decebalus.
This was no doubt the king's hope, and it may even be that he
had designedly allowed him to pass the Red Tower defile with
that object; but Trajan was too skilful a general to fall into the
trap. He accordingly divided his army, and with the main body
set out directly across the hills to capture the Mühlbach strongholds on his way. At the same time two forces were detached to
sweep up the valleys and foothills under a certain Maximus and
Lusius Quietus, a leader of Moorish irregulars whose shortcomings in peace were compensated by gifts as a cavalry commander which served Trajan well again in the Parthian War;
of these forces one no doubt was sent round by the northern route
to rejoin the Emperor somewhere near the junction of the Marisus
and the Strell[2]. The key to the success of this strategy lay in

[1] For this year's campaign, cf. especially G. A. T. Davies, 'Topography
and the Trajan column,' *J.R.S.* x, 1920, pp. 8–28.

[2] It is possible that in Maximus we should recognize the commander of
the western force outside the Iron Gate pass; but this man is probably
M'. Laberius Maximus, governor of Lower Moesia at any rate in 100
(*S.E.G.* 1, 329) and therefore a likelier partner in the eastern army, the
western being under Q. Glitius Agricola, governor of Pannonia.

Trajan's own power to take the Mühlbach fortresses within a reasonable time, and this after hard fighting he accomplished. When the last and most stubbornly defended of these, the Muncel Cetate on high ground above the upper waters of the Varosviz river, fell and the Dacian relieving army was defeated[1], the way to Sarmizegethusa lay open and the war was won. Decebalus, to save his capital the horrors of a useless siege, capitulated, and one of the most striking scenes of the Column illustrates his surrender in Trajan's camp, probably at Aquae (Kis-Kalan) on the Strell.

The terms of peace were now for Trajan to dictate; and the half-measure he adopted was perhaps the fruit of over-confidence in the effects of his recent success. At the same time he recognized both the difficulty of keeping in being throughout a Dacian winter the large army necessary for a thorough conquest of the country, and the personal value of Decebalus himself, who, if he should remain, as he no doubt professed, a loyal ally of Rome, might yet prove a most useful instrument of Roman policy. He was accordingly spared and reinstated with the position of a client-king, but he was obliged to accept a Roman garrison at Sarmizegethusa and probably in some of the Mühlbach fortresses, and to surrender Roman deserters and all his artillery and engineers and pull down his fortifications. Moreover, if this be the correct interpretation of a vexed phrase in Dio[2], the Romans retained the Banat conquests of 101 which were incorporated in Upper Moesia. A Dacian embassy was sent to Rome to secure the formal ratification of peace by the Senate[3] and in the winter of 102 Trajan himself left Sarmizegethusa to celebrate his triumph and assume the cognomen of 'Dacicus'[4]. The governors of Pannonia and Lower Moesia, Q. Glitius Atilius Agricola and M'. Laberius Maximus, were rewarded with a second consulship in 103 (which Licinius Sura had already held in the previous year), while lesser commanders received corresponding recognition[5].

---

[1] Cichorius, Scenes LXXI–III; Volume of Plates v, 38, b; in it were found relics of the disaster of Fuscus (p. 170) who had perhaps fallen into the trap set for Trajan.   [2] Dio, LXVIII, 9, 5.

[3] For the significance of this in the coin-issue, cf. Strack, op. cit. p. 108.

[4] Two imperatorial salutations, III and IV, belong to this war, probably both to the second half of 102. The title 'Dacicus' first occurs officially on coins which seem to have been specially struck in the last weeks of 102 (Strack, op. cit. p. 24).

[5] Notably Q. Roscius Coelius Pompeius Falco and L. Minicius Natalis (Dessau 1035, 1029), legates respectively of V Macedonica and VII Claudia.

The peace of 102 was not destined to last for long. Trajan had misjudged his man, and one by one the clauses of the treaty were broken. Finally, when Decebalus felt himself strong enough to annex some territory of Rome's allies the Iazyges, war was declared, and in June 105 Trajan set out again for the front. His route to the Danube on this occasion is carved in considerable detail[1], but the most divergent views have been held as to its identification. It is likely that he crossed the Adriatic from Ancona to Iader (Zara) and there are strong reasons for taking him thence south to Lissus and so across Albania to Naissus and Ratiaria, but the case is still short of proof[2]. Meanwhile Decebalus had not been idle. He determined to strike before reinforcements arrived, and when Trajan reached the river he found a serious situation. The camps in Dacia proper had already fallen, and among the prisoners was a man of consular rank, perhaps the Longinus whose capture and suicide Dio narrates[3]. Other Roman posts, either in Wallachia or even south of the Danube, were under siege and their relief occupied the campaigning season of 105, so that Trajan could not set out to reconquer the interior until 106. There could now be no doubt of his intentions; indeed the rupture of peace within three years of its conclusion left no alternative to the thorough subjugation of the country. Accordingly a strong force was collected, and crossing himself by the great Danube bridge which Apollodorus had built at Drobetae during the interval of peace, Trajan began his last campaign. Decebalus' precarious allies melted away, and after abortive attempts to conciliate Trajan or to poison him, he found himself faced by ruin. Attacked on two sides, possibly through the Iron Gate and Red Tower passes, he showed a desperate opposition, and much hard fighting was necessary before Sarmizegethusa fell to the united armies in the late summer of the year. But this did not, as in 102, finish the campaign. No such terms were now acceptable. Decebalus escaped to the north and a Roman column pressed after him, up the Marisus valley into a country yet unpenetrated. The northern chiefs, not ignorant of their certain fate, rallied to the king and gave way stubbornly, even gaining some successes. But the end

----

[1] Cichorius, *Scenes* LXXIX–XCI; Volume of Plates v, 40.

[2] This is the reconstruction of Stuart Jones, *op. cit.* pp. 448–458. It may be fairly said that the variants of the so-called Long Sea Route, involving an approach to the Danube by way of the Aegean, are less convincing than any of the proposed routes via the Adriatic and Dalmatia.

[3] Fronto, *de bello Parth.* p. 217 N; Dio LXVIII, 12, where Longinus is called στρατοπέδου ἐξηγούμενος.

was now inevitable. Decebalus was surrounded and committed suicide, preceded or followed by many of his subordinates. Others of them submitted to Trajan, and a sharp guerrilla campaign ended the war.

The difficulty of the Dacian wars may be in part appreciated from a survey of the troops involved, though any exact numerical estimate is as yet impossible. Inscriptions prove the participation of four out of the five existing Moesian legions, and that of the fifth, II Adiutrix, may be accepted as certain, though possibly it had already departed to Pannonia by 105 and took no part in the second war. After the comparative failure of the campaign in 101 (which evoked no imperatorial salutation) further reinforcements were summoned. I Minervia came from Bonn to the front and remained until after 106, while the arrival in Pannonia about the same time of another German legion, XI Claudia from Vindonissa, means no doubt that one of the existing garrisons had departed for the scene of war. Of these XIII Gemina, the future Dacian legion, certainly shared in some of the campaigns, and that the other three sent at least detachments is probable. Finally, of the two new legions, the service of XXX Ulpia is strongly suggested by its early cognomen Victrix and its subsequent movements, while the early history of II Traiana remains an open question. At any rate, from 101 there were thirteen legions at least along the Danube frontier, and the fact that none seem to have been moved away before 107 may perhaps argue Trajan's own doubts of the vitality of the peace of 102[1]. Besides the legions the Column, backed by inscriptions, records the activity of many auxiliary units, including irregulars, as well as of the Praetorian Guard and other household troops.

Trajan was now free to make a final settlement and the extreme measures which he took are a testimony to the respect with which four seasons' hard campaigning against the Dacians had inspired him. The fine motto *parcere subiectis* was indeed, as Augustus had long ago declared, not always applicable; and of Dacia Trajan found himself virtually compelled to echo Domitian's famous summary of a pettier occasion (p. 146)[2]: in the Dacian uplands, a solitude was a prerequisite of peace. The scope of his exter-

---

[1] The location of three legions, I Minervia, IV Flavia and XIII Gemina, in the years 102–5 is as doubtful as it is important. It is hard to believe with Ritterling (*P.W. s.v.*) that they were all on garrison duty in the newly conquered part of Dacia. If this were so the interpretation of the course of the second war would wear a rather different colour.

[2] Dio LXVII, 4, 6.

mination has, however, been sometimes exaggerated. Many Dacians remained, probably those who had early come to terms, and from among them were drawn the Dacian auxiliaries who now begin to appear in history. Others, whose exodus forms the dramatic conclusion to the sculptured record, trekked northwards towards Ruthenia and the upper waters of the Theiss; many lay dead; and fifty thousand stalwart prisoners marched south in chains to end their lives as gladiators and grace a Roman holiday (p. 215). A polyglot folk replaced the free. Settlers were imported from all over the empire and, bringing with them their customs and their cults, made of Dacia the most cosmopolitan of all the Danube provinces. Some came for a special purpose. We have no evidence that the Dacian gold mines were other than a subsidiary motive for the war, but they were at once re-opened with a staff of Dalmatian miners under the supervision of a *procurator aurariarum*[1] and played henceforward an important part in the imperial finances (p. 216). Of the others, the inscriptions indicate a preponderance of Orientals, though settlers of western origin are also found. The divine Zalmoxis yielded place to smaller gods, Malagbel, Bellahamon and a motley Olympus[2]. The government took a vigorous hand in the development of the country. Military needs had caused its annexation, but it was not merely to remain a camp. Besides the gold mines, salt and iron were also worked, surveyors were active and pasture lands let out on lease. Roads were opened up, and the principal interior highway from Sarmizegethusa through Apulum to Porolissum in the far north was complete in the Potaissa-Napoca section as early as 108[3]. Sarmizegethusa remained the capital, the centre of the civil government and of the Imperial worship, and was refounded by Trajan as the colonia Dacica[4]; among its original colonists were a number of veterans from Danube legions. Tsierna also became a colony, and numerous smaller settlements received an urban organization of the Roman type whence they developed into colonies or municipia.

The new province did not embrace all the land over which the

[1] *E.g.* Dessau 1593.

[2] Statistics are collected by L. W. Jones, *The Cults of Dacia*, Univ. Calif. Public. in Class. Phil. IX, 1929, no. 8, p. 245.

[3] *C.I.L.* III, 1627. The builders, *coh. I Flavia Ulpia Hispanorum c.R.* named as part of the Dacian garrison in 110 (Dessau 2004) were previously an upper Moesian unit who, from the addition to their title, had distinguished themselves in the war.

[4] *C.I.L.* III, 1443. Its full later title was colonia Ulpia Traiana Augusta Dacica Sarmizeget(h)usa metropolis.

Romans now claimed the sovereignty. On the west, portions of the Banat lying beyond the Tsierna-Teregova road were assigned to Upper Moesia, the duty of whose legions it remained to protect them against possible incursions of the neighbouring Iazyges. Some, indeed, of the territory here incorporated, whose seizure by Decebalus had been the spark to the Second Dacian War, had previously belonged to them and its retention by Rome necessitated a campaign which was entrusted to P. Aelius Hadrianus, now governor of the newly formed province of Pannonia Inferior[1]. To eastward, the Aluta formed the nominal boundary and a line of forts was soon erected along its western bank. Besides guarding the actual frontier their garrisons were available to help the police of Little Wallachia, never thoroughly pacified[2]. Beyond the river, though with the spread of civil settlement across its banks the frontier was later pushed forward some thirty miles, the plains of Wallachia and Moldavia, over which the Romans claimed a suzerainty they hardly exercised in practice, belonged to the sphere of Lower Moesia, tiles of whose legions have been found as far north as the southern outliers of the Transylvanian Alps[3]. In the far north, the line of the original boundary is harder to define; but it is probable that it was drawn roughly along the watersheds of the Bihar group in the west and the southern Carpathians in the east, including the upper waters of the river Szamos (Someş) at least as far as Porolissum, which may have been an auxiliary station from the first. The swift reduction of the Dacian garrison implies that no great difficulty was found here in establishing the determined frontier, and the process was perhaps complete in its essentials by the end of Trajan's principate. Farther east, where the Carpathian foothills approach the final bend of the Danube at Galaţi, only a short distance of a hundred miles separated the last Dacian fort at Breţcu[4] from the legionary camp at Troesmis founded about 107. A bridge was soon thrown across this gap. The fort at Barboşi north of the Danube was filled at latest in 113[5] by the lower Moesian cohort *II Mattiacorum*: from here a Roman road ran northwards up the Sereth valley to

[1] S.H.A. *Hadr.* 3, 9.

[2] Cf. Dessau 9179, recording repairs in A.D. 201 to the fort at Bumbesti, in the centre of this district.

[3] *E.g. C.I.L.* III, 12530 from Drajna de sus, north of Ploesti.

[4] Garrisoned by the cohorts *I Hispanorum* and *I Bracaraugustanorum*, both originally from Lower Moesia (cf. E. Panaitescu, *Bull. Acad. Roum.* xv, 1929, pp. 73 *sqq.*).

[5] *C.I.L.* III, 777.

Poiana, where traces of a camp have been found[1], and thence west to enter Dacia at Breţcu. This road passed through the province to Apulum and joined the main highway down the Marisus valley to the western frontier, whence a continuation still imperfectly traced seems to have crossed the intervening plain to reach the Danube again somewhere south of Aquincum, perhaps at Intercisa[2].

Meanwhile south of the river the removal of the barbarian menace of the last twenty years brought a return of prosperity to the Dobrudja. For some time after the reverses of 85 and 86 the great earth wall running from Tomi to a point north of Raşova on the Danube seems to have been the effective boundary of Roman control (p. 170). Gradually the situation improved and the heavily defended line was abandoned, but there is no certain trace of Roman occupation beyond it before the turn of the century. The auxiliary camp at Carsium (Harsova) was built after the First Dacian War[3], and the earliest signs of organized civil settlement at places such as Capidava and Ulmetum seem to belong to this period, while farther north at Histria on the coast the proceedings before the governor about the same date suggest a recent return of the Roman authority. The process of recovery may have been gradual since the nineties, but its conclusion is doubly marked. After the Dacian wars, if not in the interval between them, the legion V Macedonica took up its permanent post at Troesmis and secured not only the peace but the prosperity of the Dobrudja. By the middle of the century the country had become widely sown with small farming communities, chiefly of legionary and auxiliary veterans, and dependent for their markets as much on the camps as on the Greek coastal cities[4]. Secondly, in 109 the great monument at Adamclisi was dedicated to Mars Ultor[5], and in the valley beneath its shadow arose the small foundation of Tropaeum Traiani. A core of solid concrete, a hundred feet high and more than as much in diameter, surmounted by a trophy and ringed with sculptures, it represents a significant gesture, a counterpart to the triumphal column in the capital

[1] Probably Trajanic; cf. G. Cantacuzène, *Aegyptus*, IX, 1928, pp. 63 *sqq.* (esp. 86–96).

[2] *C.I.L.* III, 8064, 1$^{a', b', c'}$. Is this perhaps the Trajanic road, designed for quick transit between the Rhine and the Euxine and running *per feras gentes*, which is mentioned by Aurelius Victor, *Caes.* XIII, 2?

[3] V. Pârvan, *Anal. Acad. Române*, XXXV, 1913, p. 541, n. 4.

[4] Cf. Pârvan, *Ausonia* X, 1921, p. 198.

[5] See Volume of Plates v, 42; *C.I.L.* III, 12467; 12470 shows Tropaeum already municipally organized by 115–6.

itself. Had any comparable monument of victory been set up in Dacia, it is safe to say that at least the carcase would survive the years. It was no mere incident of the Trajanic campaigns, such as the raid of 101–2 or the pressure of 105, that the trophy at Adamclisi was built to mark. It proclaimed the triumphant end of the Dacian wars, on the spot where more than twenty years before the death of Oppius Sabinus had seen their sorry beginning[1]. As with Mithridates, so with Decebalus, twenty years were needed to break his threat to Rome. With the recovery of Scythia Minor and the occupation of Transylvania, the key points in the defence of the Lower Danube were held, and henceforward effectively garrisoned. There remained the intervening plains, already occupied by uncivilized and semi-nomadic tribesmen, difficult at all times to control, but now checked and all but encircled by the grapple of the new frontier dispositions. To tame and absorb them up to the shorter and easier line of the Sereth, and consequently to make firm provision against the recognized danger of westward migration from the Russian steppes, must be a gradual process: for the moment a policy of subsidy must keep them quiet[2]. That the final plan was never in fact accomplished may not detract from Trajan's credit in having dealt effectively with the first and major part of the problem.

For a time, then, a strong garrison on the Lower Danube was essential, and besides auxiliaries, who had hitherto been entrusted with the defence of the eastern sector, three legions remained between the Aluta and the sea, I Italica at Novae, XI Claudia at Durostorum and V Macedonica at Troesmis. Higher up the river the frontier advance meant a fresh alignment of troops. Oescus and Ratiaria ceased to be legionary camps, and received the status of colonies, and the two legions of Upper Moesia, IV Flavia and VII Claudia, lay at Singidunum and Viminacium. In Pannonia, where between the two wars there had perhaps been as many as six legions and which had consequently been divided into an upper and a lower province like Moesia in 86 (p. 186), there were at first probably five[3]. Dacia itself received as its permanent garrison only one, XIII Gemina at Apulum, but a

---

[1] As was long ago suggested by Davies, *op. cit.* p. 19, n. 2.

[2] S.H.A. *Hadr.* 6, 8, cf. p. 355.

[3] The exact dispositions of this force for the next few years are not yet determined and depend largely on the date of departure of XV Apollinaris from Carnuntum; but it seems probable, especially in view of the recent trouble with the Iazyges, that for a time after 108 there were two legions in Lower Pannonia.

larger force was necessary at first and there are traces of a temporary stay of I Adiutrix in the province at this time. I Minervia returned to Bonn, and II Traiana went east, if indeed it had ever been a part of the Danube forces. Finally, when XV Apollinaris left for Cappadocia and XXX Ulpia for Germany the Pannonian garrison was reduced to four legions, three in the upper province, X Gemina, I Adiutrix and XIV Gemina at Vindobona, Brigetio and Carnuntum, and one in the lower, II Adiutrix at Aquincum, leaving an establishment of ten legions along the Danube front.

Behind the border, the new Danube solution had its repercussions also in the interior, particularly in Thrace. Here the process of civil development and urbanization begun under the Julio-Claudians was rapidly pushed forward; and the city names of Augusta Traiana, Plotinopolis, Traianopolis, Hadrianopolis as well as the tribe of others, or the addition of Ulpia to their title, show new foundations or rises in municipal standing. A further mark of this progress was the elevation of Thrace about 114 to the rank of a praetorian province (p. 220). In Lower Moesia the creation of Marcianopolis and Nicopolis ad Istrum, besides Tropaeum Traiani and lesser villages, and in the upper province Ulpiana and the title Ulpia Scupi reflect the same picture, while in Pannonia the old legionary fortress of Poetovio became a colony with the title Ulpia Traiana. Trajan saw clearly that in the Danubian provinces lay the key to the prosperity of the empire of whose frontier they formed the backbone. His military solution secured their peace and in his policy of civil development lay the seeds of their future strength. In this he judged aright, and had he been content with his Danubian laurels he might claim to have done Rome service equal with the greatest. Unfortunately a wrong inference from his success turned his attention eastward, and his fruitless Parthian war upset the stability so hardly won.

II. TRAJAN IN THE EAST

Trajan's success in Dacia had been won at a cost, but the result seemed likely to justify his trouble and expense. It brought a return of confidence to an empire which at his accession had appeared uneasily conscious of decadence, and in every province fresh dedications testify to the honour in which the Emperor was held. It was otherwise with his Parthian war. One such triumph was enough for a generation and time was needed for recovery: to attempt a second major war within ten years was seriously to overtax the imperial resources. Yet it is easy to see the springs of such a miscalculation. The seeds of a conflict with the Parthians had been sown, whether consciously or not, as far back as the Flavian re-organization of the eastern frontier, which brought an effective military occupation to the banks of the Euphrates. In the north the trunk roads in Asia Minor, and especially behind the new legionary fortress of Satala, felt a keen continuance of Flavian development under Nerva and in Trajan's early years (p. 141). Farther south, facing Mesopotamia, the annexation of Commagene in 72 had brought another legion to the river and Roman arms had pressed down it as far as Sura by Vespasian's death, tightening their control over Palmyra, and building fresh roads up to the Euphrates line. One by one the remaining petty kingdoms within the provincial area were absorbed, until by A.D. 100 only the Nabataean Arabs in the south-east still preserved a client independence, and since the lapse to Rome, probably about 93, of the domains of Agrippa II beyond the Jordan the inclusion of their adjoining territories could not be long delayed. Whether there were frontier incidents we do not know, but there were sufficient grounds for the decision in the need of a provincial control of Arabia to protect the potentially rich Decapolis, and, more important, to tap effectively the trade route between the Red Sea and Syria. Accordingly, the new Syrian governor for 105, A. Cornelius Palma, was sent out with orders to annex the country.

To perform this task, he took the legion VI Ferrata[1] and auxiliary troops, but from the fact that he carried on despite the outbreak of the Second Dacian War, it is evident that little serious resistance was anticipated; and Roman coins, beginning probably in 108, which celebrate Arabia adquisita—not capta—and show on their reverse an already peaceful province, bear out this optimism. Some opposition was indeed encountered before the outlying tribesmen would accept the stricter control of Rome[2], enough together with his duties in organizing the new province to earn for Palma triumphal decorations, a statue in the Forum of Augustus and a second consulship on his return home in 108: but perhaps these very honours were in part a recognition of his success in avoiding serious disturbance; and of Arabia it may fairly be said that 'nulla pars imperii pariter inlacessita transiit.'

The new province followed fairly closely the limits of the Nabataean kingdom, though on the west some towns of the Decapolis were included in it, and in the north, where as late as

---

[1] A. H. M. Jones, *J.R.S.* xviii, 1928, p. 147.
[2] Cf. Ammian. Marc. xiv, 8, 13.

95–6 its boundaries seem to have reached the parallel of Damascus, a line drawn across the Gebel Haurân just north of Bostra assigned a large area to the Syrian administration. Bostra, which received the titles Nova Traiana, became the legionary and administrative headquarters with VI Ferrata as its garrison[1], though Petra remained the principal town and was later dignified with the name of metropolis. One legion was a sufficient protection, and its station suggests that its first duty was to comb out the Haurân country, where the nature of the ground presented difficulties comparable on a smaller scale to those of the Numidian frontier; and the pacification of outlying districts may have taken some years. The Arabian tribesmen were good fighters and auxiliary regiments were raised in time for the Parthian War, in which their familiarity with desert conditions made them specially useful.

Of prime importance, however, was the great arterial road running right through the province 'a finibus Syriae usque ad mare rubrum' which was built between 111–114 under the governor C. Claudius Severus, and of which many milestones still survive. From the Gulf of Akaba in the south, it passed through Petra, Philadelphia and Bostra and continued to Damascus and the Syrian centres, and its purpose was as much commercial as strategic. It marked a fresh stage in the progress of Roman relations with India. A Roman fleet was stationed in the Red Sea, and it was this interest rather than his Dacian successes that brought an Indian embassy to Trajan about 107. Though the province itself was peaceful, a few strong points were fortified to protect the trunk road and its caravans against marauding Bedouin raids, and it has been thought that the forts at least of El-Leggûn and Odruh are Trajanic in date[2]. But if the province owed its incorporation to its value as a highway, its internal development was not neglected, and on this ground alone the annexation was abundantly justified by results. The provision and conservation of water supplies was undertaken at once[3], branch roads spread inwards from the main artery[4], land was rapidly reclaimed for cultivation and settled, and from the Trajanic period dates the rise of many cities, besides fresh prosperity for older foundations such as Gerasa which had already benefited by the Flavian settlement of Palestine.

[1] Replaced under Hadrian by III Cyrenaica from Egypt.
[2] Brünnow-Domaszewski, *Die Provincia Arabia*, I, p. 432; II, p. 24: cf. A. Poidebard, *La Trace de Rome dans le désert de Syrie*, p. 52.
[3] *I.G.R.R.* III, 1273, 1289, 1291.
[4] *E.g. C.I.L.* III, 14176[2,3]; *Ann. épig.* 1927, no. 151; cf. no. 147.

Meanwhile, the uneasy relations between Rome and Parthia
had shown a growing tension. More than once under the Flavian
dynasty there had been at least a threat of war (pp. 143 *sqq.*). The
accession of a prince of known military ambition, who had already
taken part in operations which, if not open warfare, had earned
triumphal honours for their author, bred anxiety in a Parthia
weakened by internal rivalries which the overthrow of the Dacian
king did nothing to allay. That Decebalus and Pacorus had
been in correspondence was a fact which was probably known or
guessed in Rome long before Pliny went to Bithynia, and among
the causes of the Arabian annexation one may well have been the
closing of normal trade avenues through Parthia during the First
Dacian War. And if there was one lesson Trajan had learnt in
Dacia, it was a distaste for compromise. Moreover, from that
date, and especially from the death of Sura about 110, we may
trace a strengthening of the military element in the Emperor's
entourage, and like other great soldiers he grew bolder as he grew
older. In these circumstances the spark of war was not slow to flare.
Pacorus died about 110[1], and in the internal disputes which
accompanied the accession of the new king Osroes, Roman
prerogatives in Armenia were infringed. Trajan seized the opportunity: he had not picked the quarrel, but he was ready for the
campaign, and there is no reason to doubt that he welcomed a
chance to settle the troublesome Armenian question once for all
time[2].

The course and even the chronology of the war which broke
out in 113 are still far from clear; and if a reconstruction of
Trajan's strategy in Dacia depends on frail deductions from a
sculptured record, the historian of the Parthian campaigns must
build for the most part on scraps of late evidence which are even
more easily impeachable. The narrative which follows must be
therefore treated with reserve and many of its conclusions as at
best provisional[3]. The peace of Corbulo in 63, while it had found

[1] Suidas, *svv. ἐπίκλημα, ὠνητή*; Cureton, *Ancient Syriac Documents*,
p. 41; *B.M.Cat. Parthia*, p. 205; cf. R. P. Longden, Notes on the Parthian
campaigns of Trajan, *J.R.S.* XXI, 1931, p. 12.

[2] There is not sufficient evidence in Pliny, *Ep.* x that he had planned it
beforehand, as is sometimes alleged, *e.g.* by O. Cuntz, *Hermes*, LXI, 1926,
p. 192, cf. Longden, *op. cit.* p. 19.

[3] The whole subject is more fully discussed in the article by the present
writer cited above. The chronological problem, whether the aggressive campaigns occupied two years or three, is one which may soon be finally solved
by fresh epigraphic evidence; for the rest no demonstrable conclusions are at
present at all likely (see further, Note 1, p. 858 *sq.*).

a means for both parties to abandon without discredit the pitiful gymnastics of the previous ten years, and did much to enable them to recognize their common interests (Vol. x, p. 773), possessed one vulnerable point. To secure it Rome gave up much: she virtually abandoned Armenia to the Parthians, and perhaps her contemporary statesmen were wise enough to see that the loss was more apparent than real. But on her prestige in Armenia depended the peace of the Black Sea, over whose littoral tribes she retained the overlordship. This was to the Parthians of only secondary interest, though both powers recognized the danger from the Trans-Caucasian tribes, and the terms of peace satisfied Roman requirements by conceding her the right of enfeoffment over Armenia, which henceforth accepted its kings from the Parthian royal house. More than this Rome could not surrender, and the continuance of peace therefore rested on the willingness of Parthia to observe her side of the bargain.

How long Tiridates himself survived his co-signatory is unknown, but in due course and with the approval of Rome one Axidares, a son of Pacorus, ascended the Armenian throne, and here matters stood when, after the death of Pacorus, the new Great King Osroes took it upon himself to depose this individual and proclaim another son of Pacorus, Parthamasiris, king of Armenia in his place. The reasons which prompted Osroes to this decision are obscure. His own version, when confronted by the prospect of war, was that Axidares had proved unsatisfactory to both his masters, which means no doubt that (according to Osroes) he had failed to preserve order in his kingdom[1]; but it is probable that a more compelling motive was the need to secure a crown for Parthamasiris who, as the eldest son of the late monarch, had some title to the Parthian throne itself.

Axidares appealed to Rome and at the same time resisted his brother's invasion, which even by the summer of 114 had gained only a partial, if promising, success[2]. The affair was thus brought to Trajan's notice as a deliberate flouting of the Roman prerogative which was the mainspring of the Neronian treaty, and no responsible government could have ignored the challenge, least of all an emperor whose deeds had already recalled Rome to a sense of her imperial mission. It might have been politic to have

[1] A case against Axidares can scarcely be manufactured from the few obscure hints of trouble among the Black Sea tribes before the Parthian War (and even possibly as far back as Domitian); Suidas, s.v. Δομετιανός; Jordanes, Romana, 267; Moses Chorenensis, II, 54–5.
[2] Suidas, s.v. εὐθεῖαν; Longden, op. cit. p. 25.

stopped at small measures: a personal visit to the frontier and a firm display of force would probably, though not certainly, have restored order and coerced the Parthian king; but it is scarcely surprising that Trajan chose another way. There is no evidence that he originally intended anything more than the annexation of Armenia[1]; and for that there were persuasive reasons, even though fundamentally unsound. Armenia had been a thorn to Rome since the days of Pompey and the only thinkable solution that had not now been tried and found wanting was the clear-cut one of annexation. Such had been the fate of all the Roman protectorates one by one, generally to their material advantage. The last experiments in Dacia and Arabia were an acclaimed success, and with a like solution of the one outstanding problem Trajan might claim to have consolidated the imperial scheme of Augustus and to bequeath to his successors a State unified, respected and secure. If this were all, it had been well, however valueless Armenia might prove. But circumstances to be described drew Trajan on, and imagination—it need not be doubted —lent her wings. If eastern conquest had not yet the lure which generations of adventure, and not least his own, imparted to it, there was a glitter in the Orient even then and the success of Alexander, the failure of Crassus and Antony, were still themes to kindle one who was before all a soldier. And so, on October 27, 113, still uncertain of his final plans, the Emperor left Rome for his last and most expensive enterprise.

At Athens an embassy from Osroes met him but received little satisfaction; and, crossing through Asia and Cilicia, he reached Antioch in person at the close of the year to review the situation[2]. His arrival was greeted by envoys from Abgar, the ruler of the westernmost Mesopotamian principality of Osrhoëne, who was

[1] On this he had probably determined before he left Rome, though Suidas, *s.v.* γνωσιμαχήσας, and Dio (LXVIII, 17, 3) might be quoted to show that he still kept an open mind until his arrival in Syria.

[2] The story of Malalas (XI, 270–3), derived according to himself from Domninus, that he came to meet a Persian invasion of Syria, which had even captured Antioch, cannot be substantiated, despite attempts which have been made to throw over it the mantle of Arrian's authority; Graf von Stauffenberg, *Die römische Kaisergeschichte bei Malalas*, p. 261 *sqq.*, cf. Longden, *op. cit.* p. 29. Nor can the theory, for which there is some support in the writings of Christian authors, of an earlier war about 108 fare better. It is true that Suidas *s.v.* ἐπίκλημα seems to attest hostile manœuvres before the death of Pacorus, but at present he stands alone, although there is some evidence in the coinage of both Alexandria and Antioch that a visit of Trajan to the East was at any rate contemplated about 108.

trying, successfully as it turned out, to preserve his crown by judicious hedging between Rome and Parthia. Accepting for the moment his protest of neutrality, in the spring of 114 Trajan set out for Armenia. The composition of his army remains uncertain. There were already eight legions in the East, XII Fulminata and XVI Flavia in Cappadocia, II Traiana, III Gallica and IV Scythica in Syria, X Fretensis in Judaea and VI Ferrata in Arabia. Of these, VI Ferrata, until recently a Syrian legion, had lately seen service on campaign (p. 237) and its use in the Parthian War is proved[1]. The brunt of the fighting would naturally fall on the legions of Cappadocia and Syria, but the latter seem, as often both earlier and later, to have been of doubtful fighting capacity, at any rate at first, and tried reinforcements from the Danube were accordingly summoned. It cannot be determined at what point the new drafts were sent for, but it is likely that the first serious call came with the extension of the war in 115 and intensified with the emergencies of the following year. In response, the legion XV Apollinaris came permanently to the East, and with it portions of at least four others, I Adiutrix, I Italica, VII Claudia and XXX Ulpia, while *vexillationes* from the other two Lower Moesian legions are not to be excluded[2].

From Antioch, Trajan went first to the headquarters of XII Fulminata at Melitene, on which he conferred some privileges[3]. The place commanded the southern of the two practicable roads into Armenia, and Trajan, though his principal objective lay along the northern route, proceeded to secure his flank by sending a column up the Murad Su to take Arsamosata, one of the principal Armenian towns and the metropolis of this valley[4]. This was accomplished without fighting, and the Emperor continued his journey to Satala, where possibly the first of the Danubian troops met him. At this point, still in strictly Roman territory, he summoned an assembly of the local kings. One of these, Anchialus, king of the Heniochi, was specially rewarded, perhaps for service in a border campaign against his neighbours the Lazae; the others did homage and were confirmed in their kingdoms. The narrow valleys between the Roman frontier and the river Phasis admitted a number of separate chiefs who swelled the

[1] Dessau 2726, 9471.
[2] *I.G.R.R.* III, 173, preserves a trace of the passage of the Danubian troops through Ancyra.
[3] Procopius, *de Aedif.* III, 4.
[4] Adopting von Gutschmid's emendation of Dio LXVIII, 19, 2, cf. Dio, ed. Boissevain, III, p. 207.

gathering at Satala[1]: of more weight were the rulers of Iberia and Colchis and of the Bosporani and Sauromatae north of the Euxine who obeyed the call to give pledges of their loyalty and to receive Trajan's instructions. There was, however, one notable absentee. Trajan had come a long way to meet Parthamasiris, and his subsequent excuse that he had been prevented by his brother's troops was not well received. The march continued up the Frat Su and in the camp at Elegeia, at the strategic centre of Armenia near Erzerûm, the meeting took place[2].

Parthamasiris attempted to justify himself by incriminating Axidares. He declared that his appointment by the reigning Parthian monarch made him the rightful king of Armenia and reminded Trajan of the Neronian agreement, by which all that was necessary was his formal investiture at Trajan's hands. This he had now come voluntarily to receive, and taking off his diadem he laid it at the Emperor's feet. Trajan replied that it had been no part of the Neronian treaty that the Parthian king should depose Armenian rulers, once lawfully invested, at pleasure and without consulting Rome: if such were the case Rome's rights became a farce. But further argument was unnecessary, for it was no longer a question between Axidares and Parthamasiris; Armenia belonged to Rome, and was to have a Roman governor. Parthamasiris and his Parthian entourage were dismissed and were given an escort out of the country, but on the way he shared the fate of many Armenian pretenders before him, and the guilt of his death was imputed to Trajan himself[3]. His disappearance might doubtless be convenient, but the case is unproven; if Trajan was indeed its author he thereby closed another avenue to a reconciliation with Osroes, but against that the annexation itself had already locked the door.

After Elegeia, there was little more to do in Armenia: in the presence of Trajan's overwhelming force its inhabitants were powerless to resist and its provincial organization was undertaken at once. For the present it was to go with Armenia Minor and Cappadocia which were now separated from the Galatian complex, and the new administration was put in the hands of L. Catilius Severus, who had been consul in 110[4]. The annexation made a profound impression at Rome, and Trajan now at last consented to the inclusion of the cognomen Optimus among his official titles,

[1] Arrian, *Perip.* 11.   [2] For the Parthian War see Map 3, facing p. 105.
[3] Suidas, *s.vv.* γνῶσις, παραβαλών; Fronto, *Princ. Hist.* p. 209 N.
[4] *Ann. épig.* 1934, no. 30. Dessau 1338 records probably the first provincial procurator, T. Haterius Nepos, subsequently prefect of Egypt.

while during this year he received two and possibly three fresh imperatorial salutations. Certain details remained to be cleared up. Those chieftains who had not obeyed the summons to Satala, notably perhaps the king of the Albani, who received a new monarch at this time, reaped their reward; and Lusius Quietus with a mobile column was sent down the Araxes valley to receive the submission of the Mardi, to the east of L. Van[1]. By midsummer 114 or little later, the campaign was over.

Trajan was now faced by a new problem. The season was yet young and his army was fresh, having seen little fighting. Should he retrace his steps to Cappadocia or should he return by way of Mesopotamia, testing for himself the sentiments of those satraps who had sent their embassies to Antioch or met his advance with gifts? He chose the latter course, and thereby committed himself irrevocably. On his approach, the Parthian vassal-kings were divided. They were in a difficult position, for of Osroes there was no sign and Trajan's future intentions were uncertain. Descending from Armenia, he occupied Nisibis, which at this time probably belonged to Mebarsapes, whose satrapy of Adiabene covered a wide area on both sides of the river Tigris. A centurion named Sentius had been sent to Adenystrae with a message to this monarch, no doubt summoning him to meet Trajan. Mebarsapes, who had already had a brush with the Romans—perhaps with the column of Quietus on the borders of Adiabene and south-eastern Armenia—and had no doubt an inkling of what was to become of his kingdom, arrested Sentius; but on the approach of Trajan he retired behind the Tigris, and Sentius managed to deliver Adenystrae to the Romans, while Quietus continuing his journey perhaps from L. Van met the Emperor at Singara, which he had occupied without opposition. All northern Mesopotamia was now within Trajan's grasp and the ease of his conquest tempted him. In fact like other Roman demonstrations beyond the Euphrates it had been less a conquest than a triumphal progress, unopposed except by sporadic guerrilla warfare: and indeed the coin legend commemorating the double annexation—*Armenia et Mesopotamia in potestatem P.R. redactae*—suggests as much.

Winter was now approaching and, leaving garrisons behind him, Trajan returned towards Antioch through Osrhoëne, whose king Abgar he had yet to meet. Abgar had temporized so long as he dared, but the approach of troops made his submission inevitable and he received the Emperor at Edessa with protestations of humility which, together, so Dio says, with the personal

[1] Themistius, *Or.* xvi, p. 250, ed. Dindorf, cf. Suidas, *s.v.* ἀμφίβολοι.

recommendations of his son, succeeded in preserving his crown. Trajan was in fact in a good humour. The year's campaigning had been successful beyond all anticipation and had yielded not one but two fresh provinces to the Empire at negligible cost. On the news of the fall of Nisibis he had been popularly accorded the title of Parthicus which appears irregularly on inscriptions from the end of 114, but which was not officially assumed until after the fall of Ctesiphon in the following winter[1]. Abgar thus escaped, but a neighbouring potentate, Sporaces of Anthemusia, was not so fortunate, and fled, leaving his territory to be annexed.

Trajan now returned to Antioch, leaving a substantial army to garrison the new provinces and prepare for a fresh campaign in the following year. The rapidity of his conquest of Armenia, as well as the strategic advantage which it conferred, had made it impossible for Osroes to defend northern Mesopotamia, and there were other reasons for his absence. The disputes following the death of Pacorus II had produced that restlessness among the subordinate Parthian rulers which was a concomitant of nearly every change in the Great Kingship; and with the approach and still more with the success of Trajan, the independence of many of these vassals broke into open rebellion. This insolence was not confined to the satrapies nearest to the Roman arms; for there are traces of revolts in Persis and Elymaïs, while a rival king, another Vologases[2], issued coins from some locality undetermined, and on the shores of the Persian Gulf Attambelus V was perhaps already showing the spirit which inspired both his welcome and loyalty to Trajan in 115–6. It was vital for Osroes to establish some sort of unity within his own realm before he could encounter Trajan, and in this year 114 we find him planning a campaign against yet another princeling, Manisarus, who had taken advantage of the disturbed conditions to possess himself of some territory bordering on Armenia and Mesopotamia which Trajan had not yet reached. Manisarus attempted to negotiate with Trajan, but his ultimate fate is unknown.

But while these troubles made it impossible for Osroes to hold the line of the upper Euphrates or the Chabur, it was otherwise with the Tigris. The vassal-king of Adiabene, Mebarsapes, remained loyal and on his success in maintaining his position on the Roman left flank depended the fate of the Parthian capital at Ctesiphon, lower down the river. To subdue Mebarsapes was

---

[1] See Note 1, p. 858 *sq.* The errors of Dessau 297 testify to the difficulty experienced by the provincials in keeping pace with the rapid changes in the Imperial titles at this time.   [2] See List of Parthian Kings, p. 90.

therefore Trajan's next task, and during the winter the woods round Nisibis were heavily requisitioned for the boats and pontoons needed for crossing the river. Meanwhile, in Syria a disastrous earthquake occurred, the force of which fell most severely on Antioch, now overcrowded with court attendants and camp followers of one and another kind and during Trajan's presence virtually the seat of the Roman government. The Emperor himself was only slightly injured, but among the dead was M. Pedo Vergilianus, one of the *consules ordinarii* for 115, and a third of the city lay in ruins.

Trajan, however, was undeterred by this misfortune, and with the approach of spring departed for the Tigris. His main objective was now Ctesiphon itself, and serious opposition was to be anticipated. A further difficulty lay in the problem of communications and supply, since the invading forces must now leave the tolerably fertile land of northern Mesopotamia for desert conditions. In the circumstances, the use of the Euphrates as well as the Tigris was plainly right. That some advance had been made down this river in the previous year is likely enough, though not yet definitely proved[1]: but in any case vessels of reasonably substantial draught could navigate the river from the Syrian frontier and establish a satisfactory line of communications from that base[2], while the Euphrates expedition could hope to find supplies in the Greek riverain cities on their route. The major military problem lay before the Tigris force, and it was accordingly here that Trajan took command in person.

The river crossing was fiercely contested, but by distracting the enemy with numerous feints and covering the engineers by a barrage from infantry and archers stationed on ships anchored in the stream, a bridge of boats was eventually built and with the arrival of the Roman forces on the left bank the opposition of Mebarsapes collapsed and the whole of Adiabene lay open. Leaving a force to complete its conquest, for it was destined to be annexed also, Trajan descended the river and halted his army short of Ctesiphon, perhaps in the neighbourhood of Baghdad. Meanwhile, the Euphrates force had descended unmolested into Babylonia, possibly as far as Babylon itself[3]. Osroes was still occupied with civil troubles, but it is evident that a defence of

---

[1] The date of the triumphal arch at Doura (S. Gould, *Excavations at Dura-Europos* IV, p. 57) is unfortunately not quite certain.

[2] Cf. Dessau 9471, 2709 (?).

[3] Steph. Byz. *s.vv.* Χαξήνη, Φάλγα, Νάαρδα; cf. Jacoby, *F.G.H.* IID, p. 576 *sq.*

Ctesiphon was expected, and a further problem now arose of transferring to the Tigris the larger vessels of the Euphrates force, suitable for a siege of the city. The original idea of constructing a canal or utilizing the Naharmalcha was rejected as impracticable, and the ships were somehow dragged across the intervening desert. The exact tactics which led to the fall of Ctesiphon are obscure, but it does not seem to have held out long. Osroes himself escaped, but his daughter and his golden throne were among the Roman prizes when Trajan entered the city in triumph.

The fall of the Parthian capital was greeted with rapturous enthusiasm by the Senate, who voted to Trajan the right to celebrate as many triumphs as he wished; and the war seemed over. Into the highlands of Iran it was neither practicable nor desirable to pursue the Parthian king, and Trajan himself reluctantly disclaimed the idea of treading in the footsteps of Alexander. It remained to organize the new provinces. Their occupation lasted so short a time that it has left behind it little trace, and their governors and garrisons are alike unknown. For the latter some if not all of the Syrian legions could now be spared, but the lengthening of the frontier line and the policing of the new possessions must have meant either a permanent weakening of the Danube force, perhaps the removal of I Adiutrix from Dacia, or the raising of fresh units. Events forestalled this need, but roads could not wait; and a milestone of 115–6 has been found in the Gebel Sinjar on the road from Singara to Nisibis[1]. But before proceeding to supervise the final settlement, Trajan took one last step forward. In the winter of 115–6 he descended the Tigris to its mouth and received the personal submission of Attambelus, the king of Mesene, whose territory included the important trading centre of Spasinu Charax and who was confirmed in his dominions as a tributary client-king. With the extension of the Roman authority to the Persian Gulf, the whole of the Mesopotamian trade route to the Far East, which had perhaps been closed to Rome for some years, fell into her hands. To secure it may have been a powerful incentive towards the annexation of Mesopotamia, though that it was the original cause of the war is much more doubtful. The Emperor returned to Babylon, but while he was engaged in drawing up a fresh tariff for this trade and deciding its administration in detail[2], news was brought of

---

[1] *Ann. épig.* 1927, no. 161.
[2] Fronto, *Princ. Hist.* p. 209 N.

a very serious nature: a Parthian army had appeared in Adiabene and the whole of the conquered provinces were in revolt. Not for the first time, the Roman armies had advanced too fast and too far.

The records of the revolt which have survived are too fragmentary and obscure for any detailed reconstruction of the course of events; but enough is known to enable a bare outline to be drawn. At least three separate Roman forces were engaged in its repression, and their movements give some indication of the nature of the attack. The Parthians themselves had concentrated in Media, the strongest province still intact, and from that point launched a simultaneous offensive against Armenia and Adiabene, now the Roman province of Assyria. At the same time a sympathetic revolt broke out in Mesopotamia, where Abgar of Osrhoëne threw in his lot with the insurgents, while in the south the city of Seleuceia expelled its Roman garrison and closed its gates. Only Attambelus, moved perhaps by the proximity of Trajan himself, remained loyal.

The conflict began with a disaster for Rome. Appius Maximus Santra, a consular and perhaps the governor of either Assyria or Mesopotamia, was defeated and killed, according to a probable reading of Fronto, *ad Balcia Tauri*[1], which, if correct, implies an army of invasion descending into Mesopotamia from the northeast. This force was led by a certain Sanatruces, perhaps another brother of Parthamasiris, who after his death would become the Parthian claimant to the Armenian throne, and his son Parthamaspates: and at the same time a second son Vologases entered Armenia and was only checked by the concession of some territory[2]. Meanwhile, in southern Mesopotamia, where, it may be guessed, the bulk of the army of invasion was still encamped, the Romans were more successful and two legions under Erucius Clarus and Julius Alexander recaptured Seleuceia and burnt it. This restored order in the south, and Trajan was free to march north to the heart of the trouble.

That the successful opponents of Maximus now entered Syria, denuded of its troops, and even captured Antioch can scarcely be maintained on the authority of Malalas in view of the silence of Dio, who indeed knows nothing of Sanatruces' part in the

---

[1] Fronto, *Princ. Hist.* p. 209 N; cf. E. Hauler, *Wien. Stud.* XXXVIII, 1916, p. 167.

[2] Dio, *Exc. Ur.* 16 (cf. Boissevain III, p. 219); Suidas, *s.v.* Σανατρούκης, Malalas XI, pp. 273–4 (Bonn).

affair, and ignores the share of the Parthians altogether[1]. According to Malalas, Trajan defeated Sanatruces, who was killed,
after his son Parthamaspates had deserted to the Romans: Dio
states only that Lusius Quietus, now given command of a substantial army and probably already *adlectus inter praetorios* for his
services in 114, successfully recovered northern Mesopotamia,
retaking Nisibis and Edessa, which was sacked and burnt, while
Abgar lost his crown and probably his life also. Of Trajan's
presence in this field Dio says nothing, and it has been supposed
that Malalas here enshrines a tradition which elsewhere also
confused the deeds of the Emperor and his formidable lieutenant[2].
In any case it is not to be doubted that in northern as in southern
Mesopotamia the Romans were eventually successful in regaining
the upper hand, but the fate of Assyria is much more dubious
and Trajan's subsequent actions suggest that it was already lost
to Rome.

He had now a difficult decision to take. Whether the revolt
had been backed by a Parthian force under Sanatruces or not,
Osroes was still intact and might be expected to make a fresh
attempt to recover his losses; moreover, the outbreak of the Jews
in the Levant, which had begun in the preceding year, had
quickly spread and already assumed dangerous proportions. In
these circumstances, Trajan resigned himself to a curtailment of
his plans. Southern Mesopotamia was detached from the province
and reconstituted as a Parthian kingdom under Parthamaspates,
who was crowned at Ctesiphon as a client-king[3]. This was a
makeshift, certainly, but the Euphrates trade route was at least
nominally retained under Roman control. Armenia and northern
Mesopotamia were maintained as provinces, and Trajan himself
turned aside on his journey back from Ctesiphon to direct the
siege of Hatra, a desert stronghold where the rebels still held out.
Like Septimius Severus after him, he failed to take it by assault
and local conditions forced him to withdraw his troops and return
to Antioch. The hardships of desert campaigning and the strain
of the past few months had told heavily on his constitution—he

---

[1] Malalas xi, pp. 270–4. An invasion of Syria is at least more likely at this
point than in 113. For the second part of his account, Trajan's defeat of
Sanatruces, Malalas appears to quote the authority of Arrian's *Parthica*,
and it has therefore been accepted in the text despite the silence of Dio, who
it must be admitted is not very informative about the revolt.

[2] E. Groag, *P.W. s.v.* Lusius Quietus, col. 1880.

[3] An inscription recently discovered shows that by the end of 116 Doura
on the Euphrates had already passed back into Parthian hands; M. Rostovtzeff,
C.R. Ac. Inscr. 1935, pp. 285 *sqq.*

was now past sixty—and shortly after his return his health began
to fail.

At a severe cost, then, the bulk of Trajan's conquests had been
preserved, and their surrender is an event not of his but of
Hadrian's principate. But the shock to the Roman arms had had
a serious effect elsewhere. The most pressing diversion came from
a Jewish outbreak of savage ferocity which starting apparently
from Cyrene soon spread all over the Levant. The trouble arose
in the usual way with racial conflict between Jews and Greeks,
but rapidly developed into a desperate struggle of the Jews against
the imperial government. It began in 115 and in Cyrene the
Jews under a certain Andrew (or Lukuas) quickly gained control.
The numbers of their victims and the appalling barbarities they
committed may be an exaggeration of anti-Semite propaganda;
but it is a fact that buildings and even roads were destroyed and
the province stripped of its cultivators and reduced to ruins[1].
The fury spread to Egypt and Cyprus, and in 116, fanned by the
news from Mesopotamia, it reached alarming heights. In Egypt,
where the absence of many troops in the East made firm repression
impossible, the insurgents were less successful and in Alexandria
the Greeks won the day; but the city was badly damaged and in
many of the country districts the Jews were masters[2]. After the
failure of the prefect, M. Rutilius Lupus, to preserve order, a
failure for which he was not altogether to blame, command against
the rebels was given to Q. Marcius Turbo, commander of the
expeditionary fleet in 114[3], and peace was gradually restored,
though a trail of desolation remained and the campaign was not
over till after Trajan's death. The Jews of Cyprus, who had
destroyed the capital, Salamis, after annihilating its non-Jewish
inhabitants, were more easily coerced by troops of whom a detachment of the legion VII Claudia certainly formed part[4], and a decree
was issued forbidding any Jew ever to set foot in the island again
on pain of death. Meanwhile, the Emperor feared fresh trouble
from the numerous Jews in Mesopotamia, and Lusius Quietus,
an obvious choice, was sent back there with a mission of ruthless
pacification. On his return he was given a fresh charge. Judaea
itself, despite the presence of a Roman force[5], had inevitably

---

[1] *Ann. épig.* 1928, nos. 1, 2; 1929, no. 9; see p. 673. Orosius VII, 12.
[2] Appian, *Bell. Civ.* II, 90, 380; Eusebius, *Hist. Eccl.* IV, 2; *Chron.* ad a.
Abr. 2131–3. Cf. A. von Premerstein in *Hermes*, LVII, 1922, pp. 305–14.
[3] *Ann. épig.* 1927, no. 3.   [4] Dessau 9491.
[5] *C.I.L.* III, 13587, *vexillatio* of III Cyrenaica. The regular garrison,
X Fretensis, formed part of the Eastern expeditionary force, Dessau 2727.

shown signs of a sympathetic restlessness, and its reward in 117 was to receive as governor the sinister Moor, now promoted to consular rank and higher than ever in the imperial favour[1]. With the suppression of the Palestinian Jews the rebellion subsided; in the face of disciplined troops the fanaticism of the rebels was mere suicide.

But the eastward drain of the army and the rumours of its failure, the same causes that had inflamed the Jewish outbreak, were being felt further afield. On the lower Danube the Roxolani were restless, and away in Britain—though here from other causes—the northern garrisons were already in retreat[2]. Though by the summer of 117 order had returned in the eastern provinces, the Mesopotamian frontier was still unsettled and the precarious hold of the Roman nominee at Ctesiphon already slipping. The resources of the Empire were severely strained, and there was need of vigorous direction if the recent conquests should be maintained. But this was lacking. The Emperor was worn out, and for some months now his health had shown alarming symptoms. He nevertheless determined on a fresh campaign, but before he could leave Antioch a stroke left him partly paralysed; his dropsy was increasing, and at the end of July 117 he reluctantly set out by sea for Italy, leaving Hadrian in charge of the army in Syria. But he was not destined to see Rome or enjoy his doubtful triumph. A sudden change for the worse compelled him to halt at Selinus in Cilicia, afterwards Traianopolis, and there probably on August 9th, after declaring his long delayed adoption of Hadrian[3], he died.

In his introduction to a history of the Parthian campaigns of L. Verus, Fronto has much to say of the example of Trajan. After touching on his warlike exploits, he remarks that even Spartacus and Viriathus had considerable military ability, but that in the arts of peace 'vix quisquam Traiano ad populum, si qui adaeque, acceptior extitit'[4]. The foregoing pages illustrate the facts on which his estimate was based: and from them the man's personality gradually emerges. His personal tastes were simple: his recreations virile. Learning, as it was then fashionable at Rome, he

---

[1] For details of Lusius' activity in Mesopotamia and Judaea, cf. Groag, *op. cit.* cols. 1881–4.

[2] The withdrawal of the Scottish garrisons was perhaps already complete before Trajan's reign, cf. T. Davies Pryce and R. Birley, *J.R.S.* xxv, 1935, pp. 59 *sqq.* (see, however, Sir G. Macdonald, *ib.* pp. 187 *sqq.*); but in northern Britain the trouble was already brewing which burst out under Hadrian (p. 313).   [3] On this debated question see below, p. 299 *sq.*

[4] Cf. also Eutropius, VIII, 4, *gloriam tamen militarem civilitate et moderatione superavit.*

lacked, but he encouraged its practice and favoured philosophers, and among those closest to him Plotina, Sosius Senecio and perhaps Licinius Sura, were keen patrons of the subject[1]. In matters of religion he made no claims to personal worship, but on the death of Marciana in 112 he deified both her and his own natural father; his 'patron saint' among the gods was Hercules, the comparison of whose career with the labours of the *princeps* could not escape comment[2]. In contrast to the deviousness of some of his predecessors, he liked to be thought of as sincere and straightforward, and there is no reason to think that he wore a mask[3]: his administration and legislation show alike that he tried to foster these qualities. Yet his bluntness did not amount to rigidity: he showed himself ready to treat all matters referred to him on their merits, and his kindliness became a byword. The Emperor Julian, writing many years later, makes the gods decide that Trajan excelled all other emperors in clemency ($\pi\rho\alpha\delta\tau\eta s$)[4]. Such a man was needed in the Roman Empire when Trajan lived, a strong man and a just man; Trajan, whatever the wisdom of his military adventures, was both, and he served the needs of his time. And when in the fourth century the Senate, echoing the sentiment that had prompted Trajan's favourite title, prayed for a new *princeps* that he might be *felicior Augusto, melior Traiano*, they paid a tribute that was well deserved[5]. As subordinate and prince, in peace and in war, through fifty years of arduous service to his country Trajan had earned his proud epitaph.

[1] For Trajan's own literary studies as *princeps*, cf. Dio Chrys. *Or.* III, 3.
[2] *E.g.* Dio Chrys. *Or.* I, 84. Coins of Hercules are very frequent. Cf. Strack, *op. cit.* 95–104, 133–4. For the *ludi Herculei*, see p. 215.
[3] Cf. especially Pliny, *Pan. passim*; and Dio Chrys. *Or.* III, 2.
[4] Julian, *Symp.* 328 B.
[5] Eutropius, VIII, 5. For subsequent legends of Trajan and his admission into Heaven at the instance of Gregory the Great, cf. Paribeni, *Optimus Princeps*, II, pp. 312–16.

INDEX TO NAMES

Achaea, F 5
Africa, C–E 6, 7
Alexandria, G 7
Antioch, J 5
Aquincum, F 3
Aquitania, BC 3, 4
Arabia Nabataea, HJ 7
Arae Flaviae, D 2
Asia, GH 5
Athens, F 5
Augusta Vindelicorum, D 2

Baetica, AB 5
Belgica, CD 2
Bithynia et Pontus, GH 4
Black Sea, GJ 3, 4
Bostra, J 6
Britannia, BC 1, 2
Byzantium, G 4

Caesarea (Iol), C 5
Caesariensis, BC 5, 6
Cappadocia, HJ 4, 5
Carnuntum, E 2
Cilicia, HJ 5
Corsica, I., D 4
Crete, I., FG 6
Cyprus, I., H 6
Cyrenaica, F 7

Dacia, FG 3, 4
Dalmatia, EF 3, 4
Damascus, J 6
Decumates Agri, D 2
Deva, B 1
Durostorum, G 4

Eboracum, B 1
Egypt, GH 7
Emerita, A 5
Epirus, F 5

Galatia, H 4, 5
Gaza, H 7
Germania Inferior, CD 2
Germania Superior, CD 2, 3

Illyricum, EF 3, 4
Italy, D–F 3–5

Jerusalem (after 130 Colonia Aelia
  Capitolina), H 7

Lauriacum, E 2
Lindum, B 1
Londinium, B 2
Lugdunensis, BC 2, 3
Lugdunum, C 3
Luguvallium, B 1
Lusitania, A 4, 5
Lycia et Pamphylia, H 5

Macedonia, F 4
Mauretania, BC 5, 6
Mediterranean Sea, C–G 5, 6
Moesia Inferior, FG 4
Moesia Superior, F 4
Mogontiacum, D 2

Narbonensis, CD 3, 4
New Carthage, B 5
Nicomedeia, G 4
Noricum, E 3

Palmyra, J 6
Pannonia Inferior, EF 3
Pannonia Superior, E 3
Potaïssa, F 3

Raetia, D 2, 3
Rome, E 4

Sardinia, I., D 4, 5
Sarmizegethusa, F
Sicily, I., E 5
Sinope, H 4
Syria, J 5, 6
Syria Palaestina, HJ 6, 7

Tarraco, C 4
Tarraconensis, AB 4, 5
Thessalonica, F 4
Thracia, FG 4
Tingis, B 6
Tingitana, AB 6
Tolosa, C 4
Trapezus, J 4

Venta Silurum, B 2
Viminacium, F 3
Vindonissa, D 3
Viroconium, B 1

1 = Alpes Graiae et Poeninae
2 = Alpes Cottiae
3 = Alpes Maritimae

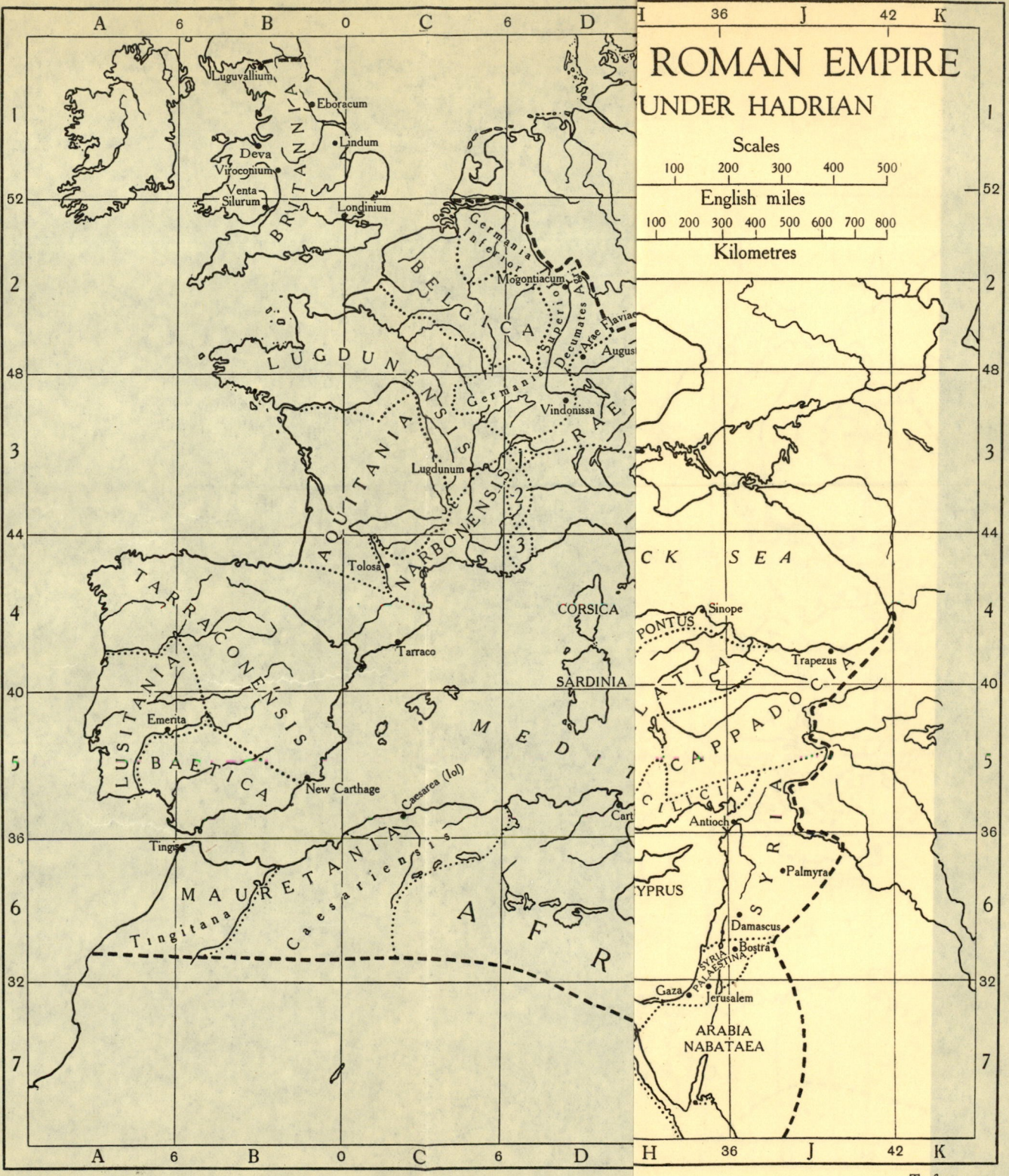

MAP 8

ROMAN EMPIRE
UNDER HADRIAN

Scales

100   200   300   400   500
English miles
100 200 300 400 500 600 700 800
Kilometres

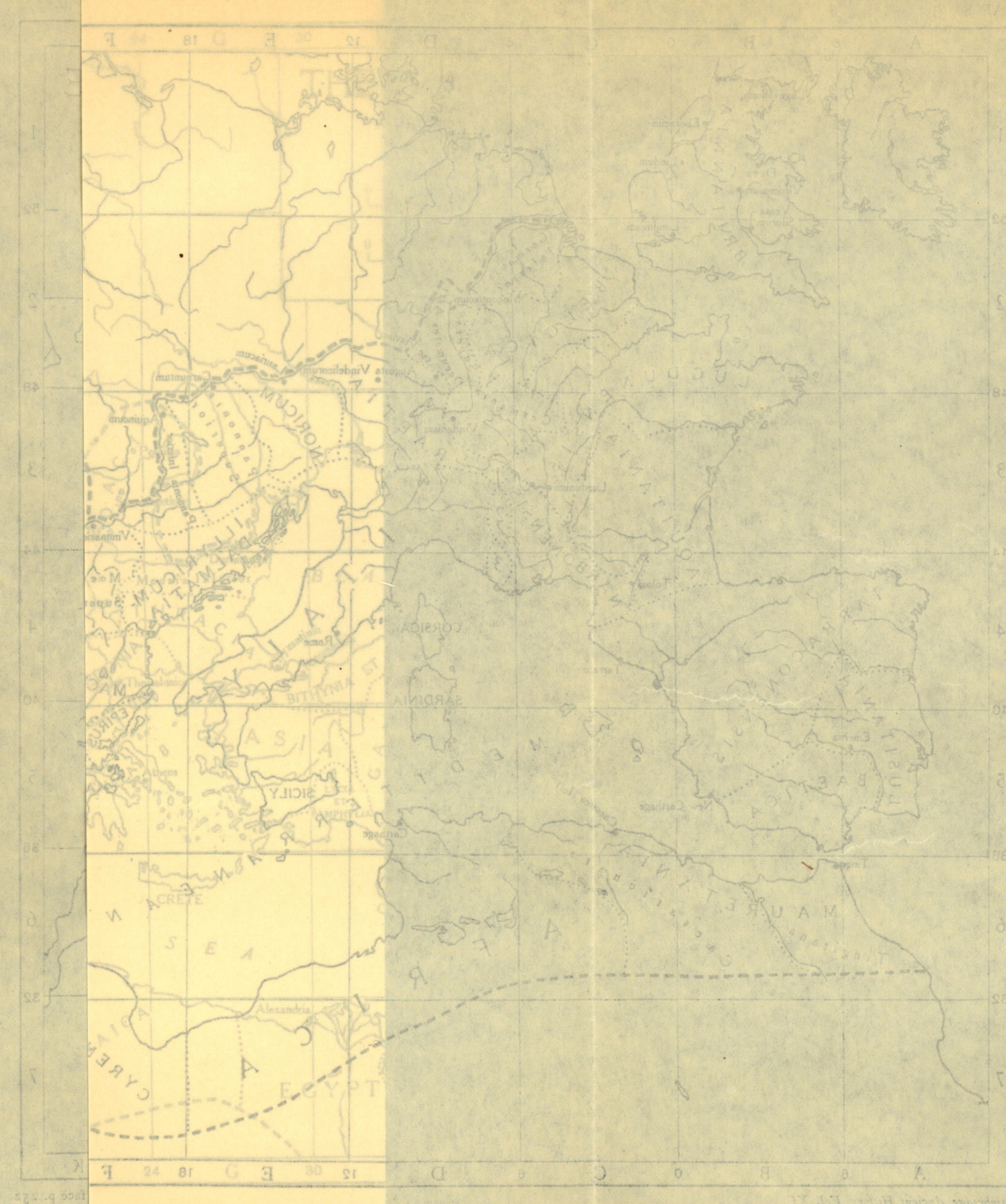

CHAPTER VII

THE RISE OF CHRISTIANITY

I. INTRODUCTION

THE death of Marcus Aurelius in A.D. 180 is for Gibbon the beginning of decline and fall in the Roman Empire. The same date may, as suitably, be taken to mark the emergence into the clear daylight of history of that highly organized World-Church which was destined to survive, and in the West to supplant, the World-State that was crumbling into ruin. Not until the sack of Rome by Alaric had inspired Augustine's vision of the *Civitas Romana* giving way to the *Civitas Dei* did the Church become fully conscious of its destiny; but already within a century and a half of the Crucifixion it had become in essential features an ecclesiastical State—with a culture fundamentally different from, and in certain ways inimical to, that inherited by the Empire from the city-states of Greece and Rome.

The rise of an institution so remarkable becomes less difficult to understand if we note the contrast between two periods. For three-quarters of a century there is intense spiritual vitality and experiment, expressing itself in an ever-increasing variety. Then follows a time of conservation and consolidation, during which the main task of the leaders was to restore a coherence, which was threatened by the legacy of diversity left by the earlier and more creative period. Of the first period the writings of the New Testament (with few exceptions) are the literary deposit; the second finds its culminating expression c. A.D. 186, in the *Adversus Haereses* of Irenaeus.

Irenaeus was the first to attempt on the grand scale a standardization of the doctrines of the Church. He is the father of Systematic Theology. He had studied the defences of Christianity addressed to the pagan world by highly-educated 'Apologists' like Justin Martyr as well as the works of simpler-minded opponents of Gnosticism like Papias and Hegesippus[1]; and he managed to unite the philosophic approach of the former with the appeal of the latter to apostolic tradition—all on the basis of the acceptance of the books of the New Testament, alongside of the Old, as inspired scripture. In the next generation Tertullian in Africa, Clement in

---

[1] See B. H. Streeter, *The Primitive Church*, pp. 288 *sqq.*, also 17 *sqq.*

Alexandria, Hippolytus in Rome, all read Irenaeus; and most of the statements they make about apostles and their writings look like slightly embroidered versions of what he says. Nevertheless they are quoted by Eusebius (and by some modern authors) as independent witnesses; nor can the possibility be dismissed that Irenaeus himself at times 'embroidered' or misunderstood statements which he in turn derived from Polycarp, Papias or Hegesippus. The survey attempted in this chapter ends with the death of Trajan in A.D. 117, but a mention of Irenaeus[1] was needed on account of a grave misconception in the traditional view of church history. What Irenaeus represents is not apostolic Christianity, but rather a critical stage in a process of standardization of beliefs and institutions, which continued to be carried on by oecumenical councils and afterwards by the Papacy, and of which the logical culmination was the Infallibility Decree of 1870.

II. ROMAN AND JEWISH EVIDENCE

To the satiric mood of Tacitus it was a congenial task to paint the picture of Rome in flames, Nero singing over it the Tale of burning Troy, and then—himself accused of ordering the fire—finding a convenient scape-goat, as well as a further opportunity for indulging his histrionic tastes, in a holocaust of Christians fantastically conceived in gardens illuminated by human torches[2]. But the very notoriety of the events of A.D. 64—which formed the grand introduction, so to speak, of the Church to the notice of the World—explains the exiguous character of the evidence concerning its early history derivable from Roman sources. A group of proletarians, condemned by an emperor for the stupendous crime of setting fire to the capital of the world, was necessarily from henceforth a secret society suspected by the police. Thus we should not expect to find Roman evidence of the doings of Christians except in the equivalent of what in modern times we should call 'Police Court News'; and precisely in the few surviving allusions to police measures or *causes célèbres* we do find references to Christianity. The most definite of these may be recalled.

Suetonius gives general summaries of police measures under various emperors. Under Nero he mentions penal measures against Christians[3]. He may refer only to the persecution described by Tacitus; but the context suggests permanent regulations of a repressive character. Sulpicius Severus derived his account of the

---

[1] See further, below, vol. XII.   [2] See vol. X, pp. 725 *sq.*, 887 *sq.*
[3] *Nero*, 16.

siege of Jerusalem from the lost portion of Book v of the *Histories*[1].
The speech by Titus on the advisability of destroying the Temple
shows that, in the view of Tacitus, the Flavian Emperors, though
quite aware that Christianity differed from Judaism, yet regarded
it as a highly objectionable 'Jewish superstition.' *In the light of
this* we must consider the charge brought by Domitian in 95
against his cousin Flavius Clemens and his wife Flavia Domitilla.
The charge, says Cassius Dio[2], was 'atheism, for which offence a
number of others also, who had been carried away into Jewish
customs, were condemned—some to death, others to confiscation
of property.' Judaism, a religion recognized by law, was not very
likely to be deemed 'atheism'; but Christians were Gentiles carried
away into Jewish customs, and they were undoubtedly styled
'atheists,' on account of their attacks on all pagan religion[3].
Moreover, the site of an inscription appears to prove that the early
Christian *Coemiterium Domitillae* belonged to this same Flavia
Domitilla[4]—described as *Vespasiani neptis, i.e.* grand-daughter of
Vespasian[5] (see above, p. 42).

   Of greater interest is the correspondence (*c.* A.D. 112) between
Pliny, when governor of Bithynia, and the Emperor Trajan.
Suetonius and Tacitus take it for granted that the unpopularity of
the Christians is deserved. To Pliny must be given the credit of
trying seriously to investigate the facts. He satisfied himself of the
truth of the statement made to him that Christians abjured criminal
acts, adultery, or breach of faith, that they ate at their assemblies
ordinary food (evidently a reference to the accusation of cannibalism) and that on certain days they met before dawn to sing
responsively hymns to Christ as to a God. The head of their
offending is their contumacious refusal to *obey*—a grave offence
in Roman eyes—when ordered by the magistrate to renounce their
religion.

   Trajan's reply to Pliny is important as revealing the attitude
adopted by the State to the Church about the end of the period
covered by this chapter. Christians are not to be sought out for
punishment, nor arrested on anonymous accusations; if openly
delated and convicted, they are to be granted a free pardon on
recantation, but, if they decline to recant, they must be punished.

---

   [1] This was shown by J. Bernays, *Die Chronik des Sulpicius Severus,*
pp. 53–7.
   [2] LXVII, 14, 2; the words are from Dio's epitomator Xiphilinus.
   [3] 'Down with the atheists' is the cry of the mob in the *Martyrdom of
Polycarp* (9) in A.D. 156.
   [4] Dessau 8306.   [5] *C.I.L.* VI, 948, 8942.

We note that both Pliny's letter and Trajan's answer take it for granted that the profession of Christianity is illegal; the point of Trajan's rescript is that, though in the last resort the authority of law must be upheld, its non-observance in this case is to be connived at so far as is decently possible. Christianity to the educated Roman was one of those oriental cults the westward spread of which was felt to be a sign of the decadence of the age; it differed from the rest in vileness of practice and criminal intent: *nova et malefica superstitio; per flagitia invisos; exitiabilis superstitio.* Seemingly the charges, mentioned later by Tertullian, of 'Oedipodean morals and Thyestean banquets' were already current. To Pliny Christ is a cult-deity; Tacitus is aware that, unlike other cult-deities, he was a historical character of recent date—having been put to death (presumably for good reason) by the Roman procurator Pontius Pilate.

Jewish sources—in effect, Josephus and the Talmud—yield, though for different reasons, less evidence than Roman. Josephus was a hellenized Jew, who wished to appear more hellenized than he was; and it was essential for him to retain the favour of the Emperor Vespasian. In the years preceding the sack of Jerusalem, A.D. 70, the Jews had managed to incur universal detestation in the Gentile world; Josephus wrote largely with the apologetic aim of lessening this impression. Obviously, then, the less he said about Christianity, the better; the Jews were unpopular enough without emphasizing the fact that they were responsible to the world for originating this 'superstition' also. There are in Josephus only three brief allusions—to John the Baptist, to Jesus and to James the brother of the Lord[1]; and unfortunately those to Jesus and James are open to the suspicion of interpolation by Christian scribes[2].

The Mishnah, the earliest portion of the Talmud, does not seem to have taken shape till after A.D. 150, and was not published in its present form before A.D. 220. The nature of the work—a collection of rulings on debatable texts of the Old Testament—is such that it has little occasion to allude to non-biblical historical events other than acts or sayings of great Rabbis; it never, for example, mentions

[1] *Ant.* XVIII [3, 3], 63–4; [5, 2], 116–119; XX [9, 1], 200.
[2] Eisler's suggestion (*The Messiah Jesus, etc.*) is interesting, that the phrases evidently of Christian origin are not mere additions to the text, but *laudatory substitutions* for remarks which in the original were hostile and offensive. But nothing can be said for his conjectural restorations of the presumed original by means of interpolations found in a Slavonic version of Josephus—which seems to have been made about the time of the Crusades. See J. M. Creed, *Harvard Theological Review*, XXV, 1932, pp. 277 *sqq.*

the name of the great national hero, Judas Maccabaeus. In the Talmud Christians (*Minim* = heretics) are rarely mentioned; and only in order to condemn some Christian usage or interpretation of scripture. The few allusions to Jesus himself are rare, and clearly originate in anti-Christian polemic; they are merely evidence of the prior existence of Christian beliefs about Jesus which they are a clumsy attempt to rebut[1].

III. CHRISTIAN EVIDENCE

Of primary importance are the epistles of the Apostle Paul. A century of critical discussion justifies us in accepting as authentic (naming them in a probable chronological order) I and II Thessalonians, Galatians, I and II Corinthians, Romans, Philippians, Colossians and Philemon, perhaps Ephesians, but only some fragments (mostly embodied in II Timothy) of the epistles to Timothy and Titus (see below, p. 290 *sq.*). The epistle to the Hebrews does not purport to be by Paul; it was already well known to Clement of Rome (it was probably originally addressed to that church), and may be dated 80–90. Chronologically the epistles of Paul are linked, on the one hand to the first generation of Christianity, on the other to secular history. Casual allusions to Peter and John, and to James and other 'brethren of the Lord' show that the author was a contemporary of Jesus; while by means of the Acts of the Apostles he can be connected with certain personages whose dates are known to us from pagan sources. Since the conjunction of the epistles with the Acts is the sheet-anchor of early Christian chronology, more must be said about that book.

The latter part of the Acts gives an account of complicated journeyings to and fro in Asia Minor and through the coast towns of the Aegean made by Paul on his various preaching tours. These bring him into contact with persons like Sergius Paulus, Gallio, Felix, Festus and Agrippa, about whom we have information from other sources; and he stays at places about which, from inscriptions and allusions in ancient authors, we know a great deal. Such is the accuracy with which the representation of Acts accords with other information, that the book must *either* have been written by a companion of the Apostle—as the employment of the first person plural 'we' in the latter part of the Acts would *prima facie* suggest —*or else* reproduces with considerable fidelity a diary kept by such a companion.

This narrative, in combination with occasional allusions in the letters of Paul, enables us to determine the place of writing, and

---

[1] See J. Klausner, *Jesus of Nazareth*, pp. 18 *sqq.*

approximately the date, of the majority of his letters. We are thus enabled to make full use of the historical evidence implied not only in these particular letters, but others which are connected with them by style or otherwise. For example, the first epistle to the Thessalonians was evidently written during the visit to Corinth described in Acts xviii, when Paul was arraigned before the proconsul Gallio. An inscription found at Delphi shows that Gallio was proconsul in A.D. 52, and that office was rarely held for more than one year. I Corinthians was written during the long residence at Ephesus (Acts xix); II Corinthians on the way from Ephesus to Achaia (xx, 1–2); Romans when again at Corinth (xx, 3); Colossians and Philemon during Paul's last imprisonment. As I Thessalonians (with the *possible* exception of Galatians) appears to be the earliest of the surviving letters of Paul, we can assign the whole series to the period 50–64. The letters, however, were clearly written in the latter part of his career, so that Paul was almost an exact contemporary of the historic Jesus; for the Crucifixion occurred under Pontius Pilate who governed Palestine A.D. 26–36[1].

The critical historian will draw a distinction between the earlier and later parts of Acts. Thus, while xvi–xxviii rests in the main on the personal reminiscences of a companion of Paul, the section i–xv appears to depend on traditions derived from Jerusalem or Antioch, of which some may well go back to circles hostile to Paul. We cannot recover the sources used; but, since the Gospel of Luke is by the same author, we can test his general fidelity to sources by the way in which in the earlier volume he uses Mark. So tested, he is seen to reproduce a source far more faithfully than does his contemporary Josephus when dealing with the Old Testament and Maccabees.

The Gospel of Luke and the Acts constitute a single work in two volumes—written for an educated public. The work is, in a sense, a 'Defence of Christianity,' in the form of an account of the origins of the religion from the birth of the founder up to the eve of Nero's dramatic attack upon it. The case of Flavius Clemens and Domitilla, if rightly interpreted above, proves the existence before A.D. 95 of interest in Christianity in some circles of the Roman aristocracy. Since the Acts ends on an exultant note, with Paul's preaching of Christianity in Rome, it is probable that the author had these circles in mind. He is naturally concerned to state a good case for the religion he professes—and that, not merely because he believed it to be true (and there was no inducement in those days

---

[1] Chronologists dispute whether the year of the Crucifixion was A.D. 29, 30 or 33. See vol. x, p. 649, n. 4.

to profess Christianity unless one was passionately convinced of its truth) but also because a secret society suspected by the police simply cannot afford 'to wash its dirty linen in public.' Hence he emphasizes the favourable attitude of Roman officials, like Pilate (Lk. xxiii, 1–25), Gallio (Acts xviii, 14–17), or Festus (Acts xxv, 25; xxvi, 31–2), who all attest their conviction that Christians are neither criminals nor political revolutionaries. For the same reason he says as little as possible about the internal feuds between Paul and the Judaizing party who stood for strict observance of the Law of Moses—feuds which, as we gather from the Epistles, nearly split the Church. Again, as appears from Paul's own summary of his toils and endurances (II Cor. xi, 24–7), there are big gaps in his story. The omission is due partly, perhaps, to lack of information, but mainly to his having less interest in an Apostle's biography than in the onward march of the Church. Lastly, being absolutely convinced of the supernatural mission of Christ and his Apostles, the canon of probability which he naturally applies in the acceptance or rejection of stories involving miracle is the opposite of that of a modern historian.

After the epistles of Paul, the earliest surviving document of primitive Christianity is the Gospel of Mark, probably produced in Rome about A.D. 65[1]. Papias (writing *c.* 135) reports 'The Elder'—a personage of an earlier generation—as saying that Mark based his Gospel on reminiscences of Peter's preaching[2]; and many, though not all, of the stories included in the Gospel may well have been derived from that Apostle.

It is generally agreed[3] that the authors of the Gospels ascribed to Matthew and Luke derived from Mark the greater part of their *narrative* material, other than their accounts of the Infancy and the Resurrection Appearances. Mark, however, contains very little

[1] The 'abomination of desolation' (Mk. xiii, 14) is not an allusion to the destruction of the Temple of Jerusalem in A.D. 70. Mark would not have used the masculine participle ἑστηκότα (contrast ἑστός in Mt. xxiv, 15) with the neuter word βδέλυγμα unless with the express intention of indicating that he interpreted this famous but mysterious phrase as the description of a *person*. The book of Daniel concludes with a prophecy (xii, 11–12) that the present world-order will come to an end 1335 days after the appearance of this βδέλυγμα; Mark takes this to mean the personal Anti-Christ who (as appears from II Thess. ii, 1–12) was expected to manifest himself *in the Temple* shortly before the Return of Christ. Mark would not have held this view unless the Temple had been still standing when he wrote.

[2] Eusebius, *Hist. Eccl.* III, 39, 16.

[3] For evidence in regard to this and other statements about the Gospels, see B. H. Streeter, *The Four Gospels.*

of the *teaching* of Christ; for this we are mainly dependent on Matthew and Luke. To the extent of about a couple of hundred verses their concurrence in material not derivable from Mark is such as to make it reasonably certain that they both used a second document, which was already *in the Greek language*. The lost document was probably older than Mark; it is commonly referred to as Q. Most of the parables, and many of the epigrammatic sayings, of Christ occur either in Matthew or in Luke only. The extent and character of the material found only in Luke makes it highly probable that (besides Mark, Q and oral tradition) he made use of a third considerable written source. This source may have already been combined with Q, and the combination (which can in that case conveniently be styled Proto-Luke) may have included a version of the Passion story. That some at any rate of the sayings and parables found in Matthew only were derived from a written source is a probable hypothesis[1].

The Gospel of Matthew is quoted in the (probably Syrian) *Didache* of perhaps *c.* 100 and by Ignatius of Antioch (*c.* 115) in a way which implies that it was the predominant Gospel, if not the only one, known to these writers. The dates which can reasonably be assigned to it vary between A.D. 80 and 100. The Gospel was evidently composed in a church where the Jewish element was strong; but the statement of Irenaeus, repeated with amplifications by later Fathers, that it was originally 'published among the Hebrews in their own language' is almost certainly an inference —and that a mistaken one—from the statement by Papias (quoted by Eusebius): 'Matthew composed τὰ λόγια in the Hebrew tongue, and each one translated them as he could[2].' Our First Gospel is based on a combination of two Greek sources, Mark and Q; it cannot therefore be a direct translation from a single work in

[1] 'Form Criticism' is a name given to a recent technique which endeavours to cross-examine the oral tradition presumed to lie behind documentary sources like Mark and Q, and to distinguish in that tradition between elements which reliably represent words or deeds of Jesus and those which reflect the point of view of the early Christian community. These endeavours are often suggestive; but, in the opinion of the writer, they are always precarious and sometimes perverse. This chapter, however, has been so planned that, even if the contrary were the case, it would not require to be re-written.

[2] *Hist. Eccl.* III, 39, 16. Some suppose that by τὰ λόγια is meant Q, others a collection of Messianic proof-texts; more probably the reference is either to our First Gospel or to the discourses contained in it. Irenaeus took it to refer to a Hebrew original of the First Gospel; but if Papias meant this, he was manifestly in error.

Hebrew. But if it was not composed in Hebrew, the inference that it originated in Palestine falls to the ground. Indeed, its dependence on Mark for narrative material, and the legendary character of its small supplements to Mark's account of the Passion, tell strongly against an origin in the country where authentic independent traditions must have longest survived. As the place of origin, a probable guess is Antioch.

The Gospel of Luke seems to have been written independently of Matthew and at about the same date. The Theophilus to whom it is addressed is saluted as κράτιστε—an honorific title, which might be rendered 'Your Excellency.' Theophilus, then, may be the 'name in religion,' as it were, of a Roman of high rank; and, as the Acts tells the tale of the march of Christianity from Jerusalem the capital of Judaism to Rome the capital of the world, it was probably written in that city. The preface implies that the work was put out under the author's own name; it was customary to give this on a kind of label which hung outside the roll. In spite of some difficulties the tradition may be accepted that the name was Luke. The Gospel of Matthew, on the other hand, may have been originally anonymous—a communal document produced for the use of a local church by a conservative combining and editing of venerated documents in the light of generally acceptable interpretations of obscure or controversial points[1].

The Gospel of John is not intended to be read as a biography, it is a mystical and theological interpretation of the life and teaching of Christ. The author draws material from Mark and Luke; doubtless also from independent tradition, though neither the extent nor the historical value of such tradition would seem great. Perhaps the most probable solution of an endlessly debated question is the hypothesis that the Gospel is by the same author as the three epistles of John, but was published posthumously, after some drastic editing. The writer of two of these epistles speaks of himself as 'The Elder,' and may be identical with 'The Elder John' mentioned in a fragment of Papias (c. 140) as 'a disciple of the Lord'—that is, presumably a person who had seen Christ but was not of the Twelve. In that case the Johannine epistles may be dated c. A.D. 90; but the Gospel, if posthumously edited, may not have been given to the Church at large for many years. Hardly otherwise can we explain why the letter of Polycarp of Smyrna, which has echoes of nearly every book of the New Testament,

---

[1] Fragments survive of *Apocryphal Gospels* current in the second century; but these appear to be of later date than Matthew and Luke, and probably than John.

including I and II John, shows no trace of a knowledge of the Fourth Gospel[1]. The book of Revelation is by a Christian prophet, who also bore the quite common name of John; his work, addressed to the 'seven churches of Asia,' c. 85–95, represents a point of view widely removed from that of the Gospel.

The epistles ascribed to Peter, James and Jude demand a brief mention. Scholars who uphold the authenticity of I Peter usually explain its apparent dependence on Paul by the hypothesis that the Silvanus (= Silas, companion of Paul) named as the amanuensis was really joint author. Its references to impending persecution are of special interest as reflecting the attitude towards a persecuting State adopted by Christian leaders. If the letter is not by Peter himself, the persecution referred to may be the one centring in Smyrna (c. A.D. 90) alluded to in Revelation (ii, 10); or it may be that carried out in Bithynia under Pliny in A.D. 112. The ascription to James of the writing which bears his name (like that of Hebrews to Paul) was probably made after the name of the real author had been forgotten; it was perhaps produced in Rome, c. 95. Jude can hardly have been written by a brother of James; but may well be the work of a Jude who was bishop of Jerusalem about 105. The authenticity of II Peter was rejected by Eusebius on the ground that it was not quoted by early Christian writers. It incorporates, almost verbatim, the greater part of Jude; it was probably composed 130–150[2].

Of the writings known as the 'Apostolic Fathers' there are three[3] which may fall within the first century, and which at one time came near inclusion in the New Testament—Clement, Hermas and the *Didache*. The letter from the Church of Rome to that of Corinth ascribed to Clement was apparently written shortly after the death of Domitian in A.D. 96. It at once acquired in many churches an all but canonical status. It is notable that, while the Old Testament alone has for Clement scriptural authority, Romans, I Corinthians and Hebrews are already religious classics. The *Shepherd* of Hermas is by a 'prophet,' who wrote in Rome. He speaks of Clement as a contemporary, from which it would appear that at any rate the first four Visions (which were published at once) are

---

[1] Cf. P. N. Harrison, *Polycarp's Two Epistles to the Philippians*, p. 257.

[2] For a detailed discussion of the dates and provenance of the Epistles, other than Paul's, and of the writings of the Apostolic Fathers, see B. H. Streeter, *The Primitive Church*.

[3] A portion of the *Ascension of Isaiah* may well fall within the first century. See the edition of R. H. Charles.

not later than A.D. 100[1]. The manual of Church Order known as the *Didache* or *Teaching of the Twelve Apostles* appears to emanate from Syria; but the date *c.* A.D. 100, which is accepted by most scholars, is hotly disputed. The epistle of Barnabas so-called and a homily misnamed the 'second epistle' of Clement are of unknown authorship. They may be dated 110–135, and are probably both products of the Church of Alexandria. In this church there was some disposition to include Barnabas in the Canon; and in the Codex Sinaiticus it forms, along with Hermas, a kind of appendix to the New Testament[2]. In the Codex Alexandrinus (probably written in Constantinople) a similar position is given to I and II Clement.

Ignatius, Bishop of Antioch, late in the reign of Trajan, was condemned to the beasts in the Colosseum. On his way to Rome he wrote letters of which there survive seven—four written from Smyrna and three from Troas. In human interest as the reflection of an individual character the letters of Ignatius are second only to those of Paul. They were collected at once by Polycarp, Bishop of Smyrna, who sent copies to the Church at Philippi with a covering letter of his own. The extant letter of Polycarp seems to be made up of two letters. The covering letter above mentioned, written before there had been time to get news of Ignatius' martyrdom, constitutes chapters xiii–xiv; chapters i–xii represent a second letter written perhaps as much as twenty years later[3].

This enumeration of Christian 'primitives' would be misleading without a warning against the error of treating the surviving literature as a representative cross-section of Christian opinion in the Sub-Apostolic Age. There must have also existed literature which at a later date was definitely branded as of a Gnostic or Ebionite tendency; this ceased to be copied, and has not survived. The severity of the struggle in the second century with extreme representatives of these tendencies is explicable only on the hypothesis that in a less extreme form they had a strong following within the Church.

[1] The statement in the Muratorianum that the *Shepherd* was by a brother of Pius, bishop of Rome (140–155), involves, among other difficulties, that of attributing to the brother of a Pope a work which internal evidence shows to have been written before the development of the monarchical episcopate at Rome. The statement is probably part of a campaign (of which there is other evidence) to eject the book from the place it had almost secured in the Canon of the New Testament.

[2] Lightfoot's dating of Barnabas before A.D. 79, though unfashionable, is not impossible.

[3] See Streeter, *op. cit.* pp. 276–8, and Harrison, *op. cit. passim.*

IV. THE FIRE FROM HEAVEN

Christianity began as a de-ossification, so to speak, of the emphatically monotheistic legalism of Pharisaic Judaism. It was as though the Lord, who spake of old by Amos and Isaiah, had awaked as one out of sleep, and like a giant refreshed with wine. The trumpet call is sounded by a strange ascetic, John the Baptist, in whom is the spirit and power of an Elijah. He summons to righteousness against the background of that hope of a catastrophic world-redemption which had been generated by two centuries of Jewish apocalyptic. But 'the law and the prophets were until John'; he is a mere precursor, there follows one who will baptize, not with water, but with fire.

'I came to cast fire upon the earth ; would that it were already kindled' (Lk. xii. 49). Jesus comes as the originator of a new epoch, but also as the climax of that unique historic process in which the prophets of the Old Testament are the outstanding figures. To him as to them, the divine initiative is paramount. His call to his appointed task is by a vision and a voice. He constantly resorts to the mountain for communion with the Divine. His whole being is 'God-centred,' but it is orientated towards a deepened and more developed conception of God than that of the old prophets. Concisely this is expressed by the choice of the metaphor of father, in substitution for that of king or judge, as the regulative description of the relation of God to man. Correlated to, and consequent on, this enrichment in the conception of God, is a reiterated insistence on absolute trust as the essence of the right attitude of man to the Father in Heaven. How futile, then, to debate whether or no Jesus went up to Jerusalem *in order to* die; he went because he felt it was God's purpose that he should go; but even in Gethsemane he was not *certain* how that purpose would work out. To summarize the essence of religion he selected two precepts from the Law, Thou shalt love the Lord thy God, with all thy heart and soul and mind and strength, and thou shalt love thy neighbour as thyself. But obedience to these, as he saw it, meant a revolutionary reversal of human values which will estimate greatness in proportion to service, 'Whosoever of you will be chiefest shall be servant of all.' Hence the paradox of the Beatitudes, 'Blessed are ye poor,' for those who have little at stake in this world may more easily adopt towards God the approach of a little child —which is the way of entry into the Kingdom of Heaven.

For nearly two thousand years Christians have wrangled over the meaning of the titles Son of Man, and Son of God, which Jesus seems to have accepted—at least when applied to him by others, even if he did not (as some think) explicitly claim one or both for himself. Had such issues been directly put before him, he would have replied, we may perhaps surmise, that in regard to intellectual problems of theology, as to the application to life of principles of ethics, light sufficient for the day is given day by day, along with 'daily bread,' to those who look upwards to their Heavenly Father; and that insight into these questions sufficient for the needs of an individual or an age is among the things that will be added unto those who seek first the Kingdom of God and His righteousness.

Be this as it may, it would be absurd to attempt, in a sub-section of a single chapter, to give an outline of the life of Jesus, to present in systematic form his teaching, to relate it rightly to that of Rabbis or Apocalyptists, to portray his character, or to appraise the significance of his person for religion. So large is the theme, so vast the literature concerning it, that it is better altogether to decline this task. Moreover, the title of this chapter demands rather that we trace the developing results of the dynamic impact of his personality as exhibited in the more striking features of the Christianity of the Apostolic Age.

The Theocentric outlook taught by the prophets of the Old Testament, and re-asserted in the teaching of Jesus, is notably characteristic of the primitive Church. Only it has become more all-pervasive, more intimate and richer in content, because it is now inextricably mingled with what we must call a 'Christo-centric' religious attitude. In the first generation, and among Jewish Christians, this was possible without any sort of theological speculation as to the person of Christ. The Palestinian Jew was the reverse of philosophically-minded; he naturally thought in pictures. Jewish apocalyptic provided the vivid picture of a supernatural personage, the Son of Man, sitting on the right hand of God until the Great Day, when he would become the divine instrument for judging the wicked and initiating the righteous into an aeon of superhuman beatitude. The belief in the Resurrection of Jesus was indissolubly connected with the identification of him with this apocalyptic Son of Man; but that was not all. The day of Pentecost which followed the Crucifixion was a moment of spiritual crisis. The little company found itself possessed by a throbbing consciousness of a Spiritual Presence—accompanied by a psychological upheaval which found expression in ecstatic utterance and a 'visualization' of tongues of fire. They *knew* themselves to be in personal contact with the Risen Christ. This mystical apprehension of 'a presence' they expressed to their own minds under the analogy of the then familiar phenomenon of spirit-possession. The vividness of the experience, combined with the Jewish lack of interest in metaphysic, made it possible for them to speak of the possessing spirit alternatively as 'the spirit of God' or 'the spirit of Christ,' or simply as 'Christ,' without feeling any need to relate these modes of expression to one another in a logical or theological way. 'Now the Lord is the Spirit; and where the spirit of the Lord is, there is liberty' (II Cor. iii, 17). Not until Christianity had invaded the Greek world, with its pre-occupation in metaphysic, did questions of this kind demand an imperative answer. Rumblings of the controversy which the attempt to give them a philosophical answer inevitably produced can be heard in Colossians; in the opening section of Hebrews, and more clearly in the Fourth Gospel, we find adumbrated the main line along which the thinking of the later Church was to develop.

Possession by the Spirit is spoken of by Paul as a phenomenon whose presence was as capable of objective verification as is that of a physical disease, save that it manifests itself not as weakness but as power (Gal. iii, 2–5). The immediate results of this experience of spirit-possession defined in terms of Christ were psychological and ethical. It produced an internal revolution in the outlook of the individual. 'If any man is in Christ, he is a new creature; the old things are passed away.' The community of disciples became a fellowship, instinct—almost hilariously so (Phil. iv, 4)—with 'love, joy, peace, longsuffering, gentleness, goodness, faith, meekness, temperance,' which were the authentic 'fruit of the spirit' (Gal. v, 22). The words are Paul's, but the quality of life they describe he had found already existent in the Church. One natural expression of this spirit was the attempt to 'have all things common'; another was that habitual submission of all problems, individual and communal, to the direction of the Holy Spirit, which is so emphasized in the Acts[1].

This communal spirit-possession has a bearing on the tradition of the sayings of Christ and stories of his deeds. Those which have come down to us have done so because they commended themselves to the spiritual insight and ethical values of the primitive community. They afford, therefore, further evidence of the quality of life in the community which selected and preserved them. Nor are they less evidential to those who accept the contention of 'Form

[1] References to this kind of 'guidance' occur even more frequently in the Western text, *e.g.* Acts, xvii, 15; xix, 1; xx, 3. This text must be as old as A.D. 150, and many of its readings look primitive. Cf. A. C. Clark, *The Acts of the Apostles*; also see *Journ. Theol. Stud.* xxxiv, 1933, pp. 232 *sqq.*

Critics' and others, that many of these sayings or stories are a product of 'the community mind.' Take, for example, the saying, 'Where two or three are gathered together in my name, there am I in the midst'; if this was not pronounced by the Master when on earth, only the more clearly is it evidence of the conviction of the community which attributed the words to him.

Yet another expression of this spirit-possession was the re-appearance of 'the prophet.' The prophets of the New Testament epoch are like those of the Old, in that they were more frequently concerned to preach righteousness than to predict the future; but there is an important difference. The Old Testament prophets arose in a small nation which felt its national deity to be close at hand; and prophecy reached its sublimest expression in the Babylonian exile, where the faithful community knew itself to be, as it were, an island of devotedness to the true God in an ocean of false religions. But later Jewish monotheism, by stressing the majesty of God and the littleness of man, had made the gap between man and God so great that belief waned in the continuance of the kind of personal contact between them which revelation implies: in the great days of old, God had spoken with man through his prophets, He would not so speak to the little men of the degenerate present. For Christians this was changed. Now that the divine spirit was thought of as being somehow one with the spirit of that gracious Jesus whom they had known on earth, this notion of the distance and remoteness of the Divine passed away. Once more it seemed natural that sons and daughters should prophesy, that young men should see visions and old men dream dreams—and had not such an outpouring of the spirit been foretold for the last days? (Acts ii, 16 *sq.*). Thus it became an everyday event for some Christian to stand forth in the community as a prophet; but instead of beginning, 'Thus saith the Lord,' his message was given as directly inspired by the Spirit of Christ.

The sublime and varied quality of this spirit of prophecy, when functioning at its best and highest, stands out in numerous passages in the New Testament. Thus in the midst of a long argument to the Corinthians, on the right use of spiritual gifts, Paul suddenly passes from prose to poetry, and, with rhythmic speech matching exalted mood, dictates the Hymn to Charity (I Cor. xiii). Again the substance, perhaps even the wording, of many of the discourses in the Fourth Gospel—so the author more than hints (John xvi, 12–14)—came to him through the spirit[1]. So, too, it was 'in the spirit on the Lord's day' that there came to the Seer in Patmos

[1] Cf. B. H. Streeter, *The Four Gospels*, pp. 365 *sqq.*

visions of the Adoration of the Lamb and of the New Jerusalem coming down from God out of heaven (Rev. iv; xxi, 2 *sqq.*).

V. JEW AND GENTILE

After the Fall of Jerusalem in A.D. 70, the membership of the Church became more and more of Gentile origin. This meant a revolutionary change of interest; and therefore the emergence of questions about which there was serious dispute. The Jew sought after righteousness, the Greek after wisdom; and philosophy to the Greek was what the Law was to the Jew. It is not surprising, then, that, while in the first century the question most hotly debated was the permanent obligation of the Law of Moses, in the second century it was the Gnostic theory of Creation, or the philosophic implications of belief in the Divinity of Christ.

But for some time even Gentiles displayed little interest in the philosophical issues raised by Christian teaching, for the simple reason that they confidently expected an immediate return of Christ in glory to judge the world and inaugurate a reign of supernatural blessedness. Indeed, this 'Advent hope' was the very core of the 'good news' which the missionary proclaimed. Paul, in writing to the Thessalonians (I Thess. iv, 15 *sqq.*) and Corinthians (I Cor. xv, 52), takes it for granted that he would himself live to witness this event. And there are sayings in the Synoptic Gospels which, whether or no they are authentic utterances of Christ, at any rate prove that Christians supposed that this belief rested on his explicit teaching. A community living thus in daily expectation of the End of the World would not make plans for future development; and it would take as little interest in questions of organization as in the philosophical implications of belief. With the Final Doom impending, what mattered was before it was too late to bring to as many as possible the message of salvation: 'Repent, for the Kingdom of Heaven is at hand.'

But from the very practical nature of this task arose a practical question. For centuries Prophets and Apocalyptists had taught the Jew to look forward to the Great Day when the yoke of the heathen would be broken and Israel would enter into its promised destiny on an earth transformed. Then was the call to repent, and so share in the glories of the coming kingdom, addressed to the Jew only—or also to the Greek? Paul tells us (Gal. i, 15 *sq.*) that from the moment of his conversion he had felt that his own duty was to preach to the Gentiles, but that James (the brother of the Lord), Peter and John were no less convinced that their mission was confined to the Jews, though (apparently only after careful consideration of the case submitted to them by Paul and Barnabas) they recognized that Paul's work was also appointed to him by God (ii, 7 *sqq.*).

A considerable party in the Church were strongly opposed to Paul's views on the importance of the Gentile mission, and still more so to his contention that Gentile converts were not to be bound by the Law of Moses. One of the earlier sources incorporated in the Gospel of Matthew evidently emanates from this 'Judaistic' party. Thus the instruction to the Twelve on the subject of their missionary duties limits these to Israel. 'Go not into any way of the Gentiles, and enter not into any city of the Samaritans: but go rather to the lost sheep of the house of Israel...verily I say unto you, Ye shall not have gone through the cities of Israel, till the Son of man be come' (Mt. x, 5–7, 23). This limitation to Israel is justified on the ground of the nearness of the End; it is not that Gentiles and Samaritans have no souls to save, but that the Jew has the first claim to hear the call, and there will not be time enough to reach both. The phrase 'the cities of Israel' has a large sound; it would naturally mean the Israelitish world, not the limited number of townships that a half-dozen pairs of Apostles could cover in an apparently brief and experimental preaching tour. It is a plausible conjecture that the Matthaean version of the commission to the Twelve is the utterance of some Jewish Christian prophet— reproducing and amplifying words of Christ preserved in oral tradition—at the time of the controversy about the admission of Gentiles to the Church. Since a prophet was regarded as one through whom the Spirit of Jesus made authentic communications to his followers, 'a word of the Lord' so received did not differ in authority from an utterance made during his earthly career.

The unexpected success of the Gentile mission forced to the front an issue far more controversial. Were Gentile converts bound by the Law of Moses? In particular, must they submit to the rite of circumcision? Political and religious causes, past and present— memories of the Maccabees, nationalistic detestation of Roman rule, the blood of martyrs and the hope of glory—had combined to make Judaism a 'Religion of the Law.' Might Gentile 'breeds without the law' inherit the 'promises of Israel,' so faithfully deserved, so long deferred; and that without submitting to the yoke which was for Israel at once its discipline, its burden and its pride?

On this point, our evidence suggests, there was a divergence of view even among the three 'reputed to be pillars' of the Church. Peter comes to Antioch, doubtless to preach to the Jews who formed one-third of the population of the third largest city in the

Roman Empire. He there finds Gentile Christians; for refugees from the persecution in which Stephen fell had been the first to preach to the Gentiles in Antioch (Acts xi, 20). He eats and drinks with them on terms of religious brotherhood. But such conduct involved Peter himself in serious transgression of the Law; for Gentiles would not be scrupulous to serve at table only what the Jew regarded as 'clean' meats. Next to idolatry the eating of unclean meats was the greatest offence which an orthodox Jew could commit. No wonder that, when news of Peter's conduct reached Jerusalem, a deputation was sent down from James to protest. So vehement were their representations that not only did Peter give way, but even Paul's fellow-worker Barnabas. Paul tells us what he said on that occasion (Gal. ii, 11–12); unfortunately, he does not tell us what effect his words produced. Did Peter resume his previous liberal conduct? Or did he decide henceforth to observe the Law, fearing that, unless he made this concession to the conscience of the weaker brethren, he would wreck the mission to the circumcision which, after all, was his special call? Probably the latter; had Peter given way to Paul, surely the mere statement of the fact would have routed Paul's opponents in the Galatian churches.

The position of Paul in regard to the Law is clear. So, at the opposite pole, is the position of James, which is known to us from Acts xxi, 18 *sqq.*, as well as from Josephus and Hegesippus. Paul held that by the death of Christ an era had been ended; the Law had indeed been divinely instituted, but only for that era; now it had been simply abrogated. This attitude to the Law was a logical deduction from what to him was the new and essential thing in Christianity, the substitution of a 'Christo-centric mysticism'— a dependence on the Christ within, spiritually apprehended—for a religion of obedience to a transcendent Deity whose will was expressed in a code of rules. On the other hand the party of James —or at least its more extreme representatives—were zealous, not merely for the Law of Moses, but also for the observance of the meticulously elaborate rules worked out by the Rabbinic inter- preters of the Law. Doubtless it is to some prophet belonging to this party that we owe 'a word of the Lord' prescribing deference to their interpretations as lawful successors of Moses: 'The scribes and the Pharisees sit on Moses' seat: all things therefore whatso- ever they bid you, these do and observe' (Mt. xxiii, 2 *sq.*). We may suspect a similar origin for the condemnation of Paul's doctrine that the Crucifixion had abrogated the Law, 'Till heaven and earth pass away, one jot or one tittle shall in no wise pass away from the law, till all things be accomplished (*i.e.* its abrogation would not be till the End of the World). Whosoever therefore shall break one of these least commandments, and shall teach men so, shall be called least in the kingdom of heaven' (Mt. v, 18–19). Here the words 'and shall teach men so' must be a reference to Paul, who, we note, is not absolutely excluded from the Church, but degraded to the rank of 'least in the kingdom of heaven.' To this party Christianity was a 'new law.'

Peter occupied an intermediate position. Left to himself, he had spontaneously taken the liberal line; for what Paul accuses him of in Galatians is not wrong belief, but 'hypocrisy'—that is of outward action which contradicted his real belief. The accusation was made in heat, and is not really fair to Peter; for Peter on this occasion behaved as did Paul on other occasions, 'To the Jews I became as a Jew, that I might gain Jews;...to them that are without law, as without law,...that I might gain them that are without law' (I Cor. ix, 20–21). Paul himself must have come to see this: for at a later date he speaks of Peter (Cephas) in quite a different tone (I Cor. i, 10 *sqq.*; iii, 22; ix, 5). He will not admit any fundamental opposition between himself and Peter, in spite of differences sufficiently conspicuous to make it possible for some at Corinth to hail them as leaders of rival sects. Paul seems to have grown more tolerant with years. To conciliate Jewish opinion he circumcised the half-Jew Timothy (Acts xvi, 3); and his discussion of food-scruples in Romans (xiv, 19–23) shows him ready to make large concessions to Jewish Christians even of the strictest school.

The degree of authenticity that can be attributed to the speeches and epistles attributed to Peter in the New Testament is not such as to make it possible to call them in as further evidence for his views. But his conduct at Antioch, until called to order by James, makes it likely that it is to his recollection that we owe three passages in Mark: Jesus' defence of his disciples for failing to observe the Pharisaic fast days (Mk. ii, 18 *sqq.*); his condemnation of Pharisaic rigour in Sabbath observance (Mk. ii, 23 *sqq.*; iii, 1 *sqq.*); his denunciation of ceremonial washings, of tricks for making void the word of God by scribal tradition, and the saying 'making all meats clean' (Mk. vii, 1–23). At any rate, it must be insisted that the practical example of Peter, rather than that of James, is the more likely to reflect the spirit of the teaching of Christ. For Peter was the leader of those who actively followed him; James was the eldest of those brethren of Jesus who, during the period of his public preaching, not only did not believe in him, but were even disposed to accept the suggestion that his mind was unhinged

(Mk. iii, 2 1). And if the position of Peter in regard to the Law was intermediate between those of Paul and James, it may well be that it was also intermediate in their conceptions of the religious relation between the believer and the Christ in Heaven.

James is named by Paul as one of those persons to whom, as to Peter himself, was vouchsafed a Resurrection Appearance. This doubtless marks the moment of James' conversion. But, once he had joined a community which believed Jesus to be Messiah, James would naturally, as the eldest male of the Messianic house, become its titular head. That, no doubt, is why the three 'pillars' of the Church are mentioned by Paul in the order James, Peter, John (Gal. ii, 9); and why James settles down as the permanent head of the Church in the sacred city of Jerusalem. On the re-constitution of that Church after the desolation of A.D. 70, Symeon, a nephew of James, became its bishop; indeed, a kind of Caliphate, hereditary in the family of Jesus, would have been a development obvious and natural to the Jewish mind. But the Jewish War had more than decimated the Palestinian church; Jerusalem was again destroyed in 135, and after that no Jew might live there. Mean-while, Gentile Christianity had become empire-wide; and, largely owing to the genius of Paul, it had taken a form which could neither be understood in, nor directed from, a centre wholly alien to the culture of the great world. Nevertheless, even in the latter part of the second century there were still Christians who wished to ascribe to James a quasi-Papal authority[1].

VI. VARIETIES OF EXPERIENCE AND BELIEF

Jerusalem, like Mecca to-day, was a pilgrimage centre to which, especially at the great feasts, came Jews from all parts of the known world. This was, at the start, a great asset to the Church. To the pilgrim, especially if he be a poor man and lives in a far country, a visit to the Holy City is an event for which he has been hoping

---

[1] In the *Clementine Homilies* Peter himself is represented as writing a letter beginning: 'Peter to James, the lord and bishop of the holy Church, under the Father of all, through Jesus Christ.' In the same work Clement writes a letter announcing his appointment as the successor of Peter as Bishop of Rome, which begins: 'Clement to James, the lord, and the bishop of bishops, who rules Jerusalem, the holy Church of the Hebrews, and the Church everywhere excellently founded by the providence of God.' At the opposite extreme was Marcion's elevation of Paul. The Twelve had so misunderstood the teaching of Christ that it had to be revealed anew to Paul; so that his epistles and the Gospel of his follower Luke—drastically revised by Marcion—constituted the sole authentic revelation of the Good God. See below, vol. XII.

and saving for years; he arrives in a state of religious exaltation. The majority carried away by the contagious enthusiasm of multitudes would depart satisfied; but there must have been many who felt strangely disappointed at the contrast between the ideal Jerusalem of their dreams and the Jerusalem of actual fact, with the crowd of swindling parasites which infests all pilgrim centres, its money-changers and sellers of beasts in the Temple courts and the crude details of a sacrificial ritual which the religious sense of the more ethically sensitive had already outgrown. In such a mood a pilgrim would be peculiarly receptive to the message of the Christian preacher. At many a Passover or Pentecost, a Jew or proselyte of the Dispersion will have caught the fire of the new religion, and returning to his distant home, become a centre for spreading the message. Often, no doubt, then as now, small parties of pilgrims from the same place travelled together; and sometimes such a group would have been converted as a whole, and so, at once on its return, there would be the nucleus of a local church. That perhaps is how it came about that already before the conversion of Paul there was a church as far afield as Damascus (Acts ix, 10). But the converts who thus became founders of churches had commonly received very little instruction; and there was no New Testament, no Creed, no written manual of theology, no accepted liturgy, which they could take with them. It is not surprising, then, that a century after the Crucifixion we discover a great diversity among persons claiming the name Christian; that is only what we should expect. What demands explanation is rather the large measure of agreement that persisted within the main body—the more so since by that time most of them were Gentiles converted from many and various types of paganism.

The continued existence of a central party, able to resist the centrifugal tendency inherent in the conditions of the first century, was due in the main to the wide circulation of, and the authority ascribed to, certain writings: (1) the Old Testament, with its emphasis on the unity of God, and on the moral standard which God requires of man; (2) collections of sayings of Christ; of which, it would seem, the oldest and most widely known was the document Q embodied in the First and Third Gospels; (3) the Gospel of Mark, whose wide circulation is proved by the fact that it formed the basis, not only of the canonical Gospels, but of the gnosticizing Gospel of Peter and perhaps of other Apocryphal Gospels; (4) certain epistles of Paul. Of these, I Corinthians seems to have been the most read, and to have got into general circulation before the rest, either alone or with Romans, and perhaps Ephesians.

In the course of time the weight and effectiveness of these documents—and therefore their influence on the Church as a co-ordinating factor—was progressively enhanced by (1) the re-organization by Matthew and Luke of the biographical material of Mark along with the teaching preserved in Q and other documents; (2) the clarification of the relation of Christianity to the Old Testament by the elaboration of the argument from prophecy. This was worked out by Matthew, Luke–Acts, and the epistle to the Hebrews in three different ways, which may respectively be named the mechanical, the historico-evolutionary, and the allegorical; (3) the increased impressiveness lent to the epistles of Paul by the fact of their being gathered into a single corpus, and then read against the background provided by the Acts, which gave definiteness to his personality and impressed upon the Church his immense services to the Christian mission.

But though this further body of literature was mainly produced between 80–95, it did not at once become authoritative in all parts of the Church. Hardly earlier than 120 would it have secured a recognition sufficiently wide to make it a powerful centripetal force. Indeed the ascription to Matthew, Mark and Luke of a co-equal and quasi-canonical authority was quite possibly the outcome of a conference held in Rome as late as 119[1]. The Fourth Gospel, though probably written before A.D. 100, was slow in securing acceptance—especially in Rome. But by 180 it had become possible with general consent to ascribe plenary inspiration to the Four Gospels, Acts, and a selection of epistles (which varied, but only slightly, from church to church) and in most churches the book of Revelation. Thus a New Testament came into being over against the Old, but organically related to it[2].

The canonization of the New Testament was a precondition of the development of the Catholic Church into a kind of inner world-state within that of the Roman Empire; for the theoretical basis of its law, discipline and philosophy was belief in a Divine Revelation contained in the sacred books. It was therefore taken for granted that the theological views of the authors of these books *must* be identical. That assumption is seen to be untenable once they are studied historically. It is, however, a little unfortunate that their individuality and variety is usually presented to the student under

---

[1] Cf. B. H. Streeter, *The Four Gospels*, p. 525 *sq.*

[2] This canonization is of importance to the historian in another way. It made the text sacred, and therefore saved it from being continually expanded or rewritten to meet the tastes of later generations—as happened to the Apocryphal Gospels and Acts and to early Buddhist scriptures.

the title of 'New Testament Theology.' The questions which the
historian will most desire to raise are psychological rather than
doctrinal. Why did people *wish* to join the Church? What was it
that made this new religion a source of comfort, power and inspiration to those who turned to it? The answer is that different
people were appealed to by different aspects. No less than seven
main types of approach can be illustrated by the documents included in the New Testament; and, since the followers of any
religious or political leader always include many who reproduce
his views in a one-sided and exaggerated form, we may reasonably
infer that the characteristic features of each of these seven types
were to be found in a far more accentuated form in different parts
of the sub-apostolic Church.

I. Even at the present day the majority of mankind is per-
petually haunted by dread of malignant spiritual powers. In India,
China and Africa, a magician may put a spell with withering and
devastating effects on a man's person, child or beast; a demon may
possess his wife or daughter; or one of the innumerable gods may
take offence at some neglect and punish it with misfortune or
disease. The religion of the Old Testament, without any assistance
from scientific knowledge or rationalistic philosophy, but by the
sheer potency of religious and ethical insight, had broken the
power of magic and witchcraft and, where possible, eliminated its
professors; it had affirmed a unity of God which made pointless the
fear of any god but one; and, by making His character predominantly Righteousness, it had removed that kind of fear of the divine
which necessarily results from belief in deities who are essentially
non-moral. But the Gentile world—outside highly educated
circles—was obsessed by the need of propitiating gods many and
capricious, convinced that the destinies of the individual are controlled (often in a malign way) by the spiritual powers inherent in
the planets, trembling before the astrologer and the magician, and
familiar in daily life with cases of insanity or neurosis raised to an
intenser pitch, and given a destructive and malicious direction, by
the belief that the cause was the possession of the patient by an
evil spirit. The early Christian was unable to counter these beliefs
with weapons drawn from the armoury of science; he did so by
maintaining that Christ, sitting on the right hand of God, yet
permeating the personality of the believer as a re-invigorating and
fortifying power, was ever waging a victorious war with all and
every spiritual power of evil—in the planetary spheres, in the
middle air where demons roam, and in the cities and villages of
earth. In Christ's power, therefore, his follower could be *sure* of

victory, whether his warfare was against 'principalities and powers and malign spirits in exalted spheres,' against the spells of the local magician, or against wandering demons seeking an opportunity to enter his body and possess his mind.

Demon-possession was common even in Palestine; and contact with a personality like that of Jesus might well result in a cure in certain cases where a psycho-neurotic disorder was diagnosed as demon-possession. But what the historian has to explain is, not how Christ might have cured demoniacs, but the relatively large proportion of space given to such cures in the very brief account which Mark gives of his career antecedent to the last week at Jerusalem. The proportion is explained by the obsession of the Gentile world with the fear of evil spirits. A similar motive explains the recounting in Acts of cases where Apostles by sheer force of spiritual personality vanquish magicians[1]. So Paul himself refers more than once to 'signs and wonders,' 'which Christ wrought through me...by the power of the Holy Spirit'[2].

II. To many converts the essence of the 'good news' lay in the words 'The Kingdom of God is at hand.' The present world-order is doomed, the Messianic age is about to dawn; only in order to participate in that glorious age, the individual must repent. This message was a gospel of hope and deliverance, not merely to Jews —who resented the domination of the 'holy people' by pagan Rome—but to the poor and oppressed, especially to slaves, in the Gentile world. Of the first Christians many, like the Communists of the present day, confidently expected themselves to live to see the mighty put down from their seats and the exaltation of the humble and meek—only this would happen, not as the result of political insurrection, but through the direct act of God in the hour of Judgment.

In Thessalonians the hope of an immediate return of Christ to end the present world-order is central even in the thought of Paul; in subsequent epistles, though never abandoned, it gradually recedes to the circumference of interest. The Lucan writings carry this process a stage further. Luke believes that Christ will return, but at a date which is vaguely postponed, 'until the times of the Gentiles be fulfilled (xxi, 24)'; and the belief scarcely affects the heart of his religion. In the Fourth Gospel the doctrine of the sending of the Spirit, the Comforter, is for all practical purposes substituted for the expectation of a visible Return. But *pari passu*

---

[1] Acts, viii, 9–24; xiii, 6–11; xvi, 16–18. For a similar conflict between a Christian Sadhu and a Hindu magician, see C. F. Andrews, *Sadhu Sundar Singh*, p. 162 *sq.*   [2] Rom. xv, 18–19; cf. II Cor. xii, 12.

with this spiritualization of the Apocalyptic hope, there went on in other circles an intensification and a progressively concrete dramatization of it. Matthew lays more stress on the Return than Mark, and adds picturesque details like the Last Trumpet; and Mark has more of this than Q[1]. But the book which consists of nothing else is the Revelation of John, one of the latest, and at the time most influential, in the New Testament. Few things more clearly illustrate the diversity in the early Church than the development side by side of tendencies so contrary to one another.

III. Paul's religion has been described as a 'Christo-centric mysticism'; that is, as one which seeks union, not like Greek or Indian mysticism, with the Absolute, but with the Divine Christ—a heavenly spiritual Being who somehow mediates or represents God Himself, in a way which Paul seems to have felt small necessity to represent in philosophical terms.

Paul shares with Jewish Christians the belief that the End is at hand, and that Christ will shortly come to judge the world. It is the problem of repentance that he conceives differently. To many, perhaps to most, religious Jews the Law was not merely an object of veneration but a source of comfort. 'Lord, what love have I unto thy law; all the day long is my study in it.' Similarly, the author of the *Imitatio Christi* found inspiration in the theology and discipline of the Catholic cloister. But the Law was to Paul what 'monkery' was to Luther; each felt that the system in which he had been bred had utterly failed him, and that the endeavour to achieve righteousness by the effort of the will is futile. But there had come to Paul, as later on to Luther, an experience—interpreted as a personal relationship to the living Christ—so vivid as to be capable of description by the metaphor of 'Christ born in me.' With this came a complete change in the orientation and inward quality of his whole personality which made the doing of the will of God no longer the grudging fulfilment of an external command, but the expression of an inward passion. Since, then, for Paul redemption is an inward change which turns what was once an irksome duty into a passionate desire, the Gospel is (from one point of view) essentially a state of mind which consists in freedom from the Law. The Law, though ordained of God for a good purpose, has now by the divine act been abrogated. Paul, theoretically at least, does not distinguish between the ceremonial and the moral law, or even between Jewish and Gentile ethic. All law, *quâ* rule to be obeyed, has been abrogated. The converted man is so completely a new man that, if he does what he likes, he will

[1] Cf. *Oxford Studies in the Synoptic Problems*, pp. 422 *sqq.*

necessarily do that which is pleasing to God, for it is no longer he that acts but the spiritual Christ that dwells in him.

To express the attitude of the believer which results in this mystical union with Christ Paul uses the word 'faith.' By it he does not mean intellectual acceptance of a creed or proposition, but loyalty, love and devotion something like what in Indian religion is known as *bhakti*. Like *bhakti* it is capable of being expressed in hymns of praise. Paul and Silas burst out into singing at midnight in the prison at Philippi (Acts xvi, 25)—in the light of which incident we should read: 'Be filled with thanksgiving. Let the presence of Christ dwell in you, a well-spring of abounding wisdom; teach and encourage one another with psalms, with hymns, and with songs of the spiritual life; making music in your hearts in gratitude to God. Indeed, whatever you say and do, let all be resting on the Lord Jesus, and through him giving thanks to God the Father' (Col. iii, 15 *sqq.*, free rendering). In the historic phrase, 'Justification by Faith,' Paul unduly strains the ordinary connotation of the word 'faith' in the hope to make it cover the *bhakti* quality in the attitude to Christ described above as that of the Christo-centric mystic.

But the idea of justification by faith was one likely to lead to practical difficulties when the doctrine expressed by it was taught to persons whose conversion had been less thorough than Paul's own. That, no doubt, is why in every epistle we find him piling up exhortations to practical morality. Nor was the precaution un-necessary. In the epistle of James—not by the brother of the Lord but by a 'teacher,' perhaps originally anonymous (Jas. i, 2)—there is an elaborate discussion of the faith of Abraham. This is evidently intended to rebut the inference drawn from Romans—and no doubt acted upon—by certain professing Christians, that, so long as you believe rightly, conduct does not matter. It is easy to see how certain schools of Gnostics could quote the authority of Paul for an antinomianism which justified grave immorality. Well might the second-century author of II Peter write of his epistles: 'Wherein are some things hard to be understood, which the ignorant and unstedfast wrest, as they do also the other scriptures, unto their own destruction' (II Pet. iii, 16).

Paul's teaching in regard to the Law, as developed in Galatians and Romans, might seem a gospel of deliverance to one brought up a Pharisee; it could have little meaning to the ordinary Gentile. At that time the Gentile world and the Jewish were suffering from opposite diseases. If the Jew had too much law, the Gentile had too little; for the old local religions, and the moral sanctions associated with them, were collapsing in the cosmopolitan scepticism of the Graeco-Roman Empire. The task of the Church was to build up a new moral law; that is why 'Paulinism,' in the Lutheran sense, simply disappears from Christian teaching until something of it was revived by Augustine. The discourses in the Fourth Gospel constantly develop Pauline themes; but the main theme of Romans is compressed into a single sentence: 'For the law was given by Moses; grace and truth came by Jesus Christ' (John i, 17). What is far more remarkable, it has accorded to it only one sentence in all the speeches ascribed in the Acts to Paul himself: 'And by him every one that believeth is justified from all things, from which ye could not be justified by the law of Moses' (Acts xiii, 39). For practical reasons it was essential for the Gentile churches to be rid of the burden of circumcision and the petty detail of the Law; it was valuable therefore to be able to point to an elaborate demonstration by a great Apostle of the abrogation of the Law. They canonized Romans, but did not understand it.

The abrogation of the Law and the rebirth of the Christian into a new and freer life, liberated from the bondage of sin and from the inward struggle of a 'divided self,' is closely associated by Paul with the Death of Christ; but it is not easy to say exactly how. He produces no theological theory, but is content to use metaphors derived from the sacrificial system of the Old Testament. Hence the exact significance which he attached to the sacrificial quality in the Death of Christ has for centuries been a matter of controversy. Much of this controversy has been beside the mark through failure to realize that his approach to the subject was not, like that of Anselm and later Western theologians, primarily scholastic and legalistic; it was rather mystical and emotional. If a rationalistic account is to be given of it, this must be sought mainly on psychological lines. It must be related to the specifically Hebrew consciousness of sin and guilt, and also to the emotional appeal made by the ancient Temple ritual to an orthodox Jew—an appeal which the mind of the twentieth century finds it peculiarly hard to approach with sympathetic insight. For that reason it would seem that Paul's meaning is far better reflected in the popular preaching of a Wesley, or in the hymns of a Toplady, than in the language of the theologians.

Paul was an educated, half-hellenized Jew like Philo, nurtured on the monotheism of the Old Testament. To retain that monotheism he needed some kind of intellectualized concept of the relation to the One God of that Heavenly Christ, whose claim to

a devotion, absolute and religious in character, he gave his life to
preaching; nor indeed could he, without some such conception,
have answered the questions which the more intelligent Gentile
converts would continually be asking. Such a concept Paul seems
to have found in a combination of the apocalyptic picture of the
pre-existent Son of Man, already found in Enoch, with an idea
derived, directly or indirectly, from Philo. Philo interpreted the
statement in Genesis that God 'made man in his own image' in
the light of Plato's doctrine of archetypal patterns or 'ideas.' God
had created man after the εἰκών or pattern which Plato would have
named ἰδέα τοῦ ἀνθρώπου. Paul's allusion to Christ as being 'the
man from heaven,' or 'in the form of God,' is thus a kind of hasty
Platonization of that apocalyptic picture of the Son of Man, which
could be taken quite literally by the less sophisticated Jewish
Christian. The conception is one which asserts with emphasis the
idea of the pre-existence of Christ. In Colossians i, 15–17 it is
given an expression far more elaborate than anything to be found
in the earlier epistles, 'Who is the image of the invisible God, the
firstborn of all creation; for in him were all things created, in the
heavens and upon the earth, things visible and things invisible,
whether thrones or dominions or principalities or powers; all things
have been created through him, and unto him; and he is before all
things, and in him all things consist.' But even here the phrase
'the firstborn of creation' shows that Paul had never faced the
philosophical difficulties which forced the Nicene Church to define
the pre-existence as eternal.

The question what, if any, influence the 'mystery religions,'
which were at that time spreading over the Roman world, may have
had on the language and thought of Paul is too large to be discussed
here. Probably Paul's own views were very slightly so influenced,
those of his converts very considerably. How far, for example, was
the meaning for him of the Lord's Supper influenced by analogies
derived from similar rites in the mystery cults in which the par-
taking of a sacred cake was held to be both a means to, and a
guarantee of, immortality? Of this there is no hint in Paul; but
by the time of Ignatius the idea has become naturalized in the
Church. Ignatius speaks quite simply of 'breaking one bread,
which is the medicine of immortality (φάρμακον ἀθανασίας) and
the antidote that we should not die but live for ever in Jesus Christ'
(*Ephes.* 20).

IV. A distinctive type of religious emphasis is found in the
Lucan writings. Luke goes further even than Paul in his pro-
Gentile sympathies; for he does not understand the Jewish case,

He insists no less on the centrality of the life 'in the spirit' which issues in love, joy and peace—which he takes for granted is only to be realized in and through the experience of fellowship found in the Christian brotherhood. Indeed, for him this fellowship, with God and with man, which accompanies the indwelling of the Spirit, would seem to be the best part of the 'good news.' His Gospel is as notable as the Acts for the abundance of its references to the Spirit; and it would seem that in his version of the Lord's Prayer the words, 'Thy Holy Spirit come upon us and cleanse us,' originally stood in place of, 'Thy Kingdom come' (xi, 2)[1].

Luke is named by Dante *scriba mansuetudinis Christi*. He stresses the message of the graciousness and loving kindness of the Divine, which is the new and the characteristic element of that which Paul the Pharisee had learnt from Christ. Luke tones down the element of Pharisaic theology which survives in the predestinarian teaching of Romans, with its subordination of the 'fatherhood' to the 'sovereignty' of God, and its sense of the need for some propitiatory sacrifice. It is often argued that the Acts could not have been written by a pupil of Paul; a pupil would have understood better 'the Augustinian' strain in Paul. Alternatively it may be suggested that Augustine largely reared his system of theology on just that element in Paul which represents a survival in the Apostle's mind of a pre-Christian conception of God. A pupil may misunderstand his master; he may also outgrow him.

At any rate, the Gospel most closely related to the standpoint of Paul is not that of Luke, but Mark. The church for which Mark wrote may have already possessed (in Q, or some other document) a summary of the ethical teaching of Christ; even so, it is still significant that Mark should make 'the Gospel' to consist, not in the teaching, but in the person of Christ, the wonder-working Son of God, and that he assigns what, from the purely biographical point of view, is such a disproportionate space to the story of the Passion. Moreover, on two occasions words of Christ are given which indicate that Mark, like Paul, saw a sacrificial meaning in his death. 'The Son of man came...to give his life a ransom for many' (x, 45). 'This is my blood of the covenant, which is shed for many' (xiv, 24).

Without doubt Luke read these words in the copy of Mark from which he derived about half of the content of his own Gospel; why then does he leave them out? The second of these sayings does occur in the ordinary text of Luke; but the 'Western' text, Westcott

[1] This reading can be traced back to A.D. 140; in most MSS. it has been 'corrected' to conform with Matthew's version. Cf. Streeter, *op. cit.* p. 277.

and Hort argue, is clearly right in omitting Luke xxii, 19 b–20, as an interpolation from I Corinthians. In the un-interpolated text of Luke, Christ gives the disciples the Cup *before* he gives them the Bread (thus reversing the order of Mark); while the sacrificial words 'given for you' or 'shed for you' are omitted. That this is not an accident, but represents an alternative ritual tradition, is shown by the fact that in the *Didache* also the Cup and the Bread appear in the Lucan order, and the forms of thanksgiving prescribed do not associate the rite with *the death* of Christ[1].

Luke's view is made still clearer by the way in which the death of Christ is, so to speak, apologized for in the speeches attributed to Peter in the early chapters of Acts. In these speeches the death of Christ, so far from being of the essence of the Gospel, is represented as an unfortunate incident which has happily been cancelled— indeed more than cancelled—by the glorious miracle of the Resurrection. Theologians frequently explain this feature in the early speeches in Acts on the hypothesis, that, at the moment of speaking, Peter had not yet had time to reflect on the real meaning of the death of Christ. Such an explanation ignores the practice of ancient historians in regard to speeches. Peter's speeches were not taken down at the time by a shorthand writer; they were either composed by Luke himself (after the universal custom of ancient historians) or they were derived by him from a written source. But whoever first committed them to writing would have done so because he regarded them as representing Peter's mature views. The Acts was written to help the spread of what its author regarded as the actual truth about Christianity; the early Christians were interested, not in the mental development of individual Apostles, but in the Gospel which they taught. A speech attributed to an Apostle is meant to be read as a summary of apostolic doctrine.

Again, the idea of the death of Christ as a sacrifice is curiously inconspicuous even in the speeches attributed to Paul in the Acts; it occurs once only, in a single phrase where he exhorts the Ephesian Elders 'to feed the Church of the Lord, which he purchased with his own blood' (xx, 28). The Gospel and Acts were obviously intended to present the case for Christianity to the Gentile world. If Luke had himself felt this doctrine to be essential, he could not have represented the Apostolic preaching as so little concerned with it. And that a large section of the Church in the sub-apostolic Age did not regard this doctrine as essential, is

---

[1] The word 'sacrifice' is used in the *Didache* of the Eucharist in another context (xiv), but evidently in the sense of communion rather than of propitiation.

proved by the fact that it is entirely ignored by Ignatius of Antioch
—who may almost be called the 'father of orthodoxy.'

Along with this—from the Pauline standpoint inadequate—
interpretation of the death of Christ, Luke exhibits an equally
elementary Christology. This is recognized by all the commentators so far as concerns the speeches attributed to Peter. But
the Christology of the speeches attributed to Paul is no more
advanced. Thus the speech to the Areopagus—the most philosophical utterance attributed to Paul—ends with the proclamation
of a final judgment 'by the man whom he hath ordained' (Acts xvii,
31). Luke was not a theologian; but, unless his general thought
of Christ had approximated to what later ages would have condemned as 'adoptionist' it is hard to explain why, in a set of speeches
presumably intended to be representative of apostolic doctrine,
the pre-existence of Christ is never even hinted at.

V. The epistles of Paul give not so much theology, as the raw
materials out of which the theology of the Church was gradually
developed. Christian theology, in the sense of an attempt to state
systematically and in due proportion the intellectual content of
religion, begins with the epistle to the Hebrews; only it is theology
lifted to the level of religious adoration, as in the *Confessions* of
Augustine. The author addresses himself at once to what was the
main problem for a thoughtful Christian. The Church accepted
as axiomatic both monotheism and the belief that the Old Testament was an inspired revelation; but it offered to Christ a loyalty
and adoration which amounted to religious 'worship,' and (by the
force of circumstances and under the leadership of Paul) had
become in the main a Gentile community, which could not observe
the Law of Moses (the most sacred part of the inspired revelation)
and had no desire to do so.

The author of Hebrews adopts, but in a more precise and clearly
thought-out form, the Pauline identification of the pre-existent
Christ with the Philonic conception of a divine emanation through
whom the primaeval God created the Universe: 'his Son, whom
he appointed heir of all things, through whom also he made the
worlds; who being the effulgence of his glory, and the very image
of his substance, and upholding all things by the word of his power'
(Heb. i, 2 *sq.*). The problem of the obligation of the Law he solves,
in a way totally different from that of Paul, by the use of the method
of allegorical interpretation—a method equally familiar to the
Greek and to the Jew and one which in that age enjoyed high
intellectual repute.

But his most original contribution to theological thinking

derives from the fact that, once an attempt is being made to get rid of the binding obligation of the Law of Moses by calling it an allegory, it becomes clear that the most conspicuous feature in that Law is the elaborate sacrificial system of the Levitical Code. When Paul discusses the Law, he is thinking of it *subjectively*, as a set of rules which the individual is asked to obey; the author of Hebrews is compelled by his method to view it *objectively*, and must therefore address his interpretation in the first place to the imposing system of sacrifices of which the Temple at Jerusalem was the centre. He probably wrote after the Temple had been destroyed by the Romans; but the books of Moses still remained. The destruction, however, of the material Temple only made the more plausible his argument that its impermanence was of the essence of the divine intention. The death of Christ was the real and eternally valid sacrifice; the offering of the blood of bulls and goats had always been, as it were, a shadow in the world of seeming of a reality of which the death of Christ revealed the substance. Look below the surface to catch the author's meaning, and it appears that in the last resort the significance of the death of Christ for him resides, not in the physical shedding of blood, but in the complete surrender of self to the divine will: 'Then said I, lo, I am come. . .to do Thy will, O God' (Heb. x, 4–9).

Actually this way of looking at it is a refinement upon, one might even say a spiritualization of, the view of Paul, at any rate as that view is expressed in some passages. Nevertheless, later theology has been more influenced by the abundance of Jewish sacrificial imagery in the epistle than by the real thought of the writer. Its sum total effect has been to exaggerate the primitive Hebraic elements which survive in the language, if not also in the thought, of the New Testament in regard to the propitiatory character of the death of Christ.

A further point should be noted. Though the author goes further than Paul in his systematic identification of Christ with an eternal creative principle primaevally emanating from the Father, he emphasizes more than any other writer in the New Testament, more even than Luke, the reality of the human nature of Christ, who was 'made like unto us in all things, sin only excepted'; and whom God did not bring to the full maturity of his moral personality except through the experience of suffering (διὰ παθημάτων τελειῶσαι, Heb. ii, 10). Strange as it may appear to a modern mind the reality of Christ's humanity and of his suffering was flatly denied by many Christians. Such teaching is already glanced at in I John; and this 'docetism' is one of the most formidable of the heresies which Ignatius is concerned to refute. 'He suffered truly, as also he raised himself truly; not as certain unbelievers say, that He suffered in semblance' (*Smyrn*. 2).

VI. In the prologue of the Fourth Gospel the problem of combining monotheism with belief in the divine nature of Christ is solved by the doctrine of an eternally existing Logos who was in him made flesh[1]. On this foundation was built the theology of the developed Catholic Church. It has been noted that the prologue reads like a hymn—it is written in the rhythmical prose used in hymns of the period—and that the same thing holds of Philippians ii, 6–11[2]. It is, perhaps, not accidental that the two passages in Paul and John which come nearest to being a theology of the Person of Christ have this almost lyric ring. Thomas Arnold said that the Creed should not be recited but sung as a hymn of praise; and, in the New Testament, theology is never found save as the impassioned expression of religion. John, a Christo-centric mystic of high intellectual power, had need of a thought-out religion; he knew that others had the same need; and there is more concentrated thought in the few verses of his prologue than in many whole treatises. But to John theology is the gateway to a temple; inside the temple is religion—the religion which in the rest of his Gospel he strives to unfold and which it is not the purpose of this chapter to obscure under the pretext of expounding it. The point of the Gospel will be missed by a reader who approaches it primarily as a historical authority. It should be read as a book of devotion, as one would the *Imitatio Christi*; and the writer's attitude of mystic adoration may at times be better apprehended by a change of pronouns in the great discourses ascribed to Christ: '*Thou* art the vine, *we* are the branches'; or '*Thou* art the Resurrection and the Life.'

VII. The Fourth Gospel marks the end of the great age of Christianity; it is by the last of the giants in the greatest religious revival in the history of man. To turn from this Gospel to the Epistle of Jude is to feel a big drop, spiritually and intellectually. This Epistle reads as if it were a 'charge' sent out by the bishop of an important church, possibly Judas (son) of James, who, according to the *Apostolic Constitutions*, succeeded Symeon (martyred under Trajan) as the third bishop of Jerusalem[3]. The writer,

---

[1] John's distinction between God and 'the Word' who from the beginning was 'with God' is comparable to that which a modern philosopher might draw between the Transcendence and the Immanence of the Divine.

[2] Cf. A. B. Macdonald, *Christian Worship in the Primitive Church*, p. 119 *sq*.

[3] See B. H. Streeter, *The Primitive Church*, pp. 178 *sqq*.

one feels, is a good old man profoundly shocked by the appearance within the Church of the teaching of an immoralism, which claims to be an expression of superior enlightenment—seemingly by Gnostics who held a docetic view of Christ. His remedy (apart from mere denunciation) is to encourage old-fashioned goodness by recalling the Church to 'the words which have been spoken before by the Apostles' (v. 17). Above all he exhorts 'to contend earnestly for the faith which was once for all delivered unto the saints.' These words might almost be called the 'slogan' of the central section of the Church during the next hundred years. In them the writer of this, otherwise rather commonplace, little note defined what shortly came to be the accepted policy of the Church throughout the second century. Doubtless that is why his was one of the first of the epistles other than Paul's to be almost everywhere accepted into the Canon. For Jude was right. In the first century the main task for a community limited by its Palestinian origins was liberation, moral and intellectual; in the second century it was consolidation and defence. The Church might no longer create, it could still conserve.

VII. PROPHET, PRESBYTER AND BISHOP

Among the major influences which have conditioned the political history of Europe has been the hierarchical organization of the Catholic Church. It was largely the political power potential in an empire-wide organization that made Decius its persecutor and Constantine its patron; it was this which turned the Germanic princedom of Charlemagne into a Holy Roman Empire. The origin, therefore, of the Christian ministry is not without interest to the secular historian. But its discussion raises questions of a highly controversial character; for it is a matter in regard to which the different denominations of Christendom inherit very diverse official theories. These theories it would be inappropriate here either to expound or to criticize; it will suffice to outline evidence for the view[1] that in church order, as in other matters, there was in the first century considerable diversity, and that even in the New Testament itself a notable evolution can be discerned.

A small community can preserve its cohesion with very little formal organization; not so one that has branches in every important city in a vast empire. In this respect the Christian Church started with one great asset. It did not have to begin, like a League of Nations or an International Labour movement, by finding some basis of union for linking together societies which already had an

[1] For the evidence in detail see Streeter, *op. cit.*

independent existence. The Church conceived of itself, not as a new body, but as the ancient 'people of God'; the inheritors of the promises given to Abraham, Isaac and Jacob. The modern historian may describe the Church as an 'offshoot of Judaism'; the early Christians took the contrary view. They were the true Israel, the 'remnant' who alone—the prophets had foretold it—would inherit the promises. Various prophecies of the Messianic age had spoken of Gentiles being gathered into this remnant; and Paul was gravely perplexed by the small proportion of born Jews alongside the relatively large number of Gentiles who had so far (c. A.D. 56) accepted Christ (Rom. xi, 25–7). Because, then, every congregation took it for granted that it was merely the local representative of the 'holy nation,' the one people of God, organization was not at first required either as a means to unity or as a symbol of it. Its necessity was first made obvious by the difficulty of coping with 'false prophets' who taught, as a word from the Lord, gnosticizing doctrine or loose morality.

Paul's advice to the Corinthians as to the use of spiritual gifts shows that the claim to spirit-possession by certain of the more egoistic or hysterical members of the community had already become a source of embarrassment when it took the form of 'speaking with tongues.' But prophesying in the congregation he strongly commends; and he speaks as if the gift of prophecy was so common that several prophets might easily be present at any ordinary meeting of the community (I Cor. xiv, 29–33, 39–40). A generation later, however, it was no longer speaking with tongues, but prophecy itself, which caused embarrassment. A prophet spoke 'in the spirit,' and therefore with divine authority; but what if he were a false prophet? Everywhere there arose the problem of discriminating between the true prophet and the false. From Asia we have the warning: 'Beloved, believe not every spirit, but prove the spirits, whether they are of God: because many false prophets are gone out into the world' (I John iv, 1). In Rome, Hermas (*Mand.* xi) has a whole section on the difficulty of distinguishing true and false prophets. While from Syria, in the *Didache*, come the most elaborate advices on this problem— a problem the more difficult because of the high peril involved in making a mistake (*Did.* xi, 7). The editor of Matthew (c. A.D. 90), in a passage clearly derived from Mark, inserts the words: 'Many false prophets shall arise, and lead many astray. And because antinomianism (ἀνομία) shall be multiplied, the love of the many shall wax cold' (Mt. xxiv, 11 *sq.*). This addition implies that among these self-styled prophets were preachers of religious a-moralism.

That some of these antinomians claimed the authority of Paul we have already inferred from the protests in James (ii, 14–21) and II Peter (iii, 15–16). Prophets seem to have been very largely itinerants. This fact made the false prophet—whether heretic, crank or mere impostor—the more formidable, in a society which believed in supernatural gifts; for to find out a pretender usually takes time. To protect themselves against false prophets the churches had to strengthen the hands of trusted local leaders.

The Church of Jerusalem, we have seen, had from the first a single head in the person of James the brother of the Lord. Presbyters are also mentioned; and it is probable, though the Acts does not explicitly say so, that the title 'deacon' was applied to the Seven who were appointed, primarily, 'to serve (διακονεῖν) tables' (Acts vi, 1 sqq.). But circumstances in Jerusalem were exceptional. At any rate, the oldest theory of the Christian ministry of which we have evidence is: 'And God hath set some in the church, first apostles, secondly prophets, thirdly teachers, then miracles, then gifts of healings, helps, governments, divers kinds of tongues' (I Cor. xii, 28). Comparing this with the actual situation at Antioch (Acts xiii, 1–3), it would seem that in an ordinary Gentile Church, the most important persons (in the absence of an apostle) were named Prophets and Teachers. The mention, however, of 'helps' and 'governments,' combined with a reference elsewhere to the 'ministry' (διακονία) and 'he who presides' (ὁ προϊστάμενος) (Rom. xii, 6–8), suggests the existence of other officers. At any rate when, a little later, Paul writes to the Philippians, he names in his opening salutation the 'Bishops' (in the plural) and the Deacons (Phil. i, 1). Ephesians, if not authentic, is a very early re-writing and elaboration of Colossians; it represents a further advance. 'And he gave some to be apostles; and some, prophets; and some, evangelists; and some, shepherds and teachers' (Eph. iv, 11). As at Corinth, Apostles[1] and Prophets still come first; but it is notable that 'Shepherd' (translated 'Pastor' in both English versions) has become a title of office, and the Shepherds are mentioned before the Teachers; and in the Old Testament the word 'shepherd' is used as a standing description of 'the rulers of Israel.'

In the Acts there is frequent mention of Presbyters. In Jerusalem (Acts xxi, 18) these form a kind of concilium to James. The

[1] The title Apostle (= delegate) is in the New Testament (and apparently also in the Didache) applied far more widely than in later usage; thus two otherwise unknown persons Andronicus and Junias were 'of note' among those who bore the title (Rom. xvi, 7). 'Evangelist' is the name given to Philip (Acts xxi, 8) and to Timothy (II Tim. iv, 5).

leaders of the Church of Ephesus are described as Presbyters (πρεσβύτεροι) but are addressed by Paul as 'Bishops' (ἐπίσκοποι) and their functions are those of shepherds, whose business is 'to feed the flock' (Acts xx, 28). As in Philippians, it is evident that a number of persons in this church bore the title 'Bishop.' So also in I Peter (v, 1–2) Presbyters are exhorted to fulfil the office of Bishop (ἐπισκοποῦντες) with zeal. This state of things still survived at Corinth, and at Rome, when I Clement was written in 96; and it lasted at Philippi till the time (c. 115) when Polycarp wrote to that Church.

The evidence of the *Didache* is very little affected by the answer given to the vexed question of its date[1]. For, if it does not emanate from some important church c. 100, it represents a survival in some out-of-the-way district of conditions which elsewhere had passed away. Its interest is that, whatever its date or provenance, it reflects a system which is in a state of incipient breakdown. It gives elaborate instructions as to the reception of 'Apostles' and Prophets. These are to be 'received as the Lord'; but tests (implying that the problem is acute) are suggested how to determine whether such an one is a true Prophet or a false. For example, he is proved to be a false Prophet if he desires hospitality for more than two days, if on departure he asks for money, or if, 'when he ordereth a table in the Spirit, he shall eat of it.' But there follows a regulation which would enable true Prophets to become, in effect, resident ministers, and to receive for their support the first fruits, 'for they are your chief-priests' (*Did.* 13). The plain intention of another injunction is to raise the status of the Bishops and Deacons: 'Appoint for yourselves therefore bishops and deacons worthy of the Lord, men who are meek and not lovers of money, and true and approved; for unto you they also perform the service of the prophets and teachers. Therefore despise them not; for they are your honourable men along with the prophets and teachers' (*Did.* 15). Evidently in the general regard, the offices of Bishop and Deacon are less esteemed than those of Prophet or Teacher; but it is, the writer insists, an honourable office, and therefore it is important that only men of high character should be appointed to it.

We have here a system like that implied in I Corinthians and in Acts xiii, 1–3—but *in a state of breakdown*. The order of precedence is still 'first apostles, secondly prophets, thirdly teachers';

---

[1] The arguments that the *Didache* quotes both Barnabas and Hermas, though reasonable, are answerable; but the contention that it is a piece of pseudo-antiquarianism is fanciful.

and the title 'apostle' has its older and wider connotation. But the prescription of set forms of thanksgiving, with a rubric allowing Prophets liturgical freedom, implies that the presence of a Prophet was by no means a matter of course. The gift of prophecy is evidently much rarer than when Paul wrote to the Corinthians; and the services once performed by Prophets and Teachers are now commonly supplied by the Bishops and Deacons.

The historical situation implied by the *Didache* is perfectly clear. The stream of prophecy, characteristic of the first age, is beginning to dry up in extent and to become muddied in quality. The leadership in worship and in instruction is beginning to pass into the hands of the Bishops and Deacons of the local churches. But these changes are only beginning; the old system is proving inadequate, the new has not yet developed.

The breakdown of the earlier system, or rather lack of system, was doubtless one main cause of the development of the monarchical episcopate. There is small gain in devising 'tests' for false prophets unless someone is made responsible for applying them. Evidence for the existence in Asia, in fact, if not also in name, of a bishop with monarchical powers is found in III John. The exact position held by the writer of the letter, who calls himself 'The Elder,' is obscure; but it is clear that the Diotrephes mentioned is not merely one who 'loveth to have the pre-eminence' in the church to which the letter is addressed; he is a person who has actually secured it. He has the power to decline to receive in the church brethren recommended by outsiders like the writer of the letter, and also to 'cast out of the church' members who differ from him; that is, he has the right of excommunication.

The evidence of the epistles to Timothy and Titus, curiously enough, points in opposite directions according as they are regarded as authentically Pauline or not. If authentic, we must say[1] that here also the terms 'bishop' and 'presbyter' are interchangeable. If, however, they are, in the main, pseudonymous writings produced somewhere in Asia *c.* 105–110, they afford evidence of the existence at that date of the monarchical episcopate. For, in that case, the advice given to Timothy and Titus must be read as advice which their actual author would like to see taken by contemporaries of his own who exercise functions in the church comparable to those once exercised by Timothy and Titus as delegates of the Apostle. Timothy and Titus are represented as in supreme command, and are instructed by the Apostle how to use their power; there would have been small point in inventing such instructions

[1] With Lightfoot (*Philippians*, p. 97).

for the benefit of church officers who, however well-meaning, had not the power to carry them out. The latest in date of these letters is I Timothy; and this unlike II Timothy and Titus does not seem to incorporate any genuine Pauline notes. But just because it is entirely the work of the editor, it is a document of great interest to the historian, as being a contemporary description (slightly idealized) of what we might call 'parish activities and organization' about A.D. 110. Ignatius, when at home in Antioch, would have occupied himself very much as Timothy is here enjoined to do.

In the letters of Ignatius (*c.* A.D. 115) we find the single Bishop, clearly distinguished under that name, a board of Presbyters and a group of Deacons. His letters also show that this system prevailed, not only in his own church of Antioch, but in the churches of Asia Minor to which he writes. The main purpose of Ignatius in writing is to exalt the office of these ministers—especially the Bishop. The language he uses is hyperbolic: 'The bishop as being a type of the Father and the presbyters as the council of God and as the college of the Apostles. Apart from these a church does not deserve to be called a church' (*Trall.* iii, 1). 'Wheresoever the bishop shall appear, there let the people be; even as where Jesus may be, there is the Catholic Church. It is not lawful apart from the bishop either to baptize or to hold a love feast; but whatsoever he shall approve, this is well pleasing also to God.... It is good to recognize God and the bishop. He that honoureth the bishop is honoured of God; he that doth aught without the knowledge of the bishop rendereth service to the devil' (*Smyrn.* viii, 2–ix, 1).

We naturally ask what was the situation at Rome at this date; for Ignatius' letter to that church does not give the title of *any* church officer. Twenty years earlier, as appears from Clement, there had been at Rome (and Corinth) a plurality of officers spoken of alternatively as bishops or presbyters, and an order of deacons. Clement emphasizes the duty of obedience to these as to persons in a succession deriving from the Apostles. This 'apostolic succession,' however, is not through a line of monarchical bishops, but is that of a corporate body; and appointment is subject to the consent of the laity (Clem. xlii, 1–4; xliv, 2–3).

Hegesippus, before A.D. 166, drew up a list of the Bishops of Rome, whom he traces back to Linus, appointed by Peter and Paul; that list should be good evidence for at least the previous fifty years. Dates, which for the later names are reasonably trustworthy, can be calculated from the terms of office of each pope given in two Latin lists apparently derived from the *Chronica* of Hippolytus. Xystus (*c.* 115–125), whose name stands sixth, is mentioned in a letter of Irenaeus[1] as the first of a succession of popes whose policy (in regard to Asian Christians) he reproaches Victor with having reversed. In Hermas, however, the rulers of the church in Rome are always spoken of in the plural—as 'presbyters,' 'rulers,' 'shepherds'—in a way which definitely excludes a monarchical bishop; though there may have been something like a chairman of the ruling elders. But if, rejecting the date assigned to Hermas in the Muratorianum, we accept his own statement that he began writing in the lifetime of Clement (c. A.D. 98), we may reasonably suppose that by A.D. 115 this chairmanship had become in practice a kind of 'managing directorship.'

The further transition to monarchical episcopate may well have taken place under Xystus, and that as a direct result of the influence of Ignatius himself, whose martyrdom in the Colosseum must have nearly synchronized with the accession of Xystus. In every letter (save that to Rome) Ignatius' farewell message to the churches is the duty of obedience to the Bishop. But Ignatius was not only a martyr, he was also a prophet; and, under seizure by the Spirit, he inculcated this same duty: 'I cried out when I was among you; I spoke with a loud voice, with God's own voice, Give ye heed to the bishop and the presbytery and the deacons.... He in whom I am bound is my witness that I learned it not from the flesh of man; it was the preaching of the Spirit who spake in this wise: Do nothing without the bishop' (*Philad.* VII, 1). It is unthinkable that such a man would have failed to give that same message in Rome. And suppose, just before he was cast to the beasts, the Spirit put into his mouth an utterance like that just quoted—the church would have given heed.

Accepting the view (p. 263) that the larger part of Polycarp's epistle belongs to its writer's later years, Ignatius is the last important figure in the period with which this chapter deals[2]. But he should be regarded, less as the last representative of the primitive period of Christianity, than as the pioneer of the next age. Ignatius is the first great ecclesiastic. It is due to him to add that the authority which he desiderated for the ministry was not claimed from love of power for its own sake, or of organization for its own sake. He fought for what seemed to him vital to unity in the Church and the protection of the flock from heresy. Nor is he merely concerned with 'sound doctrine'; he has the pastor's

---

[1] *ap.* Eusebius, *Hist. Eccl.* V, 24, 14.

[2] The Pionian life of Polycarp makes him a disciple, not of the Apostle John (as Irenaeus supposed), but of Bucolus, an obscure bishop of Smyrna. For reasons for supposing this to be correct, see Streeter, *op. cit.* pp. 265 *sqq.*

instinct. The heretics whom he denounces 'have no care for love, none for the widow, none for the orphan, none for the afflicted, none for the hungry or thirsty' (*Smyrn.* vi, 2). His letter to Polycarp, a fellow-bishop, shows the 'paternal' character of his ideal —equally kindly and authoritarian: 'Let not widows be neglected. After the Lord, be thou their protector. Let nothing be done without thy consent; neither do thou anything without the consent of God, as indeed thou doest not. Be steadfast. Let church services be held more frequently. Seek out all men by name. Despise not slaves, whether men or women. Yet let not these again be puffed up, but let them serve the more faithfully to the glory of God, that they may obtain a better freedom from God' (*Polycarp*, 4).

Neither the details of the heresies, Gnostic or Jewish, which Ignatius opposes, nor the theological conceptions with which he does so, need detain us. But it is of interest to note that the weapons which he uses include, not only the Old Testament, but the beginnings of the New. The Gospel of Matthew and a collection of Epistles of Paul are already for him more than merely Christian classics; they are an authoritative vehicle of the doctrine of the Apostles. Ignatius is clear-sightedly adopting the principle laid down by Jude, and 'contending earnestly for the faith once delivered to the saints.'

Interpenetration of religions was the fashion of the times; and without some further definition (which in practice means standardization) of doctrine, so much from the general welter of Graeco-Oriental religion would have filtered into Christianity that it would have lost its distinctive features—not by attack from outside, but by assimilation from within. A line had to be drawn somewhere; some principle of exclusion was required. The Gnostics, as their name implies, were (or at least they supposed themselves to be) intellectuals; and it was ostensibly as an intellectual issue—though one involving grave moral consequences—that the battle had to be fought. That is why the 'faith,' which the main body of the Church was concerned to defend, came to be thought of primarily as 'orthodoxy'; that is, as assent to correct opinion in regard to doctrines stated in intellectual terms. History has demonstrated the unfortunate results of the selection of this as the main principle of exclusion. But at that time no other was to hand.

Ignatius is the father of those who champion orthodoxy. For his times—though not for all time—he was in the line of next advance. He was the first ecclesiastic; but, strange as that may appear to some, his age had need for such.

CHAPTER VIII

HADRIAN

I. THE PROBLEM OF THE EMPIRE

THE year A.D. 117 marks an epoch in the history of the Mediterranean world. For in this year the Roman Empire, in which that world was politically unified, had reached its highest point of development after ages of continuous growth. From eastern Armenia to western Morocco, from northern Britain to southern Egypt, and to the borders of the Sahara and the Arabian desert, Rome and its Emperor ruled lands and seas. Only a short time before, Roman troops had beaten the might of Parthia from the field and had reached the Persian Gulf; and their victorious Imperator, Trajan, had dreamed of repeating Alexander's march to India, only to acquiesce in giving up the project on account of his age[1]. Deserts guarded almost all the southern borders; the coasts of the Atlantic Ocean were alive with Roman ships; the Northern frontier, in Britain, and from the North Sea to the northern shore of the Black Sea, was everywhere strengthened and secured; beyond that line there no longer was an empire of 'barbarians' from which danger could suddenly threaten, while behind that line the armies everywhere stood ready to attack. It is true that in the previous year, after the victorious march through Mesopotamia, serious setbacks had followed, and the rising of the Jews and Mesopotamians might well cause grave anxiety. But energetic advances and the final overthrow of the rebels had established the security of Syria and Asia Minor and the lasting safety of the whole Empire against attacks from the only great Power that lay outside the area of Roman sovereignty; and within this world Rome stands without a rival, while at the same time wide stretches of fresh territory had been won for the Empire.

The task of creating security also in this area, which had been easily acquired and long maintained by Alexander and the Seleucids, and of opening it up to Rome's authority, was of the widest range and of the highest importance: if it were successfully achieved, the idea of the world empire, the *orbis Romanus*, would seem to become a reality, the peace, the *pax Romana*, which

[1] See above, p. 247.

Rome could give to the civilized humanity of this world together with its laws and customs would be made permanent: Rome's sway over the world would be assured for ever. But if now in the primeval East, with its apparently alien and indissoluble culture, there were added to the Empire even more areas of continuous inland territory than had been gained along all frontiers since Caesar's and Augustus' days, these masses of inland territory might well outweigh the narrow coastal lands of the Mediterranean. The work of opening up, organizing and administering this region might well take up too much of the energies of the Roman-Italic ruling class of the Empire, which, even without this burden, was already far too few for the task. The body of provincial citizens, who possessed inferior rights, might be menacingly reinforced, as the old coastal empire of the Romans thus threatened to turn definitively into a continental Empire.

Almost up to the time when Trajan died (August, A.D. 117), calm and security reigned within the mighty Empire: fullness of achievement, glory of unequalled power still characterized his régime. But would succeeding emperors also be able to make good for Rome, once the true centre of the great amphitheatre of the Mediterranean nation and still its heart, its stubborn claim to be for ever mistress of the world, and to enable Italy to be the bearer of sovereignty and sharer in its profits? Or must they give place to natives of the provinces grown strong in the *pax Romana*, who will no longer stand as spectators, but will press for equality of rights with their masters? The Empire, not threatened from without, secure in itself, self-sufficient, can unfold its gigantic possibilities even to excess, can radiate its power even into scarce-known distances, if only centralization in Rome does not grow too rigid. But what if the outside world nevertheless attacks the Empire? Will it produce rulers who can meet the attack with decisive strength? These rulers must do more than talk of unity and peace within the Empire, of justice, mildness and consideration, of patience and calm, prosperity, happiness and security; they must make these things real, must exert themselves everywhere in the Empire in person, joyously and unrestingly, to awake life, to resolve oppositions, to preserve the balance of forces in healthy tension and good order; all this with the general purpose of securing that *status felicissimus*, that *status optimus civitatis* of which Augustus would have had himself named the creator (Vol. x, p. 593).

Everywhere an unexampled multiplicity was observable, as of soil and climate, so of the countless peoples, of their economic arrangements and social organization, of their languages and intellectual capabilities, of their tradition and present mental attitude. Now came the question, whether the creative power of Trajan's successors would be able to make prevail the Roman will, Roman discipline, the Greek view of life and construction put upon the world, long ago taken over by Rome and adapted to Roman purposes, in order by these means to convert the inhabitants of the Empire into Romans to the very depths of their being, and so to make the Empire grow into a complete whole, a true community of lives. Or will the attempts to form the new unity of a Mediterranean people out of a multiplicity of heterogeneous elements have only this result—that those who were once conquered and are now peacefully assimilated, educating themselves by the Graeco-Roman ideal and allowing themselves, in outward form, to be reduced to one level, actually develop and steel their own powers, in order to become victors even over the inner world of the rulers? If the rulers continue Trajan's tolerant régime, there is serious danger that the *genius populi Romani* may be transformed into something essentially foreign. The period which has been praised since Aelius Aristides[1] as the happiest in Mediterranean history is a century of external brilliance but full of grievous tragedy, a period of transition to a new world-order. One only of the rulers, Hadrian, recognized his task and strove for a great accomplishment; he failed, despite all the endeavours which he made even beyond the measure of his powers. His successors, more passive natures, did not possess his powers, did not reach the heights of his achievement, and the last of them pursued new aims. Seen from the point of view of older tradition, it is an uninterrupted sinking into the depths, a breach, the rise of something new; the power of the individual ruler can no longer effectively resist that inevitable and logical movement of forces.

The traditions concerning the five successors of Trajan are of quite different sorts and unequal in their value, but rich enough to let us describe these figures, indeed to penetrate deeply into the essential nature of almost all of them. It is true that one cannot so certainly succeed in determining their personal effect in the State, their share in the fate of the Empire. If the restless wandering and creative activity of Hadrian (A.D. 117–138) can be followed in all the provinces of the Empire, what Antoninus Pius (A.D. 138–161) did for that Empire is more difficult to grasp, since he never left Rome and Italy. The personality of Marcus Aurelius (161–180) and his struggle with the enemy in the North

[1] *Or.* XXVI K, see below, pp. 316, 333

and with all the bitter stress at home are revealed by a multitude
of most valuable pieces of evidence, among which his own *Meditations*[1], the Marcus-column in Rome, and the Roman Empire
coins are conspicuous. On the other hand, his adopted brother,
Lucius Verus (161–169), can hardly be discerned in the darkness
which enfolds him: but Marcus' own son, Marcus Aurelius
Commodus (who bore the title Augustus from 177 and was sole
ruler from A.D. 180 until 192) appears in a strong light; yet
because that light is indeed all too strong, he also sets us riddles
enough to solve.

II. THE ACCESSION OF HADRIAN[2]

P. Aelius Hadrianus (born on January 24, 76) sprang from
a family which had emigrated in the time of the Scipios from
Hadria in Picenum to southern Spain and was established in
Italica (near Seville). This family had acquired a mixture of
Iberian blood, but, like the Ulpii Traiani, who had likewise
made themselves a home there, had loyally preserved the memory
of their Italic origin. An Aelius, from whom Hadrian was directly
descended, had become, the first of his line, a Roman senator in
the late Caesarian period, no doubt because he was a partisan
of the dictator. Hadrian himself was the son of a man of
praetorian rank and of a mother whose home was in Gades: the
name of the mother, Domitia Paulina, which was passed on to
Hadrian's younger sister, attests the pro-Roman attitude of her
family too; he was also a son of Trajan's cousin, we do not know
whether on the paternal or maternal side. It is probable that his
father, the origin of whose second cognomen, Afer, remains unexplained, owed his rise to the praetorian rank to Ulpius Traianus,
who was in close association with Vespasian and Titus at a critical
period and was made a patrician in A.D. 73: similarly, Hadrian
himself owed his whole rapid career to that Trajan's son. In a
space of 250 years Spain had received a multitude of energies
from Rome and Italy; since the days of Caesar and Augustus the
romanizing of the country had made rapid progress; and now,

---

[1] This familiar title is used for convenience of reference in place of the
Emperor's own Τὰ εἰς ἑαυτόν.

[2] The main literary sources for the reign of Hadrian are what remains
of Dio LXIX, and the lives of Hadrian and Aelius in the *Historia Augusta*.
On the historical value of the *H.A.* for this and the following chapter see
below, p. 856. A collection of the relevant coins will be found in Mattingly
and Sydenham, *Rom. Imp. Coinage* (see volume of Plates V, 123), vol. II and
Strack, *Röm. Reichsprägung des Zweiten Jahrhunderts*, vol. II; of inscriptions in W. Weber, *Untersuchungen zur Geschichte des Kaisers Hadrianus*.

for a generation past, this Spain had been returning to Rome and the Empire in increasing measure what had grown out of those energies. Writers like the Senecas, Lucan, Martial and Quintilian, officers and administrative officials, amongst whom the Ulpii, Aelii, and Annii were by no means unique. Trajan and Hadrian, Marcus Aurelius (from the family of the Annii) and his son Commodus, were not merely Romans: in them the Iberian strain of their families can be seen working itself out; the devotion of Trajan to the gods of Gades, above all to Hercules Gaditanus, the attitude of Hadrian and of the others proves clearly that these 'Romans' of the provinces were other than the rulers of the Julian or even the Flavian dynasty, who had grown up in the Italic homelands of the Empire.

But the decision of Trajan to have his nephew Hadrian, early left an orphan, educated in Rome and then to set him on the career of an official, was to have great consequences. He and his fellow-countryman, the knight Acilius Attianus, afterwards Prefect of the Guard to both monarchs, had taken over the tutelage of Hadrian, who later became Trajan's nephew by marriage with his great-niece. On this relationship and education depend in the last resort Hadrian's rule, the fundamental direction of his policy, even his own decision to regulate the succession. Aelius Caesar, Antoninus Pius, Marcus Aurelius, Lucius Verus and Commodus, too, would not have been what they were without this decision. And of these, only Aelius Caesar and his son, Verus, were members of an Etruscan house, while the other three, who were immensely more important, were sprung from families in the provinces of the Roman Empire, namely the Aurelii Fulvi from Nemausus, and the Annii from Uccubis in southern Spain, and had become further interrelated among themselves. All this is the outward sign of the supersession of Italic strength by provincial elements.

The boy Hadrian was introduced to Greek education and took it up with enthusiasm. Returning to his home in 90–1 he gained early training in arms in the company of the youth of the town and became madly devoted to the chase. About A.D. 93 Trajan summoned him to Rome a second time. Now, like every one in a similar position, he began his career as an official and as a soldier from the lowest positions: in the course of his military career, as Tribune of three legions in 95–7, he came to know Lower Pannonia, Lower Moesia, and the Rhine, that is, the whole North Front of the Empire. When the childless Trajan became Emperor, his only nephew, now almost 22 years old, entered his circle;

ambitious as he was, the star of secret hopes begins to rise. In
A.D. 101, as the Imperator's quaestor, he took part in the First
Dacian War on Trajan's staff; in the Second Dacian War, having
now already become praetor, he commanded a legion; as an
ex-praetor he became governor of Lower Pannonia and fought
successfully against the Sarmatians of the plain of the Theiss.
At the age of thirty-two he was *consul suffectus*; a few years later
in his capacity as nephew of the Emperor he was a member of
high-priestly Colleges and Archon of Athens, the only private
Roman citizen who attained such distinction. A direct development leads from the first studies of the 'Graeculus,' as he was
already called when a boy, through this dignity, which the town
conferred on the most suitable person, to Hadrian's panhellenic
policy, the centre of which was his beloved Athens, in which
the Spanish 'Roman' became a Greek. He enjoyed the favour
of Plotina, the wife of his uncle, and acquired a circle of close
friends. When he went to the Parthian War in the autumn of
113 as chief of the general staff of the Emperor, in whose train
was Acilius Attianus, the Prefect of the Guard and formerly
Hadrian's guardian, the world of the East in its whole breadth
unfolded itself before him. So, before he himself became *princeps*,
he acquired a clear oversight over most of the European and Asiatic
territories of the Empire, over its energies and the tasks which
the Northern and the Eastern Fronts imposed.

How much of the credit for the victories in Armenia and
Mesopotamia should be ascribed to him can hardly be determined.
But he was at the nerve-centre of all action. When preparing to
return home, Trajan, who had now fallen sick, left his nephew
behind in Antioch as governor of Syria with orders to carry on
the war as commander of the troops. There was meanwhile a
furious revolt raging from Cyrenaica far into Mesopotamia: even
the victory over the Parthians and all the conquest of territory
were jeopardized. This was the situation in which Hadrian, now
forty-one years old, took over gigantic responsibilities. Trajan
undoubtedly valued highly his capabilities as a general and his
activity. But why at this moment, when he felt his health failing, did
he not give him more comprehensive powers, as Augustus, Tiberius,
Vespasian had done in quite different circumstances? Why did
he not summon him to a share in his power, in order to secure
for him in any event the expectation of the succession if anything
should happen to himself? Nothing of the kind was done. At
the beginning (perhaps on the 4th) of August 117 the Emperor
left Syria, and on the 9th at the latest he died suddenly, his

sickness having taken an abrupt turn for the worse, in the small town of Selinus on the Cilician coast. When, on the 11th, the news of his death reached Antioch, the Syrian army proclaimed Hadrian as his successor. This day is his '*dies imperii*.' It was but slowly that the news reached Rome that Trajan had adopted his nephew while actually on his deathbed, and that the latter had been informed of his adoption on August 9. Amid general excitement people weighed the reasons which supported this surprising fact against the much weightier ones which showed Trajan as a rigorous upholder of the Augustan conception of the Principate; and the doubts were not, and have never been, dissipated. One thing is certain: Trajan had not, up to that point, taken any step which justified the conclusion that he would propose Hadrian to the Senate as the 'best citizen.' Even assuming that at the last he had adopted him, the strict doctrine of the Principate no more entitled Hadrian than it had entitled Tiberius to regard the death of his father as the beginning of his own rule. Hadrian excused himself before the Senate, whose privilege it was to elect the '*optimus*,' by saying that 'the army had proclaimed him Imperator overhastily, because the Commonwealth could not be without an Imperator.' The secret of Selinus, kept by Plotina, by Hadrian's mother-in-law Matidia, and by the Prefect of the Guard Attianus, the persons most nearly concerned in it, cannot be discovered; the only man who might have spoken unguardedly about it, the dead ruler's personal servant, died suddenly on the 11th of August. Whether or not he died by his own hand cannot be determined beyond doubt[1].

Whether the adoption was a fiction or not, Hadrian publicly stood by it and held fast to it; for it associated him with his predecessors in the Principate, the *divus* Nerva and Trajan, who on his motion was soon promoted to be *divus*; and this gave him, as son and grandson of two gods, as it had once given to Tiberius, a tremendous authoritarian superiority over all other mortals. But neither the adoption nor Trajan's death give the date for his reign, which runs from August 11, when the acclamation of his army, and that alone, conferred power on him, as on Vespasian, a fact which the Senate could not but recognize and implement.

---

[1] The evidence for the childhood, youth and career of Hadrian till 117 is collected in *Pros. Imp. Rom.* I², pp. 28 *sqq.* no. 184. On the much discussed question of the adoption see W. Weber, *Untersuchungen zur Geschichte des Kaisers Hadrianus*, pp. 1 *sqq.*, *Traian und Hadrian*, p. 246 *sq.*, Strack, *op. cit.* II, pp. 41 *sqq.* The view of A. Stein in *Pros. Imp. Rom.* I², p. 29 *sq.* is not here adopted.

And after all, as nearest of kin, he was of the blood of the 'best citizen,' and the Senate had often enough made legitimate the succession of relatives. More than that, the armies which could assess his exploits better than the Senate had agreed to see in him the 'best citizen' himself. The Senate was confident that the new ruler would perform the task of winning back lost Mesopotamia. The Senate recognized him as the inheritor of a divine grace, as the son who secured for his father the divine honours that were his due, as the accomplisher of his father's will, who proclaimed with determination peace, justice and harmony at home; and it desired to transfer to the living man those triumphal titles which belonged to the dead. But Hadrian modestly and reverently retired behind the greater figure who, though dead, still celebrated his Parthian triumph; and refused the title *pater patriae* 'because,' he said, 'Augustus had only received it late in life[1].'

Then it was soon perceived that he had no mind to continue his adopted father's policy. The friends and helpers of Trajan, among them the Moorish chief Lusius Quietus, were soon replaced by the circle of his own friends; and from the moment when, after Attianus' return, Rome was securely in his hands, an entirely new state of affairs was revealed. It was a matter of course that the revolt of the Jews in the Eastern provinces of the Empire should be suppressed with relentless rigour: his friend Marcius Turbo, above all, quickly accomplished the task set him (p. 303). In Palestine, Egypt, Cyrenaica, calm was restored. But in Britain, too, in Mauretania, and on the Lower Danube, troubles arose or war threatened. Yet for the sake of the security of the Empire peace had to prevail. Hadrian, therefore, determined to risk all for the future of the Empire against the resistance of Trajan's supporters and of the thorough-going imperialists, left the territory that had been acquired by his predecessor to its inhabitants to look after; these latter, because the Romans were not able to hold the land, were made into client-States and commissioned to defend it. To Greater Armenia he gave back its king, the pretender whom Trajan had set up as King of Parthia he compensated with other territory, and only the pressure of his friends induced him to abandon the idea of giving back Dacia because the process of pacifying and romanizing it was so far advanced and because it was indispensable to the defence of the Empire.

In all this he was at first only doing what Augustus too had dared to do in a critical situation and Tiberius had logically carried

[1] Weber, *Untersuchungen*, pp. 60 *sqq.*; *Traian und Hadrian*, p. 247; Strack, *op. cit.* II, pp. 43 *sqq.*

out (see above, Vol. x, pp. 379 *sqq.*). To silence all resistance to this policy, he appealed to secret instructions of Trajan, of which no one knew, but which equally no one could dispute. But there was more in his decision than that: with the erection of protective rule over the client-States all was not sacrificed, the claim of Rome was maintained, the possibility of their complete annexation was only postponed to a more propitious occasion; now peace was necessary, and for the future a clear maintenance of the fundamental principle of war which, in Roman doctrine, was only possible when just. There was to be world-wide peace, the end of aggressive wars, of battles, of all piracy and all rebellion, security on all paths of the land and the sea from sunrise to sunset, as the philosopher understood it[1], prosperity for mankind. War should only be waged where the defence of the Empire demanded it.

He separated the farther East from the Empire, directing the Empire's energies to its own inner tasks. For the Romans could not protect the farther East: the power of the Empire had been over-strained; in the towns and in the country the masses were struggling for their existence and groaning under the burdens and the pressure of the bureaucracy. And he won the masses. To Italy he remitted entirely the sums due on the change of emperor, and reduced them for the provinces: to the small tenant farmers in Egypt, whose fate depended on Nile, sun, and desert, he made over arable land from the public or domain estates under new conditions; he released philosophers, rhetoricians, grammarians, doctors, from all the burdens which the State, the provinces, the towns imposed upon them, as upon all citizens; he began to make good the damage which the Jewish revolt had wrought in Cyrenaica, in Egypt, in Alexandria and in Cyprus, and granted relief to all who brought their problems to him. These are chance scraps of information taken at random concerning measures of the first days of his reign which show which way the wind was blowing. If Trajan was the 'victorious acquirer' of the Empire, as Hadrian himself had called him, he decided to be its preserver, the awakener of its forces, its social ruler and the bringer of prosperity.

When at last, in October 117, the Emperor started from Antioch, to pass by easy stages along the great military road through the lands of Asia Minor[2], accompanied by detach-

---

[1] Epictetus, *Diss.* III, 13, 9; *Orac. Sibyll.* XII, 272; see Weber, *Untersuchungen*, p. 49.

[2] Weber, *Untersuchungen*, pp. 56 *sqq.*; Strack, *op. cit.* II, p. 58; C. Bosch, *Die kleinasiatischen Münzen der röm. Kaiserzeit*, II, 1, pp. 94 *sqq.*

ments of the armies of the West, he knew that the Senate was
desiring his return home, but that it was powerless against his
new policy. He did not hurry for provincial affairs kept him
busy. He spent the winter in Asia Minor, while Marcius Turbo
crushed the rising of the Moors. In the spring he imposed peace
on the Lower Danube through negotiations with the king of
the Roxolani, and also reduced to quiet the Sarmatians of the
plain of the Theiss by a resolute converging attack from the
Danube and from Dacia. The general who had led out the
armies, had taken over the administration of Dacia, had made
preparations for war, but had died in the midst of his activities,
one highly honoured in Trajan's time, received also a triumphal
burial[1]; but Marcius Turbo finished off this war too. Hadrian
had a helper, and success with his new policy. Confidence came.
Then he journeyed hastily to Rome, arrived on the 9th of July
118, eleven months after he had taken over the rule. Anger had
broken out at Rome 'because he had permitted four men of
consular rank to be executed simultaneously,' friends of Trajan
of merit, Palma, Celsus, Nigrinus and Lusius Quietus, who, as
was stated in Hadrian's circle, had been preparing to assassinate
him[2]. The Senate, all too credulous, pliable, blindfolded, had
pronounced sentence upon them; the warrant for their death in
the hand of the executioners and their instigators (above all
Attianus) had been fatal to all four of them before Hadrian intervened. He was formally in the right, when he laid the responsibility upon the Senate itself; he even denied that it had been
done in accordance with his will; but the reproach that he
had not prevented the execution, a reproach serious enough
and yet mitigated by his absence, caused him to appear quickly,
in order to refute the harsh judgment on his behaviour.

With extraordinary bounties he bought the favour of the
people; he swore to the Senate that he would only punish senators
on the ground of a sentence pronounced by the senatorial court;
soon afterwards, 'the first and only one of all *principes* to do so,'
with unexampled generosity he made 'not only his contemporary
fellow-citizens but their descendants, too, free of debt': for he
wrote off 900 million sesterces, which were owed to the Imperial
treasury, sums of unknown but certainly not small extent, debts of
provincials, debts too to the senatorial treasury, the accumulations
of fifteen years, ordering the debt records to be burnt. Almost

---

[1] C. Julius Quadratus Bassus. Weber, *Abh. Preuss. Akad. d. Wiss.*
1932, no. 5, pp. 91 *sqq.*

[2] On this attempted assassination see Strack, *op. cit.* II, p. 166, n. 385.

directly afterwards followed the renewal and extension of Trajan's charitable work for the poverty-stricken youth of Italy, charitable bounties for impoverished senators or for women who were in distress through no fault of their own. A few weeks later Rome witnessed gladiatorial games and wild beast hunts on the largest scale. Every effort was made to obliterate the memory of his 'guilt', to free from apprehension and to lull men's fears, to be able to secure and to celebrate the return of the old 'libertas.' He desired to be a citizen among citizens, a senator among his peers and took his place in the business of the Senate, even execrated those *principes* who had curtailed its rights. Playing on Cicero's fundamental formula, he based his actions on the principle, which he often repeated before the People and the Senate, that 'he would manage the common property as conscious that it was the property of the people, not his own.'

He had reckoned boldly and had been right: the sums which the war would have devoured were free at the critical moment— ostensibly for the people and the world of the Empire, in reality for the final securing of his rule; and simultaneously he called to life the recollection of the *status felicissimus*, the *optimus status civitatis*, in which Augustus had only been the first and best of the citizens. The effect was not lacking: the Senate bowed before this selflessness, did homage to the man whose position they had only lately disputed, 'who had restored and enriched the circle of the earth[1],' who was called, thanks to the providence of the gods, to work for the prosperity of the State and of the world. But in the midst of these rejoicings the rumour suddenly went round that Hadrian desired to have the Prefect of the Guard, Attianus, murdered. Only a short time before, he had given the *ornamenta consularia*, the highest gift he could bestow, to his former guardian, his most faithful helper from the elder generation; did he now perhaps feel himself endangered by his pre-eminence and his presumption? Actually, he only compelled him to retire, and Marcius Turbo became his successor; the other Prefect of the Guard, too, was replaced by a friend. Now, and only now, with his power fully secured, Hadrian had a free course.

III. THE POSITION OF HADRIAN

Hitherto Hadrian had mastered everything with notable certainty: his usurpation had been lost in the bright glory of being son to two *divi*; the policy of renouncing war had been transformed into sympathetic care for the well-being of the masses; the

---

[1] See Strack, *op. cit.* II, p. 61 *sq.*

countries devastated by the revolt had been pacified and were now being restored; the danger along the north-eastern frontier had been exorcised; the alleged attack of the irreconcilables had been crushed with the harshest measures and the guilt transferred to other shoulders; in barely a year and a half the new ruler became the great mediator of divine blessing, the selfless lavisher of well-being, the moderate mild just pious brave Augustus, who cared only for the prosperity of the people and the world. Everyone thought he knew him, for he behaved to all simply and, as it seemed, openly, to Senators and to knights alike, and invited even freedmen to his table. He visited the sick, helped those who had fallen into distress, seemed gentle and kindly and yet suddenly spread death round him. He associated with intellectuals as one of themselves, rivalled them, showed enthusiasms, then suddenly proved that in his sobriety and strength of will he could live in such a way as to give soldiers an example of the strict discipline of their service, as if for his frame such work alone existed. Who among men had such wide interests, who was so many-sided and mobile, who thought so quickly, knew so much, surprised even those who stood nearest to him by his knowledge of their most secret thoughts? Who was in everything so supple and yet hard as steel, who so cold in calculation and determined in action? He felt the longing of men and gave it fulfilment in philosophical formulae, ideologies, and illusions, but also in deeds, so that they greeted him with exultation where he appeared. Thus he could divert their attention from that which he had to do, but could yet inspire them again with enthusiasm as soon as his new work had matured.

Hadrian understood war, was master of its conduct and means, relentlessly risked everything where the situation demanded it, and was cruel up to the moment of victory; in the Jewish war of the years 130–135 580,000 men fell in battle and there were countless others whom hunger, fire, sickness destroyed; over 1000 strongholds and villages were destroyed, and a whole nation banished and scattered. But just as out of the ruins a new and wholly different life arose, so it was everywhere: war was not fought for the sake of war, but only for the sake of peace, that is to say, on behalf of Graeco-Roman culture. The Spaniard understood the Romans, touched their inmost instincts, satisfied them, but was not a Roman. He understood and loved the Greeks, showered on them a thousand proofs of his Imperial favour, exalted them higher than even the Romans. But he was not a Greek. He did not seek the men or the curiosities of his lands to form himself by them. Since, in his abrupt rise, he had given proof of his uncanny powers, and the Senate had publicly recognized that he was divinely favoured, he was bound, now that he had become the centre of all activity, to take hold of and to irradiate the whole world of the Empire with his strength, in order to form it in accordance with his thoughts, to awaken and enhance its energies, in order that the world might become the image of his own being, all and yet one. He was worshipped and honoured as no other Emperor, a god on earth to all people. To some he appeared mighty as Zeus, beneficent as Asclepius, radiant as Helios; others feared him like Mars or the god of the Underworld himself. As he united all contrasts in himself, so he desired to compel the contrasts of the world to unity through restless activity, through being present everywhere and understanding everything, through harshness, where it averted distress, through the prodigal richness of his giving, where he had to banish death, create life, conjure up splendour and glory. His despotic striving towards the divine in all the world, the self-enhancement of his mysterious power, its setting forth for show in the image of the highest god of the Greeks and Romans, tokens of his intoxicating illusionism, offspring of his mystically dark imaginings, like his restless sweeping around the world, dissipated themselves at last in an outbreak of insanity. When he grew calm again, he found that light pleasure in trivial pursuits, that self-irony and scepticism towards all human activities and human life which wholly alienated him, lonely though worshipped as he was, from men. But no one realized that in a tragic life he had experienced in advance an example of what awaited all his people.

Hadrian, when they first got to know him in Rome, had pointedly taken as his model the image of Augustus, sacred to all. To this pattern he held fast: he literally seemed to grow into that rôle, wearing it with wonderful certainty as a mask. The preservation of moderation was to be his highest law, where his position in the State was concerned; he was the complete altruist on behalf of humanity. The official titulature of the inscriptions gives the names and titles of the emperor in the usual way down to the end of his reign, whereas on the countless honorific inscriptions of Greek cities variations are often to be observed. But the central coinage of the Empire, these highly significant pieces of evidence for the history of the time, show the official titulature only in the first year. Then from time to time occur important alterations: first 'imperator' and even the name Caesar disappear; only the office of *pontifex maximus*, the *tribunicia potestas*, the third consulate of the year 119, are given down to 123. From A.D. 123 to 128 he wished the coinage to reveal him as nothing more than 'Hadrianus Augustus,' to be compared without presumption in his personal eminence with Caesar Augustus. From 128 on appears the somewhat more comprehensive and expressive formula 'Hadrianus Augustus pater patriae consul tertium[1].' Modest in the number of his consulates, when compared with the great Augustus, since many of the higher officials of the Empire had held as many, he yet stood higher than all his contemporaries; and in that he was now equal to the august ruler following whose precedent he did not assume the title *pater patriae* till late in life when he had deserved it by the multitude and greatness of his achievements.

But there was more than that: this Spaniard, thanks to his *virtus* the first of the citizens, was now, as the exalted father of the great family of Rome, the root, centre, crown, of Rome's power, its representative towards the world, whose glance everyone who was banished from Rome's sight must avoid. Was not the stretch of road which he had traversed, to the very limits of humanity, not already almost unbearably great? A few months later he took the last step, became in Athens Zeus Olympios, the Zeus of all the Greeks (Πανελλήνιος). While to Rome he was to be *princeps*, *Augustus*, *pater patriae*, this new name was seized upon with intoxication by the world of enthusiastic Greeks: countless monuments testify to the zeal of the towns to celebrate the new Olympian. All this proves only that the boundaries between humanity and divinity were becoming shadowy, that heaven and earth were coming into contact again, that he understood the deepest longing of the world. In such images he enchanted the world, as he interpreted and covered his own activity with repeated pointings to the greatness of the past, or trimmed it with philosophical maxims. He might pose as one conscious that the common property belonged to the people, but the controller of the State, the first servant of his people, was really its master. His word was all-powerful, his word was a final decision.

Hardly any ruler of Rome pursued the cult of the past as did Hadrian. In this too he followed the example of Augustus, but he far surpassed him in energy, and his efforts no more embraced only the revival of old-Roman forms and ideas of life, but the whole of what was Greek, and they set in motion the new emergence of the manifold forces of the Provinces. Hadrian knew what tradition meant for the State and was on his guard against altering

---

[1] See for the most recent treatment, Strack, *op. cit.* II, pp. 7 *sqq. passim.*

the old forms. But these forms received ever fresh content. The 'Good fortune' of the Roman People, that every spring was to celebrate the birthday of Roma aeterna, was promised, and the new age was to bring it to pass. The People believed in it and in the fair fiction that the State belonged to it; but, as the masses of the world-capital and their standard of life had little left in common with the Republican period, so in this State they had no more power to command.

Hadrian left the Senate unassailed. Almost to the last he kept his oath to respect its right to judge senators; he honoured it and its members, allowed it to be active and so far won it to himself that for almost twenty years it gave its assent to all his edicts, and acts of State, though none the less he limited its effectiveness even in Italy. But the Senate had now changed. The men who were prominent in it, like himself, were no longer Romans; hardly three of the old Roman families were still to the fore. Spaniards, Gauls, Africans, natives of Asia Minor, who were rich and established, and possessed a strong following, composed the assembly of the illustrious, who were no longer a reflection of Rome, but a reflection of a new upper class of the Empire, divergent in their interests, world-wide in their horizon, united by the influence of a uniformly political and intellectual culture. In this Senate was concentrated the power of the provincials, made fruitful by Rome's tradition, and this power had effect on all the parts of the Empire. The Senate seemed to continue to play its old rôle, but was almost wholly a pliant tool. It may be significant that Hadrian seems only to have promoted two men to match his own tenure of a third consulship, and these his nearest relatives, Julius Servianus, the husband of his beloved sister, and the rich patrician Annius Verus, the southern Spaniard, his friend, grandfather of the boy whom he cherished, as once Augustus had cherished his Gaius, to secure him the succession. He too kept his following together: the Spanish coterie ruled Rome's Empire more strongly even than under Trajan; it was not till Marcus Aurelius and his son Commodus that it disappeared. The extrusion of the Italic element from the highest class of the Empire and the victory of the powers of the provinces proceeded unchecked, thanks to his temperament and his attitude.

Hadrian did not efface the differences between the Orders and their functions in the State as a matter of principle. But the tasks which he set his 'equestrian' friend Marcius Turbo at the beginning of his reign, and the latter's career up to the post of Prefect of the Guard, already show the tendency towards the new

state of affairs. Gradually the process of amalgamation began:
more often than formerly a man passed over from the equestrian
to the senatorial career. The rigid organization of the 'equestrian'
career in the civil service was completed[1], and this career now
became open to the bourgeoisie, no longer of Italy alone, but of
the whole empire. 'Knights' now received high posts in the
administration. Their career was regulated by means of a scale of
rank and salary and a fixed course of promotion. Civil and military
careers now take their course abreast of each other (p. 432). The
two *praefecti praetorio*, commanders of the Guard and highest
equestrian officers, whose title by itself reveals that they are the
deputies of the ruler, now take part in the re-organized *consilium
principis* (crown council), which had the duty of advising the ruler
in questions of law and administration: here they sit alongside the
senators who are called to be members of it, and one of them, now
always an eminent jurist, presides over the body. The departments
of the ruler's cabinet, the offices of the court administration, once
in the hands of freedmen, those of the domains and mines, of the
fiscal administration, of the post, now taken over by the State, of the
provincial administration—in a word all the departments to which
the career of a knight gave access, from the humblest procurator
up to the Prefect of the Praetorian Guard, attracted the ability of
those who were entitled to pursue them. These entered the service
of the ruler and, unlike the senatorial magistrates, were dependent
in everything upon his will alone. In doing this Hadrian logically
gave a new meaning to the idea that the *res publica* was the property
of the *populus*: as *princeps*, as trustee for this *res publica*, he desired
to avoid any appearance of seeking to withdraw from the State
and of making into his own servants alone this multitude of the
ruler's officials, which was acquiring a greatly increasing power
over the organization of the Empire, or of making that Empire
his 'property' or the monarchy into a hated absolutism. All the
departments of the State-administration were, at least in theory,
placed afresh under the 'sovereign' Populus Romanus.

The new order of things, in the creation of which Hadrian
carried the reforms of Augustus a long step further, clarified the
construction of the whole organization, and gave the *bourgeoisie*
of the Empire a greater share than ever before in the general
administration. In continual action and reaction that order of
things enhanced the participation of the *bourgeoisie* in the work

[1] See O. Hirschfeld, *Kais. Verwaltungsbeamten*[2], pp. 476 *sqq.*; A. von
Domaszewski, *Rangordnung des röm. Heeres*; Weber, *Traian und Hadrian*,
pp. 256 *sqq.*; A. Stein, *Der röm. Ritterstand*, pp. 361 *sq.*, 447 *sq.* and *passim*.

of government and its introduction into the prevailing form of life of the Empire. Thereby it furthered the work of resolving the contrasts of the provinces in the interest of the Empire as a whole. But it also forcefully strengthened the bureaucratic system. For it demanded a State bureaucracy which remained in effect bound to the ruler. And Hadrian trained up this bureaucracy in the principles of loyalty, fulfilment of duty, and justice, and kept it under the closest control; on his far-reaching journeys he tried to make real the theory of the ruler's omnipresence. He issued edicts in which the legal position of the civil service was further developed; he paid his officials, rewarded them, distinguished them, in order to spur on their initiative. He simplified and unified the administration, and the whole gained in clearness and continuity. But the new order of things effected in everything the opposite of that which it seemed to effect: in the hand of strong rulers it became the counterweight to the traditional powers of the aristocratic Senate, and through that weight the power of such rulers over Rome and the empire was enhanced.

IV. THE FRONTIERS AND THE EMPIRE

The security of the Empire and the interests of the Imperial power demanded that a strong army should constantly be ready to take the field, even if, and indeed, precisely because Hadrian desired peace, and none but just wars of defence. He was enough of a soldier and general to be able to judge and to deal, here too, with even the minutest details. Ancient Roman discipline, the most skilful execution of all duties from the slightest piece of drill up to the most far-reaching manœuvre, these were first commandments; the height of achievement was his goal, and on all his journeys he assured himself of these things. Relentless in his demands on his troops, he made easier the position of the soldiers in their free time, improved their legal position and their economic status, and did justice to their claims as human beings. For the soldier needed for his drill insight, character, the impulse to devote himself to his heavy task. Like the true soldier that he was, Hadrian fought against excess and luxurious living on the part of the soldiery, and trained them to hardness, simplicity, and self-discipline, in order that the army might be the embodiment of the idea of the Roman Empire and of Roman culture; and in all this he set them an admirable example of living on his journeys. He held fast to the idea of the *exercitus Romanus*, but this idea acquired a new meaning[1]. He raised the Guard to be the *élite* of the army, made it into a model regiment as the representative of Roman discipline, to which, often enough, he drew attention; he picked out its officers to be instructors and commanders of the troops of the line, in order that the technique and spirit of the line troops might all reach one level; the higher officers' posts he offered only to natives of Italy or provincials of Italic blood.

But at the same time, as a fundamental principle, he decreed that the army should be recruited from the sons of the provinces in which the several units were quartered: he allowed these provincials free access to the career of officers in them, and thereby brought it about that the portions of the army belonging to the individual provinces became wholly identified with them. To the cavalry, which was composed solely of provincials, he made concessions, permitting them un-Roman battle-cries; and he formed bodies of frontier-dwellers, who were instructed in their own camps as a militia and, as non-romanized elements, acquired nothing of the spirit of Rome. In this way the training of the army, in so far as it included the provincials, did indeed contribute to the unification of the dwellers in the empire; on the other hand, the presence of the provincial troops gave to the *nationes* a strong lever for the furtherance of their own interests, while the mere fact of the broadening of the basis shows that the way was leading towards decentralization. The *exercitus Romanus*, once the levy of the citizens of Rome and Italy for the protection of their possessions in the world, was now the imperial army along the imperial frontiers, which had to defend the interests of the disarmed population of the empire against enemies from without and within.

Its strength was secured upon the broad basis of the forces of the Empire. On these the pyramid of the army was built up, reaching its apex in the Guard. Like the bureaucracy, the army became a great instrument of power in the hand of the ruler who controlled it; and it could hardly stand any longer for the Roman idea of the lordship of Rome over the world, since the *nationes* were taking the place of Rome and Italy. But what would happen when the Guard, which was meant to hold together the whole in a Roman spirit, should no longer exist? When in 193 Severus dissolved this Roman-Italic Guard and replaced it by picked bodies of men from the provincial armies, especially the Danube army, 'He wholly ruined the youth of Italy, which

---

[1] On the reform of the army see von Domaszewski, *op. cit.* esp. p. 194; Weber, *Traian und Hadrian*, pp. 258 *sqq.*; Ritterling in P.W. *s.v.* legio, cols. 1288 *sqq.*; E. Sander in *Philol.* LXXXVII, 1932, pp. 369 *sqq.*

now had to turn to banditry and gladiatorial careers instead of
military service, and he filled Rome with a motley crowd of soldiers,
wild of aspect, dreadful in speech, boorish in behaviour[1].' The
last remnant of Roman character was then expelled from the *exercitus Romanus*, and the provincialization of the army, and simultaneously the re-arming of the provinces, was finally completed.

In harmony with the ideal of peace the army was set a new task:
instead of offensive action for the acquisition of new territory
everything was now based upon a defensive. To this idea corresponded the re-grouping of the troops in the frontier provinces,
the movement of *auxilia* right up to the imperial frontiers, which
were now sharply delimited, corrected here and there, and made
secure by Hadrian on his journeys in accordance with new points
of view, in order that in the territory behind them the culture of
the Empire might be peacefully developed. For, where no natural
barriers were interposed and the observation of the enemy was
made possible by rivers like the Rhine, the Danube, the Euphrates,
or by frontier mountain-ranges, as in North Africa, the systems
of frontier *limites* were carried straight across the country by the
surveying skill of the soldiers, in part without consideration of the
nature of the land: the Upper German *limes* of the Flavian
period and the British *limes* perhaps of the Trajanic period[2] were
examples of this (see above, p. 183). These *limites* were made into
frontier fortifications, either by means of palisades on earthen ramparts, as in Upper Germany, or by a wall such as 'Hadrian's Wall'
in Britain, which bestrode the country for a length of 80 Roman
miles (see below, pp. 522 *sqq.*). These constructions, which were
made secure by means of wide ditches pushed out in front of them
and by numerous towers and forts with their garrisons, separated the civilized empire from the 'barbarian' world outside; they
brought it about that trade from outside, which could only enter at
certain fixed points, could be watched and subjected to fiscal control; they helped to prevent raids on the part of small hostile
groups and to hold up the surprise attacks of larger masses,
until the troops from the territory behind, disposed in deep
echelon, were brought up. The new organization of frontier protection which was created in order to guarantee the security of
the empire and of the frontier provinces, which, now, were continually being more deeply permeated with its 'civilization,' had
a reflex action upon the army, which was deprived of the idea of

[1] Dio LXXV, 2.
[2] On the *limites* see E. Fabricius in P.W. *s.v.* and in *O.R.L.* A II,
Strecke 3, pp. 41 *sqq.* and above, pp. 182 *sqq.*

the offensive: on the other hand, the organization was not strong enough to prevent serious and vigorously pursued attacks upon the Empire.

Even in the few warlike undertakings which he carried out, Hadrian held to the idea of the defensive throughout. He began with the overthrow of the Jewish rebellion and of the Moors and Sarmatians in the first year of his reign; next came the crushing of the rebellious Britons, who had destroyed the legion IX Hispana in the camp of Eburacum, and the *expeditio Britannica,* which ended in 119 with the pacification of the country, and was followed, on his visit in 122, by the construction of 'Hadrian's Wall.' Then came the second Moorish revolt (122)[1], in which the *virtus Augusti* and the 'harmony of the armies' restored peace in victory 'through a fortunate success,' so that the Senate celebrated it with a festival of thanksgiving. The same idea is seen in an almost forgotten undertaking[2], in the averting of the danger of war along the Euphrates frontier by means of his appearance in person and his negotiations with the Parthian king (123), and in cases wherein he, as arbitrator, settled the quarrels of the Empire with its neighbours. When the Alani invaded Roman territory across the Caucasus in north-east Asia Minor, he was content to have them successfully repelled by the provincial governor Arrianus.

Finally, his serious war, that against the Jews, was in essence purely defensive. In it he was fully justified in taking drastic and relentless measures. On his journey through the Jewish territory (in the early summer of 130) he had ordered the building of a new town, a Roman colony with 'Greek' settlers, on the site of Jerusalem, which Titus had destroyed, and alongside the legionary camp of the X Fretensis: this town was to bear the name Aelia Capitolina, and in the place of the old temple of Jehovah he ordered one to be erected to Juppiter Capitolinus, in which he himself was to be honoured. So here also new life was to blossom forth from ruins. But the breach with the past was unavoidable. Under the protectorship of the all-uniting highest god of the Empire, and of the new founder of the town, Graeco-Roman culture was henceforth to prosper. The Jews of the country were roused by this, as were soon the Jews in every quarter of the civilized world. This excitement led to veiled opposition: a revolt was prepared but no more, as long as Hadrian still remained in the East (130–132). But when he was far away,

---

[1] Strack, *op. cit.* ii, pp. 71 *sqq.*

[2] Strack, *op. cit.* ii, p. 80 *sq.*; perhaps rather support for the wars of Cotys against the Scythians, see Weber, *Untersuchungen,* p. 151 *sq.*

there began a guerrilla war of caverns, ravines, mountain fastnesses, which the Roman army of occupation at first did not take seriously. A new Messiah, Bar Kochba, Son of the Star, led his people and stiffened their resistance. Aelia was taken by storm, soon afterwards the Egyptian legion, XXII Deiotariana, was cut up, and the troops whom Hadrian sent, above all from far-off Britain under capable leaders, whose governor was Julius Severus, had great difficulty in coping with superior numbers. The frenzy grew, the situation was so serious that in the summer of 134 Hadrian himself once more travelled from Rome to the scene of war. 985 villages of some account were taken, 50 mountain fastnesses were destroyed; 580,000 men were slaughtered, and to these must be added an incalculable number of those who perished by hunger, fire and pestilence. The Roman losses also were great. The extirpation of the fanatical race was followed by the re-organization of Syria Palaestina and its reconstruction. In December 135 the ruler adopted the title *Imperator II*, a proof that the hard victory had been definitely won.

V. LEGAL AND SOCIAL POLICY. THE JOURNEYS

Hadrian's activities in the spheres of law, economics and social life in Rome, Italy, and the empire, can only be briefly touched upon. The principles which he proclaimed at the beginning of his rule remained decisive in all that he did. He fulfilled the ruler's duty to be the supreme lord of justice often and willingly, not only in Rome, but also at many places upon his journeys, displaying the many-sided industry which characterizes his nature. And the great number of his legal decisions of which we know shows how fruitful his activity was. His decisions were famous for their clear and homely wording, pertinent pronouncements were collected and circulated in writings of his own, and the later books of law cite many of his legal interpretations and decisions. In these he created new law, in his capacity as highest tribunal of law in many matters; and the appointment of eminent jurists to be Praetorian Prefects, and so to preside over the *consilium principis*, shows what stress he laid upon the principle that his representative on this body also should be in a position to serve authoritatively and fully the idea of justice.

Often enough in Hadrian's decisions are seen the motives which determine him. Humanity, natural equity and a justice which proceeds from deep ethical sources must be the judge's supports. Not caprice, but objectivity, must rule; human nature must be respected, the will and state of mind of the doer investigated. Knowledge of mankind, the personal impression of the individual case and the judge's own conscience are to determine the judgment and the measure of the punishment, not merely formal points of view and the judge's knowledge of law. In difficult cases philosophers or doctors are referred to as authorities. And for Hadrian the slave, too, is a human being: he is only partially excepted from the protection of ordinary law; the master has to respect his humanity, must not arbitrarily torture or kill him, prostitute him, sell or mutilate him, for an unworthy purpose, and the judge must not condemn him, if he is deserving. As he himself in the *consilium principis* laid the greatest emphasis on authoritative legal counsel, so too, in other respects, he encouraged the eliciting of expert opinions, did what he could to bureaucratize the *consilium* of the judge, extended the legal authority of individual higher officials, and, by giving instructions to judges, the activity of the monarchy itself. The final redaction and codification of the Praetorian Edict[1] by the jurist Salvius Julianus[2], which he then made the Senate raise to be a norm, also shows that he desired, in legal matters as in the organization of the State, to make the creative will of the ruler prevail[3].

Hadrian's restless activity had its effect on the countless towns throughout the length and breadth of the empire. He spurred on their ambition and granted them relief: he gave them temples, baths, games, festivals, aqueducts, fountains, gymnasia: he supported in them education, instruction, theatres, furthered their autonomy, granted many of them the right to issue their own coins, strengthened their communal constitutions, gave them town regulations, looked after their budgets, and caused them, where their finances had got into disorder, to be watched over by controlling officials. Here he extended their possessions, there he increased their size by incorporating new communities within them; he founded entirely new towns or parts of towns; to many in the West he gave the *ius Latii*, to others in the East the Greek city-constitution. He took part in their life, he even became, in cities of Italy, Spain, or the Greek East, their highest honorary official or priest, did homage to their gods and often on his journeys

---

[1] See O. Lenel, *Das Edictum perpetuum*[3]; Weber, *Traian und Hadrian*, pp. 261 *sqq.*
[2] See Pfaff in P.W. *s.v.* Salvius (14), cols. 2023 *sqq.*; W. Hüttl, *Antoninus Pius*, II, pp. 90 *sqq.*
[3] See, on the judicial activity of Hadrian, S.H.A. *Hadr.* 8, 18; 21, 1; 22, 11. Dio LXIX, 7, 1; for his *constitutiones* Hänel, *Corpus legum*, 85–101.

he was himself honoured by many as their own god. He was truly solicitous for their material well-being and splendour. With him, the urbanization of the Empire reached its final heights, and was well on the way to conquer and annex economically even the most distant corners—districts hitherto closed to town-culture, survivals of primeval village-civilization in Europe and Africa, districts with widely-extended land-ownership in Asia Minor.

It is the impression of Hadrian's work that moves the pane-gyrist of Rome to say some twenty years later, that the world has become a democracy, guided by its best citizen as leader and orderer, a single city-state, in which the best men, sons of all provinces, are citizens and therefore called to rule over the masses. Thanks to these rulers and the general organization of the officials, of the armies, who are Roman citizens and all together represent the Empire, from which they derive, war only prevails now on the edges of the world; and everywhere else there is peace, prosperity, happiness, so that those who live outside are to be pitied. Rome has opened all the gates of the world; the whole earth is at work; festival on festival can be celebrated; everyone is inspired to be as noble and excellent as possible. Rome has given laws in common to all and even new gifts: all dwell in one house as members of one family...[1].

From Hadrian's attitude towards the Greek idea of the right of the city-state to freedom, autonomy, and self-sufficiency in its life, from the very idea of justice standing in opposition to might, to which he stubbornly held fast, new life was awakened in the fair fiction that the countless city-states are members, possessing equal rights, of a mighty league under Rome's selfless leadership; that consequently no one of them can be robbed of its own life, but that all together, in the organization of the Empire which stands above them, are members of the body, feel themselves one as in the 'family,' the 'house,' and thus wish to be the civilized world as opposed to barbarism. Not this dualism alone, but in real truth those panhellenic[2] ideas and fictions further the process of unifying the whole Empire; on the other hand, they also accelerate the strengthening of the provincials' self-consciousness: the claim put forward by these provincials to a greater share in the govern-ment of the Empire does not disappear, but grows quickly. But alongside and above this fiction of the league of the city-states there come to greater prominence than ever before the primeval groups of peoples, now comprehended in the Empire, the *nationes*,

---

[1] Aelius Aristides, *Or.* XXVI K, 60 *sqq.*   [2] See p. 320.

who at the Emperor's *vicennalia* pay him harmonious tribute on the Empire coins as fair symbols of his activity on their behalf. It was to local provincial spirit and cohesion that Hadrian's adoptive father Trajan, and thus Hadrian himself, owed the lordship over the world; this spirit was everywhere still alive, and it will grow ever stronger and stronger dressed in Roman forms of life; in struggle with 'Rome' it will continually give the latter new powers, but will also transform it. And so the State organization as a whole appears almost only as the outward shell, the form for the ordering of life; the army appears as the protecting, the bureaucracy as the regulating power; but all these three are taken possession of with ever increasing sureness, from now on, by these *nationes*. But if one believes the panegyrist, there arises the impression that the 'masses' in the country are only an 'object' made use of by the ruling classes, by the caprice of the officials: in reality the first beginnings of the new régime show that Hadrian, in accordance with his principles, did not overlook them either. The allotment of arable land to the Egyptian fellaheen, the fragments of his legislation concerning agricultural land, the statute concerning the African domains, and everything else which we hear, prove that he wished to prevent the land from becoming barren, to open up new areas to cultivation, to protect the small peasants from oppression and to further their prosperity. He settles them on domain-lands, where they are to be free and to earn enough to be able to exist.

In this empire of material prosperity industry and trade flourished, thanks to internal peace and to the security on all routes. Each was dependent on the other. Industry satisfied the needs of the local market, but also created enough goods for export in small and great concerns, in the manufactories owned and run by the great estates of the temples in the East, on the rapidly growing domain-lands. In this way industry was at the same time drawn from the confines of the cities also into the country. But the State, in many respects the owner of the raw materials, which for the most part carried on the production of metals, precious stones, marble, as its own monopoly, but also permitted private persons to engage in these trades, did not yet damage private trade by its own excessive power; on the contrary, it made use of private enterprise in deliveries for State undertakings. And private enterprise can hardly ever have been so powerfully stimulated during these centuries as it was by Hadrian, whose initiative spurred on the rich to imitate him, whose great building activity created work, and thereby caused money to be earned, in all the territories through which he passed; even though it may be said of him that he banded together builders of all classes in cohorts according to military practice, took them with him on his journeys, and set them to work on the erection and the decoration of walls. But trade, whether local or regional, and now for the first time really universal, was in full swing; and great distances were overcome by it, remote provinces were captured, the northern and the south-eastern frontiers of the empire were left further behind than ever before. The economic opening-up of the younger provinces, in North Africa, in the East, in the Danube area, along the Rhine, and even in such remote areas as Britain, made rapid steps forward; and in Gaul especially new forces were active and creative forces developed. Oriental trade, however, with great energy, won elbow-room in the countries of the West. From all this there results a new orientation of the driving forces in the empire: Gaul especially, but also the Rhinelands, Britain, Spain and Africa, having adopted for generations the technical achievements and the taste of Italian handicraft, and the forms of its products, drove out Italian competition from the markets of their interior territory and provided for those markets themselves. Gaul, above all, actually became Italy's competitor in other provinces and in Italy. It is true that in doing so it had given up its old native forms of goods and adapted Italian taste to its own uses, thereby deliberately contributing to the process of unifying all exterior forms of life in the empire; but in Gaul too, and not in Britain alone, the Celtic spirit was to be found, while in Africa and Spain the spirit of the old *nationes* still survived. And the East, which only needed to continue that which it had practised for thousands of years and had practised most of all in the centuries since the beginning of 'Hellenism,' betrays in everything that it had no mind to give up its own native ways. So in the economic world, too, is revealed the same picture which the political activity of Hadrian had brought about. Hadrian knew the whole empire: in efforts continually renewed he observed on his journeys the losses, the needs and wishes of the countries, towns, villages, estates, and of the men in them: everywhere he intervened in a creative spirit. His name is writ large on every region of the Roman world[1].

If one includes the first journey, mentioned already, from the East to Rome (117–8), and the journey to the scene of the Jewish War (134–5), Hadrian dedicated some twelve out of the twenty-one years of the reign to restless wanderings through the

See Weber, *Untersuchungen, passim; Traian und Hadrian*, pp. 263 *sqq.*; M. Rostovtzeff, *Soc. and Econ. Hist. of the Roman Empire*, pp. 318 *sqq.*

empire[1]. He first spent only two years in Rome and Italy (July
118 until the middle of 120); from 121 until 125, then again from
128 until 133 he was on the move, beginning with the West,
Gaul, Germany, Raetia, Noricum, hastening through Britain and
western Gaul, visiting Spain and fighting in Morocco. Travelling
eastwards along the African coast he visited Africa, Cyrenaica,
hurried by way of the islands and Asia Minor to the Euphrates;
returned through the lands of northern Asia Minor, passed
through the Balkan lands as far as Pannonia and Dalmatia, then
and then only turned to Greece, in order at last to return to
Rome after five years of wandering. He only remained there for
just three years; in 128 he crossed again to Africa, spent the winter
in Athens, passed through the territories of southern Asia Minor,
Syria, Phoenicia, Arabia and Palestine, Egypt as far as into the
upper Nile valley and once again Asia Minor, as far as up to the
districts of the Black Sea, to betake himself to Athens for a third
time in 132. He returned to the capital, perhaps not until some
time in the year 133; from late summer 134 to 135 he spent time
in Palestine; the last two and a half years were given to Rome and
its neighbourhood.

Only about four years of his period of wandering were given
to the West and the Danubian regions: the Greek-speaking East
greatly predominates. He wished to convince himself everywhere
by his own observation, by seeing and experience, how the
arrangements of the State were standing up to usage, and to
convince men that the forces of the past and present sufficed to
create a strong future. He did not go on his travels in order to
show himself to men as sovereign; he wished to win their hearts
and their enthusiasm through his presence and activity. He
inspected the officials and the troops, pronounced justice and
visited the frontiers, arranged their defence and the allotment
of the troops in their garrisons, held parades, exercises, manœuvres.
He heard the petitions of the provincials, granting what and where
he could. He gave water-systems and bridges, laid out roads,
indeed systems of road-networks, in order to open up still more
the inner regions of provinces like Africa, Spain, Galatia. He
rebuilt destroyed cities, founded fresh ones in the vicinity of
military camps, at important points; he raised the old centres of
the districts of Syria, Phoenicia, Arabia, to be capital cities, in
order to strengthen what were once the seats of independent rulers,
as the backbone of culture, and to avoid all-too-stringent central-

[1] See Weber, *Untersuchungen, passim*; *Traian und Hadrian*, pp. 264 *sqq.*;
Strack, *op. cit.* II, pp. 73 *sqq.*, 81 *sqq.*, 117 *sqq.*, 139 *sqq.*

ization. From the Euphrates and the Arabian desert to Upper
Egypt, to Mauretania, Britain and the Crimea, his helping hand
raised up this town-culture in Graeco-Roman form. Countless
buildings arose everywhere in the towns—temples, halls, baths,
town-walls and gates; in this way work was created; his example
found emulation in foundations of the competing parts of the
empire. Gods were honoured, and among them the ruler, in the
West as in the East—most of all in the latter, where life
blossomed anew as if by magic. Here he honoured a great
man of the past, there he competed in intellectual conversation
with philosophers, artists and scholars, but he also climbed
Mt Casius near Antioch and Etna, to enjoy the miracle of the
sunrise.

As was said already, the Greek Polis is once again victoriously
exalted as the form of the community, and that in the East; even
in the Egyptian countryside there arises at his command a new
town, Antinoopolis, which, colonized by veterans of Greek
blood from Egypt, glorified in the names of its tribes and demes
a skilfully artificial system, the house of the ruler, the divine
forms in which he appeared and his relations to Eleusis and
Athens (see pp. 299, 319). That is no mere chance. For his thoughts
and endeavours were directed towards Athens, towards the salvation
of the Greek world, the centre of which Athens must remain. He
showed more favour to that city than to any other town. As architect,
refounder, renewer of its cults, even of its laws, he, whose image
received a place in the Parthenon, entered upon a bond of alliance
with Athena; he became Zeus Olympios, the lord of the Olym-
pieion, at last completed; having become an initiate of Eleusis
he was raised to be a hero in the cult; he became Zeus Pan-
hellenios, who summoned all the Greeks in the world to remember
their race, to act in the consciousness of being Greek. From Pontus
and Syria as far as to their old mother-country the Greeks joined
together into a union of Panhellenes, avowing their friendship to
Rome, their gratitude to the ruler, pointing to their ancestry and
their Greek blood. Hadrian was in person the originator of a
Greek renaissance of the gods, of their cults and mythology, of
art and learning, of the whole of life. The initiator of this new
humanism[1], who now more than ever praised Rome as a Greek
town, who spoke of the noble mind of the Greek, of his glorious

[1] It has anti-Oriental tendencies. Weber, *Untersuchungen*, pp. 271 *sqq.*;
id. Handelinge van den XIII *Nederlandse Filologencongress*, 1913, pp. 42 *sqq.*;
id. Traian und Hadrian, pp. 268 *sqq.*; J. Vogt, *Alexandrinische Kaisermünzen*, 1, pp. 103 *sqq.*

language, of the charm of the barbarian, he it was who 'holds his hand over the towns, sets them up, makes free and autonomous the Best, those who have led for ages, leads the others with great consideration and care, educates the barbarians to mildness[1].' He made the nations conscious of their national life, in order to incorporate that life in the world of the Empire and wholly to permeate it with the Greek form, a federalist and a 'European' at the same time.

After these beneficent manifestations of his divinely-appointed power, Hadrian, broken by the death of his favourite Antinous, raised that Bithynian youth to godhead as Pan, as youthful Hermes, as the good god pure and simple, the bestower of fertility, the mediator between heaven and earth; he exalted him as the principle of youth and of the beauty of Greek form, caused him to be honoured in the wide circle of his Panhellenes as the symbol of his aesthetic-humanistic ideal and enthusiasm. Once in his beloved Athens one of the leaders of the still young Christian religion handed to this same Emperor a treatise which used the methods of Greek thought to refute the reproaches levelled by the world against his religion and which proclaimed the victorious truth of the new belief. The great wonder-worker and enthusiast passed it by. It never revealed itself to him in all its depths. That is strange enough, since in the end he did not close his eyes to the magic world of oriental religious images and thoughts. He had seen the sanctuaries of the gods of Asia, he knew the Alexandrian god Sarapis, honoured the Egyptian goddess Isis, listened to Egyptian thaumaturges, did honour to magi, received and accepted the pantheistic teaching of the astrologers. He shattered the fanatical fury of the new Jewish Messiah and his people; he built the Pantheon in Rome and that in Athens, in both of which his struggle to attain the divinely universal assumed shape. In his huge villa at Tivoli, as in a museum, he united the remembrances of notable places of the earth, the vale of Tempe, Canopus, Athens—an Academy, a Lyceum, a Prytaneum, a Poecile Stoa— and with them an 'Orcus' and an 'Elysium.'

One ponders vainly why he did not point the way to domination to the new religion of the Christians. Was it because it emanated from the Jewish area? Did he overlook the limitations of the effective power of his own ideal, of his new youthful god? Must the god-ruler first bow in humility before the new god? Did everything come too late to him, who indeed himself, in contradiction to his Panhellenic policy, permitted marriages between

[1] Aelius Aristides, XXVI K, 96.

Greeks and Egyptians to the inhabitants of Antinoopolis, and in the spirit of Trajan's policy of toleration rejected accusations against Christians, unless they were based on acts punishable under the criminal code? The last great impression which Hadrian received was that of the fanatical struggle of the Jews. His harshness in crushing the eternal rebels, which made a shattering impression on the world, and his unrestrained fury against his Roman circle, friends and senators, all this shows that his powers were exhausted, his ideal had paled. Men and the world passed from his ken; madness overpowered him. The constant seeker after god, who had himself become a god, the proclaimer of the new divinity, the rejecter of him who was to conquer, was himself smitten by the deity. At times he busied himself with the duties of the day; then he relapsed again, harsh towards men and the world, into brooding and trifling.

In the summer of 136, as his sickness grew worse, Hadrian suddenly arranged for the succession. He made a survey and said, at a gathering of his friends, that they should name to him the ten best men, but turned away from the suitable persons. His fate was tragic enough: he compelled his own brother-in-law, Servianus, aged 90, of whom he himself at that gathering had first thought as his successor, to die, and also Servianus' grandson, the only representative of the blood of the Hadriani; with mind darkened and unstable in judgment, even if he only desired to make him the place-keeper for a boy, he chose out and adopted, to the disappointment of all, one of the consuls for the year 136, L. Ceionius Commodus, a man of Etruscan family, who had given no proof of his suitability as 'optimus' nor, so far as we know, was related to Hadrian, and moreover was a sick man. Was it a sign of madness or is it an invention that he declared his beauty to commend him to his choice? As a matter of fact, however, he only regarded him as one to keep the place warm for his favourite M. Annius Verus, since to this latter, who was just fifteen years old, he betrothed Ceionius' daughter. He designated Ceionius for a second consulship in 137, entrusted him with the administration of both Pannonias with the imperium proconsulare, lavished great sums on soldiers and people and games, and nevertheless only leant, as he was bound to see on the 1st of January 138, 'against a fragile wall.' For when he returned from the provinces and was on that day about to deliver his speech of thanks to Hadrian in the Senate, L. Aelius Caesar, as he was called as presumptive heir, collapsed and died of a haemorrhage. Disappointments without end marked Hadrian's way; his bitterness broke out when he forbade that the dead man should be mourned, when he even lamented that he had spent so much money for nothing.

In the summer of 137, after twenty years of his reign[1], Senate and People and world praised him as the giver of blessings. In a demonstration without equal, reference was made to the peoples, the armies, the countries and towns, which, taken all together as the Empire of this ruler, had enjoyed the good-fortune of his advent, had been blessed by his activity in the re-establishment of their powers. Thanks were given to the gods who protected him and helped him to maintain peace for the world, to bring the earth into equipoise and security, who had given the Golden Age, the time of good-fortune for Rome and its world. And, now that he generously lavished presents and reported what he had done, and asserted that, with Rome's freedom secured, loyalty would continue between ruler and people, while the Senate praised him as a new Romulus, as a peaceful ruler over land and sea, he could not help seeing that at last he was wholly understood in Rome too. But now he had pleasure in nothing.

He was a tragic lonely figure in his last year of life. His hope was centred on the boy Annius Verus. He overcame the disappointment which the death of the Caesar had caused him, but preserved for the son of that Caesar his rights. When on his last birthday (January 24, 138) Hadrian, already mortally ill, summoned the most honoured senators to himself, he announced his intention of adopting the consular T. Aurelius Fulvus Boionius Arrius Antoninus, a member of his council, a long-standing friend of his house, perhaps related to Plotina, and through his wife uncle of the young Annius Verus. Four weeks later, on February 25, 138, when Antoninus, whose own two sons had died young, had adopted the young Verus and the son of the dead Aelius Caesar, and had also acquiesced in Hadrian's resolve, Hadrian took him as his son. He called himself, from now until the death of Hadrian, 'Imperator T. Aelius Caesar Antoninus trib. pot. cos.': for he received the *imperium proconsulare* and the *tribunicia potestas*, as had once Tiberius, and moreover, the first to do so, the title Imperator to be borne as praenomen. With this last act of the sick man the succession was regulated for two generations, since Hadrian (like Tiberius in former years) had intended to secure it for the two boys as well. Herein he would, like Augustus, bend the future to his will. Augustus remained, too, his model for death. He desired to die as serenely as had Augustus, after he had tried, in desperation and in vain, to lay

---

[1] Strack, *op. cit.* II, pp. 184 *sqq.*; cf. pp. 139 *sqq.*

violent hands on himself. Half mocking verses stole from his lips about his 'wandering, pleasing little soul, that now descends into the pale, cold, naked, underworld, and jests no more....' 'Hated by all,' according to his biographer, he died in Baiae, and lay in State first in Cicero's villa at Puteoli. Thanks to the energy of his adopted son, the dead man was placed in his monument on the far side of the Tiber, built after the model of the Mausoleum of Augustus, and still unfinished[1]; and, in spite of the opposition of the Senate, which at first was violent, he also entered, as *divus*, into the Heaven of the Roman State.

[1] *C.I.L.* VI, 984, dedicated towards the end of A.D. 139, S.H.A. *Pius*, 8, 2.

CHAPTER IX

THE ANTONINES

I. ANTONINUS PIUS

HADRIAN'S strength was born of the mingling in him of old-Italian and Iberian and perhaps African-Semitic blood; the ocean, the plain, now luxuriant now sun-stricken, and the sluggish river of the south-western edge of the empire left their mark on his family and his childhood. Trajan had set him in the currents of the provincial movement, and like Trajan he brought with him a nature full of contrasts: at once lively and majestic, with the play of sentiment and the pose of greatness, despising the body and full of the discipline and gravity of the soul and the spirit, with a wide outlook, a power of organization, an unshaken will to master the world of earth and of heaven, a strange almost mystical impulse to a universal embracing unity. Thus he takes his place as one of the strongest in the line of the great Spaniards rather than of 'Roman' rulers: he stands nearer to the Alphonsos and Borgias, to Ignatius, Charles V or Philip II than to Augustus whom he affected to embody. Cold to dissemble, resolute in act, he had won Rome, the Empire's centre, and from it he wandered over the whole world. He had defended it in arms at the four corners of civilization, in Britain, in Mauretania, in the South-East, on the Danube and the Black Sea. He had made the final cleavage between Orient and Occident and laid upon the West the task of defending European culture by the disciplined strength of the army and the unresting all-pervading activity of the officials, by drawing on the forces of the cities and country that made up the Empire; by ceaseless striving after a 'culture' full of life. His aim was to end barbarism, to keep the oriental world at arm's length and to strive to maintain the Greek way of life which was the bond between Rome and its empire. To that end he made of Athens a second focus of the empire, its new centre for things of the mind. His appeal, the strength and resources that he brought to the task seemed to promise success. His collapse was of evil augury. The dark days to come could only be averted by like efforts and self-sacrifice, which alone could enable the Empire

Note. Exigencies of space have made necessary in this chapter certain omissions and abridgements of a fuller text.

to revolve round Eternal Rome and not only round its ever-active Emperor.

The man whom Hadrian adopted after the sudden death of L. Aelius Caesar was cast in a different mould. T. Aelius Antoninus[1] presented the sharpest contrast to Hadrian, in his character and historical effect. His family, which originated at Nemausus (Nîmes) in Gaul, had during the last two generations risen to distinction at Rome. Though the history of the Province in his reign showed that he did not forget whence his race had sprung—or perhaps it was Nemausus that was careful not to forget—he may never have seen his home. All he knew at first was the neighbourhood of Rome, the Latin and south Etruscan countryside. After his father's death he was brought up in the house of his paternal grandfather Aurelius and then in that of his maternal grandfather Arrius Antoninus, who was still alive in A.D. 106. The property inherited from these two families made him one of the richest men of Rome and brought him estates not only in Latium and south Etruria near Lorium but farther afield in Etruria, in Umbria and Picenum and, perhaps later, in Campania. This fact was decisive for his thinking and acting. In love with the quiet and the tasks offered by his country estates he could forgo life in Rome and had no desire to travel over the world. He was happy to live in Lorium or Alsium, Lanuvium or Tusculum, Centumcellae or Signia, Baiae or Naples, and even when he became Emperor he did not care to leave Italy but left others to take charge of wars and administration in the empire. With no taste for splendour or parade, thrifty and prudential, the careful steward of his own possessions, he rebuked his wife, on becoming co-regent—'Have you not wit to see that now we have reached empire we have lost what we had before[2]?' But he, too, said 'nothing is meaner, indeed more heartless, than to nibble at the property of the State without adding to it by one's own efforts[3].' He gave lavishly of his own property but cut down the salary of the lyric poet Mesomedes. Content with little, with

---

[1] For texts see *Pros. Imp. Rom.* 1, pp. 309 *sqq.*, 118 *sqq.*, especially the life of Pius; Marcus Aurelius, *Med.* 1, 16, VI, 30, Fronto's letters, Dio LXIX–LXX. The inscriptions are collected by W. Hüttl, *Antoninus Pius* II, who does not, however, give the evidence of literature or papyri nor that of coins, which last provide very abundant evidence not only from the Empire currency (see p. 330 n. 1) but also from that of Alexandria (J. Vogt, *Alex. Kaisermünzen*, 1, pp. 111 *sqq.*) and the cities of Syria and Asia Minor (C. Bosch, *Die Kleinasiatischen Münzen der röm. Kaiserzeit*, II, 1).

[2] S.H.A. *Pius*, 4, 8.   [3] *Ib. Pius*, 7, 7.

small care for personal comfort, laborious, with a simple goodness, cheerful with an unaffected dignity, caring for integrity and piety, careful to save men and not to destroy them, bearing unjust censure without reply, calmly above calumny, he tested men by their character and their acts without distrust, without malice or ready censure. The loyal master of his servants, in honour exigent to fulfil his devoir, he strove from his chosen retreat to fashion the world so far as his duty claimed it of him.

But even there he did not as an autocrat or even with strong initiative rely upon his own powers, sure instinct and sound judgment. Never, so we are expressly told, did he allow any act of State to have effect until he had consulted his 'Friends' and had been guided by their views. This makes it hard to reach a decisive verdict on his personal share in the fortune of the Empire. Whether even his speeches were of his own composing was, it seems, a topic for jesting doubts; there are stories of pert sayings which he did not resent. This is proof of his kindliness to all the world, of his easy good nature towards his kindred and friends, with whom he did not cease, when emperor, to go fishing, hunting, making holiday for the vintage. He loved the simple pleasures of a simple citizen, admired actors, gave honour and good pay to rhetoricians, philosophers and *grammatici* because their labours were useful, though he had no touch of Hadrian's zeal to conquer the world of ideas, of knowledge and of culture. When the emotional Marcus Aurelius broke down in tears at the death of his teacher, and the palace servants would check his abandonment to grief, Antoninus found a word of sensible human comfort— 'Permittite illi ut homo sit; neque enim philosophia vel imperium tollit adfectus[1]'; nor did he lack a witty mocking thrust to bring to heel the haughty tutor of the young prince[2]. In such anecdotes is mirrored the character that can be detected as clearly in his acts of State, the *humana civilitas*, the aristocratic detachment of the rich Roman—no trace of Hadrian's daemonic restlessness.

His official career was not less significant of his character. After helping to manage the family property he won the name of a lavish quaestor and a magnificent praetor. In his thirty-third year (A.D. 120) he became consul along with Hadrian's powerful friend Catilius Severus. Probably three years before, he married Annia Galeria Faustina whose brother, M. Annius Verus, was to be the father of the future Emperor Marcus Aurelius, whom at Hadrian's wish he himself adopted. Through these connections he became the friend of Hadrian who advanced him thus early to high office.

[1] S.H.A. *Pius*, 10, 5.　　　[2] *Ib. Pius*, 10, 4.

He was made one of the four consular *iuridici* who judged matters of inheritance, guardianship and *fideicommissum*, in the towns of Italy, a duty which, doubtless not against his will, he discharged in the regions where his estates lay. In A.D. 134–5 after the usual interval from his consulship he became, like his grandfather Arrius sixty years before, proconsul of Asia, where he emulated and it was said even surpassed, as no one else had done, that eminent administrator.

Thrust into the microcosm of Asia Minor with its competing jealousies and no less its new panhellenic movement, he may have felt the effect of its ferment of life, stirred and excited by the forceful directness of Hadrian and his way of mastery and governing. He may have yielded to its influence, as when he endured patiently the brusque inhospitality of the pompous rhetorician Polemo[1], or he may have chosen in quiet devotion to an ancient ideal to fulfil his duty aloof and unmoved. After Hadrian's return from the Jewish War, Antoninus was made a member of his *consilium* not only on grounds of friendship and family connection, but because of his experience as jurist and administrator. But his horizon had been limited. He had not governed one of the Imperial border provinces, had never had to do with the army: his way had lain in lands that had long been at peace and in the care of the Senate rather than of the *princeps*. Of the problems presented by the Northern and Eastern Fronts he can hardly have known more than he could learn from the discussions at Hadrian's court, in Rome, in Italy and in Asia Minor. He was no drastic imperialist like Trajan, nor was he even strongly drawn to Hadrian's all-pervading and imaginative width of interest. He was, as has been seen, a strange compound of the *petit bourgeois* and the Italian landowner, without ambition, without elasticity of mind or the passion for greatness, without an instinct for movement, revolution or daemonic energy. He was a tenacious conservative.

More than that, he had been the closest witness of Hadrian's tragic collapse. The sight of that unquiet strength drained away to death could not well move him to desert his own quietude, even though he was certainly among those who were gravely stirred when the Emperor, with darkened judgment, adopted Ceionius Commodus to be *locum tenens* for his young nephew Annius Verus, and marked him out for the succession. But his unambitious, unsuperstitious mind could not be stirred to trust signs and wonders that proclaimed, so ran the rumour, his divine summons

---

[1] Philostratus, *Vitae Soph.* 1, 25, 3.

to the throne. He did nothing to cross the will of Heaven. When Hadrian, in his mortal sickness, summoned, on 24 January 138, the most respected senators to the Palace and saw him come supporting the steps of his aged father-in-law, the senior consular, he was touched by this filial piety. But it was not this that decided Hadrian; he had already made his choice and now he announced it and carried it through in the face of the egotistical plans of Catilius Severus though he too was near enough akin to the boy Annius. He declared his intention to make Antoninus his son, but laid on him the duty of adopting, on his part, Annius, now nearly seventeen years old and the son of Aelius Caesar, a boy of about eight. Further, he urged him to betroth his daughter to Annius, which made it plain that he wished by every means to secure him the precedence for the succession over the young Aelius. He sought to make the way sure for the Spanish line till far in the future. But would Antoninus consent to play this rôle? His personality was known to Hadrian. He was not the 'best,' but he was the richest man in Rome and all his wealth would come to the rich Annius, in whom the broken Emperor saw the man who would be *optimus*—Verissimus, as he named him at this time. Antoninus asked for time for reflection, whether in feigned modesty or from secret reluctance, like a second Tiberius. And then, by his consent to the double adoption and the betrothal, he saved the throne for the Spanish coterie. From 25 February 138—the day on which the legal formalities were completed— he was co-regent as Imp. Titus Aelius Caesar Antoninus *trib. pot. cos.* His name expressed the tie with his adopted father Hadrian and his grandfather Antoninus, and he revealed how strongly his nature responded to this ideal, though the two figures of Hadrian and Antoninus were more and more to strive for mastery in him. It is significant that, down to the fourth century when Hadrian's memory was dim, the 25th February was celebrated at Lorium as the birthday of the rule of all the Antonines.

The adoption found the usual response in the Empire in praise of his devotion as son and loyal colleague of his father. When Hadrian a few weeks later moved to Baiae, he stayed in Rome in charge of the government, though of his acts few traces are left. Then, as Tiberius had done, he hastened to his father's deathbed. On 10 July 138 Hadrian's death left him *de facto* sole ruler. He was nearly fifty-two, and still younger than Tiberius, and this stop-gap emperor retained his charge for longer than Trajan and Hadrian, longer even than Tiberius. But the patient Marcus Aurelius did not find twenty-three years too long to wait, for when

Antoninus died on 7 March 161 the son was no more than forty and in the fullness of manhood.

The filial piety of the new ruler was quickly shown. His father's body was brought from Puteoli to Rome and laid in its tomb beyond the Tiber. The State funeral and consecration, which bestowed on Antoninus the authority that went with the position of *Divi filius*, was decreed by the Senate which wished to annul Hadrian's *acta*, only after he had expended himself in urgent pleading and in threats and had consented to the release of senators whom his predecessor had arrested. This was shrewd policy, and his zeal for *pietas*, the spring of man's right conduct too towards gods, parents and dead alike, earned him the name of PIUS, which he bore, amid the applause of the world, next after his title 'Augustus.'

From 139 onwards he added the title 'pater patriae,' which he had at first, like Hadrian, refused and then accepted earlier than his predecessor had done. His full name 'Imperator Titus Aelius Caesar Hadrianus Antoninus Augustus Pius Pater Patriae' (138–9) acknowledged his adoptive father and his grandfather and, with 'Imperator Caesar Augustus Pater Patriae,' Augustus the prototype of Roman Imperial rule: he united their intrinsic properties and as Pius enriched them further. His victory over the Senate not only gave him the sanction of divine descent, but enabled him to fix the picture the world was to have of him and of his less worthy successors. Before two years had passed he set on his coins the short form 'Antoninus Augustus Pius,' which thus detached him from his predecessor. Once only, in 150–1, when he dedicated the Temple of Divus Hadrianus, he, and the Senate with him, resumed the full form of his name and had it inscribed on coins for the following months.

One thing else is significant and of consequence because the principle was rigorously carried through. On the Imperial currency[1] issued by the Emperor his consulships appear[2], as did those of Hadrian on his coins, but he went beyond him in assuming a fourth consulship, and at the same time he set himself above all other consulars, none of whom held the office more than twice. His son, Marcus Aurelius Caesar Augusti Pii filius, was an ex-

[1] For all references and allusions on the Empire currency see Mattingly and Sydenham, *Roman Imperial Coinage*, III, pp. 1 *sqq.*; Strack, *Reichsprägung*, III, pp. 1 *sqq.* with a complete catalogue of all existing types, a work which thanks to the author's kindness has here been used while still in MS. as a basis. For the titles, etc. see also the material collected by Hüttl, *op. cit.*

[2] *Cos. des.* till 1 Jan. 139; *cos.* II in 139; *cos.* III from 140 to the end of 144; *cos.* IIII from 145 to 161.

ception, attaining a third consulship in 161[1], when he was forty
years old, together with his adoptive brother, L. Aurelius Verus,
who at the age of about thirty became consul for the second time,
a visible sign of his second place. In 143–4 and at times later
Pius records his second acclamation as *imperator*, as Hadrian had
done, though not on his coins, since 135. But at first on the coins
he made as little use as his predecessor had done of the *tribunicia
potestas* in counting the years of his reign. Then at the completion
of his first decade there suddenly appears his tenth *tribunicia
potestas* (from December 10, 146 to December 9, 147), and the
series continues to the twenty-fourth tenure in 160–1, by which
time the like tenures of Marcus Aurelius had reached fifteen.

In 139 he had given to Marcus the name of Caesar and made
him consul designate. In the next year, as his colleague in the
consulship, he betrothed him to his daughter, who on her
marriage in 145 received the name of Augusta. On the birth of
their first child in 146 Aurelius was granted the *tribunicia potestas*,
to run from December 10, and *proconsulare imperium* without the
city. Now Aurelius was recognized as Pius' colleague in rule,
and the hopes of Rome and the fortunes of the dynasty rested
upon him. As Vespasian and Titus had counted their years together, so now it was made clear to all by the parallel office of Pius
and Marcus that the régime had attained a stability hitherto
unknown. What made this clearer was the steady though secondary
advancement of L. Verus. After minor distinctions he attained
the consulship at the age of twenty-four, and finally, at the end of
160, Rome witnessed an unparalleled instance of concord[2] in
the Imperial house when both the Emperor's sons were appointed
consuls together for the next year, Marcus for the third time,
Verus for the second. Thus Verus' position also in the State was
marked out.

It is plain to see how far Pius went his own way. First he speaks
of '*aequitas*,' '*felicitas*' and '*fides*' as the guiding principle of his
rule: the Senate stressed the ideas of peace, the acceptance of the
Pontificate, the care for the poor of Rome. It did not even now
admit its defeat over the consecration of Hadrian, but *aequitas*
offered a formula for agreement. In 139 the oppositions have
disappeared and these ideas have been harmonized. Now that

---

[1] He appears as *cos. des.* in 139; *cos.* on Pius' coins in 140; then after
he received the right to strike coins himself in 144 as *cos. des.* II, from 145
to 160 as *cos.* II; at the end of 160 as *cos. des.* III; 161 as *cos.* III.

[2] Cf. Strack, *op. cit.* Catalogue no. 1200 with Vogt, *op. cit.* II, p. 90,
ὁμόνοια (of like date).

Pius has taken the title 'pater patriae' the Senate speaks of 'good
success,' of the *Felicitas* and *Salus* of the ruler, of the *Libertas
publica* that leads to Security. The Emperor, too, cares for the poor
as for Victory and Peace, but he dedicated the *Clupeus virtutum*
to Hadrian and consecrated the temple of Divus Hadrianus
in the Campus Martius[1], and a temple at Puteoli and established
games in his honour, *flamines* and the Sodalitas Hadrianalis—
almost as Tiberius had once done for Augustus. On the Senate's
coins the dead Emperor still finds hardly a mention. But a series
that belongs to this time shows the representatives of the *nationes*,
Africa, Alexandria, Armenia, Asia, Cappadocia, Dacia, Spain,
Mauretania, Parthia, Phoenicia, Scythia, Sicily, Syria, and recalls
the great proclamation of two years before which extolled Hadrian
and his activity in all the provinces and on behalf of all their
peoples (pp. 323, 336). The Temple of Divus Hadrianus is to unite
them all, a visible symbol of his achievement and of Roman
pre-eminence in the world. But unsolved problems of foreign
policy were posed by the dependency of Armenia, by Parthia, still
in theory a dependency, and by Scythia (p. 313). Was Phoenicia
to be entirely separated from Syria[2], did Alexandria seek even
greater prominence?

Thus the Emperor resumed ideas that had been Hadrian's,
and like his predecessor he remitted the whole *aurum coronarium*
in Italy, the half of it in the provinces. But he and the Senate
bethought them of his ancestors and honoured the home of his
father's family in southern Gaul[3], and completed the buildings
that Hadrian had begun in Rome, in Capua and elsewhere. The
world set great hopes on him, and everywhere cities and private
people began to honour him as their benefactor and set up statues
to him and to his house. Ephesus, where he had resided as governor of Asia, declared that 'by common consent of the whole world
the most divine and pious Imperator Titus Aelius Antoninus
had assumed the sovereignty given to him by his father and restored to health the whole race of mankind[4].' In the following
years the chorus of laudation in the Empire swells in homage to
the 'best and greatest,' the 'best and most reverend,' the 'most
god-fearing and man-loving' princeps, the 'holiest of all times,'
the 'greatest and most visible of gods.' These phrases, which had
meaning when they were used of Hadrian, possessed some reality,

---

[1] H. Lucas, *Arch. Jahrb.* 1901, pp. 1 *sqq.*; Jordan-Hülsen, *Topographie
der Stadt Rom in Altertum*, I, 3, pp. 608 *sqq.*
[2] See Weber, *Untersuchungen*, p. 233 *sq.*   [3] Hüttl, *op. cit.* pp. 283 *sqq.*
[4] *O.G.I.S.* 493; Hüttl, *op. cit.* p. 351 *sq.*

but in great part were little more than the expression of an age
that was becoming more and more given up to sentiment without
ideas behind it, far removed from the Emperor's own dry style
as shown in what remains of his edicts, letters and decisions at law.

Spoilt by Hadrian, the whole world pressed on Antoninus with
petitions and demands of every kind, and there is clear evidence
that he satisfied many of them. Rome and Ostia, Lanuvium and
Tarquinii, Lorium and Caieta, Antium and Terracina, Capua
and Puteoli and other places in Campania or south Italy all owed
buildings to him. Athens, small cities of Greece and the islands,
Ephesus and distant country towns in Asia Minor, cities of Syria
and Alexandria, nor less of Africa and the Latin West and North
as far as the Black Sea enjoyed his bounty. Baths and temples
were restored or built. Not only in Italy and Narbonese Gaul but
also in Gallia Lugdunensis, Upper Germany, Pannonia, Syria and
Numidia he had roads made or repaired. In Rome, Narbo,
Carthage and Antioch he made good the damage done by fires.
Rhodes and Cos, the cities of southern Asia Minor and Cyzicus
that had been visited by two severe earthquakes received help
from the State. He induced the rich to make benefactions, but
he also was generous with his own resources[1]. Like his predecessor, he regarded it as Rome's duty to provide and maintain
employment. In the work on the frontier, the building of the new
castella on the Antonine Wall in northern Britain (p. 336) and of
a number on the Upper German *limes*, and repairs and restoration
in other parts of the Empire he was continuing and completing
his father's policy.

The panegyric of Aelius Aristides was as true of him as of
Hadrian. But there was a difference. Hadrian had made the
power and beneficence of the emperor everywhere felt and realized
by his presence; in north-west and in south-east, in villages as in
cities, the consciousness of the close bond between world-ruler
and subjects, between individuals and peoples, became a living
force, and all felt themselves members one of another, to whom
Rome was no longer a burden to be borne. But the rule of Antoninus meant that they must once more look to Rome where the
Emperor 'sat so as to be able in fact to receive messages more
quickly in the centre of the world[2].' As if, perhaps, in criticism
of Hadrian's conception of his task, he sat like a beneficent spider
at the centre of his web, power radiating steadily from him to the
farthest bounds of the empire and as steadily returning to him

---

[1] Abundant evidence on this may be found in Hüttl, *op. cit. passim.*
[2] S.H.A. *Pius,* 7, 12.

again. For the last time in Imperial history the Emperor was
wholly one with Rome and its centralization. His subjects had
nothing left them but appeals through the administration or
special embassies that were costly. But what the ruler stood for
was made fact. He slowed down the rotation of offices: many men
stayed at their posts two, three, four or more years, one of the
Urban Prefects twelve, one of the Praetorian Prefects even eighteen.
He treated them with fairness, solicitude, sometimes even indulgence, rewarded merit, and though his justice compelled him
to punish when they had erred, he protected their children from
sharing in their punishment. We can trace only a few slight
changes in the magistracies or the army, and the division of Dacia
into three in the summer of 159 is the only important measure of
organization in the government of the provinces. He kept to
his predecessor's policy, even in the admission of provincials to
advancement and to the government itself. Paradoxically enough,
he sought to secure the future of Italy and stress the unique
position, the unending fortune of Rome, while all the time the
provinces gained ground step by step.

In lawgiving he was diligent, equitable and just[1]. Careful of
the letter of the law, he was not loth to interpret it according to
the spirit: in judging disputes between cities he showed sober good
sense. He bade the Thessalian *Koinon* in the name of justice to
begin by punishing the use of violence in disputes about ownership. He called on the provincial council of Baetica, in accordance
with an old law, to exact an increased penalty for the premature
forcible appropriation of the object of a dispute. He urged the
governor of Baetica to be severe in prosecuting kidnappers, and
he referred shipwrecked men who had been robbed to the customary naval code so far as it did not clash with Roman law.
Antioch was instructed how to deal with a defendant who gave
surety and the *Koinon* of Asia was given precise direction about
the number of the physicians, rhetoricians, sophists and *grammatici*
in the different-sized cities who were to be immune from public
charges. He permitted the circumcision of the sons of Jews and
forbade the persecution of Christians for their faith. *Coloni
Caesaris* were granted direct appeal to the Emperor, minors were
protected from criminal prosecution. When a deserter was handed
over by his father he limited the punishment to loss of rank to
spare the father the reproach of causing the son's execution. He
sought to ensure a milder application of the law against the man
who killed his wife for adultery, and the release of those unfit to

---

[1] For texts Hänel, *Corpus legum*, 101–14; for inscriptions Hüttl, *op. cit.*

work who had served ten years of penal labour in the quarries
and still had relatives. He was inexorable against any master
who killed his slave. Anyone who maltreated or starved or otherwise misused a slave was deprived of him, and in other decrees
he made the laws of slavery more progressive. He sought to
prevent the prosecution of conspirators, he made punishable the
exhibition of an Imperial statue as a provocation, avoided confiscation, and imposed limits on the acceptance of bequests to the
emperor. In all this as in many other edicts on the most diverse
sides of the law, excerpts from which have been preserved, he
showed himself far removed from the rigour of old-Roman conceptions of law and developed further the liberalism of Trajan and
Hadrian.

Under his equable rule 'all the provinces flourished.' By his
strict economy he had accumulated at his death in the Treasury
a sum stated to be 675 million denarii[1]. Though he insisted on
moderation in the collection of tribute, and on nine occasions
distributed to the People of Rome money or corn to a total value
of 800 denarii to each recipient[2], though he showed his liberality
in not forgetting the soldiers, and spent large sums on games and
shows of beasts, he was not only less profuse than his predecessors
but also was a shrewd manager. Thus in providing for the care of
girls in honour of his dead wife Faustina he arranged, so far as
can be seen, that it should mainly happen on his own estates[3]. His
decree about debts[4] continued the policy of Hadrian, but it would
have been more loudly acclaimed had it been as comprehensive as
that of his predecessor. It was possible for Pius to be economical
because Hadrian in his profusion had met countless needs and
the world was in equilibrium. If the activity of Hadrian had
quickened the pulse of the Empire, Antoninus let it grow steady
of itself. The ruler was far away; his effect was due to the force
and devotion of his officials. The governed were conscious of his
remoteness, and made their own strength effective. Over all
rested the brightness of a day in late summer.

The prestige of Antoninus stood high throughout the world[5].

[1] Dio LXXIII, 8, 3; Eutropius VIII, 8.
[2] Marquardt-Dessau, *Staatsverwaltung*, II[2], p. 138.
[3] *C.I.L.* XI, 5956 (of A.D. 139 Pitinum Mergens), 5957 (A.D. 150 *ib.*),
IX, 5700 (A.D. 149 Cupra Montana), X, 6002 (Sestinum): perhaps also
XI, 5931 (A.D. 147 Tifernum Tiberinum), 5990 (Tifernum Mataurense);
cf. Hüttl, *op. cit.* pp. 281, 269; Mommsen, *Staatsrecht*, II[3], p. 1079 *sq.*
[4] A. Graf von Stauffenberg, *Unters. z. Chronik des Malalas*, pp. 318 *sqq.*
[5] See von Rohden, *op. cit.* col. 2507.

Embassies came to him from India, Hyrcania and Bactria, but they were of slight moment since the Eastern policy of the Empire renounced any offensive. He increased the domains of the King of the Caucasian Iberi, who visited him in Rome. He gave kings to the Lazae in Colchis, to the dependent Armenians and to the Quadi and admitted them afresh to allegiance. A letter from him sufficed to stay Vologases II of Parthia from an attack on Armenia; his 'authority' caused Abgar VIII of Osrhoëne to evacuate Armenia; he refused to give up to Vologases III the sacred throne which Trajan had carried off, and his firmness ensured peace until the closing months of his reign. But although he thus maintained the symbol of Parthian dependence on Rome, there was no return to the Eastern policy of Trajan. To Antoninus the Empire needed no further conquests. He decided between claimants to the throne of the Bosporan realm whose king was 'amicus Caesaris et populi Romani,' and supported the people of Olbia against the Scythians. All this continued Hadrian's policy of conciliation, but with a difference. Hadrian threw himself into the task and built up the basis from which this distant influence could be exerted, Pius used up and did not add to the Empire's reserves. While he sought peace from inertia, he justified it with the plea of Scipio and Augustus that 'he would rather save the life of one citizen than slay a thousand enemies[1],' but they had other motives, and it may be that the Empire itself suffered from his passivity. His desire to avoid wars did not save him from them, and success was due to his lieutenants, not to the Emperor who stayed in his palace at Rome.

The Empire coinage of A.D. 138–9 reveals the danger of war. As at the beginning of Hadrian's reign, so now, there were movements afoot at all the four corners of the empire. In Britain the Brigantes once more broke in, pouring across Hadrian's Wall, but were defeated thanks to the 'help of the gods' and the 'loyalty of the soldiers.' The victory was the work of Lollius Urbicus, the new governor of the province, and the Emperor received from it his second acclamation as Imperator. The strengthening of the empire's defences on the north-west by the Antonine Wall (p. 333) which Lollius carried through is significant as the necessary consequence of this invasion and victory. From A.D. 145 onwards the coin-types of almost every year suggest wars and victories. In 145–52 and also towards the end of the reign there was serious fighting in Mauretania Caesariensis and Tingitana, in which a detachment of the Sixth Legion Ferrata from Judaea and cavalry-

[1] S.H.A. *Pius*, 9, 10.

formations from Spain, Germany and Pannonia were engaged. The coins of 152 reveal the peace imposed on the rebels by the Emperor, who celebrated an *Ovatio* for his victory. There is evidence for a victorious war over Germans, but it is hardly possible to decide whether this is to be connected with the building of *castella* on the Upper German *limes* that belongs to about 146.

To the years after 152 may be assigned various conflicts, the Jewish Rebellion, a rising in Achaea (both of unknown date and extent), an insurrection of the Egyptian fellaheen which in 152–3 seriously endangered the corn-supply of Rome and led to riots in which the Emperor risked being stoned and was reduced to making a largesse of wine, oil and meal to the poor at his own expense. It was not till 154 that the 'concordia' of Nile and Tiber and the securing and peace of Rome, thanks to Fortune and the world-ruler, were commemorated. In 155 there seems to have been another victory in Britain to judge from the types of Mars, Hercules, Felicitas and, strangely enough, of the 'loyalty of the armies'—perhaps there had been a mutiny in the province. In the next year Juppiter appears as victor, and the coins again show the 'loyalty of the armies' and Victory and Peace, the providence of the gods securing for Pius Rome's mastery of the world. The literary tradition[1] records other conflicts, with the Alani, on the Borysthenes, on the Red Sea, which cannot be dated, and in the years 157 and 158 operations against Dacian tribes by the troops of the province with detachments from Africa and Mauretania. In 159, the year in which the Emperor's *vicennalia* were tardily celebrated, there was peace, but in 160–1, despite the praises of Felicitas Saeculi and Peace, there were warlike alarms, for Roma, Mars and Juppiter are hailed as victorious powers. Risings in Africa in which the Virtus of Marcus Aurelius, that had been honoured in 156 and 159, proved itself, ended in 160 with a victory for the Roman arms. All this is proof that it was no age of lasting peace, that there was not only unrest without the empire but stress within it. It was peace where there was no peace, even if men did not wake from the dream of a Golden Age[2].

Fortune herself was made the Emperor's obedient follower. He was named Pius, for like the phoenix he had cared for his father's consecration[3]. This was to be proof that a new Saeculum had begun: at his second consulship he was hailed as *optimus*

---

[1] S.H.A. *Pius*, 5, 4 *sqq.*

[2] For the Empire coins cf. Mattingly-Sydenham, *op. cit.* and Strack, *op. cit.* III; also Vogt, *op. cit.* 1, p. 125 *sq.*, II, pp. 63, 72 *sqq.*

[3] Strack, *op. cit.* II, pp. 55 *sqq.*

princeps, and the year as blessed and happy. But when on July 20, 139, the Sothic period in Egypt was fulfilled so that a new cycle began[1], hopes turned to the future. Alexandria celebrated the Emperor as the all-guiding Pantheos Helios-Zeus-Ammon (*i.e.*, Re-Amun), the lord of the new world-Era, the great bestower of fruitfulness. After the dark period of Mars and the god of the Underworld Hadrian[2] he began to appear as the god of light. In Rome the notes of *libertas publica* and *salus Populi* were struck and rose to a crescendo when Pius at last completed and dedicated the temple of Roma Aeterna and Venus Felix[3] which Hadrian had begun. The ruler under divine providence, who cared for Italy and its renewing[4], removing the *juridici* so that the old municipal rights were restored, turned the thoughts of the Romans to their primitive past, to its myths and divination and to the age of gold. Ilium, whence the city had its birth, was granted privileges, while he founded a new Pallantium in honour of the Arcadian city whence all that was Greek had sprung[5]. Thus Panhellenism received a new impulse, but Rome still more[6]. A wave of archaism swept over Rome and the Greek East. Senate and People hailed Antoninus as 'best and greatest *princeps*, the most beneficent and just for his eminent care of the State cults and for his devoutness (*religio*)[7].' Many compared him with King Numa[8].

In Alexandria, which added to all this the reference to the phoenix as the harbinger of the new Saeculum, the Prefect of Egypt, who as *praefectus annonae* at Rome had felt the magic of this worship of the past[9], caused Pius' entry on his fourth consulship on January 1, 145 to be celebrated in an especial way. Beside the Egyptian and Greek gods appeared the signs of the zodiac as rulers of the season. In A.D. 141 Hercules, the benefactor of mankind, had been advanced in honour; now the rule of the *optimus princeps* and the new year of happiness and blessing that his consulship was to bring to the capital were thus made to rest on the domination of the constellations at their fortunate conjunction by the Alexandrian divinities Sarapis and Isis, Helios and Selene. The harmony of seasons and the world's course, of the Universe and govern-

---

[1] Vogt, *op. cit.* 1, pp. 113 *sqq.*   [2] See above p. 306.

[3] Strack, *op. cit.* 11, pp. 175 *sqq.*   [4] *C.I.L.* xi, 805 (= Hüttl, 227).

[5] Pausanias VIII, 43; Weber, *Gött. Gel. Anz.* 1908, pp. 962, 977; *Drei Untersuchungen zur aegyptisch.-griechischen Religion*, p. 27.

[6] Vogt, *op. cit.* 1, pp. 120 *sqq.*

[7] *C.I.L.* vi, 1001.   [8] S.H.A. *Pius*, 13, 4; Eutropius viii, 8; Fronto, *Princ. Hist.* p. 206 N.

[9] See Hüttl, *op. cit.* pp. 7 *sqq.* for Valerius Proculus; for the coins of 145 see Vogt, *op. cit.* 11, pp. 69 *sqq.*; cf. 1, pp. 116 *sqq.* See Volume of Plates v, 128.

ment on earth were taught by the astronomers and astrologers and accepted by men, before whose belief even Rome must bow.

Alexandria in the years of the *primi decennales* hailed the Emperor anew as the world-redeemer Hercules, and loyally shared in celebrating the victories that stirred Rome. But, even if in 139 Alexandria had failed to make good its claims (p. 332), now it was perhaps presumption that Sarapis appears in the chariot as *triumphator* in celebrating the victory in Britain. Alexandrian coins show no reference to the Nine-hundredth-year celebration of the founding of Rome which coincided with the beginning of the second decade of Pius' reign[1], but in the Roman Empire coinage also there is hardly a hint of this conjunction of events or cycles of years. And apart from regular symbols or the record of current events such as the festival of the restoration of the temple of Divus Augustus at the beginning of the Emperor's third decade, these show no signs of living significance. The same is true of the coinage of Alexandria, but the insurrection in Egypt and the 'concord' between Nile and Tiber[2] alike betray how dangerous it might possibly be to the People of Rome and its daily bread. In the East on every side the sun-religion advanced ever more potently. In Rome itself and in the West offerings for the Emperor's preservation were made to the Magna Mater and to Juppiter Dolichenus. Nothing is heard of the cult of Rome, and the Panhellenic movement sank into a dream. The divinities of the East pressed on irresistibly from Egypt and Asia Minor, Mithras and Dolichenus, the sun god and the Christ; and with them Astrology. Philosophers sought new answers to life's riddles, unblinded by the brilliance of the material civilization of the time. We look in vain for the creative ideas of this quarter of a century during which Pius governed the world from Rome. He gave to the Senate what was the Senate's, he maintained the fair show that he was the 'ampliator civium,' the new *optimus princeps*, a Numa and the protector of the Greek basis of European culture. All this he did, but his sitting like a spider in the middle of the delicate web that covered the vast empire was a danger to it more than a blessing. After a short illness he died in peace, full of days, at Lorium on March 7, 161, in the dreams of his

---

[1] Aurelius Victor, *Caes.* xv, 4, A.D. 147 (cf. Tacitus, *Ann.* xi, 11 for Claudius); whereas Philip the Arabian has this festival in A.D. 248, the usual view would have it advanced to A.D. 142–3 and would make the coins of this date evidence for it, though these are sufficiently explained by the dedication of the Rome and Venus temple (see above, p. 338, n. 3).

[2] Vogt, *op. cit.* ii, p. 81; cf. i, p. 129.

delirium 'still speaking of the State and of the kings he was angered at,' and he took the peace and quiet of the Empire with him into his grave, into his temple as a fair aspiration for the future.

II. MARCUS' ACCESSION: THE TWO EMPERORS

'As the Salian priests were once casting the customary rose-garlands on the banquet-couch of the god in the temple of Mars, the crown of the young Marcus Aurelius fell upon the head of the god's statue just as though he carefully had placed it there[1].' This was taken as an omen of future rule, strangely enough the only sign that Rome discovered of the gods' early favour towards the most devout of emperors. It was the divine will that the man who did this homage to the god of the Imperial house should become a member of it. But was not this same Mars Ultor also the god of war and the army? It is one of the great paradoxes of history that the kindliest, most selfless of men, who acted only 'in accordance with reason,' modest to receive, ready to renounce, who held it the lot of a ruler to do good and be requited with ingratitude, was fated in nineteen years of his reign to give place to Mars, to die in his winter-quarters on the northern border of the empire. He had written 'A spider when it has caught a fly thinks it has done a great deed, so does one who has run down a hare, another who has caught a sprat in his net, another when he has taken a boar or a bear, another when he has captured Sarmatians. If you probe into the reasons for their acts, are they not all *robbers*[2]?' On him came war in the East, war over all the North, domestic treason, everywhere disturbance and unrest, the terrible plague that swept away peoples, the bankruptcy of cities and of the rich. It was as though a mysterious night descended on the bright day. This very Emperor, who pronounced with such logic upon his own hunting of wretched Sarmatians, amid it all desired and dreamed of quietude, of serenity, of a life of action consonant with the universe, of the harmony of the world-order.

Note. The literary tradition for the reign of Marcus Aurelius is to be found in the Scriptores Historiae Augustae—*Marcus Antoninus, Verus, Avidius Cassius,* and *Commodus Antoninus* and Dio LXX–I. For the coins, which supply further evidence, see Mattingly and Sydenham, *Roman Imperial Coinage,* vol. III, pp. 194–355; Strack, *Reichsprägung der II Jahrhunderts,* III; J. Vogt, *Die alexandrinischen Kaisermünzen,* II, pp. 64 *sqq.,* I, pp. 122 *sq.* See also Volume of Plates V, 130.

[1] S.H.A. *Marcus,* 4, 3.　　　　[2] Marc. Aur. *Med.* X, 10.

Born on 26 April 121 of the Spanish family of the Annii
Veri, Marcus[1] did not know Spain but grew up in Rome in the
circle of Hadrian's friends. When only six years of age he was
notably signalled out for admission to the Salian priesthood by
the Emperor, who set on him such hopes as Augustus had set
on his grandson Gaius Caesar, and Hadrian, more fortunate than
Augustus, was able to ensure to him the succession, though he
did not forget the son of Aelius, as Augustus did not forget his
younger grandson Lucius. There was much in the lad to attract
Hadrian. His nature was simple, direct, quietist, without any
keen penetration or depth of thought, any moving, stirring appreciation of life. Trained to bear bodily fatigues patiently, contented with the most modest satisfaction of his needs, he neither
valued nor sought anything save sincere self-understanding and
expression and truth. The Emperor found for the young Annius
Verus in jest the word 'Verissimus.' Under the spell of the lad's
untainted nature, the lonely ageing Hadrian was loyal to him and
designed him, in the ripeness of his powers, to be fulfiller of his
own work. As he himself had once done, so now Marcus longed
for knowledge and culture, and all that was needed was the right
teaching. During twenty years of steady learning, pursued often
at the cost of injury to his health, Marcus absorbed the potency
of two cultures. In his passionate embracing of the things of the
mind he did not seek to 'dangle after' poetry or rhetoric but by
'living according to nature' to be perfected as a man. Twenty-five
teachers, the best of the day, *grammatici* and rhetoricians, philosophers of different schools, jurists, even a painter, among them
men from Africa, Asia Minor, even Palestine, helped in his
education. He was devoted and loyal to them: decades later in
his *Meditations*, as he set out, as it were, the anatomy of his
intellectual being, he did not fail to mention most of them, and
to acknowledge the power of their teaching and example.

Antoninus Pius adopted him together with Lucius Aelius. He
alone became Caesar, consul at nineteen (earlier still than
Augustus) and again at twenty-four, and after hardly two years
more, as consort of his cousin Faustina 'Augusta,' son-in-law of
his adoptive father and *consors imperii*. He reached this eminence
younger than any one before, while Lucius, if only by reason of
his youth, was denied such advancement. For twenty-three years
Marcus lived at the Emperor's side, and for almost fifteen he was

---

[1] On his birth, childhood, youth and the period to A.D. 161 see von Rohden
in P.W. *s.v.* Annius (94), cols. 2281 *sqq.*; J. Schwendemann, *Der historische
Wert der vita Marci bei den Script. Hist. Aug.* pp. 1 *sqq.*

his closest helper. Long afterwards he named himself, in devotion, Antoninus' pupil[1]. In conscientious application to his high task, he cared no more than Pius had cared to 'play the emperor,' as manful to face his duty as he was gentle to his kin. As the years taught him to know, to despise or to love the ways of men, to meditate upon the mutability of life, upon rulership on earth and the divine ordering of the world, he cherished tenderly and vigorously tested again and again the nature that he attributed to the gift of the gods that passed to him from his own ancestors and his teachers, from Pius and his life of selflessness. He longed to be, like Pius, so prepared 'that his last hour might find his conscience clear.'

Antoninus appointed the two brothers to be consuls together in 161, Marcus, then forty, for the third time, Lucius, ten years younger, for the second (p. 331). Thus were made manifest his own loyalty to Hadrian's wishes and the concord that bound him to his sons and them to each other. No more than three months after they entered office, Pius died, on 7 March. At the end he commended Marcus to his friends and the Prefects of the Guard as his successor and caused the gold statue of Fortune that he worshipped to be transferred to Marcus' room and gave to the officer of the day the password '*aequanimitas*.' All he had the right to do he had done: the rest was for others to bring to pass. Marcus, now head of the family, took the cognomen Antoninus and 'as if his father[2]' conferred on his brother that of the Veri, so that Pius and the Veri were perpetuated in their names. A few months later, on August 31, twins were born to him and received the names of his brother and father as L. Aurelius Commodus and T. Aurelius Fulvus Antoninus. It was the first of them who gave the name Commodus its lasting place in history.

March 7, 161 brought a new situation[3]. Not even at the death of Augustus or of Vespasian were such powers concentrated in the hands of their heirs. Now the two sons of Pius were consuls in office, the elder indeed the senior consular and in possession of the *tribunicia potestas* and the *imperium proconsulare*, at once president and leader of the Senate and master of the armies, the treasuries and the provinces. All these powers did not cease; all that was needed was the Senate's recognition of him as the 'first,' the *princeps*. The first meeting of the Senate took its

[1] *Med.* vi, 30.
[2] S.H.A. *Marcus*, 7, 7.
[3] See for the evidence for the first period von Rohden, *op. cit.* col. 2290 *sq.*; Schwendemann, *op. cit.* pp. 128 *sqq.*

appointed course with the reading of the dead Emperor's will and the decrees for State mourning and the last honours. Of the issue of the second, which duly followed the public funeral, there could be no doubt. First came the unanimous decree for Pius' consecration and the establishment of the cult of the *divus* and his priesthood, and then the request that Marcus should assume as *princeps* the care of the State. With rigid adherence to ancient precedents he at first refused and then yielded to 'compulsion' as Tiberius had done, and took for himself alone the title of Augustus that was offered to him. So was made apparent his modesty and unselfishness, worthy of the greatest altruists of Rome. He named his brother 'Caesar' and must at once have proposed as consul the conferment on Verus of the name Augustus and the *imperium proconsulare*. Did his purpose go beyond a co-regency? In fact he claimed everything for his brother, even the *tribunicia potestas*—not merely to evade such carping criticism as Titus had to meet after Vespasian's death, but to fulfil what he believed to be the intention of Hadrian and to realize the harmony which a few months before had been so plainly proclaimed (p. 331). More than that, it was to him the guiding principle of the world-order[1], that, by the providence of the gods, those who had been recognized as 'best' by the wisest predecessors and were now acknowledged without demur or chicanery, should jointly in harmony care for the State. The Senate decreed the conferment on Verus of the *imperium proconsulare* and the title Augustus, which hitherto no man except the *princeps* himself had enjoyed. The *tribunicia potestas* was also voted in the Senate but conferred by the People some time later, as may be seen from the first issues of the Empire coinage. Whereas Marcus' coins continue to give the years of his *tribunicia potestas* as well as *cos. III*, those of Verus, though they give the accession-name Imperator Caesar L. Aurelius Verus Augustus corresponding to Marcus' Imperator Caesar M. Aurelius Antoninus Augustus, begin by giving *cos. II* alone and only later *trib. pot.* Finally, Marcus betrothed his daughter Lucilla to Verus, as he himself had once been betrothed to Pius' daughter (p. 331). The Guard and the armies in the provinces were promised donatives in proportion to their importance, a new endowment for the youth of Italy was made, and presently a bountiful largesse was distributed to the People.

Thus on Marcus' initiative Rome and the Empire had for the first time and for nearly eight years *two Augusti of equal rights*. In not leaving his brother to take second place as he himself had

---

[1] *Med.* VII, 55 and V, 30.

done he was moved by his affection for him, his belief in Verus'
worthiness and his view of his duty. As they were consuls together,
each with full and undivided powers wherever he acted, so Verus
was to be his consort in the great task of caring for the State with
equal and undivided responsibility. Thus he deduced from the
ancient institution of the consulship a new collegiality in the
'cura rei publicae,' and kept within the limits of the old Roman
ways of thinking. Piety, affection, conscientiousness, doctrinaire
ideas led him, indeed—astray. He alone had the high seriousness
to bear a burden few indeed had rightly borne and the strength
to be master of the situation. There was no opposition, and the
world rejoiced to honour his fraternal affection, though it could not
at first wholly adjust its ideas to the innovation and indeed soon
divined that a false step had been taken. Verus took his responsibility more lightly than his brother. He was indifferent, soft
when he needed to be hard as steel, no match for any high task.
Marcus was all helpfulness and consideration, self-effacing if so
his brother might be honoured, careful to give no grounds for
gossip, throughout all their joint rule patient and almost too
yielding. Rarely enough he let some serious word betray the fact
that he had borne the burden, not of responsibility alone but of
laborious effort. In calm self-mastery he had no reproaches to
make and spoke even in the Senate with restraint. He believed
men 'were made to work together,' that 'to act against each other
was against Nature.' Life was to him a coming and going, a
torrent that was past in the twinkling of an eye[1]; glory was nothing,
and to learn a new way was no fault but was his right did he only
stand 'erect not erected' (ὀρθὸν οὐχὶ ὀρθούμενον)[2] 'like a rock, on
which the waves break and break, while it stands unmoved, and
the flurry of the sea sinks to rest at its foot[3].' When Verus died
eight years later, he claimed for him honour as *divus* and kept his
memory. Nor was he made wiser; but later in his reign he
advanced his son Commodus[4], though step by step, to a like
position (see below, pp. 349, 360 *sq.*, 362)[5].

(see below, pp. 349, 360 *sq.*, 362)

---

[1] *Med.* IV, 43.   [2] *Ib.* III, 5; VII, 12.   [3] *Ib.* IV, 49.

[4] See von Rohden, *op. cit.* col. 2302; J. M. Heer, *Der historische Wert
der vita Commodi*, Philol. Suppl. IX, 1904, pp. 12 *sqq.*; Schwendemann,
op. cit. pp. 190 *sqq.*

[5] Caesar in 166 (then five years old), imperator, 176, cos. I, 177 and a
few months later *trib. pot.*, soon *trib. pot.* II, finally in the summer of 177
Augustus and *pater patriae* at the age of 16.

III. THE PARTHIAN WAR

Even on his deathbed Antoninus was visited by anxieties about the kings that had aroused his anger, and before he died troops were already marching to the Eastern Front. Few knew precisely how things stood on the frontiers. The coin-legends are of the 'joy of the people,' the 'happiness of the time,' of *hilaritas*, when the twin-princes were born, of carefree 'security.' The 'providence of the gods' guided the Empire, and its peoples rejoiced in the harmony of its rulers. Marcus 'devoted himself wholly to philosophy and sought to win the affection of the citizens.' But the felicity of the hour was transient[1]. A serious flood of the Tiber which endangered the corn-magazines of Rome and a famine that spread misery through Asia Minor fell short of causing grave anxiety. But in the spring of 162 came a sudden threat of war in Britain, Chatti invaded Upper Germany and Raetia, and the Parthian king Vologases III declared war in due form. The local troubles in the North-West and on the Upper Rhine were quickly suppressed by the governors on the spot. But in the East war soon brought disaster. The Parthian general Osroes advanced into Armenia to place the Arsacid Pacorus upon the throne and the governor of Cappadocia was defeated and killed at Elegeia. The Syrian legions, demoralized by many years of peace, scattered before the enemy, who marched into the undefended provinces and attacked the Syrian cities so that the inhabitants already had thoughts of defection from Rome. The war that Marcus had to face[2] was a just war. The Emperor's diligent teacher Fronto sought to dispel the scruples that beset his pupil. A plan of defence must be made. Was it the moment and were there the means to revive the eastern policy of Trajan that had slept for half a century? In Athens men spoke of the new 'Persian war' and of 'Xerxes,' wishing victory and health to the 'divine and brother-loving rulers.' Marcus ordered troops to the seat of war from the North, from the Rhine and the Danube, from Africa and Egypt. With the Senate's approval he commissioned Verus to set out for the East. He himself wished to stay at Rome for 'affairs in the City demanded his presence.' The reason was strange, perhaps only a pretext. Neither the flood nor any unrest meant serious danger or were beyond the capacity

---

[1] See von Rohden, *op. cit.* col. 2292 *sq.*; Schwendemann, *op. cit.* pp. 135 *sqq.*

[2] For the chronology see C. H. Dodd in *Num. Chron.* 4th Ser. XI, 1911, pp. 209 *sqq.*; Schwendemann, *op. cit.* pp. 137 *sqq.*; von Rohden, *op. cit.* cols. 2293 *sqq.*; Ritterling in P.W. *s.v.* Legio, cols. 1297 *sqq.*

of any energetic deputy. Augustus had sent his co-regent, Antoninus had stayed at the world's centre. These examples may have moved him, but was that the logic of the situation? The day was to come when he must leave the Eternal City for nearly as many years as Hadrian, and defend the Empire and the throne in the open field.

Verus was set on his way by his brother, in the spring of 162, when the news of the collapse of the Eastern Front had already reached Rome. But he was not moved to haste: it would take time before the legion from Bonn reached the seat of war. He fell ill at Canusium, and stayed there till he was restored; in the autumn he travelled to Athens, was initiated in the Eleusinian mysteries and visited his teacher Herodes Atticus. Then came a leisurely progress from island to island and from city to city in western Asia Minor until he reached Antioch towards the spring of 163. By then the deployment of the Imperial forces was complete. The defeated and demoralized Syrian army had been re-organized mainly by an Eastern Syrian, the hard-bitten Avidius Cassius[1]. Officers of proved capacity were at Verus' disposal. But the enemy had long since drawn off, and he contented himself with his first success, the regaining of Armenia. The next task was the offensive from the Euphrates line. It is characteristic of Marcus and makes his refusal of the supreme command in this war yet more perplexing that, as he did not hesitate to tell the Senate after Verus' death, 'all the strategy that defeated the Parthians was of his own devising[2].' His principles did not forbid him to engage in a war of just retribution. He had not to be anxious about Rome but to dare, as he later dared. At the head of his armies in the heart of the East defending Hadrian's legacy of panhellenism against the 'Persians,' he could have won for himself vast prestige. He had plainly studied the history of Rome's Eastern wars, appreciated the terrain and the problem and was able to devise and direct from Rome the correct strategic moves. In capacity and devotion to duty he surpassed Verus, who lacked all initiative and left his generals to act while he pursued his pleasures. He might have raised the Imperial authority high above the presumption of the ambitious and might have continued and completed Trajan's policy to his own lasting glory. It was no lack of physical energy nor contempt of fame: in later years he shunned neither hardship nor his due meed of praise.

---

[1] See *Pros. Imp. Rom.* 1², p. 282, no. 1402.
[2] S.H.A. *Marcus*, 20, 2.

No one can say how his reason counselled him. In any event his belief in the guidance of the world allowed the seed to be planted from which was to spring the dangerous rising of Avidius Cassius that brought disillusionment in its train. Verus proved no general; it was his good fortune that the officers Marcus sent to serve under him were able enough, after the long canker of peace, to seize the chance of victory. Now as so often they upheld the imperialistic policy of Rome. Nor was Verus less fortunate in that the Parthians were not stronger.

In the early summer of 163 Statius Priscus[1], who had won successes in Judaea and Britain, pressed swiftly into Armenia from Cappadocia. With his group of legions and *auxilia* he took and destroyed the capital Artaxata and founded and garrisoned a new city (καινὴ πόλις) thirty miles away. The Parthians did not defend what they had so quickly won the year before. Armenia was once more a dependency of Rome. Verus took the title 'Armeniacus,' though Marcus waited till 164, when Statius' successor Martius Verus[2] pacified the country after new raids and gave to it a king by Rome's grace in Sohaemus[3], a Roman senator born in Syrian Emesa. The offensive had followed Trajan's model in its inception and success, but its true purpose was defence, so that Armenia was not made a province but a dependent kingdom protected by Roman arms as under Hadrian and Pius. Verus had himself hailed as 'Hercules Pacifer.' He prepared to make peace, and the world believed it was attained. At this very moment the harmony between the brothers was endangered. Marcus, not ignorant of Verus' unworthy conduct, sent his daughter and uncle to have the marriage celebrated at Ephesus and to set a monitor at his brother's side. But he did not venture himself to journey to Syria, and again flinched from provoking reproach, for his heart was set on concord.

There was no peace. In the autumn of 164 one army group advanced from the Euphrates while detachments from the northern army pressed south into Osrhoëne and Anthemusia in upper Mesopotamia. There were battles at Dausara, round Edessa, where the inhabitants massacred the Parthian garrison, and near Nisibis. The king Mannus Philorhomaios VIII, whom the Parthians had driven out, was soon restored to Edessa. This thrust spelt danger to the western offensive of the Parthian main army now on the right bank of the Euphrates farther to the south and

---

[1] *Pros. Imp. Rom.* III, p. 269, no. 637.
[2] *Ib.* II, p. 350, no. 261.
[3] *Ib.* III, p. 251, no. 546.

to its retreat across the river. This was engaged with a third army, probably the main Roman force under Avidius Cassius, that plainly was working with the central group. After a hard-fought victory near Doura, this army pursued the enemy, who retired downstream, defeated them again at Sura, crossed the river and took Nicephorium. The results of this strategical masterpiece whereby the enemy forces were rolled up from north to south, northern Mesopotamia occupied and the hostile main force destroyed, opened the way for an advance into south Mesopotamia. Now the armies spread fanwise. Avidius Cassius marched down the river; Seleuceia opened its gates; next came the royal capital Ctesiphon that was reduced by siege. Both cities were destroyed from considerations of security. Like Trajan he had pressed to the heart of Parthia and taken its capital. Once again the armies of Rome had broken the hosts of Parthia; the satraps had soon been ready to change their overlords. The king of Parthia was a fugitive. The victory over his armies had conferred on Verus two salutations as *imperator* and the title 'Parthicus Maximus.' This name, too, Marcus declined at first, though as the author of the plan of campaign he had an essential right to it. He may have doubted whether the task was complete. In the next year much was achieved. The central government of the one great power of the East, the only organized State that challenged Rome, was destroyed, the whole country to the borders of Iran was defenceless before the attack of Roman armies. In 166 the forces in north Mesopotamia passed on beyond the Tigris into the highlands of Media so that Verus could receive a fourth imperatorial salutation and take the name ' Medicus.' Before his exploits the generalship and modesty of Trajan seemed to pale, and he had an itch for titles; now Marcus also accepted this appellation. The peak of victory seemed to be reached. The moment had come for ever bolder advance and the clear perfecting of Trajan's achievement.

Then suddenly the tide of fortune turned. In the autumn of 165 a plague[1] visited Cassius' troops at Seleuceia and its ravages became more and more terrible until in the next spring the army had to retreat. Only remnants returned. To the god-ridden East and the terrified soldiers it seemed as though the divine powers of the country punished, where men had failed, the presumptuous invader, the perfidious destroyer of Seleuceia. The troops carried with them into Syria the fell disease, which spread over Asia Minor and Egypt, Greece and Italy and had entered Rome before

---

[1] For the great plague see von Rohden, *op. cit.* col. 2295; Schwendemann, *op. cit.* pp. 54 *sqq.*

Verus had returned. Spreading misery and death in its progress
it advanced to the Rhine and year after year carried desolation
through the peoples of the Empire. But the honour of Rome's
arms had been cleared by the vigorous offensive of her generals;
Cappadocia and Syria were secured, Armenia and Osrhoëne with
their kings and Roman garrison were again the glacis of the
Empire. There could be no thought of annexing Parthia, nor do
we hear of a Parthian king by the grace of Rome. That was beyond
Marcus' purposes, as may be seen from his policy in the border
States. The dualism of Rome and Ctesiphon remained. Verus
might plume himself as 'propagator imperii,' but the work of
Trajan was not consummated. The time had come for peace in the
Orient, and the plague embittered even the rejoicing at what
had been achieved. Marcus, still unperturbed, received Verus, who
left his generals to govern Cappadocia and Syria and returned,
fêted by the Greek cities on his way. On October 12, 166 on the
day on which the altar of Fortuna Redux had been consecrated
to mark Augustus' return from Syria, the two Emperors celebrated their stately triumph. The boy Commodus and a younger
brother received the name of Caesar. Now at last Marcus, along
with Verus, assumed the title 'pater patriae,' which he, too,
believed he had earned by what he had done at Rome, and in all
piety made offering to win the gods' blessing for the first decade
of his reign.

IV. THE WAR IN GERMANY[1]

Loudly as the Emperors' triumph was acclaimed, there was
more and more cause for anxiety during 167. In the last few years
there had been bad harvests in Italy with famine that claimed two
largesses from the Emperor. The plague now raged in Rome itself.
Men bowed beneath the blows of fate. Prayers and resolute
administrative measures could not put a quick end to the pestilence.
Garrisons were visited by it, and the ranks of the armies were
thinned. More than that, there was danger on the frontiers of
which the masses knew nothing. Marcus declared in the Senate
that 'both Emperors were needed for the German war[2].' 'While
the Parthian war was still afoot, arose the war with the Marcomanni, that had long been postponed by the diplomacy of the
local governors[3].' Such is the curt pronouncement of Marcus'

---

[1] On this war see the works cited in the Bibliography. A critical discussion of its problems cannot be attempted here.
[2] S.H.A. *Marcus*, 12, 14.   [3] *Ib.* 12, 13.

biographer. The quickly repulsed incursion of the Chatti into Upper Germany and Raetia was clearly only the prelude to the long struggle that forced the Emperor to exchange Rome for the camp. Here, as five years earlier in the East, the crisis began with a disaster.

Along the Raetian *limes* and the upper Danube there were no legionary camps. The garrisons on the middle and lower Danube had been weakened since the beginning of the war in the East, and the troops drawn from them were still on their way back, or had been worn out or used up in four years of campaigning and in the never-ending marches in Mesopotamia or their ranks had been thinned by the plague. Doubtless the weakness was skilfully masked, but one governor at least had misread the situation, for as late as May 5, 167 time-expired soldiers in the Lower Pannonian army were granted their discharge. The German peoples from the Saale to the lower Danube[1] were kept divided, watched over, and long since pacified; some were old clients of Rome affording a passage to Roman trade to the north. These tribes, engaged in agriculture and cattle-raising in the old region of the late village-culture, who had long since occupied the northern half of that seat of the old 'Illyrian' peoples which the Danube divided, seemed to have lost their ancient valour. But once they were inspired to join their forces and strike, the Roman frontier defence was not strong enough to withstand the onset of these populous enemies, and the way was open to the provinces and to Italy. Nor could the western and northern borders of Dacia, the imperial bastion that stood out so boldly as a promontory in a sea of 'barbaric' peoples, or Moesia Inferior on the lower Danube count themselves more secure. Even Germania Inferior and Belgica were not free from danger.

A century before, the Roman frontiers had felt the shock of peoples from the North Sea to the Euxine (vol. x, p. 835); a century and again two centuries later they were to break under renewed onslaughts. Now, as the meagre records tell us, 'all the tribes from the Illyrian *limes* to Gaul conspired together[2]' and, more than that, 'other peoples came to the frontiers in flight before more northerly conquerors, and threatened war if they were not allowed entry[3].' The sole impulse of this is not to be found in the migration of the Goths from their homes on the estuary of the Vistula in north-east Germany. They had long since driven the Burgundi south-westwards, and the Vandals to Silesia (p. 351),

---

[1] See Map 4, facing p. 131.
[2] See S.H.A. *Marcus*, 22, 1.
[3] *Ib.* 14, 1.

and also subdued groups of these last. They now set out to win
new lands in the black-earth area of South Russia, passing through
Poland and along the edges of the old Dual Monarchy, thence
through Volhynia and Podolia and Bessarabia to the Black Sea.
Thus their main body, clearly of set purpose, avoided contact
with the Empire and did not even enter the country of its immediate neighbours. All they did was to alarm the tribes that
they met north and east of the Carpathians. Thus the Goths were
only one source of the movement. But no sooner was the war
begun than in 167 Langobardi and Obii crossed the Danube into
Upper Pannonia. There is no record of their earlier presence in
this reservoir of Germans north of the Danube, so that they must
have migrated soon before the war from the lower Elbe by way of
Silesia and the Western Beskid range, down the Waag to the region
of Brigetio in their search for land. These then were also the conquering peoples that drove before them other tribes on to the
borders of the Empire. The tribes of the 'Vandals' were on the
move, from the Upper Oder; the Victuali and Charii[1] reaching
the country of the Marcomanni, the Asdingi, the borders of
Dacia. About A.D. 170 Chauci from the lower Elbe pressed
across the Rhine, and perhaps by sea, into Belgica (see below,
p. 354). So widespread was the stir among the free Germans,
where long peace had made all seem to the Romans settled beyond
chance of change. Finally, there was yet a third focus of trouble.
The incursion of Chatti, the western neighbours of the northern
Hermunduri, that was repeated in 169 but was repelled by the
troops in the Mainz area, though it extended to a dimly recorded
unrest among the Sequani in Germania Superior, cannot be a mere
coincidence. For the tribes were in touch with each other and
knew well what each was about. This third focus of trouble lies
between the Elbe and Danube and it is the peoples that had
'conspired together,' clearly summoned to an alliance in arms by
Ballomar the king of the Marcomanni. The levies must have been
mobilized before the first battles were joined and have been
concentrated in 167. The first great thrust came from them, and
they bore the heaviest burden of the war.

This war, which lasted with one interruption, hardly two years
long (175–7), till 180, began about June 167 in Upper Pannonia.
The Langobardi and Obii crossed the Danube, plainly by

---

[1] In the list of the tribes in S.H.A. *Marcus*, 22, 1 the reading of the MSS.
hi aliique can only conceal the name Charii, the more as the Victuali are
mentioned immediately afterwards, the Asdingi appearing in Dio LXXII, 12.
Cf. also M. Petschenig in *Philol.* LII, 1893, p. 349.

agreement with the Quadi, through whose lands they must
have passed. They were routed by the legion at Brigetio and
two *alae*, so that perhaps 6000 fighting men escaped[1]. Peace
was negotiated at their request through the mediation of Ballomar and ten kings leagued with him, whose envoys thereupon
returned home to become themselves the insurgents. Of the
remnant of the 6000 men nothing more is heard. But at the same
time there must have been an incursion—perhaps of the Iazyges
—into Dacia, where the gold mines had to be abandoned. Then
came a short respite, until in the late summer of 167 the kings
of the Marcomanni and Quadi, reinforced by the Vandal Victuali
and perhaps also the Charii and the 6000 Langobardi, crossed the
Danube. A Roman army of nearly 20,000 men was borne down
by numbers, and the enemy pressed through the Julian Alps into
the north of Italy. They besieged Aquileia at the end of the
Alpine roads, stormed and burnt Opitergium and spread terror
as far as Verona: Rome trembled before this new Cimbric invasion. But the advance halted.

The collapse of the frontier defence, the serious threat to Dacia
and the lands south of the middle Danube, even to Italy and
southern Illyricum, coincided with the spread of the pestilence
which raged with especial violence in the camps. Nor was this all:
the Imperial treasuries were in a worse case than usual. Marcus
faced the crisis with calm determination. Rather than lay new
taxation on the impoverished provincials, he sold the golden vessels
and art treasures of the Imperial palaces. He decreed the most
far-reaching defensive measures, which were carried through in
the following year: two new legions were raised, II Pia and
III Concors; slaves, volunteers, gladiators were accepted as
recruits, as only happened in moments of the greatest danger;
even the brigands of Dardania and Dalmatia were drafted into
the local militias, the city police in Asia Minor were enrolled in
the army; new cohorts were raised[2]. To add attack to defence,
German tribal groups were hired to fight against the Germans,
and even Scythian Sacae[3]. The roads over the Italian passes were
blocked, towns in the danger zone were fortified, nor less cities
as remote as Salonae in Dalmatia and Philippopolis in Thrace. On
the lower Danube and in Dacia, Dacia Porolissensis and Dacia

---

[1] Dio LXXII, 3, 1 *a* Boissevain. The abridgment of Dio gives 6000 as the
whole body, but, in view of the Roman forces used, this is probably the
number of the survivors.

[2] Such as *I Aurelia Dardanorum, I Aurelia Pasinatum, II Aurelia nova
mil. eq. c. R.*

[3] In the *Coh. II Aurelia Sacorum* (for the form see Dessau 9165).

Apulensis were at first united with Dacia Malvensis, apparently under Sex. Calpurnius Agricola, into a single military area (III Daciae), and the V Macedonica was moved from Troesmis to Potaïssa (167). For 168 perhaps this command was extended to include Moesia Superior and was transferred to Claudius Fronto, who had distinguished himself in the Parthian War. All these are but instances from the facts that chance has preserved from the years 167–72. They reveal at once the determination of the Emperor and the wide range of the crisis, and attest once more Marcus' military and political insight. While in pursuance of Trajan's policy he sought to maintain and strengthen, so far as might be, Dacia, as the bulwark of the North-East, he not only protected the inner provinces and the communications between West and East but made secure his base for every enveloping or flanking movement that might serve the defence or even, when the time came, make possible an offensive against the enemy. Thus he was prepared to strain every nerve to restore the situation, and faced the prospect of a long war.

While all this was in hand, troops were drawn from the provinces, even as far afield as Cappadocia, Egypt and the Rhine. As an emergency measure to provide for the secure control also of the East, Avidius Cassius, the governor of Syria, was given command over all Asia Minor. But the Emperor's main care was the freeing of Italy and the regaining of the lost provinces. In this grave hour he shrank from placing Verus alone at the head of the army, so that in the early spring of 168 both Emperors took the field. Aquileia was relieved, and the pursuit of the retiring Germans was pressed. In an engagement on Italian soil Victorinus, the Prefect of the Guard, was killed, and the Romans suffered heavy losses that attest the devotion of the troops and, not less, the fighting qualities of the enemy, among whom the king of the Quadi fell in the battle. Despite the counsels of the unmanly Verus, the generals did not call a halt, while among the Germans the 'promoters of a revolt,' made scapegoats for the ill-fortune that attended their retreat, were killed. The Quadi declared that they would only recognize a king approved by the Emperors, and envoys from 'most of the tribes' pleaded for 'forgiveness for their defection from Rome.' Thus Italy and Illyricum were secured, but the provinces north of the Alps were not yet won back; and Marcus did not trust the Germans. But he was pressed to return to Rome and gave way. In January 169, Verus, as he sat by him in their carriage, suddenly died of apoplexy. Marcus brought the body home to burial and apotheosis. He was freed from a burden. In September he left Rome again, despite the death of his little six-year-old son, Annius Verus. His closest counsellor was now the former governor of Pannonia Inferior, Claudius Pompeianus, son of a knight from Antioch. He was the second Syrian to be thus trusted with great responsibility. The Emperor bound him to himself by a marriage with his second daughter, Lucilla Augusta, the widow of Verus, disregarding the cavils of mother and daughter for whom this husband was neither young enough nor aristocratic enough.

The outlook was still dark. The newly formed legions held the Alpine passes covering the roads to Comum and Tridentum. There must have been more German attacks, in which the Praetorian Prefect Macrinius Vindex was defeated and killed. But the coins of 170 attest a victory, apparently won by Pompeianus as lieutenant of the Emperor. Invasions of Chatti into Upper Germany and of Chauci, probably next year, into Belgica were repulsed by Didius Julianus (the future emperor), and insurrections in the Sequani country were quelled (p. 351). But there was heavy and prolonged fighting to hold Dacia. The Iazyges of the plain of the Theiss attacked from the west, and in 171 Claudius Fronto fell in a severe engagement, the capital Sarmizegethusa was threatened, and the country was only rescued by reinforcements from Lower Moesia. In A.D. 170 the Costoboci broke through on the lower Danube, pressed on across the Balkans and through Macedonia to the very heart of Greece, where they plundered and destroyed the Periclean temple of the Mysteries at Eleusis. They were driven out again, and after their invasion the tide began to turn.

There were isolated movements outside the Northern theatre of war in the following years. The Bucoli rose in the Nile Delta and Alexandria was in straits until, in 172–3, Avidius crushed them. Mauri from north-west Morocco harassed southern Spain, but were driven out by hastily-gathered forces in 173–4. There was a war in Britain, troubles in Armenia and on the coast of the Pontus, a rising in the new capital of Armenia which ended in the intervention of the legatus of Cappadocia and the restoration of King Sohaemus. But all this belonged to the recurrent complications in the four corners of the empire, and did not touch the main problems. These still awaited solution. Recent experience had shown how serious they were. *Restitutio in integrum* was not enough, even if the weakening of the frontiers was regarded as transient and due to the emergency caused by the plague. A like situation might arise any moment, if ever the Northern peoples

chose to attack. If the Empire was to live secure, the enemy must
be destroyed. Marcus had shown in the East that he was not
content to clear the honour of Roman arms, to make Armenia
once more a Roman protectorate. His vigorous thrust against
Parthia proved that at least an offensive-defence was in his mind.

How else could he act now? 'He meant to make the country
of the Marcomanni a province, and also Sarmatia, and he would
have done so, had not Avidius Cassius rebelled[1].' So writes his
biographer under the year 175, and his grim persistence in breaking
the power of the enemy reached a point when 'had he lived one
more year, he would have made provinces of the lands of the
Marcomanni, the Hermunduri, the Sarmatae and the Quadi[2].'
So at least declared the same writer in speaking of Marcus' death.
It is true that the ground had been prepared by his operations and
their success. He was continuing the ideas of Trajan, acting in
the spirit of all Roman imperialism, that transcended the work
of one man or one age and in many generations had created the
Empire. Parthia or even Mesopotamia might be thought too
distant from the heart of the empire to be permanently subjected
to the will of Rome, which had never failed at the decisive
moment to stay any attacks they might launch. But now it was the
vital front that must be held: if that collapsed, it meant danger,
panic, ruin for Italy. Augustus had bequeathed to his successors
the policy of keeping the Danube the northern frontier; but that
policy had been overtaken by the conquests of the Flavian dynasty
and above all of Trajan (chaps. iv and vi). The new policy had proved
itself the only possible one to meet the recent crisis. The latest plans
attributed to Caesar, the idea of allowing no independent powers
in the North, may now have suddenly revealed itself as the
Imperial strategy. The Rhine frontier and its southern glacis,
together with the Dacian bastion thrust forward from the lower
Danube, had proved strong corner-stones of the defence. But on
the upper and middle reaches of the river the frontier ran far
nearer Italy. The deep salient of the Sarmatian (Hungarian) plain
meant ever-present danger of unrest and a needless lengthening
of the Empire's frontier. Were the wars of two centuries crowned
by the annexation of the lands of the Marcomanni and then of the
Quadi, Bohemia and Moravia, the whole length of the Hercynian
mountains could be made the northern wall of the Empire. The
country of the Naristae and Hermunduri as far as the Thüringerwald could be included and fully pacified within a man's lifetime.

---

[1] S.H.A. *Marcus*, 24, 5.   [2] *Ib.* 27, 10.

Such, viewed from Rome with Rome's security as prime motive, was the logic of the situation. Rome's interests demanded the offensive, and Marcus pursued it with far-ranging strategic vision.

The goal was all but reached despite the astonishing resistance of the enemy. But the tragical intervention of two unforeseeable events twice robbed Marcus of the crown of achievement that would have set his name among the great names of Rome. The rebellion of Avidius Cassius enforced a breaking off in the earlier moment of success (p. 360); the death of the Emperor on the verge of accomplishment was followed by abandonment of his greatest purpose by his own son Commodus. In A.D. 117 Trajan had left to his nephew Hadrian the task of perfecting his work, and Hadrian had turned aside to other ends: in 180 the destiny of the first two Spanish Emperors was repeated, when Commodus, for whatever reason (p. 377 *sq.*), failed to press home the high endeavours of his father.

A detailed reconstruction of the great offensive that lasted, with only a seeming interruption in 175–7, till 180 cannot be given in these pages. The literary tradition is fragmentary; the interpretation of the Column of Marcus Aurelius presents many problems; and there is here no space for the disquisition on points of detail which must underlie such a reconstruction. The task is made harder by the fact that we have no clear knowledge of the exploits of Claudius Pompeianus save that he appears on the Column behind Marcus as Licinius Sura appeared behind Trajan (p. 221). Almost worse than that, our picture of the Emperor himself is overmuch dominated by the *Meditations* that he set down in these years. Is Frederick the Great to be judged only by his poems? The chances of Time have given us the revelation of the Emperor communing with his philosophical soul, but has denied us, almost wholly, his political decrees and his military records. Priceless as the *Meditations* are in revealing the inmost thoughts of his intellectual conflicts, the self-consciousness of the time in its level and character, yet herein they are the creations of the changing moment, while statecraft and war were more durable stuff and of lasting significance. Thus only the main events are recorded, and the Empire currency with its clear images and superscriptions is a surer guide.

With A.D. 171 the reign of Marcus ended its first decade, five years after the vows to secure its prosperous fulfilment. Grave as had been these last years, the worst was over. The divinities of Rome, Juppiter, Mars, Roma, Minerva, the patron goddess of his joint rule with Antoninus, all appear again on the coins—Salus has guarded him, Victory has been at his side. With the fulfilment of the old, new vows were made for the second decade. The armies were united in loyalty, their devotion to duty matching the Emperor's example. There was a victory in A.D. 171 which brought the sixth acclamation as *imperator* and re-established Roman control of Raetia and Noricum. Its effects were perhaps still felt in the next year, which may have witnessed the crossing of the Danube, an achievement of Marcus' '*virtus*' which emboldened the Senate to proclaim that, thanks to the foresight and good fortune of the Emperor, Germany was conquered and the day of clemency had come. In 173 the record of achievement in the last two years is received with joy. The gods had done their parts, Juppiter himself had hurled his thunderbolts against the fallen enemy. The piety (*religio*) of the Emperor dedicated in Rome a temple to the Egyptian Hermes fulfilling the vow of his priest (p. 365, n. 4). The city hoped that Marcus would return bringing peace, now 'Germany is subdued,' and honoured him as Germanicus for his victory, as '*Restitutor Italiae*' for the '*Securitas*' he had vouchsafed to it. Had not the time for his triumph come? In 174 there were like hopes, but they were vain. A new victory brought a seventh acclamation, and the expectation that Marcus would return, as Verus had done, a Hercules crowned by Victory bringing peace. In 175 yet another victory is announced, and the eighth acclamation for the Emperor's campaigns across the Danube with the gods' help. Even before this types such as *Annona Augusti*, *Concordia exercitum*, *Fides* and the like revealed the new situation created by the treason of Avidius Cassius with its threat to the corn-supply of Rome. The grant to Commodus of the right to strike coins and a largesse to the People attested the danger to the dynasty and the saving of dynasty and People alike by the exertions of the Emperor and his loyal armies. With the conclusion of the war Marcus receives the title 'Sarmaticus.' Thus the two first phases of the offensive are ended, but the Empire currency of the next two years celebrates wars and victories '*de Germanis*' and '*de Sarmatis*' and the *pax aeterna Augusti*.

Such is the outline of events given by the Empire coins, the official legend that transfigures the war into a steady ascent as from peak to peak of a mountain chain. The toils that beset the path to victory must be deduced from the rest of the tradition. The Guard was concentrated in the theatre of war and a mobile field-army was constituted of detachments from the several legions and *auxilia*, an anticipation of what was later to be the fixed practice. Thus the frontier garrisons were nowhere withdrawn. Noricum and Raetia had to be guarded against a new surprise attack, probably by the two new legions, even if the strong fortress-camp of Castra Regina (Regensburg) was not established until 179. The needs of the hour overrode the normal functions of the provincial governors. The union of Dacia and Moesia Superior in a single command continued after the severe battle in which Claudius Fronto fell and the saving of Dacia and its capital by Berenicianus. He now held command there with 'two legions and all their *auxilia* and the *ius gladii*,' though he was only *legatus legionis*. No less did the emergency dictate the allotment of posts in the field-army, where Praetorian Prefects, procurators, even the Emperor's private secretary Tarrutenius Paternus, an *eques* by birth, appear to supplant the high senatorial officers. It is possible that we may see here the hand of Pompeianus. At least he was able, despite early suspicions of Marcus, to find employment for the future ruler, Helvius Pertinax. The Emperor's bearing won the loyal service of the army.

The 'German victory' attested by the coins of 171 can hardly belong to the offensive, which did not begin till the next year. Rather it is the success that led to the regaining of Noricum and Raetia (p. 350 *sq*.). The offensive itself was based on Pannonia, and started from the legionary camp of Carnuntum with its bridgehead across the Danube. There for three years was Marcus' head-quarters, as it had been that of Tiberius in his war against the Marcomanni and of Trajan against the Suebi. In 172 the Emperor led his columns across the Danube and advanced up the valley of the March against the Quadi. The Suebi that lay in his path were quickly reduced, and those taken prisoner were executed as rebels. The campaign against the Quadi began with a deep penetration of their country, for it was the Emperor's purpose to follow his famous predecessors, and drive a wedge between the confederate powers so as to break up their coalition, to crush Marcomanni and Sarmatians separately by turning against each of them in superior force, and at the same time to block the way against German invasions from the north.

The course of the war shows his steady persistence in this strategy. The Quadi met him at a river that may be the Thaya. They assailed his camp with a siege-tower, but this Roman device against Romans was destroyed by lightning, which the soldiers greeted as the present help of Juppiter. The advance into the mountains of Moravia was attended by two further portents. One of these, the 'miraculous storm of rain,' officially ascribed to the prayers of an Egyptian priest but claimed by a Christian story as vouchsafed by their God to the petition of Christian soldiers in the Cappadocian legion XII Fulminata, broke the spirit of the enemy, who made their submission. The conditions were severe. They surrendered their cattle and horses and 13,000 prisoners and deserters carried off from Pannonia, clearly to make good the damage their invasions had inflicted on the provinces. They pledged themselves to close their borders against Marcomanni and Iazyges and to abstain from all marketing, to prevent espionage and the procuring of weapons and supplies. Then the Romans turned their arms eastwards and were joined by the German Lacringi, who agreed to supply contingents. A force under Tarrutenius Paternus reached the upper Gran, where the Cotini gave their adhesion, while farther south the main body subdued the horsemen of the Buri. At last in late autumn the victorious army returned to the Danube. The first book of the *Meditations* written during the campaign on the Gran contains the Emperor's affectionate memories of those who had shaped his intellectual being and ends with the words 'All this needs the help of the gods and good fortune.' As though in answer, Rome spent itself in thanks to the foresight, fortune, valour and clemency of its sovereign for the 'subjugation of Germany.' How different a picture from that which the Emperor drew of himself in the almost sensual minute assessment of his own qualities of mind.

But only a part of the dangerous Germans, who were the objects of vengeance, had been subdued. In 173 came the turn of the Marcomanni. The campaign will not have started from Carnuntum, but rather from Castra Regina or some point between the two. The enemy disputed the crossing of the Danube but were defeated. Marcus' biographer adds simply 'the booty was restored to the provincials[1],' which must mean that they made reparation as the Quadi had done. This was followed by a treaty of peace with other Germans, who will have been the Naristae. A further advance which must have penetrated into Bohemia won back other Germans, perhaps Hermunduri, to a treaty that needed the Senate's ratification. The Emperor's 'clemency' was justified in that he was spared conflicts with groups west of the Böhmerwald, of which we hear nothing more, and won them back to Rome. After fresh operations other Germans were bound by treaty, perhaps the Vandal Charii and Victuali (p. 351), while the Asdingi already were in Rome's service. The country of the Marcomanni was occupied, and therewith ended that war. By applying the

---

[1] S.H.A. *Marcus*, 21, 10.

principle 'divide et impera,' with steel and gold, 'Germany was subdued.'

In the next year the work of conquest was completed. Hosts of humbled enemies were transplanted to Dacia, Pannonia, Moesia, Germania and Italy to reinforce the populations thinned by the pestilence, until 'Marcomanni settled at Ravenna rose in revolt and dared to hold the city, whereupon no more barbarians were brought to Italy and those already there were ejected[1].' The Quadi were taxed with imperfect performance of their treaty duties and were once more attacked and reduced while their king was made a fugitive. Then came a new enterprise, in which the German peoples appear as auxiliaries. Its main objective was the Costoboci of Galicia to punish them for their invasion of the Empire as far as Athens and Eleusis (p. 354). In this expedition the King of the Quadi, Ariogaisus, was captured and banished to Alexandria. On the march home the war against the Sarmatians was begun which lasted until about the end of June 175. First came two victories, which brought a seventh imperatorial acclamation, and the opening of negotiations with one of their two kings, only to be frustrated by the other, so that operations continued until they were concentrated in the swampy southern plain of their territory. But no decision was reached. The news of the revolt of Avidius Cassius induced a peace on the terms granted to the Quadi and Marcomanni (end of July, 175). They ceded only a strip of land along the left bank of the Danube. Marcus showed to them the clemency he had showed to his other enemies. He received an eighth acclamation as *imperator* and assumed the title Sarmaticus. Commodus was summoned to his camp from Rome and on July 7, the day on which Romulus had vanished from men to join the gods, he assumed the *toga virilis*. The choice of the day was to have its significance (p. 390).

The scene shifts to the East. Avidius Cassius[2] had governed Syria for eight years and for almost six practically the whole of the East. He and the governor of Cappadocia, Martius Verus, had through all these grim times ensured the obedience of those provinces, though their legions had supplied large drafts to enable the wars in the North to be waged with energy and success. Now at last the results of Pius' detachment, Verus' inertia, Marcus' consideration for his brother, the Emperor's weakness and the wars in the North were plain to see. The prestige of the Imperial house was lower than it had been for a century. Harsh as he was,

---

[1] Dio LXXII, 11, 4.
[2] See *Pros. Imp. Rom.* 1², p. 282, no. 1402.

the Syrian Avidius counted for much in his own land. Men said
his *virtus* fitted him to be emperor, and, if he was the son of an
eques, so was the Syrian Pompeianus who had become Marcus'
son-in-law. Supported by a widespread conspiracy, from which
only Martius Verus held aloof, a Syrian—no Italian like Pompey,
Antony and Vespasian—dared to rise against Rome. There were
rumours that the Empress Faustina, despairing of her consort's
health, had already offered Cassius her hand, and the Empire
to preserve it for Commodus, as though the throne was in the
gift of Pius' daughter and not of the Senate and soldiers. Report
had it that Marcus was dead and that Cassius had already spoken
of him as '*divus*,' that the Sibylline oracle saw in Marcus the
'beast' of the Apocalypse, and in Cassius the legitimate ruler. It
was as though the Syrians sought to wrest from Rome world-
power to restore it to its ancient possessor, the Orient. Cassius
was proclaimed emperor, appointed a Praetorian Prefect and
established his own Chancellery. Cilicia, Syria and Judaea were
at once his, Egypt went over to him, and so threatened the food-
supply of Rome (p. 337). Cappadocia alone was held by Martius
Verus and was a make-weight against the usurper. At the news,
sent by Verus, Marcus was for a moment terrified, but he took
courage again with his philosophy as a comforter. The 'ingrate,'
as Marcus named him, was declared outlaw by the Senate. But
Commodus was hurried to the Emperor's camp. Rome itself was
restless as the rumour ran that Cassius was nearing the city.
Detachments from Illyricum had to be sent to defend the city.

Breaking off the war against the Sarmatians, Marcus prepared
in August to march against the enemy. He did not shrink from the
task of defending his lawful right. He rejected 'barbarian' help
that was offered him, that aliens might not know the reproach of
'Romans' in mutual conflict. Then came news. Cassius had been
killed by a centurion and the rebel's head was brought to the
Emperor. He refused to see those who brought it, and gave
orders for its burial. 'Who flees from his master is a runaway
slave. But Law is the master, and who breaks the Law is a runaway. . .[1].' The rule of his rival had lasted three months and six
days, from about mid-April to towards the end of July 175.

Cassius' death averted civil war and the need to maintain the
cause of legitimacy by arms. Martius Verus resolutely crushed
the movement at its centres Cyrrhus and Antioch, and administered the East till Marcus came. The Emperor at once took the

[1] *Med.* x, 25.

only path. The vitality of Roman rule must be displayed in his own presence and the provinces of the East won back to loyalty. He passed in progress across Asia Minor, through Syria and its southern neighbours to Alexandria, and then retracing his steps through Syria, journeyed by way of Athens to Rome, which he reached after fifteen months of travel in the second half of November 176[1]. Everywhere he showed clemency, even to Antioch and Cyrrhus. Disloyal officials were removed from their posts and the rule was laid down that in future no one should govern the province of his birth. When it fell to him to be judge, sentences were light, and mild judgments by the Senate were graciously approved. Among the scholars and philosophers of Alexandria he was the Stoic citizen of the world, sharing with them the franchise of their common home, the *kosmos*. As he brought his army back to Italy he gave orders that the troops should assume the toga, the garb of peace. Clemency, harmony, peace and security were his mission.

Fate had vouchsafed to him the salvation of the State from civil strife after the alarms of foreign wars, and he stood higher than those whose victories had achieved this in the past. The dynasty was preserved: he celebrated with his son Commodus, who became Imperator, the splendid triumph over Germans and Sarmatae, and a few days later, Commodus entered on the consulship. No Roman had held it so young, for he was not yet sixteen. Before many months had passed he had received the *tribunicia potestas* and was named Augustus. It was the zenith of Marcus' fame, of the man who had written of those that had attained that zenith 'What is the end of it all? Smoke and ashes and a legend— or not even a legend[2].' So he may have thought, but the world rejoiced in the Emperor's clemency and the *pax aeterna* that he promised. He was himself lonelier than ever. Faustina[3], whose obedience, simplicity and tenderness had been his pride and comfort in his quiet meditations on the Gran, was no longer at his side. She had died suddenly on the journey through Asia Minor. Deeply mourned, she received, like her mother, the title of *diva*. Her long sojourns in the field deserved the name 'Mater Castrorum' that was bestowed on her, and her portrait was placed by that of the Emperors in the chapels where the armies worshipped their ensigns.

[1] Heer, *op. cit.* pp. 39 *sqq.*; Schwendemann, *op. cit.* pp. 184 *sqq.*
[2] *Med.* v, 33.
[3] *Pros. Imp. Rom.* 1, p. 132, no. 716.

But peace was not lasting[1]. In 177 there was sharp fighting with the Mauretanians, which must have ended in a victory that year, in which Juppiter Propugnator gave his help, a victory that brought to Marcus a ninth acclamation, to Commodus a second acclamation as *Imperator*. The securing of the North was not complete, and there was new unrest on the Danube, which the provincial governors could not master. At last on August 3, 178 the Emperor and his son left Rome, but Commodus, whose marriage had been celebrated earlier than Marcus had wished, soon returned. Of the operations that followed, beyond or along the Danube, hardly any tradition has survived. Coins alone give some indications. There must have been a victory in 179, for Marcus and Commodus were again acclaimed *Imperator*. The campaign began with *vota publica* and a solemn declaration of war in the old Roman form and money was regularly allotted to it from the Treasury. In his conduct of it to victory, we hear again of 'Fortuna Augusti,' of the 'loyalty of the armies,' the Emperor's *virtus*, the vouchsafing of victory and rejoicings in Rome. On a coin of Commodus there appears his patron Romulus as conqueror (p. 360).

The Sarmatae of the Theiss valley and the Buri at first seem to have yielded, fearing that Marcus might bring in the Quadi against them. A treaty was made with them which secured some mitigation of that of 175. Only the provisions about meetings and markets, sailing on the Danube in their own boats and the possession of islands in the river were kept, and they were charged to transfer part of their population into the territory of the Roxolani. Three thousand Naristae, who declared themselves oppressed, were admitted to lands inside the Roman frontier. There must have been war with the Hermunduri, against whom was directed the building of Castra Regina in 179. But the main objective must have been the Marcomanni and Quadi. Of the operations of 177 and 178 we know hardly anything. Each of these peoples had to endure the presence of a Roman army of occupation of 20,000 men, and their envoys had to complain that their own peaceful agriculture was hampered, whereas the troops lacked for nothing, and sheltered deserters and escaped prisoners. Apparently their grievances were not redressed. Thereupon the Quadi resolved to attempt a migration with their whole population to the country of the Semnones on the middle Elbe. The Emperor discovered the plan in time and had the passes in the North barred

[1] See von Rohden, *op. cit.* cols. 2302 *sqq.*; Schwendemann, *op. cit.* p. 192 *sq.*; Heer, *op. cit.* pp. 31 *sqq.*

against them. It was now, we may suppose, that the Prefect of the Guard Tarrutenius Paternus was sent 'with a strong army to fight a decisive battle': 'the barbarians,' it is said, 'fought the whole day through, but were slaughtered by the Romans and Marcus accepted his tenth acclamation as *Imperator* (179).' 'It was his desire not to annex their country, but to punish its inhabitants[1].'

With the crushing of the last resistance of peoples that strove to be free the operations of the great war reached their end. Twelve years of struggle and of ever more drastic counter-offensive to repay the attack on Italy in its hour of distress had laid the foundations for the extension of Roman rule over the land of the peoples it had destroyed. One more year only would be needed to complete the task. During the winter of 179–180 there was no fighting but only measures of organization. Then, before the crowning operations could begin, the Emperor died on March 17, 180. On his deathbed he adjured his son, who as early as the end of 179 had come from Rome, 'not to neglect the last remainder of the war[2].' It can hardly be doubted that it was Marcus' intention to annex everything from the Hermunduri to the Sarmatae (p. 355), and he may claim the credit for having made it possible. Thus would have been achieved the protection of Italy by a wide zone of securely-held territory; the Northern frontier would be shorter, more defensible; the region in which the Northern peoples gathered from the plains of the North would be denied to them. With the decimation or transplanting of the people of this area, the dissolution of all opposition within it, the Germans would be deprived of the possibility of expansion and dammed up beyond the Hercynian forest, while the lands thus made provincial would be opened up to Mediterranean culture. Marcus and his helpers saw the problem from the angle of Rome's strength: the country between north and south must be Roman. Such was the idea he strove so steadfastly to realize. Had he been vouchsafed one more year he would have brought to consummation the policy of Caesar, of Augustus in the wars with the Pannonians and Dacians, of the Flavians and of Trajan. Marcus also preserved, one is everywhere conscious of it, the appearance of 'just' war. It did not greatly trouble him that he dealt with other men's fate as the hunter who 'catches a hare;—if you probe into the reason for their acts, are not these hunters all robbers (p. 340)?' He saw also aliens only from the Roman angle, that of the world's centre. These were appearances on the circumference, parts of that all,

---

[1] Dio LXXII, 20, 2.   [2] S.H.A. *Marcus*, 28, 1.

to whose ordinances they, like everyone, were subject. 'But when an unalterable necessity is there, why strain against it[1]?' 'All is ordained by nature to change and go under, that something other may take its place[2].'

V. THE EMPEROR AND THE AGE

It is noteworthy how in this period the coinage[3] that had hitherto reflected so many sides of the public life of Rome and the Empire, limits its range of portrayal. As with a flourish of trumpets the first issues of the reign tell of the 'providence of the gods' and 'the felicity of the age,' and the coins never tire of the story of the devout Emperor guarded by the gods. But, sincerely enough, soon no more is heard of the 'felicity of the age.' Wars and victories, triumphs, the subjugation of dreaded tribes, the saving of Italy, the safety of its people, lasting peace—these are the themes in almost bewildering abundance. They seem to proclaim almost too loudly some bloodthirsty oriental despot or the greatest warrior of Rome. Their whole thought is centred on the figure, the fame and the legend of the Emperor, though he was of all men the simplest, the farthest removed from the heroic or the divine, from the desire of a legend of glory. Of the concerns and beliefs of the Roman people, of domestic policy the coins give no more than a hint here and there. There is no trace of the panhellenic idea and but few references to the Roman myths, as though the attempts of Hadrian and Antoninus to give them life again were all forgotten. It is now the temple of the Egyptian Thoth that attests the 'religio Augusti[4]'; the currency of Alexandria is now more closely linked than ever before with the Empire coins, and there is a widespread following of its example. It would seem as though local forms of life were dying out, absorbed by the centralizing purpose of Rome. As citizenship spread more and more throughout the provinces, the peculiar character and the separate position of Rome became less and less distinct. The forces of the peoples within the Empire, that were still so strong under Hadrian, and their spiritual characteristics seem to merge into each other. But a closer view reveals how beneath the apparent uniformity there is an ever stronger growth. There arises a new dangerous power in the spiritual world of the period which seeks and accepts uniformity, but only to be 'Roman'

---

[1] *Med.* XII, 14, 2.   [2] *Med.* XII, 21.

[3] See on the coins the works of Mattingly-Sydenham, Strack and Vogt mentioned above (p. 340 *Note*).

[4] W. Weber, *Sitz. d. Heid. Akad.* 1919, Abh. 7.

as a means of wresting mastery from Rome. It would seem as though the grim days of the plague and the wars had paralysed the imagination of men and robbed them of gaiety, the love of diversity, the instinct for a real life of their own. The thoughts of men began to seek new forms and new motives. And the Emperor claims to be the centre of the world and of its life. All this cannot be mere chance; it must reveal the deepest movement of the age and the fundamental political shaping of it by the Emperor.

Marcus, as befitted a Roman, was governed by an austere soldierlike unflinching faithfulness till death. To his Stoicism all came foreordained and self-evident. Like many another of his time, he looked down upon the countless peoples and cults, the variety of existence, its ebb and flow, its rise and fall like the waves of a sea, now calm now stormy, and perceived it as a harmony. Misfortune to him was no evil but as divinely ordained as is felicity. The providence of the gods guided the world with immutable mastery. The man and the moment were transient parts of an unending process. 'Alexander and his groom are alike, for both pass and perish[1],' 'How many men do not even know thy name, how many will forget it in a moment, but how many who praise thee now will turn to censure thee[2]?' 'Asia and Europe are but corners of creation, the ocean is but a drop and Athos but a grain in respect of the universe, the whole present a point in eternity. All is petty, mutable, and transient[3].' 'Friend, thou wast made a citizen of this great commonwealth, what matter to thee if it is for five years only.... Depart content, for he that calls thee hence is content too[4].'

To Marcus the tenets of Stoicism were a hard-won faith. It was his own: he was not like the gladiator defenceless when he lost his sword, but like the pancratiast that has only to clench his fist to be ready[5]. Thus he had not Hadrian's playful pity for his soul, but hard words and rebukes when it fails in action to be worthy of his faith. In acts of State he was guided by the laws of the immutable determinism that ruled the world. The depths of his nature were not stirred by the criminal or by his nearest, by dark figure or the bright. All men were to him shadows, gratefully conjured up when he sank into meditation about himself, studied when he must know how to act, to be met with kindliness, to be urged to unity and co-operation, to be taught, chastised and led. Thus he writes his *Meditations* in Greek, and is at his ease among

[1] *Med.* VI, 24.   [2] *Med.* IX, 30; cf. IV, 6, 33; V, 33; VI, 26.
[3] *Med.* VI, 36.   [4] *Med.* XII, 36.   [5] *Med.* XII, 9.

the 'Greek' philosophers of Alexandria, like them a citizen of the
great commonwealth of reasoning men. He is at home in both
cultures, Greek and Roman, and to him Rome embodied the idea
of austerity, duty and action, but the law of Rome is but a part
of the law of the world. Anxious, pedantic almost as he was in his
Roman formalism, devoted as he was in the service of Rome, yet
he remained in mind aloof.

Rome was the capital, the central point of the world; but little
indeed of what ancient Rome had meant still clung to the Romans
or to their emperor to justify Rome's claim to be the tyrannical
mistress of the world, to compel the Emperor to be no more than
the first of the Roman stock. The Syrians Pompeianus and
Cassius had, too, the name of Roman, as had countless other
provincials, and Pompeianus had deserved and won the highest
honours of Rome, and Cassius had presumed to claim the throne
of the Roman Emperor. One of his decrees made it less necessary
for 'Roman' senatorial families to be rooted in Italian soil, and,
after Cassius' revolt, governors might no longer administer the
provinces of their birth. The Empire from being a confederation
of peoples in willing allegiance to Rome, was to be the Empire of
a united world in which all are Roman citizens, an universal
monarchy under an absolute emperor. Now is to be the fulfilment
of what Caesar and Claudius planned, and what Marcus himself
formulated. 'And I conceived an idea of a democratic State,
administered according to equality or free speech, and of a
monarchy that above all honoured the freedom of the governed[1].'
Nor less did the dynastic system which he thrust home in the face
of the ruling idea of the choice of the best show how the sovereign
powers of the ancient State were forced to serve his strong impulse
towards the hereditary principle. The city-state Empire of Rome
dissolves before the universalistic conception of Marcus. Thus
on his Stoic conception of the world he based the absolute monarchy
of Rome—and of the countries of the West. From the teaching of
the Stoic Panaetius, passed on by Cicero, Augustus had conceived
the idea of the rule of the 'optimus civis.' Now, less than seven
generations later, Marcus, almost the last of the Stoics, found Stoic
doctrines to arm an attempt to make good the ravages of time. 'For
me as Antoninus my city and fatherland is Rome, but as man the
world[2].' 'Man is the citizen of the supreme city in which the other
cities are as it were houses[3].' 'In what other universal constitution can the whole race of men have a share[4]?'

[1] *Med.* I, 14.   [2] *Med.* VI, 44.
[3] *Med.* III, 11.   [4] *Med.* IV, 4.

Thus Marcus is no longer the first citizen of Rome but of the 'Great State' of reason, the providentially guided controller of the unifying centralized Empire. Thus 'from his high tower' he surveys the multifarious world, unshaken by its crises. Now in ascetic serenity, strangely unmoved by its wild impulses, now quietist and gently understanding, now acting from deeper insight, now making good its breaches with victory, he seems to reconcile its oppositions in himself and to realize its harmony in his belief in its predestined course. He will be just and yet becomes a 'robber' (p. 340). Now he proclaims lasting peace; now he has a whole people destroyed. Now he sacrifices cheerfully all his fine possessions to meet the needs of the pestilence and war. Now he tears whole peoples from their country and plants them elsewhere, as one who roots up ancient forests and turns deserts into smiling fields. For so it is ordained. This devout patient thinker took more names from victories than any of the emperors before him. The ancient simplicity and moderation was past: the Spaniard Marcus was neither of Roman nor Greek stock. His idea of the harmony of the world was *intellectual* alone, for it rested on a culture that was international: it was the desire for a formula to resolve the confusion of an international Empire. His creative action was ever haunted by doubts. His belief was sprung from culture, not of the soul. To him the attitude of Christian martyrs was beyond understanding: 'Of what kind is the soul, that is ready, if it must be released from the body, to be quenched or scattered or to abide together. Though this readiness is to proceed from one's own judgment, not in mere headlong attack, like the Christians; but with reason and dignity and so as to convince another, without tragic show[1].' Thus he lived in thought and action, the disciple of a Stoicism that no longer sufficed even for the intellectual needs of his time. Tragic in all contradiction, which he harboured but did not feel as tragic, he saved the Empire from its perils from without, but himself, his own soul, he could not save.

VI. INTERNAL POLICY

'The universal cause is a wintry torrent: it sweeps all before it. But how paltry are both these political affairs and the mannikins who, as they think, act as philosophers. Drivellers all. What then, man? Do what now nature claims of you: strive forward, if it is granted you, and do not look round to see if anyone will know of

[1] *Med.* XI, 3.

it. Hope not for Plato's Republic. Be content if the least thing goes forward, and consider the issue even of this as no small thing. For who then changes his opinion? But apart from a change of opinion what is it all but a servitude of those who groan under it and pretend to be obedient? Come now and tell me of Alexander and Philip and Demetrius of Phalerum. Men shall see if they saw what man's common nature wished, and if they educated themselves. If they played tragedy, no one has condemned me to be their imitator. Simple and modest is the work of philosophy. Lead me not away to pompousness and conceit[1].' In his public life[2] Marcus' bearing was that of a philosopher. In his own thoughts he was no revolutionary, nor was it in his passionless nature to create Utopias. He hardly laid a finger on the existing order of things. He preserved with pedantic care the rights of the whole community, of the orders and of individuals, and their duties. When he asked for funds for the Second Marcomannic War he played on the old maxim—'res publica est res populi,' and declared simply that he possessed nothing and was even lodged by the State. Thus he made the property of the Emperor liable to be searched for runaway slaves, to make real the right of the agents of the State's authority. Though he had sold the treasures of the palace to meet the needs of the crisis and avoided enriching the *fiscus*, he did not abolish its treasuries or give away his possessions. The People did not become active again but remained the object of his constant care: Italy was more and more taken under his charge and set on a level with the provinces.

The Senate was a pliable instrument even at the time of Cassius' rebellion, when it visited him with outlawry and confiscation: Marcus allowed the Senate to decree the joint rule of Verus and of Commodus, assigned to it debate and decision on all great matters of State, such as the declaration of war on the Northern peoples and the treaties with them. He was scrupulous to maintain the Senate's jurisdiction, was careful to avoid passing sentence on senators, he requested the Senate to be merciful when, in its care for him, it would judge too harshly the rebels sent before it. Where possible, he showed it honour. He stepped down from his triumphal car in the Circus to pass on foot before it. He did not admit equestrian advisers to his *consilium* if a senator was to be tried. He was instant in forbidding marriage between a lady of senatorial rank and a freedman. It may have been at his suggestion that the Senate decreed that no one of its members might marry or retain as wife anyone condemned by a public court. De-

[1] *Med.* IX, 29.   [2] Cf. von Rohden, *op. cit.* cols. 2304 *sqq.*

spite his own wishes he would not have a senator appointed Prefect of the Guard as it would have involved a step down into the equestrian order. He entrusted new offices to senators and used senatorial magistrates as judges of appeal, as he gave the Senate the final judgment within the scope of the consular jurisdiction. He discussed with leading senators the problems of domestic and foreign policy.

All this he could do for the Senate was in his hand. When he was in Rome he was regular at its sessions and would hasten in from Campania to make proposals in person. But he did not hesitate to promote to the Senate many of his friends, even *equites*, who had done good service, or to assist senators to regain their rank if they had lost it through unmerited poverty. Men from all the provinces were allowed to reach the highest offices of State. There was one rule, that no one reached the Curia with whom the Emperor was not acquainted. Neither wealth nor illustrious descent counted with him, only merit. The future emperor, Pertinax, born 'in the Apennines,' son of a freedman, became senator and consul. Pompeianus the Syrian son of an *eques*, Petronius Sura Mamertinus grandson of an *eques*, Antistius Burrus an African, became his sons-in-law. Marcus decreed that senators need only have one-quarter of their property in Italian land. Since the days when Claudius had admitted to the Curia provincials 'who could adorn it,' things had gone so far that the high society of Rome and the aristocracy of the empire had little stake in Italy and were in only small measure of Italian birth, and even the romanized upper class of Spain was already spent. It was from Africa, the East and the Danube area that new strength came. The new senators might believe themselves the guardians of an aristocratic tradition, and have the training, education, experience and class-consciousness that gave them the name of Roman, but they were not of one blood or of one intellectual outlook. They owed all to the Emperor's favour and were his willing obedient followers. They worked in harmony with the Emperor, as, so his philosophy taught him, was the way of nature (p. 343). While the old form was kept, it received new content. The Senate was to the Emperor like a vessel in which were mingled and preserved the finest essences of the whole Empire. But the Empire was order, and of this order he was master.

The *equites* were treated with no less care. They received new strength from the army, the cities of Italy and the provinces, from intellectuals, even from freedmen. The tradition shows that Marcus granted to many the distinction of the *equus publicus*. He gave those who served him as officials precedence over the rest, distinguished the three upper classes of them and exempted the two highest from plebeian punishments, making the exemption hereditary to the third generation. He rewarded the ambition of his secretary Tarrutenius Paternus with the post of Prefect of the Guard. Others he promoted to the same rank and to his *consilium* because of their capacity as jurists and made judicial decisions 'on their authority and responsibility.' He appointed assistants to help the heads of the departments of finance and the food-supply, and equestrian procurators to assist the *praefecti alimentorum* in administering their funds. In all this may be seen the progressive organization of the magistrates and officials into a perfected bureaucracy, the promotion of the court aristocracy, the fostering of its class-consciousness, but no sign of a fundamental abandonment of the old order, no sign of revolutionary innovation.

So far as the mass of the citizens was concerned, Marcus had their prosperity at heart in good and bad times alike. Seven largesses amounting in all to 850 denarii[1] to those entitled to receive them (perhaps a total of £25,000,000), widespread provision of food, benefactions to the youth of Italy in connection with the betrothal of his daughter Lucilla and the death of his consort Faustina, grants to the Italian cities after bad harvests and famine attest his care. Throughout the empire he made efforts to alleviate the sufferings due to the plague, and gave assistance to cities that had suffered catastrophe, as Smyrna, Nicomedeia, Ephesus, Antioch and Carthage. Conquered peoples were forced to make reparations for the effects of their invasions and were transplanted to make good the depopulation of the northern provinces. Here, too, his methods were traditional, with laws, regulations and administrative action[2]. He was tireless, patient and conscientious in jurisdiction whether he was in Rome or at his headquarters at the front. To ensure continuity in dealing with litigation, he raised the number of court days to 230. In rules of law he was strictly just, humane, equitable, inflexible where grave offences were concerned. He was on his guard with informers and was careful to avoid the reproach that the *fiscus* enriched itself from their victims. In all he was concerned to preserve or revive old-established law rather than to revolutionize it.

Such novelties as he introduced fitted his character. In times of grave emergency he had used slaves, gladiators and bandits as

[1] Marquardt-Dessau, *Staatsverwaltung*, ii[2], p. 139.
[2] For his *constitutiones* see Hänel, *Corpus legum*, 114–32.

soldiers (p. 352), but he was not inspired to give freedom to their like. In the Stoic's commonwealth of man, only freemen were his equals. He might have been a great revolutionary had he boldly made fundamental changes in the legal position of slaves or freedmen or had at least made good his vision of equal rights for all (p. 367) and conferred citizenship on all non-Roman provincials. Thus he would have given internal unity as well as external security to the Empire. But between ideal and reality there was the clearest disharmony. It is true that he laid it down that the retrial of a decision declaring a man free-born might not be claimed after five years, and was ruled out by his death. But, as the jurist Marcian saw, a retrial might improve the position of a slave[1]. Marcus maintained the sharp distinctions between free-born, freedmen and slaves. He might promote freedmen to be *equites* and advance their sons to the Senate, or, continuing his predecessors' development of law about slaves, he might enable a slave to win his freedom, if he had been kept in bondage although his enfranchisement was made a condition in his sale; all that was needed was that he or a third party on his behalf should hand over to his counsel the money to buy his freedom. He might allow a man manumitted by a will to accept along with his freedom an estate so burdened with debts that no one had accepted it, if he paid the debts on it. But were these decisions due to justice or only evasions of the issue, since the wish of the emancipator needed to be reinforced by a payment on the part of the slave? So, too, Marcus allowed freedmen to have *ingenui* rather than freedmen as *patroni* only in exceptional cases. So far was he removed from any radical reforms. He was the first emperor to set up a *praetor tutelaris* for Italy and empowered him (as the governor's legate in the provinces and the Juridicus in Egypt) to appoint guardians for citizen wards who were legally compelled to act unless within a stated time they proved a right to exemption. The ancient Lex Plaetoria of 186 B.C. had pre-scribed the appointment of a *curator* to manage the property of an orphan from his majority to the age of 25 if he was extravagant or feeble-minded. This Marcus now extended to the case of all propertied citizens of this age. The person under tutelage lost his control of his property, which passed under strict rules to the *curator*, who had laid upon him responsibilities towards the State, which in turn protected his ward against his incapacity, greed or negligence. All this meant even more State interference and control in private life.

[1] Dig. XL, 15, 1.

His belief that the responsibility of an act rests only on the doer of it was the motive of his decision that a son should not be tainted by his father's crime or punishment, and that a man born while his father or mother was in exile should not be excluded from being *decurio* in any municipality in the Empire. This was 'humane' rather than Roman doctrine, and broke the bonds that bound blood-kin, and limited the operation of the *patria potestas*. Thus, too, Marcus granted soldiers who were still under *patria potestas* the right to dispose freely, and even by will, of all they had earned during their time of service. A further step towards the loosening of this powerful institution of Roman law was the *S.C.* Orfitianum of A.D. 178. In this a mother was permitted without a will to pass on her inherited property to her children, whether sons or daughters, to the exclusion of her own blood-kindred and agnates, or at least in preference to them. He also made children of a marriage that was legally invalid but accepted as valid by a husband to rank with those of a legal marriage.

In all this he may have been following his own ideals[1]. On the other hand he seems to stress the distinction between citizens and non-citizens in the setting up perhaps in 177 or 178 of a register of births, an institution of which he may have learnt in Egypt but which already existed in Africa. In future every child of a Roman citizen was to be registered within thirty days of birth, in Rome with the *praefecti aerarii*, in provinces where it did not already exist, in the record-office of the governor, 'in order that anyone born in a province could produce documentary evidence, if his free birth was challenged[2].' Here was another bureaucratic interference in private life and at the same time a further security for the privileged class in the Empire. This comprehensive measure did more than facilitate legal decisions in doubtful cases, it helped to control the present and future generations of citizens in all parts of the empire. The time had passed when the *cives Romani* were an august minority in the provinces. The granting of citizenship to soldiers and private persons had made a profound change. The new institution, indeed, points directly to the Edict of Caracalla of 212, which at the very moment when those first registered came to manhood conferred citizenship on all *peregrini* except *dediticii*. Thus may be seen a process of unification and codification which is characteristic in this as in the whole period of Marcus Aurelius. Though he did not venture to consummate

---

[1] See *Med.* x, 26.　　　　　　　[2] S.H.A. *Marcus*, 9, 8.

the process in any sphere of domestic policy, the tendency was
not to be checked. Where he would not hold it back, it passed
him by. Where his Stoic inclinations and humane impulses gave
it scope, it made them a stepping stone for further advance.

Simply brought up by his mother and, even as a child, thrifty
so that he could be generous when he would, Marcus was frugal
all his life, and was sometimes censured as miserly for his economical care of the State's finance. It is true that he matched his
predecessors in his largesses, and sacrificed his possessions to
avoid taxing impoverished provincials (p. 352). He enjoined on
his officials moderation in enforcing the claims of the *fiscus* and
taxation in times of stress. He did not lavish on buildings such
sums as Hadrian had done. He spent his money not on architectural splendour but on absolutely necessary reconstruction, or
the improvement of roads which assisted the defence of the
Empire, the advancement of commerce, of fortresses and camps
and of cities. No doubt his wars cost the State treasury dear.
But he strove manfully to be economical and to avoid extravagance.
He strengthened the control of public finances in the communities
of Italy and the provinces, making many regulations to guide the
curatores who watched over them. He forbade lavish expenditure
on actors. In a decree of 178[1], issued in the name of himself and
Commodus, extravagant prices for gladiators were prohibited, and
expenditure on games in the cities was strictly regulated according
to their wealth and importance. When he drafted gladiators in
the army, it was said in mockery 'he wished to force the people
to be philosophers.' In the time when he was far from Rome he
kept the mob in good humour by calling on the rich to provide
them with amusements. In 177 he brought himself to give games
of diverse kinds, including the baiting of wild beasts, to celebrate
his victories and the naming of Commodus as Augustus. But
he hated slaughter and made the gladiators fight with blunted
weapons. He regulated the giving of shows and limited expenditure on them. The tax payable by *lanistae* was abolished at a cost
to the *fiscus* of 20 to 30 million sesterces a year, rather than
have the Imperial treasury enriched by wealth tainted with blood.
Arrears of taxation to a total sum of 50 million sesterces were
remitted. 'We have to thank above all our great Emperors, who
by healing measures and sacrifices by the Treasury have restored
the shaken order of the communities and the property of the

---

[1] Dessau 5163 (Bruns, *Fontes*[7], 63); see Mommsen, *Ges. Schrift.* VIII,
pp. 499 *sqq.*

leading men that was on the brink of ruin.' So men spoke in the
Senate in debating the edict embodying these reforms, thus
revealing clearly an educated man's acceptance of the value of
human life and of an austerer ethical standard, the deep revulsion
of intellectual asceticism against the mob's delight in spectacles
of bloodshed and the statesman's resolution to organize relief
of distress for communities and individuals and to produce more
uniformity with stricter control. It is a part of Marcus' general
amelioration of civic life during his reign. But despite the great
expenditure and sacrifices of revenue, which must have gone far
to empty the State's treasury, could Marcus really hope that these
remedies could heal the deep wounds which the times of stress
had inflicted on the Empire and its people?

Besides this stricter control and organization of Italy more
like the provinces and the care for all the provinces, in which
indeed there was sore need of help, Marcus sought to make
Roman authority permeate the newly conquered countries,
though this proved to be a vain expenditure of strength. He
strove, as has been seen, to make good the depopulation by war
and pestilence by the forcible settlement of northern barbarians,
who were assigned to great estates as labourers, free but bound
to the soil and without land of their own, or became tenants of
small holdings or soldiers. Thus they were merged in these provincial populations and no doubt helped to bring to these regions
fresh vigour. But at the same time they added a new and strong
element in the effort of the provinces to overcome or annex to
themselves the central control of the Empire. Beneath the thin
veil of Graeco-Roman culture the forces of provincial civilization
became steadily more visible. To the claim of men to be citizens,
equal with the Romans, of a unified Empire, was added the claim
of their gods, even the gods of the obscurer corners of the provinces, to be made equal with Juppiter Optimus Maximus. The
day was near when the gods in the Imperial Pantheon were to
be organized as a unity under a single lord (p. 389). The Imperial
race of Rome and Italy, the culture of Greece and Rome were
hastening to their downfall, and it was not in Marcus' power to
hinder it, any more than it had been to conquer distress and bring
back new prosperity. The days when men spoke of the 'felicity
of the age' were past; his belief in a predestined divinely-ordained
chain of events forbade him to bring salvation. As, far from Rome,
he laid him down to die, there was still sore distress and grave
anxiety beset all men of good-will. When he was asked for the
password for the last time this was his answer: 'Go to the rising

sun, my sun is setting[1].' Ready, as he ever wished to be, Marcus died. But his farewell not only pointed a way to hope; it set to his people a final riddle.

VII. THE ACCESSION AND REIGN OF COMMODUS

Commodus, 'the rising sun,' was not nineteen when he became sole ruler of the Roman world. Born when his father was Emperor, promoted to co-regent younger than any other prince, he assumed the 'cura rei publicae' at the age at which Alexander entered on his inheritance, soon to add to it a conquered world; at which Caesar's adopted son began the conflict for his inheritance, to become Augustus and *pater patriae*. When Alexander, not yet thirty-three, lay on his deathbed, an epoch had been made in the history of the world; when the younger Caesar, not yet thirty-two, triumphed at Actium, his own strength had made sure his mastery of the Roman world; when Commodus, at a like age, gasped out his life in the clutch of the athlete[2], an opportunity of world-importance had been missed and what his predecessors had gathered, increased, guarded and sought to save had been lost[3].

Marcus Aurelius, whether yielding to Faustina or setting the dynastic principle above the old conception of the principate, had done everything to ensure the succession of his son born in the purple. On the collapse of Cassius' revolt, he had secured for him the consulship, the tribunician power, the name Augustus and co-regency for nearly three years. At the last Commodus had been summoned to the Emperor's camp, initiated into his plans, entrusted with the finishing of the war in the North, and presented to his friends as the next ruler. Ignorance of his character, hope in the good that was in him, loss of vital interest, trust that his counsellors would be strong enough to lead him, or acquiescence in divinely guided destiny and resignation before the rise of a new power, any of these may explain his action. His friends, who could control the material force of the Empire if they could not create a legitimate claim to it—above all, Claudius Pompeianus—bowed before the will of the dead Emperor, and presented his son to the army in the camp. Thus first Marcus Aurelius, who made the doer of a deed alone answerable for its effects (p. 373), then his

---

[1] Dio LXXII, 34.   [2] See below, p. 383.

[3] The literary tradition for the reign of Commodus is to be found in the Scriptores Historiae Augustae, *Marcus Antoninus* and *Commodus*, Dio LXXII–LXXIII and Herodian I. The coins which provide a parallel tradition are collected in Mattingly and Sydenham, *Roman Imperial Coinage*, III, pp. 356 *sqq.*, Strack *op. cit.* 19, III. (See also Volume of Plates V, 130.)

friends and the army, stirred to enthusiasm by a speech of the young Emperor and by his donatives, bore all human responsibility for what was soon to be lamented, opposed and condemned.

The choice of the 'best man' was long since a shadow, but the Senate in Rome must soon have formally ratified what it could not hinder even if it wished. When the new ruler, as Hadrian had done, made a gesture of respect to Rome, it hastened to wish him a prosperous and speedy homecoming and to celebrate what may have been a trifling victory as due to the *Virtus* of the Emperor, who became *imperator iv*[1]. But the Imperial coinage does not reveal that Commodus, despite the opposition of his father's helper and his own brother-in-law, Claudius Pompeianus, presently fulfilled the Senate's wish after his return by ending the war and making peace with the Marcomanni, the Quadi and the Buri. The strength of the enemy was exhausted, they 'begged for peace,' final victory was certain. But he 'longed for the pleasures of Rome'—though was it not Rome where the emperor was?—'and hated the fatigues of war[2]'—so at least his critics declared, but no one firmly opposed his act[3].

Commodus made peace on the basis of the earlier treaties, demanding the surrender of deserters and prisoners, a partial disarmament, the entry into the service of Rome of 13,000 Quadi and a smaller contingent of Marcomanni, and annual contributions of corn. The tribes must renounce war against the Iazyges, Buri and Vandals, and assemble only once a month under Roman supervision. The armies of occupation were withdrawn, and the lands along the north bank of the Danube remained in the hands of neither side. Like terms were imposed on the Buri, and the north-west border of Dacia was made secure. Gradually mitigations of the terms were granted[4]. After thirteen years of effort, in the full tide of victory, came this un-Roman renunciation of final triumph. It was a manifest denial of his father's will, whether it sprang from a long-formed purpose, or from Commodus' initiative at the moment or from the persuasions of the younger

---

[1] The number of acclamations as *imperator*, the consulships and the years of *tribunicia potestas* were continued on the Imperial currency, so that *imp.* XVIII, *cos.* VII, *trib. pot.* XVIII were reached by the end of 192, while the coins of Alexandria continued the regnal years of his father, as though the rule of father and son was conceived of as a unity.

[2] Dio LXXIII, 2; Herodian 1, 6, 4–5.

[3] See the passages cited by von Rohden in P.W. *s.v.* Aurelius (89), cols. 2469 *sqq.*; J. M. Heer, in *Philol.* Suppl. IX, 1909, pp. 7–39, 142 *sqq.*

[4] Dio LXXIII, 2–3; Herodian 1, 6, 8 *sq.*; S.H.A. *Comm.* 3, 5. See Heer, *op. cit.* pp. 39 *sqq.*

courtiers. Hadrian, too, had done the like in the despite of the old counsellors of Trajan; experience had shown that then the defeated enemy had kept the peace for decades, and here too the result might well be the same: Commodus would have been justified if he thought so and counted on thus setting free resources that he could apply to reconstruction and the relief of need, as Hadrian had done. Rome accepted the renunciation of victory without demur and with high hopes.

In autumn 180 Commodus left the seat of war and hastened, everywhere acclaimed, to the capital, which greeted him as the fortunate and victorious bringer of peace, the chosen of the gods, the protected of Juppiter the Upholder[1]. A largesse confirmed the good-will of the people; all was lulled in 'security.' Marcus received the last honour of apotheosis. But in the Senate Commodus failed to strike the due note of restrained Imperial dignity. In the triumph, which he soon celebrated, as he passed in the high state of a *triumphator*, he turned again and again to kiss the body-servant who stood behind him upholding the golden wreath above his head[2]. His words and acts seemed to aim at winning favour with the mob, and flouting Rome and all that there was held sacred, abandoning the modest dignity with which a *princeps* should be content.

The lines of cleavage were soon seen[3]. Commodus had no need of the Senate, which had repaid the indulgence of Marcus Aurelius with interested service and had sold the right to regard itself as the Assembly of the old nobility of Rome. There indeed the least real opposition lay. The Senate that never quite understood Commodus, because it was dominated by fading ideas, remained as a whole servile, flattering and trembling, without strength for attack or defence, until the day came when it could vent its fury on the murdered ruler in frenzied excitement. Far more dangerous was the malice of forces that worked in darkness, above all of his sister Lucilla and her followers. Nor could he be at ease with the elder statesmen, who cramped his freedom with admonitory claims based on the force of their policy, their services and their experience. But so long as he kept contented the masses in the world's capital, the Guard and the armies, his power was indestructible and his brightest visions could be made facts.

In the field Commodus had already rejected the counsels of his

---

[1] Heer, *op. cit.* p. 41.   [2] Heer, *op. cit.* p. 42 *sq.*
[3] For what follows see the material collected in von Rohden, *op. cit.* col. 2472; Heer, *op. cit.* pp. 43 *sqq.*; *Pros. Imp. Rom.* under the persons named.

father's old friends; in Rome he removed them from his entourage. The chief of them, Pompeianus, withdrew, embittered or ungraciously dismissed. But the Emperor did not break off all connections with this powerful group: in each of his remaining consulships he took a colleague from among them, and allowed two of them to reach a second term of office. That no higher promotion was vouchsafed to any of them during his reign is no reproach to Commodus, for the Imperial house had detached itself more and more definitely from the nobility since the time of Antoninus Pius. Thus towards the aristocracy the Emperor preserved appearances, and, further, the most eminent of the *equites*, the two Praetorian Prefects of Marcus Aurelius, Tarrutenius Paternus and Tigidius Perennis, retained their posts for some time.

The tradition hostile to Commodus declares that the city was outraged at his early introduction of new customs—drinking in public and dealing with the State treasures as though he was set on squandering an Empire. But as late as 181 the official propaganda of the coinage continued to extol the ruler whose 'providence' had brought peace, who cared for the poor and proved his generosity by a new largesse, and saved the people from anxiety and insecurity. The Senate, on the other hand, though it attributed all this to the favour of Juppiter the Upholder, now offered at the end of the first quinquennium its vows for the prosperous completion of the first decade of his tribunician power. Though the coinage, with its appeal to popular belief, stresses rather the harmony of the gods' favour and the divine creative force of the sovereign, while the Senate emphasizes the divine providence and, in its rational way, the beneficent will of the *optimus civis*, their differing interpretations do not, as yet, mark a deep cleavage between Emperor and Senate. Commodus found more and more adherents in the Senate, who went to the provinces 'as his confederates in crime' or 'commended by him[1]' and strengthened his government as his followers in offices of trust. There was nothing in this to deserve criticism, but those who had lost their power must have resented it as the beginning of the rule of favourites, as though that had hitherto been unknown at Rome. The natural result was that the opposition of forces became more keen and embittered.

The praise of the Emperor as a man of war appears also in the next year; and a success, perhaps on the Dacian border, was seized upon as the occasion for a fifth acclamation as *imperator*.

---

[1] S.H.A. *Comm.* 3, 8.

But there was soon to be a clash of ideas. While hunting in the African desert, Hadrian had once killed a lion; now Commodus showed how he could bring one down from horseback in the Roman amphitheatre before the people, to whom, in this Imperial act, he displayed the *Virtus Augusti*. The manly strength in which the Emperor, unlike the cultivated world with its lip-service to ethical values, saw the basic virtue of a ruler, was thus displayed with the instinct of a beast and the fearless elegance of a toreador to the excitable masses, and the propaganda soon celebrated it in Rome and in the empire. The lion-slayer Hercules was made the mythical symbol of his rule and the protector of the Emperor, the last of the dynasty that worshipped Hercules Gaditanus (p. 298). By such means it was his right to make himself felt and known to his people in new conceptions that meant more to them than to the anaemic intellectualism of the upper classes. But this 'grim crudity of life'[1] was made a catchword by his enemies and a pretext by his ambitious sister.

Lucilla could not forget that she had once been Empress, nor reconcile herself to a retired if not too virtuous life in the country with her husband Pompeianus, now old and suffering with his eyes. With her cousin Quadratus she set on foot a conspiracy against Commodus. One Claudius Pompeianus Quintianus was entrusted with the attempt on his life, which he made with more bombast than resolution. He was executed, and with him the guilty members of the aristocracy, while Lucilla was exiled to Capreae, where the Emperor later had her put to death. That was the penalty of the folly that had raised a hand against the sacred life shielded by the providence of the gods. To celebrate the '*salus Augusti*' a new largesse bound the people to their sovereign in the name of public security[2]. But the phrase of the would-be assassin—'The Senate sends thee this dagger[3]'—was skilfully chosen as the occasion of an offensive by the Emperor thus impiously assailed. His action was far from that of the rulers who were so careful to shield the Senate: Hadrian had had to suffer the reproach of having executed four consulars for plotting against his life. To spare criminals or their accomplices now would have been to defeat justice. The killings began, and in the next years and even till the close of his reign—as under Hadrian—more and more nobles fell before his anger. It was the sovereign's right to preserve his inviolability against all, whoever

---

[1] S.H.A. *Comm.* 4, 1.
[2] On the conspiracy of Lucilla see von Rohden, *op. cit.* col. 2473; Heer, *op. cit.* pp. 44 *sqq.* It may be set in A.D. 182.
[3] S.H.A. *Comm.* 4, 3.

and whatever they might be, who were in his eyes proved guilty or even suspect. Hercules, too, had crushed the powers of evil the world over and had so given men peace. Commodus showed his clemency in that he contented himself at first with the exile of the chief plotter and spared his own kin. For this he may have taken the name Pius, unless it was, rather, that the favour of the gods constantly proved his piety towards them.

Soon after this his chamberlain was secretly removed by the machinations of the Praetorian Prefects[1]. Of these the famous Tarrutenius Paternus was caught in the intrigues of his colleague Tigidius Perennis and removed from office. He was promoted to the Senate with the rank of consular: until charges of conspiracy, high treason and the concealment of crimes brought him to his death. Perennis, with the Guard firmly in hand, was free to work his will on his rival's followers, who were involved in his destruction. Commodus looked on. Physically strong and resolute, he lacked the cold calculation of greed for power, for he regarded his right as given by heaven, and gave free play to his instincts without care for convention or the tradition of his class. He became the instrument of his Praetorian Prefect's ambition, which followed high purposes and advanced with steady step— to his own undoing.

The new régime was now openly revealed. Perennis[2] made bold to urge his lord to follow his pleasures while he took the cares of government upon his shoulders. With this division of labour the Emperor, living in dreams rather than waking knowledge, was well content. In the palace he shared his pleasures with 300 mistresses and 300 boys of high or low degree, all of chosen beauty. Stories ran of the orgies that marked his revulsion from the old order of life, his abandonment to his senses and his imagination, and of the indolence which made him content himself with adding at most the words of greeting to his rescripts, and leaving to Perennis all the preparation of business. But after all, the work was done, and done in the name of the Emperor, so that its doing strengthened both the sovereign and his Prefect. There was even economy: no more largesse for the People, so long as Perennis was in power, no more solicitous provision for the youth of Italy. The money that had gone to this was now, so it was said, spent to satisfy the autocrat's pleasures and his vizier's greed. For now the Prefect was the omnipotent vizier of a Sultan. The

---

[1] Heer, op. cit. p. 46 sq. For the fall of Paternus, ib. pp. 47 sqq.
[2] See Heer, op. cit. pp. 55 sqq.

last of the Spanish line, monarch by grace of the gods and his
father, and the Italian who had long probed the weaknesses of his
two masters, the one in revolt against the old order, the other
intoxicated with power, did not hesitate to set up an absolutism
which no one resisted. The veil in which Marcus Aurelius had
carefully shrouded his rule had fallen. The time was ripe; and
Rome would soon have learnt to endure the brutal violation of
tradition, the more so as the Senate did not strive against it, had
only the sovereign remained himself the brain and heart of the
new order, the will that made the final decisions, whose words,
decrees, proclamations and dispositions united the forces of tradition and of the divine power that worked in and through him and
were sacred and immutable Law because they were efficient to
ensure the general weal. But what if men realized that the
Emperor spoke words that were not his own and yielded to the
influence of another? His subjects were not to feel that the judgment of him that chose such subordinates was not enlightened by
divine instinct nor that respect for the sacred institution of the
Emperor's position or the magical powers of the Emperor's personality did not exorcize the ambition of his servants. Without the
skill to understand his ministers, to promote without ceasing
to control them, to spur them on to creative efforts that would
serve the Emperor's own glory, Commodus slipped from one false
step to another. Intrigue followed intrigue; suspicion, jealousy,
despotic anger struck down victim after victim and their blood was
laid to the Emperor's charge.

The first to fall was Perennis in 185[1]. He was suspected, truly
or not, of planning a coup d'État, to be supported by the rebellious army of Britain, and the generals of this army and of the
Danube joined against him with his enemies in Rome even within
the Palace. He was denounced to the Emperor who, rousing
himself from his dreams, had him tried and outlawed by the
Senate, and delivered him with his followers to the fury of a
detachment of troops that was marching by the city. Then came
the turn of the chamberlain Cleander[1], who had come to Rome
as a Phrygian slave and had played a part in the overthrow of
Perennis. For two years he avoided becoming his successor, so
that his rivals might wear out their strength in transient tenures
of the office that ended in their fall. At last he assumed the rôle
of saviour of the State and became Prefect, thus breaking through
the *cursus honorum* of the equestrian order. With unheard-of
caprice he sold magistracies, distinctions and governorships and

----

[1] Heer, *op. cit.* pp. 75 *sqq.*

reversed decisions at law, all for money, so it was said, but perhaps
also to secure himself a following. On one occasion he named
twenty-five consuls for one year; he promoted freedmen to the
Senate, and he had senators and knights, even the Emperor's
brother-in-law whose admonitions made him unwelcome, murdered
for alleged high treason. It was perhaps at this time that his
consort Crispina was accused of adultery and banished to Capreae
where, like Lucilla earlier (p. 380), she was afterwards executed. Her
place had already fallen to the concubine Marcia, whom Commodus
had taken to himself from the household of Quadratus at his
death in 182. Marcia now ranked before all his mistresses and
enjoyed all the honours that had belonged to the Augusta and
Empress. She had leanings towards Christianity, and was
cognizant of the Emperor's crimes; until, in 192, she joined the
conspiracy that led to his death. For Cleander the 'body-servant'
(*a cubiculo*) the wit of his enemies found the new title of 'dagger-
servant' (*a pugione*), and it seemed as though a régime of murder
and ambition was to be set up by the pitiless reversal of all values
and social grades. But in A.D. 190 Commodus turned against him,
and he perished in a popular rising created in Rome by the devices
of the *praefectus annonae* which, when it had done its work, was
charmed away by a largesse, which was announced as early as 187
but had clearly not been distributed.

In one thing only was the rule of the chamberlain Eclectus[1],
an Egyptian, and of the Praetorian Prefect, Laetus[2], marked out
from that of the other holders of these offices. They set on foot
a far-reaching conspiracy against Commodus himself, in which
were enlisted the generals on the Rhine and the Danube, though
in this they served, in the first instance, the ends of another not
of themselves. Informers still had their day: citizens old and young
were sentenced to death, while the fortunes of the innocent went
to fill the Treasury together with diverted inheritances and the
property of temples, and the estates of the Emperor grew beyond
all measure. At last, almost by chance, the pair discovered a
proscription list which spelt danger to their partisans, and they
dared all. On December 31, 192, Commodus was given poison
with the help of his concubine and when it failed to take effect,
he was strangled in his bath by the athlete kept to wrestle with
him[3].

Commodus is not to be condemned for bringing in naked

---

[1] See *Pros. Imp. Rom.* ii, p. 32, no. 7; Stein in *P.W. s.v.* Eklektos.
[2] *Pros. Imp. Rom.* i², p. 56, no. 358.
[3] See Heer, *op. cit.* pp. 116 *sqq.*

despotism, but because in his dream world he was too indifferent
to exploit his opportunities in a world without illusions and to
give overmastering strength to the common efforts of master and
servants to bring to birth something great. That would have meant
the achievement at one stroke of the new order in the Empire.
For that he lacked the political gift. But even if he had gone down
in the struggle and left the way open to the strong, the man of
illusions might still have been a giant shadow. For granted that
his vizier had been the true possessor of power and architect of
achievement while his own responsibility was a fine fiction, he
would have gained the glory from it all. But Commodus was no
more than a manikin, who in this play lost all, even his own life.
His servants, without faith or conscience, were even more pitiable
than he. None of them conceived of the power of the idea which,
for all their violence, they hardly did anything to make real, even
if, like Perennis, they toiled and laboured to maintain order in
the Empire, or, like Laetus, set the stage for his overthrow to
make room for a greater. None of the chamberlains or Praetorian
Prefects made unselfishness their virtue, nor had they reverence
for the Imperial throne: no man is a hero to his valet. Even the
Prefects craned their necks too far. And all lost their heads.

In surprising contrast to the struggles and scenes of death in
Rome was the rarely broken peace maintained by the provinces[1]. There were no losses of territory. A rising in Dacia
seems to have been quickly suppressed (c. A.D. 184). The mutiny
of the armies in Britain at the end of a severe but victorious war
against Caledonian invaders from the North in the same year may
have been due to failure to provide their pay, which may explain
the rage which the soldiers vented on the 'niggardly' Perennis.
But it continued at the instigation of senatorial opponents of the
government and even led to attempts to proclaim a rival Emperor
until finally it was suppressed in 186 by Pertinax. In Germany
the provinces proved unruly, and the invasion of Imperial territory
by free Germans and the investment of the Eighth Legion[2],
perhaps in Strasbourg, produced a crisis which, for a moment,
made the Emperor contemplate visiting the seat of war in person,
until in 188 news of victory came and he was 'held back by his
Senate and People.' But more troops and more extensive and
stronger frontier fortifications were needed and were supplied.

---

[1] Heer, op. cit. pp. 48, 68 sqq., 92 sqq., 103 sqq., 129, 174 sqq.; Ritterling
in P.W. s.v. Legio, col. 1306 sq.; Vogt, op. cit. 1, pp. 150 sqq.

[2] C.I.L. xi, 6057; xiii, 6, p. 23; Ritterling, op. cit. cols. 1307, 1660,
1663.

Shortly before this a deserter, Maternus[1], who had raised bands in Southern Gaul which spread insecurity throughout Gaul and Spain so that Commodus ordered a concentration of troops against him, took the opportunity to penetrate into Italy and plan an attack on the Emperor during the procession of the Magna Mater on March 27, 188. He dared hope to seize the throne and it was only at the last moment that the plot was discovered and frustrated. In the province of Africa there were disorders which the vigour of Pertinax crushed in A.D. 190. The strengthening of the frontiers on the Upper German and Raetian *limes*, in Mauretania, Numidia, on the Danube, in Britain and in the East, the repairs everywhere even of the border military roads attest the activity of the governors who in the Emperor's name 'cared for the security of their provincial people.' It is, no doubt, their vigour and determination to preserve the Imperial organization that in general prevented more revolts and kept these wars from ending in catastrophe. The propaganda of the central government, echoed by the coinage of Alexandria[2], can hardly have had so pacifying an effect, nor was there ever a time when the radiation of power from Rome seems to have been so slight. Alexandria, Carthage and a few cities in Asia Minor boasted of the peculiar care of the Emperor. The small tenants on the great estates enjoyed his protection. Dedications for the sovereign in the most diverse parts of the Empire are fewer than before. The restoration of a bridge in Dalmatia, or of a temple in the Fayûm, and that not at the government's expense, a building inscription of the Roman garrison in Inner Armenia, work on frontier forts and on roads, baths built by Cleander in Rome—all these compare ill enough with the achievements of earlier reigns. Commodus is indeed charged with having his name inscribed on the buildings of others, with failing to complete what his father had begun. Of his legislative activity hardly a trace remains save a few decisions at law, though for this the reversal of his *Acta* at his death may be most responsible. The fact that hardly any jurist, even after the restoration of his memory by Severus, refers to Commodus' activity shows clearly enough that no attempt was made to grapple with the problems of the hard times of Marcus that awaited solution.

The passivity of the central government[3], which has its counterpart in the provincials' indifference to the struggles at Rome, became the cause of their great advance towards equality in the

---

[1] Herodian 1, 10; 11, 5. S.H.A. *Comm.* 16, 2, *Pesc. Nig.* 3, 3.

[2] Vogt, *op. cit.* 1, p. 152 *sq.*

[3] See von Rohden, *op. cit.* cols. 2479 *sq.*; Heer, *op. cit.* p. 173 *sq.*

Empire and towards the new mode of life. Everywhere armies and peoples united and the movement proceeded from both alike. As early as 184 the old deities of Dacia entered in the chief sanctuary of the Dacian army as equal powers beside the Roman gods, claiming equal devotion[1]. The Magna Mater of Asia Minor, that had preserved the Roman Emperor on March 27, 188, the Alexandrian Sarapis, who so often had proved his power and loyalty to the Imperial house, and now appeared once more as protector of the corn fleets that fed the poor in Rome and in 191 shielded Commodus from sickness, gods whom Rome had long known, now became more than Commodus' own protecting deities. With their whole train of gods and goddesses they and, like them, the Syrian Sun-god, the Juppiter of Doliche, Mithras, and Ma-Bellona from Cappadocia were received as equal citizens of the Roman Pantheon. Nor were the gods of Africa slow to find their place. In the victory of the provincial deities was reflected and foreshadowed the conflict for the victory of their provincial worshippers. Commodus was not long in his grave when the Guard in Rome, the last bulwark of Italian military tradition, was disbanded to make way for the 'barbarian' sons of the North and East, the motley *soldateska*, 'wild of aspect, dreadful in speech, boorish in behaviour' (p. 311 *sq.*). Twenty years after his death the *constitutio Antoniniana* was passed which brought this striving to fruition when the provincials were made 'Romans.' Like his father, Commodus would have saved the world the waste of much effort in this struggle, had he driven it through with a high hand.

VIII. THE POSITION OF COMMODUS AND ITS SIGNIFICANCE

The literary tradition, which measured all emperors by the ideal of Augustus, portrays Commodus in the darkest colours. Facts and gossip were intermingled, all that was hateful or ludicrous in his private life, all that was extravagant or negligent in his public acts were combined to brand him to posterity as a criminal whom the Senate first smiled at, then mocked at and finally condemned. Where the literary tradition offers only shadows or scandals or monstrous depravity, the coins describe events with growing enthusiasm. The picture given by the official propaganda of the Empire and Alexandrian coinage, shows more richness, unity and depth; much that, taken by itself, seems without motive

[1] On the provincial religions see Heer, *op. cit.* pp. 159 *sqq.*; Fr. Cumont in *Archiv für Religionswissenschaft*, IX, 1906, pp. 323 *sqq.*; Weber, *Gött. Gel. Anz.* 1908, pp. 989 *sqq.*; *Probleme der Spätantike*, pp. 67 *sqq.*

or meaning becomes significant if placed in its original setting[1].
The coins do not conceal the occasions for blame, but they persist
in seeing in the Emperor the choice and protégé of the gods.
Each new acclamation as *imperator*, the titles of honour 'Pius'
(183), 'Britannicus' (184), 'Felix' (185), and the changes of the
Imperial name are recorded, though the clear record leaves much
that is still dark to us. The illusions, the moods, the hopes that
kindled the plans and acts of the Emperor are set forth perhaps
as the government wished and so with more clear purpose and
reality than the partial caricature born of hatred. To supplement
and often to interpret this with startling clearness, the Senate
sounds an accompaniment, first forced or over-loud from fear or
interested officiousness, then on the Emperor's death breaking
out in a wild confusion of insult.

Thus in 183 the gods of Rome and the Felicity of the Emperor
were hailed by the People contented with his gifts of corn. The
Senate attested his *Hilaritas*; his *Salus* was beyond danger even
from the lions he overcame (p. 380), Peace must now reign over
the world entrusted to him by Juppiter, and the times were happy.
The victory in Britain of the next year, no less than the Emperor's
earlier munificence, was made the occasion for celebrations.
Rome has to thank its new Hercules that brought prosperity to
men (p. 390). Italy appears as the mistress of the world and the
rejoicing over victory lasts till 185. Now at last we hear of the
Felicitas Saeculi, that had seemed for two decades to be forgotten,
the Golden Age of Saturn, the gift of Juppiter. The victorious might
of the Emperor overcoming a panther posed men with the question, what divine power enabled him to strike down with a single
shaft beast after beast, himself inviolate. Was not this proof
enough of his Herculean strength and his divine sonship? Meanwhile another note is struck in the 'fidelity of the armies,' the
'concord of the soldiers,' suspiciously like an appeal to the
mutinous troops in Britain. But whatever might befall, the first
decennium of his tribunician power must end in a fortunate time.

The propaganda in 186 has the same story of these loyal
armies, of the soldiers once more in concord. Perennis had at last
fallen, the Senate could celebrate the Felicitas Publica. With a
sixth largesse to the People the hope of the coming age of happiness is described as growing and as echoed by the provinces—

[1] In the following pages the evidence of the coinage is used to show the
view of the ruler and his rule which it was desired to impress upon Rome
and the provinces. On the coins see the works of Mattingly-Sydenham,
Vogt, Bosch and Strack cited above (pp. 326, 330, 340 *Note*).

'Under King Commodus the whole world is happy.' Then, as if
ancient Rome had risen again, and the victory of the previous year
which seemed to be the fulfilment of the *vota decennalia* (p. 387)
was still celebrated, the *nobilitas Augusti* is suddenly officially proclaimed as though anyone had dared to doubt it and worshippers
in the provinces named him 'nobilissimus princeps.' Finally is
heard the exuberant enthusiasm of 'Juppiter summus exsuperantissimus,' and the Senate had already declared its glowing
aspiration after eternal peace. With the next year the gates of
Janus are closed and the lord of Time that links the past and the
future rules an earth restored to equilibrium. The Golden Age of
fancy had dawned, the happiness of the People had been achieved
by the piety, the strength and nobility, the joy and gladness, the
'providence' and munificence of the Emperor. The title of
'Father of the Senate' was added to that of Pater Patriae, thus
setting Commodus as the sole representative of the two sovereign
powers of the ancient State or, perhaps, as himself the sovereign,
endued with the *patria potestas*. Even if later the Senate was to
exalt its own piety, now it is Commodus who is the 'auctor
pietatis,' the creator of felicity.

In all this may be detected the religious movement of the time.
Commodus is the embodiment of piety viewed from the angle of
Eastern religiosity and philosophical speculation. His Juppiter
summus exsuperantissimus transcended the idea of the god of a
State and became the centre of a universal system of divinities that
restored to a divided world an elemental unity. To this system
belonged the alien gods whose rites Commodus did not shrink
from practising, although their rites were 'cruel' according to
Roman ideas and his participation in them was taken as proof of
his 'cruelty[1].' But, though old Rome might regard it as a betrayal,
the raising of the gods of the provincials into the State pantheon
of Rome was no more than the fulfilment of his whole conception,
wherein lay the essential justification of his position as ruler in the
world. In his position as devout mediator between the world of
men and the world of gods he stood raised above the political
ideas of the past, with its rational beliefs in freedom and equality.
To himself Commodus may have seemed crowned with the magic
that had attended the kings of old by divine grace. In his feats
in the amphitheatre he may have been imitating the Egyptian,
Assyrian or Persian kings, whose deeds he had seen pictured on
temples and palaces when he was a boy with his father in Egypt
and Syria. As he passionately embraced the orgiastic yet so animal

[1] See S.H.A. *Comm.* 9, 5–6, and cf. Heer, *op. cit.* pp. 154 *sqq.*

religions of the East, he may have taken as his own the philosophic speculation that at this time came in with the beginnings of metaphysic and wild religious ferment. Intrepid and fanatical, at the mercy of every illusion, he abandoned himself to his ideas and passions; but what he did seemed the monstrous abuse of power only to those who clung to the old world. It was, in fact, a new type of the pure man, and the devout ruler, an invasion of an alien strength and an alien attitude, the first triumph of the oriental and 'barbarian' alike, which found its instrument in this last of the Spanish line. As the first realization of *humilitas* before the Highest in the heathen world of Rome he stands in diametrical opposition to the political and ethical ideal of Greek and Roman *humanitas*[1]. But this new ideal was logical and deeply rooted in the aspirations of the age, and therefore genuine.

In 188 the prayers that Fortune would attend on the Emperor appear more clearly than in the past three years, until the goddess was thanked that her happy intervention had succeeded in keeping him back in Rome to make offerings for victory in Germany (p. 384). Omens and signs had been given to warn him, and as the Magna Mater helped to save him from Maternus, so did Juppiter with his thunderbolt aid him against the Germans. The abundant Empire coinage of the next year displays a host of legends that turn on the idea of eternal Rome, of eternal peace and security for the whole world provided by Juppiter juven(tus), Minerva victrix, Mars pacator, while Victory and Fortune are happy and Fortune attends on the Emperor. Over the whole Juppiter summus exsuperantissimus has sway. By the year 190, after the end of troubles in Africa, a seventh largesse to the People (see p. 383) and the just sentence of death on Cleander, the Senate too had learnt to extol the *Libertas Augusti* and his fortunate Genius, and at the end of the third quinquennium of his tribunician power vows were made for his Vicennalia. In this year was established the African corn-fleet to secure, together with the Egyptian fleet, the food-supply of Rome and in connection with it was founded the colony of Carthage that was named after the Emperor.

In the last two years of his reign the Empire coinage shows an ever richer and more consequent variety. The name of Commodus seals the unity of the Praetorian cohorts, his creative power preserves for Rome the Golden Age. Palatine Apollo and Minerva Augusta appear, Hercules takes the name and shape of Commodus

---

[1] On the idea of *humanitas—humilitas*, see Weber, *Römische Kaisergeschichte und Kirchengeschichte*, pp. 19 *sqq.*

himself, now that he has achieved the last of his labours and won the apples of the Hesperides that give immortality. Commodus has become a god in Rome. Coins and medals display further Victory, the Sun-god, Sarapis, all giving help and aid to the labours of the new divinity. The hostile tradition records that he accepted statues in the garb of Hercules and received offerings as a god. So Commodus lived in his mythical-divine world of visions. A sudden change of the Emperor's name to L. Aelius Aurelius Commodus Augustus Pius Felix seems to inaugurate a new age under a new ruler. But the official propaganda has to tell of the 'defender of the Salus Augusti,' of Juppiter Ultor. The Senate, following the Imperial coinage, adds a train of divinities, Juppiter Optimus Maximus, Mars, the Magna Mater, Sarapis, the Sol invictus of Syria to guard the Emperor, exalts the lasting felicity of Augustus, the *Salus humani generis*, and announces that 'the vows for the weal of the Roman People have been paid.' Thus all beneficent powers in Heaven and on Earth, whatever their origin or station, stand by to guard the life of the Emperor from impious attack or the peril of the pestilence before which he had withdrawn to Laurentum, and to preserve Augustus, his Roman People and mankind from mortal needs, to secure the happiness of the world and its ruler, and to banish care. Finally, Commodus appears making offerings to Felicitas or by the side of Juppiter as ruler of the world, who can claim the adoration of his children.

Belief, myth, crude reality were thus inextricably compounded together in the ecstasies of the Imperial devotee as rarely before. This great congregation of divine powers to preserve the sovereign and his beneficence would have been unthinkable in earlier times. Yet it all speaks the language of Rome, and it is still a bold venture to display himself to the People in his majesty as deified. But the ultimate climax has not yet been reached. In his last year, 192, Pietas joins the heavenly powers, the *Libertas Augusti* appears renewed and Commodus shows himself with Sarapis and Isis. Then there broke out a fire in Rome which destroyed the temple of Pax and parts of the Palace, even the temple of Vesta and some parts of the city. The order went out to found a new Rome, to be called by the name of the 'Hercules Romanus, the (new) founder of Rome.' The colossal statue that Nero set up, which later was turned into a statue of Helios, now became a Hercules with the features of Commodus, the cult-statue of the city's founder. He is to take the place of Romulus, who once vanished from the earth on the day on which Commodus assumed the *toga virilis* (p. 360), and whom the Senate still held up to him as a monitor in 178 and

180. On its pedestal his life and deeds were inscribed for men to read. The day of the edict received his name, and from the style and titles of his latest period—Lucius Aelius Aurelius Commodus Augustus Herculeus Romanus Exsuperatorius Amazonius Invictus Felix Pius—were to be named the months of the year for all posterity. Thus he is represented as the lord of the world, of its space and of its time, of mankind and of its happiness that he has created. The old Rome is dead, a new Rome comes to birth. What no man had yet ventured is represented as achieved by a single decree. He has reached the climax of his revolutionary purpose and action. Two new *congiaria*, the eighth and ninth, are to win the People, and the propaganda for the Roman Hercules becomes ever more vigorous—and then comes the sudden end.

The treason of his 'vizier,' his chamberlain, his concubine and his athlete unites as though symbolically the powers to which his breaking down of the old order gave play. The guardian of political power and the guardian of the Palace, the woman found worthy of the new deity but inclined to the god of the Christians, and the man whose office it was to steel the animal strength of the conqueror of beasts, these whom his grace had promoted, banded themselves together in their fear to destroy him. He fell, the martyr of the movement that bore him up. Rome, that he had overthrown, did not rise again despite the reproaches heaped on him and all the Senate's exultation over the 'victory of the Roman People.' The destroyer that had been swept away in its fall was to rise again as Divus Commodus when the victorious Septimius Severus, for whose ends he fell, whose good fortune it was that the athlete proved the stronger, had gained sole power. Neither fall or rise nor the expiation of timidity and treason stayed in its swift march to fulfilment what he had sought to create. Thus Commodus appears—truly the 'rising sun' that his father with the clear vision of the dying had seen in him. With a high hand he cast aside the intellectuality of the old world, its values, its spiritual and religious gradations. He crushed the pride and dispelled the sovereignty of such *humanitas*. He made the Senate his subjects, took to himself all power, and handed it to his servant to use. He preserved the privileges of the orders and the right of the nobles to hold the magistracies, but he admitted to them ever more new forces of the subject and 'peregrine' world that once was Rome's servant. He destroyed, once and for all, Rome's proud pre-eminence in the world and was himself the sole master of the Empire. Though he seemed flown with pride before his fall, he yet was humble before the highest God, the author of all being.

And from this conception of the power that dwelt in hidden supremacy, the world gained a significant direction towards a new spiritual unity and was buoyed up by the belief in the Felicity of the time, in the Golden Age. A princely prophet falls: but the Order he proclaimed abides.

The youth with his fair hair and burning eyes, whose head seemed to the people crowned with divine brilliance, stirred in the old and the moralists horror and loathing. But why judge him by our standards? A Spanish visionary, mystical, handsome, pliant, strong, now lively now indolent, now intrepid now a coward, with spirit now soaring, now sinking, a notable creature, he was in everything extreme, in obedience towards God, in power to take divinity on himself, in wild sensuality, in iron fearlessness, in animal passion. Unchecked by any laws of morality, without care whether fair boys or women serve his appetites, whether he shed the blood of strangers or of his own kin, breaking any fetters that could enchain him, he yet felt himself without guilt or stain, the source of all piety and the creator of all happiness. His life was lived beyond the world of reason, compounded of the potencies of the body, of instinct and of imagination. To the kaleidoscopic variations of his personality was added the effect of the cosmopolitan group that surrounded him, bringing to play upon him the forces that were now young, now more than old, from the far corners of the empire. Indeed Commodus became, as it were, their vessel, borne on high by their longings, prayed to by their enthusiasms, drained by their egoistic instincts, shattered by their timidly treasonable rage.

Did Commodus deserve the laughter and the scorn of the Senate as he let Rome sink to be a colony of his founding? Why did it flatter him, even outdo him in his mythical-divine attitudinizing, and then visit him with condemnation when the dreaded 'Father of the Senate' had been strangled? It was not worthy of the dreamer, for in its waking it was so cowardly, so studious of revenge, so lacking in vision. Or did it dream in its very wakefulness? In the witches-sabbath that plagued Rome in these years the Emperor stands a strange figure. He had grown out of an intellectualism that was breaking down; he guided life by instinct from its heights to its depths, gave to the forms of the old world a content of passion and enthusiasm born of a new life and sought an Empire of happiness to be guided by men of devout obeisance to piety and the supernal. Rejected by the old, pioneer for the new, far removed from Hadrian, he was the 'rising sun' of a new world.

CHAPTER X

THE PRINCIPATE AND THE ADMINISTRATION

I. THE ARMY AND THE STATE

THE problems confronting the Roman world in A.D. 68 and 69 were as grave as any since the struggle which culminated at Actium. In the days of the 'Second Triumvirate' the character of the government had been determined by the arbitrament of war: in the Year of the Four Emperors it had been submitted to the same hazard again. And on both occasions the personality of the victor was the most potent factor in setting the course which Rome should take when peace had been restored. At Actium the issue was between East and West, and victory gave power to the man who insisted that the imperial culture and the traditions of the imperial régime should be predominantly Latin. By A.D. 68 the achievement of Augustus had set a mark upon the world, and at worst its destruction could not make it as if it had never been. Though Vespasian might allow himself to be regarded as the conqueror who should come out of the East, he and all his rivals were Italians. Nevertheless, if the work of Augustus could not be destroyed, it might well be denied its full fruition. The form of government which he had framed needed time for the revelation of its merits; and by the death of Severus Alexander, when the Principate began to move rapidly and irrevocably in the direction of a Dominate, the Augustan system had endured so long as to be entitled to a place among the historical types of government which it could not have claimed if its end had come in A.D. 69. On the accession of Vespasian that system was threatened; and the threat came from the same quarter as that which finally proved fatal. In the third century the increasing importance of the army enabled it to bestow the Empire on men whose only distinction was popularity with the troops or success in military command. Against martial prowess culture ceased to count; experience in civil administration was not considered; and the Empire fell under the control of war-lords who made inevitable the process by which Principate gave way to Autocracy. This was the danger already plainly present in the sequel to Nero's death.

Five of the army-groups, in jealous rivalry[1], had taken up arms to champion the claims of various candidates for the succession; and a momentous secret had been revealed—'posse principes alibi quam Romae fieri'[2]. Then there was raised the crucial question—would the army contrive to take charge of the Empire, or not? Vespasian gave the answer. Instead of becoming its master, the army remained the servant of the State; the *princeps* was not its puppet but its commander, as before; and so were restored conditions in which the Augustan Principate, rescued from the danger of extinction, might survive in any form the *princeps* chose to give it.

When Vespasian left Alexandria in A.D. 70 the problem which awaited him in Italy was difficult. Like Octavian, he owed his position to his men; but, whereas Octavian had been at most the symbol of a cause, Vespasian was the cause himself. The armies of Syria and the Danube had intervened with no other object than to secure that he, and not the nominee of legions on the Rhine, should succeed to the Imperial position. And when their object was achieved, it still remained to see whether that brief indulgence of their vanity would be enough. They might, indeed, be content once they had placed their chosen hero on the throne. But they might, on the other hand, go farther, and demand that his tenure should be on terms of their own dictation.

According to one famous theory[3] the legions in A.D. 68 and 69 had risen to protest against the degenerate travesty of good government for which Nero had been responsible and to have done with the increasing favour shown to the Praetorians at the expense of the provincial armies. If this view could be accepted, its implications about the future aims of the soldiers would be grave[4]. Their action must have meant that they intended, if not to exercise a permanent supervision of the *princeps*, at least to place him under the threat of renewed intervention whenever his policy should give the same offence as Nero's. In such a version there is, indeed, a large element of truth; but it would be misleading if emphasis on the legionaries' jealousy of the Guards and their resentment at the unworthy performances of Nero were allowed to suggest that it was the rank and file who played the leading part in starting the campaigns of A.D. 68 and 69. A more potent factor was the fear with which Nero's brutalities, and especially his intolerance of military success, had inspired the higher

---

[1] See *e.g.* Suetonius, *Vesp.* 6, 2.   [2] Tacitus, *Hist.* I, 4.
[3] M. Rostovtzeff, *The Social and Economic History of the Roman Empire*, pp. 83 *sqq.*   [4] See *e.g.* Cicero, *Phil.* x, 9, 18.

command. There is no reason to deny the widespread resentment which Nero had aroused, but men's disgust at his behaviour need not have led to mutiny if mutiny had not found a leader. Yet, even though the armies were set in motion more by the incitement of their commanders than by their own resolve to take a hand in government, their entry into the political arena was ominous enough. Galba, the choice of the only legion in Nearer Spain, had been murdered when the Praetorians in Rome had been roused by the bribery of Otho and his own proud refusal to buy their favour[1]; Otho in turn had been driven to suicide by the victorious advance of the armies from the Rhine; and their candidate, Vitellius, had finally been butchered when Rome had fallen to the vanguard of the force whose mission it was to proclaim Vespasian. By the action of Galba the right to bestow the Principate had been made a prize for which every army-group might compete, and the competition had been severe. The armies had entered politics; and, when the issue which provoked this dangerous development had been decided, it remained to see whether they would tamely withdraw from a field in which their presence was a threat.

In the period of reconstruction much depended on the personality of the Princeps, and the attitude of Vespasian to his first great problem—the problem of restoring the army to its proper place—was the attitude to be expected of a man who had grown up under the system established by Augustus. Nowhere had Augustus' respect for the accumulated experience of the Roman Republic been more wisely shown than in his insistence that the higher posts in the civil and the military services should, so far as possible, be held in turn. With rare exceptions the greater commands were accessible to none who was held unfit for the consulship, and to none, in consequence, who had not made that intimate acquaintance with the civil traditions of the Senate which was involved by progress through the hierarchy of urban magistracies[2]. Thus the generals whom the legions might champion for the succession were all men who, however willing they might be to profit by the devotion of the troops, were familiar enough with an ideal of government which did not look to the rank and file for the inspiration of policy. Such was the class to which Vespasian belonged. At the outset he had been sparing in his promises, 'egregie firmus adversus militarem largitionem, eoque exercitu meliore[3];' and though something like a mutiny in Rome had forced Mucianus to delay demobilization in the Urban Garrison, Vespasian was not long deterred. The Guards

[1] Tacitus, *Hist.* i, 5.   [2] Dio lii, 20, 4.   [3] Tacitus, *Hist.* ii, 82.

were the hardest corps to handle; but despite the delicacy of the task their strength was soon reduced, and by A.D. 76 at latest, in place of the sixteen Praetorian Cohorts which Vitellius had recruited[1], Rome had only nine (p. 4 *sq.*).

The provincial armies, to which Vespasian himself showed no anxiety to be generous[2], called not for reduction but for a measure of reform; and the new Princeps made it one of his first objects to secure that their discipline should be maintained in those times of political crisis when it was most essential. Lack of evidence reduces us to speculation about the social character of the classes to which he looked for his recruits[3], and his motives are difficult to disentangle because there were two distinct elements in the problem with which he had to deal. Not only must the army as a whole have its interest in politics destroyed, but the forces on the Rhine in particular called for treatment which would show that disloyalty was not venial and would ensure that the lessons of the Gallo-German rising should not be lost. It was local reasons which caused four of the legions to disappear; but local reasons were probably less cogent than considerations of a more general kind in accelerating the application of principles, not wholly unrecognized in earlier days, which came in course of time to exercise powerful effects on the history of the Empire.

It was no matter for regret that henceforward the auxiliary units were more often stationed in places remote from those in which they had their origin; and if local recruits were accepted, until this practice became regular in the second century it had the valuable effect of reducing the racial solidarity of the corps to which it was applied. More questionable, however, was the increased tendency to compose the legions of provincials[4]. For a time the system was useful: it meant that the troops were largely drawn from classes whose interest in the details of political life in Rome was as slight as their knowledge. But ultimately its results were bad. In the third century, when the army finally took control of government, a defenceless Italy found itself at the mercy of forces which in origin were provincial, and whose Romanism was not even the highest which the provinces could produce. Italy in the end paid dear for her forgetfulness of the burden of empire, and Vespasian has his share of responsibility for encouraging a dangerous indifference to her military obliga-

---

[1] Tacitus, *Hist.* ii, 93.   [2] Suetonius, *Vesp.* 8, 2.
[3] See Rostovtzeff, *op. cit.* pp. 87 *sq.*, 101 *sqq.*
[4] On this, and particularly on the continued recruitment of Italians for service elsewhere than in the Guards, see p. 134.

tions, which one day would give truth to the gibe 'provinciarum sanguine provincias vinci[1].' Nevertheless, it is not to be supposed that he intended to enervate the Italian population. For many years after his time there is evidence enough to show that warlike virtues were not frowned upon in Italy, and there is no good reason to doubt the truth of Dio's word that it was left for Septimius at the end of the second century, when he made transfer to the Guards a reward for good service in the legions, to strike a heavy blow at Italian morale[2].

The risk that legions would form groups and that the groups would take up arms against one another had been familiar enough to Rome since the consequences of Marius' changes in enlistment had first become manifest. Later, when the army was made standing, Augustus had removed one frequent cause of mutiny by his momentous establishment of the Aerarium Militare, whereby the State proclaimed its responsibility for pensions and the troops were freed from the temptation to see in their immediate commander the only hope of provision for their old age (vol. ix, p. 136 *sq.*; vol. x, pp. 195, 221). But the danger that the army, instead of being one and with a single loyalty, would split into groups, that each group would regard itself, not as part of the army of the Empire, but first and foremost as the garrison of the region in which it stood, and that at length the groups would fall to fighting with one another, was more insidious and less easy to dispel. Of the one certain safeguard little use was made. Though legions were freely moved to meet the demands of war, for reasons which may be sought in the slowness and difficulty of transport, a regular and frequent change of quarters was no part of the military system in times of peace. That valuable expedient was as strange to those who followed Vespasian as to his predecessors; and Vespasian himself, after the measures which had been taken to inflame the Syrian army against Vitellius, was scarcely in a position to introduce it[3]. Nevertheless, if the legions, especially after Hadrian's time, tended to become permanent garrisons, their higher officers were still regularly changed; and, since the men rarely moved unless they were incited from above, this custom, by discouraging undue devotion by the troops to their commanders, was powerful as a safeguard against *coups de main*.

Though the army might have been better for a still more drastic treatment, Vespasian's measures beyond doubt were a success. Most valuable of all was his own firm method of dealing

[1] Tacitus, *Hist.* iv, 17.   [2] Dio lxxv, 2, 5.
[3] See Tacitus, *Hist.* ii, 80; Suetonius, *Vesp.* 6, 4.

with the men[1]; for without this the rest might have been impossible.
But hardly less useful were the efforts to weaken the ties between
auxiliary garrisons and civil population; and finally, though as an
enduring policy it did violence to the sound principle of the
Republic that a people which claims imperial position must take
its full share in fighting such battles as imperial interest may
demand (vol. x, p. 426), the increasing tendency to confine
Italians to the Guards and to depend on the provinces for legionary
recruits was above criticism as a temporary expedient to reduce
the risk that the fighting which had followed Nero's death would
be repeated. When the politically-minded population of Italy had
rare opportunity for military service outside the cohorts of
Praetorians, so far as the rank and file were concerned the legionary
forces, even if they were still recruited less from the country than
the towns, would be composed of men reasonably likely to refrain
from unwelcome interest in those questions of government which
were the proper business of the civil authorities in Rome.

So much was done to eliminate the common soldier from politics;
but the common soldier was not the only problem. Though in
eighteen months of turmoil the legionaries and the Guards in
Rome had developed sinister enthusiasms, it was only in the
Upper German army that they had taken the initiative[2]. Galba,
Otho, Vitellius with the Lower German army, and finally
Vespasian himself[3] had all owed their elevation to movements
which they or their friends had instigated. Hard as it might be,
once it had been begun, to stop military interference in affairs of
State, recent experience went to show that a beginning was not
likely to be effected unless senior officers gave a lead[4]. In the
higher command, as was often to be shown again, there was
a danger at least as great as any from the rank and file. But, for
Vespasian, measures to prevent ambitious generals from starting
a new rising were less necessary than steps to secure their acquiescence in the ending of the old; for there were at least a few who
might have seized an opportunity to challenge his position, as
Hadrian's was challenged by Trajan's discontented marshals
(p. 303). Vespasian, however, was lucky in his contemporaries.
Some, like the governors of the Danubian provinces, lacked ability;
others, like Antonius Primus, were too small to command support
commensurate with their military gifts; and others again, like

---

[1] See Suetonius, *Vesp.* 8, 2–3.   [2] Tacitus, *Hist.* 1, 8.
[3] Plutarch, *Galba*, 4, 3 *sq.*; Tacitus, *Hist.* 1, 21 *sqq.*; 52 *sq.*, 57; 11, 74 *sqq.*
[4] See Suetonius, *Dom.* 23, 1—'*miles...paratus...ulcisci (occisum Domi-
tianum), nisi duces defuissent.*'

Suetonius Paullinus, had sacrificed their chances to a losing cause. Thus there remained none but the momentous figure of Mucianus himself. To the loyalty of that complex character Vespasian owed the Principate. In the crisis of A.D. 68 and 69 Rome was well served by the two men who made the great refusal. Mucianus, like Verginius Rufus, had claims which could rival Vespasian's, and in A.D. 70 the rapid return to conditions of peace was due not a little to the fact that the one obvious alternative to Vespasian was his staunch supporter. With his help, and mainly through his efforts, the morale of the army was restored, the legions went back to their stations on the frontier, the ambitions of individuals were restrained, and discipline, which Hadrian made the object of a cult, became again the 'praecipuum decus et stabilimentum Romani imperii[1].' The lasting value of these measures it was for the future to reveal: when Domitian was murdered, neither the dangerous restiveness of the Praetorians[2] nor such facts as may have justified the mysterious rumours from Syria needed force to make them innocuous (p. 196). But whatever difficulties time might bring, the immediate results were good: for the present, at least, Rome had escaped the menace of military domination, and the new Princeps was free to do as he would—even, if so he were inclined, to renew the Principate of Augustus.

II. THE FOUNDATIONS OF THE PRINCIPATE

The Augustan principate was a system so subtle that its essence even now is hard to recapture. That its foundations were laid in the law of the constitution is a fact beyond dispute. Augustus himself was an Italian, and a champion of those Italian traditions which in his day enshrined the Hellenic conviction that law should be supreme more faithfully than did the Hellenistic world itself. Whatever may have happened in the century which lay between them, Augustus would have taken as a compliment the words in which the younger Pliny praised the age of Trajan as one when men could say not 'Princeps super leges' but 'Leges super principem[3].' The large general powers which Augustus received in 27 and 23 B.C. had even been supplemented by various minor grants (vol. x, pp. 138 *sqq.*), and it cannot be denied that for most of the acts which government involved he had express legal authorization. Nevertheless, by legal categories alone the rule of Augustus cannot be explained. The *princeps* had, indeed, been

[1] Val. Max. II, 7 *pr.*
[2] Dio LXVIII, 3, 3; Aurelius Victor, *Caes.* XI, 9; cf. Dio LXVIII, 5, 4.
[3] *Pan.* 65, 1.

grafted onto, if not into, the body of the Republican State; but when, as happened at the start, he began to exert control, his control expressed itself in something more than the mere exercise of this legal right and that.

Throughout the first three centuries of the Empire the fundamental powers of the *princeps* were unchanged, their constitutional formulation was essentially unaltered. Yet even during the Julio-Claudian age these powers had been made to justify governments of the most varied types. The unpretentious guidance of the first citizen, Augustus; the sombre rule of Tiberius, trying to emulate his stepfather and earning the name of tyrant in his own despite; the open autocracy of Gaius, whose unstable mind was fired by its own conceit and a shallow acquaintance with the forms of Hellenistic kingship; Claudius' attempted return to the ways of Augustus, an attempt which the work of Tiberius and Gaius had frustrated before it was made; and finally the crude despotism of Nero's reckless end—all these were alike in their legal basis, and in little else. Public law by itself cannot explain the Principate as it worked from day to day; for behind it lay subtler factors exercising a powerful influence on the government. Not only could every *princeps* form his own conception of his rôle, but that conception could be modified or exaggerated by the interpretations of those who for reasons of their own welcomed an opportunity to stress this aspect or that of what they regarded as a monarchy; and even the imperial cult in its provincial form could react on the outlook of the *princeps* and his neighbours in Italy. Thus there were times when a *princeps* seemed to approach the kingship which is hedged with divinity, though the legal foundations of the Principate remained unchanged; and even in the first century A.D., while these foundations still hold firm, there could be temporary anticipations in outward form of what was to be permanent reality when the Empire became an absolutism confessed and undisguised[1].

The varying conceptions of the Principate which successive rulers sought to spread, and the changing attitude towards the *princeps* adopted by the population at large, are both reflected by the material evidence—whether in official documents like the Arch of Trajan at Beneventum, or in objects of purely private origin. The interpretation of these is rarely easy; and many of the conclusions they yield concern matters commonly treated as

[1] The evidence for these factors in the history of the Principate has been collected and discussed at length by A. Alföldi in *Röm. Mitt.* XLIX (1934) and L (1935).

religion, in connection with which they will be discussed (see below, vol. xii). But here it must be emphasized that, though the constitution itself was always in essence purely legal, its working is now revealed to have been deeply affected by the influence of that popular sentiment to which monuments of all kinds give a long neglected clue. The method which yielded to Mommsen almost all its valuable results is indispensable, indeed, but still inadequate; and if a later age can in some part make good the lack, its ability is due to an advantage which the previous generation was denied. Since Mommsen's day the experience of mankind has grown, and its knowledge of the place which the theory of a constitution may take when a nation has given itself up to the guidance of an accepted hero can yield a new understanding of Augustus' meaning when he wrote 'auctoritate omnibus praestiti[1].' Augustus captured the imagination of Italy, and his reward was a position in which with increasing confidence he could count on securing the adoption of his views, not by the issue of commands in a form which might remind men of the constitutional powers in the background, but merely by indicating the course which seemed to him most suitable. In speaking to provincials he could be forthright enough: 'I order all persons from the province of Cyrene who have been honoured with citizenship to bear their public burdens...[2].' But when he was dealing with senatorial officials— and it is in the relations between *princeps* and the Senate that the view of the Principate held by its various occupants is most clearly revealed—the tone is different and the language clearly inspired by the forms which the Senate itself employed in offering advice to a holder of *imperium*[3]: 'in my opinion governors of Crete and Cyrene will in future act rightly and as the circumstances demand if they put on the jury-panel in the province of Cyrene as many Greeks of the highest property assessment as Romans...'[4]

A suggestion from Augustus was enough; for it may safely be assumed that he would not have embodied a suggestion in a *mandatum* addressed to a provincial government if there had been any likelihood that nothing less than a direct command would gain obedience. And if a hint sufficed, the reason is to be found in his *auctoritas*—that influence which made men respond to his wishes because they were his, without asking questions, either of themselves or him, about his legal right to enforce his will by commands which their own enthusiasm made unnecessary.

---

[1] *Res Gestae*, 34; see x, p. 585.
[2] H. Malcovati, *Caes. Aug. Imp. oper. frag.*[2], p. 42, c, ll. 2 *sqq.*
[3] Cf. *Dig.* xvi, 1, 2, 1.   [4] Malcovati, *op. cit.* p. 40, ll. 14 *sqq.*

So in the Roman mind the *princeps* ceased to be regarded in the first place as the holder of constitutional powers, issuing orders which the law required to be obeyed, and became instead the foremost figure in the State, the guardian of a system which had saved Rome from threatening destruction and the embodiment of such accumulated prestige that his actions passed unscrutinized because men lacked the desire to challenge them.

The prestige with which Augustus endowed his own position had consequences which reached far. It was this which enabled his successors, as it had enabled him, to make what they would of the Principate itself. Gaius could put his own unprecedented interpretation on his office because, being *princeps*, he had inherited the *auctoritas* of his place; and when his end had shown that *auctoritas* was still something less than omnipotence, Claudius for the same reason could attempt to make Augustus his model and in doing so produce yet another version of the imperial rôle. Finally, the immunity from legal checks which the emperors enjoyed in fact, though not in theory, provoked a gradual extension of their activities[1]. That increase passed almost without question. The Roman world, as Galba is made to say, had become 'unius familiae quasi hereditas[2],' and the successors of Augustus enjoyed opportunities which could be claimed by none but the heads of what Tacitus describes as 'fundata longo imperio domus[3].'

With Nero the house became extinct. Its prestige was dissipated; and, if it could be recaptured at all, so much of it as clung to the imperial position must be fostered with all care in order that the new rulers might acquire that pre-eminence among the great families in Rome which was essential to the stability of the Principate itself. It was the *auctoritas* of Augustus which had exalted the office of the *princeps*: now the office itself must exalt Vespasian and his kin (p. 4). 'Auctoritas et quasi maiestas quaedam ut scilicet inopinato et adhuc nouo principi deerat[4]'; and if at the outset something was done to make good the lack by his miracles of healing[5], a subtler method was needed to win the allegiance of those whose opinion was most valuable in Rome. For one who was regarded as a *parvenu* to array himself in the trappings of royalty and to act the god would have been disastrous, even if it had not been a course for which by character and training Vespasian was singularly unfitted. Its inevitable results must have been to alienate the Senate, to attract the resentful ridicule

---

[1] See *e.g.* Suetonius, *Claud.* 23, 2 *ad fin.*   [2] Tacitus, *Hist.* I, 16.
[3] Tacitus, *Hist.* II, 76.   [4] Suetonius, *Vesp.* 7, 2.
[5] Tacitus, *Hist.* IV, 81; Suetonius, *Vesp.* 7, 2 *sq.*; Dio LXV, 8, 1.

of Italy, and—worst of all—to throw the *princeps* back for support on that army which it was his foremost care to exclude from the business of government. He chose a better way: the power of the Flavian house was to rest on the foundations which Augustus himself had laid. Circumstances, indeed, had changed since A.D. 14; the later Julio-Claudians had left their marks; and after Gaius, Claudius and Nero *civilitas* in a *princeps* could no longer be carried to the lengths which it had reached under Augustus. Nevertheless Vespasian made Augustus his model. Even before he reached Rome, in his letters to the Senate 'ut princeps loquebatur, civilia de se et rei publicae egregia[1]'; and when he came to face the task of gaining that unrivalled eminence in the State which had been the prerogative of his predecessors, his method in its attainment was not to command obedience but to win respect. Above all in his dealings with the Senate, though that body had greatly changed in the days of the Claudian emperors, and though Vespasian himself was to change it still more, he showed throughout the consistent consideration which alone could enlist its good will.

To talk of 'Flavian absolutism' is to mislead; for, despite their differences, in the most essential quality of all the principate of Vespasian and the principate of Augustus were indistinguishable. The essence of the Augustan principate was that a man equipped with powers which in theory were great and in fact were overwhelming exercised them, not in the arbitrary manner of an autocrat, but in a way which took account of public opinion. For that reason the system of government which he devised was the nearest approach made by the ancient world to a constitutional monarchy. In it the *princeps* was the first servant of the State, holding a position near enough to that of the Stoic king for lapses to invite comparisons and for philosophy to take on some slight political significance. Indeed when Marcus brought sentimental Stoicism to the throne, though the outlook of the *princeps* was affected, the form of the Principate was not. The system was a monarchy in which the monarch, not of compulsion but of choice, exposed himself to the force of educated opinion and so guided his actions that it should not be outraged. Of that opinion the foremost organ was the Senate, and the relations between Senate and *princeps* are consequently the measure of the extent to which this emperor or that was departing from the Augustan version of the Principate in the direction of Autocracy. Of friction under Vespasian there was little or none (for Helvidius

---

[1] Tacitus, *Hist.* IV, 3.

Priscus brought his fate upon himself[1]), and in his rule may be seen a restoration of the Principate in a form as near to the Augustan as the circumstances of his age allowed. Nor was that all. The work of Vespasian had effects of long duration. For though the Imperial powers continued slowly to increase, as they had increased in the days of the Julio-Claudians, the Principate retained the essential character with which Vespasian had left it until it was changed in the chaos of the third century. The Flavian conception of government is no more to be inferred from the rule of Domitian than is the Antonine from that of Commodus. Domitian and Commodus were not typical: they were aberrations from the type which Vespasian chose to make the norm. That choice was inspired by Augustus, and thus it was that Vespasian, by extending its life for a century and a half, made the Augustan Principate not an episode in history, but an epoch.

III. THE *PRINCEPS* AND THE CONSTITUTION

Vespasian owed the principate to his troops—a fact which his forthright honesty so far confessed that, instead of following the example of Vitellius and dating his rule from the day of his acceptance by the Senate[2], he frankly admitted that it had begun when he was first acclaimed at Alexandria[3]. It was, indeed, no new experience for the Senate to be confronted with a *princeps* of the soldiers' choosing (vol. x, p. 666 *sq.*); but the Senate alone could give legality to what without it would remain a usurpation, and Vespasian, faced with the task of establishing a new Imperial house, was in no position to despise the help which he could get from that influential quarter. Accordingly he acted with deference; and the Fathers, with less misgiving than when the same grants were made to Otho[4] and Vitellius[5], voted him the customary prerogatives as soon as Vitellius was dead, when he and Titus were also designated for the ordinary consulships of the following year and Domitian was offered a praetorship, together with *consulare imperium*[6]. Thenceforward he held his position by legal right, and about his accession there would be no more to say were it not for the fortunate survival of a fragment from a series of bronze tables on which his powers were set out at length[7].

The famous document set up by Cola di Rienzi in the Basilica

---

[1] See p. 8 *sq.*
[2] Dessau 241, l. 85 *sq.*; cf. Mommsen, *Röm. Staatsrecht* II³, p. 842, n. 4.
[3] Tacitus, *Hist.* II, 79; Suetonius, *Vesp.* 6, 3.
[4] Tacitus, *Hist.* I, 47.   [5] *Ib.* II, 55.
[6] *Ib.* IV, 3.   [7] Dessau 244.

of St John Lateran, and now to be seen in the Capitoline Museum, moots questions of the first importance about the nature of the Flavian Principate. Nothing now remains but the end of a text which when complete must have been long, and in what survives there are no more than seven final clauses, with part of an eighth, followed by what describes itself as a 'sanctio' giving indemnity to all who in obeying this measure might infringe some other statute or legal enactment. Short as it is, however, this scrap has much to reveal. Despite lapses in grammar and orthography, the impressive lettering can prove that its contents were of more than ephemeral interest: it is not a draft but a statute. Yet its form is ambiguous; for though it is twice described by its own wording as a 'lex,' all except the final *sanctio* is phrased in the way appropriate, not to a law, but to a decree of the Senate. Nevertheless, its nature is not in doubt. From the middle of the principate of Augustus popular assemblies at Rome had fallen into rapid decline. Their approval of such proposals as were submitted to them became more and more of a formality, and in this law we have a measure of the length to which the decline had gone by the beginning of the Flavian age. Despite the solemnity of an occasion on which a new *princeps* was to be made, the formulation of the proposals in the preliminary senatorial decree was allowed to stand unaltered when they were submitted to the People for passage into law.

Though it is clear that the measure was what Rome of those days was content to accept as a *lex rogata*, in the absence of its most important sections the significance of the enactment as a whole is open to dispute. From the minutes of the Arval Brotherhood, whose activities during the first five months of 69 are known in detail[1], it appears that at this time the creation of a new Princeps involved repeated reference to the People: on separate occasions they conferred the *tribunicia potestas* and elected him first to his priesthoods and then to the office of Pontifex Maximus[2]. And, besides these, from some source or other he had to receive the all-important *imperium*. That this could be legally conferred by either Army or Senate, as Mommsen had supposed[3], is a view which can no longer be defended since it was demonstrated[4] that of these two the Senate alone was concerned; and it is only slightly less probable that Mommsen was mistaken, too, in maintaining[5]

---

[1] Dessau, 241.　　　[2] Cf. Mommsen, *Röm. Staatsrecht* II³, p. 1107.
[3] *Op. cit.* II³, p. 842.
[4] By O. Th. Schulz, *Das Wesen des röm. Kaisertums der ersten zwei Jahrhunderte*, chap. III.　　　[5] *Op. cit.* II³, pp. 842 *sqq.*

that the *imperium* was granted by a process in which the People had no part[1]. According to the theory of the Republic it was in the People alone that *imperium* had its origin[2]; and, if ever this doctrine was respected when the creation of a *princeps* was in question, it may well have been observed at the accession of Vespasian. For he was the first of a new line, in need of support from every quarter; and that his friends did not despise such help as could be won by deference to the traditions of the constitution is suggested by the emphasis which numismatic records lay on Libertas[3].

Nevertheless, the various attempts made to prove that the extant clauses come from a measure which in its earlier part conferred on Vespasian one or other of his main constitutional powers cannot be regarded as successful. Any such theory conflicts with Roman practice by which, when an individual was invested with authority by the State, the ways in which he should exercise it were not specified but left to his discretion; and this difficulty is not to be removed by the suggestion that after the death of Vitellius the Senate, by a bold innovation, formulated a detailed definition of the manner in which the *princeps* might use his rights in order to prevent a repetition of Nero's final tyranny[4]. The Senate was then in no condition to impose checks on a man who had fought his way to power; and the measure itself, so far from reducing his authority, in fact leaves it almost limitless. At most it may be said that, if either the *imperium* or the *tribunicia potestas* was bestowed in the missing sections, the claims of the former might be supported by the nature of the grants set out in the extant part; for two of them at least—the right to conclude treaties (and probably to declare war) and to change the course of the *pomerium*—cannot be brought into constitutional relation with the tribunician power.

There is, however, much to commend another view, which would see in this law a consolidated grant of miscellaneous rights additional to those which formed the main basis of the Imperial position[5]. Supplementary powers of this sort had from time to time been given to Augustus; for instance, the clause with which the extant fragment begins—if it is rightly assumed when complete to have authorized Vespasian to declare peace and war as well as

---

[1] See J. Kromayer, *Die rechtliche Begründung des Principats*, pp. 34 *sqq.*
[2] See *e.g.* Cicero, *de lege agr.* II, 7, 17.
[3] *E.g. B.M.C. Rom. Emp.* II, p. xlvii *sq.*
[4] O. Hirschfeld, *Die kaiserlichen Verwaltungsbeamten*, p. 475.
[5] For an approach to this interpretation see Hirschfeld, *op. cit.* p. 475 n., of which Mommsen's criticism is to be found in *Röm. Staatsrecht* II³, p. 878 n. 1.

to make treaties with whomsoever he would—to some extent
repeats a grant which there is good reason to believe that Augustus
had formally received (vol. x, p. 141). Thus, when the inscription
mentions Augustus, Tiberius and Claudius as predecessors who
had enjoyed this particular right, it may be agreed that the right
had been given them by law. Elsewhere, however, the nature of the
precedent is more doubtful. Vespasian is permitted 'to extend and
advance the limits of the *pomerium* when he shall think it in the
interests of the State, as was permitted to Tiberius Claudius Caesar
Augustus Germanicus'; but it is by no means certain that Claudius
had received any express authority to change the *pomerium* when
he did so in A.D. 49. The surviving evidence would rather suggest
that Claudius justified himself by a half-forgotten tradition of the
Republic and that, such was his *auctoritas*, no objection was raised.
But, if this is doubtful, it is harder still to believe that Augustus
had been explicitly and formally given the constitutional 'right
and power to do all such things as he may deem to serve the interests
of the State and the dignity of all things divine and human, public
and private'; and yet for this too he is adduced as a precedent,
together with Tiberius and Claudius. And to these considerations
may be added the fact that two of the rights here granted are
supported by no precedent at all.

Throughout its history the Principate was in course of development. Gradually its holders increased their powers, not so
much by securing formal authorization for acts from which their
predecessors had been debarred as by using the opportunities
afforded by their prestige quietly to assume new functions, which
thereafter were regarded as part of the imperial prerogative.
This process had gone far even before the death of Nero, when
supremacy suddenly passed to a new and undistinguished family.
Until the Flavians had acquired the pre-eminent influence of
their predecessors it was, if not necessary, at least desirable that
every act of the *princeps* should be plainly justified by law. Accordingly the past was searched, and precedents were collected in
a single act which conferred on Vespasian the right to do both
those things to which earlier emperors had been empowered by
special enactment and those other things which their *auctoritas*
had allowed them to do without fear of challenge. And finally,
to provide for those emergencies in which the *princeps* might be
required to take action of a kind not contemplated even in this
exhaustive code, an attempt was perhaps even made to formulate
the use to which *auctoritas* itself had been put. For such may well
have been the intention of the remarkable clause which formally

empowers Vespasian to take any action of whatever kind which he may deem to be in the general interest.

If such an interpretation is justified, it may well be no mere accident that the only law now partly extant about the prerogatives of the *princeps* is a law for the benefit of Vespasian. The extinction of the line which traced its descent from Julius Caesar and Augustus produced problems of a kind which had not arisen since the first establishment of the Principate, and it would not be a matter for surprise if one result of the transition to a new régime had been the codification of customs created by the old. In its turn this legal formulation of what in the past had been no more than common practice cannot have been without consequences of its own. To concentrate in Vespasian's person explicit authority to perform every act for which Augustus, Tiberius or Claudius supplied a precedent by itself was to give him powers greater than any single *princeps* had exercised before; but the attempt to find a legal substitute for the *auctoritas* which the upstart lacked went farther and did all that law could do towards turning the Principate into an autocracy. Nevertheless, the Principate survived for more than a hundred and fifty years, and for that reason the effects of the changes made on Vespasian's accession are easy to exaggerate. Henceforward it was not the constitution which stood between Rome and absolutism: as will be seen (p. 416 *sq.*), however, there were other barriers not wholly ineffective.

IV. THE IMPERIAL HOUSE AND THE TRANSMISSION OF THE PRINCIPATE

After the settlement, as before, the character of the government was determined, not by the powers with which the *princeps* had been invested, but by the use to which these powers were put. From the outset it was clear that Vespasian turned for guidance to the past, and more particularly to those of his predecessors whose outlook was least monarchical. Claudius had made Augustus his model (vol. x, p. 668 *sq.*), and Vespasian so far respected Claudius as to insist on his divinity and rebuild the temple in his honour on the Caelian (p. 19). But he could not have been content to emulate one whose reputation was so controversial as that of Claudius, and there is evidence enough to show that it was Augustus himself whom Vespasian sought to take as his example. Not only does his coinage hark back at times to Augustan themes, but in the far more significant matter of the imperial title there is a return to Augustan usage. By a decision which was not challenged while the Principate survived, he reverted to the *praenomen imperatoris*; and when he chose to follow this immediately with the name 'Caesar,' Imperator Caesar Vespasianus Augustus bore a style which had its justification and its value in the fact that 'Imperator Caesar divi filius Augustus' was its model. Yet even so Vespasian was at a disadvantage: he was not himself 'divi filius,' and there was still a need for measures which would increase, not his constitutional powers, but the distinction of the *princeps* in the eyes of the Roman world. To this end, like Vitellius before him (vol. x, p. 826), he seems to have employed the consulship. After the settlement of 23 B.C. Augustus had only twice been consul again, on each occasion for a special reason; and his successors had abstained from any frequent tenure of the office, once they had held it more often than the three times which were the most that any but a *princeps* could expect[1]. Tiberius had been consul five times before his death, though only twice since his accession; Gaius took the office four times, and Claudius and Nero five times each. But during the ten years of Vespasian's Principate the emperor and his two sons held twenty-one consulships between them; and Domitian, though he seems to have found less value in the office towards the end of his life, so far followed his father's practice as to be consul in ten out of the fifteen years of his own supremacy (p. 23 *sq.*).

This exploitation of the consulship is not difficult to interpret. That the powers it brought with it were of no account is clear from the fact that the *princeps* did not retain office throughout the year: Domitian, indeed, often abdicated on the Ides of January and his longest tenure ended on the first of May[2]. Nor again can it be regarded as an attempt to exclude senators from the highest magistracy; for there is strong evidence to suggest that suffect consulships now began almost regularly to be reduced from four months' duration to two[3], so that, even if the Imperial house had monopolized the office until the end of April, it would still have been possible for eight members of the aristocracy in general to obtain consular rank from a place in one of the four colleges which would follow between May and December. Suetonius says of Domitian '[consulatus] omnes...paene titulo tenus gessit'; and it was the title which the Flavians sought. The number of their consulships, and the number of the years to which, as *consules ordinarii*, they gave their names[4], marked them

---

[1] Pliny, *Ep.* II, 1, 2.　　　　[2] Suetonius, *Dom.* 13, 3.

[3] See H. Furneaux, F. Haverfield and J. G. C. Anderson, *Cornelii Taciti De vita Agricolae*, p. 168.　　　[4] Pliny, *Pan.* 58, 2 *sq.*

off from the rest of the nobility and so helped to gain them the unquestioned eminence which it was their urgent business to attain. But when at length the position of the house was secure and Domitian's grim consciousness of his unique responsibilities still sought titles adequate to his more autocratic conception of the Principate, a mere magistracy ceased to satisfy. After the revolt of Saturninus in 89 Domitian's consulships became less frequent, and the reason is easy to conjecture: to be consul for a few weeks and to give his name to a year were matters almost of indifference to one whose conception of his station allowed him to be addressed as 'dominus et deus' (p. 412). But when Domitian fell and the hatred of his memory provoked violent reaction towards a government of the Augustan type, in a Rome which the Flavians had made familiar with the idea that the Principate could pass from one house to another there was no need for his successors to glorify themselves by collecting titles. Trajan became consul only four times as *princeps*, Hadrian twice, Pius three times, Marcus not at all (having entered his third and final consulship nine weeks before Pius died), and Commodus only five times in the twelve years and more by which he survived his father.

If Vespasian used repeated consulships to raise his family above the rest of the aristocracy at Rome, by themselves they did not exhaust the expedients which might be invoked to serve his end. The catastrophe which had followed Nero's death was warning enough that the Flavian house must be put beyond reach of challenge, not only while Vespasian was alive, but after he had gone; and the new *princeps* found himself faced with the problem which Augustus had spent over thirty years in solving. His successor must be marked so clearly that a position still in theory elective would pass with the same certainty as under an hereditary monarchy. The choice of candidate was easy, for Titus was worthy of his father; and if his matrimonial enterprise had so far failed to produce a son, his younger brother Domitian, despite his conceit, could well be made the second string. It is not without point that Mucianus in urging Vespasian to seek the Principate is made by Tacitus to stress the value of these youths[1]. Accordingly, while Domitian was given honours with a generosity reserved for members of the Imperial house, Titus received distinctions which marked the heir apparent. Both took the name of Caesar, both at first were 'Principes Juventutis' (p. 6), and both became *sacerdotes collegiorum omnium*[2]. But already in A.D. 70 after the capture of Jerusalem Titus had been hailed as *imperator*,

---

[1] *Hist.* II, 77.   [2] Dessau 258, 267.

and, though he was denied the independent triumph which the Senate is said to have proposed [1], he was allowed to share the honour with Vespasian in June, 71. In the following month he began his tenure of the *tribunicia potestas*, and from that time not only did he keep pace with his father in the numbering of its years, as in the reckoning of imperatorial salutations, but he was the inseparable colleague of the *princeps* in all the offices, whether of consul or of censor, which Vespasian thought fit to take. Nevertheless, the principate of Titus had not begun. He was not called 'Augustus,' nor was he officially given the *praenomen imperatoris* [2]; and even his appointment to the sole command of the Praetorians, complimentary as it was to his filial devotion, emphasized his concern not with the whole army but with a single corps and put him in a position which, however powerful, had never been given to a man of senatorial rank before A.D. 70 [3]. But though he was not the equal of the first, Titus was now beyond dispute the second citizen of Rome: without exaggeration he could be called 'particeps atque etiam tutor imperii [4].'

The work of Vespasian had its reward. In A.D. 79 Titus stepped into his place unchallenged, and at once the Imperial house gained new solidity. Its head, and his brother, were now *Divi filii*. Thus the Flavians moved nearer to the position which Augustus and his successors had enjoyed, and the move is made important by the use to which it was turned by Domitian; for of Vespasian and Titus it cannot be said that they exploited their opportunities of worship [5]. There was no doubt, indeed, of Vespasian's determination to retain the Principate in his own family, even if he was not above strengthening his position by marriage ties with the nobility: not only were his sons kept prominently in the public eye, but, by a practice for which precedents were plentiful and which became normal in the second century, the distinction of the Imperial house was stressed still further by the honours bestowed on its ladies. Vespasian's only daughter, though she was almost certainly dead before he became *princeps*, was called 'Augusta' and was later deified [6], as were

---

[1] Josephus, *Bell. Jud.* VII [5, 3], 121.

[2] The sporadic monuments which seem to contradict this statement (see P.W. *s.v.* Flavius (207), col. 2709; *s.v.* Imperator, col. 1151) cannot outweigh the contrary evidence, of which the most valuable is provided by the coinage, and must be regarded as inaccurate.

[3] Tacitus, *Hist.* IV, 68.   [4] Suetonius, *Titus* 6, 1.

[5] Mommsen, *Ges. Schr.* IV, p. 269.

[6] Statius, *Silv.* I, I, 98 and Mommsen, *Röm. Staatsrecht* II³, p. 822 n. 1; and, for another view, *B.M.C. Rom. Emp.* II, p. lxxv.

Julia, the daughter of Titus[1], and Domitian's infant son[2]; and the name 'Augusta,' which may have indicated some political authority when it was borne by Livia and the younger Agrippina[3], was given by Domitian to his wife[4], as it had been by Nero to Poppaea, as a title appropriate to the consort of the *princeps*. Before long this usage was extended. Marciana, Trajan's sister[5], and her daughter Matidia the Elder[6] were both called 'Augusta' when alive, and were both, like Trajan's father, deified when dead; and their honours were not peculiar.

But for Domitian titles were not enough. With him the dignity of the Flavians was an obsession, and the knowledge that his father, his brother and his sister had been added to the number of the gods can scarcely have failed to affect the new conception which he formed of his own position. The Porticus Divorum, which he erected on the Campus Martius in their honour, and the Templum Gentis Flaviae, built on the site of the house in which he had been born (p. 34), were expressions of an outlook which found the existing accommodation on the Palatine inadequate[7]. Though the palace was not a temple, there was a great and significant difference between the unpretentious house with which Augustus had long been content and the imposing home of one who called his bed by the name proper to the couches of the gods and who could allow himself to be described as 'dominus et deus[8].' Such was Domitian's interpretation of the high prestige which the efforts of Vespasian had secured—efforts which were wasted when Domitian died at the age of forty-four,

[1] Dessau 8906; *B.M.C. Rom. Emp.* II, p. 350 *sq.*

[2] *B.M.C. Rom. Emp.* II, pp. 311, 347.

[3] Tacitus, *Ann.* I, 8; XII, 26; cf. Mommsen, *Röm. Staatsrecht* II[3], p. 821 *sq.*

[4] Suetonius, *Dom.* 3, 1.   [5] Dessau 298, 327.

[6] Dessau 327.   [7] See Martial VII, 56.

[8] Suetonius, *Dom.* 13, 1–2. This phrase, which provoked strong resentment (Martial X, 72, 8; Pliny, *Pan.* 2, 3), was objectionable because by its association with 'deus' the word 'dominus' was given a sense even more offensive than that which it bore when applied to a master by his slave or to a *patronus* by his freedman. But Domitian's innovation left no permanent result: the present writer does not accept the views expressed in *Harvard Theol. Review* XXVIII, 1935, p. 34 *sq.* On the whole subject see M. Bang, 'Über den Gebrauch der Anrede *Domine* in gemeinen Leben' in L. Friedländer-G. Wissowa, *Darstellungen aus der Sittengeschichte Roms* IV[9-10], pp. 82 *sqq.* In the same way, though the Imperial household slowly became more like a Court, Domitian did not impose new ceremonial on his successors: Pius and Marcus were still as indifferent to forms as Augustus or Vespasian (see Marc. Aur. *Med.* I, 16; VI, 13 and 30).

leaving none to follow him but two grand-nephews, whom he had, indeed, adopted but who were still no more than boys.

With the accession of Nerva, the idea that the Principate should become the possession of a natural family fell into intelligible disrepute, and Rome, whether from conviction or because chance brought the childless to power, had recourse to a principle which it had been one of the great achievements of the Republic to establish. The *populares* of the last two centuries B.C. had fought with success to secure that office should be filled by the best candidates to be found (vol. IX, p. 138 *sq.*), and this doctrine had in general been accepted by Augustus (vol. X, p. 177). But in one most vital connection he had compromised with his ideal: the overwhelming difficulty of ensuring an unquestioned succession to himself had forced him to make use of the prestige which he had communicated to his relatives and to look for an heir only among those who were in some sense members of his family. Such was the system which, well as it had worked in A.D. 14, was condemned when it gave the Empire first to Gaius and then to Nero; but, though Galba had hinted at a better way in his adoption of Piso Licinianus (vol. X, p. 814), the task of establishing a line drove Vespasian back on the same expedients as it had compelled Augustus to adopt, and the Principate was reserved for a single family even more strictly than before. When Domitian had followed Nero and a second house became extinct, change came at last. 'Imperaturus omnibus eligi debet ex omnibus[1]' are words which mark the triumph of the *populares*; for they mean that the system which, to its great advantage, had made the administration a *carrière ouverte aux talents* had now been extended to the Principate itself.

The result was a sequence of rulers without parallel in Roman history. Trajan, Hadrian, Pius and Marcus maintained for more than eighty years a level of efficiency, devotion and common-sense, which, except in a few periods both rare and brief, had not been known since the death of Augustus. Of them the first three had all passed forty when they were designated heirs, even though Trajan had shown interest in Hadrian since his marriage to Sabina in A.D. 100; and Marcus, though he was chosen young, was trained for his high destiny from the age of sixteen. It is true that even now relationship with the *princeps* may still have been a commendation; for, though Nerva and Trajan were unconnected, as probably were Hadrian and Pius, Hadrian himself was son of a first-cousin of Trajan and his nephew by marriage, as Marcus was

---

[1] Pliny, *Pan.* 7, 6.

of Pius. Yet, even so, with Trajan at least family considerations counted for so little that he did nothing to secure the claims of Hadrian until his last short illness had begun—if then (p. 300).

What told was merit, which the *princeps* recognized by adopting the man who showed it. The political consequences of this act must be distinguished from its effects in law. At a time when birth had fallen into disfavour as a claim to the Imperial place it was natural that a step which revealed the emperor's views on the succession should not be allowed to establish remoter claims in those who might now become his grandsons. The significance of adoption was confined to the adopted son alone, and no promise was made to his children. To put this beyond doubt, the name 'Caesar' was turned to the use which is normal in later history. At first a *cognomen* of the Julii, since the extinction of the Julian line it had commonly been borne by the *princeps* and his agnatic descendants, without regard to their prospects of political power; but when Hadrian adopted first L. Ceionius Commodus and then the future Emperor Pius, though each of these in turn was called 'Caesar,' Commodus, who alone had a surviving son, was not allowed to pass on the name, and the youth remained without it until he was made Caesar and Augustus simultaneously in A.D. 161. Thus it happened that only the *princeps* and his intended successor were Caesars; and, since the *princeps* himself was distinguished as Augustus—the appellation which he shared with none—Caesar, now no longer a name but a title, came in practice to be the mark of the heir-presumptive. It may, indeed, even be said that the heir was not completely designated until his adoption had been followed by the grant of this title; for though Marcus and Verus had both been adopted by Pius in A.D. 138, when Pius became emperor in the following year, Marcus was made Caesar and Verus was not; and only then was Marcus indicated as the next Augustus. The title, however, like the adoption, did no more than reveal the hopes of the *princeps*. If the Caesar was to have constitutional powers, they must still be constitutionally conferred, and this step was not necessarily an immediate sequel to the creation of a Caesar. Marcus was Caesar for seven years before he received *imperium* and *tribunicia potestas*. In his case, however, his youth was a reason for delay, and he provides no exception to the practice by which a Caesar was invested as soon as might reasonably be with the authority which Augustus had used to mark his destined successor[1].

[1] Pius seems even to have borne the *praenomen imperatoris* before the death of Hadrian: see Dessau 331.

Despite the skill with which earlier practice was thus adapted to the needs of an age when the Principate had ceased to be the possession of a single family, the enlargement of the field in which candidates might be sought inevitably increased the number of those who might seek to press their own claims, possibly by force. The only security against disputes over the succession was the personal prestige of the *princeps* who had made the choice and the reputation of the man on whom it fell; but this security was greatly strengthened when Marcus for the first time made the Principate continuous. 'Successor,' says Pliny, 'etiamsi nolis, habendus est; non est habendus socius, nisi velis[1].' A *socius* was what Marcus chose to have, and a partner in the fullest possible sense. As soon as Pius was dead he caused Verus to be appointed colleague of himself as Augustus, constitutionally not his adjutant but his equal[2]. It is true that, by the marriage of Verus to Annia Lucilla, Marcus acquired the superior position of a father-in-law, and that it was left for Pupienus and Balbinus in A.D. 238 to duplicate the office of Pontifex Maximus[3], which Marcus retained for himself[4]; but in their secular powers both were alike and the Roman world had two Augusti at once.

The motives of Marcus in taking a colleague are not recorded. The correspondence of Fronto contains ample proof that, even without the complications of war, business which ordinary routine brought before the *princeps* by now was enough to occupy the time of two[5]. Nevertheless, though this consideration may have been cogent, the functions of the two Augusti were not formally specified or distinguished, and nothing was done to make it necessary that for the future two should always be in office. So, when Verus died in A.D. 169, Marcus was left as sole ruler; and though in A.D. 166, by bestowing the title 'Caesar' on his two sons, he had given a sign that the new system was more than temporary, he remained without a colleague until A.D. 177, when Commodus became Augustus—in his seventeenth year. Three years later Marcus died, and so far as it provided for continuity of control his plan proved good. Commodus was left supreme, freed from the necessity of seeking further powers because his

---

[1] *Pan.* 9, 1.

[2] S.H.A. *Marcus*, 7, 5 sq.

[3] S.H.A. *Maximus et Balbinus*, 8, 1; Dessau, 496.

[4] The suggestion of inscriptions like Dessau 361 that Verus was Pontifex Maximus is disproved by Dessau 369, the accuracy of which may safely be assumed.

[5] *Ad Ant. Imp.* II, 1 (p. 104 N); cf. *ad Verum Imp.* I, 3 (p. 116 N).

powers were already complete. The perils of a vacant Principate were avoided and succession was no longer hazardous, because there was no succession; for now the future government was determined, not when an Augustus died, but when he secured the appointment of his colleague. As a safeguard against dangers like those of A.D. 68–9 the new system proved sound: that it left Rome in the hands of Commodus was due to the indifference of Marcus towards the methods which had chosen Trajan, Hadrian and Pius. Commodus had been promoted because he was his father's son, and Rome was to have another lesson, though not the last, in the risks to be run when holders of unrestricted power are chosen by the accident of birth.

V. *PRINCEPS* AND SENATE: THE CENSORSHIP

The various expedients by which succession to the Principate was protected from the hazards of war did nothing to increase the freedom of choice exercised by the Senate; but, though the constitutional power of that body to confer his powers on the *princeps* came to be expressed in formal votes for the benefit of a candidate to whom there was no alternative, the Senate played a leading part in determining the nature of the government. During the first three centuries of the Empire the lot of the Senate was cast in hard places: at best it enjoyed a precarious freedom, at worst it was the victim of something near to persecution. Yet all the time its thankless fortitude was exercising a decisive influence on the character of the Imperial régime. It was among the senators that the public opinion of Rome and Italy found reflection, if not open expression; and, even though the House might fawn on a Domitian with its resolutions, its members did not fail to resent a lack of *civilitas* in the *princeps*. Impotence did not reconcile it to treatment which outraged its dignity, and dignity demanded that the *princeps* should show it the deference due to a body whose history entitled it to regard the Principate itself as something new and whose individual members, filling as they did most of the chief administrative posts, could claim an experience of affairs which entitled them to a judgment of their own. Moreover, powerless as the Senate might be to impose its will on the *princeps* by formal process, its hostility remained a formidable danger. Gaius, Nero and Domitian had all given it offence; and, though the Senate was not directly responsible for their ends, it was a sobering reflection that all three had met their deaths by violence. To fall foul of the Senate was dangerous, not because the Senate habitually used the knife against its enemies, but because its ill-will was reserved for those who had forfeited their popularity with that large class of educated citizens who were the strength of Italy and the Empire. Thus an emperor's relations with the Senate supplied a measure of the degree to which his conception of the Imperial duties harmonized with those ideals of government which distinguished Principate from Autocracy. Between the accession of Vespasian and the death of Marcus it was only during the last decade of Domitian's rule that the Senate and *princeps* were dangerously estranged. Vespasian himself, indeed, had been drastic in his treatment of Helvidius Priscus, and Hadrian in the last years of his life had lost the friendship which he had enjoyed for the greater part of his career; but it was not till Commodus returned to the ways of Domitian and advanced towards the destination which he reached when he became 'invictus Romanus Hercules[1]' that the Senate, now said even to have been called 'Senatus Commodianus[2],' found itself confronted again with the threat of despotism.

If collaboration with the Senate served to keep the *princeps* in touch with opinion which was quick to resent signs of autocratic ambition, the emperor exercised an even more powerful influence on the Senate. Like other institutions in the Roman world, the Senate was threatened with atrophy by the mere presence of the *princeps*, whose superior information about the needs of government combined with his oppressive prestige to encourage the Fathers in a lazy reliance on his judgment and that of his advisers. The 'homines ad servitutem parati[3],' whom Tiberius had tried to stir into some show of independence (vol. x, p. 617) and Claudius had rated for their acquiescence in a procedure so perfunctory as to be unworthy of the tradition of the House (vol. x, p. 697 *sq.*), were always ready to make fresh surrenders of their rights and then to regret the loss. Their submissiveness to Nero[4] and their silence in the 'curia trepida et elinguis[5]' of Domitian's time may indeed have been part of prudence; nor was it strange that, despite the urgings of Helvidius Priscus, the House should have shrunk from a serious decision about public expenditure in A.D. 70 until Vespasian had been consulted (p. 7 *sq.*). But it was a sign of alarming weakness that, when judicial corruption defied the laws and its own decrees, the Senate, so far from taking the action which was its undoubted right, confessed its own incompetence by put-

[1] See Dio LXXIII, 15, 5 and Dessau 400.
[2] S.H.A. *Comm.* 8, 9.   [3] Tacitus, *Ann.* III, 65.
[4] *E.g.* Tacitus, *Ann.* XIV, 49.   [5] Pliny, *Ep.* VIII, 14, 8.

ting the whole problem in the hands of Trajan[1]; and even its best friends might pardonably have despaired when the secret ballot for elections, which Trajan had apparently introduced in order to protect the freedom and increase the dignity of the proceedings[2], was seized by some of the Fathers as an opportunity to dishonour the House by writing ribaldries and obscenities on their votes[3]. There was, indeed, no lack of evidence to prove that the Senate had learnt little and forgotten much since the end of the Republic. Nerva himself, whose sympathy was beyond dispute, found himself forced, like Mucianus before him (p. 8), to restrain the Fathers from neglecting their proper duties to open a vindictive campaign against the agents of the late oppression (p. 191); and these reminders are only two among many which survive to show how readily the Senate would have relapsed into the futile bickering of the late Republic if once the firm hand of the *princeps* had been withdrawn.

Nevertheless, under Imperial control the Senate was cast for an important part, and its responsibilities were enough to stir an active interest in its composition. In the choice of its members the influence of the emperor was increased by the growing use to which the censorship was put. Like Claudius before him, Vespasian assumed this office, and, though he and his colleague Titus seem only to have exercised its functions for the traditional period of eighteen months[4], they associated it so closely with the Imperial position that it was no great innovation when Domitian in A.D. 85 had himself made sole censor for life, or when Trajan took the final step and acted as if the rights of a censor, even though not expressly conferred, were latent in the powers of the *princeps*[5]. The result was important. The Senate needed new blood to maintain its vitality, whether from Italy or from the provinces, and the addition of a member like Agricola's father was an indisputable gain. But in the first century of the Empire there had been no permanent means by which a man of middle age could enter the Senate with a status appropriate to his years: such a one, if he was to become a member at all, could normally expect no relief from the necessity of competing for a quaestorship with young men of twenty-four born of senatorial stock and having them as his equals for the rest of his career. But the censorship opened a better way: with its help a man could be exempted from the

[1] Pliny, *Ep.* v, 13 (14), 7; cf. IV, 25, 2; VI, 19, 3; VII, 6, 14; VII, 10, 2.
[2] Pliny, *Ep.* III, 20.
[3] Pliny, *Ep.* IV, 25, 1.   [4] Censorinus, *de die nat.* 18, 14.
[5] Compare Pliny, *Pan.* 45, 4 with *e.g.* Dessau 845, 2: cf. Dessau 1054.

earlier stages of the senatorial career and enrolled in the House with the immediate seniority which became his age and qualified him for a post of the sort for which he was suited by experience.

The policy which this device was meant to serve would be a matter of dispute, even if it could be assumed that the intentions of all emperors who admitted men to the Senate by *adlectio* were the same. One plausible suggestion—that Vespasian called in large numbers of recruits from the romanized provinces to make good the failings of what had been an essentially Italian body[1]—is not confirmed by the extant evidence. If it were true, the members whom he created would have been predominantly, if not wholly, of provincial origin, whereas more than half of those recorded are Italians[2]. Nor again is it likely that even Trajan and Hadrian, who were more generous than their predecessors in opening the Curia to Greeks, sought provincial senators in order to send out as governors natives of the regions to be controlled. Such men were, indeed, freely employed in the provinces, but cases where a man is found engaged in the region of his home are too rare to justify the suggestion that what the government sought was a degree of local knowledge which only a native could possess. What may more reasonably be suspected is that men of provincial origin were welcomed in the Senate because they formed a supply of potential officials who could bring to the problems of administration in the Empire at large a general appreciation of the aims and aspirations of the provincial communities and some sense of the silent opinion which prevailed about Rome. Even if this be not the explanation, there can be no doubt about the fact that, though it was an exaggeration to suggest that Trajan was surrounded by 'unholy Jews[3],' early in the second century provincial members of the Senate had become numerous; for Trajan thought it necessary to encourage an Italian patriotism in men of this class by ordering them to invest a third of their property in Italian land (p. 212)—a rule which Marcus modified only so far as to make the fraction a quarter (p. 370).

But it was not for this reason alone that the powers of the censors were invoked. The use of adlection has a wider explanation: it was an inevitable result of the importance attained by the *equites* in public service. The more freely they were employed,

---

[1] G. Ferrero and C. Barbagallo, *A Short History of Rome*, II, pp. 251 *sqq.*
[2] This is true even when there are included such as are known of those whom Vespasian raised to the Senate immediately after his acclamation in A.D. 69 and before his return to Italy (Tacitus, *Hist.* II, 82).
[3] *P. Oxy.* x, 1242, l. 42 *sq.*

the more probable it became that the equestrian career would reveal occasional men whose proved ability might profitably be employed in posts for which senators alone were eligible; and this need for easy transfer of *equites* to the Senate was met by that process of adlection which the censorship allowed the *princeps* to perform. The cost might be high; for censorial powers gave the emperor a still stronger hold over the Senate, even if they encouraged the plebeian Fathers to hope for the honour of the patriciate, which Claudius had made it the prerogative of censors to bestow. But, at whatever price, another victory had been won by the principle for which the *populares* of the Republic had fought (p. 413), and the highest office was open to the merits even of those whose service in equestrian posts had been long.

VI. SENATE AND MAGISTRATES

The duties of the Senate whose composition was thus carefully controlled scarcely call for any long examination. As the Principate grew older, the independence of the Senate declined; and, though it remained an important part in the machine of government, its most valuable functions were to focus that educated opinion which was the strongest protection against autocracy and to maintain a supply of persons duly qualified to hold some of the highest posts in the administration. The Empire now owed more to senators than to the Senate. Trajan, indeed, might urge the Fathers 'resumere libertatem, capessere quasi communis imperii curas, invigilare publicis utilitatibus et insurgere[1],' but his words were not measurably more effective than those of Claudius on a similar occasion (vol. x, p. 697 *sq.*). A friendly *princeps* could coax the Senate into a hesitant self-confidence; but gratitude for the good-will of a Trajan was hardly less potent than the fear inspired by a Domitian in moving it to that ready acceptance of Imperial guidance which sapped its vitality as a deliberative council.

The old forms, indeed, were retained. With Hadrian's codification of the Edict, *senatus consulta*, which since Augustan times had been producing *ius honorarium*, came to be a source of Civil Law itself (see below, p. 814), even if the true source of its inspiration is revealed both by the reluctance of the Senate to act without the emperor's advice and by the custom, which appears in Hadrian's time, of quoting as the law, not the decree of the Senate, but the *oratio* in which the *princeps* had submitted the proposal to the House. In matters of the private law this was, indeed, a natural outcome of the increasing control exercised by

[1] Pliny, *Pan.* 66, 2.

the legal advisers of the court over the growth of the Ius Civile—
a control in itself desirable; but the professional jurists who sat
on the emperor's *consilium* were only a section of these experts
in all the varied aspects of government whose services the emperor
controlled and whose superior knowledge made any action difficult
without reference to the man who was their master and their
mouthpiece. And even in matters where no technical issue was
involved a diffident Senate was content to leave decisions to the
princeps: Pliny's attack on Publicius Certus produced a memorable
debate, but no trial followed because Nerva ignored the whole
affair (p. 195).

Again, though the Senate was nominally responsible for the
election of magistrates, the freedom of its choice was somewhat
circumscribed. The frequent canvassing which Pliny undertook
is evidence enough that in filling junior posts the House still
enjoyed a wide discretion[1]; but the consulships, perhaps since
the time of Nero[2], were regularly bestowed, even under the most
enlightened régimes, by what was virtually Imperial patronage[3].
Indeed the magistracies themselves were ceasing to be posts of
governmental importance and becoming, with some exceptions,
mere honours whose only other significance was the qualifications
they conferred for service in the Empire. In a letter to Pompeius
Falco, Pliny makes it plain that he himself was slightly peculiar
in refusing, as tribune, to treat the office as 'inanis umbra, sine
honore nomen[4],' and despite the extravagances of gratitude
expressed by those who became consuls it is not surprising that,
when few could hope to hold it longer than two months, the
consulship itself was regarded as an irksome distinction. Fronto,
in A.D. 143, 'stuck,' as he says, 'in Rome and bound by golden
bonds,' was not afraid to tell Marcus that he looked forward to
his release as eagerly as a Jew to the end of a fast[5]. The consuls,
indeed, had a tedious task; for their first business was with the
Senate, and the shortness of their office unsuited them for routine
of a kind which took time to learn.

Praetors, however, were in better case. It is true that their
ancient functions were being curtailed. Hadrian's concern for the
ius honorarium deprived the *praetor urbanus* of the proud right to

---

[1] Pliny, *Ep.* II, 9; VI, 6; VI, 9; VIII, 23, 1.
[2] Tacitus, *Hist.* I, 77; II, 71.
[3] Pliny, *Pan.* 62, 5; 77, 7–8; 92, 1–3; 95, 2: Appian, *Bell. Civ.* I, 103, 479.
[4] *Ep.* I, 23, 1.
[5] Fronto, *ad M. Caes.* II, 7 (p. 32 N); cf. II, 8 (p. 32 *sq.* N).

shape the 'viva vox iuris civilis[1],' and it is probable that the *praetor inter cives et peregrinos* likewise lost his power of making law. So too the praetors in charge of the *iudicia publica* were slowly yielding ground to Imperial officials in the administration of criminal justice. Yet the machinery of the *iudicia publica* which Sulla had constructed was still in active work; and even though cases in increasing numbers were heard elsewhere, in this connection praetors still had their old duties to perform[2]. Moreover, it was to the praetorship that more than one *princeps* turned when a new task of responsibility needed competent discharge. In A.D. 70 members of this college are found again in control of the *aerarium*[3], as had been the custom from 23 B.C. to A.D. 44 (vol. x, p. 195), though their restoration was brief and *praefecti* of the type instituted by Nero in A.D. 56 seem soon to have been reinstated. But at the end of the first century, after Titus had suppressed one of the two praetorships which Claudius had created to deal with cases arising out of *fideicommissa* (p. 20, n. 1), Nerva restored the number of praetors to eighteen by appointing one, who does not indeed seem to have long survived, to take charge of suits between private individuals and the *fiscus*[4]; and possibly it was when this office became superfluous through the growing activities of the *advocatus fisci* at Rome that Marcus used it to meet the need for a special magistrate to relieve the consuls of the difficult questions about *tutela* by converting its holder into the *praetor tutelaris*[5].

Despite the decay of the magistracies and the strength of Imperial influence on its proceedings, both legislative and electoral, the Senate still retained duties of the first importance, and these it was generally the aim of the *princeps* to stress. Though they were almost certainly empowered to declare peace and war (p. 406 and vol. x, p. 141), the emperors even showed deference to the ancient concern of the Senate with the foreign relations of Rome. Meaningless as the form might be, it doubtless flattered the Fathers' conceit and strengthened their good-will when Trajan consulted them about Dacian affairs[6], when Hadrian did the same about Parthia[7], and Marcus about military arrangements in the East and on the Danube[8]. But the significance of the Senate's

---

[1] *Dig.* I, 1, 8 (Marcian).
[2] For praetorian initiative in a minor matter see Pliny, *Ep.* IV, 29, 2 *sq.*
[3] Tacitus, *Hist.* IV, 9. [4] *Dig.* I, 2, 2, 32 (Pomponius): cf. Pliny, *Pan.* 36, 4.
[5] S.H.A. *Marcus*, 10, 11: cf. Dessau 1118.
[6] Dio LXVIII, 10, 4.
[7] Dio LXIX, 15, 2. [8] S.H.A. *Marcus*, 8, 9; 12, 14.

part in government is to be discerned rather in its discharge of the functions with which it had been entrusted when the Principate was first established. One of its cares was the finance of that part of the Empire for which it was immediately responsible, though since the time of Augustus the financial system had undergone a change. Within what was at first a single organization, the finances under Imperial control had grown by the time of Claudius into a separate department, and this—the *fiscus*—had been made independent of the senatorial *aerarium*, which in the end it was to absorb. But the time for that did not come until the third century, and throughout the Antonine age the two treasuries existed side by side, as they are revealed by the younger Pliny[1]. The *princeps* could, indeed, call on resources of the Aerarium Saturni at will, but if he cared for the friendship of the Senate, when its aid was needed he asked it formally to vote supplies, as Marcus did in A.D. 178[2]; and even Commodus is said so far to have followed his father's example in this respect as to use trickery instead of force to secure a grant from this quarter[3]. Again, though his *maius imperium* enabled the emperor to override or ignore the proconsuls in the public provinces, the Senate retained its immediate responsibility for the control of their administration; and even when, under Trajan, the Imperial government began its well-meant efforts to reduce the inefficiency which the Senate was unable to repress, the emperors were still content to represent their interference as exceptional and to act towards the Senate and its officials with the same regard as had been shown by Augustus and Vespasian[4].

In general, however, it is clear that even under friendly emperors the proceedings of the House were tending towards that banality which in days of oppression was a matter for complaint[5]; and against the loss of its former power the Senate had nothing to set except its increasing activity as a court of justice. The cases of Baebius Massa, Caecilius Classicus, Marius Priscus, Julius Bassus and Varenus Rufus, in all of which the younger Pliny was engaged (p. 204), are enough to show that not a little business of this sort was provided by the governors of the public provinces; and it was on the occasion of great trials like theirs that the House was more clearly conscious of its own importance[6] than at any other time save when there was a vacancy in the

---

[1] *Pan.* 36, 1–4: cf. Frontinus, *de aquaeductibus*, 118.

[2] Dio LXXII, 33, 2.   [3] S.H.A. *Comm.* 9, 1.

[4] Vol. x, p. 165 n. 6; Dessau 6092 (Vespasian); *ib.* 2927 and *I.G.R.R.* IV, 336 (Trajan).   [5] Pliny, *Pan.* 54, 3 *sq.*   [6] Pliny, *Ep.* II, 11, 18.

Principate. The judicial functions of the consular-senatorial court were not, however, confined to the hearing of such *causes célèbres*. The tribunal was competent to take civil as well as criminal cases from regions under its own control[1]; it exercised a wide discretion in interpreting, and even modifying, the law[2]; and the finality of its decisions, which may have been in doubt during the first century of the Principate, was expressly guaranteed by a *constitutio* of Hadrian[3]. One claim made for it, though without complete success before the time of Severus, deserves special notice—the claim that it alone should have the right to condemn a senator to death. According to Dio, the demand was refused by Domitian, but Nerva, Trajan and Hadrian are said to have promised that they would refrain from passing such sentences themselves[4]; and Marcus, who is not recorded to have committed himself on this matter, seems to have had difficulty in restraining the Fathers from a bloody revenge on those of their colleagues who had been involved with Avidius Cassius[5]. Mommsen observed with truth that the claim of senators facing capital charges to be tried by their peers was only respected in this period at times when they could be sure of impartial justice in a trial before the emperor himself[6]. As a High Court the Senate was not, indeed, alone; for the court of the emperor was by its side. But the equal partnership of *princeps* and Senate was nowhere more fully established than in the judicial sphere, and the consular-senatorial court was doing work of value by giving some relief to the *princeps* in that legal business which, for all its importance, could easily make excessive claims on the time of the man 'qui pro utilitate communi solus omnium curas laboresque suscepit[7].'

The decline of the Senate and the steady increase of the emperor's prestige brought with it a change in the means by which *princeps* and Senate were kept in contact. In the days when memories of the Republic were fresh Augustus had been cautious in his dealings with the House, and business in fact inspired on the Palatine had only been submitted after consideration by a cabinet which was formally constituted, regularly changed, and chosen, not by Imperial nomination, but by lot (vol. x, p. 167).

---

[1] Tacitus, *Ann.* xiv, 28; Suetonius, *Nero* 17: cf. Fronto's speech in *ad M. Caes.* i, 6 (pp. 13 *sqq.* N).

[2] Pliny, *Ep.* iv, 9, 17; vi, 5.   [3] *Dig.* xlix, 2, 1, 2 (Ulpian).

[4] lxvii, 2, 4 (Domitian): lxviii, 2, 3 (Nerva): lxviii, 5, 2 (Trajan): lxix, 2, 3; S.H.A. *Hadrian* 7, 4 (Hadrian); cf., however, Dio lxx, 1, 2.

[5] S.H.A. *Marcus* 25, 6: cf. 10, 6; 26, 13; 29, 4.

[6] *Röm. Staatsrecht* ii³, p. 962.   [7] Pliny, *Ep.* iii, 20, 12.

Such a body might command the respect due to representative members of the Senate itself, and its support was doubtless of value: indeed, in the last year of Augustus' life it was empowered in a slightly altered form to act in the Senate's name[1]. But by Tiberius its character was changed[2], and thenceforward the *princeps* relied for advice about political affairs on any of his friends whose opinion he valued. Counsellors of this kind were certainly drawn from the class of *amici Augusti*, which in the early days of the Empire included that large body of leading citizens who had acquired the right of entry to the daily levée; but in course of time the *amicitia principis* acquired a narrower sense to describe the relation between the emperor and those for whose personal service or advice he had a special use. Tiberius took with him to Capreae a carefully chosen entourage[3], and Claudius was accompanied to Britain by at least one *comes* who held rank of *legatus* without special duties[4]—an appointment of a kind which soon became more common[5]. Under the Flavians the *amici* grew in political importance[6]; in Trajan's time, if not before, their leisure was secured by exemption from certain public duties[7]; and the historian of Pius speaks as if by the middle of the second century 'amicus' had come to mean an imperial counsellor[8]. Such advisers were of two kinds—those whom the *princeps* consulted on issues of general policy, and the more technical experts on law who sat in the *consilium* which, after a history which began with the Principate, was formally constituted by Hadrian; but, though some individuals doubtless served in both capacities, the two bodies were always as distinct as the ends they had to serve, and it is in the former that we may see a link of value between emperor and Senate. Neither of these boards was composed of senators alone: indeed, it was counted for righteousness in Hadrian and Marcus that, when a senator was on trial, equestrian members of the judicial council were excluded. But senators were naturally numerous among those whom the *princeps* consulted from day to day, and in them, if their advice had been freely taken, he had spokesmen to commend their proposals to the Senate and to remind the House that they had not been framed without reference to that public opinion which senators were peculiarly qualified to express.

---

[1] Dio LVI, 28, 2 *sq.*   [2] Suetonius, *Tib.* 55.
[3] Vol. x, p. 632.   [4] Dessau 986.
[5] *E.g.* Dessau 1022: cf. Mommsen, *Röm. Staatsrecht* II³, p. 853, n. 5 and *Ges. Schr.* IV, pp. 315 *sqq.*   [6] Suetonius, *Tit.* 7, 2.
[7] Pliny, *Ep.* IV, 24, 3.   [8] S.H.A. *Pius*, 6, 11.

VII. THE DEVELOPMENT OF THE CIVIL SERVICE

The declining vitality of the Senate was in part both cause and result of the growing responsibilities of the officials under direct Imperial control. It had been among the first tasks of the Principate to supply that adequate civil service which the Republic had lamentably lacked. Julius Caesar, trying to develop the existing machine, failed before the refusal of the Senate to acquiesce in the first essential—the increase of its own numbers; and Augustus, with his unfailing deference to public opinion, had proved his loyalty to what passed as the Republic by restoring the Senate to its old dimensions. The problem thus remained, and the Augustan solution was to concentrate the public service of senators on selected kinds of office which there were senators enough to fill, and then to seek recruits among the *equites* for those of the remaining posts which were of too public a character to be held by freedmen of the imperial household[1]. In the fifty years which followed, the influence of the freedmen increased, but with the fall of Nero signs of a change appeared. Vespasian, the sturdy burgher of Reate, knew the value of the Italian *bourgeoisie* from which he came, and the *bourgeoisie* itself was eager to accept service under a *princeps* of its own class[2].

Little need be said of equestrian encroachment on senatorial posts; for this was no more than a consequence of the Senate's surrender of its functions to the *princeps*. The process had begun in Julio-Claudian times, and the contemporaries of Claudius or Nero would not have been surprised when Titus, whose Commissioners for the Devastated Area in Campania had been ex-consuls, chose *equites* to organize rebuilding in Rome after the fire of A.D. 80[3], or when Trajan—if he was the first—started the custom by which men of this class took the place of senators as census officers in the provinces[4]. But the ousting of freedmen by *equites* is of more significance. The exceptional conditions of the time make it impossible to argue that a new policy is to be seen in Otho's choice of an equestrian secretary[5] or in Vitellius' behaviour at Cologne, when he appointed Knights to a variety of posts customarily held by freedmen[6]; but a change became plain when Domitian, by whom freedmen were still indeed employed[7], gave

---

[1] See F. B. Marsh, in *Class. Journ.* xx, 1924–5, pp. 451 *sqq.*
[2] See Tacitus, *Ann.* III, 55. [3] Suetonius, *Tit.* 8, 4; Dio LXVI, 24, 3.
[4] *E.g.* Dessau 1394 (cf. 2000) and 9506. [5] Plutarch, *Otho* 9, 3.
[6] Tacitus, *Hist.* I, 58; cf. Dessau 1447.
[7] Tacitus, *Agricola* 41, 4; Suetonius, *Dom.* 7, 2.

the great office of *ab epistulis* to an *eques*[1]. Trajan, it is true, again had freedmen among his secretaries[2], though he treated his freedmen in a way which became their station[3]; but in his time an even greater prize was re-captured by the Knights when an *eques* was chosen to fill the office of Minister of Finance (p. 220)[4], long held by the famous father of Claudius Etruscus—who himself had risen to the *ordo equester* from slavery. Thus, though there was a *libertus a rationibus* again even under Marcus[5], the way was prepared for that change in the recruitment of the emperor's civil service which is particularly associated with the name of Hadrian. His biographer, indeed, is in error when he claims that Hadrian was the first to have Knights as *ab epistulis* and *a libellis*[6], but there is evidence in plenty to prove that he moved far towards substituting *equites* in all the posts of prominence which had been held in the past by freedmen[7]. The historian Suetonius, *ab epistulis* at the beginning of the reign[8], and T. Haterius Nepos, probably the *a libellis*[9], are typical of the class from which, not only great imperial secretaries, but an increasing majority of those employed by the *princeps* in administration were now regularly drawn.

The number of these was large; for they were needed not merely for the immediate business of the Palatium or in central offices at Rome but in various capacities throughout the Empire. In Rome itself their greatest influence was still to come; for the Praetorian Prefects, who were in the end to be something like deputies of the *princeps* (when they were not his masters), had not yet brought the civil service at large under their supervision, nor had they acquired those great judicial responsibilities which increased their power and compelled them to enlarge their staffs. Marcius Turbo[10], indeed, like Bassaeus Rufus after him[11], had business to do in court, but it was not till the time of Septimius that the appointment of Papinian to the Prefecture marks the beginning of its greatness as a court of civil appeal and brings the office to its full development. In other departments, however, expansion came earlier. The *praefectus vigilum* had a *subpraefectus* by the

---

[1] Compare Dessau 1519 with 1448 and *Ann. épig.* 1934, no. 154.
[2] Dessau 1667; *C.I.L.* vi, 8607.   [3] Pliny, *Pan.* 88, 1–2.
[4] *Ann. épig.* 1913, no. 143*b*, ll. 18 *sqq.*
[5] *C.I.L.* ix, 2438, l. 3; Dessau 1476.   [6] S.H.A. *Hadr.* 22, 8.
[7] Hadrian did not, however, make a clean sweep of the freedmen: in A.D. 124, for instance, a freedman was procurator of Crete (*C.I.L.* xiv, 51).
[8] S.H.A. *Hadr.* 11, 3.   [9] Dessau 1338.
[10] Dio lxix, 18, 3.   [11] Philostratus, *Vitae Soph.* ii, 1, 11.

time of Trajan[1], and before the end of the second century an
equestrian *subpraefectus annonae*[2] seems to have superseded the
freedman who served as *adiutor* in earlier days[3]. But it was outside
Italy, in the corn-bearing provinces of the Empire, that the
Ministry of Food most notably increased its activities. The government's care for the food-supply of the capital, commemorated in
Rome itself by the rebuilding of the Horrea Galbae[4] and by the
Horrea Nervae[5], is freely attested by the records of new officials
in this service abroad[6]. Even more widespread were the agents
of the new department charged with the collection of the Succession Duty. When this tax was first imposed under Augustus,
despite the obvious difficulties of such a method, *publicani* seem
to have been employed to fix the sums due and to receive them;
and, though there was a certain amount of detailed supervision
by the government[7], this system was maintained in essentials
throughout the first century[8]. But the extension of the Roman
citizenship continually increased the numbers of estates to be
taxed, and in Trajan's time equestrian procurators are found
apparently presiding over a central bureau in Rome[9], and soon
afterwards subordinates in charge of various regions in Italy and
the provinces[10]. Since Hadrian is recorded to have concerned
himself with the regulations about this tax[11], it is not improbable
that some part of the responsibility for these developments belongs
to him; and it is certain that with them came the introduction of
direct collection by the State.

Rome was now generally abandoning the use of *publicani*, and
it is clear that the old system had fallen too deep into disfavour
for it to be adopted in any new developments. Even the customs-
dues—the largest source of revenue controlled by the tax-farmers
in Imperial times—were being slowly re-organized in a way which
would make difficult abuses of the kind which had moved Nero
to the drastic proposal of A.D. 58 (vol. x, p. 712 *sq.*). In the first
century there was a tendency to give contracts for collection
no longer to large companies but to individual *conductores* of
a type early used on Imperial estates; and these were at first
supervised, and later superseded, by procurators of the permanent

---

[1] Dessau 2160.   [2] Dessau 1412.   [3] Dessau 1535.
[4] Dessau 239.   [5] Dessau 1627.
[6] Cf. Dessau 1435 (Trajanic: Africa), 5908 (Hadrianic: Lycia), 1403
(Marcan: Baetica).
[7] See *e.g.* Dessau 1546.   [8] Pliny, *Pan.* 37, 7; 39, 5; *Ep.* VII, 14, 1.
[9] Dessau 1350, 1352, 1419.   [10] *E.g.* Dessau 1381, 1092, 1454.
[11] *Cod. Just.* VI, 33, 3.

civil service. In Hadrian's time there was a procurator of the *quadragesima Galliarum*[1], as of the *quattuor publica Africae*[2], and though the latter were still let out to contract in the time of Pius[3], *conductores* are not found after the Antonines. In practice this change, which was in progress throughout the Empire, seems often to have been made by means which are attested in Illyricum, where individuals found first as *publicani* appear later to have become paid members of the administration and to have been transformed into procurators[4].

The high ideal of efficiency shown by the government before Commodus was not the only cause of the growth in the public services: business itself was increasing. Bequests to the *princeps*, which had been continuous since the time of Augustus, not only moved Trajan—if it was he who took this step[5]—to appoint a *procurator hereditatum* independent of the *procurator patrimonii*, who had probably been in charge of these matters hitherto, but also produced a steady accumulation of property for which the emperor was responsible. All this demanded a larger staff, as did the constant additions, made by purchase or penal expropriation or by the operation of the *leges caducariae*, to the already vast assets of the *fiscus*. The importance of these accessions was recognized by the creation of *advocati fisci*, officers who in fiscal matters seem to have done work not unlike that of the *procuratores hereditatum* for the *patrimonium* in the days before they too began to serve the *fiscus*. The institution of these *advocati* is ascribed to Hadrian[6], and though it is possible that at first there was only a single functionary of this kind, having his office in Rome, before long there are signs of *advocati fisci*[7], as of *procuratores hereditatum*[8], in the provinces as well. The list of departments thus developed might be prolonged, but here it will be enough, by way of final illustration, to mention the Imperial Post. The *cursus publicus*, introduced to the Roman world by Augustus to provide rapid communication with officials in the provinces (vol. x, p. 217), was at first a charge on the communities through whose territories it ran, and as early as Claudius the burden was resented. Claudius had sought remedies in vain[9], and the first unmistakable relief recorded was given when Nerva,

---

[1] Dessau 9506. [2] Dessau 1408.
[3] Dessau 1463: cf. Fronto, *ad M. Caes.* v, 34 (49) (p. 86 n).
[4] Dessau 4225 and 4244 *sq.*; 1859 and 1382 *sq.*; *Ann. épig.* 1934, no. 107.
[5] Dessau 1338. [6] S.H.A. *Hadr.* 20, 6.
[7] Perhaps implied in Dessau 1451; Philostratus, *Vitae Soph.* ii, 29.
[8] *Dig.* xlix, 14, 32 (Marcian); perhaps cf. Dessau 1449. [9] Dessau 214.

if such be the meaning of the evidence[1], transferred the cost of the service in Italy to the State. Perhaps as a result of this a small office was opened in Rome[2], and this soon had at its head an equestrian *praefectus*[3], whose duties were doubtless a result of Hadrian's decision to put the whole organization under Imperial control[4]. Thereafter, while complaints from the provinces still demanded notice[5], subordinates of this office spread outside Italy[6], and their numbers became large when Septimius[7] carried Hadrian's policy to its logical conclusion by making the government, temporarily at least, responsible for the cost of an organization which it already managed and which it alone could use[8].

Though freedmen were still employed for humble tasks, it was to the *ordo equester* that the Empire turned more and more to provide the higher officials in this growing bureaucracy. New posts were freely filled by *equites*; Knights ousted freedmen from the old; and the importance of the part they played was marked by various signs to show that they were no longer casual servants of the *princeps*, but members of an organized civil service. Already in the first century procurators were roughly graded by salary[9], but it was not before the time of Hadrian or the Antonines that they were divided into the four sharply defined classes of *trecenarii, ducenarii, centenarii,* and *sexagenarii*[10], the members of which each received 300,000, 200,000, 100,000 and 60,000 sesterces a year respectively. Even by the death of Commodus this differentiation had not reached its limits; for the *rationalis*, formerly known as *procurator a rationibus*, seems still to have been the only *trecenarius*. But evidence from the beginning of the third century makes it plain that the developments under the Severi were only an elaboration of a scheme inherited from their predecessors. The dignity of equestrian officials was also marked by formal titles, inspired perhaps by the phrase 'vir clarissimus' which had been appropriated by senators as their special appellation early in the second century[11]. Every *eques* could be addressed

---

[1] H. Mattingly and E. A. Sydenham, *Rom. Imp. Coinage* II, p. 229 *sq.*; cf. Pliny, *Pan.* 20, 4.

[2] *C.I.L.* VI, 8542–3.

[3] *E.g.* Dessau 1434.

[4] S.H.A. *Hadr.* 7, 5 (reading '*statum*').

[5] S.H.A. *Pius*, 12, 3.

[6] *E.g.* Dessau 4225.

[7] S.H.A. *Sev.* 14, 2.

[8] Pliny, *Ep.* x, 120 (121) *sq.*

[9] Suetonius, *Claud.* 24, 1.

[10] *E.g.* Dessau 1358, 1455, 478.

[11] 'Vir clarissimus' had been used even in Julio-Claudian times as an honorific description (cf. *C.I.L.* III, 12240; Dessau 6043, l. 24; 5947, l. 13), though not as a regular address of senators as such. See O. Hirschfeld, *Kleine Schriften*, pp. 646 *sqq.*

as 'vir egregius[1],' but, perhaps already in the second century, some of the more distinguished came to be known as 'viri perfectissimi,' and the most important of all as 'viri eminentissimi[2]'— a title which after slightly wider use[3] was soon confined to the Praetorian Prefects.

The class which thus obtained so prominent a place in the system of administration was one which could provide talent of the most varied kinds. Lack of traditions gave it strength; for, unlike the Senate, the *ordo equester* had no corporate conceit to be outraged when soldiers, provincials and even freedmen were added to its ranks. So, besides substantial citizens from Rome and Italy, it could absorb a centurion of humble ambition[4] or one like Bassaeus Rufus who was to become Praetorian Prefect, an Egyptian Jew like Tiberius Julius Alexander, a Smyrniote slave like the father of Claudius Etruscus, or the Greek paedagogue Nicomedes, who was first tutor to the young Verus and then advanced by stages to the second place in the Ministry of Finance. From this source the administration could draw recruits whose distinction had been earned by ability and whose status gave them qualities of value which the freedmen of earlier days had often lacked.

When large parts of the Imperial business were transacted by the emperor's household, the posts which these functionaries held belonged rather to the private establishment of the *princeps* than to the public service of the State. Gratitude for work well done was a less certain claim to advancement than the capricious favour of an individual; and the freedmen, whose fortunes rested on the good-will of their master, could count on flattery to protect them against the healthy opinion which was outraged by the audacity of their pursuit of money, their one ambition. When Knights took their place, mere servants gave way to men with a rank and honour to maintain, and at the same time what had in some degree retained its original character as the household of the first citizen became more obviously part of a public administration. In appearance at least, and perhaps in fact, this substitution of *equites* for freedmen was a success for the Republican ideals of government against the menace of autocracy. Nevertheless, the removal of freedmen from high responsibility did not mean that Rome confessed to error. Freedmen were employed by nobles of the Republic because there were many purposes

---

[1] *E.g.* Dessau 1358, 6885, 6870, IV, l. 10.
[2] *Cod. Just.* IX, 41, 11; *C.I.L.* IX, 2438, l. 9; Dessau 1346.
[3] Dessau 465, 3621.   [4] *E.g. C.I.L.* XI, 5992.

best served by the peculiar gifts of Greeks, and for the same reason
freedmen had been used by Julio-Claudian emperors. Pallas was
doubtless a peculator; but Claudius had no ground for complaint
about the state of the Exchequer. To the Greek capacity for
organization and finance Rome had cause to be grateful, and the
government did not deny itself the use of Greek ability when
freedmen were discarded. Tacitus, writing of A.D. 56, asserts that
even then the majority of the *equites* and many senators were not
without servile blood[1]; and, though epigraphic evidence suggests
that this is an exaggeration, it is clear that both by direct recruitment from the East and by the absorption of men descended from
freedmen in Italy the equestrian order in the second century was
well supplied with members whose descent enabled them to put
the shrewd competence of Greeks at the disposal of the administration.

In the salutary development of the civil service one feature may
be discerned less laudable than the rest. It had been a practice
of the Republic that men who sought to serve the State should
be qualified to hold either military command or civil office as
occasion might demand, and this custom Augustus had observed
in his incipient organization of the equestrian career no less than
in the use he made of senators. Whatever the defects of a system
which did nothing to encourage the specialist, its merits were
beyond dispute (p. 395). With Claudius, however, came a change,
when the tenure of the military tribunate was in some cases allowed
to become a formality[2]. In itself the concession was trivial, but
it deserves notice as a step towards a dangerous practice which
Hadrian seems to have made common. The historian Suetonius
may well belong to a group of several equestrian officials at this
time who appear to have served in no military capacity at all[3],
and they are the forerunners of the purely civil functionaries who
later found themselves at the mercy of the war-lords of Rome.
The separation of the civilian from the military career was
dangerous, not because it deprived men engaged in administration
of some slight acquaintance with the army, but because, if specialized service were allowed, a bureaucracy of civilians was likely
to be confronted before long with a more formidable body of men
whose occupation was wholly military. And so it befell. In the
conflict which began before the end of the second century the
civilians were helpless before the army; power passed to men whose
distinction in war was their only fame; and to its lasting harm the

[1] *Ann.* XIII, 27.
[2] Suetonius, *Claud.* 25, 1.   [3] *E.g.* Dessau 1408, 1454.

Empire found itself in the hands of soldiers whose humble origins and warlike occupations left them strangers to the arts of civil government. The needs of the frontiers in the third century gave the army that influence which is normal in time of war, and it was the conditions of the time which both enabled and constrained Gallienus and Diocletian to make a final division between civil and military services. But when at length they acted in the way which, if it saved the Empire, destroyed the Principate, their work completed a change to which Hadrian's enthusiasm for efficiency had made a small but gratuitous contribution.

Great as was the value of the *equites*, it did not move the Principate to despise the service which could be rendered by the Senate. The House contained ability and experience, increased by judicious reinforcement from the *equites* themselves, which still was enough to fill the urban magistracies and the great provincial commands and to leave men available for new posts required by the demands of government. *Equites* were adequate for any administrative routine, but when work of special responsibility had to be done abroad, like that of Pliny in Bithynia, it was in the first place to senators that the *princeps* turned[1]. Senators again played a large part in the control of the Social Services in Italy; for the alimentary system, which was sedulously tended throughout the second century, despite its foundation by Trajan with money from the Imperial treasury, had senatorial officials to supervise its complicated operations[2]; and even when this department was centralized, perhaps by Marcus, a consular was still retained at its head[3].

The intervention of Marcus has been plausibly connected with another act of his which involved the employment of senators in new appointments, and one which raises questions about the relation of the *princeps* to the Senate and its responsibilities in Italy. By a measure of a kind which would benefit a government with the interests of the country population at heart, Hadrian had chosen four ex-consuls to administer justice in those parts of Italy beyond easy reach of Rome[4]. Their duties in detail are obscure; but it is clear that their business was to free litigants of the necessity to travel far for justice, if not at the same time to relieve pressure on the courts in Rome. Such evidence as has survived suggests that it was the consuls (and later the *praetor*

---

[1] Dessau 1066 *sq.*
[2] *E.g.* Dessau 6675 (xvi), 6106, 1061, 1101.
[3] *E.g.* Dessau 1104.
[4] S.H.A. *Hadr.* 22, 13.

tutelaris[1]), the praetor in charge of *fideicommissa*[2] and the *praefectus urbi*[3] who lost some of their business to these officials; but there is no reason to believe that, even if it was criticized, their institution had been inspired by hostility towards the older magistrates or to argue that their presence reduced Italy to a level with the provinces. Their purpose was to make justice both cheaper and more expeditious—a purpose in accord with the spirit of the government and one well attested by the judicial arrangements of the Antonines[4]. They were suspended by Pius[5], though he had himself been one, but were established again by Marcus[6], with the difference that they were now, not consulars, but ex-praetors, and it was by him that they may possibly have been given some responsibility for the alimentary system.

The Principate of the second century did, indeed, concern itself with Italy more closely than the Principate of the first. The contemporaries of Augustus might have been surprised if, when war was remote, a praetorian legate had been appointed to the *regio Transpadana*[7]; and the four *iuridici* themselves were doubtless chosen by the *princeps*. Nevertheless, their revival by Marcus, whose friendship to the Senate was pronounced, is enough to prove that their institution by Hadrian was no deliberate insult to tradition, and their senatorial status is rather to be taken as evidence of respect for the past. But their creation is one among many signs of that restless passion for efficiency which was responsible for the invocation of the *equites* and for the steady expansion of the civil service which in the end gave the *princeps* control of a powerful bureaucracy with great possibilities for good or ill. The servants of the State, both high and low, were picked with honourable care; promotion was a reward for work well done[8]; and the standard of competence was high. If the sphere of government was to extend, its agents could scarcely have been better chosen. But still the one question worth the asking remained to answer. What would the State, with all its bureaucrats, contribute to the well-being of the Empire and its inhabitants? Would they be the better for its activities, or the worse? The third and fourth centuries supplied the answer.

[1] *Frag. Vat.* 205, 232, 241.   [2] *Dig.* XL, 5, 41, 5 (Scaevola).
[3] Fronto, *ad amicos* II, 7 (pp. 192 *sqq.* N), with Dessau 1118.
[4] *E.g. Dig.* XLIX, 2, 1, 4 (Ulpian).   [5] Appian, *Bell. Civ.* I, 38, 172.
[6] S.H.A. *Marcus* 11, 6.
[7] Dessau 1040.   [8] See Pliny, *Pan.* 70.

CHAPTER XI

ROME AND THE EMPIRE

I. THE ORIGINS OF ROMAN IMPERIALISM

AT the beginning of the Imperial age Rome had five hundred years of Roman history behind her. Of that history she was the outcome. If she was different from the 'suetus regibus Oriens[1],' the difference was due to her own political past: if Augustus was proud to have pacified the Alps 'nulli genti bello per iniuriam inlato[2],' his pride was the expression of an ideal for which Rome had respect enough to claim it as her own. Thanks to Augustus himself the traditions established by the experience of the Roman Republic were applied to the task of governing the united world. They were not, indeed, wholly of Roman origin. From its earliest days the city had been exposed to external influence, and its debt to Etruria, however it may precisely be assessed[3], was only an anticipation of the much greater obligation soon incurred to Greece. Yet what Rome received she assimilated and embodied in a culture which, wherever the source of its inspiration in this respect or that, remained always one and unmistakably Roman.

When the time came to organize an empire, the element in this culture which mattered most was one for which Rome's debt was least. Her political practice was of her own devising—the creation of her own good sense encouraged by the context of her history. From her earliest days the setting of Roman history had been continental. First in Latium, and then over a steadily increasing part of the Italian peninsula, Rome had grown in an environment where her enemies could unite, where numbers alone gave power, and where one State could control many only by enlisting their good-will. Rome was thus protected from the temptation to which Athenian imperialism had succumbed. Nature gave Athens an opportunity to convert allies into subjects, and her political sense was too feeble to refuse it. Exploitation yielded its brief years of brilliance; but, when Athens fell, her contribution to men's knowledge of imperial government was at most the warning which gives some slight value to even the worst of failures. In 404 B.C. the

---

[1] Tacitus, *Hist.* IV, 17.   [2] *Res Gestae*, 26.
[3] See vol. VII, pp. 383 *sqq.*

Long Walls to the Piraeus were pulled down to the sounds of music and jubilation[1]: when Alaric sacked Rome in A.D. 410 it seemed to the aged Jerome, even in the remoteness of his cell at Bethlehem, as if the end of civilization were at hand[2]. Between Athens, the 'tyrant city[3],' and Rome, 'communis nostra patria[4],' the difference was great; and some part of the reason for Rome's success is to be found in the circumstances of her early history. In the dynamics of Italy, unlike those of Greece, the dominant moment was centripetal, and this fact combined with native good sense to form the political outlook of the Romans. Living as they did in a world where the trend towards union was strong, they formed ideas markedly different from those which had prevailed elsewhere. They prized *libertas*[5] as the Greeks had prized *eleutheria*; yet so different were these two concepts that, when Rome entered the Greek world honestly claiming to preserve the first[6], she was no less honestly criticized by the Greeks for destroying the second[7]. *Libertas* was not, like *eleutheria* according to some accounts[8], an unfettered freedom, but rather, like *principatus* which was one of its constitutional counterparts, freedom from arbitrary rule[9]. In particular it did not imply a community's untrammelled control of its international relations, with the right to declare peace and war at will: whatever may have been sacrificed to the establishment of the Pax Augusta, it was not what the Romans called 'libertas[10].' For *libertas* in its wider sense was the foundation of the Imperial structure, and its employment marked the recognition of the fact, soon discovered in Italy by Rome and slowly brought home to the cities of the Greek world by the experience of the Hellenistic age, that the value of free institutions is not seriously impaired by loss of the power to take up arms against one's neighbour.

In the policy of Republican Rome there is to be seen another principle of the first importance, which again is strange to the history of Greece. Hellas was a world of small communities. When

---

[1] Xen. *Hell.* II, 2, 23; Plutarch, *Lys.* 15, 4.
[2] *Ep.* 127, 12.
[3] Thucydides I, 122, 3; 124, 3: cf. II, 63, 2; III, 37, 2.
[4] *Dig.* XXVII, 1, 6, 11; L, 1, 33 (Modestinus): *cf.* Aelius Aristides 26 K, 61.
[5] Cicero, II *in Verr.* v, 63, 163.
[6] *E.g.* Livy XLV, 18, 1 *sq.*; Ditt.³ 684, l. 15 *sq.*
[7] *E.g.* Polybius XVIII, 45 (28), 6; cf. vol. VIII, pp. 194 *sqq.*
[8] Aristotle, *Pol.* v, 1310 a, 28 *sqq.*; 1317 b, 10 *sqq.*
[9] Cf. Cicero, *Paradox.* v, 1, 34.
[10] Aelius Aristides 26 K, 29 and 36.

trade, or overpopulation, or the vicissitudes of domestic strife moved part of a city's population to seek new homes abroad, a colony was founded so loosely tied to its *metropolis* that its members were in fact lost to the place from which they came; and the result of this hiving-off was that, though cities became more numerous, their size was held in check. At Rome, on the other hand, man-power was a primary concern. Roman colonies, since they remained part of the Roman body politic, were not allowed to sap the strength of Rome; and even such Roman citizens as were enrolled in foundations of the Latin type, though they ceased to be Roman, became members of communities which were Rome's effective allies. Nor was this all. Not content with conserving her population, Rome openly sought to increase it by absorbing other peoples in the way typified by the story of Romulus and the Sabines. This concern for man-power is justly claimed by Cicero as a fundamental principle of Roman statecraft[1], and it was recognized as such by at least one acute observer abroad. When Philip V of Macedon, then at war with Rome, held up as an example the Roman practice of admitting strangers to their citizenship[2], he paid tribute to the wisdom of his enemies as well as to his own political perception.

Respect for *libertas*, a sturdy belief that freedom could be preserved even in communities which were parts of a larger whole, and an ideal of inclusiveness which led to the absorption first of Italy and later of the Empire at large into the imperial citizenship of Rome, were three outstanding features of the political technique devised by the Roman Republic. They were principles which determined the design of the administrative machine, and the machine itself ensured their maintenance until, when circumstances led to their abandonment, the machine itself was altered almost beyond recognition. Even in the last century B.C., when Italy had been united and provinces stretched from Syria to Spain, so much of the administrative business was left to local authorities that the constitution of the central power remained in essence that of a city-state. That empire should have brought changes so small was not wholly a cause for satisfaction. Not only were there difficulties presented by the armies which empire required, but the administration itself, even when private contractors, like the *publicani*, were enrolled to make good the dearth of regular officials, was an extemporization too loose in structure and too weak in

---

[1] *Pro Balbo*, 13, 31: cf. Dion. Hal. *Ant.* 1, 9, 4; Plutarch, *Rom.* 16, 5; Pliny, *Ep.* VII, 32, 1.
[2] Ditt[3]. 543, ll. 29 *sqq.*

personnel to be completely adequate. Nevertheless, though a more ample civil service was an urgent need which it was the business of Augustus to meet, even after his salutary reforms the central administration retained the best of the qualities it had developed under the Republic. Despite its expansion, its dimensions remained small, and the Roman power was still prepared to leave a province in the hands of a governor, a few adjutants, a financial officer and a small staff of clerks. With troops to protect the frontiers and to preserve internal order on the rare occasions when disturbance threatened, Rome was satisfied for the rest to receive such taxes as she claimed and to insist, so far as her restricted means allowed, on the observance of her own high standards in the administration of justice. Other business was in general left to the local communities, until in the second century Trajan and his successors, having learned by experience the difference between experts and amateurs in government, allowed themselves to intrude their agents into local affairs and thereby were forced both to enlarge the civil service to the dimensions of a bureaucracy and to begin a process which transformed the relations between Rome and the peoples of the Empire. This change had gone far before the death of Commodus, but its completion was delayed till the fourth century, and throughout the history of the Empire to the end of the Antonine age the character of the Roman control was still under the predominant influence of traditions inherited from the Republic. Lack of officiousness, reluctance to interfere, anxiety that Rome's share of the responsibility for detail should be small and that of local authorities great—such were the most striking expressions of a policy which left the governed free[1] and was content if defence, imperial taxation and the more serious judicial business were reserved for the imperial power.

II. ROME AND HER PREDECESSORS

With ideals so tolerant and with so simple an administrative machine, Rome lacked both the inclination and the means to force uniformity on the varied populations of the empire. Nothing was demanded save abstinence from unauthorized fighting, the payment of taxes and the supply of recruits to the imperial army. For the rest Rome followed the method of *laissez-faire*, helping the inhabitants, if they cared, to build on foundations laid before the Romans came and offering their own culture as a stock from

[1] Cf. Marc. Aur. *Med.* i, 14.

which peoples in the provinces might draw such ideas as seemed good, but everywhere, except in Egypt, leaving the natives to work out their own futures for themselves. If Rome may be criticized in the first and second centuries, it is for too ready an acceptance of what she found. In Africa, for instance, occasional human sacrifice to the Phoenician Saturnus seems not to have been stamped out till the time of Tertullian's father[1], and in Egypt, where a marked revival of prosperity after the Roman conquest was followed by a disastrous decline, early improvement was due to the advent of efficiency, and ultimate failure to the inherent weakness of a system inherited from the Pharaohs and the Ptolemies which was modified, indeed, but which, since it was in existence, it would have been contrary to Roman practice to destroy. Nevertheless Rome was in general justified. Egypt was unique in the hypertrophy of its organization, and elsewhere, among peoples whose institutions were the healthy result of natural growth, tolerance was vindicated by the event.

An empire on which little was imposed by the imperial power retained obvious signs of its varied composition. Gauls and Berbers, polytheists and monotheists, nomads and men whose ancestors for generations had lived in cities, peoples who spoke Latin, others who spoke Greek and those of barbarian tongues— all these, and more, were included in the 'immensum imperii corpus[2].' In every department of human affairs regional variety was to be seen, and Rome refrained from all attempts to hasten its reduction. Nevertheless, though uniformity was never attained, there were forces at work which tended by degrees to give all parts of the Empire a certain measure of resemblance. While Rome was still a petty State in Latium, the Greeks had forged a link between the two basins into which Italy and Sicily divide the Mediterranean. East and West still remained distinct; but, when Strabo calls Massilia 'a school for barbarians[3],' he rightly commemorates the service of the Greeks in bringing to Western Europe some knowledge of the culture and institutions of Hellas. Such contact, however, was with Hellas in its days of independence, and the West remained strange to the great developments inaugurated by Alexander in the East. Save perhaps for Sicily, the western Mediterranean in general lay outside the region which the

---

[1] Tertullian, *Apol.* 9, 2, following the text of Cod. Fuld. The suppression here may well have been part of Hadrian's policy; cf. Porphyry, *de abst.* II, 56, and, for another view, J. Carcopino in *Rev. de l'hist. des religions*, CVI, p. 595, n. 3. See also M. Fluss in *P.W. s. v.* Tiberius (3).

[2] Tacitus, *Hist.* I, 16.　　　　[3] IV, 181; cf. Cicero, *pro Flacco*, 26, 63.

Macedonians had veneered with a single culture and marked with signs of incipient unity. Italy in particular had been sheltered from the full force of Hellenism by the exclusive policy of Rome, and it was through Rome herself that the more valuable achievements of the Hellenistic world were slowly passed on to the West.

In the East, however, more had been done to prepare the way towards oecumenical union. Large areas had grown accustomed to the general control of the Successor Kingdoms, and the policies of Alexander and the Seleucids in Asia had been alike in encouraging the population to focus itself round centres which offered at least an introduction to that form of life best found in the cities of Greece and of the Roman Empire, even though they might not all deserve to be called *poleis* in the strict Greek sense. Many of these places had attained their full development before Rome appeared; but even the more backward held the possibility of growth to municipal stature, and their advance was a process, begun in Seleucid times, which Rome did no more than stimulate. Yet wide as Macedonians had spread Hellenic culture and Hellenic institutions in the East, the hellenization even of the lands with which Rome came to be concerned was far from uniform. Western Asia Minor was part of Hellas (p. 555); but elsewhere in the peninsula more primitive conditions survived. In the third century B.C. a large tract in Phrygia had been given to the Gauls, whose institutions were their own, and farther east the inner parts of Pontus remained wild in their isolation, while Cappadocia, touched only lightly by the Seleucids, preserved the ancient culture of Hattic Anatolia, modified only by the influence of Achaemenid Persia.[1] So too in Syria, though the rich lands of the North, the centre of Seleucid power, had become a stronghold of Asiatic Hellenism, the poorer regions had attracted less attention, and not far off were the fringes shared and disputed by the settled population and nomads like the Skenite Arabs whose sheikh St Paul had found in control of Damascus[2].

Rome's task in the East was to continue work already well begun. The Hellenistic age had at least proclaimed unity as an ideal. Save in the Egyptian sphere a single monetary standard passed from Bactria to the Adriatic; the Septuagint is a monument of the rise of Greek towards the status of a universal language; and the cities of Asia were active cells whence the Seleucids had hoped to spread Greek ways of life throughout their dominions. Yet the coming of Rome found many problems still unsolved. Beyond the limits of old Hellas Hellenism had struck root only in the

[1] See p. 606 *sq.*   [2] II Cor. xi, 32.

cities, and even there its hold was secure on none but the upper classes. Outside lay the vast country regions, where change was slight and fugitive. Though Greek had become the vehicle of culture the masses still used their native tongues, and in Asia, at least, the vitality of languages which Greek attacked in vain is a clue to the strength of the opposition which Hellenism had everywhere to meet (p. 607 *sq.*). So strong, indeed, did it prove that in the last century B.C. a momentous fact emerged. Like the earlier attempt of Alexander to blend Greek with Iranian, the efforts of the Seleucids to establish an Hellenic domination had failed before the superior numbers and the steady resistance of Semites and Iranians. Much, indeed, had been gained. The old antinomy between Greek and barbarian had given way to a salutary recognition of the value of humanity as such[1], the maintenance over wide areas of a stable peace had become something more than a Utopian aspiration, and the world had learnt that freedom might flourish even in communities which formed parts of a larger whole. But Asia had proved the grave of grandiose essays in the manipulation of culture, and the time had come for an imperial method which, whatever the means it might employ to secure the loyalty of the parts, could dispense with cultural uniformity as an essential condition of success.

III. ROME AND ROMANIZATION

The famous tribute paid to Rome in the fifth century by Rutilius—that she 'made a city what was once a world[2]'—is of value if only as a reminder that, despite the Roman tolerance of variety, forces had been at work to give the Empire a cohesion which was not least among the achievements of which Rome could boast. To produce it three factors had combined. First was the emigration of Italians. 'Ubicumque vicit Romanus, habitat[3],' says Seneca, and from the second century B.C. onwards there is evidence to prove him true. Adherbal's Italian followers massacred by Jugurtha[4] and the thousands in Asia slaughtered at Mithridates' behest[5] are only the most striking illustrations of the readiness with which, even before the Imperial age, Italians spread abroad. Their motives too are known. The inscriptions from the mart which Rome had made at Delos show that there were many whose concern was private trade to re-inforce the influence of those

---

[1] See Strabo 1, 66 [Eratosthenes].
[2] '*Urbem fecisti quod prius orbis erat*': de reditu suo, 1, 66.
[3] *Cons. ad Helviam*, 7, 7.
[4] Sallust, *Bell. Jug.* 26; cf. 47, 1.
[5] Memnon 31, 4; Val. Max. IX, 2, ext. 3; Plutarch, *Sulla*, 24, 4.

engaged on the collection of public revenue[1]. Such traders soon struck root, and before long they were scattering the seeds of the Roman civilization. To them a second class should probably be added. The evidence is admittedly scanty and its meaning a matter of dispute; but the growth of Roman influence in Provence, as in Andalusia and Tunisia, does not admit of easy explanation unless it be supposed that merchants from Italy were followed by peasants whose interest was in the soil. Indications of a readiness to emigrate among the people of the countryside— even before Italian farmers were forced to make way for veterans after the civil wars—are to be found in the history of the military foundations. It was men from the armies of the Scipios—men largely drawn from the peasant class—who settled at Carteia (Algeciras) in such numbers that by 171 B.C. the children born to them of Spanish wives presented a legal problem only solved by the grant of Latin rights to the whole community[2]; and it was soldiers again who formed the Roman nucleus in Italica[3], the home of Trajan and Hadrian. Whatever their respective numbers, traders and peasants should probably be recognized together[4] in the drift of population which had set from Italy towards the West by the beginning of the second century B.C. In at least some provincial regions these people were soon numerous enough to make their presence felt, and before long the groups in which they tended to collect became powerful agents in spreading a knowledge of Italian culture and Italian conceptions of society among the natives.

Second to this emigration in point of time, though before it in ultimate importance, must be reckoned the effects produced by the standing army. In Tunisia some small part in the romanization of the country was played by veterans who had fought under Marius himself[5], and in Gallia Narbonensis far more was due to the military colonies of Caesar and Augustus. One of them, Arelate (Arles), profiting by her position on the Rhône and on the

[1] For Transalpine Gaul see Cicero, pro Fonteio, 5, 11.

[2] Livy XLIII, 3, 4.

[3] Appian, Iber. 38: cf. Livy XXXIV, 9, 1 sqq. for the later development at Emporiae.

[4] On the question of emigration by peasants from rural Italy the present writer, though suspecting that the movement to the West began earlier than is there suggested, would otherwise agree with the remarks of M. Rostovt-zeff in his Social and Economic History of the Roman Empire, pp. 34 sqq. and 498 n. 32. For a different view see W. E. Heitland in J.R.S. VIII, 1918, pp. 34 sqq.

[5] Dessau 1334, 9405 (Uchi); 6790 (Thibaris).

route to Spain, became a great commercial centre in the first century, and in the second deposed Massilia from her control of sea-borne trade. But, potent as was the influence of such a city on the life of its neighbours, the main contribution of the army to the spread of Roman culture was due less to the foundation of colonies for veterans than to the presence of its units in the provinces and to the continuous process of recruitment and discharge. Both in the Julio-Claudian period, when the legions were composed predominantly of Italians, and later when the provincial element steadily increased, time-expired soldiers tended to settle near the camp where they had been stationed[1]; and this practice became normal when Hadrian made it regular for garrisons to get recruits from the districts in which they had their quarters[2]. Even before it became customary to give them Roman citizenship on discharge, the auxiliaries, serving with an army whose language was Latin, whose higher officers were Roman at least in outlook, and whose tone was essentially Italian, had come into contact with the surface of Roman culture; and, as Rome discovered to her cost in A.D. 69, these men soon carried a knowledge of Roman methods to their brethren at home. This result the legions reinforced, first, when their recruits were drawn from Italy, by transferring a certain number of Italians permanently to the provinces, and later by strengthening the Roman connections of soldiers locally enrolled who in their private lives had ample occasion to spread the language and ideals of the army among the natives of their province[3].

The effectiveness of the camps as centres of Roman influence was increased by the civilian settlements they provoked. A camp made heavy calls for agricultural produce on the surrounding countryside, of which part was commonly assigned to it as military land[4]; but besides this it had needs only to be met by a mart of considerable dimensions. Such was provided by the *canabae*—at first the home of traders casually come together, but soon a community with an organization of its own, capable of growth even into a city in the fullest sense. By A.D. 68 the *canabae* at Vetera in Lower Germany had become something like a town[5], and this within half a century had received the status of *colonia* from Trajan[6]. Civic development was not always so rapid

---

[1] See Tacitus, *Ann.* XIV, 27.   [2] See above, p. 311.
[3] On this see Aelius Aristides 26 K, 75 *sqq.*
[4] See *e.g.* Tacitus, *Ann.* XIII, 54 *sq.*; *C.I.L.* III, 14370[10].
[5] Tacitus, *Hist.* IV, 22: for another interpretation see *Germania* X, 1926,
p. 35 *sq.*   [6] Dessau 2907, 7064 *sq.*

or so great as here. The *canabae* at Carnuntum, not made a *muni-cipium* before the time of Hadrian[1], only gained colonial rights from one of the Severi[2]; a place so important as Moguntiacum made no progress at all until the end of the third century[3]; and Argentorate is one instance of several where the original nature of the cantonment was kept unchanged. Nevertheless, whatever their constitutions, the business of such centres served to draw men from the Mediterranean towards the frontiers, bringing with them a knowledge of that civilization which it was the abiding achievement of Rome to spread from the coasts to the inland zones and to plant throughout Europe west of the Rhine.

A similar effect, weaker perhaps but more widely felt, was produced by groups of Italians who settled in the provinces without military demands to attract them. Wherever they found themselves, Roman citizens resident among provincials regularly formed a small society of their own, with an organization capable of development into a municipal constitution. Such groups were the *conventus civium Romanorum*—collections of Roman citizens living in a community of lower status, meeting from time to time to deal with their common interests, and having as their head a *curator*, probably chosen by themselves, if possible from among the Roman citizens who had held office in the place to which the *conventus* was attached[4]. Besides these there were other types, like the *pagi* formed in Africa by veterans settled on agricultural land[5]. Of the latter a familiar example is the town of Thugga (Dougga) in the hills above the valley of the Oued Khalled, where the great Graeco-Punic mausoleum of the second century B.C.[6], the winding streets with Roman houses, the theatre, and the Graeco-Roman temple of the Semitic Caelestis (Astarte), form a memorable picture of blended cultures. Its history is its explanation. A native township which flourished in Carthaginian times became a peregrine *civitas* on the arrival of Rome; but in its neighbourhood emigrants from Italy were settled on the land, and they in turn formed a *pagus* of Roman citizens. The two communities lived side by side, both using Thugga as their social centre and steadily becoming closer in their association. Already by A.D. 48 the native *civitas* described its council as a Senate and its people as a *plebs*, though its highest magistrates at this time still

---

[1] Dessau 7121.   [2] Dessau 7122.
[3] *C.I.L.* XIII, 6727.
[4] On this see E. Kornemann in P.W. *s.v.* Conventus, col. 1192 and the literature there cited.   [5] See *e.g.* Dessau 9400.
[6] See S. Gsell, *Hist. ancienne de l'Afrique du Nord*, VI, pp. 254 *sqq.*

bore the Punic name of 'suffetes[1].' Then, as more and more of its members received the Roman *civitas*, its distinction from the *pagus* became less and less significant until at the beginning of the third century the two were united in a single *municipium*[2], which finally received the coveted title of 'colonia' from Valerian or Gallienus[3].

If emigration and the army were responsible for carrying the Roman culture abroad, its influence on the provincial populations is not wholly to be explained without reference to a third factor of importance. Though they suppressed what seemed to them barbaric, like the human sacrifice which Claudius attacked in Gaul[4] and Hadrian was forced to deal with elsewhere[5], the Romans made no attempt to press their institutions on the world. Their own attitude was receptive. They lacked the Greek consciousness of cultural superiority: as Caesar is made to say, 'imitari quam invidere bonis malebant[6].' By assuming this same attitude in the peoples of the Empire, they escaped the failure which awaits the cultural crusade and left those who became their debtors to take what they chose and cherish what they took with the tenacity reserved for a possession freely acquired. But such debts were incurred with increasing readiness, and among their many causes one stands pre-eminent. This was the prestige of Rome—earned not by the glory of Roman arms but as gratitude to the authors of the Roman peace.

The Augustan Peace had done more than mark the end of the domestic disputes which generated the Civil Wars: it had brought order to a world where war had been almost normal since the beginnings of Greek and Roman history. In earlier times warfare had not, indeed, been continuous, and for a time the Augustan Peace was mistrusted as a passing lull. Men were grateful to Augustus for a respite which soon perhaps promised to cover a human lifetime; but it was only slowly that they came to understand the full magnitude of Rome's achievement. Peace, they discovered at length, was enduring, dependent not on its creator but on Rome, and by the end of the Julio-Claudian period the condition of the new age was recognized for what it was—the abiding Pax Romana. The 'immensa Romanae pacis maiestas[7]' entitled Rome herself to the gratitude of those who enjoyed it, and

---

[1] Dessau 6797.
[2] Dessau 6796.   [3] Dessau 541.
[4] Suetonius, *Claud.* 25, 5.   [5] See p. 439 n. 1.
[6] Sallust, *Cat.* 51, 38.
[7] Pliny, *N.H.* XXVII, 3.

when the peoples awoke, as from a dream[1], to knowledge of the new age, their feelings found expression in a devotion to the imperial power whose institutions they were proud to make models for their own. Provincial cities flattered themselves by copying the civic buildings of Rome; they sought colonial rights, not because their privileges would thereby be the greater, but because the title of 'colony' suggested closer connection with Rome than any other[2]; men made the Roman *civitas* the object of ambition[3]; and in the third century their zeal for Roman culture as they conceived it led to consequences which were even embarrassing. Such was the enthusiasm of the Illyrians for the traditions of a city whose past they did not understand that they were led by an imagined duty to defend the Roman gods into persecution of the Christian Church.[4]

Though the glamour of Urbs Roma, the focus of a loyalty which grew stronger even while its administrative importance decreased, was a potent commendation of the Latin culture in the lands to which it was presented, the outward changes which it encouraged were less valuable than the attitude of mind which it implied. That 'Samian' ware came into fashion in the western provinces, that architecture fell under the influence of the Mediterranean, that Roman methods were followed in local government, and even the fact that Latin became the common language of the West were achievements of which Rome indeed might boast; but as testimony to her imperial skill they are trivial compared with that pride in membership of the Empire and that staunch fidelity to the whole of which the reverence reserved for the city on the Tiber was an expression. The solidarity of the Roman world and the unity which at first was realized and then, when the reality was destroyed, gave the West an ideal which survived the Empire itself was strengthened and symbolized by the device which was among the most notable of Rome's contributions to the art of government. Neither Semites nor Persians nor the Greeks in Hellenistic times had found an outward sign to mark the common interest of those who owed a single allegiance. Their peoples were united by nothing less precarious than loyalty to the person of the reigning king—a bond of which Rome herself came to learn the value in the first two centuries after Christ, when the 'worship of the Emperor' generally had an object worthy of the devotion it assumed.[5] But the unity of

---

[1] See Aelius Aristides 26 κ, 69.   [2] See below, p. 454.
[3] See *e.g.* Pliny, *Pan.* 39, 5.
[4] See E. Schwartz, *Kaiser Constantin und die christliche Kirche*, p. 42.
[5] See Seneca, *de clem.* I, 4.

Italy after the Social War had been secured without recourse to the popularity of an individual: the Italians had been admitted to the Roman State, and the token of their membership was the *civitas Romana*. This momentous innovation was made possible by the Republic's discovery that wider and narrower citizenships were not incompatible, and that the people of an Italian town might become citizens of Rome without sacrificing the collective life of their own community. For the first time the world was introduced to the idea of an inclusive imperial citizenship, and this it was the work of the Principate to extend to the provinces at large. Augustus and Tiberius had been chary with their gifts[1], but with Claudius the policy became more generous[2], and thenceforward special grants to individuals and communities combined with the regular enfranchisement of peregrine troops on discharge to increase the number of the Roman *cives* until Caracalla, in A.D. 212, made at least all but the most backward of the free inhabitants of the Empire 'citizens of Rome.'

The privileges of citizenship inevitably diminished as its holders grew more numerous, but throughout the second century its distinction remained. The eagerness with which the honour was sought[3] and the care with which it was bestowed[4] are proof enough of its serious significance. It marked more than the mere favour of the central government; for the *civitas* long implied some knowledge of Roman culture in those who held it, and it was left for Severus Alexander to validate Roman wills written in any other language than Latin[5]. And even when the Constitutio Antoniniana of A.D. 212 largely deprived the citizenship of legal advantage and economic value, it remained a symbol of imperial unity, with no less, so far as can be seen, of that inestimable power, on which Aristides laid stress[6], to recall the common interest of government and people.

IV. THE UNITS OF LOCAL GOVERNMENT

In a world where the central power took so modest a view of its duty and left so large a share of the administration to the inhabitants themselves, the system of local government was necessarily complex; and its complexity was the greater because

---

1 For the reason see vol. x, p. 428 *sq.*
2 See vol. x, pp. 675 *sq.*, 684 *sq.*
3 See *e.g.* Plutarch, *de tran. animi*, 10 (*Mor.* 470 B).
4 See *e.g.* Pliny, *Epp.* x, 5 (4), 6 (22), 7 (23).
5 *Studien zur Palaeographie and Papyruskunde*, xx, no. 35, 13 *sq.*; cf. P. Oxy. vi, 907, l. 2 and note, and *B.G.U.* v, 2, p. 29 *sq.*
6 26 K, 65.

Rome consistently refrained from wanton interference with the native institutions of her peoples. Development there was, but it was natural and unforced—the result less of Roman orders than of the Roman peace. Peace brought prosperity, prosperity allowed culture to progress, and, when men found themselves at once with new conceptions of a decent life and with the means for their attainment, the outward aspect of society was changed. Though Rome planted colonies even in backward lands where their influence was reflected in villages assigned to their control, and though grants of status were made by governmental acts, the most potent reason for the advance of civilization was that a demand grew up for what Rome had made available among those to whom her ways were new. The result was a movement towards city-life, of the kind familiar in Italy and Greece; but the movement was far from general, and even when begun its pace was determined by local conditions.

Romanization of society in its fullest form meant that the population was incorporated in cities, each with a *territorium* beyond its walls and each with a council and magistrates of its own. But there were vast regions of the Empire to which life of this kind remained strange, where, as in Thrace and parts of Syria, the rare cities were Roman foundations in a land which retained its village organization, or where again, as in the Tres Galliae, towns had existed even before Roman times but still failed to acquire that predominance over the surrounding country which would make them cities in the fullest constitutional sense[1]. There were great estates too, often attached to no urban unit, belonging either to private individuals, resident or absentee, or to temples, as commonly in Asia Minor, or to the *fiscus*, which penal expropriation soon made responsible for enormous areas of productive land. On the imperial *saltus* of Africa, where the survival of inscriptions has preserved some details of their economy, the land was agricultural; but the assets of the State included other forms of wealth which called for varied methods of development. Of these the mines are an instance brilliantly illuminated by the evidence from Aljustrel, where a settlement, apparently of large dimensions but without self-government, was organized and controlled by the agents of the State[2]. But though these local peculiarities all have their place in the economic history of the provinces, their relevance to romanization at large lies only in the reminder they supply of two essential facts. The first is that Rome did not lack the pliancy of method which in an imperial power is the first

[1] See p. 502 *sq.*   [2] Dessau 6891 (Bruns, *Fontes*[7], 112); see p. 493.

condition of success; and the second that the city-life wherein ancient culture reached its highest level was a life to which large sections of the people never managed to attain. For the rest, it is the cities themselves which deserve attention; for in them, if anywhere, were realized the ideals of social health and local autonomy which Rome showed to be compatible with her insistence on world-wide peace, and which were the motives of her policy even towards the rudest of the races she controlled.

When a province was formed, arrangements must be made for the permanent administration; and, since much was left to the inhabitants themselves, it was above all things necessary that the officials of Rome should know with whom they had to deal. Accordingly the local units into which the region fell were exhaustively examined, modifications which seemed expedient were made, and the status of each with its rights and obligations was defined in terms which under the Republic had by custom been considered in Rome and embodied in a 'lex provinciae.' The details of these arrangements, made at the opening of the Roman age, in general are irrelevant to the developments which followed; but in one particular their effect was of the first importance. The units which Rome recognized were destined to manage their own affairs, and the vigour of their political life was necessarily determined by its scale. If the value of freedom is to give men that zest for living without which initiative is destroyed and progress ends, and which is only to be secured when they conceive themselves to be masters of their environment, the opportunities afforded by the politics of the parish pump are less fruitful than those where issues are greater and responsibilities more extensive. Thus it is not without significance that the units of local government in the Roman empire tended to be large. Exceptions, of course, were many. In Italy itself, where the population, judged by ancient standards, was dense, and where the old units had been broken up during the Roman conquest to provide *ager publicus populi Romani*, the area over which a municipality had control was generally not wide: Pompeii, for instance, lay within sight of her neighbour Stabiae and, except to the east, her land seems not to have extended in any direction more than five miles from the walls. But in the north the territories were more impressive. Veleia, in the Apennine near the modern Bobbio, controlled an area which stretched from the frontiers of Placentia to those of Luca[1]; and between Luca and Veleia the distance is over 100 miles. In the provinces, where Rome was not constrained by the legacy

[1] Dessau 6675 (*e.g.* XIII and XVI).

of earlier times, *territoria* often attained the dimensions of a modern English county. The peoples of the Tres Galliae were grouped into sixty-four *civitates*[1], each of which, on average, must have covered a rather larger area than a Department under the Third Republic; in Pontus an important town like Amasia had control of a region which ran sixty miles from the city in one direction[2]; and in the fifth century St Augustine was moved to reflect how trivial was the domain of regal Rome, when the frontiers were nowhere more than twenty miles away, compared with the territories of the Gaetulian *civitates* in his own day[3]. Thus the business of local government was more than trivial, and those at least who controlled it were concerned with affairs which left them with no cause to fall into the lethargy which afflicts men whose opinions are of no account.

The constitutions of these urban communities and their relations to the provincial government varied in detail according to the status of their inhabitants. The least favoured of the cities— those which came into the category of *civitates stipendiariae*—were the homes of people who, save for individuals personally enfranchised by Rome either after military service or for some other reason, were foreigners (*peregrini*). Their rights in local administration and their relations with the imperial authorities were determined by the settlement made when they were brought within the Empire, and this settlement was not a negotiated treaty but an arrangement imposed by Rome and revocable by her. The same was also true of a more envied class—those commonly known as 'civitates liberae,' whose position was in fact one of independence, modified perhaps by a few small reserves. The people of Termessus Maior, for instance, whose position is partly known from the extant fragments of a *plebiscitum* in which it was defined[4], could make their own laws, administer justice for themselves without interference from the governor, even apparently in cases where Roman citizens were involved[5], manage their own finances without Roman supervision, and levy customs dues (though Roman tax-collectors could not be charged on goods in transit). Furthermore, Termessus Maior, like most *civitates liberae* until the last years of the Republic, enjoyed the valuable

[1] Tacitus, *Ann.* III, 44.   [2] Strabo XII, 561.

[3] *De civ. Dei* III, 15 *ad fin.*: cf. A. Souter in *Class. Rev.* XXXVII, 1923, p. 115.

[4] Dessau 38.

[5] Cf. *I.G.R.R.* IV, 943, l. 17 *sq.* There was, however, some limitation to this right against Roman citizens charged with more serious offences.

privilege of exemption from taxation by Rome (*immunitas*). All
that was demanded of the free cities at first was that they should
recognize the Roman supremacy and forgo the claim to a foreign
policy of their own: for the rest they were virtually outside the
provincial system and their independence was left intact, though
it rested on the somewhat precarious basis of an arbitrary grant
from the Roman People. By imperial times their position had in
one respect been changed: perhaps during Pompey's re-organization of the East, *libertas* and *immunitas* had been openly divorced[1],
and thenceforward, if *immunitas* was to be conferred, there was need
for a separate concession[2] so rarely made that the majority of cities
which called themselves 'free' were nevertheless stipendiary.
Libertas itself, however, continued, even in places with Latin or
Roman rights[3], as a privilege which the frequency of its mention
proves to have been appreciated by those who held it. It may,
indeed, have flattered their conceit more than it increased their
actual rights; for it is to be observed that in Cilicia Cicero found a
moderate measure of judicial independence, such as even *civitates
stipendiariae* enjoyed, enough to satisfy the people that they were
free[4]. But if the differences it made were trivial, the reason is not
any lack of reality in *libertas* but the extent of the freedom enjoyed
even by those communities which were not entitled technically
to be called 'civitates liberae.' With cities of this class may be
closely joined the *civitates foederatae*, which complete the list of
forms taken by urban communities of peregrine status. *Civitates
foederatae* shared the benefits of the ordinary *civitates liberae*, but in
theory their position was more secure because their freedom was
conferred, not by revocable grant, but by a bilateral *foedus*, usually
the result of service to Rome in war. The *civitates foederatae* of
the Empire kept alive in their titles the memory of gratitude
earned in days when Rome still had need of allies, but as an
instrument of international law the *foedus* in these cases retained
little of its significance. As a guarantee it lost its power; for,
whatever the method she pursued, Rome on occasion would
repudiate its terms if they were made a cover for disturbance or
disaffection[5].

Like *civitates stipendiariae* and *civitates liberae*, the *civitates
foederatae* were properly peregrine communities, but it might
sometimes happen that an earlier *foedus*, like a grant of *libertas*,

---

[1] See Mommsen, *Röm. Staatsrecht*, III, p. 683, n. 4.   [2] See below, p. 455.
[3] *E.g. C.I.L.* II, 2021, 2025; Dessau 6796.   [4] *Ad Att.* VI, I, 15.
[5] *E.g.* Tacitus, *Ann.* XII, 58; Ditt.³ 810 *ad fin.*; Suetonius, *Vesp.* 8, 4
(Rhodes).

was recalled in the style of a city[1] even after its people had risen to some higher status of the kind which must next be noticed. Between foreigners and Roman citizens in fact (though in law, like all non-Romans, they were *peregrini*[2]) stood the Latins—enjoying rights collectively described by a name which, whatever Pliny may have meant by the words 'iactatum procellis rei publicae Latium[3],' had borne many meanings in the troubled course of Rome's constitutional history—*Ius Latii* or *Latium*. In the West, though not elsewhere[4], and only to a slight extent in Africa, the more romanized communities were raised to the *Ius Latii* as a first step on the way to their final incorporation in the body of Roman citizens. These Latins[5] enjoyed various advantages— many of them included in the *ius commercii*, which as regards the law of property in Roman territory made them virtually indistinguishable from Romans; but the characteristic feature of the Latin right was that it offered to some of those who held it an avenue to the Roman *civitas*, and in the first century the conditions of entry were that a man should have held a magistracy in his city[6]. Subject to an uncertain limitation of number, at the end of his year in office the magistrate himself, his parents, his wife, his children and the children of his sons (provided that they were in *potestas*), all received *civitas Romana*. The effect of the Latin right was thus slowly to draft members of the local aristocracy into the body of Roman citizens, to be a visible link between Rome and the places where they lived. The success of this device may perhaps explain a later development which, though it may have served other ends as well[7], undoubtedly increased the speed of this incorporation[8]. *Latium maius*, which makes its first appearance

---

[1] *E.g.* Dessau 1020.　　　　　　　　　[2] Gaius I, 79

[3] *N.H.* III, 30. For a discussion of the reading in this passage and of various interpretations proposed see R. K. McElderry in *J.R.S.* VIII, 1918, p. 62 *sq.*

[4] See O. Hirschfeld, *Kleine Schriften*, pp. 88 *sqq.* with the literature there cited.

[5] The Latin right of provincial towns is to be sharply distinguished from 'Junian Latinity,' designed as a status for slaves 'informally' manumitted (see vol. x, p. 431 *sq.*). *Peregrini* who became Latins were in legal terminology 'Latini coloniarii,' and their position bore little resemblance to that of Latini Iuniani except in the one respect that Latins of both kinds had, on certain conditions, assured access to the Roman citizenship.

[6] Cf. Dessau 6088, ll. 1 *sqq.* There is no reason to qualify the statement in the text, as suggested by Mommsen (*Staatsrecht*, III, p. 639, n. 5).

[7] See below, p. 466.

[8] On this aspect of the change see L. Homo, *Le Haut-Empire*, p. 524.

between A.D. 100 and the death of Pius[1], extended to members of the town-council the Roman citizenship which hitherto, by the system now distinguished as *Latium minus*, had been withheld from all but magistrates. Still it was the local aristocracy which Rome admitted to her franchise; but the rate at which Roman citizens were recruited from towns of Latin right was now notably increased, and the institution of *Latium maius* may reasonably be said to mark a stage in the progress towards the general enfranchisement of A.D. 212.

There remain the communities of highest rank, whose members, by the mere fact of membership, were Roman citizens. The division of these cities into *coloniae civium Romanorum* and *municipia civium Romanorum* had its origins in the practice of the Republic, whereby 'colonia' was a term reserved for new foundations while 'municipium' was applied to towns which, after an earlier history of their own, were brought into the Roman system. Thus, when the Social War brought the complete enfranchisement of Italy, in a peninsula of which the whole free population had now become Roman there was no city, except Rome itself, which could not be described as either 'colonia' or 'municipium'; and so, since the colonies abroad were still few enough to be regarded as exceptions, the phrase 'municipia et coloniae' acquired the meaning which it retained even into the first century of the Empire—'the country-towns of Italy[2].' With Julius Caesar, however, when the unification of Italy was complete, Rome turned her attention to the problem of the provinces, and the progress of romanization abroad brought developments in the practice and in the terminology of government. *Coloniae civium Romanorum* in the provinces became more numerous, and at the same time cities of peregrine origin abroad began to receive either the Roman right or, as a step towards final incorporation, the *Ius Latii*. Though it was an innovation when the term was applied to a Latin community[3], provincial towns, whether Roman or Latin, began to be known as *municipia* unless some act of foundation by Rome entitled them to the name of Roman colony; and 'municipium,' used of places outside Italy, thus came to mean a

[1] Gaius (I, 96) is the earliest certain evidence for *Latium maius*, which Pliny (*Pan.* 39, 5) implies to have been unknown in A.D. 100 but which is probably to be recognized in Dessau 6680 (iii, ll. 6 *sqq.*), where the reference is to the time of Pius. The present writer does not accept the earlier dating proposed by C. Jullian in his *Histoire de la Gaule*, IV, p. 245, n. I.

[2] See *J.R.S.* XXIV, 1934, p. 59.

[3] On the lack of precedent, which has often been denied, see E. Kornemann in P.W. *s.v.* Municipium, col. 584 *sq.*

town, once peregrine, whose status had been raised by Rome, whether as yet only to the Latin stage or already to the full Roman *civitas*. Thus far the meanings of these terms had grown from their earliest sense to connote new forms generated by new needs; but their history was now confused by the fickle influence of fashion. In particular the title 'colonia' was freely given, already in the first century of our era[1], to places whether of Roman or of Latin right, which had not been founded or refounded by Rome and which sometimes were not even cities at all but merely the centre of a people whose organization remained tribal[2].

The increasing frequency of these grants, which created what have been justly distinguished as 'titular colonies[3],' was due in the last resort to the increasing prestige of Rome. Aulus Gellius[4] records a famous occasion on which Hadrian was approached by the people of his native place, Italica, with a request, like one lately come from Utica in Africa, that their city should cease to be a *municipium* and become a *colonia*. The choice between these titles had exercised local patriots on many occasions in the past, and preference was determined by the whims of taste which, after some uncertainty, finally fixed upon the colonial status as the more enviable. Since *municipia* were properly towns of alien origin, whereas *coloniae* in the strict sense were the creation of Rome, 'cuius...quasi effigies parvae simulacraque esse quaedam videntur[5],' the colonial title suggested the closer connection with the Roman People; and it was for this reason, and for this reason alone, that it was sought with an eagerness which is a clue to the good-will enjoyed by the imperial power. To the legal rights of the inhabitants and to their fiscal obligations the mere change of a city's style from *municipium* to *colonia* made no difference at all[6].

[1] There is no good reason to reject the evidence of Tacitus (*Hist.* iv, 62, 72, 77) about the colonial status of Trèves.

[2] *E.g. C.I.L.* xiii, 5685, 5693 *sq.* ('colonia Lingonum'—Langres); cf. Tacitus, *Hist.* i, 78: Dessau 7042 (Anicium Vellavorum—Le Puy-en-Velay).

[3] See E. Kornemann, *Zur Stadtentstehung in den ehemals keltischen und germanischen Gebieten des Römerreichs*, pp. 37–43.

[4] *N.A.* xvi, 13, 4 *sq.*   [5] *Ib.* 9.

[6] Hadrian, in whom ignorance in such matters cannot be assumed, did, indeed, express surprise on this same occasion that the citizens of a *municipium* should wish it to become a *colonia* when, by staying as they were, they might continue 'to enjoy their own customs and laws'; but there is no reason to suppose that he is doing more than remind his hearers of the fact that, in the early days of Rome's expansion, towns which were made *municipia* not only had been larger than the *coloniae civium Romanorum* but, by preserving many of their institutions unchanged from pre-Roman times, had retained an individuality not to be found in the small Roman colonies, which necessarily

The legal and material advantages which changes of title did
nothing to secure were conferred by the government in other ways.
The simple practice of the Republic whereby Italy supplied the
men, and the provinces the money, had indeed been modified in
detail: in Italy while recruitment diminished taxation increased,
and the demand for troops was steadily being transferred to the
provincials. But the principle that inhabitants of the provinces
should pay taxes to Rome had been maintained; and when *libertas*
and *immunitas* ceased to be inseparable[1], it was even strengthened.
Its maintenance involved the consequence that the fiscal liabilities
of provincials were determined not by their status but by their
domicile; and so by acquiring the Latin or the Roman right they
gained nothing in relief from taxation. Nevertheless, the government did not forgo the right to make exceptions. *Immunitas* was
still occasionally bestowed, though not always in the fullest form[2];
but *immunitas* itself had ceased to be the most generous concession
of which Rome was capable. The highest privilege accessible to
provincial cities was the *Ius Italicum*—a grant of great value to
the inhabitants and one which seems to have been strictly reserved
for places where circumstances were such as to demand peculiar
consideration. In general its effect was to put the territory of a
provincial city in the same legal position as Italian soil—to withdraw it from the eminent domain which Rome claimed over
solum provinciale from Julio-Claudian times, to make it capable of
individual ownership *optimo iure Quiritium*, to exempt it and its
population from direct taxation, and to leave it outside the jurisdiction of the provincial governor[3]. But the sacrifice of revenue
thus involved was one which the government made with reluctance.
In Dacia[4], as in the remoter parts of Spain[5], the grant of the *Ius
Italicum* may be explained by the need to encourage centres of
Roman influence in regions where life was dangerous as well as

conformed in some degree to a type suggested by Rome itself. The power
of Roman influence, however, was such that by the second century A.D. the
municipia, as Gellius observes, had forgotten their old distinction: if they
changed at all, it was to become more like Rome and the Roman colonies.
Thus, when origins had been obscured, *coloniae* first rivalled the *municipia* in
repute and then excelled them, because fashion favoured a style which smacked
of familiarity with Rome.

[1] See above, p. 451.
[2] Cf. *Dig.* L, 15, 8, 7 (Paul).
[3] The further consequence of this suggested by Mommsen (*Staatsrecht*, III,
p. 810) is almost certainly to be rejected: see *J.R.S.* XXIV, 1934, pp. 58 *sqq.*
[4] *Dig.* L, 15, 1, 8 *sq.* (Ulpian).
[5] Pliny, *N.H.* III, 25; *Dig.* L, 15, 8 *pr.* (Paul).

hard; and the favour of Septimius for his native land may account
for its gift, by him and Caracalla, to Leptis Magna, Carthage and
Utica[1]. To the end, however, the privilege remained so rare that it
cannot have been the serious ambition of any ordinary town, and
it deserves notice rather as an economic stimulus than as a device
to bridge the gap between Italy and the provinces.

V. THE MUNICIPAL CONSTITUTIONS

Coloniae and *municipia civium Romanorum*, cities with the Latin
right and those whose people were still *peregrini*, differed greatly
in prestige and self-esteem; but, despite the variety of detail,
urban communities of whatever status were markedly alike both
in their administrative responsibilities and in the essential features
of their civic constitutions. In the simplest form of urban organization all free citizens of a certain area were citizens of the city which
formed the centre of its life; and, if those whose work lay in the
countryside grouped their homes in villages, these villages were
mere social accidents, unrecognized by the public law. But time
brought complications, and contact between cultures increased
them. When a new city was founded in a barbarian land, the
previous inhabitants of its territory might still remain, though by
culture they were unfit to join the colonists as citizens; and when
a city had its territory extended, the people brought under its
control might likewise best be left to live as they had lived before.
Moreover, when the contrast between urban development and the
stagnation of the more distant countryside was so great that
peasants who in fact were citizens came near to forgetting their
rights[2], it ill accorded with the Greek conception of citizenship
that the mere fact of domicile should be enough to include
elements so diverse in a single polity. The problem, recognized
already in the days of Greek independence, became more insistent
when the conquest of Asia brought Greeks into contact with
peoples often far behind them in political development, and its
solution produced various features characteristic of the Hellenistic
age. None was more notable than the abandonment of the old
dichotomy by which every community was either a *polis* or politically nothing, and the substitution for it of forms in a graded
sequence through which a place might rise by stages from village
origins to the dignity of a self-governing city[3], with the result that

---

[1] *Dig.* L, 15, 8, 11 (Paul).
[2] See Dio Chrys. *Or.* VII, 49.
[3] On this see W. W. Tarn, *Hellenistic Civilisation*[2], p. 129 *sq.*

by imperial times cities are freely found controlling smaller settlements which do not share their own status. In Asia Minor, for instance, the *paroeci* were a recognized section of the population[1]; and in the West not only are there frequent signs that within the municipal areas the free inhabitants were not all of equal privilege[2] but the need for differentiation was formally recognized by the Roman practice of *attributio*.

Attributio, which had been adopted as early as the second century B.C.[3] and which was widely applied in Transpadane Gaul by the Lex Pompeia of 89 B.C.[4], was an arrangement whereby less advanced communities were placed under the control of a neighbouring city, through which they paid their *tributum* to Rome and which was immediately responsible for the maintenance of order and the administration of justice. The *attributi* were in theory a distinct and subordinate society, often with an incipient constitution of their own; and, though the land they used was sometimes included in the *territorium* of the nearby city[5], the scanty evidence suggests that it might be left outside[6]. But the feature of this institution which entitled it to notice in the story of romanization in the West is the readiness with which *attributi*, though strictly of lower status than the place to which they were attached, could mingle with its population so freely that all distinction disappeared[7]. Doubtless North Italy was a favourable setting for this assimilation, and it cannot be assumed to have happened so soon elsewhere; but even in the remoter provinces, by bringing less favoured communities into touch with more advanced, *attributio* served to spread that knowledge of municipal government which was the necessary condition of its use[8].

In the municipal constitutions, however, *attributi* had no proper place, and with them may also go the *incolae*. *Incolae*—properly residents who had their *origo* elsewhere—were indeed called

---

[1] See Rostovtzeff, *op. cit.* p. 562, n. 3.

[2] Cf. for instance, the type '*qui in ea colon(ia) intrave eius colon(iae) finis domicilium praediumve habebit neque eius colon(iae) colon(us) erit*' in Dessau 6087, tab. iii, col. iii, ll. 33 *sqq.* (xcviii) and the instances quoted by Jullian, *op. cit.* iv, p. 356, n. 5.

[3] Dessau 5946.　　　　　　　　[4] Pliny, *N.H.* iii, 138.

[5] Dessau 5946, ll. 23 *sqq.*; 206, ll. 22 *sqq.*, where this seems to be implied by Claudius' silence about an extension of Tridentine territory as a consequence of his decision on the disputed *civitas*.

[6] See Rostovtzeff, *op. cit.* p. 564, n. 6.

[7] Dessau 206, ll. 22 *sqq.*

[8] Cf. for, *e.g.*, the history of Thibilis, a *pagus* of Cirta, S. Gsell and C.-A. Joly, *Khamissa, Mdaourouch, Announa*, iiie partie: *Announa*, pp. 11–23.

upon to bear their share of civic burdens[1], just as at times
they were allowed to enjoy public benefactions[2] and, where
some form of popular assembly survived, even to exercise a
restricted right of voting[3]; but in the great days of the municipalities they seem to have been debarred from office unless they
had ceased to be *incolae* by gaining admission to full membership
of the community in which they lived[4]. Circumstances, however,
made their disabilities slight. With the decay of democracy
suffrage ceased to be an effective privilege, and admission to the
local citizenship, which opened the way to office, was less difficult
than has sometimes been supposed. It had, indeed, once been
an axiom of Roman political theory that no man could be a
citizen of two places at once[5]; but to maintain this principle in
the East after the freedom with which citizenship had been
conferred *honoris causa* and the spread of isopolity in Hellenistic
times[6], would have been impossible, as Trajan found[7], even if it
had not been the outstanding achievement of the Roman Republic
to discover that another franchise was compatible with its own.
Conservatives, it is true, seemed to have frowned on the combination of local citizenships, but even in the West the practice was
not uncommon, and Fronto, whose family came from Cirta, even
goes so far as to assume that Cirta would gain a new citizen when
his daughter found a husband[8].

　　The constitutions of the municipalities in all their variations
were developed from that combination of a popular assembly with
a council and a magistracy which was common to both Greece and
Rome. In the East democracy had been in decline even before
Rome came to throw her influence on the side of the more
substantial elements, and in Rome itself circumstances had combined to make oligarchy the one possible alternative to monarchy.
In the municipalities the same forces were at work. The size of the

---

[1] *E.g.* Dessau 6087, tab. iii, col. v, ll. 1 *sqq.* (CIII); 6680, col. iii,
ll. 3 *sqq.*; 1374.

[2] *E.g.* Dessau 6818—an inscription which reveals that, when the distinction
between town and country was marked, *incolae* resident in the town were
better treated than those resident outside. In the third century the name
seems to have been reserved for the former class: *Dig.* L, 1, 35 (Modestinus).

[3] Dessau 6089, ll. 43 *sqq.* (LIII).

[4] See, however, Dessau 6916, 6992.

[5] Cicero, *pro Balbo*, 11, 28; cf. *de legibus*, II, 2, 5.

[6] See Tarn, *op. cit.* pp. 78 *sqq.*

[7] Pliny, *Ep.* x, 114 (115) *sq.*

[8] *Ad amicos*, II, 10 (p. 200 N), reading '*habebitis*,' with Niebuhr:
cf. for instance Dessau 2688, 6624, 6953, 7005, 7159.

territoria was often such that distance alone was enough to prevent the citizens from meeting more than rarely; and so, though in towns organized by Rome the people were distributed in voting groups—in tribes at the Colonia Genetiva Julia[1] and in the more frequent *curiae* at the Latin Municipium Flavium Malacitanum[2], their part in government was small and dwindling. Rome showed no enthusiasm for democracy, and in the great *civitates* of the Tres Galliae, where the difficulties of distance were peculiar and where tradition was wholly oligarchical, assemblies make no appearance in States which, though not strictly urban, had constitutions inspired by the urban model.

In the West, where Roman influence was strongest, the assemblies were confined, like those of the Roman Republic, to a simple acceptance or rejection of proposals laid before them and to the voting on candidates for office. At first, indeed, these rights were not to be despised. The *graffiti* of Pompeii prove the vigour of election campaigns, and in A.D. 60 the people of Puteoli sent an embassy to Rome with complaints about the local aristocrats[3]. But except in Africa, where constitutional and economic development alike lagged a century or more behind events in other regions of the West, after the time of Trajan the western municipalities seem rapidly to have shed this democratic veneer and to have left everything but formalities, such as honorific decrees, in the hands of the council and magistrates. In Greek lands, however, though the public assemblies had rapidly decayed in the third and second centuries B.C., prejudice and long-standing tradition delayed their final disappearance. The judicial functions of the Athenian *demos* in the second century may owe something to the whims of Hadrian[4]; but Plutarch provides evidence enough that in his time the people were still active in politics[5], and later records[6] show that it was not till the third century that they followed the assemblies of the West into insignificance.

In the municipalities what was lost by the many was gained by the few, until finally both power and responsibility lay with the councils and magistrates alone. In the East these councils were sometimes large, and in many cases members were elected for limited periods; but the system favoured by Rome and predomi-

---

[1] Dessau 6087, tab. iii, col. iv, ll. 17 *sqq.* (CI).

[2] Dessau 6089, col. i, l. 35 *sq.* (LII) etc.

[3] Tacitus, *Ann.* XIII, 48.

[4] *I.G.* II, III, ed. minor, 1100, ll. 46 *sqq.*

[5] *Praec. ger. rei p.* 5 (*Mor.* 802 E *sqq.*)—on public speaking: cf. Dio Chrys. *Or.* XLVIII, 1 *sqq.*   [6] Cf. *e.g. O.G.I.S.* 515, 572.

nant in the West was one whereby the *ordo* consisted of a hundred *decuriones*, either co-opted or nominated[1] by the highest magistrates on the regular occasions, once every five years, when they were charged with censorial duties, and in practice holding their seats for life. As at Rome, ex-magistrates not already members of the House seem to have had first claim to vacant places[2], but there is no certain sign in the municipalities of an arrangement like that made by Sulla for recruiting the Roman Senate without the help of censors[3].

The magistracies which supplied the executive differed widely in name and nature. The Greek cities preserved forms familiar in the age of independence, overlaid with the deposit of Hellenistic times. Archons and *strategoi* were still common, but at their side appeared great figures of later origin like the permanent town-clerk (*grammateus*)[4], the *agoranomos*, whose prominence was a monument of third-century care for the social services, and the guardian of what had come to be the hall-mark of Hellenism—the gymnasiarch. In the West, where the influence of Rome commended the grouping of magistrates into colleges, from the varieties of the Italian constitutions the Romans had evolved a scheme which, in the commonest of its many forms, finally contained *duoviri iure dicundo* and two aediles, to whom a college of two quaestors might be added. Beside this there appears another arrangement, favoured for a time after the enfranchisement of Italy, by which the magistrates were a quattuorvirate, soon distinguished as two *quattuorviri iure dicundo* and two *quattuorviri aediles*; but there is evidence enough to show that this refinement, despite its prevalence, could not claim any great significance[5], and even in its absence *duoviri iure dicundo* and aediles might be treated as colleagues[6]. The duumvirate, however, though it was highest among the regular offices, was not the final reward of municipal ambition; for every fifth year it became a greater honour, when its holders, charged with various censorial powers, had to perform tasks of special responsibility—such as filling vacancies in the *ordo* and renewing leases of municipal property—and marked their distinction by adding 'quinquennalis' to their official style.

[1] See, for instance, Cicero, *pro Caelio*, 2, 5; Dessau 6085, ll. 86, 104 *sq.*
[2] Dessau 6085, l. 135 *sq.*; 6680, col. ii, l. 6 *sq.*
[3] See vol. ix, p. 286 *sq.*
[4] See Acts xix, 35.
[5] Cf. Dessau 6086, ll. 7 and 14; 6092, ll. 4 and 17.
[6] Dessau 6354; cf. Mommsen, *Ges. Schr.* i, p. 325 *sq.*

In the first century the annual elections were still generally made by the people, but the decline of the assemblies, hastened by the example of Rome, gradually transferred their choice to the *ordo*; and as early as the time of Marcus the custom had begun by which *decuriones*, to whom office was gradually confined[1], were expected to take magistracies in the order of their appointment to the council[2]. As their title would suggest, the *duoviri iure dicundo* were largely concerned with the administration of justice, and surviving records of the rules they were required to apply leave no doubt about the burden of their task[3]; but besides these duties, like the consuls at Rome they presided over the council and the assembly, and so were concerned both with the preparation of the most varied business and with the execution of the ultimate decisions. Many of these affairs were trivial, like the constant grants of honours to public benefactors, but, even if not all communities held the power enjoyed by the Colonia Genetiva Julia, to mobilize its citizens against threatened attack[4], self-government in the cities was not a sham, responsibilities were considerable, sometimes extending to powers of legislation[5], and the problems of finance, which, particularly in the East, often involved the management of a local currency, demanded competence greater than the local authorities could continuously provide. The routine of administration, especially in the town itself, fell largely to the aediles: it was their business to supervise the streets and public buildings, to control the market and to maintain order—duties for which they were equipped with judicial powers, like the aediles in Rome[6]. Quaestors, where they were found, appear to have stood in the same humble relation to the *duoviri* as the early Roman quaestors to the consuls, and in some places the quaestorship was not even regarded as a magistracy[7].

Amid all their varieties the municipal constitutions show a common characteristic which would have been inevitably developed when annual magistrates were called upon to work with a council recruited from their predecessors, even if it had not from the outset been encouraged by Rome—the strict limitation of executive freedom and an oligarchical domination which was marked at the outset and became complete when popular election

---

[1] *Dig.* L, 2, 7, 2 (Paul).
[2] *Dig.* L, 4, 6, *pr.* (Ulpian).　　　　[3] *E.g.* Bruns, *Fontes*[7], 16 *sq.*
[4] Dessau 6087, tab. iii, col. v, ll. 2 *sqq.* (CIII).
[5] Cf. *O.G.I.S.* 515.
[6] *Dig.* L, 2, 12 (Callistratus).　　　　[7] *Dig.* L, 4, 18, 2 (Charisius).

fell into disuse. Not only were the magistrates subject to the *intercessio* of their colleagues[1], but in the Colonia Genetiva Julia they were formally bound, under penalty of 10,000 sesterces for every failure, to obey the decrees of the *decuriones*[2]. Moreover, the charter of this colony, at least, enumerated the business—some of it trifling like the allocation of seats in the theatre[3]—which could not be decided without reference to the council; and even in the matter of jurisdiction, where the *duoviri* retained some measure of independence, in the Spanish municipalities given *Ius Latii* by Vespasian appeal against fines imposed by the *duoviri* or aediles lay to the *decuriones*[4]. The strength of the tendency towards oligarchy showed itself again in the development of smaller bodies either within the *ordo* itself or at its side. By the last century of the Republic leading members of the local aristocracy seem to have gained some kind of recognition in certain towns of Italy and Sicily under names such as 'decem primi[5],' and these were the forerunners of a class which, though its functions before the end of the second century are ill-recorded, subsequently gained an unenviable prominence, due perhaps in part to the fiscal changes which made the *dekaprotoi* of the East responsible for the collection of the imperial taxes in their cities. Despite their independent origin, there is little doubt that their emergence in the West was a symptom of that drift towards dependence on the few which in Greek lands was marked by the growth of the *gerousia.* In origin this institution, which is characteristic of the Roman age, may well have been purely social, but in course of time these secondary senates acquired an undoubted authority, not the less weighty because it was justified more by the reputation of the members than by the law of the constitution[6].

The strength of the oligarchies was wealth. In a world where there was no national debt and the opportunities for investment were consequently few, men parted with their money in a way which would be counted prodigal by those who know a Stock Exchange. The letters of the younger Pliny, who was only passing rich according to the standards of his day, are reminder enough that in the first two centuries munificence rose to heights rarely, if ever, attained by later ages. And when generosity is a

---

[1] Dessau 6088, col. ii, ll. 11 *sqq.* (XXVII).
[2] Dessau 6087, tab. iv, col. ii, ll. 32 *sqq.* (CXXIX).
[3] Dessau 6087, tab. iv, col. i, ll. 29 *sqq.* (CXXVI).
[4] Dessau 6089, col. iv, l. 72—col. v, l. 13 (LXVI).
[5] Cf. Cicero, *pro S. Roscio* 9, 25; *ad Att.* x, 13, 1; Dessau 139, l. 13.
[6] On the various interpretations of the evidence for the *gerousiai* see V. Chapot, *La province romaine proconsulaire d'Asie*, pp. 216 *sqq.*

tradition, the many can scarcely fail to seize their opportunity and become parasites on the few. So there grew up the system whereby the wealth of individuals was invoked to meet an expenditure which had outrun the ordinary public income.

The revenues of a municipality were derived in the first place from rents of assets belonging to the community—assets of which the accumulation was encouraged by Nerva and Hadrian when they gave these bodies the right to take legacies[1]. Land, as always in the ancient world, was the main investment, and cities held estates, sometimes remote from themselves, often of considerable dimensions. There is, indeed, no surviving record of the way in which Arpinum[2] and Atella[3] came to own property in Cisalpine Gaul, but we know that it was Octavian who gave Capua land in Crete at Cnossus, probably worth 1,200,000 sesterces a year[4]. To rents of lands and of buildings owned by the municipality in the city itself there were added miscellaneous receipts from fines, from fees, as for admission to the citizenship[5], from the lease of fishing rights on inland waters, and in some places at least from tolls and harbour dues[6]. Against the revenue had to be set an expenditure in which the only item balanced by its own returns was the water-supply, for which a rate was charged; and, though the cost of administration was not high, the ever popular games, the public cults, and in some places a food-supply subsidized in Hellenistic style, combined with the demands of local patriotism for costly satisfaction (whether in pretentious buildings or in futile embassies to congratulate the *princeps* and his agents[7] on the most trivial occasions—and incidentally to give the envoys a holiday at public expense) to raise the outgoings far beyond the limit of the normal revenue. The scale of municipal resources was large, but not large enough to allow a city to spend ten million sesterces, like Nicaea, on a theatre with foundations so waterlogged that it was found unsafe even before it was finished[8].

The resultant deficit it was the duty of the rich to meet. In places where Roman influence was strong, there did indeed survive the early institution of the *corvée* by which, at the Colonia Genetiva Julia, all free residents between fourteen and sixty, rich

---

[1] *Ulpiani Epit.* XXIV, 28.　　　[2] Cicero, *ad fam.* XIII, 11, 1.
[3] Cicero, *ad fam.* XIII, 7, 1.
[4] Vell. Pat. II, 81, 2; cf. Dio XLIX, 14, 5.
[5] At Tarsus the charge was 500 drachmae: Dio Chrys. *Or.* XXXIV, 23.
[6] The most famous case is *O.G.I.S.* 629 (Palmyra). But such privileges were by no means universal; cf. Suetonius, *Tib.* 49, 2.
[7] Cf. Pliny, *Ep.* X, 43 (52), 1 and 3.
[8] Pliny, *Ep.* X, 39 (48), 1.

and poor alike, might be called upon for five days' labour a year[1]; but regular direct taxation was contrary to Roman tradition, and the financial help of the wealthy, strict as its exaction soon became, probably had its origins in voluntary gifts. The drain on a man's purse began even before his entry into public life; for by the second century promises of benefactions to follow a successful candidature had become so common that rules of law were made to enforce performance[2]. There followed the entrance fees—not in themselves excessive, though inevitable and sanctioned by the local constitutions. The qualifications required of candidates for the *ordo* were so modest as to suggest that great wealth was not regarded as essential to public life: in Pliny's time a *decurio* at Comum had to be worth 100,000 sesterces[3]. Again, the fees charged to new members were likewise not unreasonable: Pliny found 2000 sesterces being paid by recipients of supernumerary seats in Bithynia[4], and even in the West, where such exactions were not at first kept low by the more serious demands like those of liturgies in the East, one Cn. Satrius Rufus paid only 6000 sesterces at Iguvium[5]. The *summa honoraria* for magistracies grew into a heavier burden. At the Colonia Genetiva Julia magistrates were compelled, as a minimum, to put down 2000 sesterces towards the cost of public shows, to which the city treasury also contributed[6]; but the humble resources of a colony recruited from the Roman proletariate imposed a modesty which is no clue to the practices prevailing elsewhere. In the great cities of the empire local patriotism and personal ambition made public life a continuous competition in extravagant generosity. Even in a second-class town like Turris in Sardinia a man paid 3500 sesterces for election as *quinquennalis*, and then spent more on a public fountain[7]; and at Massilia an augurate might cost 100,000[8].

To fees were added other calls. The Greek liturgies, whereby rich men were compelled, without holding office, to make themselves responsible for some public service, had their western parallel in the *munera*—an institution probably as old as Rome and one which did not become formidable till the third century A.D. But the growing interest of the jurists shows that by Antonine

[1] Dessau 6087, tab. iii, col. iii, ll. 23 *sqq.* (xcviii): cf. Bruns, *Fontes*[7], 10, ll. 79, 86. [2] *Dig.* L, 12 ('de pollicitationibus').
[3] Pliny, *Ep.* I, 19, 2. [4] *Ep.* X, 112 (113) *sq.*
[5] Dessau 5531.
[6] Dessau 6087 tab. ii, col. i, l. 6 *sqq.* (LXX *sq.*).
[7] Dessau 5765. [8] *C.I.L.* XII, 410.

times *munera* had become so essential as to win strict protection from the government, and the legal classification of these burdens is one of the main sources of information about their nature. The great majority of those recorded are of the type called 'munera personalia,' which at first were nothing more than obligations to personal service. So long as a man had merely to give his time and labour to the community, there was no great hardship; but when these tasks involved the handling of public money, the individual was first required to pledge his own property as security against defalcation[1] and then, when public funds were low, actually to meet the expenditure, wholly or in part, out of his own pocket. In cities which sold corn at a fixed rate to the inhabitants, the duty of buying grain was not onerous when money was available and prices were below the level fixed for sale; but when the treasury was empty or prevailing prices rose, the corn had still to be provided, and what the city could not pay the rich man was expected to find from his own resources. So in their financial effects *munera personalia* came to be almost indistinguishable from the direct taxes in property known as 'munera patrimoniorum'; and when these contributions took their places as a recognized source of revenue the *munera* became compulsory levies, necessarily imposed mainly on the rich. Above all it was men in public life who were expected to shoulder such burdens: magistrates bore many charges in addition to their entrance fees, and *decuriones*, whose business it was to assign the *munera*, were compelled to accept them in increasing numbers themselves.

How men thought of these inflictions is revealed by the use of their unpopularity to stimulate the birth-rate; for five surviving children brought their parents at least some measure of exemption[2]. Nevertheless, the financial demands of these duties did not become serious everywhere at once, and the system was not fully developed before Severan times. But its coming was not unheralded. Though Hadrian and the Antonines, by proclaiming that *mediocritas* was no disqualification, still maintained the ancient view that these services were calls upon the person[3], Marcus and Verus, despite the relief they gave by ruling that *decuriones* need not provide corn at less than market prices[4], were forced to confess that *paupertas* was a fatal bar[5]. Earlier still Trajan had to admit that men in Bithynia were entering the town-councils

---

[1] Cf. Dessau 6086, ll. 14 *sqq.*; 6089, col. iii, ll. 21 *sqq.* (LX).
[2] *E.g. Dig.* L, 4, 3, 6 (Ulpian).
[3] *Frag. Vat.* 244 (Paul); cf. *Dig.* XXVII, 1, 6, 19.
[4] *Dig.* L, 1, 8 (Marcian).   [5] *Dig.* XXVII, 1, 7 (Ulpian).

against their will[1], and Pliny himself had indicated some part of
the reason by asking whether, when cities could not lend idle
funds in the open market, sums so available should be offered on
loan at a rate of interest lower than the normal and, if voluntary
borrowers were not forthcoming, *decuriones* could be compelled
to take loans themselves, giving their property as security for
repayment[2]. Even the Flavians had been familiar with the
growing unpopularity of office. By itself the procedure laid down
by the charter of the Municipium Flavium Malacitanum for
filling vacancies when voluntary candidates failed[3] gives no clue to
the likelihood of such a dearth; but the urgency of the need for
such a clause is suggested, and almost proved, by a remark of
Javolenus Priscus in his abridgment of Cassius Longinus—that
exemption from *munera publica* does not release a man from his
obligation to hold magistracies; for election to a magistracy, as he
ominously observes, is still to be regarded as less a *munus* than
an *honor*[4].

The time had yet to come when town-councillors were made
personally responsible for the imperial taxes of their cities or even,
perhaps, when it was recognized by law that public relief might be
given to members of the *ordo* whose bankruptcy was due to excessive
munificence[5]; but increasing burdens clearly produced a situation,
in some parts of the empire at least, which engaged the attention
of the government from the first century and was met by a steady
stream of legislation directed with the best of motives to check
an abuse which could not be extinguished. Of such measures
it is usual to see the chief in the creation of *Latium maius*[6], and
there can be no doubt that one effect of this innovation was to
make the decurionate more attractive. Nevertheless, it is doubtful
whether such was its main intention. *Latium maius*, yet one more
step towards the Roman *civitas*, was a distinction sought by the
municipalities with an eagerness not to be expected if it was no
more than a bait to attract men to a distasteful public life, and the
enthusiasm it aroused in times and places where financial troubles
were still to come[7] must suggest that its encouragement of
candidates for the councils was only one among the purposes it
served. Nor was indifference to office, with all its burdens, the
worst enemy of municipal government: a more formidable menace
came from Rome.

---

[1] Pliny, *Ep.* x, 113 (114).
[2] *Ep.* x, 54 (62).
[3] Dessau 6089, col. i, ll. 1 *sqq.* (LI).
[4] *Dig.* L, 4, 12.
[5] *Dig.* L. 2, 8 (Hermogenianus).
[6] See above, p. 452 *sq.*
[7] See *e.g.* Dessau 6780.

VI. IMPERIAL ENCROACHMENT

The control of the cities was in the hands of men who, for all their patriotic enthusiasm, were amateurs in administration. Their lack of skill became more and more apparent as the standard of efficiency in the imperial bureaucracy rose; and this happened at a time when the central government showed signs of a growing paternalism. If Trajan could approve of interference with athletic sports in Vienne[1], it was not surprising that knowledge of the ease with which financial failings could be made good should have tempted him to well-meant intervention in that important field. Money was being wasted by incompetence, and it seemed as though nothing but good could be done if a city was saved from loss by an expert supervision which would secure, for instance, that more than 3,000,000 sesterces should not be squandered in attempts to build an aqueduct to designs which could never be completed[2]. Nevertheless in this altruism there was danger. The strength of the Empire was the conviction of its inhabitants that their interests demanded its survival; and those who mattered most—the people of the cities where self-government was a tradition—might lose their enthusiasm if encroachment by Rome destroyed all traces of autonomy. Thus, however salutary it might appear at first, interference from the centre would ultimately be condemned unless some stable balance were established between local initiative and bureaucratic control. To create such a balance is difficult, to maintain it harder still; and Rome's failure in a task which the modern world confronts with dubious success was made certain by the unprecedented strain thrown on the imperial finances during the crises of the third century.

Roman interest in the finances of provincial communities was nothing new. From Republican times the governors had exercised a certain supervision over municipal accounts[3], and their efforts were not without success: when mismanagement attracted general notice towards the end of the first century A.D., it was worst in the places normally exempt from interference—in the towns of Italy and the free cities of the provinces. To them Trajan turned his earliest attention. He sent a commissioner to Achaea 'ad ordinandum statum liberarum civitatium,' who took with him impeccable advice from Pliny on the delicacy of his task[4], and his

---

[1] Pliny, *Ep.* IV, 22, 1–3 and 7.
[2] Pliny, *Ep.* X, 37 (46) *sq.*
[3] See, for instance, Cicero, *ad fam.* III, 8, 4; *ad Att.* VI, 1, 15.
[4] *Ep.* VIII, 24; see also p. 219.

example was followed by Hadrian both in Achaea[1] and in Asia, where the free cities had Herodes Atticus as their overseer[2]. Pliny's command in Bithynia had a wider bearing; for, though one of his first instructions was to rescue the municipal finances from the prevailing chaos[3], which Trajan was determined to end in the free cities no less than elsewhere[4], his mission was really the first step towards the temporary transference to the *princeps* of a senatorial province[5] which the foreign policy of the Empire made important and where, not for the first time, there had been grievances which had lately led it twice to prosecute its governor[6]. Bithynia still received special treatment from Hadrian[7], perhaps because new difficulties had been caused by the recent earthquake, but the exceptional character of the problem which Pliny had been set to solve is proved by the suppression of his post and the return of the province to the Senate in the time of Pius[8]. In Italy, however, where the alimentary foundations[9] may have strengthened the Emperor's concern about the efficiency of local government, Trajan played a foremost part in starting an innovation which endured. Local vanity had long been flattered by imperial attention, and the *princeps* not only had allowed himself and members of his family to hold nominal office in municipalities as *duumviri*[10] but at times had exerted a mild influence on the ordinary elections[11]. With the second century, however, interference became more marked: there appeared the *curator rei publicae*, a representative of the *princeps*, who was given general supervision over the affairs of one city or more[12]. At first discretion and good taste may have restricted these intruders to friendly advice when the proposals of a town-council seemed rash; but it was inevitable that the imperial authority behind them should command a respect which made it soon difficult and finally impossible for the *ordo* and the magistrates to take any action without the *curator*'s approval[13]. At times the *princeps* invaded the municipal field even more forcibly by appointing an official of his own with duties

---

[1] Dessau 1067.   [2] Philostratus, *Vitae Soph.* II, 1, 3.
[3] *Ep.* x, 18 (29), 3.   [4] *Ep.* x, 47 (56) *sq.*
[5] Cf. Dessau 2927; 1024.
[6] Cf. Pliny, *Epp.* IV, 9, 2; V, 20, 1; for earlier signs of restiveness in this province see Tacitus, *Ann.* XII, 22 and Dio LXI, 33, 5.
[7] Cf. Dessau 8826.   [8] Cf. Dessau 8828.   [9] See pp. 210 *sqq.*
[10] Cf. Dessau 6088, ll. 19 *sqq.* (XXIIII).
[11] *Dig.* L, 3, 2 (Ulpian); cf. Dessau 964, 8902.
[12] See *e.g.* Dessau 6725 and, for possible evidence of the office under Nerva, *Dig.* XLIII, 24, 3, 4 (Ulpian).
[13] Cf. Dessau 5918*a*, especially l. 12 *sq.*

so highly specified that from the outset he was bound to withdraw some branch of business from the control of the municipality. Such was the *curator kalendarii*, whose business was to keep the public ledger with a vigilance which would see that monies due were promptly collected; and this office again is found filled by imperial nomination under Trajan[1].

The importance attached to these *curae* is shown by the choice of senators and *equites* to hold them, and the fragments preserved from Ulpian's book *De officio curatoris rei publicae*[2] are proof enough of the extent to which the institution had developed by the time of Severus Alexander. In some cities, at least, the *curatores* had become part of the constitution[3], and the stringency of their instructions even under the Antonines[4] points already to a not distant future when no public expenditure could be incurred without the sanction of the *princeps*[5]. Nevertheless, *curatores* were to be found only in a small minority of the cities before the third century, and it was not till the financial crisis broke that their activities increased to a point at which their power for evil became clear. But then at length it was apparent that the efficiency attained by the civil service of Trajan and Hadrian could only be secured in the municipalities at the cost of destroying self-government and transferring their direction to emissaries from Rome. The transference was not, indeed, made by force. Plutarch's exhortations to self-reliance and his warnings against constant reference to the provincial governors are a reminder that the Greek cities at least were like the Senate at Rome in their readiness to 'offer their heads to the halter when they were already tethered by the leg'[6]; but, so far from justifying the imperial experiment, this timid submissiveness made its victims the less suitable objects of so robust a paternalism as that which sent them *curatores* and may even have moved the honest Pius to countenance breaches of testamentary dispositions to secure its ends[7].

Over the Empire at large this intrusion was gradual: Africa, though it was a public province, remained free from *curatores* under the Antonines, and in regions under the emperor's command their appearance was slow. Even when they came, their arrival put no sudden end to municipal autonomy, and they did not

---

[1] Dessau 5502.
[2] *Dig.* XXII, 1, 33; L, 9, 4; 10, 5; 12, 1; 12, 15.
[3] *Dig.* XLIII, 24, 3, 4 (Ulpian).
[4] *Dig.* L, 8, 11 (9) *pr.* (Papirius Justus).　　[5] *Dig.* L, 10, 3, 1 (Macer).
[6] Plutarch, *Praec. ger. rei p.* 18 *sq.* (*Mor.* 814 E *sq.*).
[7] *Dig.* L, 10, 7 *pr.*—if 'noua' is to be read (Callistratus).

prevent the third century from being a time of vigorous activity in the towns of Africa. Yet from the first they were a menace to the vitality of the communities in their charge, and sooner or later circumstances thrust upon them that complete control which meant the end of self-government and changed cities with a healthy interest in life into the homes of a weary and apathetic population under the heel of the central power. Though their method was rash, Trajan and his successors meant well. But the strain of the third century, which made hopeless all attempts to preserve a successful balance between amateur direction and expert control, ruined a plan never free from risk; and in the end, by a tragic frustration of their purpose, the *curatores* did much to destroy that which they had been sent to save.

VII. GOVERNMENT AND PEOPLE

Pliny's correspondence with Trajan is a monument of the care which a conscientious *princeps* would devote to the details of administration abroad; and the evidence available does not suggest that diligence like Trajan's was rare. Yet problems calling for administrative action were not the only aspects of provincial life which could claim the attention of the central government: important as it was that such matters should receive the notice they deserved, it was more important still that Rome should be kept in touch with the general state of provincial opinion. In Roman times freedom was not, indeed, understood to involve a polity in which the executive could take no major decision without a mandate from the masses: Roman tradition was so far aristocratic that knowledge was held in respect. The value of *libertas* was rather found, not in any supposed right of the individual to a voice in the guidance of imperial policy, but in that vigorous interest in life which belongs to those who know that some of their affairs are under their own control and that the rest are directed by an authority which, though it may not depend on popular suffrage, is nevertheless ready to take public opinion into account. The provinces neither expected nor received an opportunity to thrust their views on the government whenever an issue of common interest arose: yet it was in the highest degree desirable that responsible officials in Rome should have some means of knowing the state of provincial sentiment.

The arrangements designed to give the views of the provinces an opportunity of expression have often been criticized, and admittedly they were not above reproach; but criticism, to be in

point, must not be directed on their failure to secure something at
which the Romans never aimed. A widespread franchise could
have had no value in the eyes of a people who once had given the
vox populi a hearing and then had turned away: the true measure
of Roman success in keeping contact with provincial opinion is the
strength of the conviction in the provinces that Rome was not
beyond the reach of their representations. From Republican times
the municipalities had been given means to air their opinions. By
a custom of some antiquity the founder of a colony or a general
who had received the submission of a conquered state had been
expected to represent its interests at Rome[1], and this practice had
grown into the system whereby the cities of the Empire at large
chose men of eminence, whether resident in Rome or provincials
whose occupations took them frequently to Italy, to be their
patroni. While Cicero was her sole *patronus*, the interests of Capua
would not suffer for lack of a weighty word on her behalf in the
lobbies of the Senate[2]; and later, when a rising demand caused the
distinction of *patroni* to sink, what individuals might lack in
influence was made good by an increase of their numbers. In the
time of Severus Alexander the *patroni* who head the list of the
decuriones at Canusium[3] are thirty-nine, and in the fourth century
Thamugadi seems to have had five or ten[4].

Patroni could voice the requests of separate communities. The
state of the provinces in general, which it was the business of their
governors to know, was a matter on which independent reports
might be expected from senators of provincial origin. When
Claudius so far broke with the Augustan practice as to suggest
that the Senate would be the better for a ponderable admixture of
provincials, whatever may have been his purpose at the moment he
modified the composition of the House in a way which made it
another link between Rome and the Empire at large. But the most
formal and the best assured channel of communication between
the provincial populations and the centre was provided by those
Provincial Councils whose usefulness in the first three centuries
A.D. has been disputed, but whose value was proved in the fourth,
when in a modified form they did something to fill the gap
left by the moribund municipalities as the seats of such limited
self-government as the conditions of the age allowed[5]. In the
Greek world the regional leagues of pre-Roman times were models

---

[1] Dessau 6087, tab. iii, col. iii, ll. 16 *sqq.* (xcvii); Cicero, *pro Sulla*, 21,
60 *sq.*; *de off.* i, 11, 35. See Mommsen, *Ges. Schr.* i, p. 237 *sq.*
[2] Cicero, *pro Sestio*, 4, 9; *in Pis.* 11, 25.   [3] Dessau 6121.
[4] Dessau 6122.   [5] See *e.g. Cod. Theod.* xii, 12, 11 *sqq.*

which could be adapted with ease to the needs of a Roman province, and in the case of Lycia the *Koinon* which in the second century attracted some part of the munificence lavished on the neighbourhood by Opramoas[1] was a direct continuation of the league which Rome found existing when the provincialization of the country was begun by Claudius[2]. But in the West, though federal tendencies had been strong in Italy from the beginnings of Roman history, the Concilia, which were the counterparts of the *Koina* in the eastern provinces, were less deeply rooted in native institutions[3] and owed more to their fostering by Rome.

One of the principal occupations of these Councils during the early Empire was the Imperial cult, but the easy conjecture that the maintenance of this rite was the purpose for which they were formed does not grow more plausible with inspection. In the East, the *Koina* of pre-Roman times, though their unity was regularly marked by some common worship, were primarily concerned with secular affairs; and, though it cannot be held that these eastern *Koina* directly inspired the Concilia of the West, there are signs that in the West as well the provincial Councils could claim an origin not wholly due to the demands of the official cult. In the western extension of the Empire the central episode is the conquest of Gallia Comata, and it is perhaps significant that it was Caesar's habit during his Gallic campaigns to hold an annual convention of notables from the friendly States[4]. This 'concilium Galliarum,' as he called it, served no religious end. Its purpose was merely to keep him abreast of local opinion, and also, it may be supposed, to convince men whose friendship was an asset that Rome had not come to inflict a rule which would ignore the views of the native population. Such too may have been the function for which the Councils in Imperial times were designed; and if religious occupations gradually absorbed more and more of their attention, the development may have been as little intended at the outset as was the similar process experienced by the *vici* of Augustan Rome[5].

When the institution had developed, Councils of this sort were to be found throughout the provinces, of which it was usual for

---

[1] See pp. 593 and 595.
[2] Suetonius, *Claud.* 25, 3; Dio LX, 17, 3: see P.W. *s.v.* Lykia, cols. 2276 *sqq.* and the literature there cited.
[3] On possible antecedents in Gaul, see O. Hirschfeld, *Kleine Schriften*, pp. 127 *sqq.* and Jullian, *op. cit.* IV, pp. 434 *sqq.*
[4] Caesar, *B.G.* IV, 6, 5; V, 2, 4; V, 24, 1; VI, 3, 4; cf. I, 30 *sqq.*
[5] See vol. X, pp. 459 *sqq.*

each to have its own, though there were occasional exceptions when a single assembly served several provinces, as in the Tres Galliae, and in the Tres Daciae after Marcus[1], or when circumstances demanded two assemblies for a single administrative unit, as in Crete and Cyrene (p. 660). The members of a Council were nominated, probably for a year, by the cities or *civitates* of the region which it served, and there are signs that the number of delegates sent by each was roughly determined by the size and importance of the community[2]. Its president, who with its other officers was chosen by the Council itself, after matters of cult had come to be its chief concern was called 'flamen[3],' or 'sacerdos[4],' 'Romae et Augusti' in the West and 'ἀρχιερεύς' in the East; but Eastern titles of the form Ἀσιάρχης, Γαλατάρχης and the like, though ultimately they became mere alternatives to 'ἀρχιερεύς' as appellations of the president, possibly recall a time when in Greek lands the chief official was not primarily religious. Besides this officer the Council employed functionaries with duties wholly secular, such as the *iudex*[5], and the *allectus*[6], *arcae* in the Three Gauls. These titles are not, indeed, known elsewhere, but the financial business which they imply was so indispensable to the performance of elaborate ritual that every provincial Council may be assumed to have needed at least some rudimentary staff to collect its revenues and supervise its disbursements, if not to control a coinage like those long issued by certain of the *Koina* in the East. Its income was derived partly from such property as it might have acquired, partly from the generosity of individuals, but chiefly from the regular contributions paid by the constituent communities; and its expenditure was incurred mainly in the upkeep of its religious establishment and the annual celebration of the festival, often accompanied by games, in honour of Rome and the Emperor, which became the central feature of the Councils' routine.

There was, however, another charge on the communal exchequer—the cost of embassies; and it is their use of such ambassadors to lay business before the authorities in Rome which gave the Councils a place in the political structure of the Empire. Though in the time of Augustus they had already begun to pass votes of thanks to the *princeps* for the excellence of his officials in

---

[1] Dessau 7128.
[2] Strabo xiv, 664 (pre-Roman Lycia): *C.I.L.* xiii, 3162, col. iii, ll. 22 *sqq.*
[3] *E.g.* Dessau 6964.   [4] *E.g.* Dessau 7013.
[5] *E.g.* Dessau 7017.   [6] Dessau 7020 *sq.*

a way which was found embarrassing[1], the discouragement of this practice had implied no indifference on the part of Augustus to the legitimate needs of the provincial populations[2]. The arrival of their complaints soon became a rare but recognized incident in the work of administration; the *concilia* seem even to have formally appointed *inquisitores* to investigate grievances alleged[3]; and one not infrequent result of their activities was the trial of peccant officers, generally on a charge of extortion, with representatives of the Council instructing the prosecution. Votes of gratitude to popular officials remained common[4], despite attempts to stop them, but testimonials to the honest were less salutary than denunciations of the knaves; for it was their power to arraign corruption which made the Councils a potent check on governors and a reminder to the provinces themselves that oppression was so far from being part of Roman policy that Rome would welcome help in making an example of offenders. This, however, was not all. The Councils could approach the central authorities with representations on any subject in which they wished action taken, and when Pius sent a favourable reply 'ad desideria Asianorum[5]' he gave the clearest indication of the service these bodies could render in strengthening the impression that the government of Rome was not unresponsive to the requests of the local populations. The subject of Pius' rescript to Asia was, indeed, trivial; but Asia had approached Domitian on a more serious issue when it asked for relief from his prohibition against the planting of vines[6], the local *Koinon* of Thessaly had received rulings from Hadrian or Pius on judicial procedure[7], and even the backward Thrace had been in communication with Pius about appeals to the central government[8].

Recorded incidents of this kind are not numerous, but they appear throughout the history of the first two centuries freely enough to show that cult was not the only business of the provincial councils. The great religious celebrations in honour of Rome and the *princeps* were not, indeed, without powerful effects. The whole elaborate ceremony focussed local interest on

[1] Dio LVI, 25, 6.   [2] See Suetonius, *Aug.* 33, 3.
[3] *E.g.* Dessau 7018 *sq.*; cf. Pliny, *Ep.* III, 9, 29 *sqq.* For various other accounts of this office see *C.I.L.* XIII, 1, p. 230 (O. Hirschfeld).
[4] *E.g.* Dessau 7155.
[5] *Dig.* I, 16, 4, 5 (Ulpian).
[6] Philostratus, *Vitae Soph.* I, 21, 6.
[7] *Dig.* V, 1, 37 (Callistratus); XLVIII, 6, 5, 1 (Marcian).
[8] *Dig.* XLIX, 1, 1, 1 (Ulpian).

the glory of the imperial power and thereby did something to encourage the sentiment which made the Empire one. Yet such unity was not promoted at the expense of local differences: it is hard to suppose that in the Tres Galliae the Ara ad Confluentes failed in some degree to foster that Gallic individuality which found open expression in A.D. 70 and still in the time of Gallienus was strong enough to launch the Gauls on a line of action of their own. But behind this religious façade lay machinery capable of another useful function. Rarely as they may have been employed, the means whereby provincials could lay their views before the government in Rome were a valuable element in the imperial scheme; for, so long as they remained available, the provinces might continue to believe that their hopes and desires could be brought direct to the highest authorities in the Empire, and that the government which controlled their destinies, because it was accessible to their representations, was one which left them, even outside the limits of single cities and *civitates*, with what the Roman world knew as 'libertas.'

VIII. CONCLUSION

Unity of sentiment was what Rome attained; and it was the only unity worth attainment. Uniformity was neither sought nor secured. Believing as she did in local autonomy and claiming nothing for herself but the right and the means to preserve an ordered peace, Rome could dispense with attempts to justify her imperial work by the superiority of the culture which she could offer to her peoples and be content with the knowledge that the Pax Romana enabled them the better to live lives of the kinds which were their own. The Empire had developed its essential character, and its solidity had been achieved, before a strain of paternalism became evident enough to invite reproachful reminders that good government is no substitute for self-government. Indeed Rome erred, if at all, rather on the side of remissness towards her responsibilities. It was laudable, perhaps, to leave the cities of Asia a large share in the task of maintaining public order, and in the system finally adopted, which makes its appearance in the second century, the suppression of brigandage seems still to have been entrusted jointly to local and imperial police[1]. Yet highwaymen continued to ply their trade with a persistence which would have excused far more drastic intervention by

---

[1] *Dig.* XI, 4, 1, 2 (Ulpian). On the whole subject of police in the provinces see O. Hirschfeld, *Kleine Schriften*, pp. 593 *sqq.*

the imperial power. Nevertheless, Rome's self-restraint was proved good by the result. If it encouraged local patriotism and, in the West, even tolerated that regional spirit which was the nearest approach to a sense of nationality on its modern scale to be found in the ancient world, minor loyalties did not conflict with allegiance to the Empire, since that allegiance did not demand their sacrifice. Over all the differences of race and culture, which in the Empire were many and great, there supervened a unity, not of language or religion or material civilization, but of common interest in the welfare of the whole. Remarkable as was Rome's success in consolidating the world behind her, and notable as was the determination with which her road-builders overcame the formidable obstacle of distance, from the outset she had been exempt from at least one baffling complication. Though throughout this period the West retained a certain prejudice against the Greek-speaking peoples of the Eastern Mediterranean, there was no need to evolve an imperial method of the kind which can unite races whose differences extend to colour. The colour-bar can scarcely be said to have been known in Roman times, because its conditions did not exist. Where they were present in some slight degree, ethnic divisions were generally ignored[1]; and in Western Europe, where Rome did her finest work, the predominant populations were close akin to some of the most numerous in the Italian peninsula. Indeed, it was the closeness of this connection which explains the readiness with which the Celts received not merely Roman rule but many elements in the Latin civilization, and gives its significance to the day of Actium when victory went to the side whose leader would proclaim the Latin culture, which Western Europe could accept, as the culture of the Roman power.

Though Rome asked for no uniformity, the power of prestige made her institutions a model so freely imitated that a process of limited assimilation began throughout the Empire. The limits, indeed, were somewhat narrow: with the accession of Septimius the Principate itself went to one who could not be mistaken for an Italian. Yet the general tendency was unmistakable. Local gods were identified with those of Rome; Latin spread over the West and, though pre-Roman languages long survived, struck its roots so deep that, with the assistance of the Church and its Latin versions of the Scriptures, it overcame all its rivals as the vernacular; and, even though the native peoples clung to their tribal forms of life, their towns grew to be cities scarcely distinguishable from those of the

---

[1] See *e.g.* Strabo XIII, 629.

Mediterranean world and their local administration was steadily adapted to the Roman type. Even minor institutions of the imperial people were sedulously copied. One of the most striking records left by the Augustalitas is the building which served as its head-quarters in Sarmizegethusa[1], and there is no more impressive appearance of the Juventus, which Augustus had revived in Italy[2], than the half Celtic version found at Virunum in Noricum[3]. Such developments are signs of that devotion to Rome which was encouraged and expressed by the great provincial cults of Rome and Augustus; but neither the acceptance of particular forms of organization nor the imitation of Roman fashions in the material furniture of life can claim a significance comparable to that of the imperial loyalty which was shared even by regions most con-servative of their own traditions.

The strength of the Empire was derived from the devotion of its inhabitants, and that devotion was the result of gratitude for the peace which it was Rome's primary business to maintain, for the ordered government of which the monument endures in Roman Law, and for that liberal attitude to the native populations of which the steady extension of the Roman franchise is the most notable expression. Roman methods were not, indeed, those of to-day. The aristocracy which formed the basis of the administra-tion at home looked for help to the aristocrats in the provinces, and in a world where education among the many was as back-ward as the means of disseminating news and forming public opinion the principles of democracy were neither honoured nor observed. But the age was not necessarily the worse because ability commanded esteem, nor were the ignorant necessarily the less contented for their measure of dependence on the cultured few. Though class-war has been held responsible for the fall of the Empire itself, the evidence for its existence is elusive. In places there was, indeed, an opposition between town and country; for land was always the best investment, and the countryside suffered from the notorious defects of the absentee landlord. But, though cases of every kind were to be found in an area so large as the Roman world, it is an exaggeration to suggest a general feud between peasantry and city-populations: detailed study of such rural risings as are recorded does not disclose a single cause or one affecting all regions alike. Nor is every

[1] See C. Daicovici in *Dacia*, III–IV, 1927–32, pp. 516 *sqq.*
[2] See vol. x, pp. 462 *sqq.*
[3] See R. Egger in *Jahreshefte*, XVIII, 1915, pp. 115 *sqq.*

complaint a sign of disease. When the Eastern provinces recovered
a large measure of prosperity in the first century A.D.[1], it was no
bad thing that reviving spirits found occasional expression in
grievance, even against Rome; for acquiescence and ideals go ill
together. The business of Rome was to meet such demands as she
could, and for the rest to render the world a service which
would attract loyalty of the kind which is immune from the effects
of minor discontent. And this she did. When the issue was plainly
put, men's hesitation between Rome and the alternative was
brief. It did not need Plutarch to announce that the Romans were
sympathetic to a cause vouched for by those they trusted[2], nor did
the Rhodians wait to learn from Dio that they were not so
crass and unperceptive as to want dominion over slaves rather
than the noble allegiance of the free[3]. With the easy tolerance
acquired in the long history of the Republic, Rome accepted and
even fostered the variety of customs and institutions to be described at length in the survey of the Empire which follows. Each
in its own way the provinces progressed; their advance was made
possible by the Pax Romana; and their fidelity was an outcome of the
gratitude commanded by a power which established peace throughout the world and then was wise enough, despite the growing
temptations of paternalism, to leave its inhabitants free to enjoy
the measure of self-government which they could exercise with
advantage to themselves and without danger to their neighbours—
a measure which was as salutary as it was safe because it was
fixed by a sober judgment of their capacity.

[1] Rostovtzeff, *op. cit.* p. 112.
[2] *Praec. ger. rei p.* 18 (*Mor.* p. 814 D).
[3] Dio Chrys. *Or.* XXXI, 111.

CHAPTER XII

THE LATIN WEST:
AFRICA, SPAIN AND GAUL

I. CHARACTERISTICS IN COMMON

IN the Roman Empire, Africa, Spain and Gaul form a unity in the West, a counterpoise to the hellenized lands of the East. Their conquest was begun in the second century B.C., and completed under the earliest emperors. The conditions of life in these countries prior to the Roman conquest, and, equally, the conditions under which they had been colonized by the Romans, had given them certain lasting characteristics in common, and the first task is to indicate this common heritage.

Even before the Roman conquest they had not lived in a state of complete barbarism. Their political and social life had become stabilized. The upper classes of their society expected and enjoyed the comforts of life. They had produced good work in the decorative arts, and, where circumstances were particularly favourable, more especially in certain parts of Spain, a really great art had made its appearance. Nevertheless, their political and economic horizon had remained limited, for they had produced no great or lasting State, and the radius of their commerce was not wide. Urban life had developed little, except in a few places penetrated by foreign influences. The rôle of Rome in these three countries (and this is their first point in common) lay in expanding their horizon. Rome introduced them into the vast organism of a State which covered most of the known world, into an economic system more complex than any they had known: Africans, Spaniards and Gauls came to know the products of distant lands, conceived new needs and new desires. Their civilization took a form essentially urban, of life in communities which each formed a cultural entity with collective interests and regular institutions.

The three countries have another characteristic in common. In each of them, the work of transformation accomplished by Rome was achieved by a very small minority of immigrants, directing the mass of the native population into new channels. One may say, speaking generally, that Africa, Spain and Gaul continued to be inhabited by their Berbers, Iberians and Celts, for the immigrants after the Roman conquest were few: each part of the Em-

pire needed its own labour, and was hardly in a position to send
its workpeople abroad. It is by a process of self-development,
under the influence of a small number of Romans or romanized
foreigners among them, that Africans, Spaniards and Gauls gradually conformed to the general Roman type, and became initiates of
Roman civilization.

Africa, Spain and Gaul are each the gateway to remote lands.
Before the conquest of the West, Greek and Roman history had
been made on the shores of the Mediterranean, including in this
the Black Sea, and in the valleys of the rivers that flow into it.
On these shores Graeco-Italian civilization had been perfected.
Those countries of the West which face inwards to the Mediterranean also face outwards to other worlds. North Africa extended southwards into a vast, mysterious continent, inhabited by
shadowy races of men and by creatures of fable living in a climate
almost intolerable to mankind. Beyond the Pillars of Hercules,
Mauretania and the Spanish peninsula confront the infinite expanse of the Ocean, with its daily tides and its undiscovered shores:
a sea as different as possible from the Mediterranean. Gaul, too,
is washed by the Ocean on her longest seaboard, and extends far
to the north, where the climate, vegetation and conditions of
culture were something new to the experience of the ancients; they
saw here a Europe that was damp, misty, and unattractive; but
here the long hard winters were compensated by regular harvests
in summer.

Finally, it is to be remembered that in the first two centuries
of the Empire the evolution of the three provinces followed much
the same lines. There was an increasingly thorough exploitation
of natural resources, which had as its consequence a steady advance towards economic independence. At the beginning of the
first century, Rome prescribed for every country of her Empire
a certain form of activity: she demanded from the subject countries
work for Rome, for the greater ease and comfort of the Romans,
the masters of the world. But little by little the provinces emancipated themselves. Africans, Spaniards and Gauls became Roman
citizens and members of the governing classes. The western
provinces could no longer be kept in economic subjection. Their
resources were methodically developed, and, as time passed, each
country had a wider range of products which provided it with the
means of enlarging its commerce in normal times, and of supporting itself when need arose. From the middle of the first
century to the beginning of the third, the outer regions of the
Empire gradually rose from their subordinate position. The life

of the Empire remained a unity, but it did not exclude the possibility of an autonomous life in its component parts, when the time should come for the unity to be broken.

II. AFRICA

North Africa possessed a notable racial unity. It was inhabited entirely by Berbers, for the names Libyan, Numidian, Moor, Gaetulian, which were commonly used by the ancients, corresponded to no intrinsic differences of race, but only of geographical position. The new elements which were added to this primitive and lasting foundation were not very important. Semites had occupied the harbours in very early times, but they were never more than a small ruling class. These harbours, too, and some centres of trade in the interior, had always attracted traders, at first Orientals and Greeks, later Italians; but the mass of the population remained unchanged. Nor was the number of immigrants materially increased by Roman colonization. The high officials were for the most part birds of passage. The Italians who acquired estates in Africa did not come to live there. The most numerous of the non-African elements were the bodies of veterans sent to Africa to found colonies, and the soldiers on active service in the legions or the *auxilia*, who often remained in the country after their discharge. In this way Italians, Gauls, Spaniards, Asiatics, men from the Danubian countries, established themselves in Africa and supplied to African society a certain number of small landowners. But the number of these foreign elements was in no way commensurate with their social and cultural importance. They formed a sort of aristocracy, but they were only a tiny fraction of the inhabitants, and, since many of them married African wives, their descendants were quickly merged in the mass of the Berber population. Moreover, although in the last century of the Republic, during the Civil Wars, such immigrants came fairly regularly, the pace soon slackened under the Principate, and came almost to a standstill in the course of the second century: the last colonies of veterans were founded by Nerva and Trajan. Under Hadrian and later, the army of Africa was recruited almost exclusively from the Africans themselves, with the single exception of the Syrian detachments, which were regularly recruited on the confines of the Syrian desert. As for the negroid element which, in antiquity as in every subsequent age, was introduced into North Africa by the channel of slavery, it is a curiosity worth noticing, but it is not an ethnological factor of any real importance.

Rome had not annexed the whole of North Africa at one stroke. A century had elapsed between the creation of the province of Africa and the annexation of Africa Nova, which brought a large increase of territory to the original province, towards the west and south: then more than eighty years passed before the kingdom of Mauretania became the two provinces of Mauretania Caesariensis and Mauretania Tingitana. This conquest by stages continued even after the annexation of Mauretania, in the sense that the emperors gradually extended their authority over lands which had never been truly subject to the Numidian or Mauretanian kings, lands of mountain ranges, of expanses traversed by the nomads, or of lofty plateaux adjoining the desert (pp. 146 *sqq.*). The reigns of Vespasian, Trajan, Hadrian, Commodus and Septimius Severus each saw so many extensions or consolidations of the *limes*, which reached the farthest point of its development under the Severi. Thus little by little the Roman provinces were increased by regions won from barbarism, rather by a constant process of penetration than by operations of war. The work of police, of survey, and of development proceeded side by side, and the Empire gradually approached, and at some points reached, the Sahara itself.

The several regions of Africa thus did not start abreast in the acquisition of Roman civilization. Nor were they equally endowed by nature, forming as they do a complex geographical system, with coastal plains, fertile plateaux, and inviting valleys on the one hand, and on the other, districts inaccessible and naturally poor. For these reasons, in the several parts of North Africa were to be found different degrees of civilization. The chief ports were great towns, lively and somewhat cosmopolitan, where Latin and Greek were spoken. In the fertile districts arose urban communities, possessing all the institutions of civic life and every material comfort. In some places, notably in certain valleys of Tunis, they appear thickly grouped together; but as one moves westwards the urban centres become fewer and poorer, and the population clings more closely to its primitive culture.

The existence of peaceful and civilized districts side by side with districts in which Roman influence was recent and superficial, explains the particular form which the administration of the province of Africa itself had taken. Although it was a senatorial province, parts of it were still not perfectly safe, and it was called upon to extend its frontiers progressively towards the south, breaking fresh ground among warlike peoples. Thus it needed an army, and in fact it possessed a legion (III Augusta). Authority was divided between the proconsul, representative of the Senate, and the *legatus* in command of the legion, representative of the emperor. This dual authority in a single province, this army in a proconsular province, was exceptional. In practice, from the reign of Gaius onwards (vol. x, p. 658), the *legatus* of the legion was independent of the proconsul, and governed all the territory garrisoned by his troops; but it was not until the beginning of the third century that it was decided to bring theory and name into conformity with the prevalent practice, and to make of the territory governed by the *legatus* a separate province, to be called Numidia. Meanwhile Mauretania Caesariensis and Mauretania Tingitana, except when circumstances justified a special re-arrangement of forces, were governed each by a procurator of equestrian rank.

All the African provinces were not at the same stage of development, but all alike had one basic resource, agriculture. Agriculture, and, in the second place, stock-breeding, supplied almost the whole population with its livelihood: commerce was primarily in agricultural produce. Industry was of little importance. The quarries supplied local works, and at Simitthu (Chemtou in Tunis) was produced a yellow marble with red veins which was exported; but the mineral resources were exploited in a perfunctory way[1]. Articles were manufactured for local markets only. A lamp factory at Caesarea (Cherchel in Algeria) was able to export examples of its wares to Spain, and other lamps, made in the province of Africa, went to Sardinia[2]; but, in general, African pottery stayed in Africa. The peculiar vases, with anthropomorphic decoration, which were made at El Aouja in Tunis, appear not to have spread beyond a radius of sixty or seventy miles[3]. The same is true, probably, of textiles and leather goods: usually every family supplied its own needs. Moreover, these local industries could not meet the requirements of the home market: decorated pottery was imported from Italy at first, later from Gaul; lamps and metal goods came from Italy: even the most ordinary building-materials, such as tiles and bricks, were imported from Italy, as late as the third century[4]. This feebleness of African industry, this distaste for industrial activity, is a phenomenon which re-appears in every phase of the history of North Africa. It is due partly to the fact that the natives show no aptitude in the workshop, and partly, in antiquity, to the fact that the Romans deliberately diverted their

[1] S. Gsell in *Hesperis*, VIII, 1928, pp. 1–21.
[2] *C.I.L.* VIII, pp. 2211, 2213.
[3] R. Lantier in *J.D.A.I.*, 1931, col. 566 *sq*.
[4] Dessau 8667; E. Albertini, in *Bull. archéol. du Comité des Travaux hist.* 1925, pp. ccxvi–ccxvii.

activity into a different channel: they looked primarily to Africa as a source of their food-supply.

In the early days of the conquest, what Rome demanded from Africa was wheat. The country had always produced a good supply of wheat and barley, and now the Roman administrators, abandoning barley to the peasants and their cattle, forced on the Africans an intensive production of wheat, with a view to exporting it to Italy in bulk. Pliny the Elder, writing in the latter part of the first century, records with amazement the richness of the crop and the simplicity of the methods employed[1]. He goes so far as to say that Africa is intended by nature to produce grain, and grain alone[2], although under the Carthaginians experience had shown that olives, vines and fruit trees could do very well. Nevertheless, these activities were systematically discouraged by the early emperors in favour of wheat-growing. We do not know how directly Africa was affected by the edict of Domitian limiting the culture of the vine in the provinces (p. 38), but it is certain that the spirit of this edict is reflected in the Roman administration during the first century.

In the second century, however, this policy underwent a change, and agriculture in Africa assumed a new aspect. Provincials had now attained to the highest offices of the Empire, and Rome had neither the power nor the wish to impose on the provinces restrictions and prohibitions. Moreover, she now needed other things besides wheat: there is evidence that at the beginning of the third century Italy was short of oil, and that this shortage was not something new but a familiar fact[3]. In Africa itself, continuous colonial expansion southwards brought cultivators into regions where the nature of the soil and the incidence of the rainfall are unfavourable to grain, and where the cultivation of the olive is clearly more lucrative. Thus the second century saw Africa no longer a specialist in the production of wheat. Some information about this new development in African agriculture is contained in several important inscriptions, all from Tunis in the original province of Africa[4], though the conditions to which they relate must certainly have prevailed, with some small variations, in Numidia, and probably in Mauretania also. According to this evidence a great part of the soil of Africa was taken up by large estates known as

---

[1] Pliny, *N.H.* XVII, 41; XVIII, 94 *sq.*
[2] Pliny, *N.H.* XV, 8.
[3] S.H.A. *Sept. Sev.* 23, 2.
[4] *C.I.L.* VIII, 10570 = 14464 (Soukh-el-Khemis); 25902 (Henchir Mettich); 25943 (Aïn-el-Djemala); 26416 (Aïn-Ouassel).

saltus. The most important of all the great proprietors was the emperor himself, who owned vast *saltus* in every district: other estates belonged to private individuals, mostly senators, either Italians or Africans. The proprietor did not live on his estate, but farmed out the revenue from it, either as a whole or in lots, to *conductores*, who worked sometimes as individuals and sometimes in companies. Part of the land leased in this way was cultivated directly by the *conductores* or their agents: the rest of the estate was parcelled out among *coloni* who were under contract to pay to the *conductores* a percentage of their returns, and also to work for a fixed number of days on the land cultivated directly by the *conductores* themselves.

These inscriptions are concerned most often with a procedure common enough in Africa, the clearing and development of waste land, marsh or scrub, and the reclaiming of land which had already been cleared once, but had been neglected by the cultivators, and had returned to its wild state. A measure known as the *lex Manciana*, dating either from the end of the Republic or from the first century of the Empire, conferred special rights upon cultivators who undertook to reclaim such lands: in addition to reducing, for a sufficiently long period, the rents due from them to the proprietor or the *conductores* who were his representatives, it guaranteed to them the right of occupation in perpetuity on a profit-sharing basis, and of transmission of the land to their descendants under the same conditions of tenure. The practice was confirmed by a law of Hadrian, which extended its scope and made it even more favourable to the pioneers, and this bold interference of the State in the administration of private estates ensured the extension of the productive lands and the development of new areas.

On these areas claimed or reclaimed by the plough, cereals seem to have taken only a secondary place: the most important crop was the vine, and chiefly fruit trees, especially olives. Juvenal[1], towards the end of the first century, reproaches the oil of Africa with a strong taste and smell which make it hardly fit for the table; but it is reasonable to think that, in the course of the second century, the Africans learned how to treat their oil better. Little by little African oil captured every market, and no longer lamp oil merely, but oil for the kitchen and the toilet as well. Amphorae from Tubusuctu in Mauretania have been discovered at Rome[2], and they carried there the oil of Kabylia, where to this day the olive is one of the chief sources of wealth. The same oil

[1] v, 86–91.
[2] S. Gsell, *Atlas archéologique de l'Algérie*, Sheet 7, p. 7.

travelled as far as Alexandria[1]. After the olive, the most important tree was the fig: vegetables were grown also, and especially artichokes and beans.

Naturally these new developments did not mean that the cultivation of cereal crops was abandoned: indeed, it survived as long as the western Empire lasted. The *annona* of Africa filled the same place in the food-supply of Rome at the end of the second century as it had filled in the first, and in the *stationes* of African merchants installed at Ostia wheat was always an essential commodity[2]. Barley, in the first two centuries, was consumed locally by stockbreeders, who exported notable strains both of horses and mules to Italy and the provinces; it is possible that barley, too, became an article of export to meet the needs of the armies, at the time when the cavalry had become the most important arm of the service, though this development can hardly have taken place much before the end of the third century.

Such were the primary products exported by Africa to the Roman world, and especially to Italy; the most important, wheat and oil; next, horses and mules, wine, fruit and vegetables. The list of exports included also various commodities of secondary interest: mineral products used in the manufacture of medicines or dyes; a wood, the *citrus* or thuya, in demand for high-class furniture; sponges, and rare delicacies of the table, such as jujubes and truffles. African dates were not very highly thought of in Pliny's day[3]; their reputation probably improved later, when the Romans had planted southern Tunis and the country round Biskra: but they never penetrated to the Souf or the valley of Wadi Rhir, where the date-palm flourishes best to-day. One special industry deserves a place to itself, namely the hunting of wild animals, which were captured alive and sent to Rome or elsewhere for the amphitheatre: lions, bears and panthers were most in demand. Finally, Africa transmitted to the Mediterranean world rarities which arrived by the caravan-routes from distant lands: by this means gold dust, ivory, precious stones, ostrich feathers, and black slaves made their way into the wealthy houses of Rome.

Although in the Roman world under the Empire Africa had developed her resources more widely than ever before, yet her activity remained fundamentally the same; the mass of her population underwent no change; and, inevitably, Roman Africa still presented many aspects reminiscent of her own past. The languages

---

[1] *Ann. épig.* 1922, no. 136.
[2] G. Calza in *Bull. Arch. Com.* 1915, p. 78.
[3] Pliny, *N.H.* XIII, 26.

spoken in Africa before the Roman conquest, whether Berber dialects or Punic, continued in use. The existence of these African tongues is known from Latin authors, though it is not always clear whether they refer to Berber or to Punic. Most of the inscriptions in native dialects, commonly called Libyan, date from the Empire, and, though they are certainly few in number compared with the multitude of inscriptions in Latin, it is to be remembered that these dialects were primarily spoken languages, and their use in writing or in inscriptions was exceptional. Punic, too, survived chiefly as a spoken language: it was sometimes transcribed in Latin characters, and isolated words lasted on in the vocabulary of Roman Africa. The truth of the matter probably was that in the upper and middle classes many people were bilingual or even trilingual, speaking Libyan or Punic in private and Latin in public; whereas many of the illiterate poor conversed freely in Libyan or Punic only, and knew little Latin.

In religion, too, Africa kept her own personality. The Africans accepted without resistance the Graeco-Roman cults, such as the cult of the Capitoline Triad, of Mars, patron of the military colonies, of Venus, Apollo, Mercury, Neptune, Bacchus. The Imperial cult was actively and loyally observed, and Oriental cults took their place here as elsewhere in the West. But the primitive basis still remained. The genii of springs, trees, caves and mountains were still honoured and feared: the magistrates of romanized towns or boroughs still repaired periodically to cult-centres hallowed by ancient tradition, to perform ceremonies in which the whole population probably took part[1]. Votive offerings in Latin are made to deities whose names are perfectly unknown apart from the inscriptions which contain them; they are clearly native deities under a thin Latin disguise[2]. Peculiarly deep-rooted in the hearts of the people were the Punic deities whom the natives had adopted at the time of the Carthaginian domination: the god Saturn and the goddess Caelestis have nothing Roman about them but their name, and are really African deities, the most popular in all this pantheon. Even the memory of the child-sacrifices formerly demanded by the Carthaginian Baal re-appears in dedications to Saturn when the Imperial régime was at its height[3]. African craftsmen produced many *stelae* in honour of Saturn, on which the god, his priests or his worshippers, and the

---

[1] *C.I.L.* VIII, 5504 *sqq.* and 18828 *sqq.*; 6267 *sqq.* and 19249 *sqq.*
[2] *E.g. Insc. lat. de l'Algérie*, 2034, 2036, 2053.
[3] J. Carcopino in *Revue de l'Hist. des Religions*, CVI, 1932, pp. 592–9.

sacrificial beasts, are represented in registers placed one above the other with a naive workmanship and a sincerity that give this popular art, despite its imperfections, a charm of its own[1]. In certain sanctuaries in Tunis, those of the ancient Siagu and at Bir-Derbal, statues of terracotta, of Imperial date, perpetuate a very old type, that of a lion-headed goddess who represents the 'Genius of the African land[2].'

To the Romans entering Africa for the first time the most striking characteristic which they encountered had been the nomadic life of many of its inhabitants. Nor did this habit of life disappear. Tribes which lived mainly by the rearing of stock continued to shift their quarters periodically, from winter pastures to summer pastures; but their movements were now controlled and limited by the Roman authorities. The nomadic life over wide areas was now to be found only beyond the *limes*, on those lofty plateaux in western Algeria which were never incorporated in the Roman provinces. The efforts of the Roman governors were directed towards attaching to the soil natives who had hitherto lived the life of cowboys and nomads; and the development of new lands naturally produced this same transformation. These natives attached to the soil lived, some of them, in tribes (*gentes*), with no urban settlements or municipal institutions. Such tribes were placed under the semi-military authority of a *praefectus*, in the early days of the Empire an officer of the army, but often in the second century a native chief whose loyalty was above suspicion.

But the progress of romanization was furthered above all by the transformation of the *gentes* into *civitates*, by the creation and development of urban settlements. The towns of Africa under the Empire were numerous, especially in the original Roman province and in Numidia. They were mostly small towns of a few thousand inhabitants, and very few had a population running into tens of thousands. Among these town-dwellers nearly everyone drew his livelihood directly or indirectly from the land whether as owners or as tenants or as labourers, some making the journey from town to country every day, others visiting the country at the busy seasons, and others dividing their time between their town houses and country seats. And, equally, the commerce and industry of these small towns, such as it was, depended on agriculture.

The origin of this taste for town life in cultivators of the soil

---

[1] See Volume of Plates v, 44, *a*.

[2] A. Merlin, *Le sanctuaire de Baal et de Tanit près de Siagu*; L. Carton, in *C.R. Ac. Inscr.* 1918, pp. 338–47. See Volume of Plates v, 44, *b*.

was that living in a town gave them a political and social superiority. A town was not merely an assemblage of bricks and mortar : it was an administrative unity and a cultural entity, a microcosm with its assemblies, its magistrates, its budget, its customs, and its festivals. In the application to the African provinces of the municipal system conceived by Rome for her Empire in general, the Roman authorities, who wished to mould the Africans to their own general scheme of administration, did not lack the assistance of the Africans themselves, who wished to use this means to a higher level of dignity and comfort. As soon as the peasants found themselves in easy circumstances, they wanted to become town-dwellers, and by their efforts the hamlets and villages little by little increased in size and respectability, until they became worthy of the name of town, a name which many of them did in fact acquire.

The material traces of this urbanization and, in general, of the development of the African provinces are to be found at many places in Tripoli, Tunis, Algeria, and western Morocco. On the coast, the great seaports gave access to Italy, Gaul, Spain, and the East, and the many small harbours invited a flourishing coastal trade. Inland, the absence of navigable rivers had decided the emperors to pay great attention to the road-system, which was planned, in its main lines, in the first century, and brought to completion by the Antonines and Severi. Many ingenious devices were employed to ensure that the water-supply of the country should be used to the full. The remains of Carthage give us hardly an adequate idea of this great capital, and the splendid monuments of Leptis Magna are not earlier than Septimius Severus; but there are several towns of less importance with remains sufficiently well preserved to give an accurate picture of ordinary life in Roman Africa. Such are Thugga (Dougga) and Thuburbo Maius in Tunis, pre-Roman villages which developed into towns, and in Algeria Thamugadi (Timgad) and Cuicul (Djemila), military colonies founded at the end of the first century, which soon spread beyond their walls and, in a generation or two, were provided with all the usual public buildings and places of amusement; in Morocco, Volubilis got a good start as the protégé first of Juba and later of Claudius, and did not lose ground later. Building in Africa preserved the main features of the Roman style of architecture and ornament, but adapted itself to peculiarities of African tradition or climate. The walls are sometimes of mud coated with plaster, more often of rubble with a binding of ashlar at intervals: the houses are not built round an

Italian *atrium* but round a court of the Greek type, and often contain (as at Thugga and Bulla Regia in Tunis) rooms underground in which to shelter from the heat. No part of the Roman world is richer in mosaics.

There is no doubt that during the first two centuries of the Empire the population of Africa steadily increased. The Romans had always been astonished by the longevity of Africans: nonagenarians and centenarians are frequent in the inscriptions, and even if they are not all above suspicion, they must still represent a tendency which really existed. At the same time the rate of mortality among children and the young was not low; but the birth-rate was very high. The density of the sites dating from the second and third centuries implies a corresponding density of population.

Every town was a centre of Roman culture in which the Berbers could learn the language and the manners of Rome. The thriving state of agriculture allowed African families to become rich and improve their position in the social hierarchy. A municipal *bourgeoisie* of native origin was born and grew by stages, passing from the condition of *peregrinitas* to that of *Latinitas*, from the restricted Latin citizenship to the full citizenship, and emerging finally among the privileged classes of the *equites* and the senators. In the reign of Titus an African from Cirta became consul[1]: romanized Africans were now fit for the same tasks as Romans or Italians.

It is instructive to observe the part played in the formation of this municipal bourgeoisie by service in the army. In the first century Africans served in both the legions and in the *auxilia* in Africa and abroad, and from the time of Hadrian onwards they provided the great majority of recruits for the army of Africa (p. 311). The veterans, when they were discharged after long years of service which had made them familiar with the Latin language and Roman customs, settled down either in their own country or in the neighbourhood of their old garrison, where they enjoyed prestige and authority, and were called to take part in the municipal administration. For the Berbers in general, each veteran, and especially each group of veterans, provided an encouragement and an example.

The Africans took readily to intellectual pursuits. It is true that when Juvenal speaks of Africa as 'the nurse of advocates[2],' his meaning is not so much that many Africans became advocates as that all Africans were fond of litigation. But at the same date the

---

[1] J. Carcopino in *C.R. Ac. Inscr.*, 1914, p. 32. [2] VII, 148–9.

orator Septimius Severus, the grandfather of the future emperor, gave his friends at Rome the impression of being a polished Italian gentleman[1]. Writers such as Apuleius and Fronto, representing the best in Latin literature in the second century, came from Madauros and Cirta. Salvius Julianus, Hadrian's great jurist, was an African; so too was Florus probably, and perhaps Aulus Gellius. The schools of Carthage were famous, and educated people prided themselves on as good a knowledge of Greek as of Latin. This flourishing culture came into its own with the Christian literature of the third century and later, in which Africa leads the field.

Thus archaeology and the history of letters alike suggest that towards the end of the second century Africa was effectively romanized. Nevertheless, one should beware of hasty conclusions. Outside the towns, outside the world of the aristocracy and the middle class, the world which is the concern of most of our surviving documents, lived a great country population, poor and obscure, which never comes to our notice directly, but was certainly far more numerous than the privileged classes of whom we do hear. There was a great gulf between the circumstances of the romanized bourgeoisie of landowners or capitalists and those of the country labourers living from hand to mouth. Out of this mass of the people, still ignorant of Roman manners and the Latin tongue, some individuals could emerge and rise to a higher level of comfort and culture, whether by the daily work of their hands or by means of military service; but for this process to have become general, it would have been necessary for Roman Africa after the second century to be able to look forward to a long period of peace and prosperity.

III. SPAIN

Spain was the first of the three great countries of the West to make its entry into the Roman Empire, for the Spanish provinces were in existence two generations before the formation of an African province, and three generations before that of a province in Gaul. This seniority of the Spanish provinces had lasting consequences: the vocabulary of the Latin-speaking Spaniards showed an archaism which is probably due to the fact that Latin became current in Spain in the second century B.C., and that under the Empire the Italian immigrants were too few to bring the vocabulary up to date with the Latin spoken in Rome at that time.

[1] Statius, *Silv.* IV, 5.

Before the Roman conquest Spain, more than any other Mediterranean country, contained elements of widely different origin. Each successive movement of peoples from East to West had left its deposit in the Spanish peninsula, where the Ocean barred the way to further progress. Thus the Iberians and the Celts had been superimposed on the Ligurians. On the other hand all the seafaring peoples—the Minoans, Phoenicians, Greeks, Carthaginians, and perhaps the Etruscans—had been attracted by the rich mines of the country. In this compound the dominant element was the Iberian, which had left its mark on the whole population in common. There were, however, important local differences, according to the proportion of the various ethnic groups in each district, and these differences were accentuated by the physical geography of Spain, which divides the country into regions varying in climate and products, and very much shut off from one another. Before the Roman occupation Spain presented the appearance of a series of compartments, each living its own life, and each at a different stage of civilization.

Roman rule brought unity to Spain, in so far as the natural conditions allowed it. It promoted intercourse between the different parts of the country, and introduced everywhere the ingredients of a common civilization. The division into provinces under Augustus gave the Spaniards a field of activity which was wisely adapted to the nature of the country, though no efforts on the part of the Romans could wholly banish the local disparities. In Spain, as in Africa, no great change of population followed the Roman conquest. Colonies were already in existence, some founded during the wars of conquest, but most of them by Caesar or Augustus: and a number of Italians came to seek their fortune in Spain at the time of the Civil Wars. But the native inhabitants continued to form the vast majority of the population, and Italian immigration ceased to be of importance after the earliest emperors.

The controlling factor in the economic life of Spain had always been its mineral wealth, and under the Empire its relative importance increased as the mines of Greece and Asia Minor were worked out. Spain was the land of all the metals. Gold was found in the beds of rivers such as the Tagus, the Douro and the Tader, and above all in the mines of Galicia and Asturia: the purest gold came from Galicia, but Asturia preserves the most imposing remains of Roman works for the mining and washing of the rich earth. In the time of Pliny the Elder Galicia, Asturia and Lusitania together yielded twenty thousand pounds of gold a year[1].

[1] Pliny, *N.H.* xxxiii, 78.

Silver was found usually in conjunction with lead and chiefly in two districts, on the Mediterranean coast about Cartagena, and in the Sierra Morena near Castulo, though there were also silver mines at Aljustrel in Lusitania, and silver was produced as a by-product in the gold mines. Lead was a secondary product of the silver mines, and there were lead mines in Cantabria and Baetica. Tin was mined in Lusitania and Galicia, and there was also the tin which could reach Spain from Britain, by an old route which was still perhaps not completely abandoned. Most of the Roman world's supply of copper came from Spain: the most important mines were those of the Mons Marianus in the west of the Sierra Morena, which exported their yield by way of Corduba, and other copper deposits were worked in southern Lusitania and the country of the Vettones. Iron was mined on the Mediterranean coast near Dianium, and especially in the north among the Cantabrians and Vascones. The mines of Sisapo on the borders of Baetica and Nearer Spain were the only ones known to the ancients that produced mercury: cinnabar came from them also. Finally, various parts of Spain produced materials for dyes and drugs.

Spain was thus foremost among the countries of the ancient world as a source of the precious metals and the metals in common use, and this was in fact her special function in the Imperial system. The military organization, the roads, the boundaries of the administrative areas, were alike dictated primarily by considerations of how the mines could best be exploited and their returns increased. This exploitation drew large working populations into barren mountain districts where food-supply was a problem and life was hard. Little is known of this miserable proletariate, in which there was little difference between slaves and free workers, but it formed a quite considerable part of the population of Spain.

At the end of the Republic many of the Spanish mines were privately owned, and probably in most cases the owner's title to the property had been acquired during the period of conquest, and would not bear close inspection. Under the first emperors the mines became the property of the State, that is to say of the *fiscus* or the emperor's *patrimonium*, by a gradual and varied process of acquisition by purchase, inheritance or confiscation, applied first to the gold mines, and later to the silver mines and the rest. They were then farmed out to *conductores*, who could sublet them in their turn, and the Imperial Treasury thus derived a vast revenue from them[1]. The metals from these mines

---

[1] See inscriptions from Aljustrel, Bruns, *Fontes*[7], 112 *sq.* (Dessau 6891).

were exported from the harbours of Spain in the form of ingots, and ingots of Spanish lead in particular have been found in different parts of the Mediterranean world. Nevertheless, part of the minerals was worked up in Spain itself. Several towns, such as Bilbilis, Turiaso and Toletum were famous for their steel industries, which owed their success to the special qualities of the river-water used in their processes, and which supported a flourishing export trade. Jewelry and bronze statuettes were still manufactured as they had been before the Roman occupation, but these articles hardly supplied the local demand for them. The quarries too, and building-materials, tiles and bricks, manufactured in the country, did no more than supply local needs, with the exception of the marble quarries of the Mons Marianus in Baetica, which probably produced marble for export. Mica, *lapis specularis*, was obtained in Celtiberia near Segobriga, from a vein which was originally the only one known to the Roman world; but in the time of the elder Pliny new veins had been discovered in Cyprus, Cappadocia and Sicily, and finally in Africa, though the Spanish mica continued to be the best[1]. But the growing competition of manufactured glass probably meant that mica was less used than formerly.

Although the exploitation of the mines certainly claimed the first attention of the Imperial officials, because in this respect no other province could take the place of Spain, nevertheless agriculture came a good second. Spain could do more than support her own peoples, including the thickly populated mining areas; she could also contribute to the food-supply of Rome and Italy. Spain was able to supply the three primary products of ancient agriculture, wheat, olive oil and wine. Wheat is grown all over Spain except on the north coast where the rainfall is too high. The olive, according to Pliny, had penetrated by his time *in Hispanias medias*[2], by which he means, no doubt, that it grew, as it grows to-day, not only on the west and east coast, and in the valleys of the Ebro, the Guadalquivir and the Douro, but inland as far as the central plateau of Castile, south of the Sierra de Guadarrama. Vines of one quality or another are found in every part of the peninsula. Two especially productive regions were thoroughly exploited, Andalusia, including the valleys of the Guadalquivir and its tributaries, and the coast from the Pyrenees to the south of Valencia. The harvests of Baetica rivalled those of Egypt and the best lands in Sicily: indeed their wheat was the best in weight of all wheat imported to Rome, except the African[3]. The soil that

[1] Pliny, *N.H.* xxxvi, 160.　　　　　　[2] Pliny, *N.H.* xv, 1.
[3] Pliny, *N.H.* xviii, 66 and 95.

produced the wheat supported olive trees also, and the oil of
Baetica was second in quality only to that of Venafrum[1]. The best
wines came from the Mediterranean coast, from the neighbourhood of Barcelona, Tarragona and Valencia, and from the Balearic
Isles: moreover, the most famous of the Italian vines, such as the
Falernian, were introduced into Baetica, and probably elsewhere
in Spain[2].

Wheat and oil were exported to Italy: Spain is one of the four
grain-producing provinces represented in a mosaic at Ostia in
the first century A.D. (the other three are Sicily, Africa and
Egypt)[3]. Among the broken amphorae of Monte Testaccio on
the bank of the Tiber, very many came from Spain, and more
particularly from the Guadalquivir valley, and wheat and oil were
their principal contents. From the moment when Italian oil
ceased to meet the needs of the Roman market, a fierce competition probably arose between the oil of Spain and that of Africa,
and, although it is impossible to follow its history, it seems likely
that Africa slowly gained the upper hand. The export of wine was
probably less extensive, though the fact that certain Spanish
wines gained a great name in Italy proves that Roman connois-
seurs had a chance of enjoying them.

Secondary to these staple products was the cultivation of fruit
and vegetables; honey, bees-wax and pitch were also exported.
Among exports, too, were two kinds of textiles, the raw material
being grown and treated on the spot. Flax was grown on the
Mediterranean coast and made into the finest linen at Tarraco
and Saetabis; the same crop flourished also in Galicia under the
Empire.[4] Esparto (the alfa grass of North Africa to-day) was
peculiar to Spain in antiquity, since the Romans never exploited
it in Africa: the *campus spartarius* was a plain one hundred miles
long and thirty miles across near Cartagena, and its crop was used
for many inexpensive articles of everyday use, such as ropes,
baskets and sandals, which found ready buyers among the sailors
and miners, and bulked largely in the cargoes of the ships which
sailed from Cartagena or Dianium.[5] Raisers of stock concerned
themselves principally with horses, donkeys and mules, which did
well in Lusitania, Galicia, Asturia and Celtiberia. Excellent
woollen fabrics came from the flocks of all three provinces. The
mountaineers of the Pyrenees and the Cantabrian mountains
reared pigs and exported hams which were famous. Finally, one

[1] Pliny, *N.H.* xv, 8; xvii, 94.　　　　　[2] *C.I.L.* ii, 2029.
[3] G. Calza, in *Bull. Arch. Com.* 1912, p. 103.
[4] Pliny, *N.H.* xix, 9–10.　　　　[5] Pliny, *N.H.* xix, 26–30.

very old industry, fishing, was always active on many parts of the coast, especially the oyster, tunny and mackerel fisheries, with the subsidiary industries of curing and the manufacture of *garum*. Here was a profitable opening for various commercial companies, which seem to have included a number of Orientals[1].

The trade of Spain was first and foremost an export trade of raw materials and foodstuffs to Italy, though manufactured goods were imported from Italy and Gaul. A good number of Spaniards made the journey to Italy, and even settled down in Rome or Ostia. The presence of Gauls in the neighbourhood of Tarraco and of Spaniards in southern Gaul, and the comparatively large number of Africans in the Spanish towns, indicate the close relations which normally existed between Spain and the provinces which were her neighbours[2].

As early as the period of conquest the Romans had seen possibilities in Spain beyond the mere production of minerals and foodstuffs. They had quickly recognized the military qualities of the Spaniards as cavalry and infantry. The first emperors drew heavily upon the man-power of Spain. In the legions serving in Spain in the first century many recruits came from the towns of Baetica and of Nearer Spain and Lusitania, and there were many Spaniards also in legions (such as XX Valeria Victrix) which did not belong to the army of Spain. Lusitania and Nearer Spain supplied soldiers for the praetorian cohorts. Above all, very many of the auxiliary corps bear Spanish names[3]: most of these were formed in the first century; certainly many Spaniards took part in the campaigns of this date, and Spaniards appear in the first Roman settlements in Mauretania[4]. With the progress of romanization, however, these military qualities declined. Spain was not a frontier province, and from the reign of Vespasian onwards the garrison amounted to no more than one legion (VII Gemina) supported by *auxilia*. Most of the auxiliary corps with Spanish names served in countries far from Spain itself, in Britain, on the Rhine and the Danube, or in the East, and they were recruited on the spot. Moreover, the advance of urbanization in Spain quickly narrowed the areas from which auxiliaries could be recruited.

[1] *C.I.L.* II, p. 251.   [2] E. Albertini in *Mél. Cagnat*, pp. 297–318.

[3] We know of five *alae Hispanorum*, two *Aravacorum*, four *Asturum*, one *Vettonum*; sixteen *cohortes Hispanorum* (and one *Ligurum et Hispanorum*), three *Asturum et Callaecorum*, eight *Asturum*, six *Lucensium*, seven *Bracaraugustanorum*, two *Cantabrorum*, one *Vardullorum*, two *Vasconum*, one *Ausetanorum*, two *Celtiberorum*, nine *Lusitanorum*.

[4] E. Albertini in *Bull. archéol. du Comité des Travaux hist.* 1925, pp. ccxi–ccxvi.

The Spanish contribution to the army was soon reduced practically to the legion VII Gemina, which continued to draw the great majority of its soldiers from Lusitania and especially from Nearer Spain. It even appears that under Hadrian the Spaniards in general showed a distaste for military service which attracted the displeasure of the Emperor[1], though he could still form a *cohors I Aelia Hispanorum miliaria equitata* to send to Britain[2], and about the same date Spaniards were quite numerous in the first urban cohort on garrison duty at Carthage[3]. The soldier's life kept its charm longest for the more backward peoples such as the Asturians and Cantabrians, among whom Trajan raised for his Dacian war not cohorts or *alae*, but a new type of corps known as *symmachiarii*[4], the non-Roman type described by the Pseudo-Hyginus as *nationes*, and appearing later in the second century under the name of *numeri*. These facts are symptoms of the state of culture in Spain, which was still not uniform in the second century. The veneer of Roman manners and institutions varied in thickness, but it could not change the native material underneath with all its local tendencies.

Landmarks of the old native society survived in the partition of Spain in Roman times into a great number of cities (more than five hundred in fact). This division into tiny territorial units is no more than a survival and a consequence of the Iberian political system of small independent groups, all ready to fly at one another's throats, and avoiding all save ephemeral alliances. At the height of the Imperial régime the group which exercised the strongest attraction for the Spanish mind was still often a mere fraction of a tribe, a *gentilitas*, and all the efforts of the Roman government did not wholly succeed in widening the Spanish outlook and making the Spaniards feel that they belonged to a great State; consequently the *regio*, the administrative unit for purposes of the census and of recruiting, and the *conventus*, the cultural entity associated with the Imperial cult, had a far greater significance from the Roman point of view than they possessed in the minds of the people[5]. There was however a transition to Roman manners and habits of thought among the upper and middle classes in the more highly developed parts of the country, in Baetica, on the Mediterranean coastal plains, in the Ebro valley and on the coast

---

[1] S.H.A. *Hadr.* 12, 4.　　　　[2] *C.I.L.* VII, 954; 963–5.
[3] *C.I.L.* VIII, 24619, 24629.
[4] H. Dessau in *Klio*, xx, 1925, p. 227 *sq.*
[5] E. Albertini, *Les divisions administratives de l'Espagne romaine*, pp. 105–113.

which now belongs to Portugal. But in the mining districts the working populations remained rough and barbarous. On the central plateau the old culture clung to its ground, and romanization was really effective only in a few places where cities had sprung up. The greatest resistance of all was encountered in the scattered populations of north and north-west (Vasconia, Cantabria, Asturia and Galicia); although nearly the whole of the army of occupation was concentrated here, Iberian tradition persisted most stubbornly. The native languages were in a way to becoming extinct in the richer parts of the country, but they were still spoken, by the common people at least, in central Spain and in the north and north-west; they appear, indeed, to have survived up to the present day in Basque.

In the same districts, too, the native religions kept their largest following. In Lusitania, and especially in Asturia and Galicia, a number of Latin inscriptions are dedications to gods with names which are purely barbarous except for a Latin termination, in many cases gods probably of springs or rivers. Such native gods are found also, though less frequently, in the *conventus* of Clunia and Saragossa; in the *conventus* of Cartagena they are very rare, and in the *conventus* of Tarraco and in Baetica they never appear at all. Sometimes, again, the native deities were fused with Graeco-Roman gods, and in these cases the Roman name receives as an epithet either the old Iberian name or a derivative from it: such names are Juppiter Ahoparaliomegus, Mars Cariociecus, Proserpina Ataecina[1]. The next stage is reached when the epithet disappears: then the old native deity was worshipped under its Roman name, and thus the native cults lived on, even in the most romanized districts, under their Latin disguise. Probably these cults had more vogue among the poor than among the governing classes, and probably their place in the cultural life of the Spanish people was more important than the evidence of inscriptions suggests.

The art of Spain in the Empire is, on the surface, Roman provincial art, academic and banal. The temples of the great towns, the statues of public men, and the costly monuments of the dead conform to the conventions of the age. But in the background some signs of originality are to be found in the country districts and the arts of the people. The sculptures of the mining district of Castulo[2] show an original combination of the human figure with

[1] F. Fita in *Bol. de la Acad. de la Hist.* LVI, 1910, p. 353; *C.I.L.* II, 5612; *ib.* p. 1126.

[2] See Volume of Plates v, 46, *a*.

geometric and vegetable decoration. In the neighbourhood of Clunia and Palencia, in the Pyrenees and the Cantabrian mountains, and in the Asturias, the funeral *stelae* are skilfully decorated and have their own technique, flat low-relief obtained by cutting away the background, with the stone trimmed into small slightly convex triangular surfaces, in a style reminiscent of wood-carving[1]. The painted pottery which had formerly been one of the most interesting examples of Iberian art was still manufactured in Roman times[2]. In architecture one really original feature, the Norman arch or Moorish arch, was probably invented in Spain: under the Romans it was confined to the art of the people, where it appears on *stelae* and on *terra sigillata*, but later under the Visigoths it was free to develop, and finally became prominent in the art and decoration of the Mohammedan period[3].

In Spain, as elsewhere, one must distinguish between town and country. The country remained to a great extent native, and it was the towns which were the centres of romanization. Their number increased greatly under the Empire. The Romans sometimes built a town to replace a group of villages; or they allowed or encouraged the inhabitants of a small and inaccessible acropolis to remove into the plain and build a town there[4]; or, again, they gave an urban centre to a scattered country population. This last move was particularly common in the north and north-west, where towards the end of the first century or early in the second the Roman administration formed settlements of an urban type in native cities which did not possess them, usually in the neighbourhood of a cross-road or a market or a hot spring. Native cities which in Pliny have the name of a tribe appear in Ptolemy as urban centres, and evidently the process of urbanization had gone forward in the interval. These Spanish towns were numerous, and correspondingly unimportant for the most part. In the Guadalquivir valley especially the towns were so near together that they were in close competition, and most of them numbered only a few thousand inhabitants. Those towns, too, which did attain to a greater size found themselves engaged in a competition which brought no decisive victory: in Baetica Corduba, Hispalis and Gades were rivals, on the Mediterranean coast Valentia, Tarraco and Barcino, in Lusitania the administrative capital Emerita, and the prosperous Olisipo.

[1] See Volume of Plates v, 46, *b*.　　　[2] *Ib*. 46, *c, d*.
[3] M. Gómez-Moreno, *Excursión á través del arco de herradura*, in *Cultura Española*, 1906, pp. 785–811.
[4] *E.g.* Sabora; Dessau 6092.

The communications between all these administrative and economic centres were maintained by a splendid road-system which was in essentials the work of Augustus, Tiberius and Claudius. The arterial roads were the roads from Gaul. The first came from Narbonese Gaul over the eastern Pyrenees and so through Tarraco, Valentia, Castulo, Corduba and Hispalis to Gades: a second ran over the col du Somport to Caesaraugusta (Saragossa), through central Spain from north-east to south-west, and finally reached Emerita and the Lusitanian ports: the third came down from the col de Roncevaux to Pompaelo (Pampeluna), thence through Asturia and Galicia to the ports of Brigantium (Corunna) and Iria Flavia (El Padrón, south of Compostella)— the future road of Saint James. The most important of the cross-country roads was the one which branched off from this last road at Asturica and went from north to south as far as Gades, passing through Salmantica, Emerita, Italica and Hispalis. In addition, transport by water was often possible. There was an active coastal trade, and it is certain that the towns of the *conventus* of Gades, which formed a long narrow coastal strip, communicated by sea as much as or more than by road. Boats plied constantly on the Guadalquivir (up to Corduba) and its principal tributaries, the Maenuba and the Singilis (to Astigi): other navigable rivers were the Anas, Tagus, Douro, Minius and the Ebro as far inland as Vareia near Logroño[1].

Nature had placed great obstacles in the way of modernizing the country and ensuring the free passage of men and goods, and here the Romans had their opportunity of winning great technical victories, such as the bridge at Alcantara and the aqueduct at Segovia[2]. The Roman towns of Spain, though their remains are less well preserved than those of Africa, still allow us to imagine what some ancient cities must have looked like: there is Tarragona, rising in splendid tiers on an eminence from which one surveys the Mediterranean as from a balcony, and Italica spreading its wealth of statues and mosaics over the Guadalquivir plain, and Mérida, the ancient Emerita, with its magnificent bridges, aqueducts, temples and places of amusement, all the more remarkable because the city was a creation of the Roman will in a district of no great natural wealth. In these towns lived a *bourgeoisie* which soon enough was ripe to serve the Roman State in the highest positions. As early as 40 B.C. Spain supplied a consul,

[1] Pliny, *N.H.* III, 21; this evidence is confirmed by archaeology: at Vareia have been found the rings used for mooring the boats.
[2] Volume of Plates v, 48, *a, b*.

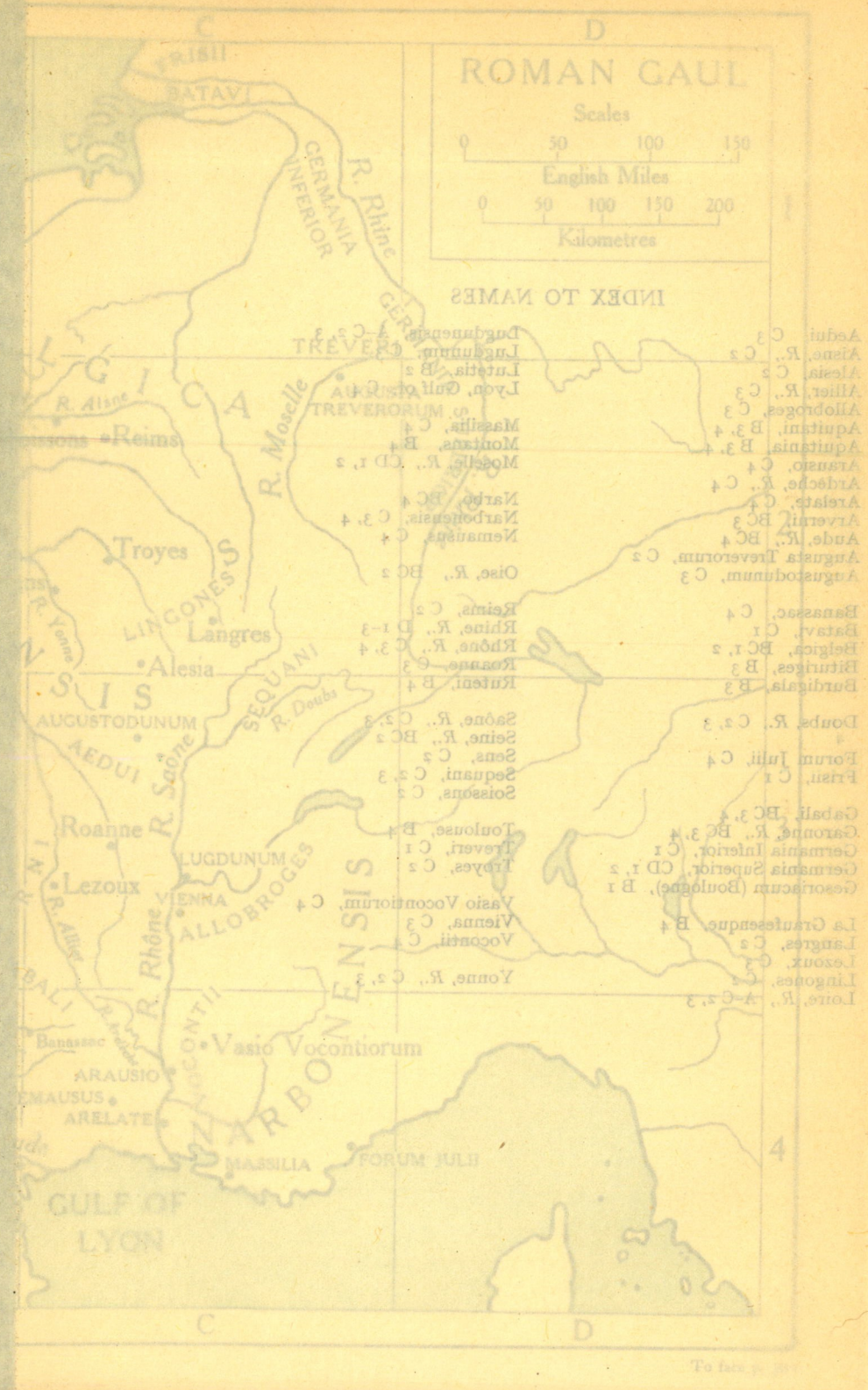

MAP 10

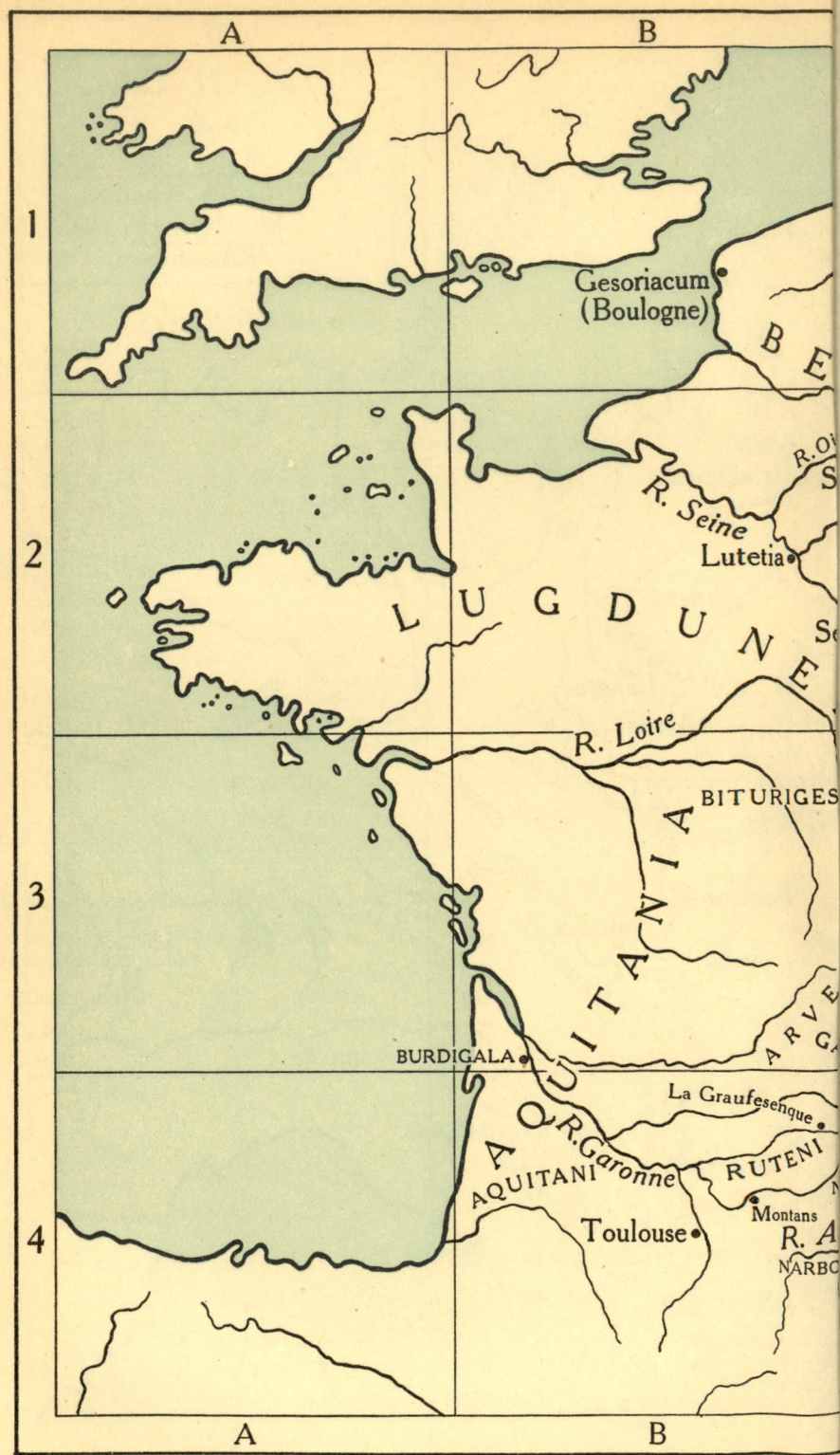

A · B · A · B

1

2

3

4

Gesoriacum
(Boulogne)

BE

R.Oi
S

R. Seine

Lutetia

L U G D U N E

Se

R. Loire

BITURIGES

A Q U I T A N I A

ARVE
GA

BURDIGALA

La Graufesenque

A
R.Garonne

RUTENI

AQUITANI

Montans

Toulouse

R. A

NARBO

the first Cornelius Balbus, and under Augustus a proconsul of
Africa who celebrated a triumph, Cornelius Balbus the second:
in the first century she produced many Roman senators, and it
was from the municipal middle class of Baetica that Trajan and
Hadrian rose to the principate. Even more remarkable is the position of Spain in the Latin literature of the first century, with
Porcius Latro, the two Senecas and Lucan, Quintilian and Martial, not to mention the technical writers such as Hyginus,
Pomponius Mela and Columella (p. 710). The excellence of the
Spanish schools is proved also by the merit of the poems among
our inscriptions, which in Spain are distinctly above the average.

Spain thus made an important contribution to the best Roman
society. But it must not be forgotten that this was only the Spanish
upper class, and beneath it there was a large population which
remained on a lower level of life, and was less receptive of Roman
influences. Above all, when Rome had done all that she could to
make the land a unity, the land remained divided, a complex of
districts which were unities in themselves, as nature and their past
history had formed them.

IV. GAUL

Augustus had begun, and Tiberius finished, a series of measures
which left Gaul divided into four provinces, with an excrescence
in the shape of the two Germanies, originally military areas, but
later provinces themselves. Of the Gallic provinces one, Narbonensis, was senatorial, comprising territory conquered by the
Romans at the end of the second century B.C. Caesar's conquests,
Gallia Comata, became the Imperial provinces of Aquitania,
Lugdunensis and Belgica, with an Imperial cult in common. The
division of Transalpine Gaul between Senate and *princeps* was
natural enough, for Narbonensis, besides being the oldest province of them all, was also geographically distinct from the others,
by reason of its Mediterranean climate and its situation. It falls
for the most part inside the zone favourable to the growth of the
olive, which never penetrated to the other parts of Gaul towards
the Atlantic, the Channel or the Rhine. Greek influences emanating from Massilia for centuries before the Roman conquest
had long since left their mark on the country's civilization. Moreover, Narbonensis lay on the road between Italy and Spain, and
offered a route which was a welcome alternative to the stormy Gulf
of Lyons; so that she not only belonged to the original nucleus of
the Empire as the rest of Gaul did not, but actually formed the

connecting link between the countries of the western Mediterranean. The prime function of the three Imperial provinces, on the other hand, was to maintain and support the German provinces, which protected the Empire against barbarism, whether from the threat of invasion or the tendency to encroach by infiltration.

These differences appeared in the character of the towns and the composition of the population. In Narbonensis there were many towns, at least on the coast and in the Rhône valley; and many of them were colonies in which had settled veterans of Caesar or of Augustus, an important Italian leaven working in the original population. Towards the end of the Republic and under the earliest Emperors, these towns were adorned with elegant monuments, embodiments of a fusion between the Greek tradition which still lived in the districts inland from Massilia, and a desire to imitate Roman manners. The *bourgeoisie* of these parts was quickly romanized, and gave to the early Empire men who shared in its government, men such as Burrus from Vaison, Valerius Asiaticus, consul in A.D. 46, from Vienne, and Agricola the father-in-law of Tacitus, from Fréjus. Roman letters, too, received their contribution. Cornelius Gallus, poet and high official, came from Fréjus; Pompeius Trogus belonged to the region of Vaison; and two of the leading orators under the Julio-Claudians, Votienus Montanus and Domitius Afer, came the one from Narbonne, the other from Nîmes. It was from Nîmes that Antoninus Pius sprang, the son and grandson of Roman consuls. Indeed, Pliny the Elder[1] was led to observe that Italy and Narbonensis were practically one and the same thing. There were parts, it is true, near the Alps, where the colonies were fewer, and the municipal territories more extensive; but, even so, smaller centres of population were there to compete with the great town of the district, and to arrive at urban status themselves by a gradual evolution. Narbonensis, in fact, was a land of towns, each dominating a rather small area round about it.

It was not so in the three Imperial provinces. There the Roman administration preserved, with few exceptions, the division by *civitates*, cities which Caesar had found in existence. In the part of Aquitania adjoining the Pyrenees the population followed the rule which we have seen in Spain (p. 497); the same local particularism resulted in a division into very small units of population, each of which lived within its own valley. But elsewhere in the three provinces the cities were comparatively few, and each city had a correspondingly large territory, varying in character

[1] *N.H.* III, 31.

and resources, and capable of an independent life of its own. The city of Gallia Comata is an economic and political entity, a sort of State in miniature. It has a central and initiative organ which is the town, the capital of the *civitas*, and also secondary organs, boroughs or villages, the centre of the *pagi* which are the subdivisions of the *civitas*. The country recognizes the supremacy and authority of the capital, but is not oppressed or effaced by it, since it contains in itself a good proportion of the most active and useful elements in the city-community. In the country districts included in each community are to be found either isolated farms, great or small, or hamlets of labourers and artisans, or centres of population which gradually spring up round a cross roads or a market or a sanctuary. Such places are focuses of industry with a function of their own, because the area of the city-community is great, and the capital a long way off. The country was subordinate to the town in Gaul as elsewhere in the Roman world; but in Gaul the opposition between the two was probably the least profound, and its effects the least marked. This population received few foreign elements superimposed on its Celtic foundation, and consequently Celtic traditions survived, traditions which made the relations between country and town not so much an affair of dependence and supremacy as of a combination between the two on equal terms.

Gaul was always rich in corn, vegetables and fruit, and under the Empire she became the richer, in that the *pax Romana* assured regular harvests and greater facilities for marketing. She thus supported her own population, and in most years had a surplus of many of her products for export to Italy or to the armies on the Rhine. The vine grew in many parts of the country, and wine was produced in latitudes well to the north of Paris. In the north, the local wines were drunk at home, but the wines of Languedoc, the Rhône, Burgundy and the Garonne were exported. Nevertheless, this industry was not always well seen by the emperors, for as long as the Italian vineyards produced enough wine for home consumption and for export, the producers demanded that the output from the provinces should be restricted, and they succeeded in moving the authorities in their favour. A measure passed about the time of the conquest of Narbonensis, restricting the growing of vines in the provinces, which had long ceased to be effective, was re-enforced by Domitian, who laid down not merely that no new vines were to be planted, but even that a part of the existing vines was to be destroyed (p. 38 *sq.*). How far this law was put into practice cannot be determined; but we know of no revolt, or even discontent, resulting from it, and may perhaps conclude that it was not rigorously enforced, and that in many instances governors and procurators were content to turn a blind eye. It seems almost certain that the legal prohibition had very largely fallen into desuetude by the time it was officially repealed by Probus in the second half of the third century,[1] and we may conclude that a long competition between Italian wines and the wines of Gaul and other provinces ended in a victory for the provincials. Olive oil, too, gave Italian producers grounds for the same fears at the time of the conquest of Gaul. Nevertheless, in the first century the growth of the olive made great strides in Narbonensis, where no doubt the presence of colonists of Italian origin counted for much, since it is difficult to stop people from growing what they have always grown, and what they like to grow. Narbonensis never came into competition with Africa or Baetica: her oil hardly travelled outside Gaul and the Germanies, and even these provinces were obliged to import Spanish oil as well, though many of the peasants probably still used their native oils, made in all likelihood from beechnuts or walnuts.

Among cereals wheat naturally took pride of place, though much barley was grown also, particularly in the north, where it was turned to good use for making beer. Flax and hemp, grown for textiles, were very profitable. The breeding of horses and mules, sheep, cattle and pigs were all flourishing industries: and Gaul was famous for its hounds. Hides, cheeses and hams were exported in great abundance.

In mineral resources Gaul was not wholly deficient, but the seams which had been freely worked before the conquest were now insignificant compared with the wealth of Spain, Noricum and Britain, and, a little later, of Dacia. Mines were closed down, except silver and iron mines: and even iron and silver were no longer exported on the old scale, but were used at home, and finally left the country, if they did leave it, in the shape of manufactured goods.

Industrial activity is the distinguishing mark of Roman Gaul, an activity embracing in its innumerable workshops articles of every kind for consumption at home or abroad. It is most often in the hands of men working at home and for their own account. A workshop is run by the members of one family, with, at the most, a few paid workmen in addition. In only a few cases, notably in the pottery and glass industries, did the industrial

---

[1] As early as the principate of Antoninus Pius, we hear of *vini olei et tritici penuriam* at Rome (S.H.A. *Pius*, 8, 11).

system develop so as to include a number of real factories employing many workmen, whether free labourers or slaves.

The output and the profits of Gallic manufacturers depended very greatly on the quality of the workmanship. There were many Gauls who were good and clever craftsmen. Trade secrets were handed down from father to son, and maintained the excellence of the finished article. An important consideration was the great forests of Gaul, which had suffered comparatively little from deforestation, and thus provided cheap and plentiful fuel. This connection between forest and industry explains the great number of ruins that have been found in the forests of France, and especially in the north: they are the sites of ancient workshops. The Gauls were metal-workers and goldsmiths, and made, besides articles of everyday use, jewelry and *objets d'art*, silver plate, bronze statuettes, *fibulae* and enamelled boxes: the *fibulae* of the Gaul Aucissa were fashionable in distant countries.[1] The products of the textile industry were greatly in demand, and especially its cloaks, as well as sails and mattresses, both well-known Gallic specialities. Of the workers in wood, the coopers, coach-builders and shoemakers of Gaul were known and respected everywhere.

But the most developed and most expansive industry was that of pottery, and its companion industry, glass-making. The Gallic potters began by imitating the potters of Italy, but later they had their own processes and their own types, less elaborate and hence less expensive than Arretine ware, and they ended by capturing nearly every market. The most famous workshops are in the Massif Central, namely, in the first century, at La Graufesenque and Montans in the territory of the Ruteni; later in the first century and early in the second at Banassac in the territory of the Gabali; and in the second century at Lezoux in the territory of the Arverni. As early as the first century great quantities of Gallic pottery had reached Pompeii, and later it is found not only all over Gaul, but in Italy, Africa, Spain, Britain and Germany:[2] in the southern parts of the Empire the vases from La Graufesenque are the most frequent, in the north those of Lezoux. In spite of the local competition and imitation encountered by Gallic wares in countries where they had originally enjoyed a monopoly, they continued to be exported abundantly and profitably right up to the crisis of the third century. The glassworkers, of whom the most famous is Frontinus in the north of Gaul, followed the example of

---

[1] M. Rostovtzeff, *Soc. and Econ. Hist.* p. 506.

[2] They have even been discovered recently in Syria (Cl. Schaeffer, *Rev. Arch.* 1935, 1, p. 269 *sq.*).

the potters, though their products, being more fragile, were less suitable for export.

All this commerce was served by a system of communications well conceived in the first place, and established for the most part since the time of Augustus and Agrippa. Here Gaul had one great advantage over every other province in its numerous river-ways, navigable nearly all the year round. Some rivers had a deeper and more regular flow than now, and the boats of that day drew little water, with the result that navigation was possible not only on the great arteries (the Rhône and the Saône, the Moselle, the Seine up to Troyes, the Loire up to Roanne, and the Garonne up to Toulouse), but also on such rivers as the Ardèche, the Doubs, the Yonne and the Allier. There were no canals joining these river-routes, but the junction was made by portages where the valleys were nearest to each other, and in this way the Doubs was linked up with the Rhine, the Saône with the Moselle and with the Seine or Yonne, the Rhône with the Allier, and the Aude with the Garonne. The corporations of boat-owners were rich and influential, and the towns situated at the junction of a river-route with important roads were the trading centres of Gaul: the prosperity of Narbonne, Arles, Bordeaux, Lyons and Trèves derived originally from this source, which indeed leads also to the future fortunes of Paris.

The mass of the population of Gaul consisted of farmers and artisans. This fact combined with the survival of the *pagi* as communities with a certain individuality of their own to assist the survival of the native culture. There was never any real conflict between the pre-Roman customs and the process of romanization. The Celts of Gaul, unlike the Berbers and the Iberians, were related to the Italians by language, with all its implications of similarity in thought and feeling, and this Indo-European relationship between the conquering and the conquered people was vital to their good understanding. The new manners brought by the Romans found no violent opposition, though they did not drive out the ancient customs completely: the civilization of Roman Gaul is in fact a combination of the two, and it is this which gives it its originality. The structure of society in general remained what it had always been; in each city there was an aristocracy of great landlords surrounded by a multitude of clients and small tenants. It was no great change for the rich noble of independent Gaul to become the Gallo-Roman senator, when under Claudius the Senate was thrown open to some of the provincial citizens of Gallia Comata (Vol. x, p. 677); and such a senator, living on the income from his estates, and controlling directly or indirectly a mass of peasants and workpeople, was a powerful conservative element in the social system, and later, when the Empire began to break up, was destined to be the most stable element in a crumbling world. He dominated, but he protected. Under his shadow peasants and workmen could live safely, if humbly, and famines and bankruptcies were rare.

In housing and dress, old habits died hard. The *toga* did not supersede the national costumes, the *sagum*, trousers and cowled cloak. The Celtic speech remained for long the popular speech of the countryside, and lawyers in the third century still recognized the validity of documents drawn up in the Gallic tongue.[1] Nevertheless, Latin gained ground daily: many people were bilingual, and in the towns there was an increasing number of Gauls who knew Latin only. Curiously enough, there are cups made for the use of tavern-keepers and their customers, that is to say, of the common people, which bear inscriptions—greetings, wishes or toasts—in Latin. The schools worked hard to diffuse the Latin speech and letters. There were famous schools at Toulouse and Trèves, at Marseilles, where the progress of Latin did more and more to efface Greek traditions, and at Autun, in that country of the Aedui which from the first had co-operated so effectively to advance Roman influence. Although few notable writers were educated in these schools under the Flavians and Antonines— Favorinus of Arles, contemporary of Hadrian and the best known Gallic man of letters, is no more than a second-rate figure—there is still no reason to doubt that the general level of the instruction which they introduced into the aristocracy and middle class was high enough.

But it is in religion, as is natural, that the tenacity of the old Celtic life is most obvious. The Druids, indeed, and their rites had been suppressed by the Imperial police (Vol. x, p. 409). But there was no incompatibility between the native cults and the cults superimposed on them by Roman influences, one of which, the semi-political cult of Rome and Augustus, assembled every year round the altar at Lyons, where the Saône joins the Rhône, the representatives of the sixty-four *civitates* of Celtic Gaul. Worshippers still flocked regularly to their ancestral sanctuaries (notably at Alesia). In many cases the native gods had been assimilated by the Romans to Graeco-Italian gods, so that by an easy syncretism the two gods were worshipped under the one name, as the great Gallic god Teutates disguised himself under the name and attributes of

[1] *Dig.* XXXII, I, II.

Mercury. Sometimes, however, the Celtic name was preserved: or a native epithet could be attached to the name of a Roman god;[1] or a Roman god could have a native goddess associated with him as his consort, a form of union which gives us the couples Mercury and Rosmerta, Apollo and Sirona; or, again, a Celtic deity could live on quite undisturbed, as did Epona, the goddess of horses, whose cult passed far beyond the frontiers of Gaul and spread throughout the Empire. The common people and peasants and soldiers clung especially to the cult of the *Matres* or *Matronae*, the ancient and popular deities of springs, rivers, forests or mountains, guardians of the land and of its inhabitants.

The same mixture of imitation and local tradition can be seen in the images of the gods, statues, statuettes and reliefs: on the one hand, the conventional Juppiter or Mercury, on the other hand gods with three heads or with the antlers of a stag. In the cities of Belgica (and also in Germany) were many columns surmounted by a giant with a serpent's tail beneath a mounted figure, where the idea is native and the execution is in the Roman style: a mythical struggle between light and darkness or between heaven and earth is expressed by forms which draw their inspiration from classical art. The architecture of the temples shows yet another example of the same process, for they are often built to a square plan derived from Celtic tradition, but they are surrounded with porticos. The sculpture which comprises the monuments of these Gallo-Roman cults is usually clumsy and uninspired. There is more originality and variety and fidelity in the funeral *stelae*, which have for their favourite theme not, as in Africa, a representation of prophylactic symbols, nor, as in Spain, a schematic picture of the world of the dead, but simply the likeness of the living man in the attitudes of his daily work and dressed for his workshop or booth. This popular realistic art is most attractive.[2] The obvious pleasure with which the Gallo-Roman sculptor treats such scenes must certainly have some connection with development of a skilled craftsmanship in Gaul. Speaking generally, the survival in this art of the Celtic spirit, which makes itself seen in a certain independence of the strict discipline of classicism, makes it alive despite all its imperfections.[3]

[1] *E.g. Mars Segomo, Mars Camulus, Mercurius Clavariates, Mercurius Iovantucarus, Apollo Cobledulitavus* (Dessau 4538, 4550, 4599, 4601, 4638).

[2] See, *e.g.*, the series of funeral monuments at Sens, in E. Espérandieu, *Recueil gén. des bas-reliefs, statues et bustes de la Gaule romaine*, IV, 1911, pp. 3 *sqq.*

[3] R. Lantier, *Monuments Piot*, XXXI, 1931, p. 37 *sq.*: *id. C. R. Ac. Inscr.* 1932, pp. 302–9: A. Grenier, *R.E.A.* XXXV, 1933, p. 46.

In the South of France, the ancient Narbonensis, monuments still standing make it easiest to imagine what the towns of Roman Gaul were like. Fréjus, Arles, Nîmes, Orange, Vaison or Vienne still possess fine ancient buildings—temples, arches, theatres, amphitheatres, aqueducts or baths—which date, many of them, from the early Empire, and the rest from the age of the Antonines. Elsewhere in France the monuments were often less soundly built, and their ruins have not lasted so well, but, even so, innumerable remains are still to be seen scattered over the land or collected in the museums.

The importance of Gaul in the Imperial system as the mainstay of the two provinces of Germany deserves to be emphasized. The close connection between the Gauls and the Germanies is illustrated even by the administrative boundaries, for the Treviri were included in Belgica, while the Lingones belonged to Upper Germany until the second century, and the Sequani until the end of the third. There were no troops in Gaul itself, except a corps of police, the urban cohort in barracks at Lyons, and several posts to maintain the safety of certain important roads: but the country was a recruiting ground for the armies of Germany. The German legions in the first century and early second century contained a rather high proportion of Gauls; and, especially, a great part of the *auxilia* of the armies of Germany in the first century was originally recruited from Gaul. They include several cohorts of Aquitani, cohorts of Bituriges and Belgae, and *alae* of Gauls which often bear the name of the officer who first formed them.[1] Later, the progress of romanization found the Gauls with less taste for military service; their numbers in the legions diminished, and the auxiliary corps which were Gallic by name and origin were transferred to more distant provinces and recruited there. But the provinces of Gaul did not cease to support and strengthen the armies of Germany, for even if the supplies of men failed somewhat, they never ceased to supply them with food, material and articles of daily use. The contractors for the armies of the Rhine were among the most important business men in the country.

Another notable function of Gaul was as the gateway to Britain and the North. The normal route from Rome to Britain was *via* Lyons, Langres, Reims, Soissons and Boulogne, the port that secured communication between the continent and Britain. Many Gauls served in the army of Britain, too, while military service was still popular. There was an active import and export and carrying trade across the Straits of Dover. From the Channel ports also,

[1] *Antiana, Indiana, Petriana, Picentiana, Proculeiana, Sebosiana.*

Gallic sailors travelled, hugging the coast, to the lands of the Batavians and Frisians and even beyond. This maritime route, no less than the newer land routes from Aquileia across the Alps and from the Black Sea up the Dnieper, brought the Romans into contact with 'the most remote of mankind,' the dwellers by the North Sea and the Baltic, and the populations of East Germany and Scandinavia (pp. 52 *sq.*, 71 *sq.*). Gaul thus contributed more than any other province to a widening of the Empire's horizon, and an extension of Roman civilization beyond its birthplace and home in the Mediterranean lands.

CHAPTER XIII

THE LATIN WEST: BRITAIN, ROMAN GERMANY: THE DANUBE LANDS

I. BRITAIN

THE impact of the Roman Empire on Britain, and its consequences, can only be understood in the light of certain geographical considerations[1].

Britain is an island large enough to have a life of its own, but close enough to the Continent to feel its influence as a constant factor in that life. This influence impinges upon it from various sides. First and foremost, there is the influence of Belgic Gaul, whose coasts are nearest and reached by the easiest sea-passage. Secondly, there is a permanent, but not always equally effective, contact along the Atlantic seaboard with Armorica, the Biscayan lands and the Spanish peninsula. And thirdly, there is a contact with Low German and Scandinavian countries outside the Imperial frontier. During the period now under review, the only positive or constructive influences were those coming from the first source, north-eastern Gaul and the Rhine-Meuse delta.

Within Britain itself, there is a broad distinction between a 'lowland zone,' including all England as far west as Dorset and Somerset and as far north as Cheshire and Yorkshire, composed of secondary and tertiary rocks, and forming a single plain where communications are almost everywhere easy, the soil almost uniformly fertile and well watered, and the climate only moderately wet; and a 'highland zone,' including Devonshire and Cornwall, Wales, and a northern region comprising the Pennines and the whole of Scotland, composed mostly of palaeozoic rocks, where communications are hard, the soil is mostly infertile, and the climate very wet.

Britain as a whole has always been a melting-pot in which racial and cultural elements, received from the Continent, have been fused into a new unity; hence her general spirit has been one of compromise and synthesis, and her contributions to the life and thought of Europe have taken the shape of old ideas and institutions, preserved there owing to her isolation, and revived in a form appropriate to a new age partly by British initiative and

[1] See Map 6, facing p. 151.

partly through the stimulus of new elements brought in from overseas. But the two functions of receiving new elements and of conserving the old have been to a certain extent divided between the two zones; the lowland zone being the more receptive, the highland the more conservative. This division is exceptionally clear during the early centuries of our era, when from the Roman point of view the sole interest of British history lies in Britain's reception of Roman influences. In the lowland zone those influences penetrated rapidly, if not very deeply, into the structure of society; in the highland zone they hardly made themselves felt at all; and consequently the lowland zone appears as the progressive and civilized part of Britain, the highland zone as a dead weight of hostile barbarism; the dividing line between the two being marked by the legionary fortresses, with a fringe of auxiliary *castella* pushed forward into the highland districts.

The population of Britain, from the physical anthropologist's point of view, was the characteristic product of such a melting-pot. Even in the Neolithic period the predominance of the 'long-barrow' type with its very long and narrow skull was by no means absolute; and the tall and massively-built broad-headed men of the Beaker period represent, not an average of the population, but an invading race soon for the most part assimilated into a normal type with less extreme characteristics. The invading Romans were especially struck by the tall, fair warriors of the Belgic aristocracy; but this, too, was a minority, lately come into the country; and modern research has established the conclusion that the average Briton in the Roman period was a man of shortish middle stature, strongly but not heavily made, with a somewhat long skull; tall and fair no doubt by contrast with Italians, but somewhat dark, and not particularly tall, by contrast with other northern Europeans. The type is one which is still common in this country, particularly (according to Sir Arthur Keith) amongst the English middle classes, and was well established here long before the Romans came.

Equally well established was the Celtic language. There is no evidence that any pre-Celtic language was spoken at the time of the Roman invasion in any part of the British isles; and philologists have abandoned the belief in an earlier, Goidelic form of that language, generally superseded by a later or Brythonic, and now hold that the peculiarities of the Goidelic form, notably the replacement of *p* by *q*, were the result of a change originating in the west, and never spreading east of the Irish sea except as carried by invaders from Ireland.

The distribution of this population relatively to the soil has undergone far-reaching changes since the Roman period, though the first hint of these changes can be traced back beyond the Roman invasion. All over the lowland zone, there are regions of light, naturally-drained soil whose geological basis is chalk, oolite, sand or gravel, and whose primitive vegetation was for the most part a thin and easily-cleared woodland; these have been called[1] the areas of primary settlement, and it is here that prehistoric man has left the relics of his occupation. There are also, however, belts of clay and heavy loams, whose wet soils were encumbered by forest with dense undergrowth, unattractive to the primitive cultivator; these, which are to-day in many places the seat of a flourishing agricultural population, were practically uninhabited in prehistoric times. During the Roman period, this prehistoric distribution was still overwhelmingly predominant, although the Belgae had already begun systematically to clear and exploit certain parts of the heavier soils, and although here and there this process went forward in Roman times; but in spite of these exceptions the broad generalization remains true that the lighter soils—mostly on chalk or oolite uplands, but also on the gravels of river-valleys—supported the main part of the agricultural population both in prehistoric and in Roman days, and that the clearing of forests and occupation of heavier soils which has given us the modern distribution of agricultural population in the lowland zone were the work of the Saxon period.

With regard to the total numbers of the population there is no direct evidence. Recent attempts at a conjectural estimate have produced figures varying from half a million to a million and a half.

The romanization of Britain, from Claudius to the Antonines, was in the main confined not only to the lowland zone, but, within that zone, to the towns; so much so, that during this period romanization and urbanization are practically synonymous. Two waves of romanization may be distinguished. The first was concentrated in the towns, and had reached its culmination by the middle of the second century; the second had its focus in the villa-system, whose 'golden age' is dated to the fourth. Here, where our chronological limit is the end of the Antonine period, we are chiefly concerned with the first; the second has hardly begun.

The development of towns went on apace from the very beginning. The figure of 70,000, given by Tacitus[2] as the number

---

[1] The phrase was used by Sir Cyril Fox when lecturing in Oxford in 1933. The idea is expressed in his *Personality of Britain*, pp. 45–49.

[2] *Ann.* x, 33.

of Romans or romanized Britons massacred by Boudicca in London, Verulam and Colchester, even if it is exaggerated, shows that these three towns grew very rapidly in the first few years of their existence. Others must have been growing with equal or almost equal rapidity. To a great extent, especially in London, their population consisted of aliens, especially those engaged in trade and industry; but it also included Britons, drawn from the upper classes, who welcomed Roman fashions and hastened to adapt themselves to the new régime, and others of humbler social standing who supplied manual labour so far as that was not provided by foreign slaves. During this first period, however, it is likely that the alien element predominated in the towns. At the same time a false sense of security led to neglect of defence, and the earliest towns were unwalled.

This state of things came to an end with the Boudiccan rebellion, after which it became the rule to fortify all towns. During the Flavian period the boom, now fostered by official advice and public subsidies, continued; the British aristocracy were increasingly led to adopt Roman ways of life, and hence, even if the influx of foreign traders fell off, the impetus resulting in the growth of towns was by no means exhausted. The romanized aristocracy adorned these towns by erecting *templa fora domos*; an urban proletariate grew up, engaged in various kinds of industry; and the force of expansion was so vigorous that by Hadrian's time, when the earlier earthen ramparts of a town like Verulam were to be replaced by stone walls, these new walls were designed to enclose twice the former area, to allow for future growth.

By this time, however, the boom period in the greater towns was already at an end. The colonies at Lincoln, Gloucester and possibly York, as well as Colchester, were by now all established; and in the tribal capitals such as Verulam, Silchester, Winchester, Cirencester, Caerwent, Wroxeter or Leicester it would seem that a condition of stability had been attained. The grandiose schemes of development for these tribal capitals, which found expression in walls like those of Verulam, never reached fulfilment. To the end of the Roman period, such walls enclosed large tracts of ground where no houses stood. The recent evidence from Verulam is here decisive, and demonstrates beyond question what a plan like that of Silchester has long made probable: namely that the defences built for Romano-British towns in the late first and early second centuries were planned to accommodate a rising population, and that the expected rise did not come. By Hadrian's time, the development of the larger towns had approached saturation-point, both quantitatively and qualitatively: not only had they almost reached their point of maximum growth, but their defences, their public buildings, and their houses, large and small alike, had attained a level of quality decidedly superior to the average of the Flavian period (this is especially true of the defences and the smaller houses) and, broadly speaking, not surpassed at any later date.

In the large towns, and to some extent also in the smaller towns which grew up at road-junctions and elsewhere, a considerable degree of romanization was attained. Native aristocrats, foreign traders, and officials of the Imperial and local administration, aided by foreign craftsmen of various kinds, set the fashion, and even the poorer town-dwellers followed it. Latin, it is clear, was generally spoken, and Roman ways of life were freely adopted. Even the small workshops of the urban artisans produced goods in which a Roman style predominated.

From these centres, romanizing influences spread into the countryside which used the towns as markets; but this diffusion was slow and its effects at this period were slight. Of the 'Roman villas' which were to become so characteristic a feature of Britain, comparatively few seem to have existed in the first century, and these mostly in Kent, on the Hampshire coast, and in the Isle of Wight. Others no doubt grew up in the second century. But it is probably true to say that at the end of the Antonine period the rural parts of Britain were still predominantly Celtic in their life and habits, and that romanization here went no further, as a rule, than the introduction of Roman coins and other portable objects from the towns.

The economic basis of this life lay primarily in agriculture. Some time before the Roman conquest, Britain had been able to export appreciable quantities of wheat, livestock and hides; Caesar was struck by the agricultural wealth of Kent; and after the conquest agriculture must have been further stimulated by the demand for grain to feed the garrison, which was very large relatively to the total population of the province. The staple crop was common wheat; and neither in cropping nor in methods is there any evidence that the Roman conquest led to extensive innovations. The old-fashioned marling still went on; draining does not seem to have been introduced on any considerable scale; and the practice of reaping the grain unripe and drying it artificially was not discontinued.

A second source of wealth was the minerals in which Britain was notoriously rich. The most important of these were the argentiferous lead-ores of Somerset (Mendips), Shropshire, Derbyshire, Flintshire, Yorkshire and Northumberland. Mendip lead was already being worked by the Romans within six years of the Claudian invasion; and by the Flavian period, when work was going forward energetically in most of the above areas, the richness of British lead was officially recognized by a regulation limiting output. It is clear that from the first there was systematic prospecting and exploitation of British lead, partly for its own sake, and even more for the sake of its silver, which was a valuable State monopoly. The facts which emerge from a careful study of details amply confirm Tacitus' suggestion[1] that the conquest of Britain was undertaken partly from a desire to exploit her mineral wealth.

Gold was mined at one place at least, in south Wales, during the late first and early second centuries. The elaborate character of the workings and of the buildings connected with them shows that a considerable return was expected; perhaps not in vain. The copper of north Wales and Anglesey, too, appears to have been exploited before the end of the Antonine period. Coal was extensively worked in Scotland, Northumberland, Yorkshire, Lancashire, south Wales and the forest of Dean, and Somerset; in most of these districts as early as the Antonine period, if not earlier. Cornish tin, on the other hand, apart from one or two experiments, was not officially exploited until later.

Probably more valuable than any British mineral except argentiferous lead was iron. By Strabo's time the Romans knew that British iron was more important than Caesar had supposed; for Strabo[2] tells us that it was a regular article of export to the Continent. The reference is no doubt to the Wealden iron; and here, as in the case of lead, the Romans laid their hands on the workings at an early date. Wealden slag-heaps contain coins as early as Nero, with those of Vespasian in especially large numbers; and the vast size and frequency of these slag-heaps show that the industry was exploited on a large scale. The ores of the forest of Dean, also, were mined extensively from the first century onwards, and smaller iron-workings existed throughout the midlands and the north. It is tempting, in the light of archaeological evidence, to identify Tacitus' *pretium victoriae* with argentiferous lead, iron, and gold; and to conclude that the yield of at least the first two amply justified expectations.

---

[1] *Agric.* 12, 6.
[2] IV, 199. See vol. X, pp. 406 *sq.*, 792.

Manufactures, during the period here under review, attained a far less important development. The pre-Roman luxury-trades that had produced the beautiful weapons and ornaments of the La Tène period died out by degrees under the influence of Roman taste, surviving in an impoverished form partly on the frontiers of the civilized region, where Celtic art still maintained something of its old genius, and partly within the civilized region itself, as a tradition of taste and craftsmanship driven underground but never quite extinguished, and ready to revive when conditions should allow it. The humbler industries, in varying degrees, felt the influence of Roman models, but always tended to interpret them in a Celtic, rather than a Roman, spirit; thus by the Antonine period the ordinary pottery and metal-work produced in Britain shows a blend of Roman and Celtic influences[1].

These and other industries were pursued for the most part in small-scale establishments, partly in artisans' shops in the towns, some towns specializing in certain industries, like the metal-working of Wroxeter or the potteries of Castor (Northants.), and partly in villages of an entirely industrial character. Such industries, small in scale and lacking in organization, confined themselves for the most part to supplying local demand, and even the most prolific of them, such as the Kentish potteries, do not seem to have found regular markets outside the limits of the province.

Thus, in the late first and early second centuries, Britain presents the aspect of a country everywhere enjoying a vigorous industrial development, and gradually becoming able to supply its own needs in respect of most manufactured articles; but not yet possessing industries comparable, for instance, with the great Gaulish potteries or able to export its manufactures to an appreciable extent.

Commerce between Britain and the Continent, before the conquest, was already considerable: Britain, as Strabo[2] tells us (and archaeology confirms at least the first part of the statement), imported luxury-goods and exported minerals, slaves, dogs, and agricultural produce. After the conquest this state of things at first continued in a greatly intensified form. There was now a very large importation of Gaulish pottery, Campanian and Gaulish metal goods, works of art, wine, oil, and in short everything required by the vigorous romanizing movement in a country still unable to meet its own demand for the material of civilized life. Exports at this time certainly included large quantities of silver and lead, probably of iron and gold; but these, as State property,

[1] Volume of Plates v, 50, *a*, *b*.   [2] IV, 199 *sq.*

cannot be reckoned in the commercial balance-sheet of the province. For that, we must look to agricultural produce, slaves, hunting-dogs, oysters and pearls. By the end of the first century, the flood of luxury-imports had declined; British industries were beginning to supply the home market. But Gaulish pottery remained a most important article of trade until the end of the Antonine period, and the same is true of wine and oil.

There was also commercial activity across the frontiers of the Empire. Traders carried Samian ware, wine, ironmongery and raw metal up the east and west coasts of Scotland, and the same country absorbed considerable quantities of Roman coin. Trade went on, too, by land across the Hadrianic and Antonine Walls. Imports from Scotland consisted chiefly, it would seem, of cattle, hides and furs. The trade with Ireland was very much smaller; Roman objects found there are practically limited to coin, and there is no such evidence as there is for Scotland of regular traffic in the hands of Roman merchant adventurers.

The political and social framework of this economic life is, in the case of Britain, poorly documented, and for the most part our conception of it must depend on analogies from elsewhere. With the extinction of the few loyal native kingdoms which at first were allowed to survive, the whole country became a single province under a single *legatus Augusti pro praetore*. The seat of government appears at first to have been at Colchester; but there are indications suggesting that, possibly after the Boudiccan rebellion, it may have been transferred to the natural centre of the country at London. By Vespasian's reign, the legions had already settled down at York, Chester and Caerleon-on-Usk, and the auxiliaries in their *castella* studding the fringe of the uplands beyond; the details and changes of their distribution are outside the scope of this sketch (see above, pp. 150 *sqq.*). Within the lowland zone peaceful conditions were by now everywhere established. Local government was organized, as in northern Gaul, on a cantonal basis, and the development of romanized tribal capitals thus had its political side in addition to its function as a measure of romanization.

Behind a façade of Roman fashions, and Roman legal and terminological innovations, the general structure of society remained Celtic. In religion, for example, the early years of the occupation produced temples in the classical style at Colchester, Chichester and Bath; in many of the chief towns exotic cults were introduced; but the old Celtic gods always retained their hold on the mind of the people, and romanization in religion took the shape of coupling their traditional names with new ones adopted

from the Roman pantheon, and thus producing forms like Sulis
Minerva, Apollo Maponus, or Mars Cocidius. The Eastern religions, of which Mithraism was the most important, that enjoyed
such popularity at a later date, have left no certain traces in Britain
as early as the Antonine age. In education, both literacy and
Latin-speaking were probably confined, with trifling exceptions,
to the towns, and perhaps approached universality only in the
larger ones. With regard to such questions as legal status and
land-tenure, it is impossible to say how far Roman technical terms
indicate a genuine romanization, and how far they cover a substantially unchanged reality of Celtic law and custom.

Communications within the province were, on the whole, an
unusually simple matter. The areas of primary occupation, as
described above, were mostly either continuous plateaux and
ridges of high, dry ground, already traversed in many cases by
pre-Roman trackways, or gravel terraces lying beside navigable
rivers; consequently they were easy of access and could be traversed
with a minimum of expenditure on road-building. The chief task
for the Roman engineers was therefore to drive roads from one
such area to another, across the intervening belts of inhospitable
country. Hence it arises that in many cases the most conspicuous
and best-known Roman roads traverse areas in which Roman
remains are infrequent and where in fact the population was
scanty: both Watling Street and the Fosse, for example, run
for many miles over the sparsely-inhabited plain of the Midlands,
Stane Street similarly through the Weald, and so forth. Roads
of this kind were of value for strategical purposes and for long-
distance traffic, whether official or unofficial; for the purposes of
local traffic they were probably of less use than the Icknield Way,
the Harroway, and the many other ridgeways that outline the
higher ground of the lowland zone.

Even so, care was taken to choose lines for the main roads
which should minimize the necessary engineering works. Watling
Street, from London to Wroxeter, never travels far from the
watershed, and crosses only the most inconsiderable streams. The
Fosse, in its whole length, encounters only one river of even
moderate size, the Avon at Bath. It seems to have been a constant
principle of Roman engineering in Britain as in Gaul that, wherever possible, roads should be built along ridges; less, perhaps,
in order to avoid the forests of the valley than in order to avoid
the necessity of crossing rivers. The geographical structure of the
British lowlands, necessitating a radial system of main roads
focussed upon London and running crosswise to the main ridges

of the country, made it less easy to apply this principle; but a detailed study of the roads themselves, as they exist on the ground, proves that it was applied wherever possible. In virtue of this principle and the comparative scarcity of large rivers in Britain, bridges of considerable size were seldom required, and where they existed they seem never to have been built completely in stone; the usual practice was to build stone piers on pile-rafts, carrying a wooden superstructure. Many such continued in use down to the twelfth century, when the art of bridge-building was brought back into this country after an interval of some seven hundred years.

The Roman road-system in Britain, as we know it, must have been completed in its main lines at an early stage of the occupation. Of this, it is true, we have no documentary evidence, the earliest extant milestones dating from the reign of Hadrian; but the main roads themselves show clear traces of systematic planning with two objects in view: the provision of direct lines of communication between the various tribal capitals and between each of these and London; and the strategic needs of armies engaged in the work of conquest. Both these objects must have been envisaged within a few years from the landing of Claudius' forces. The only fact which might induce doubts as to the early date of the main system is the emphasis laid by that system on London as the point from which the chief roads radiate; for, as has already been observed, the original administrative centre of the British province was probably at Colchester, and was moved to London, if indeed it ever was moved thither, only after the Boudiccan rebellion. But the focal position of London in the road-system was imposed on the Roman engineers by the *force majeure* of geographical facts, and might well have been the cause, rather than the effect, of making London the capital of the province.

Sea-borne traffic, as the only means of communication between Britain and the rest of the Empire, was a matter of great importance. The ancient traffic connecting south-western Britain with Armorica and the coasts beyond it was dislocated by Caesar's destruction of the Venetian sea-power, and its revival was only partial; this indeed was inevitable, for emphasis on that traffic-route belongs especially to periods in British history when the highland zone is playing a constructive part in the life of the country, and the early Roman period was emphatically not one of these. Hence the effect of Rome on British navigation was to concentrate it in the eastern part of the Channel, on the two routes already defined by Strabo[1]: one at the Straits of Dover, where the

[1] IV, 199.

early military predominance of Richborough seems before long to have yielded to the rise of Dover and especially of London as commercial ports; the other between the Seine and the Hampshire ports, among which Bitterne was especially developed by the Romans and was already used for the shipment of Mendip lead by the time of Vespasian. Coastwise traffic must have existed in plenty; many considerable Roman towns are favourably placed for it at the heads of navigable estuaries; but there is little direct evidence for a detailed account of it.

Inland navigation, though less important than in Gaul, played a certain part in the general communications of the province, especially in the east, where the Fenland waterways carried a heavy barge-traffic handling the produce of the potteries in the neighbourhood of Castor (p. 517), and where Roman engineering enterprise constructed a canal leading from the Cambridge region through Peterborough to Lincoln, and thus giving access to the Trent, the Humber basin and York.

As in agriculture, so in navigation the Romans were content on the whole to accept and develop existing practice without radically reforming it. The pre-Roman dug-out canoe, sometimes as much as 40 feet long or more, still remained in use on the eastern waterways, and the coracle was still the ordinary light craft of the coast-dwellers, especially in the west. The one Roman ship actually discovered in Britain, a sea-going sailing-vessel some 60 feet in length, seems more akin to the ships of the Veneti, as Caesar describes them, than to the ordinary Mediterranean craft.

The architectural monuments of this age, if we except the great frontier-works to be described below, lack impressiveness when compared with the Augustan buildings of Gaul or Spain, or the relics of an imperial city like Trèves. Town-walls were mostly of flint and rubble, with bonding-courses of brick or flagstones; their gates, even the fourfold gates of Colchester or Verulam, compare unfavourably both in materials and in design with the best Gaulish examples, and in spite of a certain spaciousness and magnificence in conception are intended rather as useful than as ornamental. Triumphal arches, except for two whose foundations exist at Verulam, are altogether unknown. Except at Colchester, even the fora of the chief towns were laid out on a plan derived not from the forum of an Italian town but from the headquarters building of the legionary fortress, giving a far inferior architectural effect[1]. The only known theatre is at Verulam; elsewhere public spectacles were provided only in amphitheatres, and these, wher-

[1] The writer owes this observation to Professor D. Atkinson.

ever they have been identified at Romano-British towns, were made with earth banks and wooden seats and fittings, never in solid masonry.

The finest architectural relic of the 'civil district' (to use Haver-field's phrase) is the great public baths at Bath, with a vaulted hall measuring 111 by 68 feet and several smaller baths and other rooms, the whole covering, in its original shape, half an acre of ground[1]; there is epigraphic evidence suggesting that it or the adjacent temple, or both, for the two were somewhat similar in construction and decoration, may have been built with the help of imported workmen from northern Gaul. Elsewhere too there is evidence of public baths handsomely planned during the late first century, though it may be significant that the best of them, at Wroxeter, was never finished.

Another outstanding architectural work of the first century was the temple of Claudius at Colchester, whose substructures, still existing, show that it must have measured about 105 feet long by 80 feet wide, or more than double the area of the Maison Carrée at Nîmes. This temple was of course an official building, though no doubt erected out of money collected in Britain; but as a rule the public buildings of Romano-British towns were erected by the local authorities, mainly on their own initiative and at their own expense, though both encouragement and pecuniary assist-ance were forthcoming from official quarters.

Of the military fortresses and *castella* which Britain possesses in great numbers, though much attention has been devoted by archaeologists to their study, it is unnecessary to speak here, for they belong to standard types and possess few special character-istics of their own. In the case of frontier-works, however, Britain presents features of exceptional interest. The policy expressed in these works is discussed elsewhere (pp. 153, 312 *sqq.*); here we are concerned only with their architecture and engineering.

There are two fortified *limites* in Britain: Hadrian's, on the line of the Tyne and Solway, and that of Antoninus Pius, on the Forth-Clyde isthmus. The works on Hadrian's line are strangely complicated in design. There was a continuous stone rampart[2], about 20 feet high including its embattled parapet, running for 80 Roman or 73 English miles from Wallsend to Bowness-on-Solway, where the estuary ceases to be fordable. In front was a 30-foot V-shaped ditch. The fighting garrison, consisting of auxiliary cohorts and *alae*, was housed in 17 *castella*, most of them built as part and parcel of the wall, either lying astride of it or

---

[1] Volume of Plates v, 50, c.   [2] *Ib.* 34.

attached to its southern face, a few lying a little way to the south. But this garrison was not meant to fight on the platform of the Wall; its task was to police the neighbouring countryside and engage hostile forces in the open; the Wall itself was meant as an obstacle to smugglers and raiders, and to give outlook and protection to the sentries whose duty was to patrol its top. These were quartered in the so-called milecastles, fortlets attached to its southern face a Roman mile apart, and the turrets or signal-towers, two of which stood between each milecastle and the next. Except at the forts, which were very irregularly spaced and averaged about 5 miles apart, access to the rampart-walk was provided only by a stairway at each milecastle and a ladder at each turret. Along the Cumberland coast, easily accessible to raiders across the narrow sea, the line of *castella* and signal-towers was continued for another 30 miles. At certain points provision was made for peaceful traffic passing the frontier under surveillance; and a few outlying *castella* were pushed forward to patrol what we now call the Border.

But this unity of design was only reached through a course of experiments and alterations whose history has been disentangled within the last ten years. The original plan, which was probably that of Hadrian himself, was for a Wall running from Newcastle to Bowness, a distance of 76 Roman or 70 English miles. For three-fifths of its length, from Hadrian's bridge (Pons Aelius) at Newcastle to the Irthing, it was to be built of stone with a rubble and mortar core, and was to be 10 Roman feet thick, set back for safety some 20 feet from the lip of its ditch. The remainder, from the Irthing to the Solway, was to be built of turf, 20 feet thick, and set back no more than 6 feet from the ditch. The difference of construction was due to natural causes. In Northumberland good carboniferous grit for building, and limestone for burning, were everywhere available close at hand; in Cumberland stone and lime were difficult to come by, but turf and timber were to be had in plenty.

This original design was never completed. The turf Wall had been finished, but of the stone Wall only the foundations had been laid, and part of the superstructure west of Newcastle built to its full height, when the decision was made to adopt a new plan: a stone Wall only 8 Roman feet thick running from sea to sea and extended eastward to Wallsend. The completed Wall was therefore something of a patchwork. Part of it, west of Newcastle, was allowed to stand as it had been built; thence westward to the Irthing it was built to the narrow gauge on broad-gauge foundations; parts of it were narrow-gauge work throughout; and west of the Irthing, where an intermediate gauge was adopted, the new masonry incorporated the stone turrets of the turf Wall.

The most serious complication is still to be mentioned. Close behind the Wall, sometimes almost in contact with it and sometimes a quarter of a mile or more away, lies a continuous earthwork traditionally, though incorrectly, described by British antiquaries as the Vallum. This was a ditch running from near Newcastle to Bowness, about 30 feet wide and 7 feet deep, steep-sided but (unlike a military ditch) flat-bottomed. The upcast from it was disposed in two neatly-built mounds set well back from its two sides, giving a symmetrical cross-section. Its choice of ground reinforces the inference from its tactically neutral design, that it had no military purpose and was never meant to be defended. When it approaches a fort, it aims as if to run through it, but is then abruptly diverted to southward so that the fort stands in a small recess or re-entrant, and opposite the fort it is crossed by a solid causeway provided with a gate.

Until lately, it was usual to suppose that the Vallum had formed an independent frontier, earlier than the Wall; for although it turns to avoid the Wall forts, this could be explained by suggesting either that these forts belonged to the supposed Vallum frontier and thus existed before the Wall (a view for which there was a certain amount of evidence) or that earlier forts, belonging to the Vallum frontier, had stood on the same sites. But excavation in 1935 showed that it turns in the same way to avoid at least one milecastle. It is therefore necessary to consider the problem afresh in the light of this evidence for their simultaneity. Hadrian's original plan seems to have entailed the construction of two parallel barriers: the Wall, with its military garrison, and the ostentatiously un-military Vallum close behind it. To the present writer, it appears possible that the distinction between the two works may reflect the distinction between the military administration under the *legatus Augusti pro praetore* and the financial administration under the procurators; that, in order to avoid a clash between these two services, every gate through the Wall was placed in the undivided charge of the military, and that the Vallum was a customs-barrier, whose gateways were supervised by customs-officers under procuratorial authority. Be that as it may (and this is not the place to argue it), the double system was found both inconvenient and unnecessary; soon after its original creation the Vallum was filled up in the neighbourhood of the forts; and in the Antonine frontier nothing of the kind was ever made.

Hadrian's Wall must have been completed by about A.D. 127; within 15 years from that date the decision had been made to construct a second line, in many ways similar to it, between Forth and Clyde. This, the Antonine Wall, was much shorter, only 33 miles long; it was built in a much cheaper style, of turf for the greater part of its length, its eastern part of clay; its thickness was only 14 feet, giving a conjectural height of 10 feet with a six-foot rampart-walk; and it was pierced by only a single road, serving (one supposes) the double purpose of military access to outlying forts and of admitting peaceful traffic. There was nothing corresponding to Hadrian's elaborate system of milecastles and turrets, though in certain places expansions of the structure have been recognized which would serve as bases for beacon-fires; and the forts, simpler in construction than Hadrian's—they all had mere wooden hutments for barracks, and many of them only turf ramparts—were both smaller on average and more closely spaced, so that details from their garrisons could undertake the work of patrolling the rampart-walk. As with Hadrian's Wall, a ditch defended its front and a continuous road lay immediately in its rear.

Planned and executed *d'un jet*, the Antonine Wall lacks the experimental character, the afterthoughts and alterations, of Hadrian's; and one way in which the later engineers profited by the experience of the earlier was in adopting an entirely new method of organizing their labour. Hadrian's Wall was built in short sections by individual legionary centuries, the method already established for constructing the ramparts of camps, *castella* and fortresses; but such a method, appropriate in these cases, was entirely unsuited to the construction of a frontier-work scores of miles in length, where each century, on completing one short length, would have to be moved to another, farther on; a process repeated many times over, and affording almost endless opportunity for disorganization and confusion. The Antonine builders reconsidered the whole question, and created six powerful working-parties, two from each legion, to each of which they assigned in the first instance one of six sectors together making up the first two-thirds of the Wall; the remaining or westernmost third, divided into three lengths, would then be finished off by the same six parties, united by legions into three. Sir George Macdonald, to whom we owe the greater part of what has been learnt about the Antonine Wall during the present century, has reconstructed this scheme from epigraphic evidence[1], and has shown how its time-schedule broke down over digging the ditch through the unexpected basalt of Croy Hill, so that the final stage had perforce to be reconsidered, and emergency measures adopted in order to complete the work as nearly as possible according to plan.

[1] *The Roman Wall in Scotland*, ed. 2, pp. 393 *sqq.*

II. ROMAN GERMANY AND RAETIA

Upper and Lower Germany and Raetia, although closely connected in many ways with the adjacent provinces which form their hinterland, are situated in the frontier zone, and so had a special part to play. Here the military strength of Rome was concentrated during the campaigns of Drusus and Tiberius: here the dispute dating from the time of Caesar and Ariovistus was fought out to decide whether the Upper Rhine and Danube were to be German or Gallo-Roman rivers. German tribes had occupied the west bank of the Lower Rhine long before Caesar's day[1]. Among the *Germani cisrhenani* he found the Condrusi, Eburones, Caerosi, Paemani and Segni; Pliny mentions in addition the Tungri, Sunuci and Baetasii. The Belgae and Treveri also claimed to be of German descent; the ancient authorities, however, speak with less certainty concerning their provenance. To the west of the Upper Rhine the German Vangiones, Nemetes, and Triboci still remained in spite of Ariovistus' defeat. When Tiberius pushed forward to the Upper Danube he found German settlers in that region also, holding the district which had been vacated by the Celtic Helvetii and Rauraci[2]. The occupation of this territory by the Elbe-Germans dated, however, only from the Sueban migration under Ariovistus, and hence they had not had so long a cultural contact with the neighbouring Celts, and had not struck such deep roots in the land, as their fellows in the Lower Rhine valley. Farther to the east the Romans entered into friendly relations with the southern Hermunduri, as a result of the advance through Raetia and Vindelicia under Augustus and Tiberius. Raetia was a country of Alpine foothills. Its inhabitants were Celts by birth or adoption, and, like the Gauls, though stubbornly resisting at first, they finally submitted to Roman rule and provided troops in large numbers for defending the frontier.

The defeat of Varus settled the question whether all Germany up to the Elbe was to be romanized (vol. x, p. 379 *sq.*). The provinces of Germania inferior and superior were, in fact, the outcome of this disaster, though it was not until Domitian's reign that they attained their final form. The original plan, comprising a larger province of Germany reaching to the line of the Elbe, and so securing a strategic frontier for the provinces north of the Alps, was realized in practice for a bare twenty years (12 B.C.–A.D. 9). After Augustus' organization of the four Gallic provinces, the region to the west of the Rhine belonged, strictly speaking,

---

[1] Cf. vol. VII, p. 66 *sq.*   [2] Strabo IV, 207.

to Gallia Belgica. Varus' defeat, however, resulted in the west bank being chosen as the site for the most important permanent camps, and as it was still unusual at this time for the Romans to delegate civil and military authority to separate officers, the generals commanding the armies of the Lower and Upper Rhine also administered a narrow strip of territory in eastern Belgica.

The Lower Rhine command had under its control such German cantons as those of the Batavi and Canninefates (in the Rhine delta), and of the Tungri, Cugerni, and Ubii, who lived near Tongern, Xanten, and Cologne. The cantons of the Vangiones and Nemetes, near Worms and Speyer, and the Triboci (in Alsace), and the Celtic cantons of the Rauraci (near Basle), of the Helvetii, and, farther west, of the Lingones and the Sequani (near Langres and Besançon) were subordinated to the Upper Rhine command. Cities such as Metz and Trèves, on the other hand, though in fact of greater importance for the organization of the Rhine armies, belonged to the administrative area of Gallia Belgica (cf. above, p. 509). Trèves, however, in view of its key position will be discussed in this chapter. To place the two Germanies and Belgica under separate administrations might seem an artificial political device. But it had its roots in military needs. The result was the influx of numerous new and more or less strange elements which profoundly modified the population and civilization of the frontier zone.

The inhabitants of Raetia were Celts or celticized when they first came into contact with the Romans. Many of the Rhineland peoples, on the other hand, were differentiated from the neighbouring Celts both by nation and culture even in Republican times. The native population of the Rhineland was predominantly German in origin, or, at least, strongly germanized. On the Lower Rhine these Germans had held the country from remote antiquity, and in consequence had been brought into close contact with Celtic civilization. While the Celtic tribes in this region copied German manners and customs in many ways, the material products of Celtic civilization were often the models for German imitation. It is impossible here to discuss at length the vexed question—what causes underlay the decline in German handicrafts during pre-Christian times from its zenith in the Bronze Age. It may have been due to a deterioration in economic conditions, to changes in the structure of society, or to a deliberate sacrifice of luxuries during an age of warfare and expansion, for which Spartan history offers a familiar parallel. Something of the kind is suggested by a passage in Caesar which informs us that in the first century B.C. the import of luxuries was banned by law in the great tribe of the

Suebi[1]. The handicrafts of the Celts, from the time of their migrations onwards, stimulated by the artistic achievement of the Mediterranean peoples and of the Scythians, themselves under Iranian influence, had reached a high degree of excellence, especially in the use of new technical methods. This specialized skill ensured the superiority of their products over those of the Germans (which were mostly of domestic manufacture), and facilitated the absorption of Celtic articles by the neighbouring Germans. Thus, if single objects of 'material culture' are taken as a criterion, the tribes long settled in the Rhine valley which the Romans testify to have been German are not always separable from their Celtic neighbours. Even the Vangiones, who had migrated to the vicinity of Mainz and Worms under Ariovistus, were using a pottery about the beginning of our era which we should regard as Celtic, were it not for Roman evidence[2]. Here religion and burial customs differentiated Germans and Celts. The traditional ware[3] maintained itself longer among the German tribe of the Suebi Nicretes near Mannheim, Heidelberg, and Ladenburg (Lopodunum).

The occupation of the Rhineland by the Romans brought to the river and its immediate neighbourhood a force amounting at times to more than eight legions, or approximately one-third of the Roman army. The figure of 100,000 men, as the estimated strength of these legions together with the attached *auxilia*, errs, if at all, in being too low. The troops brought many camp-followers with them, and to the superficial observer it might seem at this time that the region had been wholly romanized, or at least had become more Roman than its Gallic hinterland. The number of Roman troops in Raetia, on the other hand, was small, and the romanizing influence of the army was correspondingly less.

The question whether the Romans in Imperial times followed a deliberate policy of settlement, romanization, and economic penetration[4], is most easily answered for the frontier zone we are considering. Here it was necessary to hold a dangerous opponent in check, and in consequence the political and military demands of the situation carried more weight than economic considerations. But an examination of these military needs shows clearly that the encouragement of settlers and economic activity was thought to be the best means of securing the defences of the country. In fact the Romans had a flair for combining economic and military advantages, and were even ready to make minor strategic sacrifices to this end.

---

[1] *B. G.* IV, 2.   [2] See Volume of Plates V, 52, *a*.
[3] *Ib.* 52, *b*.   [4] Cf. vol X, p. 385.

Thus the new line taken by the *limes* in Upper Germany, a change begun under Vespasian and completed by Domitian, was primarily intended to shorten the communications between the Rhine and Danube armies, a link whose importance had recently increased. But strategical considerations do not suffice to explain the incorporation within the Empire of the fertile plain round Neuwied, and of the Wetterau, which is economically valuable but of little use for purposes of defence. The same criticism applies to the further advance of the *limes* in Upper Germany, and for that matter in Raetia, under Antoninus Pius (*c.* A.D. 155). It resulted in the occupation of a very fertile region, the Raetian part of which was also rich in iron, and which extended to the edge of the continuous Frankish pine forests. The systematic excavations carried out in the Wetterau reveal the existence of many farmhouses regularly distributed throughout the area and reaching to the immediate vicinity of the frontier. This justifies us in concluding that the Romans planned to strengthen the frontier defences by such settlements. It was an established maxim of Roman policy that a conquered province was secured only by the foundation of citizen colonies and by the settling of veterans, who in case of need could again be called to the colours. After long years of service the auxiliaries also obtained the coveted rights of Roman citizenship for themselves and their families. By means of such settlers the State built a solid wall of frontiersmen, who through their ownership of the land had a direct interest in preventing invasion. The sons of the auxiliaries could further enlist in the legions, whose personnel consisted of picked men and was limited at first to Roman citizens. It was a favourite stroke of Roman statecraft, when a people had revolted, to transplant the younger generation of warriors to some other region of the Empire, and to employ them there in the defence of the frontier. Thus after the British rebellion of 142 the *numeri Brittonum* came to the Odenwald and built *castella* and *burgi* in the architectural style of their native land (A.D. 145–6). The descendants of such frontier guards were later organized into formations of *exploratores*, whose existence on the Antonine *limes* is frequently attested.

Augustus had strictly limited the number of new citizen colonies once the problem of providing for the veterans had been solved. He was clearly unwilling to extend the privilege of Roman citizenship to insufficiently romanized provincials. The earliest colony in the Rhineland was Augusta Rauracorum (Augst near Basle). Claudius' reign saw the foundation of a colony at Cologne; Trèves also was probably colonized in his time. Trajan planted

new colonies at Ulpia Noviomagus (Nymwegen) and Ulpia
Traiana (Xanten) near old legionary camps. Augsburg's history
as a colony seems to have begun later still, under Hadrian.
Doubtless the emperors thought it essential to strengthen these
strategically vital points by the established method, namely the
foundation of colonies. In the Rhineland the Romans had found
few larger settlements, such as those, ranking almost as cities,
which they designated 'oppida' in neighbouring Gaul and elsewhere. Here the majority of the cities derived not from such
oppida, but from the garrison towns housing the *canabae* of
a legion, an *ala*, or a cohort. The larger military centres were
placed at sites chosen with a skilful eye for position on the lines
of communication. Such places attract settlers at all times, and
careful excavations in Roman cities and their immediate vicinity
reveal an increasing amount of evidence pointing to the existence
of earlier settlements. It must not, however, be assumed that such
traces always point to the existence of pre-Roman towns as large
as Oppidum Batavorum near Nymwegen. The transplantation
of whole tribes, such as the friendly Ubii, and of part of the
Sugambri, who were bitter opponents of Rome, to the west bank
of the Rhine, created favourable conditions for the foundation of
new cities. The necessary population was found by making fresh
settlements of veterans, and also, it would seem, through the
old method of synoecism; immigrants swelled the numbers. The
concentration of large bodies of soldiers on the frontier acted
as a magnet to the population of the adjacent provinces. In
particular, merchants, artisans and farmers were attracted from
other parts of the Empire into the region under military administration by reason of the economic possibilities of the frontier
zone and of the newly acquired territory.

In the rich province of Gaul, which had long suffered from
internecine quarrels, the *pax Augusta* brought an economic prosperity which was enhanced by the geographical position of Gaul
as the natural source of supply for the Rhine army[1]. This economic
development led to a marked rise in the numbers of the population.
Active and enterprising natives of the Gallic provinces found an
inviting field for their efforts in the two Germanies and Raetia.
Moreover many of the legionaries and auxiliary troops were
drawn—in the early stages, at any rate—from the provinces of
Gallia Cisalpina and Narbonensis, and most of these were naturally
of Celtic birth or civilization. Apart from the chief officers and
administrative officials, who, at first, were mostly drawn from

[1] See above, p. 509.

Italy itself, the predominantly Celtic or Celtic-Mediterranean layer of peasant settlers, artisans, soldiers, and veterans, overlaid on the old native population, had often absorbed only the rudiments of Roman culture. It was this class which set the standards in the permanent camps and in the great cities and their immediate environs, whereas in the Gallic provinces, which were almost wholly denuded of troops, it was principally civilian circles which disseminated the combined Hellenistic and Roman cultural influence. The nearer we approach to the Gallic provinces from the military frontier, the more marked this difference becomes, even as reflected in the material remains of Roman times.

The most striking monuments of Roman rule after the numerous military camps were the capitals of cantons, settlements approaching city rank and built on Hellenistic and Roman models, and further the *municipia* and *coloniae* enjoying Roman citizenship. The development of modern historical studies, and also the course necessarily followed by archaeological research in this region, explain why we are as yet best informed about the architecture and history of the military buildings, but know less about the cities and larger villas, and least about the small rural settlements. The investigation of Roman cities is generally handicapped because important medieval and modern cities have grown up on the ancient sites, as at Cologne, Trèves, Mainz, Strasbourg, Augsburg, and Regensburg. Many disconnected details have, however, been carefully observed, which, supported by the knowledge gained from the military buildings and by comparison with better preserved settlements, enable us now to reconstruct a trustworthy and vivid picture of the cities and city-life. Extensive excavations in such cities as Heddernheim (near Frankfort am Main), and Kempten in Bavaria, where there was not a continuing occupation of the Roman site, allow us to draw interesting conclusions about the planning of a provincial city. Heddernheim-Nida, a canton capital, Kempten, of the same status, which has more than Nida the appearance of a *municipium*, and Trèves, which rose to be a colony, may be briefly discussed here as types of a numerous class.

Heddernheim-Nida was the capital of the canton Civitas Taunensium. In Germany and Raetia, as in Gaul, the Romans generally left the old canton constitution untouched. They merely adapted it to their own conditions by giving each canton a capital city of the Roman type. The chief Roman features of such capitals were the public buildings and the organization of the city magistrates. Judged by our standards Nida was a city, though its inhabitants did not enjoy Roman citizenship. It developed from the so-called *canabae* of a fort along the roads radiating from an older fortress. The houses are generally of a type normally found in garrison towns, a standard architectural design which we know from the neighbouring fort of Saalburg. Nida's extensive Thermae, on the other hand, which exceed in size the public baths of modern cities many times as large, are very Roman; and there is a splendid Forum and a theatre. The walls, which are in part responsible for the impression that Nida ranks as a city, were built, here as elsewhere, in consequence of the chaos and disorders which devastated the frontier zone during and after the Marcomannic wars (pp. 349 *sqq.*). The area of Nida, as of many ancient towns, was not entirely covered with houses. Numerous factory buildings, including the important potteries, were also protected by the town walls, while the level space between them might serve to accommodate refugees, and could be used for agricultural purposes. The general impression gained is that in time of peace this town, the centre from which a net-work of roads radiated, was the focus of commercial life for a prosperous rural population. On market-days the inhabitants of the surrounding country would buy their supplies here, and among the other pleasures which the town had to offer would be a visit to the Thermae, for these in antiquity served not only as baths but also as a social rendezvous.

Kempten-Cambodunum was a similar market-town, founded under Tiberius in the land of the Celtic Vindelici. It was the capital of the Estiones and looks more like an Italian *municipium*; in consequence, its public buildings were more imposing than those of Nida. As in many cities of the south, the private houses were divided by cross streets at regular intervals into blocks—the so-called 'insulae.' In Kempten, as in Heddernheim, the public buildings are unduly large for the limited needs of those actually resident in the town; they presumably served for the other members of the canton. The number of the shops shows how much the town depended on its position as a marketing centre. The industrial quarter with numerous potteries and other factories was situated in the south of the town. There was a large inn for the convenience of travellers, who must have often passed through the town. Kempten lost its importance as a key-point in the system of communications through Vespasian's advance, which opened a shorter route between the Rhine and the Danube. This may well explain why in many parts the city was never completed as planned, and why no striking religious buildings have as yet been brought to light. Kempten's subsequent history was that of a modest provincial town in Raetia, a country which had lagged behind the Rhineland in general progress. The town fell into decay in late Roman times when its inhabitants were forced to seek a more easily defensible place of refuge.

The plan of cities continuously inhabited from Roman times, such as Augsburg and Trèves, has had to be pieced together from separate scraps of evidence which have come to light when new buildings were being erected or drains laid down. Trèves shows the regular spacing of streets which is specially characteristic of *coloniae*. This systematic planning, which was of paramount importance for its development, seems to date from the reign of Claudius, who was more disposed than Augustus to confer citizenship and to found *coloniae* in the provinces. Within the walls of this *colonia*, which followed Rome's example in possessing a Capitol crowned with the temples of the Capitoline gods, it was as difficult as at Rome itself for the gods of the native population and for foreign divinities to find a place, and a special temple enclosure outside the walls was set apart for the worship of these non-Roman gods.

Inscriptions, sculptures, and small archaeological finds combine to give a vivid picture of the life in these towns. Similar evidence from the manor houses near the city gates, or more remotely situated, attests a close connection between the city and the wealthy landed proprietors of the upper class. This is understandable in a society which still regarded the purchase of land as the most gentlemanly and secure form of investment. The landed gentry, like the prosperous citizens, decorated their residences with wall paintings of a quality which, although hardly up to the standard of the Italian models, strove in style at least to approach what was the fashion in Italy. The plan of villas, however, was often modified by the local forms of architectural design, doubtless as a result of climatic considerations.

The tombstones speak chiefly of the worldly wishes and affairs of the dead. Those who commissioned the work were, it seems, responsible for the realism of the scenes depicted, and the artists who executed it for the naturalism of the style. Whether this naturalism was limited to a local school, and is to be explained as the outcome of the same influences of environment as account for the peculiarities of Dutch art in more recent times, cannot be determined until we are able to make a wider survey of art in the Roman Empire as a whole. Some of the tombstones present scenes from everyday life in such a way as definitely to suggest that those who gave the artist his orders took a naïve pleasure in the representation of their wealth and of the pleasures it brought. Thus Menimanii, the widow of the wealthy *navicularius* Blussus from Mainz[1] (who like his wife still bears a Celtic name and wears Celtic costume), thought it desirable that her husband's riches should be symbolized on his tombstone by his purse: on her own memorial her pampered lap-dog and her jewelry must be shown. She wears a large medallion, a necklace, no less than four brooches, and numerous rings. The more aristocratic female figure on a tombstone from Nickenich[2] displays her jewelry with equal ostentation. The names on the accompanying inscription agree with the evidence of the dress in showing that this memorial was erected in Claudian times to a romanized Celtic family. As often happens nowadays in regions where national costumes are beginning to disappear, the husband is completely converted to the gala dress of the upper class—*tunica, toga,* and *calcei*. The wife still wears a Gallic robe and the Gallic necklace, though her numerous rings are borrowed from the fashions of Rome. The small son has little of the child in his face, and is the complete Roman, scroll in hand, and dressed in *tunica* and *toga*.

On tombstones from Neumagen women are shown at their toilet and waited upon by numerous maids. The sumptuous banquet, the kitchen, and the well-stocked wine-cellar often appear on tombstones from the Moselle valley. At the same time there does exist a serious desire for higher standards of culture. A scene of school life from Neumagen shows that parents were at pains to secure a tutor for their children, and to give to the next generation the classical education which they themselves may have lacked. The head of the household has his employees depicted at work, and his tenants or serfs paying their rent; he himself appears before us on a business journey, and after such exertions turns to sport, to hunting or to racing—all of this is seen on the tombstones[3]. It is no mere chance that on the most important monument we possess, the Igel pillar, the ascent of Hercules into heaven[4] is the theme chosen from among the symbolic mythological scenes which not uncommonly occur alongside the realistic ones we have been describing. Hercules was an object of special veneration in the Gallic and German provinces, and was, indeed, revered throughout the Empire as the patron of industry and enterprises. Like him, his worshippers were not averse from the pleasures which this life had to offer, and might hope through labour and effort to win the reward of a life hereafter.

[1] See Volume of Plates v, 54, *a, b*.   [2] *Ib.* 54, *c*.
[3] *Ib.* 54, *d*.   [4] *Ib.* 56, *a*.

These monuments and the other archaeological remains attest the existence of a highly developed capitalist system. The profits from a commercial enterprise, from trade in wine or textiles, and from other forms of industrial activity, were sunk in land, a safe investment and generally profitable in view of the large market for agricultural produce. In ancient commerce the cost of large-scale transport was a far more crucial factor than it is to-day (vol. x, p. 422). The clearest proof of this is the fact that the potteries which manufactured the *terra sigillata* ware (*vasa Samia*) which was extremely popular with the army, moved nearer and nearer to the frontier, where their chief customers were to be found. They won their largest markets when they succeeded, as at Rhein-zabern and Trèves, in using water transport as far as possible and then linked up with the network of roads which was especially well organized in the military zone. Carefully excavated farm-houses, like that in Müngersdorf near Cologne, show that the landed proprietors adapted themselves with great versatility to the changed economic conditions. At first, large-scale ranching on the Italian model, which demanded relatively few employees, was practised. The addition of the necessary buildings reflects the change to agriculture when corn-growing promised a higher profit. The new capitalist economic system, together with the foundation of a colony at Cologne, must at this time have driven many native peasant proprietors from their fields. During this period, however, it seems that in view of the steady increase in economic prosperity most of the peasantry succeeded in keeping their independence and winning a livelihood or acquiring new land in a less commercialized district. At a later date this was one of the regions in which the peasants and tenants, formerly free, became more and more dependent on the landowner.

It is already clear that in Roman times there was a thick population even in districts which to-day in consequence of the developments in world-trade can no longer be worked at a profit either as pasture or as arable land. Traces of settlements dating from Roman times are found in barren highlands and thick forests. Their purpose and chronology are frequently still too uncertain for us to draw any definite conclusions concerning them. Often they seem to have been small cattlesheds or barns; or they may have been situated among the sources of the raw materials for the famous cloths made at Trèves and elsewhere in the Gallic provinces. It is in such remote districts that the remains of the native civilization may be found. Their influence on the culture of the Roman provinces is so far most clearly reflected in the pottery in use during the first half of the first century. Moreover, the typical patterns of La Tène art had practically vanished under the influence of the army, which was at first strongly romanized, but these art forms began slowly to emerge again from the middle of the second century[1].

Meanwhile a part of the native population had been so romanized that in speech, writing, and pictorial representation it used Roman forms of expression. For precisely this reason we can evaluate the native element and realize how superficial most of its romanization was. In this question of the native population in the Roman provinces, we meet the difficulty that it was primarily the legionaries, the merchants, and the larger landed proprietors, who were rich enough to speak to posterity through inscriptions and sculpture. Men of this social standing, however, belonged mostly to the Gallo-Roman immigrant class. Even the names which tradition has preserved are deceptive. A number of the most famous German leaders against the Celts and Romans have names which were common to the Germans and the Celts, or even names which are to be regarded as Celtic or Roman, such as Ariovistus, Arminius, and Claudius Civilis. The Celtic name for the capital of the Suebi in the Neckar valley, Lopodunum, is an example of how Celtic names survived even in German districts, or were actually conferred for the first time by Celtic immigrants more familiar with city-life than the Germans. The racial affinities of the Treveri, who in Caesar's time played an important part as an independent people surrounded by Celts, Belgae, and Germans, is a question on which our ancient authorities disagree. An accurate analysis of all the personal names preserved to us from Roman times in the Trèves region gives the interesting result[2] that about 63·5 per cent. are of Italo-Roman provenance, though often non-Roman in construction or form, 16·5 per cent. are Celtic, and 20 per cent. non-Celtic. The last percentage must be regarded as remarkably high when we consider that the Roman and Celtic figures may be overestimated. It attests a lively survival of the native element as is known to have been the case in the neighbouring provinces (p. 508). The names show little connection with the west and with the Cologne area. They link up rather with the Mediomatrici, the Upper Rhine valley, and the northern Alpine foothills, regions from which is also derived the so-called 'Urnfield' culture of the Late Bronze Age, which was brought by the first people to settle in large numbers in the Trèves

[1] See Volume of Plates v, 52, c.
[2] L. Weisgerber in *Rhein. Mus.* LXXXIV, 1935, p. 289.

district (vol. VII, pp. 55 *sqq.*). This people cannot as yet, however, be assigned with certainty to any of the greater nations of later times[1].

It is as yet difficult to estimate the degree of romanization to be found in the region as a whole. It went deep in the cities and larger communities. Here the *graffiti* and the household utensils of the humbler citizens are more valuable as evidence than the inscriptions and the splendid funeral monuments of the upper class. The Latin language was widely known and used from the middle of the first century onwards, as is shown from its appearance on the products of small potters. Up to the reign of Claudius there is sometimes a suggestion of such knowledge in the signs resembling characters on the so-called 'Belgic ware.' The vases and goblets ornamented in relief presuppose in their users an elementary knowledge of Graeco-Roman mythology and of the Hellenistic drinking customs taken over by Rome. To judge from the finds, enthusiasm for the amphitheatre and the circus was as universal here as at Rome. In the army spoken and written Latin was definitely the rule in view of the long period of service during which it was the language of command and of written communication; and military promotion was conditional on a mastery of both. This does not, however, imply that the soldier in the company of his fellow-countrymen spoke anything but his native tongue. This bilingualism is not reflected in the use of Latin characters for transcribing the native tongues, but this process obviously takes a long while and in the Rhineland was still made difficult by the number of spoken languages (Latin, German, Celtic, and their dialects). A defective knowledge of spoken and written Latin is often betrayed by the inscriptions, and the blame cannot always be put on the stonemasons. The serviceable local costume maintained itself stubbornly, especially the cloak with hood (*cucullus*), which indeed was later adopted throughout the Empire.

Clearest of all is the survival of the native element in religion[2]. In other spheres the native contribution is not usually recognizable until it begins to adopt Hellenistic-Roman forms. In the separate phases of this development, commonly called 'Interpretatio Romana,' it is hard to say whether the Roman or the local element is more active. An 'Interpretatio Graeca' must, in the present writer's opinion, have preceded, or accompanied the 'Interpretatio Romana' in the Celtic region. It is also clear that common Indo-Germanic religious conceptions, and the beliefs of Graeco-

---

[1] See W. Dehn in *Germania*, XIX, 1935, p. 295.
[2] See above, p. 508.

Roman popular religion played a part which cannot yet be properly estimated. Thus Celtic, like primitive Greek religion, had not completed the differentiation between the highest god of heaven and the ruler of the underworld. One of the earliest stone idols from this area, the interesting image of the four divinities from Alzey[1], which dates from early Flavian times, shows how religious thought, by utilizing a variety of attributes, was struggling to express an individualized conception of each divinity. Native influence is clearly at work in the naming and representation of the gods. The distribution of divine names and types is to be explained not only through centres of artistic production, but by the geographical limits of the cantons. Side by side with the highest god, whose symbolical representation on the Juppiter pillars in partly non-Roman forms occurs just in that zone where there is a mixture of Celtic and German elements, we meet the *Matronae*, in native costume and often with native titles, and these deities are found much more frequently in the predominantly German Lower Rhine valley than in Celtic territory. The earliest datable monuments of this kind are to be placed in the Flavian era. In accordance with Roman reverence for the *numina loci*, and Roman religious policy in the provinces, high officials of the army and government (as at Bonn) were among the worshippers of the *Matronae*. The increasing worship of the Imperial ladies, and the growing religious needs of the times may have fostered this development. In these provinces as elsewhere this greater interest in religious matters led to the adoption of rites from the East. In the Rhine army, especially from the middle of the second century onwards, the worship of such deities as the Persian Mithras and the mother goddesses of Asia Minor, and later of the Juppiter from Doliche in Syria, was introduced by drafts of troops from the eastern provinces, and found most followers among the soldiery. Behind the frontier zone relatively few memorials to Oriental divinities have been found. Here, just at the time (*c.* A.D. 150) when a diminution in Roman influence first becomes perceptible, the Roman 'interpretationes' of native deities begin to appear more often. Many of these, especially on the Lower Rhine, can already be classed with certainty as German. In Britain, too, German auxiliaries clung stubbornly to their native cult.

The contribution of the German and Raetian provinces to the cultural development of the Empire was slight during this period. Their influence was felt rather in the economic and the military

[1] See Volume of Plates v, 56, *b*.

spheres. As an industrial centre the Rhine valley could show a development comparable to that of its Gallic hinterland. The superb waterway of the Rhine, and the quality of the local products made possible the export of *terra sigillata*, for example, from Rheinzabern to such distant markets as Britain and the Lower Danube. The glass of Cologne drove even Alexandrian and Italian rivals from the field. The export of bronze and metal ware to free Germany, as recent investigations have shown, was more extensive than had been supposed (p. 72)[1]. This must have been balanced by a large volume of German imports, a fact which might have been deduced already from the careful control of commerce on the *limes*, and from the existence of a special customs organization on the Rhine.

For the Roman Empire the most important contribution of these provinces was the provision of numerous auxiliary troops. These at first helped the Romans to fight their battles in Germany itself, and they were often stationed at crucial points. It was not until the Batavian revolt, when for the first time the Germans of the Lower Rhine showed signs of co-operating with the tribes of independent Germany, that the Romans thought it wiser to use larger bodies of German subjects only against foreign nations.

The subsequent rise of Germans to high positions of command in the Roman army, and the reconquest by German tribes of the region west of the Rhine and south of the Danube, lies beyond the scope of this chapter. The Marcomannic wars foreshadowed the new danger to the Empire, and left it severely shaken. The peril became more threatening when at the beginning of the third century the Alemannic league emerged as a new and vigorous power in the region flanked by the Main, Neckar, and Danube. The coalition of the German tribes into larger tribal leagues, such as those of the Alemanni and the Franks, and the intimate knowledge of Roman ways, which they had won through long contact in peace and war on the common frontier, were the necessary preliminaries to the occupation of the western Roman Empire by the Germans from the valleys of the Danube and the Rhine.

[1] See R. Uslar, *Westgermanische Bodenfunde*, Germanische Denkmäler der Frühzeit, III, Berlin, 1936.

III. THE CENTRAL DANUBIAN PROVINCES

From the time of Augustus the southern half of the Danubian basin belonged to the Empire. This area, however, flanking the river throughout its course, did not form a coherent whole. In the central region, on the other hand, where the inhabitants were of Indo-European stock, there did exist a racial and geographical unity. Illyrians, Celts and Thracians—these were the racial elements which in the constant intercourse of war and alliances throughout the centuries coalesced into a sufficiently homogeneous mixture. In Noricum, as in adjacent western Pannonia, the population was preponderatingly Celtic; next to these tribes, the Taurisci and the Boii, came yet another Gallic people, the Scordisci on the Save, who extended far into Moesia. The Illyrians, however, were predominant in parts of Pannonia, both in the east (near Budapest) and in the south (in Croatia), and still more so in Dalmatia. In the highlands of Croatia and Bosnia, whither they were driven by the Celtic tide of invasion, a peculiar civilization was maintained by the Illyrians, with singularly little modification of their Iron-age culture, until Imperial times, as the remains clearly show. In Dalmatia traces of Thracian influence also began to appear, but even in central Moesia, in Dardania, the Illyrian element was the stronger. In the north of the province, it is true, side by side with the Scordisci were settled Thracian peoples such as the Moesi. East of these tribes begins the purely Thracian sphere, in the region afterwards known as Lower Moesia, where the Odrysian client-kings ruled till A.D. 46 (vol. x, p. 678 *sq.*). This was an outpost of the Greek world, facing not westwards but east and south—a fact which the Roman government already grasped, as will be seen. A distinction must be drawn between romanization in the central group of provinces, and in this district. Even after the end of the Odrysian dynasty, only *auxilia* were stationed here, whereas even in Flavian times the legions were situated in the triangle bounded by the rivers Utus, Margus and Danube. Like Lower Moesia, the coastal strip of Dalmatia, except for its mountainous hinterland, was dissociated from the central Danubian area. Roman contractors and traders had gained a footing on the coast as early as the third century B.C., and Roman culture flourished there by the end of the Republic. A similar distinction is to be drawn between the central group of Danubian territories and Raetia, a highland country, isolated by nature, whose connections lay rather with the Rhine district (see above, p. 526 *sq.*).

Within this middle Danubian area thus delimited, a yet smaller

Danubian lands, and the fine pottery of the Gallic factories, together with other Gallic products, such as bronze-ware and glass, competed with Italian manufactures for the Danubian market. Together with this commerce, which owed its origin to Roman technical skill, much older and deeper connections with the western Celtic regions have been discovered. The astral symbolism of the native tombstones in Illyria is encountered (complete with sun-rosette, half-moon and stars, and the gate and key of heaven) in Gaul and Spain, and that in regions of those countries which were little affected by urban culture. The matres Noricae and the matres Pannoniorum and Dalmatarum represent the same trinity of goddesses that plays so important a part among the Germans and Celts, being, in fact, a relic of the matriarchal triple division of the old Indo-Germanic tribes. These goddesses were called Fatae, as in northern Italy; Campestres, Suleviae, Triviae, and the like, as in Gaul; while in the region adjacent to the east they have already assumed a Greek disguise, as Nymphs, Parcae and Graces. The later stages of Gallic religion, the deities of Imperial times, also spread in the Danubian valley: such were Sucaelus, with his hammer-sceptre; the dwarf-like protective divinity of the Celts, the *genius cucullatus*; Belenus, the Gallic Apollo; and Epona, the favourite goddess of the Illyrian cavalry. In the temple precincts of the old gods in Noricum, chapels were built, as in Gaul, with a lofty hall surrounded by a lower ambulatory on wooden pillars.

The deliberate policy of romanization naturally began under military pressure immediately after the conquest. The legions were stationed at first at the point where the great Dalmatian-Pannonian revolt burst into flame, and in Dardania. In Pannonia north of the Drave, on the other hand, and in Noricum, countries which had readily submitted, only a few auxiliary troops were placed. It was, however, an unavoidable step to place the river frontier under military control, and thus began the romanization of the region along the river, a romanism which was the result of military harshness, but of immense value to the State. As early as in Augustus' time watch-towers were erected in Moesia, and under Tiberius two legions were pushed forward to the river. So, too, in Pannonia, though here Roman legions guarded the stream only in the south-east (between the Drave and the Save) and in the north-west (near the end of the amber route from Germany). Between the two the buffer-states of the Suebi and the Iazyges Sarmatae were called into being on the river bank as a means of keeping back the Dacians (p. 85). Here, in the strate-

gically dangerous bend of the Danube, stone fortified camps were
not erected until Flavian times; but Aquincum was garrisoned,
at the latest, under Tiberius, as the sherds of *sigillata*-ware demonstrate, and *sigillata*-ware made in the Po region, dating from the
first half of the first century, is found abundantly on the central
course of the Danube, where the *auxilia* had their camps.

The great roads crossing the Alps linked the Danubian provinces to the main stream of Roman life, and they were pushed
forward under Augustus in the direction of Noricum and Pannonia, with the same eagerness as they were towards Gaul and
Spain. The point from which all these lines of communication
radiated was Aquileia. The construction of the road leading towards Virunum was begun by Caesar, but its completion was due
to Augustus, who also built the military road from Aquileia to
Emona. It was perhaps in his reign, too, that the artery of traffic
to Moesia was modernized in conformity with Roman standards
of engineering by the construction of the highway from Lissus to
Naissus. This large-scale development of the road-system was
continued under Tiberius. The military occupation of the still
unsettled Bosnian highlands was secured by a network of roads
mostly constructed between A.D. 16 and 20. The road running
across the Kasan Pass and joining the camps of Viminacium and
Ratiaria also dates from Tiberius (vol. x, p. 803). In addition,
although inscriptional evidence is still lacking, the development
of the system of communications in north Pannonia must have
begun at this time. The legionary camps of Poetovio and Carnuntum (c. A.D. 15) in themselves make this assumption necessary; and it has been rightly pointed out[1] that the most important
stations on this road, Emona, Celeia, Scarbantia and Savaria, are
Julio-Claudian foundations and must therefore have been directly
linked with each other by the middle of the first century at latest.
Moreover, at the point of intersection of the roads which run
diagonally across the Pannonian quadrilateral north of the
Drave, at the south end of Lake Balaton, traces of Roman occupation dating from Tiberius' reign have been found (p. 545).
These furnish definite evidence of the surveying of this district,
a process which involved the planning of the lines to be followed
by the main highways. Under Claudius, too, this process was
continued. It was apparently in his reign that the trade-route
joining south-western Pannonia and Trieste was converted into
a highroad. The further development of the central Dalmatian
road-system, a problem surrounded with great difficulties, was

---

[1] By A. von Premerstein-S. Rutar, *Röm. Strassen und Befestigungen in
Krain*, p. 17 *sq.*

energetically prosecuted, and the new Via Claudia Augusta ran from the plain of the Po through the Tyrol to Augsburg. The important road along the Save achieved its final form at a remarkably late stage, namely, under the Flavians, and it was not until Trajan's and Hadrian's reigns that the communications of northern Pannonia and Moesia were perfected.

The work of organization included both the exact delimitation of the several tribal territories—we have a whole series of boundary marks from central Dalmatia set up under Tiberius—and the surveying of the lands, which in Dalmatia were measured in accordance with local practice, in Pannonia by the Roman system of *centuriatio*; the fields were divided into five classes in accordance with the quality of the ground, for purposes of taxation. The duties and revenues of the *vectigal Illyrici* were also collected in all districts. The first colony of veterans, about 1500 strong, came c. A.D. 14 to Emona, but the settlements did not always result in the foundation of cities. When the mutinous Pannonian legions on Augustus' death complained that on discharge 'trahi adhuc diversas in terras, ubi per nomen agrorum uligines paludum vel inculta montium accipiant,' the truth of this protest is borne out by the archaeological evidence. Near Scarbantia the tombstones of veterans have been found who on their discharge from the Pannonian *auxilia* under Tiberius were settled here (in Walbersdorf); and at the same date legionaries whose military service was over came to the city itself. At the south-western end of Lake Balaton, the site of the future road-junction, further remains have been found of veterans discharged under Tiberius[1], and similar evidence comes from Poetovio[2]. Italian stock was chiefly brought to Pannonia by the men of the Legio XV Apollinaris. The first Roman inhabitants of Emona, and of Scarbantia, the Claudian veterans in Savaria, and many who settled of their own free will in Carnuntum came from this force. In Moesia colonization did not begin until after the legions began to be recruited from non-Italian sources.

The natives were allowed to retain their tribal associations after the conquest; the head of such a *civitas* was always the commandant of an auxiliary force situated in the neighbourhood or indeed a centurion of higher rank. The *praefectus civitatis* was also *praefectus ripae*, if the tribal area under his administration lay on the Danube: besides the force under his command he could mobilize

[1] V. Kuzsinsky, *The Archaeology of the Neighbourhood of Lake Balaton* (in Hungarian), figs. 88, 101, 108.

[2] M. Abramić, in *Jahreshefte* XVII, 1914, Beibl. cols. 133 *sqq.*

at need the young men in his district who were organized on a military basis. This provision, however, soon lost its significance: the submission of the population made armed control superfluous, and moreover higher commands were advanced up to the river itself, so that by about the time of Vespasian the prefects of the river bank gave way to the *praepositi civitatis*, who were selected from the tribal chieftains (*principes*).

The substitution of the city for the tribe as the basis of organization was undertaken or hindered by the government on general social and political grounds. In Pannonia most of the *civitates* were preserved even at a later date, and this is also true of Moesia and the Dalmatian highlands. It is, moreover, a striking fact that they were not incorporated in the city organization even when cities already existed. Most remarkable of all is the case of the *civitas Eraviscorum* which continued to exist close to Aquincum, the capital of Lower Pannonia, as late as the third century. The explanation of this fact is to be sought in the principle that the recruiting area for the *auxilia* must continue to be inhabited by *peregrini*, while the legionaries were drawn from regions which had a veneer of city civilization. It is true that the practical realization of this principle encountered ever greater difficulties, especially after the citizens of Italy and of the highly cultured western provinces were more and more excluded from an army career (p. 134). As early as the beginning of the second century this made it necessary to draft local recruits into the legions in order to maintain them at full strength. The excellent Pannonian fighting stock now won a predominant position. As, however, so few cities were in existence certain tribes were granted a privileged position, if the present writer's view is correct, in order to be able to enlist their young men in the legionary forces. Hence it was that the 'Aelii Carni cives Romani,' near Neviodunum[1], were given citizen rights *en bloc* by Hadrian. In addition, the 'cives Cotini ex Pannonia inferiore,' who in the first half of the third century served in large numbers in the Emperor's Guard, seem to have belonged to a privileged *civitas* of this kind[2],

[1] Mommsen (*C.I.L.* III, p. 496) connects them with the Carni near Trieste, but these as late as Antoninus Pius were only able to obtain the citizenship by membership of the Council of their community; see Dessau 6680. Also they belong to another province.

[2] If they came in from Slovakia as late as Marcus Aurelius (as has been supposed) they would have been treated as *dediticii* and not at once allowed to serve in the Guard. The present writer would see in them the Κύτνοι whom Ptolemy (II, 14, 2) places in the north-east of Upper Pannonia. Their territory was transferred to Pannonia Inferior under Caracalla.

which, presumably since the second century, provided recruits for the legions, and later also for the Guard. We know, besides, that the 'civitas Iasorum' provided men for the legion II Adiutrix as early as in Hadrian's reign[1]. If this slight evidence is not deceptive, the privilege of serving in the legions had been granted to certain Pannonian communities, and this break with the general rule markedly facilitated the rise of the Pannonians in the army. The Carni, Cotini and Iasi are quite small tribes; the members of the larger tribes continued to serve in the *auxilia*.

In Noricum the government adopted a very different policy. By the middle of the first century the *civitates* here had vanished with few exceptions, one of which was the Norici themselves, whose opposition to the reform seems to have brought about the destruction of their capital Noreia and the discrimination against them when city government was introduced. The rapidly urbanized population of this country accordingly became a recruiting field for the legions as early as in the first century, and was also drawn on for the Imperial Guard. Concerning the organization of the tribes, it should be added that they were divided into smaller units in order to secure easier control and utilization for defence purposes. The divisions were made in Dalmatia in accordance with the native decurial system, and in Pannonia by *gentes*, which in their turn seem to have been divided into *centuriae*. Such were the subdivisions of the *civitates*. In addition they were grouped together into large units, *conventus*, which had to attest their loyalty at the annual festivals in honour of the Caesars, and which were also entrusted with considerable political rights. These *conventus* are well attested for Dalmatia; we have as yet no evidence of their presence in Pannonia, though they must have been in existence. This makes it difficult for us to reconstruct the early history of emperor-worship in Pannonia; its centre must not be sought in Savaria, which originally belonged to Noricum, but in some city of the south.

The contrast between Noricum and the neighbouring provinces is further reflected in the foundation of new cities. The long prepared assimilation of the Norici had met with such success by Claudius' reign that their administrative regions could now be simply converted into *municipia* without bringing veteran colonies into the land. The few foundations of the Flavians and Hadrian

---

[1] For the restoration of the inscription (*Ann. épig.*1904, no. 95) see A. von Domaszewski in *Jahreshefte* VII, 1904, Beibl. col. 11. The *respublica Iasorum* of the doubtful *C.I.L.* III, 4000 (which if genuine is of Severan date) is not an argument against this view.

(Solva and Ovilava) were of this same type, with a civic population
drawn from the native peoples. Conditions were different in
Pannonia. The first military colony, Emona, and the later settlements of Claudius and the Flavians, needed a strong Italic element
to start them on their history, and the special qualities of their
inhabitants and the strategic sites on which they were built attest
their military character, which they were slow to lose. The settlements which grew up near the big permanent camps on the river
frontier were first promoted to municipal rank in Pannonia, as in
Upper Moesia, by Hadrian, who thus abandoned the old principle that camp and town must not be united. At the same time,
the military township which grew up on the *territorium legionis* and
the civic township some distance away, were kept carefully distinct:
in Aquincum, for example, the two cities remained legally separated even after the civic township had been promoted to the rank
of a colony under Septimius Severus. In general, the cities were
situated near the frontier on all four sides of the province, while
the centre was occupied by more agricultural communities. It
goes without saying that the centres of provincial administration
flourished—such as Aquincum, Savaria, and Poetovio. Still more
important was the moving of the Imperial headquarters to Sirmium. Domitian may have set the fashion of residing frequently
here during his Danubian wars, and Trajan almost certainly did
so. Later, Marcus Aurelius stayed here for long periods during
the weary years of the Marcomannic-Sarmatian war[1]. From the
time of Maximinus Thrax the city ranked as the greatest in
Illyricum, and permanent seat of residence for the emperor.

The chief cities of Dalmatia, like the old colonies, were thought
of as *praesidia et propugnacula imperii*. Their garrisons, however,
were very soon withdrawn, and when Vespasian began the
urbanization of the completely pacified province, he conferred
municipal rights on the native settlements in the highlands only.
The cities of Moesia were of purely military origin; here, however, the highly valuable Italic elements introduced by the settlements of the first century were lacking. It was only in the west,
where till Domitian all four legions of the province were stationed,
that the Roman way of life had been successfully transplanted;
and it was there that Scupi, the first colony, was created in Flavian
times. With Trajan begins in the north the urbanization of the
vicinity of the river bank, a process carried on at the same time in
Pannonia; under these circumstances the central area remained
still more backward than in Pannonia.

[1] Philostratus, *Vitae Soph.* II, I, II and 14; Tertullian, *Apol.* 25.

Decades before the conquest, the Norican and Pannonian chieftains had their names inscribed in Latin characters on their coinage, and in the words of Velleius (II, 110, 5): 'in omnibus autem Pannoniis non disciplinae tantummodo, sed linguae quoque notitia Romanae, plerisque etiam litterarum usus et familiaris animorum erat exercitatio': a testimony deriving from an officer who fought under Augustus against the Pannonians. Such, then, was the effect of the peaceful penetration into these regions. Not to mention the ancient commercial interchange, this was largely accomplished by traders who, from the second century B.C., supplied Emona and Siscia with wine, oil, and other commodities from Aquileia in exchange for cattle, hides and slaves. Still stronger was the penetration of Carinthia and the Tyrol, where iron of excellent quality could be found, and gold in such quantities that it occasioned violent fluctuations of prices on the Roman market. The contractors from the south who exploited the lead of the Jaukenberg, left behind them inscriptions in the Venetic language and script. After the occupation Aquileia became the emporium of the trade with the Danubian lands. Inscriptions[1] show how the house of the Barbii, who controlled the trading connection with the north, had agents and representatives at all the central points in the road-system: for example, on the amber route northward into Germany, on the line through Noricum to the Danube, and on the stretch Emona–Viminacium extending beyond to Moesia. By the middle of the last century B.C. at latest the Barbii had won a footing near Virunum and had dedicated fine Greek bronzes to the Norican gods. It has also been noticed, however, that the inscriptions of the Barbii are almost without exception not later than the first century of our era, a fact which must be accounted for by the advance in the trade of the Rhine district at that period. The strongest and most natural trading centre for the merchants of Aquileia was Emona. Thence the Roman business men pressed on into remote fields of activity. The 'Emonienses qui consistunt finibus Savariae' of a recently discovered inscription[2] had an association of their citizens in Savaria even before its elevation to the rank of a colony by Claudius.

Since Noricum, in view of its ancient mingling of cultures, was, in Mommsen's phrase, 'an outpost, and, to some extent, a part of Italy,' where by the last century of the Republic inscriptions were already beginning to appear, and since, in later times, fulfilling its promise, it was regarded as amongst the most advanced

---

[1] See von Domaszewski, *Westdeutsche Zeitschr.* XXI, 1902, p. 159 *sq.*
[2] A. Alföldi, *Gli studi rom. del mondo*, II, 1935, p. 275 *sq.*

culturally of the inland provinces, it naturally played a considerable part in the romanization of Pannonia. Two zones must, however, be distinguished in both countries: the south with its Italian and civilian appearance, and the north with its rougher and more military Roman aspect, which is especially marked in Pannonia. A glance at the tombstone types shows that in Noricum the normal Italian grave altar, with characteristic *bourgeois* Italian design, is common, while the military stele, which predominates in Pannonia, is absent. In the Hadrianic age these contrasts are smoothed out: the difference ceases to exist and the primitive tombstones of Celtic pattern also give way to the funeral stele with family portraits, which becomes invariable. The veneer of Imperial culture spreads still farther eastwards. But the weakening of its influence, which was established for eastern Pannonia, becomes still more marked in the mountainous region which slopes down to the Dalmatian coast, and the greater remoteness of Moesia from the cultural centre of Italy results in Latin civilization emerging here in a later, weaker, and less pure form than in the adjacent countries to the west. For this backwardness the proximity of the Graeco-Thracian area was also responsible, so much so that the government was long unable to make up its mind whether to make this boundary line the limit of the Greek or of the Roman sphere of influence. In the first century the Moesian legionaries—unlike the Pannonian—were largely drawn from Oriental peoples, and even Trajan founded in Lower Moesia cities with Greek names and of the Greek type. Moreover, the Moesian population swept away by earlier wars was very considerably replaced by barbarian settlers; in the more westerly lands such measures were not necessary until after the Marcomannic wars. Equally strong, however, was the influence of elements from Syria and Asia Minor in the whole Danube region, and through service as auxiliaries, by winning their freedom from slavery, or as contractors, these men won a footing here, both in the economic life of the country, and as spreaders of their native religions.

It goes without saying that the cities newly founded by the emperors were planned with chessboard spacing of main and transverse streets, with water-supply and drainage-system, and were adorned with Capitolia and other public buildings on the Roman model. In the towns which grew up on the sites of permanent camps, civilians and soldiers had separate amphitheatres of their own, and one of these at Carnuntum could accommodate 20,000 spectators. In the great centres of southern Pannonia and in Noricum theatres of the classical type built in stone were also found. It is not unusual to find the mansions of the aristocracy built in a tasteful style both in town and country. The peasant also adopted and benefited from Roman methods in his work. The demands of the great nobles and emperors who resided in this region, together with the nearness of the barbarian peoples, which was not without its dangers, go far to explain why the architectural type of the fortified palace is found here perhaps earlier than anywhere else.

The metropolitan standard in sculpture is chiefly known to us through the portraits of the emperors, which were produced by great central workshops and had to be set up in the residences of all officials and in the public buildings as representing the majesty of the State. In comparison, the Norican and southern Pannonian schools of sculpture reached a remarkable level of artistic ability. They worked in marble and furnished the cult-statues for the Capitolia and other important temples, together with the artistic decoration for the public buildings in other parts of Pannonia, where there flourished a somewhat primitive sculpture in lime-stone, rendered more attractive to the eye by polychrome painting. The eastern Pannonian sculpture, for all its poor quality, is historically not insignificant, because of its distribution over a wide area and its independent development. Funeral sculpture best exemplifies the way in which the general Roman and specifically Italian types take root here in the first century, while in the second the local feeling for art modifies the classical models destroying the formal balance of the composition and, by over-emphasizing the decorative and typical secondary elements (such as sacrificial scenes), setting the seal of its own individuality on its work. For the pictorial representation of the principal scene in the Mithras-cult also the Danubian land developed its own favourite design, in marked contrast to the cult reliefs of the Rhineland, a contrast which also occurs in the themes chosen for representation on tombstones in the two countries. Many wandering craftsmen are attested by the surprising quality and wide distribution of wall-paintings and mosaics. Minor articles of craftsmanship were im-ported in large numbers and show a very high standard. Besides these products, which catered for personal wishes and tastes, in-corporation in the Roman system of communications brought these provinces the mass output of the large factories in Italy, Gaul and Alexandria. However much these mechanical products injured the classical art-industry, they did bring a higher standard of personal comfort to the lower classes in the frontier provinces. *Sigillata*-ware, lamps, glass and the like poured into the nearest districts immediately after the conquest, and slowly penetrated in Pannonia and the interior during the first century. In Moesia the process seems to have been somewhat slower. Presently, however, even here local factories for such articles were built, which although they did not achieve the standard of the Italian manufactures, could offer imitations satisfying local needs, and sold their products to their neighbours on the frontier.

Education also gradually spread. More important than the *graffiti* with words of poetry is the widening knowledge of writing. To this we must add the universal demand for portraits of figures from classical mythology and from the ancient history of Rome, reflected in the provincial art of the Danubian lands, which is the best witness of the contemporary understanding for and interest in this group of ideas. The diffusion of Roman names was also rapid; at first it was often naive: thus the retired soldier often named his children Emeritus and Emerita, and names copied from those of cities are common (women being named Siscia, Solva, Sirmia, and men having corresponding names). It was, however, not until the third century that the traces of native nomenclature vanished. Tacitus still understands by 'lingua Pannonica' an Illyrian dialect, though later it was taken for granted that a Pannonian spoke Latin[1]. The advance of Latin in the east during the third century is probably to be connected with the Pannonian hegemony in the Empire.

This dissemination of Latin civilization meant a simultaneous weakening of Greek influence, a process which was very marked on the Dalmatian coast, but less immediately discernible, as we have seen, in Moesia. The limits within which the two languages were spoken in later times have been determined[2], but in the epoch under consideration the Greek element was less hemmed in and there was a broad zone in which the two areas markedly overlapped—namely, Moesia. Here the inscriptions show the linguistic developments, while the pottery attests its Greek origin; yet, to take one instance, marble sarcophagi were brought by water from Asia Minor as far as Viminacium. The religious monuments attest a very strong Thraco-Grecian influence—of which only a trace reaches Pannonia. We must distinguish these influences of the nearer East from the general impact of the Orient on the western world under the Empire, which was often retransmitted by the great emporia. Thus the cult of Herecura (Ἥρα κυρία) came from Aquileia; and the Barbii disseminated the

[1] Tacitus, *Germ.* 43; S.H.A. *Aurel.* 24, 3.
[2] See C. Jireček in *Denkschr. Wiener Akad.* XLVIII, 1902, pp. 13 *sqq.*

cult of Isis so vigorously that she became identified with Noreia. Soldiers brought the cult of Mithras from the Euphrates as early as the first century, Juppiter Dolichenus appears in A.D. 128 as the object of official worship at Carnuntum, and in the middle of the second century Mithraea are founded in Poetovio.

The limits of Roman influence on the Danube were expanded through the conquest of Dacia. The extermination of the Dacians seems to have been thorough (p. 231 *sq.*). Moreover, the numerous tribes of their kinsmen extending as far north as the Vistula provided the survivors with ample opportunity for flight. The only sites at which remains of the old population are found, apart from the natural fortress of Transylvania, are in Wallachia and on the Theiss. We may conclude from the formation of a few *auxilia* of Dacians that in the mountains also fragmentary groups of the subject people survived. Whether these troops, stationed in Britain and in the East, subsequently received drafts of Dacians is unknown. For the rest, the abundant epigraphical material, which shows only a very few names with a Dacian ring, suggests either that the Dacians vanished from this region, or that they never became literate, and in consequence had no part in romanized life. The new colonists came mostly from Asia Minor and Syria, whereas in the time of the occupation the Italian element disappeared from the army, and Italian enterprise languished. If Dacia nevertheless became a Latin country, as it did, this is to be attributed to the influence of the army, and to the Latinity of the neighbouring provinces. The garrisons were drawn, in fact, from Moesia and Pannonia, and although a special study of the subject is still lacking, we can see how the potter Pacatus, of Aquincum, and other ceramic factories of Pannonia supplied their wares, decorated with imprinted palmettes and rosettes, to Siebenbürgen. Similarly the Pannonian and Norican types of funeral sculpture (embodying the portrait medallion, tomb-chapel, and certain standard kinds of stele) took root in Dacia[1]. The tomb-altar and stone lions protecting the grave, together with the astral symbolism (p. 543) are also a legacy from the Danubian lands to the new province[2]; while the Celtic god with his hammer-sceptre accompanied by his consort were introduced by colonists from Illyricum. Equally strong was the Moesian and Thracian influence. Diana regina (Ἄρτεμις βασιληίη), the strong cult of Liber-Dionysus with typical Thracian reliefs, the Ikon portraits of the Thracian horseman-hero and the part he plays in funeral sculpture, sufficiently illustrate this. We also know of lively

[1] See Volume of Plates v, 58, *b*.   [2] *Ib.* 58, *c*.

trading connections with Thrace. But the lead in the rapid development of the country was taken by Orientals, whose foreign names and cults constantly recur on Dacian monuments.

Pannonia was largely covered with forests, in which cattle were pastured, and which supplied the capital with bears for baiting as early as in the first century. Wild boar and bison were also hunted here. There was little agriculture, and the local wines were of inferior quality. In these respects Moesia was far superior, and the fame of her rich cornlands, fruits and cattle was known in early times. There was considerable industrial development, chiefly in Noricum, but this was limited to the vicinity of the Danube. All the greater was Illyricum's importance to the Empire as a source of raw materials. At first it was one of the chief slave markets, later it was especially significant as a mining area. The iron and silver mines of southern Pannonia and Dalmatia, the iron and gold of Noricum, Moesia's mineral wealth, and Dacia's fabulously rich gold deposits were an immense source of revenue to the treasury. No less important was the fact that the provisioning of large numbers of troops, and the growing prosperity of the land itself made possible a great industrial expansion in Italy and on the Rhine. A lively commercial interchange arose, with the Danube valley in a central position, and it is to this development that the advance of northern Italy at the expense of the central and southern parts of the peninsula may be attributed[1]. Similarly, the transplantation of the Gallic *sigillata* factories from sites in the south and east to the Rhine is partly due to Illyricum. Again, the excellent military material of Illyricum, impregnated with Roman civilization during the second century, became the last bulwark, with few intellectual pretensions, but strong and sure, of Rome and of western culture in the ancient world. Before the military emperors we know of no intellectually pre-eminent native of these lands, but the standards and virility of education amongst the masses, and the political and military way of thinking engendered by this environment ripened into the 'Genius Illyrici,' which saved the Roman world from its period of weakness and crisis in the third century. For this development the deeper italianization of Noricum and the military supremacy of Pannonia were equally necessary conditions. The slower romanization of Moesia was also destined to influence the course of history: in the later days of the Empire Moesia could continue to play the part of her neighbours in Rome's service and re-awoke in Justinian the dreams the Pannonian Caesars had known of Rome's imperial mission.

[1] M. Rostovtzeff, *Soc. and Econ. Hist. of the Roman Empire*, p. 71 *sq.*

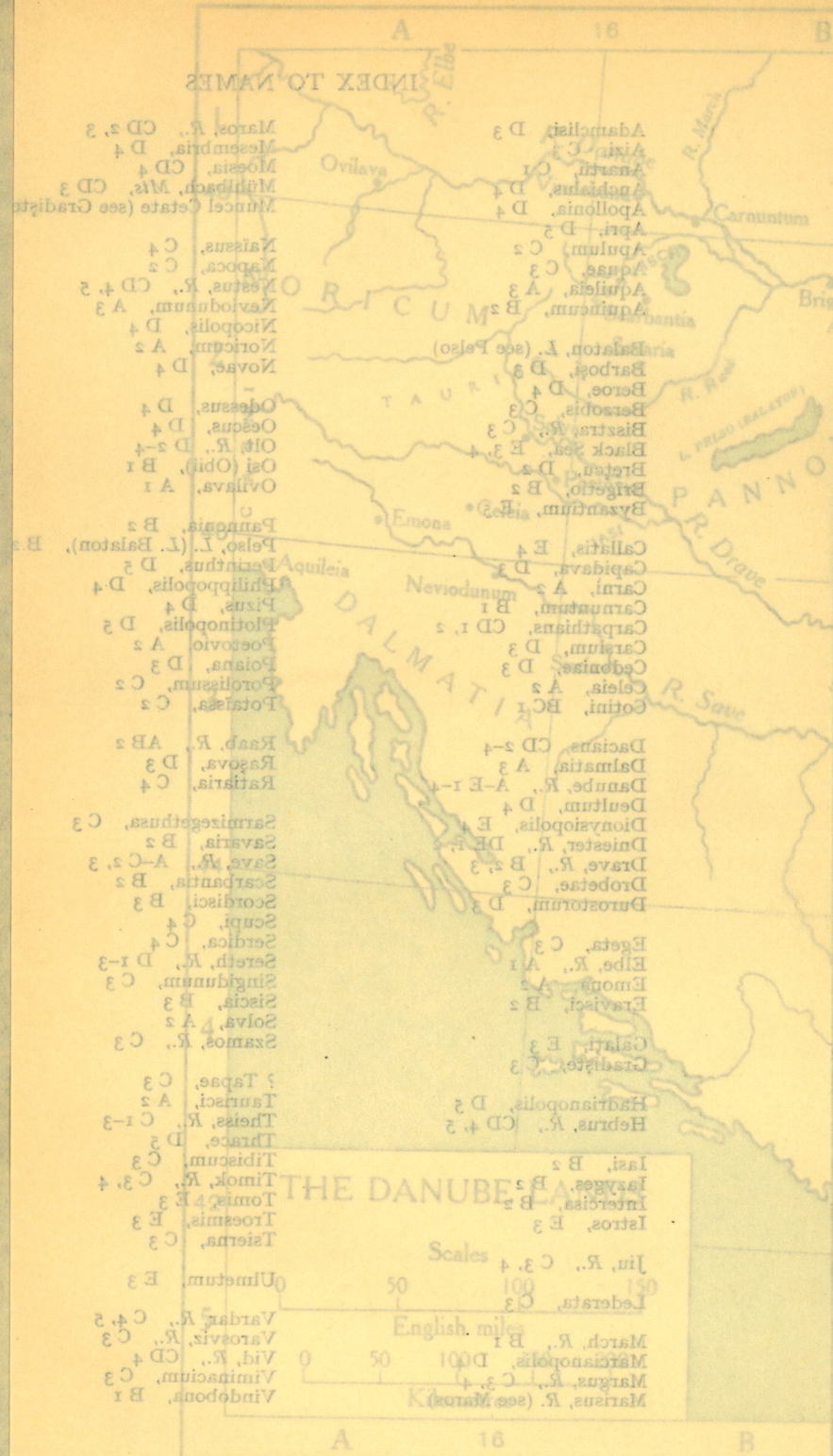

CHAPTER XIV

THE GREEK PROVINCES

I. INTRODUCTION

THE provinces Achaea, Epirus, Macedonia, Thrace, Pontus et Bithynia, Asia, Lycia et Pamphylia, Galatia and Cilicia, grouped together for consideration in this chapter, with the exception of Cilicia, in whose orientation Syria makes itself felt as the determining factor, may reasonably be described as the world surrounding the Aegean area. This area, moreover, was the first clearly defined region to be occupied by the Greeks, who had here to face the challenge of Indogermanic peoples as well as opposition from yet earlier inhabitants than these. The character of this struggle had long since changed. It was now a question not of gaining new territorial possessions to accommodate a rapidly growing Greek population, but of winning new lands and peoples for Hellenism, for the Greek way of life and Greek standards of culture. The extension of Roman rule to the East, and the unification of the whole Mediterranean world in the Roman Empire, gave a new impulse to this movement. After the recurrent and ruinous devastations of Republican times, Roman dominion during the first two centuries of our era became the strongest supporter of this hellenization, which was wholly in accordance with the aims of Imperial policy, and had to solve for it vast new problems in the opening up of fresh areas acquired by arms or peaceful means. In the solution of these problems, and in the consequent revival, Greece proper and the islands played little part, since they possessed no virgin hinterland or unexploited resources. In Macedonia, however, and still more in Lycia et Pamphylia, the situation was much more promising. Here peace and settled conditions caused a marked growth in city life to accompany the opening-up of the interior. This was still truer in the province of Asia, whose apparently unlimited resources were now for the first time fully realized, and caused an outburst of almost feverish energy affecting material and intellectual sides of life alike. The centres of this activity were the great coast cities, but it is also found in the remote interior, and, indeed, passing the boundaries of the province, contended in central Asia Minor in a fascinating way with indigenous, Celtic, and Oriental influences. It was in this period that the inland region in the northern half of the Balkan peninsula was first brought into close connection with the Mediterranean world through the advance of Roman supremacy to the Danube and on the northern confines of the Black Sea. Fresh impetus was given to this development by Trajan's conquests in Dacia, and a further contributory cause lay in the fact that this district was now traversed by the new main artery of communication between the West and the East of the Roman Empire, which was of vital importance for military transport, and acquired increasing significance for commercial purposes. It ran by land from Moesia and Thrace by way of Byzantium to Bithynia and Galatia, by sea from the cities on the western to those on the eastern shores of the Propontis and the Black Sea. In consequence, Bithynia, too, awoke to fresh activity, and the impressive advance of the Bithynian cities, Nicaea and Nicomedia, together with the growing significance of Byzantium, heralds the developments of a future age, which were to be of historic importance for the whole world, when the centre of gravity in the Aegean shifted northwards, and, at the place where the great trade-route from west to east crosses the ancient sea-passage from south to north, there arose the capital of the eastern Mediterranean, politically, economically, and culturally supreme, a tower of strength against the onslaught of Islam and the East. It is not our present task to trace the stages of this process, but the fact must be emphasized that its foundations were firmly laid in the first two centuries of our era. In these years the region which was the heart of the Byzantine Empire, comprising the countries which surround the Aegean, was bound by ties of Greek language and civilization into an indissoluble unity, within which Hellenism, in the period of the 'Second Sophistic,' experienced yet another renaissance, while Christianity found here the field for its missionary enterprises, and received in return valuable ideas, which assisted in the moulding of its doctrine.

II. ACHAEA[1]

In 27 B.C. Achaea, which had been treated as part of Macedonia since 146 B.C., was organized as an independent senatorial

[1] Only special facts are documented in what follows, general works and articles being quoted in the bibliography. It may be said here that, after the admirable fifth volume of Mommsen's *Roman History*, the present writer, as every student of the matter, is most indebted to M. Rostovtzeff's standard books. For the provinces in Asia Minor Sir W. M. Ramsay's pioneer work is invaluable.

MAP 13

GREECE

AND

MACEDONIA

Scales.

0   20   40   60   80   100
English miles

0   20 40 60 80 100 120 140
Kilometres

province under a proconsul of praetorian rank, and this form of government was maintained until Diocletian, with only two interruptions. These were from A.D. 15 to 44, when Achaea and Macedonia were placed under the control of the Imperial legate of Moesia, and from A.D. 67 to 70 or 74, when Achaea enjoyed the freedom granted her by Nero. In 27 B.C. the province embraced the whole of ancient Greece, including a strip of southern Epirus, and further the Ionian islands, the Cyclades, Euboea, Scyros, Peparethos, Sciathos, and Icos. Subsequently, under Antoninus Pius at the latest, southern Epirus, Acarnania as far as the Acheloüs, and the Ionian islands were included in the newly-founded province of Epirus, while Thessaly, with the islands off its coast, was joined to Macedonia. It was not until the third century that a separate island province was formed embracing most of the Cyclades.

Roman rule was administered by the proconsul, the legate subordinate to him, and the quaestor. The Imperial officials whose presence is attested are a procurator of the province, a procurator of the legacy-duties, and a procurator of the purple fisheries. Achaea had no military garrison.

The Romans had at first dissolved the old Greek regional leagues, but soon afterwards they decided to tolerate their existence, and they accordingly survived under the Empire, some even retaining certain executive powers binding on all cities belonging to the federation. These leagues sometimes coalesced to form larger associations: thus, in the first half of the first century, the federation of the Boeotians, Euboeans, Locrians, Phocians, and Dorians, joined with the Achaean League to form a national confederacy, in which, for a short time, a large part of the province was united[1], but this proved a transitory experiment. It seems that there was never a permanent provincial assembly of representatives from the whole of Achaea, although the Achaean League, with its seat at Argos, claimed this position in its official records, and was responsible for the organization of a cult of the Emperor. The chief official of the cult, appointed by the League, was the *Archiereus*, who often held office for life, and, from Hadrian's reign onwards, had usually the supplementary title of Helladarch.

The *Koinon* or *Synedrion* of the Panhellenes, created by Hadrian in a spirit of romantic philhellenism (p. 320), was fundamentally different in character from these leagues, for it was meant to extend far beyond the boundaries of Achaea, and to take in the

[1] *I.G.* III, 568; IV, 934 *sq.*; VII, 2711, 2878; cf. W. A. Oldfather, in P.W. *s.v.* Lokris, col. 1234; H. Dessau, *Gesch. d. röm. Kaiserzeit*, II, 2, pp. 542 *sqq.*

whole Greek world. Among the Amphictyonic religious leagues, which were formerly of political significance, the Delphic Amphictyony alone survived under the Empire as a religious association of importance, whose constitution was revised by Augustus and again later by Hadrian.

So far as we can see, all the land in the province of Achaea was divided into territories belonging to the various cities, and there were no extra-territorial estates owned by the emperor[1] or by private individuals, with the exception of the Imperial marble quarries at Carystus in Euboea and on the island of Paros. The rights and status of the various cities towards Rome showed great variety. Athens and Sparta were wholly free and independent, at least in theory, although their internal affairs, from Trajan onward, were often regulated by special *correctores* sent out by the emperor. Of the other free cities, more than forty in number, many though not all enjoyed freedom from taxation, and it is noteworthy that among them were included quite insignificant cities, the loss of whose revenue was no sacrifice. Three cities owed a brilliant rise to the Roman government: Nicopolis, founded by Augustus in memory of Actium, which derived its population from a compulsory synoecism of extensive tracts of land, and enjoyed numerous privileges; next Patrae (Colonia Augusta Aroe Patrae) established at a favourable site in 16 B.C. to accommodate the veterans of the Tenth and Twelfth legions, endowed like Nicopolis with extensive grants of land, and rising to prosperity by its vigorous textile industry, which specialized in the weaving of linens; finally, the colony of Corinth (Colonia Laus Julia Corinthus) begun by Caesar and completed under Augustus, rapidly becoming by virtue of its unrivalled position, and as the seat of the government, the first and largest city of the province. There is abundant evidence that during the first two centuries A.D. the Roman government in Achaea, as elsewhere, supported the political power of the propertied classes against radical elements, but the city constitutions were never reduced to a standard type, and throughout the province individual variations and differences of every sort survived from earlier and freer times.

The following brief survey of the province as a whole and of its parts aims principally at answering the question whether the Roman administration during the first two centuries of our era was

---

[1] Estates acquired by the emperor through inheritance or confiscation were, it seems, regularly sold by the procurators, so coming again into private hands; cf. P. Graindor, *Athènes sous Hadrien*, pp. 74, 191.

accompanied by progress or decline. The comparison must be based on conditions in the year when Augustus made Achaea an independent province, and we must avoid the error of comparing the state of affairs under the Empire with that prevailing in the third century B.C. or in classical times. Athens is the city for which we have by far the fullest information. Under Augustus it possessed besides Attica (with Haliartus and Oropus), the islands of Salamis, Ceos, Lemnos, Imbros, Scyros, Icos, Peparethos and Delos. The Emperor was none too favourably disposed towards Athens, deprived her of Aegina, a gift from Antony, and forbade her to sell the rights of citizenship and to continue to issue an autonomous coinage. Apart from imposing these penalties, however, he did not punish the city for her support of Antony, and in consequence he, together with the goddess Roma, had a special temple and cult on the Acropolis. Germanicus was overwhelmed with extravagant honours when he openly showed his respect for Rome's revered and ancient ally by entering the city attended only by a single lictor. Among the emperors of the first century, Claudius and Domitian gave proof of their sympathetic attitude towards Athens, whereas Gaius and Nero carried off her artistic treasures as plunder. Later, Trajan by dispatching an Imperial *corrector* attempted to improve the city's financial condition, which was clearly desperate. It was, however, the great philhellene Hadrian who first allowed the full radiance of Imperial favour to shine upon the city, in which it was his highest delight to stay as a private citizen, and where he had held the office of Archon as early as A.D. 112–3 (p. 299). By legislative measures, the transference to Athens of the revenues from Cephallenia, and direct subsidies, he straightened out the financial tangle, and began those splendid building schemes, which, when continued by the wealthy sophist Herodes Atticus, gave Athens an outstanding position even among the modern cities of the times[1], and so made her worthy in outward appearance of the new dignity she acquired as seat of the Panhellenic League. The consummation and crown of this advance in Athens' fortunes was attained when Marcus Aurelius added to the chair of rhetoric created by his predecessor four State-endowed permanent chairs for the great philosophical schools, thus founding the first university, and raising the '*domicilium studiorum*,' which was already

---

[1] The American excavations in the Agora have recently, surprisingly, shown that Hadrian's famous library had a predecessor in another library, dedicated to Athena Polias, Trajan and the city of Athens by a priest of the Muses, T. Flavius Pantainos; see *A.J.A.* XXXVII, 1933, p. 541.

a magnet for serious students of all nationalities, to be the educational centre of the Empire.

At the inauguration of the Empire the economic condition of Athens, which had been sacked by Sulla and thereafter, during the civil wars, was often subjected to harsh war contributions, must have been distressing, and there is no reason to assume any marked improvement during the first century. Her revenue was derived from a commerce which had sunk to mediocre proportions and had to face severe Corinthian competition, from the sale of oil, of the fine Attic marbles, and of the statues and copies worked in them, and, finally, from the money which was brought into the city by distinguished visitors and patrons, and by the young men and students of maturer age who came to complete their higher education. These resources, together with local agricultural produce and the taxes from her island dependencies, may have supported the population, and even have raised its standard of living, but the material prerequisites for a vigorous economic advance were absent, and the populace lacked the pushfulness necessary for business enterprise, since its modest mode of life had led it to concentrate rather on intellectual interests. An unscrupulous exploitation of the limited business energy that still remained to the Athenians must have been the means by which Hipparchus, the grandfather of Herodes Atticus, laid the foundations of that enormous fortune which, even after the confiscation of his estates by Domitian (p. 29), enabled his son and grandson to indulge in almost fabulous expenditure not only on Athens but also on many other cities. Yet the concentration of so vast a capital in one hand had a crippling effect on Athenian economic development. The complementary picture to the millionaire Herodes Atticus is given by the countless Athenians who were deeply in debt to his father on his death[1], and by the poverty-stricken people who wished to stone the sophist Lollianus, entrusted with the control of the market in Hadrian's reign, because of a slight rise in the price of bread beyond the normal[2].

It is not surprising that Athens with its memories of an historic past and its schools of philosophy, should have proved an unpromising field for the message of Christianity: that such it was is clearly discernible in the story of St Paul's visit. The Christian community, which counted as its first martyr Dionysius the Areopagite, must have been small. But it is characteristic that

---

[1] Philostratus, *Vitae Soph.* ii, 1, 4.
[2] *Ib.* i, 23, 1.

it was this community which produced Marcianus Aristides, the first apologist to take up the literary issue with paganism[1].

Second in rank among the free Greek cities was Sparta, which under Eurycles' leadership had supported Augustus in the campaign of Actium (vol. x, p. 100). The coast cities which, since as early a date as 146 B.C., had been grouped together in the *Koinon* of the Lacedaemonians, reconstituted as *Koinon* of the Eleutherolacones by Augustus, remained independent of Sparta; and the old quarrel with Messenia over the ager Dentheliates was settled in Tiberius' reign to Sparta's disadvantage. Hence the only possessions of the Spartan State besides the interior of Laconia were the outpost of Thuria, the port Cardamyle on the Messenian Gulf, and the island of Cythera, which was given to Eurycles by Augustus. After a temporary banishment owing to the abuses of his régime Eurycles kept his position of extraordinary power, which Strabo describes as *hegemonia*, *arche*, or *epistasia*[2], until Augustus' death. Under Gaius his son C. Julius Laco restored the dynastic succession, which had been interrupted during Tiberius' reign, and bequeathed it to his grandson C. Julius Spartiaticus, whose banishment by Nero marked the end of the line, though the lustre of the family, whose wealth was exceptional, remained undimmed for generations, and one of its members was probably the first native of Sparta to become a Roman senator. The philhellenic leanings of Hadrian benefited Sparta also. The Emperor twice visited the city, allotted her a vote in the Delphic Amphictyony, and himself held the highest office of Patronomos. The remarkable decree which orders dedications to Antoninus Pius as Zeus Eleutherios Soter to be set up in every street, or in every house[3], points to some special favour granted by that Emperor of which we do not know the details, but which seems to have done away with certain restrictions on personal liberty. It recalls memories of the distant past when we learn that the Spartan levy took part in the Parthian wars of Lucius Verus and of Caracalla. In other respects also Sparta clung with a tenacious and affectionate conservatism to the institutions of her historic past, to the old *Phylai* and *Obai*, to the *Apella*, *Gerousia*, and Ephors, even to the *Phiditia*, though these were only maintained by certain

---

[1] See Graindor, *op. cit.* pp. 211 *sqq.* Clement of Alexandria (died *c.* 215), who tried to ally Greek *paideia* with Christianity, was probably a native of Athens.

[2] VIII, 366.

[3] *I.G.* v, 1, 407–45.

colleges of officials and dining clubs. Above all the *Agoge*, the system of education for the young consecrated by long usage, was preserved, with its divisions according to age, and its severe training in physical strength and endurance, though at the same time the intellectual and moral sides of good education were not neglected. There is no evidence that this maintenance of her traditions hindered Sparta's development under the Empire, and nothing can be further from the truth than to picture the city and her territory in this period as a museum of antiquated and lifeless relics of the past. A review of the epigraphical evidence shows us a modern city, though of moderate size, with a healthy economic and social life and even a comfortable degree of prosperity which did not end until the critical years of the third century.

In the Peloponnese Messenia, although the inscriptions of its capital suggest a certain vitality, was markedly backward as compared with Sparta and the chief cities of the Eleutherolacones. The district of Elis produced crops of hemp, flax, and cotton which were used as raw materials by the factories of Patrae. The capital of the district naturally benefited most from this source of revenue, and it also derived considerable profit from conducting and preparing for the Olympic games. The north coast of the Peloponnese possessed in Corinth and Patrae, at its eastern and western ends, two of the Empire's most flourishing new foundations. In Argolis, the capital Argos, which was the meeting place of the Achaean League and the centre for the celebration of the Nemean games, maintained a considerable degree of prosperity, and this was typical of the district. Thus Hermione shows no decline, and the sanctuary of Asclepius at Epidaurus remained important and was much visited. We have to-day ample evidence on which to base a judgment on conditions in Arcadia under the Empire[1]. There can be no doubt that the population of this region as a whole, and of many cities, was now smaller than it had been when the country enjoyed its maximum prosperity, but the picture drawn by Strabo[2], who speaks of the almost universal desolation of a countryside which serves for pasturage and horse-breeding only, and who assigns a certain importance to the city of Tegea alone, seems painted in too sombre colours even as a description of the state of affairs in his day. An impartial reading of Pausanias corrects this impression, in spite of all he says about the ruinous and miserable conditions prevailing in many places, and the evidence of the inscriptions and the architectural remains

[1] F. Hiller von Gaertringen, *I.G.* IV, 1 ed. min. pp. xiii *sqq.*
[2] VIII, 388.

confirms his testimony that as early as the first century, and more particularly from Hadrian onwards, not only Tegea, but Mantinea also, and, to some extent, Megalopolis, regained a degree of prosperity, and that some other cities made an unmistakable advance.

The vitality of the population in the Central Greek districts of Acarnania, Aetolia, and also, in part, of West Locris was sapped by Augustus, who forced many of the inhabitants to settle in Nicopolis, and who further bestowed a slice of south Aetolian and of Locrian territory on his colony Patrae. Since many Aetolians evaded participation in the synoecism of Nicopolis by emigration to Amphissa, there came into being in Aetolia that wilderness, suitable for horse-breeding only, of which Strabo[1] speaks, and whose existence is strongly confirmed by the epigraphic evidence of the district[2]. The only exceptions to the general desolation are Naupactus, which survived, though subordinated to Patrae, and like Amphissa, which was originally a Locrian foundation but through the influx of refugees became Aetolian, ranks among the few Greek cities whose prosperity lasted into the Middle Ages. Phocis must also be regarded as a thinly populated area in view of Pausanias' reports, but in addition to its capital Elatea, which enjoyed the privileges of freedom and immunity, other individual towns such as Tithorea were markedly flourishing. Some light is thrown on the economic conditions of the region by a law-suit concerning the boundaries of an inherited estate which a certain Memmius Antiochus had to contest with the city of Daulis under three successive governors (116–118 A.D.), and which shows that here also single families held control over large possessions[3]. In Boeotia the unhealthy climate of the inland plain hindered a full utilization of its fertile soil and was a contributory cause in the remarkable decline in numbers of the population in this locality. While Thebes eked out a miserable existence, Tanagra and Thespiae were the most flourishing cities, and after them Lebadea, which had a special centre of attraction in the much-consulted oracle of Trophonius. Together with these cities should be mentioned Opus in Locris. We are fortunate in having Plutarch of Chaeronea as a clear witness to the high level of intellectual life attainable even in a small Boeotian country-town. Megara also won her way out of the decline which we know to have set in during the early years of the Empire.

[1] VIII, 388; cf. 450 and 460; Pausanias VII, 18, 8; VIII, 24, 11; x, 38, 4.
[2] G. Klaffenbach, I.G. IX, 1 ed. min.
[3] I.G. IX, 1, 61.

In Thessaly and on the Magnesian peninsula the league of the Thessalians and Magnetes, whose continued existence into the third century is attested, remained important. Agriculture, and horse-breeding from its famous stock, were the economic foundations of life, while the purple fisheries, and the production of salt, played their part. In addition to the flourishing capital Larisa, the cities of Hypata in Aenis and Lamia in Malis deserve mention as the most vigorous centres.

For the several islands belonging to Achaea, the general statement must suffice that on the whole we can observe a moderate development whose limits were determined by the possibilities of progress latent in the natural resources of each island, so that the picture which Dio of Prusa draws of conditions in Euboea[1] cannot be regarded as strictly in accordance with the facts. Something more must be said about the fate of the two great national sanctuaries of Greece, since these reflect with especial clearness the fortunes of the province as a whole.

The day was long past when the Delphic oracle had been a creative force in the spiritual life of the Greek nation. Yet the vitality of the sanctuary with its oracle and its great and solemn festival at the celebration of the Pythian games was by no means exhausted. Rome had brought peace and a benevolent administration, and Greece experienced a renaissance accompanied by a limited religious revival: these factors gave a new lease of life to Apollo's sacred city which only came to a definite end with the triumph of Christianity. Under Augustus and his immediate successors there was no real improvement in Delphi's condition, which in spite of some attempts at alleviation remained poverty-stricken[2]. Nero's reign was accompanied by an increase of interest and brought two glorious days when the Emperor himself appeared as a competitor for the Pythian prize, but it was also accompanied by the removal of many works of art. The patronage of the Flavians was less troubled: Titus was the first emperor to hold the office of Archon at Delphi, and Domitian restored the temple. In Trajan's reign, while Plutarch, with his literary training and religious temperament, was holding for life one of the two priesthoods after the city had been confirmed in the possession of her territory by a judicial decision against the Amphisseans[3], a vigorous building activity set in. This was continued by Hadrian,

[1] Or. VII. For social history in general, however, Dio's story is of the greatest interest.

[2] πενέστατον, Strabo IX, 420.

[3] Ditt.[3] 827.

who twice took office as Archon, and reconstituted the Amphictyony. The building programme may be said to have reached its
consummation in the rebuilding of the stadium by Herodes
Atticus under Antoninus Pius. After the repulse of the Costoboci
who had penetrated as far as Elatea in the reign of Marcus
Aurelius, Septimius Severus and Caracalla gratefully testified their
reverence towards the god who had intervened on their behalf.

The splendour of Olympia, too, revived under the Empire.
Tiberius, while yet a prince, and, later, Germanicus in the year of his
Greek tour ran four-horse teams at Olympia, and after the danger
that the sacred statue of Zeus might be removed by Gaius had
passed, there happened under Nero that unique celebration of the
festival which was subsequently declared invalid. The Emperor
appeared as driver of two four-horse teams and of a ten-horse
team, and further as citharode, tragedian, and herald, in the
musical contests introduced for his benefit: he was uniformly
successful. Later the Altis saw days of real splendour in the happy
and peaceful years of the second century, when in addition to
the athletic competitors for the most highly honoured crown of
victory in the world, the masters of rhetoric came to Olympia as
in former days, no longer to win their hearers' allegiance to a
common political policy but to move them to delight and enthusiasm by the artistry of their discourse and the contents of
their speeches, impregnated as these were with the great traditions
of ancient Greece. The excavations have revealed that the architectural setting of the Altis also underwent many changes and
additions under the Empire. The most sumptuous of these was
the aqueduct built by Herodes Atticus which at last put an end
to the shortage of drinking water. The Nymphaeum of this
aqueduct[1] in its obtrusive and showy style little in keeping with
the older buildings, is a characteristic representative of the brilliant
period of the 'Second Sophistic.' No one with any insight will
fail to recognize that this radiance is only the afterglow of a
greater past. But a radiance it remains: to overestimate its significance or to deny its existence would be equally mistaken.

III. EPIRUS AND MACEDONIA

Whereas Augustus had incorporated the land of the Epirotes
more or less completely in the province of Achaea, under Hadrian
or Antoninus Pius a separate province of Epirus was created
stretching from the Acheloüs to the Acroceraunian promontory,

[1] P. Graindor, *Un milliardaire antique*, pp. 191 *sqq.*

and accordingly embracing Acarnania also, to which the Ionian islands were appended. Presumably it had become clear that this district, which, after the vitality of the population in Acarnania and in the old colonial cities had been undermined, was sharply differentiated from the Greek world proper, needed a stricter government in order to yield better returns to the treasury. All we know concerning the organization of the province is that it was put under the control of an Imperial procurator, together with whom other special procurators are mentioned, a procurator of the purple fisheries for example, whose sphere of office extended over an area comprising Epirus, Achaea and Thessaly. We hear nothing of a provincial assembly.

The southern part of Epirus was wholly dominated by Augustus' new foundation, Actium-Nicopolis. Further to the north a few cities retained a certain limited importance, such as Cassope, Phoinice, and the colony, for which Caesar and later Augustus were responsible, Buthrotum. The Imperial government encouraged the development of city life in the interior, as may be inferred from the name of the city Hadrianopolis. Furthermore, the oracle of Dodona, which had relapsed into silence according to Strabo[1], now resumed its activity, as the archaeological evidence shows, though only on a limited scale. On the other hand, the very typical attempt of Herodes Atticus, who was forced through illness to make a prolonged stay in the port of Oricus, to recall to life this city[2], which since its sack by Pompey had sunk into insignificance, seems to have had no permanent effect. The conditions prerequisite to a vigorous economic advance, rather than a gradual progress, were lacking in a region which had been terribly devastated after the battle of Pydna. On the Ionian islands also the meagre evidence at our disposal indicates rather the maintenance of a moderate standard of living than a raising of its level.

The province of Macedonia, which was called into being after the revolt of Andriscus in 148 B.C., had from the Roman standpoint a double task: to prevent the creation of a power which should be dangerous to the southern part of the Balkan peninsula and to provide a secure line of communication by land from the coasts of the Adriatic to the northern Aegean. At the beginning of Augustus' reign after many battles and reverses, the energetic generalship of M. Licinius Crassus brought, in some measure, the attainment of this goal, so that in 27 B.C. Macedonia could be

[1] VII, 327; cf. Lucian, *Icaromenippus*, 24.
[2] Graindor, *op. cit.* p. 226.

handed over to the Senate. But even in A.D. 15, when the creation of the province of Moesia pushed forward the northern frontier of the Empire as far as the Danube, the unification of the whole of the southern and eastern sections of the Balkan peninsula under the control of one military command was again shown to be desirable, and finally, in A.D. 44, the inclusion of Thrace rounded off the system, and determined the lines which future organization was to follow. Macedonia, which was now once more a senatorial province, stretched from the river Nestus to the Adriatic, and may not inaptly be described as a broad strip of land on either side of the Via Egnatia, which ran from Apollonia or Dyrrhachium to Thessalonica, and beyond to the mouth of the Hebrus. The province included Macedonia proper together with the region which Strabo[1] designates as free Macedonia, and the Illyrian coastline on the Adriatic. Subsequently Thessaly also was separated from Achaea and added to Macedonia.

The head of the Roman administration after A.D. 44 was a proconsul of praetorian rank, supported by a legate and a quaestor. Together with these the Imperial procurator of the province is often mentioned. The seat of the Roman government was the free city of Thessalonica. There were no garrisons in the province. The official Era which dated from 148 B.C., the year of the province's foundation, remained in force under the Empire also. The provincial assembly was probably so constituted by Augustus that the representatives of the cities in each of the four regions constituted in 167 B.C. were now united to form a corporate body whose meetings were presided over by the high priest of the province's emperor-worship. The centre for meetings of the assembly and for this cult was the city of Beroea, which in consequence received official recognition under Nerva in the title 'Metropolis and Neokoros (*i.e.* protectress of the province's temple).' In addition to its usual transaction of business, the assembly from A.D. 44 to the time of Philippus Arabs maintained a very considerable issue of bronze coinage[2], which was doubtless in the first instance designed for the great provincial festival celebrated at Beroea.

For the development of city life, and also for the changes in the language and national characteristics of Macedonia, the founda-

---

[1] VII, 326.
[2] H. Gaebler, *Zeit. f. Num.* XXIV, 1904, pp. 279 *sqq.* and XXV, 1905, pp. 1 *sqq.*; *Die antiken Münzen Nord-Griechenlands*, III, 1, pp. 11 *sqq.*; cf. K. Regling in P.W. *s.v.* Koinon (2), col. 1054.

tion there of six colonies of Roman citizens in the first years of the Empire, to which must be added a number of *municipia*, was of paramount importance. Of the citizen colonies, in which principally those citizens were accommodated who had lost their property through the settlements of veterans in the Italian cities, two, Dyrrhachium and Byllis, lay in the vicinity of the Adriatic; three, namely Dium, Cassandreia and Philippi, near the Aegean; while Pella lay well inland. Denda and Scampa, near to the Adriatic, and Stobi (from Titus' reign onwards), in the upper valley of the Axius, are attested as Roman *municipia*. Among the Greek cities on the coast of the Aegean, Amphipolis and Thessalonica retained their freedom under the Empire.

The geographical character of the province of Macedonia is highly diverse. It contains several large, and many small, plains of notable fertility, but mountainous country predominates, rising in places to towering peaks, though the slopes seldom lack a covering of surface soil. Through agriculture, stock-farming, and lumbering, it provided a livelihood for a numerous peasant population, and made possible the existence of flourishing cities, which lay more especially in the coastal regions of the Aegean, towards which the country mainly faces, but were also to be found in certain of the inland plains and on the Adriatic coast. The population was as varied as the country. A pre-Indogermanic stratum had been overlaid by Thracian, Illyrian, and Macedonian tribes, while on the Aegean and Adriatic coasts Greek colonization had sought new land and trade-routes. Subsequently the vigorous Macedonian stock had forged this confusion of peoples into a unity under a strong monarchical rule, and so raised it to the position of a world power. This proud people was conquered by Rome and politically eliminated, while its country, stripped of its wealth, and sorely tried in the civil war, was now exposed to a strong influx of Italian colonists along the Via Egnatia. Thus to the earlier racial medley, whose confusion had been still further increased by immigrants from the East and Celts from the north, a new and self-assertive element was added and caused a noteworthy spread of Latin writing alongside the otherwise normal Greek. It would be intensely interesting to know in detail the foundations on which Rome built in the government of this province in particular, but the sources permit only a very fragmentary reconstruction; hence it seems more in keeping with the state of our knowledge to adduce certain inscriptions which enable us to divine conditions of life in Macedonia under the Empire.

According to the base of an honorary statue erected by the tribe

Peucastene of Beroea[1], C. Popillius Python, who held for life the office of high priest of the Imperial cult, and was *Agonothetes* of the *Koinon*, acted as envoy from Beroea to the Emperor Nerva and successfully advanced the city's exclusive claims to the Neokoria and the dignity of being entitled Metropolis. During his tenure of the priesthood he paid the whole of the poll-tax imposed on the province, roads were restored at his expense, new games including the baiting of wild beasts and gladiatorial combats were held, in times of need corn was supplied at a reduced price, there were general distributions of largesse, the whole assembly at all its sessions was entertained, while his term as gymnasiarch won him the affectionate admiration of all.

As a complementary figure to this representative of the Metropolis Beroea, may be mentioned T. Aelius Geminius[2] from the capital Thessalonica, who was gymnasiarch and protarch of his native city, and who made a gift of seven thousand yards of timber for the building of a basilica. He was appointed *logistes* of Apollonia by the Emperor, and was the first Thessalonican to be Archon of Hadrian's Panhellenic League. A stele from Heraclea in Lyncestis[3] contains the conclusion of a letter from an emperor or governor with instructions for street-building in the governmental quarter of the city. Apparently a part of the expense was to be borne by the city, a part by the people of Lyncestis, the other third by the tribe of the Antanes in so far as their dependents lived in the province. Foreign landowners are thus made to share with the city in providing funds. The decree refers to a series of regulations dealing with road-building in general. The man who set up the stele has distinguished himself as *agoranomos*, envoy, gymnasiarch, *tamias*, and politarch, and by the supply of corn at reduced rates. In return for these services he has been honoured by a resolution of the Bouleuterion, and finally by special decree has been elected to hold simultaneously the gymnasiarchy of the city and of the Lyncestian people. The fourth inscription[4] comes from the region of the 'free' Orestae, and belongs to A.D. 194. In a meeting of the people convened by the politarch of a tribe of the Orestae complaint is made against the *eparchikoi*, who find ways of getting into their hands portions of the land belonging to the community,

---

1 *Rev. Arch.* XXXVII, 1900, p. 489, no. 131.

2 *S.E.G.* II, 410.

3 P. Perdrizet, *B.C.H.* XXI, 1897, p. 162; cf. L. Robert, *Rev. E.G.* XLVII, 1934, pp. 33 *sqq.*

4 A. M. Woodward, *J.H.S.* XXXIII, 1913, p. 337; cf. M. Rostovtzeff, *Soc. and Econ. Hist.* p. 560 *sq.*, whose interpretation is here accepted as correct.

although they have not citizen rights among the Orestae. It is unanimously decided that these *eparchikoi* shall be allowed to retain only those lands in the possession of which they were confirmed by a previous decree of the governor, that their other landed property shall be taken away from them, and that any further sale of common land to them shall be a punishable offence. The Orestae alone are to profit from the yield of the common land. The decree is to be communicated to the governor by envoys from the people of the Orestae, and on receipt of his confirmation it is to be publicly displayed. The *eparchikoi* are to be interpreted as the Roman citizens who, while not possessing citizenship in the individual cities, endeavour to increase their landed properties which come under the immediate control of the governor and are, in fact, private estates. Thus we may recognize in Macedonia, side by side with the normal urbanizing process, a tendency to feudalize the land, which results in a conflict with the native system of peasant smallholdings. Furthermore, this last document is in agreement with the evidence of the numerous cult images of native deities which have survived, in showing that the interior retained its agricultural character, and maintained a vigorous and healthy population, which preserved the old tribal organization and formed under the Empire a favourite source of recruits for the Urban and praetorian cohorts.

Christianity in Macedonia derives from the Apostle Paul, who first preached in the colony of Philippi, where he was imprisoned by the '*strategoi*' and scourged, but was later set free as being a Roman citizen. Thence he went to Thessalonica, and, when he was driven out by the Jews, proceeded with his evangelical message to Beroea. In all these cities he won many converts.

IV. THRACE AND THE BLACK SEA PENTAPOLIS

The geographical character of the Balkan peninsula is such that its conquest by the Romans, which had begun with the formation of the province of Macedonia, cannot be said to have been concluded until the frontier line of the Danube was reached. The military and diplomatic activities leading to the attainment of this goal have been described elsewhere (vol. x, chaps. XII and XXIII). The final step was taken after the assassination of the last Odrysian king in A.D. 44, when Moesia was placed under the control of an Imperial governor of consular rank and Thrace, in spite of the resistance of its freedom-loving inhabitants, was converted into a province embracing the territory which extends from the Balkan range to the Nestus, with the exception of Byzantium, which belonged to Bithynia, and of the Thracian Chersonese, which was a private possession of the emperor. At the head of the province stood at first an Imperial administrative procurator of the equestrian class. From Trajan's time onwards his place was taken by an Imperial governor of praetorian rank. The financial administration was in the hands of a provincial procurator with subordinate assistants. Both governor and procurator had their seat and offices at Perinthus. Since the military defence of the frontiers was entrusted to the legate of Moesia, a relatively small garrison[1] maintained order in the country and security on the roads. A naval squadron was stationed at Perinthus.

In view of the inadequate development of city life, especially in the interior, the organization of Roman government on a basis of self-governing cities and their territories was at first out of the question. The earlier political system was taken as a model instead, and the province was divided into *strategiai*, with a *strategos*, appointed by the governor, at the head of each. The next unit in the descending scale seems to have been the tribe (*phyle*) under its phylarch, and beneath this came the associations of several villages bearing the title *komarchiai*. The urbanization of the country, which set in more strongly from Trajan's reign, conflicted with this standard organization to an ever increasing extent. Cities with their territories replaced more and more the *strategiai*, but there can be no doubt that the appointment of the chief city official, who is frequently entitled Protarch, was subject to confirmation by the governor. The villages were subordinated to the cities in whose territory they lay. As intermediate between the cities and villages the Emporia or market-towns were of especial interest. Their organization is known to us from the foundation charter of Pizus dating from A.D. 202[2]. The population here comprised some two hundered prosperous landowners from the surrounding villages; others were expected to swell the numbers, attracted by the prospect of reduced taxation. At the head of the Emporium stands, not one of its inhabitants, but a councillor of the controlling city, with the title Toparch, who, on the nomination of the city council, is appointed by the governor, and is given full powers extending also to the judicial functions which he has to discharge. A small military

1 Towards the end of Nero's reign it numbered 2000 men; Josephus, *Bell. Jud.* II [16, 4], 368.

2 Ditt.³ 880. On the *burgarii*, mentioned in this inscription, and the *burgi* see C. Schuchhardt, *Sitz. d. preuss. Akad.* 1929, pp. 450 *sqq.* and P. Kretschmer, *Glotta*, XXII, 1934, pp. 105 *sqq.*

garrison shares with the toparch responsibility for the upkeep of the praetorium and the baths. A provincial assembly for Thrace is first attested under the Emperor Antoninus Pius. The Thrakarch is to be regarded as its president, and he was doubtless at the same time high priest of the emperor-worship in the province. The seat of the assembly, and probably of the cult also, was the city of Philippopolis in the centre of the country, which held the provincial games and from Commodus' time terms itself Neokoros, and which was the only city in the province to receive the title Metropolis under Septimius Severus.

Our sources do not enable us to reconstruct an accurate picture of the economic life of the province. It is, however, certain that apart from mining, which we know to have continued under the Empire, the country was economically dependent on its agricultural output which derived from farming, vine-growing, market-gardening and cattle-breeding, supplemented on the coast by fishing and the production of salt. The demands of the army in Moesia were of crucial importance as a market for the surplus produce.

The idea of making the Thracian people, with its rich cultural inheritance, into a national unity, and of incorporating this into the Empire, lay beyond the range of Roman policy. To Rome the country was strategically important as lying on the route of communication to the military frontier of the Empire, and its people was important as furnishing excellent soldiers for the army. Moreover, the Roman government, especially from Trajan onwards, encouraged the province to develop along normal Graeco-Roman lines, which involved a process of urbanization accompanied by hellenization.

The position of the Province across the line of communication with the frontiers made it necessary for the government to pay great attention to the building and upkeep of the roads and to their security. Most important were the inland route from west to east, which ran from Upper Moesia (Naissus) by way of Serdica and Philippopolis to Hadrianopolis and beyond to Byzantium, and the two road connections running north and south from Philippopolis to Oescus and from the mouth of the Hebrus via Hadrianopolis to Nicopolis on the Ister. On these roads, to which is to be added the old coast road from Thessalonica by way of Traianopolis to Perinthus and thence to Byzantium, were situated the most important of the newly-founded cities, compared with which the old Greek ports on the Aegean and the Propontis, with the exception of Perinthus, faded into the background.

The urbanization of Thrace proceeded slowly at first, but after the tonic effect of Trajan's great achievements in the lower Danubian region, the tempo quickens. In the two colonies, which Claudius and Vespasian settled in the coastal regions of the Propontis and the Black Sea, namely Apri and Deultum, and similarly in the settlement of veterans at Philippopolis for which Vespasian was responsible, the primary motive was to strengthen the security of the province. Trajan's foundations, on the other hand,—Traianopolis, Plotinopolis, Marcianopolis, Augusta Traiana Beroë and Nicopolis ad Haemum (or Istrum)—and Hadrian's raising of Hadrianopolis to the dignity of a city aimed rather at the general opening-up of the country. All the cities in the interior of the province, despite active control by the governor, were Greek in character, although Philippopolis alone, in all probability, was completely equipped with the institutions of a Greek *polis*. Indeed, their populace was only in part composed of native elements, the rest being hellenized immigrants from the South and East. So they remained intrusive foreign bodies and did not materially affect the character of the peasant farming population, whose resistance against any kind of urbanization is attested by the privileges bestowed by the government on those peasants who consented to settle together in the Emporia. In keeping with this conservatism is the method of burial retained by the wealthier among the peasants, who down to the third century followed the old custom of interring the dead seated in their chariots under great tumuli. Similarly the native deities and rites resisted most successfully all attempts of hellenization. It cannot, moreover, be doubted that the native language was universally spoken in the country, though supplanted as a written language by Greek, which had long been diffused from the coastal cities. Compared with Greek, Latin had only a limited distribution in Thrace[1].

Christianity spread into Thrace from Bithynia, but our information concerning its advance in the first two centuries is meagre. We may assume the existence of Christian communities in Philippopolis and Hadrianopolis, besides the coastal cities, whereas the conversion of the country population must have been much later.

We may now turn to the Pentapolis or Hexapolis on the Black Sea. The Greek cities on the western shore of the Euxine, most of which were Milesian foundations, were united in a league in pre-Roman times. So far as is known, it was M. Lucullus in

[1] A. Stein, *Röm. Reichsbeamte der Provinz Thracia*, pp. 121 *sqq.*

71 B.C. who first brought them as *civitates foederatae* within the boundaries of the Roman empire, whose immediate representative for them was at the beginning the governor of Macedonia, while subsequently they formed a part of the newly created province of Moesia. The old league remained in being under the title *Koinon* of the Pentapolis (later Hexapolis), or *Koinon* of the Hellenes, and even continued to possess a federal assembly. The representatives met at the capital Tomis, which from Antoninus Pius' reign onwards bore the title of Metropolis, under the presidency of the high priest of the emperor-worship, who was entitled Pontarch. The five cities that made up the league were Istros, Tomis, Callatis, Dionysiopolis, and Odessus[1]. Apollonia, which had formerly once belonged to the league, and Anchialus, which was raised to the status of an independent city by the Emperor Trajan, were already included in the organization of Thrace, and hence played no part in the Hexapolis. The immediate protection of the cities and their sea-borne commerce was in the hands of the *praefectus orae maritimae*, who may also have had under his command the *Cohors VII Gallorum* stationed at Tomis. With the internal institutions of the cities Rome seems to have interfered little.

The period from Alexander the Great to the Roman Empire was, on the whole, difficult and dangerous for the cities on the western shores of the Black Sea, because of their exposed position and the movements of peoples in their hinterland. It was not until the extension of Roman power to include the lower Danubian region that they obtained security, and then through the vast economic advance in the hinterland, especially from Trajan's reign onwards, the possibility of a prosperity undreamed of before, though this did not benefit all the cities equally. Istros, ruined as a port by the silting up of her harbour and handicapped by tax-farmers in the free exploitation of her fisheries and of the forests in the Danubian delta, fell far behind Tomis in the race. Tomis in consequence of her favourable situation gained control of the main stream of commerce to and from the Danube, and so attained a high degree of prosperity and importance, which is attested by her epigraphical remains, and especially by the wealth of her coinage. It is further reflected in her position as capital of the Pentapolis. There can be no doubt that the foundations of this economic advance were the region's abundant output of agricultural products for export, on the one hand, and the huge demand

---

[1] The city, whose adhesion caused the temporary change of name to Hexapolis, was probably Mesembria.

of the armies for provisions, arms, and the countless other articles needed by officers and men, on the other. A similar advance, though on a more moderate scale, can be observed also in the other cities.

V. PONTUS ET BITHYNIA

This province, first constituted by Pompey, its boundaries being later revised by Antony, occupied a relatively narrow strip of territory stretching from the mouth of the Rhyndacus to the eastern boundary of the district controlled by Amisus. From 27 b.c. to the beginning of Marcus Aurelius' reign (with interruptions under Claudius and Nero), it belonged to the Senate and was governed by a proconsul, with the rank of praetor, and his attendant legate and quaestor. In 111–113 a.d., by agreement between the Emperor and the Senate, the younger Pliny was sent out as *legatus Augusti consulari potestate*[1]. There followed, doubtless at once, the rule of C. Julius Cornutus Tertullus as Imperial *legatus*; and, finally, C. Julius Severus was dispatched by Hadrian in a.d. 136–7 as extraordinary commissioner[2]. These temporary interruptions in the senatorial administration show clearly that it was necessary to put a province torn by political and social antagonisms under the immediate control of the *princeps*, especially at a time when great bodies of troops were being transported to the East. In 165 at latest the province was permanently transferred to the Imperial administration, with a *legatus pro praetore* of consular rank in charge. There is no evidence that this change involved a strengthening of the garrison, which in Pliny's time consisted of several cohorts. The Imperial procurator had a hard task in providing for the frequent transport of troops through the province and for the maintenance of communications with the Bosporan kingdom. The unsatisfactory financial condition of the cities made necessary the repeated nomination of *curatores*.

Corresponding to its two parts, the province possessed two assemblies of representatives from the cities, which met in the capitals Nicomedeia and Amastris, and were presumably presided over by the Bithyniarch and Pontarch respectively. In these capital cities were also the two temples of the Imperial cult dedicated to Rome and Augustus, that in Nicomedeia being surprisingly entitled 'the great common temple of the Mysteries[3],'

[1] M. Rostovtzeff, *B.S.A.* xxii, 1916–18, pp. 1 *sqq.*; O. Cuntz, *Hermes*, lxi, 1926, pp. 162 *sqq.*, 352.

[2] E. Groag in P.W. *s.v.* Julius (Severus), col. 817 *sq.*

[3] *I.G.R.R.* iii, 63.

and having a chief priest designated Sebastophant and Hierophant. Subsequently, further provincial temples were dedicated to Commodus and to later emperors in Nicomedeia. The whole area of the province was divided by the Romans into a relatively small number of city territories. The following were independent cities, as their exercise of the right to issue their own coinage shows: Chalcedon, Nicomedeia, Cius (Prusias ad mare), Nicaea, Apamea, Prusa, Caesarea Germanica, Prusias ad Hypium (Cierus), Bithynion (Claudiopolis), Creteia-Flaviopolis and Juliopolis (Gordiu Kome), in Bithynia; Heraclea Pontica, Tium, Amastris, Abonuteichos-Ionopolis, Sinope and Amisus, in Pontus. To this list should be added Byzantium, which despite its situation on the European shore of the Bosporus, ranks as a Bithynian city, although at the same time it stands in a close relationship to the governor of Moesia. The capital Nicomedeia had a rival in the city of Nicaea, which equally also is entitled 'first in Bithynia.' The privileges of *civitates liberae* were enjoyed in Bithynia by Byzantium and Chalcedon, while Amisus in Pontus held the status of a *civitas libera et foederata*. Colonies of Roman citizens were established by Caesar in Apamea to make good the depletion of its population due to the Mithridatic war, and in Sinope. Emperors probably owned extensive private domains in the province, but the evidence as yet is inconclusive. Altogether we are very inadequately informed of the conditions prevailing among the population living outside the cities.

Although in Pontus et Bithynia to this day no important excavations have been carried out, and although the scientific study of the province must be described as backward, yet we can win a better picture here than elsewhere of conditions in our epoch, since besides the normal testimony concerning single events furnished by the literary, epigraphical, and numismatic evidence, we possess three sources of the very highest value. First come the Bithynian speeches of Dio Chrysostom, a native of Prusa on the Olympus, which throw a flood of light on internal conditions in the municipalities; second, the correspondence between Pliny and Trajan with its abundant evidence bearing on Roman provincial administration; finally Lucian's brilliant account of the false prophet Alexander of Abonuteichos, which, rightly understood, gives us a deep insight into the state of religion in the province at that time (see below, p. 579 *sq.*).

Pontus et Bithynia comprise a country richly endowed by nature. The climate is a mean between that of the Mediterranean and that of the more temperate parts of Europe. The province, besides an adequate area for tillage, olive-plantations, market-gardening, and vine-growing, has extensive forests which provide excellent timber and the whole range of woodland produce, while splendid pasturage also exists for cattle-raising on a large or small scale. Finally must be mentioned the abundance of fish in the adjoining sea, especially of the tunny, which was caught in quantity near Sinope and Byzantium and was used not only to supply the demands of the province, but also for export. In this connection, the commercial advantages inherent in the situation of the coast cities on the Propontis, the Bosporus, and the Black Sea, should be noticed. These cities, besides assisting in the exchange of commodities between the Aegean and the Black Sea, even before the Roman conquest played the rôle of middlemen in developing trade relationships with the interior not only of the province but also, for a considerable time, of Asia, Paphlagonia, Galatia, and the Cappadocian part of Pontus. The great highways already ran from Bosporus (Chalcedon) by way of Nicomedeia and Bithynium to Gangra or Pompeiopolis, and from the Hellespont or the Propontis by way of Nicaea and Juliopolis to Ancyra, spanning the province from west to east, and crossed in their turn by a number of minor roads and tracks running north and south from the ports of the Black Sea coast to the interior[1]. As the inscriptions of the Roman era show, under Claudius and Nero and especially under Vespasian, the road-system was constantly improved and extended, a process continued in the second and later centuries in view of the growing importance which the extension of Roman rule over the northern part of the Balkan peninsula brought to the province, lying as it did on the line of communication between the eastern and the western halves of the Empire. It must not, however, be forgotten that the resulting constant passage of men and supplies, although provision was made by the State for the soldiers' commissariat, brought in its train numerous abuses, and was a severe strain on the resources of the inhabitants[2].

The long peace it enjoyed during the first and second centuries, which was only interrupted for a brief space towards the end by the decisive conflict between Septimius Severus and Pescenninus Niger, brought a marked economic advance. The intense rivalry between the cities to outdo one another in the magnificence of their architecture and in all the comforts of modern city life, which Dio records, is wholly confirmed by the many passages in Pliny

[1] J. Sölch, *Klio* XIX, 1925, pp. 161 *sqq.*; cf. J. A. R. Munro, *J.H.S.* XXI, 1901, pp. 53 *sqq.*
[2] Pliny, *Ep.* X, 77 (81).

giving particulars concerning the often feverish building activity, which might far exceed their financial resources. Inscriptions and coins tell the same tale. Despite this material prosperity political conditions in the time of Dio and Pliny were unbelievably bad. Between the cities, for example between Nicomedeia and Nicaea, or between Prusa and Apamea, there continued bitter feuds, which even affected the provincial assembly, and made almost impossible the unity of purpose which would enable a stand to be made against tyrannical administration by the governors or exactions by the procurators. Moreover, in each city the inhabitants were divided into cliques and political parties, who indulged in slander and feuds against each other; while the hatred and embitterment of the lower against the propertied classes had grown so intense that a mere pin-prick, a slight rise for instance in the price of bread, might cause revolts to spread widely throughout the province, which the governor had to repress with bloody severity. The best illustration of this is to be found in Pliny, from whom we learn that the most powerful of all Roman emperors felt constrained to veto the creation of a fire-brigade of fifty workmen in the city of Nicomedeia, because he was afraid that despite the governor's control this institution might form the nucleus of an association dangerous to the peace of the province[1].

What was the cause of such conditions? It seems that the political organization of the province cannot be wholly acquitted of responsibility. The lex Pompeia[2], on which this was based, had recognized only a few independent cities, and had subordinated all other communities to them. It may be suggested that among such subordinated communities there were included several small cities formerly independent, whose status was now much inferior. It would also seem that Pompey made no radical alteration in the particularly oppressive position of dependency, dating from pre-Roman times, in which the country population stood to some of these cities, a relationship illustrated by the Mariandyni in the territory of Heraclea Pontica, or the Bithyni in the territory of Byzantium. In the individual cities, however, with the removal of all real powers from the assembly, the government lay constitutionally in the hands of the council, whose members were not elected by the people, but were chosen by censors from those who had previously been in office or from those citizens who could show a definite property qualification. A similar property return was necessary to qualify a citizen to hold office. Such a procedure

---

[1] Pliny, *Ep.* x, 33 (42) and 34 (43).
[2] Cf. A. von Premerstein in *Z. d. Sav.-Stift. rom. Abt.* XLVIII, 1928, p. 438.

concentrated all power in the hands of the propertied class, and denied to the proletariate any chance of realizing its desires by legal means. This led to revolt by the masses, and at the same time encouraged those in office to pursue their own selfish interests at the expense of the community as a whole. The famous phrase of the Emperor Trajan 'dum inter se gratificantur[1]' is an epigrammatic description of the non-social attitude, prejudicial to the public welfare, adopted by a part of the ruling class. Trajan attempted to improve political conditions by maintaining the fundamental policy of opposition by the Roman government to revolution accompanied by lower-class violence, while fighting corruption by means of a strong central control and insisting on a reasonable financial administration in the cities. A real lessening of tension in the relations between the propertied classes and the proletariate seems, however, to have first ensued under the government of Hadrian, who had a better insight into the causes of the trouble. According to Cassius Dio[2], the administration of C. Julius Severus as commissioner of Hadrian was still well remembered in his own day (the third century). It was characterized by understanding and justice, and by the impartial advancement of the interests of the individual and the community alike.

An accurate description of the cultural background is not possible with our inadequate materials. It should, however, be pointed out that in three successive generations the province produced Dio Chrysostom, Arrian, who achieved renown both as a general and as a versatile author, and the historian Cassius Dio. Similarly, we should have no means of forming a true picture of the intense religious life of the province from the hardly characteristic list of cults furnished by the literary, epigraphical, and numismatic evidence, were it not supplemented by Lucian's account of that extraordinary character, half charlatan, half prophet, Alexander of Abonuteichos[3]. After the people of the province had been adequately prepared by wonderful prophecies, he produced in his native city a new epiphany of Asclepius in the form of a snake with human head called Glycon, and founded in this god's honour a cult, including mysteries and an oracle, which won believers and adherents not only among the superstitious local Paphlagonians, but throughout the length and breadth of Asia Minor, and even in aristocratic society at Rome, and endured long after the death of its founder. It is expressly attested that Alexander regarded

---

[1] Pliny, *Ep.* x, 38 (47).　　　　[2] LXIX, 14, 4.

[3] Lucian, *Alexandros*; cf. O. Weinreich in *N.J. Kl. Alt.* XLVII, 1921, pp. 129 *sqq.*; A. D. Nock in *C. Q.* XXII, 1928, pp. 160 *sqq.*

the Epicureans and the Christians as the two chief opponents of his god. This throws fresh light on Pliny's famous letter about the Christians, which was written in the eastern part of Pontus, not far from Abonuteichos[1]. It has recently been well remarked[2] that the numerous Christians encountered by Pliny in this vicinity need not necessarily have belonged to the orthodox Church. There can, however, be no impugning the evidence that strong and living religious forces were at work in the province about the middle of the second century. Here must be mentioned the name of the great heretic Marcion of Sinope, a contemporary and near neighbour of Glycon's prophet Alexander. His teaching of the new God, prophesied by Jesus Christ, who is only and wholly Goodness and Love, was rightly rejected by the Church as unhistorical, yet it took its rise in the deepest springs of the religious life, and when he proclaimed his message to the world, he received a widespread response[3].

VI. ASIA

In 20 B.C. Augustus himself gave the final form to the organization of the province of Asia. Arising from the legacy of the last Attalid kings, its constitution was first drawn up by a senatorial commission under the presidency of M'. Aquilius in 128–6 B.C. and was subsequently revised by Sulla in 84 B.C. From the time of Augustus to the re-division of the Empire under Diocletian no important changes were made affecting either the political administration of the province or its territorial limits within which were included the Hellespontine regions, Mysia, Ionia, Lydia, Caria, Phrygia, and the islands near the coast.

In 27 B.C. Asia was entrusted to the Senate as one of its two most valuable provinces. The governor was at that time a proconsul with consular rank, supported by three legates and a quaestor. The Emperor's financial and proprietorial interests were represented by numerous procurators. The procurator of the province had as subordinates, apparently from Vespasian onwards, especial procurators for different parts of the province[4], and beneath them the administrators of the Imperial domains and mines, who were chiefly drawn from the class of freedmen. From the first

[1] U. Wilcken, *Hermes*, XLIX, 1914, p. 120 *sq.*
[2] W. Bauer in *Beiträge zur hist. Theologie*, X, 1934, pp. 94 *sqq.*
[3] See A. Harnack, *Marcion*, ed. 2, and below, vol. XII.
[4] R. K. McElderry, *J.R.S.* III, 1913, pp. 116 *sqq.*; cf. E. Kornemann in P.W. *s.v.* Domänen, Suppl. IV, cols. 246 *sqq.*

century A.D. peace was secured in the eastern parts of the province
by a garrison comprising one or more cohorts. This was situated
in Eumeneia, thus directly protecting the two important cities of
Laodicea on the Lycus, and Apamea, while the mountainous
regions to the north and the south-east could be quickly reached[1].
In the west separate *stationarii* are attested, a reinforcement by the
State of the civil police force, whose maintenance normally devolved on the cities, which discharged this duty under the control
of the governor through the *eirenarchai* and their subordinates
(*paraphylakitai, diogmitai*). For the administration of justice the
province was divided into nine (later eleven) areas, in whose
capitals the assizes (*conventus*) were held by the proconsul or the
legates and a court of provincial judges[2]. The financial affairs of
the cities were from Trajan onwards increasingly supervised by
Imperial *curatores*.

The governor was in duty bound to set foot first in the province
at Ephesus. It remains doubtful, however, whether Ephesus or
Pergamum is to be regarded as the seat of the provincial government and the home of the central record-office. The administration
of the emperor's financial affairs was certainly concentrated at
Ephesus, where the procurator of the province had his seat, and
where the Imperial bureaux and records are often mentioned.
The most important organization of the province itself was the
assembly which was entitled 'the Community of the Greeks in
Asia' (κοινὸν τῶν ἀπὸ τῆς 'Ασίας 'Ελλήνων or alternatively
οἱ ἀπὸ τῆς 'Ασίας 'Ελληνες), and was composed of elected
representatives from the various cities[3]. The highest dignitary
of the province was the chief priest of the province's *temenos*
of Rome and Augustus at Pergamum (ἀρχιερεὺς 'Ασίας),
a sanctuary voted in 29 B.C.[4] After other cities had erected provincial temples dedicated to the Imperial cult the position was
held in rotation by whichever of the chief priests had been entrusted with presiding at the provincial festival, who in consequence
of this honour was entitled Asiarch.

Side by side with the assembly there existed the provincial
league of Roman citizens, but this never achieved any great influence. The *Koinon* of Lesbos, the community of those united in

---

[1] E. Ritterling, *J.R.S.* XVII, 1927, pp. 28 *sqq.*; Buckler-Calder-Guthrie,
Mon. Asiae Min. Ant. IV, p. 122, no. 328.

[2] Philostratus, *Vitae Soph.* I, 22, 6; cf. von Premerstein, *op. cit.* p. 442, n. 1.

[3] Buckler-Robinson, *Sardis*, VII, 1, pp. 26 *sqq.*, n. 8.

[4] On the history of the cult of Augustus at Pergamum see W. H. Buckler
in *Rev. Phil.* LXI, 1935, pp. 177 *sqq.*

the worship of the Athena of Ilium, the *Koinon* of the thirteen
Ionian cities, and the peculiar Carian religious associations which
worshipped Zeus Chrysaoreus and Zeus Panamaros, all have
purely local significance.

Sulla's reform of the constitution, the memory of which was
perpetuated in the system of dating by the provincial era, though
this was not universally adopted, divided the province as it then
was into forty-four nominal regions ($\delta\iota o\iota\kappa\acute{\eta}\sigma\epsilon\iota\varsigma$) for administrative purposes[1]. The character of these regions has not yet been
properly explained, but they must have been self-governing, since
no Roman officials were introduced in any of them. Under the
Empire the province was divided into far more numerous self-
governing areas (the exact number cannot be determined), of
which by no means all were cities ($\pi\acute{o}\lambda\epsilon\iota\varsigma$), but which can be
described as demes ($\delta\hat{\eta}\mu o\iota$) and peoples ($\check{\epsilon}\theta\nu\eta$). The course of
events was such that the demes and peoples were later themselves
organized as cities, or incorporated into the territories of cities, or
else made part of the Imperial domains which were administered
by a procurator and were not included in any city's territory. It is
doubtful if in Asia there were still self-governing temple-domains
and private estates not belonging to any city. There can be no
question, on the other hand, that temple-domains, private estates,
and villages enjoying a certain degree of local self-government did
exist within the cities' territories.

In contrast to Bithynia, where the lex Pompeia had introduced
a standard municipal constitution for all cities which retained
their independence, the Romans in Asia on the whole left unchanged the kaleidoscopic variety of the old city constitutions.
It is, however, justifiable to assume that the lex Cornelia secured
the retention by the propertied classes of decisive political power.
Thus the possession of a certain degree of wealth may well have
been a necessary qualification for the tenure of higher office and
for admission into the council. The fact that membership of the
council was for life must have conduced to the same end. The
constitution of the self-governing non-civic demes and villages
was either copied from the cities or else was evolved from old
native political organizations.

Although all self-governing districts in the province were co-
ordinated in the eyes of the Roman government, there were
nevertheless many differences between them, both actual and
nominal, the latter being no less fiercely resented and passionately

---

[1] Cassiodorus, *Chron.* ad annum urbis 670. The correctness of the number
is doubtful.

defended than the former. Strictly speaking, the free cities were wholly independent of the governor. The elder Pliny names twelve of these, but after his time their number was markedly reduced. In actual fact the freedom of these cities was not secure against encroachments on the part of Rome, nor was this necessarily accompanied by the remission of taxation, though such remission was recognized as an exceptionally valuable gift to subject cities. A special position was occupied by the only two colonies of Roman citizens in Asia: Parium and Alexandria Troas, both of which possessed the *ius Italicum* (p. 455). The privilege of being a capital with a *conventus iuridicus* was enjoyed at the beginning by nine cities only: Adramyttium, Pergamum, Smyrna, Sardes, Ephesus, Alabanda, Synnada, Apamea, and Laodicea on the Lycus, this list being later enlarged by the addition of Cyzicus, Philadelphia, and, from Caracalla's time, Thyatira. The three largest cities, Ephesus, Pergamum and Smyrna, were distinguished by the title 'first' ($\pi\rho\tilde{\omega}\tau\alpha\iota$). There were seven cities recognized as Metropoleis of the province: Sardes, Cyzicus, Tralles, and Laodicea on the Lycus, in addition to the three just mentioned. An honour eagerly coveted at first and bringing substantial material benefit was the possession of one or more of the provincial temples dedicated to the Emperor, the so-called *Neokoriai*, which were mentioned among the city-titles down to Christian times. The division of the provincial cities into Metropoleis, capitals holding assizes, and other cities, was of importance, since this classification was taken into consideration in the allocation of various privileges[1].

When the fourth book of the Sibylline oracles, composed under the Emperor Titus, makes Rome return in double measure all that she has robbed from Asia[2], this statement, if we disregard its propagandist aims and take it as referring to the province of Asia, appears to testify to the fact that the province which was so brutally plundered during the civil wars had, after a hundred years of government under the Empire, regained a prosperity surpassing her condition in pre-Roman times. This description would be still truer if applied to the developments of the next century, when the beneficent administration of the Antonines brought a still more flourishing export trade, and thus raised the standard of living to heights which were never subsequently reached again. Fortunately one of the most representative figures of this epoch, the rhetor Aristides, still speaks to us directly. Just as the ideal aims of the Roman world-empire are nowhere

[1] Dig. XXVII, 1, 6, 2.
[2] *Orac. Sibyll.* IV, 145 *sqq.*

better formulated than in Aristides' panegyric 'to Rome,' so no other passage of literature expresses more clearly the glory of Asia's development than the description of her three capitals, Pergamum, Smyrna, and Ephesus, in his speech on the concord of cities[1], or than his enthusiastic picture of Smyrna[2] and Cyzicus[3]. We should not, however, fully understand Aristides were it not that the wonderful ruins, which an extensive series of excavations has revealed, and the abundant archaeological evidence which has been collected by detailed work on journeys of exploration, have enabled us to reconstruct the appearance of a number of such cities, and have made progressively clearer the conditions of life prevailing in them.

It is not difficult to give the reasons leading to this economic revival and its happy effects. Compressing them into a sentence, we can say that now for the first time political conditions had arisen in the world at large which enabled the country and its people to develop their latent possibilities. The population was composed of many racial elements, but precisely for that reason could show a diversity of talent. The climate was particularly favourable. Geographical conditions were most propitious for the cultivation of corn, olives, and vines, and also for cattle-breeding. Together with an adequate amount of timber there were abundant outcrops of marble. In short, the territory of Asia, stretching as it did from the island world of the Aegean to the high plateau of central Asia Minor, was in itself a region of very great economic potentialities, and most favourable for an extensive commerce. Moreover, its geographical position in relation to world politics and its physical configuration alike made it resemble an open hand which the continent of Asia was stretching forward towards Europe and the Mediterranean world. All these advantages, however, could only have their full effect if the whole country was joined together to form a unity, if it was granted unhampered and peaceful progress, and if it took its place in an economic area comprising the whole Mediterranean world—conditions which were realized for the first, and, up to the present, the only time in the first centuries of the Roman Empire. It is nevertheless an amazing, though comprehensible, phenomenon that the impulse towards an increased economic output now pushed so quickly from the coastal cities up the broad river valleys to the mountainous interior, penetrating to its remotest fastnesses, and everywhere setting free a new energy. Soon the outcome of this fresh

[1] *Or.* XXIII K, 13 *sqq.*   [2] *Or.* XVII–XXI K.
[3] *Or.* XXVII K.

life flowed back to the coastal cities, which satisfied the demands
of the foreign market also, and in the highly lucrative rôle of
middlemen distributed the excess home production to the commercial centres of the Mediterranean, so developing into huge
cities with an intense commercial and intellectual activity[1]. The
great islands lying off the coast, which had no direct connection
with the hinterland, a fact which had often been to their advantage
in days gone by, now took second place: thus Rhodes ceased to
play a leading part as formerly in the affairs of the eastern Mediterranean. Her place was taken by Ephesus, the greatest market
west of the Taurus[2], and by the other cities in the coast region,
Cyzicus, Pergamum, Smyrna, and Miletus, while in the interior
at all favourably situated places regional capitals achieved an enhanced importance as centres of economic life and city civilization.
Such were Thyatira, Sardes, Tralles, Aphrodisias, Laodicea on the
Lycus, and many others. Not least among their number was
Apamea Cibotos, the eastern commercial counterpart to Ephesus[3],
situated where the route north and south from the Hellespont to
Pamphylia crosses the route east and west from the Aegean to
central Asia.

Of the material and spiritual life of Asia a few examples must
suffice. We have already indicated that the province combined a
vigorous and growing production of raw materials with manu-
facturing industries of high capacity, and hence was in the fortunate position of being a self-contained economic unit, a fact which
made for a more flourishing trade and a higher standard of living.
It is safe to say that the large demands of the population for
articles of food, clothing, and furniture, and also for oil, fuel, and
building-materials could be satisfied by the products of the land
itself, and that, quite apart from the output of marbles from
Phrygia, both agricultural produce, especially wine, oil, wool,
leather, and cattle, and also industrial manufactures, especially
textiles, could show production for export purposes markedly in
excess of local needs. The resultant profit was only in part used
for the purchase of necessary and useful articles, which could not
be furnished by the land itself (such as metalware); the remainder
served to raise the general standard of living, particularly in the
cities.

---

[1] On the other hand, as Pergamum, Smyrna and Ephesus rapidly grew,
some of the smaller old coast cities, *e.g.* Cyme, Phocaea, Erythrae, Teos,
fell still more into the background.

[2] Strabo xiv, 642.

[3] Strabo xiii, 577; Dio Chrys. *Or.* xxxv.

The economic advance was reflected in every branch of life. Physical culture enjoyed increased expenditure on gymnasiums and baths. Education became a course of study culminating in instruction by a sophist as recreator of the Greek spiritual ideals. Learning was supported by the foundation of museums at Smyrna and Ephesus, or by the endowment of medical schools at Pergamum and Ephesus. In religion we see the erection of splendid temples dedicated to the emperors, and the continued maintenance in the best condition of the great sanctuaries, such as the Artemision at Ephesus, or the Asklepieion at Pergamum, or the oracle of Claros, which now rises to the height of its reputation. In architecture the effects are: first, the excessively lavish decoration of the cities and their buildings with every kind of artistic adornment; secondly, the exaggeration of Greek forms into a baroque, among the most striking examples of which are the library at Ephesus[1], the Nymphaeum at Miletus[2], and the market-gate of the same city[3] now re-erected in Berlin; finally, the striving after an effect of vastness in the interiors, which results in an ever more grandiose style in the gymnasiums and thermae (p. 800).

It is a fascinating problem to determine the contribution of the Romans, the Greeks, and the native population, in the development we have been tracing, and in the conditions of life arising from it. There can be no doubt that in the Republican era Rome's contribution is to be entered almost wholly on the debit side of the account, since in spite of some exceptional instances, the province was then merely an object of exploitation for the Roman State and the Italian business-man. This was completely changed under the Empire. Although occasionally governors or procurator lapsed into the mentality of Republican times, and although a high taxation yield was demanded of the province as an important source of revenue for the Roman State, nevertheless, especially from the time of Trajan onwards, exploitation was replaced by a beneficent government, with the best interests of the province at heart. No historian of insight will maintain that Rome did all that was in her power for the well-being of her provinces. It would, however, be equally untrue to suppose that Rome merely created the conditions in world politics which were a necessary prerequisite to the advance we have described, but played no part in its accomplishment. It is only necessary to glance at the edicts and decrees issued by the Roman emperors and governors intended to secure an orderly system of government, administration

[1] *Jahreshefte* XI, 1908, p. 123.   [2] *Milet*, I, 5, pl. 63.
[3] *Milet*, I, 7, pl. xx.

of justice, and regulation of finance[1], to know that the Roman régime in this period did not merely adopt an attitude of *laissez-faire*, but had an active policy, pursued, on the whole, with the most happy results. The mass of epigraphic evidence in which the provincials, by no means always from servile motives or for purposes of flattery, attest their gratitude and confer honours upon the emperors and Roman officials, supports this conclusion. It is confirmed by Pliny's correspondence with Trajan, which, although concerned with Bithynia, has implications for all the provinces.

Side by side with the influence of Roman officialdom goes the effect produced by the Romans and Italians who from the province's earliest days had migrated into the country as soldiers, officials' assistants, business-men, and tax-farmers or their representatives, and had settled there. This Italian element is the core of the *conventus civium Romanorum* which we encounter everywhere; it is still clearly perceptible in the first century A.D.[2] but then quickly succumbs to hellenization. There can be no doubt that many Latin words, and also many Italian institutions (beast-baiting and gladiatorial games, for example), became naturalized in the province through this stratum in the population.

The Roman régime was based on self-government by the cities, in which we can recognize a Greek element. Though there may have been many differences in detail, yet on a general view the Greek city with its characteristic institutions and its ideal of life here knew a second flowering. Its rise was due to a prosperous, or at least comfortably off, bourgeoisie, which clung to this ideal for which it was ready to make heavy sacrifices, with an intense passion. The cities, especially the capitals, in their whole plan, with their sanctuaries and market-places, their stadiums, gymnasiums, and baths, their theatres, odeums, and lecture-rooms, their educational institutes, libraries, and residential clubs, their art treasures, public contests, and festivals, even their cemeteries and funerals, were designed to cater for the needs and the style of living of this citizen class. Yet it formed only a section of the population, and for this very reason behind all the splendour of city culture stood the spectre of the collapse which must ensue when this citizen class ceased to hold the decisive power. In our

---

[1] For a good recently restored example from the time of Claudius see F. K. Dörner, *Der Erlass des Statthalters von Asia Paullus Fabius Persicus.* Diss. Greifswald, 1935.

[2] *Forsch. in Ephesos*, iv, 1, nos. 16, 18, 20–23. C. Vibius Salutaris, known by a long boastful inscription brought from Ephesus, now in the British Museum (*ib.* ii, no. 27), belongs to this class.

period the danger is still kept at bay by the compact between the Roman government and the city *bourgeoisie*, under the terms of which Rome helps the propertied class in the cities to maintain its dominant position, and the wealthiest and most distinguished members of the class are given free access to the equestrian order and the Senate, and even to the highest official posts of the Empire[1]. Yet when, in the middle of the second century for example, Antoninus Pius sharply rebukes the Ephesians in a rescript, which has been preserved, for opposing the magnificent building activity of Vedius Antoninus, and preferring largesses and festivals[2], the historian can hear beneath such declarations the muttering of the oppressed masses who have no part in the splendour of city culture, but who are anxious how they are to earn their daily bread and long for pleasures of a kind they can appreciate.

The share of the indigenous element among the city and agricultural population in the life of the province is by far the most difficult to grasp; but it must nevertheless not be underestimated. It is among this stratum of the population that such of the native tribes' national tradition as survived is to be sought; these are the men who after the disappearance of the hellenized ruling class were to be the bearers of the new cultural development. It is well known that of the ancient Asiatic languages from this region none has survived in a literary work, and the Phrygian district alone has epigraphic evidence reaching down to our era. We may accordingly conclude that the native tongues in the coastal area, and far into the interior, were driven out by Greek, and were only spoken among the more remote localities in the mountains. But this disappearance of languages does not in the least imply an analogous change in the racial composition of the population, and the survival of personal names belonging to the various languages as well as the no less characteristic individuality of the monuments from the separate districts, shows that no such change actually occurred. It is, however, in religion that the importance of the native element in Asia Minor is most clearly revealed. We

---

[1] As an instance of these wealthy men and women, who played the first rôle in their cities and among the provincial aristocrats, may be mentioned the family of the Vedii at Ephesus (*Forsch. in Ephesos*, III, p. 166), famous, before all, for its magnificent buildings, which gave a new aspect to the city. The last heiress of the family's fortune, Vedia Phaedrina, married the celebrated and no less wealthy sophist Flavius Damianos, whose enormous possessions and public works for Ephesus are praised by Philostratus (*Vitae Soph.* II, 23) and have been already partly rediscovered together with his portrait-statue (*Jahreshefte*, XXVII, 1931, Beibl. cols. 40 *sqq.*).

[2] *Ditt.*[3] 850.

are still far from a full utilization even of the material already at our disposal, but the state of religion in Caria, Phrygia, and Lydia is by now very well known. The worship of the Divine Mother, a cult of great antiquity in Asia Minor, still survived in Lydia with surprising strength[1], and a religious jurisdiction, reaching back into immemorial antiquity, was actually practised in the village sanctuaries of Maeonia as late as the third century A.D.[2]

There can be no doubt that the widespread religious longing of the population was also an important influence in the triumph of Christianity, which acquired in Asia the impetus that assured its success. It would, however, be misguided to ignore the social and, generally, the intellectual forces, which, no less than the religious factors, were at work in this movement. The new teaching won greatest support among the lower classes of the city population, whether slaves or hired labourers, sailors, retail tradesmen, or artisans, who in the struggle for the bare necessities of life could have no real share in those cultural treasures to whose maintenance the policy of the official leaders of the State was directed. It would be mistaken to suggest that the city governments and the propertied classes did not realize the needs of the poor population or took no heed of them. Yet all that was done to secure for them a sufficiency of food, or bread at a low price, all the very significant expenditures which were privately or officially made in the interests of the community at large, could not do away with the sharp social contrast, and could not open to the oppressed masses the kingdom of Greek culture, that kingdom of which the sophists spoke in such enthusiastic tones, but which was, in reality, barred to all except a limited circle even among the propertied classes. Hence it was that the great majority of the population regarded the ideal of the *Polis* with estrangement, full of resentment towards the ruling class, which represented this ideal, and towards Rome, which frustrated all opposition to it, and full of longing for a new way of life more in keeping with its own wishes and thoughts. The existing religions could bring no real aid in this need, since the official cult was bound up with the city, and, through emperor-worship, which made difficult any deep religious feeling, with the Roman dominion. Then it was that the enthusiastic preachers of the new doctrine raised their voice, men who from the beginning turned with their gospel of salvation not to the upper, but expressly to the lower classes.

[1] *Anatolian Studies, presented to Sir W. M. Ramsay,* pp. 250 *sqq.*
[2] J. Zingerle, *Jahreshefte,* XXIII, 1926, Beibl. cols. 1 *sqq.*; cf. W. Schepelern, *Der Montanismus und die phrygischen Kulte,* pp. 79 *sqq.*

Their message proclaimed a high ideal of the brotherhood of all mankind without distinctions of birth or condition, and replaced the complicated intellectualism of hellenic culture, which was no longer intelligible to the man in the street, by a simpler and less pretentious interpretation of the world. Christianity thus won the cities first, while the country folk, who lived under more primitive conditions, clung more tenaciously to their traditional cults. This fact not only made the victory more easy, but was also not without effect on the form taken by Christian theology and ritual.

VII. LYCIA ET PAMPHYLIA

In the province of Lycia et Pamphylia, constituted by Vespasian in A.D. 74, three distinct regions, each with a separate geographical configuration, population, and history, were joined to form an administrative unit. These were the territory of the old Lycian league (with only slight alterations), the coastal strip of Pamphylia stretching from Phaselis to Syedra, and the Pisidian mountain area which surrounds this coastal strip on the north and at the same time links it with the inland plateau of Asia Minor. The experiment of Claudius should be regarded as a forerunner of Vespasian's province. In A.D. 43 Claudius put an end to the freedom of the Lycian league, which had formerly been spared, and joined its territory to the Pamphylian coastline which had come under Roman sway as early as 103 B.C. and was counted as part of Cilicia. This creation of Claudius lasted only a short time, however, as the Lycians regained their freedom, and Pamphylia was temporarily joined to Galatia. With the new limits imposed on the province by Vespasian it lasted until the reform of the Empire by Diocletian and Constantine, at first under a governor of praetorian rank, appointed by the Emperor as *legatus Augusti pro praetore*, assisted by the procurator of the province, subsequently as a senatorial province with a proconsul of praetorian rank as head of the administration, with a quaestor in charge of the finances. The province had at the beginning no permanent garrison; but under Marcus Aurelius a military diploma of A.D. 178[1] mentions the *Cohors I Flavia Numidarum*, 'quae est Lyciae Pamphyliae.'

The two parts of the province were linked solely by the fact that both governments had at their head the same official. In all other respects, however, each was fully independent, and here they must, accordingly, be dealt with separately.

[1] *C.I.L.* III, p. 1993, n. LXXVI; cf. Josephus, *Bell. Jud.* II [16, 4], 368; Tacitus, *Ann.* II, 81.

Internal dissensions were adduced as the reason why Claudius put an end to the freedom of the Lycians in 43, and Roman citizens appear to have been among those who lost their lives[1]. At that time Lycia was a federal State. Its constitution is described by Strabo[2], whose source is here Artemidorus. There were, he says, twenty-three cities comprising the league, divided into three classes in such a way that each of the largest cities had three votes each, of the moderate-sized two and each of the smallest one. In accordance with this formula they sent their representatives to the federal assembly (κοινὸν συνέδριον), which met in whatever city was chosen for each occasion. In the assembly first the Lyciarch, then the officials of the league, were elected, and arrangements were made for dispensing justice, each city receiving consideration in accordance with the number of its votes. Deliberations and resolutions followed concerning matters of common interest.

It is exceptionally interesting to observe that the Romans, when they converted Lycia into a province, left the old political organization of the country (of course under the governor's supervision) almost undisturbed, and so conceded to Lycia a measure of provincial self-government such as was not granted anywhere else. The executive bodies of this self-governing league are well known to us from an abundance of inscriptions. The federal assembly (κοινὴ ἐκκλησία) met each autumn in one of the provincial cities for the purpose of elections. It comprised, so far as we can see, the league officials, the members of the league council, and an unknown number of delegates chosen to vote at the elections (ἀρχοστάται), who were dispatched by the several cities, doubtless in accordance with some fixed formula. Besides holding the elections, this federal assembly passed resolutions concerning the granting of honours, embassies to the emperor and the governor, the apportionment of the taxation imposed on the league, financial expenditure on behalf of individual cities, and the religious affairs of the league, including the conduct of its sanctuaries, the celebration of festivals and sacrifices, and similar business. The league council (κοινὴ βουλή) had as its principal task to meet at an appointed time and place in order to deliberate beforehand as to the resolutions to be introduced at the federal assembly. No doubt it also held extraordinary meetings when

---

[1] Suetonius, *Claud.* 25; Dio LX, 17. It may be suspected that Roman business-men who arrogated rights not due to them were the real offenders.

[2] xiv, 665. G. Fougères, *De Lyciorum Communi*, Thèse Paris, 1898; cf. Kornemann, in P.W. *s.v.* κοινόν, Suppl. IV, cols. 927 *sqq.*

necessary. We have no information concerning its composition, but it may be suggested that it was made up of the league officials and a number of delegates drawn from the city councils. Among the federal officials the chosen representative of the league, the Lyciarch, ranked highest. Next to him came the priest of the emperor-worship, who had charge of the cult of all the emperors, and was not associated with any specific sanctuary (ἀρχιερεὺς τῶν Σεβαστῶν), and the priest of Apollo Patroos, the chief divinity of the nation. An inscription from Rhodiapolis[1] shows that the old organization of justice by the league remained in being, at least to some extent. The actual functioning of this instrument of federal self-government was secured by the fact that the cities which were members of the *Koinon* represented the whole country, and that each city had a similar constitution and was ruled by a social class with the same interests at heart.

We may assume that in Lycia, even before the formation of the province, the whole territory of the country was divided between the various cities, and we have no reason to think that this division was largely altered under Roman rule by the creation of extra-territorial Imperial or private domains. Among the cities a certain distinction of rank is to be observed, since the largest bear the title of Metropolis, the medium-sized exist as units, while the smallest are joined by *sympoliteia* to one of the regional capitals[2]. Within the city-territories there were certainly villages, also with a limited self-government, but it is nevertheless characteristic that few villages are mentioned in the many hundreds of Lycian inscriptions[3]. The constitution of the cities was standardized in so far as each had a popular assembly with the right of voting, and a council whose members (*Bouleutai*) held office for life. It is noteworthy, in this connection, that in Xanthus[4], and perhaps in other cities also, the official posts were divided into those open to any citizen and those reserved for the *Bouleutai*, and that in Sidyma[5], by permission of the governor, there existed a *Gerousia* comprising 101 members, 51 being *Bouleutai* and 50 *Demotai*. It is clear that the propertied families, from whom the *Bouleutai* were drawn, had the power in their hands not only in the several cities but in the country as a whole. Thus many inscriptions

---

[1] *I.G.R.R.* III, 736.

[2] See *e.g. I.G.R.R.* III, 646; 692.

[3] Heberdey-Kalinka, *Denkschr. Akad. Wien*, XLV, 1897, II, 69, belongs to the Cibyratis, *i.e.* not to Lycia properly so-called.

[4] *Tit. Asiae Min.* II, 301.

[5] *Ib.* 175. Among the 50 *Demotai* occur three freedmen and one πατρὸς ἀδήλου.

testify to the custom whereby a distinguished inhabitant of one city might simultaneously enjoy citizenship in a plurality of cities, or even in all the cities in the league, and in consequence might hold office and supply funds in these other cities, receiving in return honours and distinctions.

The policy of the Roman government towards this federal organization was limited to securing the revenues from taxation, and to exercising everywhere the ultimate power of control by making all elections and resolutions of the *Koinon* subject to confirmation by the governor. It goes without saying that the supreme judicial power of the province was vested in the governor, and this is confirmed by a series of inscriptions which expressly describe him as 'dispenser of justice' ($\delta\iota\kappa\alpha\iota o\delta\acute{o}\tau\eta s$). On the other hand, an inscription already referred to[1] shows that pre-Roman courts of justice survived into the second century A.D. Again, in another inscription[2] it is said of Opramoas from Rhodiapolis that in A.D. 125 as Archiphylax of the league he conscientiously and skilfully carried out the judicial responsibilities and governmental duties entrusted to him by the governor. There is little evidence in Lycia of that supervision of city finances by *curatores* sent out by the emperor, so necessary elsewhere. It is significant that in an inscription from Termessus near Oenoanda[3] the Lyciarch appears as auditor of the city's finances ($\lambda o\gamma\iota\sigma\tau\grave{\eta}s$ $\kappa\alpha\grave{\iota}$ $\tau\hat{\eta}s$ $\mathring{\eta}\mu\epsilon\tau\acute{\epsilon}\rho\alpha s$ $\pi\acute{o}\lambda\epsilon\omega s$). The granaries established by Hadrian at Patara and Andriaca were doubtless intended in the first instance to secure food for troops in transit, although the emperor could naturally draw on them also to supplement the province's resources in years of bad harvest. Antoninus Pius was most generous in his relief measures when in 144 the cities of Lycia were devastated by a terrible earthquake[4].

Lycia, a country wholly shut in by lofty mountain ranges, lay on no trade-routes of great importance, and was unhappy in its climate with its rapid fluctuations between extremes of temperature. On the other hand, it must be observed that the mountain slopes afforded much excellent timber for building houses and ships, and were also suitable for pasturage and, to some extent, for vineyards and olive-plantations. Moreover, scattered between the mountains were valley plains and table-lands, which furnished a high yield from the cultivation of corn. Finally, there was a considerable commercial intercourse between the interior and the coast cities, which for their part afforded welcome stopping-places

---

[1] *I.G.R.R.* iii, 736.   [2] *I.G.R.R.* iii, 739 iii, l. 91 and v, l. 30 *sq.*
[3] *I.G.R.R.* iii, 491.   [4] Pausanias viii, 43, 4.

for ships following the southern shore of Asia Minor. Thus Lycia, while lacking the conditions necessary for any startling economic development, had yet sufficient resources to support its not very numerous inhabitants. Its marked isolation from the outside world tended to promote the creation of a unified federal State, and in connection with the country's limited possibilities of expansion to favour the maintenance of a conservative organization of society.

The data we have mentioned reflect this development, which derives from the geographical character of the country. After becoming a part of the province of Lycia et Pamphylia, Lycia remains as it was before the days of Rome's supremacy, a self-contained unity, within which social conditions prevail that in many respects remind us of the old Greek aristocracies. It is surprising in this connection how closely the Lycian people copied Greek models in the most varied spheres of public and private life, although the contribution of the Greek immigrants to the racial mixture had not been strong. In the fourth century B.C. the Lycians had indeed substituted Greek script for their native alphabet, and subsequently, in the cities at any rate, Greek had displaced the native language. A still more significant fact is that in their political life, just like the Greeks, they achieved the full development of the *Polis*, and transcended this system in a federal organization reminiscent of the Aetolian and Achaean Leagues. Their architecture and sculpture were instinct with Greek artistic feeling, and they had an intense liking for every sort of contest whether physical or intellectual competition was involved[1]. The Epicurean philosophy found here a most enthusiastic follower[2], and the Lycian religion, in contrast to the cults of other countries in Asia Minor, contained very little that was strange, and much that was akin to Greek religion.

The *pax Romana* brought the land into closer contact with the outside world during the first and second centuries—a development which proved happy in its effects, but did not seriously affect the social foundations of life. It is not by chance that in Lycia we do not hear of social antagonisms or conflicts in these years, and that the abundant epigraphical evidence seldom makes allusion to a man's profession. On the other hand, there is an abundance of inscriptions concerning the propertied and wealthy citizens, preserved especially on the bases of the honorary statues or on the walls of the sumptuous and beautiful sepulchral buildings.

[1] *Tit. Asiae Min.* II, 25–27; *I.G.R.R.* III, 467.
[2] Diogenes of Oenoanda; cf. Philippson in P.W. *s.v.* Suppl. V, cols. 153 *sqq.*

These men, moved by an almost morbid ambition, strove to outdo one another in services, on behalf not only of their native cities but of many, or even all, the cities in the country, or on behalf of the *Koinon*. It was they who held office, built buildings, in times of bad harvests saw to the relief of the poor, organized the games, often actually shouldered the burden of the taxation and so on. Opramoas, who has been mentioned above (p. 593), about the middle of the second century commemorated on his Heroon in twenty long columns all his public services and the distinctions bestowed on him for them[1]. In the first half of the third century Licinnia Flavilla of Oenoanda immortalized the genealogy of her family in eight such columns on the family sepulchre[2]. These figures are remarkable less as individuals than as the representatives of a social class which stamped its character on the life of Lycia. We are justified in assuming that the greater part of the land was owned by members of this class, that the country population largely lived in patriarchal dependence on them, and that the leadership in city politics lay in their hands.

Jewish communities are attested for many cities in Lycia. For Christianity in the first two centuries reliable evidence is lacking, though something can be learnt from the *Acts of Paul and Thekla*.

The second part of the province, comprising Pamphylia and Pisidia, stands in sharpest contrast to the self-contained unity of Lycia. The joining, under Vespasian, of the two different parts, neither of which ever before achieved unity, was a somewhat arbitrary step. Moreover, it was taken so late that the usual provincial institutions never developed here. Although a Pamphyliarch is mentioned in several inscriptions[3], we hear next to nothing of the activities of a provincial assembly, and a unified organization of Caesar-worship was probably never attained. Moreover, a united upper class, the mainstay of the political and cultural life of the country, like that in Lycia, was wholly lacking[4]. There is, rather, a sharply differentiated individuality in the various cities and village settlements. The most fundamental of the innovations and reforms introduced by the Roman dominion was carried out by Augustus shortly after A.D. 6 when he established

[1] R. Heberdey, *Opramoas*; see *I.G.R.R.* III, 739.
[2] *I.G.R.R.* III, 500.
[3] *I.G.R.R.* III, 475. *Tit. Asiae Min.* III, 127 and 138.
[4] From *I.G.R.R.* III, 800–802, we learn that in Sillyum public gifts were distributed according to the following division of the populace: (1) βουλευταί, (2) γεραιοί, (3) ἐκκλησιασταί, (4) πολεῖται, (5) οὐινδικτάριοι (men freed in the life-time of their masters), (6) ἀπελεύθεροι, (7) πάροικοι.

five colonies of veterans in the Pisidian mountains with the aim of
finally pacifying this disturbed district (vol. x, p. 272). The three
colonies which were handed over to Lycia et Pamphylia at Vespasian's re-organization, namely Olbasa, Comama and Cremna, are
sharply marked off during our period by their Italo-Roman constitution and their use of Latin in official, and to some extent in
private documents, though they could make no permanent resistance to the hellenization imposed by their environment. We may
deduce from an inscription at Pogla[1] that part at least of the estate
formerly belonging to King Amyntas of Galatia was converted
into an Imperial domain.

The researches, organized under Austrian and later under
Italian leadership, into this country, with its abundance of ruined
sites, have brilliantly provided a detailed and brightly coloured
picture of the general conditions, and have revealed the clear-cut
individuality of the city and village settlements. We know the
character of the comfortable and prosperous cities of the Pamphylian coastal plain, such as Side, Attaleia, Perge, or Aspendus;
of the proud capitals of mountainous Pisidia, on their precipitous
crags, such as Termessus maior, Sagalassus, or Selge; of the
humble Lyrboton Kome[2] belonging to Perge, and equally well
of the small town Pednelissus[3] in its mountain fastness. The ruins
and monuments of all these sites are at one in attesting that the
first, and especially the second and early third, centuries were an
era in which city-life flourished as never before. When with the
pacification of the mountain tribes the exploitation of the latent
possibilities of the district began[4], it brought a natural increase
in the stream of trade flowing to the coast cities, which in their
turn were stimulated by the *pax Romana*. A good part of the
newly acquired capital was re-invested in the improvement of the
cities and their buildings. There resulted on the other hand a
widespread improvement in the means of livelihood for the poorer
classes, and on the other the high degree of civilization and culture
which is encountered even in remote mountain districts[5]. The
leaders in this development were doubtless the cities in the coastal

---

[1] *I.G.R.R.* III, 409.
[2] *Jahreshefte* XXIII, 1926, Beibl. cols. 93 *sqq.*; cf. A. M. Woodward in
Class. Rev. XLVI, 1932, p. 9.
[3] Paribeni-Moretti-Pace, *Annuario*, III, pp. 73 *sqq.*
[4] Strabo XII, 569 *sq.*
[5] A vivid and detailed picture of Termessus maior, based on the whole of
the available evidence, has recently been drawn by R. Heberdey in P.W. *s.v.*
Termessos (2) cols. 732 *sqq.*

area, which were of ancient Greek foundation or had been early hellenized, so that it is no cause for surprise if the culture of the country bears on the whole a Greek stamp, and the native element is pushed far into the background in all spheres, even in religious matters. The existence of a Jewish community is proved, up to the present, in Side only. Paul, the apostle of the people, visited Perge on his voyage from Cyprus to Pisidian Antioch, and then crossed the country from south to north, but as yet there is no evidence that Christianity gained a strong footing in the first two centuries.

VIII. GALATIA

The Imperial province of Galatia, which was brought into being in the year 25 B.C. (vol. x, p. 261), included not only Galatia proper (the home of the three Galatian tribes) but also regions which had from time immemorial been separate by virtue of the nationality of their inhabitants, Lycaonia, Pisidia, and Isauria, and its area was still further increased in 6 B.C. by the addition of the inland district of Paphlagonia, which bordered on the northern Galatian frontier. The territorial limits thus defined were temporarily still further expanded to the north-east, as, before the protection of the frontiers was definitely transferred to the province of Cappadocia (c. A.D. 110) the governor of Galatia was given control over Pontus Galaticus (2 B.C.), Pontus Polemoniacus (A.D. 64), Cappadocia and Armenia minor (c. A.D. 74). To the south, on the other hand, the province was permanently reduced in size by Vespasian who gave (in A.D. 74) the greater part of Pisidia to the newly-formed province of Lycia et Pamphylia, and by Antoninus Pius who added southern Lycaonia and Isauria to Cilicia. The mountainous region of Paphlagonia and Galatia, the central steppe, and the Taurus range impinging on it to the south, including the strip of land through which runs the Via Sebaste (by Egerdir and Beyshehr Geul), remained the established limits of the province of Galatia until the division of the Empire under Diocletian, which again called into being many of the old traditional frontiers.

The first and most pressing problem in the new province was to carry out the pacification of the bandit tribes in the mountainous area of Pisidia, Lycaonia, and Isauria, which the last Galatian king Amyntas had essayed in vain. It was solved by Augustus, who first broke the resistance of the Homanadenses and then made the district secure by founding five new colonies of veterans, in addition to the colony of Antioch in Pisidia, established soon after

25 B.C. The Via Sebaste, built in 6 B.C., provided an exceptionally important link between Apamea Cibotos, the great market at the eastern frontier of the province of Asia, and Iconium, thus connecting with the old military highway leading through the Taurus passes to Tarsus in Cilicia. After the province had been pacified, its organization was changed in accordance with the changes in its size. At first the government was entrusted to Imperial legates, generally of praetorian rank. These were replaced at the time of the great Galatian military commands[1] by consulars supported by two officers of praetorian rank in command of the two legions at the governor's disposal, and assisted in the administration of justice by a third legate of praetorian standing. With the permanent transference of the responsibility for frontier defence to the governor of Cappadocia the province lost its military importance though it retained a strategic significance as lying on the line of communication with the frontier. It was now defended by *auxilia*[2] only, and governed once more by a legate of praetorian rank whose seat was in the capital Ancyra. We are insufficiently informed concerning the organization of the financial administration. In addition to the procurator of the province, procurators of separate districts are mentioned, to whom the government of the Emperor's domains was no doubt principally entrusted. Such domains[3] were especially numerous in the central and southern parts of the province (in the vicinity of Laodicea Combusta and Antioch in Pisidia). Deriving in part from the extensive private estate of King Amyntas[4], in part, perhaps, from secularized temple property, they were governed in much the same way as the not very remote Imperial domains in the east of the province of Asia. Those on the steppes were chiefly used for cattle-breeding.

Soon after Galatia had been constituted a province, a temple was dedicated at Ancyra to Rome and Augustus, which has subsequently become world-famous, for on its walls were carved the Latin text and Greek translation of the *Res Gestae* of Augustus. On the left-hand *anta* of the same temple is preserved a list of benefactions made in the time of Tiberius[5] which shows that

---

[1] E. Ritterling, *Jahreshefte* x, 1907, pp. 299 *sqq.*

[2] W. M. Ramsay and A. M. Ramsay, *J.R.S.* XVIII, 1929, pp. 181 *sqq.*

[3] W. M. Calder, *Mon. Asiae Min. Ant.* I, p. xiii; E. Kornemann, P.W. *s.v.* Domänen Suppl. IV, col. 247.

[4] Strabo XII, 568; Cicero, *pro rege Deiotaro*, 9, 27.

[5] *O.G.I.S.* 533; M. Rostovtzeff, *Mél. Boissier*, pp. 419 *sqq.*; F. Stähelin, *Gesch. der Kleinasiatischen Galater*, p. 101, n. 3 and 102; a new emended edition by M. Schede in Krencker-Schede, *Der Tempel in Ankyra*, pp. 52 *sqq.*

the cult, in its early days at any rate, was less the concern of the province as a whole than of the three Galatian tribes, and that these quarrelled over the matter so that the Trocmi completely withdrew for a time. Later the chief priests of the Emperor-cult, appointed annually, and the organizers of the yearly festival and games, appear as functionaries of the *Koinon* of the Galatians which is mentioned on coins struck under Nero. It is not certainly known how the *Koinon* was organized[1], to what extent representatives from the different parts of the province had a share in its proceedings, and how such representatives were appointed. After Ancyra, the capital of the Tectosages, which was raised to the position of principal city in the province, Pessinus, the centre of the Tolistoagii, ranks second, famous for its old Anatolian sanctuary of the Great Mother of the Gods, taken over by the Phrygians at an early date, in whose hierarchy it is significant that the Galatians could only obtain the sixth to tenth position after the high priest[2]. Compared with Ancyra and Pessinus, Tavium, the capital of the Trocmi, for all its importance as a centre of converging trade-routes, and despite the fertility of its environs, lagged behind. Here Zeus Tavianos was worshipped at a sanctuary possessing the right of asylum: the bronze statue of his cult is mentioned by Strabo[3], and appears upon the city's coinage. Whether political motives lay behind the foundation by Augustus of Germe, the only colony of Roman citizens on the soil of Galatia proper, is uncertain. He may merely have wished to utilize a royal estate which was at his disposal, and which originally, perhaps, belonged to the sanctuary of Pessinus.

Paphlagonia had its traditional centre at Gangra, and this was the residence of its last rulers. Here in the year 3 B.C., three years after the Roman occupation, the people of Paphlagonia and the Romans who had settled in the land swore an oath of allegiance to Augustus, the exact wording of which has been preserved for us in an inscription[4]. In the second century A.D. the city of Pompeiopolis in the remote north also designated herself Metropolis of Paphlagonia. A separate *Koinon* of Paphlagonia is not yet attested.

Similarly in Lycaonia, the district bordering on Galatia to the south, it is not until after the reign of Antoninus Pius that we first encounter such a *Koinon*. It is confined to those cities which

---

[1] For an attractive reconstruction of the history of the *Koinon* see Sir W. M. Ramsay, *J.R.S.* XII, 1922, pp. 154 *sqq.*
[2] *O.G.I.S.* 540 *sq.*; cf. Strabo XIII, 567.
[3] XII, 567.   [4] *O.G.I.S.* 532; *Studia Pontica*, III, 1, no. 66.

can be shown to have been added by that emperor to Cilicia, where they formed a separate group in the provincial assembly. The capital city of the *Koinon*, according to the numismatic evidence, was Laranda. Among the Lycaonian cities which remained in Galatia the following are especially important and merit mention here: Laodicea Combusta, with its abundant epigraphical remains, and its significance as a centre for the administration of the emperor's domains[1]; Iconium, already in Strabo's time a populous city in a fertile territory, patronized by Claudius, and raised by Hadrian to be a colony; finally, the colony of veterans settled by Augustus at Lystra. Less important, though not without an enduring vitality of their own, were the cities in the neighbourhood of Lake Trogitis and Lake Caralis—Pappa-Tiberiopolis, Misthia, Vasada and Amblada.

The name Isauria was used within the province of Galatia in a limited sense referring only to a small part of the Taurus slopes facing towards Lycaonia, together with the two cities Old Isaura and New Isaura. It regained, however, something of its earlier wider application when this region was allotted to Cilicia by Antoninus Pius: it was evidently joined to a part of the former Cilicia Tracheia, and, like Lycaonia, constituted a special part of that province.

An exceptionally important part of Galatia was the narrow strip of land between the Taurus district of Pisidia, and the mountain range of the Sultan Dagh, which makes communication with Apamea Cibotos possible. Here lay the city of Apollonia, which prided itself on being a colony of Lycians and Thracians, and which now attained to a new prosperity. Above all, here was situated the 'splendid Metropolis' Antioch, which Augustus founded as the first and largest of the Pisidian colonies, bestowing upon it rich estates formerly belonging to a famous sanctuary of Mēn; now it rose to wealth and power. Both these cities, like Ancyra, had the *Res Gestae* of Augustus, to whom they owed their new foundation, recorded and publicly displayed in his honour[2]. The Augustan colony of veterans at Parlaïs was probably situated in the same region.

This brief survey shows that the central plateau of Asia Minor, where the Romans created an artificial unity in the province of Galatia, displayed a colourful variety of very different countries

[1] W. M. Calder, *Mon. Asiae Min. Ant.* I, pp. xiv *sqq.*
[2] 'Monumentum Antiochenum': von Premerstein und Ramsay, *Klio*, Beih. 19 (1927); 'Monumentum Apolloniense': Buckler-Calder-Guthrie, *Mon. Asiae Min. Ant.* IV, pp. 49 *sqq.* no. 143.

and peoples; that here at the beginning of the Roman supremacy a close network of cities with a common culture based on Greek standards was still lacking; and that the development which ensued was very strongly influenced by the policy of the Roman government[1]. In the Hellenistic age a ruling upper class was imposed on the old national groups through the advent of the Celtic Galatians from Europe. In the sphere of religion the Galatians, as we can clearly see in the case of Pessinus, widely assimilated the native religious cults[2]. Yet they retained the language which they brought with them down to the fifth century A.D., and a like conservatism led them to preserve their political institutions, in which the tribe rather than the *Polis* was the basis of organization, their family jurisdiction with its strong emphasis on a Celtic *patria potestas*, and their custom whereby the princes and nobles dispensed a lavish hospitality to the people. The Romans found them loyal subjects, whose warlike temperament made them especially suitable for service in the legions or in *auxilia*[3]. At quite an early date cadets of the ancient princely houses or aristocratic families began to embark with comparative frequency on an official career in the Empire, and actually attained to high positions of command in the West[4].

Among the Galatians it was not until the second century A.D. that the capitals of the three tribes, which Strabo[5] describes as *phrouria*, first became cities in the Greek sense of the word. Similarly in the inland region of Paphlagonia the foundation of cities was consequent on the establishment of the Roman dominion. It was otherwise in the southern part of the province. Here even before the Roman occupation of that area there existed several cities of much the same kind as those in Pisidia. As the Romans, however, did all in their power to encourage the development of these cities, raised a number of other settlements to the status of cities on the Greek model, and founded a whole series of veterans' colonies with a strong Italian element in their population, they gave an exceptional impetus to the development of the

---

[1] The aims of Roman policy in Galatia are expounded by Ramsay, *J.R.S.* XII, 1922, pp. 147 *sqq.*; cf. *St Paul the Traveller*, xv, pp. 130 *sqq.*

[2] A single Celtic god, Ζεὺς Βουσσουρίγιος, seems to be attested by inscriptions of the province; J. G. C. Anderson, *J.H.S.* xxx, 1910, p. 164 *sq.* nos. 1 and 2; cf. Dessau, III, 2, p. clxxxii *sq.* (*ad* 4621).

[3] H. Dessau, *Gesch. d. röm. Kaiserzeit*, II, 2, pp. 246 *sq.*; E. Ritterling in P.W. *s.v.* Legio, col. 1791.

[4] C. S. Walton, *J.R.S.* xix, 1929, p. 56 *sq.*; A. von Premerstein, *Sitz. d. bay. Akad.* 1934, p. 46 *sq.*; E. Groag in E. Ritterling, *Fasti des röm. Deutschland*, p. 68. [5] XII, 567.

land and its economic resources. The use of Greek as the written and spoken language of the educated classes, which slowly but surely won the day in these cities, including the colonies, did not indeed convert them into truly Hellenic cities, but did give them a veneer of common culture sufficient to bridge the differences of nationality—and this was the goal of Imperial policy. It would, however, be a mistake, in making an historical study of the province, to examine only the overwhelming evidence for this uniformity of civilization and in consequence to neglect the other group of witnesses to the stubborn persistence of traditional native culture and custom, especially among the peasant population, which was less exposed to foreign influence.

In the early annals of Christianity also Galatia played an important part. The cities in the south of the province along the great road leading from Cilicia to Apamea Cibotos contained since the Seleucid period Jewish communities which were doubtless in communication with the Jews of Tarsus. Here Paul preached on three missionary journeys and won great successes despite intense opposition by orthodox Jewry. He founded a number of communities which were of decisive importance in the subsequent spread of Christianity in this district. After the Acts of the Apostles there is silence until nearly the end of the second century. At about that date the *Acts of Paul and Thekla* were written which, though fictitious, give an illuminating picture of the conditions that prevailed at the time of their composition.

IX. CILICIA

The province of greater Cilicia created by Pompey after his victory over the pirates and the disappearance of the Seleucid kingdom, embraced nearly the whole of southern Asia Minor, stretching roughly from the Salbacus range to the boundaries of Syria and including after 58 B.C. also the island of Cyprus. It was, however, not of long duration. While the eastern plain part of Cilicia proper (Cilicia Campestris) was joined to Syria, the mountainous western part (Cilicia Aspera), after a short-lived domination of Cleopatra and of King Amyntas, was handed over in 25 B.C. to King Archelaus of Cappadocia, who built himself a residence on an island near Elaeussa between Seleuceia on the Calycadnus and Soli-Pompeiopolis. On his death and the annexation of Cappadocia in A.D. 17 the Cilician kingdom alone remained to his son, until in 38 or 41 either Gaius or Claudius gave it to Antiochus IV of Commagene, who was restored to power. This monarch, as co-regent with his sister and wife Iotape, maintained a vigorous administration conducive to the progressive development of the country until A.D. 72, in which year he was dethroned by Vespasian (p. 139)[1]. At about the same time the client-state of Olba was abolished. The last ruler of Olba seems to have been Polemo II of Pontus who in A.D. 41 was compensated for the loss of his Bosporan kingdom by this territory, to which he may well have withdrawn completely on the appropriation of his Pontic kingdom in A.D. 64–5[2]. We may presume that Vespasian did away with this client-state also and raised the Olbian sanctuary, at this occasion, to the status of an independent city under the name of Diocaesarea[3]. The third client-state on Cilician territory, the kingdom of Tarcondimotus in the district of Amanus, with its capital Hieropolis-Castabala, also disappeared, perhaps even at an earlier date. We do not know whether it was joined at first to Commagene or added to the province of Cilicia immediately. The supervision over all these client-states, as long as they existed, was, in the first instance, the duty of the Imperial governor of Syria[4].

After Vespasian, by reuniting Cilicia Campestris and Aspera, restored an independent province of Cilicia[5], its limits were once more materially expanded, when under Antoninus Pius, southern Lycaonia and Isauria, which had previously belonged to Galatia, were incorporated.

At the head of the province stood Imperial legates, a number of whom are known to us. The governor had no legion at his disposal. The provincials had to pay a poll-tax, assessed at one per cent. of their properties' capital value[6]. By virtue of their military proficiency many inhabitants of the mountainous areas of Cilicia Aspera were attracted to enlist in the Roman army, as is shown by the numerous inscriptions and stone reliefs portraying warriors[7].

The provincial assembly, at whose head stood the Cilicarch, met at Tarsus, a city with the rights of autonomy, and originally the only Metropolis of the province, which after the addition of

---

[1] It is possible that a part of Antiochus' Cilician territory was restored by Vespasian to his daughter Iotape and her husband Alexander; see Josephus, *Ant.* XVIII [5, 4], 139 *sq.*; cf. A. Wilhelm, *Arch.-epigr. Mitt.* XVII, p. 389.

[2] See above, vol. X, p. 774, n. 1.

[3] *Mon. Asiae Min. Ant.* III, p. 44 and p. 71, no. 73.

[4] Tacitus, *Ann.* VI, 41; XII, 55.

[5] G. A. Harrer, *Studies in the hist. of the Roman province of Syria*, Diss. Princeton, 1915, pp. 72 *sq.*; cf. *Jahreshefte* XVIII, 1915, Beibl. col. 57.

[6] Appian, *Syr.* 50; cf. Tacitus, *Ann.* VI, 41.

[7] *Mon. Asiae Min. Ant.* III, p. 97, no. 108; p. 98, no. 111; p. 99 and 118, etc.

southern Lycaonia and Isauria styled herself 'capital of the three provinces' (προκαθεζομένη τῶν γ' ἐπαρχειῶν), and from Commodus' time 'guardian of two temples of the Emperors.' Later Tarsus found a keen rival in the city Anazarbus, which claimed almost the same titles, won the privilege that meetings of the assembly should be held within its walls, and actually ranked before Tarsus in possessing the honour of freedom. Next to these two Metropoleis are ranked Mopsuestia[1] and other cities enjoying the rights of freedom, autonomy, *asylia*, and the like.

Any attempt at describing the development of the province of Cilicia under the Empire must take account of the fact, which immediately forces itself upon the notice of any historically-minded visitor, that this country does not belong to the Aegean circle of culture, but looks towards Syria. In this connection, however, we must not forget that Cilicia is composed of two parts with marked geographical and ethnographical divergences. There is first the rugged mountainous area of Cilicia Aspera with its deficiency of surface soil, and, to some extent, also of water, its population fused into a unity by language, tradition, and the same hard conditions of life, and free from sharp social distinctions. Second come the broad and exceptionally fertile plains of Cilicia Campestris, in which a medley of peoples, with marked social disparities, is herded together in populous cities. To both these regions Roman dominion, and the settled conditions which it imposed everywhere, brought unparalleled prosperity, in which the chief feature was that the civilization which had formerly been largely confined to the coast cities now had an increasingly stimulating effect on the interior. All other cities in Cilicia Aspera, whatever their architectural beauties, paled into insignificance by comparison with Seleuceia on the Calycadnus[2], the proud foundations of the first Seleucus. From the beginning, Seleuceia grasped the nature of her mission as a spreader of culture, and she had an advanced outpost and ally farther inland in the priestly state of Olba. The best evidence for her further development under the Empire and also for her increasedly awakening and fertilizing influence on the interior, is to be found in the surprisingly large number of splendid funeral monuments which are still standing in the mountainous district to the north of the city, a district now almost deserted by man because of shortage of water, but at that

---

[1] This city enjoyed the title of ἱερὰ ἐλευθέρα ἄσυλος αὐτόνομος φίλη καὶ σύμμαχος Ῥωμαίων; I.G.R.R. III, 915.

[2] *Mon. Asiae Min. Ant.* III, pp. 3 sqq.; cf. V. Schultze, *Altchristliche Städte und Landschaften*, II, 2, pp. 223 sqq.

time studded with flourishing villages and settlements of an urban character[1]. A number of new cities and a colony were founded in this period; road-systems were laid out in this otherwise almost impassable country; most important of all, the building of a splendid series of aqueducts and reservoirs made it possible for the land to support a greatly increased number of men and beasts.

Tarsus occupied a corresponding position in Cilicia Campestris to that of Seleuceia in Cilicia Aspera. Strabo[2], in about A.D. 19, and Dio of Prusa[3], in about 110, are moved to enthusiasm in depicting the high intellectual and cultural standards no less than the economic prosperity of this city, which was especially favoured by Augustus. This evidence is supported and confirmed by the almost unparalleled richness of the city's coinage. Small wonder that such a rapid advance provoked the envy and hatred of her neighbours, particularly the old coastal cities of Mallus and Aegaeae, now sinking more and more into the background, and that among the city populace, swollen by many newcomers, political and social antagonisms began to appear, just as they did in the Bithynian cities, and led to the intervention of the governor, and so, at times, to strained relationships between the city and the Roman government. From the second century onwards, however, the capital of the upper Cilician plain called Anazarbus rapidly grew in importance and began to challenge Tarsus' supremacy —a sign of the steady penetration of culture into the interior of the country.

In the Cilician religion there is an unmistakable native element in which the subterranean powers, worshipped in sacred grottos, and also Helios and Selene, with far-famed country sanctuaries, are prominent. On this stratum were superimposed strong, and, in part, very old Greek and Syrian influences, with an occasional contribution from Rome. By winning adherents among the numerous Jewish communities Christianity spread rapidly in Cilicia, as the Acts of the Apostles[4] show, but we have no trustworthy information as to its progress in the first two centuries.

[1] *Mon. Asiae Min. Ant.* III, pp. 23–43.
[2] XIV, 672–4.   [3] *Or.* XXXIII and XXXIV.
[4] XV, 23 and 41; cf. Gal. i, 21.

CHAPTER XV

THE FRONTIER PROVINCES OF THE EAST

I. CAPPADOCIA. LESSER ARMENIA. COMMAGENE

PERHAPS no country in the Roman Empire was more isolated by nature and more cut off from the great centres of ancient culture than the provinces of Cappadocia and Lesser Armenia in the eastern part of the Anatolian plateau. In the north three chains of mountains parallel with the coast, and separated by the double moat of the Iris and the Lycus, formed a kind of triple rampart making communication difficult between the high bastion and the Black Sea. The impassable forests of the extensive mountain-ridges of Pontus were still in the second century A.D. held by savage tribes which Rome had left under the rule of native chiefs. In the south, the massive wall of the Taurus, through which the Euphrates, the Pyramus and the Sarus forced their way in narrow gorges, with the tracks across it unusable for the whole of the winter, all but denied Cappadocia access to the Mediterranean. The easiest pass, the famous Cilician Gates, which was the route of every army, came out at the extreme western frontier of the province. Between it and the Aegean lay the Lycaonian desert and half the length of the whole peninsula of Anatolia. In the east, on the other hand, beyond the Euphrates, rose the maze of snow-clad mountains of Armenia proper, that almost impregnable fortress which dominated the Black Sea, Mesopotamia and Media alike. It is not surprising that a district so difficult to reach and almost set apart from the Mediterranean world did not see the development of any very active commerce, or that it long retained the forms of its old Asiatic civilization which were elsewhere forsaken.

Cappadocia was Iran on a small scale. The continental climate of its high plateau, where, except in the neighbourhood of Mt Argaeus, the rainfall is slight, was subject to violent changes and resembled the climate of Media; in both countries extensive pastures favoured the rearing of horses. The Hittites had in the past owed many of their military successes to the excellence of their cavalry, skilfully trained according to rules laid down in treatises on horsemanship (vol. II, chap. XI). Under the Achaemenid dynasty Cappadocia, like Armenia and Pontus, attracted

Persian settlers. The estates of the old aristocracy fell to the conquering race, and a landed nobility of Iranian stock lorded it over the native population reduced to serfdom. These lords or 'satraps,' hereditary chiefs of their clans, seized or built strong castles with deep slanting tunnels for the supply of water, and they were the real masters of the land, their power in the Hellenistic period severely limiting that of the kings.

This feudal organization was supplemented by that of the ecclesiastical domains. The high priests of the old national shrines, such as Comana or Venasa, cultivated enormous tracts of sacred land and had authority over thousands of temple slaves. But by the side of the native priests were settled many Iranian Magi, or, to give them the Semitic name by which they were known, Magusaeans (μαγουσαῖοι), who were to keep their traditional rites faithfully until the Byzantine era. The most important temple of the Persian gods was at Zela in Pontus, but the 'fire-kindlers' (πύραιθοι) had lit their altars in large sacred enclosures all over Cappadocia, on which they had imposed the Mazdaean calendar, and the religious ideas of Zoroastrianism strongly influenced the native cults (p. 612).

At the same time the language used, or, at all events, the language written by the Iranian settlers of Asia Minor was not their old Aryan speech but Aramaic, a Semitic dialect, which was employed, since before the Great Kings, for diplomatic and business purposes in all countries west of the Tigris. Semitic influence was very old in these parts: as early as the third millennium Assyrian traders had founded busy guilds there. Throughout the Hellenistic period Aramaic remained the literary language of the aristocracy in Cappadocia and probably the liturgical language of worship. From the Taurus to Armenia the people continued to speak their Cappadocian dialect but as a vulgar *patois*.

However, after Alexander, the Hellenism which was so strong on the coast of Pontus (vol. IX, p. 212) began to make itself felt at the court of the Cappadocian rulers. From the time of Ariaramnes (third century) Greek replaces Aramaic on the royal coinage. Two towns, both named Eusebeia, Mazaca (Caesarea) and Tyana, were founded in a district hitherto cityless by one of the kings Ariarathes who bore the surname Eusebes, probably Ariarathes V (163–130 B.C.), the friend of philosophers[1]. He had the former of these towns, the Eusebeia near Mt Argaeus, governed by the ancient Greek laws of Charondas[2] interpreted by a *nomodos*, but as a royal

[1] Diodorus XXXI, 19, 7. See also vol. IX, p. 235.
[2] See vol. IV, p. 355 *sq.*

residence it could not be surrounded by a wall for fear of rebellion, and it was placed under an official acting for the king. On the other hand the old Hittite settlement of Kaniš, a little to the north, was named Anisa and granted a municipal constitution with Greek temples and festivals; but the town soon disappeared. It was only a princely caprice, and Hellenism planted thus artificially did not take firm root in the east of Anatolia. Greek no more became the language of the country than the French spoken at the court of Catherine II became that of Russia. Bilingual inscriptions, which enable us to see Greek and Aramaic in competition, prove that the latter did not drop out of use until the Empire.

The civilization of the small kingdom of Commagene, sandwiched between the Euphrates and the Taurus, was similar. It was ruled by a dynasty which traced its descent both from Darius, son of Hystaspes, and from the Seleucids, and which fostered the traditions of this double pedigree. The official religion was a hellenized Mazdaism, as is shown by the monumental sculptured tomb which Antiochus I (64–38 B.C.) set up on the Nimrud-Dagh, a spur of the Taurus. The funeral worship that he established combined Persian ritual, handed down from legendary forefathers, with Greek practice, just as the names of Avestian deities were associated with those of the gods of Olympus. The religion of the Magi modified no less the worship of the sky-god of Doliche, who later under the name of Juppiter Dolichenus was to be venerated as far as the camps and cities of the West (p. 613). But the great majority of the population remained true to its old customs and beliefs just as it continued to speak its old Anatolian or Semitic dialects. Lucian, who was born at Samosata, the capital of the country, knew only Syriac in his childhood.

Such then was the position when the Romans took possession of this country. In A.D. 18 Tiberius annexed Cappadocia in order to be able to assert himself more effectively against Armenia, which was ruled by a Parthian prince (vol. x, p. 745). This poverty-stricken province, without permanent garrisons, was at first governed simply by a procurator. But in 72 Vespasian also annexed Commagene, which was placed under the legate of Syria, and Lesser Armenia, which had been governed by Aristobulus (p. 139). Thus the Roman frontier was extended, as in Syria, as far as the upper waters of the Euphrates, and, farther north, where the river was too narrow to provide an adequate defence, it had the protection of the high mountains of the Pontic chain, where the passes are blocked by snow during the winter. The reason for the suppression of those three petty client kingdoms was thus primarily military, whether for the purposes of defence or offence against Armenia and the Parthians and they were strongly garrisoned (p. 140). Of especial importance, as has already been pointed out (p. 141), was the making of roads under the Flavians after the campaign of Corbulo had shown the difficulty of supplying food to armies in Armenia. These emperors placed under the same government not only Galatia and Cappadocia but most of the adjoining provinces of the Anatolian peninsula, and undertook the construction of great strategic roads to link up the coast of the Aegean and the Propontis with the far eastern frontier, and especially to facilitate transport across Asia Minor and the movements of troops and convoys from the camps on the Danube. In its effects this vast work of military engineering is in some degree comparable with the transcontinental railways of the nineteenth century. The Antonines had only to complete this road system, which in Cappadocia received its final elaboration from the Severi.

The security and speed of communication thus brought about explains the overwhelming success of the expedition of Trajan against Armenia. The creation of a new province with this name, surrounded by small satellite kingdoms, meant the Empire's furthest extension towards the Caucasus at the time when it was reaching towards the Persian Gulf (p. 617). But here the prudence of Hadrian abandoned conquests which would be difficult to control and to defend (p. 301). Armenia proper was given up, and Cappadocia, which Trajan had separated from Galatia, was placed under a consular legate, whose authority included also Lesser Armenia, Galatia Pontus and Pontus Polemoniacus together with the fortresses on the coast, which ran as far as Dioscurias (Sebastopolis) at the foot of the Caucasus.

The improvement in the communications of a district which had hitherto not been easy to reach brought new life to it, and the presence of numerous garrisons in the midst of a people whose way of life was very primitive, naturally spelt prosperity and progress. Corn from South Russia was probably brought by way of the ports on the Black Sea as far as the encampments on the Euphrates. Caesarea, where the emperors minted coins, enjoyed a flourishing trade and carried on business with Amisus and Sinope in the north and received goods from the south by the route through the Cilician Gates and Tyana. Cappadocia was certainly never a country with a large trade nor of great wealth. Except for a few more favoured districts, like Melitene, where the olive and vine grew, the bare soil was poor in fruit-trees. In barren ground and under an unfriendly sky corn did not grow well and enormous steppes were left as pasture for the rearing of cattle and especially of horses (p. 606). The studs of Cappadocia, which the emperors inherited from the kings of the past, kept their renown until the end of antiquity. Its quarries yielded rock-crystal, onyx, *miltos* (red lead or cinnabar); possibly mines in the neighbourhood produced the silver that was coined at Caesarea (vol. x, p. 746). But the chief article of export after horses was slaves. A hard climate had formed a dull-witted but sturdy peasantry, and the landed proprietors made money by the sale of the children of their serfs, who were conveyed by slave-traders to Rome, just as in recent times Turkish beys trafficked there in the daughters of their tenants who went to fill the harems of Istambul.

On the southern slopes of the Taurus the winter was less severe and rainfall more plentiful. In spite of its altitude, Commagene, which was amply watered by streams from the mountains, was a 'very rich' country if we may trust Strabo[1], and its immense forests supplied abundant timber, which, as in modern times, could be floated down the Euphrates to the countries down stream which had none.

Cappadocia was not, like the civilized provinces of the Empire, made up of a collection of city-states; its population, which was almost entirely rural, was divided under the kings into ten 'areas of command' or prefectures ($\sigma\tau\rho\alpha\tau\eta\gamma\iota\alpha\iota$) which the Romans maintained, and, as before the annexation, it continued to be subject to the landed aristocracy or to the temple-priests. The chief difference was that the royal estates passed to Tiberius and his successors and formed imperial domains, administered by agents of the Caesars, who became the most important land-owners in the country, and that, instead of being governed by weak princes, the landed nobility had to obey first a procurator, then a legate, who had at their backs troops to enforce their orders. But here, as everywhere, the gradual urbanization which marks this period of history changed political and social conditions, though less rapidly than elsewhere. To the two settlements enjoying municipal franchise which existed at the time of the annexation, the capital Caesarea and Tyana, others were added from time to time. Archelaïs, a foundation of the last king, became a colony under Claudius; Comana or Hieropolis, like other market-towns which grew up near frequented temples, freed itself from ecclesiastical control and obtained a communal charter at least by the time of Vespasian. As on all the frontiers the *canabae* which sprang up round the camps developed into cities;

[1] xvi, 749.

Melitene became a *municipium* under Trajan. Similarly in Lesser Armenia, the military town of Satala took its place by the side of Pompey's foundation Nicopolis; so, too, of the *quattuor civitates*[1] in Commagene—Samosata, Perrhe, Germaniceia, and Doliche—, Doliche owed the grant of a privileged political status to the existence of an important shrine, while Samosata owed it to the existence of a legionary camp. The same process went on under the Antonines—the village of Halala, where the wife of Marcus Aurelius died, became Faustinopolis—and it continued under the Severi. In the Christian age the east of Asia Minor hardly fell behind the rest of the Empire in the number of its cities and bishoprics.

On these strongly held frontiers, the Latin of the army naturally spread in the neighbourhood of the garrisons. As the traveller approaches the frontier of the Euphrates, he sees an increasing number of Latin inscriptions. It may, too, have been in official use in military foundations like Satala and Melitene. But it extended very little beyond the border districts. Elsewhere the cities were Greek in civilization, and each new city lit a new hearth of Hellenism. Thus Rome continued the work begun by the kings. Aramaic disappeared quickly as a literary language. The native dialects were not driven out and we have proof of their continued existence until the close of antiquity. The people continued to speak Cappadocian, or, farther to the east, Armenian, but these forms of speech, which were not used in writing, were looked down upon as barbarous jargon.

All culture became Greek, though the low-bred pronunciation of the Cappadocians kept a strong accent of the soil. Although Lucian asserts that it is harder to find a reputable orator in Cappadocia than a white crow, examples could be quoted as early as Augustus[2]. The Muses were cultivated as far as Lesser Armenia, and we possess the metrical epitaph of a doctor-poet who was born at Nicopolis, and whose ashes were brought back to his native land[3]. This part of Asia Minor is an area which Hellenism snatched from Iranism, which successfully resisted it beyond the Euphrates. It is characteristic that the Church, which was democratic in spite of its hierarchy, because it addressed itself to the people, brought no new life to the common tongue here as in Armenia proper or Syria. The great Cappadocian bishops of the

[1] Dessau 7204.
[2] Lucian, *Epigr.* 32 = *Anth. Pal.* xi, 436. Cf. Glaucippus Cappadox, P.W. Supp. iii *s.v.*
[3] *S.E.G.* vi, 798.

fourth century, the Basils and the Gregorys, preach to their flocks and write to their correspondents in Greek.

Religion, like all the civilization of the country, was composite in character and its stratification can be detected. Its primitive foundation was very much older than the Persian conquest, and went back to the Hittites and even further. The cult of the mountain, which was widespread through the Nearer East, had remained strong. The veneration in which the volcanic cone of Mt Argaeus, the highest peak in Asia Minor, was held is attested by the coinage of Caesarea. The great native divinity, Ma, was the goddess of Mother Earth, whose fertility was aided by temple prostitution. She was also the mistress of the wild animals of the forest, for whom she assured progeny, and hinds were sacrificed to her by hunters. Lastly, as the protecting goddess of warriors, she delighted in the bleeding gashes which her votaries inflicted upon themselves in their frenzy. By her side was worshipped as supreme being, a sky-god, lord of the thunderbolt. At the same time, in Cataonia the Sun ranked highest in the Anatolian pantheon, about which otherwise very little is known.

As a result of the Persian conquest, as we have seen (p. 607), colonies of Magi were settled all over the country. They were to maintain themselves in it, obstinately faithful to their sacred traditions, throughout the Empire, even after the triumph of Christianity. The description given by Strabo[1] of the sacrifices offered by them to the 'ever-burning Fire' shows how scrupulously they observed the directions of the Mazdaean liturgy. The teachings of Zoroastrianism, especially its regard for moral purity and its doctrine of immortality and future retribution, transformed the doubtless rudimentary theology of the old native religion.

Finally Hellenism, when it triumphed, profoundly altered the religious beliefs of these barbarian peoples. The gods were assimilated to those of Olympus. Ma, after having been looked upon as a form of Astarte in the Aramaean age, now became Artemis or, as a warrior-goddess, Athena or Enyo. The Lord of Heaven took the name of Zeus and the Sun that of Apollo. Suitable stories attributed the foundation of temples to heroes of mythology: Orestes had introduced the cult of Artemis Tauropolos at Comana. The liturgical language was no longer Aramaic but Greek; the temple statues showed the influence of Greek artists; and a Mazdaean sect, which worshipped Mithras, gave its cult the form of mysteries with successive initiations as among the Greeks. In the same way, south of the Taurus, the god of the

[1] xv, 733.

thunderbolt who was worshipped at Doliche on the top of a mountain where the Magi served Ahura-Mazda, was called Zeus under the Seleucids and for the Romans became Juppiter Dolichenus, protector of armies, and the funeral cult founded by king Antiochus shows a curious combination of Iranian and Greek elements (p. 608).

Roman influence scarcely modified the hybrid religion of eastern Asia Minor. Undoubtedly the ancient kings of Cappadocia had been deified by their subjects, and the imperial cult did no more in this country than perpetuate an existing tradition. A 'Cappadocarch,' an 'Armeniarch,' a 'Pontarch' presided over the provincial assemblies which belonged to them, Lesser Armenia forming for this purpose a separate unity, like Pontus Galaticus and Pontus Polemoniacus, although it was, like them, subject to the legate of Cappadocia. It was, on the contrary, the religion of these distant lands which, as will be seen elsewhere, had an appreciable influence on the western world. Ma, identified with Bellona, had been worshipped at Rome with her cruel rites since Sulla; the mysteries of Mithras and the practice of the *taurobolium* spread from the heart of Anatolia to all the Latin provinces. Thus the old Oriental spirit took its revenge for the Roman conquest (see above, p. 386 and further, vol. XII).

II. SYRIA, ARABIA AND THE EMPIRE

The economic and social conditions of Syria present a complete contrast to those which we have found north of the Taurus. Washed on the west by the Mediterranean, adjacent in the north-east to the fertile plains of Mesopotamia, bounded on the south by Egypt, she gave wide scope for the exchange of foreign products, and her prosperity more than that of any other Roman province depended on the activity of a considerable international trade. She was always the natural way of communication by land between the east and west. But her old Semitic civilization was never wholly extinguished by the dominant Hellenism, and though the hilly character of the country which broke up the population into districts and clans, exposed an enfeebled people to the assimilating action of a central power, this did not endure for ever. At long last she awoke to a feeling of national solidarity and was able to throw off a culture that was foreign to her.

As a kind of dyke raised by Nature between the desert and the sea, with a parallel double chain of mountains, bordered on the north by the Taurus and on the north-east by the headlong course of the Euphrates, Syria seems to have the great advantage of well-protected frontiers; but this geographical advantage is only apparent. The history of the country was at all times that of a struggle, now secret now open, between settlers tilling the soil and nomads roving the desert. A constant impulse urges the tribes of the arid plateaux of Arabia northwards, and tends to drive the occupants of the *ḥamād* towards the 'fertile crescent' of Syria and Mesopotamia. When a strong government overawes the *Skenitae*, the 'men of the tent,' and does not allow their raids, they content themselves, when the heat of the summer burns up the desert pasture and dries up the wells, with leading their numberless flocks to fields where the harvest is over or to the green banks of streams. The extent of the migrations, kept within bounds by authority, is reduced, and regulated, and nomadism becomes a periodic exchange of land. The Bedouins, gradually taking up a fixed abode on the land, either from choice or from necessity pass from a pastoral to an agricultural life, and these new settlers then extend the cultivated area bordering the desert. This is what Herod brought about in Transjordan, and it is noticeably what occurred elsewhere when the *pax Romana* guaranteed centuries of security, and the traveller is surprised to find countless traces of ancient settlements in districts which are now desolate. But when a weak government shows itself incapable of controlling tribal movements, the chiefs oppress the peasants, impose ruinous taxes on them, fleece them and plunder them, making life intolerable for village-dwellers. The desert then extends its borders, while the sheikhs establish their power in the populous centres.

This process is seen at work during the decline of the Seleucid kingdom. From the close of the second century it was involved in the confusion of hopeless anarchy, the incessant struggles of pretenders, the revolts of governors of cities, and civil wars leading to the establishment of local tyrannies. The old decaying empire, progressively reduced by insurrection, broke up more and more. The tribes of Arabia took advantage of this growing weakness. While certain 'phylarchs' made themselves masters of 'Parapotamia[1],' and all along the Euphrates levied exorbitant dues on caravans for their right of way, another sheikh, Sampsiceramus, seized Emesa and Arethusa; Damascus fell into the hands of Nabataeans, and Ituraeans from beyond the Jordan set themselves up at Chalcis, south of Heliopolis, pushed across the Lebanon,

[1] The geographical and doubtless official name for the irrigated and peopled zone that lies between the Euphrates and the desert. Strabo XVI, 753, cf. 748; Polybius V, 48, 16.

threatened the ports of Phoenicia and extended their plunderings all over the south of Syria[1].

Such was the anarchy that confronted Pompey in 64 when he annexed Syria, wishing both to expel from their final lairs the pirates whom he had conquered, and to drive away for good and all the Parthians from the Mediterranean, where their presence might have been a constant threat to Rome[2]. But the direct administration of the new province was reduced to the minimum. The only districts placed under the immediate authority of the proconsuls were, in the north, apart from the towns on the coast, the well-watered table-land eastwards from Mt Amanus as far as the great bend in the Euphrates—consisting of the old *tetrapolis* of Antioch, Seleuceia, Laodicea, and Apamea—further south the flourishing riviera irrigated by the streams from Mt Lebanon together with the wealthy harbours of Phoenicia, and, beyond the coastal mountain chain, part of the valley of the Orontes. In this region, the centre of the former Seleucid State, powerful Greek towns, which were granted autonomy, could serve as a strong support to the new government. For the same reason Pompey separated from the Jewish kingdom the ports on the coast belonging to the Philistines and added them to the new province together with the cities of the Decapolis east of the Jordan. Here also the kings of Antioch had founded urban centres of Greek culture. The remainder of the country was left in the hands of native vassals, phylarchs or tetrarchs, subject to tribute like the towns which enjoyed municipal liberties. As guardians of the frontiers of the Republic these petty chiefs ruled over districts that served as buffer-states between the province and the desert, and they protected the land belonging to the towns from the incursions of nomads. In this way from the very beginning that policy took root by which Rome was always to abide, the policy of maintaining Hellenism and of strengthening the city-states, which were its home, against the threat of the 'barbarians.'

In spite of the violent changes which marked the history of the East during the next fifty years, and in spite of falls and restorations of dynasties and adjustments of their frontiers, Pompey's organization survived in its main features until the time of Augustus. Proof of this can be seen in a semi-official document, the geographical lists which the Elder Pliny took from the com-

---

[1] Strabo XVI, 753–755; cf. Dessau 2683.
[2] On this cf. J. Dobiaš, *Archiv Orientalni*, III, pp. 215–56, and the present writer's note in *Syria*, XII, 1931, p. 382.

mentaries of Agrippa, which shows that there were still in Syria more than a score of vassal States[1]. These kingdoms lay between the territories of republican cities, which sometimes formed enclaves in them. The political map of the country was a mosaic almost as checkered as that of eighteenth-century Germany.

Thus the valley of the Orontes was occupied by the petty kings of Chalcis in the Lebanon and of Abila, Emesa and Arethusa. To the south between the ports of the Philistines and the Decapolis lay the Jewish kingdom of Herod the Great, which was to be partitioned in 4 B.C. between his three sons under the control of Roman procurators (vol. x, p. 338). Further east, on the edge of the desert, from Damascus to the Red Sea stretched the crescent-shaped territory of the Nabataeans of Petra, caravan-dwellers whose trade had brought them wealth (p. 630). The dynasty of the Obodae and the Aretae had imposed their authority upon northern Arabia. Nabataea became with Judaea the most powerful and also the most nationalist of the States that had given their allegiance to Rome; as it was a desert country with an almost inaccessible capital, its submission to its conqueror was always doubtful and precarious. A tribe of merchant Arabs, whose literary language was Aramaic, was converted into a kingdom with officials bearing Greek titles. But Greek civilization was only skin deep, and under the native princes they kept their own alphabet, their own religion and traditional laws, and remained faithful to their ancestral customs as to their Semitic rites.

In the north on the Syrian frontier lay Commagene, ruled by a dynasty of Graeco-Iranian stock (p. 608), but the immediate authority of the proconsuls probably extended, from the reign of Augustus to A.D. 73, over the eastern part of Cilicia with the capital Tarsus as headquarters. All along the Euphrates the province marched with the principality of Osrhoëne in Mesopotamia, which was officially subject to the Parthians, but came to be one of the dependencies of the Caesars. Further south behind the curtain of small States which were dependent on the Empire, the desert remained unsubdued. Its nomad tribes lived as in modern times, pitching their tents of dark mohair in the sandy plain. Their countless flocks of sheep and camels provided food in the form of milk and meat, and clothes from their wool and hair, which was woven by the women. These *Skenitae*, however, never settled, 'a tribe of brigands and shepherds, readily moving from one place to another when pasture and booty fail them,' as they are described

[1] Pliny (*N.H.* v, 81 *sqq.*) gives the name of six and adds *praeter tetrarchias in regna descriptas barbaris nominibus XVII.*

by Strabo[1], did not all live by plunder and smuggling. Accustomed as they were to traversing the lonely steppes, where they knew the tracks and disputed for the watering-places, they undertook the conduct of transport and became the carriers of the desert. At the oasis of Palmyra, a rest stage for the caravans, grew up an association of merchants which was to attain to an amazing wealth (p. 631). Its riches aroused the cupidity of Antony, who sent cavalry to raid it without success (vol. x, p. 40): this is the earliest evidence we have of its growing prosperity.

During the first century of the Christian era the emperors followed a policy of absorption, which caused the gradual disappearance of local dynasties, and incorporated their principalities with territory under the immediate control of Roman authority. The process of securing uniformity was completed by Trajan, who in A.D. 106 made of Nabatene the new province of Arabia with Bostra as its capital, and who probably annexed Palmyrene[2] as far as the Euphrates, before he extended beyond the river his vast and impermanent conquests which were abandoned by himself or by Hadrian[3] (see above, p. 609). Only northern Mesopotamia was recovered and made a separate province by Lucius Verus (see above, p. 349). On the other side, after the capture of Jerusalem all connection was broken between Syria and Judaea, which after the year 70 no longer obeyed procurators but its own legates, and in A.D. 73 Cilicia was re-organized in the same way under separate government. But from the second century, Syria from the Taurus to beyond Carmel and the mountain wall of the Haurân and from the Mediterranean to the Euphrates, was one continuous area where the *ius gladii* of the imperial legates was exercised with full military and judicial authority. This populous frontier-province, which was second to none in the size of its army and its economic importance, was one of the largest and most important spheres of government in the Empire. Among all the offices of a consular legate none ranked higher than that of governor of Syria, and it was often held by outstanding men as the crown of their career. It was not until A.D. 194[4] that Septimius Severus divided this enormous territory in two—Syria Coele in the north and Syria Phoenice in the south—

---

[1] XVI, 747.

[2] See above p. 139 and Note 2, p. 859 sq.

[3] An inscription of A.D. 116/7 found in 1935 at Doura proves that the city was evacuated before the death of Trajan, probably together with all lower Mesopotamia. See M. Rostovtzeff in *C.R. Ac. Inscr.* 1935, pp. 285 sqq.

[4] Cf. H. Ingholt in *Syria*, XIII, 1932, pp. 284 sqq.

whereby the city of Antioch ceased to be the sole capital of all the old Seleucid territory.

The defence and military occupation of Syria under Augustus and his successors down to the time of Trajan has been described elsewhere (vol. x, pp. 219 *sqq.* and above, pp. 137 *sqq.*). The troops had the duty not only of making good the frontiers but of controlling the nomads and suppressing brigandage. An imperial fleet, the *classis Syriaca*, had its base at Seleuceia in Pieria. Of no Roman army is our knowledge, however, so slight as of the army of the East, although the discoveries at Doura are beginning to penetrate the darkness for the time of the Severi. One fact is certain, namely that Syria supplied the imperial forces with many special bands of archers, often mounted on horse back or on camels (*dromedarii*), of which Rome made effective use not only in their own native land but on all the other frontiers both in Africa and in Europe. No troops were more skilled than these Orientals in discharging their arrows at full gallop, nor more fitted to harass the enemy in time of war or to pursue bands of robbers in time of peace.

Thanks to aerial exploration[1] we can now form a reasonably clear picture of the system of defence adopted by the emperors for the protection of the eastern frontier. In the east it had the support of the Euphrates, and, strictly speaking, there was no *limes*. The broad and swift river was almost impossible to cross, and on the hills commanding it ran a series of camps and *castella*, which, to use an expression of Herodian[2], were like 'the shields covering the Empire of the Romans.' At the end of the second century the right bank of the Euphrates was thus held by Roman or Palmyrene troops at least as far as Anah in the south[3]. After the conquest of Mesopotamia this line was extended along the Chaboras and ran across the spurs of the Singar to join the Tigris.

On the Roman side of the Euphrates, castles set at the watering-places of the caravan routes across the desert maintained communications and kept watch on the Arab phylarchs, and in the west on the borders of the *ḥamād* a line of small forts was sufficient to keep the villages and cultivated lands of Syria free from nomad raids. Only in the extreme south of the Roman territory where it was necessary to keep back the powerful tribes of the Nejd, who were always on the move, was the *limes* of the new province of Arabia more strongly fortified by Trajan and a whole legion, III

[1] See A. Poidebard, *La Trace de Rome dans le Désert de Syrie.*
[2] VI, 2, 5.
[3] See Note 3, p. 860.

Cyrenaica, stationed at Bostra, was assigned to its defence to-gether with *auxilia*.

The Sassanid invasion was to force the Romans much later to draw back their frontier and alter its arrangement. Against the incursions of the formidable cavalry of the successors of Ardashir, Diocletian had to strengthen and increase the fortifications on the road—the famous *strata Diocletiana*—which went from the camp at Sura on the Euphrates to Damascus and crossed the desert in the centre. The vast tracts which destructive wars had desolated now supplied a glacis for the military works with which the new frontier was equipped. The organization of the *limes*, here as elsewhere, was changed in the course of centuries from a system which was primarily offensive, intended to serve as a base for operations against the enemy, into a strong defensive line fixed and immutable.

To make possible the movement of troops and military trans-port good roads were needed, and, whenever the Romans estab-lished themselves in a new province, it was their first care to build them. They did not fail to devote themselves to road-making in Syria. Even before the official annexation of Palmyrene, Trajan's father built the road from Palmyra to Sura through Aracha (p. 859). No sooner had Trajan himself conquered Mesopotamia than he secured his communications by driving a road to the Tigris over the slopes of the Singar[1]. So too when he annexed Arabia, he boldly had a road constructed (A.D. 111–114) *a finibus Syriae usque ad mare Rubrum*[2]. We do not know how far the Seleucids had already seen to the making of roads in their empire. But the new masters of the country introduced those solidly built highways, provided with rest-stages and lodging-places, which were one of their great achievements in all the Mediterranean world. The paving of thick blocks, the bridges with their enduring arches, the deep cuttings through mountain ridges, still attest the perfection of these works, the technique of which was skilfully adapted to the nature of the ground. Until the third century the emperors steadily increased the range and drew closer the web of this road-system, and to the end of the Turkish régime communica-tions in Syria were never again as good as they had been in antiquity. The successive restorations which have altered the names carved on the milestones make it impossible to follow the historical de-velopment of this great undertaking of the State, and they tell us more about repairs than about construction. But, in all probability,

---

[1] R. Cagnat, in *Syria*, VIII, 1927, p. 53 (milestone).
[2] Dessau 5834, 5845 *sqq.*

the governors first secured communication between the coast towns subject to their authority by building the highway along the seaboard from Antioch to Palestine. It was supplemented by the road which ran between the Lebanon and Antilebanon. Later, when provincial territory extended into the desert, there was added the road, which we have already mentioned, from Sura to Damascus, while, finally, a military road linked up the stations and camps on the right bank of the Euphrates. But besides these, other broad highways, the importance of which was at once strategic and commercial, ran from west to east to the Euphrates, across which there was a bridge at Zeugma, and continued through Mesopotamia to the Tigris or else, at Palmyra, Damascus or Bostra, led into the caravan tracks of the desert.

By all these measures Rome imposed on Syria security and the almost unbroken enjoyment of the *pax Romana* for nearly three centuries, and by its expert administration it gave it the benefit of stable institutions. In conformity with its universal practice, Rome left the Greek cities in Syria a large degree of autonomy, requiring from them in return the management of most of those public services which in modern times are kept in its own hands by the central authority. These small States with independent administration were given an aristocratic constitution, which reserved the exercise of political rights to those possessed of a certain census. This was more necessary in Syria than elsewhere. The municipal middle class was the only class which was hellenized, which had, that is to say, a culture comparable with that of Italy, and which was considered worthy to enjoy a certain amount of civic freedom. It was also the only class from which capable administrators could be recruited, the Semitic population being debarred from education by its ignorance of Greek.

The civic constitution remained broadly what in the Hellenistic age had been common to all the Seleucid colonies. The executive power was in the hands of a body of magistrates or archons, of whom the chief were sometimes an eponymous president ($\pi\rho\acute{o}\epsilon\delta\rho o\varsigma$), sometimes two eponymous *strategoi*, and the government of the city was divided between them and two deliberative bodies, the Senate ($\beta o\upsilon\lambda\acute{\eta}$) and the assembly of the people ($\grave{\epsilon}\kappa\kappa\lambda\eta\sigma\acute{\iota}a$). In some cities like Gerasa a college of rich senators (the $\delta\epsilon\kappa\acute{a}\pi\rho\omega\tau o\iota$) levied the taxes and possibly superintended the census[1]. But we are very ill informed concerning the functions of these different institutions of municipal life; we have not yet at our disposal for

[1] R. Boecklin and J. P. Myatt in *Am. Journ. Arch.* XXXVIII, 1934, pp. 517 *sqq*.

this country the wealth of epigraphic documents left us by the Greek towns of Asia Minor. In particular we do not know whether at the beginning of the Christian era the people (δῆμος), that is to say the citizen body, still possessed real power and was not restricted to ratifying by acclamation the laws passed by the *boulê* and to electing magistrates whom it proposed. The general tendency under the Empire for these magistrates to become more powerful at the expense of the citizen body, because the Roman officials could more easily manage them, and to reserve to themselves the parliamentary initiative which had been taken from private persons, is seen in Syria as in other provinces.

The autonomy solemnly conferred on cities by Pompey involved them in hardly any other obligation towards Rome than the payment of tribute and the sending of military contingents. But in actual fact the decrees voted by the towns under the Seleucids had often been only the expression of a monarch's will translated into republican language. In practice the power of the Roman governors over them was hardly less extensive, and as disorder in the municipal finances invited, or rather demanded, the intervention of the Imperial officials, these city-states ended by retaining no more of autonomy than the name. The more of a reality the unification of the Empire became and the more the distinction between *cives* and *peregrini* disappeared as the latter were absorbed into the former, the more the Greek republics found a place in the constitutional system of Rome.

Compared with Asia, Syria had but few towns, and consequently these possessed extensive territories, sometimes including hundreds of villages: that of Cyrrhus had an area of about 160 square miles and in the time of the bishop Theodoret 800 parishes. The total population was considerable. In the time of Augustus the census of Quirinius showed 117,000 citizens of Apamea of both sexes not counting slaves and the labouring classes[1]. Most of the land belonged to large landowners who lived in the towns and who had their vast estates cultivated by small farmers or paid workmen. Though we do not hear of *coloni* or serfs bound to the soil in Syria, the rural plebs, denied the rights of municipal citizenship and excluded from all part in public life, were harshly exploited by the owners of the *latifundia* and often lived in extreme poverty. But the appearance of the villages whose remains have survived forces us to suppose that by the side of the towns where the citizen noblemen came to reside in the summer, there existed a numerous class of well-to-do peasants

[1] Fr. Cumont in *J.R.S.* XXIV, 1934, pp. 187 *sqq.*

cultivating their plots of land. Beside the estates of the aristocracy stretched the sacred land of the temples, the revenue from which was used to maintain their worship. Even when these temples were in towns, they had their estates, their own treasuries and their financial administration, which in practice made them nearly independent of civil authority. Sometimes, as at Hierapolis or Emesa, the high priest had been lord of the city, and even when he no longer ruled over the civil population, he retained an almost regal rank and dress. But other shrines, like that on the Nimrud Dagh in Commagene or that of Baetocaece on Mt Bargylus, formed outside the cities definite ecclesiastical principalities, whose head was served by a host of temple slaves and possessed numerous villages from which he received revenue. Finally the old 'royal land' of the Seleucids had passed at least in part to the emperors, who exploited it through their agents. They were the owners particularly of the forests of Lebanon which Hadrian delimited. Some of the imperial *saltus* continued to exist by the side of urban territory until the Arab invasion[1].

The villages (κῶμαι), whether they belonged to the municipal aristocracy, a temple or the emperor, had a local administration, entrusted to a mayor, who was called a *comarch* or by some other title, and presided over a communal council. On him devolved the policing of his village and the management of its property. Occasionally, in areas which remained essentially rural, several villages were grouped together under the chief village of the district (μητροκωμία).

In Syria the contrast between the towns and the country was not only social but also one of language. Although in the urban centres Macedonian colonists had quickly mixed with the native population and although constant marriage with the women of the country had profoundly altered the ethnic quality of the dominant race, the latter strove to preserve through the centuries, together with the political system which assured its supremacy, the laws, religious worship and language on which its proud position depended. The education given in the schools and by teachers of rhetoric was as Greek in the colonies, even in those of the Far East, as it was in Greece itself. Hellenism was at that time synonymous with culture. If a man wished to be educated, he had to learn Greek, if he wished to better himself he could do so only with its help. Official documents, literary works, religious dedications are in Greek. On the coast Phoenician dies out, and in every city Aramaic ceases to be a written language and

[1] Cf. Georgios Cypr. *Descriptio*, nos. 981, 994 *sqq.*

becomes the *patois* of the common people. It is no more spoken by the educated classes than Celtic in Gaul or Britain. If a child of the people rose to a higher social standing he hastened to hellenize his name, like Malchus of Tyre, son of Malchus, who became the philosopher Porphyry. Hellenism prevailed more perhaps at Antioch than at Alexandria. But people spoke Aramaic at the gates of the town, and it was the language of the whole of the open country. One sign of the bilingualism of the population was the fact noticed by Ammianus Marcellinus[1] that the cities often had a double name, one Macedonian, which was due to the Seleucids, and the other native, which was older than the period of hellenization and survived it. Beroea, which had been called Chalybon, shows a reversion to its old name in the form Aleppo.

If in the heart of Roman Syria the native tongues are no more than despised *patois*, they remain on the circumference of the province, in districts long unsubdued, written languages which are not only those of conversation and business but also of government and religion. Jews in Palestine, Nabataeans in Arabia, Safaïtes in the Haurân, Palmyrenes in the desert, each have their peculiar Semitic dialect and their own alphabet. In Mesopotamia Bardesanes of Edessa in the second century formulates his religious speculations in Syriac, just as in the third Mani uses it for his sacred books[2].

In seeking everywhere the support of the urban middle classes and in preserving an aristocratic character in the social organization, Rome was also helping Hellenism and it certainly spread in Syria, as it did north of the Taurus (p. 611) during the first centuries of the Empire. Variety of tongues tended to give way before a world language. In the cities Greek gradually gained ground among the lower strata of the population. At the same time it widened its field of action and pushed forward its borders as urbanization extended. The process common to all the provinces acquires a special character here. Syria proper and the Decapolis had been widely colonized by the Seleucids, and the emperors founded there hardly any new cities. They contented themselves for the most part with restoring the existing ones which acquired a new dignity under their rule. But it was otherwise on the borders of the province in districts hitherto rural and Semitic. Sometimes groups of dwellings which depended on temples were transformed into cities, as happened with Emesa; sometimes, as in Palestine where Herod had led the way, monarchical absolutism was replaced by the system of independent

[1] XIV, 8, 6.   [2] See below, vol. XII.

cities; sometimes, as in Ituraea, growing villages (κῶμαι) were organized so that they hardly differed from cities, or existing settlements were raised to the rank of Roman colonies, as was done by the Severi as far afield as Mesopotamia. The continual spread of Greek language and customs can nowhere be better observed than at Palmyra, as this business republic comes more within the legal framework of imperial administration. But the old tribal organization of the Semites was so powerful that in the outlying districts, in Nabataea, Transjordan and Palmyrene, it was more or less preserved under a western form. The tribes (φῦλαι) among which the population was divided according to Greek custom, were often in Arab country simply the old nomad clans, and the head of the community, who was called the ethnarch or president (πρόεδρος), was the direct descendant of the former sheikhs.

How far did Rome, the furtherer of Hellenism, also introduce her own culture into Syria? Nowhere did she impose by force her language, customs or beliefs on the peoples subject to her rule. She did not open schools in which young Syrians were made to learn Latin. Greek was the second official language of the Empire, and as early as the reign of Augustus the *princeps* and his officials used it in their correspondence with Eastern cities or for the publication of edicts. But naturally the Latin language and the customs of Italy spread to some extent in a country in which so many Italians found themselves resident.

At the same time those who in other parts were the most active instruments of romanization played only a small part in Syria. Rome, unlike modern Europe, did not send overseas millions of the lower classes to inhabit large continents, but she encouraged the emigration of capitalists, large and small, those *negotiatores* who were everywhere the most active pioneers of Latin civilization. When the new province had been created by Pompey, it saw a swarm of traders settle down on it, who were, as elsewhere, readily given protection by the governors. But from the beginning of the Empire these Italian traders become fewer or disappear. The Syrians were such adroit dealers that they made foreign competition impossible. The associations of *negotiatores*, which are so common in Asia Minor, are almost unknown in Syria.

The many Latin inscriptions which have been found in Syria and Arabia give a sufficiently accurate picture of the factors which made for partial latinization. They come partly from Roman officials. But the number of servants of the State scattered over this vast province was exceedingly small, for almost all the administration was left in the hands of local authorities (p. 620). If Latin

was the language of the legates resident at Antioch and of their
entourage, it was as little the language of this capital as French is
that of Damascus to-day.

More important was the influence of the army. In the first
century when the legions consisted largely of volunteers recruited
from Italy and were commanded by officers drawn from the
Italian aristocracy, their camps were very definite centres of
romanization in Semitic countries, as they were on the Danube or
the Rhine. They were indeed more so, for contrary to the practice
in the West, the troops were often quartered in or near to the towns
(vol. x, p. 280)[1]. But after Hadrian local recruitment meant the
predominance of native peasants even among the legionaries, and
as the territory was extended, it meant an increase in the number of
auxiliaries recruited from peoples who were half barbarians. An
army which became more and more oriental counted for less and
less in the spread of latinization. The customary speech of the
soldiers and officers of lower rank,—the language which they used
for everyday purposes—was either their Semitic dialect or Greek.
None the less, everywhere, even on the banks of the Euphrates,
the official language, used in commands and at military offices,
was exclusively Latin, as is shown by the archives of the *praetorium* of Doura. So that during their long service with the
colours the barbarian recruits obtained a rough knowledge of it.
The jargon they write is occasionally a trooper's Latin, like the
English of sepoys, but a feeling of *esprit de corps* made them take a
pride in using it. It was probably a soldier who carved on a rock
on Mt Sinai this faulty but proud appeal: 'cessent Syri ante Latinos
Romanos[2].' Thus all along the frontier, in the neighbourhood of
the garrison towns, the language spread which was spoken by the
masters of the world. When a village is formed, grows and becomes a town, the town is trilingual, Greek, Latin and Semitic[3].
Military even more than commercial influence is responsible for
filling with Latin words the Syrian *koine*, such as is written, for
example, by Ignatius of Antioch, and for causing them to find
their way in large numbers even into the Hebrew of the Talmud
and literary Syriac.

---

[1] Tacitus' statement (*Ann.* xiii, 35, 3) *militia per oppida expleta* is confirmed by the most recent discoveries at Palmyra (H. Seyrig, *Antiquités
syriennes*, 1934, pp. 70 *sqq.*) and at Doura, where the soldiers' quarter is
inside the fortification but separated from the rest of the city by a wall.

[2] *C.I.L.* iii, 86.

[3] Cf., for example, Waddington no. 2136 and the note on Eaccaea in
Batanea.

The change in the composition of the army necessarily affected that of the colonies of veterans. Only those which had been founded at the beginning of the Empire had a population of Italian origin and were really like Latin islands in the Semitic ocean; such were Berytus and Heliopolis (Baalbek) under Augustus, Ptolemaïs Ace under Claudius. The numerous *coloniae* of the Severi, even when they did not receive a purely honorific title, had their lands assigned only to oriental soldiers.

The only one of all these cities that matched Gellius' definition of a colony as 'effigies parva, simulacrumque[1]' of the Roman State, was Berytus, which was thickly populated by the veterans of two legions. It is typical that this distant Phoenician city saw the birth, under Nero, of a famous grammarian, Valerius Probus, who was an enthusiastic defender of the ancient classics, of which he published valuable editions, and was all the more anxious to preserve the purity of the language because he had seen it threatened in his native land. At Berytus, probably in the second century, was instituted the celebrated school of Law in which the teaching continued to be given in Latin and not in Greek until the end of the fourth century, and which attracted students from all over the East. About the year 233 the instructor of Gregory Thaumaturgus taught him Latin in Cappadocia together with the elements of the science of Law and strongly advised him to complete his studies at Berytus[2]. In proportion as the *ius civitatis* was granted to an increasing number of Syrians, the application of Roman law among populations hitherto governed by Greek laws or native customs, multiplied the questions that had to be settled, both those that concerned the laws dealing with the family and with inheritance and those concerning obligation. Rome had found in the East a highly developed Hellenistic law, which, in the cities, served as the rule for judicial practice, and a well perfected system of compulsory registration of deeds in the official and carefully kept archives ($\chi\rho\eta\mu\alpha\tau\iota\sigma\tau\dot{\eta}\rho\iota\alpha$). It is still a matter of controversy how far Roman civil law, which in theory applied to all citizens, was substituted for the Hellenistic law that was a legacy from the Seleucid monarchy, and how far the latter was modified by it or whether on the contrary the latter modified the former. But it is certainly true that the distinguished school of Berytus played a considerable part in the development of juridical doctrine under the Empire and the old science of the Scaevolas and Labeos was cultivated with brilliance in this Levant-

---

[1] *N.A.* xvi, 13, 9.
[2] Greg. Thaum. *Paneg. ad Origen*, 5 (Patr. Gr. x, 1065).

ine port, which was to remain until the time of Justinian a nursery of officials for the imperial administration.

In Law then there was give and take between Rome and Syria. Was it the same in Art? The terms of this disputed question can be better expressed when the economic position of the country, which explains the magnificence of its monuments, has been indicated.

III. INDUSTRY AND TRADE

In Syria luxuriant vegetation borders on the desolate wilderness. Wherever the rainfall, as on the riviera of Lebanon, or else irrigation, as along the rivers, provided a sufficiency of water, the soil was fertile, and the construction of aqueducts under the Empire increased the arable land. Droughts were less severe than they are to-day, for the country, which had not been made bare by the cutting down of trees, still possessed enormous forests. The cedars and cypresses of the imperial domains of Lebanon could be used for the building of the fleets of the emperors, as they had been three thousand years before for those of the Pharaohs. Immense plateaux which to-day are bleak deserts with rock everywhere on the surface, were then covered with a deep soil suitable for agriculture and tree-growing. In northern Syria cereals grew abundantly, and the Haurân was then, as now, a great granary. Syrian wines, strong in alcohol, were exported to Persia and India no less than to the West. Some Phoenician wines were esteemed even in Rome and they still reached Gaul under the Merovingians. Olive-plantations surrounded the villages everywhere and supplied oil in plenty. Many presses have been found in districts now abandoned by man. This oil was chiefly used with food, but it was also employed in the making of scent and balsams, for strongly smelling aromatic plants throve under the strong sun as did medicinal plants. The towns and market-villages were, as in modern times, surrounded by fruit gardens with pears, apples, pistachio-nuts. The figs and damsons of Damascus which were dried for export were famous. Vegetables were so various that their number became proverbial[1]; to Ascalon particularly we owe the shallot (*ascalonia*). Even uncultivated tracts did not fail to contribute to the prosperity of this wealthy country. The desert fed and clothed Syria. The meat from its large flocks was the citizens' food and their wool was used for the weaving of cloth.

Weaving, indeed, was one of the important industries of the

---

[1] πολλὰ Σύρων λάχανα.

country. It produced not only ordinary plain stuffs but many-coloured textures with varied designs worked into the woof. Linen clothes were also made of extreme fineness suitable for the hot climate. They were particularly the compulsory dress of the native priesthood, and they were an important article of export. Finally, the Syrians had learned to work in silk, the most precious of textile materials. From China, which then alone knew how to rear caterpillars on the mulberry, raw silk reached them across Turkestan and Persia or by boat from India, and the *sericarii* of the Phoenician towns worked it into luxurious materials. Syrian workers were equally clever at metal-work; their armourers supplied Arabia, their bronze-workers cast and hammered well-finished plate for distant Persia, their silversmiths and goldsmiths chased elaborate jewelry with which women adorned themselves. Inscriptions give us the names of numerous specialist workmen who formed clubs in the cities.

But the two characteristic industries of Syria were glass-making and purple-dyeing (vol. x, p. 400). The chief centre of the former was Sidon, which discovered a process for making translucent the opaque vitreous impasto and learned to blow it in moulds; and every cemetery in the province can show numerous glass vases of all shapes, either transparent or coloured, worked with a delicacy and taste that is often amazing. They spread all over the Roman world and as far as Germany. Tyre and the neighbourhood had a monopoly of purple-dyeing; this colour which was so prized by antiquity and became the sign of sovereign power, was obtained from the secretion of one, or rather two, shell-fish, the murex and the trumpet-shell, which were fished on this coast.

This country where the land produced abundant fruits and busy towns provided work for a mass of artisans, supported a population very much larger than that of to-day. Its density was the result not only of the size of the towns—the ruins of Apamea cover about 250 hectares (= about 615 acres)—but of the number of villages whose stone dwellings are still scattered about in districts now uninhabited. Lack of adequate statistics makes it difficult to estimate the total figure, but probably Syria and Palestine together had at least ten million inhabitants[1]. This

---

[1] See Fr. Cumont in *J.R.S.* xxiv, 1934, pp. 187 *sqq.* M. Schlumberger's exploration in 1934 of the region north-east of Palmyra, which to-day is wholly barren and uninhabited, has revealed remains of some twenty-five temples, and has shown that all this part of the desert was once covered with pastures where the horses for the famous Palmyrene cavalry were reared. See that writer's report in *C. R. Ac. Inscr.* 1935, pp. 250 *sqq.*

density of population explains how the country was an important source both of slaves for the markets of the West and of recruits for the imperial armies.

If the produce of its fields and workshops placed Syria on a level with, or little below, Egypt, nevertheless it owed its economic importance above all to its commerce. A nation of traders, highly gifted for business, made great profits as transport contractors and brokers between Asia and the Mediterranean world.

The camel was not introduced to North Africa until the Roman period, but Syria had been using it as a beast of burden from the beginning of its history. The caravans did not visit only the market-towns which were stocked by them on the edge of the desert, Bostra, Gerasa, Damascus and Emesa. As to-day, they carried the commodities of the hinterland to the ports on the coast, whence Phoenician ships bore them to all the shores of the Mediterranean. But only these caravans could cross the melancholy wastes of the ḥamād, for nature and man alike beset it with dangers. Success depended on a knowledge of the tracks which led to the watering-places and oases and on ability to repel the attacks of nomads. The financial organization of these costly expeditions needed considerable capital, which was advanced by bankers or merchants in the business towns, who shared largely in the profits of the venture. The traders formed great convoys and submitted themselves to the instructions of a leader ($\sigma\upsilon\nu\omega\delta\iota\acute{\alpha}\rho\chi\eta\varsigma$), who was always an important person in the city. These convoys, often of hundreds of camels strongly escorted by mounted bowmen to intimidate the rovers of the desert, resembled an army on the march[1] whose only care was the protection of its baggage. For safe travel an understanding was necessary with the phylarchs of the tribes through whose pasture the caravans had to go, and they had an interest in the profits of a regular traffic in so far as they received dues in return for their protection. These expenses heavily increased the net cost of merchandise. Pliny tells us that the carriage of incense from the Gebbanitae of southern Arabia to Gaza passed through sixty-five stations and cost some 688 denarii for a camel-load[2], which can be estimated at about 300 lb. Only goods of great value in small bulk could bear such costs, and in this respect the caravan traffic had its limitation.

Two desert towns in succession, by coming to an agreement with the Arab sheikhs, succeeded in running convoys across these inhospitable districts and in securing for themselves for a time the

---

[1] Strabo XVI, 781.   [2] N.H. XII, 65.

profitable monopoly of the land trade with foreign countries. They were Petra and Palmyra.

Half-way between the Dead Sea and the Gulf of Akaba, Petra, the capital of Nabataea (p. 616), grew up in a circle of steep rocks to which the only approach was through narrow gorges which could be defended by a handful of men. The safety of this mart which was so well fortified by nature and in which inaccessible caves gave merchants protection from robbery, was the chief cause of its prosperity. By the end of the Hellenistic period these dauntless and clever traders had concentrated in their hands the trade with the Arabian peninsula, from which the caravans brought gems and perfumes, especially myrrh and incense, of which an enormous quantity was used by the temples of the whole ancient world. Ships also carried the scents, precious woods and fine muslins of India across the ocean to Aden, whence the coasting-trade of the Red Sea brought them to Leuke Kome, the port of the Nabataeans, who then loaded them on their camels. But their fearless caravaners also made their way across the whole breadth of the Nejd to the harbour of Gerrha on the Persian Gulf, which was renowned for its pearl-fisheries, or even boldly set their course for Forat, a port near the mouth of the Tigris, where fleets from the sea of Oman could put in. The precious wares produced or imported by Arabia poured into Petra, which saw to their spread through the Roman world. To the north a busy road took them to Damascus, which distributed them in the rest of Syria, and this important commercial highway brought life to the towns of Trans-jordan, which lay on its course, such as Philadelphia and Gerasa. In the east the merchants of Petra discharged their precious loads at Rhinocolura on the Egyptian frontier whence they reached Alexandria or at Gaza where they could be shipped direct to Italy. As in the Hellenistic age the Nabataeans carried on business at Delos, so at the beginning of the Empire they had a flourishing colony at Puteoli, which then served as a port for Rome.

This constant stream of business brought Petra a wealth which is still attested by the remarkable rock tombs of which the façades, rising tier above tier, form a scene from fairyland on the precipitous sides of the mountains, while on the tops stood temples dedicated to the Nabataean gods, of whom the chief were Dushara (Dusares), assimilated with Dionysus, and Allath, a warrior goddess identified with Athena. The annexation of Arabia under Trajan (p. 617) was to strike a fatal blow to the trade of Petra. Bostra, the political centre of the province, became the commercial centre also, and until the end of the Empire it was the meeting-place of caravans from Medina and Mecca. But above all Petra could not withstand the successful competition of Palmyra. When Palmyra opened up easier routes to the Persian Gulf, it deprived Petra of the Indian trade.

Two abundant springs, gushing forth like a miracle in a burning country, have since time began made Tadmor a stage in the passage of the desert half-way between the valley of the Euphrates and the towns of Syria. In the time of Antony, who hoped to surprise it by a cavalry raid (p. 617), Palmyra was still an open straggling village of caravaners of so little importance that Strabo does not even mention it. But the peace between Augustus and the Parthians, which allowed Palmyrene to remain as an independent republic between its two great neighbours, greatly favoured the extension of its trade. In the reign of Tiberius it was already rich enough to build a magnificent temple to the supreme trinity of its pantheon, Bel, Yarhibol (Sun), and Aglibol (Moon). Like Petra it succeeded in gaining the co-operation of the nomad sheikhs and its authority was recognized by the oases of the desert, of which it made a State. It thus re-opened for traffic the way to the Euphrates which had been impossible for traders since the Seleucid anarchy, and this was the source of notable prosperity. It could, in fact, make use of a route to lower Mesopotamia that was much easier and safer than the long crossing of the Arabian desert, which was infested by robbers but had to be risked by the people of Petra, or than the route which made a détour to the north round the sands of the *ḥamād*, crossed the Euphrates at Zeugma and went diagonally across Mesopotamia to the Tigris in twenty-five stages. The caravans of Palmyra either went due east until they reached Doura[1] and then descended the valley of the Euphrates along the right bank of the river, or else by a track that has been traced, which was shorter and provided with wells, they reached the river in a straight line at Hit. They could then comfortably continue their way as far as Seleuceia on the Tigris, which was the meeting-place of the convoys bringing Persian tissues or Chinese silk[2]. But the Palmyrenes travelled particularly to the ports of the lower Euphrates, Babylon, where

[1] The discoveries of 1935 at Doura have shown that the Palmyrenes had a factory there as early as the first century B.C., when their wealth was a temptation to Antony. These inscriptions are the earliest known Palmyrene inscriptions.

[2] Not only raw silk (p. 628) but also Chinese tissues reached Palmyra. Characteristic fragments have been found in one of the tombs. R. Pfister, *Textiles de Palmyre*, 1934, pp. 39 *sqq.*

their merchants founded a prosperous colony as early as A.D. 24[1], and Vologasia, where they had an important staple and a temple, or proceeded beyond the river to the small kingdom of Characene on the shores of the Persian Gulf, where ships from India unloaded their cargoes in the port of Spasinu Charax.

The trade from India, whence were obtained spices and sweet-smelling herbs, ivory, ebony and sandal-wood, pearls and precious stones, cotton and fine muslins, brought huge profits. The elder Pliny[2] puts the amount of money which the Roman Empire paid annually to India, Arabia and China at a hundred million sesterces on the lowest estimate (see however, vol. x, p. 417). At least half this sum went to India. That, adds the moralist, is what luxury and women cost us. The gains of the middlemen were enormous. According to Arab writers before Islam, merchandise brought from Mecca to Gaza or Bostra could easily be sold at a hundred per cent. net profit, and bankers who made advances to the caravans guaranteed interest of fifty per cent. on the capital invested in the enterprise. Pliny could say with some exaggeration that between India and Rome prices increased a hundredfold.

From Palmyra, now become the great mart for the products of the East, many roads led to the towns in Syria from Damascus in the south to Antioch in the north. But Rome's authorization was needed if the bales of foreign merchandise were to enter the Empire, and an understanding with her was an absolute necessity for the commercial republic of the desert. On the other hand the emperors, like the Ptolemies before them, were anxious to assure for themselves the control of the profitable trade with Persia and India. At the same time as the discovery of the monsoon made it possible to establish regular communication by sea between Egypt and the coast of Malabar, the Romans worked their way into Palmyra and drew it closer and closer to the Empire. Annexation came not later than Trajan (p. 617). The expedition of the mighty conqueror against Parthia certainly had, over and above political aims, an economic purpose, the complete domination of the route to the Persian Gulf and Iran, and the collection of heavy customs dues on goods crossing Mesopotamia. Hadrian gave up his predecessor's conquests, but not his plan. When he re-established peaceful relations with the Parthians he was careful to make sure of the free passage of Roman caravans. After the reign of that emperor who was looked upon by Palmyrene, which bore the title Hadriane, as its second founder, the traffic across the

---

[1] J. Cantineau, *Inv. des inscr. de Palmyre*, IX, 1933, p. 11.
[2] *N.H.* XII. 84; cf. VI 101.

desert underwent a new development. A tariff dated A.D. 137 shows that Palmyrene formed a closed district with customs, where, with the stipulation that a quota was to be paid to the treasury, the town levied taxes on imports and exports for its own profit and through its own officials. Steadily favoured by the emperors, who granted it the title of colony and the *ius Italicum*, it increasingly adopted Greek civilization. As though in defiance of nature there grew up under an unfriendly sky and in the midst of inhospitable lands a proud city whose ruins still arouse the wonder of travellers and inspired Volney to his thoughts on the decline of empires. In the middle of the third century it was even to aspire to become the capital of an important oriental state on the eve of its destruction by Aurelian.

The fabulous wealth accumulated by these large-scale business men was due to the ease with which they could dispose of their goods in the Mediterranean world. The whole Roman Empire was open to their enterprise, and we see them extending their connections and founding banks in Egypt and Rome and as far off as Dacia. But they played only a minor part in the sea trade of the Syrians, which was as vigorous in the West as their caravan trade was in the East.

The Phoenicians had long ago filled the shores of the Mediterranean with their colonies and flooded them with their wares. Their descendants remained enterprising sailors and their ship-owners and sailors formed powerful bodies in the ports all along the coast. A citizen of the small town of Rhosus did good service to Octavian as admiral (ναύαρχος) during the civil wars[1]. As soon as the Roman fleets, one of which had its base at Seleuceia in Pieria (vol. x, p. 236), had secured the safety of the sea, close relations were established between these ports and Italy, Gaul and Spain. Syria sent all round the Mediterranean crafty merchants, whose aptitude for profit-making became proverbial. In all important commercial centres they set up not only factories but real colonies. Even in the Hellenistic age they were numbered by the thousand at Delos, and Juvenal complains that the Orontes has flowed into the Tiber[2]. But they did not confine themselves to the coast; their mercantile activities took them far inland wherever they found profitable traffic. This foreign element was particularly strong in Gaul and reached the northern capital of Trèves. Even barbarian invasions did not prevent its immigration in the West: only the ruin of Mediterranean trade by Saracen pirates put a stop to it. These Syrian strongholds had a marked influence for six

---

[1] P. Roussel in *Syria*, xv, 1934, pp. 33 *sqq.*   [2] III, 62.

centuries on the economic life of the Latin provinces as on their
moral and religious life. As bankers and moneylenders the
Syrians secured a share of the money market and their merchants
had a monopoly in the importation of the wares of the Levant.
They sold its dried fruit, its wines, its spices and seasonings, its
perfumes, its papyrus, its glass, its silk, its purple stuffs, its
precious stones and also its jewelry which was imitated by native
craftsmen in the West. At the same time they introduced the
worship of their foreign gods and attracted the devout to the
temples of Adonis or Atargatis, the *dea Syria*.

But this dispersal, recalling that of the Jews, was no less important for the economic development of Syria itself. The remains
of fine villages, bearing witness to a wide distribution of wealth in
districts which do not seem marked out by nature for such
prosperity, show that what is happening to-day in Lebanon must
have happened in antiquity: emigrants returned home built themselves large and substantial residences out of the savings which
they had amassed. Colonization of the West in this way led to a
constant accretion of capital in Syria which added to the wealth
accumulating there as a result of an extensive export trade. The
rôle of middleman between the East and Europe which was later
to be the greatness of Genoa and Venice fell in antiquity to Syria.
Not without good reason did the emperors set up at Antioch one
of their chief mints for silver and gold, and a second at Tyre.

IV. SYRIAN CULTURE

The wealth of Syria under the Empire is revealed to us above
all in the magnificence of its towns. The monuments of which
remains are still to be seen almost all date from the Roman period,
a period marked by a fever of building in cities that compete
in improvements to which the private purses of the well-to-do
contributed as much as the municipal exchequer. The ruins of
Antioch are still buried under the deposits of the Orontes, and we
can form some idea of its magnificence only from the enthusiastic
account of writers; but those of Apamea, Gerasa, Palmyra and of
other towns still testify to the splendour of their past. They are
usually built on a regular plan with a system of parallel streets
meeting one another at right angles in accordance with the
teaching of Hippodamus of Miletus (vol. v, p. 19). This type of
city seems to have been adopted by the Seleucids for all the
colonies founded by them. A broad avenue starting from a gate
in the encircling wall and bordered by a double covered colonnade

giving the shops protection from sun and rain, a large-scale prototype of the modern *souks*, ran past the buildings from one side to
the other. At Antioch its length was thirty-six stades. The wide
lateral porticos were paved in marble or mosaic; arcades were
inserted to give access to transverse streets, and at the intersection
of two colonnaded avenues were set up four-sided archways
decorated with columns and statues. Sumptuous public buildings,
rectangular or circular, temples, baths, theatres, basilicas, gymnasiums, stadiums and exedras lined the principal streets. The
descriptions which we possess of the buildings of Herod at
Jerusalem and of their gorgeous decoration in which marble,
bronze, gold and precious stones were combined, can give us
some idea of the luxurious interiors of some of them. But thought
was taken also for the comforts of life and the science of town-
planning had reached a high degree of perfection. A double
system of conduits ran under the streets: large pipes distributed
under pressure clear and healthy water, which had been brought
from a distance by aqueducts, to the baths and to the storeys of the
houses, and drains carried out of the city flood-water and sewage.

The best preserved are the temples, of which the oldest still
standing is that of Palmyra dedicated in A.D. 32 to the supreme
trinity (p. 631). Inside a large outer rectangular wall decorated
with pilasters and porticos which fixed the boundary of the
harăm, stood the sanctuary which was closed by bronze doors and
of which the columns supported bronze capitals. The rather drily
sober style which characterizes its sculptural decoration and
recalls the Neo-Attic school, contrasts with the luxuriant foliage
which runs over the walls of the two temples at Heliopolis on which
work proceeded from the time of Nero to the third century. The
temple of Artemis at Gerasa, on a terrace overlooking the town, to
which one ascended by a broad stairway, still has thirteen columns
standing out of the 260 which surrounded it. These are the most
impressive of the buildings still left among a countless number of
others to which time has been less kind. The streets and buildings
were ornamented with many statues in marble and bronze.
Sidon in particular had bronze-founders of repute[1]. The oriental
taste for dazzling polychromy is seen in the abundance of mosaics
(an art in which Syrians have always excelled) and of paintings,
which were sometimes ranged one above another and covered the
entire surface of the wall. Series of pictures in temples were
intended to instruct the illiterate and took the place for them of

---

[1] Philo, *Leg. ad Gaium*, 31, 222.

the sacred books which their ignorance prevented them from reading.

Questions about the characteristics of Syrian art and of the influence which it had or was subject to, provide matter for endless discussion since the powerful pleas of Strzygowski on behalf of oriental originality. But out of a mass of doubtful points certain facts emerge.

When the Seleucids established themselves in Syria the country possessed a Syrian art which was the result of a technique a thousand years old, and which, if it was not inventive, was at least very productive. The influence of the Greeks in the Nearer East had long preceded their conquest of it. In Persia the Achaemenids of the sixth century had already combined types borrowed from Ionia with those of their Semitic or Iranian subjects. New combinations resulted from the native art, which was already composite, and that which the kings of Antioch caused to prevail. Syro-Persian elements modified more or less according to the district the genuine Greek traditions. The difference was not only in the means employed and the forms adopted, but even in the conception of subject. In pagan times, as later in the Christian period, Greek idealism was opposed by the realism of the Syrian school, and in religious iconography the subtle spirit of the East delighted in an abstruse symbolism which was alien to the aesthetic of the direct genius of the Greek. Art had not only to elevate the soul by its beauty but to instruct the mind.

In the Phoenician ports, at Antioch and in the neighbouring towns, where Hellenism reigned supreme, work seems to have been produced which was not fundamentally different from that turned out by the workshops of Athens or Ephesus[1]. But native traditions remained stronger and counted for more in the countries where the conquering Macedonians had left only a few scattered colonies or had exercised only a loose control. And besides, there was a distinction, as in the case of language, between the different classes of society, for the popular works remained more oriental than those which conformed to the taste of the aristocracy. The sculpture of Palmyra, isolated by the desert, was a hellenized offshoot of Aramaic stock, and always retained a very pronounced savour of its country (p. 633). The façades at Petra

[1] The discovery in 1934 of a potter's studio at Gerasa with thousands of fragments of statuettes is instructive. 'All the pieces show strong Greek influence, many of the terra-cottas being copies of well-known classical Greek statues' (*Am. Journ. Arch.* XXXIX, 1935, p. 120). Gerasa was a Seleucid colony and it never forgot the fact.

enable us to see the introduction of 'Ptolemaic' forms to a native architecture, and the paintings at Doura[1], which was removed from Mediterranean influence by Parthian invasion, allow us to study better than anywhere else the fusion of Greek and Oriental elements which prepares the way for medieval Christian art.

Had the Roman conquest and the foundation of colonies of veterans an influence on art comparable with that on language (p. 624)? Some scholars maintain that in this sphere as in that of government Italy imposed her supremacy above all, and that the architecture of Syrian towns and their sculptural decoration derive from buildings already existing in the capital of the Empire. The neo-classicism of the Augustan age was reproduced throughout the whole Mediterranean world and was the source from which the provincial schools and notably that of Syria were derived. Other scholars on the other hand hold the view that Syria in this respect was in advance of Rome and was her pattern, and that it far surpassed her in inventive genius and in the technical knowledge and skill of its workmen. It has been supposed, in particular, that Apollodorus of Damascus, the famous architect of the forum and market-place of Trajan, copied the buildings of his native country on the slopes of the Quirinal (p. 781).

It cannot wholly be denied that Italian architecture, introduced in the colonies of Berytus and Heliopolis or made use of by military engineers, may have modified in the first century certain formulas of construction as it had hitherto been practised in Graeco-Semitic countries. But in all probability this influence was very limited and did not last long. At the same time the question of priority as between Italy and Syria will often remain insoluble as long as we do not know what the buildings of the Seleucids were like. The champions of Oriental dependence on the West take too little account of an essential fact: Antioch, which was the capital of a vast kingdom before it was that of a Roman province, was the second Greek town in the Roman Empire and only a little behind Alexandria in importance[2]. It was adorned by its kings with magnificent buildings and was famous for its beauty. It appears highly probable that its temples and public buildings served as a model for Syria in pagan times, as later in the Christian period, and the form of its churches and their decoration were to be followed at a distance in the surrounding countries.

The ascendancy of Antioch in all northern Syria showed itself also in buildings on a more modest scale, in private houses and

---

[1] See Volume of Plates v, 26, *a*; 28, *b*.

[2] Strabo xvi, 750. Cf. Josephus, *Bell. Jud.* iii [2, 4], 29.

tombs. In no other province of the Empire is the humble architecture of the countryside represented by so many ruins, so well preserved and of so many different types. They enable us to reconstruct exactly the picture of the domestic life of the large and small country landowners. In the districts of Syria where stone in square blocks was used to build solid walls, whether the grey limestone from the mountains of the north or the dark basalt of the Haurân, we can follow through the first six centuries of the Christian era the continuous development of this series of buildings: separate villas with a portico in front and outhouses set round a large court, houses set along the streets of villages, monumental and rock tombs, rustic temples of villagers, and the baths which preceded the hammāms of the Moslems. In this incomparable collection can be studied in detail how Greek technique modified or sometimes took the place of the technique handed down by ancient local tradition.

Syria contained within its borders a motley crowd of people in whose social standing, more or less advanced, was to be found a complete contrast of culture and barbarism. Between the shepherds of the desert or the troglodytes of the mountains with their savage ways and the cultured town-dwellers, large landowners or wealthy shipowners, eloquent rhetoricians or acute thinkers, there was a great gulf. In the upper classes a luxurious private life corresponded to the splendour of their aristocratic residences. If a wretched member of the lowest agricultural class, clad in a fleece or simple loin-cloth, lived exposed to the weather practically in a state of nakedness, the well-to-do middle classes loved to dress in fine linen or silken materials, dyed in bright colours and embroidered in gold or braided, and women of fashion loaded their head, neck and arms with a mass of jewels. The fertility of the country ensured to landed families a life of abundant leisure. According to Posidonius[1] his countrymen were great lovers of jovial gatherings and of good cheer. They spent the day at the gymnasium anointing themselves with scented oil as at the bath, or at endless banquets where they lingered drinking freely to the sound of instruments. Their love of music and dancing showed itself in secular merrymakings as well as in religious festivals. During the *Brumalia*, which lasted nearly all the month of December, the whole of Antioch, so a Syriac writer tells us[2], resembled a tavern, and the streets rang all night long with the noise

---

[1] *F. Gr. Hist.* 87, 10 (II, p. 228).

[2] Isaac of Antioch, ed. Bickell, I, p. 295. The piece is really by Isaac of Edessa (Baumstark, *Syr. Lit.* p. 147, n. 7).

of singing and of serenades to the magistrates and leading men under the windows of their palaces. The pursuit of sport took the place of the martial exercises which the *pax Romana* made superfluous. For the aristocracy the most manly sport was hunting, which was exciting in a country where big game was abundant and even the lion had not disappeared. The people in the towns thronged to the *venationes* of the amphitheatre, where the Romans had also introduced their cruel contests of gladiators. The mob showed an equal passion for the chariot-races of the hippodrome, the athletic contests of the stadium and the performances of the theatre. Syria produced in superabundance and exported abroad charioteers, athletes, actors, dancers, flute-players, harpists, performers on the sambuca, and tumblers and rope-walkers of both sexes. It is significant that Publilius Syrus, who in the time of Caesar introduced to the Latin stage the sparkling dialogue of the mime, had come to Rome from Antioch. Jockeys and boxers carved the story of their victories in marble that their glory should not perish with them. If the superintendents of the public games in all the cities vied with one another in the money lavished upon them, those of Antioch surpassed all the others in magnificence. Nowhere did the joys of life so far outdo serious matters as in this city of pleasure and dissipation, and its loose morals seemed shocking even in an age when prostitution flaunted itself everywhere. Licentiousness extended even to certain religious festivals, like the Maïouma, the occasion of great depravity.

At the same time Antioch was a great centre of liberal studies, and letters were held in honour[1]. The course of study, about which we are enlightened especially by the autobiography of Nicolaus of Damascus[2], was in Syria what it was at that time throughout the Greek world. Education began with grammar, which was particularly necessary for children whose mother tongue was often a Semitic dialect (p. 622). A curious funeral bas-relief from Palmyra shows us a schoolboy in national dress holding a stylus in his hand and writing on tablets on which can be read the last letters of the Greek alphabet $\phi \chi \psi \omega$. The memorial was to recall his keenness in learning the foreign language[3]. After grammar the pupil proceeded to poetics and exercises in verse composition, and that is why these Orientals, with their heads filled with reminiscences from school, have had engraved in marble even in the heart of Susiana so many sorry efforts in verse.

[1] Cicero, *pro Archia*, 3, 4; cf. Philostratus, *Vitae Soph.* II, 5 and Eusebius, *Hist. Ecc.* VII, 29.   [2] *F. Gr. Hist.* 90, 132 (II, p. 421).

[3] M. Rostovtzeff, *Caravan Cities*, pl. XXII, 3; Volume of Plates V, 62, *a*.

The adolescent next passed on to rhetoric, the mistress of the ancient world, and was initiated into music and mathematics, the essential preparation, in the prevailing theory[1], for the understanding of philosophy, which was the crown of a liberal education.

Did the quality of the intellectual life of the Syrians correspond to the refinement of their material life? Historians of note have doubted it. These hellenized Semites have been represented as a vivacious people, witty, quick in the uptake and of ready repartee, but superficial, frivolous, living for the day and lacking in depth and seriousness; and certainly they cultivated with success the lighter forms of literature. In the Alexandrine age Meleager of Gadara and Antipater of Sidon were distinguished among the bright spirits who turned epigrams of studied elegance with a dash of sentiment. The epic poems of Archias of Antioch, who was fortunate enough to have Cicero as his counsel, seem to have been works of respectable mediocrity and we may imagine the four poems of Seleucus of Emesa[2] on angling are no great loss. But if the Syrian was hardly successful in this stately *genre*, he secured a triumph in satire. His bantering humour, always on the alert, quick at seizing on the ridiculous and not sparing even the emperors with its merciless jests, made him excel in the criticism of manners. In the third century B.C. the cynic, Menippus of Gadara, had furnished the model which was to be imitated under the Antonines with more asperity and bluntness by his compatriot Oenomaus. He was also the model of Lucian of Samosata, who throughout the ages has been the most popular of the ancient pamphleteers. His mordant irony, his winged fancy, his grace and ease of style, all the qualities of the writer which he put to the service of a robust common sense, would have made of him a great man if his jeering criticism had not been purely negative and destructive. More curious is the case of a Christian, Tatian 'the Assyrian,' who mocks the Greek science on which he was brought up, in language which is up to all the tricks of the sophistic art. The fertile imagination which distinguishes Lucian comes out in other writers of his race and puts them in the company of the story-tellers of the Thousand and One nights. The *Babylonica* of Iamblichus, whose nationality was as Syrian as his name, was a novel of adventure in which through thirty-nine books tragic or paradoxical situations succeeded one another in order to keep up the interest as in a serial story; and a grave priest of Emesa, Heliodorus, did not despise this artificial genre in

[1] Cf. e.g. Justin Martyr (of Nablus), *Dial. c. Tryph.* 11, 4.
[2] The Ἀσπαλιευτικά, see P. W. *s.v.* Seleukos (43), col. 1251.

which an amorous intrigue serves as the pretext for fantastic incidents and moral lessons.

A talkative, ready-tongued people (as they still are to-day), the Syrians seemed born for rhetoric. Theodorus of Gadara, who was the head of a school of sophists, numbered Tiberius among his pupils at Rhodes; under Trajan Isaeus had at Rome a period of resounding fame. Maximus of Tyre was likewise a successful lecturer, a mere phrase-maker, in spite of his pretensions to being a philosopher, and his banal eclecticism was hardly more than a brilliant ornament for his addresses to people of quality. If these talented men were by no means geniuses and if their skill in popularizing the ideas of others stood in the way of their originality, they show at least that the schools of rhetoric continued to flourish in Syria, and some of their pupils, like Hadrian of Tyre under Marcus Aurelius, Fronto of Emesa and Apsines of Gadara in the third century, became famous professors at Athens and were loaded with honours by the emperors. These orators herald the masters of profane and sacred eloquence who were to be the glory of Antioch in the following age: Libanius and John Chrysostom.

But to forget all but this brilliant futility would be to underrate the Syrian mentality. The close mixture of Semitic and Greek blood produced minds eager to know and conspicuously gifted for philosophic speculation. None of the hybrid races of the Empire exercised so strong an influence on its intellectual and moral development by its merits as well as by its defects. It gave to the world distinguished doctors, like Archigenes of Apamea, who under Trajan was one of the leaders of the eclectic school, and lawyers eminent among those of any age such as Papinian and Ulpian (p. 817). But above all and most important, Greeks and natives laboured together at theoretical problems and worked out ideas which forced themselves upon the whole ancient world. As early as the Seleucids, Zeno of Citium and many of his chief disciples, such as Diogenes of Babylonia and Antipater of Tarsus, had been Orientals, and it may be said that Stoicism was largely a Semitic philosophy not only in respect of its teachers but of its doctrines also. Its pantheism which deifies all the elements of Nature, and its acceptance of the fatalism of astrology side by side with the retention of belief in the active intervention of God in earthly matters, link the Porch with the Syro-Babylonian temples. Later there were many Syrians among the leading savants who initiated the Romans into the precepts of the various schools. The eclectic Platonist Antiochus of Ascalon accompanied Lucullus to

Asia; Antipater of Tyre converted the younger Cato to Stoicism; the sensual epicurean Philodemus of Gadara, who has become famous through the discoveries at Herculaneum, had the consul Calpurnius Piso and Virgil as his pupils. Boethus of Ascalon was the head of the Peripatetic school at Athens in the time of Augustus. The names could be multiplied. But the renown of all these disputants was eclipsed by the glory of Posidonius of Apamea, the scholar with the widest range and the most influential philosopher in the Ciceronian age. Greek in the constructive power of his genius for speculation and the rich harmony of his glowing style, he is oriental in his singular combination of the most exact knowledge with a religious mysticism and in his complaisance towards astrology and daemonology. Like Posidonius, a philosopher and writer on many subjects and, like him, a learned man interested in the study of customs and manners, Nicolaus of Damascus, the protégé of Herod the Great, succeeded in writing a hundred and forty-four books of a universal history which was superficial and moralizing. The blending of Greek thought with elements borrowed from old oriental theories was to go farther with the Syrian thinkers of the imperial age. In the second century the Pythagoreans Nicomachus of Gerasa, an expounder of the symbolism of numbers, and Numenius of Apamea, a champion of the wisdom of the Brahmins, of the dualist Magi and of Moses, whose disciples Pythagoras and Plato were supposed to have been, were the forerunners of the Neo-platonist teachers of the following age, Porphyry of Tyre and Iamblichus of Chalcis, whose school had a long life at Apamea. These Syrians guided the lofty and lonely mysticism of Plotinus more and more towards an alliance with the established forms of worship and the occult practices of theurgy.

These epigoni of Platonism constantly appeal in support of their speculations to the revelations of the 'Chaldaean Oracles' which were composed in the East probably about the year 200. They were the sacred book of a sect which prided itself on assuring the salvation of its initiates, and their verses reveal a strange mixture of fantastic mythology and metaphysical doctrines, such as is also found in Christian gnosticism. The title of the collection is a tardy sign of the prestige which continued to be enjoyed by the wisdom of the 'Chaldaeans.' This reputation was by no means ill-deserved, and the regard expressed by Strabo[1] for

[1] XVI, 739; cf. XVII, 806. The title Chaldaean occurs no less than four times in inscriptions of Palmyrene as the designation of an astronomer and astrologer. Cf. H. Ingholt, *Berytus*, I, p. 39.

the Chaldaei, that is to say for the Babylonian priests of the Hellenistic age and of his own day, is found to be justified by a study of the cuneiform texts. To this priesthood indisputably belongs the glory of having founded scientific astronomy, which in Babylonia reached its highest point under the Seleucids (vol. VII, p. 195). The Greeks till Ptolemy made use of the observations which had been patiently noted by the Chaldaeans from remote antiquity. Their follower Seleucus, of Seleuceia on the Red Sea, seventeen centuries before Copernicus held that the earth revolved about the sun. Oriental astronomers were the first to establish the primordial part played by the sun in the system of the universe which surrounds us and recognized it as the mover of the planets. At the same time they fastened on it as the arbiter of destiny, the master of nature and of humanity, for all, or nearly all, believed in astrological determinism. The Syrians took over from them both astronomy and its bastard sister, and they worked with the Egyptians for the spread of the pseudo-science. Apocryphal writings passing under the name of Zoroaster, who was turned into the head of the 'Chaldaeans,' are the oldest evidence of this propaganda. The most extensive of the astrological treatises which have come down to us is the work of a writer from Antioch in the second century A.D., Vettius Valens. In the nine books of his *Anthologiai* this compiler, whose polemical spirit ill conceals his mediocrity, interpolates in his formulae for the casting of horoscopes digressions in which he expresses in vulgar language a philosophy still more vulgar.

The solar theology of the 'Chaldaeans' had a decisive effect upon the final development of Semitic paganism, and this is the last point with which we are here concerned. Syrian religion in the imperial age was a collection of singularly complex beliefs, into which in the course of a very long history there had come a combination of the most diverse elements. A profound faith to which a large number of temples and dedications everywhere bears witness, and a fervour which might reach the most extreme forms of mysticism—the ecstatic expression of some of the faces in the frescoes of Doura is striking—prompted a credulous people to accept an infinite number of cults and superstitions. The corner of the world inhabited by the Semites, from the Tigris to the Red Sea, has always been a land of fervent devotion. From there have come four great religions: Judaism, Christianity, Manicheism and Islam.

The oldest religious conceptions of the Semitic tribes survived especially in country districts; relics of a primitive nature-worship

which have not entirely disappeared even to-day: the worship of
high places and steep rocks, of health-giving water which wells
forth to sustain life or flows in genial streams, of sacred trees
which no axe may touch, and, above all, of meteoric stones in
which God resides, of animals, and especially of doves and fish.
On the other hand, veneration of the divine pair Baal and Baalat,
masters of the land made fertile by them and of man who is their
slave, heads of clans who become protectors of cities—and also
adoration of Baal-Shāmīn, lord of heaven, who speaks and hurls his
thunderbolt in the crash of the storm; finally the superstitious
dread of countless local spirits, now kindly, now malignant,
abounding in all nature.

But it is not easy to grasp even the essential features of these
primitive beliefs because in the course of the ages they had become
so overlaid with foreign ideas. Syria was a land with a very busy
trade, always exposed to the enterprises of conquering kings, and
from the beginning of its history open to outside influence. The
influence of Egypt was felt in Phoenicia, notably at Byblus and as
far as Heliopolis beyond Lebanon[1]. That of Babylonia was particularly strong in the east and the north of the country, where it
introduced the worship of Bel and prompted the grouping of
powerful gods in trinities, like that worshipped at Palmyra
(p. 631). Later, under the Achaemenids, the dualist Magi came
from Persia; their conception of a Principle of Good, Ahura-
Mazda, reigning in the upper light, tended to raise the Aramaean
god of Heaven above all the rest of the pantheon, and they made
the confused throng of demons into an army of devils subject to
the supreme spirit of Evil. The unbending monotheism of the
Jews, who had communities scattered all over Syria and Mesopotamia, reacted on the pagan conception of the supreme God, and
the anonymous divinity of the dedications of Palmyra, 'he whose
name is blessed in Eternity,' borrows this title from the formulary
of Judaism, which was as strong in this commercial town as it was
at Antioch and at Doura. Still more profound was the influence
of Hellenism after Alexander the Great; the ancient temples were
often rebuilt in the Greek style; the native gods were assimilated
to the Olympians, Bel and Baal-Shāmīn being identified with
Zeus, Atargatis with Hera and Allath with Athena; Greek art
humanized and beautified their representations; local myths were
told after their own style by Greek poets and in this way Syro-
Babylonian legends reached even the *Metamorphoses* of Ovid.
Mysteries were introduced into Syria in imitation of those of

[1] Macrobius, *Sat.* I, 23, 11.

Greece: the commemoration of the death and resurrection of
Adonis, old rustic ceremonies which were held at the beginning of
the Sothic or canicular year (July 19), henceforth assured the
salvation of the initiated; Dionysus brought his secret rites; the
Aramaeans put him by the side of their local Baals, the Arabs of
Dusares, and the Bacchic worshippers even as far as the desert,
where the vine did not grow, met at holy feasts to drink wine as the
draught of immortality. Finally Greek philosophy tried to explain
the myths and rites of the past; Stoicism, the power of which in
the East has already been pointed out (p. 641), interpreted the
gods as personifications of the elements of nature or physical
forces, while Euhemerism regarded them as great men to whom
after their death a cult was dedicated in gratitude by their people.
This system was adopted by Herennius Philo of Byblus (c. A.D.
64–140) in his account of the Phoenician theogony in which, as
can no longer be doubted after the discovery of the mythological
poem of Ras Shamra, he made use of an old narration in Phoenician attributed to Sanchuniathon.

As a result of so many varied blendings the religion of Syria
formed a singularly incongruous conglomeration; and, as the
number of inscriptions grows, one is more and more struck by the
host of Aramaean, Phoenician, Arabian, Babylonian and Greek
deities of which it consisted. But the theology of the priests regarded all these gods as different forms of a single divinity and
they were easily confused because none had a strongly marked
personality of his own. Scholars have rightly spoken of the
'fluid' state of the Semitic religions in which the conception
formed of a divine power and the function attributed to him is
easily transferred to some power with another name; and in which
the *mal'ak*, the messenger or 'angel,' of a god is substituted for
the god himself, whose representative borrows his character and
becomes, to employ philosophical terms, his emanation or
hypostasis. Syria was acquainted with this wholesale syncretism,
which triumphed when paganism declined, before it reached
Rome.

The same diversity which characterized theology likewise prevailed in religious worship. Lucian's valuable essay on the
Syrian goddess of Hierapolis, on which recent excavations have
shed new light, gives some idea of this. Round the temple, as
at Palmyra and elsewhere, a large encircling wall marked off
the sacred ground on which, by a survival of ancient zoolatry,
animals of different kinds lived at large. The sanctuary was
Greek, rebuilt by Stratonice, the wife of Seleucus I, but at the

entrance stood gigantic phalli, and in the *naos* the statue of the goddess Atargatis, covered with gold and jewels and loaded with emblems which recalled the multiplicity of her functions, had a foreign look, while her consort Hadad was more like a Greek Zeus. In accordance with tradition archaic rites were practised in this great sanctuary whose meaning was no longer understood and of which an attempt was made to give an historical or rational explanation. Very many of these practices perpetuated under the emperors the customs of a barbarian past. The Galli of Atargatis continued to dedicate themselves to their goddess by castration. Elsewhere temple prostitution went on until the end of paganism, and human sacrifice, especially the sacrifice of children, continued to be performed in certain places until the time of Hadrian, by whom it was everywhere forbidden.

From this religion which was in so many respects obscene and cruel and which in the midst of Roman civilization kept alive the habits of untamed and bloodthirsty tribes, was to arise, by a singular contrast, the most scientific theology known to paganism, which was to force itself in the third century upon Rome herself. In the great temples an educated priesthood which meditated on the nature of divine beings and the meaning of the traditions inherited from far-off ancestors, could not escape from the influence of the science of the Chaldaeans. At the same time as it accepted their astrology and their fatalistic view of the world (p. 643), it followed them in seeing in the sun the directing power of the cosmic system. All the Baals were thenceforward turned into suns, the sun being the mover of the other stars, like it eternal and 'unconquerable,' whose revolutions together determined the succession of the phenomena of the universe according to the cycles of 'great years.' As the heart of the universe ($\kappa\alpha\rho\delta\acute{\iota}\alpha$ $\tauο\hat{υ}$ $\kappa\acute{ο}\sigma\mu\omicron\nu$) the sun was the seat of the divine energy pervading this vast organism to its extremities; as intelligent light ($\phi\hat{\omega}\varsigma$ $\nu\omicron\epsilon\rho\acute{ο}\nu$) it was the creator of the human mind, and just as it attracted and repelled the planets, so it sent to their birth the souls in the bodies which they animated and after death caused them to ascend to its bosom. This celestial immortality, in which the soul is victorious over death and participates in the eternal life of the stars that are always being reborn, was the great hope offered by the cults of Syria to the faithful. On tombs is often to be seen sculptured an eagle with outspread wings, the bird of the Sun charged with the duty of carrying the souls of the dead to its master.

Such was the final form reached by the religion of the pagan Semites, and, following them, by that of the Romans when

Aurelian, the conqueror of Palmyra, had raised *Sol invictus* to the rank of supreme divinity in the Empire. The same Semitic race which precipitated the fall of paganism was also the race which made the strongest effort to save it.

It can easily be realized how a pagan theology so close to monotheism prepared the ground for Christian propaganda. It was helped also by the presence in a large number of cities, and especially at Antioch, of many Jewish settlers, who were far from all being strict in the observance of their religion. If in the first two centuries the new faith hardly succeeded in taking root in Phoenicia at all, except in the ports along the coast, and if Lebanon and the rest of the hinterland, except Damascus, remained all but closed to evangelization, Antioch on the other hand, where the burning words of Paul had resounded, as early as the apostolic age became the mother of the Church of the Gentiles in opposition to the Judaïzers of Jerusalem (pp. 269 *sqq.*). It is here that pagans had first been converted in crowds, that they had first received the name of 'Christians,' and from here that the first missions had radiated which had so greatly advanced the work of the faith. The queen of the East thus acquired a moral supremacy which was recognized long before the patriarchate was officially established, not only in Syria but in Asia Minor and Mesopotamia and as far as Armenia and Persia. The religious authority of Antioch grows all through the history of the early Church; it was the leader and teacher in dogmatics, liturgy and art alike.

The extravagant fervour of the newly converted caused to spring up by the side of orthodoxy, 'like mushrooms[1],' a swarm of gnostic sects, fantastic systems in which the unbridled imagination of the East gave itself free play, and the captious brains of a Graeco-Syrian race, doubly friendly to disputation, were bound to multiply heresies. Montanists, Docetists, Marcionites, Novatians and others contended for men's souls before the great schisms of Nestorius and Eutyches. But if the fervent devotion of the oriental spirit shows itself in unrestrained mysticism and the development of extreme asceticism, on the other hand the best Syrian controversialists preserve a sobriety of judgment which still bears the mark of the scientific rationalism of the Greeks. The preference of Syrian art for realism rather than for allegory (p. 636) distinguished also the teaching of the school of Antioch as compared with that of Alexandria, whose priests it rivalled in culture.

Like the great mother-city herself the Church was Greek, and the Christian communities of the other Syrian cities round her

----

[1] Irenaeus *c. Haer.* i, 29.

were also Greek. Propaganda tended therefore to maintain or strengthen the predominance of Hellenism, as it did in Cappadocia (p. 611). But Christianity was a popular movement and soon also won initiates in country districts which had remained Aramaean. As early as the middle of the third century it had spread across the desert as far as the banks of the Euphrates, as is proved by the recent discovery of a chapel at Doura. From that time the priests had no choice but to use for their catechism and preaching the vulgar tongue which was all their flocks understood. In the middle of the second century Tatian 'the Assyrian' wrote his *Diatessaron* or harmony of the Gospels, which was translated into Syriac and remained in liturgical use until the fourth century (see further, vol. XII).

The centre of this propaganda in Aramaic, which extended to Mesopotamia and Iran, was Edessa, which under a superficial Greek polish had remained at bottom Semitic. About the year 204 it followed the example of its kings and went over entirely to Christianity. The gnostic Bardesanes (born A.D. 154) there exalted, in prose and verse, a dialect which was still crude, and was the true creator of literary Syriac. This was adopted by the national churches of the Monophysites and Nestorians separated from Byzantine orthodoxy and was to produce in abundance throughout the middle ages a series of works both sacred and profane. In this way the intellectual activity of the Christian Semites was to be continued, but outside the tradition to which their past greatness had belonged. Under the domination of Islam Arabic was gradually substituted for Greek even in the liturgy of the orthodox patriarchate of Antioch. And so the last trace of Hellenism disappeared from Syria.

CHAPTER XVI

EGYPT, CRETE AND CYRENAICA

I. EGYPT

THE administrative and financial system of Egypt as organized by Augustus and his successors was sketched in chapter x of the preceding volume; and though the picture there drawn was intended to represent primarily the first century of Roman rule it is applicable also in the main to the Antonine Age. Such changes as occurred between the death of Nero and the accession of Septimius Severus were due rather to the development of existing principles than to any fundamental alteration in the system itself or its details. All that is necessary now, therefore, is to note the principal differences, to attempt some characterization of the tendencies operative during the second century, and, in conclusion, to mention the much more drastic and momentous innovations introduced by the Severi.

The political status of Alexandria remained during the Antonine period as it had been under the early Empire: the coveted senate was still withheld, and the Alexandrines maintained in consequence their attitude of factious opposition, a perpetual thorn in the side of the prefect. Yet there was in one respect a change in the character of this obstructiveness. The Jewish revolt in Cyrene (see above, p. 250), which spread also to Egypt, had been disastrous to the Jewish community of Alexandria. Greatly diminished in numbers and probably still more reduced in wealth and consideration, the Jews appear to have lost much of their former importance; and after a series of anti-Semitic disturbances which occurred partly during the later stages of the Jewish revolt and partly after its suppression we hear of no more conflicts between Greek and Jew at Alexandria. A disturbance which occurred in A.D. 122 was connected with the installation of a new Apis bull; and the only surviving specimen of the class of literature known as 'Pagan Acts of the Martyrs' which refers to events of a later date than Hadrian[1] contains no reference to the Jews.

The disturbances occasioned by the Jewish revolt must have greatly impaired the prosperity of the city, portions of which were destroyed; and a regular programme of rebuilding was undertaken

[1] Wilcken, *Chrestomathie*, 20.

under Hadrian. It may have been as part of this that Hadrian established the so-called 'Library of Hadrian' as a central Record Office for the custody and registration of documents. The natural advantages of Alexandria, however, and the industry which, no less than their turbulence, distinguished its inhabitants seem to have repaired its losses. Trajan had renewed the canal from Babylon (Cairo) to the Gulf of Suez (thenceforward known as the 'River of Trajan'), which was doubtless intended in part to improve the water communications between Alexandria and the Red Sea; and the indications point to considerable commercial prosperity during much of the second century. An active trade with India continued, and there is some evidence for the existence of a Roman fleet in the Red Sea[1].

Of Naucratis and Ptolemaïs even less is known in the second century than in the first; but the small group of Greek cities in Egypt was increased by a new foundation concerning which we have a fair amount of information. This was Antinoopolis, founded by Hadrian 30 October A.D. 130 on the east bank of the Nile opposite Hermupolis in honour of his favourite Antinous, who was drowned in the river. Hadrian, with his philhellenic tendencies and his urbanizing policy, was a great founder of cities, and it was natural that he should choose this method of honouring Antinous, and should give to his new foundation a Hellenic character. Its laws were taken from those of Naucratis, though, unlike the Naucratites, its citizens enjoyed the right of *connubium* with the Egyptians, and it used, like Naucratis, the Milesian calendar, Poseideon being equated with Thoth, the first month of the Egyptian year[2]. Its inhabitants were drawn from various quarters, some from Ptolemaïs, whose people had guarded with special care the purity of their Greek blood and Greek traditions, while others were recruited from the less pure-blooded Greeks of the Fayûm and were known officially as 'settlers from the Arsinoite nome, of the Greek men[3].' Some of these latter, though willing enough to accept the privileges which citizenship bestowed, seem to have been less ready to become effective settlers; and we can trace the continued connection of one or two such families with their old homes through successive generations. Under Antoninus Pius the citizen body was strengthened by the settlement of many discharged veterans, some at least of whom

[1] *Bull. de l'Inst. fr. d'arch. or.* XXXI, 1930, pp. 1–29; M. Rostovzev, *Storia economica e sociale dell' impero romano,* p. 181 *sq.*

[2] Mary E. Dicker, *Arch. Pap.* IX, 1930, p. 226 *sq.*

[3] P. Lond. Inv. No. 1896, *Aegyptus,* XIII, 1933, p. 523 *sq.*

probably received allotments of land, and whose inclusion, since they were originally recruited from the Greek or Graeco-Egyptian elements in the population, did not violate the principle expressed by the official designation of the citizens, *Antinoeis Neoi Hellenes*. The constitution was on familiar lines, with a senate and popular assembly, the usual civic magistrates and a division of the population into tribes (apparently ten in number) and demes (probably five to each tribe). The citizens were exempted from all offices and liturgies, and from the obligation to undertake guardianships[1], outside their own city—privileges not always respected by local officials—as well as from the *enkyklion* or tax on transfers of real property[2]; and by a further bounty of the founder their children, if registered within thirty days of birth, were entitled to maintenance from funds appropriated by Hadrian to this purpose[3]. Ptolemy seems to be in error in asserting[4] that an Antinoite nome was created: we hear in the second century only of an Antinoite nomarchy, apparently part of the Hermupolite nome, but occupying a special position inasmuch as it formed the territory of the free city and the nomarch had authority in State affairs alike in city and nomarchy. Later, perhaps under Diocletian, this nomarchy became a nome[5].

The city was built on the plan characteristic of Hellenistic foundations, with straight streets intersecting at right angles, two of which, running respectively from north to south and from east to west, were of special importance. Thus were formed numbered quarters (*grammata*) and blocks (*plintheia*). With what initial difficulties the new foundation had to struggle we do not know, but it certainly justified its existence, becoming a place of importance and eventually, in Byzantine times, the capital of the Thebaid and the residence of the Duke.

No radical change had occurred in the position of the *metropoleis* or nome-capitals, but tendencies already noticeable by the end of the first century were further accentuated during the second. It is uncertain how far in early days the municipal magistrates formed a college or corporation (*koinon*), but they are found acting in a clearly corporate capacity during the Antonine period, when we hear also of some sort of popular assembly (*demos*), and by the

---

1 For this last exemption see P. Mich. Inv. No. 2922, *Journ. Eg. Arch.* XVIII, 1932, pp. 69 *sqq.*
2 P. Lond. Inv. No. 1890+1892 (*Aegyptus*, XIII, 1933, pp. 515 *sqq.*).
3 P. Lond. Inv. No. 1905 (*Aegyptus*, XIII, 1933, pp. 518 *sqq.*).
4 IV, 5, 61.
5 Wilcken, *P. Würzb.* pp. 53–8; P. Iand. 140, 12 *sqq.* note.

end of the century the word *koinon* was employed alike for the whole body of *archontes* and for the groups of particular magistrates which it included. In fact the *metropolis*, though still juristically no more than a part of the nome, a mere village indeed, had acquired *de facto* something comparable to municipal status. But this dignity was bought at a heavy cost. The liturgical system (see vol. x, p. 301 *sq.*), fully established in principle for the *munera* by the beginning of the second century, was extended to the *honores* or municipal magistracies as well. At Hermupolis about A.D. 115 the gymnasiarchy was still normally, though clearly not always, voluntary; but the fact that Hadrian granted the Antinoopolites as a special privilege exemption from both *honores* and *munera* outside their own city shows that compulsion was already a regular practice; and in the reign of Antoninus Pius we find a man of Oxyrhynchus commended for undertaking the gymnasiarchy of his own accord. By the end of the century there was no distinction, save in name, between *honores* and *munera*, and they had become a crushing burden to the middle class, upper and lower alike[1]. In A.D. 202 we find an Alexandrine making a charitable foundation for the support of liturgists in certain Oxyrhynchite villages which were 'extremely impoverished owing to the demands of the yearly liturgies for the *fiscus* and the policing of the district[2].' Even earlier than this we have evidence of the disastrous effects of the system, not least in the revolt of A.D. 153–4, since the prefect, in an edict of amnesty, speaks of the avoidance of liturgies as among the causes which led men to abandon their homes[3]; and an unpublished papyrus in the British Museum shows that at Arsinoe the exhaustion of the municipal middle class led to the expedient of impressing even villagers into the service of the magistracies; a practice forbidden, though with no lasting effect, by Septimius Severus[4].

Yet it would be rash to infer a general impoverishment of the middle class, urban or rural, in the second century. There is plenty of evidence which points to some degree of well-being. Civic pride, which in the third century led to the adoption by the *metropoleis* of high-sounding titles and to ambitious schemes of town-planning, is evident enough in the second. Membership

---

[1] Even the distinction in name disappeared in the third century (P. Lond. Inv. No. 2565).

[2] Wilcken, *Chrestomathie*, 407.   [3] *Ib.* 19.

[4] P. Lond. Inv. No. 2565. For the privilege of using this papyrus the writer is indebted to the kindness of Mr T. C. Skeat and Miss Wegener, who are to edit it.

of the 'gymnasium class' was a privilege jealously guarded, ready
advantage was taken of educational facilities, the ephebic and other
festivals were celebrated at times with a considerable outlay, and
the numerous literary papyri which date from this century indicate
a fairly high level of culture. In times of desperate need and
economic crisis, art and literature usually receive short shrift; and
if there was in towns like Oxyrhynchus a public not merely for
the more popular classics but for difficult authors like Aeschylus
and Pindar, the poets of the Old Comedy, Sophron and Archilochus
and Callimachus, we may be sure that people of means and leisure
were still to be found there. Nor were the less wealthy classes
without their recreations in the form of mime and farce, dance
and music and gymnastic displays.

In the land categories and the method of their administration
there was little change. One or two private estates (*ousiai*) are
known from papyri of the second century, but the great majority
had become part of the *patrimonium*[1] and were under the supervision of the *procurator usiacus*. The department had in some respects its own special methods of administration[2], and the conditions attaching to leases of patrimonial land would appear to
have been specially burdensome. The katoikic land retained its
identity and its separate registers; and the fact that on transfers
of this land women paid higher rates than men[3] shows that its
originally military tenure was not forgotten.

It may be due to the accident of discovery but is perhaps evidence of an improvement caused by the reforms of the capable
prefect Ti. Julius Alexander that in the latter part of the first
century we hear less of depopulation and economic distress than
in the middle of the century[4]. In the reign of Trajan however
the Jewish revolt caused heavy losses and widespread devastation,
and produced an economic crisis, which Hadrian at the beginning
of his reign sought to remedy not only by special concessions to
the tenants of the various domain lands and possibly to others,
but apparently also by sales of the less fertile royal land to private
purchasers. In A.D. 136, when a bounteous harvest succeeded

---

[1] The οὐσία Φιλοδάμου seems, for some unexplained reason, to have
been incorporated in the domain (βασιλική) land; see Kalén, *P. Berl.
Leihgabe*, p. 68[2].

[2] Kalén, *op. cit.* p. 114.　　　　　[3] P. Iand. 137.

[4] There is, however, a striking instance in A.D. 103 (P.S.I. 1043). An
unpublished papyrus in the British Museum (Egerton Pap. 13) shows that
just before the Jewish revolt under Trajan many of the dykes and canals
were in a very neglected state.

a succession of bad ones, he again issued a 'benevolent' edict in relief of the exhausted peasantry; but it was sadly limited in scope, consisting merely in a permission to pay the money dues (as opposed to those payable in kind) for the current year in a series of annual instalments. If an Emperor like Hadrian was so grudging of his favours the tax-payer could hardly hope for much consideration from less liberal rulers; and a study of the Gnomon or rules of the department of the *Idios Logos* (vol. x, p. 289 *sq.*) will give some idea of the ruthless thoroughness with which Imperial Rome turned to profit her Egyptian estate. The same spirit, that of the exploiter rather than the ruler, is seen everywhere, in the liturgical system, supported by the principle of collective responsibility, under which the liabilities of a defaulting tenant or liturgist were transferred to the members of his group, in the methods employed for the collection of the taxes, in the treatment of state debtors, and even in such petty meannesses as delay in paying the transport agents their dues, and their payment, when payment was at last made, in old grain[1].

The spirit of Roman rule appears also in a feature of the agrarian policy which played a growing part throughout the second century and, in the third and fourth, was to produce far-reaching consequences. Even in Ptolemaic times the Government had never scrupled to apply compulsion when tenants of the domain lands were slow to offer themselves; but under Roman rule this practice, at first resorted to sporadically, grew into a regular institution. Three different methods were employed. The land to be let might be distributed among the domain tenants by lot (*diairesis*); it might be assigned to a whole village, to be then divided among the tenants (*epimerismos*); or parcels of it might be attached to the holdings of neighbouring owners, the liability to cultivate it passing thenceforward with the land (*epibole*)[2]. Naturally, the land thus treated was likely to be the less productive soil, for which it was difficult to find voluntary tenants, and the burden was the greater. The three methods were not all equally indicative of economic difficulties; *epimerismos*, for example, may have been originally merely a method of equalizing the responsibility as between village and village in view of varying agricultural conditions; but it is fair to assume that increasing frequency of such practices was in general a symptom of decline, and there is no

---

[1] See, e.g., *P. Berl. Leihgabe*, p. 84; P. Würzb. 10, intr.
[2] Responsibility for the *epibole* land was probably communal; cf., e.g., P. Mich. Tebt. 123 recto, XII, 43, ὁμο(λογία)...διαιρέ(σεως) ἐπιβολῆ(ς) κώμη(ς). This (A.D. 46) seems to be the earliest instance of *epibole*.

doubt that *epibole* was always felt as a hardship, since sales of land
frequently contained a clause specifying that the land was free
from 'the village *epibole*' or 'free from the cultivation of royal,
usiac or sacred land or any other category.' It is significant
therefore that these institutions, already known in the first century,
grew ever more regular in the second; and as we advance further
into the century we hear more and more of the flight of peasants,
that expedient which in all periods has been the last resort of the
long-suffering Egyptian fellah. Individual cases of depopulation[1]
may perhaps be attributable to plague or other temporary or
local causes, but the total weight of evidence is overwhelming,
and such conditions as are revealed by the edict of Sempronius
Liberalis[2], conditions which led to the revolts of 152/3–4 and 172,
speak a language which cannot be misinterpreted. It is clear that
the policy of Rome, aimed at extracting the maximum revenue
from the soil of Egypt, imposed on the cultivators a burden which,
always heavy, grew progressively more burdensome with every
period of agricultural depression.

Yet there is danger of exaggerating the darker side. Such
evidence as that of the papyri may easily mislead; for it is abuses,
difficulties and irregularities, rather than the normal working of
the system which such documents record[3]. That the land offered
for sale by the Government found buyers, that private estates,
sometimes extensive, continued to be formed, that voluntary
tenants were usually forthcoming even for the less productive
land, and that purchasers of land from the State and tenants of
domain land were still apt to be ousted by rival bidders who offered
more favourable terms, are facts proving that agriculture could
even yet be made to pay. Documents, such as private letters
and accounts, which illustrate social life, show that existence in
a village community was by no means an unbroken round of
unremunerative toil, and archaeological finds reveal a reasonable
degree of prosperity. At Karanis, in the Arsinoite nome, which
has been more thoroughly excavated than any other Graeco-
Roman site, at Soknopaiou Nesos and Tebtunis, there is no
evidence of a really serious decline till the third century; and if
an advocate at Arsinoe in the reign of Decius could refer to the
Septimian period as a time 'when the cities were still prosperous[4],'
while we must allow for rhetorical exaggeration and the rosy haze

---

[1] E.g. S.B. 8.   [2] Wilcken, *Chrestomathie*, 19 (A.D. 154).
[3] It is worth pointing out too that the second century is better documented, so far as papyrus evidence goes, than any other period of Egyptian
history.   [4] P. Lond. Inv. No. 2565.

of distance, we may fairly assume that conditions, even at the end of the second century, were far from intolerable.

On the whole the conclusion to be drawn from all the evidence, urban and rural, is that the Antonine period was one in which, while the natural resources of Egypt and an efficient administration still secured a fair measure of general prosperity, the effects of a fundamentally mistaken policy were becoming gravely sensible, and that from this point the decline of the country proceeded at a quickening pace. This decline was probably rather accelerated than retarded by the measures of the Severi; and the present chapter would not be complete without some account of these, though considerations of space forbid any detailed discussion.

Septimius Severus visited Egypt with Caracalla towards the end of A.D. 199 and remained there for a year, travelling up the Nile as far as the southern frontier. During his visit, besides a good deal of building at Alexandria, he made far-reaching changes in the administrative system. It was very likely he who established in Egypt the important office of *rationalis* (*katholikos*) as a central authority in finance. Whether this official, who is mentioned in many documents of the third century and became still more prominent in Byzantine times, was in part intended, as has been suggested[1], to lessen the power of the prefect is uncertain; but one object of the innovation was no doubt to increase the efficiency of the financial system, for Severus was clearly impressed by the gravity of the economic position and did his utmost to devise remedies. Thus, he settled veterans on the land, and efforts were made by his prefect, Subatianus Aquila (*c.* A.D. 202–210), to bring about a return of fugitive cultivators to their homes. The same intention no doubt inspired the most notable of Severus' measures, the grant of a senate not merely to Alexandria but to the nome-capitals as well, an enlargement of the concession which must have deprived it, for Alexandrian pride, of much of its value. Increasing difficulty had for some time been felt in filling the municipal magistracies, even under compulsion, and Severus probably hoped to widen the circle of choice, while at the same time, through the system of collective responsibility, he secured an additional guarantee against default. In this way the whole body of the wealthier citizens was drawn into the net of the financial organization; for though the nucleus of the senate presumably consisted of the existing magistrates and ex-magistrates it was augmented by the enrolment of private citizens who possessed the necessary qualification. The senate, which was

[1] By M. Rostovtzeff, *Social and Econ. Hist. of the Rom. Empire*, p. 610.

presided over by a *prytanis*, was responsible both for the financial administration of the metropolis and for the appointment and warranty not only of the municipal but also of many of the higher state officials. The duties of the *strategos* were proportionately lessened; but the senate, whose powers were strictly circumscribed, was subject to his authority, and the position of the *metropoleis* fell considerably short of municipal status. The popular assembly retained some shadowy place in the system, and the urban population was divided into tribes, which were responsible in rotation for supplying the liturgies. The magistrates were normally senators, but non-senators (*idiotai*) might also be nominated, at least later in the century. The burden on the metropolis was the heavier because Severus forbade the nomination of villagers to municipal offices; but he confirmed the right of exemption to persons over seventy years of age and that of *cessio bonorum*, by which those nominated to office could escape the liability by a surrender of their property.

It was probably in connection with his grant of senates that Severus established in Egypt the *decemprimi* (*dekaprotoi*), liturgical officials charged with a general supervision over the collection of the taxes, both in money and in kind. The office continued all through the third century but disappeared about A.D. 307 with the introduction of the *praepositus pagi*. The sphere of duty of the *decemprimi* was geographically determined by toparchies, and they had authority over the state granaries, the *sitologoi*, who had previously been in charge of these, becoming their subordinates. A change was also made in village administration by placing the chief authority in the hands of comarchs; and finally it seems to have been Severus who instituted, on the Alexandrian model, the office of *nyktostrategos*, as chief of police in the *metropolis*[1].

In the year 212 Caracalla, by his famous Constitution, extended the Roman citizenship to all the free inhabitants of the Empire. There has been much controversy whether the first of the three edicts contained in a mutilated papyrus at Giessen is the Constitutio Antoniniana, what is the meaning of a clause excepting the *dediticii*, and whether the native Egyptians belonged to this class and were therefore excluded from the scope of the measure. The result of recent research is to make it almost certain that this text is indeed the Constitutio Antoniniana; and in the present writer's

---

[1] The author wishes to express his indebtedness to Miss Wegener of Leyden, who has kindly allowed him to consult her unpublished thesis on the senates of Egypt; and to Mr E. E. Turner for a similar service with regard to an unpublished article on the *dekaprotoi*.

opinion it seems clear that the Egyptians as a whole received the citizenship. The change probably made little practical difference. The new citizens do not appear to have been exempt from poll-tax; and though they were now subject to Roman law, in practice wide concessions were made to existing usage, and a hybrid law arose, combining Roman and Graeco-Egyptian elements. Enfranchisement entailed liability to the *vicesima hereditatum*; but it is going too far to suppose that this result was the main reason for the measure.

Whatever Caracalla's motives for his edict, there can be no doubt that his father's reforms were intended to remedy the state of Egypt, tightening up the existing system, preventing evasion of responsibilities on the part of any class, and securing, by improvements in technique, a more equitable distribution of burdens. The policy was however a failure. The papyri of the third century, which are fairly numerous, though less so than those of the second, speak, in language which cannot be misinterpreted, of a rapid and continuous decline. The *metropoleis* became progressively impoverished; the number of those qualified for magistracies and senatorial rank was so reduced that the rural population was again drawn on, in defiance of Severus' edict, and in certain places some magistracies were suppressed altogether. Lands fell out of cultivation; neglect of the canals caused serious desiccation of the soil and the beginning of that process which in the fourth century led to the abandonment of many once populous villages, to the profit of modern archaeology but to the economic loss of Egypt; and the debasement of the coinage produced a dizzy rise in prices and finally a slump in the old currency comparable only to that which in several European countries followed the Great War. It was high time that an attempt at reform should be made; but Diocletian's measures, which substituted a simpler and more rough-and-ready system of taxation for the complex and highly articulated methods in force were themselves a confession of the bankruptcy of the Roman government; and they only made matters worse. Without a complete change in the spirit of the administration, an abandonment of the idea that Egypt was a cow to be milked for the benefit of the Empire, no real improvement was possible; and the Byzantine Servile State, in which an exhausted country was divided between almost feudal nobles, powerful enough to set the Imperial government at defiance, and a semi-servile peasantry, and in which the *metropoleis* had become little better than big villages under the heel of the noble houses, was the outcome of an inexorable evolution.

II. THE PROVINCE OF CRETE AND CYRENAICA

Crete and Cyrenaica became a single Roman province under the Republic. It was convenient to join them together, since they were near to one another, their cultures were similar, and they had come under the direct rule of Rome at about the same time. Under Augustus this union was maintained, or rather restored, after its breakdown during the Civil Wars. And now to the purely practical reasons in its favour there was added the more general desire to return to tradition, and also, perhaps, a concern for the special circumstances of Cyrenaica, which was less fitted than Crete to be a separate province. For while the great island was in a way self-contained, enjoying, and able to enjoy, a uniform and homogeneous life of its own, Cyrenaica, like Africa proper, shared both the life of the Mediterranean, which had reached the height of material development and culture, and the life of the interior of the African continent, which was still in a state of savage barbarism. This contrast had given rise to struggles between the Greek colonists in the cities and the native population in the distant past of Cyrenaica's freedom and perhaps under the Ptolemies. Now it gave rise to wider and more difficult problems, as Roman rule and civilization tended to expand southwards, leaving the narrower sphere of the cities within which Greek colonization had traditionally confined itself, and as, with the unification of government along the north of Africa, the problem of the conquest and pacification of the interior became more extensive and complex.

It would have been Augustus' normal policy to deal with such differences in the political and social conditions of the two parts of Cyrenaica, either by separating them administratively, as in Africa proper, or by joining the whole province with Africa. It is not unlikely that such a union was established, at least partially, for a short time under Augustus (p. 667), but it was impossible to maintain it; Cyrenaica was too far distant from Africa, and separated from it by the inhospitable deserts of the Syrtes region, and quite different in its political and cultural character. On the other hand, the setting up of two administrative centres within so small an area would have given rise, even earlier than it did in Africa, to all those difficulties which actually arose there, and which necessitated in practice the separation of the military and civil powers. These considerations, together with those already mentioned, probably induced Augustus to maintain the union of Cyrenaica with Crete. But this union was purely administrative, inasmuch as both were under the same proconsul: they remained quite separate in their economic, cultural, and political development, each retaining its own peculiar life and character; and even in matters of administrative organization each was considered apart from the other, as a self-contained unit.

Thus it is certain that each region had its own provincial assembly. Of the Cretan *Koinon*, we have ample evidence in inscriptions and coins; it was in existence before the Roman conquest, and continued after it, assuming that combination of political and religious aspects which we find generally among the provincial assemblies of the Empire. In Cyrenaica we have no record of a *Koinon* under the Empire, but we may infer its existence both from analogy with Crete and with the other provinces, and from evidence of prosecutions and actions brought by the people against some of their governors[1]: for such actions were normally set on foot by these assemblies. The Cretan provincial assembly cannot ever have represented also the interests of the cities of Cyrenaica, for in all texts and coins of the Roman period it is consistently called the *Koinon* of the Cretans, *Commune Cretensium*.

The division between the two regions may be observed also in their adoption of provincial Eras. In Cyrenaica the Era in general use after Augustus is the Actian of 31 B.C.; the Era previously in use is also followed, but it occupies a subordinate position. Crete followed neither of these. And finally, the division of the province, each part of which clung to its autonomy, is exemplified in the coinage. Sometimes the governor issued two series of coins, one for circulation in Crete, the other in Cyrenaica; sometimes the same coin bears on its two sides the symbols of the two regions, distinct from one another. And though such coins for the most part belong to the pre-Augustan period, they are not on that account less valuable as evidence for the later ages.

In view of this division between the two parts of the province, it will be better to examine separately their life and development under the Empire.

III. CRETE

Crete was annexed after its conquest by Q. Caecilius Metellus in 67 B.C. For more than a century it had contacts with Rome or her allies and enemies; and in the last age of the Republic it shared the life of the Roman State. The island was populous, rich in

---

[1] Tacitus, *Ann.* III, 38, 70; XIV, 18; *Hist.* IV, 45.

natural resources, situated on the route to Egypt and Asia, and it could neither be forgotten nor neglected. In the decades that followed the conquest it was settled by groups of veterans, who found excellent land for cultivation and were the first centres from which spread the influence of Rome. The triumvir Antony, seeking for allies in his war with Caesar's murderers, had granted financial exemptions to the cities, and had conferred Roman citizenship on some of the inhabitants, while Octavian assigned to Capua land in the territory of Cnossus. Thus at the beginning of the Empire peaceful and profitable relations existed between Rome and the island, and these relations now became closer and more firmly established. As a result, Crete enjoyed the advantages of material prosperity and of internal peace, which had been destroyed in the past by continual internal struggles. This fuller participation in the life of the Empire could only come slowly, not only because this was the general policy of Rome, but also because all islanders cling to their traditions, the Cretans even more than others on account of their splendour and the halo of mystery and legend that surrounded them. For these reasons, a complete and profound romanization of the Cretans was not possible.

Roman citizenship had already been granted on a fairly large scale by the later governors under the Republic. Antony, as we have said, was especially liberal, and his gentile name is very often found in Cretan inscriptions. The older gentile names of the Republic are relatively common too: Caecilius, from the first conqueror, Junius, Marcius, Octavius, Cornelius and the like. Compared with these, and allowing for the difference between the durations of the Republican and Imperial dominations, Imperial names are relatively rare, except those of Flavius and Tiberius Claudius. But after the third century the name of Aurelius, which was spread to all provinces by the Edict of Caracalla, is also uncommon. There is, in general, a noticeable variety of names in Cretan inscriptions of the Roman period; and this shows that citizenship, except in certain particular periods, cannot have been granted in the island *en bloc* or on a large scale.

From the *cognomina*, some of which are of a purely local character, while the rest are all, or nearly all, of Greek origin, it is clear that the population of the island was homogeneous; and in this it differed greatly from Cyrenaica. Foreign elements in the ports and towns, coming from Egypt, Cyrenaica, or Asia Minor, had not touched the mass of the population, which remained compact, resisting any infiltrations from outside. Nor does it seem that the Jewish communities, which were established there in the Hellenistic period, ever assumed much importance: if we may judge from the sources, the fall of Jerusalem and of the rising of the Jews in the neighbouring regions of Egypt and Cyrenaica had no repercussions in Crete.

The Roman conquest, then, brought to Crete, and especially to those towns which were centres of the provincial government, a certain number of Romans and Italians—colonists, officials, merchants, and landowners—but it seems that they had not changed the nature and character of the native population. At Gortyn these Romans formed a *conventus*, governed by *curatores*, and provided with its own revenues. But there is no record of other *conventus*, nor of other similar organizations (*pagi, vici*). And there is no trace in the inscriptions or literary sources of the Imperial age of the colonists that settled under the Republic. Inscriptions record only the property of an Augusta, perhaps an empress, while Statius refers to a great landowner, Flavius Ursus[1].

The distribution of the population remained unchanged under Rome. The government assisted the development of agriculture, both by securing peace, and by improving the land and by works of engineering; and for political or other reasons, some cities were especially favoured, while others, which had flourished previously, suffered a decline. But the general aspect of the island remained the same, with the population and influence concentrated in the towns.

The communal constitution did not change, though perhaps it became a little simpler, as a result of the decrease of civic autonomy; but its organization remained the same. The supreme magistrates are the *kosmoi*, presided over by a *protokosmos*, and assisted by a *Boule*. The lower magistrates are the *grammateis* who are in charge among other things of the archives and of the record offices. The people continues to be divided into tribes, which keep their old organization. The only city with the constitution of a colony is Cnossus (Colonia Julia Nobilis Cnossus), which is ruled by duumvirs. Cnossus, Gortyn, and the other principal cities have the right of coining money, and the mints seem to have been particularly active under Tiberius, Gaius, and Nero. But only a few are still working towards the beginning of the third century; most of them came to an end under the first Antonines. Compared with these city currencies, the coins issued by the provincial *Koinon* are much more numerous. We do not find many *patroni*

---

[1] *Silv.* II, 6, 67.

in Crete, nor do we yet know of any *curatores* there (see above, p. 219); a fact which suggests that the cities were much wiser in their financial administration than they were, for example, in Asia Minor. Another indication of good order in the island is the total absence of those struggles between cities over honorific titles (πρώτη, μητρόπολις, λαμπροτάτη κ.τ.λ.) which were the reproach of the Greeks in Asia Minor. This is the more noteworthy in that before the Roman domination the island was continually disturbed by wars between the cities. But now we find only one *metropolis*, the capital, Gortyn; and neither in the inscriptions nor in the coinage is there any trace of the other titles.

The conservative character of the island is particularly clear in those forms of life which are most intimately connected with the people and express their most profound feelings, language and religion. Greek is still everywhere spoken; indeed, in some parts the older language, the so-called Eteo-Cretan, remains in use, and expressions derived from it are found in some inscriptions together with words of Greek. Latin is never more than the official language, and does not pass into popular usage; it is found only in inscriptions in the capital, or on public monuments, and even there is often displaced by Greek, or combined with it. Only Cnossus produced a coinage with Latin inscriptions.

The same is true of religion. We find in Crete all the various forms of religion by means of which the provinces expressed their loyalty to the Empire: there is the cult of Rome and of Augustus, with its *sacerdos provinciae* (ἀρχιερεύς) and a communal priest at Gortyn, the cults of the Imperial family, and of the Senate. But all this, with its celebrations of dynastic events, is purely official, and never penetrates deeply among the natives, who remain faithful to their ancestral religion. Emperors and governors pay respectful homage to the most venerated divinities of the island, above all to those whose cults are connected closely with myths and primitive legends. Zeus and Hermes are worshipped at Ida, where the cult of the Curetes is also very strong. Dictynna and Asclepius are widely honoured, and patronized by the Emperors, as is the temple of Zeus Skylios at Rhythium[1]. The sanctuary of Dictynna became the centre of a small community with its own coinage, while the temple of Asclepius at Leben ranked with Cos and Epidaurus as a sanctuary-hospital, to which came pilgrims from Cyrenaica and Egypt and even from Rome. Most of the

---

[1] A fragmentary inscription of A.D. 120 (*Inscr. Cret.* I, p. 304) refers to an earlier document, perhaps of the Neronian period, and to ordinances of Metellus, clearly the conqueror of the island, and of the earlier emperors.

dedications for healings belong to the time of Hadrian. Artemis enjoys widespread veneration, and is sometimes confused with Dictynna, sometimes with Britomart, another indigenous goddess. Kore and Demeter maintain their character of earth-goddesses, and are therefore connected with burial. On coins, the Cretan myths and legends are much used: the Labyrinth, the infant Zeus nursed by the Nymph, Zeus Cretagenes, Europa on the bull, local heroes, Gortys and so on.

The cults of Ephesian Artemis and of Cybele, and that of the Egyptian gods are observed here as fervently as they are in the rest of the Empire. But they cannot be considered as a Roman importation, for they were held in honour before the conquest. Only one Italian deity seems to have been introduced into Crete, *Fortuna Primigenia*, and it would seem that this cult declined after the Republican period. Christianity spread in the island easily and quickly. It was propagated by Jewish communities, some of whose members were in Jerusalem at the time of the Crucifixion. Churches seem to have been formed very early, according to the evidence of the Apostle Paul, and the disciple Titus was left there to organize them; with him the first bishopric comes into existence, and others follow until the beginning of the second century. Probably the religions which were then rivals of Christianity were also spreading in the island—for example Orphism, of which there is evidence in a gold tablet found at Eleutherna. So far no trace has been found of Mithraism, but it is hard to believe that it had no adherents. On the other hand, this cult was mainly propagated through the army, and since Crete never had a permanent garrison, it would not be surprising if it prospered very little there, if at all.

The history of the island in the early centuries of the Christian era contains no happenings worthy of note, nor does it seem that much interest was taken in outside events, in Rome, in the rest of the Empire, or in the neighbouring regions. We have already noticed that there is no evidence of any repercussions in Crete of the rising of the Jews in Egypt and Cyrenaica (p. 662). There is, it is true, one inscription to the Numen and Providentia of the Emperor and of the Senate, on the anniversary of the death of Sejanus; but it is set up by the proconsul, and can only be interpreted as the expression of ostentatious loyalty on the part of the magistrate towards the Emperor. Perhaps it was this isolation from outside events, as well as its geographical position, which led to the selection of the island as a place of refuge for fugitives and suspects[1].

[1] Tacitus, *Ann.* IV, 21.

Once peace, both external and internal, was assured, the immediate concern of the emperor was to encourage its material welfare. And as agriculture was the main resource of the population, the Imperial government took care that it should develop as fully as possible, with the assistance of those technical improvements of which the Romans were masters, and by means of which they could remedy or minimize natural obstacles and deficiencies. In this work, they were unhampered by any of those difficulties which could arise where there was no regular system of landownership.

The ownership of land, it seems, was mainly in the hands of large proprietors, among whom, besides private persons, were Italians, even members of the Imperial family, and also temples and the several Cretan cities. But as a result of the internal struggles before the conquest, and of the administrative disorganization caused by the Civil Wars, there must have been a good deal of confusion in the system of ownership. This required and received the attention of the government, which restored rights usurped from the cities by private individuals, and settled questions of boundaries between one city and another[1].

The technical works undertaken by the Romans to deal with natural difficulties seem to have been much the same as in the other provinces of the Empire: roads facilitating internal communication, aqueducts, reservoirs, protection against floods, and the like. Similar improvements were made in the cities, for whose development the emperors of the first and second centuries provided liberally. It is true that there are no great centres of Roman remains, comparable with those in other provinces, and this cannot be entirely due to the destructive agencies of time and man. But it cannot be doubted that some of the cities, especially the capital, received notable attention from the emperors.

In Gortyn some efforts had been made before the time of Augustus to give the city an appearance worthy of its new dignity as seat of the provincial government, and the new rulers were favourably disposed towards it because it had taken the side of Rome during the conquest (vol. ix, p. 375 n. 2). But Augustus pushed on the work with greater vigour, and under him the Odeon was rebuilt for the first time, and its surroundings re-organized:

---

[1] *E.g.* a fragmentary inscription at Arkades (*Inscr. Cret.* i, p. 13) describes a settlement of a boundary dispute with Cnossus. The governor L. Turpilius Dexter restored certain lands to Gortyn, the boundary-stones being dated 63 (*ib.* pp. 288, 302). But it is likely that the preparations for this work were undertaken under Claudius, who, through the quaestor Q. Paconius Agrippinus, did much to settle such disputes in the island (*I.G.R.R.* i, 1013 *sq.*)

the earliest praetorium was constructed, and perhaps the great defences against the floods of the river Lethaeus. Inscriptions at Cnossus, Heracleum, and Polyrrhenium show that Augustus did not confine his care to Gortyn, and his work seems to have been continued by Tiberius.

Under Claudius, in 46, severe damage was done in Crete by a violent earthquake, recorded in Suidas[1] and in Philostratus[2]. It was not the only earthquake suffered under the Empire, but it was perhaps one of the most violent, and the damage caused by it was apparently still being repaired in the time of Trajan and Hadrian[3]. But as Claudius and Nero were chiefly concerned with communications and the condition of the land, the phase of active building in the cities must have begun under the Flavians; it reaches its height under Trajan and Hadrian, and continues under the earlier Antonines and up to the end of the second century. The temple of the Egyptian deities at Gortyn belongs to the Flavian period; on the other hand, the copious and instructive series of Imperial dedications found at Lyttus begins with one to Divus Titus, goes on to Domitia, wife of Domitian, and reaches its climax between 105 and 117 under Trajan. It continues under Hadrian, Marcus Aurelius, Lucius Verus, and Septimius Severus, but with steadily decreasing energy. And throughout this period, activity in the cities must have been on the wane. With this halt in their progress decadence set in, as yet unnoticed. Both Trajan and Hadrian (who certainly visited the island to see those places in which so many of the oldest legends of the Greek world had originated) are honoured by the erection of statues in many cities. It is interesting to note that the images of Hadrian reproduce a convention invented, probably, in some Athenian workshop, but spread throughout the Aegean, which expresses in the appearance together of the Capitoline Wolf and the Palladium[4] the union in the Emperor of Roman power with Greek wisdom.

In all this constructive activity, only technical and engineering work is carried out according to Roman principles; all work of the artistic type follows the traditional forms of Greek architecture, with the addition of certain decorations derived from Asia Minor and Syria. We find everywhere the imprint of that artistic style which was common to the whole Aegean basin: nor is this surprising, for the signatures preserved on Cretan sculptures show

---

[1] *S.v.* Δίκτυς.　　　　　　　　　　　[2] *Vita Apoll.* IV, 34.
[3] An inscription set up by Trajan in 100 in the Odeon at Gortyn (*Ann. épig.* 1933, no. 7) records its reconstruction 'ruina conlapsum.'
[4] See Volume of Plates v, 62, *b*.

that the artists came from Athens, Paros, Miletus, and Aphrodisias. There are no paintings, and good mosaics are rare.

The archaeological remains confirm the impression received from the general study of the life of the island. It seems to have remained secluded, self-contained, enjoying the material prosperity which resulted from the Roman rule, but without any renewal of energy and life, clinging to the old traditions. And when, with the decline of the Empire as a whole, its own prosperity declined, the Cretans probably did not notice any signs of decadence: certainly they did nothing to arrest its progress.

IV. CYRENAICA

The life of Cyrenaica in the Roman age is much more varied and disturbed, much more closely connected with events in the rest of the Empire. This was the result of the complex ethnical composition of the country, its geographical position, and its close connections with its neighbours, Egypt and Africa, two of the most important provinces in the Empire both politically and economically.

The part of Cyrenaica nearest the sea, containing the narrow band of coast itself and behind that the mass of the plateau where most of the cities are situated, is clearly separated from the neighbouring regions both to east and west by wide areas of desert, Syrtica and Marmarica. But further south, the country joins up with, and is inseparable from, the regions on its border; and here the nomad population, though divided into tribes, forms a single, complex, and shifting whole, so that the problem of the conquest and protection of the south is really one problem, arising in all parts of the African provinces, though varying in urgency from time to time and from one place to another.

At the beginning of his reign, Augustus dealt with the problems of Cyrenaica and Africa together. A series of campaigns from Africa against the southern nomads opened in 21–20 B.C. with the great expedition of L. Cornelius Balbus, and closed in A.D. 6 with the victories of Cossus Cornelius Gaetulicus, to be followed by a period, at least, of peace[1]. At some date before A.D. 6 P. Sulpicius Quirinius made an expedition from Cyrenaica against the Marmaridae and Garamantes, and we have in two

---

[1] This period of unrest may be reflected in the repairing of the gate and wall of the Acropolis at Cyrene completed by Q. Lucanius Proculus, governor in the reign of Augustus later than 12 B.C. (*Doc. Afr. Ital., Ciren.* I, 2, no. 54 = *Ann. épig.* 1934, no. 256).

inscriptions from Cyrene, one undated[1] though of the Augustan period, the other dated A.D. 2[2], references to war with these tribes. The latter records, indeed, the end of the war, but whether this refers to the war in which Quirinius had been engaged, or to some other, we cannot say; nor is it possible to decide whether it records the real termination of hostilities, or merely some indecisive victory, interpreted as final by the optimism of the man who set up the inscription. However, it is quite clear that immediately after the beginning of the reign of Augustus, the province, which had been governed by the Senate and a proconsul of praetorian rank, was involved in a long and difficult war, the conduct of which must of necessity have been co-ordinated with the campaigns undertaken in the west by the governors of proconsular Africa. Possibly Augustus was led to depart for a time from his usual policy, and to entrust Cyrenaica to the rule of a magistrate of higher rank, uniting at the same time the whole region between the Syrtis Major and Syrtis Minor—modern Tripoli. It has been suggested that Sulpicius Quirinius was governor of Cyrenaica not after his praetorship, but after his consulship, and therefore after 20 B.C.; and certain geographical texts[3] deriving from the Map of Agrippa seem to show that, when that map was made, the province stretched westwards as far as the northern entrance of Syrtis Minor. But if this expansion of the province took place, it was reduced again not only before the death of Augustus, but in the first few years of the Christian era—perhaps after the successful conclusion of the campaigns against the nomads.

No more wars against the nomads are mentioned up to the end of the third century. But that is not in itself sufficient to prove that there was no further trouble in Cyrenaica arising from that quarter. Certainly the government had to keep constant watch, and though we have no evidence of fortifications proper on the frontiers, such as there were in Africa, for example, or in Numidia, and other provinces, we must suppose that there were border-garrisons to protect the more prosperous parts of the country against invasion. One such garrison was situated at Agedabia, in Syrtica, as we know from the names of the Syrian soldiers carved on the rocks[4]. Other garrisons probably occupied the numerous forts, some of which are certainly of Roman construction, found

---

[1] O.G.I.S. 767.   [2] Doc. Afr. Ital., Ciren. II, 1, no. 67.
[3] Pliny, N.H. v, 38; vi, 209. See S. Gsell, Hist. anc. de l'Afrique du Nord, VIII, pp. 164 sq. Granted the official character of the Map this evidence is strong, but it is not confirmed by any other notices.
[4] Ann. épig. 1927, no. 157, 157 bis.

in the semi-desert region of the south. Evidently these garrisons were composed of auxiliaries rather than of legionaries, probably combined, as in Africa, with irregulars enrolled on the spot from among the friendly tribes. Besides these, we have reference to two other bodies, a *cohors Lusitanorum* and a *cohors Hispanorum*: since the soldier who belonged to the latter is an *eques*, it must have been composed of cavalry and infantry together. On the other hand, this inscription dates from the second half of the second century, and this cohort may possibly have come to Cyrenaica at the time of the Jewish War, whereas the *cohors Lusitanorum* may have come in the reign of Tiberius.

From the time when Cyrenaica came into the possession of Rome through the will of its last king (96 B.C.), until the accession of Augustus, it received no real benefit from its new rulers, except the suppression of piracy on the coast (and some at any rate of the inhabitants had been gainers rather than losers by it). The province was, in fact, left very much to itself, and after only a few years of regular government it felt the effects of the Civil Wars. Some partisans of Pompey landed there after Pharsalus, and Antony gave it to a daughter of Cleopatra. Through neglect and disorganization, both political and administrative, the country suffered serious harm, some of it perhaps irreparable; and only with the advent of Augustus were its affairs put into order, and its proper development made possible. It is no mere chance that has preserved in the Agora of Cyrene the record of acts of Augustus in the sphere of administration and jurisdiction.

These famous decrees bear the dates 7–6 B.C. and 4 B.C., years in which the war against the Marmaridae was raging in the southern part of the province, but evidently that did not prevent the Emperor from turning his attention to the cities, and to that part of the population which had already been pacified. Those which refer more particularly to Cyrenaica are, in their general tendency, inspired by a policy favourable to the Greek population, intended to protect it from being oppressed by the small minority which already possessed Roman citizenship. The *senatus consultum de repetundis*, which applied to the whole Empire, was of concern to Cyrenaica as much as to Crete; for the province had suffered in the preceding period from the rapacity of its governors, and continued to do so. Tacitus records three actions brought by the province against governors, under Tiberius, Nero, and Vespasian; all three were successful, a proof that the benevolent policy of Augustus was maintained by the later emperors in their dealings with the province.

The general policy of Rome in all countries of Greek language and culture which had reached a high level of civilization, and which did not need to be held down by armed force, was to protect the Greek spirit, and to bring it as near as possible to the spirit of Rome, thus making it more fruitful, without dissipating or destroying it. And this was the policy followed in Cyrenaica, where no racial or administrative changes were made by the Romans, save such as were absolutely necessary to adapt it to the new government. No colony was settled there, except after the Jewish War; no lands were assigned to Italians; Cyrene itself and Teucheira were given the title of *colonia*, but they probably acquired this rank quite late, and merely as an honour, or for the sake of the financial privileges which went with it. Roman and Italian immigrants appear not to have been numerous—there is no mention of their *conventus*—and Roman citizenship, granted slowly and gradually among the Greek population, was prevented by a decree of Augustus from detaching the recipient from the Greek community. Caesar, Antony, and Octavius had granted rights of citizenship in the province, and their gentile names are found in inscriptions, but the number of such citizens was not large[1]. The only enfranchisements on a large scale are under Tiberius, or, more probably, under Claudius, to judge from the frequency of their names in inscriptions. At the beginning of the third century, about half the population were Roman citizens[2], and in later inscriptions the name Aurelius becomes the most common, reflecting the effect of the Edict of Caracalla.

But as Roman citizenship did not detach the recipient from the Greek community, he was still able to take a full part in the administrative and religious activity of the city, together with those who were not Roman citizens. The Greek *polis*, indeed, had retained under the Romans its autonomy and old system of government; but as the former was rather nominal than actual, the latter was naturally simplified and reduced. At Cyrene, the city for which there is considerable evidence, the magistrate who

---

[1] From the Augustan *stele* it appears that in 7 B.C. there were only 215 Roman citizens with a census of not less than 2500 denarii in all Cyrenaica; most of the Roman settlers must have been men of some substance, and those who secured the Roman citizenship by favour would normally be members of the upper classes who sought thus to evade the liturgies that went with membership of the Greek body politic.

[2] A list of 22 priestesses of Artemis (*Doc. Afr. Ital., Ciren.* 1, 2, no. 49 = *Ann. épig.* 1934, no. 255, dated A.D. 215) shows 14 Roman gentile names; in a list of ephebes (*Doc. Afr. Ital., Ciren.*, 1, 2, no. 53, A.D. 224), of 60 with a Roman gentile name, 30 are Aurelii.

gave his name to the year continued to be the priest of Apollo; inscriptions later than Hadrian mention a *hiereus kallietes*, perhaps the head of a tribunal with civil and religious competence. A *strategos* appears in the list of ephebes of 224, the only reference to the office which, as a college of six members, was the highest civil magistracy of Cyrene in the third century B.C. The *nomophylakes* retain the number of nine, and there are secretaries and a 'watcher of the gate' (πυλοκλειστής) for the sanctuary. No *gerousia* is recorded, but there exists a *boule* to reflect the will of the people. Time had not changed some of the old institutions; there are the ephebes with their ephebarchs and the *gymnasia* with their gymnasiarchs, offices sometimes bestowed on women as honorary distinctions. We may deduce that the other cities enjoyed similar institutions, except as regards the worship of Apollo. In some of them, then, the *polis* of Greeks had by its side a *politeuma* of Jews, who were distinguished, by their numbers and by privileges bestowed on them since the time of Caesar and Augustus, from the other foreigners (μέτοικοι). They may have copied the organization of the Greeks[1].

To the citizens, Jews and metoecs may be added a fourth class —the *georgoi*[2], who are Libyans engaged in agriculture and stock-farming. Despite their contacts with the Greeks they remained distinct and may have partly kept their own tribal organization and in part shared in the life of the Greek villages (κῶμαι), which seem to have been at once quasi-municipal in character and administrative districts, to judge from a recently discovered inscription[3].

The Roman administration, then, respected the rights and independence of the cities, but on the other hand it took very particular care of the country. It seems that Cyrenaica never enjoyed a period of great commercial activity. Its coasts were inhospitable, and its geographical conformation unsuitable for commerce; moreover, the great port of Alexandria must have diverted much of that traffic which Cyrenaica had enjoyed before its foundation. Agriculture was the main resource of the province, and the Romans, by ensuring security from the nomads, and by undertaking works of irrigation, provided the conditions under which it could develop most fruitfully.

During the years of neglect and disorder which preceded the

---

[1] An early Imperial inscription from Berenice (*I.G.R.R.* I, 1024, perhaps of 21 B.C.) shows that the Jewish *politeuma* of that city was governed by nine archons.   [2] Strabo *ap.* Josephus, *Ant.* XIV [7, 2], 115.
[3] *Doc. Afr. Ital., Ciren.* II, 1, no. 135.

accession of Augustus, the plundering of the barbarians, and the rapacity of the *publicani* and governors had denuded the country of silphium, hitherto its main source of wealth. Plants were now so rare that when one was found, it was given to the Emperor, as a remarkable and precious rarity[1]. Cyrenaica was therefore compelled to fall back on other products, especially cereals, with which it had assisted Greece formerly in times of scarcity. By a better system of land valuation, and a return to a regular system of landowning, the province could soon become very prosperous, for it was more favoured by nature than some of the neighbouring regions in proconsular Africa which acquired great wealth through the same resources.

The care taken by the Romans to promote agriculture is shown by the numerous works of irrigation and communication which are found both in the coastal regions, in the plateau, and in the southern part of the province, down to the edge of the semi-desert belt, where the Greeks had certainly never established themselves. We have no exact dates for these works, save in the case of some milestones on the road from Apollonia to Cyrene; these, for the period anterior to the Jewish rising, bear the names of Claudius and Trajan. On the other hand, certain inscriptions and authorities[2] mention the provisions made by Claudius and Nero in Cyrenaica, as in Crete, for the regulation of the problems caused by the usurpation of property by private individuals.

But here the rights of ownership violated were not, as they were in Crete, those of the cities, but those of the Roman State itself, acquired as heir of the last kings. On the death of Apion, the Senate, basing its claim on his will, had hastened to take possession of the *agri regii*, while it allowed the cities to retain their autonomy. The crops had been let out to the *publicani*, but gradually a part of these lands had come to be regarded as the property of the individuals who occupied them. It does not appear that the question interested Augustus or Tiberius, but it forced itself on the attention of Claudius. Even so, the problem was not finally settled until the reign of Vespasian, for it was not easy to alter a state of affairs which had been consolidated by time, and every effort was made not to disturb the delicate economic organization of the country.

Claudius entrusted this work to a special legate, L. Acilius Strabo, but it was not completed at the time of the Emperor's death: the boundary-stones bear the name of Nero and the date 55.

[1] Pliny, *N.H.* XIX, 38 *sqq.*
[2] Tacitus, *Ann.* XIV, 18; Hygin. *de cond. agr.*, ed. Lachmann, p. 122.

Tacitus says that the decisions of Strabo encountered the opposition of those who believed themselves penalized by them, as might be expected, and that they appealed to the Senate. The Senate laid the matter before the Emperor, who, though he approved the decisions of Strabo, left the usurped property in the hands of the occupiers. But boundary-stones and texts which survive seem to indicate that the evidence of Tacitus must be interpreted as meaning that while Nero confirmed the decisions of the legate by revising the boundaries, he mitigated the effect on private individuals, by remitting the arrears which they owed to the treasury. But the lands in dispute were so numerous and so widely spread throughout the province that Strabo could not finish the work: other stones are found bearing the date A.D. 71–2 and the name of the legate Q. Paconius Agrippinus, the same who, as quaestor, had taken charge of the re-organization of the roads in Crete under Claudius, and had perhaps carried out similar revisions of property boundaries there.

After the construction of the various works of engineering, and after the regulation of these questions of land ownership, the province was on the way to a period of peace and prosperity, evidence of which can be found in the activity of municipal building, when its progress was interrupted by the Jewish rising in the last years of the reign of Trajan (see above, p. 649).

This war was the second main disturbance which the province suffered under the Empire, and its effects were very much more serious than those produced by the continual danger of the nomads (see above, p. 667 sq.). The way it was conducted both by the rebels and the Romans who conquered them, was such that the loss of life was very heavy, even if the figures given by Dio[1] are exaggerated; and the damage done in the cities and in the country to public and private property was so great, and had such an effect on the political and economic life of the province, and perhaps even on its government[2], that the war must be regarded as a turning-point in the history of Cyrenaica.

Once the rebels had been crushed with unrelenting vigour Hadrian turned his attention to repairing the damage suffered by the country. Groups of colonists were brought from other parts of the Empire; a new city, Adrianopolis, or Adriana, was founded on the coast between Teucheira and Berenice; the roads were

[1] 220,000, LXVIII, 32, 2.

[2] In a new Vatican papyrus (*Studi e testi*, no. 53) the district of Marmarica appears as an Egyptian nome, and it is possible that it was transferred from Cyrenaica to Egypt in consequence of the Jewish rising.

re-opened for traffic, and the buildings in the cities, beginning with Cyrene, were rebuilt and restored. For his activity in this matter, the Emperor earned from the inhabitants the title of 'founder' (*Ktistes*). The work was carried on under the succeeding rulers, but with steadily decreasing energy. Undeniably, the country enjoyed certain advantages of this kind as a result of the rebellion, but they were not long-lived; and on the other hand, other forces of a more general nature now supervened, which involved Cyrenaica in the common decadence of the Empire.

The decline in political and civic life which followed the rebellion did not fail to produce effects in the cultural and spiritual activities of the province. From this point of view, Cyrenaica had received more openly than Crete the forms of civilization imported by Rome, but at the same time it had remained very closely bound to its own tradition and to the Hellenic spirit. Perhaps if the renewal of prosperity and of energy brought about by Rome had been permitted to develop, and if the new civilization grafted on to the old traditions had been allowed to bear fruit, Cyrenaica might have become, like Egypt and Asia Minor before it, though to a lesser extent, a centre of Mediterranean culture. As it was, it remained until the end of the ancient world, and until it was overrun by the invading Arabs, a humble and obscure country, unable either to transcend, or to give new life to, the old traditional forms.

The language most in use was Greek, and Latin was confined to official documents, even there almost always combined with Greek. Earlier, the religious life of the province centred around the cult of the founder-god, Apollo. But later his sanctuary, though it remained the focus of life in Cyrene, was overshadowed by the construction of baths above the altars, which were no longer venerated. The ancient gods and local heroes kept their priests and the festivals, which were distributed through the year in the months indicated by their names. Artemis was worshipped in close connection with Apollo; we have a reference to the priestess of Hera; there were temples of Zeus Olympios, Demeter, Asclepius and Aphrodite; and we have statues and votive inscriptions which show the continuance of the cults of Zeus Ammon, Isis, the nymph Cyrene, Aristaeus, and Libya.

On the other hand, the Imperial cult was widespread in the province, and was not, as in Crete, simply an official religion, but penetrated deeply into the mass of the populace. The cults of Rome and of Augustus are found very early; the *strategeion* of Cyrene, formerly consecrated to Apollo, was dedicated to Tiberius;

the victories and prosperity of Nero, Trajan, and Hadrian are often celebrated, both in inscriptions and in ritual observances.

Immediately after the Jewish rising, and during the work of reconstruction which followed it, there is a noticeable revival of the older cults, in accordance with the policy of the ruling Emperors, and with the spirit of the time, but the revival does not seem to have had any roots in the populace itself. The works of religious reconstruction are both extensive and considerable— for example, all the temples of the sanctuary of Apollo were restored. But on the other hand, the economic depression of the country and its changed condition can be observed very clearly in these works. The chief temple of Apollo, for example, arose from the ashes left by the Jewish incendiaries, but its appearance was very different from that of the older building, being far removed from the principles of classical architecture. Moreover, after the first short period of intense activity, due probably to the assistance of the Emperor, building proceeded very slowly amid the rivalries of priests and laymen: the temple was not finished even under Commodus, and work still continued on it at the beginning of the third century, as was also true of the temple of Zeus Olympios. New ideas and new cults have penetrated into the province, giving rise on the one hand to the first Christian churches, on the other to syncretism, of which we have clear evidence in the so-called sanctuary of the Alexandrine deities, after the period with which we are dealing. But the general lack of energy prevented these importations from producing anything living and vital.

As in Crete, the works of engineering, both before and after the Jewish rising, are of Roman workmanship, while the works of artistic character are under the general influence of that style which was found also in Crete, and which was common to the whole Aegean. At the same time, however, they prove, especially in the early period, a certain refinement of taste, and the local artists show some Alexandrian influences. But after the time of Hadrian there is progressive decadence and barbarism; a hybrid style of architecture takes elements from many styles, without combining them into an organic whole; in sculpture, the formulae of Greek classicism are repeated, but without sympathy or comprehension, or there is unharmonized eclecticism of styles derived from Rome, from other parts, or from traditional practice.

In the third and fourth centuries, Cyrenaica has no share in the life of the Mediterranean world, from which it is cut off not so much by geographical position as by its own feeling of isolation.

CHAPTER XVII

GREEK LITERATURE, PHILOSOPHY AND SCIENCE

I. POETRY

WHILE the Hellenistic Empires ran their courses and Rome's power advanced erratically over the East, poets and philosophers, historians and satirists, scientists and compilers, were covering their pages of papyrus; many of their names were recorded by a posterity which did not save their works from oblivion. But for us Greek literature comes to life again with the establishment of the Roman Empire. In mere bulk the surviving writings of the first two centuries of our era may well exceed those from the fifth and fourth centuries B.C., despite the fact that verse is almost negligibly represented.

The composition of tragedies came to an end about the beginning of the first century A.D., and even the classics disappeared from the stage, except in so far as isolated scenes were sometimes performed. The old myths were now represented to the public in a form which appealed more to the eye and ear than to the intellect. The silent dancer, miming to the accompaniment of music and chanting, to whom Italy first gave the name of *pantomimos*, rose about the beginning of our period to a popularity he retained as long as paganism survived. His art, which called for the most highly developed physical control, was bewailed by those who disliked all mass enthusiasm or were revolted at its erotic element; but probably it was as salutary and as harmful as are most forms of popular entertainment.

Comedy, too, was dead, though complete plays were sometimes revived as late as the beginning of the second century. Its popular successor was that old dramatic form, the *mime*, short scenes by one or more actors, not always in verse. Our specimens are sentimental and romantic rubbish; but sometimes living persons were attacked and some mimes were sententious enough to win the approval of Seneca. Drama succumbed so quickly because it had required a certain unity of education, feeling, and interest, among its vast audiences; when that unity was enfeebled by the decay of the city-state, no one arose to convert what had been a public festival into a private entertainment for a select few; accordingly, what dramatic performances there were made the least possible demand on the spectator.

Yet the poor showing made by verse is not entirely due to the disappearance of old forms; epics were still composed, and didactic poetry was written even on twice-used subjects. But fortune and the labours of a series of anthologists have seen to it that for us the poetry of this period means the epigram; and probably nothing better could have survived; the poetic inspiration worked best within a narrow compass. Yet when we compare the epigrammatists of this time with their predecessors, we are aware of a change; there is less desire to convey a sentiment, more to make a point. The most attractive of them is the earliest, Meleager of Gadara (born *c*. 130 B.C.), whose Menippean satires, moralizing in jesting form, are lost, but who secured immortality for his erotic epigrams by making them the kernel of an anthology, his 'singing garland.' There had been anthologies before; Meleager's may have been the first to aim at being in itself a work of art. For the sake of unity only poems in the elegiac metre were admitted, and they were arranged with reference to schools and subjects. Variation on a theme by an earlier poet or by oneself had long been a practice among writers of epigram. Much of Meleager's own work we know, and more we may suspect, to have been of this kind. But neither this nor his command over the devices of rhetoric and metre condemn him as a poet. His best work has such certainty of word and such life in its movement as may give him an assured place. The strength of his passion for Heliodora or Zenophila is as irrelevant as it is unknown.

Perhaps in the time of the Emperor Gaius, Philippus of Thessalonica issued a supplement to Meleager's *Garland*, containing the work of later poets. His own poems are as mechanical as the alphabetical arrangement of his *Garland*. The most important of his supplementary authors are Philodemus, the Epicurean, who continues the erotic tradition, Antipater of Thessalonica, and Antiphilus of Byzantium, both of whom display gifts more rhetorical than poetical. Crinagoras, who in his younger days had written a bitter comment on Caesar's new settlers at Corinth, broke new ground by composing flattering poems on the great achievements or trivial experiences of the Imperial house. A conceit on the death of a slave was another favourite form with him. A representative, perhaps, of a side of Greek letters which Greeks deservedly forgot, he foreshadows some of Martial's less attractive poems. Another epigrammatist in a very different style was certainly known to Martial—Lucillius (*c*. A.D. 50), who together with his imitator Nicarchus from Egypt specialized in the satirical epigram, mainly at the expense of the stock butts—doctors, artists, physical peculiarities.

Beyond the epigram there is not much worth mention: Babrius' pleasantly colloquial fables, the versified geography of Dionysius 'Periegetes,' and the two poems which go under the name of Oppian the Cilician (*flor.* 170–80). The *Cynegetica*, on animals and hunting, is falsely ascribed to him, being in fact by an unknown Syrian, a generation later in date, and far inferior in merit; pretentious, unrestrained in the use of epithet, and proud of the resources of his vocabulary, he is a representative of what was to become the predominant poetic style. But the *Halieutica*, which contains a vast amount of information, true and fancied, on the habits of fish as much as on methods of catching them, is a pleasant book. It contains little poetry, to be sure; but Oppian writes cleanly, without excessive ornament, and knows how to make a scene vivid. He was praised in antiquity for his similes; their application is often mechanical, but their subjects had obviously struck his imagination. Snow in a garden, a boy with a mousetrap, the footpad's rough way with a benighted reveller, all these are admirably done (i, 792, ii, 156, ii, 408); or, again, there is good observation in the description of the wild-beast fighter in the amphitheatre, standing half-sideways as he waits with his long-bladed spear for the leopard maddened by the cracking of whips (ii,350). These similes give, all too occasionally, what we generally miss in the poetry of this period, namely, relation to contemporary life; a fresh observation or new emotion brings a thrill through its very rarity. Books, not life, inspire these poets; the burden of the past has become too great for a literature in which innovation had never ranked high. The ordinary Greek looked to poetry for instruction rather than an extension of his experience, and that attitude was fatal to its continued existence.

II. ATTICISM AND THE SECOND SOPHISTIC MOVEMENT

The degradation of prose in the hands of the careless, the tasteless, and the vulgar, has been sketched in an earlier chapter (vol. vii, p. 255 *sq.*). But the great Athenian masters of eloquence had always had their admirers, particularly at Athens, and the practitioners of the new styles had to meet their hostility. The Atticists in style were important enough to be an influence on Roman oratory as soon as it became self-conscious and in need of theoretical

active in local politics and generous benefactors of the town; his mother received heroic honours after her death. Dio seems to have paid an early visit to Italy in the practice of his profession as a sophist. A lost speech *Against the Philosophers* is plausibly attributed to his stay there; according to Synesius, it improved on Vespasian's edict of expulsion from Rome (see above, p. 9) by demanding that they should be driven from the face of the earth. But there was in Dio a strain of seriousness and a desire to preach which led him to dissociate himself from the sophists. We have a number of speeches, presenting many unsolved problems[1], which take the form of advice to various cities. Some are placed in the mouth of imaginary and idealized philosophers, a device which betrays an unresolved division within Dio himself. The *First Tarsian Oration* is only a comically exaggerated vituperation of the men of Tarsus for their habit of snorting, but the *Alexandrian*, if really a single speech, alternates between abuse and more measured criticism of the Alexandrians for their devotion to the theatre and the games. The *Rhodian* begins by an elaborate attack on the heinousness of currying favour by inscribing Roman aliases on old statues, but passes into a heartfelt appeal to the Rhodians to preserve Hellenic civilization. The old days of greatness are gone for ever, and the so-called freedom which the Romans allow to favoured cities is but a phantom. It is a mistake to struggle for a shadow out of the past, when a real danger threatens the Greek world, a danger which by its insidiousness calls for higher qualities than the dangers of war; it is that they will be assimilated to their barbarous neighbours, Phrygians, Mysians, and Thracians. The *Second Tarsian* speech is serious throughout: philosophers and politicians neglect their duty of telling the people the truth; what is needed is social reform at home, patience with their neighbours abroad, readiness to overlook minor faults in the Roman administration, but determination to fight for matters of importance with all their power.

> The spectator of our present disputes, which bring us into ill favour, might well be ashamed. He sees fellow-slaves contending for distinction and primacy among themselves. What? Is there nothing good in these times to deserve our efforts? There is, as there was formerly and always will be, the most important and only worthy objects of effort, which no one has power to give or take away. (xxxiv. 51.)

---

[1] A. Lemarchand, *Dion de Pruse*, is here followed in his view of the date and sophistical character of these speeches, though his discovery in them of different recensions appears doubtful.

Dio had therefore already passed beyond the usual limits of the sophist when about A.D. 82 his friendship with T. Flavius Sabinus brought on him a sentence of exile from Italy and Bithynia (p. 24, n. 4). It was not a heavy sentence, but it seemed so to Dio: his ambition had brought disaster, his local patriotism was forbidden. He disappeared, and led a wandering life supported by manual labour. But many, who could see that he was no ordinary tramp, supposed he must be one of those philosophers who carried about the spiritual comfort there were no priests to give. He was gradually forced into this rôle, and even came to dramatize himself as a second Socrates. Some reports of his talks during this period survive. Sometimes they start with a conversation with an unnamed individual; a crowd collects and Dio ends with a continuous speech. Others start with a speech and develop into a discussion. They seem to be as genuine as Arrian's reports of Epictetus' conversation (see below, p. 694), which show these same features. They are for the most part intended for uneducated men and very dull; any historical allusion is explained, and points are elaborated to bring them home to the slowest witted.

The murder of Domitian and the annulment of his acts brought the possibility of restoration and return. Invited by Nerva to Rome, Dio soon obtained leave to retire to Prusa, where he spent some years engaged in public affairs. A series of speeches of this time, together with an earlier one, delivered after a mob, suspecting him of hoarding corn in a time of scarcity, had made a raid on his house, throw an interesting light on the internal politics of a Greek Asiatic city. Later he went to Rome at the request of Trajan, who grasped the importance of enlisting the goodwill of the Greeks. Here he did some propaganda in favour of the monarchy: the emperor is the unremitting servant of his people, the laborious shepherd of his flock.

Several other speeches of this period, composed in a deliberately wandering style, contain the fruits of Dio's experience. The picture of Borysthenes at the mouth of the Dnieper, an isolated outpost of Greeks among Scythians, and the story of his wreck on the coast of Euboea, though doubtless owing much to imagination as well as to memory, show a remarkable power of making a scene live. The one serves as an introduction to a talk on the unity and harmony of the universe; the other to a discussion of the economic relations of town and countryside. Dio remembers enough of his earlier days to take care to be eloquent and entertaining, but his preoccupation is with the matter, not with the manner. The same style characterizes the speech delivered at Olympia (still a centre

of Hellenism) on the sources of our knowledge of God. He is
perhaps never an original thinker, though his moving attack on
prostitution[1] strikes an unfamiliar note; but his varied contact with
contemporary life and his romantic, if slightly priggish, personality
make his best work delightful reading and his psychology a
fascinating problem.

Aelius Aristides (117–c. 185), the son of a prosperous but
undistinguished inhabitant of Mysia, received his youthful literary
education from Alexander, the teacher of the Emperor Marcus
Aurelius. From him he learnt a genuine admiration for the great
classics, whom he determined to emulate rather than imitate. Then,
like many ambitious young rhetoricians, he travelled, visiting
Athens, Egypt (with more thoroughness than the ordinary tourist),
and Rome, where he delivered the famous panegyric on Rome's
power, wisdom, and benevolence. It may contain rhetorical conceits, as that if Indians or Arabians want any of their own produce
they must come and beg it at Rome; it may flatter in representing
the perfection of the provincial government and the willing
co-operation of the ruled; it may be blind in ascribing pitiable
insignificance to the barbarian fringe outside the *pax Romana*; but
it is an inspiring picture of the Antonine ideal, shortlived, partly
illusory, of world-wide peace and a universal civilization.

If Aristides had thought of a political career, he was debarred
from it by a lengthy illness which determined the course of his life.
Where doctors failed, the god Asclepius brought alleviation, and
thereafter, through many relapses, Aristides was Asclepius'
devoted admirer, whom the god favoured by frequent dream-visits.
In these, though he did and said much to satisfy Aristides' ever-
growing vanity, yet he also commanded him the most drastic of
cures, which were faithfully carried out. The six *Sacred Discourses*,
in which part of the story is told in detail, are of great interest to
students of religion and of psychology.

Aristides was far too self-conscious not to write apologies for his
art; an interminable one-third of his surviving writings is occupied
with polemic against Plato's disparagement of rhetoric. In it he
assumes that rhetoric is the ally of justice and a worker of edification
in a manner which, creditable though it may be to his heart, shows
that he had no conception of the argument of the *Phaedrus*. And
when, in the tradition of Isocrates and Dionysius, he thinks of
rhetoric as bound up with the practical life of politics, the assumption bears little relation to the facts of the time. He himself attacks
his contemporaries who profane their art to tickle the ears and

---

[1] *Or.* VII, 133 *sqq.*

catch the plaudits of the mob. 'Alone of all the Greeks I have approached Eloquence, not to win wealth, or glory, or honours, or a rich marriage, or political power, or any advantage whatsoever, but as her true lover' (*Or.* xxxiii κ, 19). So it comes about that his style is more Attic and restrained than was common, though in his prose-poems, both in the hymns to divinities and above all in the lament for the destruction of Smyrna by earthquake, he falls into the short phrases and metrical elaboration of one type of Asianism; so too that his *meletai* on historical subjects show a remarkable historical conscience, which goes beyond what even a historian of that era would have thought necessary in the composition of his speeches. As far as a vain man who thought in commonplaces could be, he was a follower of truth and beauty, writing for posterity; the next fourteen centuries rendered him an exaggerated homage and the present day redresses the balance by forgetting him.

The third figure of more than transitory importance thrown up by the sophistic movement was Lucian (*c.* 120–after 180), a native of Samosata, whose mother-tongue was not Greek but Syriac (p. 608). Determined, however, to become a sophist (*rhetor* is his own word), he acquired a good, though not pedantically accurate, knowledge of Attic Greek, and travelled in the exercise of his profession to Rome and even to Gaul, where the Roman culture spread Greek among the educated classes. Unlike Dio and Aristides, he had little of the age's love of self-revelation, and what he tells of himself is not much, nor free from irony and inconsistency; moreover in his dialogues he never introduces himself except under a pseudonym, which may excuse any artistic re-arrangement of the facts. If we may believe the account in *Twice Accused* he was already forty when, deciding that the art he was practising was meretricious, he invented his great contribution to the resources of literature, the comic prose dialogue. The Atticists had long found authority for their language in Comedy as well as in prose; it was Lucian's inspiration, all the greater for the distinctness in antiquity of literary forms, to blend some of its spirit with the dialogue, supposed to be the possession of philosophy. Further he resuscitated his countryman Menippus, now borrowing his Cynic moralizing, now imitating his medley of prose and verse. With these elements, mixed in changing proportions, he constructed the infinite variety of his dialogues.

The dialogue form may be used as a device to introduce a continuous essay, or as a framework on which are disposed a series of short stories; it may approximate to the mime, as in the *Courtesans' Dialogues*, or, with the addition of an element of mockery, in the

Dialogues of the Gods, which treat well-known incidents of mythology with a bourgeois realism.

> *Poseidon:* Is it possible to see Zeus just now?
> *Hermes:*   Impossible, Poseidon.
>   — All the same, tell him I'm here.
>   — Don't bother him, I tell you. It's inconvenient, you can't see
>   him at present.
>   — Oh, is he with Hera?
>   — No, it's something of a different kind.
>   — I understand. Ganymede is there.
>   — No, not that either. He's not well.
>   — What is the matter with him, Hermes? This is alarming.
>   — I'm ashamed to tell you—it's so dreadful.
>   — You mustn't be shy with your uncle.
>   — Poseidon, he's just had a baby.
>
>   (*Dialogues of the Gods,* 9.)

But the most characteristic of Lucian's dialogues serve to display
all his versatile powers—his wit, his fantastic invention, his gift
of description and paradox, his ability to combine variety with
unity. Many of them are not mere frothy entertainment; Lucian
adds solidity by having a point of view to express. Unfortunately
it is just in this that he fails. Lucian is one of those clever persons
who refuse to be impressed by what stands out above the general
level. Power and wealth are his constant butts, as bringing nothing
but trouble in this life, while they will be annihilated in the grave;
science and metaphysics seem to him pretentious nonsense, though
when it suits his turn he professes regard for *true* philosophers.
And he has a fundamental contempt for the dreams of the poets:

> Then tell me first about the Trojan War. Was it like Homer's
> description?
>   How could he have known anything about it, seeing that he was at
> the time a camel in Bactria? But I will tell you this much, that nothing
> extraordinary happened and that neither was Ajax so large nor Helen so
> beautiful as men think. I saw a white woman with a long neck, so that
> you could guess her to be a swan's daughter, but she was quite old, nearly
> the age of Hecuba. (*The Cock,* 17.)

The only ideal Lucian can offer is to have neither hopes nor fears,
and to laugh at the follies and pretensions of others. But taken as
the entertainer it was his main object to be, he rarely disappoints.
His style may be a little too full of Attic idioms, his polemics may
have lost some of their savour, yet he has amused the world not
only with his dialogues, but also with the other genres he employed
—introductory speeches like *You talk like a Prometheus* or that skit

on travel-books, *A True Tale*. Baron Munchausen himself could not improve on the impudent plausibility of this description of a river of wine:

> Desiring to discover the river's source, I marched up its bank, and found no spring, but many large vines covered with clusters of grapes. From the root of each tree flowed a trickle of sparkling wine, and from them came the river. In it we could see many fish, very like wine both in colour and in taste; having caught some of them and having eaten of them, we became drunk; and on cutting them open we found them full of lees. Afterwards we devised the plan of mixing other fish from fresh water with them and thus tempered our excessive wine-eating. (1, 7.)

But that Lucian was born out of time in a solemn age is revealed by the apologetic preface, which argues that serious readers must have their relaxation, and that the relaxation he has to offer combines profit with pleasure.

Lucian is interesting also for the light he throws on the life of his time. There pass through his pages the haughty rich man and those who scramble for his insulting favours, ignorant pedants, lecherous, quarrelsome and superstitious philosophers, together with an occasional recipient of praise, like Demonax the Cynic—or Panthea, the mistress of L. Verus. It must be admitted that part of his picture is traditional, but then much in his surroundings had suffered little change for centuries. No doubts arise with regard to his biographies of the false prophet Alexander of Abonuteichos and of the unstable half-mad Peregrinus, the one battening on the prevailing desire among the masses for new and direct religious experience, the other its pitiable victim. Contemporary historians are depicted in the essay on *How to write History*, which describes a recital by several authors who had composed an account of Verus' Parthian War. One imitated Thucydides, plague, funeral speech, and all; another composed a pastiche in Herodotean dialect and style; a third padded his book with long descriptive passages and marvellous stories; a fourth decorated his slipshod prose with poetic phrases.

Lucian's butts were ephemeral nonentities; but even those who inherited the spirit of the great historians of old took it for granted that they should reflect their manner also. This conscious modelling on the past is particularly clear in Flavius Arrianus of Nicomedeia (*c.* 95–175). Actually calling himself 'the Second Xenophon,' he wrote supplements to Xenophon's *Cynegeticus* and to his cavalry manual; he set alongside the *Memoirs of Socrates* the *Conversations of Epictetus* (see below, p. 694) and alongside the old *Anabasis* an *Anabasis of Alexander*. This is the best history of Alexander we possess;

it is written very simply, as becomes an imitator of Xenophon: such speeches as he allows are of the shortest exhortatory kind. Arrian chose his sources well, following mainly Aristobulus and Ptolemy, of whom he quaintly observes that it would be particularly disgraceful for a king to tell lies. He may have imitated Xenophon so successfully because he too was a soldier like his model. His own life is interestingly illuminated by a fragment on the military dispositions to be adopted against the Alani, and by the *Circumnavigation of the Black Sea*, being in part taken from books, but as regards the eastern half from Trebizond to Sebastopol a record of his own voyage. He also fell in with the fashion of writing in the extinct Ionic dialect, which he used for his account of the voyage of Nearchus, prefaced by a short description of India.

Herodotus, but without the dialect, was the stylistic inspiration of Pausanias; but in trying by a sedulous avoidance of any parallelism of expression to imitate his freshness, he often becomes hard to understand. A native of Lydia, he wrote in the second half of the second century a guide to Greece, which is in fact a handbook to its antiquities rather than a collection of itineraries for that unreality, the ideal tourist. He must have taken the bulk of his historical matter from books, but his descriptions seem to be mainly from his own notes of what he had seen and been told. He was much more interested in religious than in civic monuments. Superstitions, ritual, and relics, fascinate him. He has a simple faith in the traditional gods, combined with a naïve Herodotean incredulity about many of the traditional stories. He is fond, too, of digressions on curiosities of nature even when, as is true enough of the silkworm of China or the frozen wastes of the North, he had not seen them himself. The love of the age for such stories is attested not only by the works of Aelian (born *c.* 170) or Phlegon of Tralles *On Wonders* but also in the pages of the sober Plutarch. Pausanias, as is shown also by his unfortunate style, intended his book to be readable, not a mere work of reference. But it would be a mistake to suppose that he meant to be read in the study rather than on tour; even the tourist likes a change from a diet of measurements and dates.

In this sketch of Greek literature under the Romans, dominated as it is by the art of rhetoric, we have found much that seems false and hollow. Pausanias, even more than Arrian, may serve to remind us that there was still conventional ability working with honest diligence. He does not reach that height of scholarship which is dissatisfied with anything less than truth where truth might be discovered; but he is widely read and on occasion shows

independent critical judgment. In his preference for archaic and
early classical art he follows contemporary fashion; but his sparing
individual commendations show a discriminating taste. He deserves credit for his knowledge of early literature, even if he read
it as being richer and more trustworthy in mythology; and we
cannot but admire his persistence and accuracy in collecting his
facts. But it may be doubted whether he had any idea of the needs
of his time, though he deplores its wickedness. Antiquarianism is
a good hobby, but all too often it blinds its devotees to what goes
on around them.

III. PHILOSOPHY

Whatever differences separated the schools under the early
Empire, on one point they were agreed: the philosopher is the
physician of the soul. Though not enjoying the universally accepted
status of the 'straighteners' in Butler's *Erewhon*, yet in some
quarters philosophers came to receive a respect and exercise an
influence which thirty years ago could be compared with that of
the clergy; too often, however, complains Dio[1], men wait for
adversity before summoning a philosopher, even as they foolishly
wait for sickness before adopting the rules of health. 'It is owing
to their wonder that men begin to philosophize... pursuing science
in order to know, and not for any utilitarian end'; Aristotle's
famous words must have seemed meaningless to these later
generations.

The Academy, occupied for a hundred and fifty years in a sterile
dispute with its younger rivals, had been rescued by Antiochus of
Ascalon (died *c.* 68 B.C.) from the disrepute into which it was
falling. Abandoning the sceptical position, he boldly declared that
the true doctrine of the Academy was essentially compatible with
that of the Stoic and Peripatetic schools. The common origin of
their ethics from Socrates, the Platonizing of such Stoics as
Panaetius and Posidonius, and the growing disregard for metaphysics, lent a certain colour to his claim. This perversion of
history did not hold the field, but it exercised a determining
influence on the next two centuries by allowing Platonism to revive
and by the encouragement it gave to eclecticism. The typical
philosopher no longer hunts, like Chrysippus or Carneades, for
arguments to defend his dogmas; he reads the writings of others
for profit, not for controversy. Diodotus, described as a Stoic,
studies Pythagorean literature[2], a combination also attempted by

---

[1] *Or.* XXVII, 7 *sqq.*   [2] Cicero, *Tusc.* v, 39, 113.

the short-lived school of the Sextii; Favorinus follows the sceptical Academy but allows 'the greatest probability to the Peripatetics[1]'; even the disreputable Epicurus is laid under contribution by the Stoic Seneca. In the third century a man can actually be described as 'the Platonist and Stoic[2].'

Yet there were still men to maintain the study of the old systems, men to whom the old issues were still living, whether because they realized their importance or through mere pedantry. Plutarch, who yields to none as a practical moral teacher, is a most damaging controversialist when he thinks ethical standards or common sense are endangered. His criticism is directed against the early generations of Stoics and Epicureans, because their writings were still studied and admired. The survival of traditional scholastic Stoicism, regarding Chrysippus as its oracle, is vouched for not only by such attacks, but also by the exasperation of the adherents of the newer, exclusively moral direction: 'Is virtue no more than a knowledge of Chrysippus?' cries Epictetus[3]. Epicureanism did not admit of innovation at all; in one of Plutarch's dialogues the Epicurean states his case and then goes[4]: there is no room for discussion and accommodation with an Epicurean. Even the Diogenes who, towards the end of the second century, inscribed the Epicurean message for all to read on a colonnade in his native town of Oenoanda in Pisidia included a noteworthy amount of polemic against other schools. In fact Epicureanism's strength lay in opposition; it thrived by combating superstitious credulity and religious feeling[5], though it was doomed to fail in the unequal struggle.

Among the exponents of Platonism there were different currents. Some were strongly affected by the ideas of Antiochus, like the anonymous commentator on the *Theaetetus*, or like Albinus (late second century), whose *Introduction to Platonism* not only ascribes to Plato the Aristotelian logic and the theory of virtue as a mean, but also confounds the Platonic Forms and Aristotelian Form. Yet many maintained the true distinctions: an example is provided by Atticus, whose polemic against Aristotle, written in excitable Alexandria, goes beyond modern limits of taste in philosophical controversy. Among the Peripatetics themselves there seems to have been less eclecticism: with the re-discovery of the lost Aristotelian books in the time of Sulla the period of multifarious research comes to an end, and that of commenting on the Master begins.

---

[1] Gellius, *N.A.* xx, 1, 9; Plutarch, *Quaest. Conv.* viii, 10 (*Mor.* 734 D *sqq.*).
[2] Porphyry, *Vita Plotini*, 17.   [3] *Diss.* I, iv, 7.
[4] *de sera numinis vindicta*, 1 (*Mor.* 548 B).   [5] Lucian, *Alexander*, 25.

The father of the great series of Aristotle-commentators is Andronicus of Rhodes (*c.* 70 B.C.), and the line leads through Nicolaus of Damascus, Aspasius, Adrastus of Aphrodisias, and Herminus, to Alexander of Aphrodisias (*flor. c.* 200), who was later called 'the Second Aristotle.' The value of this scholastic philosophy to its own age must not be unduly depreciated; the man who had understood the outlook of Plato or Aristotle had a better-balanced and deeper insight into the world than contemporaries whose insistence on a confined line of thought caught them the ear of posterity.

After Posidonius of Apamea (*c.* 135–50 B.C.), who taught in Rhodes, and, standing out against the prevailing tendency to concentrate on ethics, won some reputation as an authority on science and history, the centre of development in Stoicism moved to Rome. The insistence on duty and the subjection of the personality to the will of heaven were congenial to a people who had idealized the subordination of the individual to the good of the State; and the belief that the world was directed by an all-embracing Providence may have been attractive to the governing classes of a ruling nation. But though addressed mainly to Romans this Stoicism is written for the most part in Greek, still, for all Cicero's efforts, the natural language for philosophy. The single notable exception is that of Seneca[1], whose choice of the more difficult tongue may have been due to pride in his Latin style. He is indeed more a rhetorician than a philosopher, a sounding-board for other men's ideas.

In general he adopts the current view that the concern of the philosopher is with his own and other people's morals; he is the master of deportment (*paedagogus*) for the human race. And so Seneca writes treatises *On Anger, On Clemency, On Life's Shortness,* and so on, in which he argues, exhorts, gives historical examples, suggests practical rules, with all the resources of his rhetoric—and to the great benefit of many succeeding generations. This concentration on moral precept is his usual tone; but he does not neglect the philosophical structure on which Stoic ethics rested; and occasionally, under the influence of Posidonius, he finds that no life is better than that of the scientist. In the preface to his *Problems of Natural Science* (*Quaestiones Naturales*) he writes:

> What do you think it worth to learn all this, to set limits to nature, to find how much God can do: whether He makes his own matter or uses what He is given; whether matter or mind came first; whether God can

[1] Cf. below, p. 731, and vol. x, p. 509 *sq.*, where some account will be found also of Cornutus and Persius.

do all he wishes or does his material often betray him...? Are not such studies an outleaping of mortality?...'What good,' do you say, 'will it do you?' This, if naught else: I shall know all things' narrowness when I have measured God (16–7).

But as he goes on he finds many opportunities for moral harangues; typical of this, as of his exaggerations, is his prophecy of the march of science:

> The people of the coming generation will know much that we do not know; much is reserved for ages which will have forgotten our names: the world is a tiny thing, except that it contains questions enough for all the world....Great discoveries come slowly, especially when the work goes slow. We have not yet perfected the one thing to which we apply ourselves with all our mind—our complete badness. Advance is still being made in vice...we have not gone far enough in throwing away all that is good...we outdo feminine neatness in smoothing and polishing our bodies, we men use cosmetics that even our wives should avoid...we no longer walk but step, we adorn our fingers with rings and put a jewel on every joint.... (VII, 30–31.)

Though Seneca often expresses the orthodox Stoic belief in an immanent pantheistic God, at other times he so much stresses the divine Providence that God is felt to be personal and transcendent. 'The Gods have held and hold us very dear[1]' and so our prayers are not requests, but reminders[2]. 'God has a father's feelings towards good men and dearly loves them[3].' The same feeling is found in Epictetus and in Marcus Aurelius; it is an expression of the desire, widespread in this age, to stand in a close personal relation to the divine. Seneca also tempers the chill of Stoic psychology. Following Posidonius, he adopts the Platonic tripartition of the soul, according to which a divine rational element must control two irrational elements. The image of the battle in the soul between the good and the bad is more inspiriting than the orthodox Stoic view of the soul as single and diseased; and the community of mankind becomes something more real: it had been a community of non-existent sages, all others having in common only folly, which, theoretically, alienated them from their fellows; to Seneca all mankind are brothers because all contain an element of pure divinity: 'God is near you, He is with you, He is in you[4].' An upright soul is nothing but God dwelling as a guest in a human body; and such a soul may descend equally into a Roman knight, into a freedman, and into a slave[5].

---

[1] De benef. II, 29, 6.   [2] Ib. V, 25, 4.
[3] De Prov. 2, 6.   [4] Epist. Mor. 41, 1.
[5] Ib. 31, 11.

A less imaginative but more respected teacher was C. Musonius
Rufus (*flor. c. 65*). Fragments of his discourses, recorded by one
Lucius, are preserved in Stobaeus, and show a concern almost
entirely with the practical details of life. For 'philosophy is nothing
else than investigating what is fit and proper and then performing
it.' Girls should receive the same education as boys; the philosopher will not resent an injury; marriage should aim at a joint life
in which husband and wife care for one another, in health and
sickness, for all time; men should live by the same sexual code that
they demand of women. These are noble ideals, but the arguments
by which they are supported are purely intellectual and theoretical.
It is particularly evident that Musonius is not speaking from
experience when he advises the philosopher to live by agriculture.
He also shows a bias towards asceticism, attributable partly to the
example of the Cynics, partly to reaction against the rampant self-
indulgence of the age. When else could a moralist have declared
that the pleasures of the table are the most dangerous? 'If God
had made food to be a means of pleasure, he would have made
digestion pleasant.' So too the only excuse for sexual intercourse
is procreation; 'what pursues mere pleasure is wrong and perverse
even inside matrimony.' Many parallels are to be found in the
fragments of Hierocles (early second century); a more theoretical
treatment of ethics by him has come to light on papyrus, and serves
to remind us that the systematic study of Stoicism was not neglected
even by those whose main interest was in particular topics.

So it was with Epictetus (*c. 50–120*), a Phrygian slave of Nero's
freedman Epaphroditus. After being manumitted he set up a
school in Rome, which he transferred, when expelled along with
other philosophers from Italy by Domitian, to Nicopolis over
against Brundisium. Systematic exposition was done by lectures
and study of Chrysippus and Zeno; but he also gave many special
discourses, some of which were set down 'word for word as far as
possible' by his faithful pupil Arrian. Thus they are in living
speech, not literary Attic, and give a vivid picture of an intense
personality, who had achieved the narrow magnificence of renouncing the world without rejecting it. His leading idea is that
we must attain indifference towards everything which is not in our
complete control, that is towards everything except our moral
purpose. Since he to all intents abandoned the doctrine of
'preferred' things, the keystone of Zeno's ethics, this moral
purpose assumes the negative aspect of avoiding fear, desire, anger
and grief. 'Do not admire your clothes, and you will not be angry
with the thief; do not admire your wife's beauty and you will not

be angry with the adulterer[1].' 'Behave in life as at a banquet:
a dish comes to you—stretch out your hand and take a portion
politely; it passes on—do not detain it; it has not yet reached you—
do not anticipate it in desire[2].' However immoral this teaching
may be, one cannot help admiring Epictetus for his earnestness,
for the vigour of his style, for his closeness to life, which appears
in many an illustration—the soldier in mufti who plays the *agent
provocateur*, the man who covered his face when the horse he
favoured was running and fainted when it won, the procurator
shouting and jumping from his seat in enthusiasm for a comic
actor[3].

The effect of Stoicism on a man of affairs may be seen in the
Meditations of the Emperor Marcus Aurelius. He recognizes as
his principal benefits from his instructors Rusticus and Sextus that
he had learnt to be kindly, to avoid affectation and superficiality,
to consider his friends, to bear with the unlearned, to be affectionate
and free from evil passions. But he learned other and more peculiarly Stoic lessons, which make his *Meditations* melancholy reading.
He is always insisting on the beneficence of Providence and the
all-pervading God; yet he can find no joy in the world. Every day
he wakes to guard against sin, to bear with sinners, to prevent
himself from attaching any value to what may escape him. 'What
bathing is, if you think,—oil, sweat, dirt, greasy water, everything
disgusting—such is every part of our life and every object[4].' It is
a tragedy that the man who had seen beauty in the slaver of an angry
boar should imagine he was getting to grips with reality by thinking
of roast pork as a pig's corpse or of a fine robe as sheep's wool
steeped in shell-fish blood[5]. God had called him to be an emperor;
that is, to preserve the worthless lives and properties of his subjects;
he will endure, longing that his soul should attain a life free from
earthly trammels, but telling himself that if it is extinguished at
death, as seems probable, that is God's will and for the best[6] (see
further, above, chap. IX).

Stoicism was most important in Rome, but in every town
throughout Italy and the East there swarmed adherents of the sect
from which it had partially derived and towards which such teachers
as Musonius and Epictetus were returning. These were the Cynic
philosophers, a ragged, begging, preaching fraternity. Some of
those attracted to the movement were anti-social ruffians. Epictetus
represents a possible convert as saying to himself:

[1] *Diss.* I, 18, 11.   [2] *Encheiridion*, 15.
[3] *Diss.* IV, 13, 5; I, 11, 27; III, 4, 4.
[4] *Med.* VIII, 24.   [5] *Med.* III, 2; VI, 13.   [6] *Med.* XII, 5.

> I wear a poor cloak now and shall then; I sleep hard now and shall then: I shall take a wallet and a stick and start walking round and begging from those I meet and reviling them. And if I see someone who uses a depilatory or with a fancy coiffure or strolling about in purple, I shall pitch into him. (*Diss.* III, 22, 10.)

Such false Cynics, as vicious as those they rail at, are also portrayed by Lucian. The true Cynic has a vocation from God, whose messenger he is. He gives up everything to devote himself to telling men that spiritual welfare is all that matters; he goes his rounds like a physician overseeing the rest of men: 'who treats his wife well? who treats her ill? who is quarrelsome? what household is stable? which is not?' He does not call on all men to follow his way of life; for it is not the ideal life, but only the one necessary to cure the wickedness of the world. Things being as they are, the Cynic must be as free from distraction as the soldier in the battle line, entirely devoted to the service of God, able to go about among men, and not tied down by private duties. 'Who do more good, those who bring into the world two or three ugly-snouted children to replace themselves, or those who are overseers of all mankind?' His 'patients' are not necessarily to imitate his poverty, but they will learn from his example that they need not fear it.

> Look at me, I am without house or city, property or slave. I sleep on the ground. I have no wife, no children, no official residence, but only earth and sky and my bit of a cloak. And what do I lack? Am I not without distress or fear? Am I not *free*? (*Diss.* III, 22, 47.)

The Cynics' mockery of authority, of wealth, in fact of the whole structure of society, made them unpopular with autocratic rulers. The Stoics did not mock; yet they would at any time support conscience against authority. They were perhaps less dangerous as only appealing to an educated few; but both were on more than one occasion in the first century expelled from Rome by an undiscriminating decree against philosophers. Mild persecution did nothing to check the Cynics, who continued to flourish till they were absorbed among the Christian friars.

IV. PLUTARCH

The inherited millions of Herodes Atticus are no sign that old Greece had been prosperous in the first century: the country was poor and even at Athens there seem to have been hardly any men of distinction. But at this lowest ebb dull Boeotia produced a man who embodies beyond all others the Greek spirit. Plutarch (*c.* 46–126) came of a prominent family of Chaeronea; as a student he

went to Athens and found there in Ammonius, the head of the
Academy, a teacher who gave him a thorough training in philosophy.
He was soon sent on a political mission to Rome; he returned
there to teach—and to learn, and there he spent considerable periods
of the prime of his life, making friends with many Romans. Later
he settled in Chaeronea; some sort of philosophic circle grew up
round him; his eminent Roman friends came to visit him and were
surprised to find him busied, as Epaminondas had once been, in
the minor municipal offices of a little town, which he was 'striving
to prevent from becoming yet smaller[1].' This was also a period of
astonishing literary activity; not only the *Lives* but also most of
that portion of his other writings that has survived seem to date
from after the death of Domitian.

The miscellaneous writings go under the misnomer *Moralia*,
a title proper to barely one-third of a collection which includes
among other things literary criticism, an attack on Herodotus'
bona fides, interpretations of Plato, and controversy with Stoics and
Epicureans; archaeological notes and queries, discussions on
points of physical science, collections of anecdotes, and common-
sense medical advice; essays and dialogues on politics, on the soul,
and on God; an old man's relaxation entitled *Are Land or Water
Animals More Intelligent?* and rhetorical efforts on *The Glory of
Athens* and *Alexander: Luck or Genius?* which date from his youth.
'I cannot easily do without Plutarch,' wrote Montaigne, 'he is so
universal and so full, that on every occasion, however extraordinary
your subject, he is at hand to your need.' Plutarch's memory was
a richly filled storehouse and he commanded a style perfectly
adapted to a mind which disposed of so much treasure: similes and
illustrations press upon one another; the period, crowded with the
unessential but picturesque, with synonyms and quotations, moves
slowly and smoothly to its goal; and the interwoven order of words,
adopted partly for reasons of rhythm, suits an intelligence which is
never focussed on a single fact, but sees it in relation to many others.
The richness of Plutarch's mind is illustrated by his nine books
of *Table Talk*, which contain many an interesting *mise-en-scène* to
illuminate the cultured and good-tempered milieu in which he
liked to live; every topic under the sun is discussed; rather too
frequently the fatal Greek preference of *a priori* reasoning to experiment obtrudes itself, a fault easily forgiven to the brilliant talker
over the cups, who hardly takes himself seriously, but one a little
wearisome when committed to paper.

Yet the name *Moralia* indicates the truth that Plutarch's central

[1] *Life of Demosthenes*, 2.

interest is in helping people to lead good lives. Some of his ethical writings, e.g. *The Love of Riches*, have a rhetorical appeal to the emotions; others, like those on *False Shame* or *How to distinguish Friend from Flatterer*, are in a graver and ampler style. But throughout he remains in touch with reality; he has no thesis to uphold or impossible ideal to proclaim; he writes to help the men he knows with all their weaknesses and passions. It is instructive to compare his consolatory work *On Exile* with that by his friend Favorinus, a Gaul who attained contemporary fame by his equal eloquence in Greek and Latin and who was held to be in the front rank at once of sophists and philosophers. Plutarch is humane and practical; Favorinus is a debater, supporting the paradox that 'Exile is no hardship' with complete disregard for intellectual or emotional truth. Perhaps no work gives better proof of the understanding that Plutarch had won from experience than the dialogue *On Love*, which shows how false is the common opinion that 'romantic' love between the sexes is the product of Western Christianity. The earlier speakers in the dialogue bring out the old-fashioned views: man's love for woman is like that of the fly for the milk; virtuous women can neither love nor be loved. But Plutarch protests that without the persuasion and delight of love it is only shame and fear that keep the married together: physical union is the way to spiritual unity, which is far more to be valued than the immediate pleasure: love is an ennobling influence even on the bad, and for the good its powers are almost unlimited. His panegyric takes up many of the ideas of the *Symposium* and *Phaedrus*, but with the essential difference that he has not Plato's need to disparage the physical.

Nor when we turn to the *Lives* are we outside the moral sphere, for they neither are, nor are intended to be, history: they are biography and moral biography at that. 'The noble immediately produces an impulse to action, forming the character of him who contemplates it, not by leading him to reproduce what he admires, but because the knowledge of the noble deed produces in him a moral tendency. And so I have decided to spend much time in the writing of lives.' One or two of his subjects are on the whole bad men, but Plutarch excuses himself with the plea that they will provide useful warnings. Most of the lives are arranged in pairs, a Greek matched with a Roman. Occasionally the comparison is illuminating, that, for example, of Agis and Cleomenes with the Gracchi; but often the coupling is merely ingenious, and it is not surprising that the set comparison with which some pairs end usually disappoints by its superficiality. But the device seems intended to teach the Greeks that Roman history is worth their attention, and that an outlook and purpose common to both peoples might come about if they would share their pasts. At the same time he reminds his countrymen, and the Romans too, that they had had warriors and patriots who might be compared with those of Rome.

It must be said at once that Plutarch has no conception of dynamic biography. It is curious that one so busied in the formation of character should make so little attempt to depict its development. When he tells stories of his heroes' youth it is to show that the adult character was already there. But to anyone who accepts this limitation the best of the biographies make the most fascinating reading. It is hard to say why. Does Plutarch, with his interest in almost any fact, a man to whom one thing immediately suggests another, show consummate skill in the selection of his subject matter? Everywhere we are faced with what seems to discredit the idea. There are long purely historical passages, especially in those lives where little personal was known of the subject, which do something to excuse those critics who have thought to deal with Plutarch by attaching the label 'bad historian.' There are irrelevant digressions. There are passages of almost pedantic learning, for example, the account of Themistocles' relations. Yet this very passage closes with a magnificent effect. After saying that Themistocles' tomb was in the market place of the Magnesians, and after dismissing two accounts of the disposal of his relics, he ends the Life thus:

> But Diodorus the guide in his *Monuments* says, appearing to guess rather than to know, that at the great harbour of the Peiraeus a kind of elbow reaches out from the promontory of Alcimus, and that when you round this, inside, where the sea begins to grow calm, there is a large base and on it the tomb of Themistocles, shaped like an altar. And he claims the support of Plato the comedian, who writes:
>
>> Thy monument, piled up high in a fair place
>> Where merchants all will give it greeting,
>> Shall see the comers in and goers out
>> And watch whene'er one ship shall race another.
>
> Yet there were certain honours for the descendants of Themistocles preserved among the Magnesians to our own times, and they were enjoyed by Themistocles the Athenian who was my friend when we were fellow-students under Ammonius the philosopher (32, 5–6).

Is that design or accident? Again, a comparison of the end of the *Life of Antony* with *Antony and Cleopatra* will show that Shakespeare hardly needed to select from or rearrange Plutarch's story.

Surely there were times when Plutarch was possessed by the Muses. Perhaps the real secret of his success is that he was deeply interested in people, and always ready—too ready, he confesses—to find good in them. (It is typical of him that, as befitted one who lived by 'Ares' dancing-floor,' he is always quick to admire military prowess, regardless of its aims.) His heroes always appear to him as particular examples of general human behaviour. We are never enabled to see them as products of their times and circumstances. He rarely makes the effort to grasp the historical background. But for that very reason his people come nearer to us; we have the illusion of entering into their feelings, and are moved, just as he wished, to act not unworthily of them.

Plutarch's ethical teaching found reinforcement not only in the past, but also in the unseen present. His sympathy with human nature must have turned his eyes to heaven; for nothing was more characteristic of his time than a readiness to believe in the intervention of divine powers in this world. When in A.D. 98 he became one of the priests at Delphi, it was not through mere archaeological interest in the venerable tradition. He threw himself into speculation—more emotional than systematic, and much of it therefore rightly cast in the form of dialogue and myth—on the nature and relations of God and man. In essence this speculation is an interpretation of Plato, owing much to Xenocrates and to a sect in which Plutarch often evinces an interest—the Pythagoreans. The Pythagorean revival, which began in the first century B.C. (vol. x, p. 507), presents a strange compound of magic, mysticism, astrology, philosophy, and forgery. Its influence during the next two centuries was probably greater than the literary remains suggest; they are scanty because it did not find its best expression till the third century, when Philostratus wrote his account of the prophet Apollonius of Tyana, about whom had grown up a legend of wisdom, sanctity, and miracle-working, while the more speculative side found its way through Numenius (c. 160) to Plotinus and Porphyry. Plutarch is swayed by two opposed needs: a philosophical need to elevate his God as Pure Being and Unity and Intelligence above the contamination of the world's confusion, and a human desire to feel close to the divine care. The gap is filled, following a hint in the *Symposium*, by the introduction of an intermediate class of beings, the *daimones*, through whom God acts. They are compact of intelligence and passionate soul, and the good ones care for men, give oracles, and appear in visions; they seem to include the gods of popular religion. There are bad or imperfect *daimones* also, responsible for what is bad in the supernatural; for

Plutarch does not ascribe evil to the recalcitrance of matter, but to an evil world-soul. When intelligence and soul are separated, the *daimon* dies, as man dies when his body is separated from his soul and intelligence. But these elements are of the same nature as a *daimon*, and if the man's life has strengthened and purified them, they may not be reincarnated in a human or animal form, but exist alone and perform a *daimon*'s functions. And when a *daimon* dies, may not the intelligence escape recombination with soul and rejoin the Highest Being? 'The world is full of gods, ascending the golden stairs, although your feeble vision cannot see them. Rising out of the deep abyss, the long ascent of life reaches up into the heaven of heavens; and of that chain you, on your little step, are but one small link.' The words which Lowes Dickinson[1] puts into Plato's mouth may justly be borrowed to express the vision of Plutarch.

V. SCIENCE

Science was during these two centuries by no means at a stand-still. But outstanding discoveries were few. Men did not in general aim at more than the completion and better arrangement of the work of their predecessors. Yet there were now written books of the greatest importance in the history of Western civilization. With the third century there sets in a decline in science, the symptoms of which are already visible in the second and even the first. And so the great writers of the earlier Empire came, in their original texts, in re-arrangements, or in translations, to enjoy an authority which was undisputed for twelve centuries and to exert on the revival of learning an influence which is not exhausted to-day.

Thus most that the Middle Ages knew of botany was preserved by Dioscorides (first century), a Cilician who served with the army as a doctor. His book was properly a *materia medica*, and the plants were arranged according to the effects of the drugs prepared from them. But besides the method of preparation and the effect of the drug he gives a description of the plant and sometimes of its habitat, often vague and inaccurate, for though he claims to have seen on his professional travels many of the plants he describes, he himself admits that he was at times solely dependent on earlier writers. Manuscripts of Dioscorides were early adorned with illustrations which derive, in part, from those attached to the works

---

[1] *After Two Thousand Years,* p. 212.

of Crateuas (c. 100 B.C.), and the estimation in which he was held is shown by one of the earliest existing Greek codices, a magnificent illustrated copy given, as a memento of her foundation of a church in Constantinople, to Julia Anicia, a lady once thought worthy of betrothal to Theodoric the Ostrogoth.

Dioscorides is as unscientific in medicine as in botany, for his drugs are intended to cure symptoms, not diseases. Medicine was indeed suffering from not being a profession which could impose standards on its practitioners. The absence of orthodoxy did not so much encourage a search for the truth as the flourishing of ill-qualified charlatanry. Doctors who desired to know how the human system functioned were probably not hard to find; even the so-called Empiricists, who confined themselves to the observations of experience, were in a sense scientific in their refusal to accept undemonstrated theories of causation. But the 'Methodist' school, who refused to pay any attention to individual factors, but laid the blame for all diseased conditions on 'congestion' or 'flux,' which were to be remedied by counter-measures without regard to the part of the body affected, were neither good scientists nor good doctors. Only the fact that they did not always adhere to their theory can have made plausible their witty motto, *ars brevis, vita longa*[1]. The best-known member of the school, Soranus of Ephesus, reached a high level in obstetrics, a subject, significantly enough, to which the peculiar views of his school had little application. His surviving book gives striking testimony to the thought devoted by some doctors to infant welfare.

The pneumatist school was more important; they followed the Stoics in holding that the body was maintained by a 'breath of life,' on whose condition depended that of the body. Their most eminent representative was Archigenes of Syria (c. A.D. 100), some of whose works survive, rewritten by Aretaeus of Cappadocia (second century) in a would-be Hippocratic style. His accounts of diseases have been much praised for their keenness of observation and vividness of description; he also made valuable researches in dietetics.

But all these doctors were eclipsed in industry, in learning, and probably in originality, as they were in influence and fame, by Galen of Pergamum (129–c. 200). A man of an enquiring mind, he travelled for study in his earlier years, then took a post as gladiatorial surgeon in his native town; later he went to Rome, and soon established his eminence both in the art of healing and in that of professional controversy. He strenuously maintained the necessity of a broad and scientific approach to medicine, which was to

[1] Galen, περὶ αἱρεσέων τοῖς εἰσαγομένοις, 6, p. 14, Helmreich.

be ensured by a training in philosophy; he himself wrote with competence, though at excessive length, on various philosophical topics. He further stressed the importance of anatomy, which had been practised with some success by Soranus and his contemporary Rufus of Ephesus. But Roman sentiment, though it allowed vivisection[1], was more delicate than that of the Ptolemies, in that dissection of the human body was illegal, and many mistakes were made through an unwarranted use of analogy from other animals. In physiology Galen established a theory destined to be of great importance. The principle of life is a breath or spirit, which takes three forms: *natural spirits* (πνεῦμα φυσικόν), whose seat is the liver, are carried thence in an ebb and flow to all parts of the body by the hepatic vein (a vessel not in fact to be found in man) and its offshoots; some part of the venous blood filters through into the left ventricle of the heart, where the *natural spirits* with which it is charged become *vital spirits* (πνεῦμα ζωτικόν); these are distributed by the arterial system, some of the blood in which reaches the brain; as it filters through the (again non-human) *rete mirabile* the *vital spirits* become *animal spirits* (πνεῦμα ψυχικόν), to be distributed to the body by the nerves. These phrases, still living at the beginning of the nineteenth century, when Coleridge can write to Humphry Davy 'But still my animal spirits bear me up, though I am so weak...,' have now lost their meaning; but we still speak of sanguine, phlegmatic, melancholic and choleric temperaments, because Galen handed on the Hippocratic doctrine of the four humours: blood, phlegm, black and yellow bile. More valuable was his insistence on what he calls Nature: man is a living *organism* not a mechanical complex of parts; and we must recognize as a characteristic of the organic a highly developed power of repulsion and attraction.

Though verbose and often conceited and egotistical, Galen's writings deserve praise for their clarity and accuracy of statement. But it was not these merits that made him so popular with later ages, but his all-pervading teleological outlook, which saw in the human body a divinely and perfectly fashioned instrument of the human soul. For example, after explaining, with acknowledgements to Hippocrates, the marvellous efficiency of the combination of nail and pulp of finger in picking up various objects, he continues:

Why then did Plato, in spite of his admiration for Hippocrates, from whom he borrowed his most essential doctrines, give such an idle account of the use of nails? Why did Aristotle, whose brilliance is nowhere more

[1] E.g. *On Natural Faculties*, 1, 13, p. 127, Helmreich.

evident than in his explanation of Nature's skill, overlook this important fact about the nails' utility? The former treats the gods who fashioned Man as bad workmen, declaring that as they had previously arranged that there should be nails in other animals where their existence served a purpose, they therefore planted nails on the tips of the human finger also. And Aristotle says that the nails come into existence 'for protection'; from what they should protect, cold, heat, wounds, or bruises, he does not explain. (*On the Use of the Parts of the Body*, 1, 8.)

While Asia Minor produced doctors, Alexandria remained the home of mathematics, or at least of those branches which were connected with astronomy. Geometry appears to have languished until revived by Pappus at the end of the third century, and we know of no great arithmeticians until we come to Diophantus (*c.* 250), who invented a system which was a long step towards algebraic notation. The unknown (x) is called *arithmos* and represented by a sign, variously written in our manuscripts: there were further signs for all powers to the sixth and for reciprocals. The unit is represented by μ, subtraction by $\wedge$, and addition by juxtaposition. Thus $\delta^{\upsilon}\ \iota\epsilon\wedge\mu\lambda\varsigma\ \acute{\epsilon}\nu\ \mu\omicron\rho\acute{\iota}\omega\ \delta^{\upsilon}\delta\alpha\mu\lambda\varsigma\ \wedge\delta^{\upsilon}\iota\beta$ would in our notation be $(15x^2 - 36)/(x^4 - 12x^2 + 36)$. The great disadvantage of the system is in problems involving more than one unknown; ingenious elimination and the assignment of arbitrary *pro tempore* values to all unknowns but one evade some of the difficulties. Hero, an encyclopaedic writer, mainly on practical applications of mathematics, who provided convenient text-books which were re-edited for centuries in Greek, in Latin and in Arabic, is probably also to be placed in the later third century[1]. But astronomy and mathematics useful to astronomers seem always to have aroused interest. We possess an Arabic translation of the excellent spherical trigonometry of Menelaus, an astronomer who was observing at Rome in A.D. 98. From Theon of Smyrna (*c.* A.D. 130) we have an introduction to mathematics which pays particular attention to the astronomy of the Academics and the Peripatetics. But most important historically is the work of Ptolemy (*c.* 150), whose *Mathematical Collection*, known to commentators as the 'Great Collection,' transliterated into Arabic as Al-majisti, and familiar to the later world as the *Almagest*, was till Copernicus the standard text-book of astronomy. In his preface he claims no more than to systematize the work which had been done since Hipparchus had shown the inadequacy of contemporary theory to explain all the movements of the planets. The movements of some of the planets had been worked out before Ptolemy, but he seems to have been

[1] T. L. Heath, *History of Greek Mathematics*, II, pp. 298 *sqq.*

the first to complete, in terms of eccentrics, a theory that covered them all. He was apparently a mathematician rather than an observer, for his catalogue of 1022 fixed stars is taken from Hipparchus and Menelaus and brought up to date by a calculation (actually incorrect) of their change of position since last observed.

A firm reliance on mathematics appears also in Ptolemy's *Geography*. Hipparchus had pointed out that scientific map-making was impossible without the taking of astronomical observations at numerous places in all parts of the inhabited world; but no one had undertaken the work. The rulers of the Roman Empire might have had a use for maps, but were too ignorant to know the process, or even the value, of scientific cartography. In the absence of astronomical observations Marinus had set to work a generation before Ptolemy, to collect material obtained by a critical study of itineraries and travellers' tales. Without his labours Ptolemy's geography could not have been written; what Ptolemy supplied was the mathematical competence necessary to reduce them to order. Two fundamental errors, which might have been avoided had Ptolemy not been content to work with material already available, vitiated his results. First, the only known method of determining longitude astronomically was by recording at different places the time of an eclipse. The only eclipse of which Ptolemy made use was that which accompanied the battle of Arbela, five hundred years before his day; popular reports recorded its time there and at Carthage; trusting to these he greatly exaggerates the distance between the two places. Secondly, instead of making an original attempt to determine the earth's circumference, he accepted the lower of Posidonius' estimates, based on a single observation and considerably below the truth. Thus any distance determined astronomically is less than it would have been if measured on the ground. Ptolemy gives the estimated latitude and longitude of all the places he mentions; thus the user of the book might be his own cartographer; various projections are discussed; it is uncertain what maps, if any, accompanied the original edition, but maps were soon attached. The knowledge of different countries even within the Empire is unequal and often out of date; rivers and mountains are little mentioned and ethnography is deliberately ignored. The old idea of the circling river of Ocean, the belief of a thousand years, is abandoned; for the next millennium men were to believe Asia and Africa to be joined by an equally mythical Southern Continent.

VI. CHARACTER OF THE AGE

Among all the figures who have appeared in the preceding pages
three only were born in old Greece. Greek intellectual life draws
its recruits from wherever the Greek tongue is spoken; Favorinus
comes from even beyond that limit. But the influence of non-Greek
ideas on these intellectuals who lived among or were even drawn
from the native populations was negligible. Their eyes were fixed
on the Greek past. Philo[1] and Josephus[2] must be excepted; but
they remained essentially Jewish and have therefore been passed
over in this chapter. The non-literary sources tell another story:
in religion, superstition, popular thought, the marriage of Greece
and the East was not proving sterile.

Rome on the other hand exercised a fascination which drew
many Greeks thither. The better of them fully recognized the
Roman genius for administration and admired the *pax Romana*;
but no Greek looked to gain any intellectual or artistic benefit from
Rome; no one read Latin for pleasure: even Plutarch did not learn
the language until middle age. The educated Greek preferred his
own culture to its bastard offspring, an attitude which aroused
resentment in Roman breasts[3]. From the time of Trajan it becomes
official policy to encourage Greek culture; while Hadrian is an
enthusiastic philhellene. Towns receive benefactions; new games
are instituted; chairs of philosophy and rhetoric impartially established. All these favours are received by the Greeks as merely their
due; they give no impulse to new intellectual life. The greatest
literary figures are those who were shaped before the sun shone
so steadily and benevolently: 'Longinus,' Dio, Plutarch, have all
learnt in national adversity to look below the surface[4]. The typical
produce of the second century is the self-satisfied Aristides. Lucian
is an original genius, but his laughter can lead to nothing constructive. Further, since this official philhellenism was, if not
with Trajan, at any rate with Hadrian, mostly sentimental, due to
regard for the glories of the past rather than hope for present
assistance, the Greeks were encouraged in their existing tendency
to look backward and imitate the old. And naturally the old began
to be a burden as well as an inspiration, and convenient summaries
and anthologies came to take the place of the original texts. By the
end of the second century the decline of reading was in full course.
Now and again we are reminded that these men had to struggle with

[1] See vol. IX, p. 431.   [2] See vol. X, p. 874.
[3] Cf. W. Kroll, *Studien zum Verständnis der römischen Literatur*, pp. 1–10.
[4] Cf. Plutarch, *Praec. ger. rei* p. 32 (*Mor.* 824 c).

the perverse failings of ancient manuscripts[1]; even well-educated
men did not read very much more of the *classical* Greek authors
than we do, and these were all their classics. If this was true
of the educated, how slight a hold must the higher Greek culture
have had on the masses, or on all but a very few at Rome, where
Dio can say to Trajan 'Socrates, an old and poor Athenian, of
whom you too have heard[2].'

Philosophy and science, the most living parts of the Greek
inheritance, attracted relatively few men in the greatly enlarged
world of Greek culture. What the ordinary man cared for was none
of these things, but astrology and the new Eastern religions; and
in this he was supported by those who should have been the
enemies of superstition. Diodorus Siculus, hostile like most historians to philosophy, compares it unfavourably with Babylonian
astrology: 'the barbarians, by holding always to the same views,
keep a firm hold on every detail, while the Greeks, aiming at the
profit to be made out of the business, keep founding new schools[3].'
Even the great Ptolemy was a believer in astrology and wrote
four books on the subject, once rejected as spurious by those who
could not associate science and superstition. But however it may
be at other times, they went together in that age, when Galen
ascribed many of his cures to divine instruction. Belief in divine
revelation by dreams was in fact almost universal, and, like
astrology, a symptom of the importance attached to the individual.
The State had become so vast that men concentrated their attention
on themselves, whether to seize what they could or to enquire
How shall I be saved? Hence comes the concentration of philosophy
on ethics, hence comes the impression that a self-righteous minority
was desperately maintaining some standards of decency in a rising
tide of selfishness. Such conditions favoured religious movements
more than literature; and it is significant that the only literary
form of the time which would show much power of development
was the romance, which appeals largely through its opportunities
of self-identification with hero or heroine. But though we can and
must trace the elements of disintegration in Greek intellectual life
of this age, we must also recognize that it could still produce a
literature which, though it may not dazzle or thrill, has been for
the Western world a quiet and steady source of knowledge and
inspiration.

---

[1] Epictetus, *Diss.* ii, 18, 2; Dio Chrys. *Or.* xviii, 6; Galen, περὶ τῶν
ἰδίων βιβλίων, *Praef.* p. 91 Müller.

[2] *Or.* iii, 1.   [3] ii, 29, 6.

CHAPTER XVIII

LATIN LITERATURE OF THE SILVER AGE

I. GENERAL CHARACTERISTICS

AUGUSTAN literature decayed, if it did not actually die, before Augustus. Virgil and Horace predeceased their patron, and Livy, though surviving him for three years, had done his work. Of the greater figures, only Ovid remained, still pouring out his lamentable tale in exile. But Ovid really stands between two periods; and, if his best work entitles him to a place among the Augustans, in his characteristic defects he is plainly the forerunner, and indeed the model, of the post-Augustan age.

For the doctrine of Models continued as powerful in the Silver as in the Golden age, with the difference that, whereas the Augustans had mainly borrowed from the Greek, the post-Augustans felt that Latin literature was now strong enough to stand on its own merits. Cicero, Sallust and Virgil had served their apprenticeship in Greek workshops; it was time for them, in their turn, to become masters. It is true that Greek influence, at first hand, was still dominant: neither in form nor thought could Rome dispense with her original source of inspiration; but she had now acquired a tradition of her own, and Roman *exempla*, both historical and literary, were now to be preferred. Although, from time to time, a Seneca or a Statius may appear to derive inspiration from Greek sources, we shall always find that the clear stream has been mixed (and often muddied) by Latin waters. The debt of Seneca, for example, to Greek tragedy was no more than an initial impulse: his real starting-point, no doubt, was the *Medea* of Ovid and the *Thyestes* of Varius.

The epithet 'Silver'—loosely used as a label for all post-Augustan literature—must be understood with qualification. If the term refers primarily to linguistic 'decadence,' it is obvious that change is inherent in all languages, and the difference between the Latinity of Cicero and Tacitus is less than the development of English from Shakespeare to Tennyson. If, again, the Silver age is to be distinguished by the lack of great writers, as Tacitus himself thought, when he deplored that, after Actium, 'magna illa ingenia cessere,' we may well ask whether Tacitus was not a 'genius' equal, or even superior, to any Augustan historian.

Nevertheless, the distinction between the two ages is patent to us, and was recognized, at least in certain aspects, by the post-Augustans, even if their sympathies were sharply divided into two camps—the Ancients and the Moderns. Pliny the Younger (to take a single instance) holds the balance evenly: 'sum ex iis qui mirantur antiquos, non tamen, ut quidam, temporum nostrorum ingenia despicio[1].' But Pliny missed the real difference. In form, Augustan art was perfectly symmetrical and harmonious—in a word, simple, classical. The post-Augustans had lost the symmetry and harmony, and tried to replace these essentials by a forced brilliance. Moralists like Seneca and Persius, assuming the decline of letters, explained it by pointing to the increase of luxury and depravity, as if Lucullus or Apicius had not lived a century before. Others, including Tacitus[2], with more reason attributed the corruption of oratory, as well as literature in general, to political causes. Even under Augustus, as the Flavian author of the *Dialogus* remarks, the imperial system had 'pacified'—a striking euphemism—the eloquence of the Forum and Senate[3]. If, in the sphere of oratory, this pacification was true for the early Empire it became still truer, and extended to other forms of literature, in the Terror of Nero or Domitian. The fate of Lucan and Seneca, victims of imperial fear or jealousy, is supported by the express declarations of Tacitus and Pliny that tyranny was then, as it still is, incompatible with free speech.

But this truism must not be pressed too far. The theory cannot explain everything. Indeed, it can explain very little, beyond the tautology that tyrants will not brook opposition. It is not necessary, however, for a great poet to flaunt opposition, as Virgil showed by accepting his environment. Genius, if thwarted in one direction, will break out in another. We should therefore look beyond the political cause (however important that may be) for a further explanation of the acknowledged Decline. And here a more modern view was at least suggested by Velleius Paterculus, himself a minor historian in the reign of Tiberius. Velleius, it will be noticed, starts from the theory (implicit in Aristotle) of the Imitation of Books. So far, there is nothing new. Latin practice amply justified the doctrine, although the Romans preferred to explain it as a form of Rivalry—first with the Greeks, and, later, with their own Latin models. It was just here that the danger lay, as the Augustans had already recognized. Virgil himself complained in the *Georgics* that all themes had been worked out—*omnia iam volgata*. But Virgil and his contemporaries at least claimed—and

[1] *Ep.* VI, 21.   [2] *Hist.* I, 1.   [3] 38.

made good their claim—to have been the first to sow the Greek seed in a Latin soil. Velleius saw that no such boast could properly be made by the post-Augustans, whose gleaning, after the abundant harvest of their predecessors, was bound to be scanty. After observing that men of genius in any branch of art or literature are apt to be contemporary—he gives Attic drama and philosophy as examples—Velleius points out that emulation fosters talent; it is a law of Nature that perfection, once achieved, cannot long be maintained: 'at first we are zealous in following those who we think are ahead of us; but, as soon as we despair of passing or equalling them, our interest dies with our hope, and ceases to follow what it cannot attain and seeks a new province, as though relinquishing a subject already appropriated.' As long as Imitation —that is, an exaggerated love of Tradition—held the field, no fresh advance could be expected. On the contrary, we find that certain avenues, which the Augustans had opened with conspicuous ability, were now closed. In particular, the impulse of the Horatian lyric was no longer felt. Quintilian[1] is right in his estimate of Horace, as *fere solus legi dignus*; in personal lyric, at least, he had no successors.

It might be thought that the remarkable influx of provincial blood into Roman culture, during the first century, would have stimulated new ideas, just as northern Italians—Catullus and Virgil—had revivified the poetry of their own generations. Spain had now been completely romanized, and literary Spaniards, including the Senecas, Lucan, Columella, Quintilian and Martial, were crowding to the capital. Gaul was not far behind; and, by the end of the first century, Africa—Juvenal's *nutricula causidicorum*— had already entered the Roman bar. But it is hard to detect any marked results from this expansion in the Roman world of literature. The provincials, on leaving their province, seem at once to have adopted their new home with all its traditions unimpaired. We have to wait for Ausonius, in the fourth century, to strike a true provincial note.

Meanwhile, Rome continued to stand on the ancient ways, with the difference that Virgil succeeded Homer as the supreme ideal of imitation. Here, surely, lay one of the chief causes of the decadence, even more powerful than the social or political environment. In itself, the Greek genius was unexhausted—it is inexhaustible; but its particular Roman expression was limited, and the limit had almost been reached. Statius, one of the cleverest of later epic poets, still handles Greek subjects, trying conscien-

[1] x, 1, 96.

tiously to recapture the old spirit. But Virgil has intervened, and Statius takes the *Aeneid* as his guide, although with becoming modesty (only too well justified) he 'follows at a distance':

> nec tu divinam Aeneida tempta,
> sed longe sequere et vestigia semper adora.
>
> (*Theb.* xii, 815.)

This adoration, it is true, was very partial, since, with other epic poets, Statius preferred the smoother, tamer versification of Ovid to the strong and sonorous rhythm of the *Aeneid*.

The spell of the great poet who was to become the magician of the Middle Ages was not confined to verse. It dominated prose as well as poetry, and succeeded in turning a pedestrian writer on agriculture into a rather second-rate poet. Columella, after writing nine books *de re rustica*, remembered that Virgil had left horticulture 'to be sung by others'; and the result was a tenth book in verse, respectable enough, if rarely inspired, either by Nature or Virgil.

'Maronolatry' even included a close imitation of the *Bucolics*. Calpurnius Siculus believed that the Golden Age of which Virgil sang had really arrived with the advent of a young Emperor, who may have been Nero; and his rustics, in their pursuits, their language and sometimes their names, follow the Virgilian model. Political flattery had not been absent from the *Idylls* of Theocritus himself; but the founder of the *genre*, no less than his Roman follower, might well have been scandalized by Calpurnius, whose seventh eclogue brings a countryman to Rome, where he visits the Arena, and is astonished by the magnificence of the building and the beast-shows, while he is of course chiefly impressed by a distant view of the presiding 'god.'

Not only the poets but the prose-writers succumbed to the lure of Virgil. He was *Romanus*, 'our' poet, and—whether by quotation, as in Seneca, or by imitation of language or construction, as in Tacitus—all serious literature was henceforward in his debt. If the whole character of post-Augustan literature could be summed up in a single word, that word would be 'Virgilian.' No doubt, if Imitation was to continue as the watchword of the poets, they were wise in their choice of the highest model. But they showed little wisdom in the manner of their following. As has just been mentioned, the poets could not reproduce his metrical effects; in reproducing his language they succeeded only too well. Virgil, after all, had never shrunk from the 'common' word; in the *Georgics* he moved easily among the garden-rollers and the manure.

But the essential purism of the *Aeneid* worked disaster on the Roman theory of poetic diction. Republican poets had done well to broaden the base of their (not too rich) vocabulary; but Virgil's successors only made it narrower. Petronius[1] gives a true index of post-Augustan practice. He applies the Horatian tag—'odi profanum volgus et arceo'—to poetry, warning the young poet 'to choose expressions remote from the herd.' His castigation could hardly have been intended for Lucan, who was quite blameless in this respect, since his diction is so 'pure' that, in describing a sea-fight at the length of several hundred lines, he successfully avoids the word *navis* (which Virgil and the other Augustans had freely used), preferring its 'poetical' equivalents—*puppis, carina, ratis* and the like. The result was as deplorable as that of the poetic language in the French and English Augustan ages; but there is this much excuse for the Romans, that, as the diction of poetry had now invaded the domain of prose, the poet, who in Cicero's time, had 'spoken another language,' must now in self-defence refine and purge, in order to protect his shaky barriers.

It is pathetic to contrast the meagre results of Neronian and Flavian poetry with the very real devotion of the poets to their art. Boissier believed that in no other period was literature loved so much; Seneca, indeed, thought that it was loved too much: 'litterarum intemperantia laboramus'[2]. Poetry claimed a large share of this enthusiasm, even in an age when liberal education was still mainly a training for oratory. But it was precisely here that the real trouble lay. After making due allowance for the political causes of decline, we are forced to the conclusion that, whatever the government, neither great poetry nor great prose could often be achieved by a system of education which was almost wholly rhetorical.

Hard things have often been said, and not unjustly, about rhetoric, especially by English writers who, as a rule, have little sympathy with its ideals. The system was a late-comer at Rome, where the first attempt to open a school of rhetoric in 94 B.C. met with little favour[3]. Even Cicero is rather apologetic on his study of the Greek art to which he owed so much, and Virgil, in an early poem, protested against the tricks of rhetoricians, yearning for philosophy as an alternative. But Ovid fell to the lure; and, by the time of the early Empire, no author (except such realists as Petronius and Martial) was free from one or other of the defects which we must roughly class under the convenient head of 'rhetoric.' This is not the place to discuss the details of Roman education;

---

[1] *Sat.* 118.   [2] *Epist. Mor.* 106, 2.   [3] *Dial. de clar. or.* 30.

but the character of post-Augustan literature cannot be understood without some acquaintance with a training which so profoundly influenced the expression of prose and poetry alike. The staple feature of the schools was declamation on a thesis, whether *suasoria* (deliberative), or *controversia* (argumentative), and ancient critics of the system (who were, however, only voices in the desert) complained that declamations had lost touch with real life. The subjects and their treatment can be found in the elder Seneca; for the criticism, we need go no further than a passage in Petronius[1], who ridicules the stock themes of imaginary law, with pirates in chains on the shore, and tyrants issuing edicts for sons to behead their fathers. Youths had not been so corrupted, he adds, when Sophocles and other great poets taught them to speak. Parents are to blame for submitting their sons to this turgid Asianism. No doubt this was a pertinent criticism of an abuse, but it hardly touches the actual system, which the Romans seem to have accepted the more readily in that they had nothing to put in its place. Quintilian makes much the same point as Petronius: he objects to declaimers who draw on their own imagination for a subject, instead of choosing a real law[2]; but he has no qualm about the training itself.

With declamation treated as the staple of a school curriculum, it followed as a matter of course that any new work, whether in verse or prose, was recited to an audience. The practice, initiated by Asinius Pollio in the Augustan age, had developed so rapidly that, by the time of Nero (who loved to hear himself recite), it had become, apparently, the normal process of publishing a book. Virgil rarely adopted this form of publication, and Horace complained of the lack of readers since he feared to recite[3], but Ovid found it suited to his taste, and missed it during his exile[4]. The craze for recitation reached its height during the first century, when Pliny could speak of the 'crop of poets' whose audience were more or less unwilling listeners[5]. Juvenal's *semper ego auditor tantum* had become a commonplace of satire, only too well justified by the *Theseids* of the age.

There may be nothing inherently vicious in the practice of recitation; but, in the mouth of a poet, educated from earliest youth in the declaimer's art, corruption was bound to result. School-declamations were to a great extent competitive, and it was the ambition of every boy to outvie his fellows in new phrases and ideas. A trite theme could be made striking only by fresh and often

---

[1] *Sat.* 1.   [2] V, 12, 17; X, 2, 12.   [3] *Sat.* 1, 4, 22.
[4] *ex Pont.* IV, 2, 34; *Trist.* III, 14, 39.   [5] *Ep.* I, 13.

bizarre treatment. Hence arose the love of the *sententia*—the commonest feature of post-Augustan literature. The word itself has no single exact equivalent in English. According to various shades of meaning and usage, it may be translated by 'epigram,' 'paradox,' 'maxim,' 'point,' or (in older English) 'conceit.' Like the Greek *gnome*, the *sententia* was properly used to express maxims applicable to moral life. Gnomic wisdom is of course not confined to any language or period: in Latin literature, examples of 'point' could be found in every author. But, for occasional and sparing epigrams, the post-Augustans substituted a style which (at least in the prose of Seneca) depended almost wholly on their employment. Sallust and Ovid had set a fashion that exactly suited the Roman temperament, tired of Ciceronian verbosity. No doubt there were other causes for the love of epigram and point than a natural reaction from Ciceronianism: on the moral side, the Stoics aimed at impressive apophthegms as concisely summing up their views of human life. Both of these motives are clearly seen in the prose of Seneca. That author, here followed by Lucan, must be given the credit of making Stoicism a literary creed, which may be fairly called the one new feature in the almost exhausted stock of literary ideas. Unfortunately, Stoicism became political, and suffered after the breakdown of the Pisonian conspiracy; moreover (as we shall see from Quintilian) the rhetoricians disliked its training; princes and average people alike suspected philosophy, as little better than astrology. It is significant that Agrippina would not allow her young son to learn philosophy from Seneca[1]. Vespasian, on political grounds, relegated all philosophers (except Musonius) to the islands, and Domitian expelled both classes impartially. Stoicism, therefore, while adding a certain dignity of thought, became, at least to the poet, a doubtful blessing. The old antagonism between philosophy and poetry took on a fresh significance when Seneca, at some uncertain period in his career, turned the Roman stage into a platform for Stoic aphorisms and attitudes.

II. TRAGEDY

Tragedy must be reckoned among the literary forms which became atrophied in the Empire; it had ceased to attract a public whose taste was now more and more the art of the *pantomimi*; moreover, the most guarded public reference to Atreus or Agamemnon was liable to be resented by a Gaius or a Nero. Hence

---

[1] Suetonius, *Nero*, 52.

such tragedies as continued to be written were mainly intended
for private recitation. The dramas of Seneca, at all events, could
never have been performed. None the less, they will repay
examination, not so much for any intrinsic merit, as for their
negative value in illustrating certain defects of post-Augustan
verse.

It is unfortunate that the subjects are all derived from the Greek,
so that we can scarcely avoid comparisons between Seneca and
Euripides. Even if that Greek poet is too 'forensic' for modern
fashion, the rhetorical whips of his *Medea* are harmless in contrast
with the scorpions of Seneca. Seneca is undeniably clever, but the
cleverness is too often misplaced. All his persons speak much the
same language, with abundance of 'point,' but with little regard
for the light and shade of character. His heroes and heroines are
uniformly Stoic, and the expression of willingness, or even anxiety,
to meet death becomes monotonous. A still more serious fault is
Seneca's love of horrors. Obviously, he wishes to make the flesh
creep, and this effect was not easy to produce among the Romans,
inured to the real bloodshed of the Arena. Seneca was therefore
bound to force the note, as a single illustration may be enough to
show. Euripides had recounted the death of the young Astyanax
with simple and restrained pathos: 'he was cast from the battle-
ments'—says the herald Talthybius—'and gave up his life[1].' In
the Senecan version the boy is turned into a Stoic, proudly leaping
to his death, while the messenger expatiates on his mangled body[2].
Even this horror is outdone by the description of the dead Hippolytus, whose scattered limbs must needs be 'collected on every side
for his pyre and assembled for the funeral.' As if that were not
enough, both the chorus and his father Theseus enlarge on the
gruesome theme. After this, we open the *Thyestes* with apprehension, to find that Seneca outdoes Shylock in demanding every
pound of flesh from the cannibal feast of Atreus. Less painful,
perhaps, but hardly less repulsive is the long description of an
unfavourable sacrifice in the *Oedipus*, where 'the signs of terrifying
rites' are discussed in eighty lines (303–383). For prolixity is
quite as characteristic of Seneca as exaggeration. He knows, for
example, the poetic power of names, but, unlike Milton, he does
not know when to stop. The chorus of captive women in his
Troades may be pardonably anxious to know their final destination,
but this is hardly a good excuse for their exhaustive catalogue of
towns and districts from Tempe to Ithaca (814–860).

Yet Seneca's lack of proportion should not blind us to his good

---

[1] Euripides, *Troades*, 1134–5.   [2] Seneca, *Troades*, 1110 *sqq.*

qualities. Like his nephew Lucan, he may not be a poet—it depends on our conception of poetry—but he was at least a fine writer in a *genre* which he had made peculiarly his own. His purpose was no doubt to satisfy a private audience who admired the rapier-thrust of rhetoric, as presented in the staccato style of vivid dialogue. Even in recitation, such an audience, however jaded in taste, must have experienced a thrill from the great 'curtain' of the *Medea*, when Jason utters his last passionate cry to his wife in the chariot of the Sun:

> per alta vade spatia sublimi aethere,
> testare nullos esse, qua veheris, deos.

Some of the choruses, too, are at least on the border-line of poetry, although they rarely, if ever, strike a new note. There is imagination in the chorus of the *Medea*, ending with the famous prophecy:

> venient annis saecula seris,
> quibus Oceanus vincula rerum
> laxet, et ingens pateat tellus,
> Tethysque novos detegat orbes,
> nec sit terris ultima Thule.   (*Medea*, 375 *sqq.*)

Again, the song of Dawn[1] has a distinct charm, while the speech of Hippolytus[2] in praise of country life—the original state of man —is effective, though perhaps not more poetical than Seneca's own prose description of early man in his ninetieth letter.

But, whatever place we may assign to these dramas, their influence has been quite out of proportion to their intrinsic merits. Although the Christians, in classing him almost with sacred writers, may have thought of Seneca the philosopher rather than of Seneca the tragic writer, it is instructive that Boethius, while rejecting the aid of the meretricious Latin muses for his *Consolation*, adopted the metres, with much of the phraseology, of these tragedies. They were at least *naturaliter Christianae*, like the *Consolation* itself. In another and later sphere, the influence is conspicuous, if less pleasing. For it cannot be denied that Seneca is directly or indirectly responsible for the 'blood and bombast' of Elizabethan tragedy, just as he influenced the early drama in Italy and France. Dates are here decisive, since the original plays of Seneca were being studied and revived, together with imitations produced by schools, Inns of Court and Universities, when *Gorboduc* was acted in 1561–2. Marlowe's *Tamburlaine* (about 1587) and Kyd's *Spanish Tragedy* (about 1590) are only the best-known examples of a fashion which lasted well into the seventeenth century. It may

---

[1] *Herc. Fur.* 125 *sqq.*   [2] *Phaedra*, 483 *sqq.*

be doubted whether Shakespeare himself was directly influenced; but, in any case, his debt to Seneca at second-hand can hardly be disputed. He took his good—or, sometimes, his bad—wherever he found it; and, as we have just seen, Senecan ghosts and gore were already in possession of the English stage. He was forced to cater for a superstition and a savagery in Tudor times at least comparable with the Roman. The fires of Smithfield would not have disgraced the Colosseum; and, if Seneca, with all his own contempt for the Arena, had to follow the gladiatorial taste of his age, Shakespeare was no less constrained to please the groundlings.

III. LUCAN (A.D. 39–65) AND OTHER EPIC POETS

The French critic, Nisard, held Lucan to be the typical poet of the Decadence—an age of 'learned versifiers' which succeeded that of 'literary poets,' and his indictment of the *Pharsalia* is so damning that it may be wondered why Lucan has ever been regarded as a poet. Even the Romans had their doubts: Martial wrote an inscription for a present of Lucan's works:

> sunt quidam qui me dicant non esse poetam,
> sed qui me vendit bibliopola putat.   (XIV, 194.)

Apparently, even in an age of rhetoric, Lucan was thought to overstep the bounds of poetry. Such, at least, is the considered judgment of Quintilian, who places him among the orators rather than the poets. Servius, too, agreed, though on the different ground that his 'poem' was really history[1]. Others thought otherwise. Even if we discount the opinions of Statius and Martial, whose eulogies on Lucan may be regarded as compliments to his rich widow[2], there remains a passage of the *Dialogus* (20), where Lucan is mentioned in the same breath as Horace and Virgil for *poeticus decor*—the beauty or propriety of language selected from the educated use of the day. In the age of the Antonines, however, criticism became more acute. Fronto, the archaist, launches a devastating attack on one of Lucan's worst faults—the excess of repetition. He chooses (and the choice is admirable) the Proem of the *Pharsalia*, where the theme *bella plus quam civilia* is worn threadbare by rhetorical variations. Fronto's words are too long to quote, but the raillery, as Mr Heitland well remarks, is worthy of Swift[3].

[1] *ad Aen.* I, 382.
[2] Statius, *Silv.* II, 7; Martial VII, 21, and elsewhere in his epigrams.
[3] Introd. to Haskins' ed. p. xx.

But this criticism, though it goes to the root of the matter, and
might have killed a weaker poet, still leaves Lucan very much
alive. His poem *On the Civil War* may be a failure, but is at least
a magnificent failure. In a world of poetic imitators Lucan alone
dared to be original. He broke with the convention of divine
machinery at a time when the gods were in full possession of the
epic field; and he thereby incurred the censure of Petronius[1] for
neglecting the *deorum ministeria*. The boldness of this innovation
may be measured by the fact that no later writers of Latin epic
followed the break with tradition. His own reasons seem to have
been partly historical, but mainly philosophical. The Civil War
was too near the Neronian age, and the motives of the combatants
too clearly mundane for 'divine ministration.' Even if the gods
could have fitted into a scheme tolerable for Ennius or Virgil, there
remained the ban of philosophy. Lucan had learnt too much from
his uncle to countenance the departmental gods of Olympus. Here
and there, no doubt, he lapses into Epicureanism, as when he cries
that either no gods exist, or they care nothing for mankind. His
references to *dei* or *superi* are largely conventional, as in the most
famous of his apophthegms—'victrix causa deis placuit sed victa
Catoni'—but they were also a poetic concession to current beliefs,
like the address to Venus in the *de Rerum Natura*, or the presence of
the Spirits in *The Dynasts*.

No less than Lucretius or Hardy, Lucan must have felt the need
of some higher Force to pull the strings of his human puppets on
the epic stage. So Juppiter, behind the scene, remains; but the Stoic
god is really identified with Destiny—Fortuna or Fatum. Lucan
has moved far from the tender regard for Roman and Italian religion
in the *Aeneid*. To foreign beliefs he is indifferent or hostile. He
dislikes Oriental cults, and is scornful about the apotheosis of
emperors; the God of Judaism is dismissed as *incertus*[2]; and,
although he is interested in Druidism, the interest is plainly that
of horror and repulsion[3]. But he contrives to make up for the lack
of Olympian machinery by a plentiful use of superstition—a
growing sign of the times. Of his many overdrawn passages, none
is perhaps more ridiculous than the description of a Thessalian
witch, consulted by Sextus, Pompey's son, about the event of the
war. The witch, in true Endor tradition, calls up a dead man to
prophesy; and finds that he cannot fully read the fates, and only
asks for a second death. This, however, the fates cannot grant, as
they have 'used up their power,' and finally the dead man is obliged

---

[1] *Sat.* 118.   [2] II, 592.
[3] I, 444 *sq.*; III, 399 *sq.*

to walk to his own pyre and to be duly burned[1]. Lucan can do better than this; but the long passage illustrates one of his commonest faults—a complete lack of proportion and (one may add) of humour.

It would be an easy, if ungrateful, task to point out other faults in the plan and execution of Lucan's epic. The poet belongs to an age in which Stoicism was the fashionable creed, and Rhetoric the means of expressing it. The 'crime' of civil—or worse than civil— war is the keynote, struck at the outset of the first book and continued at the end of the seventh: the poet seems obsessed with words like *nefas, crimen, scelus*. This central motive gives a certain unity to the poem, and may help to explain the want of a 'hero,' whose presence is not only the focus of sympathy but secures continuity[2]. The fault of the *Pharsalia* is that there are too many heroes—and they are not heroic enough. Neither Caesar nor Pompey can fill the rôle. Lucan was on the side of the Senate; but, by the beginning of the war, Pompey had become *magni nominis umbra*, and readers are fobbed off with a recital of his former greatness. He is the champion of (Senatorial) 'Liberty'; and it has been suggested that Lucan thought of a personified *Libertas* as his real hero[3]. Caesar can only be called the hero in the Miltonic sense—he has often been compared with Satan, and at most extorts Lucan's unwilling admiration. From the Rubicon to Pharsalus, Caesar never falters:

nil actum credens cum quid superesset agendum;

but he is on the wrong side, and Lucan misses no chance of blackening his character as that of a bloodthirsty tyrant. This attitude (for a Stoic) was common form; but there is no reason to believe that the poet would have preferred the despotism of Pompey. Of course there was Nero to be considered. Lucan's suggestion, that the 'crime' was justified by paving the way for that emperor, may be dismissed as merely a monumental piece of gross flattery; but at least there is no evidence that he believed a return to senatorial rule either possible or even desirable. After all, Fate had decreed Caesar's victory.

There remains Cato, as a candidate for the part of hero. Even Horace, who was neither Stoic nor Republican, had been impressed by his noble death, which both Manilius and Seneca exalted as the

---

[1] VI, 642–827.

[2] The authentic title *de Bello Civili* (in the *Lives* and some MSS) is here instructive.

[3] See H. C. Nutting in *A.J.P.* LIII, 1932, p. 41.

ideal of political independence[1]. But history required that the stern, impracticable philosopher should only become prominent at a later stage of the war. Hence, although we are treated, in advance, to a eulogy of his character[2], his main action, in the Libyan desert, is deferred until the ninth book. If Lucan had lived to complete his work, Cato's death would certainly have inspired the Stoic poet to expend his best rhetoric on the loss of liberty at Utica. For, with all its drawbacks of bombast and artificiality, over-cleverness and paradox, Lucan could be moved to a high flight of rhetorical sublimity. The famous apostrophe to Thessaly is a splendid conclusion to the seventh book—the whole of which, if it stood alone, might well give pause to the most censorious critic. In the eighth book, the descriptions of the plot against Pompey, his murder and the reflections on his character and fate, are hardly less remarkable. The speeches in the work generally, smack too much of the declaimer, and are often very inappropriate to the speakers; but Cato's lines before the oracle of Ammon—an epitome of Stoicism—have a dignified sincerity which makes the speech 'worthy of the oracle[3].'

Of Lucan's technique little need here be said. The *Pharsalia* has lost the fine cadence of Virgil, with his periodic structure, his effective use of elision, his subtle assonance and alliteration. Decay had already set in with Ovid's facile smoothness and showy glitter. Lucan, however, has mannerisms from which Ovid is comparatively free. 'Golden,' or semi-golden lines of the type of

Assyrias Latio maculavit sanguine Carras

are all too common[4]. But this defect, though it becomes monotonous, is not perhaps so formidable as the pointed brevity so well described in verses (almost certainly ancient), which draw attention to the trick of 'striking like a thunderbolt[5]':

haec vere sapiet dictio quae feriat.

Quintilian, in mentioning Lucan as *sententiis clarissimus*, appears to be referring rather to this brevity of form than to any particular merit in the *sententiae* themselves, since, although in verse and therefore more quotable, they are inferior, both in number and vigour, to the famous 'epigrams' of Tacitus.

Lucan stands alone, for his Flavian successors add little to the sum-total of epic poetry, or—it must be confessed—to poetry at all.

[1] Manilius I, 796; Seneca, *Epist. Mor.* 24, 71; 95, 104.
[2] I, 128; II, 276 *sqq.*   [3] IX, 564 *sqq.*
[4] See Heitland, *op. cit.* p. xcix *sq.*
[5] Quoted by Heitland, *op. cit.* p. xx.

Three of these have survived—Valerius Flaccus, Statius and Silius Italicus, each of whom has an interest to the professional scholar, but hardly deserves more than a passing mention in this place.

They have certain features in common: all are permeated with rhetoric; all are Alexandrine in their love of erudition, both geographical and mythological; and all seem incapable of saying a simple thing simply. Valerius Flaccus has indeed his own merits in dealing with the well-known theme of the Argonauts; but his eight books—twelve were probably intended—are a doubtful improvement of the Greek story as handled by Apollonius; and even if it is claimed that his psychology of Medea is superior to the love-interest in the Third Book of the Greek *Argonautica*, we must assign part of the credit to Ovid. Statius was also concerned with Greek themes, in the *Thebais* and the unfinished *Achilleis*. He was more successful in a different *genre*—the *Silvae*, a name which implied a rough poem 'thrown off' with great facility and rapidity[1]. Such verses might be in various metres, though all the collection (except for a few pieces in Horatian lyrics and hendecasyllabics) are hexameters. The subjects are various, and some of the poems, at least—for they are of very different merit—are not only admired but read: the invocation to Sleep, though to our minds rather disfigured by the affectation of learning, seems to be a genuine *cri du cœur*[2]; and the hendecasyllabic address to Polla, Lucan's widow, is a neat and vigorous encomium of that poet.

Impromptu verses—if indeed such *Silvae* were really impromptu, since, in this *genre*, Quintilian allows for revision—are not to be judged too severely; and it is fair to add that some modern scholars (but not all) have rated these occasional pieces very high among Flavian poems. Whatever their value as poetry, the *Silvae* of Statius at least reveal a man of pure character and refined sensibility, devoted to his parents, his wife, his adopted son and his friends. He never mentions Martial, nor Martial him, though they moved in the same circles; and—apart from the jealousy of rival clientship—it has been suggested that the characters of these poets were too dissimilar for any feeling but mutual dislike.

The famous legend that the poet was converted to Christianity belongs rather to the study of Dante than to that of Statius, as there is no argument to be drawn from anything known either in the life or the works of the poet himself. He was quite as 'pagan' as Seneca, whom the early Christians tried to adopt.

---

[1] Quintilian x, 3, 17.
[2] Translated by W. C. Summers, *The Silver Age of Latin Literature*, p. 126, and E. E. Sikes, *Roman Poetry*, p. 87.

IV. PERSIUS, JUVENAL, MARTIAL

When Quintilian said that 'Satire is wholly ours,' he was thinking of Lucilius, Horace and Persius, although he goes on to mention another kind of Satire, which Varro modelled on the Greek Menippus. Even so, we have now learnt that Quintilian was unduly patriotic, since Roman Satire was quite as much derived from the Cynic 'diatribes' of Timon and other Greeks as from native genius[1]. But, in quite a different sense, not of course intended by Quintilian, the remark has a wider application: Latin poetry, when least influenced by Greece, was a 'criticism of life,' and many Roman poets, who could not be technically classed as satirists, often give support to Arnold's definition, however inadequate it may be to explain the poetic process. Some of the finest passages in Lucretius and Virgil are no less satiric because their criticism on luxury and ambition is not, like that of Lucilius, directed against named persons. In the Empire personal attacks and, indeed, all politics were impossible, as we know from Horace's practice and Juvenal's express confession. But there was still room for comment on many aspects of Roman life under fictitious names; and here Horace led the way. That genial soul, who 'spoke the truth with a smile,' found a devoted admirer and constant imitator in Persius. The young and earnest Stoic, however, forgot (as Stoics were apt to forget) the Horatian smile, and only succeeded in making Horace more difficult.

The themes of Persius are all those of the Schools—on literary corruption, on right and wrong prayers, tyranny, wise spending, and the folly of all the world except Stoicism. The same material was to be handled by the greater pen of Juvenal, and Persius will hardly stand the comparison. Yet there are times when he reaches a Juvenalian eloquence, sometimes in a single monumental line, as on the tyrants who (he prays) may look on Virtue and pine away for the loss of her

virtutem videant intabescantque relicta   (III, 38.)

—sometimes in whole passages inspired by his loved philosophy, as in the famous praise of his teacher Cornutus in the fifth satire.

To pass from Persius to Juvenal is to exchange an academic lecture-room, with a bookish, if enthusiastic, lecturer, for the society of a man of the world, taught, in his own words, by Life, and inspired by 'savage indignation' over the vices of Rome. With

---

[1] Quintilian was perhaps misled by Horace (*Sat.* I, 10, 66) where *Graecis intacti carminis* refers to primitive Latin satire.

Juvenal, two questions inevitably arise: Were these vices as wide-spread as the satirist believed or would have his audience believe? and, Is this indignation genuine, or mainly a pose? Perhaps we may be content with the answers that Rome was not quite so vile, nor Juvenal quite so indignant, as he would lead us to think. For it has been well remarked that 'if society at large had been half as corrupt as it is represented by Juvenal, it would have speedily perished from mere rottenness[1].' Pliny's Letters, as well as Quintilian and even Tacitus, give a different set of facts. Martial, while corroborating much of the depravity, also shows that life was liveable in Rome no less than in the provinces. It seems, then, that if Juvenal was one-sided in his selection of these facts, they were lurid enough to warrant the most scathing condemnation.

But, as it is the business of Satire to choose the abnormal, so it was the essence of Rhetoric to exaggerate the abnormality; and Juvenal, however sincere in feeling anger, cannot be acquitted of over-emphasis in expressing it. No doubt he could hardly condemn vice without describing its character, but too often the description seems merely an excuse for gloating over the vice. The poet has only himself to blame if we question his sincerity. In any case, his sense of proportion is often at fault. After making all allowance for different scales of value in ancient and modern ethics, we can hardly share his indignation at the 'muleteer consul' driving past the tombs of his ancestors at full speed, and then applying the brake 'with his own hands.' 'True,' he comments, 'it is at night, but the moon sees, and the stars strain their eyes in witness[2].' In the sixth satire, again, though a Messallina or an Agrippina may not have been unique among Roman ladies, it is difficult for us to understand why a mere blue-stocking deserves to share the vituperation accorded to the murderess or adulteress. It might almost seem as if Juvenal, in spite of his express disclaimer of following a particular sect[3], had held the Stoic view that all sins are equal, and therefore equally to be condemned. But he was no Stoic, although he had absorbed those principles of the Porch that were accepted as rules of common morality in paganism. In giving expression to these, Juvenal has hardly an equal. The thirteenth satire, with its emphasis on the anxiety of a bad conscience, deserves to be reckoned among the noblest sayings of Stoicism. Another subject of the school was the question of prayer, which Horace and Persius had already discussed. This rather outworn theme becomes, in the tenth satire,

---

[1] S. Dill, *Roman Society from Nero to Marcus Aurelius*, p. 2. See further below, chap. XIX.

[2] VII, 146 *sq.*   [3] XIII, 120.

one of the masterpieces of literature. Here, at least, the indignation is less in evidence than elsewhere; the keynote is rather pity for the vanity of human wishes, and sympathy with the doom, not doubtful to Juvenal, of human kind. It may be true that the pity and sympathy are not Virgilian. Instead of Virgil's *mentem mortalia tangunt*, we find a hard Stoicism which takes little account of nobler impulses and higher aspirations. Too much stress is laid on the physical and mental disabilities of old age with its attendant sorrows; the whole picture is gloom unrelieved. But the pessimism need not blind us to the power of a satire in which Juvenal has himself shown all the *eloquium* that ruined Demosthenes and Cicero. Yet, though not conspicuous for humour, he does not pitch the note too high, remembering to be a realist, concerned with life— *quidquid agunt homines*—rather than with ideal morality. So, in the fine conclusion of the satire, he prefers to interrupt a passage of splendid rhetoric on the Limits of Prayer with a quaint line of intentional bathos

candiduli divina tomacula porci—

where 'the sausages of a little white porker' follow the noble aphorism that man is dearer to Heaven than to himself, and immediately precede the famous line

orandum est ut sit mens sana in corpore sano.

Perhaps Juvenal had learnt the trick—if it can be called a trick— from Horace and Seneca, but he made it magnificently his own.

Possibly the great Roman satirist may not appeal to the twentieth century as he certainly appealed to the early eighteenth, when 'discourses on morality' were less suspect, or to the later years when Dr Johnson thought him worthy of translation or adaptation. But his modern critics seem to lay too much stress on his weaker satires—some of them can be very weak—as well as on satires like the sixth, where the power of its denunciation hardly compensates for its indecency. Judged, as he should be, by his best work, Juvenal could give a new significance to Quintilian's proud boast that Roman satire owed nothing to the Greeks.

It is no small credit to Domitian who, much more than Augustus, had 'pacified' so many kinds of literature, that a new *genre* survived his reign of terror. For, as has often been pointed out, there were many epigrams before Martial, but (in the modern sense of the word) no epigrammatist. The Greek epigram, as typified by Simonides, Leonidas and Meleager, had all the Hellenic grace of brevity, but the quality of humour and wit was not characteristic.

Martial was very much the child of his age, which (as we have amply seen) required the *sententia* for any form of literature. He never fails to make his point, although this may sometimes seem hardly worth the making. But, as he confesses,

> sunt bona, sunt quaedam mediocria, sunt mala plura,
>   quae legis hic: aliter non fit, Avite, liber.   (I, 16.)

He even writes one or two 'poems' of a single line, which are all point, as in the brief *sententia*

> pauper videri Cinna vult, et est pauper.

Here the epigrammatic 'bee' only exists for the sting in its tail, and the epigram has reached its usual modern connotation. Whether long or short, however, his verses have always the sting, except when he is writing occasional poems for friends or patrons, where it would hardly be in place. Even so, professional humour will out; witness the glaring want of taste in his otherwise charming lines on the death of the little Erotion—his 'love and joy and playmate'—ending with a satiric reference to a widower, who complains of Martial's excessive grief for a mere slave-girl when he himself still survives the loss of a rich and noble wife:

> quid esse nostro fortius potest Paeto?
> ducentiens accepit et tamen vivit.   (v, 37, 21–2.)

But Martial need not be blamed for a rare lapse. A much more serious offence is his Aristophanic and Rabelaisian obscenity, which he shares with Petronius and Juvenal. The grossness may be a legacy from Fescennine verses—or from the bestial side of human nature. Anyhow, 'Latin frankness' was traditional in certain classes of literature, and even the respectable Pliny confessed to erotic hendecasyllables. It is perhaps no excuse to urge that less than a quarter of Martial's epigrams are obscene, as statistics may here be thought irrelevant. The poet himself was from time to time rather nervous about his 'sportive Muse,' and not only made traditional excuses—'lasciva est nobis pagina, vita proba est'—but, in dedicating two of his books to Domitian, as censor, he is careful to observe almost perfect propriety.

When Martial came to Rome, the vogue of literary poems was rampant, rhetoric was universal, and recitations were becoming a bore. The young Spaniard had no patience with the Gorgons and Harpies of epic or the banquets of Thyestes in tragedy. More than once[1] he protests against these stock themes, claiming that his own page is true to Life—'vitam pagina nostra sapit.' This 'taste of

---

[1] IV, 49; X, 4.

life' implied abstention not only from the material of current poetry, but from the rhetoric of its practitioners. Martial disliked all bombast, and never desired to be recited—and hated—by 'big girls and nice boys[1].' His own style was admirably clear—too often much too clear; and it is very rare for him to fall, no doubt quite unconsciously, into an involved or tortuous expression, as when he speaks of unrolling *nostrarum tineas ineptiarum,* 'the worms of my trifles,' which seems to mean trifles fit only for worms to eat[2].

Generally, he is as straightforward as his model, Catullus, and as 'easy' as his other pattern, Ovid, although there was certainly no Lesbia, and perhaps no one Corinna, in his life. When he likes, he can be personal enough, but more often he sinks his own individuality in representing his class, and it is largely owing to his epigrams that we are so familiar with the status of Roman clients. In this connection, readers have often deplored Martial's servility. His 'begging letters' are a stumbling-block to critics who have themselves no need to write them, and who fail to recognize that the cringing of the Senate itself to Domitian was reflected in the general abasement of other ranks to their superiors. As a matter of fact, Martial often redeems his servility by a wit, at least equal to that of the begging scholar in later ages. His request for a 'good' cloak is a pretty piece of humour—his own bad cloak had puzzled a stranger who asked him if he were the celebrated Martial:

> subrisi modice, levique nutu
> me quem dixerat esse non negavi.
> 'cur ergo' inquit 'habes malas lacernas?'
> respondi, 'quia sum malus poeta.'
> hoc ne saepius accidat poetae,
> mittas, Rufe, mihi bonas lacernas. (VI, 82.)

There is plenty of this sly humour in the epigrams, even if it here turns on a verbal point. Indeed, Martial is not above the pun— *non nautas puto vos sed Argonautas,* he says of idle bargees—but his range of both wit and humour is really much wider. Sometimes it depends on exaggeration, like the 'American' humour of Mark Twain: an estate (not necessarily his own) is so small that a cucumber could not lie straight, and a single mouse can ravage it like a Calydonian boar[3]. But most often he anticipates the wit of a Voltaire rather than the humour of a Dickens. Indeed, there are those who, while of course granting Martial plenty of wit, would deny him humour; and he may well lack the geniality of Horace, who, in the phrase of Persius, 'could play round the heart.' There is too much of the satirical in his make-up, without, however, the

---

[1] VIII, 3, 16.   [2] X, I, 13.   [3] XI, 18.

(rather doubtful) standards of Juvenal. It would be difficult, indeed, to credit Martial with any standard at all, unless it be admiration of *urbanitas*, good form. Pliny, however, praises him not only for the wittiness of his points, but for a certain quality which he calls *candor*. This 'candour' has been explained by a severe critic as 'simply that of a sheet of paper which is indifferent to what is written upon it, fair or foul' (J. W. Mackail). But Pliny, who liked Martial and helped his return to Spain, meant something far more laudatory. No less than Virgil to Horace, Martial was to Pliny a 'white soul,' fair and generous, not a man to hit under the belt. We may not agree with Pliny, but Martial's poems to his intimates—Julius Martialis and the rest—seem to justify the praise. It is to this side of his character that poets such as Herrick owed most; and R. L. Stevenson, although he was forced to call Martial a 'sorry jester,' is almost equally in his debt.

V. PROSE SATIRE AND ROMANCE
The Apocolocyntosis: Petronius

There are two documents, belonging to the age of Nero, which may be classed together, since, although they are of very different importance, both are realistic in style, and illustrate the strong vein of satire so characteristic of Roman taste, from the days of Ennius and Lucilius[1]. The first of these—the *Apocolocyntosis* or *Ludus de morte Claudii Caesaris*—is a political squib, attributed to Seneca himself, who is said by Tacitus to have composed the funeral speech delivered by Nero, when the whole Senate smiled at a reference to the late Emperor's 'foresight and wisdom.' We learn from Dio that Seneca afterwards wrote a satire called the 'Pumpkinification of Claudius'—a parody on the official 'deification' (apotheosis). But there are serious difficulties in assuming that Seneca was the author of the present pasquinade. Apart from doubts of a more or less subjective kind—that the satire is unworthy of the philosopher, and the style different from that of his other work—the actual ascription is made uncertain by the absence of the keyword— pumpkin—in the text, even if this is mutilated. Negatively, an anonymous squib was likely to be attributed to the most important writer of the period, whose life and death were so closely linked with the successor of Claudius, just as the play of *Octavia* was (however impossibly) added to the genuine tragedies of Seneca.

The *Ludus* is a mixture of prose and verse, obviously of the

---

[1] The author of the *Apocolocyntosis* imitates the *Concilium deorum* in Lucilius i, i. See E. Bolisani, *Lucilio*, p. 67.

Menippean *genre*, and the sole surviving example of the kind, unless we include the *Satyricon* of Petronius, which, however, is more of a Romance, if technically, perhaps, a Varronian satire. Some of the humour is a little heavy, and the author is too anxious to blacken the character of Claudius; but the scene in which the Emperor is introduced into the Senate of the Gods, to stand his trial, is a clever parody of the proceedings in the Roman *curia*, not unworthy of Lucian, whose *Council of the Gods* may conceivably have been indebted to the *Ludus*. In the end, Claudius is condemned and more or less appropriately punished.

The *Ludus* has been rather unkindly treated by modern critics. It is stigmatized as a 'venomous political satire' by Teuffel, and even Mr Mackail calls it a 'silly and spiteful attack.' It may be spiteful, but it is certainly not silly. More than one Renaissance scholar admired the work; and Byron's *The Vision of Judgment* (no doubt independent) may give a fair idea of its character and scope, although Byron was kinder to the King, whom he leaves in Heaven, practising the hundredth Psalm.

If there is some dispute about the authorship and value of the *Ludus*, the *Satyricon* leaves no doubt on either point. Few will question either its merits or the identity of the writer with the Petronius Arbiter whose life and death are so graphically described by Tacitus[1]. Only excerpts from the fifteenth and sixteenth books remain, but one of these—the *Banquet of Trimalchio*—is of considerable length; and the fragments sufficiently prove the general character of the work. This is primarily a Menippean satire, though it seems also to have affinities with other Greek sources, of which we know very little—Milesian tales (the famous story of the Milesian widow is incorporated) and Greek romances. Whatever its origins, the *Satyricon*, as we find it, is intensely Roman, and in many respects the most interesting document of its time. The reader is reminded, now of *Gil Blas* or *Tom Jones*, now of Casanova's *Mémoires*, or of *Candide*, while its central theme—a series of scandalous adventures by land and sea—has been thought a parody of the *Odyssey* (without its poetry, like Joyce's *Ulysses*), the wrath of Priapus being substituted for that of Poseidon. Angry gods, however, are a common motive in folk-tales, and Petronius need not have looked as far afield as Homer. Anyhow, the much-enduring Odysseus has been put in commission, to become a party of disreputable characters, of whom one, Encolpius a Greek freedman, tells the story. The longest fragment, on the Banquet of Trimalchio, is too well known to need detailed description. That

[1] *Ann.* XVI, 18 *sq.*

vulgar, upstart freedman is obviously a type, but he has also a
well-marked individuality, from the moment when he is carried
in a *lectica* to the dining-room, till the end of the dinner, which he
is drunk enough to turn into his own funeral feast. His ill-bred
ostentation is incredible, but the author makes us believe it.

There is so much of value in this earliest extant Romance, that
a critic finds it difficult to know where to begin—or stop. In form,
its most striking feature is the diction. Educated speakers speak
with all the 'urbanity' of polite conversation; but Trimalchio
himself, as well as slaves and other members of the lower classes,
uses the *sermo plebeius*, full of proverbs, slang, and bad grammar.
The rich parvenu drops easily into such solecisms as *caelus*, *fatus*,
pudeatur, in stark contrast with his affectation of culture.

Petronius was himself a poet, more or less in the Ovidian tradition, and between thirty and forty epigrams or short poems (possibly
from lost parts of the *Satyricon*) are assigned to his pen, showing—
for a Roman—rather unusual powers of imagination. But these
powers are hardly conspicuous in the two longer poems inserted
in the body of his prose. The verses (nearly 300) on the Civil War
are of special interest in so far as they have a bearing on Lucan,
whose first three books must have been already known by recitation.
Petronius clearly intended, not to parody, but to improve on Lucan,
but it cannot be said that he succeeded. His main criticism (see
above, p. 718) refers to the absence of *deorum ministeria* in the
de Bello Civili, and this supernaturalism is amply supplied. But,
although Petronius is commendably free from the tricks of rhetoric
in his own prose, his verse is here as rhetorical as Lucan's, and often
as frigid. The carnage in the war leads to the distressing result that
Charon will need a whole fleet to ferry the dead: *classe opus est*—
a remark that almost surpasses Lucan in his unhappiest moments.
In general, this epic fragment, though possibly smoother, is much
tamer than the poem which it would correct.

VI. SENECA (A.D. 3–65)

Seneca was one of the most voluminous writers of the Neronian
period. Besides the tragedies (which, as we have seen, show him
at his worst) he composed a large number of moral essays, as well
as various works on physical science and natural history, none of
which has survived, except the *Quaestiones Naturales*. This book,
in the true Stoic way, combines queries about certain natural phenomena (such as thunder, wind, earthquakes) with the moralizing
inevitably suggested by Roman 'science.' It is clear that for

Seneca, as for Persius, the 'causes of things,' which interested Lucretius and Virgil for their own sake, had ceased to appeal, except as mere texts for a diatribe or sermon (p. 722).

Seneca has met with serious and often indignant critics, both ancient and modern. The objections of his Roman censors may partly be discounted. Quintilian, the champion of Cicero, not unnaturally condemned a prose which, of set purpose, had renounced the Ciceronian 'period,' with the substitution of verbal conceits expressed in terse epigrammatic sentences, and of vulgar words mixed with the dignified speech of earlier Roman oratory. To the teacher of rhetoric, Senecan eloquence was 'corrupt and the more dangerous in that it was full of attractive faults[1].' Such faults —Quintilian proceeds—endeared him to the youthful taste; and Tacitus agrees[2]. Seneca, in fact, was a modernist, in the secular quarrel between Ancients and Moderns[3]. In the archaizing fashion of the Antonine age, Fronto is no less severe. He would like to 'root out Seneca's eloquence, as full of unhealthy plums '—'mollibus et febriculosis prunuleis'; his aphorisms are repeated a thousand times in various dresses; his style is vulgar, its modulations effeminate. Aulus Gellius[4] records a difference of opinion between those who rejected Seneca both as philosopher and stylist, and those who could see merit in his matter while denying his elegance. On the general question of Seneca's place in literature, Gellius refrains from judgment; but he resents the philosopher's attitude towards Cicero and (of course) Ennius.

Adhuc sub iudice lis est. There are still Ciceronians and Taciteans. But here the question is not so much between the rival merits of classical and 'silver' Latin, as on the actual style of Seneca. Some of the charges brought forward by his ancient critics must be allowed. His inordinate love of point, his monotonous rhetoric, his flashy antitheses, are all perhaps as offensive to the modern reader, as they seemed to Quintilian or Fronto. There may be many who will agree with Macaulay's often-quoted criticism that to read Seneca straightforward is 'like dining on nothing but anchovy sauce.' Yet, in one important part of style—the choice of words—Seneca will hardly be blamed at the present day. His service to Latin prose, by widening the vocabulary, was immense. Hitherto, serious literature, when not technical, had eschewed the colloquial word; Seneca, not only in his letters, but in his full-dress prose, loves to intermingle technical or humble words with the language of the forum[5].

---

[1] Quintilian x, 1, 129.   [2] *Ann.* XIII, 42.

[3] See further, p. 734, and cf. J. F. D'Alton, *Roman Literary Criticism.*

[4] *N.A.* XII, 2.   [5] See Summers, *op. cit.* pp. xlii *sqq.*

The modern critic, much as he may object to Seneca's peculiar style, must at least admit the importance and interest of his matter. Whether in his Consolations on bereavement, or in his treatises on Clemency and Anger, he presents a sane and moderate Stoicism which led early Church Fathers to reckon him as a Christian and a saint. We may dispute the value of his code—it has been thought, by some, too narrow, by others, too impracticable—but his earnestness can hardly be denied. Addressed to Lucilius, his letters are a complete 'guide to philosophic life,' issued for the instruction of his pupil in the art of living. Only, for Seneca, this art has nothing to do with ordinary personal life, as in Cicero—Seneca himself notes the difference (108)—still less are the letters a social record, as in Pliny. Their closest analogy is to be found in the philosophic letters of Epicurus; and as Seneca greatly admired that philosopher, and often finds points of contact between his own eclectic creed and Epicureanism, it is possible that there was some conscious imitation. Not that Seneca wrote at all in the manner of Epicurus. He was too good an artist to imitate the dull pedestrian style of the Greek master; and his letters have a charm that Epicurus generally lacks. They have all the grace of Pliny, without his vanity. For, if Seneca is too much inclined to wrap himself in his own Stoic virtue, he writes as one who has not yet attained. Most of his letters are 'protreptic'—to awaken in Lucilius the love of philosophy: but he never places himself on a pedestal; he is a learner— 'non sum tam improbus ut curationes aeger obeam' (27, 1). Both his reader and himself are 'in the same nursing-home.'

The plan of the letters is fairly uniform. Each is introduced by a kind of text—a remark on his own or his friend's health, on the public games, old age, physical exercise, travel, slavery, suicide, indeed on all the pursuits, attitudes and interests of Roman life. But, whatever the nominal subject, the treatment is invariably that of a Stoic. A sea-trip, with its attendant sickness, starts with a vivid and witty description of the sufferer's distress, which can hardly be paralleled in ancient literature; but the description soon passes into an encomium of philosophy, the sovereign remedy for all ills, including nausea—Seneca does not mention a philosopher's toothache—and the letter (53) ends with a series of aphorisms. The sermon is always imperfectly disguised.

VII. PLINY THE ELDER (A.D. 23 OR 24–79)

If the Flavian epoch had contributed nothing else to prose literature, the age would be remarkable for the *Natural History* of C. Plinius Secundus. The work itself is conceived on wrong principles, but it is so full of information on various aspects of the ancient world—its beliefs, its history, its science and art—that we could better spare many a better book. Pliny himself belonged to a type, of which Varro was the most striking instance—soldier, administrator and admiral turned scholar. His (doubtless) early work, a manual on the use of the javelin for cavalry, would seem a curious preparation for the author of an encyclopaedia on Universal Knowledge. For the *Naturalis Historia*, in thirty-seven books, purports to be nothing short of encyclopaedic, since it starts with cosmography, passes through Man to zoology and botany (which suggests a long account of *materia medica*), and then, through mineralogy, deals with the history of art.

Something of the kind had been attempted before, notably by Celsus in the preceding generation; but nothing, apparently, on the same scale. Pliny was justly proud of his immense industry and, in a preface to Titus, claims to have consulted 2000 *volumina*, mentioning his use of a hundred select writers—*exquisiti auctores*, his 'hundred best authors'; while his secondary authorities greatly exceed that number. And Pliny has the merit, rare among Roman historians, of acknowledging his debts: it is only generous, he says, *fateri per quos profeceris*. But enormous learning does not necessarily imply good judgment, and Pliny seems to be completely wanting in discrimination. It is true that, discussing were-wolves in Arcadia, he protests against 'Greek credulity'—'impudens mendacium est ut teste careat' (VIII, 82). This sounds promising; but in the previous book (VII, 32) he has already qualified his scepticism: such monstrosities as Sciapodes, and men with eyes in their shoulders, are no doubt due to Nature in a humorous mood— 'haec et talia ex hominum genere ludibria sibi, nobis miracula, ingeniosa fecit natura.' We need not perhaps expect a saner disbelief from Pliny than from Augustine[1], who guardedly remarks that whole races—if they exist—may be as monstrous as certain individuals.

Yet, of the twenty thousand 'noteworthy facts' (*viginti milia rerum dignarum cura*) which Pliny claims to have mentioned, a large proportion are such as to make the work—in his own words— a treasure-house rather than a book. He extracted the wisdom, as well as the errors, of all antiquity, including Aristotle and Theophrastus among the Greeks, Cato and Varro among the Romans, down to Columella in the generation preceding his own. There is no trace of a scientific method—the elephant is mentioned after man, as the biggest animal—and his cosmogony, being Stoic,

---

[1] *de civ. Dei*, XVI, 8.

passes over the Epicurean alternative; so that, even judged by the standpoint of his contemporaries, Pliny cannot be regarded as up-to-date. But he has an unfailing eye for the curious and uncommon item of information, and the encyclopaedia must have been as interesting to his first readers as it still remains to us. Who would willingly miss his remark (VIII, 68) that there are fifty flavours in that *materia ganeae*, the pig, while every other animal can give only one; or, again, his note on the ostrich—the foolish bird which thinks itself safe, if it can find a bush to cover its head (x, 2)? A zeal for investigation, which directly caused his death in the eruption of Vesuvius, was bound to leave a mark, even if it was not quite that which Pliny intended. If for no other reason, his chapters on painting and sculpture are invaluable, as the chief extant account of ancient art.

Of his style—or rather, styles—little can here be said. The bulk of his work is succinct and almost Tacitean in brevity. Like Vitruvius and Columella, he often uses technical language, which a Roman historian was careful to avoid. But, where Pliny is not hampered by technology, he is as rhetorical as the worst rhetorician. Not only in the preface, but in many parts of the Natural History, he finds room for moralizing, though his Nature does not suggest the same plethora of Stoic comments that we find in Seneca's *Questions*. Pliny, one suspects, was but a half-hearted philosopher: it was enough to describe the wonders of the world with no more than an occasional pointing of the moral.

VIII. QUINTILIAN (*c.* A.D. 35–95)

It is probable that few of even professional scholars do more than dip into the *Institutio Oratoria* of Quintilian; and the latest editor of his first book can justly complain that 'seldom have sixty pages of equal importance and interest lain so long neglected[1].' The favourite of the Humanists, from Poggio (who discovered the complete copy in 1416) to Erasmus and Pope, seems now, at least in English-speaking countries, to eke out a precarious existence by virtue of a single chapter in the tenth book. This chapter, however, although important as a summary of first-century criticism, is the merest excrescence in the sum-total of the *Institutio*, which is concerned with the training, not only of the orator, but of every educated Roman. As the elder Seneca claimed, rhetoric educates even those whom it does not employ[2].

[1] F. H. Colson, pref. to his *First Book of Quintilian*.
[2] *Contr.* 2, pr. 3.

The reason for this present-day neglect is no doubt largely due
to the odium of the word 'rhetoric'—a reaction from the spacious
days of English eloquence between Burke and Gladstone. There
may be other contributory causes: Quintilian, though perfectly
readable, has been largely dethroned by his own ideal—Cicero—
in the more-than-Byzantine contraction of the Classics rendered
necessary by the modern curriculum. For Quintilian's main object
was to return to Cicero. Naturally, he did not quite succeed,
because the language and idiom of prose had changed; because
the modern taste revolted from the Ciceronian 'periods,' and not
least, perhaps, because—in spite of his remarkable ability—he was
not strong enough to wield the club of Hercules. Anyhow, he was
well aware that the art of Cicero could never be recaptured, but
although the model was unapproachable, it was at least an ideal.
If Quintilian could have had his way, Seneca would have been
impossible. The roots of the new prose went back as far as Sallust,
for whose 'immortal brevity' Quintilian has very faint praise,
saying that it may be intelligible to the educated reader, but it is
a dangerous weapon to the speaker[1]. In this respect Quintilian
himself is not quite blameless. He sometimes bowed to the prevailing cult of the *sententia*—the only grace in which Cicero was
deficient—but he seldom allowed brevity to interfere with lucidity.
His own aphorisms are as full of common sense as they are infrequent. Nothing could be truer, or more tersely put, than the
familiar 'cito scribendo non fit ut bene scribatur; bene scribendo
fit ut cito' (x, 3, 10), or than 'philosophia enim simulari potest,
eloquentia non potest' (xii, 3, 12)—an epigram which has had a
new lease of life—at least in academic circles—with the substitution of 'piety' for 'philosophy' and 'scholarship' for 'eloquence.'

Before he wrote the *Institutio*, Quintilian had been the most
successful rhetor in a rhetorical age, numbering amongst his pupils
not only the younger Pliny and probably Tacitus, but the two sons
of Domitilla, sister of Domitian, who gave him consular rank. His
fame marked him out as the first holder of the chair of rhetoric
established by Vespasian about A.D. 72. After his retirement, he
wrote a (lost) treatise *de causis corruptae eloquentiae*; and the
Institutio itself, which followed, was intended to supply the remedy
for this corruption. Rhetoric is the art of speaking well, but this
is possible only for a good man—Cato's definition, *vir bonus dicendi
peritus*, is in fact the text on which the whole work is founded,
although the character required for the good orator is specially
drawn in the twelfth book. But who is the good man? Quintilian

---

[1] *Inst. Orat.* IV, 2, 45; X, 1, 32 and 101.

had here to reckon with the philosophers, who claimed a monopoly of goodness. He retorts that philosophy has usurped ethics[1] and is only a trespasser on a field abandoned by the orator, who is now the true *homo sapiens*. We have here an echo of the conflict between two ideals of education which (in default of a really scientific view) divided the Roman world. The expulsion of philosophers from Rome on two occasions (in 89 and 94/5) marks the temporary triumph of rhetoric, and indeed the tables were not completely turned until the reign of a Stoic emperor. Yet Quintilian himself is not an extremist, since he allows that an eclectic philosophy may have value in the training of an orator[2]. But he is Roman enough to value the practical *exempla* of real life before the *praecepta* of Greek theory—'illum quem instituo, Romanum quendam velim esse sapientem.'

The *Institutio* itself gives the best picture of its author's character. He was obviously kindly and humane, with admirable sense, and an absence of the vanity which hampers our enjoyment in reading his pupil Pliny. His attitude towards his art shows that the teacher could be remarkably free from the faults that vitiated nearly all the literary work of the period. For, although he is in general severely technical, and devoted to the Rules, he can rise to passages of real dignity and pathos—notably in his touching reference to the loss of his wife and sons (praef. 6)—while his discussion of wit and humour (founded on Theophrastus) has a fund of anecdotes dealing with the lighter side of Roman oratory (VI, 3). But the *clou* of the whole work, at least for a modern reader, is to be found in the twelfth book, which contains a penetrating contrast between Greek and Roman styles, and incidentally discusses the capacities of the two languages—'non possumus esse tam graciles? simus fortiores. subtilitate vincimur? valeamus pondere.' Not, of course, that Quintilian is merely, or mainly, concerned with the linguistic side of education. *Eloquentia*, as has been well observed[3], 'always carried with it wealth of thought as well as wealth of words, and the rhetorical ideal is not so narrow as we are wont to think.' Quintilian himself is the best antidote for this mistaken view of ancient education.

IX. PLINY THE YOUNGER (A.D. 62–*c.* 113)

Pliny, following his teacher, was also a determined Ciceronian. His obvious ambition was to emulate his model, not only as an orator, but as a letter-writer. He succeeded—with a difference.

---

[1] *Praef.* 10 *sq.*; *Inst. Orat.* II, 15, 33, and 16, 11.
[2] *Inst. Orat.* XII, 2, 26 *sq.*　　　　　　[3] Colson, *op. cit.* p. xxii.

Like Cicero, he lived to become consul and augur (at a much
younger age, he blandly notes), although the consulship under
Trajan gave no opportunity to save his country. In early life he
had attended the lectures of Musonius Rufus and other Stoics;
but he had neither the temperament nor the ability to follow Cicero
in philosophic writing. He imitated, again, the author of the
Verrines by prosecuting a corrupt proconsul before the Senate; his
main activity, however, was before the *centumviri*, a minor court
in which the cases were mainly trivial. Martial, in a well-known
epigram, which Pliny quotes with satisfaction[1], suggests that posterity will bracket his pleadings with the pages of Arpinum.
Undaunted by the very dubious reputation of his model in poetry
—Martial[2] might have warned him here—he even tried his hand
in erotic verse, 'not beneath the dignity of M. Tullius,' although
the 'Ciceronian' epigram which he quotes must be spurious. His
own epigrams—only one or two survive in his correspondence—
hardly justify the boast that even Greeks learned Latin in order
to sing his hendecasyllables. His panegyric on Trajan, however
interesting to the historian of that Emperor's reign, has no value
to the student of literature. Pliny's letters, therefore, alone remain
to challenge comparison with those of his great *exemplar*; and here,
too, the comparison becomes a contrast. It is not merely that Cicero
did not intend his letters to be published (though in later life he
contemplated their publication); the real difference is that he wrote
for his correspondent alone, whereas Pliny's letters, like Seneca's,
are written *urbi et orbi*. They are, in fact, little essays, each devoted
to a single subject. But, whatever his subject, his extreme vanity
is apparent. This inordinate self-consciousness is the more to be
regretted, inasmuch as Pliny's moral and intellectual qualities were
very high. Kind to his inferiors, with many friends and few enemies,
a generous benefactor, devoted to his wife, conscientious in the
performance of public and private duties, he has been described
as the best type of Roman gentleman. It is needless to say that his
letters are of the greatest value for evidence on the manners and
social life of the age; but the most that can be claimed for them as
literature is that their style is not corrupted by the worst faults of
Seneca—a far abler writer—and that, even if Pliny jokes with
difficulty, his Latinity is always clear and graceful, neither too
condensed, nor too copious. His place is in the eighteenth century,
where his greatest translator, Melmoth, found him a congenial
subject; and, among the finest letter-writers of that century, the
spirit of Pliny has often been recognized in William Cowper.

---

[1] *Ep.* III, 21, 5.   [2] Cf. Martial II, 89, 4.

X. TACITUS (*c.* A.D. 55–120)

There remains the great name of Cornelius Tacitus, whose genius might well redeem the Silver (or any other) age from the charge of mediocrity. His reputation—not particularly striking in the next few centuries when Roman culture still survived—has steadily grown since the Renaissance; and, in spite of some recent carping criticism, it may safely be maintained that Pliny was right in predicting 'immortality' for his friend. The twentieth century, at least, is so largely 'Tacitean,' both in outlook and expression, that we cannot wonder if his pessimism is accepted and his style admired. Tacitus, in fact, has a double claim on modern interest. He is both historian and artist; and if these aspects are largely fused in classical theory and practice, they may, for convenience, be considered separately.

Any attempt to pass judgment on Tacitus as a historian[1] must, of course, start from his theory on the function of history. Here he is in direct line with previous Roman thought. The purpose is moral, to illustrate virtues and vices by concrete examples: in his own words,

> ne virtutes sileantur utque pravis dictis factisque ex posteritate et infamia metus sit.　　　　　　　　　　　　　　　(*Ann.* III, 65.)

This definition, in the latest work of Tacitus, not only repeats his object in the Histories—*non tamen adeo virtutum sterile saeculum ut non et bona exempla prodiderit*—but precisely represents Livy's attitude in his preface. The 'truth' of history is assumed—only poets might dispense with strict veracity—but how is the truth to be discovered? Tacitus claims to write *sine ira et studio*; modern methods lay more stress on research than on mere 'impartiality,' which quality, indeed, is perhaps superhuman. He does not often mention his authorities by name, although he certainly consulted various kinds of official documents, as well as earlier historians; but it is one thing to 'consult' an authority; quite another, to estimate his credibility; and, if Tacitus refuses to accept stories told *odio magis quam ex fide*—his researches may have gone no further than this modified scepticism.

But, whatever may be the limitation of his craftsmanship as historian, his supreme value as an artist remains untouched, and it is with his art that we are here chiefly concerned. The first problem that naturally arises is his relation to Cicero's style. It has been usual to remark that Tacitus started with a Ciceronian bias

---

[1] See also vol. x, pp. 871 *sqq.*

from which he shook himself free. This theory depends on the
assumption that the *Dialogus* is his earliest work. But there is
absolutely no external evidence for the Tacitean authorship. The
single manuscript from which later copies are derived gives no
indication of the writer's name, although the *Germania* and
Agricola, which follow, are both definitely assigned to Tacitus. But
even critics who deny that the work can be attributed to him with
any confidence[1] allow that it was written in his day, so that it is still
open for lovers of the *Dialogus* (and the present writer is one) to
argue that the author whom we must call Anonymous may possibly
have been no other than Tacitus himself.

It follows from this uncertainty that the *Dialogus* can supply no
evidence on the usual belief in a 'Ciceronian' period for Tacitus.
We know that he was a distinguished orator—according to Pliny[2]
he spoke with dignity (σεμνῶς)—but there is nothing to prove that
this dignity was Ciceronian. Others, besides Quintilian, were in
favour of returning to Cicero. The peculiar style of the *Dialogus*,
with its admixture of *sententiae* grafted on a Ciceronian stock, is just
what Quintilian himself affected, although his own responsibility
for the treatise (a theory doubtfully advanced by Lipsius) seems
to be negatived on chronological grounds[3]. Whoever the author,
he was a student of Cicero (especially of the *de oratore*), and there
is no difficulty in assuming that the treatise, in a sense, was
archaistic: Cicero had settled the *genre* of dialogue, and a Flavian
imitator must needs follow the model. The servility of imitators
is shown by the ingenuous admission of Pliny, who is naïve enough
to take credit for using several styles in the same speech (*plures
dicendi species*) in order to attract various tastes.

It is therefore in the *Agricola* and *Germania* that we must look
for the first certain traces of a development in Tacitean style. Here,
too, a model was required, and Tacitus found it in Sallust. The
subjects of these treatises are too well known to need discussion,
and their stylistic features are equally familiar. Every schoolboy
is taught the main characteristics of Silver Latin prose—its variations from Cicero's norm of *concinnitas* in rhythm and structure,
its tendency to introduce poetic words and forms, its Graecisms,
its developments of grammar and syntax, its love of archaism. This
is common to all writers of the period, and need not be further
examined. But, beyond the common changes, there is the personal

---

[1] See R. Sabbadini, *Storia e critica di testi latini*, p. 41 *sq.*; C. Marchesi,
Tacito, p. 301 *sq.*
[2] Pliny, *Ep.* II, 11.
[3] See Peterson, Tacitus, *Dialogus*, p. iii *sq.*

style of Tacitus. Here, he has not escaped modern detraction. He is accused of straining the resources of Latinity beyond even the much freer scope and wider possibilities of the language, as naturally extended in the Flavian epoch. Only a Flavian, perhaps, could criticize him with finality. A modern is excluded from the mere fact that Tacitus can only, or mainly, be judged by himself. But if the final test of style is pleasure and ease of reading, we can hardly deny the success of his work, from the opening of the *Agricola* to the last extant chapter of the *Annals*. That there was development between the two is undisputed; but, substantially, in the *Agricola*, Tacitus had already found himself. Writing a eulogy, he could hardly avoid some echo of Ciceronian amplitude, so that we are not surprised to find that his great peroration owes something to the third book of the *de oratore*[1], just as Macaulay, in his turn, modelled his description of Warren Hastings—'he looked like a great man and not like a bad man'—on 'bonum virum facile crederes, magnum libenter.' In the main, however, it was Sallust, not Cicero, who provided the *exemplum* of monographs, and both in the *Agricola* and the *Germania* the brevity and conciseness of Sallust as well as the arrangement are predominant. But in both treatises there are certain rhetorical features, which Tacitus pruned away in his later works. We find too many 'doublets'—*quiete et otio, ignavis et imbellibus*, and many others, as signs of the orator's desire to drive his point home.

But it is in the *Histories* and (still more) in the *Annals* that we chiefly look for 'Taciteanisms.' There Latin is reduced to the barest bones of its structure, while the nature of the subject required, above all things, variety of expression. The author was conscious of a certain sameness in his subject-matter—*nobis in arto et inglorius labor*—compared with the broad field in which Livy worked. His *Annals* is almost entirely concerned with a single phase of history—the lives of successive emperors and the fortunes of the senatorial order. Lucan's epigram—*humanum paucis vivit genus*—might be the text of the whole work. On other aspects of social life he has little to say. His contemptuous view of the plebs 'habituated to the circus and theatre' is precisely that of Juvenal's 'food and the games.' The life of the municipia, the social and economic system of the Empire, the government of the provinces, are all outside his sphere[2]. In so narrow an area, it was the artist's prime need to avoid monotony. Hence—as has long been recog-

---

[1] *Agric.* 43, 1.
[2] This is not to say that he viewed them with indifference. Cf. e.g. *Ann.* XVI. 5, 1.

nized—his search for variety of synonyms to express death or suicide, which bulk only too largely in the *Annals*.

One other side of his art seems less tolerable to modern taste: the dislike of the 'vulgar' word, which is most conspicuous in his reference to spades and shovels as things 'per quae egeritur humus aut exciditur caespes' (*Ann.* 1, 65). We are reminded of the *mouchoir* in French tragedy, and indeed history has here repeated itself with fair accuracy; for, if Tacitus was not a poet, there was now, as we have seen, no clear line of demarcation between the dignity of prose and verse, in spite of the Senecan attempt to broaden the vocabulary, at least of prose. A writer, who borrowed so abundantly from poetry, could not be expected to neglect the first poetic principle of the age—'ab omni verborum vilitate refugiendum.'

How far was this art successful? At the present day, readers are not particularly moved by the Figures. Anastrophe, Chiasmus, Hendiadys and the rest are apt to leave us cold. Yet we cannot fail to be impressed by the genius that has wielded so much art. Tacitus was admittedly a pessimist, and pessimism often jades. But, instead of producing the tedium which he feared, his *Annals* is one of the supreme achievements of historical writing. Utterly remote, in style, from Gibbon, Tacitus is still akin to the historian of later Rome in his biting comments on human weakness and depravity, and his penetrating insight into human psychology. His complex and saturnine Tiberius—'torvus aut falsum renidens voltu'—is a wholly different creation from the typical stage-tyrant of Seneca. The last four books, with their monotony of murders, are sad reading, but the reader's interest never flags while the tragedy 'ira numinum in res Romanas' is moving to its predestined end.

When we have exhausted all that can be said about his art, we find that it is the mind—the *ingenium*—of Tacitus that really counts. His greatness may be seen by a contrast with his coevals, with the facile self-satisfaction of Pliny, or the eulogistic commonplaces of Florus, or the curious admixture of learning and scandal that makes the gossiping biography of Suetonius. Tacitus was equipped with very different qualities, so that any comparison with these three contemporaries must be invidious. He has naturally some of the faults of his age: he is not entirely free from rhetoric, but in the main it may be said that he, alone of Silver Age historians, can make rhetoric a servant instead of a master. His famous *sententiae* would have satisfied Petronius—they do not 'stand outside the body of his speech, but shine with a colour woven into its garment[1].' So far from suggesting a rhetorical commonplace, they express, in a brief and pregnant summary, the 'inwardness' of the situation. And these thoughts—even when he appears to borrow —are his own. He may formally owe the apophthegm 'non esse curae deis securitatem nostram, esse ultionem' (*Hist.* ɪ, 3) to Lucan:

> Felix Roma quidem...
> si libertatis superis tam cura placeret
> quam vindicta placet;

but he lifts the idea to a higher level by the substitution of *securitas* for the merely political *libertas*. Even in his nominal 'borrowings' from Seneca and others—for it must be repeated that to borrow was to be in the tradition of Latin literature—Tacitus cannot help showing the individuality of a great artist, as well as a great thinker.

XI. C. SUETONIUS TRANQUILLUS (*c.* A.D. 75–140)

To mention Suetonius after Tacitus may seem something of a bathos. An account of post-Augustan literature might well conclude with its greatest name. Yet the biographer of the Twelve Caesars has a secure place, *proximus* if not *secundus* to his more famous contemporary. The son of a military tribune, he was befriended by Pliny, who admired his character and learning, and obtained for him the *ius trium liberorum* from Trajan. But he survived Pliny by many years, and lived to become private secretary (*magister epistolarum*) to Hadrian, who dismissed him for lack of respect to the Empress. His further career seems to have been literary and antiquarian, but of his extensive output only the *Lives* (*de vita Caesarum*) remains, together with fragments of his *Illustrious Men*.

To the historian, the *Lives* is a very important document, if only to confirm or supplement Tacitus, while from the literary point of view, Suetonius is at least an interesting figure. He suffers from faults common to his age: while generally affecting the fashionable brevity, he sometimes lapses into long, sprawling and rather formless sentences packed with participial additions. On the whole, however, his style is clear and straightforward, with no attempt at the false brilliance of Seneca or the real brilliance of Tacitus. It may be held that his style is the expression of a rather commonplace mind, almost destitute of any psychological subtlety, and occupied with the *minutiae* of biography. Suetonius paints on a large canvas, but it is over-crowded with details. Some of these are petty enough, but unlike Tacitus, who passes over the unessential, the biographer

---

[1] Petronius, *Sat.* 118.

is Terentian—nothing human is outside his range. The result is that his readers, being also human, will always turn to Suetonius, to learn the 'private lives' of the emperors, for which Tacitus had little taste or room.

Suetonius, though the son of a soldier, has no skill in describing wars and battles, no political discrimination, no care for strict chronology or the sequence of events. He presents, not the times, but the man; and if the man's life is scandalous, he has no hesitation in exposing the scandal, without comment, unless the *infamia* of an emperor is worse than was to be expected of even a Tiberius[1]. For such enormities, he must no doubt have depended on common talk and tradition; but, for the rest of his narrative—and there is little libellous in the biographies of Julius and Augustus—we know him to be careful and scrupulous in research. By virtue of his office he had access to the imperial archives; and he seems to have made good use of his documents, since he often transcribes autograph letters of Augustus, notes the peculiarities of his hand-writing[2], and remarks that Nero's manuscripts, with their erasures, prove his verses to be genuine[3].

So far, it may appear that Suetonius was a biographer of more industry than distinction; and if his merits were confined to the preservation of famous sayings—'iacta alea est,' 'veni, vidi, vici,' 'qualis artifex pereo,' 'marmoream se relinquere quam latericiam accepisset,' 'vae, puto, deus fio,' and a hundred others—or of the appearance and personal habits of the emperors, the *Lives* might without injustice be 'epitomized' or 'excerpted'—and then put aside. But, as a matter of experience, few who take up the *Lives* will content themselves with a single reading. Suetonius may not be a great artist—he is certainly not a great historian—but he is always good to read, and sometimes enthralling. Again and again he rises to the occasion, and that without a trace of rhetoric which he, almost alone in his day, seems to have despised. Literature would be poorer, without the fine account of Caesar at the Rubicon[4], or the really moving description of Nero's last hours[5]—a passage so dramatic as almost to rouse the reader to some feeling of sympathy with that bane of the human race.

It is not without significance that Suetonius wrote some of his multifarious works in Greek. The day was coming when even native Romans and Italians ceased, for a time, to express themselves in Latin, and the language of Hadrian yielded more and more ground to the hellenizing age of the Antonines.

[1] Cf. *Tib.* 44. [2] *Aug.* 27. [3] *Nero,* 52.
[4] *Div. Iul.* 31 *sq.* [5] *Nero,* 47-9.

CHAPTER XIX

SOCIAL LIFE IN ROME AND ITALY

I. CHARACTERISTICS AND CHANGES

SOCIETY during the Neronian period and two or three generations thereafter has its characteristics recorded in a literature copious and sometimes apparently conflicting. In this respect it differs from Ciceronian society, whose salient features may be reconstructed from the voluminous correspondence of Cicero alone. But for a picture of Imperial society, besides illuminating excavations in Italy and a mass of inscriptions testifying to significant facts of social standing, public service, private occupation, individual munificence, domestic affection, or religious belief, we have a large number of Latin writers who range in date from Seneca and Petronius to the *Historia Augusta*. Greek sources also are valuable, particularly in estimating the ethical thought of the times.

In the grades of this society, among outstanding features are the gradual emergence of an Imperial court supported by a garrison in Rome; the deterioration of the old senatorial order and its replacement, to a large extent, in official duties by members of other classes, resulting in a marked withdrawal of many Romans from public service; new phases in the importance of the *equites*, who rose in esteem as successful business men and as civil servants; and the much greater part taken in administrative and commercial life by emancipated slaves. This prominence of freedmen was responsible for the admixture of alien blood which now profoundly altered Rome racially, just as innumerable foreign elements from Greece and the Orient affected its culture and religion. The common folk, at least in Rome, dropped still further in the social scale, demoralized by loss of political privilege, by poverty and by doles. In spite of their material advantages under Hadrian and the Antonines they failed to satisfy the criteria of a complete civilization. They did not greatly contribute to their own civilization: they did not maintain a conception of honourable service for the State or care to defend it themselves; while the existence of slave-labour as ever kept some citizens from working at a craft. Content with free food and free amusements, they did not learn the lesson, which always comes slowly, how to use leisure well. In their general want of self-reliance and enterprise lay the seeds of decay.

The very comfort of the Antonine age, an era of reputed felicity under enlightened and unchallenged rulership, tended to produce a certain stagnation of ideas. It was not a time of striking originality. Yet in its society, owing to the business abilities of knights and freedmen, there was a notable diffusion of wealth, by no means always dissipated in luxury, but often devoted to the betterment of cities in Italy and the provinces. This sense of the obligations of wealth is among the healthy symptoms in the period, and is of a piece with that growing humanitarianism which made a foil to the cruelties of slavery and the arena.

The culture of the age, reflected in literature, is also unmistakable in the enthusiasm for rhetoric and for literary *séances*. The higher learning was pursued by many women, who, if they no longer influenced politics, had reached a stage of emancipation from much that was inherent in ancient Roman conventions. Scraps of Virgil and Tibullus on the walls of a small town like Pompeii indicate the spread of literary knowledge, presumably disseminated by local rhetorical schools. Vespasian established for Quintilian the first chair of literature and rhetoric (p. 734), and in the next century Antoninus Pius endowed chairs at Rome and elsewhere for rhetoricians, who were held in high honour and sometimes entrusted with diplomatic missions. This Imperial interest in education was akin to the welcome accorded to Greek sophists, even though from time to time philosophers suffered expulsion from the capital. Teachers of morality were eagerly listened to and the quest after cults more satisfying than the State formalism of Rome prepared the soil for the growth of the Christian creed.

II. THE SOCIAL GRADES

One feature of society impossible in Republican days was the evolution of an Imperial court. At first, the family of the *princeps* was not elevated by ceremonial above other families of rank. The preference of Augustus was for simplicity; but by degrees the institution of a body-guard, the presence in Rome of the Praetorians, the interposition of State-officials, the maintenance of a *cohors amicorum* or *comites* with an accompanying elaboration of ceremony tended to assimilate routine in the palace to that of Oriental monarchies, though the process was not completed till under Diocletian late in the third century. Claudius' principate, by virtue of its efficient secretariate and increased centralization, had gone some way towards absolutism. The Imperial family was thereby set over ordinary citizens. This is not, however, to say that it was entirely isolated. Imitation is the sincerest flattery; and the manners observed in an emperor's household inevitably affected formalities and fashions among the upper ranks at Rome. His tastes, high or low, set a social standard, as Nero's did, whether in rhetoric or luxury; and after Nero's extravagances came Vespasian's old-fashioned thrift, which produced at least a temporary effect upon some circles. Another illustration is the way in which Hadrian's Hellenism caused a renascence of Greek studies. His passion for travel could not pass unobserved: even his wearing of the beard reduced the number of the close-shaven. But it is not suggested that everything in an emperor was followed as a pattern: sometimes the very departure from aloofness might give offence; for nothing in Nero's conduct more deeply outraged aristocratic taste than his unabashed indulgence of his artistic temperament so far as to appear on a public stage.

The gulf severing emperor from community became patent when a ruler arrogated to himself divine honours. Whereas Vespasian had made access to himself easy, all the characteristics of a ruler-cult were exhibited in Statius' adulation of Domitian as *dominus* and *deus*. Another mark of differentiation and a barrier against free access to the monarch can be seen in the institution of a Privy Council. Burlesqued for Domitian's time by Juvenal[1], it was well developed in the Antonine age. On questions of State Antoninus Pius regularly consulted his conclave of *amici*[2], and Marcus made a habit of discussing home and foreign policy with a *consilium* of *optimates*: 'it is fairer,' he explained, 'that I should follow the advice of my many excellent friends than that my excellent friends should follow my single will[3].' The sentiment does him credit; but a Council chosen by the emperor signalized a certain severance from the rest of the State machinery. So too the consort of the *princeps* was elevated more and more over other women. It is not merely that a Messallina's birthday was celebrated publicly or that an Agrippina assumed still greater regal airs (vol. x, p. 699 *sq*.); but the fashion of deifying the women of the Caesars increased, until we find Marcus Aurelius, when his empress Faustina died in Asia Minor, asking the Senate to

---

[1] IV, 64—the nobles, shut out themselves, gaze at the huge turbot admitted as fit to set before an emperor. Pliny, *Pan*. 47, contrasts Domitian's inaccessibility with the free approach to Trajan.

[2] S.H.A. *Pius*, 6.　　[3] S.H.A. *Marcus*, 22.

decree to her divine honours and a memorial temple, while his eulogy implied ignorance, real or simulated, of her notorious depravity[1].

The Senate, the *amplissimus ordo*, whose members once enjoyed exalted prestige for services rendered to the Republic by themselves or ancestors, had fallen on evil days. The attitude of different emperors to the Senate is a matter for political history: here it emerges mainly for its social significance. Prolonged civil warfare and the proscriptions towards the end of the Republic had killed off many of the nobility and ruined others. The infertility of race-suicide also operated. Many bearing names of ancient families are found in menial occupations; some, in dire penury, felt driven to apply for subventions from the emperor. A Corvinus might work as a hireling on a sheep-farm[2], and Valerius Messalla accepted a yearly allowance of 500,000 sesterces in alleviation of his 'blameless poverty' in A.D. 58, when also two impoverished spendthrifts were financed[3]. By Hadrian's time there were only about thirty senators who bore names of the old nobility. The senatorial order was being recruited from a recent official class including wealthy parvenus, often provincials or descendants of freedmen, who could not command, or indeed fully appreciate, the reverence secured in older days by the optimates. After the loss of life in the struggle among the four emperors in 68–69, replenishment of an attenuated Senate became necessary. Italy and the provinces were drawn upon for members, and this fresh blood, though more widely representative, was more directly subservient to the emperor who made the selection. It is, therefore, scarcely a matter for surprise that the treatment of senators by some emperors was cavalier and by a Domitian tyrannical.

The liberty regained after Domitian's death was liberty in opinion and speech[4], not in government; for Trajan enacted laws and declared war at his pleasure: and in the composition of the Senate changes continued because of the more habitual inclusion of Greeks and Orientals under Trajan and the philhellene Hadrian. Senators saw their old place in the State usurped under the Imperial constitution, and they were debarred by their rank from engaging, openly at least, in trade. They could still hold magistracies at home, even as colleagues in the consulship with the *princeps*, or governorships abroad under his surveillance; but at best this meant a division of executive function rather than of

[1] S.H.A. *Marcus*, 26; Dio LXXII, 31.   [2] Juvenal I, 106 *sqq.*
[3] Tacitus, *Ann.* XIII, 34.   [4] Tacitus, *Hist.* I, I *ad fin.*

real power. Many consequently found outlet for their energies, in reckless expenditure (for some still possessed great wealth), or in conspiring against the government (though they never quite formed an organized opposition), or in the study of the fortifying consolations of Stoicism. Hence, too, with fewer opportunities for public distinction than the Republic had offered, with less hold upon government in a weakened patriciate, and without the old invigorating conflicts in political oratory, the senator, whether newcomer or of noble lineage, often contented himself with a round of social engagements, forum, games, baths, banquets, authors' *recitationes*, light gossip or serious discussion as temperament might prefer. Life uninspired by any definite purpose became for some a rudderless drifting among the *ardeliones*, those fussy wasters of time whom Phaedrus satirized in one of his few Roman anecdotes[1]. A recurrent note is the complaint that work worth doing gets hindered by trivial inroads upon leisure. Seneca reminds us that people gaily rob us of our time, the one thing that no one can repay; Martial grumbles that he might have written a poem but for the duty of attendance upon a patron; and Pliny finds a day gone, its hours squandered on the ceremonial entanglements of social life.

When it is remembered that the patrician order had been diluted first with wealthy *equites* and plebeians of the city raised in rank by Augustus and Claudius (vol. x, pp. 122 and 499), then widely in ever-increasing numbers with the Italian and provincial *bourgeoisie*, the *novi homines* of whom Cicero had been a notable instance, and with a new military aristocracy as well, it will be seen that the upper class constituted a compact record of the imperial expansion of Rome. Like the capital itself, now a caravanserai of many nationalities, its nobility had grown cosmopolitan and vastly altered since the days when the *patres* had been custodians of a traditional lore accepted as a touchstone in custom, morality, law and religion. That there was deterioration in moral tone is undeniable. Pliny, for instance, comments on the misuse of ballot-papers by senators so lost to self-respect as to scribble on them irrelevancies, jokes and even indecencies. And yet the senatorial order showed extraordinary resilience after oppression, and extraordinary power of recovering a part of its ancient prestige. In spite of clipped authority and alien admixture, the Senate was still a great arena for achieving through eloquence a *succès d'estime* rather than much political result. In Nero's time the nobleman

---

[1] *Fables* II, 5.

praised in the *Laus Pisonis* was listened to with hushed attention[1]; in A.D. 100 Pliny's *Panegyric* on Trajan was delivered on what was felt to be a great occasion; and nearly half a century later it was of high significance in Fronto's eyes to produce an impression by an official speech of thanks to Antoninus Pius as *consul suffectus* for two months of the year 143. His oration was a refined appeal to the culture of the day and testified to the Antonine view that, despite all change, the Senate remained by conservative tradition a dignified caste in command of social prestige. There was at least an attempted resuscitation of bygone glory.

The equestrian order, on the other hand, throve because it was less exposed to an emperor's jealousy and suffered from no bar in pursuing commercial vocations. Our business here is not with its re-organizations by Augustus (vol. x, p. 185) and by Claudius or with Hadrian's re-organization of his civil service so as to secure a strong equestrian personnel (pp. 426 *sqq.*). It should, however, be made clear that Augustus saw in the *equites* no longer the political order conceived by C. Gracchus nor merely the money-making class of the later Republic, but a class from which the Empire could be supplied with the lower officers for its army and men of experience for civil service posts in the provinces and in administrative departments at Rome. Provincial procuratorships, prefectures such as those of the Praetorian Guard, the urban police, the fleet and *annona*, as well as the governorships of Egypt, Noricum and Raetia, were regularly held by knights. Membership of the order was conditional on a census of 400,000 sesterces, and among its best types were middle-class Romans willing to use their abilities in patriotic service when many of senatorial rank shirked such a career from laziness, disaffection, or philosophical prejudice against sharing in public life. The order continued to be the financially successful class recruited from business men, tax-farmers, and moneylenders; in some cases Imperial freedmen too were given equestrian status. The position of *equites* as officials in the Imperial household was conspicuous during the brief reign of Vitellius and again under Domitian, Hadrian and Antoninus Pius. In the second half of the first century equestrian rank was granted over-lavishly. Many new knights were army veterans settled in Italian and provincial towns, and, while some were public-spirited men who deserved the honorary priesthoods and magistracies recorded in inscriptions, others exhibited so

[1] *Laus Pisonis*, 65–71. Its authorship is undetermined: see *Minor Latin Poets*, ed. J. Wight Duff and A. M. Duff.

much self-assertive vulgarity that they merit the ridicule of Martial and Juvenal. According to the latter[1] the fourteen equestrian rows in the theatre accommodated persons who had reached the legal census but whose past might be of the shadiest kind. His contemptuous phrase *equites Asiani*[2] is a parody on *equites Romani* in sarcastic allusion to the riff-raff who came as slaves from the East and by profits from sordid occupations qualified as knights.

Within the order itself gradations existed of social as well as of moral status. There was a vast difference between a Maecenas, the herald of equestrian importance in Imperial times, and some who by undesirable methods scraped enough for admission. Within the order too there were the extremes of capitalist wealth and grinding poverty. Martial's honorary tribuneship, carrying the title of *eques*, left him too poor to pay for his final journey back to Spain; and Gellius[3] tells of a knight driven to subsist on bran-bread and the poorest wine. But for the mass of middle-class citizens, though the order lacked the prestige due to senators, equestrian rank, outwardly marked by *anulus* and *angustus clavus*, was an object of ambition. Many inscriptions record success in attaining it: some men claimed the distinction of having sons who were *equites*[4]: others fraudulently made pretence of being entitled to the equestrian ring or equestrian seats. Hadrian's con-ferment of his household secretaryships upon knights, instead of freedmen, ensured respect for these intermediary officials and heightened the general dignity of the order. Besides high and confidential appointments, other factors enhanced its status, such as the rule that sons of senators must pass through it as a pre-liminary in their *cursus honorum*, the matrimonial alliances occa-sionally contracted with the Imperial family, the purging of its register of unworthy members, and enactments—not uniformly observed—against a knight's appearance on the stage or in the arena. Its moral reputation was consulted when, under Tiberius, a decree forbade any woman whose grandfather, father or husband was an *eques* to make a living by immorality. Professional learning was represented in the grade. Rubellius Blandus was the first *rhetor* of knightly standing; later, *equites* appeared among the *grammatici* and physicians[5]. There is a pleasant picture of an *eques* who, after military service and administrative work as pro-curator in Narbonensian Gaul, took up agriculture and literature,

[1] Juvenal III, 153 *sqq.*   [2] Juvenal VII, 14.
[3] *N.A.* XI, 7, 3.
[4] See A. Stein, *Der römische Ritterstand*, p. 424.
[5] Stein, *op. cit.* p. 437.

thus turning his farm, as Pliny remarks with admiring exaggeration, into an Athens[1].

As for the plebeians, their protector was nominally the emperor, the holder of tribunician power. But their political importance had vanished with the transference of elections to the Senate under Tiberius. From this standpoint they were worse off than citizens in the *municipia*, and Cicero's contemptuous phrase *faex Romuli* is matched by Juvenal's *turba Remi*. Yet from a purely civic standpoint their status was unimpaired: the toga remained as much in evidence as ever, and regulations were devised to stem the swamping of the body of free Romans caused by unrestricted emancipation of slaves. By the beginning of the second century a greatly diminished percentage of free plebeians could prove unmixed Italian descent: the proportion of foreign blood has been stated as high as 90 per cent.[2]. On the surface, the lot of the common folk seemed one of comparative comfort: years of peace brought freedom from many anxieties: games were provided for all, and free food for 150,000 to 200,000. Of the passion for games we still have a reminder in the Flavian amphitheatre, the Colosseum (p. 33 *sq.*), and of the corn distribution, in the remains of capacious granaries and offices of importing firms at Ostia. For men engaged in trade and industry the guilds rendered some of the services of modern friendly societies; and, while in the army plebeian status opened no higher rank than that of centurion, there was still left the chance of a rise to equestrian status and of consequent promotion. But a large portion of the *plebs* avoided work at a trade or industry in which slaves and freedmen were employed. They felt strongly the temptation to be content with the two objects of desire, *panem et Circenses*[3]. Augustus and others saw the risk for a *plebs urbana* whose popular ideals were unearned food and free amusements; but it remained State-policy to subsidize idleness without attempting systematically to create employment or, apart from spasmodic drafts of *coloni*, to introduce the workless to unworked land. *Frumentationes* alone could not support citizens handsomely, and widespread poverty[4] forced plebeians upon devices whereby to increase their means.

The cleavage between social ranks is nowhere better illustrated

[1] *Ep.* VII, 25.
[2] See Tenney Frank, 'Race Mixture in the Roman Empire' in *Amer. Hist. Rev.* XXII, 1916, pp. 689–708.
[3] Juvenal x, 79–81; cf. Persius v, 73 *sq.*
[4] See S. Dill, *Roman Society from Nero to M. Aurelius*, pp. 94–7.

than in the relation of poor clients to their patron—the burdensome etiquette of the morning call (*salutatio*), the possibly daylong
attendance as escort, the dependence on the private *sportula* to
supplement the public dole, the hopes of an occasional invitation
to dinner, where the superciliousness of host and lackeys was
often made very evident[1]. Many clients had little home life, but
led a parasitic existence out of doors. Most were too poor to
ingratiate themselves with rich childless people, as professional
captatores[2] did, by handsome gifts in hopes of a legacy; for, as
Juvenal[3] asks, *quis pauper scribitur heres?* Martial might see something funny in the concealed poverty of a dandy who pawned his
ring to get a meal while he posed as 'the A1 in cloaks' (*alpha
paenulatorum*), but for many impoverished Quirites there was
nothing more painful than the shaft of ridicule[4]. Educational
and professional skill did not in themselves raise their possessors
above this third class. Doctors, jurists, teachers belonged to it as
much as jockeys, auctioneers, artisans and dancers, unless they
acquired money sufficient to raise their status. And here the
prospects were not rosy; for auctioneers, builders, undertakers,
musicians, even men of evil life, had more chance of making
profits than the ill-paid teacher or the literary man[5]. The latter's
best hopes lay in catching that rarity, a generous patron.

The poorer folk were most exposed, without any break, to the
drawbacks and dangers of the city—to rickety homes in unhealthy quarters, and to risks from conflagrations, night roysterers
and footpads. The housing problem was serious, because much
of the city space was occupied by public edifices and the Imperial
fora. Dwellings for the masses could not be conveniently erected
in the outskirts when means of transport were so inadequate as
compared with those in modern cities. High site-values resulted
in the increase of tenement-blocks (*insulae*), often jerrybuilt
lodging-houses of as many storeys as possible. Wealthy men
could, if they visited the heart of the city, return at what time
they chose in a slave-borne *lectica* to mansions on the high ground
of Rome, but the central districts offered little cessation of noise.
Juvenal[6] says 'many a sick man meets his death by being kept
awake' and 'It costs a fortune to get a sleep in the city.' Though

---

[1] Contrast the considerate treatment of guests by Piso (*Laus Pisonis*,
109–32) with Virro's arrogance (Juvenal v, 37 *sqq.*).
[2] See below, p. 767.   [3] III, 161.
[4] Martial II, 57; Juvenal III, 152 *sqq.*
[5] Petronius, *Sat.* 46; Martial IV, 5; V, 56; Juvenal VII, 104.
[6] III, 232 and 235.

carriage traffic for private individuals was forbidden during the day, yet the din in narrow streets resounding to hawkers' cries and rumbling waggons was to sensitive ears often unbearable.

III. WOMEN

The women of the period show the variety incidental both to human nature and to a developed civilization. As history, it will not do to join with satirist or epigrammatist in overstressing their immorality: equally it will not do to regard them solely in the light in which they appear among Pliny's letters. One change strikes us at once. The grand dames now mainly belong to the Imperial circle. In the later Republic a married woman of rank often exercised a powerful effect upon public affairs in virtue of the influence of her family (vol. IX, p. 782 *sq.*); but under the Empire constitutional changes had robbed her of value as a political asset. So women ceased to be either active players or mere marionettes in a game where a marriage engagement subserved family policy or party schemes. Other views of matrimony had their advocates. Following Stoic tenets on the moral equality of woman to man and the wisdom of giving the same education to both, Musonius Rufus[1] emphasized the importance of character, rather than name or riches or beauty, in a match, and asserted the identity of ethical standard for both sexes. In general, the break-up of many established relations in life during the civil wars contributed to greater freedom for women of the higher circles. This freedom some used well, others ill. The honourable State-service of the Vestal Virgins under a vow for a long period of their lives still kept high an ideal of pure womanhood and a breach of these vows could still be punished with an archaic severity (p. 37). Convention guaranteed a careful surveillance of unmarried girls. But divorce and re-marriage, which had increased towards the close of the Republic, continued under the Empire to betray so much slackness of regard for the matrimonial tie as to render parts of Augustus' moral legislation nugatory. Despite the fact that Augustan enactment had made adultery a crime, emperors like Gaius and women of the imperial family like Augustus' own daughter Julia or Claudius' consort Messallina had set scandalous examples of sexual licence. The infidelities of married women, the breach of vows by some Vestals, the flaunted shame of *meretrices* in tell-tale finery combined to lower the moral

[1] Ed. O. Hense, 1905, pp. 67–76: cf. Ch. Favez, 'Un féministe romain, Musonius Rufus,' in *Bull. de la Soc. des études de lettres,* Lausanne, 1933.

standard. That prostitution was widespread over Italy is clear
from the evidence of Pompeii and from the brothels in Petronius'
Satyricon. But it was unusual for anyone to protest against this
degradation as Dio Chrysostom did[1]: more comment would be
aroused if a woman fought in the arena or went hunting scantily
clad[2].

There was, therefore, considerable ground, though not complete justification, for the invectives of Juvenal's sixth satire. It
is a nightmare of bad women, and formulates an indictment
unrelievedly depressing, unless taken with requisite allowances.
Some feminine types pilloried are incurably vicious and richly
deserve castigation, but others are rather of the 'impossible' type
in society—the loud-tongued termagant, the blatant 'new woman,
the she-pedant who talks literary 'shop' at table—objectionable,
no doubt, but undeserving of an equal measure of Juvenal's
wrath. His keynote, in virtual defiance of the Augustan legislation against celibacy, is the insanity of any man's contemplating
wedlock so long as he could procure the alternative of a rope to
hang himself. The whole catalogue, illogically arranged, jumbles
in one medley moral delinquents with ladies whose faults lie in
using Greek or citing Virgil. Juvenal's prejudices are against
the higher learning for a woman: logic, history, grammar, rhetoric
will train her to be a nuisance by quoting unfamiliar lines or cor-
recting a friend's grammatical mistakes. Others satirized are the
mistress who is cruel to her slaves, votaries of Oriental cults,
smugglers of supposititious infants, users of magic spells, or, worse
still, poison. Wealthy shirkers of motherhood, too, come under
the lash for practising birth-control and abortion:

> Childbirth is rare upon a gilded bed:
> So great the skill and drugs of her that makes
> A woman barren, killing men unborn
> For hire. (VI, 594–7.)

Underneath its rhetorical exaggeration, the satire reveals dark
places in social life, just as Martial's epigrams expose much of
its nauseating vice.

But this is not the whole story. Apart from the fact that
married happiness is less apt to provoke comment or inspire protestations, inscriptions prove that wedded couples all over Italy
in this very period led lives of loyal affection. It was, as of old,
the ideal of many a diligent wife that she should respect the virtues

---

[1] *Or.* VII, 133: see Dill, *op. cit.* p. 77.
[2] Juvenal I, 22 *sq.*

of piety and chastity, that she should be literally a housekeeper by staying at home to mind the wool-work: hence epithets like *lanifica, pia, pudica, frugi, casta, domiseda*[1]. Martial sends a pretty greeting[2] to a bride and bridegroom wishing them years of harmony and picturing them, towards the close of their days, as a sort of Darby and Joan:

> May bride love husband in his eve of life
> And she, though old, still seem his youthful wife.

There were memorable instances of faithful wives who accompanied their husbands into exile or shared their doom of compulsory suicide, as the elder Arria did when she stabbed herself and uttered the famous words *Paete, non dolet*.

A pleasant example of a happy marriage is the mutual devotion of the younger Pliny and his third wife Calpurnia. This inexperienced girl-wife was granddaughter of one of his elderly correspondents Fabatus. In one letter we discover Pliny nervously waiting news of Calpurnia, who has had to go away to Campania for her health. This and two others[3] are love-letters: 'I lie awake a great part of the night, conjuring up your face: in the day-time my feet lead me to your room at the hours when I used to visit you.' Another letter describes her keenness for literature[4]. She was a clever and thrifty housewife, whose affection extended to studying her husband's compositions and even getting them off by heart. When he gave a *recitatio* to his friends she was an affectionate audience behind a curtain. 'She sings my verses,' he adds, 'and sets them to her lyre with no other master of the craft than Love, and Love is the best teacher.' This model helpmate was with Pliny in Bithynia under his special commission from Trajan. Our last glimpse of her is through a letter from her husband to the Emperor, explaining that he had issued an exceptional warrant authorizing her to travel back to Italy by the Imperial post, as news had come of her grandfather's death and she was needed to console her aunt[5]. We have Trajan's reply[6] in approval; but we do not know if the loving couple ever met again; for there is no proof of Pliny's home-coming from his province. We can only picture the parting when she started in the post-chaise along some dusty road leaving her husband to continue his scrutiny of the shaky finances of Bithynian towns.

---

[1] *C.I.L.* VI, 11602 (age of Hadrian). For examples in verse of varying quality see Buecheler and Riese, *Anthol. Lat.* II, i, ii, iii (*Carmina Latina Epigraphica*).   [2] IV, 13.

[3] *Ep.* VI, 4; VI, 7; VII, 5.   [4] *Ep.* IV, 19.

[5] *Ep.* X, 120 (121).   [6] *Ep.* X, 121 (122).

History and literature open a gallery of different types—bad women in plenty down the whole social scale from a Messallina or a Faustina; good women doing domestic duties unexceptionably; the two imperious Agrippinas; Trajan's consort Plotina, whose strength lay in nobility of character; the learned Helvia, the elder Seneca's mother; other wise mothers such as Agricola and Aurelius had; Marcia, daughter of Cremutius Cordus, brave enough to publish some of her dead father's proscribed writings; Fannia, in days of nerve-racking espionage, courageously maintaining the Stoic tradition of her mother and grandmother, the two Arrias; Ummidia Quadratilla, a go-ahead old lady who died at the age of 80 in Trajan's reign and who scandalized her straightlaced grandson, a friend of Pliny's[1], by keeping a troupe of *pantomimi* for performances at home; hardworking *libertinae*; concubines in the Imperial household like Nero's Acte or Vespasian's Caenis; women drawn to Egyptian and other cults, and suspected, some of them, of Judaism or Christianity; vulgar and intemperate creatures like those depicted in the *Satyricon*; and frail traffickers in vice. No one formula will fit so much variety, and the list might be greatly expanded. But it may be said of family life that, though brightened by much natural affection, it had still to reach a higher general standard of respect for womankind. The truth had yet to be realized that not only the *matrona* but the *ancilla* was entitled to respect.

IV. SLAVES AND FREEDMEN

Both slaves and ex-slaves played important parts in Roman households, the Imperial household included. Before we survey these two classes, certain changes from Republican days must be observed. Home-breeding of slaves and, to some extent, organized kidnapping compensated for the falling-off in war-captives during the comparative peace of the Empire. With thoughtful citizens, partly owing to the Stoic doctrine of the fraternity of man, humaner views gradually spread and made for amelioration in the lot of servitude, and for so much readiness in masters to liberate slaves that Augustus, recognizing the serious infiltration of alien blood into the body politic, introduced restrictions upon manumission[2]. Yet this proved but a slight check, and Tacitus[3] records a significant remark that 'if freedmen were marked off as a sepa-

[1] *Ep.* VII, 24.
[2] See A. M. Duff, *Freedmen in the Early Roman Empire*, pp. 30–4.
[3] *Ann.* XIII, 27.

rate grade, then the scanty number of the free-born would be evident.' The rise of successful freedmen to riches made a social change[1] of the utmost moment, and the wealth amassed by a Narcissus or a Pallas gives point to Martial's use of *libertinae opes* as something proverbial[2].

Slaves still came from all parts of the world; they fulfilled all sorts of duties, many menial, others demanding high secretarial, musical, medical or literary skill. They remained, in the eyes of the law, chattels without personal rights and were subject not infrequently to the cruellest scourging, branding, or even crucifixion at an owner's command. When the Emperor Claudius issued an edict protecting, if they recovered, sick slaves exposed in the temple of Aesculapius (Vol. x, p. 694), he was in this, as in much else, ahead of his time, and it was not until the reign of Hadrian that masters were deprived of the right to put slaves to death (p. 315). The evidence of slaves was always elicited by torture. Juvenal comments scathingly on their maltreatment by some owners, on gambling masters so mean as to grudge proper clothes to a shivering slave, and on a capricious dame sentencing a slave to death. There were Romans who grimly declared that a man had as many enemies as the slaves he possessed, and in Nero's reign the Senate by a majority sentenced to death all the slaves of a city prefect who had been murdered by one of them[3]. In the debate a speaker argued:

As nowadays we have in our households nations with customs different from ours, with foreign worships or none at all, it is by fear alone that you will restrain scum of that sort (*conluviem istam*).

Popular anger ran high at the decision, and only by lining the streets with soldiers could the authorities carry out the execution. Long afterwards, the younger Pliny, himself a kind-hearted master, was horrified at the murderous attack made on Macedo by slaves in his Formian villa[4]: even indulgent masters, he felt, were no longer safe. Certainly slaves did not always bear estimable characters. Many imported from their native land an unscrupulous smartness: they were often dishonest and treacherous. Their manners and morals were such that Quintilian counselled extreme care before giving them charge of Roman children, and Juvenal detests the pampered lackeys who deny a master to a client at the morning call.

But there is a brighter side to this picture. Most masters per-

---

[1] *E.g.* Martial II, 29; III, 29.   [2] Martial V, 13, 6.
[3] Tacitus, *Ann.* XIV, 42–5. See vol. x, p. 705.   [4] *Ep.* III, 14.

mitted and indeed encouraged slaves to save a *peculium* towards the ultimate purchase of independence. Many were emancipated gratis under their owner's will, and, as Persius sardonically observes 'Citizens made yesterday shoulder their master's corpse'; yet Stoic-like he insists that true freedom is freedom of the mind. Gradually, respect was bound to increase for the better sort of slaves. Some, intellectually superior to their masters, could instruct them in literature and philosophy. We read in Seneca of an ignorant freedman who bought highly-educated slaves to coach him in learning which he might parade at dinner. Some possessed qualities of soul fine enough to compel grief for their death, as Statius felt over the slave of Ursus. If, as Tacitus says of civil turmoil in Rome[1], slaves were bribed to betray masters, and freedmen to betray patrons, he adds of others that their fidelity bade defiance to torture. There rises to the mind the touching faithfulness of the women slaves of Octavia, Nero's ill-used wife: no torments could wring from them false witness against their mistress. Fortunately humanitarian ideas were growing. Seneca urges the duty of kindness to slaves, nay rather he would call them 'our humble friends or even our fellow-slaves'; for to a Stoic way of thinking what ordinary man is free[2]? He realizes that he may offend snobs by his teaching[3], and that he is propounding revolutionary ideas in the handling of slaves[4]. Martial seldom shows more feeling than in his elegy over the dead slave-boy, Alcimus: and Columella in plain prose assures us that for farm-work encouragement is most efficacious with slaves, while the younger Pliny was so considerate that he had one of his villas planned with a private study in such a position as to save him from any temptation to interfere with the rowdy revelry of his slaves at the *Saturnalia*[5]. In one letter[6] he offers to induce an official friend to make a detour on his way to Baetica in order to visit Fabatus, and so enable him to emancipate certain slaves in due form. Later[7], we learn that Fabatus had taken this chance, and that Pliny thought it made a desirable addition to the citizen body.

A great rôle in Roman life, social, commercial and political, was played by the ex-slave. Circumstances determined whether the *libertus* was to remain in the household controlling part of its work, or go out into the world to conduct a business, usually

---

[1] *Hist.* I, 2–3.　　　　　　　　　[2] Seneca, *Epist. Mor.* 47, 1.
[3] Seneca, *Epist. Mor.* 47, 13.　　　[4] Seneca, *Epist. Mor.* 47, 18.
[5] Pliny, *Ep.* II, 17, 24.　　　　　　[6] Pliny, *Ep.* VII, 16; cf. 23.
[7] Pliny, *Ep.* VII, 22.

under a financial arrangement with his previous master. In the latter case, and increasingly under the Empire, freedmen left a mark on commerce and industry. They ran a factory or *officina*, where the employees were largely slaves, to make goods like pottery, bricks, glass, pipes, metal-work, jewellery, clothes. Thus many clay lamps in archaeological museums bear a maker's name indicating servile descent[1]. A freedman who followed such callings joined a trade-guild (*collegium*), a friendly or burial society in which he rubbed shoulders with freeborn citizens; even if he incurred their dislike, he might occasionally rise to be master of his guild. Some became builders, grain-merchants, or, by irony of circumstance, slave-dealers. The wine-trade and agriculture attracted others. Very many, proving successful business men, amassed considerable wealth. Trimalchio is pictured as having increased his riches by lending money. Freedmen also entered the professions—teaching, medicine, painting and, in a few cases, architecture and sculpture. The typical Roman magistracies and priesthoods were closed to them, though the conferment of technical *ingenuitas* through the presentation of the symbolic gold ring could open the avenue towards equestrian rank (vol. x, p. 616). In the municipalities freedmen were, as a rule, excluded from the duumvirate, with the result that they could not rise into the local order of the *decuriones*, unless they had been honoured with the *anulus aureus*. Priesthoods of foreign cults, such as that of Isis, were within their reach, and they were not infrequently concerned with emperor-worship as *seviri Augustales*.

Etiquette demanded from a *libertus* grateful respect (*obsequium et officium*) towards his emancipator. Normally, the tie was close. Freedmen often set up statues and inscriptions in honour of their patron, the converse also holding good, where a patron recognized years of faithful and affectionate service. A similar sense of obligation prompted a patron's legacies. The younger Pliny entertained warm feelings towards his consumptive freedman Zosimus, and was at pains to arrange for him a home on the Riviera near Fréjus, where he could benefit by health-giving air and milk suitable for his treatment. One of Pliny's bequests was for the maintenance of 100 poor freedmen in North Italy. Not every freedman could afford to build luxuriously appointed marble baths like those of Claudius Etruscus in Statius' *Silvae*; nor could every freedman rival the career of Trimalchio. Left by his master a princely inheritance (as co-heir with the emperor), he lost heavily through shipwreck in his first enterprise, but more than

---

[1] See A. M. Duff, *op. cit.* pp. 109 *sqq.*

recouped his losses in a second venture with a cargo of wine, bacon, beans, perfumes and slaves: 'A single voyage,' he boasts, 'brought me in a round ten million': then he turned to landowning and later to moneylending. Freedmen had attained their maximum of political influence during Claudius' reign, when a few favourites held the chief secretaryships at court. Succeeding emperors varied in the amount of trust reposed in them, until Hadrian restricted such posts to Knights (see further, p. 427). Their bad name for arrogance, although not unconnected with the intolerable parade of wealth by other freedmen, was largely earned by the offensive behaviour of these imperial officials, before whom senators had to cringe (vol. x, p. 700). Such was the insolent condescension of Pallas, one of Claudius' secretaries, when the senate demeaned itself by offering him praetorian insignia and fifteen million sesterces. Through the Emperor he sent a message accepting the honour but declining the money; upon which this multi-millionaire was thanked for his old-fashioned frugality[1]. When Claudius in the *Apocolocyntosis* applies for admission to Heaven, he is so angry with the goddess Malaria (*Febris*) for her intervention that he makes his customary sign to indicate 'Off with her head!' but 'nobody paid the slightest attention: you might have taken them for his freedmen![2]' By way of contrast, Pliny in his *Panegyric* is clear that Trajan could control his freedmen: 'greatness in freedmen,' he observes, 'is the pre-eminent sign of littleness in a prince'; and Tacitus notes as a merit in Germany that freedmen count for little among the tribes, except those ruled by kings[3]. It is noteworthy that, though Juvenal is recorded (but not proved) to have been the son or foster-son of a rich freedman, he assails the class with venomous contempt. The wealthy ex-slave is loathed for his ostentatious airs[4]. The vulgarity of a retired barber displaying a special summer ring matches the absurd extravagance of Trimalchio's dinner-party and its ill-bred, ungrammatical chatter, when one of the guests chaffs Agamemnon, an authority on rhetoric, in bad Latin: 'The likes of you that's able to speak, doesn't (*tu qui potes loquere non loquis*): you don't belong to our set (*fasciae*), and so you jeer at the talk of we poor folk (*pauperorum*)...'' and so on. There the cloak of literary style is lifted and we hear the actual conversation of common people in the early Roman Empire.

---

[1] Tacitus, *Ann.* xii, 53; cf. xiii, 23.			[2] *Apoc.* 6.
[3] *Germ.* 25.						[4] Juvenal i, 24 *sqq.*

V. ECONOMIC FACTORS

This is not the place for a full survey of economic conditions in town and country. The economic unification of the Mediterranean region at large has been described for the early Empire (vol. x, chap. XIII), and many of its characteristics hold good for the Flavian and Antonine age. To several economic facts allusion has already been necessarily made in considering the grades of society, but a few special aspects may now be glanced at.

Agriculture, as of old, remained a source of wealth, though the remedial measures adopted from time to time were symptomatic of something amiss. Vespasian's restoration of financial equilibrium after his accession in 69 helped the recovery of districts which had just felt the ravages of civil war. In 91, a year of bad corn-harvest but good vintage, Domitian sought, with better intention than success, to aid corn-growing by an edict forbidding new vineyards in Italy and putting down half the existing vineyards abroad (p. 38). Nerva's alimentary scheme lent money to small farmers on interest payable to local municipalities for the maintenance of poor children (p. 210 *sq.*). This implies the existence of owners on a small scale borrowing on the security of their farms. Alongside of this type of farm, itself very different from extensive estates worked by slave-gangs, there developed in Trajan's time a system of tenancy, instead of ownership, by humble cultivators, free-born or emancipated. Like other emperors, he settled groups of free tenant-farmers (*coloni*) on the land; and to the same period belongs the ordinance whereby senatorial candidates for office were required to have one-third of their property invested in Italian real estate (p. 212). We cannot here enter into the intricate question whether Italian agriculture in the century from Nero to Aurelius was prosperous or the reverse. It has been argued[1] that agricultural colonies were mere palliatives incapable of curing the disease of rural Italy, and stress has been laid on the elder Pliny's familiar 'latifundia perdidere Italiam[2].' On the other hand[3], it is argued that emperor after emperor would not have organized colonies, if the small farmer uniformly failed; and Pliny's letters show that, although he had bad vintages and impoverished tenants, he yet derived both pleasure and profit from his estates let out in different parts of Italy. We find him in one case proposing a half-profits arrangement, so anticipating the *mezzadria* of Tuscany.

[1] W. E. Heitland, *Agricola*, pp. 272–4, 299–300.   [2] *N.H.* XVIII, 35.
[3] M. Rostovtzeff, *Soc. and Econ. Hist. of the Roman Empire*, pp. 94–7, 180–93, 545; B. W. Henderson, *Five Roman Emperors*, p. 230.

Pliny was wealthy and his wealth came very largely from the land (*sum prope totus in praediis*).

The development of land in its yield of corn, wine, oil, oxen, sheep, hides, fleeces and timber offered solid chances of gain. From inscriptions giving the names of *mercatores* and *negotiatores* we learn that many served the imperial *annona* or the needs of great cities as transporters of foodstuffs; for merchants were often shipowners and warehouse-proprietors. The money so acquired was constantly invested on the security of land. Our concern is not here, however, with interprovincial trade but with that of Italy. In this age, when wealth was no longer concentrated in few hands, as in the days of senatorial ascendancy, but distributed among capitalists over the Empire, there remained many avenues to fortune. The middle class, including knights, descendants of the old citizen farmers and of soldiers, with a large number of freedmen, were drawn to trade and industry (vol. x, p. 388). The decline of speculative tax-farming had partially restricted the careers of knights, and those who pursued trade with success rose gradually above the disesteem once fostered by aristocratic convention. Yet in imperial inscriptions so many of the wholesale dealers (*negotiantes vinarii, olearii, materiarii* and others) appear with Greek *cognomina* that they lend colour to the contention that Romans were not at heart enthusiastic traders as were Southern Italians of Greek descent and freedmen of alien breeds[1]. Inside the peninsula there went on a vigorous interchange of products, especially foods, stone and wood. Campanian wines and oils were sent all over the Roman West, and Italian wines found a sale in Egypt and India. Pompeii testifies to the business energy of Campania in wines, oil, fish-sauce, pottery, glass and attar of roses (vol. x, pp. 394–6). But by degrees Puteoli, once the most flourishing seaport of Italy, was eclipsed by Ostia—a change due less to Claudius' harbour improvements at Ostia than to the fact that other parts of the world were learning to supply themselves with products which Campania had formerly provided as return cargoes for ships unloading at Puteoli. In the second century Ostia became the chief harbour for imports needed by Rome, though she had little to export in exchange; for Rome never was the productive centre of her Empire. Because she developed comparatively little of a factory system, she could not add to conquest the more permanent bond of a common economic interest among her dominions.

---

[1] T. Frank, *An Economic History of Rome*[2], p. 322.

Yet in industry capitalistic enterprise had organized a measure of mass production (vol. x, p. 391). This held good of the manufacture of pottery, metal articles and, what was often of metal, furniture, glass, paper, leather, bread. The maker's signatures[1] on products of typical industries have been examined to procure data regarding scale of production, extent of market, and class of workmen[2]. The work absorbed large numbers of employees, mainly slaves, with an admixture of free labour. Freedmen were often in control as representatives of a patron or as actual employers, and they took a prominent part, as we have seen, in the trade guilds[3]. The free wage-earner found his pay depressed by the co-existence of slave-labour: he had also less direct claim on a patron for financial help than a *libertinus*, and his inducement was therefore the less to aim at starting even a small business on his own. Upon the spirit of the workers slave-labour acted as a handicap: individual industrialists relying mainly on it could not count on hearty and inventive co-operation. It is not, then, surprising that industrial progress beyond the stage reached in the early Empire was tardy, if indeed appreciable. Besides, the workshops of Rome had their custom diminished through the production of articles by slaves in private houses: tailoring, shoemaking, fulling, carpentry and much else could be done at home.

Another handicap on industry was the shifting of centres of production which followed the extension of city life to the Western provinces. That was inevitable where transport by road and sea was slow and expensive. The red pottery of Arretium was once an Italian ware which accompanied the legions to distant frontiers; but Southern Gauls took to imitating it and their *terra sigillata* was in turn imitated by Germans. This was one of several cases where Italy lost to Gaul her predominance in industrial output. Other provinces also competed in this replacement of her manufactured goods. Italian glass, formerly made by skilled Campanians on Syrian methods, had its sales restricted, when Cologne took up its manufacture. The earthenware lamps of Italy were first supplanted by copies made in Carthage, which was afterwards ousted from some markets in Africa by lamps of local make. But in face of this competitive movement Italian industry seemed less able even than agriculture to secure a preferential position. The

---

[1] Collected *C.I.L.* vol. xv, *Inscriptiones urbis Romae Latinae—Instrumentum domesticum.*   [2] T. Frank, *op. cit.* chap. XIII.
[3] For the *collegia* see A. M. Duff, *op. cit.* pp. 115–17; G. Kuehn, *De Opificum Romanorum condicione privata quaestiones,* Halle, Diss. 1910, p. 74.

central government, which tried means of helping agriculture
and commerce, did nothing to protect industry, and the inference
is that industrialists had no political influence, because industry
was mainly undertaken by producers in a small way, not by great
factories[1]. One aesthetic disadvantage ensued: cheap imitations
by local artisans meant standardized goods, in which the sense
of beauty bequeathed by the Hellenistic age gradually withered
away in the industrial products of the second century A.D.[2]

VI. EXTERNAL CONDITIONS OF LIFE

Housing, often miserable, as we have seen, for the poor, was
palatial for the rich. The former, in low-lying slums, had to put
up with dark hovels or with rooms close under the roof of a
tenement-building, an added danger in case of fire, and yet at
least an unlikely harbourage for citizens worth an emperor's while
to arrest[3]. But on the Palatine there rose magnificent palaces
and on other of the Hills, above the sweltering parts of the city,
sumptuous mansions, though even there the heat could be oppressive. 'What a gain,' is Seneca's sigh of relief, 'after the
stuffiness of town to feel myself among the vines![4]' This lure
of the country ensured the continuance of the villa-habit of the
Ciceronian age (vol. IX, pp. 793–5). Sometimes it was the residential villa that drew a man through a desire for change, fresh
air, rest, or study: sometimes it was the productive farm whose
accounts or prospects had to be examined. Pliny, like Cicero a
connoisseur in villas, had country homes, selected, some as invest-
ments, others for their position, as were his 'Villa Comedy' and
'Villa Tragedy' on the Lago di Como. Of his villa at Laurentum
his description is so detailed[5] that it makes a virtual ground-plan;
and there one of the specified attractions was the view from the
dining-room—a broad sweep of sea, a long stretch of coast and
very pretty country-houses to look at. In a quiet room Pliny could
be happier over books and speeches than in superintending, as
he did on occasion, his vintages reinforced by a detachment of
town-servants. Such *villegiatura* fostered a holiday spirit highly
beneficial for over-serious or over-worked Romans. So a re-
freshing note runs through the brief correspondence of Fronto
and Aurelius about the latter's vacation at Alsium on the Tuscan
coast. Fronto hopes he may picture his pupil, not fasting, not

---

[1] Rostovtzeff, *op. cit.* p. 165.   [2] Rostovtzeff, *op. cit.* pp. 166–8.
[3] Juvenal III, 200–2, 225; cf. Martial I, 117, 7; Juvenal X, 18.
[4] Seneca, *Epist. Mor.* 104, 6.   [5] Pliny, *Ep.* II, 17.

working hard, but enjoying a complete break, reading Plautus, Accius, Lucretius and Ennius; taking a walk on the sea-shore or an excursion by boat; bathing and then dining on a royal repast (*convivium regium*) of all sorts of shellfish and other fish, fat capons, delicacies, fruit, sweets, confectionery, and 'happy' wines. The reply shows Marcus content with a light evening meal and an interval of rest[1].

Excavations and literature combine to place before us the dwellings of the time. The ordinary houses of a small town are best understood at Pompeii: its ruins, many of them now scientifically restored, with the exhibits in the Museo Nazionale at Naples, present a mirror of life in the first century. Pompeian houses are of a type then usual in Italy, not so high as in Rome or at Ostia, but many with a staircase to a second floor and with projecting balcony, and running back from the street to an elegant *peristylium*, the painted wall-decorations falling into at least four well-defined styles, the mosaic pavements representing, often in *tesserae* of different colours, geometric or floral designs or such elaborate pictures as Alexander at Issus. The trades of the town can be reconstructed from the remains of shops and bakeries and even from paintings of Cupids executing tasks as fullers or vintners; its enjoyments from the theatres and gladiatorial barracks; its local politics from appeals on the walls to vote for this or that candidate; its business methods from waxed tablets containing a banker's bonds and receipts; its religion from niches for household gods and from temples like that of Isis; its pious affection from sepulchral inscriptions; its superstition from its protective emblems; its immorality from the houses of ill fame. The *graffiti* on stucco surfaces, some in Oscan, some in Latin correct or illiterate, some quoted, others parodied from poets, are great aids towards the reconstitution of the everyday experience of the inhabitants. So plentiful are they that they prompted somebody to scribble an elegiac in pity for a wall burdened with so much balderdash:

> Admiror, paries, te non cecidisse ruinis
> qui tot scriptorum taedia sustineas.

There are charming products of fancy from other cities within the zone of destruction. A graceful painting is the so-called Flora from Stabiae, her face averted, as she fills a *calathus* with blossoms[2]. And humour takes the form of caricature and parody. From Herculaneum came a green parrot pulling a brownish red go-cart

---

[1] *De Fer. Als.* IV, p. 230 *sq.* N.   [2] M. H. Swindler, *Anc. Painting*, Pl. I.

driven by a grasshopper[1]: the suggestion has been gravely made
that this symbolizes Seneca controlling Nero! From Stabiae there
is another caricature burlesquing the flight of Aeneas, Anchises
and Ascanius from Troy by giving dogs' heads to all three; and
among the wall-scribblings is that of someone whose theme is the
fullers and their sacred screech-owl—no 'arms and the man' for
him! ('fullones ululamque cano, non Arma Virumque').

But for impressive literary pictures of lavish domestic appointments Statius' *Silvae* are unrivalled. His pages make the reader
dwell in marble halls. A bride's home is portrayed as rich in
marbles, onyx and porphyry, its wood-work agleam with Dalmatian metal, its gardens freshened by crystal springs and welcome
shade under immemorial trees—cool at midsummer but warm in
winter, controlling the season at choice. Describing a residence
at Tivoli, Statius praises the natural beauties of the Anio and,
inside the mansion, its gilded beams, Moorish lintels, veined
marbles, pictures, statues in bronze, ivory, silver and gold—a
haunt of peace for leisure and study. The baths of Etruscus,
where the torches of winged Loves are fancied to kindle the
heating apparatus, are similarly resplendent. Another poem pictures a mansion near Sorrento with steaming bath-house, rooms
within earshot of the waves, others full of countryside peace, and
a hall gorgeous in the whites, reds, greens and yellows of marbles
from many lands[2]. Roman taste in art had by Ciceronian times
travelled far beyond the standard of Mummius: now it was still
more widespread. Statius' recollections of the art-treasures of
Vindex[3] turn on 'a thousand shapes of classic ivory and bronze'
possessed not by a mere collector but by an expert in the work
of different masters. Pliny was proud of his purchase of a
Corinthian bronze representing realistically an old man[4], and he
mentions Silius Italicus[5] as a connoisseur ($\phi\iota\lambda\acute{o}\kappa\alpha\lambda os$) who carried
expensive vagaries to an excess. Silius had a craze for buying
villas, books, statues, and busts—above all, a worshipful reverence
for his bust of Virgil.

Domitian's fishponds (*vivaria Caesaris*)[6] represent the well-
stocked *piscinae* of rich Romans which continued the fashion of
days when Cicero marked the wealth of nobles by styling them
piscinarii. Slightly later, we have Pliny's commodious Laurentinum
as well as his country house in Tuscany, of which he naïvely

---

1 *Real Museo Borbonico*, VII, 5.
2 For these see Statius, *Silv.* I, 2, 147 *sqq.*; 3; 5; II, 2.
3 Statius, *ib.* IV, 6.   4 Pliny, *Ep.* III, 6.
5 Pliny, *Ep.* III, 7.   6 Juvenal IV, 51.

argues that a big villa needs a long description[1]; his account of Trajan's seaside residence[2] amid green fields overhanging the shore; and his interest in a friend's building projects at Baiae[3]. And nothing could be more elaborate than the enormous villa of Hadrian, a city in itself under the slopes of Tivoli.

Little wonder that the persistent attacks on luxury were directed as much against domestic equipment as against Apician banquets or dishes of gold and silver or costly dress demanding sumptuary restriction. Seneca, simple in his tastes for all his wealth, was staggered at the transparent windows, heating pipes and superb ornamentation of houses. These inventions he considers might be due to the wit of any ingenious slave, but are paltry compared with true wisdom[4]. Roof gardens are in a similar condemnation[5]. Mosaics make him feel that Romans have grown so fine that they will have nothing but precious stones in their flooring to tread upon[6]. Modern bathrooms, he notes, have mirrors, marble slabs, silver taps: 'baths once up-to-date are in view of the latest improvements scouted as back-numbers (*in antiquorum numerum reiciuntur*)[7].'

This looks like an unbroken chronicle of selfish parade. Yet not entirely so. Juvenal[8] comments on the rich man who spends freely on baths, *gestatio*, colonnades, dinner-parties, but will not support education. Others, however, did: the younger Pliny, for example, advanced one-third of the cost for a school in North Italy. Many opulent men in Flavian and Antonine times realized the obligations of wealth, and their liberality was a pleasing revival of a tradition in Hellenistic cities. Intellectual men of abundant means, like Polemo and Herodes Atticus, were noted for their benefactions (p. 559). Pliny gave to Comum a library worth one million sesterces with a tenth more for upkeep; as a rent-charge on part of his property, half a million for the maintenance of boys and girls of free birth; an equal amount for a bath establishment; nearly two millions for pensions to freedmen and an annual dinner to the common people. To Comum he presented a temple, as he did to Tifernum on the Tiber; and his private generosity was lavish[9].

The streets, already glanced at, were among important external conditions of city life, as so much of each day was spent out of doors. The bustle along narrow thoroughfares supplied a satirist

---

[1] Pliny, *Ep.* v, 6, 44.   [2] Pliny, *ib.* VI, 15–17.
[3] Pliny, *ib.* IX, 7, 31.   [4] Seneca, *Epist. Mor.* 90, 25.
[5] Seneca, *ib.* 122, 8.   [6] Seneca, *ib.* 86, 4–7.
[7] Seneca, *ib.* 86, 8.   [8] VII, 178 *sqq.*
[9] See *C.I.L.* v, 5262 (= Dessau 2927); 5263; 5267; Pliny, *Ep.* I, 8; 19; II, 4; III, 6; IV, 1; 13; V, 7; VI, 32; VII, 18; IX, 39; X, 8 (24).

with incomparable opportunities[1]. Foot-passengers might be knocked against by porters or trodden on by soldiers: a waggon-load of marble or timber might collapse and kill people, or a block between herds of cattle stir the drovers into torrents of abuse[2]. Men and women who could afford to be carried in their *lectica* through the crowd sometimes flaunted a wealth gained by the shadiest practices. At night[3] there was risk from slops thrown out of open windows or from drunken bullies or robbers, who grew more active in town as often as the authorities drove them off the highroads to protect travellers; and the danger on these roads may be illustrated by two cases of mysterious disappearance recorded by Pliny[4]. The narrow Roman streets were narrowed still more by booths and projecting shops which curtailed the available space to a wayfarer's discomfort. It was set to Domitian's credit that he cleared off the trespassers:

> Indoors cook, barber, merchant, butcher stay:
> What late was one big shop is Rome to-day[5].

The engagements of a Roman day are summarized by Martial[6] —the morning call of etiquette, thereafter the forum for law or business, the siesta about noon, then exercise and bath before dinner at the ninth hour, possibly prolonged by junketing and carousals, or followed by the performances of dancers or other entertainers, or by a *recitatio*. It was a comfortable society with well-regulated customs. But there were drawbacks in the ostentation of upstarts, in the pestering attentions of *captatores* on their legacy-hunt (vol. x, pp. 437–9), and in the apprehension, when *delatio* was a paying profession, lest a festive company might be entertaining a spy unawares. Delation, always the treacherous sycophant's homage to tyranny, flourished under the worst emperors: Titus might punish the informers of the past (p. 20); but it was not always so. Pliny relates the following story[7]. At a dinner given by the Emperor Nerva, Veiento, who had been a notorious informer under Domitian, was an honoured guest next to the host. The conversation turned on another informer who was dead, the pitiless, though blind, Messallinus, and the Emperor's question 'What would have happened to him, if he'd lived?' was answered at once by one of the company: 'he would be dining with us!'

---

[1] Juvenal i, 63–72. [2] Juvenal iii, 235–8; 243–8; 254–61.
[3] Juvenal iii, 268–308. [4] Pliny, *Ep.* vi, 25.
[5] Martial vii, 61, 9–10. [6] Martial iv, 8.
[7] Pliny, *Ep.* iv, 22, 4–6.

VII. MORAL, INTELLECTUAL AND RELIGIOUS FEATURES

It is easy to frame an indictment against the luxury, gluttony, fraudulence, gambling and unclean living of the times. Much revolts us in the selfish extravagance of mean patrons' dinners, in the Neronian and Vitellian artifice of a second appetite secured by emetics, in people whose sole reason for living was their palate[1]. Anger is stirred against unscrupulous defrauders of a ward, and pity for the cheated *pupillus*: too often 'probitas laudatur et alget[2].' The Roman, by no means immaculate himself, yet had ground for complaint against the cheats and charlatans in a city where he was eclipsed by the cleverest of the alien immigrants, the versatile, dishonest, cringing Greek[3]. Gaming became a mania with some: it could begin early, for Persius mentions truancy from the recitation lesson in favour of dice[4]. Nor can anyone overlook the existence of infanticide, the callousness of the slave system, the cruelty in the arena to man and beast, barbarities of punishment like the *tunica molesta* and crucifixion, and the sexual immoralities and perversions to which Juvenal and Martial bear witness.

But moral obliquities were not universal, nor did they pass unchallenged. Denunciations of contemporary vice by writers in prose and verse were so many reminders of a higher moral standard, and leavens of Stoicism and Christianity were working. Nowhere is this heightening of standard more noticeable than in the tendency towards humanitarianism. Nerva's *alimenta*, as well as private charities, proved that the cry of poor children was being answered. Though exposure of newborn infants was so traditional that it seemed to Tacitus a distinguishing custom among the Jews to forbid it, and though it survived long enough to be denounced by Lactantius, yet Pliny in Bithynia felt bound to consult Trajan regarding foundlings who, after abandonment by free parents, had been rescued and reared in servitude[5]. Slaves, however maltreated by some, were to many masters what Seneca called them, *humiles amici*; and it is Seneca who comments on the impiety of gladiatorial *spectacula*: 'man—for man a sacred thing—is nowadays butchered to make a sportive holiday[6].' In Juvenal's

---

[1] Juvenal v, 24 *sqq.*; iv, 137–8; xi, 11.
[2] Juvenal i, 45–8; xv, 135; i, 74.
[3] Juvenal iii, 58–125.   [4] Juvenal i, 87–93; Persius iii, 44–50.
[5] Tacitus, *Hist.* v, 5; Lactantius, *Div. Inst.* vi, 20; Pliny, *Ep.* x, 65 (71) and 66 (72); see Daremberg-Saglio, art. *expositio*.
[6] *per lusum ac iocum occiditur*, Seneca, *Epist. Mor.* 95, 33; cf. 47, 1.

eyes man's inhumanity to man runs counter to nature; for nature by her gift of tears declares that she has given to mankind tender hearts: hence the emotion at a friend's danger, a maiden's death, or the burial of a baby too little for the funeral pyre[1]. Wisely, too, Juvenal lays his finger on home influence as a cardinal factor in morality. Cruelty is one of the vices which is learned along with gambling, gluttony and wantonness through bad domestic example: wherefore 'maxima debetur puero reverentia[2].'

It is a cheering social feature that several factors which, like flagrant immorality, frequency of divorce, and preference for celibacy, wrought as solvents of family life, were counterbalanced by the steady piety, virtue, diligence and affection which, as is evident in scores of inscriptions, held households united. Literature also gives the impression of a normal and efficient routine in well-conducted homes both urban and rural. Hospitality could be shown at country-houses by capable slaves even in an owner's absence[3]. The apportionment of Pliny's summer day in Tuscany proves he was as economical of time as his uncle—rising about daybreak, keeping windows closed to aid reflection, opening them to dictate a composition, and sandwiching exercise and literature till the hour for dinner with his wife and a few friends, after which there might be a domestic performance of a light play or music. It is well to realize the importance of the *cena* as the principal private relaxation for Romans: they had not such evening entertainments of modern times as balls, conversaziones, public concerts or the cinema: theatrical performances and contests in circus or arena belonged to the daytime. Dining with guests at home or meeting fellow-guests elsewhere afforded an opportunity for the cultivation of friendship, interchange of thought, and improvement of critical taste, if the occasion permitted the reading of recent literary work. The lady of the house might be present, exercising on the recumbent guests a restraining influence, as (unlike the women at Trimalchio's banquet) she maintained her dignity by sitting and by avoiding wine. Pliny's ideal at dinner was good conversation and sobriety, and, along with reasonable amusements, a *recitatio* or music[4]. In one of his letters[5] we get a peep at an evening entertainment for the imperial circle in Trajan's villa at Centumcellae, some 47 miles from Rome: it consisted of talk and a programme by various artistes.

The culture of the period is best represented in its literature,

---

[1] Juvenal xv, 131 *sqq.*
[2] Juvenal xiv, 1–43; 47.
[3] Pliny, *Ep.* i, 4; vi, 28.
[4] Pliny, *Ep.* iii, 12; i, 15; viii, 21.
[5] Pliny, *Ep.* vi, 31.

which is separately surveyed (chap. XVIII). Here it is appropriate to mention two typical circles, that of Pliny[1] and that of Fronto. Pliny's set included Tacitus (eleven letters to him are preserved), Martial, Silius Italicus, Frontinus and Suetonius. He was, by exchange of correspondence and by fostering *recitationes*, able to spur other authors towards composition in Latin and Greek and, despite his flattering estimates of works by friends, to maintain standards in prose and verse. Along with his learning and talent went that gentlemanly openhandedness which makes Pliny representative of the courtesy of the age at its best. Punctilious in duties, considerate for others, he had a heart easily touched by the death of the young[2]. His liking for young people comes out in a letter about a betrothal[3], in his generous contribution to the marriage portion of a certain Quintilian's daughter[4] and in his grief over the death of a promising youth whom he admired for his deference towards seniors in contrast with the cocksureness of many of the rising generation[5]. He urges on a father forbearance towards a son's faults, reminding him he had been a boy himself[6], and he recognizes that true social manners depend on due regard for different ranks—all men cannot be treated alike[7].

The surviving letters, some in Greek, between Fronto and his pupil Aurelius throw light on the culture of the court. Couched in affectionate terms, they mark Fronto's characteristic interest in eloquence and in words carefully chosen, especially from old Latin, though to the teacher's disappointment Aurelius felt drawn away from rhetoric by that philosophic bent to which we owe his famous *Meditations*. We read of the prince in his twenties studying for five hours in the morning before paying his respects to the Emperor, then, after an unsuccessful boar-hunt, returning in the afternoon to two of Cato's speeches borrowed from the Apollo Library in Rome, and retiring early because of a chill. In another letter he mentions gargling with honey-water, but significantly hesitates over the word *gargarissavi*, though Novius, he believes, uses it. He lunched that day on a little bread while others gorged beans, onions and herrings with roe: then he sweated hard among the grape-gatherers, next, at home, after trying to study without result, enjoyed a chat with his 'little mother' about absent friends. Later came a bath and supper in the oil-press room with the diversion of listening to the peasants chaffing each other, and

---

[1] See J. Wight Duff, *A Lit. Hist. of Rome in the Silver Age*, pp. 555–8.
[2] Pliny, *Ep.* v, 16; 21 (9).   [3] *Ep.* vi, 26.   [4] *Ep.* vi, 32.
[5] *statim sciunt omnia, neminem verentur, Ep.* VIII, 23.
[6] *Ep.* IX, 12.   [7] *nihil est ipsa aequalitate inaequalius, Ep.* IX, 5.

finally a literary task to complete and an account of the day to write to Fronto 'before turning over in bed to snore.' His literary likings appear in his request for something written by Fronto himself, something in prose by Cicero, Sallust or Gracchus, and in poetry by Ennius or Lucretius. An undercurrent of simple feeling runs through the correspondence on points like health and illness or manners in eating; and the affection for children is very human. Fronto kisses 'the tiny hands and plump little feet' of Aurelius' baby-girl; and Aurelius talks to his mother about Fronto's little Gratia. To the same period belongs Aulus Gellius' haphazard miscellany, entitled *Attic Nights* because partly written at Athens. The author was in Fronto's circle and his notes form an interesting index to the learning of the day. Favorinus, the Gallic philosopher, is a prominent contemporary figure in several of Gellius' sketches, censuring an archaism, attacking astrologers, advising a lady of rank to suckle her child herself, or refuting, *more Socratico*, a self-confident grammarian amid a group of scholars waiting in the entrance hall on the Palatine to pay their respects to Antoninus Pius.

Recitationes appealed to a limited and cultured circle. What reached a wider audience was the homily delivered at a street-corner or from temple-steps, particularly the preaching of Cynic missioners. They met in part, however vulgarly—and Dio Chrysostom hated their chicanery[1]—a growing popular desire for guidance in conduct, as the masses seemed to grope after some evangel, and the Antonine age witnessed a movement towards their moral elevation. Oratory in its ethical and religious aspect suited this restlessness of spirit. The 'second Sophistic' was Atticist in style by preference and epideictic in its ingenious speeches not only on serious subjects but often on such trivialities as a gnat or hair or the want of it. The itinerant professor was a familiar figure in the Greek portion of the Empire, but his wanderings frequently brought him to Rome, where his performances were social and fashionable occasions. Because of the influence on society and culture, we may cite a few examples of this imported eloquence taken from several generations[2].

Epictetus, Phrygian and freedman, whose championship of goodness survives in compilations by his pupil Arrian, taught Stoicism impressively at Rome before Domitian's edict expelled philosophers. Plutarch (*c.* 46–126) stayed several times in Rome

[1] Dio Chrys. *Or.* xxxii, 9; cf. Dill, *op. cit.* p. 349.
[2] See above, pp. 681 *sqq.* These sophists are sketched by Philostratus. For their influence on life see Dill, *op. cit.* Book iii.

after his first visit in Vespasian's time as a Boeotian delegate. He knew leading personages in the capital and lectured in Greek under Domitian. His famous *Lives* do not come under our purview; but his philosophy, as seen in the range of his *Moralia*, has the interest of using eclecticism to help his fellowmen with good advice (see p. 698). With Platonic and Aristotelian conceptions he blended elements from Stoicism and Epicureanism, although both these systems fell under his censure. His treatise on *Isis and Osiris* marks the syncretism in religion; and his expansion of the theory of daemons, good and bad intermediary beings, was intended to explain seeming defects in the divine management of the world. Dio of Prusa, expelled from Rome under Domitian (p. 684), returned under Nerva, and became a welcome guest at Trajan's table. Eclectic in his eighty orations, he combined, as a popular teacher of morality, Platonic, Stoic, Cynic, and even Epicurean principles in his advocacy of an ideally noble life as against the life of the senses. But the Roman world depressed him: he felt that its materialistic and sensual self-complacency lacked the true guarantees for permanent cohesion. In the Antonine age, Maximus of Tyre, though he lived chiefly in Greece, visited Rome, and delivered discourses animated with a serious purpose and a religious spirit. Forty-one of his dissertations have survived. Lucian, by his own claim a *rhetor*, travelled to Rome and even further west (see p. 686). He is our authority for the theatrical suicide of Peregrinus, a wandering scholar who broke away from a Christian fraternity in the East and was banished from Rome for injudicious attacks on Antoninus Pius.

Some sophists possessed great riches, like the Laodicean Polemo, a frequent visitor to the capital and a favourite with Trajan, Hadrian and the Antonines. He won Hadrian's interest for Smyrna, as Aristides did that of Marcus Aurelius later. Another wealthy man was the antiquary Herodes Atticus (p. 560), renowned for benefactions of public buildings and race-courses in Greek cities. He had studied under the best rhetoricians, including Fronto's friend, Favorinus. Herodes in turn taught at Athens and Rome, and had Marcus for an admiring pupil. He and Alexander the Phrygian, another of the Emperor's instructors, trained the celebrated P. Aelius Aristides (see p. 685), whose description of the earthquake at Smyrna in 178 moved Aurelius to tears and practical generosity. What most concerns us is his activity at Rome. A true imperial spirit breathes through his laudatory oration *To Rome*[1]. Sometimes condemned outright for

---

[1] See Rostovtzeff, *op. cit.* pp. 125–29.

rhetorical extravagances, it yet expresses the Antonine belief in the service which Rome was rendering to the world and a less well-founded confidence in the durability of the imperial peace.

In religion, amid a welter of ideas, official, literary, philosophic and popular, it is possible to isolate certain outstanding developments. The formal State-ritual had been strengthened under Augustan auspices, and to it was added emperor-worship, which tested loyalty rather than orthodoxy. Interest grew in Eastern religions which had made their appearance at Rome in Republican days—the cults of Magna Mater, Isis, Mithras and Judaism; and this interest enabled the mystery religions to reach an acme of proselytizing power. But potentially the great new factor was Christianity. Its latent strength, however, was as yet little realized; for its appeal even to an investigating magistrate like Pliny remained almost as slight as that of Judaism to Tacitus in his confused account of Jewish history and religion (see above, p. 254 *sq.*). The old Roman religion, rustic in its far distant origins, but overgrown with Italic, Etruscan, Greek and oriental accretions, was always a matter less of belief than of ritual performance. Yet it was by no means dead. Many still viewed its age-long antiquity with reverential affection, as is clear from much that is not purely conventional in inscriptions. Citizens of Rome could feel pride in the antique ritual that marked the laying of the foundation-stone of the Capitoline Temple in A.D. 70 (see p. 5) and in the cryptic Salian litany punctiliously recited by the young Marcus Aurelius nearly a hundred years later. It was a religion which formed a bond in public affairs and was expected to confer a benison in answer to rites duly performed; and yet it contained no promise of purification from sin, no consistent explanation of a divine purpose in regard to man, no kindly consolation in trouble. While its rigid formality served for State machinery, it could not satisfy religious aspirations and emotions. People of pious or even excitable instincts were therefore often impelled towards a worship involving mystic or orgiastic ceremonial, especially if its esoteric doctrine prophesied a continued existence, and conceivably a happier one, for the human soul after release from the body. The Eastern cults had far more spiritual aid to give than the heterogeneous polytheism of Rome: and the moral sense responded to ideas of cleansing from guilt, closer relationship with deity, ascetic renunciations, and the final appraisal of a human life according to its good and bad deeds.

In literature it may be discerned that, however sceptical and hesitant the views of some writers, the ferment of noble conceptions in religion was at work. Elevated views were inseparable from Stoic tenets regarding deity, which abandoned the absurdities of mythology and which could, as Seneca did, declare true worship to consist not in a Sabbath lighting of lamps (*accendere aliquem lucernas sabbatis prohibeamus*) but in knowing the gods aright and following them in goodness[1]. Seneca has his inconsistencies admittedly. On immortality, like Marcus Aurelius after him, he wavers. He is at times as cautious in his hypothetical postulate of a life beyond as are the frank phrases on tombstones *si quid sapiunt inferi*[2] or *si sunt di Manes*: 'if the account given by sages is true,' he says, 'and there is some abode which receives us, then the friend we think lost has been only sent on before[3].' But in moments of exaltation he trusts a larger hope: 'this weary mortal existence is but a prelude to a life better and longer . . . and one day darkness will be dispelled' in what he prophesies will be a beatific vision of celestial light[4]. Here he is at one with dogmas in the creeds of Isis and Mithras. If Juvenal makes flippant references to mythology[5], he has also serious thoughts. The keynote of the conclusion to his *Vanity of Human Wishes* is faith in the gods instead of foolish and wicked prayers: 'dearer is man to them than he is to himself.' In Stoic vein he insists that an upright life is the path to happiness[6]. He would, then, agree with the growing recognition of a good conscience as outweighing costly sacrifice, in the spirit of Statius' declaration that a handful of meal and a little salt on a turf altar can please the gods, if the worshipper's heart be right[7]. This echoes what Persius said, that spirituality must be brought by the worshipper to the temple and then the handful of meal would win acceptance (*farre litabo*[8]). In literature, as in popular feeling, appears a critical attitude towards mere formalism. Needs had arisen which the Christian faith ultimately met, and it is one of the ironies of history that the Caesar-worship which Christians rejected at the peril of martyrdom was in its attainment of official universality an actual harbinger of the victory of Christianity.

[1] Seneca, *Epist. Mor.* 95, 47–50.
[2] Buecheler and Riese, *op. cit.* ii, nos. 179, 180, 1057.
[3] Seneca, *Epist. Mor.* 63, 16.
[4] Seneca, *ib.* 102, 22 and 28.
[5] Juvenal xiii, 38–52.   [6] Juvenal x, 350; 363.
[7] Statius, *Silv.* i, 4, 130 *sq.*   [8] Persius ii, 71–5.

CHAPTER XX

ART FROM NERO TO THE ANTONINES

I. NERO TO TRAJAN

AUGUSTUS had been one of the greatest builders of all time and could boast that he had changed Rome from an *urbs latericia* into an *urbs marmorea*. Yet, despite this, Roman architecture made no decisive advance in the Augustan age, and in a description of the art of that age the buildings rightly come last. Augustan architecture freed itself from the defects of provincialism that still clung to the Republican buildings of Rome; it combined tactfully and with taste a classic faultlessness of proportion and ornament with elegance of materials, travertine and marble. Yet it failed to evolve fresh architectural conceptions. The subdued temper of the Augustan period repressed the dynamic force that was peculiar to Roman architecture. The first great creative period had lasted from about 200 B.C. to the end of the Republic. The aim of the Greek builder had been the perfecting of the single edifice, satisfactory and self-contained, and he ventured only with hesitation on composition by means of architectural complexes. The Roman, on the other hand, inclined to strong movement and combined buildings and squares into unities that were grandly conceived. The gift and passion for organization, that had brought greatness to the Roman State, found its direct visible expression in architecture. The political significance of architecture is formulated in characteristic Roman fashion by Vitruvius[1] when he applauds Augustus for his care: 'ut civitas per te non solum provinciis esset aucta, verum etiam ut maiestas imperii publicorum aedificiorum egregias haberet auctoritates.' In Rome architecture and architects enjoyed the place of honour among the arts and artists, and the most eminent architects were generally Romans.

About the middle of the first century the energy of Roman architecture, that had been subdued by Augustan classicism, burst out afresh, inaugurating a second golden age which lasted down to the reign of Trajan. Finally, after a long interval of slow development, there came the third and final emergence of architectural creative force in the late classical buildings of the age of Diocletian and Constantine.

[1] *De Arch* I, 2.

Except for disconnected portions of the *Domus Transitoria* and a part of the *Domus Aurea*, preserved in the foundations of the Baths of Trajan, we have no means of envisaging Neronian Rome. Its historical significance must be deduced from brief references in our texts, laborious reconstructions, and buildings that reflect its character or show its influence. At Vetera near Xanten on the Rhine two types of architecture are exemplified in the Neronian permanent camp for two legions. The ground-plan, revealed by accurate and careful excavation, enables us to reconstruct the elevation also. In the centre of the camp is the Praetorium[1], which combines organically a Forum-like court with a Basilica. Next to this are the palaces of the two *legati*, one of which has been completely excavated and can be reconstructed[2]. This rectangular building-area, flanked on two sides by colonnades, is occupied by a well-designed complex of roofed chambers and open courts. Minor asymmetrical variations occasioned by the internal economy of the rooms were skilfully adjusted by means of heightened walls and pitched roofs. Along the shorter main axis, which divides the whole block into two symmetrical halves, there is the suite of principal rooms. From the vestibule one passes through a hall into the central peristyle. Next to this comes a second hall, which takes the place of the *tablinum* and which opens on to a garden laid out on the plan of a hippodrome. This central axis is crossed at right angles by two others. One of these—architecturally the more important—runs through the middle of the central court, which thereby becomes the central point of the whole enclosed residential block of buildings, and also separates two side-courts and their adjoining rooms. The second axis is formed by the central line of a garden which is itself surrounded by a colonnade. The elevation must have produced a façade suggesting life and movement, developed, as it was, out of the various roof-levels of the different portions of the broad edifice. There can be no doubt that the palaces of the *legati*, no less than the long colonnades of Vetera, show the direct influence of the most recent contemporary buildings in Rome. We must assume that the general plan of Nero's palaces on the Palatine was conceived in similar fashion. Perhaps the Palatine buildings of Tiberius and Gaius had supplied the prototypes.

The same style of massive structure, planned with a shorter central line and one or two intersecting axes, recurs in the Baths of Titus and thereafter in other Imperial Roman Thermae, of which the well-preserved Baths of Caracalla and Diocletian are

[1] Volume of Plates v, 64, *a*.   [2] *Ib.* 64, *b*.

naturally most prominent in our minds. When did the Romans first evolve this structural conception which was one of the most magnificent inventions of classical architecture? The difference between the palaces near Xanten and the Roman Imperial Baths lies in this: in the latter the main hall, in the middle of which the axes intersect, was spanned by a mighty cross-vault. Titus, who resided in a villa that was part of the *Domus Aurea*, built next to this the small Baths which prove that this type of structure was already in existence in the Flavian age. It is only a theory, but most probably a correct one, that this architectural conception was first realized in the famous Baths which Nero dedicated in A.D. 62. If so, we may assume that the ground-plan—not known with sufficient precision—of the Thermae which Severus Alexander reconstructed, may go back in essentials to the time of Nero. An architect who could plan rooms and courts with such sure mastery may well be credited with the epoch-making invention of the hall spanned by the cross-vault. There is, indeed, evidence to show that cross-vaulting was employed during Nero's reign, for a seventeenth-century drawing shows a room in the *Domus Aurea* spanned by a cross-vault resting upon free-standing columns.

Nero's 'Golden House,' the Imperial residence constructed after the fire of A.D. 64, was a gigantic system of parks, stretching from the Palatine over the Velia to the Oppian and Caelian, within which there were built palaces of varying sizes, as later in Hadrian's Villa at Tivoli. One of these buildings is partially preserved beneath the Baths of Trajan[1] and presents a contrast to the massive type of structure which we may assume to have characterized the palace on the Palatine. It takes the form of a rambling villa, the main façade of which faced the artificial lake which occupied the place where the Colosseum now stands. There was a central block flanked by wings set obliquely, and to these there were attached corresponding pavilions. Such buildings are familiar from contemporary wall-paintings found at Pompeii and from the Roman provinces[2]. The choice of an oblique plan betrays a certain turning towards a novel tendency, which had for its aim the displacement of the regular ground-plan of rectangle and circle; and by the time of Domitian this tendency had developed into a preference for flat curves in place of straight lines and semicircles. The Neronian Villa aims at adding to the official palace a princely country house in the heart of the Capital. At the same time a desire for monumental style found effective expression in the colonnades and porticos which led in a fine sweep from the

---

[1] Plan 1; Volume of Plates v, 66, *a*.   [2] *Ib.* 66, *b*.

venerable irregularity of the ancient Forum to the great entrance
hall of the 'Golden House' on the crest of the Velia. The rising
ground helped the forcefulness of line and direction, while the
colossal statue of the Emperor drew all eyes with a fascination
enhanced by its position. The whole design was celebrated in its
time for its spacious lavishness. Nero's megalomania afforded
really great architects the opportunity of realizing their grandiose
ideas. Their names, Severus and Celer, still live.

Roma vetus was replaced after the great fire by *forma aedificiorum
urbis nova*[1]. The ground-plan and elevation of the houses in
second-century Ostia are impressive in their contrast with those
of Pompeii, though the very latest Pompeian buildings foreshadow
the new style. This Ostian style is rightly supposed to go back
to the Rome that was rebuilt after the fire. In place of the house
rambling in leisurely fashion round atrium and peristyle, there
now appeared in the Capital the house of many floors with its
storeys ranged round an arcaded central yard. Shops and porticos,
windows and balconies now fronted on wide, straight streets.
For all this, too, prototypes can be adduced, but the decisive step
was plainly taken in Nero's time. After the intelligent and measured
caution that marks the maturity of the Augustan style, Roman
feeling in Neronian architecture strives with youthful enthusiasm
after great and impressive form. Its true achievements first become
apparent to our eyes in the surviving Flavian and Trajanic structures that are on the same high level.

The greatest task of the builder in the Imperial, as in the
Republican age, remained the construction of *aedificia publica* that
ministered to the common life of the citizens. Even Nero had not
failed in his duty in this respect, though he had appropriated for
his own sumptuous dwelling an area so large as to offend public
opinion. Vespasian, with his old-fashioned middle-class tastes, revived the Augustan tradition and handed back a part of Nero's
Golden House to the Roman People. His temple of Peace no
longer exists; but it stood as a symbol of the restored *pax Augusta*,
and its court and adjoining halls completed the designs of the
Fora of Julius and of Augustus. At the opposite end of the Forum
Romanum, in the hollow between Velia, Oppian, and Caelian,
there arose the Amphitheatrum Flavium, to which medieval Rome,
associating it with the tradition about Nero's colossus, gave the
name 'Colosseum[2].' To our day its façade is probably still the
most imposing symbol and monument of *maiestas imperii*. We

[1] Suetonius, *Nero*, 16.
[2] Volume of Plates v, 68, *a*.

may suppose that the early Augustan amphitheatre of Statilius had anticipated the main structural form with its elevation of three tiers of arches, and that this was a form developed on Italic soil. The façade itself in all probability had its Republican prototype in the Theatre of Pompey. In the Colosseum however, quite a new technique appears in the cross-vaulting employed both for the inner *foyer* of the second storey, and for the third storey. The whole construction is presumably bolder and stronger than that of its early Augustan prototype. An original touch, perhaps characteristic of Flavian architecture, appears in four places at the end of each main radius on the ground floor: this is the construction of triple entrance-halls, in each of which the nave and aisles narrow as they approach the interior. The addition of the topmost storey was a structural alteration that took place under Titus and Domitian, and it gives us a deep insight into the architectural fashion and feeling of the time. In order to achieve its effect in the interior the colonnade which crowned the building was raised to a fantastic and dizzy height[1]. In consequence the exterior aspect of the building was completely altered by the exaggerated height of the top storey with its engaged pilasters. This not only leads the eye upwards but also acts as a grand coping that unifies the whole structure. We are so familiar with the pictures of the Colosseum that it requires an effort to grasp the force and power of its elevation as compared with that of the theatre of Marcellus with its three storeys[2]. Instead of a mere piling of three tiers, one upon another, we have a dominating co-ordinated whole. Greek architects had built halls of two storeys[3]; Republican Rome added a third as well as the embellishment of the arch; but here in the Colosseum the ultimate stage of romanization was attained.

The arch dedicated to Divus Titus[4] on the crest of the Velia shows the same sure hand of a great master-builder. Augustan architects had often worked at combining the vaulted arch with a façade of engaged columns[5]. The master of the Arch of Titus had almost all these motives ready to his hand. Yet whereas Augustan architects experimented with caution and hesitation, he, with his touch of genius, combined the various parts in such fashion that the result became a pattern to his contemporaries as to us. Here too the emphasis is on the parts that unite and bind the whole. The actual arch is pressed together while its supporting walls face inwards. Powerful piers at the sides hold the whole

---

[1] Volume of Plates v, 68, *b*.
[2] *Ib.* IV, 188, *b*.   [3] *Ib.* III, 182, *c*.
[4] *Ib.* V, 70, *a*.   [5] *Ib.* IV, 192.

structure together like pylons. The base for the statuary is set directly over the building like an *attica* crowning the whole. When the Senate and People decreed in A.D. 114 the setting up of an arch in honour of the *Optimus princeps* Trajan at the starting point of the Via Traiana at Beneventum, the Arch of Titus served as model. But the simple strength of its exterior decoration was replaced by ornamental reliefs, almost excessively elaborate and full of political symbolism,—reliefs of the kind that exemplify the Roman love of imparting knowledge through a pictorial medium. Another contemporary arch, erected in A.D. 115 beside the port of Ancona in Trajan's honour, presents a variant on the original theme and shows the elasticity of architectural practice in that age.[1] The arch tops a great flight of steps, and, soaring upwards like a tower above the harbour, is visible from afar to incoming craft. There is emphasis on the plastic value of the grouping of its columns and of the base for the statuary; the columns themselves appear to strive and strain upwards, and their markedly offset plinths make them derive their motion from the ground, while the powerful angle-blocks of the statue-base above prolong the upward sweep of the whole.

Martial's friend, the architect Rabirius, built to Domitian's order on the Palatine the palace that became thenceforward the Imperial residence. The most recent excavations have supplied more accurate details of the main lines of the ground-plan[2]. The State and private apartments are set side by side and are organically joined by a uniform arrangement of their storeys. For the ground floor the hollow between the humps of the Palatine hill had to be filled in, and the made earth obliterated some older houses as well as the unfinished portions of Nero's *Domus Transitoria* and of his *Domus Aurea*. The garden laid out in the shape of a hippodrome was probably designed in Nero's time. The bare rectangular ground-plan is relieved at intervals by flattened curves. Dome and cloister-vault are employed in the private apartments. The State apartments are divided into two groups separated by a peristyle, and either group consists of only three halls, but these are most impressive. In the centre of the front group is the throne-room which has no antechamber but is entered straight from the columned portico in front. This throne-room was finely decorated with niches, a worthy setting for ceremonial receptions. Its vast barrel-vault with a span of over a hundred feet was considerably greater than that of the nave of St Peter's.

---

[1] Volume of Plates v, 70, *b*.
[2] See Plan 2.

Parallel to the throne-room was a smaller hall on either side. Beyond the peristyle there was a Triclinium, lying in the same axis as the throne-room, and from this there opened out on either side a Nymphaeum alive with fountains. These were the Imperial banqueting halls. The plan of Rabirius was naturally adapted to the needs of the Court and to the forms of ancient ceremonial; and the main hall with its barrel-vault must have made an overwhelming impression upon the beholder as he entered. Parthian and Sassanian palaces contained reception halls of similar type and a possible relationship suggests itself. Did Rabirius translate the oriental *liwan* into terms of Roman architecture?

The Baths of Trajan, but little inferior in size to their successors, the Thermae of Caracalla and Diocletian, were the work of Apollodorus of Damascus, the only Greek practising architecture in Rome at this period. Consequently his buildings have often been claimed as examples of Hellenistic architecture. But the East supplies no prototype for the Imperial Baths, while we have seen that they possibly originated in Neronian Rome. If this is correct, then Apollodorus merely carried on a tradition that had grown up in Rome. But whether he contributed anything materially fresh to this tradition cannot be ascertained owing to the uncertainty of our knowledge of the oldest Thermae. In those of Trajan, as in the later Baths, the cross-vault of the central hall was carried on free columns abutting on the walls.

Apollodorus owed his fame mainly to the Forum of Trajan which was admired down to the close of antiquity as an incomparable achievement, and which has now been made to stand clear and so come to life again. There was a street that ran between the Fora of Julius and Augustus and Vespasian's temple of Peace, and Domitian altered this street into the long, narrow Forum Transitorium which owed its peculiar shape to the configuration of the ground[1]. Its final completion was reserved for his successor Nerva. It was probably also Domitian who remodelled the simple Julian temple of Venus Genetrix, transforming it into a richly decorated structure of marble, though it was left to Trajan to dedicate it in A.D. 113[2]. Trajan outdid all former Imperial Fora when he planned his, which formed a link between the old Rome and the Campus Martius. To this end large blocks of houses were removed and the top of the Quirinal was levelled. The Forum Traianum[3] with its bordering shops presents one of the grandest architectural compositions ever realized, and is characteristically and completely Roman. A great centre-axis runs from the entrance

[1] See Plan 3.   [2] *Ann. épig.* 1934, no. 30.   [3] Plan 3.

gate to the Temple of Trajan. In its middle is set transversely the Basilica Ulpia, the central hall of which is surrounded by two colonnades and which has an apse at either of its narrower sides. This linking of the Forum court with the Basilica has its closest prototype in the Praetorium of a Roman camp, and especially in that of the camp at Vetera (p. 776). It is not surprising that a soldier-emperor like Trajan should instruct his engineer-architect, Apollodorus, who had built the Danube Bridge in the second Dacian campaign, to lay out his Forum after the manner of the central section of a Roman camp. In attaching apses to the court Apollodorus was reviving a motive found in the Forum of Augustus. But, whereas in the latter the apses flank the temple and are near the end of the forum, in the Trajanic forum they lie on a short axis that intersects the long main axis of the whole court, and lead up to the motive of the Basilica. Beyond the Basilica lies a small court with the Column on which a ribbon-like frieze narrates in relief the history of the Dacian campaigns[1]. Flanking the Column were the Greek and the Latin Libraries, and the whole plan reached its end and climax with the shrine planned from the first to be the temple of Divus Traianus, though only built by Hadrian.

The Forum and the Basilica as public buildings, as festal places of assembly for the Roman People, were decorated with every conceivable splendour and costly material. The adjoining market halls were simpler buildings of utilitarian type loosely linked with the Forum. A building of two storeys follows the curve of the north-eastern apse behind a street that runs along the outer walls of the Forum, and this building masks the cutting of the Esquiline. Its façade is one of the earliest examples of the plain brick frontage of the type destined to full development in the course of the second century both in Ostia and Rome. Perhaps this style of building is also to be traced back to Nero's rebuilding of the City after the great fire. The large central hall of the *mercato di Traiano* is roofed with cross-vaults. In a practical building of this type such a characteristically Roman feature is more marked than in the State buildings which are more under the influence of tradition. In the decoration employed in the Forum of Trajan there is a reaction from the over-elaboration, from the nervous fussiness, and from the contrasting play of light and shade that characterized the Flavian decoration of architectural members and funerary altars. And with this return to a calmer feeling there comes a revival of classic Greek simplicity of plastic form. Here, perhaps,

[1] See Volume of Plates v, 36, 38, 40, and above, p. 224.

in the sphere of decoration the Greek sensibility of Apollodorus made itself felt, just as it did in his avoidance of any vaulting in the construction of the Basilica Ulpia. But when we begin to encounter similar phenomena in sculpture and portraiture, we may perhaps conjecture that Apollodorus was not personally responsible for this tendency, but that the new classicism of the Hadrianic age was already at hand.

In the solid world of architecture flights of fantasy are sternly limited, not so however in the realm of wall-painting. Imaginative pictures of buildings ignored the laws of gravity and filled the living-rooms with a kind of lively gracefulness that was a counterpart to the *maiestas* in Roman monumental architecture. Changes of style in wall-painting, as in architecture, go back to a period long before the beginning of the Flavian age. Our conceptions of Neronian-Flavian painting are derived almost entirely from the walls of Pompeii and Herculaneum. From these we learn not only that the most fully matured Pompeian style was alone practised after the earthquake of A.D. 63, but that it had been previously in vogue. After what has been observed in other arts we may assume that immediately after the Augustan-Tiberian, or 'third style,' in the second quarter of the first century there followed the 'fourth style' which reached its prime during the reign of Nero and continued into the Flavian period.

As Neronian architecture carried forward the development which had been interrupted at the end of the Republican age, so the wall-painting of the 'fourth style' is linked to that of the 'second style' that belonged to the late Republican and early Augustan periods. Such a harking back by contrast may be observed in almost every period of art-history. The painters of Nero's day had before them a plentiful supply of examples on surviving walls of the second style. The emotionalism and temperamentalism of the Neronian age disdained alike the stern formalism of the early second style and the sober planes of the third style, but turned with enthusiasm to those graceful architectural creations of the late second style which the philistine Vitruvius had condemned. No new system of mural decoration was evolved, but the delight in blending motives, inherited from Italic art, produced a lively use and variation of older themes. Architectural members, which in the painting of the third style had become mere two-dimensional ornaments, now regained the effect of recession in space though their proportions were far from realistic. Between the restful surfaces of the main wall, and in the frieze above it, there are now painted glimpses of fantastic struc-

tures[1]. It seems as though the elaborate architecture of a proscenium with its stucco and paint work were copied but at the same
time translated into a thing of lightness and grace, unreal in its
delicate proportions. Here and there 'views' remind us of the
architectural fantasies of Piranesi—the most ingenious from a wall
panel in Herculaneum[2]. The same touch that dared to raise the
fourth storey of the Colosseum soaring into the air is apparent
here, creating poetic structures bold beyond belief. Pavilions and
gables seem to be piled one on the other until they reach away
into the recesses of a fading distance. Beams bend away in impossible curves; ornamental designs and figures appear to move;
decorative members flash in sudden patches of light against sombre
backgrounds; the contours of rising columns are circled by vines;
and beside the fantasy of these structures and the glitter of these
lights there is the suggestion of an approaching storm which
already stirs the heavy curtains. Yet a certain artistic limitation
is apparent from the fact that on Pompeian walls select portions
and details generally afford us more satisfaction than any whole
composition.

As the structural design of fourth-style wall-decoration differs
from that of third style, so do the painters' palette and technique.
The impression of cool reserve in the colouring of the third style
is produced by the whitish narrow stripes that separate the large
clear colour-areas. The restless movement that fills the frescos of
the fourth style results from a certain bold gayness of colour which
is intensified by emphatic intermediate strokes of yellow. A painter
of the third style always set himself with accurate care to draw
exact outlines, and to round off each delicate detail. An artist of
the fourth style records his impressions with easy brush-work and
produces the greatest charm just in those places where he paints
most fluently. Both in this illusionistic technique and in the
imaginary decorative creations we seem to see rising to the surface
an element of the same baroque character that appears in some of
the vase-painting of early Italy of the fourth and third centuries
B.C.

The same liking, apparent in decorative designs, for blending
varied types re-appears in the subject-pictures that decorate the
central panels of walls. These differ essentially from the pictures
of the third style both in content, composition and feeling and in
stylistic form. In the third style there was a preference for the
presentation of restful existence and restrained feeling; the artist
favoured figures detached from one another, plastically clear, painted

in clean tones against the spacious plane of a neutral background. But when the fourth-style artist makes a composition of a figure-subject, like that of Pan and Cupid wrestling in the House of the Vettii[1], he fills the whole picture with thrust and movement. The protagonists are boldly set in diagonal composition, and from the background the Thiasos surges forward, while curtains flutter and restless lights flicker on bodies and objects alike. Even when Greek panel-pictures are copied with approximate truth the subjects preferred are those with great dramatic force, like Achilles in Scyros, the death of Pentheus, and the punishment of Dirce, or else those that are tense with mental suspense, like the surrender of Briseis, and the meeting of Odysseus and Penelope[2]. Odysseus is seated in the courtyard; an almost uncontrollable emotion seems to shake him. The questioning, wondering glance of Penelope rests on his passion-ridden head as she stands beside him. Here the feelings of the fourth-style painter have made him heighten the emotive content of the original with the aid of the hard lights upon the knife-edge folds of Odysseus' cloak, and the mysterious restlessness of the veil's pleats flickering like little flames round Penelope's head.

The most notable achievements of the fourth style are, however, not the large figure-paintings but the small friezes with Cupids and Psyches[3], the floating visions of deities, satyrs, and maenads, and the animals[4] moving gracefully on ornaments and tendrils lit up by brilliant high-lights against sombre backgrounds. In such subjects the painting is full not only of excitement but also of wit, irony, and humour like contemporary literature, and its feeling seems to run the whole gamut from nervous restlessness to tragic suffering. The happiest creations of the brush correspond to the best products of the mason's chisel like the rose-pilasters of the tomb of the Haterii.

Pliny has recorded the names of a few painters of this period: the *eques* Turpilius, Titidius Labeo, proconsul and dilettante, the two artists Cornelius Pinus and Attius Priscus whom Vespasian commissioned to decorate the temple of Honos and Virtus, and Famulus, monopolized by Nero for work in the Golden House. It is not without significance that they were all Romans. Moreover the old popular tradition of realistic representative painting also flourished. We have information about certain pictures of gladiatorial shows painted on the walls of public halls by a freedman of Nero's *omnium veris imaginibus redditis*[5]; while Josephus

[1] Volume of Plates v, 74, *a*.   [2] *Ib.* v, 74, *b*.   [3] *Ib.* 76, *a, b, c*.
[4] *Ib.* 76, *d*.   [5] Pliny, *N.H.* xxxv, 52.

refers to the pictures with scenes from the Jewish war that were carried in the Triumph of Titus. Nero had a colossal portrait of himself painted on linen.

In the surviving frescos of the villa beneath the Baths of Trajan we should expect to recognize the art of Famulus displayed in Nero's Golden House, and therefore to be confronted with the masterpieces of the fourth style. What we can see there on walls and ceilings is of the fourth style. The Italian Masters of the late quattrocento and the early cinquecento revelled in the cheerful grace of these designs and evolved from them what they called 'grotesques,' after the '*grotte*,' as this ruin was popularly termed. But if we expect to find that the achievements of the small provincial town were far surpassed by the works of the Capital, we are doomed to disappointment. The rather monotonous mural decorations show no rich imagination, the panel pictures lack playful lightness of touch. The ceilings, like the famous *Volta Dorata*, are the best thing. There the painting and technique are more careful and restful. An accurate estimate is not however possible until we possess the published report of the recent excavations. Possibly the decoration of this portion of the Golden House was only carried out by Titus, who probably made it his residence. In that case the frescos would seem to point towards that development which strove for the modification of fevered *pathos* and florid fantasy. Priscus, whom Vespasian employed, is called by Pliny *antiquis similior*[1]; and from Trajan's time we have a few paintings, in a loggia of the so-called 'bridge of Caligula' on the Palatine, that demonstrate a return to quiet reserve in the system of decoration and to painstaking carrying out of detail.

Interior decoration, whether of the palace or the home, is an intimate art; in turning to the historical reliefs of the period we enter the stage of public life. Augustan art created a type of monumental relief founded on Greek relief sculpture but Roman in its subject-matter and feeling, with certain Italic elements apparent in its form. The treatment of plastic forms was one end and perfection of Greek relief. On Roman soil new problems, those of space and the effect of line in the figures, are added. Space and line are in their turn intimately linked with the Italic attitude to the realism of the actual world and the Italic zeal for expressiveness such as calls for the reinforcing of emphasis. Roman relief cannot be truly appreciated if it is only studied from its several formal angles; subject-matter, space, expression, line, all combine to give meaning to the whole. The different periods are distinguished from one

---

[1] *N.H.* XXXVI, 120 *sq.*

another by the degree of similarity to or divergence from classical Greek art.

No historical relief of the Neronian age survives. We encounter the new style suddenly on the Arch of Titus, of which the interior reliefs are masterpieces that overshadow the creative achievements of Nero's time. The subject consists in two phases of the triumph of Titus over the Jews. First there is a part of the procession bearing along the sacred furniture captured in the Temple at Jerusalem and the *tituli* that label these objects[1]. What a contrast to the ceremony, harmony and dignity of the procession on the Ara Pacis[2]! No mood of *favete linguis*, but the deafening uproar of a great triumph that we can almost hear. In the centre of the panel the procession comes quite close to the spectator and then in the distance turns off to the right towards an arch. It does not move parallel with the plane but seems to curve before our very eyes. The bearers of the booty advance with no ceremonial precision, but hurry along eagerly while their companions stand rigidly looking on. Figures are massed into groups between which gaps appear. The upper outline of the whole procession seems to defy rules of composition as much as the arrangement of the mass. The slanting lines of the *tituli*, the long trumpets crossed in the air, the arch seeming to float in the background, these things carry the feeling of restlessness into the space over the figures. Light seems to catch the golden furniture, and the garments have deep-cut folds parted by sharp ridges. Light and line seem to fill the picture with throbbing restlessness.

The feeling of the second relief is more restrained, with its picture of Titus crowned by Victory in his chariot led by Honos and Virtus[3]. In this, too, the chariot comes forward out of the depth of the relief; the horses have just turned to one side. The heavy, short figure of the Emperor is almost facing, but his head is turned away towards the goal of the procession, the Capitol. But here too a wealth of emotion is diffused over the picture by the movement of figures, the stirring of garments, and the slanting fasces. There are no soft, rounded, flowing lines, but forceful clash and discord. It is not so much a greater faithfulness to nature that differentiates these pictures from classical or classicizing reliefs as the realization of a mood that is inimical to any classical norm. That kind of strong feeling, which in decorative painting was often merely wasted on minor subjects, found here

[1] Volume of Plates v, 78, *a*.
[2] *Ib.* IV, 114–116.
[3] *Ib.* v, 78, *b*.

a worthy historical theme. Content and form are each worthy of the other; hence the reliefs on the Arch of Titus are as true an expression of the style of the Flavian age as are those of the Ara Pacis of Augustan art.

The characteristic Flavian style for reliefs is just as clear when older prototypes are employed, as, for example, on the fragment of a battle scene in Mantua, or on another architectural relief which uses the motive of the Alexander mosaic to depict a battle against barbarians. The style persists, though more restrained, in a series of important reliefs of Trajan's time. Those closest in feeling to the Flavian style are the panels of a frieze with pictures of the Emperor now in battle, now crowned as victor, which are built into the Arch of Constantine. The enemy breaks before the onset of Trajan and his cavalry[1]. The composition may be cut by a diagonal: above on the left the victors, below on the right the vanquished. In the victory panel Rome guides the Emperor, Victory swoops down to crown him, the light seems to concentrate on his figure, and the picture acquires something of the visionary character of some baroque painting. Roman relief, like painting, could contain not only a historical narrative significance, but also a certain political value as a record and as a source of instruction. This is the character of the interior reliefs of the screens of the Rostra in the Forum Romanum. One represents the destruction of the debt-rolls, the other the founding of *alimenta*[2], both of them acts by means of which the Emperor sought to combat the bankruptcy of the farmers and the depopulation of Italy. Both reliefs were intended to be companion-pieces; they are of the same period and must certainly be referred to Trajan. Even if the feeling of restlessness has gone there still remains enough of the old liveliness and of the shrinking from the harmonies of the Classical.

The sculptures of the Arch of Beneventum present a political manifesto in symbolism. Upon the side of the Arch facing towards Rome there are well-conceived and finely designed scenes referring to the blessings of the Imperial rule for Italy; upon the other side the reference is to the benefits bestowed on the provinces. The subject-matter in itself calls for a quiet manner of presentation. Of three principal groups among these reliefs that of the right-hand pier, on the cityward side, is nearest in style to the Flavian with the nervous rendering of its draperies[3]. Soft flowing curves, rounded in section, show the sculptor of the other pier as a man approaching to later art. It is surely no mere chance that here—still within the ambit of the strong expressiveness of the period—the figure of the

[1] Volume of Plates v, 80, *a*.   [2] *Ib.* 80, *b*.   [3] *Ib.* 82, *a*.

Emperor is for the first time presented on some of these carvings as of superhuman size. The reliefs of the *attica* by reason of their position require more emphatic modelling[1]. We may then perceive here the work of a sculptor who already belongs to the Hadrianic age and who is influenced by the new classicism.

Quite another side of Roman art survives in the reliefs of Trajan's Column. In Rome there was always a popularly expressive art cultivated side by side with the art that was subject to Greek artistic influence. Its real continuity was preserved through painting. Occasionally it was translated into stone as in tomb-reliefs like the slabs of the Flavian monument of the Haterii. Possibly the notion of unfurling the long roll of some painted chronicle of a campaign round a column was at first an improvisation adopted for some procession. But the idea proved a success. With its transference to a monument of enduring material we are suddenly face to face with a kind of popular presentation with which the Roman people had already grown familiar during the Republican age, though examples of it have not survived. Deeds of war were set among landscapes and views of castles and townships[2]. A long tradition had been formed of typical scenes: the address to the troops, sacrifice, the submission of the vanquished, marches, battles; scenes that probably recurred in every triumph. But the Column of Trajan shows the lively freshness of a new and effective originality. One magnificent scene shows the submission of the Dacians at the end of the first campaign[3]. Behind the captive imploring mercy stands the figure of Decebalus, menacing, erect, a hint of the new struggle to come. The companion picture to this scene is the exposure of the enemy commander's severed head, at the end of the war.

If the primitive Roman had a passion for the historical narrative picture he had an equal passion for portraiture of the most realistic kind. In this his interest, in contrast to that of the Greek, was centred from the very beginning upon the features of the face. Augustan art had failed to find a real compromise between the Roman desire to reproduce incidental, temporary, even momentary conditions and the Greek organic, plastic style that strove to seize upon the essential character of the subject. Thus the classicizing portraiture of the Court and the realistic portraiture of the *petite bourgeoisie* stand side by side, unrelated. In both Italic feeling and Greek schooling are inextricably bound up together; only in the former it is the Greek element that predominates, in the latter it is the Roman. A real synthesis was only achieved in the develop-

[1] Volume of Plates v, 82, *b*.   [2] *Ib.* 38, *b*.   [3] *Ib.* 84.

ment of portraiture during the reigns of Nero, the Flavians, and
Trajan; and the phases of this development can be worked out in
more detail than can be described in these pages. The portrait
of Domitius Corbulo[1] combines Classical plastic form with a
greater emphasis on individuality of character and Roman racial
quality than is found in portraiture of the Augustan or Claudian
age. More picturesque and emotional, but just as sharp in its
characterization is the head of Nero in the Museo dei Terme[2].
Vespasian's worthy *bourgeois* character comes out in his portraits
as something much more human than that of any of the Julio-
Claudian Emperors, who always appear to be viewed from a point
of indeterminate remoteness. The Flavian portrait, which carries
through the reign of Trajan to Hadrianic times, favours heads in
attitudes expressive of sensibility, as for example the male head
from the tomb of the Haterii. It is able to render the charm of
a young girl[3] as well as the character and ugliness of an old
woman[4]; and the dramatic quality of the style comes out in the
elaborately theatrical coiffures.

In full length portrait-statues a tendency towards the new style
is already apparent in two works of about A.D. 50—the Claudius[5]
and Agrippina at Olympia. A masterpiece like the Titus of the
Braccio Nuovo[6] differs from Augustan or Claudian togate figures
not only in the actual realism of the rendering of the plump face
and figure, but also in the restlessness of the contour and in the
play of light and shade on and among the sharp folds of the garment. With Augustan armed figures we may contrast another
figure in the Braccio Nuovo clad in a cuirass and probably rightly
combined with the head of Domitian[7], for here too is the same
flickering restlessness. Lastly there is an armed statue of Titus
in Olympia full of animation, the very leather fringes of the breast-
plate appearing to be stirred by some strong wind. Beginning
from these portrait statues it will one day be possible to discover
where the rest of the sculpture of this period sought its models
and how it transformed themes of different kinds so that they might
conform to the feeling of the time.

---

[1] Volume of Plates v, 86, *a*.   [2] *Ib.* 86, *b*.
[3] *Ib.* 86, *c*.   [4] *Ib.* 86, *d*.
[5] *Ib.* 88, *a*.   [6] *Ib.* 88, *b*.
[7] *Ib.* 88, *c*.

II. HADRIAN TO COMMODUS: ROME AND
THE LATIN WEST

If the age of Hadrian was to be represented by a single work of art, the choice would most naturally fall upon a statue of Antinous. This expresses at once the predominance of sculpture and of Greek classicism and the intimate connection with the Emperor's own misfortune in the death of his favourite. Certain essential elements coincided to produce Hadrianic art, among them the exhaustion of the Neronian-Flavian style and a consequent inevitable reaction, secondly, a fresh productive energy in the Hellenic world which had taken on a new lease of life since the first century, thirdly, the Empire's external prosperity founded on a shrewd policy of peace, fourthly, the Emperor's personal sympathy for the creative arts. As henceforward Greeks and Romans were equal partners in all matters political and economic, so from this time onwards Greek and Roman art advanced abreast of each other.

No century saw as much building as the second, the most flourishing age of the urban culture that the Empire knew. Hadrian himself by building in every province of the Empire gave a tremendous stimulus to the erection of public edifices. Yet with Hadrian architecture lost the primacy among the arts. Even the second most definitely Roman art of historical relief-carving slipped into the background, for the great original achievement of the Hadrianic renaissance lay in sculpture in the round and the Greek relief. The picture of Antinous is no mere presentation of the Emperor's Bithynian favourite in the flesh, but rather of the new god Antinous. Greek classical tradition summons up all its force once more in order to give form to a divine Ideal. There is more here than the fortuitous coincidence of an Imperial command, a clever artist, and the abject flattery of subjects. Stirred with genuine devotion, the Greeks sought and found a worthy expression of their gratitude when they created, as solace for a ruler bereaved by a mysterious death, the Being of the divine Antinous for their own age and for all time. A lucky star has guarded the likeness of Antinous. Beside many mediocre copies there have survived in the villas of the Emperor himself and in those of Roman nobles statues, heads, and reliefs which we may venture to describe as originals of the first rank. In spirit and form they are purely Greek; the Roman art of portraiture has no part in them. Their forms are derived solely from classical prototypes, and yet they are conceived with such newness and unity that we

can truly term them a fresh creation. We have no hesitation in
placing the Naples Antinous Farnese[1], the once acrolithic statue
of Antinous-Dionysus in the Vatican Rotonda[2], the relief of the
Villa Albani[3], and the Mondragone head in Paris[4] beside masterpieces of classical art. And yet we stand before them with mingled
feelings. In the face of Antinous there are combined pure classical
forms with features of barbaric beauty, like the shock of snake-like
locks, the low level eyebrows, and the curve of the nose. It is this
mixture that must have endowed the favourite himself with a
strange fascination. Then there is evident a kind of formal antagonism between the desire to express his brooding sensual
beauty and the wish to let the fineness of the marble produce an
effect like some carved gem. We can admire the masterly creation
of form, our knowledge of the story enables us to share the tragic
meaning behind it; but an unbridgeable gulf divides us from the
emotions beneath.

One relief of Antinous is signed by a master from the Carian
city of Aphrodisias. This was the home of a school of Sculpture
that continued to flourish down to a late period, and supplied both
Rome and the East. In Hadrian's Villa at Tivoli there were found
works by Aristeas and Papias of Aphrodisias, centaurs which are
showy copies in black marble of Hellenistic models. The use of
coloured marbles, often hard to work, was only occasional in the
Greek and Roman world, but now became fashionable. In Trajan's
forum there was a *porticus porphyretica*, from which perhaps come
the extant porphyry figures of captive Dacians[5]. Other types of
stone that now came into use were Egyptian basalt, *rosso antico*,
diorite, polychrome marble, and, for Egyptianizing works, granite
from Assuan. Statues and busts were made of different kinds of
stone fitted together; even when white marble was used the artist
tried to let the beauty of the material itself have its effect. Greek
originals were not merely translated mechanically into some new
material, but acquired a peculiar charm from the careful adaptation of colours and light effects. Yet this latest flowering of
classical sculpture is no healthy natural growth, but a product of
the hot-house. The emphasis is on the costliness of the material,
wherein lies a feeling unfamiliar to the classical work but congenial
to the East.

Hadrian's portraits are in the same changed sphere. His features,
simplified in classical fashion, are framed by hair worn in large

1 Volume of Plates v, 90, *a, c.*   2 *Ib.* 90, *b.*
3 *Ib.* 92, *a.*   4 *Ib.* 92, *b.*
5 *Ib.* 94, *a.*   6 *Ib.* 94, *b.*

locks and a finely curled beard[1]. The artistic effect is attained by
the contrast between the warm colour of stirring locks and the cool
marble of the face. This fundamental motive is maintained as a
remarkably fixed tradition for the portraits of all the Antonines
down to Commodus, and beyond him to Septimius Severus. The
cut and stylization of hair and beard change. In the face the
character and development of the personality of Antoninus Pius,
of Marcus Aurelius[2] and of Commodus, are expressed with appreciable reserve. The fine portrait of Lucius Verus, with his unplea-
sant sidelong glance, is much more of a personal thing, perhaps
on account of some stronger Roman influence[3]. A new split is
apparent in the art of portraiture in Rome itself under Hadrian,
for beside the classicism of the Imperial Court, the more individual, lively, Roman art of the Neronian-Flavian epoch continues.
One of its best achievements, enhanced by the plastic skill of the
period, is a head which formerly was mis-named Vitellius[4].

The influence of Greek classicism upon the Roman relief was
especially interesting and powerful. A fashion arose for combining
the marble-incrustation of whole wall-surfaces with large decorative mural reliefs which combined Greek prototypes and a classical
style with the surviving motives of purely Roman reliefs. Of far
greater historical importance was, however, the rise of a new type
of monument that promised to monopolize the activities of the
stonemasons' yards in Rome—the sarcophagus decorated with
reliefs. Reasons founded in religion or faith have been sought in
vain to explain the change that took place from cremation to
inhumation. It seems that about the beginning of the second
century the sarcophagus came into use first in Asia Minor (see
below, p. 801), and the use passed thence to Greece, Syria, and
Egypt. This type, at first decorated with garlands, was soon enriched with reliefs that replaced the simpler type of ornament. The
fact that the Romans adopted the custom of inhumation simultaneously with the form of the monumental sarcophagus was due
to something less than a change in their conceptions about death
and to something more than a mere passing fashion. It was rather
an essential result of the spiritual and artistic influences of the
Greek East that were affecting Rome at this period. But Rome
made no passive surrender to this new artistic form. From now
on sarcophagi were doubtless imported into Italy from Greece and
Asia Minor, but the Roman workshops from the very beginning
gave a turn of their own to the craft. An Italic-Roman feeling

[1] Volume of Plates v, 96, a.   [2] Ib. 96, c.
[3] Ib. 96, d.   [4] Ib. 96, b.

expressed itself in the shaping of the stone coffin. The oldest type of Roman garland-sarcophagus shows the Greek influence in the retention of *kymatia*, though these are of Roman shape. But the Roman desire to tell a story is apparent from the insertion of pictorial scenes above the garlands and from the figures decorating one front moulding of the lid[1]. On the one hand it is a love of representation, and on the other it is a poverty of structural sensibility, that distinguishes the typically Roman sarcophagus. The Greeks of the East retained right into the Byzantine age the architectural shape for the sarcophagus, and its relief-work, even when over-elaborated, remained subsidiary. The Roman sarcophagus, faintly influenced by the distant tradition of the Etruscan sarcophagus, became a box, the relief-carving of which was finished off above and below by a smooth moulding. The narrow ends of this box are neglected and its back remains quite plain, the gable roof of the lid becomes insignificant behind a plank-like moulding along the front. One of the oldest Hadrianic sarcophagi shows the wedding of Peleus and Thetis; the lid has still got a low-pitched roof and the tooth pattern above the relief still retains a remnant of Greek structure. The unity of the presentation is Greek too. While Eastern sarcophagi, thanks to their purely Greek tradition, display a comparatively slow and simple development, the story of the Roman sarcophagus is one of extraordinary movement. During the second century subjects are mainly borrowed from Greek mythology; but the Roman gives preference to the lively picture that tells a continuous story over mere unity of presentation. He introduces the Roman personification Virtus into the midst of Meleager's hunting party. He is always adopting fresh motives from the East; but he mingles the revived Roman taste with these Greek influences. We may observe two contemporary sarcophagi in the Lateran which belong to the transition from the Hadrianic to the Antonine age: the style of relief on the one with the story of Orestes is Greek and Hadrianic[2]; that of the other with the death of the Niobids betrays, both in the spatial grouping of the figures and in the picturesque restlessness of the design, the age-old Italic taste for the baroque[3]. Standing before such a relief one is inevitably reminded of some Etruscan ash-chest.

In the later Antonine age the emotionalism in the sarcophagus reliefs grows more intense, culminating in works like the Medici Judgment of Paris[4]. Here there develops a kind of renaissance of the Flavian style, but more slowly and without the eruptive force

[1] Volume of Plates v, 98, *a*.
[2] *Ib.* 98, *b*.   [3] *Ib.* 98, *c*.   [4] *Ib.* 100, *a*.

of the Neronian age. It is comprehensible that the stonemasons should adopt for a series of battle-sarcophagi[1] the peculiar character of the Roman historical relief which had risen to new heights in the Column of Marcus Aurelius. From Rome the sarcophagus was gradually exported in the course of the second century to the provinces of the West. North Africa, where there was no old Greek tradition, imported all its sarcophagi from Rome; Cyrenaica drew its supply from Greece. In Gaul there were both Roman and Greek imports. Northern Italy with its harbours of Ravenna and Aquileia looked eastwards; there a special type of sarcophagus was developed under Greek influence, though perhaps not long before the end of the century.

The Roman historical relief, with its tradition firmly embedded in the Roman spirit, was governed by its own laws also in this period. Types, composition, and symbolism were as conservative as the shapes of the monuments which they were employed to decorate. Greek influence was only perceptible in the plastic style and in the calmer moods. Examples of Hadrianic historical reliefs are the scene of public sacrifice in the Louvre, which probably comes from the Forum of Trajan, a relief at Chatsworth with a theme related to that of one of Trajan's rostra-screens, and two reliefs in the Palazzo dei Conservatori, which were once on some triumphal arch. There are rondos on the Arch of Constantine made during the latter part of Hadrian's reign. One series of these is of typical classical Greek style[2]; but there are others, in sharp contrast to the clear restfulness of the former, with objects diagonally placed, with emotional movement, and with violent play of light and shadow on restless garments[3]. In these, as in portraiture, the tendencies of Flavian art lived on as a type form. Two groups of reliefs survive from the time of Marcus which must have adorned two different triumphal arches. The earlier group, consisting of three slabs in the Palazzo dei Conservatori, has figures plastically restful and the soft flowing line of the Hadrianic style, though a new element of fluttering movement intrudes itself in the hair and beards and the manes of horses[4]. On the eight reliefs which now decorate the *attica* of Constantine's Arch the same movement affects figures and garments as well; architectural elements recede in depth, standards flutter in the breeze[5]. But the new style culminates in the reliefs of the Column of Marcus Aurelius[6] which was constructed under Commodus and completed about A.D. 193.

[1] Volume of Plates V, 100, *b*.　　　[2] *Ib.* 102, *a*.
[3] *Ib.* 102, *b*.　　　[4] *Ib.* 104, *a*.
[5] *Ib.* 104, *b*.　　　[6] *Ib.* 106, *a*.

Trajan's Column was the pattern, but the artist transmuted it to suit a different taste. The Roman temperament comes through once again in the emotional content of the representation. The reliefs of the Arch of Titus are in spirit related to these. A Flavian column would have been more like the Column of Marcus than the Column of Trajan, the reliefs of which are already affected by the coming Classical revival. But on the Column of Marcus some essentially new and peculiar elements, unknown to Flavian or Trajanic art, are apparent. In place of broad presentation there is a concentration of action, Roman pride of conquest, helpless barbarian submission[1], the solemn representation of the Emperor himself are strongly stressed, and a transcendental element comes into the scene depicting the Miracle. The Italic centralizing method of composing single scenes and the un-classical repetition of identical figures, like those of marching legionaries, are employed to intensify effect. Lines and alternations of light and shadow heighten the expressive character of the whole work, the merit and artistic significance of which has for long been underrated. It is no transition, but rather a prelude to the last phase of ancient art. Its roots are struck deeper in the spiritual heritage of Rome than those of Trajan's Column, and yet it points towards the art of the future.

We can only assume that there was a fresh and flourishing production of Roman historical painting corresponding to the achievements of Roman relief sculpture. The victory-paintings which Septimius Severus placed on exhibition must have been of this kind. The scanty remains of second-century painting that survive fulfil our expectations and show that between Flavian and late Antonine illusionism there was a phase of neo-classic style. From disconnected fragments it appears that one of the important arts of the last classical phase, the use of mosaic decoration for vaults, had its beginnings at this period.

In view of the overwhelming impression made by the Pantheon, it may seem paradoxical to assign the last place in this period to architecture, the art which Hadrian himself practised. In this edifice which Hadrian rebuilt completely, replacing the Pantheon of Agrippa, he seems to have employed Roman engineering to effect a synthesis of the Greek and the Roman feeling for spatial content. The exterior of the Pantheon[2] is an inorganic compilation of three parts, a domed chamber, an anteroom, and an entrance hall. The interior[3], which was the one thing that concerned the

[1] Volume of Plates v, 106, b.
[2] Ib. 108, a.   [3] Ib. 108, b.

architect, has a perfection of form and a restful sense of space that is without equal in the whole world. There are two storeys to the interior wall, the flatness of which is emphasized by columns and pilasters, and upon it there rests miraculously the coffered dome. Through the round opening in its centre light streams down, filling the whole space with cheerful brightness. There is but a slight architectural movement between the entrance and raised central niche. Here are no mystic shadows or patches and spears of light. This perfectly restful round chamber had for its precursors the round Greek *tholoi* with their coffered tent-like ceilings. But it needed Roman engineering skill to give a round building monument size and the unifying effect of the vaulted dome. As long as critics sought to ascribe some structural significance to the brick ribs and the curves of the dome, they might presume to discern a conflict between structural and decorative values. They analysed the building from the gothic angle as though it were a ribbed vault carried upon eight piers. To-day we know that the dome is simply bound together by the consistency of its mortar; it is, to quote Auguste Choisy's apt definition of the Roman vault, 'un monolithe artificiel.' Consequently we must envisage the substructure as a strong wall in the inner side of which eight niches have been scooped out. A gothic edifice strains heavenwards, but the Pantheon stands there in a self-contained peacefulness founded on the harmony of science and aesthetic.

The fame of this achievement will ever be linked with the name of Hadrian. Yet it does not mark the attainment of a new stage in the history of Roman architecture. It is probable that Hadrian's building surpassed that of Agrippa in size and consequently in boldness of construction and splendour of decoration. But in the essentials of shape and construction Agrippa's Pantheon will have resembled the present building. We can trace the general type back through the early Augustan age into Republican times. Within the precincts of his far-flung Villa at Tivoli Hadrian employed vaulted constructions of new and extravagant kinds, but these were ingenious experiments rather than historically significant creations. The so-called Piazza d'Oro in the Villa combines in an original way a ground-plan copied from some Hellenistic-Roman Gymnasium of the East with a propylon and a main hall with the boldest of vaulted roofs. Maxentius completed the vaulting of the temple of Venus and Roma which Hadrian himself had designed, and which, with its exterior plan of a pseudo-dipteral building providing a front of ten columns situated inside a relatively small *peribolos*, was copied from purely Greek models.

But the Tomb of Hadrian carries on a traditional Roman form on a gigantic scale.

The temple dedicated to Divus Hadrianus by his successor stood on a Roman podium ornamented with reliefs of the Provinces and trophies of Victory, but took the form of a Greek peripteral temple. The shrine of Antoninus and Faustina in the Forum Romanum marked a return to the Italic-Roman type. Otherwise Antonine architecture seems to have developed steadily and carried on the architectural ideas of the Neronian and Flavian period. In the urban dwelling-houses of Rome and Ostia the type evolved under Nero prevails and dictates the street-planning. The use of rough brickwork on street façades[1] and on tomb buildings[2] in the environs of Rome acquired a charm through its details and colour shades that was thought worthy of imitation in the Middle Ages and the Renaissance.

Provincial architecture in the West was completely under the influence of Rome. Some day it will certainly be possible to establish the peculiarities of each separate Province in the form and decoration of its architecture. Cities in ancient Narbonese Gaul, the monumental buildings of which began at the end of the Republic, showed more originality and confidence in their art than the cities of North Africa which owed their rapid growth to the period after Trajan. At Nîmes the so-called 'Bath of Diana' shows a hellenizing type of barrel-vault continuing down to the Antonines. The *Tetrapyla* of Tripolitania are perhaps inspired from the East. But generally all the Western provinces show forms that are not only stylistically related, but also similar in type and almost entirely absent in the East. Among them are the *Capitolia* of Roman colonies, copies of Italian prototypes, like the well-preserved examples at Dougga and Sbeitla in North Africa, as well as triumphal arches, Fora, Praetoria, and Basilicas, also theatres and amphitheatres of Italic-Roman type, and Baths formed on the Roman four-square style[3]. The provincials not only copied *exempla Romana*, but sometimes improved on them as in the Basilica of Leptis Magna[4]. Its connection with the forum shows a general plan that goes back to the Forum of Trajan in Rome or directly to a Roman camp. But the huge hall of the Basilica provides a new impression of spaciousness because the apses of the nave are not cut off by colonnades, but are joined on to it. The vast cross-axis, over 300 feet in length, suggests a double sense of movement from the centre to both ends because the apses are

---

[1] Volume of Plates v, 110, *a*.   [2] *Ib.* 110, *b*.
[3] *Ib.* 112, *a*.   [4] *Ib.* 112, *b*.

included. In place of two colonnades round a rectangular space in the middle there are two aisles. The unity of the Civilization and Art of the West is effectively demonstrated by the close similarity between the Baths of Leptis Magna built by Hadrian and the St. Barbara Thermae in Trèves that also belong to the second century. This development is continued without a break after the Antonine age.

III. HADRIAN TO COMMODUS: THE GREEK EAST

The art of the Greek East is more uniform and more governed by tradition than that of the Roman West. It has none of the divided purpose, partly destructive partly constructive in its effect, that springs from a conflict between Roman instincts and Greek education, and there is less trace of the pendulum swinging from the classic to the baroque and back again. In the West violent movement and restless striving prevail, in the East a development quiet and self-confident, but less interesting. Every Greek copy, every head, relief, and ornament contains within itself a bit of the unbroken tradition of Classical art. The transition to Augustan classicism, which followed parallel lines in West and East, supplied Hellenism also with a fresh artistic platform, but the step to this was not so great as in Italy. The tidal waves of Flavian and late Antonine art are felt, but with less force, in the East. The problem of reaching a compromise with the art of the reinvigorated Orient had not yet arisen in this period. Some Roman elements in the art of the West are carefully adopted, others are rejected with unhesitating instinct.

Masonry and vaults in the Roman style appear in the East and are there subject to certain modifications. Linked with these is the adoption of domes and barrel-vaults as structural forms of artistic merit. Occasionally the Roman podium turns up in the East, especially when the shrine upon it happens to be a temple dedicated to an Emperor, like the Traianeum of Pergamum. Augustan Asia Minor had already transformed the Roman arched gateway into something of a Greek type. The composite capital was adopted together with temperamental Flavian architectural decoration. In the case of theatres, like the one at Aspendus and the Odeum of Herodes Atticus in Athens, the auditorium and stage building are welded together, as in Rome, into an organic whole. But, following the ancient Greek tradition, the *cavea* is sunk into the sloping hillside and the effect of a façade is avoided. Amphitheatres, adopted in the East together with gladiatorial and

wild-beast shows, were also preferably sunk within natural depres-
sions. Yet it is even more characteristic of the Greeks that they
deliberately rejected certain types, partly on cultural grounds,
partly for aesthetic reasons. There are no commemorative arches
of the distinctive Roman type; no Imperial Thermae. The place
of the latter was filled by Gymnasia which were developed on the
grand scale. The East in general declined to take over the Roman
cross-vault although its prototype was a product of Hellenistic
architecture. The Greeks clearly felt the cross-vaults in the Halls
of the Thermae to lack an organic character. While Greek sarcophagi were constantly employed in Rome and the West the un-
architectural Roman sarcophagus proved distasteful to the Greek.
In the East the Roman historical reliefs found no place; and it
was foreign to the Greek to thrust a Roman personification, like
Virtus, into the midst of a mythological scene. We may likewise
be sure that the bourgeois paintings of battles, gladiatorial shows,
and judgment scenes were lacking. Thus, for all the unity of the
combined styles of antiquity, a Greek city must have had a
markedly different artistic aspect from a Roman one.

The history of the art of the Roman provinces, Eastern and
Western alike, has not yet been written, and its realization will
demand much toil and preparation. In this sketch only a few
points can be touched upon. Hadrian bestowed a deep devotion
on the city of Athens, where he evinced tremendous energy in
building. An Olympian himself he completed the Temple of Zeus
Olympios. The ground-plan of the surviving stoa and library
shows a connection with the Hellenistic Gymnasium. Between
the old city of Theseus and the new city of Hadrian a monumental
gateway was erected in his honour. The conception of such a gate
and the shape of its curved arch are Roman; and yet the gate is
an edifice that is pronouncedly Greek. The clumsy way in which
the archivolt of the arch cuts into the horizontal architrave shows
that the builder was naïvely wrestling with an untried problem that
had long been solved in the West. The columns in front are not
engaged in the wall; the substructure does not support a base for
some great monument but simply a second storey, a wall with
piers and an aedicula protruding in the centre. A Roman arch has
a distinct depth; walls flank the passage through it, for that is the
predominating idea of the march through which arises from the
religious significance that a Roman attached to a gateway. The
Athenian gate is just a thin wall broken by a doorway. We get
the impression of a cross-wall in front of which are free-standing
columns. This is no city gate but the propylon of a temenos and

merely carries on the Hellenistic tradition of the propylon of two storeys.

Hadrian's devotion did not, however, succeed in filling Athens and Greece with anything that could be termed new and creative life. Herodes Atticus, the great patron whom Greece produced, might put up decorative structures at many a famous site such as impressed the beholder, but he called no fresh bloom of architecture into life. Greece was and remained a museum that was visited and appreciated by cultured men of the day; Athens was a home of learning. The Neo-Attic workshops which had prospered during the first century now found a fresh clientèle in the flourishing cities of the second century and were able to develop the wholesale manufacture of copies of classical statues which were supplied to Asia Minor, Rome, and the provinces of the West. Attic sarcophagi were turned out, not so much for use by impoverished Greeks as for export, and in these a shape derived from Asia Minor was ornamented in accordance with classical Attic tradition[1]. In one field at least second-century Greece made a truly notable contribution to art. Attic portrait heads have survived from the Antonine period, and these are at least as good as the very best contemporary Roman products, perhaps even a good deal better[2]. Herein a new task challenged the skill of the Athenian sculptor.

Yet the land of the most vital Hellenism was certainly Asia Minor, which during this period enjoyed both economic and artistic prosperity. The school of sculpture at Aphrodisias has already been mentioned in connection with the Hadrianic renaissance. South-western Anatolia was the original home of the sarcophagus[3], and its employment, like its shape, spread quickly during the second century to every province that was linked to Asia Minor by maritime trade. Anatolian sarcophagi display great variety, for in addition to the common types there are original and unique representations. In the Antonine period and later the column-sarcophagi that link on to contemporary Anatolian architecture are especially significant[4] with their restless architectural niches and aedicula and their rich figure-ornamentation. Here even more than in Athens there is a feeling that a sarcophagus must be something that is equally finished off on all sides. When Marcus and Verus were honoured in Ephesus by the erection of a frieze full of figures it did not occur to anyone to copy the Roman type of historical relief: Hellenistic models were followed for a work of art in the spirit and form of a Greek relief.

[1] Volume of Plates v, 114, c.　　　[2] Ib. 114, a, b.
[3] Ib. 116, a.　　　　　　　　　　　[4] Ib. 116, b.

The Antonine reconstruction of the Asclepieum at Pergamum reveals the influence of the Pantheon's ground-plan and elevation upon the small round temple, but for the rest the traditions of the general lay-out, of the shape of the Propylon, and of the theatre backing on the hillside, are Greek. After the Corinthian Trajaneum at Pergamum comes the Hadrianic temple at Aezani, which revives Hellenistic-Ionic and rests on a wide podium of a Hellenistic type known from earlier examples such as the temple at Ancyra and the Great Temple of Heliopolis. The large agoras and periboloi reveal the continuity of Greek town-planning. During the first century the Hellenistic type of gymnasium had developed along more complex and elaborate lines, and it seems to have reached its most brilliant development in the gymnasia of the provincial metropolis, Ephesus; the gymnasia of Miletus were less pretentious. They were axially symmetrical constructions which retained their originality despite the existence elsewhere of Imperial Thermae. A preference for long barrel-vaulted rooms may have had its later influence on the type of the Anatolian Christian Basilica.

In Asia Minor there developed for use in State buildings an original and remarkable kind of façade. The Library of Celsus at Ephesus[1] dates from the latter part of Trajan's reign. Its composite capitals and ornament are influenced by Flavian art, but its component parts and structural spirit are Greek. This kind of art appears to reach its climax with the market gateway of Miletus[2]. Its three archways resume a Roman motive and it has composite capitals. The *aediculae* stand out from the wall sharply and yet with a restful effect. The side-wings form a strong enclosing frame. The spectator grows aware of a wealth of movement in the broken roof-lines. The meagre two-storied Hellenistic *propylon* has here grown, under the influence of theatrical proscenium design, into a decorative structure of brilliant effectiveness. Its restoration, in spite of numerous weaknesses of detail, is surprisingly impressive in its effect. It shows that this is no degenerate art of a late age, no piece of theatrical decoration. Its effect derives from the force, size, and nobility that permeate the architecture.

Syria, Palestine, Transjordania, and Egypt cannot vie with Anatolia in artistic matters although an abundance of decorative buildings arose in them all (see above, pp. 634 *sqq.*). The great precinct of the temple of Bel at Palmyra and the sanctuary of Heliopolis belong to the age before Nero. But work continued at these places. The original and magnificent architecture of the tomb-fronts at Petra ceased with the place's incorporation by

---

[1] Volume of Plates v, 118, *a*.   [2] *Ib.* 118, *b*.

Trajan in the Empire. The shapes of the capitals are evidence for an unbroken Hellenistic tradition. Isolated Roman influences may be detected in the temple at Heliopolis, in the sanctuary of the Roman Colonia Heliopolitana, and in the construction of some theatres. Syria is comparatively poor in sculpture and relief. Apart from a few insignificant local products there was no Syrian production of sarcophagi. These articles were imported from Asia Minor, Greece, and, remarkably enough, from Rome. Lacking as it was in any vital artistic fertility of its own, Syria was, as ever, receptive of manifold external influences (see above, p. 636). It is possible that the vanished wall-paintings of Syria were achievements of more significance.

Though doomed to extinction the Egyptian style still survived in the Egypt of this period. In Alexandrian cemeteries strange but remarkable hybrids of Greek and Egyptian motives have survived. The sarcophagi that are derivatives from Anatolian models are devoid of artistic merit. On a higher level is the portraiture which developed under Roman influence but still showed the influence of Hellenistic sentiment and an occasional Egyptian element as well. A fortunate chance has also preserved for us in Egypt the art of portrait painting. A combination of ancient Egyptian practice and Graeco-Roman style brought about the custom of inserting painted portraits of the deceased into mummy-cases. A whole series of portraits of this provincial *genre* survive and their artistic range is such that they may be placed beside contemporary sculptural likenesses.

IV. ART ON THE FRONTIERS OF THE EMPIRE

In conclusion, a problem of art history that became acute during this period must at least be touched on briefly. Both in the central nuclei of ancient civilization and in the provinces the art of the Roman Empire is borne on the two streams of Greek and Roman tradition and is inspired by the vitality of Greek and Roman nationality. The Greeks in the dim past, and the Romans through long centuries of development, had both absorbed groups of other peoples and unfamiliar races, and had fused them into their own historical nations. In the provinces, however, there dwelt a quantity of widely differing peoples, folk who understood Greek or Latin but clung to their mother tongue and treasured many of their customs and religious beliefs. Even in Italy we can perceive beneath the crust of romanization something of the Celtic tradition in the north and of the Greek in the south. It was only in the East that the native population possessed an ancient artistic tradition or bordered on some foreign nation of artistic capacity. Elsewhere there were barbarians. The younger the civilization of a province and the further it lay from the centres of culture, the weaker was the influence upon it of ancient classical tradition. Thus Greek and Roman prototypes became barbarized; and this meant that they did not merely deteriorate in quality, but that an unschooled but quite original artistic sensibility of a primitive kind permeated them. Research will presently enable us to grasp the more positive merits of this provincial art.

The decline towards the primitive tends to give the monuments of different provinces a certain family likeness when contrasted with purely classical art. But close study reveals perceptible differences. The reliefs of the great Trajanic monument at Adamclisi have stylistic peculiarities that do not recur in Gaul, but that point to the East. If Phrygian reliefs appear related to Lycian, Palmyrene, and Parthian art this may be due to the influence of old and new connections. The West differs from the East in the fact that it takes greater pleasure in the realistic representation of the actualities of urban and country life. It seems that in this respect there is a definite spiritual relationship between Italic, Celtic, and Germanic taste. When we find a similar tendency in the original North African mosaic art, then we face the unsolved puzzle whether this art is due to the Italian immigrant or to the native.

Many a provincial form of art shared the fate of the land and people and left no historical influence behind it. The art of a province was only significant if it rose above the average to monumental proportions, and when there were forces at work in it that we can meet and recognize again in the later course of history. This happened in two places on the edge of the Empire, in the East and in the North, at Palmyra and in the land of the Treveri.

The architecture of Palmyra is predominantly Greek. Beside this there grew up during the second century an art of painting and relief work founded on first-century models, and this art evolved a very characteristic style from the mixture of diverse elements. There is no lack of purely Greek and of Syrian influence; beards are worn in Roman fashion. But more than mere traces of oriental garb and ornament come in, a far-reaching orientalization of form is evident in the severe lines of the folds of garments, in hair, in features, and especially in the shape of the eyes with their lids and brows. This hybrid style, and one of its most impressive motifs, the frontality of gods and donors on votive reliefs[1], finds

[1] Volume of Plates v, 120.

its closest parallel in the frescoes of another city whose fate was bound up with that of Palmyra—the Parthian frontier-city of Doura Europus, the excavations of which widen our knowledge year by year (pp. 115 *sq.*, 120). In the fresco with Conon sacrificing[1] from the temple of Baal at Doura, though it is of first-century date, this frontal composition is already established. It expresses something foreign to ancient painting and relief, a spiritual link between the subject painted and the spectator; in fact, reverence. From this a historical line runs to the late classical and early Byzantine subject pictures. Even if Palmyrene relief-work ceased after Aurelian captured the city, the art movement to which it belonged still exerted its influence on such classical art as was developing kindred tendencies.

An actual as well as a spiritual world divides the orientalizing and hieratic art of Palmyra from the profane and realistic representations of life on the tombstones in the land of the Treveri, the development of which can best be followed in the finds of Neumagen. Up to the time of Hadrian the relief work on the tombstones offers nothing that is particularly superior to the products of other provinces. Then in the Antonine age there suddenly appears a speedily evolved style which presents with surprising boldness the life of the wealthy landowners of the Moselle region, and gives new formal value to the material of soft sandstone. The famous relief in which a school-scene[2] is presented with fresh *naïveté* and delight in detail dates from about the time of Commodus. The picturesque heads are full of character and expression. This baroque type of art reached its climax in the course of the first half of the third century; and was then destroyed by the invasion of the Alemanni *c.* 259–60. In contrast to the art of the Eastern frontier, which was founded in ancient tradition wedded to the new forces of the Orient, the art of the Treveri perished and its influence with it. It was only in the art of the Middle Ages and the baroque that that western-European sensibility, which had ventured here on too bold a stride, at last found the way to an organic development.

[1] Volume of Plates v, 28, *b*.　　　　[2] *Ib.* 122, *a, b, c.*

CHAPTER XXI

CLASSICAL ROMAN LAW

I. CHARACTERISTICS OF THE PERIOD

HOWEVER we interpret the constitutional changes made by Augustus and his immediate successors, they did not, of themselves, greatly affect private law, though, indirectly, they were of vast importance to it. An age of continuous, devastating, civil war was succeeded by one of order, internal peace and at least apparent prosperity. It is in such an age, when law is respected and lawcourts work without fear of tumult, that law makes most steady progress. A crisis may indeed compel the adoption of a reform long overdue, but the effect of these rare occasions is negligible, when compared with that of the slow, almost silent, but continuous, evolution of law in the traffic of the courts. Decisions were commonly inspired by jurists, whose business it was to mould the law according to the notions and needs of the time. In an earlier chapter[1] attention was called to the struggle between rigid and flexible interpretation, *verba* and *voluntas*, *strictum ius* and *aequitas*, which, stimulated, but not originated, by study of Greek thought, through the rhetoricians, whose teaching was a great part of the education of a Roman gentleman, marked the last century of the Republic. But this struggle was not ended: it is never ended. In all ages we can find one lawyer contending for the strict view, another for that which corresponds with expressed intent. It was only, for instance, in this age that Mistake (*error*) became an important rubric in law.

The new conditions called for much new law. Rome was now not merely a city State, not merely a capital: she was becoming the commercial centre of the world. Communications were greatly improved. All roads led to Rome, the chief mart for all commodities, including brains, and by these roads men of all races flocked thither, bringing new ideas and new needs. One result, in the legal world, was the appearance of a great literature of which enough survives to show its character, a literature in which legal notions, as applied to concrete facts, were submitted to an analysis which has no parallel in the ancient world. Many of the writers were provincials, as were an increasing proportion of those for whom they wrote. In such conditions some foreign, especially

---

[1] Vol. IX, pp. 869 *sqq.*

Hellenistic, ideas inevitably crept in. The impetus given by the rhetoricians to the tendency to more equitable interpretation of the law had the effect of modernizing or humanizing existing rules, making *aequitas*, in the sense of fairness, a dominant principle, just as it was their successors, the Christian theologians and the philosophers of the later Empire, who caused the lawyers to apply *aequitas* in a new sense, that of *benignitas*, with results not always admirable. But we have also to consider another influence, not a mode of thought but a way of trade, the habits and ingrained notions of the provincials who did business at Rome. The effect however of these imported notions proves to be less than might have been expected: throughout the period the law remains essentially Roman.

The merits of Augustus will probably be debated so long as history is written, but the student of legal institutions must see in him one who honestly sought to adapt the law to the needs of the time and, by his legislation on marriage, tried, if unsuccessfully, to restore something of the nobility of ancient manners, and to maintain the purity of the Roman race (see above, vol. x, pp. 434 *sqq.*). If he began his career with ideas of enlarging the Empire, these were soon abandoned, and the whole period was more concerned with organizing the Empire than with extending it. This involved the loss of one great source of supply to the slave market, but not a smaller number of slaves. If these no longer came in the train of conquering generals they came in increasing numbers by the trade routes, from the borders of the empire. But the change affected the quality of the slaves. Rome's early wars were with kindred races, and when, in the second half of the Republic, she went farther afield, her wars were mainly with races whose culture, though different, was not inferior. Many, if not most, of the slaves acquired in these wars were of such races, and it was this fact which enabled the slave to become the important figure he was in commercial life, a thing impossible if we think of slaves in terms of North America. The slaves acquired from without the Empire were mostly of an inferior culture, who could not be utilized in the way in which the Greek slaves were[1]. Greek slaves and their like were, however, still plentiful, and their importance is shown by the fact that the law on the effect of trans-

---

[1] Tacitus (*Ann.* xiv, 44) makes C. Cassius Longinus compare the new state of things with the old: 'postquam vero nationes in familiis habemus quibus diversi ritus, externa sacra aut nulla, sunt, conluviem istam non nisi metu coercueris.' Though slaves bred freely and *vernae* were an important source of supply, this source alone would have been quite inadequate.

actions by slaves is one of the most carefully elaborated parts of the whole system, an elaboration almost entirely the work of the first two centuries of our era.

The traditional division of the law is into *ius civile*, in one sense of that term, and *ius honorarium*, the former being that part of the law which is enforced by actions asserting a legal right or obligation (*meum esse, dare oportere*, etc.), the latter consisting of the institutions protected by praetorian actions of the types mentioned in an earlier chapter[1]. The *ius gentium* is not a third element. It is a reforming influence rather than a branch of law: of its institutions some are accepted by the *ius civile*, the rest are part of the *ius honorarium*. In the new conditions the dichotomy becomes difficult. New modes of legislation appear: new institutions are created by the emperor's authority. Of these the most important is the *fideicommissum*, a disposition of property at death, free from most of the formal and substantial restrictions which affected legacies. These new institutions were not left to the ordinary courts. Questions affecting them were tried by *cognitio* (*extraordinaria*), by the Consul, an administrative officer, or by officials appointed for the purpose. In this administrative procedure the carefully framed *formula*, the reference to a *iudex privatus* for decision[2], had no place. It was an inquisition by an imperial officer and as it fitted better into the imperial scheme (for over the *iudex privatus* there was little control) it is not surprising that it was rapidly extended. These new institutions and the body of law created by new legislative agencies are here and there in the texts called *ius novum* or *extraordinarium*, and this is sometimes held to be a third body of law, neither *ius civile* nor *ius honorarium*[3]. But the Jurists still seem to follow the old lines, using the term *novum* merely to indicate that some law is newer than other[4], and the few references to *ius extraordinarium* are on this view merely stating a point of procedure. *Ius novum* is *ius civile novum*: the same law is sometimes called *leges novae*[5]. But it has been shown that though the distinction may not be clearly formulated it is real and important. Changed economic conditions had rendered archaic the narrow civil, and even the praetorian, law. The need for new law was met by new agencies. The new procedure, not bound by the *formula* and ignoring the formal differences

---

[1] Vol. ix, p. 865.   [2] See vol. ix, p. 862.

[3] On the various senses of the term *ius civile*, P. F. Girard, *Manuel*[8], p. 47, n. 3.

[4] M. Wlassak, *Kritische Studien*, pp. 51 *sqq.*

[5] *Dig.* iv, 5, 7, *pr.*

between civil and praetorian law, facilitated reform and rendered inevitable the later fusion[1]. And it is in this part of the law that will be found the beginnings of that looser conception of *aequitas* which finds so important expression in later times.

Though Hadrian was probably the first emperor openly to claim legislative power, and Justinian's Code contains no enactment before his time, the emperors had in fact been making law from the beginning, obviously in administrative matters, but hardly less so in private law. From Augustus came *fideicommissa* and the organization of *peculium castrense*, acquisitions in connection with military service, which a *filiusfamilias* held like a *paterfamilias*, the first step in legislation which by Justinian's time had revolutionized the economic position of *filiifamilias*. Many other changes were made by emperors before Hadrian, and, as having *imperium*, often consuls and always proconsuls, they had the right to sit in judgment in matters triable by *cognitio*. They did so mainly in constitutional and criminal matters, but Claudius loved to try civil suits, showing, says Suetonius, sometimes sagacity, sometimes almost insanity, and 'nec semper praescripta legum secutus[2].' If this had been habitual it might have much affected the law, but it was not till late in the second century, when the emperors had unquestioned right to legislate as they would, that their judgments became an important factor.

II. SOURCES OF THE LAW

We need consider only two senses of this expression: the influences, the facts of life, which suggest new ideas to the law, and the mechanism which makes them part of the law. Of the first sense it may be said that while it is sometimes, but rarely, possible to show the origin of an institution, it is impossible, so cosmopolitan had Rome become, so diverse were the contacts of everyday life, to catalogue the influences at work. What must be emphasized is the stubbornness with which a denationalization of law, to some extent inevitable, was resisted. The notion of *ius gentium* in the practical sense, rules applicable to *cives* and *peregrini*, had, to some extent, spent its force: the tale of *iure gentium* institutions was complete by the time of Augustus, though some of them, till much later, were protected only by the Praetor.

---

[1] S. Riccobono, *La Formazione di uno 'novum ius' nel periodo imperiale*, Atti del I° Congresso Nazionale di Studi Romani, 1928.

[2] Suetonius, *Claud*. 14–5.

In the 'philosophical' sense, rules the presumed universality of which rests on the view that they were based on *naturalis ratio*, it is similar to *ius naturale*, and it has been said that for the classical lawyers the notions were the same—the trichotomy, *civile, gentium, naturale*, being post-classical. This may be true of texts like *Dig.* 1, 2, 2, which treat *ius gentium* and *ius naturale* as two elements in the existing law, but it involves too drastic treatment of many texts. It implies also that the jurists always use the term *ius gentium* in the 'philosophical' sense, whereas the other is more common. Slavery is *iuris gentium*, and conflicts with *ius naturale*, and it is not easy to see why texts which say this should not have been written by the men whose names they bear. No juristic text assigns to *ius gentium* any rule not contemplated as part of the law, though civil law may cut down its field, as in the law of marriage[1]. But the slavery texts show a *ius naturale* which is no part of the law. One notion based on *ius naturale* and appearing at the beginning of the Empire, is that of *obligatio naturalis*, the idea that there may be duties not such as law will directly enforce, but such nevertheless as to need indirect recognition, as by refusal to allow recovery where such an obligation has been fulfilled, even in error. The first cases, perhaps the only cases in classical law, were of transactions of slaves and obligations between members of the same family, between whom there could be no legal process, but the notion was destined to much wider application in later law.

That remarkable phenomenon of later law, the persistence of local law, in practice, in regions the inhabitants of which were Roman *cives* and, in theory, 'lived Roman law' was vividly shown from the documents by Mitteis[2], and the other aspect of the same phenomenon, infiltration into Roman law of ideas from alien systems, forms an important part of the history of later law. It is essentially an Eastern influence: only hellenized regions had a culture which could effectively resist the Roman[3]. But the great extension of *civitas* comes at the end of the classical age of law and the topic has little importance for this chapter. Not till late in the third century is the pressure insistent: not till the fourth has it any success. For the earlier centuries of the Empire, such evidence as exists, for Europe, suggests, not a tendency for Romans to adopt foreign law, but for *peregrini* to apply Roman law. We find them transferring property by *mancipatio*, from which they were excluded, and even for provincial land to which it did not apply[4].

---

[1] See also *Dig.* 1, 1, 6, *pr.*   [2] *Reichsrecht und Volksrecht.*
[3] Mitteis, *op. cit.* pp. 8, 85.   [4] Bruns, *Fontes*[7], 1, pp. 329 *sqq.*

In Egypt the more plentiful evidence suggests that at least for civil law transactions the Romans observed Roman forms. Even in *iure gentium* transactions, *e.g.* Sale, there is little sign of difference due to local conditions[1]. No doubt differences did occur, here and there: they have no real bearing on the evolution of the Roman law.

Passing to the mechanism of legislation we must note that the old sources survive, but with diminished importance. '*Mos*,' '*consuetudo*,' '*diuturnus usus*' often appears as a source of law, but, local customs apart, this means only the unwritten *ius civile*, the traditional common law. It raises a question on which Justinian preserves apparently contradictory texts: could a contrary custom or long disuse repeal a statute? We are told that just as popular consent created a *lex*, so tacit consent could repeal it, but also that no custom was good against a *lex*[2]. When we remember that the talk in juristic texts about tacit consent comes from a time when the People had long ceased to be concerned in legislation, the most likely view seems to be that it is only recognition of the fact that some *leges* had passed into disuse and that no one would have thought of applying the idea to imperial enactments, though these are sometimes called *leges*.

Leges and *plebiscita* had never been important sources of private law. Of the hundreds of recorded *leges*, not more than 40 were of importance in everyday life. The powers of the Assembly (by this time always the Tribual Assembly) were not those of a Parliament on the British model. Apart from the indeterminate control of the Senate, the possible veto of a magistrate and the luck or trickery of the auspices, so far as those applied, there was no initiative in the body. It voted only on what was submitted by the president—there were no private member's bills—and without alteration—there were no amendments. Under Augustus no real meeting of the Assembly was possible: a full Assembly would have depopulated Italy.[3] It had now no real control of the choice of the magistrate to preside, and it is surprising to find in it such a power of resistance to the legislation on marriage, finally forced on it by Augustus. The use of the sur-

---

[1] Mitteis und Wilcken, *Grundzüge und Chrestomathie der Papyruskunde*, II, Juristischer Teil, Einleitung, pp. xvi *sqq.* See, however, for a somewhat different view, R. Taubenschlag, *Studi Bonfante*, I, pp. 377 *sqq.*

[2] *Dig.* I, 3, 32, 1; *Cod. Just.* VIII, 52, 2.

[3] This is not to say that the Tribual Assembly might not, by manipulation, have been made into a reasonable representative of the Roman People, if Augustus had so desired. See vol. IX, p. 8 *sq.*

viving reverence for ancient institutions was a convenient piece of window-dressing, but this simulacrum of a popular assembly could not endure. For a short consolidating period it was useful to the emperor, but, that ended, no one wanted it. There are few enactments of the Assembly after Augustus: none is certainly later than the first century. But some, especially those of Augustus, left a deep mark on the law, notably the legislation on marriage, the *leges Iuliae iudiciariae*, which revolutionized procedure, and the laws on manumission of slaves[1].

The Edicts of the magistrates continued, but the great age of praetorian activity was over. Augustus made indeed little nominal change. Praetors were appointed till the end of the classical age. The Urban Praetor still controlled ordinary litigation. His Edict still appeared annually, and, for a century and a half, he retained, nominally, the power of making changes in it. And changes there were. Some transactions, *e.g.* deposit, became protected only under the Empire by actions with civil *formulae*, and this must have been in form the work of the Praetor. There are changes in the Edict which are due to C. Cassius Longinus. Though, in some cases, he may be only the jurist who suggested the change, the point is indifferent, for it took effect in the Edict. No one, however, is more likely than he to have been able to make changes. A member of a great Republican family hostile to Caesar, but himself a supporter of the new régime, a *rallié*, he had great lawyers in his ancestry and was himself probably the greatest lawyer of his time. He had a great public career and held the Praetorship before it had lost its ancient dignity—he was consul in A.D. 30. But changes were few and the fact that the Edict was used in the first century as a means of effecting changes desired by the Senate, itself, in such matters, little more than a mouthpiece of the emperor, suggests that the Praetor would make no changes that were not certain to be approved by him.

We know that the Edict of the *Praetor peregrinus* still existed, and was needed, since the new conditions did not lessen the flow of peregrines to Rome, but we know no more. The ascendancy of *ius gentium* meant that so far as commercial law was concerned the two Edicts would be much alike, but the peregrine Edict must have contained special rules on procedure, and if it contained rules on succession they were not those of the Urban Edict. Caracalla's grant of *civitas* to '*in orbe Romano qui sunt*,' whatever its exact scope, must have made this Edict unimportant, and the last trace of a *Praetor peregrinus* is little later.

[1] See also vol. x, pp. 429 *sqq.*

A Provincial Edict or Provincial edicts existed, but such borrowings of foreign law as appear are probably not due to infiltration from this document. Apart from administrative matters, especially procedure, this Edict seems only to have extended to the provinces the protection which the Praetorian Edicts, of no force in the provinces, gave to those within the jurisdiction of the Praetors. Such borrowing as there was was through provincial practice, local law left in force, but not embodied in the Edict.

The end of the Edict as a Source of law came when Hadrian, late in his reign, further consolidated imperial power by calling on Julian to put it into permanent form. Nothing shows that Julian did this as Praetor: more probably it was while he was ' *Quaestor principis*' and received double pay *propter insignem doctrinam*. The completed work was confirmed by senatusconsult, and Justinian says in the Latin *constitutio* '*Tanta*' confirming the Digest[1] that according to Hadrian further necessary changes would be made by '*nova auctoritas*,' *i.e.* the emperor. The Greek version[2] seems to allow the magistrates to make necessary changes, but '*Tanta*' is the original and appears in the Code, and no later change in the Edict has been proved.

Julian, whose work is treated as of great importance—he is '*ordinator*,' '*conditor*' of the Edict—re-arranged the *formulae*, dropped obsolete rules, added at least one new clause and no doubt amended others. But the great change was that the Edict was now permanent and the name *Edictum Perpetuum* acquired a new meaning, though its common use in this new sense seems to be later. The change was no fusion of civil and Praetorian law. The Praetor still issued his Edict, though he could make no change. Praetorian rights had still their specially formulated remedies. With the Romans, as with us, procedure profoundly affected legal thinking, and it was not till the *formula* disappeared that real fusion began.

III. THE SENATE AND THE EMPEROR

Of the ways in which the Senate had formerly influenced legislation that which concerns us is its practice of issuing instructions to magistrates: it was from this that its power of legislation proceeded. It does not seem that any further power was ever expressly granted, and the doubt expressed as to the basis of its power[3] is evidence that no definite authorization

[1] *Cod. Just.* 1, 17, 2, 18.   [2] Δέδωκεν, 18.
[3] Gaius, 1, 4; cf. *Dig.* 1, 3, 9 'non ambigitur.'

existed. The earlier *senatus consulta* of the Empire are instructions
to magistrates and there is definite movement from language of
request to that of command. It may be not till Hadrian's time
that the Senate directly lays down private law, for though some
earlier *senatus consulta* seem to do this, they can all be otherwise
explained.

Senatus consulta were, for a time, enacted side by side with *leges
latae*: apparently the more fundamental reforms were made by the
latter. When we note that *senatus consulta* seem not directly to have
affected private law till the emperor was asserting power of
legislation, that he practically controlled the membership of the
Senate, that it could vote only what the president submitted,
and that in the first century the emperor commonly presided, it
becomes clear that the Senate was only in form the legislative
authority, but was used, like other old institutions, to mask, and
assist, the concentration of power in the hands of the emperor.
Many *senatus consulta* bear, unofficially, the names of magistrates
in office when they were enacted, but none is ever said to have
been passed by the authority (*auctore*) of anyone but the emperor.
There is also the significant fact that the jurists in the second
century often cite as the authority, not the *senatus consultum*, but
the *oratio principis* in which the proposal was submitted to the
Senate. A piece of legislation is not framed in a moment: it needs
deliberation. The Senate was a consultative body to which matters
of importance, including projects of legislation, were submitted,
but it had now little to do with the preliminary discussions. The
emperors, from Augustus onwards, worked with a *consilium*[1], at
first informal, but fully organized by Hadrian: it was with the help
of this body that proposals were framed. And though, at first, it
may have consisted solely of senators, it soon began to contain
others, chosen by the emperor. Claudius tried to interest the
Senate in such matters[2]; but rarely, and probably never in the
second century, did the Senate criticize the projects or resist, as
the Assembly did, distasteful legislation. When the Edict had
been made permanent, the Assembly had ceased to act, and the
emperor had assumed full legislative power, there was no longer
need of the Senate as a cover, and by the end of the second
century the ignominious history of the Senate as a legislative body
was at an end.

[1] On the relation of this *consilium* to the Council of State for political
business, Mommsen, *Staatsrecht*, II[3], p. 992.

[2] *B.G.U.* 611. See J. Stroux, *Sitzungsber. d. Bay. Ak. d. Wiss.* 1929, VIII,
pp. 70 *sqq.*

As we have seen, the emperors from Augustus onwards made what were in effect laws[1], and Gaius does not scruple to cite *constitutiones* of the first century as valid laws. It is not, however, till late in the second century that imperial enactments become numerous. It is easy to overestimate the importance of the *constitutiones* of this age. Nearly all those preserved are rescripts, answers to enquiries by officials or private persons, issued through one or other of the official bureaux, settling doubts submitted. Mostly, these say nothing new: they are explanation, rather than legislation, though there is a large residue of cases in which the emperor either tacitly changed the law or took the opportunity to lay down a new rule. To some extent, though the hand is that of the emperor, the voice is that of the *consilium*, but the character of the emperor told: there is a marked difference between the innovating activity of Pius and the caution of his successor[2]. Edicts of the emperor affecting private law are few, though some, *e.g.*, that of A.D. 212, extending *civitas* to the whole Empire, had very important effects on it. Edicts raise an interesting question. Issued by virtue of proconsular *imperium* they applied to all provinces, as the *imperium* did, but, on principle, they should expire with the *imperium*, *e.g.* by death of the emperor. There is no reason to think they did so after the emperor claimed full legislative power, but for the earlier period the evidence is conflicting[3].

The principle of our law, under which a decision is binding in later cases raising the same point, had no place in Roman law: it was impossible under the *formula*, the *iudex* being an untrained private citizen. But, since the emperor could make law as he liked, he could do so by decisions, and in the second century these *decreta* appear as sources of law. But where they (or rescripts) say what is inconsistent with existing law, there is often doubt whether they were meant to do so. They may have been errors: they may have been favours, not for general application. As to rescripts, it is possible that only those intended to make law were promulgated, posted up (*proposita*[4]), the others being simply

---

[1] The Cyrene inscriptions (A. von Premerstein, *Zeitschr. d. Sav.-Stift. Rom. Abt.* XLVIII, 1928, pp. 419 *sqq.*; J. Stroux-L. Wenger, *Abh. d. Bay. Ak. d. Wiss.* XXXIV, 2, 1928) have little bearing on private law but they show Augustus legislating freely. See also the Διάταγμα on violation of sepulture in Palestine, F. de Zulueta, *J.R.S.* XXII, 1932, pp. 184 *sqq.*

[2] E. Cuq, *Conseil des Empereurs*, Partie I, chap. v.

[3] P. Krüger, *Gesch. d. Quell.*[2], pp. 113 *sqq.*; for the view that they were always permanent, L. Wenger, *Abh. d. Bay. Ak. d. Wiss.* 1928, Abh. 2, p. 70.　　　　[4] Girard, *Textes*[5], p. 206.

communicated to the applicants. But there were real difficulties met by much legislation in later times.

Rescripta and *Decreta* are important only late in this age, and the emperor is always acting with his *consilium*. Hadrian's re-organization of this body, with its importation of the leading lawyers of the time, made it more effective for these purposes, and gave some guarantee of consistency: no one could have made precedents of the decisions of Claudius. But the Rescript, the *Decretum*, was in a real sense the act of the emperor. Justinian preserves rescripts and decrees which show that the emperor did not think himself bound by the opinion of his advisers: his decision is sometimes against the advice of the lawyers, and some decisions, especially in the law of Wills, savour of cadi justice. They may have been fair in the circumstances, but, though they appear in Justinian's compilations, it is hard to see how some of them could be used as precedents: they are in direct conflict with principles elsewhere laid down in the same compilations.

Though most imperial enactments of this age are on detail, some are important. *Longi temporis praescriptio*, in practice a great extension of the law of acquisition by long possession, was established as a definite system by a rescript addressed to a woman who was not a *civis*. The few Edicts affecting private law deal with important matters. The most far-reaching in its effects was that of Caracalla, giving *civitas* to everyone, but that is not very significant: the emperors seem always to have had the right of giving *civitas* to persons or to communities, and Edicts of this kind, though less wide, are found from Claudius onwards[1].

Thus the most important legislation of this age is nominally the work of the Assembly or the Senate, though it ends with the emperor in possession of full, and sole, legislative power. But legislation is not everything: the main progress was made, not by express legislation, but by the interpretation of the Jurists.

IV. THE JURISTS

The Republican jurist had no official position, and the founding of the Empire made, of itself, no change. The increased literary output only continues the scientific study of the law begun by Quintus Mucius and Servius Sulpicius, stimulated by increased commerce and resulting complexity in Roman life. Augustus, 'ut maior iuris auctoritas haberetur' says Pomponius, meaning, no

[1] Suetonius, *de Gramm.* 22, quotes as addressed to Tiberius the words 'tu enim, Caesar, civitatem dare potes hominibus, verbo non potes.'

doubt, in order to attach to his name an influence he could not control, declared that he would give to certain jurists the right to give sealed *responsa* 'ex auctoritate eius.' Gaius tells us that Hadrian made opinions so given binding on the *iudex*, if unanimous. What this *ius respondendi* really meant is a much discussed question, rendered all the more obscure by the facts that the privilege is recorded of only two Jurists, nearly three hundred years apart, the first under Tiberius, though it was probably held by all jurists in the *consilium* from Hadrian onwards, and that *responsa* (which could still be given by non-privileged Jurists) are rarely mentioned in surviving juristic texts independent of Justinian. Of the diverse views, the most probable is that Augustus gave only honorific distinction, tending to become *de facto* authority with lay judges, and that Hadrian first gave such *responsa* binding force, if unanimous, but only for the case in which they were given. They could be cited in later cases, but so could any opinion: only when there were no more great Jurists did their writings, as such, acquire authority.

Law, in the Republic, was an aristocratic profession; not only did most of the great lawyers hold high office, they came of great houses. Alfenus, said to have been a cobbler, consul in 39 B.C., is an exception. In the Empire there is a change. Law still attracts intellect, perhaps more than ever, for the orator is not what he was and law is almost the only career not dependent on the emperor's will. 'The King can make a belted Knight' but he cannot make a great lawyer. Few great Jurists of the first century are of the great houses: a growing proportion are provincials, and of most of them we know little but their works and their careers. Many held the consulate and other Republican posts, less important than they had been, but few held the new and increasingly important Imperial posts. With Hadrian came a change, perhaps to be associated with his handling of the *ius respondendi*. Jurists fill the *consilium* and begin freely to hold Imperial posts. Julian was deep in the confidence of Hadrian. Papinian, Paul and Ulpian, somewhat later, were all Praetorian Prefects. The provincial origin of the jurists becomes noticeable: of these four, the greatest lawyers of their times, Julian was from Hadrumetum[1], Papinian, it may be, from Emesa, Ulpian a Syrian, and Paul's origin is unknown. Able men found their way to Rome and were welcome: it would be surprising if the dwindling stock of the old houses had been much represented.

It might have been expected that such men, of Hellenistic

[1] See, however, E. Kornemann, in *Klio*, vi, 1906, p. 182.

origin and exercising great influence, would have remodelled the
law on Hellenistic lines. Nothing of the sort happened. Importations there were. Forms were relaxed and there was a
tendency, of Greek origin, to set down transactions in writing,
and, possibly, though this may be later, to let the record of a
formal transaction stand for the form itself. But, in the main, the
law was still Roman: it is inadmissible to speak as yet of denationalization of the law. The stimulus given by rhetoricians to
rational interpretation only hastened what was already under
way, and the recognition of intent as against form, and of the
need for real assent in voluntary transactions, would have found
full expression in the law though no Roman soldier had ever
crossed the Adriatic or the Mediterranean. It was not a provincial, but a Roman of the old stock, who said about the end of the
first century: 'ius est ars boni et aequi[1].' For him, law was an art as
well as a science. He did not mean that law was always equitable,
but that it was for the lawyer to do what in him lay to make it so.
The view that the great Jurists were formalists, rigidly adhering
to ancient principle, a view few admit, but many seem to hold, is an
error. Pedants, no doubt, there were, and everyone is a pedant sometimes, but these men made the law of a primitive agricultural society
fit for a commercialized community without sacrificing anything
of value. Much of their work consisted in advice to officials, and
there is little doubt that many of what appear as civil rights in the
Digest, and, from the difficulty of reconciling them with strict
civil principle, have been called Byzantine, originated as praetorian rights, suggested by the Jurists. The suppression of the
formula made the distinction meaningless and the stigmata of
praetorian origin have disappeared[2].

The stiff resistance to infiltration is, in the circumstances, a fact
to be explained. Pride in the national heritage, recognition of the
fact that the law was better than those with which it came into
contact are enough to explain the wish, but not its fulfilment.
What gave Roman law its strength was what saved the Common
Law when the Roman law bid fair to conquer the world. It had
long been taught. 'Taught law is tough law' said Maitland.
Everywhere young lawyers learn from their elders, but in Rome,
as with us, the teaching of budding lawyers was an important part
of the system. Even in the Republic we often hear of a lawyer as
studying under another. Servius, probably the greatest Re-

[1] *Dig.* 1, i, *pr.*

[2] S. Riccobono, *Arch. für Rechts- und Wirtschaftsphilosophie*, XVI, pp.
503 *sqq.*; *Mél. Cornil*, II, pp. 237 *sqq.*

publican lawyer, was a great teacher and we are told that he learnt the rudiments from one lawyer but was '*maxime instructus*' by another. This was probably unsystematic, but early in the first century we find teaching organizations, modelled, it seems, on schools of philosophy, each with a succession of Heads, always great lawyers. What part these notable and busy men took in the teaching is not clear. Elementary work was no doubt left to humbler professors, but we cannot doubt that the great men took a real part in the instruction. They may have lectured; Tiberius Coruncanius, the first plebeian *pontifex maximus*, had given public instruction[1], but their main part was probably giving consultations in the presence of students at the *stationes docendi* and sharing in the discussion of knotty points[2]. It was the continuous succession of trained men which gave the law that solidity and consistency which enabled it to resist the doctrines of rival systems without these qualities.

We hear in the texts of two rival schools, not only schools in a technical sense, but also *sectae*, adherents to particular bodies of doctrine. Beginning in rivalry between Labeo and Capito under Augustus, they later became definite schools bearing the names Proculian[3] and Sabinian (or Cassian) after famous leaders[4]. They cannot be traced as definite schools after Hadrian, for though Gaius calls himself a Sabinian and speaks of '*praeceptores nostri*' this implies adherence to doctrines, but not continuance of definite organizations. Many of the disputes are recorded and much effort has been devoted to the discovery of any difference of principle. It is tempting to think of one as representing literal interpretation, *verba* against *voluntas*, the other as adopting equitable interpretation. But, in fact, most of the disputes have little obvious significance. A few rest on difference of philosophical position (p. 821). While there is no agreement, most historians regard the Sabinians as the more conservative, and, as Sabinian doctrine was dominant in later times, this opinion, so far as it is justified, confirms the view that legal development was essentially from within. Though the schools apparently ended under Hadrian, their respective doc-

---

[1] *Dig.* 1, 2, 2, 35, 38.

[2] Gellius, *N.A.* XIII, 13, 1; Pomponius says (*Dig.* 1, 2, 2, 47) that Labeo 'totum annum ita diviserat ut Romae sex mensibus cum studiosis esset, sex mensibus secederet et conscribendis libris operam daret.'

[3]. For the statement, found here and there, that this school was sometimes called Pegasian there seems to be no authority in the sources.

[4] For the Heads and their order of succession see H. F. Jolowicz, *Hist. Introd. to Roman Law*, pp. 384 *sqq.*

trines were still maintained, and the disputes are not completely adjusted even by Justinian.

Disputes did not begin with Labeo or end with Justinian. Q. Mucius Scaevola, and a little later, Servius, the greatest lawyers of their time, did not always agree. Servius seems indeed to have written a book in criticism of Quintus Mucius[1]. It has been maintained that Mucius takes the rigid view, as he certainly did in the case of Curius[2], and Servius the equitable, this difference being represented by followers throughout the classical age. There is some evidence for this view.

The lawyers influenced their own time by their advice to consultants, official and private, and by their manipulation of the law as officials, but their influence on later Rome and the later world is due to their writings, of which, in mutilated form, a great mass survives. There were general treatises and monographs in the Republic, but there was a much larger output in the Empire, and the great treatises which form the backbone of Justinian's Digest were written after the Edict had been stabilized. The works are of many types, but, a few elementary books apart, they are all casuistic in form. They discuss the law, with much illustration from facts, in an order, or orders, due to historical causes, but looking, to modern eyes, not much more rational than the alphabetical arrangement which was thought adequate in our law till modern times. None of them states the law as a system based on assignable fundamental principles. Even the intelligible, if not wholly logical, arrangement under Persons, Things and Actions, first found in Gaius but certainly older, is not adopted by the great masters. They theorize little: any text which has a generalizing discussion is apt to be suspected of interpolation. They reason from case to case with an eye to modifications called for by the needs of the time. Indeed some modern critics seem to hold that they were acute reasoners but no more, so that most of the relaxations from strict principle, making for justice, which we find in the Digest are due not to them but to their successors. On this it must suffice to express the opinion that the Jurists are far more worthy of our admiration than they would be if this were true.

The question has been much discussed how far the doctrines of the lawyers are affected by their philosophical views. It has been said that they were, as a body, of high philosophical attainments. What is left of their work does not justify this view. Signs of philosophical conceptions there are, but not such as to suggest

[1] Gellius, *N.A.* IV, I, 20.
[2] See vol. IX, p. 870.

that these matters were in the forefront of the lawyers' minds or to require more than that modicum of philosophy which, through rhetoric, was part of the equipment of all educated Romans. We have noted the impetus given by rhetoric to the revolt of ἐπιείκεια against *strictum ius*. Alfenus quotes 'the philosophers' on the identity of a body notwithstanding change in the atoms which compose it[1], but we may doubt whether the cobbler of Cremona was deeply versed in philosophy. The influence of philosophy is clear in the discussions of the effect on ownership of change of form. If I make a box of your wood, is it yours or mine? Is the εἶδος or the ὕλη to prevail?[2] For Proculus and his followers the form was the essence and the thing went to the maker. For Sabinus and Cassius the material was the essence and ownership was unchanged[3]. Nothing suggests profound study: the illustrations are the common school illustrations. Here, as in the cognate question of the effect of joinder of elements belonging to different owners ('*accessio*'), the Romans fell back on philosophy, as Bracton fell back on Roman Law, because there was nothing in native sources on the unimportant topic. Philosophy influenced the discussion of '*corpus*' and '*animus*' in possession, of impossibility, of reality of consent, of degrees of liability in contract and of the different kinds of *corpora*. Similar things have been pointed out on the ethical side, but what can be read into a text is not necessarily there: a man may be of stout heart and sound morals without having studied the doctrines of the Stoa. It seems hardly credible, if the Jurists were of high philosophical culture, that none of them should have felt the urge to express the law in a more philosophical form[4].

It was formerly held that what the Digest said, apart from a few Byzantine accretions, the Jurists had said, that this was a coherent body of doctrine and that the individuality of the Jurists was immaterial. It is now clear, apart from the question of interpolation, that the law was, as it must have been, continually changing, and that the Jurists not only have marked personal characteristics, but represent different stages of legal development. Ulpian's outlook under Caracalla is not that of Labeo under Augustus. Fortunately for legal historians, but inconveniently for his practitioners, Justinian's compilers were not critical, and admitted representa-

---

[1] *Dig.* v, 1, 76.

[2] P. von Sokolowski, *Philosophie im Privatrecht*, i, pp. 69 *sqq.*, sees here the conflict between Peripatetic and Stoic conceptions.

[3] Gaius, ii, 79.

[4] Cicero saw the need, Gellius, *N.A.* i, 22, 7. So did Bacon.

tives of all these stages, though giving most prominence to the later men. Of the great names of this period a few need mention.

M. Antistius Labeo, a staunch Republican, of sardonic humour, of which many tales are told[1], was a liberal in law, who maintained the spirit against the letter, consistently enough with his opposition to the changes of Augustus, who maintained the letter of the Constitution but not the spirit. His example led to the recognition of Codicils, but no great new principle is traceable to him, though his conflicts with the courtier, Capito, led to the foundation of the Schools already mentioned. Of so early a writer, little is directly quoted by Justinian, but he is more often cited by others than is any other first-century writer. His seems to be the earliest extensive commentary on the Edict[2].

Masurius Sabinus (after whom, but rather late, the followers of the school originating with Capito came to be known as Sabinians), a man of unknown origin, who held no office and had, it is said, no income but his fees, is the only classical jurist known to have had the *ius respondendi*. He is not directly quoted in the Digest, but often cited by later writers, even by leaders of the other school. His chief work, a small book on the *ius civile*, acquired great authority, so that works by Pomponius, Paul and Ulpian, which are in fact general treatises on the civil law, are entitled 'ad Sabinum.' It seems that his reputation grew. Aulus Gellius, nearly a century after his death, often cites him, and the first of the three commentaries mentioned is of about the same date: it seems to be about then that 'Sabinian' supplants 'Cassian' as the name of the School. Perhaps the conservative tendency attributed to the School as a whole may be more fairly assigned to Sabinus himself.

C. Cassius Longinus, whose origin and work have been already mentioned, a favourite in imperial circles, seems to be one of the earliest jurists to hold both the consulate and Imperial posts. It is to his credit that Nero suspected him, but he saved his neck, and, recalled from exile, died peacefully under Vespasian. The Digest contains no direct extracts, but many citations. Though, to judge

---

[1] H. J. Roby, *Introd. to Digest*, p. cxxv. Gellius, *N.A.* XIII, 12, says that when the tribunes sent a messenger to summon him to them he told him to tell his masters that they could seize him, but not summon him. Kipp observes (*Gesch. d. Quell.*[4], p. 115) that this marks him as a doctrinaire, a judgment which seems to lack humour.

[2] Servius had written a short work (*brevissimum*) on it. Ofilius had also dealt with it in some way, *Dig.* 1, 2, 2, 44.

from Tacitus[1], a severe man, he was a liberal reformer in law, responsible for many innovations. He dispensed, in his Edict, with the *exceptio metus*, a defence on the ground of duress, holding that the *exceptio doli*[2] would cover this[3], a wide conception of *dolus* not accepted by successors. His chief work, on *ius civile*, was annotated by Javolenus, but never equalled that of Sabinus in authority.

Proculus, whose full name is unknown, was important enough to give a name to the Proculian School, but the use made of him in the Digest is less than might have been expected, though two texts of his on Partnership and Sale[4] are interesting. Both transactions give *bonae fidei iudicia*, and these texts show that the words of the *formula*, to the effect that the defendant must pay whatever ought in good faith to be paid, meant in the later part of the first century, not only that he must not be fraudulent, but that he must do what a fairminded man would do in the circumstances. The genuineness of the second text, and the existence of the principle in classical law, are disputed, as it seems without reason.

Salvius Julianus (L. Octavius Cornelius Salvius Julianus Aemilianus), from Africa, but clearly of good family, the last and greatest Head of the Sabinians, was probably the greatest of all the Jurists. In the list of jurists prefixed to the Digest, the roughly chronological order is broken so as to give primacy to him and Papinian. His revision of the Edict is only a small part of his achievement. Justinian preserves much of his chief work, *Digesta*, essentially a treatise on the whole law. The work of his follower Africanus is mainly an account of his *Responsa*. Thus, so much is left that, allowing for interpolations, we get a picture of the law as it was in the middle of the second century. It is often difficult to say what a jurist is merely recording and what he is himself settling: we can better judge his effect on the law from later citations of him, and we can see by the frequent references to him by Paul and Ulpian how many points were settled by his opinion. What has been said of Papinian is more true of Julian, that his greatness united all schools. Disputes remain, but there is no later head of either school. No other lawyer left so great a mark on the law. He gives the impression of a clear-minded and equable man. The fact that he never cites his senior rival Celsus has suggested that there was personal feeling, but he cites rarely and no such inference is just. The Sabinian ascendancy in later law is mainly due to him.

[1] *Ann.* XIII, 48; XIV, 42 *sq.*   [2] See vol. IX, p. 851.
[3] *Dig.* XLIV, 4, 4, 33.   [4] *Dig.* XVII, 2, 76–80; XVIII, 1, 68, *pr.*

Gaius (no more is known of his name), a professed Sabinian, later than Julian, though unimportant in himself, plays a great part in legal history. Probably no answer can be given to the question whether he was a provincial or an Italian. Apparently an undistinguished teacher, of the middle of the second century, he is nowhere cited or mentioned till he appears in the famous 'Law of Citations'[1] as one of the five who may be cited in Court, and is so mentioned as to suggest that he had not, while the others had, the *ius respondendi*. The explanation is that he wrote a lucid elementary manual which found favour, of which recently discovered fragments testify to the wide dissemination. When the later men became incapable of handling the great treatises, elementary books grew in importance, and this book, with others of the same type, mostly abridged, sufficed for them. The book seems to be based on an earlier work: the famous classification into Persons, Things and Actions is not his. It may be added that it has had much more effect on modern arrangements of the law than it ever had among the Romans. Justinian preserves passages from several of his works, including his commentary on the provincial Edict from which we get most of what we know of that mysterious document. Accident had not done with Gaius. Apart from a very bad late abridgment his book was lost from Roman times till about a century ago, when it was found as the under writing of a palimpsest. Some parts are indecipherable, but most of it has been read and it has greatly added to our knowledge of principle. In particular, it has made clear, for the first time, the working of the formulary procedure. Further fragments recently discovered have added greatly to our knowledge of the *legis actio*.[2]

Aemilius Papinianus, most of whose work seems to have been done under Severus and Caracalla, was murdered by the latter's orders, apparently for refusing to applaud the murder of Geta. He was the first lawyer to be Praetorian Prefect, now an office of greater administrative than military importance, and in that capacity had Paul and Ulpian as assessors. Traditionally he disputes with Julian the claim to be the greatest jurist: in the fifth century he held the palm. The Law of Citations, which declared what authors might be cited, and defined their authority, directed *iudices* to follow the majority, and, in case of equality, Papinian, 'qui ut singulos vincit, ita cedit duobus,' and adopted a rule of a century

---

[1] *Cod. Theod.* I, 4, 3; A.D. 426.

[2] *P.S.I.* 1182. Edited by V. Arangio Ruiz, *Frammenti di Gaio*; E. Levy, in *Zeitschr. d. Sav.-Stift. Rom. Abt.* LIV, 1934, pp. 258 *sqq.*; F. de Zulueta in *J.R.S.* XXIV, 1934, pp. 168 *sqq.*, XXV, 1935, pp. 19 *sqq.*; P. Collinet, *Rev. Hist. de Droit*, 1934, pp. 96 *sqq.*

earlier excluding certain notes of Paul and Ulpian on Papinian. It is strange that men capable of such absurd legislation should have appreciated Papinian. Justinian so far followed this estimate as to continue the special prominence given to Papinian in the scheme of legal education. He often adopts suggestions of Papinian: in one case he notes that Papinian cites in support 'sublimissimum testem Salvium Iulianum[1].' Papinian's main works, *Opiniones* and *Responsa*, are notable for precision, close reasoning and sense of Equity. He is a little more given to generalization than his contemporaries are. He wrote no general treatise and thus had less effect on his successors than might have been expected. Ulpian cites him freely, but much less than he does the earlier Julian. Paul, who cites Julian freely, hardly ever mentions Papinian, notwithstanding their close relations, and, though he annotates Papinian's *Responsa*, this seems to be mainly with a view to correction. Papinian's reputation endured. A thousand years later, Cujas, the greatest lawyer of his age, makes Papinian the greatest lawyer of any age.

Julius Paulus, of unknown origin, junior to Papinian, but, it seems, senior to Ulpian, whom, however, he outlived, was also Praetorian Prefect, perhaps with Ulpian. About a sixth of Justinian's Digest is from him: only Ulpian provides more, and of him there is nearly twice as much. Though we have much of Paul's work he is something of an enigma: every possible judgment of his merits, as lawyer and as writer, may be found in current literature. He is given to abstract reasoning, so that it has been said that he is 'here and there' primarily philosopher, only secondarily jurist[2], but the texts are better evidence of mental habit than of training. Much of his work is critical, sometimes captious. His mind seems acute rather than constructive, but this may be due to the fact that, in the Digest, his work is usually treated as supplementary to Ulpian. The only important topic on which his views have primacy is Possession, and the emphasis on the mental element in the possession which the law protects, *animus sibi habendi*, which appears in the Digest, and has influenced law ever since, may well be due to him. He may also have had much to do with the disentangling of the notion of '*culpa*' in contract, the rule that one who benefits is liable for negligence, from those of '*custodia*' and '*bona fides*' with which it had been involved. Of Paul there survives, in mutilated form, but independent of Justinian, a work, the *Sententiae*, of which something will be said later.

Domitius Ulpianus, of Syria, had a career similar to that of

---

[1] *Cod. Just.* IV, 5, 10, I.   [2] von Sokolowski, *op. cit.* I, p. 13.

Paul, but cut short when, in A.D. 228, he was murdered by his own Praetorians. Like Paul, he annotated Papinian's *Responsa*, but, in general, he is less given to criticism. His work, even more than Paul's, is largely compilation, setting forth the creative work of two centuries. Unlike Julian and Papinian, he quotes freely: every important earlier jurist appears. Sometimes he seems to have been giving a history of doctrine, though the Digest obscures this by the piecemeal form of the texts. But there is more than compilation. Earlier writers presented a vast mass of conflicts. In the Vatican Fragments, a practitioner's commonplace book, much is from Ulpian. We see him citing opinions and adopting one, with or without modification: if the passage appears also in the Digest, we get usually only the final solution. He was not himself a great forwarder of the law. We learn more from him than from any other, but that is because we have so much of him, owing not to his merits, but to his being the latest and most encyclopaedic of the great jurists. Of him too, or purporting to be of him, we have part of a book independent of Justinian, the *liber singularis regularum*.

The great achievement of Paul and Ulpian was that they garnered for us the results of legal evolution in the classical age. They seem to have been preparing for the débâcle which was soon to come. For, with them, the great line ended. There are later names, but they are not important. Marcian contributed new ideas which affected later law, notably the conception of servitudes as of two classes, personal and praedial, but his notions do not suggest a very clear mind, and, for this reason, but without justification, they are sometimes said to be later interpolations. These later men show the tendency to schematization and definition which is a sign of the end of the creative age and was to become an obsession with their Byzantine successors. The question why the line ended then has as many answers as have been given to the question why the Roman Empire decayed. It does not seem necessary to go beyond the social and political conditions. The Pax Romana was over. Increasing poverty, unrest, civil war, threat of invasion—these do not make for scientific evolution of law. Add to this the supersession of the old procedure by an administrative process the manipulators of which had, under strong emperors, no independence and, under weak emperors, no responsibility, and we can see that law is not likely to be well administered, except under the rare combination—an emperor both powerful and just. It was natural that able men should turn to other fields than law.

V. THE PRIVATE LAW

A general account of the movement of law between Augustus and Alexander ought, it seems, to be a simple matter, as Justinian preserves much juristic literature and much legislation of the 'classical' age, and we have works purporting to be of that age, untouched by him. It is however very difficult. So many institutions were obsolete, so many distinctions obliterated, and the new surroundings were so different, that the texts could not be made available to sixth-century practitioners without drastic changes, omissions and additions. These alterations have gained the name of 'interpolations' and much of the work of the last fifty years has been devoted to the study of them. Controversy still rages. On one hand are those who hold that the Digest expresses an Oriental system, set out in a classical framework. For these not only is every text under suspicion, as, in a sense, it must be, for the compilers were told to bring the work up to date, but the suspicion is apt to become rejection on what, to others, seem inadequate grounds. Many of the alterations are held to be due, not to the compilers, who could not have done so much in the time, but to Oriental glosses, mainly from Berytus. But there is another, and, as it seems, better view, that though there are many interpolations and glosses, Justinian's aim was essentially conservative, to keep what could be kept of classical doctrine. In fact he kept too much, for there is much obsolete matter in the Digest, a fact explained in part by hasty work, in part by reverence for the old masters. On this view the evolution was from within, affected indeed by the surroundings, especially by Christianity, but offering a resistance, steady, though not always successful, to orientalization. On this view, much that is called Byzantine is Western, sometimes post-classical, but often late classical, and the Digest is more trustworthy than it is for those of the other opinion.

Some check is provided by the texts independent of Justinian, the *Institutes* of Gaius, the *Sententiae* of Paul, the *liber singularis regularum*, and so on. But the manuscripts are late and corrupt. They are nearer the source than those of most of the lay literature, but the cases are not parallel. Holders of manuscripts purporting to state the law, are apt to add marginal notes where the law has changed, and these get into the text. That temptation does not assail the holder of a manuscript of the *Aeneid*. That, however, is not the whole story. The *liber singularis regularum*, attributed to Ulpian, of which we have part, is an epitome, and it is doubtful what it epitomizes. It has been said that its original was a second edition of Gaius, and, also, that it makes no use of Gaius. Its latest editor[1] makes it an epitome of an epitome, the latter post-classical, and derived from various authors. The book appears to follow Gaius closely: it is hard to believe it the work of Ulpian, who elsewhere shows no knowledge of Gaius. It contains post-classical elements, but their extent is matter of controversy. The *Sententiae*, a collection of brief statements of law more or less in the order of the Edict, treated by Constantine as certainly Paul's, is suspect. The opinion is growing, and is consistent with Constantine's words[2], that it was not written by Paul in its present form, but is a selection from his works, put together late in the third century. It has recently been maintained that its source is not even mainly Paul. There are certainly contaminations, but their extent is disputed. Even Gaius, the earliest and most important of these works, has been much attacked. We have been told that it represents only fifth-century tradition and that it is the most heavily glossed of all the texts. It is difficult to accept this, but the manuscript is not earlier than the end of the fourth century and glosses must be expected. Recently discovered fragments in the main confirm the Veronese manuscript; but one shows that it has omissions, though these may be accidental. A valuable authority is the so-called Vatican Fragments, put together in the fourth century, containing extracts from jurists and imperial legislation. Its special value is that the extracts are not from elementary books, but from larger works, dealing with difficult points. Though it seems on the whole faithful, its date is against it. Documents are few except from Egypt, and these are unsafe guides for Roman Law. The other documents show laxity in the provinces in the use of Roman forms, a laxity not necessarily, or probably, to be found in Italy itself at this time.

In the following brief account of the law little can be said of the machinery by which the changes were effected, but it may be well to point out here that over the greater part of the law the main agency is the Praetor. It is no exaggeration to say that, in the fields of property (in a wide sense) and of obligations, the classical age saw the supersession of civil law notions by those of the *ius honorarium*.

The period begins with additional complication in the law of personal capacity, caused by the introduction of grades of freed-men who are not *cives*, i.e. *Latini Juniani* and '*qui in numero dediticiorum sunt*,' slaves whose manumission, for one of various reasons, had only a limited effect. The end of it brings what looks

---

[1] F. Schulz, *Die Epitome Ulpiani* (1926).   [2] *Cod. Theod.* 1, 4, 2

like a great simplification. In the Empire, *civitas*, now of small import in the law of property and contract, but still important in family relations and succession, was conferred with increasing readiness. In A.D. 212 Caracalla made a great change. Many writers, contemporary and later, tell us, with some inaccuracies, that he gave Roman citizenship to all in the Roman world. One main aim was fiscal, to widen the range of the succession duties, recently doubled; but there were others. It was a step towards unification. There was also no doubt a desire to win popularity, much endangered by the terrible accompaniments of his accession. A Papyrus[1] contains what seems to be a Greek translation of the Edict, which suggests other possible motives. But the effect of the enactment is still not wholly clear. It was a personal benefit: it gave *civitas* to existing persons and therefore to their issue, but it did not abolish any inferior status or affect slaves. Those afterwards defectively manumitted would still be Junian Latins. Barbarians afterwards settled in the Empire would be at best *peregrini*. Persons afterwards deported would not be *cives*. But here obscurity begins. The papyrus is fragmentary and its interpretation uncertain. We cannot here consider the various hypotheses which have been offered as to the nature of the document and its interpretation. It seems most probable that *dediticii* of all types were excluded, and it may well be that most of the free non-citizens who certainly existed after this change were of this class, not easy to define for the third century. But if there were any large number the rule would hardly have served Caracalla's purposes, and the emphatic way in which the texts speak of the universality of the gift would be inexplicable. There is much on which to exercise the *ars nesciendi*, but it may be taken that the Edict did so far extend the class of *cives* that, thereafter, the Empire was in the main one of *cives* and slaves.

The subjection of women, in the old Roman law, is in apparent variance from the traditional dignity of the Roman matron. But if, in the looser manners of the Empire, something of that dignity was lost, much of the subjection was gone also. The old *manus*-marriage, which put the wife, whatever her previous status, into that of a daughter, with no property rights beyond a precarious right of succession and a provisional right in her marriage portion (*dos*), disappeared, and the only marriage in late classical law was the '*liberum matrimonium*' which did not affect the proprietary rights of the spouses, apart from *dos*, and was so loose that either party, if *sui iuris*, *i.e.* not under a *paterfamilias*, could

[1] *P. Giess.* 40, ed. P. M. Meyer, first published in 1910.

end it at will. The rule that women *sui iuris*, of whatever age, were under *tutores*, without whose authority they could not bind themselves by contract or alienate property, still existed, but hardly more than formally. For, when Claudius had abolished the *tutela* of women by their agnatic relatives (vol. x, p. 694), *tutores* of women were in general compellable to give the necessary *auctoritas*, and the only *tutor* of a freeborn woman (*ingenua*) who retained real power was her *paterfamilias* who had released her from the *patria potestas*.

The main legal aspect of marriage was not the relations between the parties, which were little affected in law, but the position of issue, who were in the *potestas* of the husband or his *paterfamilias*. Thus a marriage needed consent of the *patresfamilias* on both sides, and, just as either party could divorce at will, at least if *sui iuris*, so either *paterfamilias*, subject to an obscure restriction under Pius, could end the marriage. Logically the *paterfamilias* should have been able to compel a marriage. No doubt he could, in early law; the consent of the *filius*(*a*) was not needed. This seems obsolete in the Empire, though the old rule may have survived for *filiae*.

Lifelong *patria potestas* over issue remained, shorn of its old severity. In later classical law the father could no longer kill his son with impunity or sell him into slavery, but the only exception as yet admitted to the rule that a *filius* could have nothing of his own was the *peculium castrense* already mentioned. In relation to this fund he had—it must have seemed a paradox—the rights of a *paterfamilias* even against his own father.

Artificial filiation by adoption, in one or other of its forms, is ancient in Rome. It differs from the Greek system: the element of State control, prominent in Rome, is not Greek, and the consent of the phratry, required in Greece, was, if it had ever existed, obsolete in the Roman classical law. There are signs, about the beginning of the Christian era, of an attempt to introduce the Greek adoption by will, but in Rome this seems only to have been a desire that the beneficiary should take the testator's name: it did not transfer the person affected from one agnatic group to another, which was the essential effect of adoption both in Greece and in Rome.

Guardianship, in early Rome, as in all early law, is for the protection of the family interest in the property rather than for protection of the child. Thus it ends, for males, at puberty, since they can then have issue to succeed them, and the relatives, who cannot prevent marriage, have no further interest. The age varies, but the principle seems universal. Long before the end of the Republic, however, this view was giving way to that of guardianship in the modern sense, so that a jurist of Cicero's day describes it as 'ad tuendum eum qui propter aetatem suam se defendere nequit.' A boy of fourteen cannot manage his own affairs, but there was, for a long time, no further protection, except against clear fraud, with a power of setting aside transactions into which a minor had been led by his 'inconsulta facilitas' and a possibility of prohibiting spendthrifts of any age from dealing with their property. These remedies might be too late. It was not till the middle of the second century that a general system was introduced under which a *curator* might be appointed to consent to the dealings of one under twenty-five. It was not very effective, for the minor had lost no powers and could still act alone, subject to the old safeguards. Gradually, but not fully till post-classical times, the position of a minor under a *curator* was assimilated to that of a *pupillus* under fourteen, with a *tutor*.

Mancipatio, conveyance by ritual sale, was obsolete under Justinian, and references to it are altered in the Digest. The evidence suggests that in classical times men were becoming satisfied with the praetorian ownership which could be acquired, even in *res mancipi*, by Delivery (*traditio*). This became the most important mode of direct transfer and was carefully analysed. There is a profound difference between the two modes. In *mancipatio*, form is everything and its purpose appears on its face. Delivery is colourless: a thing may be handed over on loan, or in pledge, or for care, or to transfer ownership, and only the circumstances, of which expressed intent is the most important, can determine which is meant. Thus we get the rule that there must be a *causa*, a pre-existing fact showing intent to transfer and receive ownership. Hence arise many questions, discussed by the lawyers. Must the previous transaction really have existed, or did belief that it existed suffice? If it was shown that one party meant a gift, the other a sale, did ownership pass? If *A*, intending a gift to *B*, sent *C* with it, and *C* gave it as from himself, did ownership pass? If *A*, acting as agent for *B*, delivered to *C* what was supposed to be *B*'s but was *A*'s, did ownership pass? If I took delivery from one whom I did not think to be owner, but who in fact was, did I become owner? We need not consider the solutions: the point is that the lawyers are discussing, but with no display of philosophy, what are really philosophical questions. Without using this language they are asking whether, as the transaction needs *causa*, there must be an objective *causa*, or a subjective *causa* suffices, and, on the latter view, whether the subjective *causae* must be the same. They are also determining, though they do not expressly raise the point, how the necessary intent is to be defined, a point on which modern scholars are not agreed, but though this may be called subjective, it is always intent shown in the transaction. Only external elements can come into account, so that the attitude is practically objective.

The term set by Roman Law for acquisition by long possession is very short to modern eyes, but dates from a time when the State was very small and long absences were no part of life. It was made fitter for a larger State by adding other requirements to the fact of possession, but was unchanged till Justinian. Apart from moveables, however, it applied only to Italic land, and this, in the Empire, is a small part of the territory. For provincial land, for two centuries of the Empire, Hellenistic ideas seem to have been applied, and long enjoyment, with no fixed limit, was taken, not as itself a root of title, but as *prima facie* evidence that there was a title. In A.D. 199 Severus and Caracalla fixed a definite term of ten or twenty years, according to circumstances. The rule differed in its working from the Greek but its origin seems clear.

Decline of constructive thought and tendency to schematization are evident towards the end. Usufruct, the right of enjoyment for a limited period, commonly life, would be, for us, limited ownership. To the Romans it was not ownership, but a right *sui generis*. Marcian, noting similarity in the remedies for, and modes of creation of this right and the corresponding rules for rights of way, etc. (servitudes), grouped them together, usufruct and its derivatives as 'personal' and the other class as 'praedial' servitudes. They make unhappy yokefellows, so much so that some modern writers think the scheme Byzantine, apparently on the view that anything unsatisfactory must be Byzantine. But the last of the classical jurists were not the equals of their predecessors.

No branch of law underwent more rationalization in the early Empire than the law of Succession. The old law of intestacy, irrational to modern eyes, excluding as it did persons with obvious claims, was little improved by the Praetor. He gave emancipated children of a man a claim, with safeguards against unfairness, but a woman's children, and a mother, received no rights if there was any civil claim. It was not till Hadrian that the s.c. Tertullianum gave some mothers, but not all, a reasonable place in succession to their issue, and not till A.D. 178 did children get the first claim in succession to their mother. It was not till after the classical age that succession through women was rationalized. So, too, the Will had formalities which to modern eyes look aimless. The

Praetor gave some effect to Wills which ignored them, if substantial requirements were satisfied, but only in the second century were they made effective against civil claims.

Though children took on intestacy, they were at their father's mercy, and could be completely excluded by suitable words in the Will (*exheredatio*). The praetor applied similar rules to *emancipati*, but went no farther. Very late in the Republic signs appear of more effective protection, *Querela inofficiosi testamenti*, but perhaps not till the second century did this become a settled scheme, under which a man's issue excluded, a woman's issue omitted (there was no question of *exheredatio* in a woman's Will), and some other relatives, could attack the Will, unless there was ground for their exclusion. This indefeasible claim, accepted by many systems, but not by ours, marks a great inroad on paternal power: it expresses the notion of *condominium* in the family property, heard of before, but, hitherto, at least in historical times, of small import. Though sometimes called customary, the rule does not look Roman. Both the limit on paternal power and the claims of other than issue look Greek, and the system first appeared when Greek influence was very strong. In Attic law it seems, though the nature of the Sources forbids dogmatism, that a father with legitimate sons was restricted in his power of testation, and that, if there was no issue, collaterals could attack the Will on the ground that the testator must have been insane (δίκη μανίας). Roman texts speak of 'color insaniae' but it is only a word; the partial effect sometimes left to the Will is inconsistent with insanity of the testator. This is borrowed: possibly the whole institution is.

The introduction of *fideicommissa* as a legal institution was notable in more ways than one. It was quite usual in the last century of the Republic for a testator to request the *heres* to make a specified provision for some person, commonly one who could not be a beneficiary under the will, e.g. a *peregrinus*, especially a man who had been proscribed. Such requests were not enforceable: they were, strictly, *fideicommissa*. Augustus, however, in some cases in which *fideicommissa* had been imposed on him as *heres*, and others in which the failure of the *heres* to obey the injunction appeared to him peculiarly shocking, directed the consuls to see that the *fideicommissa* were performed. These were merely individual cases: there is no trace of legislation making such things valid. But Justinian[1] tells us that 'quia iustum videbatur et populare erat,' they were accepted as valid, and a special court

---

[1] *Inst.* II, 23, 1.

was soon set up to deal with them. The consuls seem to
have treated the emperor's direction as establishing a general
rule, so that it is difficult to say what is the technical basis
of the validity of these gifts, though in actual fact they rest on
the authority of Augustus. Earlier law had given free power of
devise, but little power of Settlement: the absolute interest must
vest in someone conceived at the time of death. The *fideicommissum*
changed all this: its introducers either did not see the change they
were making, or realized that the existing restrictions were intolerable. For these gifts were subject to hardly any of the old
rules of form or substance. They might be given to almost anyone, even not yet existing. Land could be left to *X* with a *fideicommissum* to give it on his death to his son, and so on in perpetuity.
The Roman liked to exercise power after death, as Englishmen
do. Such perpetuities were created: we have a record of one[1].
But reaction came. One after another restrictions were put on
fideicommissa, and Hadrian made perpetuities impossible. But old
severity was not restored: it remained possible to make a family
settlement in favour of grandchildren not existing in the testator's
lifetime.

Augustus, with the aim, amongst others, of encouraging marriage and improving the birth-rate among *cives*, procured the
passing of two *leges*, the Lex Iulia de maritandis ordinibus and the
Lex Papia Poppaea, the exact contribution of each of which is not
clear, and which, though they were twenty-seven years apart, are
often cited in the texts as the Lex Iulia et Papia[2]. Of their many
provisions that which most affected private life was the rule
excluding, from direct benefit under a Will, unmarried adults,
and cutting down, by half, gifts to childless married people. Relatives were, substantially, excepted, and the rule could be evaded
by making the gift as a *fideicommissum*, but this was stopped in
A.D. 73. It did not affect intestacy, but the *leges* also contained
complex rules on succession to freedmen (an important topic, as
liberti were often wealthy) which made claims of manumitters
(*patroni*) and their issue largely dependent on the number of
children the parties had.

In Cicero's time a *hereditas* is regarded as a mass of property,
and Gaius, in the second century, speaking of acquisition '*per
universitatem*' means no more than 'as a whole.' But his theoretical views, in his Institutes, are borrowed and of an earlier age.
Already lawyers were thinking of *hereditas* as an ideal unit, a *res*,

---

[1] *Testamentum Dasumii*, ll. 95 *sqq.* (Bruns, *Fontes*[7], I, p. 307).
[2] See above, vol. x, pp. 448 *sqq.*

independent of its content. Texts credited to Gaius and Julian say that 'hereditas nihil aliud est quam successio in universum ius quod defunctus habuit[1].' Several jurists tell us that it is *iuris nomen*, and exists though there be nothing in it: 'hereditas sine ullo corpore iuris intellectum habet,' says Papinian[2]. Many writers however hold, with varying degrees of confidence, that these texts are interpolated, the notion of an ideal unit being Byzantine, express-ing an oriental tendency to abstraction. But that it is Western is shown by its appearance in the Autun paraphrase of Gaius[3] and that it is classical is shown by Seneca, who chides the lawyers for thinking a *hereditas* is anything else but what is in it[4].

It may be noted as evidencing the little importance attached in law to the tie of marriage, apart from *manus*, that the Praetor gave the spouses no right if there were any relatives to claim, and that classical law made no change in this. The spouse's succession was in his or her own family.

An age of increasing commerce would naturally see develop-ment of the law of obligations, especially in contract. The very notion of obligation—in the sense of the law of enforceable under-takings, tacit or express (contract), and of liability for infringement of private right (delict)—itself underwent a change. Early in the Empire it was still a purely civil notion: the Praetor could no more create a contract than he could create *dominium*. He could give actions and defences, but not, technically, make or destroy an obligation. The action he gave asserted no right or obligation (*oportere*): his defences left to the civil claims which they paralysed a notional existence. Gaius, whose theory is often belated, gives this view under M. Aurelius. But, before he wrote, the Edict had been made permanent; and, apart from differences in form of remedy, which lasted so long as the formulary system did, prae-torian rights were just as stable and effective as those of civil law. It would not therefore be surprising if later jurists gave the name of obligations to praetorian rights; indeed, they often do: for the view that the texts are all interpolated there seems no adequate basis.

Absolutely new institutions are few. The old principle still holds that an undertaking, as such, is not enforceable: only those in a certain form or in certain specifiable groups are binding. But, already, the principle is making way—to be generalized only later —that any agreement for mutual services can be enforced by one who has done his part, the so-called Innominate Contract. It is a significant development, foreshadowing the modern view that

---

[1] *Dig.* L, 16, 24; L, 17, 62.   [2] *Dig.* V, 3, 50, *pr.*
[3] *Par.* 62.   [4] *de benef.* VI, 5.

promises are binding unless the law excludes them, as opposed to the old view that they are not binding unless law makes them so.

There was, however, much advance in refinement of analysis. In contract and the like, questions of conduct arise, and there was much evolution, especially in what may be called *bonae fidei* transactions, Cicero's 'sine lege iudicia in quibus additur "ex fide bona[1]."' In these, one who thought himself entitled to claim that the obligation had not been properly fulfilled claimed 'whatever, *ex fide bona*, ought to be paid.' *Bona fides* suggests, as breach of it, *dolus*, fraudulent or wilful failure to do what was required, and it is clear, whatever texts say, that in some of these cases the starting-point is a liability only for what can be called *dolus*. A commercial society could not, however, be content with this: carelessness must be brought into account. But classical law, like all rational law, is concerned with conduct, external facts, not, directly, with states of mind; it is objective. In the texts we find a system in which one who benefits by the transaction is liable for '*culpa*' and for failure in '*diligentia*.' That is not a state of mind: it is failing to behave, as in the circumstances a reasonable man would behave.

Many writers, however, impressed by the objective attitude of the jurists, as compared with the words '*culpa*,' '*diligentia*,' etc., which seem to express states of mind, reject the texts for classical law and set down their present form to glossators or Justinian. This would not really mean liability for *dolus* only. In the first place it seems that the classical jurists treated utterly reckless conduct (*culpa lata*) as in practice indistinguishable from *dolus*, though only their successors said that it actually was *dolus*. Again, there were rules, in some cases determining where the risk of damage should fall, which helped to make the notion of *culpa* unimportant in those cases. And there was the principle of *custodia*, under which, in some transactions, the holder was liable if the thing was lost, or, as some say, damaged, without reference to culpability. But it is not clear that liability for *custodia* covered many cases, and it does not seem to have covered damage, so that it seems better to hold that the theory of *culpa* and the 'utility' principle, that one who benefits is liable for *culpa*, were known to the Severine jurists. Paul seems to use it most. Its genesis is obscure. It may have arisen naturally from the notion of *bona fides* and the formulation of the action: the claim is not in respect of breach of contract in bad faith, but of damage suffered which good faith requires the other party to make good. That is not the same thing. An upright man may be careless, but, in commercial dealings, he may be

[1] *de off.* III, 15, 61.

expected to make good the damage his carelessness has caused. Perhaps not till the second century did this become a rule that in such cases a party is liable for *culpa*.

A similar attack has been made on texts which speak of *animus, mens, voluntas,* and here also it seems to have gone too far. Lawyers in any reasonably developed system must deal with intent, and these words occur often in Gaius and also in the other pre-Justinian sources. It is true that the classics often speak of '*quod actum est*' rather than the '*mens*' of which this is an index, and that the compilers often insert references to *voluntas* in explanatory clauses. But there is a difference. The classics mean by such words an intent to be gathered from the facts of the transaction: the compilers use them, seemingly, without reference to the evidence. But the view that the compilers often make the *voluntas* with which the act was done material where the classics did not, is to be received only with caution.

The principle of the old law, that no contract between *A* and *B* could affect the rights of *C*, so that there could be no Agency in the modern sense, and no third person could acquire rights under a contract, remained in form that of classical law. But acquisitions by subordinate members of a *familia*, children or slaves, had always vested in the *paterfamilias*; and the Praetor, by a system of actions created in the Republic, but greatly elaborated by the classical lawyers, though not probably basing his rule on any notion of representation, imposed on him a liability on their contracts, limited or not, according to circumstances. And to some extent, though to what extent is much disputed, classical law allowed a remedy by *actio utilis* to some third persons contemplated or interested in a contract.

Whatever actual institutions may be borrowed, the practice which appears in this age of putting everything into writing, is certainly Greek. In Roman private law, apart from one sophisticated way of giving credit (*expensilatio*), there was never legal need of writing. Wills, for obvious reasons, were usually written, but an oral will was good. In general, evidence of witnesses sufficed, and, in transactions involving acted ritual, it was required by law. But in Roman theory, and to a great extent in practice, a man's word was his bond. In hellenized lands there was less faith in a man's word—*Graeca fides* is ready money. Lies were to be expected, and no transaction was binding without writing. Roman law never had such a rule, but the habit of getting a written note of the transaction made rapid headway. Commerce was so widespread, the people so mixed, that confidence in the old *fides* was no longer possible. Thus we hear much of *cautiones*, here meaning memoranda of the contract, of *syngraphae* and *chirographa*, in Rome mere evidence, not, as they may have been in Greece, of contractual force. With this came inevitably a tendency to confuse the sign and the thing signified. *Stipulatio* was oral, but a written note became usual. There are texts, professedly of the late classical age, which say that where presence is proved, and a *cautio* alleges a *stipulatio*, the oral question and answer may be presumed[1]. The texts are suspected of alteration, but this is far from proved. So too, *mancipatio* was an oral transaction of transfer, but a written record became usual, and men may have sometimes contented themselves with this. A later age treated the document as itself the *mancipatio*: it no longer recorded the fact that *B* had received by *mancipatio* from *A*; it said that, by the document, *A* mancipated to *B*.

On the face of the texts, *Stipulatio*, by question and answer, underwent much change in this period. In the Republic, question and answer must be in exact verbal agreement and in Latin. According to the Digest, any language, even different languages, may be used. It suffices if there is substantial agreement: '*quidni?*' is a good answer, though a nod is not. Useless verbiage is immaterial: '*arma virumque cano, spondeo*' is good. We are told, but there is some apparent conflict, that even if there is not substantial accord, the transaction stands for what is common: if one party says ten and the other five, it is good for the five. The classicality of all this is disputed. On one view it is nearly all post-classical, but as *stipulatio* is *iuris gentium*, and some other departures from strict rule are in Gaius, it seems probable that the classical law admitted most of these relaxations.

It may be a result of *Romana fides* that personal guarantee was preferred to pledge, as security. There was indeed a very formal type of real security (*fiducia*) from early times, and, also, undertakings not otherwise enforceable were very early made so by giving a pledge, to be forfeited if the undertaking was broken. But the contract of Pledge, to reinforce a contract, though due to a Republican praetor and protected by his possessory remedies, was not protected at civil law till the end of the classical age, and possibly later. Security by giving a right to seize the thing wherever it was, without present taking (hypothec), appears about the beginning of the Empire, and, as it resembles a Greek institution of the same name, has been thought to be borrowed, but it is now generally held that it is Roman, only the name, adopted later, perhaps much later, being Greek.

[1] Paul, *Sent.* v, 7, 2; *Cod. Just.* VIII, 37, 1.

The chief point of interest in the law of Delict, liability to a penalty payable to the aggrieved person, for interference with private right, is a refinement of detail which the law undergoes to meet the needs of a more advanced civilization. Greater precision is given to the notion of Theft, treated mainly as a private delict though it is also a crime. There is much evidence of dispute and change of doctrine, but the story of the evolution of the rules in the Empire has still to be written. The law of damage to property, at first very narrow, based on a brief ancient statute, was early rationalized, mainly by the Praetor, but there was still refining and extension to be done. Some of this, *e.g.* the giving of the action where the damage was not to property but to the person, may be post-classical.

The most interesting evolution is that of *Iniuria*, outrage on personality. The Twelve Tables had only a crude set of fixed penalties for assault. The Praetor substituted an action for a penalty assessed by the Court, covering only the same cases, no doubt inspired by the Greek action for injury (δίκη αἰκίας) which closely resembles it. Before Augustus the Praetor added similar provisions for less crude insults, such as would be felt in a more advanced society, inspired, here too, probably by the similar actions of Greek law (δίκη κακηγορίας, etc.). Under Augustus, Labeo held that the word *iniuria* in the first edict was wide enough to cover these, and it was soon made to cover much more. The action required intent to insult, readily implied where the act was wilful, and thus it became the remedy for any wanton or wilful interference with another's rights. No action lay for trespass to lands, but an entry made knowingly against prohibition was an *iniuria*. For damage, the penalty was the same whether it was wilful or negligent, but if it was wilful there was also an *actio iniuriarum*. This flexible instrument went far beyond the Greek model.

The Formulary procedure[1] remained, throughout the period, nominally, the normal form of civil remedy, but from Augustus onward it was fighting a losing battle. Trial by '*cognitio*' of an official, with no reference to a *iudex privatus* over whom there was no direct control, was clearly better suited to the new régime. Thus, as provision was made for new needs, the protection was normally by *cognitio*, not by an action in the old form. We saw this in relation to *fideicommissa* and there were other cases. So far, there was no supersession, but, in the second century, the process began of removing matters from the formulary process and having

---

[1] See vol. IX, pp. 862 *sqq.*

them tried by the new administrative method. The change was helped by the fact that, though the *formula* was used in at least some provinces, it was early superseded there. It lasted little longer in Rome: the last trace of a *iudex privatus* is said to be in A.D. 261.

The formula did not disappear with the *iudex privatus*: issues were framed in the old way, with *de facto* retention of the old conception of the issue joined as a contract *inter partes*[1] till the *formulae* were abolished in A.D. 342[2]. No doubt this conception and the consequent lack of power to amend claims (the abolishing enactment speaks of '*aucupatio syllabarum*') had led to miscarriages of justice, but increased power of amendment might have served better than abolition of the *formula*, for the old method had the merit, lacked by the new, of compelling a clear statement of the issue, so that litigation became longer and more costly.

More than change of procedure was involved, more than a further rivet in the emperor's armour, though this was important, as judges now held office practically at his pleasure. For the legal historian another fact is more important. While the *formula* lasted, the difference between civil and praetorian law was strongly marked: when this was gone there was no distinction practical or formal. The way was clear for the unitary system of later law.

The mixed population of Italy probably did not feel that they lost much by the abolition of the *iudex privatus*. They were accustomed to autocratic government and, though no doubt proud of being Romans, they had little in common with the privileged class from whom *iudices* in important cases were still drawn. The change may have been welcome for another reason. The *iudex* not being an official, his judgment was not appealable: for some forms of misconduct an action lay against him, but in general his judgment stood. Its force could be destroyed only indirectly, *e.g.* by inducing a magistrate to veto further proceedings under it, which must often have depended on influence and hardly made for justice. The new judge was in principle an official, one in a hierarchy, responsible to superiors, so that his acts could be called into question. There was in fact an elaborate, over-elaborate, system of appeals. It is possible that towards the end appeal was applied to formulary cases, but there is no good evidence of this.

---

[1] M. Wlassak, *Die Litiskontestation im Formularprozess*; *Die klassische Prozessformel*, p. 104.   [2] *Cod. Just.* II, 57, 1.

VI. THE CRIMINAL LAW

From what survives of the criminal law it may be inferred that it never underwent the close analysis applied to civil law. The accounts we have of cases before the Assembly or the *quaestiones* suggest that the orator was more important than the jurist, but the recorders are historians, and these are usually cases which aroused public feeling. It may be that in the more numerous un-recorded cases law was applied with due attention to principle but, even so, and in the later period, if we may judge from legal texts, juristic analysis was less active in criminal law than else-where.

The criminal jurisdiction of the Assembly, under the presi-dency of the Consul, was not obsolete at the accession of Augustus, but it had little life, and he made no attempt to reinvigorate it and use the Assembly as he used it in legislation. Its place was taken by the Senate, earlier than in legislation, the transfer being no doubt aided, and its practical field perhaps defined, by the fact that in the last days of the Republic the Senate had exercised jurisdiction in important constitutional cases[1]. The jurisdiction so assumed, though politically important, did not greatly affect everyday life, for it was confined in practice to political offences, and, after the first century, to those charged against men of high rank. The Senate was essentially an administrative tribunal, with an inquisitorial procedure, but, in practice, it seems usually to have waited for an accuser to take the initiative.

Legislation, partly under Julius Caesar, and mainly inspired by him, promised to the *quaestiones perpetuae*[2] an even greater importance than they already had. By various Leges Iuliae the field of existing *quaestiones* was redefined and enlarged, with the effect of destroying what was left of comitial jurisdiction[3]. Thus the Lex Iulia Maiestatis brought within the field of the *quaestio* not only facts approximating to *perduellio*, but also facts actually amounting to *perduellio*, previously tried by the Assembly. New *quaestiones* were created, *e.g.* by the lex Iulia de vi privata and the Lex Iulia de adulteriis coercendis, which for the first time brought conjugal infidelity, at least on the part of the wife, under statutory criminal law. And, by a Lex Iulia Iudiciaria, more uniformity was given to the procedure under the different *quaes-tiones*. It seems therefore that Augustus contemplated the main-

---

[1] On the Senatorial jurisdiction in general, see also vol. x, p. 169 *sqq.*
[2] Vol. ix, pp. 876 *sqq.*　　　[3] See above, vol. x, p. 147 *sq.*

tenance of these as the definitive form of criminal process. But this was not to be. Though they existed till late in the second century, they were gradually superseded by a new administrative process, *crimina extraordinaria*, a jurisdiction of the emperor, exercised mainly by delegates. The history of the *ordo iudiciorum publicorum* in the Empire resembles that of the *ordo iudiciorum privatorum*[1], though the triumph of the administrative tribunal is earlier in criminal law. Though Mommsen's view, that the system of *quaestiones* is, essentially, adopting for criminal law the conceptions of civil procedure, is now discredited[2], it shared with that procedure characteristics which would not commend it to the new régime. The *iudices* were private citizens, and the lists from which they were taken were so large and the method by which the actual jury was struck was such that there could be no effective administrative control. This would explain what happened, but there is also the fact that they were unsatisfactory tribunals. The juries were too large, and the system under which, when a potential jury was reached, the parties could strike out a large number without reason assigned, resembles the method formerly applied in election petitions in this country, not unfairly described as 'knocking the brains out of the Committee.'

The *crimina extraordinaria*, which were to be the normal criminal process, may originate in the emperor's *tribunicia potestas*, and so be rooted in Republican institutions. There was development in two directions. At first it was the emperor's court, in which he himself (with a *consilium*) or a delegate, heard and decided, decision by a delegate being in theory decision by the emperor; but in course of time the officials to whom such things were commonly delegated came to be regarded not as mere delegates but as having a jurisdiction of their own. Again, the system began as an intervention by the emperor in cases which, for various reasons, the existing law did not reach, where, *e.g.*, the facts were not quite covered by the terms of the Statute erecting a *quaestio*. Here it was analogous to the *coercitio* of Republican magistrates, which, though primarily only a means of compelling obedience to magisterial orders, did in fact constitute, especially in the provinces, where there was little check on the magistrate, an ill-defined supplement to the criminal law. *Crimina extraordinaria* were soon regulated by many *senatus consulta* and *rescripta* creating offences. By the second century the administrative

[1] See above, p. 839 *sq.*
[2] See above, vol. IX, p. 877; Wlassak, *Anklage und Streitbefestigung in Kriminalrecht der Römer* (1917); *Anklage und Streitbefestigung* (1920).

tribunal had begun to take over cases hitherto in the hands of *quaestiones*: by the end of the century these had ceased to act.

The new process was inquisitorial. The whole matter was in the hand of the official. The court was private, normally, but there were exceptions, there was no need of formal *accusatio*[1]: there was usually a *denuntiatio*, a *delatio*, but the accusers were in general mere informers, not prosecutors. The death sentence, a dead letter in the late Republic for *cives*[2], was restored to practice by Augustus. The *ius gladii*, not a part of the ordinary powers of a governor, could be conferred on him, so that he could impose a death sentence, but usually he could not carry it out upon a *civis* without reference to the emperor. It had always been possible to evade the death sentence (the only punishment of early criminal law) by voluntary exile. This, in the form of *aqua et igni interdictio*, had become a definite punishment by Cicero's time, to be replaced by *deportatio* under Tiberius, and penal slavery was added by Hadrian. All these were capital in the sense of involving loss of *civitas*, but the Lex Julia had introduced a lesser, non-capital, punishment for adultery. *Relegatio*, without loss of *civitas*, appeared in the Empire, and other minor punishments were borrowed from the methods of magisterial *coercitio*. Under the *quaestiones* each crime had its statutory punishment: under the new law, the punishment might vary with the circumstances of the crime, the accused's part in it, his previous history, his civil standing and the standing of the Court. Much of this was prescribed by Statute, but, clearly, the judge had now a wider discretion. Imprisonment was not even now a normal punishment: 'carcer enim ad continendos homines, non ad puniendos haberi debet[3].'

Restrictions of the early Empire on the power of the *paterfamilias* and the domestic tribunal[4] brought within reach of the courts many offences by women, *filiifamilias* and slaves, hitherto dealt with privately. From the *quaestio*, or the Assembly, there had been no appeal. Naturally there was none from the Emperor, and the same rule applied, logically, to his delegates. But when jurisdiction was extended to many officials, and was seen as original, not delegated, an elaborate system of appeals, culminating in the Emperor, soon appeared.

It is impossible to consider here the changes in the substantive law, but two points of interest must be noted.

---

[1] At least as to the new offences. *Accusatio* remained for the old statutory offences, even though they were dealt with in the new way.

[2] See above, vol. IX, pp. 874 *sqq.*

[3] *Dig.* XLVIII, 19, 8, 9.

[4] Vol. IX, p. 875.

Under the Twelve Tables wilful homicide was capital, while
negligent or even accidental homicide called for a propitiatory
sacrifice. That distinction was generalized and remained throughout the Republic: criminal law is for wilful, not for negligent,
wrongdoing. The act must be done *scienter*, *dolo malo*. This
remains, in general, true for the Empire. There are indeed texts
which deal with punishment for negligent homicide[1], but these
are cases of *coercitio* rather than of true criminal law. A more real
exception is provided by criminal punishment of negligent
officials, but there is little of this in classical times. The *scientia*
and *dolus* have to do with the facts. Other views are held,
but the probable opinion is that ignorance of the law was, in the
classical age, no defence, even where the crime was not '*turpe*' or
against *ius gentium*[2]. But there is some evidence that in this type
of offence, which corresponds to what came in later times to be
called *mala quia prohibita*, ignorance of the law was a defence to
some classes, *e.g.* women and soldiers.

Modern systems have found it necessary to develop a doctrine
of criminal attempts, making an attempt at crime itself a crime.
For the view that Rome had this conception from very early times
there is no evidence. For the view that such a doctrine appeared
in Hadrian's time, there is some evidence, but it is unconvincing.
Most of it deals with homicide, and it must be remembered that
the legislation on homicide contained express provisions dealing
with specific forms of attempt and preparatory acts, and there
were similar provisions for other crimes. Such propositions as:
'in lege Cornelia dolus pro facto accipitur[3]' seem to be merely sum-
mations of these specific provisions and not to indicate any
general doctrine that an attempt as such is a crime. Such texts as:
'in maleficiis voluntas spectatur, non exitus[4]' are concerned with the
need for actual intent, not with a supposed absence of need for
the *factum*. When we note that there is nowhere discussion of
what amounts to an attempt, a question prominent wherever
there is such a rule, it is difficult to think that classical law had a
general conception of an attempt[5].

---

[1] *Dig.* xlviii, 8, 4 = *Coll.* i, 11, 1 (the last words of which are more
general); Paul, *Sent.* v, 23, 12 and 19; E. Costa, *Crimini e Pene*, p. 172.
[2] E. Volterra, *Bull. Ist. Dir. Rom.* 1930, pp. 75 *sqq.*
[3] *Dig.* xlviii, 8, 7; cf. Paul, *Sent.* v, 23, 3.   [4] *Dig.* xlviii, 8, 14.
[5] To create criminal liability the act must come within some specific
provision. C. Ferrini, *Opere*, v, pp. 51 *sqq.* But it is obvious that there is
here a field for magisterial *coercitio*.

CONCLUSION

The foregoing chapters have described the course of Roman Imperial history between the crisis that accompanied the fall of the Julio-Claudian dynasty and the crisis that was to follow the assassination of the last of the Antonines. The first crisis posed the question who should be *princeps*; but what mattered more, it might have ended in the effective domination of the army. Fortunately for the world the answer to the question was Vespasian, and Vespasian, like Augustus, intended the Principate to be civilian, not military in character. Himself a victorious general, he had no intention of seeing the seat of power occupied by others with no better claim than his own. His two sons provided successors who could not be challenged, and on the death of Domitian the new *princeps*, Nerva, was chosen as 'the best citizen,' the choice of statesmen and not of legions. But the secret of empire had been revealed, and the danger that the armies might impose some general on Rome had to be averted. The Praetorian Guard was still powerful enough to coerce an emperor, so that there was recourse to a homoeopathic treatment of the threatened malady. By the adoption of Trajan Rome received an emperor who was an active soldier, so that his reputation satisfied the mood of the legions, while, at the same time, as ruler in Rome he held to the civilian order. He suffered no military ambitions save his own, and when he died his successor Hadrian prevented the policy of the State from being guided by Trajan's generals, re-organized the Empire for defence and strengthened the position of the *princeps* by intense personal activity in all the provinces. How far the elevation of Hadrian was the deliberate choice of Trajan cannot be told, but Hadrian, after one unlucky venture, secured the succession for an emperor who could fulfil the conception of the *princeps* as the centre of an all-pervading and beneficent machine of government. As will be seen, this conception, which indeed weakened the fibre of local self-government,[1] did not meet to the full the needs of the future, but the reign of Antoninus Pius seemed at the time, and has seemed since, to be the most secure hour in the history of the Empire.

The position of the *princeps* received a philosophic aura which

---

[1] The consummation of this process was to be reached when, to the late Greeks, the emperor becomes a universal providence so that his πρόνοια can be used to describe in a word the government of the Empire.

was appropriate to the personality of Antoninus' successor, Marcus Aurelius, whose training for rule, no less than his intellectual equipment, came through philosophy. Whereas Antoninus' sense of duty was guided by the instincts of a Roman gentleman and administrator, the ideals of Marcus were rationalized in ethical speculation, which was born of the Graeco-Roman culture of his day[1]. He set by his side his adoptive brother L. Verus, whose character, if we may trust the tradition, was not worthy of the ideal that inspired his promotion. For a time Rome saw two Augusti equal in all legal standing, but the prestige of Marcus kept him, almost in his own despite, the first man in the State, so that the refutation of the root idea of the Principate, the pre-eminent *auctoritas* of one citizen, was apparent rather than real.

External dangers and the ravages of a prolonged and wide-spread plague robbed the Empire of its margin of prosperity and its heritage of peace. For a moment the East produced a rival to the *princeps* in the person of Avidius Cassius, but the great services of Marcus and his prestige kept the loyalty of his subjects. With Verus dead Marcus raised his own son Commodus to be the partner and successor of his rule. The ideal of 'the choice of the best' was sacrificed, and the breach with a conception that had been the moral foundation of the Principate for nearly a century was widened by the personality of Commodus himself. As has been seen, there were movements in the region of religious ideas that challenged the ethical and social ideas of Rome, and broke with the traditions of the Imperial government (p. 391). In so far as these new movements found a prophet in Commodus, he was the destroyer of the old order, but he had not the strength to create a new form of rule. He outraged Roman sentiment without securing the triumph of provincial ideas, winning for himself the hatred of the Senate, which stood for the old conceptions of government and of social ethics, and though these conceptions did not match the true needs of an Empire which was beginning to outgrow the grasp of Rome, the break with them destroyed the conventions that underlay the Principate. Marcus Aurelius on his deathbed had named Commodus 'the rising sun,' but his day was brief and was followed by the twilight of the Empire. In that twilight may be discerned the rise of the army to triumph over

---

[1] In this speculation may be dimly seen an undercurrent of justification of enlightened absolutism which springs from Greek thought earlier than the Augustan period. To the Greek East, it is to be remarked, the *princeps* was from the first little else than a *basileus*, whatever he might be in Rome.

the civilian conceptions of the Principate, and the intrusion of Eastern religious ideas into the very seat of power.

It is not surprising that the crisis which followed the death of Commodus did not find its solution in the form taken by the rule of Vespasian. The factors in the problem had suffered change. The extravagances of Nero were external and episodic, and the Augustan conception of the Principate, like the Flavian, could find room for aberrations without having its essence destroyed. But the autocracy of Commodus, whether direct or exercised by Prefects and Chamberlains without hindrance from the emperor, cut more deeply at the roots of government. The machine of empire continued to work, revolts were suppressed, the person of the emperor was consciously made the object of adulation and of worship and was exalted in propaganda; but there was not the impulse of an active ruler whose will was the driving force of the machine, nor was there the full strength of a tradition that had its roots in the past. The Principate was becoming something different, or almost nothing. The Senate, which had at least represented the public opinion that supported the Imperial order, had been reduced to an aristocratic *fronde*, impotently hostile to the autocracy, less able to stand for the tradition of Rome, despite occasional championship of the ideals of the Principate, yet unwilling to assist in the conversion of the Imperial system so as to welcome and make fruitful the growing influence of the provinces. The bureaucracy, though strongly knit and professionally efficient, was not anchored to the centre of government. It was more and more a web without a centre. The army itself had changed. Hadrian's defensive policy had made of the legions permanent garrisons on the frontiers, recruited from the frontier peoples, with a romanization that was only professional and technical. The plague had greatly diminished the population of the empire, and shifted the balance towards the soldiers and away from the civilian population. During the long wars of Marcus the Empire had been driven to put into the field its fighting strength drawn from any source that showed military qualities. The Praetorian Guards and a part of the officer class alone retained a specifically Latin tradition. Rome had discovered among the provincials soldierly material of high value, but material that had only the slightest tincture of Roman political ideas or of Graeco-Roman culture.

Granted that the barbarization of the legions cannot be proved to have been as complete as has been alleged,[1] it remains true that the army was drawn far less from those with Roman or any other

[1] M. Platnauer, *The Life and Reign of Septimius Severus*, pp. 164 *sqq.*

civilized political instincts than at the time of Vespasian. In the darkest days of the third century the Empire was to owe its salvation to the great soldiers of Illyricum, but the people from which they sprang, though convinced defenders of the traditions of Pagan Rome, had small understanding for the constitutional conventions of the Principate. Further, Hadrian's reforms had carried far the separation of the military from the civil career so that even the higher officers, despite their Roman birth and training, had no experience in civil government. On the other hand, the civilian bureaucracy had no hold upon the army, before whose power it was to be helpless in an age in which the dangers of the State gave to soldiers the initiative that falls to those who are plainly needed.

A further change in the relation of Rome to the Empire was implicit in the spread of provincial cults and influences, religious and secular. The full sweep of this will be described in the next volume; it is enough to observe that there were symptoms which showed that the dominantly Western trend that Augustus gave to the mind of the Empire was being replaced by motives which fitted less well the political ideas of the free city-state or of an Empire led by the first citizen of a dominant community. The great benefit which the Principate had bestowed upon the Mediterranean world was freedom to live its own life, to retain its own variety of customs and institutions. The extent of this and the return made by the provinces have been described in the review of the Roman world that has been given earlier in this volume (chaps. xii–xvi). The achievement of Rome and of the Empire as a whole is not to be belittled because it did not last for ever. But the benefits of Roman rule did not accrue equally to all those who lived within the Empire's borders. Latin culture in the West and Greek culture in the East belonged most to those classes that gained most, but meant less to masses of people whose national modes of thought continued. When the plague and the famine that followed it under Marcus Aurelius undermined the prosperity of the well-to-do, the need of the less urbanized people could no longer be met by benefactions whether Imperial or local. The Imperial bureaucracy, in its search for efficiency, had already done something to destroy the local self-government that was the strength of the Empire's unity.

In the region of the intellect, Roman, as Hellenistic, culture was living on its capital. Even as early as the Julio-Claudian age a flagging of intellectual vitality may be observed. Under the Flavians and their successors we find great names, but their genius was not fruitful for others. After Tacitus *magna illa ingenia cessere*. The lively mental stir of the Second Sophistic marked no such deep currents of thought as ran in the days of the first Sophists. What was achieved—the spread of education and of what may be called cultural amenities—must not be discounted or dispraised. Roman jurisprudence reached its maturity. In many spheres men became more humane in both senses of the word. All this has been described and has not been overrated. But there was no intellectual trend upward, and, as the age of the Antonines became darkened by stress and troubles, men sought escape or courage in new religions or in religions that came new to some parts of the Empire. Christianity, the faith that was in the end to prevail, to pass from opposition to government, from outlawry to giving law, had already laid the foundation of an organization which later was to be both the pupil and teacher of the Imperial régime. It had already seen in Ignatius the first great ecclesiastic (p. 292). But other religious movements that can be detected as astir in the reign of Commodus, with the great divine names of the East advanced to predominance over their fellows, were to play their part in exalting the person of this or that emperor and in stressing phases of the Imperial power that were alien to the whole conception of the Principate.

When account is taken of these factors, it may well seem to us, with our knowledge of what the third century was to bring forth, that the change which came over the Empire was inevitable and even plain to foresee. Yet, for most, at least, of the period described in the present volume, the order of things must have seemed marked by the legend that appeared on the coins of Vespasian—*Aeternitas Populi Romani*. Even during the reign of Commodus men did not cease to speak of the *Felicitas Saeculi*, as though all that seemed to deny it was transient—clouds that would pass and leave the world in the bright sunshine of security and prosperity. Gradually through the Flavian period there had developed a system of defence, which under Hadrian reached a stability that promised permanence. Trajan had broken the power of Dacia and, for a moment, beaten the Parthians from the field. A new province beyond the Danube became a bastion of power in eastern Europe; and if Hadrian abandoned newly-won territory that might have been hard to hold and might have made the Empire more continental and more Eastern than suited its character (p. 295 *sq.*), he showed how long was the arm and how heavy the hand of Rome if it was challenged by rebellion. The prestige of the Empire was not abated under Antoninus, and Roman generals contrived to re-assert Roman power against the Parthians at his death. Despite the visitation of the plague and the sudden impact of barbarian peoples on the northern borders of the Empire, Marcus Aurelius was able to do more than restore the shaken front, and was twice within sight of further conquests that would at least deny to the restless peoples of northern and central Europe ready access to the heart of the Empire. The 'great refusal' of Commodus to complete his father's work was ominous; but for the time the potential loss was, so it seems, not to be detected. Our scanty tradition reveals here and there a doubtful loyalty in the armies, but as men looked at coins with the legend *Concordia Exercituum*, they may well have seen the fulfilment of a prayer rather than an anxious aspiration.

From province to province the material benefits of Imperial rule and of local enterprise, permitted and encouraged by Rome, took forms that seemed to promise lasting life. Great roads, built to shorten the marches of the legions, knit the Empire together in trade as well as in arms. As men travelled on these roads they came to towns and cities in which stately public buildings combined an Imperial unity of architectural ideas with conformity to the needs of artistic traditions of the provinces where these traditions existed. Provincial cities sought in their buildings to copy Rome as they strove to be associated with her in the status of 'colonies.' The presence of armies was fruitful in works of peace. Where troops were posted or veterans were settled there was romanization, and where Romans went abroad on their lawful occasions they embodied in their *conventus* the spirit of the new Roman People that Augustus had done so much to make living and permanent. The gradation of right that had so greatly assisted the unification of Italy under the Republic played its part in unifying the world under the Empire. At the same time, the readiness of Rome to acknowledge the *poleis*, the leagues, the *civitates* and *municipia* of the East and of the West showed a readiness to admit now tradition, now development. Throughout the provinces as the period advances can be detected the strain on local public spirit that material amenities and the satisfaction of civic pride increasingly imposed. Equally may be seen signs of the encroachment of the central power on local self-government, though the encroachment was justified by increased efficiency and, in general, by benevolence. But as yet public spirit had not reached its breaking-point nor had bureaucracy deadened the sense of responsibility. When all deductions are made and the growth of a provincial reaction is not overlooked, the keynote of

the period covered by this volume was loyalty to Rome, not
merely because this loyalty had no rival, but because Rome
deserved to receive it (p. 477 *sq.*) and because an order of things
which almost all men confidently hoped would be permanent
seemed to rest upon the 'eternity of the Roman People.'

Finally, in this period the Empire shows a cohesion, though not
a uniformity, of culture. The romanization of the West, its most
lasting achievement, was due to men in whom the native qualities
of Italy and Rome had been enriched by judicious borrowing from
the intellectual heritage of Greece. The spread of trade brought
natives of one province into another far removed, and countless
inscriptions that reveal their clinging together are not to be interpreted as revealing them in precarious alienation from their neighbours. In Italy Latin culture kept its traditions, but not to the
exclusion of Greek letters or of the influence of Greek art. Greek
philosophers were at home by the Tiber, and the one Roman Emperor who can claim to be a great figure in letters meditated to
himself in Greek, which was, after all, the language of the Epistle to
the Romans. The social life of the capital shows, despite a partial
reaction under the Flavians, a progressive sophistication that is due
in part to the influence of the non-Italian elements that made the
City a microcosm of the Empire. In the Danube lands may be
detected a partial romanization which blended with earlier elements and inspired traditions that helped to make these people
later the defenders of the Empire. The hellenism of Greece itself
and of Western Asia Minor is not the antithesis but rather the
complement of the culture of the West. To Hadrian panhellenism
seemed a natural counterpart to the preservation of Roman
tradition. And, as we pass farther eastwards, the border provinces
show a civilization in which hellenistic ideas live side by side with
the Eastern culture to which they give a speech and language.
Especially in the sphere of religion these provinces have their own
contribution to make, but the following of the Eastern gods was
not a form of Dissent. The contribution that these provinces had
to make to the art of the Empire is not easy to assess, but whatever
the elements that were fused in Imperial art and whatever their
proportions, of the fusion there is no doubt (pp. 799 *sqq.*). Even
in the sphere of Roman Law,—the most characteristic intellectual
achievement of Rome,—natives of the provinces, as Julian,
Papinian, Ulpian, were to take a high place. From Egypt, which
itself gained so little from the Empire, and from Cyrenaica the
Empire gained less: by policy or by nature both provinces
remained comparatively isolated, and shared unequally in the

benefits of Roman government. Of Crete it is known, and of
Cyprus, Sicily, Sardinia and Corsica it may be assumed, that their
inhabitants lived the life of the Empire in almost unbroken
tranquillity.

The western Mediterranean was a Roman lake, and within
sight of its waters romanization was dominant, though the
provinces of Africa preserved a native life that gave a special
colour to the Latin civilization that spread through its borders.
In Spain and Gaul this civilization advanced to form the basis
of their national culture, despite the invasions that later centuries
had in store for them. Spaniards and Gauls repaid to Rome the
intellectual debt they owed her and the Empire knew the first of
the great Spanish rulers (p. 325). These countries, though, are
not Mediterranean alone: the great rivers of Gaul drew men
outwards from *mare nostrum*. Rome had already sent legions into
Britain, and the great landmark of Imperial rule in this island still
stands between Tyne and Solway. Here, too, men received from
Rome a heritage that did not perish beyond recall. New actors were
entering the stage of history, and their characters were becoming
discerned: the tribes of free Germany had been described by
Tacitus, and archaeology can supplement and correct what ancient
writers have told us of the peoples of the North. Before the age
of the Antonines was past, movements beyond the sight of Rome
had impelled the Empire's neighbours to be the Empire's enemies.
Dacia rose to be a danger and fell to be a province; beyond the
Euphrates the Parthian Empire continued through vicissitudes
to be an Empire, though the rule of its Arsacid kings was soon
to give way to the more vigorous power of the new Persian
dynasty. In Sarmatian and Parthian culture may be seen elements
that are drawn from lands far from the Mediterranean world.
But though Northern and Eastern peoples had their own person-
alities, distinct and persistent, the world that mattered most, then
and for the future, was the world of the Empire whose fortunes
were governed by the Roman fate.

It may be said, indeed, that the Empire at its zenith was
governed by the upper middle classes for the upper middle
classes. There was, we may grant, some divergence of interest
between the cities and the countryside; for the countryside had
not an equal share in the material blessings of Roman rule, and
was in a degree exploited by the towns. So far as the later triumph
of the army marked a victory over the civilian conception of the
Empire, it was a triumph over the urban civilization that was
especially fostered by the Empire of the Principate. But it may

be doubted whether the army, in asserting its own claims, consciously asserted the claims of others, or whether, apart from the working out of the destructive influences that have been traced, the Empire was fated to be divided by a kind of social revolution. It is difficult to detect a conscious policy that would produce such an effect, or to discover in the economic diversity of the Empire, which has been described in the chapters of this volume, a steady trend which (apart from the stress of wars and the destruction they brought) would have broken down the unity-in-diversity which seems to underlie the social structure of the Empire. Yet it cannot be denied that overspending so weakened its financial and economic resources that the crises that were to come in the third century were in part the price that the world had to pay for the gilding of the golden age of the Antonines.

The price had to be paid, and there was loss as well as gain during the hundred and twenty years that follow the accession of Vespasian. It may be a historian's duty to point to the seeds of decay present in the most vigorous of growths and to foretell, with the assurance of afterknowledge, the fall of the strongest institutions. The famous verdict of Gibbon that the period which elapsed from the death of Domitian to the accession of Commodus was the period in which the condition of the human race was most happy and prosperous must suffer deductions in the light of evidence then still unrevealed. Thus we can now detect the draining away of the prosperity of Egypt recorded in the documents that its sands have yielded up. The age of the Flavians, of Trajan, Hadrian and the Antonines entered into the heritage of the Augustan Principate. The summer of the Empire had its debt to the spring. Greatest of all its debts was that the fundamental political problem of the Ancient world, the problem how communities might live together and yet live their own lives, had found a solution within the framework of the Empire.

What is witnessed in this volume is not so great an achievement as that which was described in its predecessor. But it does not reveal an age of passive possession only. It was not inevitable, it was the reward of unresting endeavour and wise restraint in action, that so great a part of mankind enjoyed for so long safety and contentment, secure of justice and fair treatment, able to continue its own traditions, to speak its own languages and to follow its own religions, yet learning of Rome and every day conscious of the *immensa Romanae pacis maiestas*.

APPENDIX ON SOURCES

In the period covered by the present volume, A.D. 70–192, there is a marked decline both in the bulk and the quality of the literary material, which is so plentiful for the closing years of the Republic and for the first century of the Principate. The great names disappear: though inscriptions are more numerous, and though coins are increasingly informative (see below, p. 857), though the jurists and the Digest reproduce edicts and decisions of the emperors with greater frequency, the student of this period of Roman history has fewer literary authorities upon whom he can rely. This being so, all that will be given here is a brief account, mainly in chronological order, of the most important, and little notice will be taken of secondary or of non-surviving sources. It should be borne in mind that the value of an author may vary greatly according to the period with which he is dealing, and the estimates here given apply to the history contained in this volume only; for comparison the reader should consult the Appendices upon the Literary Sources in the two previous volumes (IX, pp. 882 *sqq.* and X, pp. 866 *sqq.*).

First should be mentioned some prose-writers: Pliny the Elder in his *Encyclopaedia*, the moralist and biographer Plutarch in his *Moralia*, Quintilian in his *Institutio Oratoria*, and the Jewish historian Flavius Josephus, all supply occasional items for the Flavian age. Later in date come the antiquarian Pausanias, whose guide-book to Greece is full of evidence for the beneficence of Hadrian to the country he loved, and another antiquarian, Aulus Gellius (*flor.* 150), whose *Noctes Atticae* in twenty books (of which the eighth is missing) contain much miscellaneous information. The Letters of M. Cornelius Fronto, the rhetorician and tutor of Marcus Aurelius, are valuable for the picture they give of life in the Antonine period, while many of the orations of Dio of Prusa (*flor.* 100) and of Aelius Aristides of Smyrna (*flor.* 170) not only throw light upon the state of the Greek provinces of the Empire during this period, but also give the reaction of the cultivated Greek mind to the advantages (and disadvantages) of the *pax Romana*. Plutarch lived in the past, Lucian in the world of the satirist or critic, though both reflect the ideas of their day. Among the poets, Valerius Flaccus, Silius Italicus and Juvenal have scattered references to contemporary events, as have Statius and Martial, who are even more valuable for the picture they give of the personnel of Domitian's court and of the flattery which that Emperor demanded. Yet all these authors, helpful though they are, in their sum total simply give references to incidents or persons rather than chronicle events themselves; for narrative we must turn to the historians proper[1].

CORNELIUS TACITUS (*c.* 55–*c.* 120) wrote and published, during the early years of Trajan, his *Historiae*, an account of the Flavian dynasty and of the Civil Wars that led to it. It was probably in twelve books, but the only portions left dealing with our period are Book IV and a fragment of Book V, and they are mostly concerned with the Batavian and Jewish revolts and do

---

[1] For a selection of literature on the historical sources in general see the General Bibliography below, p. 865.

not carry the chronicle of events in Rome beyond June, A.D. 70. The rest is lost, and the loss is a grievous one: though some chapters of Tacitus' *Agricola* give glimpses of events in Rome, we are left without his annalistic treatment of the years between 70 and 96, and the few surviving fragments are not enough to enable scholars to give any answer to the question whether the *Histories* were a source for Cassius Dio.

A contemporary of Tacitus, who shared his views, PLINY THE YOUNGER (*c*. 61–*c*. 114), in his *Letters* gives an interesting commentary upon many of the persons of his age. Two of these letters (16 and 20 in Book VI), addressed expressly to Tacitus, describe the part that Pliny and his uncle played in the great eruption of Vesuvius, but perhaps the most valuable are those which, as Special Commissioner for Bithynia, he wrote to Trajan regarding affairs there. Not only do they afford first-hand evidence for the state of the province, including the earliest pagan description of the new sect of the Christians (x, 96 [97]), but the short, decisive and sensible replies of Trajan show that Emperor at his best. Pliny's *Panegyricus*, which he delivered in 100 (p. 200), is important not only for its lurid glimpses of life under Domitian and its rather idealized portrait of Trajan, but also because it gives expression to the creed of those who strove for a non-hereditary Principate with a ruler chosen for merit: 'imperaturus omnibus eligi debet ex omnibus.'

SUETONIUS TRANQUILLUS (*c*. 71–*c*. 150) is represented by his Lives of Divus Vespasianus, Divus Titus and Domitian, which three make up volumes VII and VIII of his *Lives of the Caesars*. They are some of his best and very much to the point, but unfortunately very brief; the three together take up less space than the Life of Tiberius. In this short compass, however, Suetonius furnishes many facts and details, the value of which would be even higher had he but strung them on some chronological string, e.g. if only he had given us a clear account, with dates, of the conspiracies against Vespasian and Domitian.

The would-be historian of the second century, deprived of the help of Tacitus and Suetonius, has a hard task. It would have been lightened had chance but been kinder to the writings of two men. One was Ammianus Marcellinus, who in the fourth century began his history with the principate of Nerva and carried it down to the death of Valens in 378, continuing not unworthily the tradition of Tacitus. The other was Marius Maximus, who after a career in which he rose to be *Praefectus Urbi* in 218, took as his model Suetonius and compiled (*c*. 230) a series of biographies of emperors, from Nerva to Elagabalus, which retained their popularity for many years. But the first thirteen books of Ammianus (covering the years A.D. 96–352) have perished, and Maximus is now known to us mainly through the use made of him in the *Historia Augusta* (see below). Apart from Dio of Prusa and Aristides there is unfortunately an almost complete absence of contemporary literary material for the second century: one solitary surviving sentence of Trajan's *Commentarii* and a few sentences from the self-revelation of Marcus Aurelius are all that can help for political history.

With CASSIUS DIO COCCEIANUS we reach the one historian of consequence who helps towards a connected narrative for the whole period from 70 to 192. He was a man who, in the service of the Empire, had held important posts both in the provinces and in Rome: he twice attained the consulship, the second time as colleague of Severus Alexander in 229. He spent ten years in collecting material and twelve years in writing a complete 'annalistic' history of Rome (LXXIII, 23, 5)[1]. This was in eighty books: what sources he used for the period between Vespasian and Marcus Aurelius cannot be conjectured with any profit; of events after 180 he was himself a contemporary and eyewitness (LXXIII, 4, 2). Unluckily, of the relevant books (LXV to LXXIII) we do not possess a complete text, but excerpt and epitome only. Still the bulk of these is not inconsiderable and their usefulness is great: they derive from a connected narrative, of a somewhat anecdotic character, with dates, names, and places, which make it possible to draw up a chronological framework, into which we can fit other pieces of information.

For the reign of Commodus and onward we can rely upon a new author, a Syrian Greek named HERODIANUS, who wrote (c. 240–250) a history of the years from 180 to 238 in eight books. He has a keen eye for a dramatic situation or a picturesque incident, though his style is flat and repetitive. He did not apparently use Dio as a source, and one of his main merits is that he enables us to fill up the gaps in Dio (e.g. the episode of the deserter Maternus, see above, p. 385) and to correct and control the *Historia Augusta*.

There follows a blank of some hundred years or more and then we are faced with the problem of the *Historia Augusta*. This is a collection of *Lives*, professedly by six authors, of emperors and pretenders from Hadrian down to Numerian (117–284), though the *Lives* from 244 to 253 are missing. This collection was supposedly compiled by these six authors in the reigns of Diocletian and Constantine. It is now widely held that the *Historia Augusta* in its present form is a product of the second half of the fourth century, or even of the beginning of the fifth, and that the attribution of the separate biographies to different writers is only a literary artifice. In this volume we are concerned with lives which are in general based upon excellent sources. But there is an admixture of biographical material, partly of value partly mere fabrication, which it is more difficult to control. In the chapters on Hadrian and the Antonines the view has been adopted that this biographical element, in its less valuable form, is most marked in the subsidiary lives, especially of Aelius but also of Avidius Cassius, whereas the life of Verus is compounded of good material (taken from the life of Marcus) and of evidence of far less value. Thus it is the task of the historian to separate out and make use of what is good and disregard the remainder. For the purpose of this volume the questions at what precise date the *Historia Augusta* was produced, and how far and in what way it may be called 'tendencious,' are of slight moment. A discussion of these matters will be given in the following volume.

There remain several epitomes or short summaries of Roman history. Sextus Aurelius Victor wrote a *Historia abbreviata* from Augustus to Constantius (usually referred to as *Liber de Caesaribus*), and published it some time shortly after 360. Eutropius, who was Magister Memoriae to the emperor Valens, A.D. 364–378, dedicated to him a *Breviarium ab urbe condita* in ten books. Both these, together with an *Epitome* professedly of Aurelius Victor, are short works of small value for the period under consideration and are rarely used in this volume as evidence. Much later still come some Greek

---

[1] References from Dio are given according to Boissevain's edition, books being cited by the numbers on the left-hand pages of that work.

compilers and historians. John Malalas of Antioch in Syria compiled in the sixth century an universal history in twelve books, with its main interest in Eastern affairs. Though he does occasionally provide some item of information which appears to rest upon genuine city-tradition, he apparently blunders even on a matter so interesting to him as the date of the disastrous earthquake at Antioch in the winter of 114–15 (p. 858), and he rarely adds anything of genuine importance to knowledge. Among works of Byzantine scholars we possess excerpts from the great *Encyclopaedia* of historical extracts which the emperor Constantine Porphyrogenitus had drawn up in the tenth century, and to the same century probably belongs the *Lexicon* of Suidas, which includes articles on the emperors. In the eleventh century John Xiphilinus compiled (from books XXXVI to LXXX of Dio Cassius) an account of the Roman 'monarchs' from Pompey the Great to Alexander Severus, which he called '*An Epitome of the Roman History of Dio of Nicaea*' and which is the main base for the reconstruction of the contents of the last books of Dio. In the twelfth century another Byzantine, John Zonaras, made considerable excerpts from Dio for his own *Epitome of Histories*, but as from the reign of Trajan onwards he follows Xiphilinus closely his work has little independent value for our period.

In view of these facts the historian of the period is necessarily dependent upon the evidence afforded by inscriptions and coins. Inscriptions gathered together in the *Corpus Inscriptionum Latinarum* and other collections, such as that of Greek Inscriptions which refer to Roman History (*I.G.R.R.*), supply information for institutions and life of the several provinces, for the Imperial administration and army and for the prosopography of the Empire together with chronological indications. The last-named are also provided by coins, both those of the Emperor and of the Senate and of cities which retained the right of striking currency for themselves. On these we find given fixed points of time which can be connected with historical events. But, more than that, the coins may reflect the policy and attitude of emperors, of the Senate and of communities, and are valuable evidence for the religious, emotional and cultural movements of the time.

NOTES

1. THE CHRONOLOGY OF THE PARTHIAN WAR OF TRAJAN

It is now generally accepted that the first campaign, against Armenia, began in spring 114, and the combination of Xiphilinus, 235 (= Dio LXVIII, 18, 3ᵇ–23, 1, ed. Boissevain) with *C.I.L.* III, p. 1975, a diploma of September 1, 114 showing the titles *Optimus* and *imp.* VII, seems to prove that it was over by about midsummer of that year. At the other end, a new inscription from Doura[1] shows that that city had already passed back into Parthian hands by the end of 116.

The question then arises whether the conquest of Mesopotamia, as has in recent years been widely maintained, occupies 115, leaving for 116 the whole of the final advance to the Persian gulf, including the capture of Adiabene and descent of the Tigris and Euphrates, as well as the revolt and its partial suppression, or whether northern Mesopotamia was annexed along with Armenia in 114 and the subsequent operations spread over two years instead of one.

In favour of the former hypothesis is the fact that the famous earthquake at Antioch which undoubtedly occurred, if Dio can be believed, after the capture of Mesopotamia and during Trajan's personal presence in the city, is dated by John Malalas to Sunday, December 13, 115. If this were unimpeachable evidence, it would be conclusive; but Malalas, though himself an Antiochene, is so untrustworthy a writer that we cannot be sure he would even copy down a date correctly from the city records[2]. It is therefore necessary to examine other sources, and the following considerations tell against his evidence and in favour of the dating adopted in the text.

(1) The run of Xiphilinus' abridgment which, when stripped of editorial insertions of the actual extracts from Dio made by order of Constantine Porphyrogenitus, shows clearly that he reckoned only two years of aggressive campaigning divided by a winter at Antioch.

(2) The absence of any coins proclaiming the single annexation of Armenia (cf. p. 244) which would surely have been struck if the first year had closed with this success.

(3) The difficulty of accounting for Trajan's movements. For example, had his invasion of Mesopotamia begun in 115, he would have approached

---

[1] M. Rostovtzeff, *C. R. Ac. Inscr.* 1935, pp. 285 *sqq.*; other evidence of probability also confirms this terminus.

[2] December 13, 115 was not in fact a Sunday; but that mistake, which is in any case unimportant, was ingeniously explained away by A. von Gutschmid (*ap.* Dierauer, *Beiträge zu einer kritischen Geschichte Trajans*, p. 154, no. 4) by exchanging the day of the week with that given by Malalas for his other precisely dated event, the entry of Trajan into Antioch on January 7, 114, where it is also wrong. A different explanation has been given by Graf von Stauffenberg, *Die römische Kaisergeschichte bei Malalas*, p. 277, who interprets Malalas' date as December 30 (cf. Longden, *J.R.S.* XXI, 1931, p. 34).

Osrhoëne from Syria, whereas the sources indicate that he did so from the east or north-east.

(4) Trajan received seven imperatorial salutations in these years (VII–XIII) and of these at least five before the end of 115; it is hard to attach so large a proportion to the events prior to the crossing of the Tigris[1].

(5) The fact that M. Pedo Vergilianus, *cos. ord.* for 115, who is known to have perished in the earthquake, vacated office before the normal end of his *nundinum*[2] (of two or four months) suggests a date early in that year for the disaster, but is not in itself conclusive, since there may have been other reasons for his laying down office.

(6) The title of Parthicus which Dio says was bestowed unofficially after the capture of Nisibis and Batnae, and confirmed officially on the fall of Ctesiphon (LXVIII, 28). Now a new fragment of the *Fasti Ostienses* gives the official date of conferment by the Senate as February 20, 116 and this is virtually conclusive[3]. For, granted the time necessary for the news to reach Rome, it implies that Ctesiphon had fallen by the end of January, at latest.

For these reasons, pending further discoveries the following chronology has been adopted in the text; 114, annexation of Armenia and northern Mesopotamia; winter of 114–5 (? January), earthquake at Antioch; 115, annexation of Adiabene and southern Mesopotamia, culminating in the fall of Ctesiphon in the winter of 115–6; 116, journey to the Persian Gulf, revolt of the conquered provinces and its suppression.   R. P. L.

2. THE ROMAN OCCUPATION OF PALMYRENE

The date of the annexation of Palmyrene is difficult to determine exactly. On the one hand a well-known passage in the elder Pliny, who finished his *Natural History* in A.D. 77, makes Palmyrene a separate State between the Romans and the Parthians (v. 88 *privata sorte inter duo imperia summa Romanorum Parthorumque*). On the other hand a recently discovered milestone (H. Seyrig, *Syria*, XIII, 1932, p. 271) informs us that in 75 a legate, the father of the future emperor Trajan, was building the great military highway from Palmyra to Sura on the Euphrates. Does it follow that the capital of the desert was Roman by the time of Vespasian? Not necessarily. Rome did

---

[1] For details cf. Longden, *op. cit.* pp. 5–6; S. Gould, *Excavations at Dura-Europos*, IV, pp. 57–65, who discusses the whole matter. Unfortunately neither the inscription over the triumphal arch at Doura nor *Ann. épig.* 1927, no. 147 (improved by W. F. Stinespring, *Bull. Amer. Soc. Orient. Research*, LIV, 1934, p. 22) provides definite evidence of value.

[2] *Ann. épig.* 1911, no. 95. His successor was presumably *not* L. Catilius Severus, who is now known to have been consul in 110, *Ann. épig.* 1934, no. 30.

[3] G. Calza, *N.S.A.* XII, 1934, p. 248. The date is in any case fatal to the view that official confirmation followed the capture of Nisibis (and that Dio's ἐβεβαιώσατο (LXVIII, 28, 2) means merely 'justified'). Nisibis must *at latest* have fallen in the summer of 115 and the news must have reached Rome by the autumn.

not get possession of it by force of conquest but by a patient policy of peaceful penetration, which in exchange for substantial advantages and efficient protection gradually tightened the bonds which joined the Semitic town to the Empire. Certainly it was part of the Empire in the second century. Appian, about 160, enumerating the countries which were subject to Rome, expressly includes Palmyrene among them (*Prooem.* 2 Παλμυρηνοί τε καὶ ἡ Παλμυρηνῶν ψάμμος ἐπ' αὐτὸν Εὐφρατὴν καθήκουσα). At least from the time of the Parthian wars of Lucius Verus, perhaps from the time of Hadrian, it had a Roman garrison, as is proved by recently discovered inscriptions (H. Seyrig, *Syria*, XIV, 1933, pp. 152 *sqq.*). The *praefectus* plays a part in the administration of the city and sits with the local magistrates. But side by side with the Imperial troops Palmyra kept its own militia, under a native commander, of mounted bowmen whose task it was to protect the caravans. In 198 it honours a general 'who had restored peace' in its territory (H. Ingholt, *Syria*, XIII, 1932, pp. 279 *sqq.*). In 225 another Palmyrene general was guarding the forts of Anah and Gamlah on the caravan route (see Note 3). These native troops do not seem to have been incorporated with the regular army until the beginning of the third century. They then formed in it the *cohortes Palmyrenorum* of which the twentieth did garrison duty at Doura.

FR. C.

3. STATIONS ON THE EUPHRATES

The letter of Marius Maximus, written between 202 and 207 and brought to light by a papyrus from Doura (M. Rostovtzeff, *C. R. Ac. Inscr.* 1933, p. 316), mentions two stations Eddana and Biblada situated to the south of this town. It follows that Roman rule extended at least as far as these. Perhaps it extended farther, for the general's letter may indicate only the posts which depended on the fort of Doura and not the others. It only gives us a section of the Euphrates *limes*. Palmyrene troops occupied the line of the river below this point. This is proved by two inscriptions from Palmyrene, one of which mentions in A.D. 132 a Nabataean 'who was a cavalryman at Hirtha and in the camp at Anah' (Chabot, *Répert. épigr. sém.* I, no. 285; on the site of Hirtha cf. R. Dussaud, *Syria*, XIV, 1933, p. 77). The other text, which belongs to A.D. 225, bears the name of someone 'general at Anah and at Gamlah' (*Syria*, XIII, 1932, p. 289; XIV, 1933, p. 179). According to M. Cantineau Gamlah is to be identified with Gmeylah four kilometres below Anah. But these points may have been occupied solely by Palmyrene troops and not by regulars of the Imperial army. Prof. Rostovtzeff (*Röm. Mitt.* XLIX, 1934, pp. 197 *sqq.*) argues that these troops were not Palmyrene, but Arab militia recruited by the municipal authorities. It appears to the present writer more probable that the road to the Persian Gulf was marked by *fondouqs*, guarded by Palmyrene archers and serving as posting-houses for the mounted troops that escorted the caravans. The question will only be decided by excavations in the plains of Iraq.

FR. C.

LIST OF ABBREVIATIONS

[See also General Bibliography, Parts ii, iv, and for papyri the
bibliography to vol. x, chapter x and below, p. 927]

Abh. Arch.-epig.	Abhandlungen d. archäol.-epigraph. Seminars d. Univ. Wien.
Aeg.	Aegyptus. Rivista italiana di egittologia e di papirologia.
Afr. Ital.	Africa Italiana; Rivista di storia e d'arte a cura del Ministero delle Colonie.
A.J.A.	American Journal of Archaeology.
A.J. Num.	American Journal of Numismatics.
A.J. Ph.	American Journal of Philology.
Ann. épig.	L'Année épigraphique.
Arch. Anz.	Archäologischer Anzeiger (in J.D.A.I.).
Arch. Pap.	Archiv für Papyrusforschung.
Arch. Relig.	Archiv für Religionswissenschaft.
Ath. Mitt.	Mitteilungen des deutschen arch. Inst. Athenische Abteilung.
Atti Acc. Torino	Atti della reale Accademia di scienze di Torino.
Bay. Abh.	Abhandlungen d. bayerischen Akad. d. Wissenschaften.
Bay. S.B.	Sitzungsberichte d. bayerischen Akad. d. Wissenschaften.
B.C.H.	Bulletin de Correspondance hellénique.
Berl. Abh.	Abhandlungen d. preuss. Akad. d. Wissenschaften zu Berlin.
Berl. S.B.	Sitzungsberichte d. preuss. Akad. d. Wissenschaften zu Berlin.
B.J.	Bonner Jahrbücher.
B.M. Cat.	British Museum Catalogue.
B.S.A.	Annual of the British School at Athens.
B.S.R.	Papers of the British School at Rome.
Bull. Comm. Arch.	Bullettino della Commissione archeol. comunale.
Bursian	Bursian's Jahresbericht.
C.I.L.	Corpus Inscriptionum Latinarum.
C.J.	Classical Journal.
C.P.	Classical Philology.
C.Q.	Classical Quarterly.
C.R.	Classical Review.
C.R. Ac. Inscr.	Comptes rendus de l'Académie des Inscriptions et Belles-Lettres.
Dessau	Dessau, Inscriptiones Latinae Selectae.
Ditt.[3]	Dittenberger, Sylloge Inscriptionum Graecarum. Ed. 3.
D.S.	Daremberg et Saglio, Dictionnaire des antiquités grecques et romaines.
Eph. Ep.	Ephemeris Epigraphica.
F.Gr. Hist.	F. Jacoby's Fragmente der griechischen Historiker.
F.H.G.	C. Müller's Fragmenta Historicorum Graecorum.
Germ.	Germania.
G.G.A.	Göttingische Gelehrte Anzeigen.
Gött. Abh.	Abhandlungen d. Gesellschaft d. Wissenschaften zu Göttingen.
Gött. Nach.	Nachrichten von der Gesellschaft der Wissenschaften zu Göttingen. Phil.-hist. Klasse.
Harv. St.	Harvard Studies in Classical Philology.
H.Z.	Historische Zeitschrift.
I.G.	Inscriptiones Graecae.
I.G.R.R.	Inscriptiones Graecae ad res Romanas pertinentes.
Jahreshefte	Jahreshefte d. österreichischen archäologischen Instituts in Wien.

J.D.A.I.	Jahrbuch des deutschen archäologischen Instituts.
J. d. Sav.	Journal des Savants.
J.E.A.	Journal of Egyptian Archaeology.
J.H.S.	Journal of Hellenic Studies.
J.P.	Journal of Philology.
J.R.S.	Journal of Roman Studies.
Mél. Beyrouth	Mélanges de l'Université Saint-Joseph, Beyrouth.
Mém. Ac. Inscr.	Mémoires de l'Académie des Inscriptions et Belles-Lettres.
Mem. Acc. Lincei	Memorie della reale Accademia nazionale dei Lincei.
Mem. Acc. Torino	Memorie della reale Accademia di scienze di Torino.
Mnem.	Mnemosyne.
Mon. Linc.	Monumenti antichi pubblicati per cura della reale Accademia Nazionale dei Lincei.
Mus. B.	Musée belge.
N. J. f. Wiss.	Neue Jahrbücher für Wissenschaft und Jugendbildung.
N. J. Kl. Alt.	Neue Jahrbücher für das klassische Altertum.
N.J.P.	Neue Jahrbücher für Philologie.
Not. arch.	Notiziario archeologico del Ministero delle Colonie.
N.S.A.	Notizie degli Scavi di Antichità.
Num. Chr.	Numismatic Chronicle.
Num. Z.	Numismatische Zeitschrift.
O.G.I.S.	Orientis Graeci Inscriptiones Selectae.
Phil.	Philologus.
Phil. Woch.	Philologische Wochenschrift.
P.I.R.	Prosopographia Imperii Romani.
P.W.	Pauly-Wissowa-Kroll's Real-Encyclopädie der classischen Altertumswissenschaft.
Rend. Linc.	Rendiconti della reale Accademia dei Lincei.
Rev. Arch.	Revue archéologique.
Rev. Belge	Revue Belge de philosophie et d'histoire.
Rev. E. A.	Revue des études anciennes.
Rev. E. G.	Revue des études grecques.
Rev. E. L.	Revue des études latines.
Rev. H.	Revue historique.
Rev. Hist. Rel.	Revue de l'histoire des religions.
Rev. N.	Revue numismatique.
Rev. Phil.	Revue de philologie, de littérature et d'histoire anciennes.
R.-G. K. Ber.	Berichte der Römisch-Germanischen Kommission.
Rh. Mus.	Rheinisches Museum für Philologie.
Riv. Fil.	Rivista di filologia.
Riv. stor. ant.	Rivista di storia antica.
Röm. Mitt.	Mitteilungen des deutschen arch. Inst. Römische Abteilung.
Sächs. Abh.	Abhandlungen d. sächs. Akad. d. Wissenschaften zu Leipzig.
S.B.	Sitzungsberichte.
S.E.G.	Supplementum Epigraphicum Graecum.
Symb. Osl.	Symbolae Osloenses.
Wien Anz.	Anzeiger d. Akad. d. Wissenschaften in Wien.
Wien S.B.	Sitzungsberichte d. Akad. d. Wissenschaften in Wien.
Wien. St.	Wiener Studien.
Z. D. Pal.-V.	Zeitschrift des Deutschen Palästina-Vereins.
Z. d. Sav.-Stift.	Zeitschrift d. Savigny-Stiftung f. Rechtsgeschichte, Romanistische Abteilung.
Z.N.	Zeitschrift für Numismatik.

BIBLIOGRAPHIES

These bibliographies do not aim at completeness. They include modern and standard works and, in particular, books utilized in the writings of the chapters. Some technical monographs, especially in journals, are omitted, but the works that are registered below will put the reader on their track.

The first page only of articles in journals is given.

GENERAL BIBLIOGRAPHY

I. General Histories

Albertini, E. *L'Empire romain*. (Vol. iv in the *Peuples et Civilisations* Series directed by L. Halphen and P. Sagnac.) Paris, 1929.

Barbagallo, C. *Roma Antica*, ii. *L'Impero romano*. (Vol. ii of *Storia universale*.) Turin, 1932.

Boak, A. E. R. *A History of Rome to* A.D. 565. Ed. 2. New York, 1929.

Bury, J. B. *A History of the Roman Empire from its Foundation to the death of Marcus Aurelius* (27 B.C.–A.D. 180). 6th Impression. London, 1913.

Chapot, V. *Le monde romain*. Paris, 1927.

Dessau, H. *Geschichte der römischen Kaiserzeit*, ii, ii. (*Die Länder und Völker des Reichs im ersten Jahrhundert der Kaiserzeit*.) Berlin, 1930.

von Domaszewski, A. *Geschichte der römischen Kaiser*. 2 vols. Ed. 3. Leipzig, 1922.

Duruy, V. *Histoire des Romains depuis les temps les plus reculés jusqu'à l'invasion des Barbares*. Nouv. Éd. Paris. Vol. iv, 1882; vol. v, 1883; vol. vi, 1883.

Frank, T. *A History of Rome*. London, n.d. [1923].

—— *An Economic History of Rome*. Ed. 2. Baltimore, 1927.

Gibbon, E. *The History of the Decline and Fall of the Roman Empire*, edited by J. B. Bury. London, vol. i, 1896.

Henderson, B. W. *Five Roman Emperors. Vespasian, Titus, Domitian, Nerva, Trajan*, A.D. 69–117. Cambridge, 1927.

Homo, L. *Le haut-empire*. (Vol. iii of *Histoire romaine* in the *Histoire générale* directed by G. Glotz.) Paris, 1933.

Kornemann, E. and J. Vogt, *Römische Geschichte* in Gercke-Norden, *Einleitung in die Altertumswissenschaft*. Ed. 3, iii, 2. Leipzig-Berlin, 1933.

Miller, S. N. *The Roman Empire in the first three centuries*. In *European Civilization: its origin and development* (ed. E. Eyre), vol. ii. London, 1935, pp. 279–522.

Mommsen, Th. *The Provinces of the Roman Empire from Caesar to Diocletian*. (English Translation by W. P. Dickson in 1886, reprinted with corrections in 1909.) London, 1909.

Niese, B. *Grundriss der römischen Geschichte nebst Quellenkunde*. 5te Auflage neubearbeitet von E. Hohl. (Müller's *Handbuch der klassischen Altertumswissenschaft*, Band iii, Abt. 5.) Munich, 1923.

Nilsson, M. P. *Imperial Rome*, translated by G. C. Richards. London, 1926.

Parker, H. M. D. *A History of the Roman World from A.D.* 138 *to* 337. London, 1935.

Rostovtzeff, M. *The Social and Economic History of the Roman Empire*. 1926. Ed. 2, *Gesellschaft und Wirtschaft im römischen Kaiserreich*. Leipzig, n.d. [1930]: ed. 3, *Storia economica e sociale dell' impero Romano*. Florence, 1933.

Rostovtzeff, M. *A History of the Ancient World*. Vol. ii, *Rome*. Oxford, 1927.
Schiller, H. *Geschichte der römischen Kaiserzeit*. Gotha. Vol. i, ii, 1883.
Stevenson, G. H. *The Roman Empire*. London, 1930.
Stuart Jones, H. *The Roman Empire*, B.C. 29–A.D. 476. 3rd Impression, London, 1916.
Wells, J. and R. H. Barrow, *A Short History of the Roman Empire to the death of Marcus Aurelius*. London, 1931.

II. Works of Reference, Dictionaries, etc.

Abbott, F. F. and A. C. Johnson, *Municipal Administration in the Roman Empire*. Princeton, N.J., 1926.
Daremberg, Ch. and E. Saglio, *Dictionnaire des antiquités grecques et romaines d'après les textes et les monuments*. Paris, 1877–1919. (D.S.)
De Ruggiero, G. *Dizionario Epigrafico di Antichità romane*. Rome. 1895– . (Diz. Epig.)
Friedländer, L. and G. Wissowa, *Darstellungen aus der Sittengeschichte Roms*. Edd. 9 and 10. Leipzig, 1919–21.
Gercke, A. and E. Norden, *Einleitung in die Altertumswissenschaft*. Ed. 2, Leipzig-Berlin, 1914. Ed. 3 in course of publication. (Gercke-Norden.)
Hirschfeld, O. *Die kaiserlichen Verwaltungsbeamten bis auf Diocletian*. Ed. 2. Berlin, 1905.
Klebs, E., H. Dessau, P. von Rohden, *Prosopographia Imperii Romani Saec. I, II, III*. Berlin. Vol. i, ed. E. Klebs, 1897; vol. ii, ed. H. Dessau, 1897; vol. iii, edd. P. de Rohden et H. Dessau, 1898. Vol. i of the 2nd edition, edd. E. Groag et A. Stein, Berlin-Leipzig, 1933 (P.I.R.).
Lübker, Friedrich. *Reallexikon des klassischen Altertums für Gymnasien*. Ed. 8 (by J. Geffcken and E. Ziebarth). Leipzig, 1914. (Lübker.)
Marquardt, J. *Römische Staatsverwaltung*. Leipzig. Ed. 2. Vol. i, 1881; vol. ii, 1884; vol. iii, 1885.
Mommsen, Th. *Römisches Staatsrecht*. Leipzig. Vol. i (ed. 3), 1887; vol. ii, 1 (ed. 3), 1887; vol. ii, 2 (ed. 3), 1887; vol. iii, 1, 1887; vol. iii, 2, 1888.
von Müller, Iwan. *Handbuch der Altertumswissenschaft*. (In course of revision under editorship of W. Otto.) Munich, 1886–   (Müllers Handbuch.)
Platner, S. B. *A Topographical Dictionary of Ancient Rome*. (Completed and revised by T. Ashby.) Oxford, 1929.
Sandys, Sir J. E. *A Companion to Latin Studies*. Ed. 3. Cambridge, 1929.
Stuart Jones, H. *A Companion to Roman History*. Oxford, 1912.
Wissowa, G. *Pauly's Real-Encyclopädie der classischen Altertumswissenschaft*. Neue Bearbeitung. (Under editorship of W. Kroll.) Stuttgart, 1894– . (P.W.)

III. Chronology

Bickermann, E. *Chronologie*, in Gercke-Norden, Band iii, Heft 5. Leipzig-Berlin, 1933.
Griffin, M. H. and G. A. Harrer, *Fasti Consulares*. A.J.A. xxxiv, 1930, pp. 360*sqq*.
Kubitschek, W. *Grundriss der antiken Zeitrechnung*, in Müllers Handbuch, i, 7. Munich, 1928.
Leuze, O. *Bericht über die Literatur zur Chronologie (Kalendar und Jahrzählung) in die Jahren* 1921–1928. Bursian, ccxxvii, 1930, pp. 97–139.
Liebenam, W. *Fasti Consulares imperii Romani von 30 v. Chr. bis 565 n. Chr.* Bonn, 1909.

IV. Numismatics

Bernhart, M. *Handbuch zur Münzkunde der römischen Kaiserzeit.* Halle a.S., 1926.

Cohen, H. *Description historique des monnaies frappées sous l'empire romain.* Ed. 2. Paris, 1880–92.

Mattingly, H. *British Museum Catalogue of Coins of the Roman Empire.* London. Vol. ii (Vespasian to Domitian). 1930. Vol. iii (Nerva to Hadrian), 1936.

Mattingly, H. and E. A. Sydenham, *The Roman Imperial Coinage.* London, vol. ii (Vespasian to Hadrian), 1926. Vol. iii (Antoninus Pius to Commodus), 1930.

Milne, J. G. *Catalogue of Alexandrian Coins in the Ashmolean Museum.* Oxford, 1932.

Schulz, O. Th. *Die Rechtstitel und Regierungsprogramme auf römischen Kaisermünzen, von Caesar bis Severus.* (Studien zur Geschichte und Kultur des Altertums, xiii, 4.) Paderborn, 1925.

Strack, P. L. *Untersuchungen zur römische Reichsprägung des zweiten Jahrhunderts.* Stuttgart. Teil ii, 1933, Teil iii (in publication).

Vogt, J. *Die alexandrinischen Münzen: Grundlegung einer alexandrinischen Kaisergeschichte.* Part i, Text; Part ii, Münzverzeichnis. Stuttgart, 1924.

V. Source Criticism

Leo, F. *Die griechisch-römische Biographie nach ihrer litterarischen Form.* Leipzig, 1901.

Peter, H. *Die geschichtliche Literatur über die römische Kaiserzeit bis Theodosius I und ihre Quellen.* Leipzig, 1897. 2 vols.

Rosenberg, A. *Einleitung und Quellenkunde zur römischen Geschichte.* Berlin, 1921.

Wachsmuth, C. *Einleitung in das Studium der alten Geschichte.* Leipzig, 1895.
(For treatment of particular portions of the Sources see the bibliographies to the relevant chapters.)

Schwartz, E. Art. in P.W. *s.v.* Cassius (40) Dio Cocceianus.

Schultz, H. Art. in P.W. *s.v.* Herodianus (3).

Enmann, A. *Eine verlorene Geschichte der römischen Kaiser.* Phil. Suppl. iv, 1884, p. 337.

De Sanctis, G. *Gli Scriptores Historiae Augustae.* Riv. stor. ant. i, 1896, p. 90.

Dessau, H. *Über Zeit und Persönlichkeit der Scriptores Historiae Augustae.* Hermes, xxiv, 1889, p. 337. Cf. ib. xxvii, 1892, p. 561.

Tropea, G. *Studi sugli Scriptores Historiae Augustae.* Messina, 1899.

Lécrivain, C. *Études sur l'Histoire Auguste.* Paris, 1904.

Seeck, O. *Politische Tendenzgeschichte im 5 Jahrhundert.* Rh. Mus. lxvii, 1912, p. 591.

Mommsen, Th. *Die Scriptores historiae Augustae.* Ges. Schrift. vii, pp. 302–52.

Hohl, E. *Das Problem der Historia Augusta.* N.J. Kl. Alt. xxxiii, 1914, p. 698.

von Domaszewski, A. *Die Personennamen bei den Scriptores Historiae Augustae.* Heid. S.B. 1918, 13 Abh.

Baynes, N. *The Historia Augusta, its date and purpose.* (With Bibliography.) Oxford, 1926.

Funaioli, G. Art. in P.W. *s.v.* Suetonius (4).

Macé, A. *Essai sur Suétone.* Paris, 1900.

CHAPTER I

THE FLAVIANS

A. Ancient Sources

(1) *Inscriptions*

The inscriptional evidence for the Flavian era is very large. Down to the year 1900 it has been well collected in a monograph by H. C. Newton, *The Epigraphical Evidence for the Reigns of Vespasian and Titus*, Cornell Studies in Classical Philology, xvi, 1901. Many of these inscriptions, together with some later material, will be found in Dessau, Dittenberger[3], I.G.R.R. and O.G.I.S.: material later than this can usually be tracked down in *L'Année épigraphique* (Latin) and in *Supplementum Epigraphicum Graecum* (Greek). Reference is made to the more important of these documents in the footnotes to this chapter, and also in the footnotes to the chapter on the Flavian Wars and to the chapters on the provinces.

Edict of Domitian concerning the immunity of veterans: G. Lefebvre, *Bull. de la Soc. archéol. d'Alexandrie*, 12, 1910, p. 39: see U. Wilcken in Arch. Pap. v, 1913, p. 434, and F. Schehl in Aeg. xiii, 1933, p. 136.

(2) *Coins*

Laffranchi, L. *Sulla numismatica dei Flavii*. Riv. ital. di num. xxvii, 1915, p. 139.
Mattingly, H. and E. A. Sydenham, *The Roman Imperial Coinage*. Vol. ii, London, 1926. Pp. 1–213.

(3) *Texts*

Codex Justinianus (rec. P. Krueger, ed. 9, Berlin, 1915), viii, 10, 2.
Corpus Agrimensorum Romanorum, ed. C. Thulin, vol. i, i, Leipzig, 1913.
Digesta (rec. Th. Mommsen, ed. 14, Berlin, 1922), i, 2, 32; xl, 15, 1 and 4; 16, 1; xlviii, 3, 2, 1; 22, 1; l, 4, 18, 30.
Dio lxv–lxvii, ed. U. P. Boissevain, vol. iii, Berlin, 1901.
Epictetus, *Dissertationes ab Arriano digestae*, iterum rec. H. Schenkl, Leipzig, 1916.
Festus, *Breviarium* (ed. W. Förster, Vienna, 1894), 10.
Gaius, *Institutiones* (ed. E. Poste, ed. 4, Oxford, 1904), i, 85; ii, 286, 286a.
Juvenal, ed. A. E. Housman, Cambridge, 1931.
Martial, *Epigrammata*, rec. W. M. Lindsay, Oxford, 1903.
Orosius, *Historiae adversus Paganos* (ed. C. Zangemeister, Leipzig, 1889), vii, 9, 1–15; 10, 1–7.
Pliny the Elder, *Historia Naturalis*, ed. C. Mayhoff, Leipzig, 1892–1909.
Pliny the Younger, *Epistulae* and *Panegyricus*, rec. M. Schuster, Leipzig, 1933.
Quintilian, *Institutio Oratoria*, ed. L. Radermacher, Leipzig, 1907–35.
Statius, *Silvae*, ed. J. S. Phillimore, ed. 2, Oxford, 1918.
Suetonius, *de vita Caesarum libri viii*, ed. M. Ihm, ed. maior, Leipzig, 1907, ed. minor, 1908.
　　C. Suetoni Tranquilli Divus Vespasianus, with an introduction and commentary by A. W. Braithwaite. Oxford, 1927.
　　C. Suetoni Tranquilli Vita Domitiani, J. Janssen, Amsterdam Diss., The Hague, 1919.
　　C. Suetoni Tranquilli de vita Caesarum Libri vii–viii, with Introduction, Translation, and Commentary by George W. Mooney, London, 1930.
　　C. Suetoni Tranquilli de vita Caesarum Liber viii Divus Vespasianus. Suetonius' Life of Vespasian with Notes and Parallel Passages. H. M. T. Skerrett, Pennsylvania Diss., Philadelphia, Pa., 1924.

Tacitus, *Historiae*, rec. J. van der Vliet (cum fragmentis et supplementis), Groningen, 1900: rec. C. D. Fisher, Oxford, 1910.

—— *Agricola*, edd. H. Furneaux, F. Haverfield, J. G. C. Anderson, Oxford, 1922.

Occasional references are to be found in Aulus Gellius, Dio of Prusa, Frontinus, Josephus, Pausanias, Philostratus (*Life of Apollonius of Tyana*), Silius Italicus and Valerius Flaccus: where they are important they are cited in the notes to the chapter.

For the later tradition see Aurelius Victor, Malalas, and Suidas (*s.vv.* Βεσπασιανός, Τίτος and Δομετιανός).

B. Modern Works

(a) *Criticism of the Sources*

In addition to the relevant pages in the works of Funaioli, Leo, Macé, Peter, Rosenberg, Schwartz and Wachsmuth (see General Bibliography, p. 865) the following should be consulted:

Groag, E. *Zur Kritik von Tacitus Quellen in die Historien.* Jahrb. f. class. Phil. Suppl. Bd. xxiii, 1897, p. 711.

Mesk, J. *Zur Quellenanalyse des Plinianischen Panegyricus.* Wien. St. xxxiii, 1911, p. 71.

Meyer, Joh. *Der Briefwechsel des Plinius und Traian als Quelle römischer Kaisergeschichte.* Diss. Strassburg, 1908.

Weber, W. *Josephus und Vespasian.* Stuttgart, 1921.

von Wölfflin, E. *Zur Komposition der Historien des Tacitus.* Münch. S.B. 1901, pp. 3–52.

—— *Plinius und Cluvius Rufus.* Arch. f. Lat. Lexikographie, xii, 1903, p. 345.

(b) *Books and articles on the Flavian period*

In addition to the relevant pages of the histories cited in the General Bibliography (p. 863 *sq.*), the following should be consulted:

Bang, M. *Die Steuern dreier römischer Provinzen.* In L. Friedländer, *Darstellungen…* (ed. 9 and 10, Leipzig, 1921), iv, pp. 297–300.

Bücheler, Fr. *Prosopographica*, xii. Rh. Mus. lxiii, 1908, p. 194.

Cantarelli, L. *La Lex de imperio Vespasiani.* Studi Romani e Bizantini, Rome, 1915, pp. 99–123.

Charlesworth, M. P. *Providentia and Aeternitas.* Harvard Theol. Rev. xxix, 1936, p. 107.

Colson, F. H. *Quintilian, the Gospels and Christianity.* C.R. xxxix, 1925, p. 166.

Constans, L. A. *Les jardins d'Épaphrodite.* Mélanges d'Arch. et d'Hist. xxxiv, 1914, p. 383.

Erman, A. *Obelisken roemischer Zeit.* Röm. Mitt. viii, 1893, p. 210: see also Zeits. f. ägypt. Sprache und Altertumskunde, xxxiv, 1896, pp. 149–158.

Gardthausen, V. *Ein Vizekönig von Aegypten.* Phil. lxvi, 1907, p. 481.

Groag, E. *Zum Konsulat in der Kaiserzeit.* Wien. St. xlvii, 1929, p. 143.

Gsell, S. *Essai sur le règne de l'empereur Domitien.* Paris, 1894.

Hahn, L. *Römische Beamte griechischer und orientalischer Abstammung in der Kaiserzeit.* Festgabe zur 400-Jahrfeier des alt. Gymn. Nürnberg, 1926, pp. 9–64.

Harrer, G. A. *The Latin Inscription from Antioch.* A.J.A. xxix, 1925, p. 429.

—— *Inscriptions of Legati in Syria.* Ib. xxxvi, 1932, p. 287.

Herzog, R. *Urkunden zur Hochschulpolitik der römischen Kaiser.* Berl. S.B. xxxii, 1935, pp. 967 *sqq.*

Lugli, G. *La villa di Domiziano sui colli Albani*. Bull. Comm. Arch. XLV, 1918, p. 29; XLVI, 1920, p. 3; XLVII, 1921, p. 153; XLVIII, 1922, p. 3.

McElderry, R. K. *Some Conjectures on the Reign of Vespasian*. J.R.S. III, 1913, p. 116.
—— *Vespasian's Reconstruction of Spain*. Ib. VIII, 1918, p. 53, and *Addenda*, IX, 1919, p. 86.

Marucchi, O. *Di alcuni frammenti dell' obelisco di piazza Navoni, ora nel museo egizio vaticano*. Bull. Comm. Arch. XLV, 1918, p. 103.

Mickwitz, G. *Zu den Finanzen Trajans*. Arctos, III, 1934, p. 1.

Nock, A. D. *Religious Developments from Vespasian to Trajan*. Theology, March, 1928.

Otto, W. *Zur Lebensgeschichte des jüngeren Plinius*. Bay. S.B. 1919, no. 1.
—— *Zur Prätur des jüngeren Plinius*. Ib. 1923, no. 4.

Pichlmayr, F. *T. Flavius Domitianus (Ein Beitrag zur römischen Kaisergeschichte)*. Amberg, 1889.

Schehl, F. *Zum Edikt Domitians über die Immunitäten der Veteranen*. Aeg. XIII, 1933, p. 136.

Schönbauer, E. *Zur Erklärung der lex metalli Vipascensis*. Z. d. Sav.-Stift. XLV, 1925, p. 352; XLVI, 1926, p. 181.

van Sickle, C. E. *The Repair of Roads in Spain*. C.P. XXIV, 1929, p. 77.

Sizoo, A. *Paetus Thrasea et le Stoïcisme*. Rev. E.L. IV, 1926, p. 229; V, 1927, p. 41.

Stech, B. *Senatores Romani qui fuerint inde a Vespasiano usque a Traiani exitum*. Klio, Beiheft 10, 1912.

Stein, A. *Balbillus*. Aeg. XIII, 1933, p. 123 (esp. pp. 134 *sqq.*).

Syme, R. *The imperial finances under Domitian, Nerva and Trajan*. J.R.S. XX, 1930, p. 55: and cf. C. H. V. Sutherland, *ib*. XXV, 1935, p. 150.

Thiele, G. *Die Poesie unter Domitian*. Hermes, LI, 1916, p. 233.

Valdenberg, V. *La théorie monarchique de Dion Chrysostome*. Rev. E.G. XL, 1927, p. 142.

Walton, C. S. *Oriental Senators in the Service of Rome*. J.R.S. XIX, 1929, p. 38.

Weinreich, O. *Studien zu Martial*. Stuttgart, 1928.

Wissowa, G. *Vestalinenfrevel*. Arch. Relig. XXII, 1923, p. 211.

Arts in P.W. *s.vv.* T. Flavius Vespasianus (Flavius, 206), Imperator T. Flavius Vespasianus Augustus (Flavius, 207), and T. Flavius Domitianus (Flavius, 77), all by Weynand: in Diz. Epig. *s.v.* Domitianus by Corradi.

(c) *The deification and titles of Domitian*

Beurlier, E. *Le culte impérial*. Paris, 1891, esp. pp. 43–54.

Case, S. J. *Josephus' anticipation of a Domitianic persecution*. Journ. Bibl. Lit. XLIV, 1925, p. 10.

Charlesworth, M. P. *Some observations on Ruler-Cult, especially in Rome*. Harvard Theol. Rev. XXVIII, 1935, p. 5 (esp. pp. 31–35).

Dölger, Fr. *Die Kaiservergöttung bei Martial und 'Die heiligen Fische Domitians.'* Antike und Christentum, I, 1929, p. 163.

Kubitschek, W. *Des Grafen Klemens Westphalen Münzsammlung und Münzforschung*. Num. Z. (N.F.), VIII, 1915, 2. dominus et deus *als Titel des Kaisers*, p. 167.

Merrill, E. T. *The Alleged Persecution by Domitian*. Essays in Early Christian History, London, 1924, pp. 148–173.

Sauter, F. *Der römische Kaiserkult bei Martial und Statius* (Tübinger Beiträge, no. 21). Stuttgart-Berlin, 1934 (with full Bibliography).

Schütz, R. *Die Offenbarung des Johannes und Kaiser Domitian*. Forschungen u. Fortschritte, X, 1934, p. 141.

Scott, K. *Statius' Adulation of Domitian*. A.J.Ph. LIV, 1933, p. 247.
—— *The Elder and Younger Pliny on Emperor Worship*. Trans. Amer. Phil. Assoc. LXIII, 1932, p. 156.

CHAPTER II

THE PEOPLES OF NORTHERN EUROPE

A. Sections i—v

The aim of this bibliography is to supply a select list of works which have been used by the writer of this chapter and which seem to him specially useful in illuminating the ethnographic conditions and geographical distribution of the Germanic peoples during the two first centuries after Christ. A † set against an entry indicates encyclopaedias, dictionaries, works of general reference, etc.

For the literary sources, e.g. Caesar, Strabo, Tacitus, and for commentaries upon them consult generally the relevant articles in Bursian's *Jahresbericht* and *Bibliotheca Philologica Classica*. Special reference is here made to vol. ccxxiv (Suppl. vol. 1929), pp. 303 *sqq.*: H. Drexler, *Tacitus für die Jahre* 1913–1927. Among recent editions of Tacitus' *Germania* that of W. Reeb (unter Mitarbeit von H. Klenk, mit Beiträgen von A. Dopsch, H. Reis, K. Schumacher), Leipzig and Berlin, 1930, is recommended.

Almgren, O. *Zur Bedeutung des Markomannenreichs in Böhmen für die Entwicklung der germanischen Industrie in der frühen Kaiserzeit.* Mannus, v, 1913, p. 265.
—— *Studien über nordeuropäische Fibelformen der ersten nachchristlichen Jahrhunderte.* Ed. 2, Mannus-Bibliothek, xxxii, 1923.
—— and Nerman, B. *Die ältere Eisenzeit Gotlands.* Stockholm, 1914–23, pp. 16–151.
Anger, S. *Das Gräberfeld von Rondsen.* Graudenz, 1890.
Antoniewicz, W. *Archeologja Polski.* Warsaw, 1928, pp. 155 *sqq.*
Beltz, R. *Die vorgeschichtlichen Altertümer des Grossherzogthums Mecklenburg-Schwerin.* Text, Tafeln. Schwerin i. M., 1910, pp. 312 *sqq.*
Beninger, E. *Die Germanenzeit in Niederösterreich von Marbod bis zu den Babenbergern.* Vienna, 1934.
Blume, E. *Die germanischen Stämme und die Kulturen zwischen Oder und Passarge zur römischen Kaiserzeit.* i–ii, Mannus-Bibliothek, viii, xiv, 1912, 1915.
Bolin, S. *Fynden av romerska mynt i det fria Germanien.* Lund, 1926.
—— *Die Funde römischer und byzantinischer Münzen im freien Germanien.* R.-G. K. Ber. xix, 1929.
†Bremer, O. *Die Ethnographie der germanischen Stämme.* Grundriss der germanischen Philologie. Hrsg. von Hermann Paul. iii, ed. 2, 1900, pp. 735 *sqq.*
†Capelle, W. *Das alte Germanien. Die Nachrichten der griechischen und römischen Schriftsteller.* Jena, 1929.
Congressus secundus archaeologorum Balticorum Rigae 19–23, viii, 1930. Acta Universitatis latviensis, Philologorum et Philosophorum ordinis series, Tomus I, Supplementum 1. Rigae, 1931, pp. 167 *sqq.*, 395 *sqq.*, 437 *sqq.*
Dopsch, A. *Grundlagen der europäischen Kulturentwicklung.* 2 vols., ed. 2, Vienna, 1923–4.
Ekholm, G. *Zur Geschichte des römisch-germanischen Handels.* Acta Archaeologica, vi, 1935.
—— *Forntid och fornforskning i Skandinavien.* Stockholm, 1935.
Engel, C. *Führer durch die vorgeschichtliche Sammlung des Dommuseums.* Riga, 1933.
—— *Aus ostpreussischer Vorzeit.* Königsberg, 1935, pp. 73–86.
Gaerte, W. *Urgeschichte Ostpreussens.* Königsberg i. Pr. 1929, pp. 162 *sqq.*

Girke, G. *Die Tracht der Germanen in der vor- und frühgeschichtlichen Zeit.* Mannus-Bibliothek, XXIII–XXIV, 1921–2.

Hackman, A. *Die ältere Eisenzeit in Finnland.* I, Helsingfors, 1905.

—— *Die ältesten eisenzeitlichen Funde in Finnland.* Mannus, V, 1913, pp. 279 *sqq.*

Hamberg, P. G. *Zur Bewaffnung und Kampfesart der Germanen.* Acta Archaeologica, VII, 1936.

Hostmann, Chr. *Der Urnenfriedhof bei Darzau.* Braunschweig, 1874.

Jahn, M. *Die Bewaffnung der Germanen.* Mannus-Bibliothek, XVI, 1916.

—— *Der Wanderweg der Kimbern, Teutonen und Wandalen.* Mannus, XXIV, 1932, p. 150.

†Karsten, T. E. *Die Germanen.* Grundriss der germanischen Philologie. Hrsg. von Hermann Paul. Ed. 3, IX, 1928.

Katalog der Ausstellung zur Konferenz baltischer Archäologen i Riga, 1930. Riga, 1930.

†Kaufmann, Fr. *Deutsche Altertumskunde.* Hälfte I–II. Munich, 1913–23.

Kiekebusch, A. *Der Einfluss der römischen Kultur auf die germanische im Spiegel der Hügelgräber des Niederrheins.* Studien und Forschungen zur Menschen- und Völkerkunde, III, 1908.

Kossinna, G. *Germanische Kultur im I. Jahrtausend nach Christus.* I, Mannus-Bibliothek, L, 1932.

—— *Die Karte der germanischen Funde in der frühen Kaiserzeit (etwa 1–150 n. Chr.).* Mannus, XXV, 1933, p. 6.

Kostrzewski, J. *Wielkopolska w czasach przedhistorycznych.* Posen, 1923, pp. 167 *sqq.*

Kunkel, C. *Pommersche Urgeschichte in Bildern.* (2 parts, Text and Plates.) Stettin, 1931.

La Baume, W. *Vorgeschichte von Westpreussen.* Danzig, 1920.

†Lindenschmit, L. *Die Alterthümer unserer heidnischen Vorzeit.* I–V, Mainz, 1858–1911.

†Montelius, O. *Den nordiska järnålderns kronologi,* I–II. Svenska fornminnesföreningens tidskrift, IX, 1894–6, p. 193.

Moora, H. *Die Vorzeit Estlands.* Veröffentlichungen der Archäologischen Kabinetts der Universität Tartu, VI, 1932, pp. 29 *sqq.*

†Müllenhoff, K. *Deutsche Altertumskunde.* Vols. I–V, Berlin, 1870–91. (New impressions of vols. IV and V appeared in 1920 and 1908; IV: *Die Germania des Tacitus,* with commentary by K.M., is invaluable.)

†Müller, S. *Ordning af Danmarks Oldsager.* Système préhistorique du Danemark. [Résumé en français.] Vol. II. Copenhagen, 1888–95, pp. 12 *sqq.*

—— *Nordische Altertumskunde.* Vol. II, Strassburg, 1898, pp. 50 *sqq.*

—— *Juellinge-Fundet og den romerske Periode.* [Résumé en français] Nordiske Fortidsminder, II, 7, 1911.

—— *Oldtidens Kunst i Danmark.* III. *Jernalderens Kunst.* [Résumé en français.] Copenhagen, 1933.

Nerman, B. *Die Herkunft und die frühesten Auswanderungen der Germanen.* K Vitterhets Historie och Antikvitets Akademiens Handlingar, XXXIV, 5, 1924.

Norden, E. *Die germanische Urgeschichte in Tacitus' Germania.* Ed. 2, Berlin, 1922.

Noreen, A. *Nordens äldsta folk- och ortnamn.* Fornvännen, XV, 1920, p. 23.

Petersen, E. *Die frühgermanische Kultur in Ostdeutschland und Polen.* Vorgeschichtliche Forschungen, II, 2, 1929.

Pič, J. L. *Die Urnengräber Böhmens.* Leipzig, 1907.

Plettke, A. *Ursprung und Ausbreitung der Angeln und Sachsen.* Die Urnenfriedhöfe in Niedersachsen, III, 1, 1921.

†*Reallexikon der germanischen Altertumskunde.* Hrsg. von Johannes Hoops, I–IV. Strassburg 1911–19. (Hoops, *Reallexikon.*)

†*Reallexikon der Vorgeschichte.* Hrsg. von Max Ebert, I–XV. Berlin, 1924–32. See especially the articles *Finnland, Ostpreussen, Südostbalticum.* (Ebert, *Reallexikon.*)

†Rygh, O. *Norske Oldsager. Antiquités norvégiennes.* Christiania, 1885. Le premier âge de fer.

†Schmidt, L. *Geschichte der deutschen Stämme bis zum Ausgang der Völkerwanderung.* [I] Die Ostgermanen. Ed. 2, Munich, 1934.

Schroeder, A. *De ethnographiae antiquae locis quibusdam communibus observationes.* Halis Saxonum, 1921.

Schulz, W. *Das germanische Haus in vorgeschichtlicher Zeit.* Mannus-Bibliothek, XI, 1913.

Schumacher, K. *Die Germania des Tacitus und die erhaltene Denkmäler.* Mainzer Zeitschrift, IV, 1909, p. 2.

Schütte, G. *Ptolemy's maps of northern Europe.* Copenhagen, 1917.

†——— *Our forefathers, the Gothonic nations.* (Trans. by Jean Young.) Vols. I and II, Cambridge, 1929–33.

Shetelig, H. *Préhistoire de la Norvège.* Instituttet for sammenlignende kultur-forskning, Ser. A, 5, 1926. (A new book on Scandinavian Archaeology, in English, by Prof. Shetelig, will be published by the Clarendon Press, Oxford, in 1936.)

Stocký, A. *La Bohême à l'âge du fer.* Prague, 1933.

Tackenberg, K. *Zu den Wanderungen der Ostgermanen.* Mannus, XXII, 1930, p. 268.

Voss, A. and G. Stimming, *Vorgeschichtliche Altertümer aus der Mark Brandenburg.* Ed. 2, Berlin, 1890. Abt. V–VI.

Wadstein, E. *Die nordischen Völkernamen bei Ptolemaios.* Göteborgs högskolas årsskrift, XXXI, 1925, p. 189.

Weibull, I. *Uppsachten av den skandinaviska Norden.* Scandia, VII, 1934, p. 150.

ERRATA

P. 870 l. 40 *for* II, 7, *read* II, 1.
P. 871 l. 27 *for* 'Uppsachten' *read* 'Upptäckten'.
Ll. 32–3 should be transferred to l. 12 to follow '1909, p. 2.'

B. SECTIONS VI AND VII

I. ANCIENT SOURCES

A comprehensive collection of the ancient sources relating to the Getae and Dacians is being prepared by Th. Rados, *Fontes Historiae Dacicae,* to be published in *Dissertationes Pannonicae.*

II. MODERN WORKS

1. General

Brandis, C. G. Art. *s.v.* Dacia in P.W.

Kazarow, G. I. *Beiträge zur Kulturgeschichte der Thraker.* Sarajevo, 1916.

Müllenhoff, K. *Deutsche Altertumskunde.* III, Berlin, 1892.

Pârvan, V. *Getica, o protoistorie a Daciei.* Bucharest, 1926. (Roumanian, with French résumé.)

——— *Dacia.* Cambridge, 1928.

Tomaschek, W. *Die alten Thraker,* I. Wien S.B. CXXVIII, 1893, Abh. 4; II, I, *ib.* CXXX, 1894, Abh. 2; II, 2, *ib.* CXXXI, 1894, Abh. I.

2. *Archaeological Evidence*

Childe, V. G. *The Danube in Prehistory*. Oxford, 1929.

Cichorius, C. *Die Reliefs der Traianssäule*. Berlin, 1896.

Nestor, J. *Der Stand der Vorgeschichtsforschung in Rumänien*. R.-G. K. Ber. XXII, 1933, pp. 11–181.

Tocilescu, G., Benndorf, O. and G. Niemann, *Das Monument von Adam-Klissi, Tropaeum Traiani*. Vienna, 1895.

de Tompa, F. *Zwanzig Jahre Urgeschichtsforschung in Ungarn*. R.-G. K. Ber. XXIV, 1934–36.

3. *Linguistic Evidence*

Kretschmer, P. *Zum Balkan-Skythischen*. Glotta, XXIV, 1935, p. 1.

Mateescu, G. G. *I Traci nelle epigrafi di Roma*. Eph. Dacoromana, I, 1923, pp. 57–290.

—— *Nomi Traci nel territorio Scito-Sarmatico*. Ib. II, 1924, pp. 223–238.

Pârvan, V. *Getica*, pp. 200 *sqq.*

Tomaschek, W. *Les restes de la langue dace*. Louvain, 1883.

4. *Special Topics*

(a) *The Cimmerians on Daco-Getic territory.*

Gallus, S. and T. Horváth, *Das Auftreten der Reitervölker in Ungarn*. Diss. Pann. 2nd series, fasc. 4: in preparation.

Nestor, J. *Ein thrako-kimmerischer Goldfund aus Rumänien*. Eurasia Septent. Antiqua, IX, 1934, p. 175.

Reinecke, P. *Ein neuer Goldfund aus Bulgarien*. Germ. IX, 1925, p. 50.

(b) *The Scythians.*

See also the books and articles listed under the bibliography to Chapter III, Part I, Section II, A and B.

Kovács, I. *Station préhistorique de Marosvásárhely*. Dolgozatok, VI, 1915, pp. 226 *sqq.* and 310 *sqq.* (Hungarian and French).

Minns, E. H. *Scythians and Greeks*. Cambridge, 1913.

Patsch, C. *Die Völkerschaft der Agathyrsen*. Wien Anz. 1925, pp. 69–77.

Rostovtzeff, M. *Skythien und der Bosporus*. I, Berlin, 1931: esp. pp. 494–529 (*Bestand der skythischen Altertümer Ungarns*, by N. Fettich), and pp. 530 *sqq.*

(c) *Relations with the Greeks.*

Borzsák, St. *Die Kenntnisse der Griechen über das Gebiet von Ungarn*. Diss. Pann. 2nd series, fasc. 6: 1936.

Kleinsorge, J. *De civitatium Graecarum in Ponti Euxini ora occidentali sitarum rebus*. Diss. Halle, 1888.

Pârvan, V. *La pénétration hellénique et hellénistique dans la vallée du Danube*. Bull. de la section hist. de l'Acad. roumaine, X, 1923.

Pick, B. *Die antiken Münzen Nordgriechenlands*. I, Berlin, 1898.

(d) *The Celtic Period.*

Andrieşescu, I. *Piscul Crăsani*. Acad. Română, Mem. sect. ist. 3 (Ser. 3), Mem. 1, Bucharest, 1924 (Rumanian).

de Márton, L. *Die Frühlatènezeit in Ungarn*. Arch. Hungarica, XI, 1933.

—— *Das Fundinventar der Frühlatène-Gräber*. Dolgozatok, IX–X (Szeged), 1933–34, p. 128.

Pârvan, V. *Considérations sur les sépultures celtiques de Gruia*. Dacia, I, 1924, p. 35.

de Roska, M. *Keltisches Grab aus Siebenbürgen*. Praehist. Zeits. XVI, 1925, p. 210.

Vulpe, R. and E. *Fouilles de Poiana*. Dacia, III–IV, 1927–32, p. 351.

(e) The late La-Tène Period.

Bahrfeldt, M. *Über die Goldmünzen des Dakerkönigs* ΚΟΣΩΝ. Berlin, 1911.

Dessewfy, (Count) M. *Barbarian coins in the Collection of Count M. Dessewfy.* Budapest, 1913 (Hungarian and French).

de Finály, G. *The Dacian fortresses of Grădişte.* Arch. Értesitö, 1916, pp. 11–43 (Hungarian).

Gohl, E. *Contributions to the Dacian Coinage.* Numerous articles in *Numizm. Közlöny,* from vol. II, 1903 to vol. XV, 1916 (Hungarian).

Pârvan, V. *La Dacie à l'époque celtique.* C.R. Ac. Inscr. 1926, p. 86.

Ruzicka, L. *Die Frage der dacischen Münzen.* Bulet. Soc. numism. romăne, XVII, 1922, p. 5.

Theodorescu, D. N. *Cetătile antice din munţii Hunedoarei.* In Publicat. Comis. Monument. Istorice, sect. p. Transylvania, II, 1923, pp. 7 *sqq.* (Rumanian).

—— *Cetatea dacă dela Costeşti.* Anuarul Comis. Mon. Ist. sect. p. Transylvania pe 1929, pp. 265 *sqq.* (Rumanian).

—— *Cetatea dacă dela Gradiştea.* Ib. 1930–31, pp. 45 *sqq.* (Rumanian).

(f) First Contacts with the Romans: War and Commerce.

For campaigns against the Dacians G. Zippel, *Die römische Herrschaft in Illyrien bis auf Augustus,* Leipzig, 1877, is still valuable: it should be supplemented by the books and articles cited in the Bibliography to Chapter XII in Volume x, v, B. 1, 2, 3 and 4 (p. 939 *sq.*), especially those of C. Patsch, A. von Premerstein and R. Syme. For commercial and cultural penetration see V. Pârvan, *Inceputurile vieţii romăne la gurile Dunării,* Bucharest, 1923 (Rumanian) and *I primordi della civiltà Romana alle foci del Danubio,* in *Ausonia,* x, 1921, pp. 198 *sqq.*

CHAPTER III

THE SARMATIANS AND PARTHIANS

PART I. THE SARMATIANS

I. ANCIENT SOURCES

A. *Literary Texts*

(*a*) *Greek and Roman*

Our main information about the Sarmatians is derived partly from geographers and partly from historians, who often add to their narrative geographical and ethnographical excursuses. The earliest evidence comes from Ephorus, Pseudo-Scylax and Eudoxus of Cnidus. Later geographers, Posidonius, Pseudo-Scymnus and the late Hellenistic sources of Strabo, especially Artemidorus of Ephesus, and finally Strabo himself know the Sarmatians well. In most of the Roman geographers, however, hopeless confusion reigns between the Sarmatians of the present and the Sauromatians of the past, but Mela, Pliny, Lucan, Valerius Flaccus (the two last depend on some geographical treatise) and Dionysius Periegetes need consulting. Of great importance are the *Peripli* of the Pontus Euxinus of Arrian and of an anonymous writer and, of course, the descriptions of Ptolemy. Good sources were used by Ammianus Marcellinus for his geographical and ethnographical excursuses.

Among the historians Polybius, Posidonius, Polyaenus and Josephus must be consulted for the Hellenistic period. The best information for early Roman times is contained in Tacitus, *Annals* and *Histories* (cf. *Germania*), supplemented by scattered notices in Suetonius and Dio. For the later period Dio and the *Scriptores Historiae Augustae* (cf. Eutropius) mention the Sarmatians from time to time. Quite apart stands the report of Arrian on his expedition against the Alans, of which we have one chapter, Ἔκταξις κατ' Ἀλανῶν. Ovid gives in his *Ex Ponto* and *Tristia* (cf. *Ibis*) valuable pictures of a Greek city surrounded by barbarians, while the *Borysthenicus* of Dio Chrysostom shows another Greek city on the Black Sea (Olbia) already half-Sarmatized. Finally, a novelistic picture of the life of Bosporus in the Hellenistic age is presented by Lucian's Scythian dialogue—*Toxaris*; cf. the Scythian episode in a novel discovered recently, Pap. Soc. Ital. vol. VIII, no. 981; see R. M. Rattenbury, in J. U. Powell, *New Chapters in the History of Greek Literature*, 3rd Series, Oxford (1933), pp. 240 *sqq.*; and cf. Fr. Zimmermann in Phil. Woch. LV, 1935, cols. 1211 *sqq.*

The literary evidence on the Sarmatians of the Classical period has been carefully collected by B. Latyschev, *Scythica et Caucasica*, etc., I: Scriptores Graeci, II: Scriptores Latini, St Petersburg (1906) and illustrated by M. Rostovtzeff, *Skythien und der Bosporus*, I, Berlin (1931), pp. 1–139.

(*b*) *Chinese.*

Shi Ki, ch. 123 (F. Hirth, in Journ. Am. Orient. Soc. XXXVII, 1917, pp. 89 *sqq.*).
Ch'ien Han Shu, ch. 96 (Wylie, in Journ. of the Roy. Anthr. Inst. X, 1881, pp. 21 *sqq.*).
Heou Han Shu, ch. 98 (Chavannes, in T'oung Pao, VIII, 1907, pp. 195 *sqq.*).

B. *Inscriptions*

The inscriptions of South Russia are collected by B. Latyschev, *Inscriptiones Orae Septentrionalis Ponti Euxini*, I² (1916), II (1890), IV (1901), cf. vol. VIII, bibliography to ch. XVIII. Of inscriptions found outside Russia the most important texts are: *Res*

Gest. 31; Dessau 852–53, 986, 1017, 1098, 1117, 1326, and 1327, 2719, 9197.
Cf. the coins of M. Aurelius and Commodus and of later Emperors with the title *Sarmaticus, C.I.L.* XII, 1122*a* (Alan horse). One *numerus* and several *alae Sarmatarum* were incorporated into the Roman army, see Cichorius in P. W. *s.v.* ala, cf. D. Árpad, *Inscriptiones ad res Pannonicas pertinentes extra provinciae fines repertae*, Budapest, 1932. Sarmatian slaves and their descendants called Sarmates are not infrequent in Greek and Latin inscriptions and papyri; cf., for example, Preisigke, *Namenbuch*, *s.vv.* Σαρμάτας and Σαρμάτης.

C. *Archaeological Material*

Rostovtzeff, M. *Skythien und der Bosporus.* 1, Berlin, 1931 (with bibliography).

II. Modern Books

A. *History*

Berthelot, A. *L'Asie ancienne centrale et sud-orientale d'après Ptolémée.* Paris, 1930.
Bleichsteiner, R. *Das Volk der Alanen.* Ber. des Forschungsinstitut für Osten und Orient, II, 1918, p. 4.
Herrmann, A. Arts. *s.vv.* Jaxartes, Jaxamatae, Massagetae, and Tanais in P.W.
Kretschmer, K. Arts. *s.vv.* Sarmatae, Sarmatia, and Sirakes in P.W.
Kulakovsky, J. *The Alans according to the Information derived from Classical and Byzantine Writers*.* Kiev, 1899.
Minns, E. H. *Scythians and Greeks.* Cambridge, 1913, pp. 113 *sqq.*
Müllenhoff, K. *Deutsche Altertumskunde.* III, Berlin, 1892.
Niederle, L. *Slovanské Starožitnosti,* Dil. I. Svazek I, ed. 2. Prague, 1925, pp. 127 *sqq.*
Patsch, C. *Beiträge zur Völkerkunde von Südosteuropa.* I. *Agathyrsoi.* II. *Banater Sarmaten.* Wien Anz. LXII, 1925, pp. 181 *sqq.* (Jazyges). III. *Die Völkerbewegungen an der unteren Donau.* Wien S.B. 208, 2, 1928. IV. *Die quadisch-jazygische Kriegsgemeinschaft im Jahre 374/75. Ibid.* 209, 5, 1929 (cf. Rostovtzeff in Gnomon, VI, 1930, pp. 625 *sqq.*). V. *Aus 500 Jahren vorrömischer und römischer Geschichte Südosteuropas:* 1. Bis zur Festsetzung der Römer in Transdanuvien. *Ibid.* 214, 1, 1932 (cf. Rostovtzeff, Gnomon, X, 1934, p. 1).
Rostovtzeff, M. *Iranians and Greeks in South Russia.* Oxford, 1922, pp. 113 *sqq.*
Stein, A. Art. *s.v.* Sarmaticus in P.W.
Täubler, E. *Zur Geschichte der Alanen.* Klio, IX, 1909, p. 144.
Tomaschek, W. Art. *s.v.* Aorsoi in P.W.
Treidler, H. Art. *s.v.* Jazyges in P.W.
Werner, J. *Fund Bosporanischer Münzen in der Dzungarei.* Eurasia Septentr. Antiqua, VIII, 1933, p. 249.

B. *Archaeology and Art*

Alföldi, A. *Die theriomorphe Weltbetrachtung in den hochasiatischen Kulturen.* Arch. Anz. 1931, pp. 394 *sqq.*
Anderson, J. E. *The Hunting Magic in the Animal Style.* Bulletin Ostasiatska Samlungana, 1932.
Appelgren-Kivalo, H. *Alt-Altaische Kunstdenkmaeler.* Helsingfors, 1931.
Borovka, G. *Scythian Art.* Transl. V. G. Childe, London, 1928.
Dalton, O. M. *The Treasure of the Oxus.* Ed. 2, London, 1926.
Ebert, M. *Reallexikon der Vorgeschichte.* XIII, 1929, pp. 98 *sqq.*
Griaznov, M. P. *The Pazirik Burial of Altai.* A.J.A. XXXVI, 1933, p. 30.

* An asterisk denotes works written in Russian.

Hentze, C. *Beiträge zu den Problemen des eurasischen Tierstiles.* Ostas. Zeitschr. VI, 1930, pp. 150 *sqq.*

Kondakov, N. P. *Essays and Notes on the History of Medieval Art and Civilization*.* Prague, 1929.

Kümmel, O. *Chinesische Kunst.* (Ausstellung Chinesischer Kunst.) Ed. 2, Berlin, 1929, nos. 1216–1272 (finds at Noin-Ula).

Minns, E. H. *Scythians and Greeks.* Cambridge, 1913.

Rau, P. *Die Hügelgräber römischer Zeit an der unteren Wolga.* Mitt. d. Zentral- museums Pokrowsk, I, Pokrowsk, 1926, p. I.

—— *Praehistorische Ausgrabungen auf der Steppenseite des Deutschen Wolgagebietes.* Ib. II, Pokrowsk, 1927, p. I.

Rostovtzeff, M. *Ancient Decorative Wall Painting in South Russia*.* St Petersburg, 1913.

—— *Iranians and Greeks in South Russia.* Oxford, 1922.

—— *Une trouvaille gréco-sarmate de Kertsch.* Mon. et Mém. Piot, XXVI, 1923, pp. 99 *sqq.*

—— *Sarmatian and Indo-Scythian Antiquities*.* Recueil Kondakov, 1926, pp. 239 ff. (With a résumé in French.)

—— *The Animal Style in South Russia and China.* Princeton, N.J., 1929.

—— *The Great Hero of Middle Asia and his Exploits.* Artibus Asiae, IV, 1933, p. 99.

—— *L'Art Gréco-Iranien.* Rev. d. Arts Asiat. 1933, pp. 202 *sqq.*

—— *Some new aspects of Iranian Art.* Semin. Kond. VI, 1933, pp. 161 *sqq.*

Salmony, A. *Sino-Siberian Art in the Collection of C. T. Loo.* Paris, 1923.

Tallgren, A. M. *Inner Asiatic and Siberian Rock Pictures.* Eurasia Septentr. Ant. VIII, 1932, pp. 174 *sqq.*

—— *Zum Ursprungsgebiet des sog. Skythischen Tierstils.* Acta Arch. IV, 1933, pp. 258 *sqq.*

Toll, N. P. *Chinese Silk Stuffs found at Panticapaeum*.* Semin. Kond. I, 1927, pp. 85 *sqq.*

Zakharov, A. *Antiquities of Katanda (Altai).* Journ of the Roy. Anthr. Institute, LV, 1925, p. 37.

PART II. THE PARTHIANS

This Bibliography should be taken in conjunction with the other bibliographies upon Parthia in Vol. IX to chapter XIV, p. 947, and the following sections of biblio- graphies in Vol. X; chapters I–IV, Part II, E, p. 912, chapter IX, 3, p. 921, and chapter XXII, 2, p. 985. See also the bibliography to chapter IV in this volume, B. II, p. 882 *sq.*

I. Ancient Sources

A. *Greek and Roman Literary*

From late Hellenistic times onward there is scarcely an author in Greek or Latin, whether poet or prose-writer, who does not contain references (of varying value) to Parthia and the Parthians. The most valuable are Strabo, Justin, Isidore of Charax (*Parthian Stations*), the Elder Pliny, Josephus, Tacitus, Arrian, Lucian, Herodian, Ammianus Marcellinus and the Scriptores Historiae Augustae. The most important references are given in the footnotes to the text of the chapter.

B. *Oriental Literary*

Addai. *The Doctrine of Addai the Apostle.* Ed. and trans. by G. Phillips, London, 1876.

Agathangelos. Langlois, V. *Agathange, Histoire du Règne de Tiridate.* F.H.G. V, 2, pp. 99 *sqq.*

CHINESE CHRONICLES. Chavannes, E. *Trois Généraux Chinois de la Dynastie des Han Orientaux.* T'oung Pao, VII, 1906, pp. 210 *sqq.*: and *Les Pays d'Occident d'après le Héou Han Chou.* Ib. VIII, 1907, pp. 109 *sqq.*

CHRONICLE OF ARBELA. Messina, G. *La Cronaca di Arbela.* La Civiltà Cattolica, 83 (III), 1932, pp. 362 *sqq.*: Peeters, P. Le 'Passionnaire d'Adiabène.' Analecta Bollandiana, 43, 1925, pp. 302 *sqq.*: and Sachau, E. *Die Chronik von Arbela.* Berl. Abh. 1915, 6.

JOHN OF EPHESUS. Tr. J. M. Schoenfelder. Munich, 1862.

MANI. Andreas-Henning, *Mitteliranische Manichaica aus Chinesisch-Turkestan.* Berl. S.B. 1933, pp. 301 *sqq.*: Schaeder, H. H. *Iranica.* Gött. Abh. (III Folge), x, 1934: Schmidt, C. and H. J. Polotsky, *Ein Mani-Fund in Aegypten.* Berl. S.B. 1933, 12 (cf. E. Peterson, Byzant. Zeits. XXXIV, 1934, pp. 379 *sqq.*).

MIRCHAND. Muehlau, F. and A. von Gutschmid, *Zur Geschichte der Arsaciden:* I. *Geschichte der Arsaciden aus Mirchand übersetzt.* Zeitschr. d. d. morgenländ. Gesell. XV, 1861, pp. 664 *sqq.*

Cf. also the works of J. Marquart listed below in section II, B and D.

C. Inscriptions, Papyri, Cuneiform Tablets, Coins

(a) Inscriptions.

Persis-Media. S.E.G. VII, nos. 35–36. *Susiana.* S.E.G. VII, nos. 1–33; on the letter of Artabanus III see A. Wilhelm, Wien Anz. 1934, pp. 45 *sqq.*; C. B. Welles, *Royal correspondence in the Hellenistic period,* New Haven, 1934, no. 75, pp. 299 *sqq.* *Assyria* and *Babylonia.* S.E.G. VII, nos. 37–40 (on no. 37 see M. Rostovtzeff, Πρόγονοι, J.H.S. LV, 1935, p. 56). *Dura.* S.E.G. VII, nos. 331–800, cf. *The Excav. at Dura-Europos.* Preliminary Rep. of vth Season, Oct. 1931–March 1932, 1934 (Report on the vith Season in the press). *Palmyra.* S.E.G. VII, nos. 132–185 (cf. M. Rostovtzeff, in *Berytus,* II, 1935, pp. 145 *sqq.* See also Gardthausen, V. *Die Parther in griechisch-römischen Inschriften,* Orient. Studien Th. Noeldeke gewidmet, Giessen, 1906, pp. 838 *sqq.*).

(b) Parchments and Papyri.

Rostovtzeff, M. *Les archives militaires de Doura.* C.R. Ac. Inscr. 1933, pp. 309 *sqq.*: *Das Militärarchiv von Dura.* Münch. Beitr. z. Papyrusforschung, XIX, 1934, pp. 351 *sqq.*: and Welles, C. B. *Die Zivilen Archive in Dura.* Ib. pp. 379 *sqq.*

(c) Cuneiform tablets.

Krueckmann, O. *Babylonische Rechts- und Verwaltungsurkunden aus der Zeit Alexanders und der Diadochen.* Weimar, 1931.

(d) Coins.

De la Fuye, A. and J. M. Unvala, *Inventaire des monnaies trouvées à Suse.* Mém. d. l. mission arch. en Perse, XXV, Mission en Susiane, 1934.

Gholam-Reza Kian, *Introduction à l'histoire de la monnaie et histoire monétaire de la Perse. Des origines à la fin de la période parthe.* Thèse Paris, 1934.

McDowell, R. H. *Coins from Seleucia on the Tigris.* Univ. of Michigan Stud. (Hum. Ser. XXXVII), Ann Arbor, 1935.

de Morgan, J. *Manuel de Numismatique Orientale de l'Antiquité et du Moyen Age.* Paris, I, 1923.

Catalogue Naville, Monnaies grecques et romaines, no. XII (Coll. A. de Petrowicz), Geneva, 1926.

II. Modern Books and Articles

A. *Political and Dynastic History*

Articles in P.W. and the Encyclopaedia Britannica on the several kings of Parthia and on vassal kingdoms.

Anderson, A. R. *Alexander's Gate, Gog and Magog and the enclosed nations.* Monogr. of the Mediaeval Academy of America, 5, Cambridge, Mass. 1932.

Boissevain, U. P. *Ein verschobenes Fragment des Cassius Dio* (LXXV, 9, 6). Hermes, XXV, 1890, p. 329.

Dobiaš, J. *Seleucie sur l'Euphrate.* Syria, VI, 1925, p. 253.

Ensslin, W. *Die weltgeschichtliche Bedeutung der Kämpfe zwischen Rom und Persien.* N.J. f. Wiss. IV, 1928.

Guey, J. in C.R. Ac. Inscr. 1934 (Séance du 23 Mars), p. 72.

Günther, A. *Beiträge zur Geschichte der Kriege zwischen Römern und Parthern.* Berlin, 1922.

Herzfeld, E. *Sakastan.* Arch. Mitt. aus Iran, IV, 1932, p. 1.

Kunzmann, W. *Quaestiones de Pseudo-Luciani libelli qui est de longaevis fontibus atque auctoritate.* Leipzig, 1908.

Olshausen, J. *Ueber das Zeitalter einiger Inschriften auf Arsacidischen und Sassanischen Monumenten.* Monatsb. d. Berl. Akad. 1878, pp. 172 *sqq.*

Roos, A. G. *Studia Arrianea.* Leipzig, 1912.

Ruehl, F. *Die Makrobier des Lukianos.* Rh. Mus. LXII, 1907, p. 421.

Schachermeyer, F. Art. *s.v.* Mesopotamia in P.W. cols. 1133 *sqq.*

Schur, W. *Die Orientalische Frage im röm. Reiche.* N.J. f. Wiss. II, 1926, p. 270.

Stauffenberg, A. Schenk, Graf von, *Die römische Kaisergeschichte bei Malalas.* Stuttgart, 1931.

von Wesendonck, O. G. *Kusan, Chioniten und Hephtaliten.* Klio, XXVI, 1933, p. 336.

B. *Organization, Social and Economic Conditions, Law, Religion*

Andrae, W. *Hatra*, vols. I, II, Leipzig, 1908, 1912.

Barthold, W. W. *On the problem of feudalism in Iran.* New Orient, XXVIII, 1930, p. 108. (Cf. S. Transkij, ib. p. 117.)

Christensen, A. *Die Iranier.* Müller's Handbuch, III, 1, 3, p. 301.

—— *L'Empire des Sassanides, le Peuple, l'État, la Cour.* Det K. Denskab. Selkskabs Skrifter, VII, 1, 1903.

Clemen, C. Art. *s.v.* Magi in P.W. cols. 905 *sqq.*

Cumont, F. *Les Religions Orientales dans le Paganisme romain.* Ed. 4, Paris, 1928, pp. 125 *sqq.* (La Perse).

Ensslin, W. Review of Yale Classical Studies II in Phil. Woch. 1933, cols. 266 *sqq.*

Herrmann, A. *Lou-lan.* Leipzig, 1931.

Herzfeld, E. *Paikuli.* Berlin, 1924.

Kornemann, E. *Die römische Kaiserzeit.* Gercke-Norden, ed. 3, III, 2, 1933, pp. 139 *sqq.*: Neurom und Neupersien.

Koschaker, P. *Ueber einige griech. Rechtsurkunden aus den östlichen Randgebieten des Hellenismus.* Sächs. Abh. XLII, 1, 1931.

—— *Die Rechtsgeschichtliche Bedeutung d. griech. Pergamenturkunden aus Dura.* Chronique d'Égypte, nos. 13–14, 1932, p. 202.

—— *Keil-schriftrecht.* Zeits. d. d. morgenländ. Gesell. XIV, 1935, p. 1.

Manandjan, J. A. *Notes on the feudal structure and the feudal army in Parthia and in Arsacid Armenia*.* Mem. of the hist.-ec. Section of the Academy of U.S.S.R., Caucasian Inst. of Research, 1932, p. 19. Cf. F. D., Byzant. Zeits. XXXIII, 1933, pp. 195 *sqq.*

Marquart, J. *Beiträge zur Geschichte und Sage von Eran.* Zeits. d. d. morgenländ. Gesell. XLIX, 1895, p. 632.

—— *Eranshahr nach der Geographie des Pseudo-Moses Xorenacei.* Gött. Abh., N.F., III, 1901.

—— *Osteuropaeische und Ostasiatische Streifzüge.* Leipzig, 1903.

—— *A Catalogue of the Provincial Capitals of Eranshahr.* Rome, 1931 (Analecta Orientalia III).

Meyer, Ed. *Blüte und Niedergang des Hellenismus in Asien.* Berlin, 1925.

Noeldeke, Th. *Geschichte der Perser und Araber zur Zeit der Sasaniden.* Aus der arabischen Chronik von Tabari übersetzt, Leyden, 1879.

—— *Aufsätze zur Persischen Geschichte.* Leipzig, 1887.

Rostovtzeff, M. *Social and Economic History of the Roman Empire.* Oxford, 1926; German edition, 1931; Italian edition, 1933; especially Ch. VII.

—— *L'Hellénisme en Mésopotamie.* Scientia, LIII, 1933, p. 120.

Schaeder, H. H. *Der Orient und das griechische Erbe.* Die Antike, IV, 1928, p. 236.

Schönbauer, E. *Paramone, Antichrese und Hypothek.* Z.d. Sav.-Stift. LIII, 1933, p. 422.

Stein, E. *Ein Kapitel vom Persischen und vom Byzantinischen Staate.* Byzant.-Neugriech. Jahrbuch, I, 1920, p. 59.

C. *Art and Archaeology*

Details of publications dealing with excavated and illustrated ruins of the Parthian times in and outside of Iran, especially in Mesopotamia, will be found in M. Rostovtzeff, *Dura and the Problem of Parthian Art,* Yale Classical Studies, V, 1935. Various contributions to the history of Parthian art and life by P. V. C. Baur, C. Hopkins and M. Rostovtzeff will be found in the yearly Reports of the Yale Dura Expedition quoted in section D.

The list which follows contains books and papers illustrating Parthian Art in general or points bearing on Parthian art and material life.

Andrae, W. and H. Lenzen, *Die Partherstadt Assur.* Leipzig, 1923.

Andrews, F. H. *Catalogue of wall-paintings from ancient shrines in Central Asia and Sistan.* Delhi, 1933.

Cumont, F. *Fouilles de Doura-Europos* (1922–23). Paris, 1926.

Debevoise, N. *Some Problems of Parthian Architecture.* Journ. Amer. Orient. Soc. XLVIII, 1931, p. 357.

—— *Parthian Pottery from Seleucia on the Tigris.* Univ. of Michigan Studies (Hum. Ser.), XXXII, Ann Arbor, 1934.

Dieulafoy, M. *L'Art antique de la Perse.* V, Monuments Parthes et Sassanides, Paris, 1884.

Furlani, G. *Sarcofaghi Partici di Kakzu.* Iraq, I, 1934, p. 90.

Herzfeld, E. *Am Tor von Asien, Felsendenkmale aus Irans Heldenzeit.* Berlin, 1920, pp. 55 *sqq.*: Die Arsakiden Denkmale.

—— *Hatra,* Zeitschr. d. d. morgenländ. Gesell. LXVIII, 1914, p. 655.

Ingholt, H. *Quelques fresques récemment découvertes à Palmyre,* Acta Arch. III, 1932, p. 1.

Jordan, J. *Uruk-Warka nach den Ausgrabungen durch die Deutsche Orient-Gesellschaft.* Leipzig, 1928.

Pézard, M. *La céramique archaïque de l'Islam et ses origines.* Paris, 1920.

Pfister, R. *Textiles de Palmyre.* Paris, 1934.

Reuther, O. *Die Innerstadt von Babylon* (Merkes), pp. 39, 178 *sqq.,* 279 *sqq.,* 1926 (Wiss. Veröff. d. d. Orient-Ges. XLVII).

Rostovtzeff, M. *Das Mithraeum von Dura*. Röm. Mitt. XLIX, 1934, p. 190.
—— *Dura and the Problem of Parthian Art*. Yale Class. Stud. v, 1935, pp. 157–304.
—— *Die Synagoge von Dura*. Röm. Quartalschrift, XLII, 1934, p. 203.
Sarre, F. *Die Kunst des alten Persien*. Berlin, 1922, pp. 25 *sqq.*
—— *The Problem of Parthian Art*. In the forthcoming *Survey of Persian Art*
    edited by A. U. Pope, I, Oxford, 1935.
Seyrig, H. *Antiquités syriennes*. 1 Série (Extrait de Syria 1931–1932–1933 corrigé
    sur certains points). Paris, 1934, esp. pp. 36 *sqq.*
—— *Bas-reliefs monumentaux du temple de Bel à Palmyre*. Syria, XV, 1934, p. 155.
Stein, Sir Aurel. *Innermost Asia*. II, Oxford, 1928, pp. 909 *sqq.*
Strzygowski, J. *Griechischer Iranismus in buddhistischer Bildnerei*. Artibus Asiae, IV,
    1933–4, p. 5 and p. 185 and v, 1935, p. 5.
—— *Asiens bildende Kunst in Stickproben*. Augsburg, 1930, p. 267.
—— *Die altslavische Kunst. Ein Versuch ihres Nachweises*. Augsburg, 1929, pp.
    33 *sqq.*
Waterman, L. *Report upon the Excavations at Tel-Umar, Iraq*. I, Michigan, 1931;
    II, Michigan, 1933.
Zahn, R. *Silber-Emblem der Sammlung Loeb*. Festschr. für James Loeb, Munich,
    1930, pp. 131 *sqq.*

D. *Vassal States and Cities* (cf. I, sect. B and C)

(a) *Armenia and Georgia.*

Amirashvili, A. *Greek inscription from the region of Mtskhet (Iberia)**. Bull. of the
    Acad. of Mat. Culture, v, 1931, p. 409.
Djavakhov, Pr. *The constitution of ancient Georgia and Armenia**. St Petersburg, 1905.
Kakabadzé, S. *Problème de l'origine de l'État Géorgien*. Bull. Hist., Tiflis, 1924.
Lehmann-Haupt, C. F. *Armenien einst und jetzt*. Berlin, I, 1910, II, 1931.
Manandjan, J. A. *Materials for the economic history of ancient Armenia**. Izvestija
    of the State Univ. of Armenia, IV, 1928, pp. 43 and 73.
—— *Feudalism in ancient Armenia*. Erivan, 1934 (in Armenian).
Marquart, J. *Südarmenien und die Tigrisquellen nach griech. und arabischen
    Geographen*. Vienna, 1930.
de Morgan, J. *Histoire du Peuple arménien*. Paris, 1919.
Romanov, K. K. *Remains of a temple of Graeco-Roman type at Bash Garni**. Bull.
    of the Acad. of the History of Mat. Culture, No. 100 (Marr volume), 1933,
    p. 635.
Rostovtzeff, M. *New Latin inscriptions from S. Russia** (Armenia). Bull. de la Comm.
    Imp. Arch. XXXIII, 1909, p. 1.
von Wesendonck, O. G. *Zur Georgischen Geschichte*. Klio, XXI, 1927, p. 125.
    For current bibliography see Revue des Études Arméniennes.

(b) *Babylonia.*

Heuzey, L. *Découvertes en Chaldée*. II, Paris, 1912, p. 56.
Kirste, J. *Orabazes*. Wien S.B. 182, 2, 1917.
Art. *s.v.* Mesene in P.W. cols. 1082 *sqq.*

(c) *Dura.*

Baur, P. V. C., Rostovtzeff, M. and A. Bellinger, *Excavations at Dura-Europos.*
    Preliminary Reports, I–V, 1929–34, New Haven.
Cumont, F. *Les fouilles de Doura-Europos (1922–3)*. Paris, 1926.
Johnson, J. *Dura Studies*. Philadelphia, 1932.
Rostovtzeff, M. *Caravan Cities*. 1932.

(d) Edessa.

Torrey, Ch. C. *A Syriac Parchment from Edessa of the Year* 243 A.D. Zeitschr. f. Semitistik, x, 1935, p. 33.

Bellinger, A. R. and C. B. Welles. *The third century contract of sale from Edessa in Osrhoene.* Yale Class. Stud. v, 1935, pp. 93–154.

(e) Palmyra.

Février, J. G. *Essai sur l'histoire politique et économique de Palmyre.* Paris, 1931.

Ingholt, H. *Deux Inscriptions bilingues de Palmyre.* Syria, 1932, p. 278.

Mouterde, R. and A. Poidebard. *La voie antique des Caravanes entre Palmyre et Hit au II Siècle apr. J.-C.* Syria, XII, 1931, p. 101. (Cf. the memoirs of P. Poidebard quoted in section 2, 1).

Rostovtzeff, M. *Les Inscriptions caravanières de Palmyre.* Mél. Glotz, Paris, II, 1932, pp. 793 *sqq.*

—— *Hadad and Atargatis at Palmyra.* A.J.A. XXXVII, 1933, p. 58.

—— *The Caravan Gods of Palmyra.* J.R.S. XXII, 1932, p. 107.

—— *Caravan Cities.* Oxford, 1932.

Seyrig, H. *L'incorporation de Palmyre à l'empire romain.* Syria, XIII, 1932, p. 266.

—— *Textes relatifs à la garnison romaine de Palmyre.* Syria, XIV, 1933, p. 152.

(f) Sakastan.

Herzfeld, E. *Sakastan.* Arch. Mitt. aus Iran, IV, 1932, p. 1.

CHAPTER IV

FLAVIAN WARS AND FRONTIERS

A. Ancient Sources

The more important parts of the literary and epigraphical evidence are referred to in the footnotes to the chapter.

B. Modern Works

See also the Bibliography to chap. VI, and below, under the respective provinces of the Empire. The following Bibliography is rigorously selective.

I. *Military and General*

von Domaszewski, A. *Beiträge zur Kaisergeschichte*, 4. *Die Inschrift des Velius Rufus*. Phil. LXVI, 1907, p. 164.
Fabricius, E. Art. *s.v.* Limes in P.W.
Klose, J. *Roms Klientel-Randstaaten am Rhein und an der Donau*. Historische Untersuchungen, Heft 14. Breslau, 1934.
Kornemann, E. *Die neueste Limesforschung*. Klio, VII, 1907, p. 73.
Ritterling, E. *Zu den Germanenkriegen Domitians am Rhein und an der Donau*. Jahreshefte VII, 1904, Beiblatt, col. 23.
—— *Zu dem neuen Militärdiplom Vespasians*. Westdeutsche Zeitschr. XXV, 1906, Beiblatt, col. 20.
—— Art. *s.v.* Legio in P.W.
Syme, R. Review of Klose in *J.R.S.* XXIV, 1934, p. 95.

II. *The Eastern Frontier*

Anderson, J.G.C. *The Road System of Eastern Asia Minor*. J.H.S. XVII, 1897, p. 22.
Chapot, V. *La frontière de l'Euphrate*. Paris, 1907.
Cumont, Fr. *Le gouvernement de Cappadoce sous les Flaviens*. Bull. de l'ac. royale de Belgique, 1905, p. 197.
—— *L'annexation du Pont Polémoniaque et de la Petite Arménie*. Anatolian Studies presented to Sir W. M. Ramsay, Manchester, 1923, p. 109.
Février, J. G. *Essai sur l'histoire politique et économique de Palmyre*. Paris, 1931.
Gwatkin, W. A. *Cappadocia as a Roman Procuratorial Province*. Univ. of Missouri Studies, V, no. 4, 1930, pp. 55–62.
Harrer, A. *Studies in the History of the Roman Province of Syria*. Diss. Princeton, 1915, pp. 72–7.
Hogarth, D. B. and J. A. R. Munro, *Modern and Ancient Roads in Eastern Asia Minor*. Supp. Papers of the Roy. Geogr. Soc. III, 1893.
Jones, A. H. M. *Inscriptions from Jerash*. J.R.S. XVIII, 1928, p. 144.
Marquart, J. *Iberer und Hyrkanier*. Caucasica, Fasc. 8, 1931, p. 78.
McElderry, R. Knox. *The Legions of the Euphrates Frontier*. C.Q. III, 1909, p. 44.
Munro, J. A. R. *Roads in Pontus, Royal and Roman*. J.H.S. XXI, 1901, p. 52.
Reinach, Th. *Le mari de Salomé*. Rev. E.A. XVI, 1914, p. 133.
Ritterling, E. *Zu zwei griechischen Inschriften römischer Verwaltungsbeamten*. Jahreshefte X, 1907, p. 299.
Schürer, E. *Geschichte des jüdischen Volkes im Zeitalter Jesu Christi*. Edd. 3 and 4. Leipzig, 1901, I, pp. 642–61.
Seyrig, H. *Antiquités syriennes*. 9. *L'incorporation de Palmyre à l'empire romain*. Syria, XIII, 1932, p. 266.

Täubler, E. *Zur Geschichte der Alanen.* Klio, IX, 1909, p. 14.

Wroth, W. *Parthia.* B.M. Cat. of Greek Coins, 1903, pp. lii–lvii.

Yorke, V. W. *A Journey to the Valley of the Upper Euphrates.* Geogr. Journ. VIII, 1896, pp. 462–72.

III. *Africa and Mauretania*

Cagnat, R. *L'armée romaine d'Afrique.* Ed. 2, Paris, 1913.

—— *La colonie romaine de Djemila.* Mus. B. XXVII, 1923, p. 113.

De Pachtere, F. *Les camps de la troisième légion en Afrique aux premiers siècles de l'empire.* C.R. Ac. Inscr. 1916, p. 273.

Gsell, S. *Inscriptions latines de l'Algérie.* I, Paris, 1922, pp. 286 sqq.

Pallu de Lessert, A. C. *Fastes des provinces africaines.* I, Paris, 1896.

Poinssot, L. (Inscrr. from Ammaedara.) Bull. arch. du comité des trav. hist. et scient. 1927, p. 199.

Syme, R. *Notes sur la légion III^a Augusta,* Rev.E.A. XXXVIII, 1936, p. 182.

Articles in P.W.: Cn. Suellius Flaccus (Groag): Mauretania (Weinstock): L. Minicius Natalis, L. Munatius Gallus (Groag).

IV. *Britain*

1. *General.*

Cary, M. *La Grande-Bretagne romaine.* Rev. H. CLIX, 1928, p. 3.

Collingwood, R. G. *The Archaeology of Roman Britain.* London, 1930.

Furneaux, H. and J. G. C. Anderson, *Cornelii Taciti De vita Agricolae.* Oxford, 1922.

Haverfield, F. and G. Macdonald, *The Roman Occupation of Britain.* Oxford, 1924.

Macdonald, Sir G. *Agricola in Britain.* London, 1932.

—— *Roman Britain* 1914–1928. British Academy Supp. Papers No. VI, 1931.

—— *Forschungen im römischen Britannien* 1914–18. R.-G. K. Ber. XIX, 1929, p. 1.

McElderry, R. K. *The Date of Agricola's Governorship of Britain.* J.R.S. X, 1920, p. 68.

2. *Wales.*

Haverfield, F. *Military Aspects of Roman Wales.* London, 1910.

Pryce, T. Davies. *The fort at Caersws and the Roman occupation of Wales.* Montgomery Hist. and Arch. Coll. 1931, p. 17.

Wheeler, R. E. M. *Prehistoric and Roman Wales.* Oxford, 1925.

3. *Northern England.*

Birley, E. *An introduction to the excavation of Chesterholm—Vindolanda.* Arch. Aeliana⁴, VIII, 1931, p. 182.

Bushe-Fox, J. P. *The use of Samian Pottery in dating the early Roman occupation of the north of Britain.* Archaeologia, LXIV (2nd ser. XIV), 1912/3, p. 295.

Collingwood, R. G. *Hardknot Castle.* Cumberland and Westmorland Trans. (C.W. Trans.), XXVIII, 1928, p. 314.

—— *Roman Ravenglass.* C.W. Trans.², XXVIII, 1928, p. 353.

Gibson, J. P. and F. G. Simpson, *The Roman fort on the Stanegate at Haltwhistle Burn.* Arch. Aeliana³, V, 1909, p. 213.

Haverfield, F. and D. Atkinson, *The first days of Carlisle.* C.W. Trans.², XVII, 1916/7, p. 235.

Miller, S. N. *Roman York: Excavations of 1926–1927.* J.R.S. XVIII, 1928, p. 61.

Richmond, I. A. *The four Roman camps at Cawthorn in the North Riding of Yorkshire.* Arch. Journ. LXXXIX, 1932, p. 17.

Simpson, F. G. *Excavations on the line of the Roman Wall in Cumberland during the years* 1909–12: *The Stanegate.* C.W. Trans.², XIII, 1913, pp. 381–9.

4. *Scotland.*

Birley, E. and T. Davies Pryce, *The First Roman Occupation of Scotland.* J.R.S. xxv, 1935, p. 58.

Christison, D. *Earthworks between Ardoch and Dupplin.* Proc. Soc. Ant. Scot. xxxv, 1900/1, p. 15.

Curle, J. *A Roman Frontier Post.* Glasgow, 1911.

Haverfield, F. *Ancient Rome and Ireland.* Eng. Hist. Rev. cix, 1913, p. 1.

—— *Agricola and the Antonine Wall.* Proc. Soc. Ant. Scot. lii, 1917/8, p. 174.

Macdonald, (Sir) G. *Roman coins found in Scotland.* Proc. Soc. Ant. Scot. lii, 1917/8, p. 203; lviii, 1923/4, p. 325.

—— *The Agricolan Occupation of North Britain.* J.R.S. ix, 1919, p. 111.

—— *The Romans in Dumfriesshire.* Trans. Dumfries Ant. Soc. viii, 1920/1, p. 96.

—— *The Dating-Value of Samian Ware.* J.R.S. xxv, 1935, p. 187.

—— *The Roman Wall in Scotland.* Ed. 2. Oxford, 1934.

Richmond, I. A. *The relation of the fort at Newstead to Scottish history.* Proc. Soc. Ant. Scot. lviii, 1923/4, p. 309.

V. *The German Frontier*

The standard work is *Der obergermanisch-rätische Limes des Römerreiches,* edited by E. Fabricius (almost complete). Of special value is the same writer's article *Limes* in P.W. The following represents a brief selection from the enormous literature of the subject, arranged under three heads.

1. *General and comprehensive works.*

Brogan, O. *The Roman Limes in Germany.* Arch. Journ. xcii, 1935, p. 1.

Fabricius, E. *Die Besitznahme Badens durch die Römer.* Heidelberg, 1905.

Hertlein, Fr., P. Goessler and O. Paret, *Die Römer in Württemberg,* i–iii. Stuttgart, 1928–32.

Koepp, Fr. *Die Römer in Deutschland.* Ed. 3. Bielefeld-Leipzig, 1926.

Pelham, H. *Essays on Roman History.* ix, *The Roman Frontier in Southern Germany.* Oxford, 1911, pp. 179 *sqq.*

Ritterling, E. *Fasti des römischen Deutschland unter dem Prinzipat.* Vienna, 1932.

Schumacher, K. *Siedelungs- und Kulturgeschichte der Rheinlande.* ii, Die römische Periode. Mainz, 1923.

Sprater, F. *Die Pfalz unter den Römern.* i, Speier, 1929.

Stade, K. *Der römische Limes in Baden.* Badische Fundberichte, ii, i, 1929.

Stähelin, Fr. *Die Schweiz in römischer Zeit.* Ed. 2, Basel, 1931, pp. 189–230.

Stein, E. *Die kaiserlichen Beamten und Truppenkörper im römischen Deutschland unter dem Prinzipat.* Vienna, 1932.

Wagner, Fr. *Die Römer in Bayern.* Ed. 4, Munich, 1928.

Wolff, G. *Die südliche Wetterau.* Frankfort, 1913.

Germania Romana: ein Bilder-Atlas. Ed. 2. i, *Die Bauten des römischen Heeres.* Bamberg, 1924.

2. *Special studies.*

Barthel, W. *Die Erforschung des obergermanisch-raetischen Limes in den Jahren 1906–1907/8.* R.-G. K. Ber. iii, 1909, p. 167.

—— *Die Erforschung des obergermanisch-raetischen Limes 1908–1912.* R.-G. K. Ber. vi, 1913, p. 114.

Bersu, G. *Kastell Burladingen.* Germania, i, 1917, p. 111.

—— *Das Kastell Lautlingen.* Württembergische Studien. Stuttgart, 1926, pp. 177–201.

Fabricius, E. *Mainz und der Limes.* Mainzer Zeitschr. ii, 1906, p. 4.

Goessler, P. *Arae Flaviae*. Rottweil, 1928.

Goessler, P. and R. Knorr, *Cannstatt zur Römerzeit*. Stuttgart, 1921.

Hertlein, Fr. *Der Alblimes*. Blätter des Schwäb. Albvereins, xxxvii, 1925, p. 217.

Herzog, E. *Kritische Bemerkungen zu der Chronologie des Limes*. B.J. cv, 1900, p. 50.

Lachenmaier, G. *Die Okkupation des Limesgebietes*. Württ. Vierteljahreshefte für Landesgesch. xv, 1906, p. 187.

Rau, R. *Das Alter der Neckar- und Albkastelle*. Württembergische Vergangenheit (Festschrift Goessler). Stuttgart, 1932, pp. 47–71.

Wolff, G. *Zur Geschichte der römischen Okkupation in der Wetterau*. Nassauische Annalen, xxxii, 1901, p. 1.

—— *Zur Geschichte des obergermanischen Limes*. R.-G. K. Ber. ix, 1916, p. 18.

3. Miscellaneous.

Gebert, W. *Limes*. B.J. cxix, 1910, p. 158.

Hesselmeyer, E. *Decumanusstudien*. Klio, xxviii, 1935, p. 133.

Kahrstedt, U. *Die Kelten in den decumates agri*. Gött. Nach. 1933, p. 261.

Norden, E. *Alt-Germanien*. Leipzig and Berlin, 1934.

Oxé, A. *Der Limes des Tiberius*. B.J. cxiv, 1906, p. 99.

Pichlmayr, F. *L. Norbanus Appius Maximus*. Hermes, xxxiii, 1898, p. 664.

Riese, A. *L. Appius Norbanus Maximus*. Westdeutsche Zeitschr. xxvi, 1907, p. 129.

Ritterling, E. *Zur römischen Legionsgeschichte am Rhein*. II, *Der Aufstand des Antonius Saturninus*. Westdeutsche Zeitschr. xii, 1893, p. 203.

VI. *The Danubian Wars*

Alföldi, A. *Studi ungheresi sulla romanizzazione della Pannonia*. Gli studi romani nel mondo, II, 1935, p. 267.

Cichorius, C. *Die römischen Denkmäler in der Dobrudscha*. Berlin, 1904.

von Domaszewski, A. *Die Heimat des Cornelius Fuscus*. Rh. Mus. lx, 1905, p. 158.

Drexel, Fr. *Altes und Neues vom Tropaeum Traiani*. N.J. Kl. Alt. xxv, 1922, p. 330.

Filow, B. *Die Legionen der Provinz Moesia*. Klio, Beiheft 6, 1906.

Gnirs, A. *Die römischen Schutzbezirke an der oberen Donau*. Augsburg-Vienna, 1929.

Köstlin, E. *Die Donaukriege Domitians*. Diss. Tübingen, 1910.

Kubitschek, W. and S. Frankfurter, *Führer durch Carnuntum*. Ed. 6, Vienna, 1923.

Kuzsinszky, V. *Aquincum: Ausgrabungen und Funde*. Budapest, 1934.

Nowotny, E. *Römische Forschung in Österreich* 1912–1924. I, *Die Donaugegenden*. R.-G. K. Ber. xv, 1923/4, p. 121.

Pârvan, V. *Getica*. Bucharest, 1926.

Patsch, C. *Zum Dakerkriege des Cornelius Fuscus*. Jahreshefte vii, 1904, p. 70.

Paulovics, S. *Nuovi scavi e scoperte nella Ungheria romana*. Aevum, viii, 1934, p. 242.

von Premerstein, A. and N. Vulić, *Antike Denkmäler in Serbien und Macedonien*. Jahreshefte vi, 1903, Beiblatt, cols. 44 *sqq*.

Ritterling, E. *Rheinische Legionare an der unteren Donau*. Germ. ix, 1925, p. 141.

Schuchhardt, C. *Die sogennanten Trajanswälle in der Dobrudscha*. Berl. Abh. 1918.

Syme, R. *Rhine and Danube Legions under Domitian*. J.R.S. xviii, 1928, p. 43.

Szilágyi, J. *Inscriptiones Tegularum Pannonicarum*. Budapest, 1933.

Der römische Limes in Oesterreich, xvi, 1926, p. 51.

CHAPTER V

NERVA AND TRAJAN

I. Ancient Sources

The most important inscriptions are cited in the footnotes to the chapter, but it would take too much space to give even a selective list here out of the great number relevant to the period.

(a) Papyri

B.G.U. I, 50, 341; III, 832; IV, 1068; V, 1210, § 1 (Gnomon of the Idios Logos= Meyer, P. M. *Juristische Papyri*, no. 93): P. Bad. 37: P. Brem. 34, 40: P. Fay. 20, 36, 296: P. Giess. 24, 27, 41: P. Lond. I, 227: P. Oxy. 46, 74, 483, 705, 1022–3, 1189, 1242, 1434: P. Par. 68: P. Ryl. 191, 329: P. Tebt. 391: Mitteis-Wilcken, *Grundzüge und Chrestomathie*, II, 2, 15–18, 205, 316, 352, 453.

(b) Coins

Besides the works of Mattingly, Sydenham and Strack cited in the General Bibliography, see

Durry, M. *Le règne de Trajan d'après les monnaies*. Rev. H. LVII, 1932, p. 316.
Kubitschek, W. *Nervas römischen Münzen*. Wien Anz. 70, 1933, p. 4.
Mattingly, H. *The restored coins of Titus, Domitian and Nerva*. Num. Chr. 4th series, XX, 1920, p. 177.
—— *The restored coins of Trajan*. Num. Chr. 5th series, VI, 1926, p. 232.
Merlin, A. *Les revers monétaires de l'empereur Nerva*. Paris, 1906.

(c) Literary Sources

Ammian. Marcell. XVI, 10, 15; XXIV, 2, 3; XXVII, 3, 7.
Arrian, *Perip. Maris Euxini*, 11; *Parthica*, ed. Roos, pp. 228–31, 236–48 (Fragm. 5–17, 35–85), cf. Jacoby, F. Gr. Hist. II B, pp. 858–63, 872–8.
Chronographer of 354, svv. *Nerva, Traianus*. Ed. Mommsen, *Chronica Minora saec.* IV–VII (Mon. Germ. Hist. Auct. Ant. IX).
Digesta. I, 2, 2 (32); II, 12, 9; V, 3, 7; XXVI, 7, 12; XXVII, 1, 17 (6); XXVIII, 5, 1; XXIX, 5, 10; XXXVI, 1, 30 (5); XXXVII, 12, 5; XL, 5, 26 (7) (=Bruns, *Fontes*[7], 58); XLI, 4, 2 (8); XLVII, 11, 6; 21, 3; XLVIII, 16, 10; 18, 1 (11–2, 19, 21); 19, 5.
Dio LXVII, 15–6; LXVIII; LXIX, 1–2 (ed. Boissevain).
Dio Chrysostom, *Or.* I; III; XXXII, 60, 95; XXXIV, 25; XL, 15; XLVII, 13.
Eusebius, *Hist. Eccles.* IV, 1–2; *Chronici Canones* (Jerome) ol. CCXVIII–CXXIIII (pp. 274–9 ed. Fotheringham).
Frontinus, *de Aquaeductu urbis Romae.*
Fronto, pp. 204–10, 217 (ed. Naber).
Jordanes, *Getica* 93, 101; *Romana* 217, 266–8 (ed. Mommsen).
Malalas, X–XI, pp. 267–77 (ed. Bonn).
Martial, *Epigrammata*, V, 28; VIII, 70; IX, 26; X–XII.
Or. Sibyll. V, 40–6; XII, 142–63.
Philostratus, *Vit. Apoll.* VII, 8, 132; VIII, 7, 160; *Vit. Soph.* I, 7, 206; 18, 217.
Pliny Minor, *Epistulae; Panegyricus* (ed. M. Schuster).
S.H.A. *Hadr.* 1–9, 21; *M. Aurel.* 11; *Avid. Cass.* 8; *Macrin.* 13; *Alex. Sev.* 39, 65; *Tyr. Trig.* 6.
Tacitus, *Annals*, II, 61; XV, 72; *Agricola*, 3; *Germania.*
Occasional references will be found in Gaius, *Instit.* I, 34; Julian, *Convivium* (*Caesares*), 311 C, 327 A–328 B; Pausanias, V, 12, 6; Priscian, *Inst. Gram.* VI, 13 (=Peter, *Hist. rom. rel.* II, p. 117); Themistius, *Or.* XVI, p. 250 (Dindorf); Ulpian,

Epit. XXIV, 28 and *Frag. Vatic.* 233; see also the relevant sections in Aurelius Victor, Eutropius, and Orosius.

(d) Modern Works on the Sources

von Arnim, H. *Leben und Werke des Dio von Prusa.* Berlin, 1898.

Cantarelli, L. *Le fonti per la storia dell' Imperatore Traiano.* Studi e Documenti di storia e diritto, 1895, p. 185.

Hardy, E. G. *Pliny's Correspondence with Trajan.* London, 1889. (Cf. the works of Mommsen and Otto cited in II (*f*) below, and for full bibliography of Pliny see ed. Schuster, Leipzig, 1933, pp. xix–xxvi.)

Lightfoot, J. B. *The Apostolic Fathers,* II², Part II, pp. 436–46.

Morr, J. *Die Lobrede des jüngeren Plinius und die erste Königsrede des Dio von Prusa.* Diss. Troppau, 1915.

Roos, A. G. *Studia Arrianea.* Leipzig, 1912, pp. 30–64. Cf. for the fragments of the *Parthica,* Jacoby, F. Gr. Hist. II D, pp. 567–80.

Stauffenberg, A. Schenk, Graf von. *Die römische Kaisergeschichte bei Malalas,* pp. 255–94. Stuttgart, 1931.

II. Modern Works

(a) General: in addition to the relevant pages in works cited in the General Bibliography

de la Berge, C. *Essai sur le règne de Trajan.* Paris, 1877.

Dierauer, J. *Beiträge zu einer kritischen Geschichte Trajans,* in M. Büdinger's *Untersuchungen zur röm. Kaisergeschichte,* I. Leipzig, 1868.

von Domaszewski, A. *Die Politische Bedeutung des Traiansbogens in Benevent,* in *Abhandlungen zur römischen Religion,* pp. 25–52. Leipzig, 1909.

Groag, E. Art. in P.W. s.v. *Licinius* (167) *Sura.*

—— *Prosopographische Beiträge* V; *Sergius Octavius Laenas Pontianus.* Jahreshefte XXII, 1924, Beibl. col. 425.

Gsell, St. *Étude sur le rôle politique du sénat à l'époque de Trajan.* Mél. d'arch. et d'hist. de l'école française de Rome, VII, 1887, p. 339.

Paribeni, R. *Optimus Princeps.* 2 vols. Messina, 1926–7.

Rubel, J. *Die Familie des Kaisers Trajan.* Zeitschr. für die Oest. Gymn. LXVII, 1916, p. 481.

Stein, A. Art. in P.W. s.v. *Cocceius* (16) *Nerva.*

Stuart, D. R. *The point of an Emperor's jest.* C.P. III, 1908, p. 59.

Weber, W. *Traian und Hadrian* in *Meister der Politik,* I². Stuttgart, 1923.

—— *Untersuchungen zur Geschichte des Kaisers Hadrianus.* Leipzig, 1907 (esp. pp. 1–75).

(b) The Alimenta

Ashley, A. *The alimenta of Nerva and his successors.* Eng. Hist. Rev. XXXVI, 1921, p. 5.

Carcopino, J. *La Table de Veleia et son importance historique.* Rev. E.A. XXIII, 1921, p. 287.

de Pachtere, F. *La table hypothécaire de Veleia.* Paris, 1920.

Kubitschek, W. Art. in P.W. s.v. *alimenta.*

Mommsen, Th. *Die italische Bodentheilung und die Alimentartafeln.* Hermes, XIX, 1884, p. 393, reprinted in *Ges. Schr.* V, p. 1908.

(c) Finance

Carcopino, J. *Les richesses des Daces et le redressement de l'Empire Romain sous Trajan,* Dacia I, 1924, p. 28 (reprinted in *Points de vue sur l'impérialisme romain,* Paris, 1934, p. 73).

Heichelheim, F. *Zu Pap. Bad. 37, ein Beitrag zur römischen Geldgeschichte unter Trajan.* Klio, xxv, 1932, p. 124.

Mickwitz, G. *Zu den Finanzen Trajans.* Arctos, III, 1933–4, p. 1.

Sutherland, C. H. V. *The state of the Imperial treasury at the death of Domitian.* J.R.S. xxv, 1935, p. 150.

Syme, R. *The imperial finances under Domitian, Nerva and Trajan.* J.R.S. xx, 1930, p. 55.

(d) Public Works

See in particular the full account in Paribeni, *op. cit.* II, chaps. XIV–XVI and the notes in Strack, *op. cit.*, on the works represented in the coinage, and add:

Ashby, T. *The Aqueducts of Ancient Rome*, pp. 26–33 (Frontinus), 55–8 (Anio Vetus), 252–3 (Anio Novus), 299–307 (Aqua Traiana). Oxford, 1935.

Ashby, T. and R. Gardner, *The Via Traiana.* B.S.R. VIII, 1917, p. 104.

Lehmann-Hartleben, K. *Die Antike Hafenanlagen des Mittelmeeres.* Klio, Beiheft XIV, 1923, pp. 192–9.

Lugli, G. and G. Filibeck, *Il Porto di Roma imperiale e l'Agro portuense.* Rome and Bergamo, 1935.

Platner, S. B. and T. Ashby, *A Topographical Dictionary of Ancient Rome.* Arts. *Forum Traiani, Naumachia Vaticana, Thermae Suranae, Thermae Traiani.*

(e) Personnel and Administration

Carcopino, J. *Lusius Quietus, l'homme de Qwrnyn.* Istros, I, 1934, p. 5.

Groag, E. *Zu einem neuen Fragment der Fasten von Ostia.* Jahreshefte XXIX, 1935, Beibl. col. 177.

Heberdey, R. *Die Proconsules Asiae unter Trajan.* Jahreshefte VII, 1905, p. 231.

Kornemann, E. Art. in P.W. s.v. *curatores.*

Lacey, R. H. *The Equestrian Officials of Trajan and Hadrian: Their Careers, with some Notes on Hadrian's reforms.* Diss. Princeton, 1917.

Mancini, G. Art. in Diz. Epig. s.v. *curator reipublicae et civitatis.*

von Premerstein, A. *C. Iulius Quadratus Bassus.* Bay. S.B. 1934, 3.

Stech, B. *Senatores Romani qui fuerint inde a Vespasiano usque ad Traiani exitum.* Klio, Beiheft x, 1912.

Stein, A. *Ser. Sulpicius Similis.* Hermes, LIII, 1918, p. 422.

Walton, C. S. *Oriental Senators in the service of Rome.* J.R.S. xix, 1929, pp. 48–54.

Wilcken, U. *Plinius Reisen in Bithynien und Pontus.* Hermes, xLIX, 1914, p. 120.

Cf. also the relevant sections of:

Ritterling, E. *Fasti des römischen Deutschland unter dem Prinzipat,* and

Stein, E. *Die kaiserlichen Beamten und Truppenkörper im römischen Deutschland unter dem Prinzipat.* Vienna, 1932.

(f) Chronology

Holzapfel, L. *Römische Kaiserdaten. 5. Nerva und Traian.* Klio, xvII, 1921, p. 82.

Hülsen, Ch. *Neue Fragmente der Fasti Ostienses.* Rh. Mus. LXXXII, 1933, p. 362.

Lightfoot, J. B. *The Apostolic Fathers,* II², Part II, pp. 391–418.

Longden, R. P. *Tribunicia Potestate, a note.* J.R.S. xxi, 1931, p. 131.

Mattingly, H. *Tribunicia Potestate.* J.R.S. xx, 1930, pp. 76–81.

Mommsen, Th. *Zur Lebensgeschichte des jüngeren Plinius.* Hermes, III, 1869, p. 31 (reprinted in *Ges. Schr.* IV, p. 366).

Otto, W. *Zur Lebensgeschichte des jüngeren Plinius.* Bay. S.B. 1919, no. 1.

CHAPTER VI

THE WARS OF TRAJAN

I. Ancient Sources

The following inscriptions may be noted here as specially relevant to this chapter:

Ann. épig. 1923, 28; 1927, 3, 147, 161; 1928, 1, 2; 1929, 8, 9; 1934, 225, 268; 1936, 167.

C.R. Ac. Inscr. 1935, p. 287.

C.I.L. ii, 2424; iii, 777, 1004, 1443, 1627, 1940, 6273, 10336, 12467, 13587; vi, 32933; x, 5829; xi, 3100, 5992; xii, 5899.

Dessau, 289, 292, 297, 301, 308, 1019, 1021ᵃ, 1022, 1023, 1029, 1035, 1041 (cf. A. Merlin in Rev. E.A. xiii, 1913, p. 268), 1046, 1350, 1352, 1419, 1465, 2004, 2081, 2083, 2417, 2647, 2654, 2660, 2661, 2665, 2720, 2723, 2724(?), 2727, 4081, 4393, 5035, 5834, 5863, 6523, 7134, 8863, 9107, 9471, 9491.

I.G.R.R. iii, 173, 739, 831, 1026, 1140, 1273, 1283, 1291, 1319, 1346, 1434. For literary sources see the bibliography to chap. v.

For coins, in addition to the relevant pages of works cited in the General Bibliography and in the Bibliography to chapter v, 1(*b*), see:

Hill, G. F. *B.M. Cat. Coins of Arabia, Mesopotamia and Persia.* London, 1922.

Wroth, W. *B.M. Cat. Coins of Parthia.* London, 1903.

Head, B. V. *H.N.*² p. 720 (Epiphaneia, Selinus), 802 (Diocaesarea-Sepphoris), 812 (Bostra): and for changes in the Danube and Balkan provinces (*supra*, p. 236) Head, *op. cit.* p. 275 (Marcianopolis, Nicopolis ad Istrum) (cf. E. Seure, *s.v.* Rev. Arch. 1907, p. 257), 277 (Anchialus), 287 (Pautalia, Nicopolis ad Mestum), 288 (Plotinopolis, Serdica, Topirus, Augusta Traiana, Traianopolis).

II. Modern Works

In addition to the relevant parts of the works of de la Berge, Dierauer and Paribeni cited in the Bibliography to chapter v, ii(*a*), consult the articles in P.W. *svv. Legio* (E. Ritterling) and *Limes* (E. Fabricius) and also the following:

(*a*) The Dacian Wars

Brandis, G. Art. in P.W. s.v. *Dacia.*

Cantacuzène, G. *Un papyrus latin relatif à la défense du bas Danube.* Aeg. ix, 1928, p. 63.

Cichorius, C. *Die Reliefs der Traianssäule.* 2 vols. Berlin, 1896–1900.

—— *Die römischen Denkmäler in der Dobrudscha.* Berlin, 1904.

Davies, G. A. T. *Topography and the Trajan column.* J.R.S. x, 1920, p. 1.

—— *Trajan's first Dacian war.* J.R.S. vii, 1917, p. 74.

von Domaszewski, A. *Die Dakerkriege Traians auf den Reliefs der Säule.* Phil. lxv, 1906, p. 321.

Feliciani, N. Art. in Diz. Epig. s.v. *Dacia.*

Florescu, G. *Le camp romain de Arcidava.* Istros, i, 1934, p. 60.

Furtwängler, A. *Adamklissi.* Bay. S.B. 1897, p. 247.

—— *Das Tropaion von Adamklissi und provinzialrömische Kunst.* Bay. Abh. xxii, 1905, p. 455.

Jung, J. *Fasten der Provinz Dacien.* Innsbruck, 1894.

Lehmann-Hartleben, K. *Die Trajanssäule. Ein römisches Kunstwerk zu Beginn der Spätantike.* Berlin, 1926.

Panaitescu, E. *Le Limes dacique.* Bull. Acad. Roum. xv, 1929, p. 73.

Pârvan, V. *I primordi della civiltà Romana alle foci del Danubio.* Ausonia, x, 1921, p. 198 (summarising earlier articles in Anal. Acad. Române).

Petersen, E. *Trajans dakische Kriege.* Leipzig, 1899–1903 (2 vols.).

Richmond, I. A. *Trajan's army on Trajan's column.* B.S.R. xiii, 1935, p. 1.

Schuchhardt, C. *Die sogenannten Trajanswälle in der Dobrudscha.* Berl. Abh. 1918, xii.

Stuart Jones, Sir H. *The historical interpretation of the reliefs of Trajan's column.* B.S.R. v, 1910, p. 435.

Studniczka, F. *Tropaeum Traiani, ein Beitrag zur Kunstgeschichte der Kaiserzeit.* Sächs. Abh. xxii, 1904, p. 152.

Tocilesco, G. (with O. Benndorf and G. Niemann). *Das Monument von Adamklissi, Tropaeum Traiani.* Vienna, 1895.

—— *Fouilles et recherches archéologiques en Roumanie.* Bucharest, 1900.

Vaschide, V. *La conquête romaine de la Dacie.* Paris, 1907.

(b) The East

Brünnow, R. E. and A. von Domaszewski, *Die provincia Arabia.* Strassburg, 1904–9 (3 vols.).

Cuntz, O. *Zum Briefwechsel des Plinius mit Traian.* Hermes lxi, 1926, p. 192.

Gould, S. *The triumphal arch,* in *Excavations at Dura-Europos,* iv, 1933, pp. 57–65.

Groag, E. Art. in P.W. s.v. *Lusius* (9) *Quietus.*

von Gutschmid, A. *Geschichte Irans und seiner Nachbarländer.* Tübingen, 1888.

—— *Untersuchungen über die Geschichte d. Königreichs Osroëne.* Mém. de l'Acad. des Sciences de St Pétersbourg, vii series, xxxv, 1887, pp. 25–8.

Hauler, E. *Zu Frontos Principia Historiae.* Wien. St. xxxviii, 1916, p. 166.

Longden, R. P. *Notes on the Parthian campaigns of Trajan.* J.R.S. xxi, 1931, p. 1.

Poidebard, A. *La trace de Rome dans le désert de Syrie; le limes, de Trajan à la conquête arabe.* Paris, 1932.

Rostovtzeff, M. *L'Empereur Trajan et Doura.* C.R. Ac. Inscr. 1935, p. 285.

Sills, H. *Trajan's Armenian and Parthian wars.* Cambridge, 1897.

Warmington, E. H. *The Commerce between the Roman Empire and India.* Cambridge, 1928, pp. 91–100.

(c) The Jewish Question

von Premerstein, A. *Alexandrinische und jüdische Gesandte vor Kaiser Hadrian.* Hermes, lvii, 1922, p. 266.

Schürer, E. *Geschichte des jüdischen Volkes im Zeitalter Jesu Christi,* i⁴. Leipzig, 1901, pp. 659–68.

Weber, W. *Eine Gerichtsverhandlung vor Kaiser Traian.* Hermes, l, 1915, p. 47.

Wilcken, U. *Ein Aktenstück zum jüdischen Kriege Trajans.* Hermes, xxvii, 1892, p. 464.

—— *Zum alexandrinischen Antisemitismus.* Sächs. Abh. xxvii, 1909, pp. 792–821.

CHAPTER VII

THE RISE OF CHRISTIANITY

As far as possible this list is confined to books accessible in the English language: commentaries on the books of the New Testament are not included.

GENERAL

Anderson Scott, C. A. *Dominus Noster*. A Study in the Progressive Recognition of Jesus Christ our Lord. Cambridge, 1918.

Angus, S. *The Mystery Religions and Christianity*. London, 1925.

—— *The Religious Quests of the Graeco-Roman World*. London, 1929.

Cumont, F. *Les religions orientales dans le paganisme romain*. Ed. 4, Paris, 1929. (Eng. trans. from 2nd ed. by Grant Showerman, Chicago, 1911; German trans. from 4th ed. (Gehrich-Burkhardt) with supplementary material, Berlin–Leipzig, 1931.)

Deissmann, A. *Light from the Ancient East*. Eng. trans., London, 1927.

Glover, T. R. *The Conflict of Religions in the Early Roman Empire*. London, 1909.

Harnack, A. *The Expansion of Christianity in the First Three Centuries*. (Trans. and ed. by J. Moffatt.) London, 1904.

—— *The Constitution and Law of the Church in the First Two Centuries*. (Trans. by F. L. Pogson, ed. by H. D. A. Major.) London, 1910.

Kennedy, H. A. A. *Philo's Contribution to Religion*. London, 1919.

Lake, K. *The Text of the New Testament*. Ed. 6 (revised by Silva New), London, 1928.

Lawlor, H. J. and J. E. L. Oulton, *Eusebius Bishop of Caesarea*. The Ecclesiastical History and the Martyrs of Palestine. (Trans. and Notes.) London, 1927.

Lietzmann, H. *Messe und Herrenmahl*. Bonn, 1926.

Lightfoot, J. B. *Dissertation on the Christian Ministry*. (In his edition of St Paul's Epistle to the Philippians.) London, 1894.

Macdonald, A. B. *Christian Worship in the Primitive Church*. Edinburgh, 1934.

Meyer, E. *Ursprung und Anfänge des Christentums*. Stuttgart and Berlin, I–III, 1921.

Micklem, E. R. *Miracles and the New Psychology*. A Study in the Healing Miracles of the New Testament. Oxford, 1922.

Moffatt, J. *An Introduction to the Literature of the New Testament*. Ed. 3, Edinburgh, 1918.

Nock, A. D. *Conversion*. The Old and the New in Religion from Alexander the Great to Augustine of Hippo. Oxford, 1933.

Oxford Society of Historical Theology. *The New Testament in the Apostolic Fathers*. Oxford, 1905.

Streeter, B. H. *The Primitive Church*. London, 1930.

Swete, H. B. (ed.). *Essays on the Early History of the Church and the Ministry*, by Various Writers. London, 1918.

Wellhausen, J. *Einleitung in die drei ersten Evangelien*. Ed. 2, Berlin, 1911.

SPECIAL TOPICS

(a) *The Gospels.*

Thompson, J. M. *The Synoptic Gospels, arranged in parallel columns*. Oxford, 1910. [English of Revised Version: coincident words in italics.]

Huck, A. *A Synopsis of the First Three Gospels*. Ed. 9 (revised by Hans Lietzmann; Eng. ed. by F. L. Cross). Tübingen, 1936.

Bacon, B. W. *The Fourth Gospel in Research and Debate.* New York, 1910.

Burkitt, F. C. *The Gospel History and Its Transmission.* Edinburgh, 1906.

—— *Jesus Christ. An Historical Outline.* London, 1932.

Burney, C. F. *The Poetry of Our Lord.* An Examination of the Formal Elements of Hebrew Poetry in the Discourses of Jesus Christ. Oxford, 1925.

Cadbury, H. J. *The Making of Luke-Acts.* London, 1927.

Carpenter, J. E. *The Johannine Writings.* London, 1927.

Dibelius, M. *From Tradition to Gospel.* (Eng. trans. in collaboration with the author by B. L. Woolf.) London, 1934.

von Dobschütz, E. *The Eschatology of the Gospels.* London, 1910.

Dodd, C. H. *The Parables of the Kingdom.* London, 1935.

Gardner, P. *The Ephesian Gospel.* London, 1915.

Grant, F. C. *Form Criticism* (Translation of *The Study of the Synoptic Gospels* by R. Bultmann, and *Primitive Christianity in the Light of Gospel Research* by K. Kundsin). New York, 1934.

Harnack, A. *The Sayings of Jesus.* The Second Source of St Matthew and St Luke. (Eng. trans. by J. R. Wilkinson.) London, 1908.

Hawkins, J. C. *Horae Synopticae.* Ed. 2, Oxford, 1909.

Hoskyns, (Sir) E. C. and N. Davey, *The Riddle of the New Testament.* London, 1931 [with good Bibliography].

Howard, W. F. *The Fourth Gospel in Recent Criticism and Interpretation.* London, 1931.

Klausner, J. *Jesus of Nazareth, His Life, Times and Teaching.* (Eng. trans. by H. Danby.) London, 1925.

Manson, T. W. *The Teaching of Jesus.* Studies of its Form and Content. Cambridge, 1931.

Montefiore, C. G. *The Synoptic Gospels.* I and II, Ed. 2, London, 1927.

—— *Rabbinic Literature and Gospel Teachings.* London, 1930.

Sanday, W. *Oxford Studies in the Synoptic Problem.* Oxford, 1911.

Schweitzer, A. *The Quest of the Historical Jesus.* (Eng. trans. by W. Montgomery.) London, 1910.

Scott, E. F. *The Fourth Gospel, Its Purpose and Theology.* Edinburgh, 1906.

Stanton, V. H. *The Gospels as Historical Documents.* 3 vols., Cambridge, 1903–1920.

Streeter, B. H. Essay *The Historic Christ* in *Foundations*, by Seven Oxford Men (ed. B.H.S.). London, 1912.

—— *The Four Gospels.* (A Study of Origins. Treating of the Manuscript Tradition, Sources, Authorship, and Dates.) 4th Impression revised, London, 1930.

Taylor, Vincent. *The Formation of the Gospel Tradition.* London, 1933.

(b) Acts and Epistles.

Anderson Scott, C. A. Essay *What Happened at Pentecost* in *The Spirit* (ed. by B. H. Streeter), 1919.

Clark, A. C. *The Acts of the Apostles.* A Critical Edition with Introduction and Notes on Selected Passages. Oxford, 1933. A reconstruction of the Western text.

Deissmann, A. *Paul. A Study in Social and Religious History.* Eng. trans. by W. E. Wilson, Ed. 2, London, 1926.

Foakes-Jackson, F. J. and K. Lake, *The Beginnings of Christianity.* Part I, The Acts of the Apostles, vols. II and V. London, 1922 and 1933.

Goodspeed, E. J. *New Solutions of New Testament Problems.* Chicago, 1927.

Harnack, A. *Luke the Physician.* The Author of the Third Gospel and the Acts of the Apostles. Eng. trans. by J. R. Wilkinson, ed. by W. D. Morrison, London, 1907.

Harnack, A. *The Acts of the Apostles.* Eng. trans. by J. R. Wilkinson, London, 1909.

Harrison, P. N. *The Problem of the Pastoral Epistles.* Oxford, 1921.

Kennedy, H. A. A. *St Paul and the Mystery-Religions.* London, 1913.

Lietzmann, H. *Petrus und Paulus in Rom.* Bonn, n.d.

Morgan, W. *The Religion and Theology of Paul.* Edinburgh, 1917.

Ramsay, W. M. *St Paul the Traveller and the Roman Citizen.* Ed. 3, London, 1897.

(c) *Apostolic Fathers and Apocryphal Gospels.*

Bell, H. I. and T. C. Skeat (eds.), *Fragments of an Unknown Gospel and Other Early Christian Papyri.* London, 1935. (Cf. review by F. C. Burkitt in *Journ. of Theol. Studies,* July, 1935.)

Connolly, R. H. Arts. in *Journ. of Theol. Studies,* April and July, 1934.

Gebhardt, O., A. Harnack and T. Zahn, *Patres Apostolici.* Leipzig, 1875–77.

Harnack, A. *Die Lehre der Zwölfe Apostel.* Leipzig, 1884.

Harrison, P. N. *Polycarp's Two Epistles to the Philippians.* Cambridge, 1936.

James, M. R. *The Apocryphal New Testament.* (Being the Apocryphal Gospels, Acts, Epistles and Apocalypses, with other Narratives and Fragments newly translated by M. R. James.) Oxford, 1924.

Lake, K. *The Apostolic Fathers.* Text and translation (Loeb Series). London, 1912–13.

Lightfoot, J. B. *The Apostolic Fathers.* (*St Clement of Rome,* vols. I and II.) Ed. 2, London, 1890.

—— *The Apostolic Fathers.* Part II (*S. Ignatius and S. Polycarp,* vols. I, II, III). Ed. 2, London, 1889.

Lightfoot, J. B. and J. R. Harmer, *The Apostolic Fathers.* Text and translation, London, 1893.

Maclean, A. S. *The Doctrine of the Twelve Apostles.* London, 1922 (Text and commentary).

Robinson, J. A. *Barnabas, Hermas and the Didache.* London, 1920.

Souter, A. Art. *s.v. Gospels* (Uncanonical) in Hastings' *Dictionary of the Apostolic Church.* Edinburgh, 1915.

Streeter, B. H. *The much-belaboured Didache.* Journ. of Theol. Studies (forthcoming).

Watt, H. Art. *s.v. Didache* in Hastings' *Dictionary of the Apostolic Church.* Edinburgh, 1915.

CHAPTERS VIII–IX

HADRIAN: THE ANTONINES

A. Ancient Sources

(*a*) *Literary*: see Notes on pp. 297, 326, 340. For legislation see S. Hänel, *Corpus legum ab imperatoribus Romanis ante Justinianum latarum.*

On the sources see the bibliography on p. 865 and the following works:

Heer, J. M. *Der historische Wert der Vita Commodi in der Sammlung der S.H.A.* Phil. Supplbd. ix, 1904.

Kornemann, E. *Kaiser Hadrian und der letzte grosse Historiker Roms* (see E. Hohl in *N.J. Kl. Alt.* xxxiii, 1914, p. 698).

Schulz, O. Th. *Das Kaiserhaus der Antonine und der letzte grosse Historiker Roms.* Leipzig, 1907 (see reviews by K. Hönn in *Deutsche Literaturzeitung*, xxix, 1908, col. 1002 and W. Weber in *G.G.A.* 1908, pp. 945–1004).

Schwendemann, J. *Der historische Wert der vita Marci bei den Scriptores Historiae Augustae.* Heidelberg, 1923.

Stauffenberg, A. Schenk, Graf von. *Untersuchungen zur Chronik des Malalas.* Stuttgart, 1931, pp. 307 *sqq.*

Tropea, G. *Studi sugli S.H.A.* Riv. stor. ant. vi, 1901–2, p. 185.

(*b*) *Epigraphical.*

See for epigraphical material the relevant articles in *P.I.R.* For Hadrian see especially:

W. Weber, *Untersuchungen zur Geschichte des Kaisers Hadrianus.* Leipzig, 1907.

For Antoninus Pius:

Hüttl, W. *Antoninus Pius,* ii. *Römische Reichsbeamte und Offiziere unter Antoninus Pius. Antoninus Pius in den Inschriften seiner Zeit.* Prague, 1933.

(*c*) *Numismatic.*

Bosch, C. *Die kleinasiatischen Münzen der römischen Kaiserzeit.* Stuttgart, 1931.

Kubitschek, W. *Zur Abfolge der Prägungen der Kaiser Marcus und Verus.* Wien S.B. 212, 5, 1933.

Mattingly, M. *British Museum Catalogue of Coins of the Roman Empire.* Vol. iii (Nerva to Hadrian). London, 1936 (appeared after these chapters were in print).

Mattingly, H. and E. A. Sydenham, *The Roman Imperial Coinage.* London, vol. ii, 1926, pp. 314 *sqq.*; vol. iii, 1930.

Strack, P. L. *Untersuchungen zur römischen Reichsprägung des zweiten Jahrhunderts.* Stuttgart, vol. ii, 1933; vol. iii (in publication).

Vogt, J. *Die alexandrinischen Münzen: Grundlegung einer alexandrinischen Kaisergeschichte.* Part i, Text; Part ii, Münzverzeichnis. Stuttgart, 1924.

B. Modern Works

(*a*) *Hadrian.*

Dürr, J. *Die Reisen des Kaisers Hadrian.* Vienna, 1881.

Henderson, B. W. *The Life and Principate of the Emperor Hadrian* A.D. 76–138. London, 1923.

Lacey, R. H. *The Equestrian Officers of Trajan and Hadrian: Their Careers with some Notes on Hadrian's reforms.* Diss. Princeton, 1917.

Mancini, G. and D. Vaglieri, Art. *s.v.* Hadrianus in Diz. Epig.

Perret, L. *La titulature impériale d'Hadrien.* Paris, 1929.

Pringsheim, F. *The Legal Policy and Reforms of Hadrian.* J.R.S. xxiv, 1934, p. 141.

von Rohden, P. Art. in P.W. *s.v.* Aelius (64).

Sander, E. *Die Hauptquelle der Bücher* i–iii *der* epitoma rei militaris *des Vegetius.* Phil. lxxxvii, 1932, p. 369.

Schulz, O. Th. *Leben des Kaisers Hadrians.* Leipzig, 1904.

Weber, W. *Untersuchungen zur Geschichte des Kaisers Hadrianus.* Leipzig, 1907.

—— *Traian und Hadrian* in Meister der Politik, i², Stuttgart, 1923, pp. 244 *sqq.*

(*b*) *Antoninus Pius.*

Bryant, E. C. *The reign of Antoninus Pius.* Cambridge, 1895.

Dodd, C. H. *The cognomen of the Emperor Antoninus Pius.* Num. Chr. xi, 1911, p. 6.

von Rohden, P. Art. in P.W. *s.v.* Aurelius (138).

Toynbee, J. *Some 'programme' coin-types of Antoninus Pius.* C.R. xxxix, 1925, p. 170.

(*c*) *Marcus Aurelius.*

For earlier literature see von Rohden, art. in P.W. *s.v.* Annius (94).

Dodd, C. H. *Chronology of the Eastern Campaigns of the Emperor Lucius Verus.* Num. Chr. xi, 1911, p. 209.

—— *The Danubian Wars of Marcus Antoninus.* Ib. xiii, 1913, p. 162.

—— *On the coinage of Commodus during the reign of Marcus.* Ib. xiv, 1914, p. 34.

von Domaszewski, A. *Der Völkerbund des Marcomanenkrieges.* Serta Harteliana, Vienna, 1896, pp. 8–13.

Franke, Art. in P.W. *s.v.* Marcomanni.

Günther, A. *Beiträge zur Geschichte der Kriege zwischen Römern und Parthern.* Berlin, 1922, pp. 113 *sqq.*

Lambrechts, P. *L'Empereur Lucius Verus. Essai de réhabilitation.* L'Antiquité classique, iii, 1934, p. 173.

Mommsen, Th. *Der Marcomanenkrieg unter Kaiser Marcus.* Ges. Schriften, iv, pp. 487 *sqq.*

Napp, E. J. *De rebus Imp. M. Aurelii Antonini in Oriente gestis.* Bonn, 1879.

von Premerstein, A. *Untersuchungen zur Geschichte des Kaisers Marcus.* Klio, xi, 1911, p. 355; xii, 1912, p. 167; xiii, 1913; p. 70.

Sedgwick, H. D. *Marcus Aurelius, a Biography.* Yale Univ. Press, 1921.

von Wilamowitz-Moellendorff, U. *Kaiser Marcus.* Berlin, 1931.

(*d*) *Commodus.*

For earlier literature see von Rohden in P.W. *s.v.* Aurelius (89), cols. 2464 *sqq.*

Cumont, F. *Jupiter summus exsuperantissimus.* Arch. f. Rel. Wiss. ix, 1906, p. 323.

von Domaszewski, A. *Geschichte der römischen Kaiser.* Leipzig, 1914, vol. ii, pp. 233 *sqq.*

Mommsen, Th. *Perennis.* Ges. Schriften, iv, p. 514.

von Premerstein, A. *Protest des Gymnasiarchen Appianos gegen seine Verurteilung durch Commodus (C).* Phil. Suppl. xvi, 1923, 2, p. 28.

Rostovtseff, M. *Commodus-Hercules in Britain.* J.R.S. xiii, 1923, p. 91.

Stein, A. *Das Todesjahr des Gardtepraefekten Perennis.* Hermes, xxxv, 1905, p. 528.

Weber, W. *Probleme der Spätantike.* Stuttgart, 1930, pp. 67 *sqq.*, 87.

—— *Römische Kaisergeschichte und Kirchengeschichte.* Stuttgart, 1929, pp. 19 *sqq.*

CHAPTER X

THE PRINCIPATE AND THE ADMINISTRATION

The following works may be specially mentioned, whether in addition to those enumerated in the bibliographies to chapters I, V, VIII–IX or on account of the writer's particular indebtedness. The ancient authorities are not set out here because a reference to the evidence for every important statement in these chapters appears in a footnote. Books recorded in this and the following bibliography are arranged in groups; the order of the groups is that in which they become relevant to the argument of the text; and within each group works of wider bearing precede those concerned with more restricted problems.

I. General Works

Hirschfeld, O. *Kleine Schriften*. Berlin, 1913.
Schiller, H. *Geschichte der römischen Kaiserzeit*: 1, 2, *Von der Regierung Vespasians bis zur Erhebung Diokletians*. Gotha, 1883.
Hahn, L. *Das Kaisertum* (*Das Erbe der Alten*, Heft VI). Leipzig, 1913.
Rostovtzeff, M. *The Social & Economic History of the Roman Empire*. Oxford, 1926.
—— *Storia economica e sociale dell' impero romano*. Florence, 1933.
Homo, L. *Les institutions politiques romaines. De la cité à l'état*. Paris, 1927.
Hirschfeld, O. *Zur Geschichte der römischen Kaiserzeit in den ersten drei Jahrhunderten*. In *Kleine Schriften*, p. 901.
Kornemann, E. *Die römische Kaiserzeit*, in *Einleitung in die Altertumswissenschaft*, herausgegeben von A. Gercke und E. Norden, dritte Auflage, III, 2 (Leipzig-Berlin, 1933), p. 55.
Cary, M. *A History of Rome down to the Reign of Constantine*. London, 1935.
Ferrero, G. and C. Barbagallo, *A Short History of Rome*: II. *The Empire from the Death of Caesar to the Fall of the Western Empire*. New York-London, 1919.
Friedlaender, L. *Darstellungen aus der Sittengeschichte Roms in der Zeit bis zum Ausgang der Antonine*. Neunte...Auflage, besorgt von G. Wissowa. Leipzig. Vol. I, 1919; vols. II–III, 1920; vol. IV (Anhänge), 1921.
Hüttl, W. *Antoninus Pius*: II, *Römische Reichsbeamte und Offiziere unter Antoninus Pius. Antoninus Pius in den Inschriften seiner Zeit*. Prague, 1933.
Kubitschek, W. *Zur Abfolge der Prägungen der Kaiser Marcus und Verus*. Wien S.B. CCXIII, 1932, 5.

II. The Constitution

(a) General Works

Mispoulet, J. B. *Les institutions politiques des Romains*. 2 vols. Paris, 1882–3. (Appendix on *La lex regia* in vol. I, p. 367.)
Karlowa, O. *Römische Rechtsgeschichte*, I. Leipzig, 1885.
Mommsen, Th. *Römisches Staatsrecht*. Leipzig. II, 2³, 1887; III, 1888.
Herzog, E. *Geschichte und System der römischen Staatsverfassung*: II, *Die Kaiserzeit von der Diktatur Cäsars bis zum Regierungsantritt Diocletians*. Leipzig. 1. *Geschichtliche Übersicht*, 1887. 2. *System der Verfassung der Kaiserzeit*, 1891.
De Francisci, P. *Storia del diritto romano*, II, 1. Rome, 1929.

Schulz, O. Th. *Das Wesen des römischen Kaisertums der ersten zwei Jahrhunderte.* Paderborn, 1916.

Siber, H. *Zur Entwicklung der römischen Prinzipatverfassung.* Sächs. Abh. XLII, 1933.

Kromayer, J. *Die rechtliche Begründung des Principats.* Strassburg Diss. Marburg, 1888.

Pelham, H. F. *On some disputed Points connected with the Imperium of Augustus and his Successors.* J.P. XVII, 1888, p. 27 (*Essays by Henry Francis Pelham* (Oxford, 1911), p. 60).

Kornemann, E. *Doppelprinzipat und Reichsteilung im Imperium Romanum.* Leipzig-Berlin, 1930.

Volkmann, H. *Zur Rechtsprechung im Principat des Augustus.* Munich, 1935. (*Münchener Beiträge zur Papyrusforschung und antiken Rechtsgeschichte,* XXI.)

Chambalu, A. *De magistratibus Flaviorum: adiecta est appendix de Titi nomine imperatoris.* Bonnae, 1882.

(*b*) The '*Lex de imperio Vespasiani*'

von Reumont, A. *Geschichte der Stadt Rom.* Berlin. I, 1867, p. 397 *sq.*

Cantarelli, L. *La Lex de Imperio Vespasiani.* Bull. Comm. Arch. Com. di Roma, XVIII, 1890, pp. 194, 235 (*Studi romani e bizantini* (Rome, 1915), p. 99).

Hellems, F. B. R. *The lex de imperio Vespasiani.* J.P. XXVIII, 1903, p. 122.

—— *Lex de imperio Vespasiani.* Diss. Chicago, 1902.

Mattingly, H. *Tribunicia Potestate.* J.R.S. XX, 1930, p. 78.

(*c*) The Position of the Princeps

Heinze, R. *Auctoritas.* Hermes, LX, 1925, p. 348.

Nock, A. D. *Religious Development from Vespasian to Trajan.* Theology, XVI, 1928, p. 152.

Charlesworth, M. P. *Some Observations on Ruler-cult, especially in Rome.* Harv. Theol. Rev. XXVIII, 1935, p. 5.

Schulz, O. Th. *Die Rechtstitel und Regierungsprogramme auf römischen Kaiser-münzen (von Cäsar bis Severus).* Paderborn, 1925.

Alföldi, A. *Die Ausgestaltung des monarchischen Zeremoniells am römischen Kaiser-hofe.* Röm. Mitt. XLIX, 1934, p. 1.

—— *Insignien und Tracht der römischen Kaiser.* Röm. Mitt. L, 1935, p. 1.

Koch, L. G. *De principe Iuventutis.* Diss. Lipsiae, 1883.

III. THE ADMINISTRATIVE SYSTEM

Hirschfeld, O. *Die kaiserlichen Verwaltungsbeamten bis auf Diocletian*[2]. Berlin, 1905.

Mattingly, H. *The Imperial Civil Service of Rome.* Cambridge, 1910.

Liebenam, W. *Beiträge zur Verwaltungsgeschichte des römischen Kaiserreichs:* I, *Die Laufbahn der Prokuratoren bis auf die Zeit Diocletians.* Jena, 1886.

Rostowzew, M. Art. *s.v.* ab epistulis in P.W.

von Premerstein, A. Art. *s.v.* a libellis in P.W.

Cagnat, R. *Étude historique sur les impôts indirects chez les Romains.* Paris, 1883.

Holmberg, E. J. *Zur Geschichte des Cursus publicus.* Uppsala, n.d. [1933].

IV. THE SENATE

Marsh, F. B. *The Roman Aristocracy and the Death of Caesar.* C.J. XX, 1924–5, p. 451.

Gelzer, M. *Die Nobilität der Kaiserzeit*. Hermes, L, 1915, p. 395. On this
    see

Otto, W. *Die Nobilität der Kaiserzeit*. Hermes, LI, 1916, p. 73.

Hirschfeld, O. *Die Rangtitel der römischen Kaiserzeit*. Berl. S.B. 1901, p. 579.
    (*Kleine Schriften*, p. 646.)

von Premerstein, A. Art. *s.v.* Legatus in P.W.

Rosenberg, A. Art. *s.v.* Iuridicus in P.W.

Dessau, H. *Die Herkunft der Offiziere und Beamten des römischen Kaiserreichs
    während der ersten zwei Jahrh. seines Bestehens*. Hermes, XLV, 1910, pp. 1,
    615.

Lully, G. *De senatorum Romanorum patria*. Rome, 1918.

Stech, B. *Senatores Romani qui fuerint inde a Vespasiano usque ad Traiani exitum*.
    Klio, Beiheft X, 1912.

Hahn, L. *Römische Beamte griechischer und orientalischer Abstammung in der
    Kaiserzeit*. In Festgabe des alten Gymnasiums, Nürnberg, 1926.

Walton, C. S. *Oriental Senators in the Service of Rome*. J.R.S. XIX, 1929, p. 38.

Gsell, S. *Étude sur le rôle politique du sénat romain à l'époque de Trajan*. École
    française de Rome: Mélanges d'archéologie et d'histoire, VII, 1887, p. 339.

V. THE ORDO EQUESTER

Belot, E. *Histoire des chevaliers romains*, II. Paris, 1873.

Kübler, B. Art. *s.v.* Equites Romani in P.W.

Stein, A. *Der römische Ritterstand. Ein Beitrag zur Sozial- und Personengeschichte
    des römischen Reiches*. Munich, 1927.

Lacey, R. H. *The Equestrian Officials of Trajan and Hadrian: Their Careers, with
    some Notes on Hadrian's Reforms*. Diss. Princeton, 1917.

CHAPTER XI

ROME AND THE EMPIRE

The more important publications concerning particular regions will be found in the bibliographies to chapters xii–xvi. Those cited here are mainly those mentioned in the notes to the chapter. The following list contains only a brief selection of more general studies, with a short set of works on the municipalities in which references to the more detailed literature may be found, and such other books and articles as have laid the writer under a special debt. On the order of works see note above, p. 896.

I. General Works

Mommsen, Th. *Römische Geschichte:* v, *Die Provinzen von Caesar bis Diocletian.* Berlin, 1885. (*The Provinces of the Roman Empire*². 2 vols. London, 1909.)

Chapot, V. *Le monde romain.* Paris, 1927.

Tarn, W. W. *Hellenistic Civilisation*². London, 1930.

Haverfield, F. *Some Roman Conceptions of Empire.* Occasional Publications of the Classical Association, No. 4. Cambridge, n.d. On this see

Fowler, W. Warde, *Aeneas at the Site of Rome* (Oxford, 1917), p. 103 *n.*

Bryce, J. *The (Ancient) Roman Empire and the British Empire in India* and *The Diffusion of Roman and English Law throughout the World,* in *Studies in History and Jurisprudence,* 1 (Oxford, 1901), pp. 1 and 85 (published together as *The Roman and the British Empires* (Oxford, 1914)).

Cromer, Lord, *Ancient and Modern Imperialism.* London, 1910.

Lucas, Sir C. P. *Greater Rome and Greater Britain.* Oxford, 1912.

Heitland, W. E. *The Roman Fate.* Cambridge, 1922.

—— *Iterum, or a further Discussion of the Roman Fate.* Cambridge, 1925.

—— *Last Words on the Roman Municipalities.* Cambridge, 1928.

—— *Repetita. An unwilling Restatement of Views on the Subject of the Roman Municipalities.* Cambridge, 1930.

Gelzer, M. *Gemeindestaat und Reichsstaat in der römischen Geschichte.* Frankfurter Universitätsreden, 1924, xix.

Judeich, W. *Der Reichsgedanke im Altertum.* Jenaer akademische Reden, ix, 1930.

Schwartz, E. *Weltreich und Weltsfriede.* Strassburg, 1916.

Wenger, L. *Von der Staatskunst der Römer.* Bay. S.B. 1925.

Kloesel, H. *Libertas.* Diss. Breslau, 1935.

Snellman, W. I. *De interpretibus Romanorum deque linguae Latinae cum aliis nationibus commercio.* Lipsiae. Pars i: *Enarratio,* 1919. Pars ii: *Testimonia veterum,* 1914.

Hahn, L. *Rom und Romanismus im griechisch-römischen Osten. Mit besonderer Berücksichtigung der Sprache. Bis auf die Zeit Hadrians.* Leipzig, 1906.

Kahrstedt, U. *Die Kultur der Antoninenzeit.* Neue Wege zur Antike, iii. Leipzig-Berlin, n.d.

Mitteis, L. *Reichsrecht und Volksrecht in den östlichen Provinzen des römischen Kaiserreichs.* Leipzig, 1891.

Schwartz, E. *Kaiser Constantin und die christliche Kirche.* Leipzig, 1913.

II. The Municipalities

(a) Selected Authorities and their Interpretation

Mommsen, Th. *Lex Municipii Tarentini*. Eph. Ep. ix, p. 1. (*Ges. Schriften*, i, p. 146.)
—— *Lex coloniae Iuliae Genetivae Urbanorum sive Ursonensis*. Eph. Ep. ii, p. 108. (*Ges. Schriften*, i, p. 194.)
—— *Legis coloniae Genetivae c. LXI–LXXXII*. Eph. Ep. iii, p. 91. (*Ges. Schriften*, i, p. 240.)
—— *Die Stadtrechte der latinischen Gemeinden Salpensa und Malaca in der Provinz Baetica*. Sächs. Abh. iii, 1855, p. 361. (*Ges. Schriften*, i, p. 265.)
Hardy, E. G. *Six Roman Laws*. Oxford, 1911.
—— *Three Spanish Charters and other documents*. Oxford, 1912. (Published together as *Roman Laws and Charters*. Oxford, 1912.)

(b) The Municipal System in General

Marquardt, J. *Römische Staatsverwaltung*, i². Leipzig, 1881.
Kornemann, E. Art. *s.v.* Coloniae in P.W.
—— Art. *s.v.* Municipium in P.W.
Rudolph, H. *Stadt und Staat im römischen Italien. Untersuchungen über die Entwicklung des Munizipalwesens in der republikanischen Zeit*. Leipzig, 1935.
Kuhn, E. *Die städtische und bürgerliche Verfassung des Römischen Reiches bis auf die Zeiten Justinians*. Leipzig. Erster Teil, 1864: zweiter Teil, 1865.
Liebenam, W. *Städteverwaltung im römischen Kaiserreiche*. Leipzig, 1900.
Reid, J. S. *The Municipalities of the Roman Empire*. Cambridge, 1913.
Abbott, F. F. and A. C. Johnson, *Municipal Administration in the Roman Empire*. Princeton, 1926.
Berger, A. Art. *s.v.* Incola in P.W.
Kornemann, E. Art. *s.v.* Conventus in P.W.
Schulten, A. *De conventibus civium Romanorum*. Berolini, 1892.
Zumpt, A. W. *De propagatione ciuitatis Romanae*, in *Studia Romana* (Berolini, 1859), p. 325.
Dorsch, E. *De civitatis Romanae apud Graecos propagatione*. Diss. Vratislaviae, 1886.
Kornemann, E. *De civibus Romanis in provinciis imperii consistentibus*. Diss. Berolini, 1891.
Henze, W. *De civitatibus liberis quae fuerunt in provinciis populi Romani*. Diss. Berolini, 1892.
Souter, A. *The Extent of Territory belonging to Cities in the Roman Empire*. C.R. xxxvii, 1923, p. 115.

(c) Ius Latii

Steinwenter, A. Art. *s.v.* Ius Latii in P.W.
Hirschfeld, O. *Zur Geschichte des Latinischen Rechtes*, in *Festschrift zur fünfzigjährigen Gründungsfeier des Archäologischen Instituts in Rom* (Wien, 1879), p. 1. (*Kleine Schriften*, p. 294.)
Mommsen, Th. *Latium maius*. Z. d. Sav.-Stift. xxiii, 1902, p. 46. (*Ges. Schriften*, iii, p. 33.)

(d) Municipal Officials

Spehr, F. *De summis magistratibus coloniarum atque municipiorum*. Diss. Halis Saxonum, 1881. [Largely antiquated.]

Mommsen, Th. *Die Erblichkeit des Decurionats*, in *Festschrift zu Otto Hirschfelds sechzigstem Geburtstage*. Berlin, 1903, p. 1. (*Ges. Schriften*, III, p. 43.)
Seeck, O. *Decemprimat und Dekaprotie*. Klio, I, 1902, p. 147.

III. The Provinces, their Councils, and the like

Kornemann, E. Art. *s.v.* Concilium in P.W.
Guiraud, P. *Les assemblées provinciales dans l'Empire romain*. Paris, 1887.
Fougères, G. *De Lyciorum communi*. Diss. Lutetiae Parisiorum, 1898.
—— *Encore le Lyciarque et l'archiéreus d'Auguste*, in *Mélanges Perrot* (Paris, 1903), p. 103.
Ruge, W. Art. *s.v.* Lykia in P.W.
Kornemann, E. Art. *s.v.* Κοινόν in P.W. Supplbd. IV, col. 914.
Hardy, E. G. *The Provincial Concilia from Augustus to Diocletian*, in *Studies in Roman History*, First Series[2] (London, 1910), p. 235.
Hirschfeld, O. *Le Conseil des Gaules*, in *Recueil de Mémoires publié par la Société des Antiquaires de France à l'occasion de son Centenaire* (Paris, 1904), p. 211. (*Kleine Schriften*, p. 127.)
van der Mijnsbrugge, N. *The Cretan Koinon*. New York, 1931.
Tod, M. N. *Greek Inscriptions from Macedonia: 1. Thessalonica and the Panhellenion*. J.H.S. XLII, 1922, p. 167.
Mommsen, Th. *Die römische Provinzialautonomie*. Hermes, XXXIX, 1904, p. 321. (*Ges. Schriften*, V, p. 552.)
Hirschfeld, O. *Die Sicherheitspolizei im römischen Kaiserreich*. Berl. S.B. 1891, p. 845. (*Kleine Schriften*, p. 576.)

IV. Regional History

(a) Italy

Friedlaender, L. *Städtewesen in Italien im ersten Jahrhundert*. Deutsche Rundschau, XIX, 1879, p. 210. (*Petronii Cena Trimalchionis*, mit deutscher Übersetzung und erklärenden Anmerkungen von Ludwig Friedlaender[2] (Leipzig, 1906), p. 23.)
Willems, P. *Les élections municipales à Pompeii*. Paris, 1887.

(b) Spain

McElderry, R. K. *Vespasian's Reconstruction of Spain*. J.R.S. VIII, 1918, p. 53; IX, 1919, p. 86.
Albertini, E. *Les divisions administratives de l'Espagne romaine*. Paris, 1923.
Pidal, R. M. (ed.), *Historia de España*. II. *España Romana*. Madrid, 1935.

(c) The Gauls

Jullian, C. *Histoire de la Gaule: IV, Le gouvernement de Rome*. Paris, n.d. [1913].
Constans, L. A. *Esquisse d'une histoire de la Basse-Provence dans l'antiquité*. Marseilles, 1923. (Extrait du Tome II des *Bouches-du-Rhône, Encyclopédie départementale*.)

(d) Rhine, Danube and Balkan Lands

Kornemann, E. *Zur Stadtentstehung in den ehemals keltischen und germanischen Gebieten des Römerreichs*. Giessen, 1898.
Bohn, O. *Rheinische "Lagerstädte."* Germ. X, 1926, p. 25.

Lehner, H. *Vetera. Die Ergebnisse der Ausgrabungen des Bonner Provinzial-museums bis* 1929. Römisch-Germanische Forschungen, IV. Berlin-Leipzig, 1930.

Wagner, F. *Die Römer in Bayern*. Munich, 1924.

Stähelin, F. *Die Schweiz in römischer Zeit²*. Basel, 1931.

Schober, A. *Die Römerzeit in Österreich an den Bau- und Kunstdenkmälern darge-stellt*. Baden, Vienna, n.d. [1935].

Egger, R. *Eine Darstellung des Lusus iuvenalis*. Jahreshefte XVIII, 1915, p. 115.

Box, H. *Roman Citizenship in Laconia*. J.R.S. XXI, 1931, p. 200; XXII, 1932, p. 165.

Daicovici, C. *Fouilles de Sarmizegethusa: deuxième compte-rendu (1925–1928)*. Dacia, III/IV (1927–1932), p. 516.

(*e*) *Asiatic Lands*

Chapot, V. *La province romaine proconsulaire d'Asie depuis ses origines jusqu'à la fin du Haut-Empire*. Paris, 1904.

Broughton, T. R. S. *Roman Landholding in Asia Minor*. Trans. Am. Phil. Ass. LV, 1934, p. 207.

Ramsay, Sir W. M. *Studies in the Roman Province Galatia*: III, *Imperial Govern-ment of the Province Galatia*. J.R.S. XII, 1922, p. 147.

(*f*) *North Africa*

Toutain, J. *Les cités romaines de la Tunisie. Essai sur l'histoire de la colonisation romaine*. Paris, 1896.

Broughton, T. R. S. *The Romanization of Africa Proconsularis*. Baltimore, 1929.

Gsell, S. and C.-A. Joly, *Khamissa, Mdaourouch, Announa*. Algiers-Paris, 1914–1922.

Mommsen, Th. *Die Stadtverfassung Cirtas und der Cirtensischen Colonien*. Hermes, I, 1866, p. 47. (*Ges. Schriften*, V, p. 470.)

Besnier, M. *Les Augustales de Timgad*. Constantine, 1903.

Carcopino, J. *Survivance par substitution des sacrifices d'enfants dans l'Afrique romaine*. Rev. Hist. Rel. CVI, 1932, p. 592.

Fluss, M. Art. *s.v.* Tiberius (3) in P.W.

CHAPTER XII

THE LATIN WEST: I

I. AFRICA

A. Ancient Evidence

Corpus Inscriptionum Latinarum. Berlin. Vol. VIII, Inscriptiones Africae Latinae, 2 parts, 1881; Supplementum, 4 parts, 1891–1916: *Inscriptions latines de l'Algérie.* Tome 1er, Inscriptions de la Proconsulaire, by S. Gsell, Paris, 1922: *Inscriptions latines d'Afrique* (Tripolitaine, Tunisie, Maroc), by R. Cagnat, A. Merlin and L. Chatelain, Paris, 1923: *Inscriptiones Graecae ad res Romanas pertinentes,* I, fasc. 4, by R. Cagnat and J. Toutain, Paris, 1906: *Atlas archéologique de la Tunisie,* Paris, 1st series, by E. Babelon, R. Cagnat and S. Reinach, 1892–1913; 2nd series, by R. Cagnat and A. Merlin, from 1914: *Atlas archéologique de l'Algérie,* by S. Gsell; Algiers and Paris, 1902–1911: *Inventaire des mosaïques de la Gaule et de l'Afrique,* Paris. t. II (Tunisie), by P. Gauckler, 1910; Supplément, by A. Merlin, 1915; t. III (Algérie), by F. de Pachtere, 1911; plates, 3 fasc., 1913–1925: *Inventaire des mosaïques du Maroc,* by L. Chatelain. Publications du Service des Antiquités du Maroc, fasc. 1, Paris, 1935, p. 67: *Musées et collections archéologiques de l'Algérie et de la Tunisie,* 30 fasc., Paris, 1890–1928.

B. General Works

Albertini, E. *L'Afrique romaine.* 3rd impression, Algiers, 1932.

Barthel, W. *Zur Geschichte der römischen Städte in Afrika.* Greifswald, 1904.

—— *Römische Limitation in der Provinz Africa.* B.J. cxx, 1911, p. 39.

Bartoccini, R. *Le antichità della Tripolitania.* Milan, 1926.

Besnier, M. *La géographie économique du Maroc dans l'antiquité.* Archives marocaines, VII, 1906, p. 271.

Broughton, T. R. S. *The Romanization of Africa Proconsularis.* Baltimore, 1929.

Cagnat, R. and P. Gauckler, *Les monuments historiques de la Tunisie. Les temples païens.* Paris, 1898.

Cagnat, R. *L'armée romaine d'Afrique et l'occupation militaire de l'Afrique sous les empereurs.* Ed. 2, Paris, 1912.

—— *L'annone d'Afrique.* Mém. Ac. Inscr. XL, 1915, p. 256.

Carcopino, J. *L'inscription d'Aïn-el-Djemala. Contribution à l'histoire des saltus africains et du colonat partiaire.* Mél. d'arch. et d'hist. XXVI, 1906, p. 365.

Dessau, H. *Geschichte der römischen Kaiserzeit,* II, 2. Berlin, 1930, pp. 462–480.

Gsell, S. *Les monuments antiques de l'Algérie.* 2 vols. Paris, 1901.

—— *L'Algérie dans l'antiquité,* in *Histoire d'Algérie,* by S. Gsell, G. Marçais and G. Yver. Paris, 1927, pp. 1–82.

Julien, Ch. A. *Histoire de l'Afrique du Nord.* Paris, 1931, pp. 143–218.

Monceaux, P. *Les Africains.* Paris, 1894.

Pallu de Lessert, A. C. *Fastes des provinces africaines sous la domination romaine.* Vol. I. Paris, 1896.

Romanelli, P. *Vestigia del passato, monumenti e scavi (Le colonie italiane di diretto dominio).* Rome, 1930, pp. 1–56.

—— *La vita agricola tripolitana attraverso le rappresentazioni figurate.* Afr. Ital. III, 1930, p. 53.

Rostowzew, M. *Studien zur Geschichte des römischen Kolonates.* Leipzig and Berlin, 1910, pp. 313–402.

Schulten, A. *Das römische Africa*. Leipzig, 1899.
Thieling, W. *Der Hellenismus in Kleinafrika*. Leipzig, 1911.
Toutain, J. *De Saturni dei in Africa Romana cultu*. Paris, 1894.
—— *Les cités romaines de la Tunisie*. Paris, 1895.
—— *Le cadastre de l'Afrique romaine*. Mém. Ac. Inscr. Sav. étrang. XII, 1907,
   p. 341.
—— *Les cultes païens dans l'Empire romain*. Vol. III. Paris, 1917.

C. SPECIAL WORKS

Audollent, A. *Carthage romaine*. Paris, 1901.
Aurigemma, S. *I mosaici di Zliten*. Rome, 1926.
Boeswillwald, E., R. Cagnat and A. Ballu, *Timgad, une cité africaine sous l'Empire
   romain*. Paris, 1892–1905.
Cagnat, R. *La colonie romaine de Djemila*. Mus. B. XXVII, 1923, p. 113.
Carton, L. *Dougga*. Tunis, 1929.
Gsell, S. and C.-A. Joly, *Khamissa, Mdaourouch, Announa*. Paris, 1914–1922.
—— *L'huile de Leptis*. Rivista della Tripolitania, I, 1924, p. 41.
—— *Promenades archéologiques aux environs d'Alger*. Paris, 1926.
Merlin, A. *Le sanctuaire de Baal et de Tanit près de Siagu*. Paris, 1910.
—— *Le forum de Thuburbo Majus*. Paris, 1922.
Romanelli, P. *Leptis Magna*. Rome, 1925.

II. SPAIN

A. ANCIENT EVIDENCE

Corpus Inscriptionum Latinarum. Berlin. Vol. II, Inscriptiones Hispaniae Latinae,
   1869; Supplementum, 1892: *Ephemeris Epigraphica*. Additamenta ad Corporis
   vol. II. Vol. VIII, fasc. 3, 1898, p. 351; IX, fasc. 1, 1903, p. 12. Wickert, L.,
   *Bericht über eine Reise zur Vorbereitung eines Supplementum Hispaniense des
   C.I.L.* Berl. S.B. 1929, p. 54, and *Bericht über eine zweite Reise zur Vorbereitung etc.* Berl. S.B. 1931, p. 829: *Inscriptiones Graecae ad res Romanas pertinentes*,
   Vol. I, fasc. 1, by R. Cagnat and J. Toutain, Paris, 1901: Serra-Ráfols, J. de C.,
   Forma conventus Tarraconensis, I. Memòries del Institut d'Estudis catalans,
   vol. I, fasc. 4, 1928: Albertini, E., *Sculptures antiques du conventus Tarraconensis*.
   Anuari de l'Institut d'Estudis catalans, IV, 1911–12, p. 323: Lantier, R., *Inventaire des monuments sculptés pré-chrétiens de la péninsule ibérique. Lusitanie,
   conventus Emeritensis*, Bordeaux-Paris, 1918: de Serpa Pinto, R., *Inventario
   dos mosaicos romanos de Portugal*. Anuario del Cuerpo de Archiveros, I, 1934
   (homenaje á J. R. Mélida), p. 161.

B. GENERAL WORKS

Albertini, E. *Les divisions administratives de l'Espagne romaine*. Paris, 1923.
Besnier, M. *Le commerce du plomb à l'époque romaine d'après les lingots estampillés*.
   Rev. Arch. 1920, 2, p. 211; 1921, 1, p. 36; 1921, 2, p. 93.
Blázquez, A. and several contributors. *Exploraciones y excavaciones en vias romanas*.
   Memorias de la Junta superior de excavaciones, 1916–1925.
Cuq, E. *Le développement de l'industrie minière à l'époque d'Hadrien*. J. d. Sav. 1911,
   p. 296 and p. 346.
Dessau, H. *Geschichte der römischen Kaiserzeit*, II, 2. Berlin, 1930, pp. 445–462.
Hübner, E. *La arqueología de España*. Barcelona, 1888.
Leite de Vasconcellos, J. *Religiões da Lusitania*. Vol. III, Lisbon, 1909–1913.

Marchetti, M. *Le provincie romane della Spagna.* Rome, 1917 (Offprint from Diz. Epig.).

Mélida, J. R. *Arqueología española.* Barcelona, 1929.

Mesquita de Figueiredo, A. *Les monuments romains du Portugal.* Rev. Arch. 1913, 1, p. 347.

Pellati, Fr. *I monumenti del Portogallo romano.* Historia, v, 1931, p. 198.

Pidal, R. M. (ed.), *Historia de España*, II. *España Romana.* Madrid, 1935.

Puig i Cadafalch, J. *L'arquitectura romana a Catalunya.* Barcelona, 1934.

Rickard, T. A. *The mining of the Romans in Spain.* J.R.S. XVIII, 1928, p. 129.

Sutherland, C. H. V. *Aspects of imperialism in Roman Spain.* J.R.S. XXIV, 1934, p. 31.

Toutain, J. *Les cultes païens dans l'Empire romain.* Vol. III, Paris, 1917.

West, L. C. *Imperial Roman Spain: the objects of trade.* Oxford, 1929.

C. Special Works

Amador de los Rios, R. and Conde de Aguiar, *Excavaciones en Itálica.* Memorias de la Junta superior de excavaciones, 1916–1926.

Conde de Aguiar. *Itálica.* Barcelona, 1929.

Bosch Gimpera, P. and J. de C. Serra-Ráfols, *Emporion.* Barcelona, 1929.

Cazurro, M. *Terra sigillata. Los vasos aretinos y sus imitaciones galo-romanas en Ampurias.* Anuari del Institut d'Estudis catalans, III, 1909, p. 296.

Mélida, J. R. *Excavaciones en Mérida.* Memorias de la Junta superior de excavaciones, 1916–1932.

—— *Mérida.* Barcelona, 1929.

de Navascués, J. M. *Tarragona.* Barcelona, 1929.

III. GAUL

A. Ancient Evidence

Corpus Inscriptionum Latinarum. Berlin. Vol. XII, Inscriptiones Galliae Narbonensis, 1888. Vol. XIII, Inscriptiones trium Galliarum et duarum Germaniarum, 1899–1933: *Inscriptions latines de Gaule (Narbonnaise)*, by E. Espérandieu, Paris, 1929: *Inscriptiones Graecae ad res Romanas pertinentes*, Vol. I, fasc. I, by R. Cagnat and J. Toutain, Paris, 1901: *Carte archéologique de la Gaule romaine*, under the direction of A. Blanchet, Paris, from 1931: Espérandieu, E., *Recueil général des bas-reliefs statues et bustes de la Gaule romaine*, 10 vols., Paris, 1907–1928: *Inventaire des mosaïques de la Gaule et de l'Afrique*, Paris, vol. I, by G. Lafaye and A. Blanchet, 1909; plates, 3 fasc., 1911–12: Reinach, S., *Catalogue illustré du Musée des Antiquités nationales à Saint-Germain-en-Laye*, 2 vols., Paris, 1917–1921 (vol. I, ed. 2, 1926).

B. General Works

Blanchet, A. *Étude sur la décoration des édifices de la Gaule romaine.* Paris, 1913.

Bloch, G. *La Gaule romaine* (in Lavisse's *Histoire de France*). Paris, 1900.

Bonnard, L. *La Gaule thermale.* Paris, 1908.

—— *La navigation intérieure de la Gaule à l'époque gallo-romaine.* Paris, 1913.

Carcopino, J. *Ce que Rome et l'Empire romain doivent à la Gaule.* Oxford, 1932 (and in *Points de vue sur l'impérialisme romain*, Paris, 1934, pp. 201–256).

Cumont, Fr. *Comment la Belgique fut romanisée.* Ed. 2, Brussels, 1919.

Déchelette, J. *Les vases céramiques ornés de la Gaule romaine.* 2 vols., Paris, 1904.

Desjardins, E. *Géographie historique et administrative de la Gaule romaine.* 4 vols., Paris, 1876–1893.

Dessau, H. *Geschichte der römischen Kaiserzeit*, II, 2. Berlin, 1930, pp. 480–529.

Fustel de Coulanges, N. D. *Histoire des institutions politiques de l'ancienne France. La Gaule romaine*. Ed. 5, Paris, 1922.

Grenier, A. *Manuel d'archéologie gallo-romaine*. Paris, 1st part, 1931: 2nd part, 2 vols., 1934.

Jullian, C. *Histoire de la Gaule*. Vols. V and VI, Paris, 1920.

Oelmann, Fr. *Zum Problem des gallischen Tempels*. Germ. XVII, 1933, p. 169.

Toutain, J. *Les cultes païens dans l'Empire romain*. Vol. III, Paris, 1920.

West, L. C. *Roman Gaul: the objects of trade*. Oxford, 1935.

C. Special Works

Chatelain, L. *Les monuments romains d'Orange*. Paris, 1908.

Clerc, M. *Massalia. Histoire de Marseille dans l'antiquité*. Vol. II, Marseilles, 1930.

Constans, L. A. *Arles antique*. Paris, 1921.

—— *Arles*. Paris, 1928.

Donnadieu, A. *La Pompéi de la Provence: Fréjus*. Paris, 1927.

—— *Fréjus: le port militaire de Forum Julii*. Paris, 1935.

Drioux, G. *Les Lingons*. Textes et inscriptions antiques. Paris, 1934.

—— *Cultes indigènes des Lingons*. Paris, 1934.

Espérandieu, E. *Répertoire archéologique du département du Gard. Période gallo-romaine*. Montpellier, 1934.

Germain de Montauzan, C. *Les aqueducs antiques de Lyon*. Paris, 1908.

Hermet, F. *La Graufesenque*. 2 vols., Paris, 1934.

Héron de Villefosse, A. *Deux armateurs narbonnais*. Mém. de la Soc. des Antiquaires de France, LXXIV, 1914, p. 153.

Krencker, D. *Das römische Trier*. Berlin, 1926.

Sautel, J. *Vaison dans l'antiquité*. 3 vols., Avignon, 1927.

Toutain, J. *La Gaule antique vue dans Alésia*. La Charité-sur-Loire, 1932.

—— *Alésia gallo-romaine et chrétienne*. La Charité-sur-Loire, 1933.

CHAPTER XIII

THE LATIN WEST: II

PART I. BRITAIN

A. Ancient Sources

The evidence from the literary sources is not large: it has been collected in *Monumenta Historica Britannica,* vol. I (all published), 1848.

The inscriptions were collected by E. Hübner in vol. VII of *C.I.L.* Supplements and additions to this were published by Hübner in Eph. Epig. vols. III and IV, and by F. Haverfield, *ib.* vols. VII and IX. A new Corpus of the inscriptions, edited by R. G. Collingwood, is in preparation. Since 1921 an annual report upon Roman Britain, summarizing the results of excavations and publishing the new inscriptions, has been given in J.R.S. by R. G. Collingwood and Miss M. V. Taylor. On all economic questions, such as Agriculture, Commerce and Communications, Industry, etc., the evidence will be found collected and translated by R. G. Collingwood in a forthcoming volume of Tenney Frank's *An economic Survey of Ancient Rome,* Baltimore.

B. Modern Works

I. *General*

Collingwood, R. G. *Roman Britain.* Ed. 3. Oxford, 1934.
—— *The Archaeology of Roman Britain.* London, 1930.
Haverfield, F. *The Romanization of Roman Britain.* Ed. 4 (revised by George Macdonald). Oxford, 1924.
—— *The Roman Occupation of Britain.* (Revised by George Macdonald.) Oxford, 1924.

II. *Special Topics*

The topics are given in the order in which they are discussed in the text.
Geography. Sir Cyril Fox, *The Personality of Britain,* ed. 2, Cardiff, 1932 (*passim*).
Physical Anthropology. J. Beddoe, *Races of Britain,* Bristol and London, 1885; G. Rolleston, *Scientific Papers and Addresses,* Oxford, 1884; Sir Arthur Keith, Archaeologia, LXXI, 1921, pp. 159–163; L. H. Dudley Buxton, J.R.S. XXV, 1935, pp. 35–50.
Language. I. C. Peate, *The Kelts in Britain.* Antiquity, VI, 1932, pp. 156–160.
Distribution of Population. Fox, *op. cit.* pp. 55 *sqq.*
Density of Population. R. G. Collingwood. Antiquity, III, 1929, p. 276; R. E. M. Wheeler, ib. IV, 1930, p. 95.
Romanization. Haverfield, *Romanization...,* pp. 29 *sqq.*
Growth of Towns. Royal Commission on Historical Monuments, *Roman London,* London, 1928; R. E. M. Wheeler, *London in Roman Times,* London, 1930; J. P. Bushe-Fox, *Wroxeter Excavation Reports,* London, 1913–1916; R. E. M. Wheeler, *Verulam Excavation Report* (in preparation).
Minerals. Haverfield's appendix in Anderson's edition of Tacitus, *Agricola,* Oxford, 1922 (pp. 173–182); G. C. Whittick, *Roman Mining in Britain,* Transactions of the Newcomen Society, XII, 1931–2, pp. 1–28; O. Davies, *Roman Mines in Europe,* Oxford, 1935, Chapter V (*The British Isles*), pp. 140–164.
Political and Social Structure. Haverfield, *Romanization...,* pp. 57 *sqq.*

Architecture. Haverfield, *Romanization...*, pp. 36 *sqq.*; Haverfield, *Roman Occupation...*, pp. 204 *sqq.*
   Bath: W. H. Knowles, Archaeologia, LXXV, 1925, pp. 1–18.
   Colchester: R. E. M. Wheeler and P. G. Laver, J.R.S. IX, 1919, pp. 139–169.
The Hadrianic Frontier. R. G. Collingwood, J.R.S. XI, 1921, pp. 37–66, and XXI, 1931, pp. 36–64; J. C. Bruce, *The Handbook to the Roman Wall*, ed. 9, edited by R. G. Collingwood, Newcastle, 1933. Recent and forthcoming excavation reports in Transactions of the Cumberland and Westmorland Antiquarian and Archaeological Society, and in Archaeologia Aeliana.
The Antonine Frontier. Sir G. Macdonald, *The Roman Wall in Scotland*, ed. 2, Oxford, 1934.

PART II. THE GERMAN PROVINCES AND RAETIA

In addition to the sources and modern works given here the reader should consult those cited in Section V (The German Frontier) of the bibliography to Chapter IV, p. 884, and in Section III (Gaul) of the bibliography to Chapter XII, p. 905 *sq.*

A. ANCIENT EVIDENCE

Corpus Inscriptionum Latinarum. Berlin. Vol. XIII, Inscriptiones trium Galliarum et duarum Germaniarum, 1899–1933: Vol. III, Inscriptiones Illyrici, 1873–1902: Byvanck, A. W., *Excerpta Romana*. De Bronnen der Romeinsche geschiedenis van Nederland. 2 vols., 's-Gravenhage, 1931/35. *Inscriptiones Baivariae Romanae*, ed. F. Vollmer, Munich, 1915: Riese, A., *Das rheinische Germanien in den antiken Inschriften*, Leipzig, 1914: also *Das rheinische Germanien in der antiken Literatur*, Leipzig, 1892: Espérandieu, E., *Recueil général des bas-reliefs statues et bustes de la Germanie romaine*, Paris and Brussels, 1931. *Germania Romana*. Ein Bilderatlas, ed. 2, 2 vols. Bamberg, 1924/30.

B. GENERAL WORKS

Dopsch, A. *Wirtschaftliche und soziale Grundlagen der europäischen Kulturentwicklung.* 2 vols. Ed. 2, Vienna, 1923–24.
Dragendorff, H. *Westdeutschland zur Römerzeit.* Ed. 2, Leipzig, 1919.
Evelein, M. A. *De resultaten der Prov. Rom. Archaeologie voor de geschiedenis der Gallo-Germaansch provincies van het Romeinsche keizerrijk.* Zutphen, 1931.
Holwerda, J. H. *Nederlands vroegste geschiedenis.* Amsterdam, 1918.

C. SPECIAL WORKS

Aubin, H. *Der Rheinhandel in römischer Zeit.* B.J. CXXX, 1925, p. 1.
Behn, F. *Das Mithrasheiligtum zu Dieburg.* Römisch-Germanische Forschungen, I, Berlin, 1928.
Behrens, G. *Neue Funde von der Westgrenze der Wangionen.* Mainzer Zeitschrift, XXIX, 1934, p. 44.
—— *Zur Frage der Juppitergigantensäulen.* Germ. XVI, 1932, p. 28.
Dragendorff, H. and Krüger, E. *Das Grabmal von Igel.* Römische Grabmäler des Mosellandes, I, Trier, 1924.
Drexel, Fr. *Die Götterverehrung im römischen Germanien.* R.-G. K. Ber. XIV, 1923.
—— *Bauten und Denkmäler der Brittonen am Limes.* Germ. VI, 1922, p. 31.
Ferri, S. *Arte Romana sul Reno.* Milan, 1931.
—— *Arte Romana sul Danubio.* Milan, 1933.

Hagen, J. *Die Römerstrassen der Rheinprovinz.* Ed. 2, Bonn, 1931.

Kahrstedt, U. *Die Kelten in den decumates agri.* Gött. Nach. 1933, p. 261.

Koethe, H. *Neue Daten zur Geschichte des römischen Trier.* Germ. xx, 1936, p. 27.

Lehner, H. *Orientalische Mysterienkulte im römischen Rheinland.* B.J. cxxix, 1924, p. 36.

Loeschcke, S. *Römische Gefässe aus Bronze, Glas und Ton im Provinzialmuseum.* Trierer Zeitschrift, iii, 1928, p. 69.

—— *Denkmäler vom Weinbau aus der Zeit der Römerherrschaft an Mosel, Saar und Ruwer.* Trèves, 1933.

Norden, Ed. *Die germanische Urgeschichte in Tacitus Germania.* Ed. 3, Leipzig and Berlin, 1923.

Oxé, A. *Germanen des linken Niederrheins auf römischen Inschriften.* Die Heimat (Krefeld), xiv, 1935, p. 175.

—— *Redende Sigillatastempel.* B.J. cxxxix, 1934, p. 94.

Reinecke, P. *Cambodunum, ein römischer Marktort im heutigen Südbayern.* Neue Deutsche Ausgrabungen herausg. von G. Rodenwaldt, Münster, 1930, p. 229.

Schmitz, H. *Zur wirtschaftlichen Bedeutung des römischen Gutshofes in Köln-Müngersdorf.* B.J. cxxxix, 1934, p. 80.

Siebourg, M. *Der Matronenkult beim Bonner Münster.* B.J. cxxxviii, 1933, p. 103.

Vermeulen, W. *Een Romeinsch Grafveld op den Hunnerberg te Nijmegen.* Amsterdam, 1932.

Woelcke, K. *Neue Ergebnisse über die Stadtbefestigung von Nida-Heddernheim.* Germ. xv, 1931, p. 75.

PART III. THE DANUBE LANDS

(The geographical area once covered by the Roman provinces of Noricum, Pannonia, Dacia and Moesia does not fall under one government, and accordingly the literature on its history and archaeology is scattered and not easy to control. Hence a fuller, though even so selective, bibliography is given than for Britain and Roman Germany.)

A. Ancient Sources

Epigraphic

The epigraphical material down to 1902 has been published in the *Corpus Inscriptionum Latinarum*, iii and Supplements. A new edition of the Pannonian inscriptions by A. Alföldi is in preparation: see also A. Barb, *Die römischen Inschriften des südlichen Bürgenlandes*, Bürgenlandische Heimatblätter, i, 1932, pp. 75 *sqq.*: J. Brunšmid, *Roman Stone Monuments in the Croatian National Museum*, Vjesnik hrvats. arheol. društva (new series), vii, 1903/4 to xi, 1910/11 (Croatian): Á. Dobó, *Inscriptiones ad res Pannonicas pertinentes extra provinciae fines repertae*, Diss. Pann. Ser. 1, fasc. 1, 1932: D. Sergejevski, *Rimski spomenici iz Bozne*, Spomenik Srpski kralj. Akad. lxxvii, 1934, p. 1: and N. Vulić, *Antiki spomenici naše zemlje*, ib. lxxi, 1931, p. 1, lxxv, 1933, p. 1 and lxxvii, 1934, pp. 31 *sqq.*

The literary sources for the history of Dacia will be collected in a forthcoming fascicule of Dissertationes Pannonicae, *Fontes historiae Dacicae*, by Th. Rados.

B. Modern Works

1. *General Surveys*

Alföldi, A. *Studi ungheresi sulla romanizzazione della Pannonia.* Gli Studi Romani nel Mondo, ii, 1935, pp. 267 *sqq.*

Alföldi, A. *Die Vorherrschaft der Pannonier im Römerreiche und die Reaktion des Hel-lenentums unter Gallienus.* 25 Jahre R.-G. K. Frankfort, 1929, pp. 11 *sqq.*
—— *The Romanism of Pannonia and its historical frame.* Századok, LXX, 1936 (Hungarian).
Daicovici, C.–M. Macrea, *Contribuţii la bibliografia Daciei Romane (Beiträge zur Bibliographie des römischen Daciens)* 1920–1935. Cluj, 1936.
Dobiáš, J. *I Romani nel Territorio della Cecoslovacchia odierna.* Gli Studi Romani nel Mondo, II, 1935, pp. 61 *sqq.*
Fluss, M. Art. *s.v.* Moesia in P.W.
Kuzsinszky, V. *The Archaeology of the Neighbourhood of Lake Balaton.* Budapest, 1920 (Hungarian).
Nowotny, Ed. and W. Schmid, *Römische Forschung in Österreich* 1912–1924. R.-G. K. Ber. XV, 1925, pp. 121 *sqq.*
Panaitescu, E. *Momenti della civiltà romana nella Mesia.* Gli Studi Romani nel Mondo, II, 1935, pp. 223 *sqq.*
Pârvan, V. *Inceputurile vieţii Romane la gurile Dunării.* Bucharest, 1923.
—— *I primordi della civiltà Romana alle foci del Danubio.* Ausonia, X, 1921, p. 198.
Patsch, C. *Archäologisch-epigraphische Untersuchungen zur Geschichte der römischen Provinz Dalmatien.* Wissenschaftliche Mitt. aus Bosnien u. d. Herzegowina, IV–XII, 1896–1912. (Cf. Wien S.B. CCXIV, 1932, Abh. I.)
—— *Bosnien und Herzegowina in römischer Zeit.* Sarajevo, 1911.
Saria, B. *Vor- und frühgeschichtliche Forschung in Südslavien.* R.-G. K. Ber. XVI, 1927, pp. 86 *sqq.*
Schober, A. *Die Römerzeit in Österreich, an den Bau- und Kunstdenkmälern darge-stellt.* Baden (Vienna), n.d. [1935].
A useful map is that of G. de Finály, *Forma partium imperii Romani intra fines regni Hungariae,* Budapest, 1911.

2. *Special Topics*

(a) *Native population: language and dress*

Columba, G. M. *Le sedi dei Triballi dell' età romana.* Studi storici, IV, 1911.
Fluss, M. Art. *s.v.* Illyrioi in P.W. Supplbd. V, cols. 311 *sqq.*
Geramb, V. *Die norisch-pannonische Tracht.* Graz, 1933.
Gronovszky, I. *Nomina hominum Pannonica certis gentibus adsignata.* Diss. Pann. Ser. 1, fasc. 2, Budapest, 1933.
Jokl, N. Art. *s.v.* Illyrier in Ebert's *Reallexikon für Vorgeschichte.*
Kerényi, K. *Über den heutigen Stand der Illyrierforschung.* Revue internat. des études balcaniques, II, 1936.
Krahe, H. *Die alten balkanillyrischen geographischen Namen.* Heidelberg, 1925.
—— *Lexikon altillyrischer Personennamen.* Heidelberg, 1929.
Láng, M. *Die pannonische Frauentracht.* Jahreshefte XIX/XX, 1919, Beiblatt, cols. 207 *sqq.*
Mateescu, G. G. *I Traci nell' epigrafi di Roma.* Ephemeris Dacoromana, I, 1923, p. 57.
Novak, G. *La nazionalità dei Dardani.* Archiv za arbanaski starini, jezik i ethno-logiji, IV, 1929, p. 72.
Vulić, N. *Le sedi dei Triballi.* Studi Romani, I, 1914, p. 233.
Weisgerber, L. *Die Sprache der Festlandkelten.* R.-G. K. Ber. XX, 1931, pp. 147 *sqq.*

(b) *Topography, cities, principal monuments*

Brunšmid, J. *Colonia Aelia Mursa.* Vjesnik hrv. arh. dr. (n.s.) IV, 1899/1900, pp. 21 *sqq.*: *Colonia Aurelia Cibalae,* ib. VI, 1902 (both in Croatian).

Buday, Á. *Excavations at Porolissum.* Dolgozatok, II, 1911–VI, 1915: *Roman Towns in Transylvania,* ib. IV, 1913, p. 109. (Hungarian, with French résumés.)

Daicovici, C. *Fouilles et recherches à Sarmizegetusa.* Dacia, I, 1924, p. 224: III/IV, 1927–1932, p. 516.

Decei, A. *Le pont de Trajan à Turnu-Severin.* Anuarul Inst. stud. clas. I, 1932, p. 140.

Egger, R. *Das zweite Amphitheater (von Carnuntum).* Der röm. Limes in Öster-reich, XVI, pp. 69 *sqq.*

Gráf, A. *Die antike Geographie von Pannonien.* Diss. Pann. Ser. 1, fasc. 5, 1936.

Kubitschek, W. *Die Römerfunde in Eisenstadt.* Vienna, 1926.

Kuzsinszky, V. *Aquincum.* Ausgrabungen und Funde. Budapest, 1934.

Nowotny, Ed. *Das römische Wien und sein Fortleben.* Mitt. d. Vereins f. Gesch. d. Stadt Wien, IV, 1923, p. 5 (and cf. E. Polaschek, ib. XV, 1935, p. 1).

Paulovics, St. *Intercisa.* Arch. Hung. II, 1927.

Pichler, F. *Austria Romana.* Vienna, 1902–1904.

Schmid, W. *Emona.* Jahrb. f. Altertumskunde, VII, 1913, pp. 61 *sqq.*: *Flavia Solva,* Graz, 1915.

Also the following Guides to sites and museums, published at Vienna: *Poetovio* (Abramić), 1925: *Klagenfurt* (Egger), 1921: *Teurnia* (Egger), ed. 2, 1926: *Iuvavum* (Klose and Silber), 1929: *Carnuntum* (Kubitschek and Frankfurter), ed. 6, 1923.

(c) Provincial administration

See the Bibliography to Chapter XII in Vol. X, Part V, sections 1, 2, 3, and 4 (p. 939 *sq.*) and especially the works by A. von Domaszewski, J. Jung, A. von Premerstein and R. Syme there cited. In addition:

Dessau, H. *Zur Reihenfolge der Statthalter Moesiens.* Jahreshefte XXIII, 1926, Beiblatt, col. 345.

Jung, J. *Die Fasten der Provinz Dazien.* Innsbruck, 1894.

Patsch, C. *Die römische Grenzwehr der Balkanhalbinsel an der Donau.* Rev. internat. des ét. balc. I, 1935, p. 82.

Peaks, M. B. *The general civil and military administration of Noricum and Raetia.* Diss. Chicago, 1907.

Ritterling, E. *Die Statthalter der pannonischen Provinzen.* Arch.-Epig. Mitt. XX, 1897, p. 1.

—— *Die* Legati pro praetore *von Pannonia inferior seit Traian.* Arch. Ért. 1927, p. 281.

Stout, S. E. *The Governors of Moesia.* Diss. Princeton, 1911.

(d) Art and the Applied Arts

Drexel, F. *Römische Paraderüstung.* Strena Buliciana (Zagreb, 1925), pp. 55 *sqq.*

Ferri, S. *Arte romana sul Danubio.* Milan, 1933.

Hekler, A. *Forschungen in Intercisa.* Jahreshefte XV, 1912, p. 174.

—— *Kunst und Kultur Pannoniens in ihren Hauptströmungen.* Strena Buliciana, pp. 107 *sqq.*

Iványi, D. *Die pannonischen Lampen.* Diss. Pann. Ser. II, fasc. 2, Budapest, 1935.

Juhász, G. *Die Sigillaten von Brigetio.* Ib. fasc. 3, 1935.

Kuzsinszky, V. *Das grosse römische Töpferviertel in Aquincum.* Budapest Régiségei, XI, 1932.

—— *Die ältesten verzierten Terrasigillata-Gefässe auf pannonischem Boden in Ungarn.* Arch. Ért. 1923/26, pp. 295 *sqq.*

Nagy, L. *Die römisch-pannonische dekorative Malerei*. Röm. Mitt. XLI, 1926, pp. 79 *sqq.*

—— *Hungary in Roman times*. Extract from Vereczkétöl napjainkig, Budapest, 1928 (Hungarian).

—— *Das Peltamotiv in der Ornamentik der pannonischen Steindenkmäler*. Ib. 1928, pp. 68 *sqq.*

Saria, B. *Zur Entwicklung des mithrischen Kultbildes*. Mitt. d. Vereins klass. Phil. in Wien, IV, 1927, p. 53.

Schober, A. *Zur Entstehung und Bedeutung der provinzialrömischen Kunst*. Jahreshefte XXVI, 1930, p. 9.

—— *Die römischen Grabsteine von Noricum und Pannonien*. Sonderschriften des Österr. Arch. Inst. X, Vienna, 1923.

Weigand, E. *Die Stellung Dalmatiens in der römischen Reichskunst*. Strena Buliciana, pp. 77 *sqq.*

Zingerle, J. *Kyknos-Relief in Wien*. Jahreshefte XXI–XXII, 1922/24, pp. 229 *sqq.*

(e) Social and economic history: trade routes

Alföldi, A. *Siscia*. I, Budapest, 1931.

Ballif, Ph. and C. Patsch, *Die römischen Strassen in Bosnien und der Herzegowina*. Vienna, 1893.

Christescu, V. *Viaţa economica a Daciei romane*. Piteşti, 1929 (with French résumé).

Cuntz, O. *Ein Reskript des Septimius Severus über die Centonarii in Solva*. Jahreshefte XVIII, 1915, p. 98.

Daicovici, C. *Gli Italici nella provincia Dalmatia*. Ephem. Dacorom. V, 1932, p. 57.

von Domaszewski, A. *Die Beneficiarierposten und die römischen Strassennetze*. Westdeut. Zeits. XXI, 1902, p. 158.

—— *Die Grenzen von Moesia Superior und der illyrische Grenzzoll*. Arch.-Epig. Mitt. XIII, 1889, p. 129.

Egger, R. *Eine Darstellung des* Lusus iuvenalis. Jahreshefte XVIII, 1915, p. 115.

Elmer, G. *Der römische Geldverkehr in Carnuntum*. Num. Z. 1934, p. 55.

de Finály, G. *Le vie romane nell' Ungheria transdanubiana*. Mem. Acc. Lincei (Classe di Scienze fisiche, matematiche e naturale), CCCXI, 1914, p. 409.

Nagy, L. *Cives Agrippinenses in Aquincum*. Germ. XV, 1931, p. 260; XVI, 1932, p. 288.

—— *Die Orgel von Aquincum*. Budapest, 1933.

Patsch, C. *Die Saveschiffahrt in der Kaiserzeit*. Jahreshefte VIII, 1905, p. 139.

Pink, K. *Der Geldverkehr am österreichischen Donaulimes in der Kaiserzeit*. Jahrb. f. Landeskunde von Niederösterreich, XXV, 1932, p. 49.

von Premerstein, A. and S. Rutar, *Römische Strassen und Befestigungen in Krain*. Vienna, 1899.

Rostovtzeff, M. *La vie économique des Balkans dans l'antiquité*. Rev. internat. des ét. balc. I, 1935, p. 49.

Saria, B. *Eine Emonenser Landmannschaft in Savaria*. Pannonia, I, 1935, p. 171.

On mines and mining see O. Davies, *Roman Mines in Europe*, Oxford, 1935, p. 173 *sq.* (Noricum), pp. 182–197 (Illyrian provinces), pp. 198–208 (Dacia), and pp. 209–225 (Moesia).

(f) Religion

Buday, Á. *Das Problem des sogenannten thrakischen Reiters*. Dolgozatok, 2nd Series (Szeged), II, 1926–VI, 1930.

Dobiáš, J. *Les influences orientales dans le bassin du Danube sous l'empire romain*. Bidluv sbornik, 1928, p. 15 (Czech, with French résumé).

Egger, R. *Genius cucullatus*. Wien. Präh. Zeits. xix, 1932, p. 311 (but cf. F. M. Heichelheim, *Genii cucullati*, Arch. Aeliana, xii, 1935, pp. 187–194).

Floca, O. *I culti orientali in Dacia*. Ephem. Dacorom. vi, pp. 204 *sqq*.

Jones, L. W. *Cults of Dacia*. Univ. of Calif. Publ. in C.P. ix, 1929, no. 8.

Kerényi, K. *Telesphoros*. Offprint from Egeyetemes Philologiai Közlöny, 1933, Heft 7–8.

Láng, N. *The Dolichenum of Brigetio*. Klebelsberg-Festschrift, Budapest, 1925, pp. 93 *sqq*.

Nagy, L. *Astral symbolism on the tombstones of the autochthonous population in Pannonia*. Pannonia, i, 1935, p. 151 (Hungarian).

Paulovics, St. *Der dionysische Thiasos auf ungarländischen Steindenkmälern*. Arch. Ért. 1936 (forthcoming).

Wigand, K. *Die Nutrices Augustae von Poetovio*. Jahreshefte xviii, 1915, Beiblatt, cols. 189 *sqq*.

CHAPTER XIV

THE GREEK PROVINCES

1. ACHAEA

For the Sources and for the general history see G. F. Hertzberg, *Die Geschichte Griechenlands unter der Herrschaft der Römer*, Vol. II (Von Augustus bis auf Septimius Severus), Halle, 1868: also the articles *s.v.* Achaia in P.W. (Brandis) and in Diz. Epig. (E. Ruggiero).

Special Regions

(*a*) ATHENS. P. Graindor, *Athènes sous Auguste*, Univ. Égyptienne. Recueil de travaux publ. par la fac. d. lettres, fasc. 1, 1927; *Athènes de Tibère à Trajan*, Cairo, 1931; *Un milliardaire antique. Hérode Atticus et sa famille*, Cairo, 1930; *Athènes sous Hadrien*, Cairo, 1934. W. Judeich, *Topographie von Athen*, ed. 2, Munich, 1931. Reports on the American Excavations in the Agora are published in *Hesperia*, Vol. I, 1932, onwards.

(*b*) SPARTA. The Testimonia for Sparta and Messene are conveniently given by W. Kolbe in *I.G.* v, i, pp. vii *sqq.*, 1913. The results of the British Excavations are given by A. M. Woodward in *B.S.A.* XXVI–XXIX (1922–28). See also E. Kornemann, *Neue Dokumente zum lakonischen Kaiserkult*, Breslau, 1929, and the article *s.v.* Sparta in P.W. (Bölte, Ehrenberg, Ziehen, Lippold).

(*c*) CORINTH. The results of the American Excavations are published in a series of volumes entitled *Corinth*, Harvard University Press, Cambridge, Mass. (Vol. VIII, i, Greek Inscriptions; ii, Latin Inscriptions, 1932). A comprehensive guide is given by R. Carpenter, *Korinthos*, ed. 2, Cambridge, Mass. 1933. See also the article *s.v.* Korinthos in P.W. Supplbd. IV (Lenschau) and Supplbd. VI (de Waele).

(*d*) THESSALY. The Testimonia are given by O. Kern in *I.G.* IX, ii, pp. xviii *sqq.*, 1908. See also F. Stählin, *Das hellenische Thessalien*, Stuttgart, 1924, and art. *s.v.* Thessalia in P.W. (Stählin-Hiller von Gaertringen).

(*e*) DELOS. P. Roussel, *Délos, colonie athénienne* (Bibl. école franç. 111), Paris, 1916; see also W. A. Laidlaw, *A History of Delos*, Oxford, 1933.

(*f*) DELPHI. Besides the monumental French publication of the excavations, *Fouilles de Delphes*, the reader should see E. Bourguet, *Delphes*, Paris, 1925, art. *s.v.* Delphi in P.W. (Hiller von Gaertringen), and the survey of the monuments in P.W. Supplbd. IV, cols. 1189 *sqq.* and v, cols. 61 *sqq.* (H. Pomtow and F. Schober).

(*g*) OLYMPIA. Besides the monumental publication of the results of the German excavations, *Olympia*, Berlin, 1890–97, see also E. N. Gardiner, *Olympia, its History and Remains*, Oxford, 1925.

2. MACEDONIA

A useful general Bibliography will be found in S. Casson, *Macedonia, Thrace and Illyria*, Oxford, 1926; see, for example, the titles listed there under the names of M. G. Dimitsas, L. Heuzey and H. Daumet, and Th. Tafel. For reports upon journeys and excavations, mainly by French scholars (P. Collart, P. Perdrizet, Ch. Picard, A. Plassart and A. Salač), see *B.C.H.* passim and *B.S.A.* XXIII, 1918–19; also A. M. Woodward in *J.H.S.* XXXIII, 1913, A. J. B. Wace-A. M. Woodward in *B.S.A.* XVIII, 1911–12, M. Rostovtzeff in *Bull. inst. arch. russe à Constantinople*, IV, 1899 (cf. Rev. Arch. 1900 (ii), p. 789); L. Robert in *Rev. E.G.* XLVII, 1934, etc. On coins see H. Gäbler, *Zur Münzkunde Makedoniens*, Z.N. XXIII, 1902, XXIV,

1904, XXXVI, 1926, XXXIX, 1929, and *Die antiken Münzen Nord-Griechenlands*, Berlin, III, i, 1906, III, 2, 1935; but see the remarks of K. Regling in P.W. *s.v. Koinon*, col. 1054.

See also W. Baege, *De Macedonum sacris* (Diss. Phil. Hall. XXII), Halle, 1913, C. Praschniker, *Muzhakia und Malakastra*, Jahreshefte XXI–XXII (1922–24), (Beiblatt), col. 1, and C. Praschniker and A. Schober, *Archäologische Forschungen in Albanien und Montenegro*, Vienna, 1919. See also C. Patsch, *Beiträge zur Völkerkunde von Südosteuropa*, v, Wien S.B. 214, 1932. (Very valuable.)

Art. in P.W. *s.v.* Makedonia (F. Geyer and O. Hoffmann).

3. THRACE

Many of the articles listed in the Bibliography to Volume VIII, Chapter XVII (p. 781), will be found useful; see, for example, the titles cited under the names of A. Dumont and Th. Homolle, E. Kalinka, G. Kazarow, M. Rostovtzeff, and G. Seure. An admirable general survey is provided by G. Kazarow, *Beiträge zur Kulturgeschichte der Thraker*, Sarajevo, 1916: to this may be added D. Kalopothakes, *De Thracia provincia Romana*, Diss. Berlin, 1893; F. Münzer and M. L. Strack, *Die antiken Münzen von Thrakien*, Vol. I, part i (only the cities of Abdera, Aenus and Anchialus), Berlin, 1912; A. Stein, *Römische Reichsbeamte der Provinz Thracia*, Sarajevo, 1920; G. Seure, *Archéologie Thrace*, Rev. Arch. 1921 (i), 1922 (i), 1923 (i), 1925 (ii), 1926 (ii), and 1929 (ii); and the article by C. Patsch cited above.

Art. *s.v.* Thrake in P.W. (Lenk, Beetz, Kazarow).

4. PENTAPOLIS

B. Pick and K. Regling, *Die antiken Münzen Nord-Griechenlands*, Berlin, Vol. I, 1898, Vol. II, i, 1910: J. Weiss, *Die Dobrudscha im Altertum*, Sarajevo, 1911: V. Pârvan, *La pénétration hellénique et hellénistique dans la vallée du Danube*, Bull. sect. historique Acad. roumaine, x, 1923, and *I primordi della civiltà Romana alle foci del Danubio*, in Ausonia, x, 1921—both these contain full bibliographical references: O. Tafrali, *La cité pontique de Callatis*, Rev. Arch. 1925 (i), p. 238.

5. PONTUS AND BITHYNIA

The exploratory journeys of many European scholars through this area during the last seventy years have brought a rich harvest of inscriptions: among important publications should be mentioned—G. Perrot, E. Guillaume and J. Delbet, *Exploration de la Galatie et de la Bithynie*, Vols. I and II, Paris, 1872: W. von Diest, in *Petermanns Mittheilungen*, Erg.-Heft 94, 1889, and *ib.* 116, 1896 (with M. Anton): G. Mendel, in *B.C.H.* XXIV, 1900, XXV, 1901, and XXVII, 1903: J. G. C. Anderson, *Studia Pontica*, Brussels, I, 1903: F. Cumont and E. Cumont, *Studia Pontica*, II, 1906; III, i, 1910: E. Kalinka, *Aus Bithynien und Umgebung*, Jahreshefte XXVIII, 1933 Beiblatt, col. 45: L. Robert, *Voyages dans l'Anatolie septentrionale*, Rev. Arch. 1934 (i), p. 88.

Books and articles—H. von Arnim, *Leben und Werke des Dio von Prusa*, Berlin, 1898: D. M. Robinson, *Ancient Sinope*, A.J.Ph. XXVII, 1906, p. 125: M. Rostovtzeff, *Pontos, Bithynia and Bosporus*, B.S.A. XXII, 1916–18, p. 1: J. Sölch, *Historisch-geographische Studien über bithynische Siedlungen Nikomedeia, Nikaia, Prusa*, Byz.-Neugr. Jahrb. I, 1920, p. 263; *Bithynische Städte im Altertum*, Klio, XIX, 1925: V. Schultze, *Altchristliche Städte und Landschaften*, II, i, Gütersloh, 1922: Art. in P.W. *s.v.* Bithynia (G. Brandis).

Coins: W. H. Waddington, E. Babelon and Th. Reinach, *Recueil général des monnaies grecques d'Asie Mineure*, 1, 2, Paris, 1906: C. Bosch, *Die kleinasiatischen Münzen der römischen Kaiserzeit*, 11, Vol. 1, part i, Stuttgart, 1935.

6. ASIA

Of general works should be noticed V. Chapot, *La province romaine d'Asie*, Paris, 1904, V. Schultze, *op. cit.* 11, i, 1922 and ii, 1926, and L. Robert, *Villes d'Asie Mineure*, Paris, 1935. See also the articles *s.v.* Asia, by D. Vaglieri in Diz. Epig. and by G. Brandis *s.v.* Asia (Provinz) in P.W.

The following short list gives a selection merely from the vast body of literature upon different sites and cities:

Aphrodisias. M. Collignon, *Les fouilles d'Aphrodisias*, Rev. de l'art anc. et mod. XIX, 1906, p. 33: R. Vagts, *Aphrodisias in Karien*, Diss. Hamburg, 1920.

Claros (with Notion and Colophon). Th. Macridy, in *Jahreshefte* VIII, 1905 and XV, 1912: Th. Macridy-Ch. Picard, *B.C.H.* XXXIX, 1915: R. Demangel and A. Laumonier, *B.C.H.* XLVII, 1923, and XLIX, 1925: Ch. Picard (see Ephesus).

Cyzicus. F. W. Hasluck, *Cyzicus*, Cambridge, 1910.

Ephesus. O. Benndorf (and others), *Forschungen in Ephesos*, I–IV, Vienna, 1906 onwards: reports on the excavations by R. Heberdey and J. Keil have appeared in *Jahreshefte* since 1898: Ch. Picard, *Éphèse et Claros* (Bibl. école franç. 123), 1922: J. Keil, *Führer durch Ephesos*, ed. 2, Vienna, 1930.

Hierapolis. C. Humann, C. Cichorius, W. Judeich, F. Winter, *Altertümer von Hierapolis*, J.D.A.I. Erg.-Heft, IV, 1898.

Iasus. G. Jost, *Iasos in Karien*, Diss. Hamburg, 1933.

Magnesia ad Maeandrum. C. Humann-Kohte-Watzinger, *Magnesia am Maeander*, Berlin, 1904.

Miletus. Th. Wiegand (and others), *Milet. Die Ergebnisse der Ausgrabungen und Untersuchungen*, Berlin, 1906: periodical reports on the excavations by Th. Wiegand appeared in *Berl. Abh.*

Nysa. W. von Diest, *Nysa ad Maeandrum*, J.D.A.I. Erg.-Heft, X, 1913: K. Kuruniotis, Δελτίον, VII, 1921/2, pp. 1–88 and 227–246.

Pergamum. A. Conze (and others), *Altertümer von Pergamon*, Berlin, 1885: reports on the excavations of the German Archaeological Institute by W. Dörpfeld and his colleagues have appeared in Ath. Mitt. XVII, 1902 onwards: occasional reports on the most recent excavations by Th. Wiegand, Berl. Abh. 1928 (no. 3) and 1932 (no. 5, Asklepieion).

Priene. Th. Wiegand, H. Schrader, *Priene*, Berlin, 1904: M. Schede, *Die Ruinen von Priene*, Berlin, 1934.

Rhodes. Art. *s.v.* Rhodes in P.W. Supplbd. v (F. Hiller von Gaertringen).

Sardes. *Sardis* (Publications of the Amer. Soc. for the Excav. of Sardis) Leyden, 1916 onwards; Vol. VII, i, Greek and Latin Inscriptions, edd. W. H. Buckler and D. M. Robinson, 1932, is important.

Smyrna. W. M. Calder in Aberdeen Univ. Studies, no. 20, Aberdeen, 1906.

Regional Exploratory Work

Caria. O. Benndorf, G. Niemann, *Reisen in Lykien und Karien*, Vienna, 1884: A. Laumonier, *Inscriptions de Carie*, B.C.H. LVIII, 1934, pp. 291 *sqq.*

Lydia. J. Keil, A. von Premerstein, *Berichte über drei Reisen in Lydien*, Denkschrift. Akad. Wien, LIII, 2, 1907, LIV, 2, 1911, and LVII, 1, 1914. J. Keil, *Die Kulte Lydiens*, Anatolian Studies presented to Sir W. Ramsay, Manchester, 1923, p. 239, and art. *s.v.* Lydia in P.W.

Mysia. C. Schuchhardt, *Altertümer von Pergamon*, no. 1, i, Berlin, 1912.
Phrygia. W. M. Ramsay, *The cities and bishoprics of Phrygia*, Oxford, 1, i, 1895,
  1, 2, 1896: W. H. Buckler, W. M. Calder, W. K. C. Guthrie, *Monumenta
  Asiae Minoris Antiqua*, IV, Manchester, 1933: W. Schepelern, *Der Montanismus
  und die phrygische Kulte*, Tübingen, 1929.
Rhodes. F. Hiller von Gaertringen, art. *s.v.* Rhodos in P.W. Supplbd. v.
  Of future volumes of *Monumenta Antiqua Asiae Minoris* v will deal with
Doryleum and Nacolea, VI with Acmoneia, Apamea and the cities of the Lower
Lycus, and VII with Southern Caria.

7. LYCIA AND PAMPHYLIA

Among publications of inscriptions see Benndorf-Niemann, *op. cit.*, E. Petersen,
F. von Luschan, *Reisen in Lykien, Milyas und Kibyratis*, Vienna, 1889: K. Graf
Lanckoroński-Niemann-Petersen, *Städte Pamphyliens und Pisidiens*, Vienna, I, 1890
and II, 1892: Heberdey-Kalinka, *Bericht über zwei Reisen im südwestlichen Klein-
asien*, Denkschr. Akad. Wien, XLV, i, 1897: Kalinka, *Tit. As. Min.* II, i, 1920 and II,
ii, 1930. There are valuable articles by Italian scholars—A. Anti, G. Moretti, B.
Pace, R. Paribeni, P. Romanelli, and V. Viale—published chiefly in *Monumenti
Antichi* and in the *Notiziario* of the Italian School at Athens.
  For books and articles see O. Treuber, *Geschichte der Lykier*, Stuttgart, 1887:
R. Heberdey, *Opramoas. Inschriften vom Heroon zu Rhodiapolis*, Vienna, 1897:
G. Fougères, *De Lyciorum communi*, Paris Diss. 1898: V. Schultze, *op. cit.* and
R. Heberdey, *Termessische Studien*, Denkschr. Akad. Wien, LXIX, 3, 1929, and art.
s.v. Termessos in P.W. Supplbd. v.

8. GALATIA

Among books and articles—G. Perrot, *De Galatia provincia romana*, Paris Diss.
1867: F. Stähelin, *Geschichte der kleinasiatischen Galater*, ed. 2, Leipzig, 1907:
W. M. Ramsay, *Studies in the Roman province Galatia*, in J.R.S. VII, 1917 onwards
in addition his *Historical Commentary on St Paul's Epistle to the Galatians*, London,
1899, and innumerable other articles and papers from the greatest authority on the
country. R. Leonhard, *Paphlagonia*, Berlin, 1915, V. Schultze, *op. cit.* II, 2
W. M. Calder, *Mon. As. Min. Ant.* I, 1928, and E. Swoboda, J. Keil, and F. Knoll,
Denkmäler aus Lykaonien, Pamphylien und Isaurien, Brünn, 1935.
  Articles *s.v.* Galatia in Diz. Epig. (D. Vaglieri) and in P.W. (L. Bürchner and
G. Brandis): *s.v.* Galatie in Cabrol-Leclercq, *Dict. d'arch. chrétienne*, VI, p. 46
(V. Chapot): *s.vv.* Isauria and Lykaonia in P.W. (W. Ruge), and many others by
Ruge on the various cities of the province in P.W.

9. CILICIA

Collections of inscriptions in Th. Bent, *J.H.S.* XII, 1891, p. 206, and in *Proceedings Roy. Geog. Soc.* (N.S.), XII, 1890, p. 445: R. Heberdey, A. Wilhelm,
Reisen in Kilikien, Denkschr. Akad. Wien, XLIV, 6, 1896: R. Paribeni, P. Romanelli,
in *Mon. Ant.* XXIII, 1915: J. Keil, A. Wilhelm in *Jahreshefte* XVIII, 1915 Beiblatt,
col. 5: E. Herzfeld, S. Guyer, *Meriamlik und Korykos*, Mon. As. Min. Ant. II,
1930, and Keil-Wilhelm, *Denkmäler aus dem Rauhen Kilikien*, ib. III, 1933.
  See also V. Schultze, *op. cit.* II, 2: F. X. Schaffer, *Cilicia*, Petermanns Mitt.
Erg.-Heft 141, 1903: and art. *s.v.* Cilicia in Diz Epig. (D. Vaglieri).

CHAPTER XV

THE FRONTIER PROVINCES OF THE EAST

PART I. CAPPADOCIA AND ARMENIA MINOR

A. Ancient Sources

(*a*) *Writers.* The only extant description of the civilization of this region is the invaluable one by Strabo (XII, 533 *sqq.*, 555 *sqq.*; XV, 733), who knew it well since his birthplace was Amasia. A few details can be gleaned from others (esp. the Elder Pliny, *Hist. Nat.* VI, and Philostratus, *Vita Apollonii*, I) and in the works of the Fourth-Century Cappadocian bishops there are statements which are applicable to the earlier period.

(*b*) *Inscriptions.* Greek inscriptions are relatively few. The most notable, the Anisa decree (Michel, *Recueil*, 546), is before the Roman period; the others are scattered in various publications: W. H. Waddington, *B.C.H.* VII, 1883, p. 125; H. Grégoire, *ib.* XXXIII, 1909, p. 1 and p. 437; V. W. Yorke, *J.H.S.* XVIII, 1898, p. 317; E. Chantre, *Mission en Cappadoce*, Paris, 1898, pp. 133 *sqq.*; J. R. S. Sterrett, *An epigraphical journey*, Boston, Mass., 1885, pp. 231 *sqq.*; G. de Jerphanion and L. Jalabert, *Mél. Beyrouth*, V, 1911; *O.G.I.S.* nos. 350–364. The Latin inscriptions are collected in *C.I.L.* III and Supplements. For some interesting Graeco-Aramaean inscriptions see F. Cumont, *C.R. Ac. Inscr.* 1905, p. 93; Th. Reinach, *Rev. E.G.* 1905, p. 159; H. Grégoire, *C.R. Ac. Inscr.* 1908, p. 434; Ch. Clermont-Ganneau, *Rec. arch. orientale*, VIII, p. 296 and *Répert. épig. sémitique*, II, no. 966. A remarkable Aramaean inscription from Arabissus: J.-B. Chabot, *Répert. épig. sémitique*, III, no. 1785.

(*c*) *Coins.* Th. Reinach, *Trois royaumes d'Asie Mineure*, Paris, 1888, pp. 1–89 (Cappadocia); also in *Rev.E.A.* XVI, 1914, p. 1 (Armenia Minor); W. Wroth, *B.M. Cat. Galatia, Cappadocia*, 1899, pp. 29 *sqq.*; E. Babelon, *Traité des monnaies grecques*, Paris, 1910, II, ii, pp. 431 *sqq.*; K. Regling, *Dynastenmünzen von Tyana Morima und Anisa in Kappadokien*, Z.N. XLII, 1932, p. 1; E. A. Sydenham, *The Coinage of Caesarea in Cappadocia*, London, 1933.

B. Modern Works

Cappadocia

1. *General.* Th. Mommsen, *Römische Geschichte*, V, p. 316; J. Marquardt, *Staats-verwaltung*, I², pp. 365 *sqq.*: art. *s.v.* Cappadocia by D. Vaglieri in Diz. Epig. The best account of the condition of Cappadocia at the time of the Roman conquest is still that of Th. Reinach, *Mithridate Eupator*, Paris, 1890, pp. 15 *sqq.*, 23 *sqq.*, 89 *sqq.* and 257 *sqq.* For Cappadocia in the first century see the excellent monograph of W. E. Gwatkin, *Cappadocia as a Roman procuratorial province* (Univ. of Missouri Stud. V, 4, 1930), and F. Cumont, *Le gouvernement de Cappadoce sous les Flaviens*, Bull. Acad. de Belgique, 1930, pp. 197–227.

2. *Geography.* W. M. Ramsay, *Historical Geography of Asia Minor*, 1890, pp. 267–317; D. Hogarth and J. A. R. Munro, *Modern and Ancient Roads in Eastern Asia Minor*, Roy. Geog. Soc. Suppl. Papers III, 1893, pp. 643 *sqq.*; W. Ruge, art. in *P.W. s.v.* Kappadokia (and the travellers cited there), and G. de Jerphanion, *Les églises rupestres de Cappadoce*, Paris, I, 1895, pp. 1–52.

3. *Feudalism and Hellenization.* E. Kuhn, *Die städtische Verfassung des römischen Reiches*, Leipzig, 1865, II, pp. 231–244; K. Holl, *Volkssprachen in Kleinasien*,

Hermes, XLIII, 1908, p. 24; M. Rostowzew, *Studien zur Geschichte des röm. Kolonates*, Berlin, 1910, pp. 271 *sqq.* and 297 *sqq.*; G. de Jerphanion, *Mél. d'arch. anatolienne*, 1928, pp. 24–40 (strong places); F. Cumont, *A propos d'un décret d'Anisa*, Rev. E.A. XXXIV, 1932, p. 135: also the article by Regling in A (*c*).

4. *Commerce.* B. Landsberger, *Assyrische Handelscolonien in Kleinasien aus dem dritten Jahrtausend* (Der alte Orient, XXIV), 1925; M. Rostovtzeff, *Soc. Econ. Hist. Rom. Emp.* pp. 146, 241, etc., and Gwatkin, *op. cit.* pp. 22 *sqq.*

5. *Horse-raising.* Gothofredus, Commentary on the Codex Theodosianus, X, 6 (Vol. III, pp. 440–3, ed. J. D. Ritter, 1731); H. Grégoire, *Saints jumeaux et dieux cavaliers*, Paris, 1905, pp. 55 *sqq.*; B. Hrozný, Archiv Orientální, II, no. 3, Prague, 1931 (a Hittite manual of horsemanship from the xivth century B.C.); and article by G. Lafaye *s.v.* Equitium in D.S.

6. *Roman occupation.* V. Chapot, *La frontière de l'Euphrate*, Paris, 1907, pp. 347–355; E. Ritterling, art. *s.v.* Legio in P.W. cols. 1707 *sqq.*, 1754 *sqq.*, 1765 *sqq.*

7. *Religion.* A. M. Levidis, Ἱστορικὸν Δοκίμιον, I, Athens, 1885; F. Cumont, *L'archevêché de Pedachtoë et le sacrifice du faon*, Byzantion, VI, 1931, pp. 525 *sqq.*; *Les religions orientales dans le paganisme romain*, ed. 4, Paris, 1929, pp. 50 *sqq.* and 134 *sqq.* (Persian magi); and art. in P.W. *s.v.* Ma (Hartmann).

Armenia Minor

See Strabo, XII, 555 *sq.*, and for modern works: V. W. Yorke, *Roman roads on the Upper Euphrates*, The Geogr. Journal, VIII, 1896, p. 470; F. Cumont and E. Cumont, *Voyage archéol. dans le Pont et la Petite Arménie*, Brussels, 1905, pp. 296–330: on the annexation, Th. Reinach in *Rev. E.A.* XVI, 1914, p. 1, and F. Cumont in *Anatolian Studies presented to Sir W. Ramsay*, 1923, pp. 109 *sqq.*

Commagene

C. Humann and O. Puchstein, *Reisen in Kleinasien und Nordsyrien*, Berlin, 1890; Th. Reinach, *La dynastie de Commagène*, Rev. E.G. III, 1890, p. 363; F. Cumont, *Études syriennes*, Paris, 1917, pp. 153 *sqq.*; and art. *s.v.* Kommagene in P.W. Supplbd. IV (Honigmann).

PART II. SYRIA

A. ANCIENT SOURCES

(a) Writers

1. *Geographers.* The most detailed description of Syria that we have is Strabo, Book XVI, his principal source both for Syria and Palestine being Posidonius (J. Morr, *Phil.* LXXXI, 1925/6, p. 256): the precise statements of Pliny, *N.H.* V, derive partly from the *Commentarii* of Agrippa (cf. Honigmann in P.W. *s.v.* Syria, col. 1633): the lists of Ptolemy, V, 14–17, are (here as elsewhere) of considerable value, and can be completed and corrected by the Roman *Itineraria*, the Peutinger Table (Honigmann, *loc. cit.* 1646), the *Descriptio Orbis* of Georgios Kyprios (ed. H. Gelzer, 1890), and the *Notitia Dignitatum* (ed. O. Seeck, 1876). The *Expositio totius mundi et gentium* (commentary by G. Lumbroso, 1903) has some curious pages about Syria (29–43).

2. *Historians.* Of the works of the great Syrian historians, the *Historiae* of Posidonius of Apamea in 52 books, the *Universal History* (in 144 books) and the *De Vita sua* of Nicolaus of Damascus, there remain only fragments: *F.H.G.* III, pp. 240–277 and 348–456, and Jacoby, *F. Gr. Hist.* II A, pp. 225–430. Josephus,

Ant. Jud. XIII–XIV and *de Bello Judaico*, in dealing with Palestine has some incidental treatment of the neighbouring regions. The late compilation of Malalas has some interest because he used a local chronicle of Antioch. The sources for the Parthian Wars of Nero, Trajan, Lucius Verus and Septimius Severus, whose base of operations was in Syria, are given in the relevant chapters: the only continuous account we have, that of Julian's expedition by Ammianus Marcellinus (XXII–XXV), belongs to a later epoch. In this dearth of information we must sometimes turn to writers of the fourth and fifth centuries such as Julian (*Misopogon*, Letters 82 *sqq.*) and Libanius, and among ecclesiastics above all John Chrysostom and Theodoretus of Cyrrhus.

(b) Inscriptions

1. *Latin and Greek.* L. Jalabert and R. Mouterde, *Inscriptions grecques et latines de la Syrie*, 1 (Commagène et Cyrrhestique), Paris, 1929, will form a complete Corpus: until its completion we must turn to W. H. Waddington, *Recueil des inscriptions gr. et lat. de la Syrie*, Paris, 1870 (with an Index by J.-B. Chabot, Paris, 1897); J. J. E. Hondius, *S.E.G.* (esp. vol. VII) contains the inscriptions discovered between 1925 and 1933. Among the numerous archaeological expeditions special mention must be given to W. K. Prentice, *Greek and Latin Inscriptions* (Amer. Arch. Expedition to Syria in 1899), Part iii, 1908; E. Littmann, D. Magie and D. R. Stuart, *Greek and Latin Inscriptions* (Princeton Arch. Exped. to Syria, 1904–1905), Southern Syria, and W. K. Prentice, Northern Syria, Leyden, 1907–1921; G. Lucas, *Griech. und Lat. Inschriften aus Syrien und Mesopotamien*, Byz. Zeits. XIV, 1905, pp. 1–72 and 755 *sqq.*

2. *Semitic.* The volumes of the *Corpus inscriptionum semiticarum* that are most relevant are Pars II, vols. I and II (Inscriptiones aramaicae, 1889–1907), and vol. III (Inscriptiones Palmyrenae), ed. J.-B. Chabot, 1926. Among other collections should be mentioned: the Marquis de Vogüé, *Syrie centrale, Inscriptions sémitiques*, Paris, 1868–1877; R. Dussaud and F. Macler, *Voyage arch. au Safâ et dans le Djebel-el-Druz*, Paris, 1901, and *Mission dans les régions désertiques de la Syrie moyenne* (Nouvelles archives des missions, vol. x), Paris, 1903; Q. Pognon, *Inscr. sémitiques de la Syrie et de la Mésopotamie*, Paris, 1908; E. Littmann, *Semitic inscriptions* (Amer. Arch. Exped. to Syria in 1899), Part iv, 1905, and *Nabataean inscriptions from the Southern Hauran* (Princeton Arch. Exped. to Syria), part iv, A, 1914; J.-B. Chabot, *Choix d'inscriptions de Palmyre*, Paris, 1922; J. Cantineau, *Inventaire des Inscriptions de Palmyre*, Publications du Musée National de Damas (9 fascicules published), Beyrouth, 1930–1933; M. Lidzbarski, *Ephemeris für semitische Epigraphik*, 3 vols., Giessen, 1902–1915; J.-B. Chabot, *Répertoire d'épigraphie sémitique*, 6 vols., Paris, 1900–1935.

(c) Coins

B. V. Head, *Historia Numorum*, ed. 2, 1911, pp. 755–816; E. Babelon, *Catal. des monnaies de la Bibl. Nationale*, Les Perses Achéménides, 1893 (Monnaies phéniciennes, pp. 122–354); *B.M. Catalogues*—Galatia, Cappadocia, Syria (Wroth), 1899: Phoenicia (Hill), 1910: Arabia, Mesopotamia, Persia (Hill), 1922; R. Dussaud, *Numismatique des rois de Nabatène*, Journ. Asiatique, 1904, pp. 129–238; A. Dieudonné, *Les monnaies grecques de Syrie du Cabinet des Médailles*, in Rev. N. 1926–1929. For the imperial mints at Antioch and Tyre see A. Dieudonné, *Du droit de monnaie à Antioche à l'époque impériale*, *Mélanges Numismatiques*, Paris, 1909; H. Mattingly, *Coins of the Roman Empire in the British Museum*, 1, p. xxvi; 11, pp. xiii *sqq.* and *passim*; J. Maurice, *Numismatique Constantinienne*, III, 1912, p. 143.

B. Modern Literature

I. *General Works*

Th. Mommsen, *Römische Geschichte*, vol. v, pp. 423–429 (Palmyra), 446–486 (Syria and Nabatene); E. Schürer, *Geschichte des Jüdischen Volkes*, vol. i, ed. 4, 1901: M. Rostovtzeff, *Soc. Econ. Hist. Rom. Emp.* pp. 244–255 (in the Ital. trans., 1932, pp. 311–324) and *passim*: also *La Syrie romaine*, Rev. H. CLXXV, 1935, p. 1; J. Dobiaš, *Dějiny Římské Provincie Syrské* (History of the Roman Province of Syria), in Czech with French résumé: vol. i, to A.D. 70, has so far appeared, Prague, 1924: also *La Donation d'Antoine à Cléopâtre*, Mél. Bidez, Brussels, 1934, pp. 287–314; E. S. Bouchier, *Syria as a Roman Province*, Oxford, 1916; R. Dussaud, *Les Arabes en Syrie avant l'Islam*, Paris, 1907. E. Honigmann, Art. *s.v.* Syria in P.W.

II. *Geography*

E. Honigmann, *Historische Topographie von Nordsyrien im Altertum*, Z.D. Pal.-V. XLVI, 1923, pp. 149–193; XLVII, 1924, p. 1–64; U. Kahrstedt, *Syrische Territorien in hellenistischer Zeit*, Gött. Abh., N.F. XIX, 1926; R. Dussaud, *Topographie historique de la Syrie antique et médiévale*, Paris, 1927 (fundamental); A. Musil, *Palmyrena*, New York, 1928 (cf. Dussaud in *Syria*, x, 1929, pp. 52–62); E. C. Semple, *The geography of the ancient Mediterranean region*, London, 1932, pp. 180–210 and *passim*.

For the travels of archaeologists and explorers see the full list in Honigmann, in P.W. *l.c.* cols. 1723 *sqq.*: special mention may be made here of the works of E. Sachau, C. Humann and O. Puchstein, P. Perdrizet and C. Fossey, M. von Oppenheim and Gertrude Bell. See also sections IX(*b*) and XI.

Reference may be made to the guide to Syria, Palestine, Iraq and Transjordania in Hachette's *Les Guides bleus*, Paris, 1932. See also the *Carte des États du Levant sous mandat français*, published by the Bureau topographique, Beyrouth, 1928 (on a scale of 1 : 500,000): a map on a scale of 1 : 50,000 is also in preparation.

III. *Administration*

J. Marquardt, *Staatsverwaltung*, I², 1881, pp. 392–430 (Syria), 431–438 (Arabia, Mesopotamia); G. A. Harrer, *Studies in the History of the Roman Province of Syria*, Princeton Diss. 1915, and in *A.J.A.* XXXVI, 1932, p. 287 (additions to the list of legates); G. M. Harper, *Village administration in the Roman Province of Syria*, Yale Class. Stud. I, 1928, pp. 105–168; A. H. M. Jones, *The urbanization of the Ituraean principality* and *The urbanization of Palestine*, in J.R.S. XXI, 1931, p. 78 and p. 265; V. Tscherikower, *Die hellenistischen Städtegründungen von Alexander d. G. bis auf die Römerzeit*, Phil. Supplbd. XIX, 1927.

IV. *Roads: Defence*

P. Thomsen, *Die römischen Meilensteine der Provinzen Syria, Arabia und Mesopotamia*, Z.D. Pal.-V. XL, 1917, p. 1; A. Poidebard, *Coupes de la chaussée Antioche-Chalcis*, Syria, x, 1929, p. 22; M. Dunand, *La Strata Diocletiana*, Rev. Biblique, XL, 1931, p. 227, and *La voie romaine du Ledja*, Mém. sav. étr. Ac. Inscr. XIII, 1933, pp. 521–557; E. Honigmann in P.W. *s.v.* Syria, cols. 1645–1680. Route from Gaza to Petra; *Quart. of the Dept. of Antiq. Palestine*, III, 1933, p. 132: from Petra to Bostra; G. Beyer, Z.D. Pal.-V. LVIII, 1935, p. 159.

V. Chapot, *La frontière de l'Euphrate*, Paris, 1907; A. Schulten, *Masada; die Burg des Herodes und die römischen Lager*, Z.D. Pal.-V. LVI, 1933; A. Poidebard, *La* trace de Rome dans le désert de Syrie, 2 vols., Paris, 1934 (indispensable): see also G. L. Cheesman, *The auxilia of the Roman Imperial army*, Oxford, 1914, pp. 87 *sqq.* and 160 *sqq.*; R. Cagnat, in *Syria*, IX, 1928, p. 26; G. Cantacuzène, in *Mus. B.* XXXI, 1927, pp. 157–172; J. Carcopino, in *Syria*, VI, 1925, pp. 30–57 and 118–149, and XIV, 1933, pp. 20–55. On the *praetorium* at Doura see Preliminary Report IV, pp. 215 *sqq.* (see below, XI (*c*)).

V. *Romanization*

L. Hahn, *Rom und Romanismus im griechisch-römischen Osten*, Leipzig, 1906, and *Romanismus und Hellenismus bis auf die Zeit Justinians*, Phil. Supplbd. X, 1907, pp. 697–718. For the absence of *negotiatores* see J. Hatzfeld, *Les trafiquants italiens dans l'Orient hellénique*, Paris, 1919, pp. 142 *sqq.*: for Roman and native Law see L. Mitteis, *Reichsrecht und Volksrecht in den östlichen Provinzen des römischen Kaiserreichs*, Leipzig, 1891; E. Sachau, *Syrische Rechtsbücher*, 3 vols., Berlin, 1907–14; P. Collinet, *Histoire de l'école de droit de Beyrouth*, Paris, 1925; L. Wenger, *Der heutige Stand der Rechtswissenschaft; Erreichtes und Erstrebtes*, Munich, 1927; M. Rostovtzeff and C. B. Welles, *Parchment contract of loan from Dura-Europos*, Yale Class. Stud. II, 1931, p. 1 (and cf. other articles cited by Rostovtzeff in *Soc. Econ. Hist. Rom. Emp.* Ital. trans. pp. 220 *sqq.*); P. Koschaker, *Ueber griechischen Rechts-Urkunden aus den östlichen Randgebieten des Hellenismus*, Sächs. Abh. XLII, 1931, p. 1; C. A. Nallino, *Sul libro siro-romano e sul presunto diritto siriaco*, in Studi Bonfante, I, p. 201 n. 1, and in *Rend. Linc.* 1925, p. 721.

VI. *Industry*

For cloth etc. found at Doura and Palmyra see F. Cumont, *Fouilles de Doura*, Paris, 1926, p. 252 and plates XCII, XCIII; R. Pfister, *Textiles de Palmyre*, Paris, 1934; on Syrian glass see A. Kisa, *Das Glas im Altertum*, 2 vols., Leipzig, 1908; A. de Ridder, *Collection de Clercq: Catalogue*, vol. VI, pp. 117 *sqq.*; R. Dussaud, *Un verrier sidonien*, Syria, I, 1919, p. 230 and cf. X, 1929, p. 82; D. B. Harden, J.R.S. XXV, 1935, p. 163: on silk see below, VII (*c*).

VII. *Commerce*

See L. C. West, *Commercial Syria under the Roman Empire*, Trans. Amer. Phil. Ass. LV, 1924, p. 159, and cf. R. Mouterde, *Mél. Beyrouth*, XII, 1927, p. 288.

(*a*) *Caravan trade.* H. Lammens, *La Mecque à la veille de l'Hégire*, Beyrouth, 1924 (Mél. Beyrouth, IX); F. Cumont, *Fouilles de Doura*, pp. xxiii–xli; M. Rostovtzeff, *Caravan Cities*, Oxford, 1932; J. G. Février, *Essai sur l'histoire politique et économique de Palmyre*, Paris, 1931, pp. 46–63; A. Schmidt, *Drogen und Drogenhandel im Altertum*, ed. 2, Leipzig, 1927.

(*b*) *Commerce with India.* E. Fabricius, *Der Periplus des Erythräischen Meeres*, Leipzig, 1883 (cf. M. P. Charlesworth, in *C.Q.* XXII, 1928, pp. 92–101); M. P. Charlesworth, *Trade Routes and Commerce of the Roman Empire*, ed. 2, Cambridge, 1926, pp. 36–73; E. H. Warmington, *The Commerce between the Roman Empire and India*, Cambridge, 1928.

(*c*) *The Silk-trade.* A. Herrmann, *Die alten Seidenstrasse zwischen China und Syrien*, I, Berlin, 1910; and *Lou-lan*, Leipzig, 1931: cf. R. Hennig, *Byz. Zeits.* XXIII, 1933, p. 295. See also Pfister, above, VI.

(*d*) *Sea-borne trade and Syrian emigration.* The Phoenician fleets: G. Contenau, in *Syria*, I, 1920, p. 35 (cf. Ch. Picard, *ib.* XIV, 1933, p. 318); P. Scheffer-Boichorst, *Zur Geschichte der Syrer im Abendlande*, Mitt. d. Inst. f. Oesterr.

Geschichtsforschung, IV, 1885, pp. 520–550; L. Bréhier, *Les colonies d'Orientaux
en Occident au commencement du Moyen Âge*, Byz. Zeits. XII, 1903, pp. 1–39;
V. Pârvan, *Die Nationalität der Kaufleute im römischen Kaiserreiche*, Breslau,
1909, pp. 10 *sqq.*; A. Solari, *Delle antiche relazioni commerciali fra la Siria e
l'Occidente* (I, Roma e Gallia), Ann. d. Università Toscane, N.S. 1, 6, 1916;
F. Cumont, *Les Syriens en Espagne*, Syria, VIII, 1927, p. 330, and X, 1929, p. 281,
and XIV, 1933, p. 86; H. Pirenne, *La fin du commerce des Syriens en Occident*,
Mél. Bidez, 1934, pp. 677–687.

VIII. *Literature and Science*

There is no general work on the intellectual movements in Syria either in the
Seleucid or Roman era: the following works deal with particular points.

(*a*) *Literature.* P. Perdrizet, *Légendes babyloniennes dans les Métamorphoses d'Ovide*,
Rev. Hist. Rel. CV, 1932, p. 193; M. Hadas, *Gadarenes in Pagan Literature*,
Class. Weekly, XXV, 1931, p. 25.

(*b*) *Influence of Chaldaean doctrines.* F. Cumont, *Astrology and Religion among the
Greeks and Romans*, New York, 1912, pp. 78 *sqq.*, and art. in D.S. *s.v.*
Zodiacus; H. Gressmann, *Die hellenistische Gestirnreligion*, Leipzig, 1925;
J. Bidez, *Les écoles chaldéennes*, in Mél. Capart, Brussels, 1935, pp. 41–89.

(*c*) *Stoicism and Semites.* E. R. Bevan, *Stoics and Sceptics*, Oxford, 1913, pp. 20 *sqq.*;
J. Bidez, *La cité du monde et la cité du soleil chez les Stoiciens*, Paris, 1932.

(*d*) *Neo-Platonists.* H. Ch. Puech, *Numénius d'Apamée*, Mél. Bidez, 1934, pp.
749–778; J. Bidez, *Iamblique et son école à Apamée*, Rev. E.G. XXXII, 1919,
p. 31; and *Vie de Porphyre*, Ghent, 1913.

IX. *Art and Archaeology*

(*a*) *General Works.* Ch. Clermont-Ganneau, *Études d'archéologie orientale*, 2 vols.,
Paris, 1895–1897; *Recueil d'archéologie orientale*, 8 vols., Paris, 1888–1924
(with full index); E. Littmann, *Die Ruinenstätten und Schriftdenkmäler Syriens*
(Länder und Völker der Turkei, N. F. Heft II), 1917; P. Perdrizet, *Syriaca*,
Rev. Arch. 1898, I, pp. 34–49: 1899, II, pp. 34–53: 1903, I, pp. 392–400:
1903, II, pp. 399–401: 1904, I, pp. 234–244; F. Cumont, *Études syriennes*,
Paris, 1917; R. Dussaud, P. Deschamps and H. Seyrig, *La Syrie antique et
médiévale illustrée*, Paris, 1931; J. Materne, *A travers les villes mortes de la
Haute Syrie* (Mél. Beyrouth, XVII), 1933, p. 1; and H. Seyrig, *Antiquités
syriennes*, 1st series, Paris, 1934.

(*b*) *Architecture.* The Marquis de Vogüé, *Syrie centrale. Architecture civile et
religieuse du Ier au VIIe siècle*, 2 vols., Paris, 1865–1877; H. C. Butler,
Architecture and other arts (Amer. Exped. to Syria, 1899–1900, II), New York,
1904; *Ancient Architecture* (Princeton Univ. Arch. Exped. to Syria, 1904–5),
Division II, Leyden, 1919; *Early Churches in Syria, fourth to eleventh centuries*
(ed. by E. Baldwin Smith), Princeton, N.J. 1929. For city plans see M.
Cultrera, *Architettura Ippodamea*, Mem. Acc. Lincei, XVII, pp. 403 *sqq.* and
575 *sqq.*, and see section XI for monographs on Palmyra, Doura, Baalbek, etc.

(*c*) *Sculpture.* R. Foerster, *Skulpturen von Antiochia*, J.D.A.I. XIII, 1898, pp. 179–
191; V. Müller, *Zwei syrische Bildnisse römischer Zeit* (Winckelmanns-
programm LXXXVI), Berlin, 1927; H. Ingholt, *Studier over Palmyrensk Skulptur*,
Copenhagen, 1928 (the dated monuments), and Berytus, II, 1935, p. 57.

(*d*) *Painting.* (For a complete list of paintings discovered before 1926 see F.
Cumont, *Fouilles de Doura*, pp. 165 *sqq.*) H. Ingholt, *Quelques fresques
récemment découvertes à Palmyre*, Acta Archeologica, III, Copenhagen, 1932:

for the paintings of the Christian chapel see P. V. C. Baur in Excav. of Doura-Europos, Report v, pp. 254–289: the paintings of the synagogue will be published in Report vi.

(*e*) *Goldwork*. L. Bréhier, *Les trésors d'argenterie syrienne*, Gaz. d. Beaux Arts, 1920, I, pp. 173–196; Ch. Diehl, *L'école artistique d'Antioche et les trésors d'argenterie syrienne*, Syria, II, 1921, p. 81, and *Un nouveau trésor d'argenterie syrienne*, ib. VII, 1926, pp. 105–122, and cf. XI, 1930, p. 209; G. de Jerphanion, *Le calice d'Antioche* (Orientalia christiana, VII), Rome, 1926, and *La voix des monuments*, Paris, 1930, pp. 121–137.

(*f*) *Mosaics*. J. Chamonard, *Exploration archéologique de Délos*, XIV, Paris, 1933; E. de Lorey, *Les mosaïques de la mosquée des Ommeyades*, Syria, XII, 1931, pp. 326–349. For mosaic work in Syria before the Arab period see esp. the chapter by M. von Berchem in K. A. C. Cresswell's *Early Muslim Architecture*, vol. I, Oxford, 1932, pp. 151–252. For Antioch see Elderkin, below, XI (*a*). (The mosaics found at Apamea have not yet been published.)

(*g*) *Syria and the West*. The controversy roused by the books of J. Strzygowski (*Orient oder Rom*, 1901; *Hellas in der Orientumarmung*, 1902, etc.) is no nearer settlement. From the enormous mass of literature a few titles only can be cited. Roman influence on Syrian architecture: E. Weigand, *Baalbek und Rom*, J.D.A.I. XXIX, 1914, p. 37, and also in Th. Wiegand, *Palmyra* (see below, XI (*b*)), chap. XVI, pp. 151–166: cf. M. Rostovtzeff in *A.J.A.* XXXVII, 1933, p. 183; D. Schlumberger, *Formes du chapiteau corinthien*, Syria, XIV, 1933, pp. 282–317; G. de Jerphanion, *Le rôle de la Syrie et de l'Asie Mineure dans la formation de l'iconographie chrétienne*, Mél. Beyrouth, VIII, 1922, pp. 331–379 (reprinted in *La voix des monuments*, pp. 201 *sqq.*); O. M. Dalton, *East Christian Art*, Oxford, 1925; J. Ebersolt, *Orient et Occident*, Paris, 1928.

X. *Religion*

W. von Baudissin, *Studien zur semitischen Religionsgeschichte*, 2 vols., Leipzig, 1876–1878; W. Robertson Smith, *The religion of the Semites*, ed. 3 (with notes by S. A. Cook), London, 1927; M. J. Lagrange, *Études sur les religions sémitiques*, ed. 2, Paris, 1905; R. Dussaud, *Notes de mythologie syrienne*, Paris, 1903; S. A. Cook, *The religion of ancient Palestine in the light of Archaeology*, London, 1930; F. Cumont, *Les religions orientales dans le paganisme romain*, ed. 4, Paris, 1929, pp. 95–124, 248–270, and *La théologie solaire du paganisme romain*, Mém. sav. étr. Ac. Inscr. XII, 1909, 446–479; S. Langdon, *Semitic mythology*, Boston, Mass., 1931.

Survivals in the beliefs of to-day. S. J. Curtiss, *Primitive Semitic religion to-day*, Chicago, 1902; A. Jaussen, *Coutumes des Arabes au pays de Moab*, Paris, 1908, pp. 287 *sqq.*; R. Dussaud, *Histoire et religion des Nosaïris*, Paris, 1900.

Temples and countries. HIERAPOLIS. E. Strong and J. Garstang, *The Syrian goddess*, London, 1913 (trans. of Lucian with notes); F. Cumont, art. in P.W. *s.v.* Dea Syria; P. V. C. Baur, in *Excavations at Dura*, III, pp. 100 *sqq.* and plate XIV. DOLICHE. A. H. Kan, *De Iovis Dolicheni cultu*, Groningen, 1901 (see below, XI (*a*)). CARRHAE (Harran in Mesopotamia). D. Chwolsohn, *Die Ssabier und der Ssabismus*, 2 vols., St Petersburg, 1856. PALMYRA. J. G. Février, *La religion des Palmyréniens*, Paris, 1931 (with bibliography up to date); H. Seyrig, *Hiérarchie des divinités à Palmyre*, Syria, XIII, 1932, pp. 190–195, and *Le culte de Bel et de Baalshamin*, ib. XIV, 1933, pp. 238–282. HELIOPOLIS (see below, X (*a*)). R. Dussaud, *Jupiter héliopolitain*, Syria, I, 1920, pp. 3–15, and ib. II, 1921, p. 40.

PHOENICIA. The discovery at Ras Shamra of a very ancient Phoenician mythological poem (see articles by Ch. Virolleaud in *Syria*, x–xix) appears to raise the credit that Herennius Philo of Byblus (A.D. 64–140) deserves as a translator of Sanchuniathon (*F.H.G.* III, 560 *sqq.*): see R. Dussaud, *Rev. Hist. Rel.* CIV, 1931, p. 356: CV, 1932, p. 245, CVIII, 1933, p. 1 and CXI, 1935, p. 5; W. von Baudissin, *Adonis und Esmun*, Leipzig, 1911; Sir J. G. Frazer, *Adonis, Attis, Osiris*, ed. 3, London, 1919; S. Ronzevalle, *Venus Lugens et Adonis Byblius*, Mél. Beyrouth, xv, 1931; F. Cumont, *Adonis et Sirius*, Mél. Glotz, Paris, 1932, I, pp. 257–264. (Works on Adonis-cult outside Syria are omitted.)

ARABIA. J. Wellhausen, *Reste Arabischen Heidentums*, ed. 2, Berlin, 1897 (new impression in 1927); Th. Nöldeke, art. *s.v.* Arabs in Hastings' *Encyclopaedia of Religion and Ethics*; D. Nielsen, *Zur altarabischen Religion*, Handbuch der Altarabischen Altertumskunde, Munich, 1928, pp. 176–250; H. Lammens, *Les sanctuaires préislamiques dans l'Arabie occidentale*, Mél. Beyrouth, xi, 1926, and *L'Arabie occidentale avant l'Hégire*, Beyrouth, 1928, pp. 101–236. (See also below, *Monographs*.)

XI. *Monographs*

(a) *Syria*.

ANTIOCH. K. O. Müller, *Antiquitates Antiochenae*, Göttingen, 1839 (and in Kunstarchäol. Werke, v, 1873, pp. 1–132) is still indispensable; E. S. Bouchier, *A short history of Antioch*, Oxford, 1921; V. Schulze, *Antiocheia* (Altchristliche Städte und Landschaften, iii), Gütersloh, 1930; I. Guidi, *Una descrizione araba di Antiocheia*, Rend. Linc. VI, April, 1897; G. W. Elderkin, *Antioch on the Orontes* (The Excavations of 1932), Princeton, N.J., 1934.

APAMEA. F. Mayence, *L'Antiquité classique*, I, 1932, p. 233 and IV, 1935, p. 199.

BEYROUTH. L. Cheiko, *Beyrouth. Histoire et monuments*, Beyrouth, 1927; Cte du Mesnil du Buisson, *Syria*, II, 1921, pp. 235 and 317 *sqq.*

CHALCIS ad Belum. P. Monceaux et L. Brossé, *Syria*, VI, 1925, p. 339.

CYRRHUS. F. Cumont, *Études syriennes*, pp. 221–239; E. Honigmann, arts. in P.W. *s.v.* Kyrrhos, Kyrrhestike.

DAMASCUS. G. Watzinger and K. Wulzinger, *Damaskus, die antike Stadt*, Berlin, 1922 (cf. R. Dussaud, *Syria*, III, 1922, pp. 219–250).

DOLICHE. F. Cumont, *Études syriennes*, pp. 174–202, and in *Syria*, I, 1920, p. 183.

HELIOPOLIS (BAALBEK). Th. Wiegand (and collaborators), *Baalbek. Ergebnisse der Ausgrabungen in den Jahren* 1898–1905, 3 vols., Berlin, 1921–25; H. Thiersch, *Zu den Tempeln und zur Basilika von Baalbek*, Gött. Nach. 1925, p. 1; H. Seyrig, *La triade héliopolitaine et les temples de Baalbek*, Syria, x, 1929, p. 314 (cf. R. Dussaud in *Monuments Piot*, xxx, pp. 78 *sqq.*).

HIERAPOLIS. D. G. Hogarth, *B.S.A.* xiv, 1907, pp. 183–196.

LAODICEA. For the three towns of this name see E. Honigmann in P.W. *s.v.*, cols. 712–721; M. Hartmann, *Das Liwa el-Ladkije*, Z.D. Pal.-V. xiv, 1891, p. 151; J. Sauvaget, *Le plan de Laodicée sur mer*, Bull. d'ét. orient. IV, 1935, p. 83.

SELEUCEIA IN PIERIA: V. Chapot, *Séleucie de Piérie*, Mém. soc. antiquaires de France, LXVI, 1906, pp. 149–226; E. Honigmann, *s.v.* Seleuceia in P.W. cols. 1185–1200.

ZEUGMA. F. Cumont, *Études syriennes*, pp. 119–150: cf. J. Dobiaš, *Séleucie sur l'Euphrate*, Syria, VI, 1925, p. 253.

(b) *Palmyrene*.

PALMYRA. J. Partsch, *Palmyra, eine historisch-klimatische Studie*, Verhandl. Akad. Leipzig, xxiv, 1922, p. 1; A. Gabriel, *Recherches à Palmyre*, Syria, vii, 1926, p. 71; J. G. Février, *Histoire de Palmyre*, Paris, 1931; Th. Wiegand (and collaborators), *Palmyra. Ergebnisse der Expeditionen von* 1902–1917, 2 vols., Berlin, 1932; H. Seyrig, *Antiquités syriennes*, Paris, 1934, pp. 36–55, 70–132; D. Schlumberger, *Berytus*, ii, pp. 149–167.

RESAFA. S. Spanner and H. Guyer, *Rusafa* (Forschungen zur Islamischen Kunst, herausg. von Sarre, iv), Berlin, 1926. E. Honigmann in P.W. *s.v.* Sergioupolis.

(c) Mesopotamia and Parapotamia.

P. Sarre and J. Herzfeld, *Archäologische Reise im Euphrat- und Tigrisgebiet*, 3 vols., Berlin, 1911.

AMIDA. M. von Berchem and J. Strzygowski, *Amida*, Heidelberg, 1910.

DOURA. F. Cumont, *Fouilles de Doura-Europos* (1922–1923), Paris, 1926; M. Rostovtzeff (and collaborators), *The excavations at Dura-Europos*. Preliminary Reports. Five vols. have so far appeared, covering the excavations from 1923 to 1932, Yale Univ. Press, 1929–1934. A sixth is in the press.

HATRA. W. Andrae, *Hatra*, 2 vols., Leipzig, 1908–1912.

(d) Phoenicia.

E. Renan, *Mission en Phénicie*, Paris, 1864.

SIDON. F. C. Eiselen, *Sidon. A study in oriental history*. (Univ. Columbia Oriental Studies, iv), New York, 1907; O. Hamdy Bey and Th. Reinach, *Une nécropole royale à Sidon*, Paris, 1892; Th. Macridy Bey, *Le temple d'Eshmoun à Sidon*, Rev. Biblique, 1902, p. 489: 1903, p. 69: 1904, p. 390; G. Contenau, *Mission archéologique à Sidon* (1914), and *Deuxième Mission archéologique à Sidon* (1920), Paris, 1921 and 1924 (offprints from *Syria*): and art. *s.v.* Sidon in P.W. (Honigmann).

TYRE. D. A. Le Lasseur, *Syria*, iii, 1922, pp. 1–26, 116–133.

(e) Decapolis and Transjordania.

H. Guthe, *Die griechisch-römischen Städte des Ostjordanlandes*, Leipzig, 1918; C. Steuernagel, *Der 'Adschlun nach den Aufzeichnungen von Dr. Schumacher*, Z.D. Pal.-V. XLVIII, 1925, pp. 1 and 201; N. Glueck, *Explorations in Eastern Palestine*, Ann. Amer. Schools for Oriental Research, XIV, 1934, pp. 1–114; M. Dunand, *Mission archéol. dans le Djebel-el-Druze*, Syria, VII, 1926, p. 326.

GERASA. G. Schumacher, *Dscherasch*, Z.D. Pal.-V. XXV, 1902, pp. 109–178; H. Guthe, *Gerasa*, Leipzig, 1919; M. Rostovtzeff, *Caravan cities*, pp. 57–90; R. O. Fink, *Jerash in the first century*, J.R.S. XXIII, 1933, p. 109. Archaeology of the Haurân: M. Dunand, *Le Musée de Soueïda*, Paris, 1934.

(f) Arabia.

E. Schürer, *Geschichte des jüdischen Volkes*, ed. 4, 1, pp. 726 *sqq.*; A. Musil, *Arabia Petraea*, 4 vols., Vienna, 1907–1908; R. E. Brünnow and A. von Domaszewski, *Die Provincia Arabia*, 3 vols., Strassburg, 1904–1909; A. Jaussen and R. Savignac, *Mission archéologique en Arabie*, 3 vols. and 2 vols. of plates, Paris, 1909–1922; A. Kammerer, *Petra et la Nabatène*, 2 vols., Paris, 1929–1930.

MSCHATTA. J. Strzygowski, *Mschatta*, Jahrb. d. Preussischen Kunstsammlungen, XXV, 1904, pp. 205–373.

PETRA. G. Dalman, *Petra und seine Felsheiligtümer*, Leipzig, 1908; W. Bachman, G. Watzinger, and Th. Wiegand, *Petra*, Berlin, 1921; Sir A. Kennedy, *Petra: its history and monuments*, 1925; M. Rostovtzeff, *Caravan Cities*, 1932, pp. 1–53.

The excellent bibliographies for Palestine furnished by P. Thomsen in *Die Palästinalitteratur*, Leipzig, i (1908), ii (1911), iii (1916) and iv (1927) include parts of the neighbouring countries.

CHAPTER XVI

EGYPT, CRETE AND CYRENAICA

A. Egypt

A comprehensive bibliography of Graeco-Roman Egypt was given in Volume x, pp. 922–931. Below are noted a few works which have appeared since that bibliography was compiled, but no attempt is made at completeness.

Documents

A. *General*

Otto, W. and L. Wenger. *Papyri und Altertumswissenschaft: Vorträge des 3. internat. Papyrologentages.* (Münchener Beiträge zur Papyrusforschung u. ant. Rechtsgesch., 19. Heft.) Munich, 1934.

B. *Papyri*

P. Iand. = *Papyri Iandanae*, fasc. 7 (D. Curschmann). Leipzig-Berlin, 1934.
P. Milan Univ. = *Dal Iº volume dei papiri della R. Università di Milano.* (Pubbl. d. R. Univ. di Milano.) Florence, 1935.
P. Ross.-Georg. V. *Varia.* Tiflis, 1935.
P. Vars. = G. Manteuffel, L. Zawadowski, and C. Rozenberg, *Papyri Varsovienses* (Univ. Varsoviensis, Acta Facultatis Litterarum). Warsaw, 1935.

C. *Ostraca*

Amundsen, L. *Greek Ostraca in the University of Michigan Collection.* Ann Arbor, 1935.
Préaux, Claire. *Les ostraca grecs de la collection Charles-Edwin Wilbour au Musée de Brooklyn.* New York, 1935.

Modern Literature

Avogadro, S. *Le ἀπογραφαί di proprietà nell' Egitto greco-romano.* Aeg. xv, 1935, p. 131.
Bell, H. I. *Diplomata Antinoitica.* Aeg. xiii, 1933, p. 514.
Calderini, A. *Dizionario dei nomi geografici e topografici dell' Egitto greco-romano.* Cairo, 1935– .
Gercke-Norden. *Einleitung in die Altertumswissenschaft*, iii. Band, 2. Heft, ed. 3, Leipzig and Berlin, 1933. E. Kornemann, *Die römische Kaiserzeit*, pp. 55–186 (for Egypt in the period covered by this chapter see especially pp. 97–105).
Henne, H. *Liste des stratèges des nomes égyptiens à l'époque gréco-romaine.* Cairo, 1935.
Leider, E. *Der Handel von Alexandreia.* Hamburg Diss. 1933.
Lumbroso, G. *Testi e commenti concernenti l' antica Alessandria.* (Pubbl. di 'Aegyptus,' Serie Scient. iv.) Fasc. 1, Milan, 1934.
Reinmuth, O. W. *The Prefect of Egypt from Augustus to Diocletian.* (*Klio*, 34tes Beiheft.) Leipzig, 1935.

B. Crete

In the first two centuries of the Empire Crete was happy in being a province almost without a history, and references to it in literary authors are few. Those of importance, for this and the following section, are cited in the text. But the epigraphical evidence is large; the first collection of inscriptions appeared in *C.I.G.* II, in 1843, and in *C.I.L.* III, in 1873, but since those years numerous important additions have been made, chiefly owing to the excavations of American, French and Italian scholars, among whom the late F. Halbherr holds an honoured place. Among the chief reports by Halbherr are those in *Museo italiano di antichità classica* II, 1888, cols. 689 and 913, III, 1890, col. 559; in *A.J.A.* XI, 1896, p. 525, I (Series II), 1897, p. 159 and II, 1898, p. 79; and in *Rend. Linc.* X (Series V), 1901, p. 291. In more modern times Italian scholars, Bendinelli, M. Guarducci, Maiuri, Oliverio, Pace, Perali and Pernier, have published reports, mainly in the *Annuario* of the Italian School at Athens, I, 1914, II, 1916, and VIII–IX, 1929, in *Rivista R. Istit. di Arch. e storia dell' arte*, I, 1929, II, 1930, and in *Bull. Comm. arch. com. di Roma*, LVI, 1928, and LVIII, 1930. All this work is now in process of being gathered up into a comprehensive Corpus, *Inscriptiones Creticae opera et consilio F. Halbherr collectae*, of which the first volume, *Tituli Cretae Mediae praeter Gortynios*, edited by M. Guarducci, was published at Rome in 1935.

Among the most valuable publications may be cited: B. Haussoullier, *Inscriptions de Crète*, B.C.H. IX, 1885, p. 1; L. Mariani, *Antichità cretesi*, Mon. Lincei, VI, 1896, col. 135; L. Savignoni and G. De Sanctis, *Esplorazione archeologica delle provincie occidentali di Creta*, Mon. Lincei, XI, 2, 1902, col. 285; L. Savignoni, G. De Sanctis and R. Paribeni, *Nuovi studii e scoperte in Gortina*, Mon. Lincei, XVIII, 2, 1908, col. 177; A. Taramelli, *Ricerche archeologiche cretesi*, Mon. Lincei, IX, 2, 1900, col. 285.

Coins

Svoronos, J. N. *Numismatique de la Crète ancienne.* Vol. I with text and plates, Mâcon, 1890. (Supplement in Ἐφημερὶς Ἀρχαιολογική, 1889, col. 193.)

General works

Cardinali, G. *Creta nel tramonto dell' ellenismo.* Riv. Fil. XXXV, 1907, p. 1.
Paribeni, R. Art. *s.v.* Creta in Diz. Epig.

C. Cyrenaica

The literary evidence about Cyrenaica, too, is scanty, but the epigraphic, thanks especially to recent Italian excavations, plentiful. In 1864 two Englishmen, R. Murdoch Smith and E. A. Porcher, published the results of their discoveries, but little more work was done until 1914–15. Since then Italian archaeologists, Anti, Ferri, Ghislanzoni, Guidi, Oliverio, and Pernier, have published the results of excavations, chiefly in the *Notiz. arch. min. col.*, the *Rend. Linc.*, the *Rivista della Tripolitania*, *Africa Italiana*, *Documenti antichi dell' Africa Italiana*, and in reports of the excavations (*Campagna di Scavi a Cirene*) from 1925 onwards. Chief among these reports are: E. Ghislanzoni, *Notizie archeologiche sulla Cirenaica*, Notiz. arch. min. col. I, 1915, p. 65; L. Pernier and G. Oliverio, *Campagna di scavi a Cirene nel 1925*, Africa Italiana, I, 1927, p. 126; C. Anti and G. Oliverio, *Campagna di scavi a Cirene nell' estate 1926*, ib. I, 1927, p. 296; G. Oliverio, *Campagna di scavi a Cirene nell' estate 1927*, ib. II, 1928–29, p. 111; *...nell' estate 1928*, ib. III, 1930, p. 141. For literature upon the Augustan Edicts from Cyrene see Vol. X, p. 913.

Papyri

Norsa, M. and G. Vitelli. *Il papiro vaticano greco II* (Studi e testi no. 53). Città del Vaticano, 1931.

Gallavotti, C. and G. La Pira. *Un registro catastale e un libro processuale della Marmarica nel nuovo papiro vaticano.* Bull. Ist. Diritto Rom. 1931, fasc. iv–vi, p. 19.

La Pira, G. *Esegesi del Papiro Vaticano* (Documento della Marmarica). Ib. 1933, fasc. i–vi, p. 103.

Coins

Robinson, E. S. G. *British Museum Catalogue of the Greek Coins of Cyrenaica.* London, 1927.

GENERAL WORKS

Ferri, S. *Contributi di Cirene alla storia della religione greca.* Rome, 1923.

—— *Il telesterio isiaco di Cirene.* Studi e materiali di storia delle religioni, III, 1927, p. 233.

Oliverio, G. *Federico Halbherr in Cirenaica* (Luglio 1910–Aprile 1911). Afr. Ital. IV, 1931, p. 229.

Paribeni, R. Art. *s.v.* Cyrenae in Diz. Epig.

Pietrogrande, A. L. *Sarcofagi decorati della Cirenaica.* Afr. Ital. III, 1930, p. 107.

Rossberg, W. *De rebus Cyrenarum provinciae Romanae.* Diss. Frankenbergae s.a. 1876.

Rostovtzeff, M. I. *Storia economica e sociale...* pp. 361–63.

Vitali, L. *Fonti per la storia della religione cyrenaica.* Padua, 1932.

CHAPTER XVII

GREEK LITERATURE, SCIENCE AND PHILOSOPHY

I. General Works

(a) Literature and Culture

Aly, W. *Geschichte der griechischen Literatur*, Bielefeld-Leipzig, 1925, pp. 295–369.
Dill, S. *Roman Society from Nero to Marcus Aurelius*. London, Ed. 2, 1905, fifth reprint, 1925, pp. 289–528.
Geffcken, J. *Geisteskämpfe im Griechentum der Kaiserzeit*. Kantstudien, xxx, 1925, p. 23.
Hahn, L. *Rom und Romanismus im griechisch-römischen Osten*. Leipzig, 1906.
Hirzel, R. *Der Dialog*. 2 vols. Leipzig, 1895.
Mahaffy, J. P. *The Silver Age of the Greek World*. London, 1906.
Norden, E. *Die antike Kunstprosa*. 2 vols. ed. 2, Leipzig, 1909.
Reich, H. *Der Mimus*. 2 vols. Berlin, 1903.
Rohde, E. *Der griechische Roman*. Ed. 2, Leipzig, 1900.
Rose, H. J. *A handbook of Greek literature from Homer to the age of Lucian*. London, 1934.
Schmid, W. *Der Atticismus in seinen Hauptvertretern von Dionysius von Halikarnass bis auf den zweiten Philostratus*. 5 vols. Stuttgart, 1887–97.
Sikes, E. E. *The Greek View of Poetry*. London, 1931, pp. 183–244.
Wendland, P. *Die hellenistisch-römische Kultur in ihren Beziehungen zu Judentum und Christentum*. Tübingen, 1913, pp. 1–127.
von Wilamowitz-Moellendorff, U. *Die griechische Litteratur des Altertums*. Hinnebergs Kultur der Gegenwart, i, viii, Leipzig, 1912, pp. 144–5, 218–258.
—— *Asianismus und Attizismus*. Hermes, xxxv, 1900, p. 1.

(b) Philosophy

von Arnim, H. *Arius Didymus' Abriss der peripatetischen Ethik*. Wien S.B. cciv, 1926.
Arnold, E. V. *Roman Stoicism*. Cambridge, 1911.
Bréhier, E. *Histoire de la philosophie*. Vol. 1, 2, Paris, 1931, pp. 401–448.
Carcopino, J. *La basilique pythagoricienne de la Porte Majeure*. Paris, 1927.
Chaignet, A. E. *Histoire de la psychologie des grecs*. Vol. iii, Paris, 1890.
Diels, H. *Doxographi graeci*. Berlin, 1879, reprinted 1929.
Gomperz, H. *Die Lebensauffassung der griechischen Philosophen und das Ideal der inneren Freiheit*. Ed. 3, Jena, 1927.
Martha, C. *Les moralistes sous l'empire romain, philosophes et poètes*. Paris, 1865.
Méautis, G. *Recherches sur le pythagorisme*. Neuchâtel, 1922.
Praechter, K. *Überwegs Geschichte der Philosophie*. Vol. 1, ed. 12, Berlin, 1926.
Rohde, E. *Psyche*. 7th and 8th imp. Tübingen, 1921. Eng. trans. London, 1925.
Strache, H. *Der Eklektizismus des Antiochus von Askalon*. (Phil. Unters. xxvi.) Berlin, 1921.
Theiler, W. *Die Vorbereitung des Neuplatonismus*. (Problemata, i.) Berlin, 1930.
Zeller, E. *Die Philosophie der Griechen*. Vol. iii, ed. 5 (a reprint of ed. 4), by E. Wellmann. Leipzig, 1923.

(c) Science

Allbutt, Sir T. Clifford. *Greek Medicine in Rome*. London, 1921.
Berger, H. *Geschichte der wissenschaftlichen Erdkunde der Griechen*. Ed. 2, Leipzig, 1903.
Boll, F. *Sternglaube und Sterndeutung*. Ed. 4 by W. Gundel, Leipzig, 1931.
Bouché-Leclercq, A. *L'Astrologie grecque*. Paris, 1899.
Bunbury, Sir E. H. *A History of Ancient Geography*. 2 vols. London, 1879.
Deichgräber, K. *Die griechische Empirikerschule*. Berlin, 1930.
Garrison, F. H. *An introduction to the history of medicine*. Ed. 4, Philadelphia, 1929.
Haeser, H. *Lehrbuch der Geschichte der Medizin und der epidemischen Krankheiten*. Ed. 3, vol. 1, Jena, 1875.
Heath, Sir T. L. *A History of Greek mathematics*. Oxford, 1921.
—— *A Manual of Greek mathematics*. Oxford, 1931.
Heiberg, J. L. *Geschichte der Mathematik und Naturwissenschaften im Altertum*. Munich, 1925.
Kubitschek, F. Art. *s.v. Karten* in P.W.
Neuburger, M. *Geschichte der Medizin*. Trans. by E. Playfair. London, 1910, vol. 1, pp. 208–275.
Thorndike, L. *A History of Magic and Experimental Science*. Vol. 1, London, 1923, pp. 39–286.
Tozer, H. F. *A History of Ancient Geography*. Ed. 2, by M. Cary, Cambridge, 1935.
Wellmann, M. *Die pneumatische Schule bis auf Archigenes*. (Phil. Unters. XIV.) Berlin, 1895.
—— *Der Physiologos*. Phil. Supplbd. XXI, 1930.

II. INDIVIDUAL AUTHORS

(a) Poetry

THE GREEK ANTHOLOGY. Text, H. Stadtmüller (Leipzig, 1894–1906, Books I–VII, IX only); F. Dübner and E. Cougny (3 vols. Paris, 1864–90, complete). Text and translation, W. R. Paton (5 vols. London, 1916–18); P. Waltz (Paris, 1928– , in progress). See also C. Cichorius, *Römische Studien*, Berlin, 1922, pp. 295–374; C. Radinger, *Meleagros von Gadara*, Innsbruck, 1895; R. Reitzenstein, Art. *s.v. Epigramm* in P.W. and M. Rubensohn, *Crinagorae Mytilenaei Epigrammata*, Berlin, 1888.
BABRIUS. Text, O. Crusius (Leipzig, 1897). Text and notes, W. G. Rutherford (London, 1883).
DIONYSIUS PERIEGETES. Text in C. Müller, *Geographi graeci minores*, vol. II, p. 102. No critical edition.
OPPIAN. Text, translation and notes, A. W. Mair (London, 1928).
    For other verse, mostly fragmentary, see U. von Wilamowitz-Moellendorff, *Griechische Verskunst*, Berlin, 1921, pp. 595–607 (Mesomedes); the same author's *Marcellus von Side*, Berl. S.B. 1928, p. 3; P.Oxy. 1085 (Pancrates); P.Oxy. 1383; W. Kroll, *Catalogus codicum astrologorum graecorum*, VI, pp. 91–113 (Dorotheus of Sidon); the Didot volume, *Poetae bucolici et didactici*, Paris, 1851, pp. 165–174, 90[II]ff., 115[III]ff. For the mime see O. Crusius, *Herondae mimiambi*, Leipzig, 1914, pp. 101–149; J. U. Powell and E. A. Barber, *New Chapters in the History of Greek Literature*, Oxford, 1921, pp. 120–3; A. Koerte, in *Arch. Pap.* X, 1932, p. 62.

(b) Literary Criticism

DIONYSIUS OF HALICARNASSUS. Text, C. Jacoby, H. Usener, and L. Radermacher (6 vols. Leipzig, 1885–1929). Text, translation and commentary, W. Rhys Roberts, *Dionysius of Halicarnassus, The Three Literary Letters* (Cambridge, 1901), *Dionysius of Halicarnassus on Literary Composition* (London, 1910); see also M. Egger, *Denys d'Halicarnasse*, Paris, 1902.

DEMETRIUS. Text and notes, L. Radermacher, *Demetrii Phalerei qui dicitur de elocutione libellus* (Leipzig, 1901); W. Rhys Roberts, *Demetrius on Style* (with translation, London, 1902). See also F. Solmsen, *Demetrios περὶ ἑρμηνείας und seine peripatetisches Quellenmaterial*, Hermes, LXVI, 1931, p. 241.

'LONGINUS.' Text, A. O. Prickard (Oxford, 1906); J. Vahlen (Leipzig, 1910). Text and notes, W. Rhys Roberts, *Longinus on the Sublime* (Cambridge, 1907). Translations, A. O. Prickard (Oxford, 1906), T. G. Tucker (Melbourne, 1935). See also H. Mutschmann, *Tendenz, Aufbau, und Quellen der Schrift vom Erhabenen*, Berlin, 1913.

CAECILIUS. Fragments, E. Ofenloch (Leipzig, 1907).

(c) The Sophistic movement

For text of Herodes see E. Drerup, [Ἡρώδου] περὶ πολιτείας (Paderborn, 1908), of Polemo H. Hinck (Leipzig, 1873); two speeches of Favorinus are preserved among the works of Dio Chrysostom, *Or.* XXXVII, LXIV; for a third (*On Exile*) see M. Norsa and G. Vitelli, *Il papiro vaticano greco* II, Studi e testi, LIII (Città del Vaticano, 1931), for fragments see F.H.G. III, pp. 577–585. Fragments of the sophists are to be found in Philostratus, *Vitae Sophistarum* (ed. C. L. Kayser, Leipzig, 1870; text and translation, W. C. Wright, London, 1922) and Seneca the Elder (ed. H. J. Müller, Vienna, 1887). See also P. Graindor, *Un milliardaire antique: Hérode Atticus et sa famille*, Cairo, 1930, pp. 137–177.

DIO CHRYSOSTOM. Text, H. von Arnim (2 vols. Berlin, 1893–6); G. de Budé (2 vols. Leipzig, 1915–19). Text and translation, J. W. Cohoon (London, 1932– , in progress). See also H. von Arnim, *Leben und Werke des Dio von Prusa*, Berlin, 1898; and L. Lemarchand, *Dion de Pruse, les Œuvres d'avant l'exil*, Paris, 1926.

ARISTIDES. Text, G. Dindorf (3 vols. Leipzig, 1829); B. Keil (vol. II only, Berlin, 1898). Text and notes, J. Amann, *Die Zeusrede des Ailios Aristides* (Stuttgart, 1931). A new verse fragment in Berl. S.B., R. Herzog, 1934, p. 753. See also A. Boulanger, *Aelius Aristide et la sophistique dans la province de l'Asie au IIᵉ siècle de notre ère* (Bibliothèque des écoles françaises d'Athènes et de Rome, 126), Paris, 1923; J. Mesk, *Zu den Prosa und Vershymnen des Aelius Aristides*, Raccolta di scritti in onore di Felice Ramorino, Milan, n.d., p. 660; and U. von Wilamowitz-Moellendorff, *Der Rhetor Aristeides*, Berl. S.B. 1925, p. 333.

LUCIAN. Text, C. Jacobitz (4 vols. Leipzig, 1836–41, ed. min. 1866–72); J. Sommerbrodt (3 vols. Berlin, 1886–99); F. N. Nilén (3 fasc. Leipzig, 1900–23, suspended). Text and translation, A. M. Harmon (London, 1913– , in progress). Translation, H. W. and F. G. Fowler (4 vols. Oxford, 1905). Among works on Lucian see J. Bernays, *Lucian und die Kyniker*, Berlin, 1879; M. Croiset, *Essai sur la vie et les œuvres de Lucien*, Paris, 1882; R. Helm, *Lukian und Menipp*, Leipzig, 1906; B. P. McCarthy, *Lucian and Menippus*, Yale Class. Stud. IV, 1934, p. 3; O. Schissel von Fleschenberg, *Novellenkränze Lukians*, Halle, 1912; and Th. Sinko, *De Luciani libellorum ordine et mutua ratione*, Eos, XIV, 1908, p. 113.

(d) Historians, etc.

ARRIAN. Text, A. G. Roos (2 vols. Leipzig, 1907–28). Text and translation of *Anabasis* and *Indica*, E. T. Robson (2 vols. London, 1929–33). Translation with notes, E. J. Chinnock (London, 1893).

PAUSANIAS. Text, F. Spiro (3 vols. Leipzig, 1903). Text and commentary, H. Hitzig and H. Blümner (3 vols. in 5, Leipzig, 1896–1910). Translation and commentary, J. G. Frazer (6 vols. London, 1898. Ed. 2, New York, 1913). See also W. Gurlitt, *Über Pausanias*, Graz, 1890; G. Pasquali, *Die schriftstellerische Form des Pausanias*, Hermes, XLVIII, 1913, p. 161; and C. Robert, *Pausanias als Schriftsteller*, Berlin, 1909.

OTHER HISTORIANS, ETC. *Appian* is edited by L. Mendelssohn, 2 vols. (Leipzig, 1879); vol. II, ed. 2 by P. Viereck (Leipzig, 1905); *Chairemon* by H. R. Schwyzer (Leipzig, 1932); *Phlegon of Tralles* by O. Keller in *Rerum naturalium scriptores* (Leipzig, 1877); *Polyaenus* by J. Melber (Leipzig, 1887); *Dionysius of Byzantium* by R. Güngerich (Berlin, 1927). See also F.H.G. and F. Gr. Hist.

(e) Philosophy

DIOGENES OF OENOANDA. Text, J. William (Leipzig, 1907): see also R. Philippson, Art. *s.v. Diogenes Oenoandensis* in P.W. Suppl. v.

PLATONISTS. Text of *Albinus* by C. F. Hermann in vol. VI of his Plato (Leipzig, 1853), of the commentary on the *Theaetetus* by H. Diels and W. Schubart (Berl. Klassikertexte, 2, Berlin, 1905), of *Apuleius'* philosophical works by P. Thomas (Leipzig, 1908), of *Maximus Tyrius* by H. Hobein (Leipzig, 1910); the fragments of *Atticus* collected by J. Baudry (Paris, 1931). See also J. Freudenthal, *Hellenistische Studien*, vol. III, Berlin, 1879, and K. Praechter, *Nikostratos der Platoniker*, Hermes, LVII, 1922, p. 481.

PERIPATETICS. Fragments of *Andronicus* published by F. Littig (Erlangen, 1894–5); of *Nicolaus* in F. Gr. Hist. IIA, pp. 324–430 and T. Roeper's *Lectiones Abulpharagianae*, pp. 37–42 (Danzig, 1844); *Aspasius* and *Alexander of Aphrodisias* in Comm. in Aristot. Gr. XIX, I–III, and Suppl. Aristot. II.

SEXTUS EMPIRICUS. Text, H. Mutschmann (Leipzig, 1912–14, vols. I and II only); I. Bekker (Berlin, 1842); text and translation, R. G. Bury (3 vols. London, 1933–6, not complete): see also A. Goedeckemeyer, *Die Geschichte des griechischen Skeptizismus*, Leipzig, 1905, and W. Heintz, *Studien zu Sextus Empiricus*, Halle, 1932.

POSIDONIUS. Incomplete collection of fragments, J. Bake (Leyden, 1810); the historical fragments in F. Gr. Hist. IIA, pp. 222–317. The following is a selection from the immense literature which has gathered round Posidonius: W. Capelle, *Die Schrift von der Welt*, N.J. Kl. Alt. xv, 1905, p. 529; J. F. Dobson, *The Posidonius Myth*, C.Q. XII, 1918, p. 179; I. Heinemann, *Poseidonios' metaphysische Schriften*, 2 vols. Breslau, 1921–8; W. Jaeger, *Nemesios von Emesa*, Berlin, 1914; M. Pohlenz, *De Posidonii libris περὶ παθῶν*, Jahrb. f. klass. Phil. Suppl. XXIV, 1898, p. 535; *Poseidonios' Affektenlehre und Psychologie*, Gött. Nach. 1921, p. 163; K. Reinhardt, *Poseidonios*, Munich, 1921; *Kosmos und Sympathie*, Munich, 1926; *Poseidonios über Ursprung und Entartung* (Orient und Antike, 6), Heidelberg, 1928; G. Rudberg, *Forschungen zu Poseidonios* (Skrifter. k. hum. Vetenskapssamfundet, Uppsala, xx, 3), Uppsala, 1918; and A. Schmekel, *Die Philosophie der mittleren Stoa*, Berlin, 1892.

EPICTETUS. Text and notes, J. Schweighäuser (5 vols. Leipzig, 1799–1800); text, H. Schenkl (ed. 2, Leipzig, 1916); text and translation, W. A. Oldfather (2 vols. London, 1926–8). Translations: Elizabeth Carter (London, 1758), G. Long

(London, 1877), P. E. Matheson (2 vols. Oxford, 1916). See also A. Bonhoeffer *Die Ethik des Stoikers Epictet*, Stuttgart, 1894; *Epictet und die Stoa*, Stuttgart, 1890; *Epictet und das Neue Testament*, Giessen, 1911; and W. A. Oldfather, *Contributions toward a bibliography of Epictetus* (Illinois Univ. Bulletin, 25, xii), Urbana, Ill. 1927.

MUSONIUS. Text, O. Hense (Leipzig, 1905).

HIEROCLES. Text, H. v. Arnim (*Berliner Klassikertexte*, 4, Berlin, 1906); see also R. Philippson, *Hierokles der Stoiker*, Rh. Mus. LXXXII, 1933, p. 97.

MARCUS AURELIUS. Text, J. H. Leopold (Oxford, 1908); H. Schenkl (Leipzig, 1913); text and translation, C. R. Haines (London, 1916); A. I. Trannoy (Paris, 1925). Translation, G. H. Rendall (London, 1898).

PYTHAGOREANISM. The most important pseudepigraphal works are 'Ocellus Lucanus' (ed. R. Harder, Neue Phil. Unters. 1, Berlin, 1926) and 'Timaei Locri' περὶ ψυχᾶς κόσμω (ed. C. F. Hermann in vol. IV of his edition of Plato, Leipzig, 1852). The fragments of Nigidius Figulus (ed. A. Swoboda, Leipzig, 1889) are of little philosophic interest. Fragments of Numenius in K. S. Guthrie, *Numenius of Apamea* (Grantwood, N.J. 1917). See also F. C. Conybeare, *Philostratus: the Life of Apollonius of Tyana, etc.*, text and translation, 2 vols. London, 1912; J. Hempel, *Untersuchungen zur Überlieferung von Apollonius von Tyana* (Beitr. z. Religionswiss. 4), Stockholm, 1920; G. R. S. Mead, *Apollonius of Tyana*, London, 1901; E. Meyer, *Apollonios von Tyana und Philostratos*, Hermes, LII, 1917, p. 371; and J. S. Phillimore, *Philostratus' Life of Apollonius of Tyana*, 2 vols. Oxford, 1912.

PLUTARCH. (*a*) *Morals*. Text, G. N. Bernardakis (7 vols. Leipzig, 1888–96); C. Hubert, W. Nachstädt, W. R. Paton, M. Pohlenz, W. Sieveking, J. B. Titchener, J. Wegehaupt (Leipzig, 1925– , in progress). Text and translation, F. C. Babbitt (London, 1927– , in progress). Text and unfinished commentary by D. Wyttenbach (Oxford, 1795–1830). Translated by several hands, revised by W. W. Goodwin (Boston, 1870). See also *Selected Essays of Plutarch* by T. G. Tucker and A. O. Prickard (2 vols. Oxford, 1913 and 1918).

(*b*) *Lives*. Text, C. Lindskog and K. Ziegler (4 vols. in 7, Leipzig, 1914–35). Text and translation, B. Perrin (11 vols. London, 1914–26). Translations, by Sir Thos. North (1579) from the French of Amyot (1559); by Dryden and others, revised by A. H. Clough. See also H. von Arnim, *Plutarch über Dämonen und Mantik* (Verh. d. k. Akad. v. Wet. te Amsterdam, N.R. XXII, 2, 1921); N. I. Barbu, *Les procédés de la peinture des caractères et la vérité historique dans les biographies de Plutarque*, Paris, 1934; W. Hamilton, *The myth in Plutarch's de facie*, C.Q. XXVIII, 1934, p. 24; *The myth in Plutarch's de genio*, C.Q. XXVIII, 1934, p. 175; R. Hirzel, *Plutarch* (*Das Erbe der Alten*, IV), Berlin, 1912; R. Jeuckens, *Plutarch von Chaeronea und die Rhetorik*, Strassburg, 1907; J. Oakesmith, *The Religion of Plutarch*, London, 1902; R. C. Trench, *Plutarch, his life, his lives, and his morals*, London, 1873; R. Volkmann, *Leben, Schriften und Philosophie des Plutarch von Chaeronea*, Berlin, 1869; A. Weizsäcker, *Untersuchungen über Plutarchs biographische Technik*, Berlin, 1931; and U. von Wilamowitz-Moellendorff, *Plutarch als Biograph*, in *Reden und Vorträge*, vol. II, p. 247, Berlin, 1926.

(*f*) Science

DIOSCORIDES. Text, introduction, facsimiles, etc., J. de Karabacek (2 vols. Leyden, 1906). Text, M. Wellmann (3 vols. Berlin, 1906–14). Translation, J. Goodyer (XVIIth cent., Oxford, 1934). See also C. Singer, *The Herbal in Antiquity*, J.H.S. XLVII, 1927, p. 1.

SORANUS. Text, J. Ilberg in *Corpus medicorum graecorum* IV, Leipzig, 1927.

ARETAEUS. Text, C. Hude in *Corpus med. graec.* II, Leipzig, 1923.

RUFUS. Text, C. Daremberg and E. Ruelle in *Collection des médecins grecs et latins*, Paris, 1879. A Latin version of *de podagra* edited by H. Mørland, Oslo, 1933. There are also extracts in Oribasius, *Corpus med. graec.* VI. See also J. Ilberg, *Rufus von Ephesos*, Sächs. Abh. XLI, 1931.

GALEN. Uncritical text in C. G. Kühn's *Medicorum graecorum opera*, vols. I–XX, Leipzig, 1821–33; four parts have appeared of *Corpus med. graec.* V (= Galen), and eight volumes in the Teubner series. Fragments of a commentary on the *Timaeus* were published, together with an essay on Galen, by C. Daremberg (Paris, 1848), the fragment of the *Protrepticus*, by E. Wenkebach, *Quellen u. Studien z. Gesch. d. Naturwissenschaften*, IV, 1935, p. 240; of *de placitis Platonis et Hippocratis*, ed. I. Müller, only vol. I appeared (Leipzig, 1874). Translations, C. Daremberg, *Œuvres anatomiques, physiologiques et médicales de Galien* (Paris, 1854–6), A. J. Brock, *Galen on the Natural Faculties* (London, 1916). Arabic versions (with German translations) of lost works: *Anatomy*, books 9–15, by M. Simon (2 vols. Leipzig, 1906); *Medical Nomenclature* by M. Meyerhof and J. Schacht, Berl. Abh. 1931; and see R. Walzer, *Galens Schrift über die medizinische Erfahrung*, Berl. S.B. 1932, p. 449. See also J. Ilberg, *Aus Galens Praxis*, N.J. Kl. Alt. XV, 1905, p. 276.

DIOPHANTUS. Text and Latin translation, P. Tannery, 2 vols. Leipzig, 1893–5. See also Sir T. L. Heath, *Diophantus of Alexandria*, ed. 2, Cambridge, 1910.

MENELAUS. Latin translation, E. Halley, Oxford, 1758. See also A. A. Björnbo, *Studien über Menelaos' Sphärik*, Abh. Gesch. Math. Wiss. XIV, 1902, p. 1.

THEON. Text and translation, J. Dupuis, Paris, 1892.

PTOLEMY. Text of *Syntaxis mathematica* and *Opera astronomica minora*, J. L. Heiberg, 3 vols. Leipzig, 1898–1907; German translation of the former, K. Manitius, 2 vols. Leipzig, 1912–13. Text of the *Geography*, C. F. A. Nobbe (2 vols. Leipzig, 1843); of the first five books, with Latin translation and notes, C. Müller (2 vols. and atlas), Paris, 1883–1901. Latin translation (from the Arabic) of the *Optics* by Eugenius (12th-cent. Sicilian admiral), ed. G. Govi, Turin, 1885. Text of the *Harmonics*, I. Düring, *Die Harmonienlehre des Klaudios Ptolemaios*, Gothenburg, 1930, of the *Tetrabiblos*, J. Camerarius, Nuremberg, 1535. See also O. Cuntz, *Die Geographie des Ptolemaeus, Galliae Germania Raetia Noricum Pannoniae Illyricum Italia, Handschriften, Text und Untersuchung*, Berlin, 1923: J. L. E. Dreyer, *History of the Planetary Systems from Thales to Kepler*, Cambridge, 1906, pp. 191–206; I. Düring, *Ptolemaios und Porphyrios über die Musik*, Gothenburg, 1934; F. Gisinger, Art. *s.v.* Geographie in P.W. Supplbd. IV; F. Kubitschek, Art. *s.v.* Erdmessung in P.W. Supplbd. VI; P. Schnabel, *Die Entstehungsgeschichte des kartograpischen Erdbildes des Klaudios Ptolemaeos*, Berl. S.B. 1930, p. 214; and G. Schütte, *Ptolemy's maps of Northern Europe* (with bibliography), Copenhagen, 1917.

CHAPTER XVIII

LATIN LITERATURE OF THE SILVER AGE

The following Bibliography makes no attempt to cover the vast amount of literature that has appeared upon the Silver Latin writers: what follows is a list of texts and books that have been found helpful in writing the chapter. Full references to the literature will be found in the various reports upon authors contained in the Bursian *Jahresberichte* and in the articles upon poets and prose-writers that have so far appeared in P.W.

A. General Works

Butler, H. E. *Post-Augustan Poetry*. Oxford, 1909.
Dill, S. *Roman Society from Nero to Marcus Aurelius*. Ed. 2. London, 1905, 5th reprint, 1925.
Dimsdale, M. S. *A History of Latin Literature*. London, 1915.
Kroll, W. *Studien zum Verständnis der römischen Literatur*. Stuttgart, 1924.
Nisard, D. *Études sur les poètes latins de la décadence*. 2 vols. Paris, 1849, 1888.
Plessis, F. *La poésie latine*. Paris, 1909.
Sabbadini, R. *Storia e critica di testi latini*. Catania, 1914.
Schanz, M. *Geschichte der römischen Literatur*. II, ed. 4, revised by C. Hosius, Munich, 1935.
Sikes, E. E. *Roman Poetry*. London, 1923.
Summers, W. C. *The Silver Age of Latin Literature*. London, 1920.
Terzaghi, N. *Per la Storia della Satira*. Turin, 1933.
—— *Storia della Letteratura latina da Tiberio a Giustiniano*. Milan, 1934.
Wight Duff, J. *A Literary History of Rome in the Silver Age*. London, 1927.

B. Authors and Editions, etc.

Under the name of each author are given (*a*) texts and editions, (*b*) English translations, and (*c*) books or articles upon the author.

1. *Calpurnius Siculus*

(*a*) H. Schenkl, Prague, 1885: same editor in J. P. Postgate's *Corpus Poetarum Latinorum*, II, London, 1905 (cited hereafter as *C.P.L.*): C. Giarratano, Turin, 1924. (*b*) Verse: E. J. L. Scott, London, 1890. Prose: J. Wight Duff and A. M. Duff, in the Loeb series, *Minor Latin Poets*, 1934. (*c*) E. Cesareo, *La poesia di Calpurnio Siculo*, Palermo, 1931: C. Chiavoli, *Della vita e dell' opere di T. Calpurnio Siculo*, Ragusa, 1921.

2. *Columella*

(*a*) In *Scriptores Rei Rusticae Veteres Latini*, Leipzig, 1735: Book x only, ed. V. Lundström, Uppsala, 1902, and ed. J. P. Postgate in *C.P.L.* London, 1905. (*c*) W. Becher, *De L. Iunii Moderati Columellae vita et scriptis*, Leipzig, 1897.

3. *Juvenal*

(*a*) J. E. B. Mayor, xiii Satires with commentary, 2 vols., London, 1853–95: E. G. Hardy, xiii Satires, London, 1883: L. Friedländer, 2 vols., Leipzig, 1895: J. D. Duff (omitting ii and ix), Cambridge, 1898: A. E. Housman, London, 1905, ed. 2, Cambridge, 1931: S. G. Owen, ed. 2, Oxford, 1907: O. Jahn, ed. 5 by F. Leo, Berlin, 1910: P. de Labriolle and F. Villeneuve, *Les Satires de Juvénal*

(Text and French trans.), ed. 2, Paris, 1932. (*b*) Verse: J. Dryden (and others), London, 1693: W. Gifford, London, 1802. Prose: G. G. Ramsay (with Persius), in the Loeb series, 1918. (*c*) J. de Decker, *Juvenalis declamans*, Ghent, 1913.

4. *Lucan*

(*a*) C. E. Haskins (Introduction by W. E. Heitland) with commentary, London, 1887: C. Hosius, Leipzig, 1892, ed. 3, 1913: C. M. Francken, 2 vols. (with bibliography), Leyden, 1896: W. E. Heitland, in *C.P.L.* London, 1905: A. E. Housman, Oxford, 1926. (*b*) Verse: Sir E. Ridley, London, 1905. Prose: H. T. Riley, London, 1903: J. D. Duff, in the Loeb series, 1928.

5. *Martial*

(*a*) L. Friedländer, 2 vols., with introduction and German notes, Leipzig, 1886: W. M. Lindsay, Oxford, 1902: J. D. Duff in *C.P.L.* London, 1905: W. Heraeus, Leipzig, 1925. Selections with English notes: F. A. Paley and W. H. Stone, London, ed. 2, 1890: H. M. Stephenson, London, ed. 4, 1899: R. T. Bridge and E. D. C. Lake, 2 vols., Oxford, 1908. (*b*) Verse: J. H. Pott and F. A. Wright, London, 1924. Prose: W. C. A. Ker, in the Loeb series, 2 vols., 1919–20. (*c*) G. Boissier, *Tacite* (chapter on 'Le poète Martial'), ed. 4, Paris, 1923. (Eng. trans. of 2nd ed. by W. G. Hutchison, London, 1906): K. Flower Smith, *Martial the Epigrammatist*, Baltimore, 1920: O. Weinreich, *Studien zu Martial*, Stuttgart, 1928.

6. *Persius*

(*a*) J. Conington and H. Nettleship, text and translation, ed. 3, Oxford, 1893: S. G. Owen (with Juvenal), Oxford, 1902: Fr. Bücheler, Berlin, ed. 4, 1904 (rec. F. Leo, 1910): W. C. Summers in *C.P.L.* London, 1905: A. Pretor, Cambridge, 1907. (*b*) Verse: J. Dryden, London, 1693. Prose: G. G. Ramsay (with Juvenal), in the Loeb series, 1918: J. Tate, Oxford, 1930. (*c*) R. C. Kukula, *Persius und Nero*, Graz, 1923: F. Villeneuve, *Essai sur Perse*, Paris, 1918, and *Les satyres de Perse*, Paris, 1918.

7. *Petronius*

(*a*) Fr. Bücheler, ed. maior, Berlin, 1862; ed. minor (6th ed.), Berlin, 1922: L. Friedländer (*Cena Trimalchionis*), Leipzig, 1891: A. Ernout (*Satiricon* and Fragments), Paris, 1922. (*b*) W. D. Lowe, with text. Cambridge, 1905: M. Heseltine, in the Loeb series, 1913. (*c*) F. F. Abbott, *Petronius* (in *Society and Politics of Ancient Rome*), London, 1914: E. Collignon, *Étude sur Pétrone*, Paris, 1892: R. Heinze, *Petron und der griechische Roman*, Hermes, xxxiv, 1899, pp. 494–519: E. Paratori, *Il Satyricon di Petronio*, 2 vols., Florence, 1933: H. Stubbe, *Die Verseinlagen in Petron*, Leipzig, 1933: P. Thomas, *L'âge et l'auteur du Satyricon*, Ghent, 1905.

8. *Pliny the Elder*

(*a*) L. Jan, Leipzig, 1854–65, ed. 3, C. Mayhoff, 1892–1909: K. Jex-Blake and E. Sellars (Chapters on the History of Art), London, 1896: K. C. Bailey (Chapters on Chemical Subjects), Dublin, 1929. (*b*) Philemon Holland, London, 1601: J. Bostock and H. T. Riley, London, 1898. (*c*) Joh. Müller, *Der Stil des älteren Plinius*, Innsbrück, 1883.

9. *Pliny the Younger*

(*a*) H. Keil, ed. minor, Leipzig, 1853, ed. maior, Leipzig, 1870: C. F. W. Müller, Leipzig, 1903: R. C. Kukula, Leipzig, 1908, ed. 2, 1912: M. Schuster, Leipzig, 1933. E. G. Hardy (The letters to Trajan), London, 1889: E. T. Merrill

(Letters), Leipzig, 1922. There are numerous editions of separate books of the letters, of which the following may be noticed: Book III, J. E. B. Mayor, London, 1880: VI, J. D. Duff, Cambridge, 1906: X, E. G. Hardy, London, 1889, as well as various selections. (*b*) Wm. Melmoth's translation of 1746 revised by W. M. L. Hutchinson in the Loeb series, 2 vols., 1915. (*c*) A. M. Guillemin, *Pline et la vie littéraire de son temps*, Paris, 1929: see also Bursian, CCXXI, 1929, pp. 1–63.

10. *Quintilian*

(*a*) C. Halm, 2 vols., Leipzig, 1868–9 (ed. 5, 1913): E. Bonnell, Leipzig, 1884–9: L. Radermacher, Leipzig, 1907–35: Book X, W. Peterson, Oxford, 1891 (with introduction and notes): Book I, F. H. Colson, Cambridge, 1924 (with introduction and notes). (*b*) H. E. Butler, 4 vols. in the Loeb series, London, 1921–2. (*c*) See Bursian, CXCII, 1922, pp. 215–308.

11. *Seneca the Philosopher*

I. *Philosophical Works.*

(*a*) Vol. I. 1, E. Hermes, Leipzig, 1904; I. 2, C. Hosius, ed. 2, 1914; II, A. Gercke, 1907; III, O. Hense, ed. 2, 1914. (Vol. IV containing Fragments and Index is in preparation.) W. C. Summers, *Select Letters*, London, 1910. (*b*) J. Clarke and Sir A. Geikie, *Quaestiones Naturales* (Physical Science in the time of Nero), London, 1910: Letters, R. M. Gummere, 3 vols. in the Loeb series, 1917–25: Moral Essays, J. W. Basore, 3 vols. in the Loeb series, 1928–35: E. P. Barker, *Letters to Lucilius*, 2 vols., Oxford, 1932. (*c*) See Bursian, CXCIII, 1923, pp. 109–214.

II. *Tragedies.*

(*a*) R. Peiper and G. Richter, Leipzig, 1867; ed. 2 by R. Peiper, Leipzig, 1902. (*b*) Verse: F. J. Miller, Chicago, Ill., 1907. Prose: W. Bradshaw, London, 1902: F. J. Miller, in the Loeb series, 2 vols., 1916–17. (*c*) H. E. Butler, *Post-Augustan Poetry*, Oxford, 1909: T. S. Eliot, *Selected Essays* (Chapter on Shakespeare and the Stoicism of Seneca, pp. 126–140). Ed. 2, London, 1934: L. Herrmann, *Le Théâtre de Sénèque*, Paris, 1924: F. L. Lucas, *Seneca and Elizabethan Tragedy*, Cambridge, 1922: E. M. Spearing, *The Elizabethan translations of Seneca's Tragedies*, Cambridge, 1912.

III. *The Apocolocyntosis.*

(*a*) Fr. Bücheler, Bonn, 1864–7; ed. minor (with Petronius), 1871; ed. 6 by W. Heraeus, Berlin, 1922: A. P. Ball (with commentary and translation), New York, 1902: O. Weinreich (with commentary and translation), Berlin, 1923. (*b*) W. H. D. Rouse (with Petronius), in the Loeb series, 1913.

12. *Silius Italicus*

(*a*) L. Bauer, 2 vols., Leipzig, 1890–2: W. C. Summers in *C.P.L.* London, 1905. (*b*) J. D. Duff, in the Loeb series, 2 vols., 1934.

13. *Statius*

(*a*) *Thebais* and *Achilleis*: A. S. Wilkins in *C.P.L.* London, 1905: H. W. Garrod, Oxford, 1906. *Silvae*: F. Vollmer (with German commentary), Leipzig, 1898: G. A. Davies in *C.P.L.* London, 1905: J. S. Phillimore, Oxford, 1905, ed. 2, 1918: A. Klotz, ed. 2, Leipzig, 1911. (*b*) Verse: Alexander Pope (*Thebaid* I), 1712. Prose: D. A. Slater (*Silvae*), Oxford, 1908: J. H. Mozley (*Silvae* and *Thebais*), 2 vols. in the Loeb series, 1928. (*c*) L. Legras, *La Thébaïde de Stace*, Paris, 1905.

14. *Suetonius*

(*a*) C. L. Roth, Leipzig, 1858, ed. 3, 1904; M. Ihm, ed. maior, Leipzig, 1907; ed. minor, Leipzig, 1908. (Vol. 1 only, *de vita Caesarum libri viii*.) (*b*) J. C. Rolfe, 2 vols. in the Loeb series, 1914: Philemon Holland, London, 1606, ed. by J. H. Freese, London, 1923. (*c*) A. Macé, *Essai sur Suétone*, Paris, 1900: see also Bursian, CCXXVI, 1930, pp. 207–232.

15. *Tacitus*

(*a*) *Annals:* W. Pfitzer, Gotha (4 vols.), 1885–93: H. Furneaux, Oxford, 2 vols., ed. 2, 1896–1907: C. D. Fisher, Oxford, 1906: E. Köstermann, Leipzig, 1932–4. *Histories:* C. Heraeus, Leipzig, ed. 4, 1885: E. Wolff, 2 vols., ed. 2, Berlin, 1914–26: C. Halm, ed. 5 (G. Andresen), Leipzig, 1916. *Agricola:* A. J. Church and W. J. Brodribb, London, 1869, ed. 2 (with *Germania*), 1881: H. Furneaux, Oxford, 1898 (revised by J. G. C. Anderson, Oxford, 1922). *Germania:* H. Furneaux, Oxford, 1894: W. Reeb, Leipzig, 1930. *Dialogus:* W. Peterson (with commentary), Oxford, 1893: A. Gudeman, Leipzig, ed. 2, 1914. (*b*) *Annals:* G. G. Ramsay, London, 1904: J. Jackson, in the Loeb series, 1931– . *Histories:* W. H. Fyfe, 2 vols., Oxford, 1912: G. G. Ramsay, London, 1915: C. H. Moore, in the Loeb series, 1925–31. *Agricola* and *Germania:* M. Hutton, in the Loeb series (with the *Dialogus*), 1914. *Dialogus:* W. Peterson, in the Loeb series, 1914. (*c*) (A select list only.) G. Boissier, *Tacite*. Ed. 4, Paris, 1923; Eng. trans. of the 2nd ed. by W. G. Hutchison, London, 1906: E. Courbaud, *Les procédés d'art de Tacite dans les Histoires*, Paris, 1918: N. Eriksson, *Studien zu den Annalen des Tacitus*, Lund, 1934: C. Marchesi, *Tacito*, Messina-Roma, 1924: E. Norden, *Die Germanische Urgeschichte in Tacitus Germania*, Leipzig, ed. 2, 1922: R. Reitzenstein, *Tacitus und sein Werk*, Leipzig, 1926.

16. *Valerius Flaccus*

(*a*) G. Thilo, Halle, 1863: P. Langen, 2 vols. with commentary, Berlin, 1896–7: J. B. Bury in *C.P.L.* London, 1905: O. Kramer, Leipzig, 1913. (*b*) J. H. Mozley, in the Loeb series, 1934. (*c*) W. C. Summers, *A Study of the Argonautica of Valerius Flaccus*, Cambridge, 1894.

CHAPTER XIX

SOCIAL LIFE IN ROME AND ITALY

A. Ancient Sources

The footnotes to the text of this chapter give many of the more important references to ancient authors who have been drawn upon. In Latin, they include Seneca and Petronius; the elder Pliny and Quintilian; Statius, Juvenal and Martial; Tacitus, the younger Pliny and Suetonius; also, as the survey is extended to the Antonine period, Apuleius, Fronto and Gellius, and, later, the *Historia Augusta*. In Greek, the chief available sources are Musonius Rufus, Plutarch (*Moralia*, especially *De Educatione Puerorum, De Iside et Osiri*), Dio Chrysostom and Dio Cassius, Maximus Tyrius (*Dissertationes*), Polemo (*Declamationes duae*), Arrian's Ἐπικτήτου Διατριβαί and Ἐγχειρίδιον, Aelius Aristides, Philostratus and Marcus Aurelius' *Meditations*.

In addition, evidence from inscriptions is furnished by *Carmina Latina Epigraphica* in Buecheler and Riese's *Anthologia Latina*, II. i. ii. iii (including Lommatzsch's *Supplementum*), Leipzig, 1897–1926, and by the *Corpus Inscriptionum Latinarum*, especially vols. IV, VI, IX–XI, XV; and archaeological evidence by *Notizie degli Scavi di antichità* (Accademia Nazionale dei Lincei, 1877 *sqq.*).

B. Modern Works

Most of the general histories of the Empire and of the monographs on individual emperors contain chapters on social life and customs; for these reference should be made to the General Bibliography, especially the works of Duruy, Friedländer, Gibbon (ch. ii), Nilsson and Rostovtzeff, and to the Bibliographies on the Flavians (Chapter I), Nerva and Trajan (Chapter V), and Hadrian and the Antonines (Chapters VIII and IX). For works on Lucian, Plutarch and the 'Second Sophistic' see the Bibliography to Chapter XVII.

Abbott, F. F. *Society and Politics in Ancient Rome.* London, 1914.

Allain, E. *Pline le jeune et ses héritiers.* 4 vols. Paris, 1901–2.

Bardt, C. *Römische Characterköpfe in Briefen vornehmlich aus Caesarischer und Traianischer Zeit.* Leipzig, 1925.

Barrow, R. H. *Slavery in the Roman Empire.* London, 1928 (with Bibliography).

Boissier, G. *La Religion romaine d'Auguste aux Antonins.* 2 vols., ed. 4, Paris, 1892.

—— *L'Opposition sous les Césars.* Paris, 1875.

Brassloff, S. *Staat und Gesellschaft in der römischen Kaiserzeit.* (Zwei Vorträge.) Vienna-Leipzig, 1933.

Brock, D. *Studies in Fronto and his Age.* Cambridge, 1911.

Cagnat, R. and V. Chapot, *Manuel d'archéologie romaine.* Paris, 1917–20.

Chapot, V. *The Roman World.* Eng. trans., London, 1928. [The study of local life and economic conditions in the provinces is illuminating by way of parallel or contrast to Rome itself.]

Cumont, F. *After-Life in Roman Paganism.* Yale Univ. Press, 1927.

—— *Astrology and Religion among the Greeks and Romans.* New York and London, 1912.

—— *Les Mystères de Mithra.* Ed. 2, Brussels, 1902; ed. 3, Paris, 1913. [Trans. of earlier ed., Chicago and London, 1903.]

—— *Les religions orientales dans le paganisme romain.* Ed. 4, Paris, 1929.

—— *Textes et monuments figurés relatifs aux mystères de Mithra.* Brussels, 1896–9.

Davis, W. S. *The influence of wealth in imperial Rome.* New York, 1910.

Denis, J. *Histoire des théories et des idées morales dans l'antiquité.* Paris, 1879.

Dieterich, A. *Eine Mithrasliturgie.* Leipzig, 1903; ed. 2, 1910.

Dill, S. *Roman Society from Nero to Marcus Aurelius.* Ed. 2, London, 1905, 5th reprint, 1925.

Duff, A. M. *Freedmen in the Early Roman Empire.* Oxford, 1928 [with Bibliography].

Duff, J. Wight. *A Literary History of Rome in the Silver Age.* London, 1927.

Esser, J. J. *De Pauperum cura apud Romanos.* Diss. Kampen, 1902.

Gasquet, A. *Essai sur le culte et les mystères de Mithra.* Paris, 1899.

Gelzer, M. *Die Nobilität der Kaiserzeit.* Hermes, L, 1915, p. 395.

Glover, T. R. *The Conflict of Religions in the Early Roman Empire.* London, 1909.

Greene, W. C. *The Achievement of Rome.* Cambridge, Mass., 1933 [esp. the final chapter].

Gusman, P. *Pompei: the city, its life and art.* Eng. trans., London, 1900.

Gwynn, A. *Roman Education from Cicero to Quintilian.* Oxford, 1926.

Heitland, W. E. *Agricola: A Study of Agriculture and Rustic Life in the Greco-Roman World from the point of view of labour.* Cambridge, 1921.

Kromayer, J. *Staat und Gesellschaft der Römer* in Hinneberg's *Kultur der Gegenwart,* ed. 2, Leipzig-Berlin, 1923.

Lafaye, G. *Histoire du culte des divinités d'Alexandrie (Sérapis, Isis, Harpocrate et Anubis) hors de l'Égypte.* Paris, 1884.

Marquardt, J. and Th. Mommsen, *Handbuch der röm. Alterthümer,* in which Marquardt's *Das Privatleben der Römer* is vol. vii, Leipzig, 1887.

Martha, C. *Les moralistes sous l'empire romain, philosophes et poètes.* Paris, 1865; ed. 8, 1907.

Mau, A. *Pompeii: Its Life and Art.* (Trans. by F. W. Kelsey.) London, 1899.

Nock, A. D. *Conversion: the Old and the New in Religion from Alexander to Augustine.* Oxford, 1933 [esp. chaps. vi–ix].

Renan, E. *Marc-Aurèle et la fin du monde antique.* Ed. 5, Paris, 1883.

Showerman, G. *Rome and the Romans.* New York, 1931.

Stein, A. *Der römische Ritterstand.* Munich, 1927 [esp. ch. vi].

Toutain, J. *Les cultes païens dans l'empire romain.* Paris, 1908–11 [esp. II, ch. iv, Le Culte de Mithra].

Tucker, T. G. *Life in the Roman World of Nero and St Paul.* London, 1910.

Waldstein, C. and L. Shoobridge, *Herculaneum: Past, present and future.* London, 1908.

Wilkins, A. S. *Roman Education.* Cambridge, 1905.

Wissowa, G. *Religion und Kultus der Römer* in Müller's Handbuch, ed. 2. Munich, 1912.

C. Articles

In Daremberg-Saglio: *collegium* (G. Humbert), *expositio* (G. Humbert), *fabri* (C. Jullian), *Isis* (G. Lafaye), *mercator* (R. Cagnat), *mercatura* (R. Cagnat and M. Besnier), *negotiator* (R. Cagnat), *religio* (J. Toutain).

In *Encyclopaedia of Religion and Ethics,* ed. J. Hastings: *education, Roman* (J. Wight Duff), *Isis* (G. Showerman), *Mithraism* (H. Stuart Jones).

In Pauly-Wissowa: *Collegium* (Kornemann), *Industrie und Handel* (Gummerus), *Religio* (Kobbert).

In Roscher's *Ausführliches Lexikon der griech. und röm. Mythologie: Isis* (in Egypt), E. Meyer; *Isis* (outside Egypt), W. Drexler.

CHAPTER XX

ART FROM NERO TO THE ANTONINES

A. General

The reader should consult the Bibliographies to the Chapters on Art in Vol. ix, p. 965, and in Vol. x, p. 957.

Rodenwaldt, G. *Römisches in der antiken Kunst.* Arch. Anz. xxviii/ix, 1923/4, p. 365.
—— *Die Kunst der Antike (Hellas und Rom).* Propyläen-Kunstgeschichte, iii, 2, Berlin, 1930, pp. 501 *sqq.*
Strong, E. *Art in Ancient Rome.* 2 vols., ed. 2, London, 1930.

B. Nero-Trajan

On the importance of Nero's reign in the history of Imperial art see G. Rodenwaldt in *Gnomon,* ii, 1926, p. 337.

(i) *Architecture*

Bartoli, A. *Scavi del Palatino (Domus Augustana),* 1926–28. N.S.A. 1929, p. 1.
Boethius, A. *Appunti sul Mercato di Traiano.* Rome, 1931.
—— The Neronian 'nova urbs.' Corolla Archaeologica, Lund, 1932, p. 84.
Choisy, A. *L'art de bâtir chez les Romains.* Paris, 1873.
—— *Histoire de l'architecture.* Paris, n.d.
van Deman, E. B. *Methods of determining the date of Roman concrete monuments.* A.J.A. xvi, 1902, pp. 250, 387.
—— *The* sacra via *of Nero.* Mem. Amer. Acad. in Rome, v, 1925, p. 115.
von Gerkan, A. *Das Obergeschoss des flavischen Amphitheaters.* Röm. Mitt. xl, 1925, p. 11.
—— Review of Krencker and Krüger (see below) in *Gnomon,* viii, 1932, p. 31.
Krencker, D. and E. Krüger, *Die Trierer Kaiserthermen.* Augsburg, 1929.
Lehner, H. *Vetera.* (Römisch-Germanische Forschungen, iv.) Berlin, 1930.
Leopold, H. V. R. *Colosseum.* Med. d. Nederl. Hist. Inst. te Rome, iv, 1934, p. 39.
Lugli, G. *La villa di Domiziano sui colli Albani.* Bull. Comm. Arch. 1918–1922.
—— *I Monumenti antichi di Roma e Suburbio.* 1, Rome, 1931.
Noack, F. *Triumph und Triumphbogen.* (Vorträge der Bibliothek Warburg, 1925/6.) Leipzig, 1928.
—— *Die Baukunst des Altertums.* Berlin, n.d. (1910).
Oelmann, F. *Die Ausgrabung des römischen Lagers von Vetera.* B.J. 136/7, 1932, p. 273.
Ricci, C. *La Via dell' Impero.* Rome, 1932.
Rivoira, G. T. *Architettura romana.* Milan, 1921. (English trans. by G. McN. Rushforth, Oxford, 1925.)
Rostowzew, M. *Pompeianische Landschaften und römische Villen.* J.D.A.I. xix, 1904, p. 103.

(ii) *Painting*

Diepolder, H. *Untersuchungen zur Komposition der römisch-kampanischen Wandgemälde.* Röm. Mitt. xli, 1926, p. 1.
Ippel, A. and J. Schubring. *Neapel.* (Berühmte Kunststätten, Bd. 77/78.) Leipzig, 1927, pp. 123 *sqq.*

Mau, A. *Geschichte der dekorativen Wandmalerei in Pompeji.* Berlin, 1882.
Rodenwaldt, G. *Die Komposition der pompejanischen Wandgemälde.* Berlin, 1909.
Wirth, F. *Der Stil der kampanischen Wandgemälde.* Röm. Mitt. XLII, 1927, p. 1.

(iii) *Relief*

von Domaszewski, A. *Die politische Bedeutung des Traiansbogens in Benevent.* Jahreshefte II, 1899, pp. 173 *sqq.*
Lehmann-Hartleben, K. *Die Traianssäule.* Berlin, 1926 (cf. review by F. Koepp, in *G.G.A.* 1926, pp. 370 *sqq.*).
Michon, E. *Bas-reliefs historiques romains.* Mon. Piot, XVII, 1910, pp. 145 *sqq.*
Philippi, A. *Über die römischen Triumphalreliefs.* (Sächs. Abh. VI.) Leipzig, 1872.
Rizzo, G. *La battaglia di Alessandro.* Boll. d'Arte, V, 1925/6, p. 529.
Rostovtzeff, M. *Gesellschaft und Wirtschaft im römischen Kaiserreich.* Leipzig, 1930, I, pp. 206 *sqq.*; II, pp. 248 *sqq.*
Sieveking, J. *Das römische Relief.* Festschrift P. Arndt. Munich, 1925, pp. 14 *sqq.*
Snijder, G. A. S. *Der Traiansbogen in Benevent.* J.D.A.I. XLI, 1926, p. 94.
Wace, A. J. B. *Studies in Roman historical reliefs.* B.S.R. IV, 1907, p. 227.
Wickhoff, F. *Römische Kunst* (Die Wiener Genesis). Berlin, 1912. (English transl. by E. Strong, London, 1900.)

(iv) *Portraiture*

Hekler, A. *Greek and Roman Portraits.* London, 1912.
Sieveking, J. *Zum Bildnis des Kaisers Vitellius.* Habich-Festschrift, Munich, 1928.
West, R. *Römische Porträt-Plastik.* Vol. II, Munich, 1933.

C. HADRIAN-COMMODUS

(a) *Rome and the Latin West*

The works cited in section B under Choisy, Hekler, Krencker, Michon and Sieveking should also be consulted.

Altmann, W. *Architektur und Ornamentik des antiken Sarkophagreliefs.* Berlin, 1902.
Bartoccini, R. *Il Foro Imperiale di Leptis.* Africa Ital. I, 1925, p. 53, II, 1926, p. 30.
—— *Le Terme di Lepcis* (*Leptis Magna*). Africa Ital. IV, 1929.
Buschor, E. *Die hadrianischen Jagdbilder.* Röm. Mitt. XXXVIII/IX, 1923/4, pp. 52 *sqq.*
Calza, G. *Ostia. Guida storico-monumentale.* Rome, 1925.
—— *La preminenza dell' Insula.* Mon. Ant. XXIII, 1914, p. 541.
Delbrück, R. *Antike Porphyrwerke.* Berlin, 1932.
Hekler, A. *Studien zur römischen Porträtkunst.* Jahreshefte XXI/II, 1922/24, p. 172.
Lantier, R. *Les grands champs de fouilles de l'Afrique du Nord.* Arch. Anz. 1931, p. 461.
Lippold, G. *Kopien und Umbildungen griechischer Statuen.* Munich, 1923.
Michon, E. "*Extispicium.*" Mon. Piot, XXXII, 1932, p. 61.
Nock, A. D. *Cremation and Burial in the Roman Empire.* Harv. Theol. Rev. XXV, 1932, p. 321.
Robert, C. *Die antiken Sarkophag-Reliefs.* II, III, 1–3, Berlin, 1890–1919.
Rodenwaldt, G. *Gemälde aus dem Grabe der Nasonier.* Röm. Mitt. XXXII, 1917, p. 1.
—— *Stilwandel in die antonin-Kunst.* Berl. Abh. 1935.
Rosi, G. *Pantheon.* Bull. Comm. Arch. LIX, 1931, p. 227.
Toynbee, J. *A Roman Sarcophagus at Pawlowsk and its fellows.* J.R.S. XVII, 1927, p. 14.
—— *The Hadrianic School.* Cambridge, 1934.
Wegner, M. *Die kunstgeschichtliche Stellung der Marcussäule.* J.D.A.I. XLVI, 1931, p. 61.

von Wilamowitz-Moellendorff, U. *Der Glaube der Hellenen.* Berlin, ii, pp. 428 *sqq.*
Wirth, F. *Römische Wandmalerei vom Untergang Pompejis bis Hadrian.* Röm. Mitt·
   xliv, 1929, p. 91.

(*b*) The Greek East

Breccia, E. *Alexandria ad Aegyptum.* Bergamo, 1922.
—— *Le musée gréco-romain,* 1922–32. Alexandria, 1924–33.
Corinth. *Corinth. Results of Excavations conducted by the American School of Classical
   Studies at Athens.* Vols. i–x. Cambridge, Mass. 19– onwards.
Drerup, H. *Die Datierung des Mumienporträts.* Paderborn, 1933.
Dussaud, R., P. Deschamps and H. Seyrig, *La Syrie antique et médiévale illustrée.*
   Paris, 1931.
Keil, J. xii–xvii *vorläufiger Bericht über die Ausgrabungen in Ephesos.* Jahreshefte
   xxiii–xxviii, 1926–33.
von Massow, W. *Führer durch das Pergamonmuseum.* Berlin, 1932.
Miletus. *Milet.* Die Ergebnisse der Ausgrabungen und Untersuchungen, heraus-
   gegeben von Th. Wiegand. Berlin, 1906 onwards.
Morey, C. R. *The Sarcophagus of Claudia Antonia Sabina.* Sardis, Vol. v, i,
   Leyden, 1924. Cf. review by G. Rodenwaldt in *Gnomon,* i, 1925, pp. 121 *sqq.*
Neugebauer, K. A. *Herodes Atticus.* Die Antike, x, 1934, p. 92.
Poulsen, F. and K. Rhomaios, *Erster vorläufiger Bericht über die dänisch-griechischen
   Ausgrabungen von Kalydon.* Danske Videnskab. Selskab. Hist.-Fil. Med. xiv,
   1927.
Rodenwaldt, G. *Der Klinensarkophag von S. Lorenzo.* J.D.A.I. xlv, 1930, p. 116.
—— *Sarcophagi from Xanthos.* J.H.S. liii, 1933, p. 181.
Ronczewski, K. *Description des chapiteaux corinthiens et variés.* Acta Universitatis
   Latviensis, xvi, 1927.
Schede, M. *Ausgrabungen in Ankyra und Aezani.* Gnomon, v, 1929, p. 60.
Schlumberger, D. *Les formes anciennes du chapiteau corinthien.* Syria, xiv, 1933, p. 283.
Weigand, E. *Propylon und Bogentor in der östlichen Reichskunst.* Wiener Jahrb. f.
   Kunstgesch. v, 1928, p. 71.
—— *Die kunstgeschichtliche Stellung der palmyrenischen Architektur.* Palmyra,
   herausgegeben von Th. Wiegand, Berlin, 1932, vol. i, pp. 151 *sqq.*
Wisson, M. A. *The stoa of Hadrian at Athens.* B.S.R. xi, 1925, p. 50.

(*c*) Art on the borders of the Empire
(see also the Bibliography to chap. xv, Part II, B ix)

Breasted, T. *Oriental forerunners of Byzantine painting.* Chicago, 1923.
Cumont, F. *Fouilles de Doura-Europos.* Paris, 1926.
Dura. *Excavations at Dura-Europos.* Preliminary Reports i–v, 1929–1934.
Ferri, S. *Arte Romana sul Reno.* Milan, 1931.
—— *Problemi di arte Pannonica.* Boll. d' Arte, 1931/2, p. 307.
—— *Nuovi monumenti plastici dello Zeus di Bitinia.* Historia, vi, 1932, p. 238.
Ingholt, H. *Studier over Palmyrensk Skulptur.* Copenhagen, 1928.
von Massow, W. *Die Grabmäler von Neumagen.* Berlin, 1932.
Rodenwaldt, G. *Zeus Bronton.* J.D.A.I. xxxiv, 1919, p. 77.
—— *Neumagener Köpfe.* Arch. Anz. 1927, p. 192.
Schlosser, J. *Zur Genesis der mittelalterlichen Kunstanschauung,* in *Präludien* (Vor-
   träge und Aufsätze von J. Schlosser), Berlin, 1928.
Schober, A. *Zur Entstehung und Bedeutung der provinzialrömischen Kunst.* Jahres-
   hefte xxvi, 1930, p. 9.
Seyrig, H. *Trois bas-reliefs religieux de type Palmyrénien.* Syria, xiii, 1932, p. 258.
Thiersch, H. *An den Rändern des römischen Reichs.* Munich, 1911.

CHAPTER XXI
CLASSICAL ROMAN LAW

(This bibliography is merely supplementary to that appended to Chapter XXI of Vol. IX.)

I. Texts

Codex Iustinianus, rec. P. Krueger (= Vol. II of the stereotyped Berlin *Corpus Iuris Civilis*). Berlin, 1915.

Kuebler, B. *Gai Institutionum libri quattuor.* Ed. 7, Leipzig, 1935 (containing the new fragments).

Schulz, F. *Die Epitome Ulpiani.* Bonn, 1926.

Hunt, A. S. *Oxyrhynchus Papyri* XVII, no. 2103.

Editions of the new fragments of Gaius:

Arangio Ruiz, V. *Pubblicazioni della Società Italiana per la ricerca dei papiri Greci e Latini in Egitto.* No. 1182. Florence, 1933. See also "*Il nuovo Gaio. Discussioni e Revisioni*," Bull. del Ist. di Diritto Romano, XLII, 1935, p. 571.

Levy, E. *Z. d. Sav.-Stift.* XLVIII, 1928, p. 536 and LIV, 1934, p. 258.

de Zulueta, F. *J.R.S.* XXIV, 1934, p. 168 and XXV, 1935, p. 19 (with references to the literature on the fragments).

Collinet, P. *Les nouveaux fragments des Institutes de Gaius (PSI 1182).* Rev. Hist. de Droit Français et Étranger, 1934, p. 81.

II. Sources and History of Jurisprudence

Arnò, C. *Cassio.* Memorie della R. Accademia di Scienze, Lettere ed Arti in Modena, IV, Modena, 1925; *Nuovi Studi su Cassio,* Modena, 1925; *Le due grande correnti della giurisprudenza Romana,* Modena, 1926; and other writings.

Baviera, G. *Le due Scuole dei giureconsulti Romani.* Scritti giuridici, vol. I, Palermo, 1909, pp. 109 *sqq.*

Berger, A. Art. *s.v.* Iurisprudentia in P.W.

Bremer, F. P. *Die Rechtslehrer und Rechtsschulen im römischen Kaiserreich.* Berlin, 1868.

Buckland, W. W. *Marcian.* Studi in onore di Salvatore Riccobono, I, p. 275. Palermo, 1935.

Buhl, H. *Salvius Iulianus.* Vol. I, Heidelberg, 1886.

Costa, E. *Papiniano.* Vol. I, Bologna, 1894.

Fitting, H. *Alter und Folge der Schriften römischer Juristen.* Ed. 2, Halle, 1908.

Guarneri Citati, A. *Indice delle parole, frasi e costrutti ritenuti indicio di Interpolazione.* Milan, 1927: *Supplemento,* Palermo, 1934.

Kalb, W. *Roms Juristen nach ihrer Sprache dargestellt.* Leipzig, 1890, and other writings.

Kniep, F. *Der Rechtsgelehrte Gaius.* Jena, 1910.

Kornemann, E. *Der Jurist Salvius Julianus und Kaiser Didius Julianus.* Klio, VI, 1906, p. 178.

Kuebler, B. Art. *s.v. Rechtsschulen* in P.W.

Lenel, O. *Das Sabinussystem.* Strassburg, 1892.

Nordeblad, J. B. *Gaiusstudien.* Lund, 1932.

Pernice, A. *Ulpian als Schriftsteller,* Berl. S.B. 1885, pp. 443 *sqq.*

Rechnitz, W. *Studien zu Salvius Julianus.* Weimar, 1925.

Sokolowski, P. *Die Philosophie im Privatrecht.* Halle, vol. I, 1902, vol. II, 1907.

See also articles in P.W. on the different jurists, especially on *Gaius* (2) Kuebler, B; *Paulus* (*s.v.* Iulius [382]) Berger, A. and *Ulpianus* (*s.v.* Domitius [88]) Jörs, P.

Interpolations and Glosses

This question arises in nearly all recent Romanistic work. A good general account of the methods used for the discovery of interpolations will be found in H. Appleton, *Des Interpolations dans les Pandectes*, Paris, 1895, and of the whole question in E. Albertario, *Introduzione storica allo studio del Diritto Romano Giustinianeo*, Milan, 1935; P. Bonfante, *Storia del diritto romano*, II, pp. 126–171, Milan, 1923 (French trans. by J. Carrière and F. Fournier, revised by the author, Paris, 1928); and F. Schulz, *Einführung in das Studium der Digesten*, Tübingen, 1916.

The following is a selection from works specially devoted to the subject:

Levy, E. and E. Rabel. *Index Interpolationum quae in Iustiniani Digestis inesse dicuntur.* I, *ad libros Digestorum* I–XX *pertinens.* II, *ad libros Digestorum* XXI–XXXV *pertinens. Supplementum* I, *ad libros Digestorum* I–XII *pertinens.* Weimar, 1929, 1929, 1931.

Albertario, E. *La Crisi del Metodo interpolazionistico.* Studi in Onore di P. Bonfante, I, pp. 609 *sqq.*, Pavia, 1930; *Glossemi e Interpolazioni pregiustinianee* (Atti del Congresso Internazionale di Diritto Romano, Rome, 1933), I, p. 385. Pavia, 1934; and many other writings.

Beseler, G. V. *Beiträge zur Kritik der Römischen Rechtsquellen.* 5 Hefte, Tübingen, 1910, 1911, 1913, 1920; Leipzig, 1931; and many other writings, especially in Z. d. Sav.-Stift.

Buckland, W. W. *Interpolations in the Digest.* Yale Law Journal, XXXIII, 1924, p. 343.

Chiazzese, L. *Confronti testuali. Parte Generale.* Cortona, 1933.

De Francisci, P. *Premessi storiche alla Critica del Digesto.* (Conferenze per il XIV Centenario delle Pandette.) Milan, 1931, pp. 1–38.

Felgentraeger, W. *Die Literatur zur Echtheitsfrage der römischen Juristenschriften.* Symbolae Friburgenses in honorem Ottonis Lenel, p. 357. Leipzig, n.d. (*c.* 1935).

Gradenwitz, O. *Interpolationen in den Pandekten.* Berlin, 1887.

Pringsheim, F. *Die archaistische Tendenz Justinians.* Studi in Onore di P. Bonfante, I, p. 549, Pavia, 1930; *Animus in Roman Law*, Law Quarterly Rev. XLIX, 1933, p. 43 and p. 379 and many other writings.

Riccobono, S. *Nichilismo critico-storico nel campo del diritto romano e medievale.* Annuario della R. Università degli Studi di Palermo. Palermo, 1930. *Origine e Sviluppo del Domma della Volontà nel Diritto.* Atti del Congresso Internazionale di Diritto Romano. Rome, I, p. 177, Pavia, 1934; *La Verità sulle pretese Tendenze Archaiche di Giustiniano*, Milan, 1931, and many other writings.

Solazzi, S. *Glosse a Gaio* I, II. Palermo, 1931; Pavia, 1933. (In course of publication.)

Wenger, L. *Der heutige Stand der römischen Rechtswissenschaft.* Munich, 1927.

III. General and Miscellaneous Works

Betti, E. *Diritto Romano. Parte Generale.* Padua, 1935.

Chiazzese, L. *Introduzione allo Studio del Diritto Romano privato.* Rome, 1931.

Costa, E. *Storia del Diritto Romano Privato.* Ed. 2. Turin, 1925.

Huvelin, P. *Cours Élémentaire du Droit Romain.* Paris, 1927–1929.

Jörs-Kunkel-Wenger, *Römisches Privatrecht, auf Grund des Werkes von P. Jörs.* Berlin, 1935.

Monier, R. *Manuel Élémentaire de Droit Romain.* I, Paris, 1935.

Riccobono, S. *Corso di Diritto Romano.* II, III, Milan, 1933–1935.

Schulz, F. *Prinzipien des Römischen Rechts.* Munich, 1934.

IV. Special Works on Civil Procedure

Arangio Ruiz, V. *Cours de Droit Romain* (Les Actions). Naples, 1935.
von Beseler, G. *Juristische Miniaturen*. Leipzig, 1929, pp. 113 *sqq*.
Jolowicz, H. F. *Procedure in iure and apud iudicem*. Atti del Congresso Internazionale
    di Diritto Romano, Bologna, 1933. II, pp. 59 *sqq*., Pavia, 1934.
Mazeaud, J. *La Nomination du Iudex Unus*. Paris, 1933.
Pringsheim, F. *Natura Contractus* und *Natura Actionis*. Studia et Documenta
    Historiae et Iuris, 1, Rome, 1935.

V. Special Works on Criminal Law

Costa, E. *Crimini e Pene*. Bologna, 1921.
Ferrini, C. *Il tentativo nelle Legge e nella Giurisprudenza Romana*. Ateneo Veneto,
    1884 (= *Opere*, v, pp. 51–73, Milan, 1930).

VI. Collected Works

Albertario, E. *Studi di Diritto Romano*. 1, Milan, 1933 (in course of publication).
Baviera, G. *Scritti Giuridici*. 1, Palermo, 1909.
Rotondi, G. *Scritti Giuridici*. 1, 11, 111, Milan, 1922.
Segrè, G. *Scritti Giuridici*. 1, Cortona, 1930 (in course of publication).

VII. Periodicals

Rivista Italiana per le Scienze Giuridiche. Rome, 1926–1932.

Among the published volumes of communications to Congresses of recent years
may be mentioned:

Conferenze per il XIV Centenario delle Pandette, Milano, 1930. Milan, 1931.
Atti del Congresso Internazionale di Diritto Romano, Bologna, Roma, 1933. Pavia,
    1934–1935.
Acta Congressus Iuridici Internationalis VII *saeculo a Decretalibus Gregorii IX et XIV*
    a Codice Justiniano promulgatis, Romae, 1934. Rome, 1935.

GENERAL INDEX

Where the only mention of a name does not record a fact of historical importance, the name is usually omitted. Romans are indexed under the most familiar part of their name, whether *praenomen, nomen,* or *cognomen.* If there is doubt, a cross-reference is given. All dates given are A.D. unless otherwise stated.

Apollodorus of Artemita, historian, 126
— of Damascus, architect, Danube bridge
  of, 209, 230; his work in Rome, 206 *sq.*,
  637, 781 *sqq.*
Apollonia, in Cyrenaica, 672; in Epirus,
  569; in Galatia, 600; in Thrace, 574
Apollonius of Tyana, 700
Appian, 10
Appuli of Marisus valley, 85
Apsines of Gadara, Syrian rhetor, 641
Apuleius, 491
Aquileia, 352 *sq.*, 542, 552, 795; centre of
  roads and commerce, 510, 544, 549
Aquincum in Pannonia, 544, 546, 548,
  553
Aquitania, Aquitani, 501 *sq.*, 509
Ara ad Confluentes in Gaul, 475
Arabia, annexed by Trajan, 237 *sq.*, 617;
  roads in, 238; organization of, 238;
  trade of, 628 *sqq.*; Arabs and worship
  of Dionysus, 645; Arabic in church
  services, 648; translation of Ptolemy,
  704
Aracha, 619
Arae Flaviae (Rottweil), 160 *sq.*
Aramaic language in Cappadocia, 607 *sq.*,
  611 *sq.*, 622 *sq.*; sculpture, 636; Aramaean
  deities, 645
Arcadia, Strabo and Pausanias on the con-
  dition of, 562; werewolves in, 732
Archelaus of Cappadocia, 602
Archias of Antioch, epic poet, 640
archiereus (Helladarch), and Imperial cult,
  557, 663; and provincial *concilia*, 473
Archigenes of Apamea, medical writer, 641,
  702
Architecture, see chap. xx *passim*; in Africa,
  489 *sq.*; in Britain, 521 *sqq.*; in Danubian
  Provinces, 550; Gallic, 508 *sq.*; in
  Roman Germany, 531 *sq.*; Parthian,
  127 *sq.*; in Rome, 206 *sqq.*, 775 *sqq.*;
  Spanish, 499; in Syria, 634 *sqq.*
Aretae, Arabian dynasty, 616
Aretaeus of Cappadocia, medical writer,
  702
Arethusa in Syria, 614, 616
Argaeus, Mt, 606 *sq.*; venerated in Cappa-
  docia, 612
Argos, meeting-place of the Achaean
  League, 562
Ariogaisus, king of Quadi, 360
Ariovistus, 526, 528, 536
Aristaeus, cult of in Cyrenaica, 674
Aristeas of Aphrodisias, sculptor, 792
Aristides, P. Aelius, rhetor, 447, 682, 706,
  854; his works, 685 *sq.*; his panegyric
  on Rome, 583 *sq.*, 772 *sq.*
Aristobulus of Chalcis, 139; governs Lesser
  Armenia, 608
— biographer of Alexander, 689

Aristotle, 436 *n.*, 690; philosophy of, under
  the Empire, 691 *sqq.*; commentators on,
  692; Galen on, 703 *sq.*; Pliny and, 732;
  in Plutarch, 772
Arkades, inscription at, 665 *n.*
Arles (Arelate), 506 *sq.*, 509; importance of,
  442 *sq.*
Armenia, Roman and Parthian policy in,
  105 *sqq.*, 608 *sq.*, see also vol. x; policy of
  Trajan, 108, and of Hadrian, 108 *sq.*; re-
  conquered by Vologases III, 109; appeals
  to Rome against Parthia, 240 *sq.*; annexed
  and organized by Trajan, 242 *sqq.*, 858 *sq.*;
  revolt of, 248; abandoned by Hadrian,
  301; Armenia Minor, 220 and chap. xv,
  606 *sqq.*
"Armeniarch," 613
Arminius, 56 *sq.*, 156, 536
Armorica, 511, 520
Army, in Africa, 481 *sq.*, 490; in Cyrenaica,
  688 *sq.*; in Danubian Provinces, 546;
  of the East, 618; in Gaul, 509; of the
  Rhine, 396, 527 *sq.*, 537 *sq.*; Roman, and
  Vespasian, 5, 7, 132 *sq.*, 394; pay and
  terms of service, 134; provincial recruiting, 134; discipline, 135; generals
  and specialization, 136; change in legions
  and *auxilia*, 131 *sq.*; Hadrian's reforms,
  310 *sqq.*, 847; and the State, 393 *sqq.*, 845,
  847 *sq.*; its influence towards romanization, 442 *sq.*; as regards language, 625;
  in Spain, 496 *sq.*; of Syria, 397
Arpinum, 463
Arretium, pottery of, 505, 762
Arria, wife of Thrasea Paetus, 31, 754
  sq.
Arrian (Flavius Arrianus), historian (cos.
  146), 579; Alani defeated by, 111, 313;
  works of, 684, 688 *sq.*, 694, 771
Arsinoe, 652, 655
Arsinoite nome, 650, 655
Art, see ch. xx; in Africa, 488; in Britain,
  517; in Crete, 666; in Cyrenaica, 675; in
  Danubian Provinces, 533; in Gaul, 508;
  Parthian, painting and sculpture, 128 *sq.*,
  minor arts, 129 *sq.*; Sarmatian, 102 *sqq.*;
  early Scandinavian, 105; in Spain, 479,
  498 *sq.*; in Syria, 636 *sq.*; sculpture of
  Trajanic age, 89; under the Empire,
  775 *sqq.*; in the provinces, 800 *sqq.*, 851
Artabanus III of Parthia, 90, 107
— V, 90, 110
Artemis, worship of, in Cappadocia, 612;
  temple at Gerasa, 635; worshipped in
  Crete, 664, 670 *n.*, in Cyrenaica, 674
Arulenus, L. Junius Rusticus, *see under*
  Rusticus
Arval Brethren and Domitian, 25 *sq.*, 173;
  minutes of, 404 *n.*, 405
Arverni, 14, 505

peace without conquest, 175 *sqq.*; revolt of Saturninus, 172 *sqq.*; Flavian frontier policy, 178 *sqq.*

Flavium Amphitheatrum, *see* Colosseum

Flavium Malacitanum, *municipium*, 459, 466

Flavius, Roman name found in Crete, 661

— Archippus, informer, 27 *n.*

— Damianos, sophist, 588 *n.*

See also under Sabinus, Ursus

Fleet, Italian fleet, 134; Rhine fleet, 174; of Syria, 618, 633; in Red Sea, 650

Florus, 491, 740

Fora built by the Emperors, 781 *sq.*

Forat, port on the Tigris, 630

Formula in Roman law, 808, 812, 815, 839; re-arranged under Hadrian, 813; disappearance of, 818, 840

Fortuna Primigenia, cult of in Crete, 664

Fosse Way, the, 519

Franks, 56, 539

Freedmen, high office given to by Domitian, 40 *sq.*; and civil service, 220 *sq.*, 309, 426 *sq.*, 430; under Marcus Aurelius, 372; private employment of, 757 *sq.*, 762; social character of, 758 *sq.*; status of, 829

Fréjus, 502, 509, 758

Frisii, 53 *sq.*, 158, 510

Frontinus, P. Calvisius Ruso L. Julius, 10 *n.*, 28 *n.*, 40

— Sex. Julius, 27 *sq.*, 423 *n.*, 770; subjugates Silures, 152, 198, 222; *curator aquarum*, 193 *sq.*

— glassworker in Gaul, 505

Fronto, C. Caristanius, 10, 40 and *n.*

— Claudius, 353 *sq.*

— M. Cornelius, tutor of M. Aurelius, 345; African birth of, 458, 491; on Lucan, 717, on Seneca, 730; speech to Antoninus, 748; correspondence with M. Aurelius, 415, 421, 763, 770 *sq.*, 854

— Q. Pactumeius, 18

— Ti. Catius, 191, 194, 198 *n.*

— of Emesa, 641

Fulvius, C., Lupus Servilianus, 10

Fuscus, Cornelius, 41, 170 *sq.*

Gabali, 505

Gadara, 640 *sq.*, 677

Gades, 499 *sq.*

Gaetulians, 450, 481

Gaetulicus, Cossus Cornelius, 667

Gaius, Emperor, 559, 714, 752, 776; autocracy of, 400, 402 *sq.*; and consulship, 409; and Senate, 416

— Roman jurist, 452 *n.*, 815, 817, 819 *sq.*, 824, 827 *sq.*, 834 *sq.*, 837 *sq.*; on *Latium maius*, 453 *n.*

Galatia, 597 *sqq.*; regions included in, 597; pacification of bandit tribes by Augustus, 597; the Via Sebaste, 597 *sq.*; government

of, 598; variety of countries and peoples in, 600 *sq.*; religion in, 601; conservatism of Galatians in language and political institutions, 601; Roman influence in southern cities of, 601; Christianity in, 602

Galatia-Cappadocia, *see under* Cappadocia

Galatia-Pontus, *see under* Pontus

Galba, Emperor, 395, 398, 402, 413

Galen of Pergamum, 702 *sqq.*, 707

Galerianus, Calpurnius, 4

Galicia (in Spain), mines in, 492 *sq.*; flax grown in, 495; Iberian institutions in, 498

Galli, Syrian devotees, 646

Gallia Belgica, 527

— Cisalpina, 530

— Comata, 472, 501, 503, 506

— Lugdunensis, 501

See also under Gaul *and* Narbonensis

Gallienus, Emperor, 433, 445, 475

Gallus, Annius, general under Vespasian, 5

— A. Didius, informer, 27

— Rubrius, governor of Moesia, 169

Gamaliel II, rabbi, 42

Garamantes, 3, 145, 667

Garonne, R., 503, 506

Gatalas, king of Sarmatians, 92

Gaul, common characteristics with Spain and Africa, 479 *sqq.*; agriculture in, 504; importance of, 509 *sq.*; in literature, 710; Councils of, 472 *sqq.*; individuality of, 475; industries in, 496, 505, 551; pottery of, 483, 518, 762; provinces of, 501 *sqq.*; religion in, 507 *sq.*; rivers in, 506; towns in, 502

Gaza, 629 *sq.*, 632

Gebbanitae, 629

Gellius, Aulus, 454, 455 *n.*, 491, 626, 749, 771, 822, 854

Geminius, T. Aelius, gymnasiarch and protarch of Thessalonica, 569; gift for the building of a basilica, 569; *logistes* of Apollonia, 569; archon of Panhellenic League, 569

Genetiva Julia, Colonia, 459, 461 *sqq.*

Gentile Christians and the Law, 269 *sqq.*

Gepidae, 61

Gerasa, 238, 629 *sq.*, 634; Greek statues at, 636; local government in, 620; temple at, 635

Germania, Germani: original home of, 48; civilization of, 68 *sqq.*; physical characteristics, 69; dwellings, 69 *sq.*; clothing, 70; tribal and family feeling, 70 *sq.*; coinage, 71 *sq.*; trade and industry, 71 *sqq.*; and Roman culture, 72 *sq.*; religion, 73 *sq.*; political and social structure, 74 *sqq.*; kingship, 74 *sqq.*; methods of government, 76; military system, 76 *sq.*

For Roman Germany *see* Germany

Germania of Tacitus, 68 *sqq.*, 738

INDEX TO MAPS

Maps have each their own index, and reference is here made only to the number of the map. The alphabetical arrangement ignores the usual prefixes (lake, etc.).

INDEX OF PASSAGES REFERRED TO

(Classical authors p. 984; biblical texts p. 992; inscriptions p. 993; papyri p. 997.
References to pages include the notes at the foot of the page)

[1] References in Books LXI–LXXX are to the books given on the left-hand pages of Boissevain's edition.

CAMBRIDGE: PRINTED BY
W. LEWIS, M.A.
AT THE UNIVERSITY PRESS

A.D.	Rome and Ital[y]	Literature, Philosophy and Art	A.D
70	69 Accession of Vespasian 70 Vespasian reaches Rome (about O	of foundation stone of the Capitoline Temple 21) which is completed in the following year	70
	71 Titus returns from the East (Sprin imperium and shares tribunician Banishment from Rome of astrol		
75	73–4 Censorship of Vespasian and Ti 75 Visit of M. Julius Agrippa II and	blication of Josephus, *Bell. Jud.*	75
80	78 Conspiracy of A. Caecina Alienus 79 Death of Vespasian (*June* 24). A tion of Vesuvius (*Aug.* 24) 80 Fire at Rome	of the Elder Pliny ration of Colosseum. Destruction of Capitoline le by fire istle to the Hebrews	80
	81 Death of Titus (*Sept.* 13). Access 83 Domitian's triumph over the Cha	ospel of Matthew. Gospel of Luke tion of restored Capitoline Temple	
85	85 Domitian *censor perpetuus*	velation of John	85
90	86 Inauguration of the Capitoline Ga 88 Ludi Saeculares held 89 Edict against *astrologi* and *philoso*	nine epistles on the Palatine completed	90
95	93 Death of Agricola (*Aug.* 23). Tri Baebius Massa 95 Philosophers expelled from Italy Acilius Glabrio put to death	lication of Josephus, *Antiquities* of Arrian of Quintilian tle of James	95
100	96 Assassination of Domitian (*Sept.* 97 *Lex agraria* to provide distribut measures of social improvement. 98 Death of Nerva (*Jan.* 25). Access 99 Trajan enters Rome	tion of Forum Nervae *rmania* of Tacitus he Younger's *Panegyricus* *e* (see p. 289)	100
105			105
110		tion to Mars Ultor of monument at Adamclisi	110
115		tion of the Forum Traiani (*Jan.*) h of Pliny the Younger h of Dio of Prusa	115
	117 Accession of Hadrian 118 Hadrian reaches Rome (*July* 9)	f Aelius Aristides	